With Best Compliments of

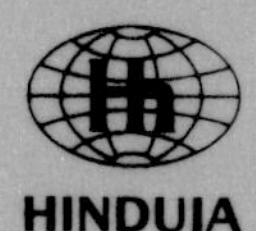

The Hinduja Foundation is privileged to sponsor the *Dictionary of Indian Art & Artists* by Pratima Sheth. We hope that the years of meticulous research that Pratima has put into compiling it will help artists to establish their credentials. We hope the dictionary will reach out to young people in schools, colleges, libraries, universities and will provide a complete reference to Indian art and artists.

Our father and the founder of Hinduja Foundation and Group, Shri Parmanand Deepchand Hinduja was a great visionary who believed strongly in India's cultural values. He always led by example and today we continue to practice his five guiding principles: 1. Duty to Work; 2. My Word is my Bond; 3. Act Local, Think Global; 4. Partnership for Growth and 5. Advance Fearlessly.

The support extended toward the publication of this dictionary is symbolic of Hinduja Foundation's commitment to the cause of promoting art and cultural initiatives.

Srichand Hinduja • Gopichand Hinduja • Prakash Hinduja • Ashok Hinduja
Sareeta Srichand Hinduja • Harsha Ashok Hinduja

Hinduja Foundation
Hinduja House, Dr. Annie Besant Road, Worli, Mumbai 400 018
Tel: 022-2496 0707

With Best Compliments of

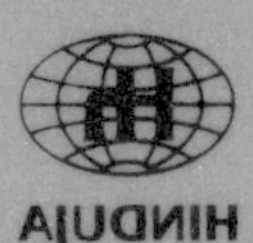

The Hinduja Foundation is privileged to sponsor the *Dictionary of Indian Art & Artists* by Pratima Sheth. We hope that the years of meticulous research that Pratima has put into compiling it will help artists to establish their credentials. We hope the dictionary will reach out to young people in schools, colleges, libraries, universities and will provide a complete reference to Indian art and artists.

Our father and the founder of Hinduja Foundation and Group, Shri Parmanand Deepchand Hinduja was a great visionary who believed strongly in India's cultural values. He always led by example and today we continue to practice his five guiding principles: 1. Duty to Work; 2. My Word is my Bond; 3. Act Local, Think Global; 4. Partnership for Growth and 5. Advance Fearlessly.

The support extended toward the publication of this dictionary is symbolic of Hinduja Foundation's commitment to the cause of promoting art and cultural initiatives.

Srichand Hinduja • Gopichand Hinduja • Prakash Hinduja • Ashok Hinduja
Sareeta Srichand Hinduja • Harsha Ashok Hinduja

Hinduja Foundation

Hinduja House, Dr. Annie Besant Road, Worli, Mumbai 400 018

Tel: 022-2496 0707

Dictionary
of
Indian Art & Artists

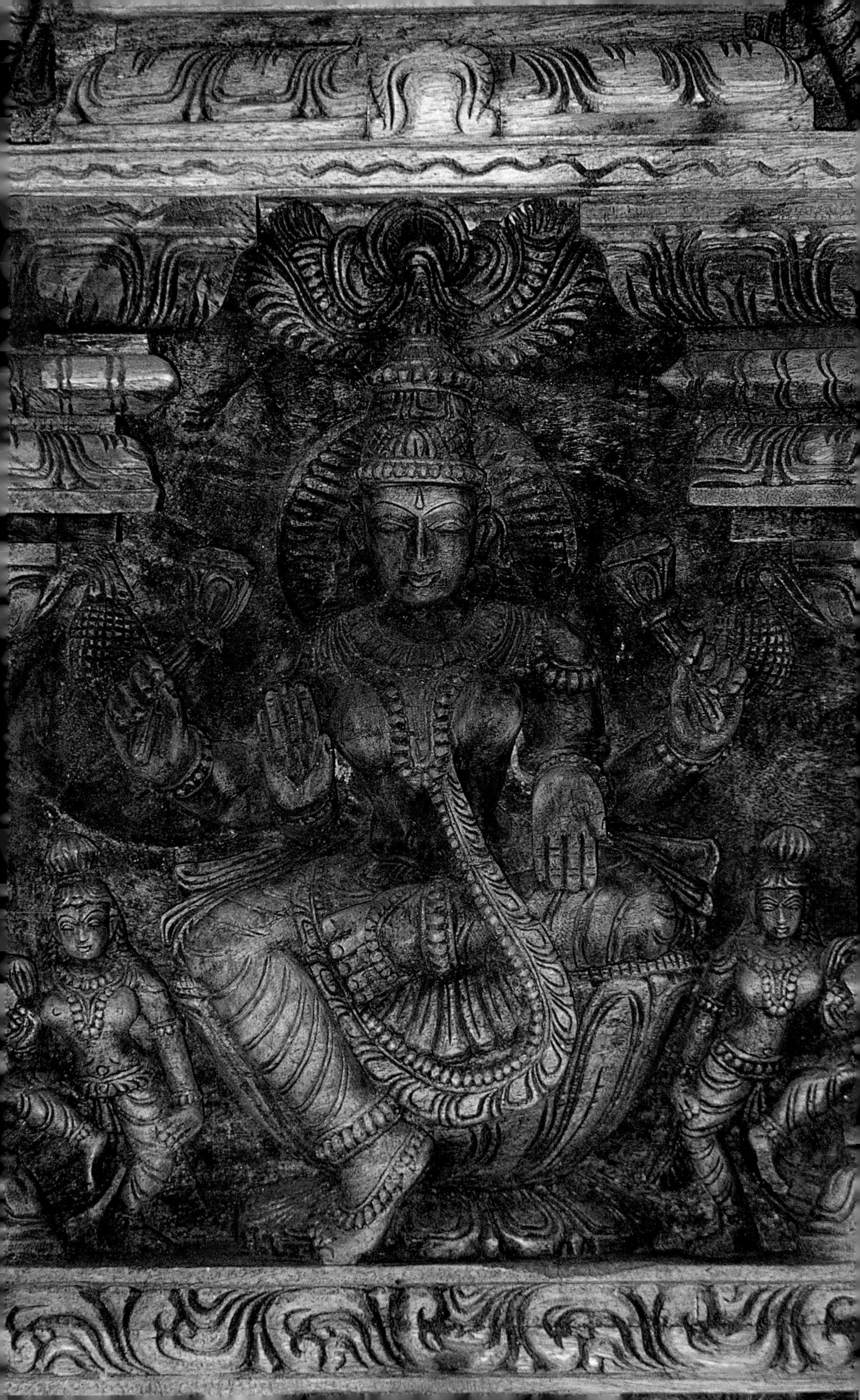

Dictionary
of
Indian Art & Artists

including
TECHNICAL ART TERMS

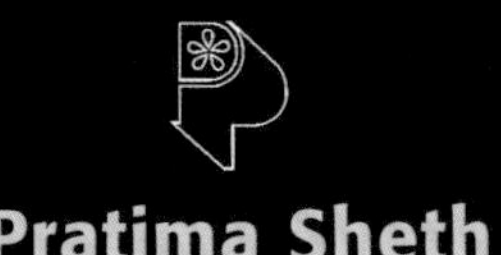

Pratima Sheth

Mapin Publishing

First published in India
in 2006 by
Mapin Publishing Pvt. Ltd.

Simultaneously published in the
United States of America
in 2006 by
Grantha Corporation
77 Daniele Drive, Hidden Meadows, Ocean Township, NJ 07712
E: mapinpub@aol.com

Distributed in North America by
Antique Collectors' Club
East Works, 116 Pleasant Street, Suite 60B
Easthampton, MA 01027
T: 800-252 5231 • F: 413-529 0862
E: info@antiquecc.com • www.antiquecollectorsclub.com

Distributed in the United Kingdom, Europe
and the Middle East by
Art Books International
Unit 200 (a), The Blackfriars Foundry, 156 Blackfriars Road
London, SE1 8EN UK
T: 44 (0) 207 953 7271 • F: 44 (0) 207 953 8547
E: sales@art-bks.com • www.art-bks.com

Distributed in South-East Asia by
Paragon Asia Co. Ltd.
687 Taksin Road, Bukkalo, Thonburi Bangkok 10600 Thailand
T: 0066-2-877 7755 • F: 0066-2-468 9636
E: rapeepan@paragonasia.com

Distribution in rest of the world by
Mapin Publishing Pvt. Ltd.
31 Somnath Road, Usmanpura, Ahmedabad 380013 India
T: 91-79-2755 1833 / 2755 1793 • F: 91-79-2755 0955
E: mapin@mapinpub.com • www.mapinpub.com

ISBN: 81-85822-90-5 (Mapin)
ISBN: 1-890206-33-4 (Grantha)
LC: 2001090906

Edited by Diana Romany/Mapin Editorial
Editorial Consultant: Krishen Kak
Designed by Mapin Design Studio
Processed by Reproscan, Mumbai
Printed in India at Pragati, Hyderabad

For future editions: If you have any corrections or additions please write to pssheth@vsnl.net

Page 2
Lakshmi: ***mural detail.***

Dedication

To tread on an unexplored path requires tremendous courage,
For only courage can surmount hurdles, resolve difficulties.
–C.R. Srinivasan

Thanks, Srini

A Note to the Reader

The original criterion for selecting artists was that they should have held at least five solo shows in reputed art galleries and a reasonable number of group participations as well. However, as the compilation work progressed, a few new facts came to light. Pre-Independence artists rarely held solos as there were very few galleries and it was a drain on their limited financial resources. Therefore, the criterion was modified to include those artists whose output was large by any standard—to which I can personally attest.

As for contemporary artists, a few have been chosen despite having fewer shows because of the avant-garde nature of their work and the impact it made on the Indian art scene. There are some omissions of some rather senior artists, because of lack of or no response from them despite many efforts.

While providing factual information and explanations there is no attempt at a qualitative evaluation. The Dictionary contains over 1700 entries with 320 visuals in colour and black and white. Extensively using cross-references, the Dictionary enables the reader to comprehend the full context in which artists' works or art terms are applied. There are many common words or technical terms covered in this Dictionary which may be adequately defined in common English dictionaries. They are reiterated here with specific reference to or in the context of their relevance to Indian art. A deliberate attempt has been made to make entries as simple as possible, for the Dictionary to be popularly understood.

The need to remain factual, not to provide any form of critique, very often flies against the very attempt to bring out qualitative aspects of art works and styles. Further, several interpretations exist in the various treatises available. The myriad influences on Indian art and the total lack of any authentic documentation of it made the job that much more daunting. Thus, some deficiencies could have inadvertently crept in, with the emphasis sounding different and so on. These should be viewed in the context of the vastness of the task at hand.

A discerning viewer may also notice, despite our best efforts, a certain discrepancy in colours of the visuals used vis-a-vis the true representation of art works on printed matter. This arose because colour photographs, negatives or slides provided were of varied professional standards. Therefore, in some cases, it is likely that the printed colour may not truly represent the artist's true expression. This was beyond our control.

Talking about artists is a complex job. It is pertinent to note that irrespective of what one may write, it is not going to please everyone. This is an occupational hazard involved in the effort. However, the author has been acutely aware that this is the single most important area that will lend credibility to the Dictionary. Therefore, great care has been taken to remain factual, base the comments on evidence and stay away from making any kind of analytical or qualitative statements and value judgements. Despite this caution, some description is required, if only to ensure that entries do not sound totally sterile. Thus, an effort such as this requires fine tuning, careful balancing and juxtaposing of facts and assessments. All entries have been read and reread keeping this litmus test in mind.

How to read this Dictionary:

- Bold words are new entries.
- Italicized words are those that are defined in this Dictionary for cross reference.
- Capital words represent Indian words, without diacritical signs. These are sourced from Sanskrit and other Indian languages.
- An artist's bio-data uses many short forms. For clearer understanding, refer to "Abbreviations", which are used constantly throughout the book.
- Most of the schools, museums, galleries, institutions, etc., are named in abbreviated form followed by the names of the cities/towns in which they are located.
- Entries are arranged alphabetically with the artist's surname coming first.
- Information provided is based on artist's own contributions or as provided by art galleries, museums or libraries.

Contents

Acknowledgements

Pheroza Godrej, eminent art historian and Director of the Cymroza Art Gallery, Mumbai, who encouraged me to prepare this book.

Barbara Bayani, Italian lecturer and editor at Wetzlar, Germany, who inspired me first with the idea of preparing this Dictionary.

Dr. A.P. Jamkhedkar, retired Director of Archaeology and Museums, Government of Maharashtra, who helped with all the Sanskrit words.

Veena Thimmaiah, art historian, ex-faculty at Sir J.J. School of Arts, Mumbai and guest faculty at NIFT, Mumbai and Bangalore, who helped prepare detailed notes.

My husband Shailesh who helped in all matters, big and small, be it as a sounding board for my plans and ideas or otherwise facilitating my innumerable meetings and all that these entailed.

To my respected late in-laws, and my mother who encouraged me even as the idea was only begining to take shape, and also to late Professor Malathi Bolar for her constant encouragement and support.

My Jyothsnaphiya, Kakiso and Rashmikaka, Shailesh's sisters, my sister Rashmi and my two daughters Ushma and Sneha, helped at different stages. Lastly I thank all the staff members, who have worked for the book.

Preface

At present there is no dictionary available in India covering contemporary Indian art as well as the terms popularly used in Indian art. This has resulted in the fact that contemporary African and Japanese art is generally better known in the U.S. and Europe than the works of contemporary Indian artists. In most countries, Indian art only generally covers traditional art such as miniature paintings, Ajanta frescoes and Ellora sculptures etc.

This Dictionary provides comprehensive coverage of Indian fine art and artists, art terms, galleries and Institutions. The period covered is from approximately 1890 to the present day. The purpose of this Dictionary is to act as a companion to an art inquirer as well as serve as a useful reference book for students of art and for everyone connected with the field of Indian art. Its scope is restricted to paintings, drawings, prints and sculpture. Thus, by providing extensive information on contemporary Indian art and artists not conveniently accessible elsewhere, together with full examination of historical styles and movements in arts on a national scale, it is a useful compendium of the contemporary Indian art scene.

The Dictionary has been in preparation since 1993. Comprehensive research, spanning several institutions all over India, contacts with nearly 2000 artists through detailed questionnaires, personal calls and visits covered this period of trial and tribulation.

The genesis of the Dictionary lies in my discovery of a lack of any authentic source of information on contemporary Indian art and artists. There were many coffee-table books covering specific artists or art forms, but none that could become an art inquirer's companion or a reference book for students and art lovers alike. Such dictionaries do exist but most contain too general or broad a coverage and are focused on European art. I have travelled extensively, visiting galleries and collecting information. India is home to paintings, graphics and sculpture, each in their own style, changing through the decades to the Indian contemporary world, starting with Raja Ravi Varma from southern India and Tagore from Santiniketan. However, all these remain as yet largely unexplored because of a lack of information available upon which a student, a layperson or a buyer could fall back on.

My exhibitions held in Germany in 1991 and 1994 gave me the inspiration to prepare a book about contemporary Indian art. Indian art and artists, who are only just beginning to be appreciated outside India, needed reference material that could be of use to artists, art students, buyers, tourists, art dealers, critics, historians and connoisseurs alike. This was the primary inspiration behind my taking on such a monumental task.

It has not been easy but, all in all, it is hoped that this Dictionary will fill the vacuum that currently exists and it is intended that future editions will handle these inherent contradictions and give this Dictionary a permanent place in the collection of everyone connected with art in general, and contemporary Indian art in particular.

Pratima Sheth

Abbreviations

AAI	National Airport Authority of India
ABC	ABC Art Gallery, Varanasi
ACB	Acharya Chitrakala Bhavan, Bangalore
AD	Anno Domini (After Death of Christ)
AFA	Academy of Fine Arts
AGC	Academie de la Grande Chaumiere, Paris
AIC	Aurobindo Institute of Culture
AIFACS	All India Fine Arts and Crafts Society, New Delhi
AIKS	All India Kalidas Samaroha, MP
AIR	All India Radio
AP	Andhra Pradesh
ASI	Art Society of India, Mumbai
ATG	Art Today Gallery, New Delhi
b.	born
B.A.	Bachelor of Arts
B.FA.	Bachelor of Fine Arts
B.Sc.	Bachelor of Science
BAAC	Birla Academy of Art and Culture
BAG	Bajaj Art Gallery, Mumbai
BARC	Bhabha Atomic Research Centre, Mumbai
BAS	Bombay Art Society, Mumbai
BB	Bharat Bhavan, Bhopal
BC	Before Christ
BHU	Banaras Hindu University, Varanasi
BKB	Bharat Kala Bhavan
bth.	breadth
BVB	Bharati Vidya Bhawan, Guntur
CAG	Contemporary Art Gallery
CCACM	Chaze Centre for the Arts & Crafts, Margao
CCAG	Centre for Contemporary Art Gallery, New Delhi
CCMB	Centre For Cellular & Molecular Biology, Hyderabad
CFA	College of Fine Arts
CHAG	Chitram Art Gallery, Cochin
Cholamandal	Cholamandal Artists' Village, Chennai
CIMA	Centre of International Modern Art
CKAG	Chitrakoot Art Gallery, Kolkata
CKP	Chitrakala Parishad, Bangalore / Karnataka Chitrakala Parishad, Bangalore / Karnataka
CMC	Computer Manufacturing Company Limited
CNCFA	Sheth C.N. College of Fine Arts, Ahmedabad
COAG	Cholamandal Art Gallery, Chennai
Co-op.	Co-operative
CRAR	Crimson (the Art Resource), Bangalore
CSMVS	Chhatrapati Shivaji Maharaj Vastu Sanghralaya (earlier Prince of Wales Museum of Western India (PWM) (Mumbai, MAHA))
CTAG	Chitrala Art Gallery, Thiruvananthapuram
CTC	Craft Teacher's Certificate
CVA	College of Visual Art
CYAG	Cymroza Art Gallery, Mumbai
d.	died
D.Litt.	Doctor of Literature
DAE	Dasera Art Exhibition
DATG	Delhi Art Teachers Group
Dept./dept.	Department
DG	Designscape Gallerie, Mumbai
Dhoomimal	Dhoomimal Art Centre / Dhoomimal Art Gallery, New Delhi
Dip./dip.	Diploma
Dir.	Director
ENSBA	Ecole Nationale Superieure des Beaux Arts, Paris
EZCC	East Zone Cultural Centre
FA	Fine Arts
FAC	Fine Arts and Crafts
FAIM	Federation of Artists Institution of Maharashtra
FAR	Forum of Art and Research, Kolkata
FFA	Faculty of Fine Arts, M.S. University, Vadodara
G88	Galerie '88, Kolkata

GAC Garhi Artists' Centre, New Delhi
GAG Genesis Art Gallery, Kolkata
GBP Gallery Bose Pacia, New York
GC Gallery Chemould
GCA Government College of Arts
GCA&D Government College of Art and Draftsmanship
GCAC Government College of Arts and Crafts
GDA Government Diploma Arts
GDFA Government Diploma in Fine Arts
GE Gallery Espace, New Delhi
GG Gallery Ganesha, New Delhi
GK Gallerie Katayun, Kolkata
GMAG Government Museum and Art Gallery, Chandigarh
Godrej Godrej and Boyce Mfg. Co. Ltd.
Govt. Government
grad. graduate / graduation
GSA Government School of Arts
GSAC Government School of Arts and Crafts
GSFAC Government School of Fine Arts and Crafts
GUJ Gujarat

HAS Hyderabad Art Society, Hyderabad
HCVA Hutheesing Centre of Visual Art, Ahmedabad
HG Habiart Gallery, New Delhi
HoD Head of Department
Hon. Honour
HP Himachal Pradesh
HRD Human Resources Development Ministry, Govt of India
ht. Height

IAFA Indian Academy of Fine Arts
IAPC International Art Promotion Centre, New Delhi
ICA&D Indian College of Art and Draftsmanship
ICCR Indian Council for Cultural Relations, New Delhi
IFAS Ideal Fine Art Society, Gulbarga
IGNCA Indira Gandhi National Centre for the Arts, New Delhi
IIC India International Centre, New Delhi
IIT Indian Institute of Technology
IMTMA Indian Machine Tools Manufacturing Association, New Delhi
INTACH Indian National Trust for Art and Cultural Heritage
INTACR Indian National Trust for Art and Culture Resources
ISCA Indian Society of Contemporary Art, Kolkata
ISCC Indo-Soviet Cultural Centre
ISOA Indian Society of Oriental Art, Kolkata
ISOAS Indian Society of Oriental Art School, Kolkata

J&K Jammu and Kashmir
JAG Jehangir Art Gallery, Mumbai
JJIAA Sir J.J. Institute of Applied Arts, Mumbai
JJSA Sir J.J. School of Arts, Mumbai
JMI Jamia Millia Islamia, New Delhi
JNAG Jehangir Nicholson Art Gallery, Mumbai
JNM Jehangir Nicholson Museum, Mumbai
JNTU Jawaharlal Nehru Technological University, Hyderabad

KAR Karnataka
KB Kala Bhavan

LCAG Lakeeren-The Contemporary Art Gallery, Mumbai
LKA Lalit Kala Akademi
LKC Lalit Kala Centre, New Delhi
LKK Lalit Kala Kendra
LSRSA L.S. Raheja School of Art, Mumbai
LTG Little Theatre Group Art Gallery, New Delhi

M.A. Master of Arts
M.FA. Master of Fine Arts
MAHA Maharashtra
MKKP Maha Koshal Kala Parishad

MMB	Max Mueller Bhavan
MP	Madhya Pradesh
MPCVA	Mohile Parikh Centre for the Visual Arts, Mumbai
MPKP	Madhya Pradesh Kala Parishad
MSU	Maharaja Sayajirao University, Vadodara
NCAG	Nehru Centre Art Gallery, Mumbai
NCPA	National Centre for the Performing Arts
NDA	National Diploma of Arts
NDFA	National Diploma of Fine Arts
NGMA	National Gallery of Modern Art
NID	National Institute of Design, Ahmedabad
NKM	Nootan Kala Mandir, Mumbai
NZCC	North Zone Cultural Centre
PAG	Progressive Artists' Group
PG	Prithvi Gallery, Mumbai
PUAG	Pundole Art Gallery, Mumbai
PUJ	Punjab
PWM	Prince of Wales Museum, Mumbai
RAA	Royal Academy of Arts
RAG	Raffic Art Gallery, Madurai
RAGM	Rainbow Art Gallery, Mumbai
RAJ	Rajasthan
RB	Rabindra Bhavan
RBM	Rabindra Bharati Museum, Kolkata
RBU	Rabindra Bharati University, Kolkata
RCA	Royal College of Arts, London
RG	Renaissance Gallery, Bangalore
Roopankar	Roopankar Museum, Bhopal
RPG	R.P.G. Enterprises
RSA	Rajasthan School of Arts, Jaipur
SAG	Sista Art Gallery, Bangalore
SAI	Sarala's Art International, Chennai
Sanskriti	Sanskriti Art Gallery, New Delhi
SC	Shilpi Chakra, New Delhi
SCA	Society of Contemporary Artist, Kolkata
SG	Sakshi Gallery
SJM	Salar Jung Museum, Hyderabad
SKP	Sahitya Kala Parishad, New Delhi
SNSPA	Sarojini Naidu School of Performing Arts, Fine Arts
sq. ft.	square foot (feet)
SRAG	Sridharani Art Gallery, New Delhi
SUG	Surya Gallery, Hyderabad
SUSA	Sarada Ukil School of Arts, New Delhi
SZCC	South Zone Cultural Centre
TAG	Taj Art Gallery, Mumbai
TG	The Guild, Mumbai
THAG	Thanjavur Art Gallery, Thanjavur (Tanjore)
TIFR	Tata Institute of Fundamental Research, Mumbai
TKS	Triveni Kala Sangam/Triveni Art Gallery, New Delhi
TN	Tamil Nadu
UGC	University Grants Commission
UK	United Kingdom
UNESCO	United Nations Educational, Scientific and Cultural Organization
UP	Uttar Pradesh
USA	United States of America
USIS	United States Information Service
V&A	Victoria and Albert Museum, London
VAG	Vadehra Art Gallery, New Delhi
VBU	Visva Bharati University, Santiniketan
VEAG	Venkatappa Art Gallery, Bangalore
VG	Village Gallery, New Delhi
VMM	Victoria Memorial Musuem, Kolkata
WB	West Bengal
WBAF	West Bengal Artists' Federation
WBSA	West Bengal State Academy
WSC	Weavers' Service Centre
wth	width
WZCC	West Zone Cultural Centre
YBCAG	Y.B. Chavan Art Gallery, Mumbai
YWCA	Young Women's Christian Association

Glimpses of the Evolution of Indian Art

Art in India was a means to an end and this was to nurture the spiritual side of its patrons; to guide them to experience that rich, bountiful and overwhelming feeling, abstract in many ways. The entire creative energy was born from the intuitive vision to tap this subtle feeling in a way that the individual would comprehend the intangible. There was a constant probe to realize the ultimate meaning of life and existence. This led to the ideas of religious philosophers who created intense doctrines, highly esoteric and metaphysical in many ways. But the artist through his creativity, using either brush or chisel, attempted to give these abstract ideologies imbedded in the teachings of philosophers and seers a visual and a multi-dimensional form. As a result, great transformations took place. Stones began to speak, brushes and paints narrated a story, huge structures with remarkable grace and dynamism blossomed.

Hence, be it the frescoes of Ajanta or the mammoth architectural creations of the temples or the sculptures, they all were strung in a common thread of purpose.

Each epoch in the history of India has left its classic imprint on the walls of caves, or in architectural and sculptural creations of time. Diverse shades of India's bustling life were captured by the creators to tell the pulsating story of that time.

These inimitable works of art, done most of the time by artistes who decided to merge their individuality in their creations, also act as a definite source for historical studies.

Based on the content, style and also the larger frame of chronology in the panorama of Indian architecture, writing, sculpture, miniature paintings, murals and calligraphy are classified into definite periods of creations. The aspects in focus are sculpture, painting and writing.

Indian Sculpture:

Sculpture in stone and metal as an art form has been known in India since the Indus Valley Civilization. Through the ages, the materials used have varied from solid rock to clay, limestone, sandstone and marble and alloys such as bronze, brass and steel. Classic examples seen along the progress of time are the creations during the Mauryan and Kushan period. The former was known for its famed capitals and the latter for the depiction of Buddha in the Gandhara and Mathura schools. Timeless pieces were also developed during the period of the Gupta, Pala and the Sena kings. In the south the contribution of the Cholas and Pallavas was also noteworthy. In the 20th century, cement/concrete and plaster of Paris became popular. Forms and styles too have evolved from the impressive curvilinear "Dancing Girl" of Harappan culture to the modern abstract and impressionist works making use of found objects and scrap metal for installations.

Historic landmarks	Year/Circa	Milestones in art
Prehistoric–Stone Age, Paleolithic Age, Neolithic Age	9000–3000 BC	Primitive caves, rock-cut paintings, sculpture
Tantra	circa 3500 BC	Tribal in origin, Indian civilization, Sanskrit roots
Indus Valley Civilization, Mohenjo Daro, Harappa	circa 2300–1750 BC	Terracotta, pottery, seals, statues, use of bronze
Indo-Aryan, Vedic age	circa 1800–500 BC	Pastoral society, rituals, Vedic religion, *Rigvedas*
Early Jainism, Buddhism, Hinduism and transition	circa 600–322 BC	Early Buddhist art, development of philosophy, books of law
Maurya dynasty, Greek invasions, Sunga dynasty	End of 4th–1st century BC	Mauryan sculpture, Ashoka pillars, representations of Buddha, Graeco-Roman sculptures, stupas
Kushan dynasty, Andhra dynasty	1st–4th century BC	Graeco-Buddhist sculpture, stone sculptures of Buddha, Mathura style, Amravati style
Gupta dynasty	4th–6th century BC	Golden age of art, Gupta style, free-standing temples
Beginning of Arab invasions	8th century AD	Post-Gupta style, Pallava style, Pala style
Delhi Sultanate	12th century AD	Late Pala style, Dravidian style
Deccani Muslim period, Vijayanagar rule	14th–16th century AD	Indo-Persian style, Dravidian style
Moghul empire	16th–18th century	Indo-Persian style, Dravidian style, Moghul and Rajput miniatures
British rule	18th–19th century AD	Company School of painting
Contemporary	19th–Present	Indian modern art

Indian Paintings:

In Indian art, historical paintings may be divided into murals and miniatures. Murals are generally large wall paintings depicting historical subjects such as the life of Buddha at the Ajanta and later at the Ellora caves; and Hindu gods and goddesses from epics such as the *Ramayana* and the *Mahabharata*. In murals the paint adheres to the background which is made of lime plaster and is applied to a durable support such as rock or stone. The pigments in the paint need a binding substance which preserves it and prevents it from flaking. Murals are naturally bigger than miniature paintings where the name itself implies smallness. The support of these miniatures are more perishable and smaller in size than in the case of murals.

Important murals		
Bhopal	Palaeolithic age Neolithic age	Rock-cut paintings; Bhimbetka caves
Ajanta and Bagh	200 BC–AD 200 4th–6th century AD 5th–6th century AD	Frescoes depicting previous lives of the Buddha
Badami	circa AD 578	Brahmanic frescoes
Ellora	5th–8th century AD	Buddhist, Brahmanic, Jain frescoes
Panamalai, Kanchipuram	7th–9th century AD	Jain frescoes, Pallava style
Sittanavasal	9th century AD	Jain frescoes
Thanjavur	10th–11th century AD	Temple frescoes
Tiruparutikundram	14th century AD	Temple paintings
Hampi, Lepakshi	16th century AD	Vijayanagar paintings
Indian miniatures		
Bengal, Bihar, Orissa	circa AD 1175–8th century	Buddhist palm leaf manuscripts, Pala and Sena style
Gujarat	11th–14th century AD	Jain palm leaf manuscript paintings
Mandu	11th–15th century AD	Paper manuscripts
Mughal	circa AD 1526–AD 1707	Persian influence
Deccani Islamic	16th–18th century AD	Combined influence of Hinduism and Islam
Rajput	16th–19th century AD	Illustrated poems with musical compositions–Raga-Ragini
Pahari	17th–19th century AD	Basohli, Kangra.
British Raj, Renaissance Period, Independent India	19th & 20th century AD	Western influence from 1757, development of various styles such as Bengal School, Bombay School, Southern School, Naturalism, Tantricism, Abstract

Writing in India:

Writing is the visual representation of language and therefore a secondary means of communication. The first true writing was in the form of pictures representing objects. However, the limitation of this form in depicting abstract ideas led to the combined use of ideograms i.e. sense signs, and phonograms i.e. sound signs.

Most modern alphabet systems derived from two major off-shoots of the one basic source known as Proto-Semitic. These two streams were the Phoenician and the Aramaic. A branch of Aramaic then spread to the Indian subcontinent by the 7th century BC where it became the basis of Brahmi, Devnagari, Pali and other scripts used throughout South-East Asia. Indian scripts have undergone many changes in the design of the graphemes due to the variety of writing materials in use such as rocks, pillars, clay tablets, gold plates, silver plates, copper plates, palm leaves, birch-bark and cloth.

Sanskrit of the Indo-Aryan group of languages, first found manifestation in the Vedic treatises such as the *Rigveda* (4th century BC). It is considered to be the most scientific and a language composed with comprehensive grammar.

Stone and metal were used for engraving, rock was the principal writing material in ancient India. Gold and silver were used for engraving and casting–yantras engraved on gold and silver were used for Tantric worship. Palm leaf from the palm trees known as *tada-patra* was used in the south and birch-bark i.e. the inner bark of the Himalayan birch tree known as *burja-patra* was used in the north. Wood and bamboo written on with chalk was known as *phalaka* and *sataka*. Bricks were stamped and scratched before being baked but were rarely used. Earthernware and seals were used for inscriptions as well as clay tablets, dried or fired, for documents. Another metal used as writing material in ancient and medieval India was copper plate known as *tamra-patra*. Brass, bronze and tin were rarely used. Use of cloth for writing dates back to AD 1361. The manuscript of Dharmavidhi of Sriprabhasura has been discovered in Patan in Gujarat. The manuscript contains 93 13-inch wide leaves. Cloth was prepared for writing by sizing it with rice or wheat pulp and polishing with conch-shell after drying. Black ink was used for writing on this cloth. Cloth known as *kadatam*, sized with tamarind seed powder and blackened with charcoal was in use in Karnataka till the 19th century. Chalk was used for writing on this cloth. The earliest reference to paper dates to the 11th century by Raja Bhoja in Central India. The oldest manuscript written in Sanskrit comes from Gujarat dating from the early 13th century. However, paper manuscripts written in the Gupta script of the 5th century AD have been found at Kashgar and Kugier. Paper used for these manuscripts was coated with gypsum. Indigenous paper factories existed before the advent of mill-made paper. Paper leaves were cut out in the shape of palm leaves and birch-bark and were written on with ink made from pulverized charcoal, gum and sugar mixed with water. Red, green and yellow made from vegetable dyes were also used. Gold and silver inks were employed for writing illuminated manuscripts. The various instruments used for writing were reed pens known as *kalama*, wooden sticks called *varnika*, coloured pencils or *varna-vartika*, brushes known as *tuli* or *tulika* and the engraver's tool *salaka*.

Aban Amroliwalla, B.Com., B.L.Sc., Mumbai.
Radha Kumar, M.A. Ancient Indian History, Culture, Archaeology, Mumbai.

Art, Nation and Identity: Colonial India—the First Phase

As the dust raised by the collapse of the vast edifice of colonialism begins to settle in this post-colonial era, writers in the East and West have started dissecting the global impact of colonial empires, the implications of Western technology and ideas of modern nationalism for the Third World. One of the most powerful and transformative, yet relatively unexplored, impacts of Westernization has been on artistic taste. A close scrutiny of Indian art during the Raj reveals the complex clash of cultures between the Western universal canon—a colonial legacy taken for granted by us contemporary Indians—and pre-colonial taste that was lost with the spread of British rule. The only exceptions were Mewar and a few Rajput courts which continued to produce traditional miniatures. Victorian academic art and the idea of artistic progress grew deep and firm roots in India during the late 19th century, (1850–1922), as part of a grand imperial design.

The infiltration of Western taste in India, which began with the British victory in Bengal in 1757, was mainly confined to the Indian nobility for a century. In 1851 the pace quickened because of changes taking place in British imperial ideology. With immense confidence, the Raj announced its grand design of improving Indian artistic taste as part of Westernization centering on English as the medium of instruction. While Indian miniature paintings, it was argued, were "pretty" they were merely decorative, lacking the high moral content of Victorian art, particularly history painting.

The Western model art schools founded in the 1850s in Madras, Bombay and Calcutta, wrought profound changes in artistic practice and production in India. Originally founded to train artisans, they became centres for the dissemination of European fine arts. Previously in India, there was no distinction between artists and artisans. After his apprenticeship under a master, the artist became part of the royal entourage, the best-known examples of whom are the Mughal masters. The new graduates of impersonal art schools now looked to the public for patronage which was provided by art exhibitions organized by art societies, a Victorian cultural institution imported into India. Two further elements in this diffusion were modern journalism and cheap prints which helped in the wide diffusion of Western academic art. The new elite artists now sought inspiration in artistic individualism, in European romanticism and, above all, in the image of the artist as a lonely outsider.

However, no one embodied the new idea of artistic genius more strikingly than Raja Ravi Varma (1848–1906), a minor prince from Kerala who took the unprecedented step of choosing this hitherto lowly profession. Varma set up his studio as a business enterprise, making his reputation with fashionable portraits which won him clients among the British rulers and the Indian aristocracy throughout India. However, it was history painting that secured his lasting fame. Varma engaged in a systematic invention of the Hindu past, based on a close reading of the Sanskrit classics, while borrowing the "vocabulary" of Victorian salon painters. Ravi Varma's artistic project was part of a burgeoning national consciousness, as improved communication and printing technology brought India together as never before. A shrewd entrepreneur, Varma released cheap prints of his celebrated history paintings, thus winning a permanent place in the nation's affection. Indeed, no Indian painter has been able to match his popularity at all levels of society.

When Varma died in 1906 he was acclaimed as a nation-builder, and yet within six months his works were denounced as debased and un-Indian. What went wrong? The emerging cultural nationalism rejected academic art as a proper vehicle for expressing Indian aspirations: the Indian "decorative" style of painting embodied a spirituality denied to the materialist art of Europe. Nationalist art was aided by a growing disenchantment with English education and a renewed confidence in Hindu civilization, symbolized by Swami Vivekananda's historic address to the World Parliament of Religions in Chicago. The cultural nationalists, led by the Tagore family of Bengal, found valuable allies among European theosophists and a host of romantic critics of Victorian industrial society. The final ingredient in this heady cultural nationalism was a powerful "pan-Asian" sentiment that brought Indian and Japanese intellectuals together.

In 1905, the first widespread nationalist protest in India was precipitated by the Partition of Bengal. The nationalists demanded self-rule (Swaraj) and boycotted British products in a bid for economic and cultural self-sufficiency (Swadeshi). Abanindranath Tagore, who founded the nationalist Bengal School, provided a blueprint for "the recovery of India's artistic past" based on a rejection of Western nationalism and a synthesis of different Asian painting traditions. Abanindranath Tagore's first target was naturally Raja Ravi Varma. The Keralan artist's imaging of India's past, based as it was on Victorian salon art and not on any Eastern artistic tradition, was rejected as being the product of a hybrid colonial culture.

During the Swadeshi agitation of 1905, the urgent objective of the cultural nationalists was the replacement of academic art at the Calcutta Art School with indigenous teaching. This campaign was led by its English Principal, E.B. Havell, who put Abanindranath in charge of inculcating oriental art in the Calcutta art school students, many of whom, notably Nandalal Bose, Asit Haldar, Surendranath Ganguly and K. Venkatappa, later became leading nationalist artists. While the use of Sanskrit epics, such as the *Ramayana* and the *Mahabharata*, as artistic sources by his group was similar to Varma's, the quest for an indigenous expression was entirely their own. Also, unlike Varma's unquestioning optimism, the orientalist works exuded a deep sense of degeneration and despondency. Often in these paintings, the figures were bent double with the burden of history, a sentiment that was in accord with the nationalist sense of loss that had attended the British subjugation of Indians.

The years 1900–1920 saw the relentless rise of the nationalist oriental art. Abanindranath's pupils, who were appointed heads of all major government art schools in India, came to exert a powerful influence on the direction that art took. But ironically, at the very moment of its almost total triumph, the Bengal School lost its impetus. By the 1920s, pan-Asianism was on the wane, as embarrassing differences between different Asian nations surfaced. Tagore was particularly critical of Japanese imperialism and Tagore himself was criticized by the Chinese intellectuals for extolling the feudal past. The arrival of Western modernism in India blunted the conflict between academic artists and orientalists; after all, academic art was so thoroughly discredited in the West that it was no longer worth bothering about in the colonies. But above all, with the launching of the mass non-cooperation movement by Mahatma Gandhi, the role of artistic nationalism was relegated to a secondary place. Although oriental art inaugurated by the Bengal School faced increasing challenges from different quarters, not least from powerful individual artists like Rabindranath Tagore, Amrita Sher-Gil and Jamini Roy in the late 1920s and the 1930s, its engagement with colonialism and Indian cultural identity has continued to influence all subsequent art in India. That is arguably its lasting legacy as the first art movement in India.

Partha Mitter
Professor in History of Art
University of Sussex

Dictionary
A to Z

A

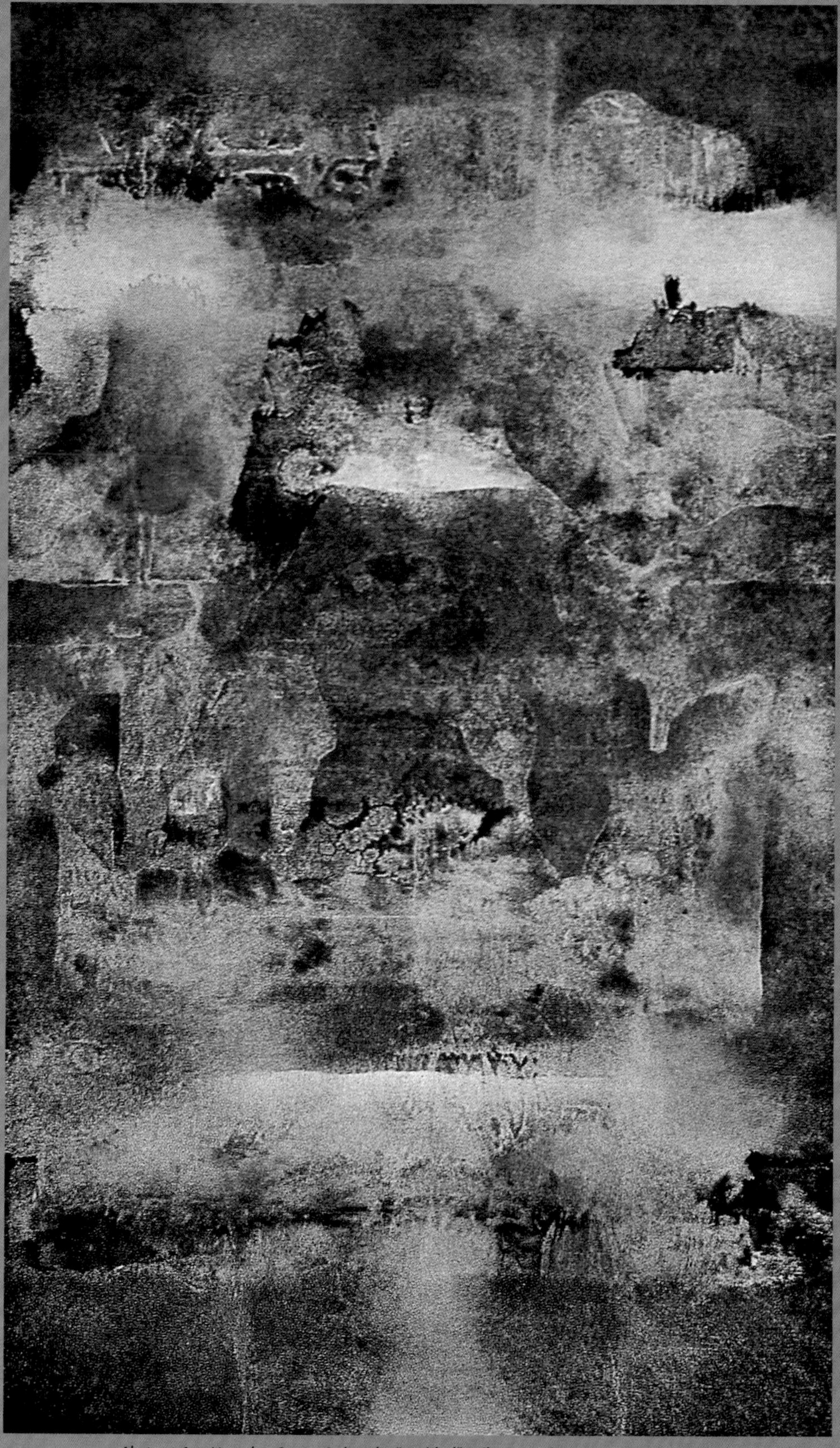

Abstract Art: *Vasudeo Santu Gaitonde*, "Untitled", *Oils*, 1997. (See notes on page 23)

AAJ=today. AAJ Society of Visual and Performing Arts was founded in 1979 in Udaipur, to evolve an indigenous *idiom* for *contemporary* Indian *Art*. Apart from an individualistic pursuit of *art* by its members, AAJ has organized camps, seminars and workshops. AAJ has acquired a Haveli (mansion or villa) in Udaipur, a theatre, a *graphic* workshop and *folk* and *tribal art* documentation centre in *Mewar*, RAJ. Members of the society include *P.N. Choyal*, *Shail Choyal*, *Prabha Shah*.

ABC Art Gallery (ABC) (Varanasi). ABC was established in 1991 by Anand Agarwal to promote young *artists*. An average number of 25 shows are held each year. There is also a permanent *museum* that includes works of *Madhavi Parekh*, *Badri Narayan*, *Suhas Roy*, *Bikash Bhattacharjee*, *Latika Katt*, *Deepak Shinde*.

Abhaya=fearless. Refer MUDRAS.

Abhisarika One of the eight specific types of NAYIKAS mentioned by ancient Indian writers and poets. The Abhisarika is usually depicted as a young woman braving the terrors of the night in order to meet her lover. There are two types of these NAYIKAS. The KRISHNA-Abhisarika, who meets her lover on a dark, new moon night. She wears dark coloured garments in order to blend with the surrounding forest. The Shukla-Abhisarika, who meets her lover on a full moon night, is dressed in *white* and is usually depicted at the door of her palace or midway through the jungle replete with snakes and other perils. Refer ASHTANAYIKA.

Abhushana=ornaments. Elaborate jewellery worn by men and women, seen today in Indian *sculpture* and *miniature paintings*, varies from region to region and from period to period. Some of the more common ornaments are the MUKUTA, the HARA (necklaces in different *patterns*), the KEYURA (armlet worn above the elbow), KANKANA (bangle or bracelet in several *patterns*), the Channavira (a flat disc-shaped ornament worn on the MUKUTA, or suspended around the neck to lie against the chest), the Yajnopavitam (a jewelled sacred thread worn over one shoulder and resting on the opposite hip), the KAMARPATTA or Katibandha (a waist belt sometimes holding the unstitched lower garment in place), the KUNDALA (ear ornaments in various shapes—loops, discs, pendants), and the Nupura (anklets, worn above or below the ankles).

Certain ornaments are associated only with specific deities, e.g., the BHUJANGA-VALAYA (a snake-shaped KEYURA) worn by SHIVA; the Srivatsa of VISHNU, also seen on BUDDHA. In *sculpture* this is represented by a four-petalled flower or a simple triangle and is placed towards the right side of the chest; Vaijayanti worn by VISHNU, each group of five gems supposedly composed of the five elements and is therefore called the elemental necklace (the five gems being the pearl, ruby, emerald, sapphire and diamond, signifying water, fire, air, earth and ether, respectively). PRABHAVALI (a *Halo*) or ring of *light* that surrounds the entire *figure* of a *God*. It is represented as an ornamental oval or circular ring with a number of Jwalas (*lights*, flame, *illumination*).

Abstract That which is non-factual and frequently abstruse in *terms* of being unrelated to the real world. In the Indian context, spirituality (symbolized by YANTRA, CHAKRA, SWASTIKA, etc.) is at the core of dematerializing the *form* from the viewing *impression*, *Rabindranath Tagore's sketches* in *ink* e.g. of 1928, *Ramkinkar Baij's cement forms* in *sculpture* at *Santiniketan*—are but a few examples of early abstraction. Refer *Abstract Art*, *Abstract Expressionism*, *Abstract Impressionism*, *Abstract Landscape*, *Abstract Movement*, *Abstract Painting*, *Abstract Symbolism*, *Abstraction Figurative*, *Abstraction Geometric*, *Abstraction Lyrical*, *Abstraction Organic*, *All-Over*.

Abstract Art *Art* which is completely non-representational and non-figurative. The *forms* and *colours* used by the *artist* are not readily identifiable as belonging to the existing world. Instead the *forms* are conceptual and are mostly seen as relationships between *patterns*, symbolically reduced to *ciphers*. Though Indian *artists* here are exposed to Western *Art*, abstract art in India is generally rooted in Indian *culture* and *tradition*. The *symbolic figures* and geometric *forms* used in Indian religion YANTRA, CHAKRA, SWASTIKA, etc., *form* the base from which intuitive ideas emerge, and the traditional *art* influences abstract art in India. Refer *Figurative Art*, *Abstraction Geometric*, *Ambadas*, *Biren De*, *Vasudeo Santu Gaitonde*, *Ghulam Rasool Santosh*, *Rabindranath Tagore*, *Balbir Singh Katt*, *Mahendra Pandya*, *Sayed Haider Raza*. (See illustration on page 22)

Abstract Expressionism Though this *term* was first used in 1919 to describe V. Kandinsky's work, it is now popularly used to describe the *abstract* works produced in the United States after World War II. Though the influence of Europe is undeniable, through the teachings of H. Hoffman and the exposure to the works of P. Picasso, P. Mondrian and the Surrealists, Abstract Expressionism is an American phenomenon. Though the *styles* were as diverse as the frantic gestural movements of J. Pollock and M. Rothko's vast, calm fields of glowing *colour*, the large scale is typically American. American *sculptors* like D. Smith, too incorporated large, *abstract* shapes in the three-dimensional *medium*. In India the *term* can be applied to the *drawings* of *Rabindranath Tagore*, and *paintings* of *Ambadas*, *Sayed Haider Raza*, the *colour prints* of *Krishna N. Reddy* and others.

Abstract Impressionism A *term* used specifically to describe the last great works by the French Impressionist, C. Monet. The brushstrokes in the works, "The Water Lilies" series are interwoven to form a luminous *abstract* mesh of *paint*. Viewing such *paintings* from a distance often enhances their effect.

Amrita Sher-Gil and the *PAG* Mumbai, were among the first *artists* to use this *style* in India. Using *translucent colours*, *tempera*, and short brushstrokes, they created shimmering *landscapes* and *portrait* studies. Also refer *K.M. Adimoolam*, *P.T. Reddy*, *Shiavax Chavda*.

Abstract Landscape An *abstract painting* in which the elements suggest *vignettes* from *nature* or *landscapes*. Some *artists* term it as semi-abstract; *Artists* like *Akbar Padamsee*, *Ram Kumar* and *Laxman Shreshtha* have captured abstractions of *nature* by their *technique* of *colour* application; While *Setlur Gopal Vasudev's* abstractions, owe their landscape-like look to the rippling brushstrokes that he uses. Refer *Harkrishan Lall, Bimal DasGupta, Abstract, Abstract Art, Abstract Painting.*

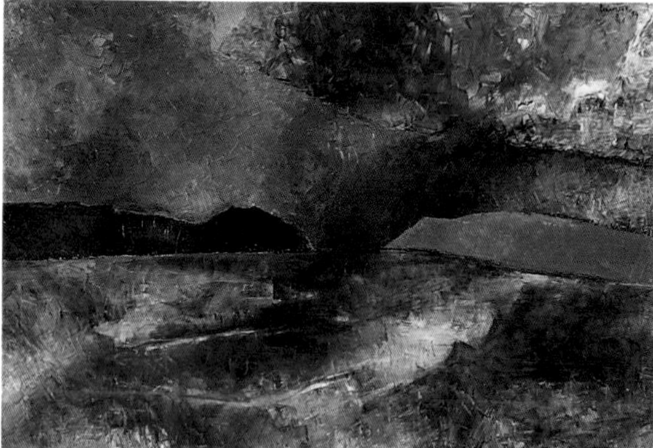

Abstract Landscape: *Akbar Padamsee*, "River", *Oil* on *Canvas*, 1994, 108x161 cm.

Abstract Movement The trend towards abstraction which began during the last decades of the 19th century in the West, culminating in what is widely regarded as the first "*abstract*" or "non-objective" *painting* around 1910 by the Russian V. Kandinsky. Various *forms* of abstraction quickly appeared throughout Europe, along with justifications in the *form* of manifestos. Suprematism, *neo-Plasticism*, Rayonism and Orphism were a few of these relatively short-lived movements. Abstraction in general continues to this day, making its appearance in India relatively late in the *post-Independence* era. Most of these *artists* began by taking direct inspiration from the West. In recent years, Indian *artists* have increasingly displayed an originality of vision and conception in their *abstract* works. Refer *Bengal School, Rabindranath Tagore, Ramkinkar Baij, Setlur Gopal Vasudev*, Illustration–*Ambadas.*

Abstract Painting Non-representational art's original source, e.g., *landscape* or *still life* becomes simplified or geometrical on the two-dimensional surface of the *canvas* or *paper* with *oil paint, ink, watercolour, gouache, collage* and many other *mediums*. Refer *Vasudeo Santu Gaitonde, Homi Patel, Natvar Bhavsar.*

Abstract Sculpture Non-representational art in three-dimension. The *form* conveys the inner relationship of the *artist* with his or her work. *Artists* express themselves in simplified or geometrical *forms* in various *media*. These could be *mixed media, cement concrete, clay, bronze, wood, metal, hemp, weaving* or any other. The *size* may vary from the very small to large building-sized *sculptures*.

Arriving in India in the 20s, it influenced the works of *artists* such as *Debi Prasad RoyChowdhury*, S. Pansare, *Vinayak Pandurang Karmarkar, Ramkinkar Baij, Vivan Sundaram* and *Shankar Nandgopal*. Refer *Abstract, Abstract Art, Abstract Expressionism, Abstract Impressionism, Abstract Symbolism, Abstraction Organic.*

Abstract Symbolism When *abstract forms* stand for certain symbols with specific meaning as in the neo-Tantric works of *Biren De* and *Ghulam Rasool Santosh*. Tantricism is however an ancient way of life in India, exploited by *painters* mainly in the latter half of the 20th century. Refer *Neo-Tantricism, Symbolic Art, Symbolism, Tantric Composition*; Illustration–*Madhukar B. Bhat, Prafulla Mohanti.*

Abstraction Figurative A *term* used to describe works in which the *figure*, entirely or in fragmented *form*, still appears, e.g., H. Moore, P. Picasso. The first *artist* in India to adopt this *style* was *Ramkinkar Baij*, others are *Maqbool Fida Husain, K.K. Hebbar, Rabin Mondal*; Refer Illustrations–*Aku, Manjit Bawa, Dhanraj Bhagat, Arpana Caur, Francis Newton Souza.*

Abstraction Geometric It is when the *forms* in the work of *art* have a geometric character as opposed to the soft flow of Organic Abstraction. *Gaganendranath Tagore* was the first Indian *artist* to adopt geometric *construction* of *forms* and cubist *style* in the works of *art*. *Sayed Haider Raza's* works, after the 70s especially are demonstrative of this *style*. Refer *Art*, Tantric, *Gaganendranath Tagore, Dipak Banerjee, Shobha Broota, V. Viswanadhan.*

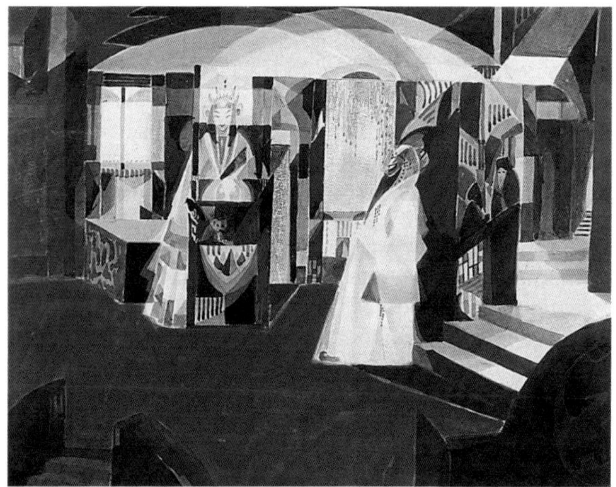

Abstraction Geometric: *Gaganendranath Tagore*, "Magician", *Watercolours*, 27x34 cm.

Abstraction Lyrical The European version of *Abstract Expressionism*, associated particularly with the delicate *calligraphic paintings* of H. Michaux. The *modern* works of the Kolkata *painter*

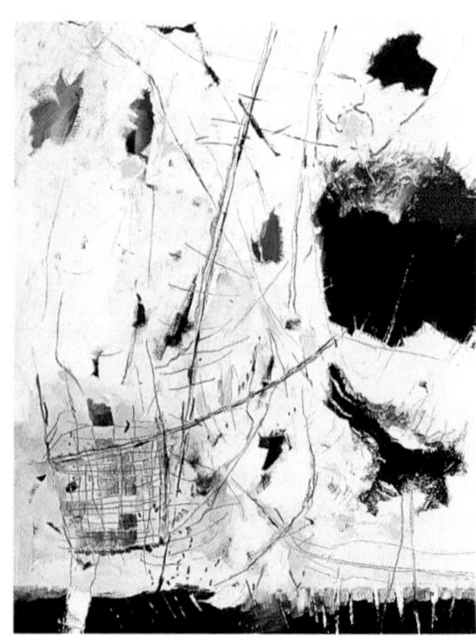

Abstraction Lyrical: *Sudhangsu Bandhopadhyay*, "Colour Shadows", *Oil* on *Canvas*, 102x76 cm.

Sudhangsu Bandhopadhyay using strokes of *black* against a *white background* can be termed as lyrical abstraction.

Abstraction Organic The *forms* in such works, though still non-representational, evoke associations with organic *forms*, *forms* of *nature*. V. Kandinsky's works of 1910–15, e.g., when a splash of blue could variously mean the flow of water, or the spread of the sky over the *horizon*. In India, this *form* can be seen in the works of *Ambadas* and *Setlur Gopal Vasudev*, both of them exploiting this *genre* to create meandering *forms*, that could also be seen as *landscapes*. Refer *Abstract Expressionism*.

Abu-Dilwara Temples The Vimala Vasahi and the Luna Vasahi are the main *Jain* temples erected at Mount Abu, RAJ. In the Solanki era the former was dedicated to the first Tirthankara, Adinath, and built by Vimala Shah, the minister of King Bhimadeva in 1032. The Luna Vasahi was built later in 1231, by Vastupala and Tejpala in memory of their brother Lunige.

The delicate *marble carvings* and *sculptures* in both these shrines illustrate the general Solanki tendency towards a high level of ornamentation. The shrine was dedicated to the 22nd Tirthankara, Neminatha. The outward aspect of these temples contrasts sharply with the profusely decorated interiors, the *carvings* having delicate *filigree* work. The domes, though plain on the outside, are decorated with concentric rings and suspended pendants on the inside and are filled with repeated *patterns* of elephants, lotus flowers and dancers. Bracket *figures* of goddesses further embellish these domes. The Luna Vasahi also has an elephant stable with ten *marble* elephants carrying attendants on their backs. The cells around the periphery of the temples also show elaborate *carvings*. The *sculptures* are gently stylized, with sharp features and flattened limbs, pointing to the use of the file rather than the *chisel* in *carving*.

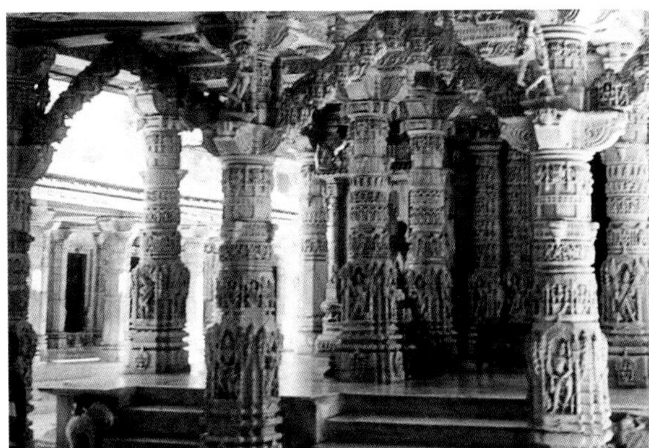

Abu-Dilwara Temples: Dilwara temple *style*, Mount Abu, RAJ.

Academic Art This originally meant the traditional or conventional *style* of *art* taught at official Academies of Art from the 16th century onwards. Academic Art flourished in India with *Raja Ravi Varma* (1846–1906). Today it is a pejorative *term* meaning *art* which is non-innovative, unoriginal. In the 70s when abstraction became popular, *figurative art* was called academic; today any conventional *painting* or *sculpture* including *realistic landscape* and *portrait* is termed academic. Refer *John Fernandes*, *Suhas Bahulkar*, *Vinayak Pandurang Karmarkar*, *Gajanan Narayan Jadhav*.

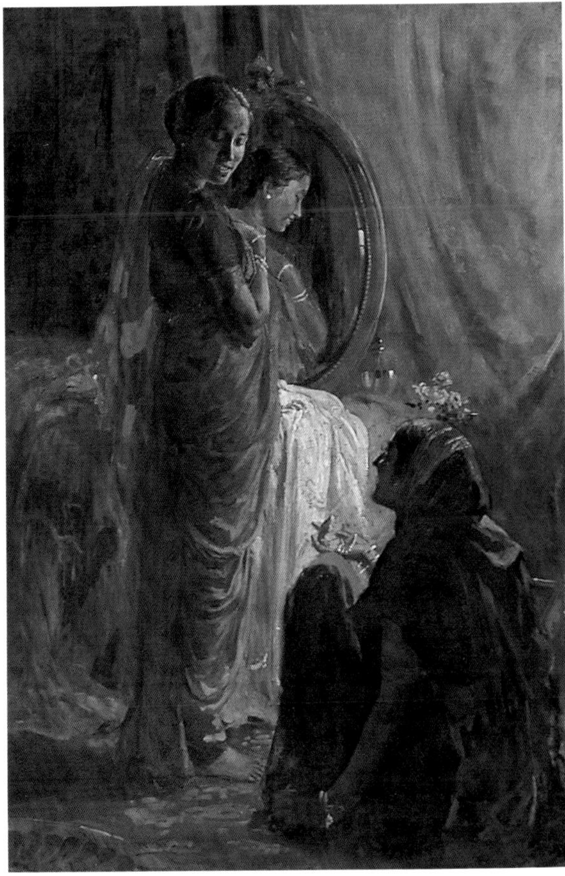

Academic Art: *Muralidhar R. Achrekar*, "Toilet", *Oils*, 1929, 105x73 cm.

Academy An institution, organization or association dealing with the promotion or teaching of the *arts*. The word can be traced to *classical* Greek (the Athenian grove where Plato discoursed with his students) Plato's Academy. In 15th- and 16th-century Italy, the *term* referred to groups of humanists meeting for discussion. These gradually became formalized and the first Academy of Fine Arts was founded by Gallery Vasari in Florence in 1563. Academies were subsequently founded in Paris, the French Academy in 1648 and the RAA in London in 1768. Today the *term* is widely used to denote a teaching institution in the field of the *arts*, including music, drama, etc. In India this *term*, sometimes spelled Akademi, includes schools such as *AFA* Kolkata, *JJSA* (*Bombay School*), *GCAC* & *Madras School of Art* Chennai, *KB* in *Santiniketan*, *AFA*, *RBU* & *RB* Kolkata and associations like *LKA* & its branches.

Academy of Fine Arts (AFA) (Kolkata). AFA was founded in 1933 by Lady Ranu Mukherjee for the promotion of *art* and *culture* in India. It is an educational institution offering dip. courses in *FA* and *Applied Art*. It houses a *museum*, with nine galleries devoted to different *themes*, including the Rabindra Gallery, a CAG, with *paintings* including some by the Tagore family, *Nandalal Bose*, *Asit K. Haldar*, *Benode Behari Mukherjee*, *Paritosh Sen*, *Gopal Gosh* and *contemporary sculptures*, one displaying old *ivory* works, Indian *sculptures*, old textiles and carpets, others displaying *miniature paintings*, RAGAMALA, and old *engravings* of Kolkata by British *artists*. The *academy* has five exhibition halls and two airconditioned auditoriums. It also has a mobile *art* van.

Accidental Light Any source of artificial *light* depicted in a *painting*, e.g., candle-light, the *light* from a fire, a *charcoal* brazier or a lantern.

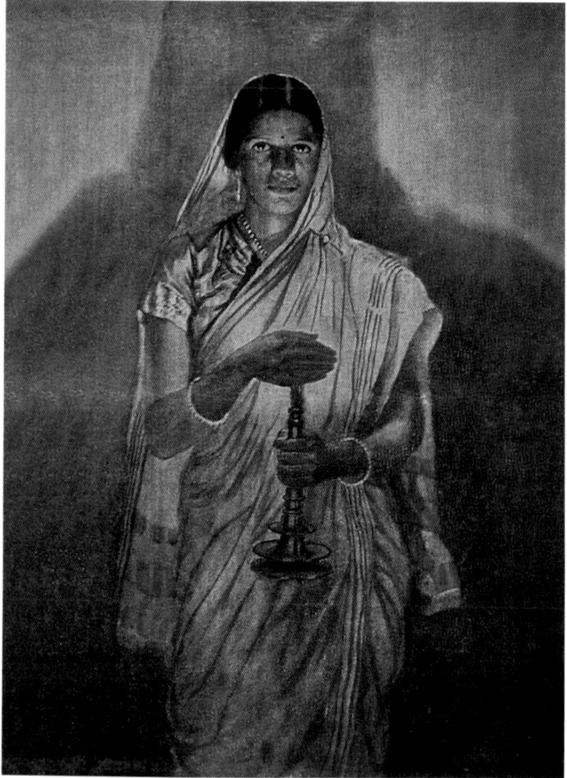

Accidental Light: *Savlaram L. Haldankar*, "Glow of Hope", *Watercolours*, 96x75.5 cm.

Acharya Chitrakala Bhavan (ACB) (Bangalore). This institution was founded in 1969 by the *artist M.T.V. Acharya*, to spread *art education* among the masses. The ACB courses were planned around the individual need of students to supplement their knowledge of *art* in a shorter period than the conventional five-year course. However, direct coaching classes for local candidates in *FA* started in 1976. Correspondence courses which include cartooning and *commercial art* are also available at the Bhavan. Refer *Adiveppa Murigeppa Chetty*.

Acharya, M.T.V. (1921–1992) b. Mysore. Education: Dip. in *art* Sri Chamarajendra Technical Institute Mysore. Solos: *JAG*, *VEAG*, later in Chennai, Mysore, Hassan, Shimoga, Bhadravati. Group participations: Mumbai, Bangalore, Chennai, Kolkata, Mysore; International: Minsk. Awards: *AFA* Kolkata, Mysore DAE Gold Medal. Founder member: *ACB*. Appointments: Secretary and Principal of *ACB* till 1992; Organized lectures, demonstrations and held *art* camps for students in the State of KAR; Held students *exhibitions VEAG*, Mysore DAE. Publications: "Art and Myself" by the *artist*. Collections: Govt. Museum KAR; International: State Art Museum Minsk, & pvt.

Known as KAR *Raja Ravi Varma*, M.T.V. Acharya's forte was mythological and historical *painting*, including 80 *watercolours* based on the MAHABHARATA of which "Gadayuddha" is best known. Many of his *masterpieces* like "Village School Master", "Farewell from the Doorway" and "Offspring of the Unknown" were created during 1940 –1950. He was known for his *portraits*, and throughout India for his cover *designs* for the children's magazine "Chandamama". Dir. of *Painting*, Indian Institute of FA Chennai, Assistant Cartoon Film Dir. in TN Talkies Chennai, and Founder Principal of *ACB*.

Achrekar, Chandranath K. (1949–) b. Puttur, KAR. Education: Dip. KAR School of Art Bangalore, Post-Dip. in *printmaking Santiniketan*. Solos: *Art Heritage* New Delhi, *SAI*, *CRAR*. Group participations: Contemporary 80 Kolkata, National Exhibition *LKA* New Delhi, *Images Art Gallery*, Hebbar Festival, 50 Years of Independence & *LKA* Bangalore, *RG*, *VEAG*, *JAG*, *SAI*; International: London, *Biennale* Bangladesh, Festival of India USA. *Art* camps & workshops: *Krishna N. Reddy's printmaking* workshop, All India artists' camps Hyderabad, KAR *LKA* Srirangapatna, KAR Mela Bangalore, *CKP*; International: Singapore, Bangkok. Awards: *LKA* & International Book Fair New Delhi, KAR *LKA* Bangalore and *graphics* in Chandigarh. Appointments: Art Dir. & Chief Artist of newspapers including Deccan Herald KAR. Collections: *LKA* New Delhi & Bangalore, pvt. & public.

Earlier his works were based on dream *imagery*. Today he affects a *realistic style* of *painting* in the *manner* of KAR *artists Ramesh Rao* and *Bhaskar Rao*. The subjects mostly seem to be from the underprivileged section of society, especially adolescent boys making a living in the street. He has in addition worked as an Art Dir. for films.

He lives and works in Bangalore.

Achrekar, Muralidhar R. (1907–1979) b. Mumbai. Education: Trained in *art* Mumbai & RCA. Solos: Moscow. *Auction*: Osian's Mumbai. Awards: Padma Shri 1968. Member: Elected President *ASI* 1947. Appointments: Visited Russia as Art Dir. of film "Pardesi" in 1957. Publications: Books "Skyscrapers" & "Flying Gandharvas" are a *visual* record of his visit to USA.

Though he was an excellent portraitist, he was best known for his illustrated books on famous places in India, including *Ajanta*, *Elephanta*, *Ellora*, Karla and *Khajuraho*. These books were studied by *art* students, not only for the monuments, but also for the *handling* of *line* and delicate *colour washes*. Interested in the female *form*, especially *nudes*, printed a portfolio of *nude pencil sketches*. Refer *Academic Art*; Illustration–*Life-Drawing*.

Acid A chemical solution used mainly by photographers and printmakers. The printmakers use acid for *etching* into *metal plates* of *copper* and *zinc*, i.e. different acids are used for different *metals*. As acids are extremely dangerous in their concentrated form, only dilute versions should be used. *Mukul Chandra Dey* was the first *modern* Indian *artist*, who learnt the *art* of *etching* in London and America 1916–1917. Refer *Acid Bath, Acid Resist, Bite, Biting in, Etching, Krishna N. Reddy.*

Acid Bath A tray or deep dish filled with dilute solutions of *acid*, used for *etching zinc* or *copper plates*. Hydrochloric *acid*, nitric *acid* and ferric chloride are commonly used now. This new process was introduced by visiting European *artists* to a group of Indian *artists* in the early 19th century. Refer *Aquatint, Bidri, Bite, Biting in, Etching, Krishna N. Reddy, Mukul Chandra Dey.*

Acid Resist A *ground* applied to the *zinc* or *copper plate* to withstand the corrosive effects of the *acid* used for *engraving*. In India, this *technique* was initally used by *artist* Ramachand Roy and others in Calcutta around the second half of the 19th century. Refer *Bite, Biting in, Etching, Hard Ground, Intaglio, Soft Ground, Varnish, Amitabha Banerjee, Jyoti Bhatt, H.R. Kambli.*

Acrylic Plastic A *synthetic* plastic both lightweight and durable, available in different forms, colourless, coloured, *transparent*, *opaque* and used by both *sculptors* and *painters*. Acrylic plastic in sheet form is used in the place of glass for framing, and *painting* on the reverse side, as (*Back-Glass Painting*) by *Madhu Champaneria*. *Shakuntala Kulkarni* has lately used *acrylic* sheets in her *compositions*. Refer *Glass Painting, Installation.*

Acrylics A relatively new *medium* in *painting*, acrylic *paints* are *pigments* suspended in *synthetic* resin. The advantage they have over *oil*-based *paints* is that they dry almost immediately, thus permitting a more spontaneous "mode of expression". *White* acrylic is versatile and can be applied on *canvas*, *wood*, *paper*, cardboard, fibreboard, *plaster* as well as on *metal*, *stone* and *concrete* (over a primer). Both *matte* and glossy *finishes* are possible with acrylics. However, if used carefully, the advantages are considerable. Acrylic was first developed around 1920 and was used by *artists* in the West by the 40s. In India it was first used in the 70s. Many Indian *painters* use this *medium* these days but the pioneer was *Amrut Patel*, who had the first all acrylic show in 1971–72. He also wrote instructions for the use of acrylics for a *paint* manufacturer. *Bal Wad*, an employee at Camlin, then gave public demonstrations of this new material. *Tyeb Mehta, Francis Newton Souza, Maqbool Fida Husain, Shamshad Husain, Krishen Khanna* have also used this *medium*. Acrylic is also sometimes used in *mixed media*. Refer *Overlapping.*

Action Painting A *term* coined by critic H. Rosenburg to describe the *abstract* expressionist works of J. Pollock. It denotes a *style* of *painting* in which the *canvas* is usually laid on the floor and *paint* and other materials (including sand, glue and powdered glass) are dripped, flung or sprayed over it. The action of the *painter* thus creates the *painting*, which is *abstract*, though often with accidental effects. Tachisme is the French *term* for action painting. In India *Homi Patel* has used this *style* of working, at times seeking these effects deliberately. Refer *Abstract Expressionism, Blot Drawing, Cinema, Drip Painting, Gestural Painting, Video Art*; Illustration–*Homi Patel*, Pratima Sheth (*drip painting*).

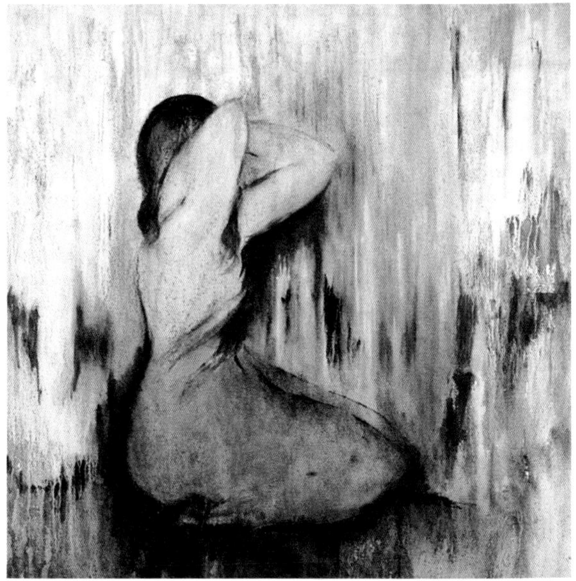

Action Painting: Pratima Sheth, "Secluded", *Oil* on *Canvas*, 1992, 77.5x77.5 cm.

Adalja, Jivan (1931–) b. Karachi. Dip. *JJSA*, Education: Dip. in *graphic art* Warsaw Poland. Solos: *Art Heritage* New Delhi, University Museum Chandigarh, SKP, *JAG*. Group participations: *Biennale*–1962, 64, 65, 67; International: *Graphic Prints* exhibitions in Poland by UNESCO, Manila, Cuba & later in London by *AIFACS* 1984 & 88, Mexico & Cuba by *LKA*, *Painting* Tokyo; Group show: *JAG*. *Art* camps & workshops: USIS & *LKA* New Delhi, International *Graphic* workshop Bhubaneshwar, *Drawing* workshop Chandigarh, others at *GAC* & SKP workshop. Awards: MAHA State, GUJ State, Poland magazine cover *design*, National New Delhi, Silver Medal at *Biennale* Chandigarh, *AIFACS* Hon. Fellowship: Senior in *painting* by Dept. of Culture, Govt. of India. Collections: *LKA* & *NGMA* New Delhi, SKP; International: National Museum Warsaw Poland, & pvt.

Jivan Adalja's compositional *style* derives from P. Klee's work and Indian folk *tradition*. The *figures* that he uses are primarily frontal, with large staring eyes and solemn expressions done in *watercolours*. However, his colouring is more modernistic, compared to the basic primaries that the folk *artist* affects.

He works in New Delhi. Refer *Frontality.*

Adimoolam, K.M. (1938–) b. South India. Education: Dip. *GCAC* Chennai. Over 22 solos: Chennai, Mumbai, New Delhi, Hyderabad, Bangalore, Kolkata, *Art Heritage* New

Delhi; Retrospective: Chennai & Drawing 1962–96, Bangalore 1997. Group participations: National Exhibition, 25 Years of Indian Art, *Triennale*, *LKA* & 50 Years of Indian Art *LKA* New Delhi, *CIMA* & Annual Show *BAAC* Kolkata, *CRAR*; International: *Biennale* Sao Paulo, South Indian Painters Australia; Group show: by *SAI* in Japan. *Art* camps & workshops: Pondicherry, Kanpur, *LKA*–TN, KAR & Andaman, SZCC Gwalior, *BAS*. *Auctions*: Heart Mumbai & New Delhi, Osian's Mumbai. Awards: *LKA* New Delhi & Chennai, *AFA* Kolkata, *CKP*, *BAS*. Member: Modern Tamil Writers Group. Commissions: *Mural paintings* in New Delhi, Bangalore & Chennai. Publications: "Between the Lines" *drawings* done between 1962–1966, illustrated books & book jackets for the Modern Tamil Writers Group. Collections: Bangalore, Mumbai, Hyderabad, Regional Centre, National Art Gallery, Orion Nunkalai Kulu, *LKA* Chennai, *NGMA* & *LKA* New Delhi, Kerala & KAR, *CIMA* & *BAAC* Kolkata, *PUAG*, *Dhoomimal*, *G88*, *SAI*; International: Singapore, Hong Kong, Air India office at London airport.

K.M. Adimoolam is basically a colourist, *handling* pure *pigment* with his *palette knife* to recreate *nature* in the *manner* reminiscent of both C. Monet and M. Rothko, blurring the distinction between abstraction and reality. He makes a sophisticated use of *colour*, never stepping into the fauvist nightmare of clashing uncoordinated *colours*.

He lives and works in *Cholamandal*.

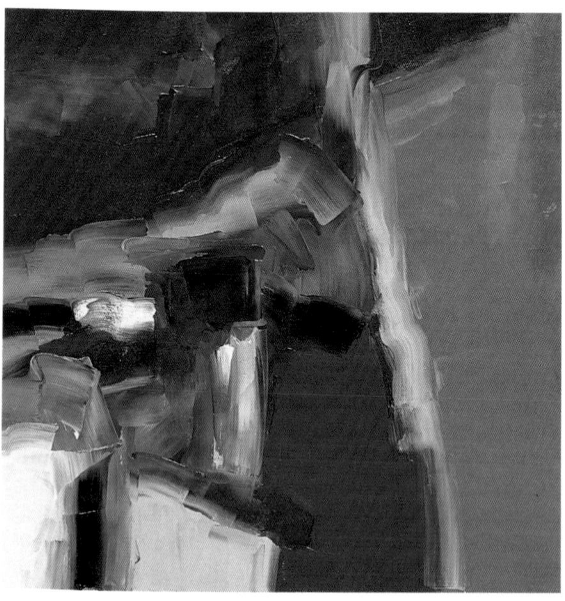

Adimoolam, K.M.: "Red, Orange, Grey", *Oil* on *Canvas*, 110x110 cm.

Adivrekar, Gopal S. (1938–) b. Ratnagiri, MAHA. Education: GDA in *painting JJSA*. Solos: TAG, *PUAG*, *JAG*, *Dhoomimal*, *CRAR*. Group participations: National *LKA* New Delhi, Veteran *artists* of India *BAAC* Mumbai, *VAG*, *JAG*, *PUAG*, *DG*; International: Geneva, Singapore, London, Belgium. *Art* camps: Bangalore, Panjim. *Auction*: Sotheby's in India. Awards: *LKA* Award–Eminent *Painter* New Delhi, *BAS*. Member: General Council *LKA* New Delhi, Art Council Govt. of MAHA State Mumbai, Managing Committee of *JAG* 1995, Life member *Artists' Centre* Mumbai & *BAS*. Appointments: Designer at the *WSC* Mumbai for 22 years, exhibiting his tapestries at various international shows *LKA* VII *Triennale*, New Delhi, International: *Biennale* Turkey. Collections: *NGMA* & *LKA* New Delhi, *BB*, pvt. & corporates.

Gopal S. Adivrekar's *imagery* is relatively *abstract*, depending mainly on the use of a heavy *impasto*. From the grid-like *landscapes* of the 60s, he has moved towards a *composition* that is relatively asymmetric and is based on the dichotomy between the terrestrial and the aquatic. It is the lash of the white-topped waves breaking against the rough-hewn coastline of his native Konkan region that inspires him. His *palette* chiefly comprises beige and brown with flashes of bright *primary colours*.

He lives and works in Mumbai.

Adurkar, Vasudeo (1907–1992) b. MAHA. Education: Dip. in *painting* & *sculpture JJSA*; Studied at Westminister Technical School, Dip. in *painting* & Certificate in *etching*, *aquatint* & *dry-point-engraving* RCA; Certificate in *drawing*, *design* & *painting* Slade School of Art London. Solos & group shows: British Museum and other galleries London, RCA. Awards: Prize, Medal for *painting JJSA*; International: RCA Exhibitions. Commissions: *Murals* for the palace of the ruler of Vadodara. Appointments: Dean of *JJSA* 1947–1953, First Dir. of *JJSA*; International: Prof. of *painting* RCA & visited Italy, Switzerland, Holland, Belgium, France & Germany. *Restoration* works on *portraits* in Indore, & on Hon. Judges in the room of the High Court Building and *painting* of Battle of Basantor. Publications: Study books Free Drawing I, II, III & Nature Drawing.

Vasudeo Adurkar, a *portrait painter* and an academician, specialized in "*Nature*" and "Free" *drawing*. Apart from commissioned works of *portraits*, his portrayal of flowers in *pencil*, *brush* and *colour* were plentiful. His commissioned *portraits* were strongly coloured but his flower studies were in pale and pleasing *colours*. His greatest contribution, however, was in the academic field. He authored "Free Drawing"–Parts I to III, which provided students of *art* with a compilation of a high order of perfection in norms of *aesthetics*, a strain of English *Romanticism* and chaste *line drawings* and *compositions* with pale *colour washes*. Refer *Pastel Shades*.

Advancing Colours *Warm colours* (red, yellow, orange etc.) which appear to advance from the picture plane as opposed to *cool colours* (blue, violet, green etc.) that appear to recede. Refer *Colour Wheel*, *K.M. Adimoolam*, *K.V. Haridasan*, *Chittrovanu Mazumdar*, *Sayed Haider Raza*.

Aerial Perspective 1. A *term* used in representational or *figurative painting*, in traditional Indian *art*, when the *landscape* elements are seen as if viewed from above. Aerial perspective was traditionally used in the depiction of water-bodies (e.g., lakes, rivers, fountains) terraces and floor *spaces*, including carpets in certain *schools* of Indian *miniature painting*. Refer *Mughal Miniature*. **2.** A *term* used in representational *landscape painting*, in Western *Art*, when the features are seen as receding into the distance by using tonal changes. This will be especially evident in *landscapes* with trees, rivers, lakes, mountains and skies with clouds.

Aesthete Generally, a lover or connoisseur of the *arts*, or one who enjoys artistic sensations. In Hindi, the *term* "Rasavant" or "Rasika" would be used. Refer RASA.

Aesthetic Movement A *style* in England in the 1880s dictated by the doctrine of *"Art for Art's Sake"*, advocated first by the French writers T. Gautier & C. Baudelaire and the English writers W. Pater & O. Wilde. It denied the moral value of *art*, concentrating instead on simplified decorative & evocative *motifs*. E. Burne-Jones & J. Whistler were chief exponents of the movement. It had a greater impact on *Applied Art* rather than on *FA*.

It was epitomized by *ISOA* and, until the nationalist movement overtook the *Bengal School*, it was considered as *art* of an Indian pedigree. It found its forum in the *art* journal "Rupam", Kolkata which represented the *aesthetics* of young Indians.

Aesthetics The philosophy and appreciation of the beautiful, especially in relation to *art*. Several aestheticians strove to set the various parameters governing beauty and sensitivity to the *ideal* in *art* and its related fields. In India, the NAVA RASA i.e. the nine emotions, though essentially meant to define drama, was adapted to suit the *visual arts* as well. The CHITRASUTRA (the rules of picture making), a chapter in the ancient treatise, the Vishnudarmottara PURANA, also sets down the SHADANGA, the six canons of *painting*. The SHADANGA clearly states that it is grace (Lavanya), similitude (Sadrisyam), emotion (BHAVA) and *colour* (Varna) in addition to *form* (Rupa) and *proportion* (Pramanani) that makes a perfect picture (CHITRA).

In the 19th century, with the setting up of *art* academies in the major cities, aesthetics became a subject of study for *art* students. It was not just the theories of Western aestheticians that were studied, Indian literature was also scoured for information on the appreciation of *art*. *Abanindranath Tagore* was one of the first to translate the CHITRASUTRA. Refer *Aesthetic Movement*, *Art for Art's Sake*, *FFA* (Vadodara), *GCAC* (Chennai), *KB Santiniketan*, *Dhruva Mistry*, *Ratan Parimoo*, *Shankar Patil*, *Sohan Qadri*, *Murlidhar Nangare*.

African Art This *term* refers to the *conceptual art* created by the indigenous peoples of the continent of Africa, excluding Egypt. It particularly denotes *sculpture* that was later used as source material by 20th-century *artists* in the West. Refer *Mask*, *Santiniketan*, *Somnath Hore* and *Rabin Mondal*.

After-Image The *image* retained (though in a *complementary colour*) of a particular object on which the eye is focused for sometime. This *complementary colour image* appears when the eye moves to a neutral *background*, especially *white*. It is a scientific phenomenon, exploited by *Op Artists*. It can be experienced in the works of *Manjit Bawa*, *Sayed Haider Raza*, *Chhaganlal D. Mistry*, *Ghulam Rasool Santosh*, *Ali J. Sultan* and many others.

Agarwal, Rajendra (1939–) b. Gurgaon, Haryana. Education: NDA in *applied art College of Art* New Delhi. Over 16 solos: Bhopal, Chandigarh, *AIFACS*, TKS, *JAG*, SRAG. Group participations: Over 47 shows Mumbai, Chandigarh, Hyderabad, Lucknow, Guwahati, Chennai, *LKA* annuals New Delhi, Kala Mela SKP, *AIFACS*; International: World Art Fair Mexico, Through *AIFACS* Cuba, London, Sharjah. *Art* camps & workshops: Chandigarh, *LKA* New Delhi, camp to Goa & Screen printing workshop by *AIFACS*, *GAC*; International: Sketching camp Nepal by *AIFACS*. Awards: Kala-Shri 1991, Five awards in All India Annual Exhibition. Fellowship: in *painting* by Dept. of Culture HRD Ministry 1991–1993. Member: *LKA* New Delhi, *AIFACS*. Publications: Broadcasted—"Paintings on Seasons" by BBC and "A Face in The Crowd" by New Delhi Doordarshan. Collections: *LKA* New Delhi, Museum in Chandigarh & Bhopal, *AIFACS*, TIFR, pvt. & public.

After his early naive renderings of *Sher-Gil*-like *compositions*, he shifted to *painting landscapes*. His later works are *figurative* with simplified *forms* juxtaposed against decorative *landscapes*.

He lives in New Delhi.

Agarwalla, Balbhadra (1937–) b. India. Education: Self-taught *painter*, basically studied under Indra Dugar, an eminent *painter* of the *Bengal School*. Solos: *CKAG*, TKS, *LTG*, *SAI*, *JAG*. Group participations: *BAAC* Kolkata, *Santiniketan*, National Exhibitions. Collections: pvt. & corporates.

His chosen mode of expression is *landscape*. The early academic works have now given way to an observation of the play of *light* in *nature* in the *manner* of *Paramjit Singh*.

He lives in New Delhi.

Agashe, Vasant D. (1937–) b. India. Education: Dip. in *FA*. *JJSA*. Solos: *AFA* Kolkata, FA. Institution Indore, *JAG*, TAG, SRAG; International: USA. Group participations: National Exhibitions and All India Exhibitions New Delhi, Mumbai, Kolkata & Bhopal. *Art* camps: AIKS, *Printmaking* camp *BB*. Awards: *LKA* MP, AIKS. Founder member: Spectrome Progressive Painter's Group Indore. Collections: *Roopankar*, *BB*, pvt. & corporates.

His recent *drawings* and *paintings* are a departure from earlier *abstract* ones, being *figurative* with an academic use of *warm* and *cool colour* schemes. The work is built up in a *collage form* with *paints*, and fragmentary *figures* composed in a decorative *manner*.

He lives and works in Indore, where he retired from the post of *Artist* in the Office of the Labour Commissioner.

Aggregate The chemically stable, i.e., not subject to structural weaknesses or weathering ingredient used in *casting cement*, which should bond well with the main material used. It is used primarily for reasons of economy. Refer *Cast Stone*, *B. Vithal*, *Ramkinkar Baij*, *Dhanraj Bhagat*, *Vinayak Pandurang Karmarkar*, *Balbir Singh Katt*, *Kanayi Kunhiraman*, *Pilloo Pochkanawalla*.

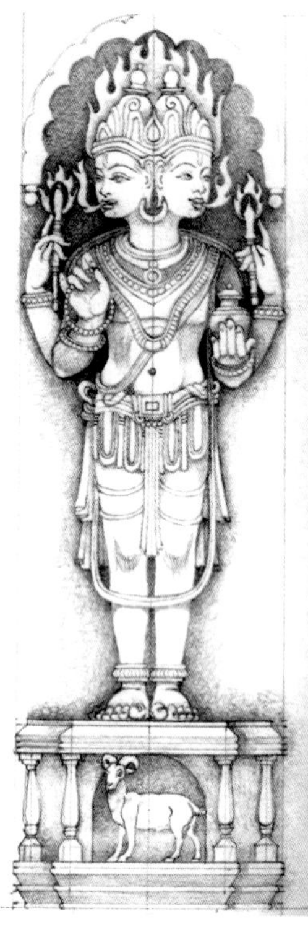

Agni=fire, the Fire *God*. **1.** A *weapon* commonly seen as an attribute of SHIVA. **2.** A vehicle for making a sacrificial offering, represented as flames rising from a bowl. **3.** One of the chief Vedic deities, a personification of the *ritual* fire, he is represented with seven tongues, each with a distinct name, used for licking up the clarified butter (ghee), used in sacrifices. He is the guardian of the south-eastern quarter. **4.** An eternal source of all energy. Fire has been represented in temple *sculptures* and *miniature paintings*. Agni, in the *form* of *warm colours* is used to convey energy, especially in TANTRIC *art*. Refer NATARAJA, *Madhukar B. Bhat, Savlaram L. Haldankar*.

Agni: *Nagesh B. Sabannavar, Drawing* (1990), *Pencil* on *Paper*.

Ahimsa=non-violence. The world views Buddhist, Hindu and *Jain* religions as the chief proponents of Ahimsa; hence, the *themes* of Hindu, *Jain & Buddhist art* are often centred around it. Refer *Hinduism, Jainism & Buddhism*.

Ahivasi, Jaganath M. (1900–1973) b. Baldeo, Mathura. Education: Porbunder, GUJ, Dip. in *painting JJSA* (1926); Studied *murals* under Govt. scholarship. Solo: Only solo at BHU 1940. Group participations: *LKA* New Delhi, *BAS*. Awards: G. Solomons Medal 1935 Mumbai, Gold Medal *LKA* New Delhi. Commissions: By *LKA* to *copy frescoes* from Badami & Sittanvasal; *Murals* Vidhan Sabha UP, Rashtrapati Bhavan, Parliament House. Appointments: HoD in *painting JJSA* until he retired in 1956, Lecturer in Dept. of *Painting* BHU & HoD until 1968. Publication: Painted for German Gita. Collections: BKB Museum Lucknow, Parliament House, *LKA* & *National Museum* New Delhi, BHU Museum Varanasi, Maharaja of Patiala, TATA Mumbai, *CSMVS* (*PWM*); International: for Queen of England, Museum of Moscow, pvt. England & Germany.

Jaganath M. Ahivasi's contribution to *modern* Indian *art* lies in the fact that he preferred going to the traditional roots of Indian *miniature painting* and using bright, flat *colours* with a *flat application* in his decorative *compositions* and *murals*, rather than the pale washed-out layers of *colours* used by the *artists* of the *Bengal School*. Some of his famous works include "The Message", "Subhadra and Arjuna", and "Departure of Meera" which was presented by the then Prime Minister of India, Pandit Jawaharlal Nehru to Chou-En-lai, the Prime Minister of China.

Ahire, Umesh (1955–2000) b. MAHA. Education: GDA *painting* & Post-Dip. *JJSA*. Solos: *Artists' Centre* Mumbai, Treeshant Art Centre Jammu (Tawi), *JJSA, JAG, SAI*. Group participations: Mumbai, Chennai, Bangalore, Kolkata, New Delhi, Jaipur, Patna, Jammu, 1st *Biennale BB*, 4th Asian Art *Biennale* Dhakka, 7th *Triennale* New Delhi. *Art* camps & workshops: Godrej Mumbai, All India Artists at Goa & Jammu, *BAS*. Awards: *Artists' Centre*, "Rajya Puraskar", MAHA State, Nasik Kala Niketan, All India Art *Exhibition* Patna, *BAS, JJSA*; Gold Medal—*JJSA*; International: *Biennale* Dhakka; Fellowship: *JJSA*. Member: *BAS*. Appointments: Workshop on Pictorial Aesthetics and Design Education Pune; Lectures in *drawing* & *painting* S.N.D.T. College Mumbai. Collections: *LKA* & *NGMA* New Delhi, Dir. of State MAHA, *NGMA* Mumbai, pvt. India and International.

Ahire believed that *art* and life were interrelated. In the early 80s his works were small-sized and playfully *abstract* in the *manner* of Paul Klee; later his *paintings* increased in *size*. Fragmented pieces of textured reality float against a flat, tinted *background*. Ahire's affinity for the downtrodden is clearly seen in his *compositions*. He worked with several *media*, including *pen* and *ink*, *mixed media* and *acrylics* in addition to *oils* and *watercolour*. He passed away in August 2000.

Ahuja, Krishan (1943–) b. India. NDA & lecturer at *College of Art* New Delhi. Solos: TAG; International: Canada. Group participations: *LKA* New Delhi, *AIFACS*, SKP; International: *Biennales* France, Intergraphics 87 Berlin, *Graphic prints* Cuba & Australia. *Art* workshops: *Printmaking* New Delhi, Chandigarh, Udaipur. Awards: For *printmaking* & photography New Delhi, All India Graphics Exhibition Chandigarh, Annual Awards *AIFACS*, SKP. Member: Group 8, an association of printmakers New Delhi, SC, *AIFACS*. Appointments: Demonstration & talks on Indian *graphics* Canada. Collections: *College of Art*, *NGMA* & *LKA* New Delhi, Directorate of Archaeology Museum Jaipur, pvt. & corporates.

Krishan Ahuja has experimented with many *mediums*, including printing, *printmaking* and photography. However, he is essentially a printmaker using *serigraphy*, *colour* viscosity printing and *collography* to render his *themes* and concepts. He simplifies organic *forms* found in *nature* using *texture* to enliven his *compositions*.

He lives and works in New Delhi.

Ahuja, S.C. (1948–) b. Kapurthala, PUJ. Education: B.FA. & M.FA. in *sculpture College of Art* New Delhi. Solos: Juneja Art Gallery Jaipur, Museum of FA. PUJ, *JAG*; International: California. Group *artists* shows: Jharokha Art Gallery New Delhi, SRAG, *AIFACS*, *JAG*, BAG, *NCAG*. Group participations: Kala Melas by *LKA* New Delhi in Bangalore, Kolkata & New Delhi & *LKA* Exhibitions Lucknow, Bangalore, Chandigarh & New Delhi, SRAG, *AIFACS*, *JAG*. *Art* camps: by SKP at *LKA* New Delhi. Awards: *College of Art* New Delhi for *sculpture*, Rajiv Gandhi Memorial Prize, *AIFACS* by Kala Mela; Senior Fellowship by Dept. of Culture HRD Ministry. Collections: *NGMA* & *LKA* New Delhi, pvt. & corporates.

S.C. Ahuja is a *sculptor*, working with *bronze* and *aluminium* to make his small-sized *figurative* works. His *imagery* is culled from rural India, depicting the simple villager travelling to the city in search of the perfect dream.

He lives and works in New Delhi.

AIFACS (New Delhi). The All India Fine Arts and Crafts Society was founded around 1925 by prominent Indian *artists* in order to decorate India House in London. Three *Ukil* brothers, Sarada, Barada and Ranada contributed towards forming the society. One of the first *exhibitions* held by AIFACS was organized to select *paintings* for the Viceregal Palace (now Rashtrapati Bhavan). The society's first All India Art *Exhibition* was sent to London, later toured various European countries and returned in 1932. AIFACS sponsored the first World Art Conference and regularly sponsors international *exhibitions*. It has annual *exhibitions* throughout India and since 1984 it has been honouring veteran *artists* over the age of 60, by awarding the President of India's Silver Plaque for the best exhibit each year. Awards given are Kala Ratna, Kala Vibhushan and Kala Shree and *artists* who have won include *Sardar Gurcharan Singh*, *Bimal DasGupta*, *Manohar Kaul*, *Anupam Sud*, *Ranvir Singh Bisht*, *Paramjeet Singh*. The society moved to its Delhi premises in 1953, housing four galleries, a theatre, a library and a conference room. In 1994 it established its Regional Centre at Panchkula, Haryana, with galleries and *artists* camps. AIFACS has been regularly publishing an *art* journal "Roop-Lekha" and a monthly bulletin "Art News" since 1928. Other publications are books, "Studio Potters of India", "Glimpses of India" 1947–97, several *portfolios* and *monographs* on *art*. Its secretary, Late S.S. Bhagat was also the President of Asia Pacific Regional Committee of International Art Associations of UNESCO.

Air Brushing A method of *painting* by using a mechanical spray gun or a sprayer to achieve a smooth flat *finish*, with none of the "personal marks" left by the *brush*. It has been used mostly by the *artists* connected with Pop and photo *realistic styles*. In India, this *style* is associated with the *artists' style* and *technique* of collection, e.g. *Ganesh Pyne*'s "Girls" in *watercolours* on *paper* 1960; "Still Life" *mixed media* on *paper* 1989. Refer *Action Painting*, *Art Deco*, *Stencil*, *Jaganath M. Ahivasi*.

Air Vents Used in the *cire perdue* or *lost wax process* of *casting metal*. They are essentially long tubes of *wax* attached to the main *sculpture* and are meant to melt away and allow air and gases to escape from the hot *metal* as it is poured into the *cast*. This process has been used by *Meera Mukherjee* and *Somnath Hore*. Refer *Bronze*.

Ajanta A series of 28 caves excavated in horseshoe formation in central MAHA, near the city of Aurangabad. The caves were excavated for the purpose of providing shelter to the Buddhist monks in the monsoon. During the *Gupta* era (the golden age of Ancient Indian Art) these caves were decorated with *wall paintings* and *sculptures* describing the Buddhist way of life. They were rendered over a long period of *time*, circa 200 BC to AD 728.

The *style* of *painting* at Ajanta, developing over a period of *time*, is dominated by graceful flowing *lines*, depicting slender-waisted, heavy-breasted women with downcast modest eyes, and wearing intricate costumes and jewellery. The *form* and *proportions* of the *figures* closely adhere to the theory of *painting* as set down in the CHITRASUTRA.

The *pigments* used were extracted from excavated mineral rock, powdered and mixed with glue to the plastered wall of the cave. The addition of vegetable fibre and perhaps cowdung and animal hair, to the *plaster* has rendered it unstable and large amounts of painted *plaster* continue to peel away from the rough cave wall, rendering the stories incomprehensible.

The earlier caves, No. 9 and 10, represent Hinayana Buddhism, in which only JATAKA stories about the BUDDHA in his previous incarnations were depicted. The later caves belong to MAHAYANA *Buddhism* where the BUDDHA himself is depicted in a variety of situations, including preaching and performing miracles.

The earliest *image* is one of the standing BUDDHA in cave No.16. The caves show similar *styles* of rendering but large contrasting vigorous *forms* like flying figures, dwarfs, musicians, female figures and BODHISATTVAS are added.

The most compelling *images* at Ajanta are BODHISATTVA Vajrapani and BODHISATTVA Padmapani in cave no.1. BODHISATTVA is called the Padmapani because of the lotus (PADMA) held in his right hand. He inclines gracefully to the right in the TRIBHANGA posture, his entire bearing being regal and modest. His complexion is enhanced by the placing of a dusky princess on his right. A common trait of the *composition* at Ajanta was the use of *hieratic scaling*, increasing the scale of the most important personage in the story.

The caves were rediscovered in 1819, prompting visits by *artists* and students from Bombay School of Arts in 1875 (now *JJSA*) and *Santiniketan*, especially *Nandalal Bose* and *Mukul Chandra Dey* for the purpose of copying the *frescoes*. The *style* was to play a major role in influencing *artists* from the *Bengal School* in the early part of the 20th century *Amrita Sher-Gil* was one of the *artists* influenced by the compositional devices at Ajanta. Refer *Bombay School*, ASANAS, *Terracotta*.

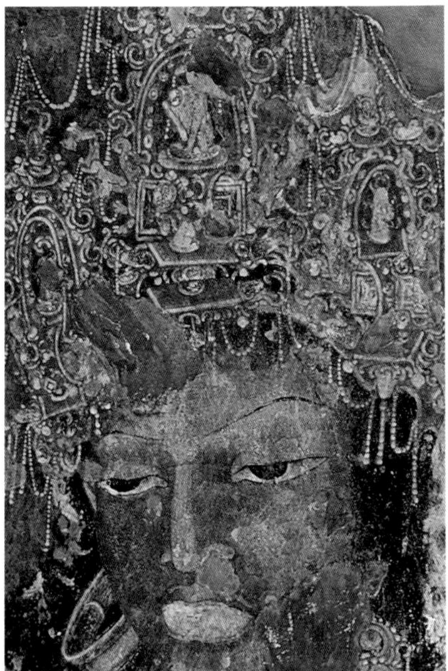

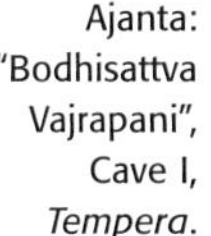

Ajanta: "Bodhisattva Vajrapani", Cave I, *Tempera*.

Akbar-Namah The biography of the Mughal Emperor Akbar (1556–1605) written by Abul Fazl in the 16th century, and it was later illustrated in *folio form* by Mughal miniaturists.

Akhilesh (1946–) b. Indore, MP. Education: NDA Indore School of Art. Over 15 solos: Mumbai, Bhopal, Kolkata, Chennai, New Delhi. Group participations: *Biennale BB*, XAL Praxis Foundation Print Exhibition, Indian Painters *GC* & Black Group Exhibition Mumbai, 100 years of Modern Art *NGMA's* collection curated by Geeta Kapoor New Delhi, *Serigraphy* Jaipur, *Abstract* Expression *SUG*; International: *Tribal art* for Festival of India Japan. *Art* camps: CMC New Delhi, International Artists Weaving Camp by MMB Chennai in Baypore Kerala, other camps in Varanasi, Bhopal, Hyderabad, Jaipur, Udaipur, Ujjain; International: Museum & *design* camps organized by British High Commission V&A. Awards: State Award 84 Gwalior, *Biennale BB*. Fellowship: Govt. of India New Delhi 1994–95. Member: Founder member "Black Group" Bhopal, General Council *LKA* New Delhi. Appointments: Established Museum of Urban *Folk* & *Tribal Art* of Malwa at Lal Baugh Palace Indore. Collections: CMC, *NGMA* & *LKA* New Delhi, *GC* Mumbai, NZCC Allahabad, *BB*.

Akhilesh's interest in textile *design* led to a series of *canvases* with an architectonic, yet free-flowing sense of textural *pattern*. His recent works contain an asymmetric element, that opens up the shallow space of his earlier *painting*. "Ek Patang Anant Mein" (A Kite in Infinity), one of the few titled works provides the tenuous link between the real world and his abstraction of it.

He lives and works in Bhopal.

Akki, Shivananda P. (1900–1980) b. Gadag, KAR. Education: *Art* Master *JJSA*. Solos & group participations: Kolkata, Shimla, New Delhi, Vijaya Kala Mandir (*Vijaya FA. Society*) Gadag, *BAS*. Awards: Maharaja of Patiala. Collections: Maharaja of Patiala, pvt. Bijapur.

His *paintings* were realistically rendered. A lover of *portraits*, *nature* and places of historical importance, his *watercolours* captured the glory of many historical monuments all over the country, and views of the *Ghats* at Khandala, MAHA. In 1924, he opened an Art School in Mumbai which, unfortunately, closed within a few years due to lack of students.

Akki, Takappa P. (1908–1994) b. Lakshmeshwar, KAR. Education: *Art* Master *JJSA*. Solos: GUJ, KAR. Group participations: Delhi, Mumbai, Bangalore. Member: Honorary Member—Mysore State Govt. Board of Art Education and Deputed to *LKA* Bangalore, Elected member of the Central *LKA* KAR CKP. Appointments: Secretary of KAR Art Society; Examiner, Controller & Adviser to Bombay Govt. in the field of *Art Education* for two decades; Chairman for State KAR *LKA* for three years; Chairman of the Art Teachers Association of the State & for eight years as President of Art School of the State; Served State *LKA* as member for 10 years; Served as an *art* teacher in Mumbai, Bassein & Navsari and settled in Gadag in 1935.

Takappa P. Akki was basically a *nature* lover and *landscape artist*, practising an impressionistic approach in *watercolours*. A major contribution was the setting up of *Vijaya Kalamandira* in Gadag, KAR to offer a degree in *art* in North KAR. It is now run by his son Ashok Akki, who is also an *artist*.

Akkitham, Narayanan (1939–) b. Kerala. Education: Dip. in *painting GCAC* Chennai; International: studied *Monumental art* and *engraving*. Solos: *SAI*, TKS, *PUAG*, *CKAG*; International: Paris, Hanover, Bonn, Frankfurt, Tokyo. Group participations: *BAAC* Kolkata, All India Print & *LKA Triennale* New Delhi, *LKA* Chennai, *AIFACS*, *Biennale BB*; International: *Biennale* in France, Bulgaria, Vienna & Germany, Modern Art Museum Saitama & Indian Art Sogo Museum Japan. Awards: Indian Govt. Scholarship *LKA* Chennai, All India Print New Delhi; International: Scholarship French Govt., Festival of Painting France. Member: *Cholamandal*, Founder member & Honorary Secretary of Artists Handicrafts Association Chennai. Collections: *NGMA* New Delhi, National Art Gallery Chennai; International: Paris, Wilhelmshaven, Glenbarra Museum Japan.

Narayanan Akkitham practises a *geometric abstraction* that is essentially Indian in *nature*. It could be the influence of the new *Tantricism* of *K.C.S. Paniker* who was his master. He admits that each of the elements has a *symbolic* undertone, mostly connected with man's relationship with *time* and *space*. The *treatment* of the *composition* however, is not hard-edged and minimalistic but *painterly* and expressionist.

Narayanan Akkitham lives in Paris.

Aku (1953–) b. Varanasi, UP. Education: B.FA. & M.FA. BHU, Higher studies at *VBU*. Solos: *AFA* Kolkata, *JAG*. Group participations: Litho print *AFA* & Open air Sculpture *BAAC* Kolkata, *LKA* New Delhi & Kolkata, *Biennale BB*, *GAC*, *GMAG*; International: *Biennales* Bangladesh & Seychelles. *Art* camp: BHU. Awards: 6th *Biennale BB*. Fellowship: HRD in the field of *Visual Art*. Member: ASSO (Art Mission India) Kolkata. Appointments: Supervisor in *sculpture* Dept. Rashtriya *LKA* Kolkata. Collections: *BAAC* Kolkata, *NGMA* New Delhi, *GMAG*, *Roopankar*.

Aku started working with *mixed media assemblages*, using *metal* chiefly, in conjunction with *wood* and *ready-made* objects. Later, he was introduced to the creative possibilities of working with *leather*. After a visit to the *leather* factories in Kolkata, he started incorporating it into his wooden boxes and *metal creations*. He has begun exploiting the inherent qualities of the material,

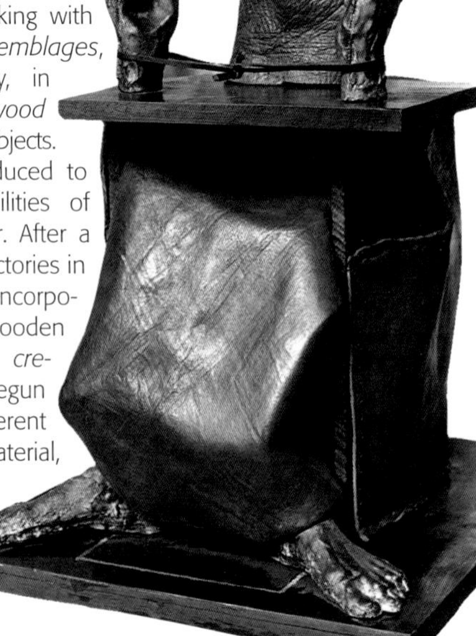

Aku: "M-3", *Leather, Wood, Alum*, 1997, 75x67x55 cm.

stitching it, folding and draping it to create surreal *sculptures* based on organic *forms* and shapes.

He lives in Kolkata.

Albumen The *white* of an egg, is a solution used as a binding *medium* for *pigments* in *tempera painting* and also for *gold* dust in gilding. In *tempera painting*, the egg-white is diluted with water and mixed with colour, resulting in a thin, insoluble *film*. *Artists* prefered to draw and *paint* in *egg-tempera* on cloth pasted on hardboard or ply board either coated or uncoated. The *egg-tempera technique* was extensively used in *miniature painting*, *frescoes* and *painting* on silk depicting mythology and literary subjects. Refer *Bengal School, Wash (Technique), Egg-Tempera, Egg-oil emulsion, Media, Mixed Media, Oil, Transparent, Paresh C. Hazra, Ved Pal Sharma, Sarada Chandra Ukil, Vidya Bhushan, Subhogendra Tagore, Nathu Lal Verma.*

All'antica Meaning "after the antique", it implies an *art* object, *painting* or *sculpture* which is based on the *classical model*. It is also a form of teaching which became common in *art* schools in India, e.g., *Raja Ravi Varma* and *Ganpatrao K. Mhatre* who followed the *neo-classical style*. Refer *Rameshwar Singh*.

Alla prima Italian phrase for completing a *painting* in a single session with no preparatory under *drawing*, glazes or later retouching.

The works of *Pralhad A. Dhond* in *watercolour landscape* and Pratima Sheth's *oil* and *watercolour*, semi abstract *landscapes* and *compositions* fall in this category.

Allegory A story in which the parallel meaning is more important than the literal one. An allegorical *painting* would thus be interpreted mainly through symbols. Though this *style* was more popular in the West especially during the Medieval or *Renaissance* periods, several *modern* Indian *artists* have displayed a fondness for it. Refer *Symbolic, Symbolic Art, Bhupen Khakhar.*

All-over A *term* specifically used to remark on the non-use of the traditional *values* of *balance*, *harmony* and *composition* in *modern*, specifically *abstract* works, which have no central focus or dominant area of interest. Indian *artists* who practised the all-over *technique* are *Vasudeo Santu Gaitonde, Sudhangsu Bandhyopadhyay, K.M. Adimoolam, Ambadas, Chittrovanu Mazumdar*. Refer *Abstract, Abstract Art.*

Alloy A homogeneous mixture of two or more *metals* to create a compound with physical properties that differ from those of the "parent" *metals*, e.g., the material for *casting* bells was called bell-*metal*. It is an alloy produced by fusing *copper* and tin in the *proportion* of 4:1. Refer *Pilloo Pochkanawalla, Mrinalini Mukherjee.*

Almelkar, Abdul Rahim Appabhai (1920–1982) b. Ahmedabad, GUJ. Education: *NKM* & received his GDA in *drawing & painting* in 1948 & later became principal. Over 44 solos: India & the Far Eastern countries, Sri Lanka, Malaysia, Singapore, Bali, Thailand. Awards: National *LKA exhibitions* & All India *Exhibitions* in Kolkata, New Delhi, Hyderabad, Chennai, Amritsar, Mysore, Ahmedabad winning 20 Gold & 24 Silver Medals, including *BAS*. Collections: India including *NGMA* & *LKA* New Delhi; International: USA, Japan, Germany, Switzerland, Russia.

Abdul Rahim Appabhai Almelkar began his career as a landscapist in the Impressionist *manner*. In this, he was inspired by the works of W. Langhammer and *Narayan S. Bendre*. A detailed study of *miniature paintings* led to him evolving a personal *style* based on an amalgamation of the *colour*, *theme* and *pictorial* quality of Indian and Persian miniatures from the mid-50s. His *style* can be described as folk, with its decorative *linearity* and grey *colour* schemes with emphasis on the eyes and facial features of his subjects. His *themes* ranged from NAYAKAS and NAYIKAS to tribal and adivasi life. There is a use of foliage and other decorative *details* of pots, huts and tribal paraphernalia in almost all the works. His earlier works were in *opaque watercolours* and *oils*; after 1955 he used cardboard as a base for his *watercolours*, with bits of cloth, shells and outlining of the *figures* with *India ink*.

Altaf (Mohammedi) (1942–) b. Vadodara. Education: various *art* schools England. Solos: *JAG*, *PG*, TAG, *TG*, Retrospective *JAG* 1988, *SG* Mumbai 2002; Jointly with *Navjot Altaf*, *SG* Chennai & Bangalore, *JAG*, *NCAG*, TKS; International: Kunst Galaria Dedeke Germany. Group participations: *SG* Art Plaza, 50 years of Indian Art *NGMA* & *JAG* 50 years of Indian Art Mumbai, CMC Gallery & Glenbarra Art Museum Collection

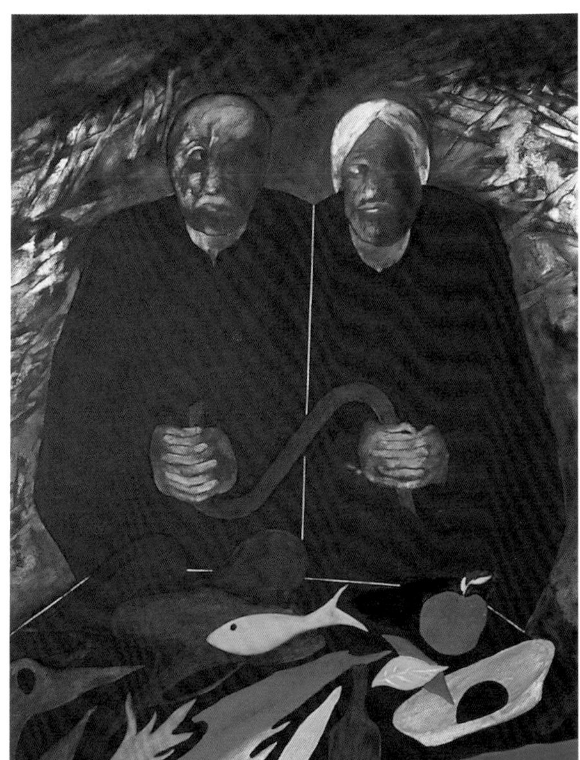

Altaf: "Untitled", *Oil* on *Canvas*,1997, 152x122 cm.

in *NGMA* New Delhi, *BAAC* Kolkata, *Biennale BB*, *JAG*, *VAG*, Harmony *NCAG*; International: "Artists from India and Pakistan" at Martini Gallery Hong Kong. Participated: In Film Divisions Documentary "The Young Canvas". *Art* workshops: Organized *painting* workshops Goa. *Auctions*: Heart Mumbai. Commissions: *Mural* for a high school in Mumbai (jointly with *Navjot Altaf* & other *artists*). Collections: *SG* Mumbai, Husain Ki Sarai New Delhi, *BAAC* Kolkata, RPG, *JAG*.

Altaf's works comprise of the gestural *figurative paintings* of the late 60s to the simplified shapes and *forms* in the 90s. A strong Marxist sense of oppression has always pervaded his *compositions*, aptly coloured in sombre *shades* of *black*, brown and beige. Sharp accents of bright vermilion and cobalt provide the requisite point of interest in his recent jigsaw shaped fragments of the human body. There is an affinity to the *imagery* of F. Bacon. The phallic "necktie" is a recurring *motif* in the works of the 90s, providing a break of *space* with its *colour* and *form*.

He and his wife, *Navjot Altaf*, also an *artist*, live in Mumbai.

Altaf, Navjot (1949–) b. Meerut, UP. Education: Dip. in *FA*. & *applied art JJSA*, *Graphics GAC*. Solos: *Gallery 7* Mumbai, *JAG*, *PG*; Jointly with *Altaf SG* Chennai & Bangalore, *JAG*, *NCAG*, *PG*, *TG*, TKS; International: Germany. Group participations: *Art Heritage* New Delhi, *Arts Acre* & *BAAC* Kolkata, *GC* Mumbai, *VAG*, *LTG*, *JAG*, *PG*, *CYAG*, *Tao Art Gallery*, Harmony–*NCAG*, "Years of India's Independence"–*NGMA* Mumbai, *JAG* & *CYAG*, "Ways of Resisting 1992–2002" curated by *Vivan Sundaram*–Safdar Hashmi Memorial Trust New Delhi, RB New Delhi, *Biennale* & *Triennale BB*; International: *Biennale* UK, Sao Paulo, *Graphic Biennale* England, Japan, Poland, Berlin & USA, Fukuoka Asian Art *Triennale* Japan, RPG Collection of Indian Contemporary Art–Germany. *Art* workshops: *Graphics* Urja Art Gallery Vadodara, *Paintings* workshop CMC Kolkata, Arts Trust Mumbai, *JJSA*, GAG. *Auctions*: Cry Charity Dubai, Heart, Osian's, Christie's, Sotheby's & Timeless Art Mumbai. Awards: *BAS*, *AIFACS*. Commissions: *mural* jointly with *Altaf* & other *artists*. Publications: Designed book, "Nasreen in Retrospect" along with *Bharati Kapadia*.

Navjot Altaf began *painting* in *oils* on *canvas* and later experimented with *acrylics* and *printmaking*. Since the 90s her focus has been on the three-dimensional *medium* of *installation*. From the 1994 environment with *"found objects"*, she has moved on to figuration and adding *photographs*, audio and video to her *installations*. Navjot has constantly challenged traditional notions of normal communication presenting her own *narrative* of cultural displacement. Fighting social injustice, promoting the cause of feminism and inspired by socialistic ideologies, her explorative and experimental works with material and *medium* attempt to integrate trajectories of memory, history and *culture*. She makes effective use of materials such as *iron*, *steel*, plastic, cotton, Xerox *paper*, map based works and *soft-sculpture*. Due to her emphasis on integration of *form*, her *art* works seem to communicate with each other.

She lives and works in Mumbai.

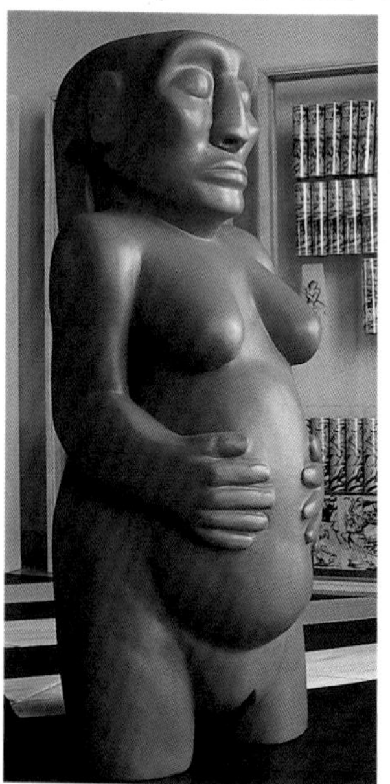

Altaf, Navjot:
"Across the Crossing",
Painted *Wood*, 110x43x45 cm.

Altarpiece A work of *art* with a religious *theme*, originally made to be placed on, above or behind the altar in a church or chapel. It may be either sculpted, carved, or often painted. Medieval altarpieces were often composed in several panels, hinged together and depicting various scenes from the Old and New Testaments. They are known as *diptychs*, *triptych* or polyptychs depending on the number of panels. Some Indian churches were built in the Mannerist and *Baroque style* introduced by the Portuguese in Goa. The *Baroque style's* decorative impulse is thus visible in altarpieces one finds in these areas. Refer *Christian Art*.

Alto-Relievo (Italian)=*high relief*. Refer *Relief*.

Alum 1. *Painters* from the Mughal school dipped *paper* in a solution of alum (a double sulphate of potassium and *aluminium*), before drying and burnishing it with an agate to make the surface smooth. This is also used in *leather* tanning. Refer *Miniature Painting*. **2.** A solution of alum with nitric *acid* is used to clean *zinc aluminium plates* in the lithographic process.

Aluminium A lightweight silvery-white *metal*. It can be *cast*, or welded and has a high *tensile strength*. Seldom corrodes, since a protective oxide *forms* on its surface, thus making it ideal for both indoor and outdoor *sculpture*. Today lightweight *frames* are also being made in aluminium. Recent trend is painted or powder coating on aluminium with the required *colours*. Different *alloys* of aluminium such as magnalium (90% aluminium–10% magnesium) and aluminium *bronze* (90% *copper*–10% aluminium) are also being used today. *Sculptor Sanko Chaudhuri* has used *aluminium* sheet for his *sculpture*. Refer *Janak J. Narzary*.

Amateur Artists A *Sunday painter*, one for whom *art* is primarily a hobby–a creative activity; may not exhibit professionally. Amateur artists may have had academic training.

Ambadas (1922–) (Ambadas Khobargade) b. Akola, MAHA. Education: Dip. in *FA*. *JJSA*. Solos: Indore, Bhopal, *Art Heritage* New Delhi, *GC* Mumbai, *Dhoomimal*, *PUAG*, *VAG*; International: Copenhagen Zurich, Gallery Surya Germany, Gallery Alana, Gallery LMN & Kunstner for Bundet Oslo, State University of Art California, State University Stanislaus. Group participations: *LKA* New Delhi, *GC* Mumbai, *GE*, *Roopankar*; International: Japan, Teheran, London, *Biennale*–Japan, Brazil

& Menton, Contemporary Indian Art Ben & Abbey Foundation USA. *Auctions*: Heart Mumbai & New Delhi, Osian's Mumbai. Awards: National *LKA* Award, *Biennale* Bhopal; International: Stipened in Norway 1994, 1996. Member: *Group 1890*, Jury Member *Biennale* Bhopal. Collections: *NGMA* & *LKA* New Delhi, *Chandigarh Museum*, *BAAC* Kolkata, TIFR; International: Ben & Abbey Grey Foundation USA & pvt.

Even though he has been living in Norway, a country quite different in character to his own, Ambadas' work has always had a close affinity to Indian *nature* and philosophy. At first his work appears influenced by the *Abstract Expressionism* of American *painters* like J. Pollock or even gestural like R. Motherwell's, but soon one realizes the stylistic differences, so acute that Ambadas seems to echo the frenzied agony of Van Gogh's strokes. Ambadas speaks of *nature*, moving innately and rising towards its optimal expression–this, he says, remains his continual source of inspiration. Together with his late *artist* friend *J. Swaminathan*, he was a founder member of *Group 1890*.

He lives in Oslo, Norway.

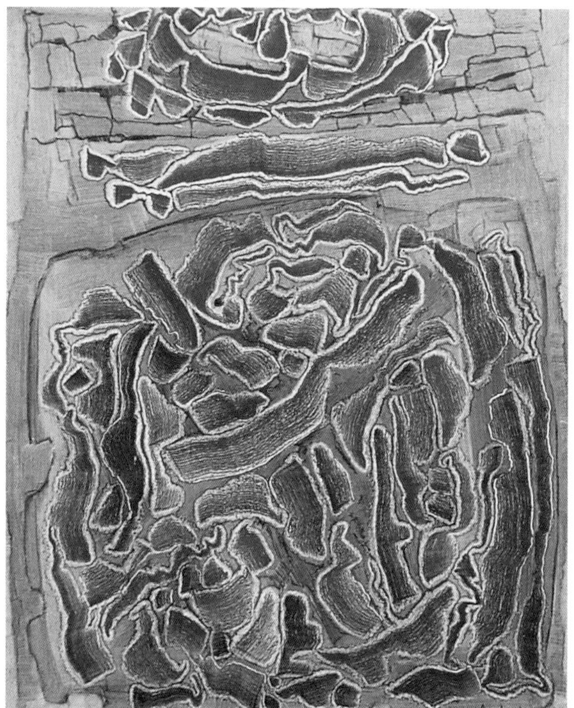

Ambadas: "Abstract Movement", *Oil* on *Canvas*, 81x65 cm.

Ambalal, Amit (1943–) b. Ahmedabad, GUJ. Education: under *Chhaganlal R. Jadav*. Solos: *GC* Mumbai, *Amdavad ni Gufa & Herwitz Gallery*, Sangath, Sanskar Kendra Gallery, CAG Ahmedabad, *AFA* Kolkata, *JAG*, *GE*, TKS, HCVA. Group participations: 6th *Triennale* & Artists Alert New Delhi, Harmony Show & Art for Cry Mumbai, Marvel Art Gallery Ahmedabad, *Painting Biennales BB*, *GE*; International: Utsava–Festival of India Perth Australia, Schoo's Gallery Amsterdam. Member: Founder member secretary of "Contemporary Painters Ahmedabad". Publications: "Krishna as Shrinathji: Rajasthani Paintings from Nathdvara". Collections: *NGMA* & *LKA* New Delhi, GUJ *LKA* Ahmedabad; International: British Museum & V&A UK.

Amit Ambalal works with *watercolour* and *pastels*, using these materials for their spontaneity and freshness. His *imagery* is both playful and naive, being inspired in part from the Nathdwara *images* of KRISHNA. Much of the sophistication is derived from his use of *textures*, *patterns* and certain *key motifs*, like the tiger skin and the cow.

He lives and works in Ahmedabad.

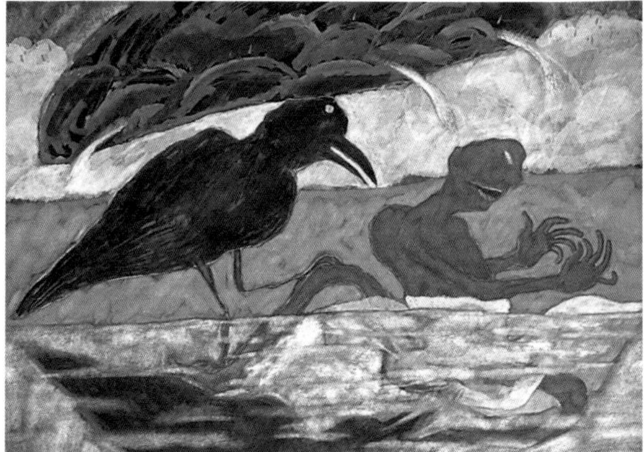

Ambalal, Amit: "You carry the burden I will play the flute–I", *Watercolours*, 1994, 55x75 cm.

Amberkar, Vasant R. (1907–1988) b. Mumbai, MAHA. Education: Studied *painting* under the guidance of *Savlaram L. Haldankar*, completed a 16-lesson course in *art* through correspondence from the Press Art School in London. Had a studio. Solos: *JAG*. Group participations: *BAS*, *ASI*, & others in Chennai & Kolkata. Awards: for his *paintings*, known more for his work in the field of *art education*. Fellowship: *LKA* Felicitation at *CSMVS* (*PWM*). Member & appointments: several such committees being instrumental in forming the *art education* courses at *MSU*, in forming the *LKA* at the National level, First Joint Secretary (Hon.) along with Dr. Mulk Raj Anand, President of the *ASI* until 1954, Member of the Senate & Visiting Prof. at the *MSU*, Chairman of the MAHA State Art Education Advisory Board, Member of Art Review Committee & The University Board Mumbai & Thiruvananthapuram.

Vasant R. Amberkar's *style* ranges from the *academic* to the *abstract*, with his early impressionist *landscapes* giving way to *gestural* and *calligraphic paintings* similar to R. Motherwell and *Shankar Palsikar*.

Amdavad ni Gufa & Herwitz Gallery (Ahmedabad, GUJ). Formally named as the Husain-Doshi Gufa, the Amdavad ni Gufa and Herwitz Gallery is an interactive project between *artist Maqbool Fida Husain* and architect B.V. Doshi. The building, designed by Doshi, the architect and painted by *Maqbool Fida Husain*, serves as a promotional centre for the *arts*, by inculcating an *art* and architectural awareness among people. It also serves as a platform, for the display of the works of prominent *artists* and architects. The Gufa has a collection of rare books and videos on *art*, *architecture* and other subjects.

Amin, Narendra (1934–) b. GUJ. Education: M.FA. in *painting MSU*. Solos: Albert Museum Jaipur; International: Edinburgh College of Arts Gallery UK. Group participations: GUJ *LKA*, Baroda Group of *Artists* Vadodara, Citi Utsav *Exhibition* Mumbai, *Triennale LKA* & All India Art *Exhibition* New Delhi, Ujjain, Ahmedabad, Jaipur, Chandigarh & Hyderabad; International: Contemporary Indian Art Australia. *Art* camps: Jaisalmer, Udagamangalam, Bhubaneshwar, New Delhi. Awards: National Award, RAJ State *LKA*. Senior Fellowship: *MSU* by HRD Ministry. Member: RAJ University 1970–80, *LKA*–RAJ, GUJ, Lucknow & Central; Organized workshops, camps & was in Judging committee of *Art Exhibitions* in GUJ State, RAJ & National New Delhi. Appointments: Slide shows & *Art* talks–*RSA* Jaipur, Udaipur University, *Art* purchase committee Jaipur; Worked as an Examiner, Paper-setter; Lecturer for 16 years College of Education Govt. of RAJ Jaipur, Principal *RSA* & Kala Kendra CFA Vallabh Vidyanagar GUJ; International: Slide shows & *Art* talks–Tokyo University, Nihon University, School of FA. Glasgow & Duncan of Jordastone, College of Arts Dundee UK. Publications: *Monograph* on *P.N. Choyal*. Collections: *LKA* in New Delhi, Jaipur, Chennai, Orissa, Gandhinagar GUJ, J&K & Lucknow.

Narendra Amin has experimented with *still life*, *landscapes*, *pastoral* scenes and socially relevant *themes* before moving on to abstraction in 2001. Running through all these various inspirations is a love of simplification and stylized distortion. His works were never *narrative*, it was always predominantly emotional. His *technique* is based on the spontaneous *handling* of *pigments* and *pallette knife*.

He lives and works in Vadodara, GUJ.

Anaglyph Refer *Relief*.

Analogous Colours *Colours* that lie next to each other on the *colour wheel*. Yellow, yellow-green and green would form an analogous *harmony*. Refer *Local Colours*, *Impressionism*, *Pointillism*, *Narayan S. Bendre*, *Ganesh Haloi*. Illustration–*Colour Wheels*.

Ananta Shayana Ananta=endless, Shayana=sleeping. The *image* of VISHNU reclining on Ananta in the cosmic sleep state is known as Ananta Shayana. The group can also be termed the Sheshasayi VISHNU, literally VISHNU on Shesha (snake). A beautiful example of this is the panel on the ruined DASAVATARA temple at Deogarh (Jhansi District), MP.

Anatomy Literally, the science of studying the body, especially the human body. Anatomy lessons became especially popular during the *Renaissance*, though there is no doubt of the *classical* Greek interest in studying the flexions of the body. However, the Greeks developed a composite *ideal* type of anatomy, whereas the *Renaissance artists* were more true to *nature*. There are many accounts of these *artists* resorting to robbing graves to indulge in their quest for studying anatomy. In India, anatomy lessons in *art* were introduced by the British in their *art* school, with the introduction of *drawing* from *antique plaster reproductions* of *classical* Greek *sculpture*. Today, in India also, *drawing* from the *nude* (live *model*) is one of the main subjects in the curriculum of *art* schools. Refer *Art Education*, *Figure Painting*, *Greek Art*, *Nude*, *Realistic*, *Renaissance*, *Samhita Basu*, *Savlaram L. Haldankar*, *Debi Prasad RoyChowdhury*, *K.M. Shenoy*, *Yagneshwar Kalyanji Shukla*, *Anupam Sud*, *Abanindranath Tagore*, *Raja Ravi Varma*.

Andani, V.G. (1947–) b. Keerangai, KAR. Education: GDA in *painting* Ideal FA Institute (*IFAS*). Experimented with *fresco Banasthali Vidyapith* RAJ. Solos: Shahbad, Gulberga, KB Hyderabad, TAG, TKS, *JAG*, *VEAG*, *CKP*. Group participations: *IFAS*, *LKA* Rashtriya Kala-Mela New Delhi KAR *LKA* Chennai, Bangalore, Jaipur, Mumbai, Chandigarh, Kanpur & Lucknow, All India Graphic Exhibition Gulberga, 50 years of Indian Independence *BAAC* Kolkata, *RG*, *CKP*; Group shows: "Art Alive" New Delhi, *JAG*, *CKP* & *RG*. *Art* camps & workshops: *IFAS*, KAR *LKA* in Dharwar, Hampi & *CKP*, All India camp *CKP*, *AIFACS*. Awards: *LKA* New Delhi & Bangalore, HAS. Fellowship: Junior Fellowship by HRD Ministry. Member: KAR *LKA* Bangalore and New Delhi, *INTACH*; Founder & Principal of the CVA Gulbarga. Appointments: Served as Convener & Dir. at camps organized by Central & State *LKA* & Zonal Art Centres, University Exhibition & Convenor International Painter's & Sculptor's symposium Gulbarga. Collections: *LKA*–AP, Chennai, Bhuvaneshwar, Bangalore, *Folklore Museum* Mysore, Govt. Museum KAR, *CKP* & pvt., national & international.

V.G. Andani has moved from an earlier *Realism* to the use of marked definite *lines* with soft *colour washes*, and a *figurative* abstraction in his recent works. However, *figure* relationships continue to interest him.

At present he lives and works in Gulbarga.

Anjali=offering. **1.** Bringing the two palms together to make a bowl, with the palm facing upwards and the fingers pointing down as if to make an offering. It is a gesture of reverence made to *God*. It is also one of the MUDRAS to be used in the beginning of a dance performance. **2.** Anjali Karman=Namaste. Bringing the palms together in the *manner* of the Indian greeting Namaste. Refer NAMASKARA.

Annealing The blacksmiths' process used while working with *metal*, especially *repousse* work. The hard and brittle *metal* is fired to red heat, then rapidly plunged into water. This process makes the *metal* malleable and easier to work on. Refer *Tempering*, *Embossing*, *Sculpture*, *Dhanraj Bhagat*, *Raghav Kaneria*, *Chandrakant N. Mhatre*, *Bishamber Khanna*, *Leela Mukherjee*, *Shankar Nandagopal*, *Pilton Kothawalla*.

Anti-Art *Term* first used by Dadaist and Futurist *artists*, while describing their position on *art*. One of the first anti-art works was the exhibition of a *ready-made* urinal under the *title* "Fountain" by a man already known as an *artist*, Marcel Duchamp. *Dadaism* became one of the first anti-art movements.

In India, *Rabindranath Tagore's* non-figurative experiments with scribbling and *Gaganendranath Tagore's* geometric splintering of *forms* and cubist stylizations come close to it. Refer Illustration–*Abstraction Geometric*.

Anti-Cerne An *outline* created by leaving the *canvas* bare, between two areas of *colour*. A favourite device of the French fauve *painters* leading to the *composition* appearing sketchy and unfinished.

Practised, to a certain extent, by Indian *artists* such as *Tyeb Mehta*, *Satish Gujral*, *Ram Kumar*, who depicted social violence & terror through the *technique* of splitting the *painting* into two *colour* area and yet maintaining equilibrium.

Antique 1. A *term* used to refer to *Greek* and *Roman art*, specifically *sculpture*. **2.** Today, also used in the *applied arts* to denote objects, mostly furniture, *silver*, *stone* work, *ceramics*, more than a century old. In India the same 100 year rule applies to legally classify objects as antique. Refer *Anatomy*, *Art Education*, *National Museum*, BRAHMA, ASANAS.

Appasamy, Jaya (1918–1984) b. Chennai. Education: Dip. in *FA*. *KB VBU*, Dip. College of FA. Beijing China, M.A. Oberlin College Ohio. Solos: 30 National & International *Exhibitions*. Group participations: National *Exhibitions*. Awards: *AIFACS*. Fellowship: Indian Institute of Advanced Study Shimla and Research on *Thanjavur Paintings*. Member: SC. Appointments: Lecturer at *College of Art*, *National Museum*, MMB & University Art Dept. New Delhi; *Critic* The Hindustan Times & Editor *LKA* New Delhi. Publications: *LKA* New Delhi—*Contemporary Monographs*, catalogues & newsletters; other publications include, "Abanindranath Tagore & the Art of his Times", "An Introduction to Modern Indian Sculpture", "Thanjavur Painting of the Maratha Period", "Indian Paintings on Glass" (*Glass Painting*); Articles in various publications, including, "Visva-Bharati" quarterly, "Kalashetra", "Indian Horizons", "Roopa-Lekha", Fulbright Newsletter. Collecter: *antiques* & *folk art* now housed in "Rasaja Foundation's Manjusha Museum" New Delhi. Collections: *NGMA*, *LKA* & Parliament House New Delhi, *AFA* Kolkata, Madras Art Gallery Chennai, PUJ University Museum Chandigarh.

Jaya Appasamy was well known as an *art critic* and writer, documenting the early years of *modern* Indian *Art* through her many books and articles. She was also a *painter*, having worked in *oils*, *watercolour* and *ink*. Admiring the Chinese *style* of *wash painting*, she mastered it during her sojourn in Beijing. Her *oeuvre* is marked by a fondness for creative *landscapes*. They are heavily stylized, with an inherent stillness and serenity, akin to Chinese *painting*. Refer *Rasaja Foundation*.

Apparao Galleries Formerly called "The Gallery", was founded by Sharan Apparao in 1984 in Chennai (Madras) to promote Contemporary Indian *Art*, Apparao Galleries stocks a comprehensive range of *artists* in Chennai and has had the distinction of having *exhibitions* of some of the renowned Indian *artists*, such as *Laxma Goud*, *Sakti Burman*, *Anjolie Ela Menon*, *Sayed Haider Raza*, *Jehangir Sabawala* in cities across the world. Apparao has its representatives in New Delhi and Mumbai; International Hong Kong, Singapore, New York, London, and San Francisco.

It appeals to the *aesthetic* needs of the Indian Diaspora and provides a window to the exciting trends that are emerging from South Asia, to promote Indian *art* overseas.

Applied Art Also known as *craft*, the *term* is used to describe functional or *decorative art* as opposed to *fine arts*, but with an *aesthetic* appeal. Earlier the *term* was limited to furniture, *metal* work, textiles, book-binding etc.; it now includes certain types of *commercial/graphic art*, i.e. photography, advertising etc. It evolved from *fine arts* with the advent of the Machine Age. Broadly speaking in India circa 1850, is the turning point, prior to which there was no distinction between *fine arts* and applied art. Refer *Design*, *JJIAA* & *LSRSA* Mumbai, *AFA*, *GCAG* & *RBU* Kolkata, *College of Art* & *SUSA* New Delhi, *CFA* Thiruvananthapuram, *FFA* (*MSU*) Vadodara, *GCAC* Chennai.

Apsara Beautiful nymph, born of the ocean according to Indian *mythology*. They are graceful dancers and are specifically sent by the *gods* to test the morality of saintly men. A good example is Menaka, who seduced Viswamitra and gave birth to Shakuntala. Other examples, Urvashi and Rambha were the chief dancers in the court of INDRA, the ruler of heaven. Apsaras are also the wives of GANDHARVAS, another mythical species. Refer *Demons*.

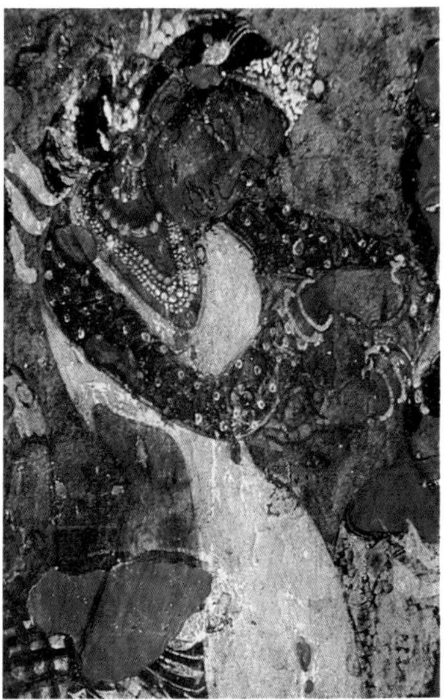

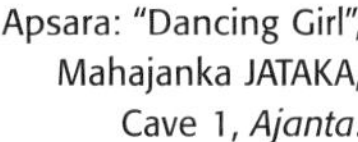

Apsara: "Dancing Girl", Mahajanka JATAKA, Cave 1, *Ajanta*.

Apte, Dattatrey D. (1953–) Education: Dip. in *drawing* & *painting* Pune Govt. of MAHA 1974; B.A. Hons.: *Art* Master Govt., of MAHA; Post-Dip. in *Printmaking MSU* Vadodara. Solos: *Art* Heritage New Delhi, *CYAG*, *JAG*, *GE*, *SAI*. Group shows: *CYAG*. Group participations: MAHA State *Exhibition*, GUJ State *LKA*, Village Gallery, Gallery Aurobindo & *Triennale* New Delhi, "Indian Printmakers' Guild". Established and exhibited in New Delhi Bangalore, Kathmandu, Kolkata; Mini Prints show and "Beyond The Surface" *Exhibition* of *paper* and works on *paper-pulp casting GE*, *Biennale* *BB*, Baradari *GAC*, *JAG*, *AIFACS*, others in Chandigarh and Bangalore; International: *Biennale*—former Yugoslavia, Netherlands & Bangladesh; *Triennale*—Norwegian, Poland; Festival of India USA, Contemporary Indian Artists in Dubai, Peru; others in Hungary, Canada, Germany, Seoul and Norway. *Art* camps & workshops: Graphics—Vadodara, *Viscosity Printmaking* by *Krishna N. Reddy GAC*, *wood cut* workshop *GE*. Awards: Govt. of MAHA, *CKP*, *AIFACS*; International: Charles Wallace India Trust Award to work under Prof. Jack Pery at Glasgow School of Art Scotland UK. Senior Fellowship: HRD; Honorary mention *Biennale BB*. Collections: *Art Heritage, NGMA* & *CFA* New Delhi, *FFA*; International: Library of Congress USA.

Apte has experimented with several *media* in *printmaking*, including *wood* blocks, plywood and *zinc plate*. In the *FFA*, where he specialized in *printmaking*, he created a series on automobiles, working in *lithography* as well as *etching* and *engraving*. His silk screen series were based on the display windows of shops in Delhi. Later, with the birth of his son, his *imagery* underwent a radical change. Now it is the beauty of *nature* as seen through the wondering eyes of a child that inspires him. Since the later 90s Apte has made *paper-pulp casts* using *wax* sheets, *found objects*, liquid latex (milky fluid of rubber tree) and coloured *handmade paper*. These works are highly textural, collaging fragments of man-made environment into an *aesthetic* ensemble. Refer *Colour, Creation, Paper-Pulp Casting, Screen Printing, Silk Screen Printing*.

Aquarelle A *painting* executed in *transparent watercolours*. Also a *term* used for *watercolour* sticks and pans. The *"wash" technique* created by *Abanindranath Tagore* and his encounter with Japanese *paintings* brought aquarelle into Indian *paintings*.

Aquatint A *term* used in *printmaking*. An aquatint is a *print* made through a specialized *technique*, involving a *metal plate* coated with a fine layer of powdered resin, that is heat bonded. Later, stop out *varnish* is applied after which it is placed in *acid* for *biting in* the *image*. *Patterns* and *images* are created by stopping out certain areas of the *plate* with *acid*-resistant *varnish* or *ground*, before reimmersion in the *acid bath*. The resin and *varnish* are later washed off with certain chemicals e.g., benzene. The *plate* is then inked for printing.

W. Daniells, British printmaker of the 18th century was the earliest practitioner in India. He trained the local *artists* in this *technique*. In the *modern* period, several Indian *artists* have used the *painterly* quality of the aquatint, to their advantage. They include *Jyoti Bhatt, Anupam Sud* and *Rini Dhumal*. Refer *Acid Bath, Sugar Lift, Tone, Vasudeo Adurkar, Lalitha Lajmi, Laxma Goud*.

Ara, Krishnaji Howlaji (1914–1985) b. Bolarum, Hyderabad AP. Education: Studied *art* informally with Prof. W. Langhammer. Solos: Hyderabad, Bombay Art Society Salon,(*Artists' Centre*) Roop Gallery for defence fund Surat & Rander, *PWM, JAG*, TAG; International: several national & international shows. Group participations: *LKA* New Delhi, *PAG* Mumbai, Marvel Art Gallery Ahmedabad, *BAS, PWM, NCAG* & others in Kolkata, Vadodara, Jamshedpur, Hyderabad; International: London, Paris, Tokyo, Milan, New York, Moscow, Sofia Galarie, Sturchler Basle. *Auctions*: Christie's, Bonhams, Sothebys and Bowrings; Heart New Delhi, Osian's Mumbai. Awards: Simla FA. Society, *BAS* annual prize, Governor's prize MAHA, *AFA* Kolkata, Sir Henry Knight Prize & UNESCO International *Exhibition* prize. Fellowship: *LKA* AP. Member: General Council *LKA* New Delhi, Founder member Bombay Group & *Artists' Centre* Mumbai, *ASI, PAG*. Appointments: Lent a helping hand to young struggling *artists* in the country. Collections: Bangalore, Jehangir Nicholoson's Collection (*JNAG*), *NGMA* New Delhi, Tata & Govt. of Mumbai, Thiruvananthapuram Museum, *FFA* (*MSU*), AP Museum, *CSMVS* (*PWM*), *JAG*; International: Yale University USA, UNESCO Museum Paris.

Krishnaji Howlaji Ara, one of the most influential *post-Independence artists* in India, had no formal education in *art*. It was during the course of earning a living—first as a domestic help, then as a car cleaner, (he was also sent to jail for participating in the freedom struggle) that Ara began to paint. Unlike *painters* with an academic background, Krishnaji Howlaji Ara's *art* was truly intuitive. He painted only those objects familiar to him. Influenced by Prof. W. Langhammer, C. Gierrard and R. von Leyden, his subject was *still life*, mainly pots and pans; flowers and fruits; jars and vases. Later when he became interested in the female *form*, he began *painting* female *nudes*, with dark skin *tones* and caressing touches similar to A. Renoir or P. Rubens. His favourite flowers and *still life* still lingered in the *form* of *background* in these *nude compositions*.

For sometime he attempted *painting* in constructivist *style*, making *collages* on the *canvas* with strings, silks, wires and slashing it with bold strokes of the *palette knife*. However in the end, he maintained that he was not in favour of *abstract art* because he was deeply in love with

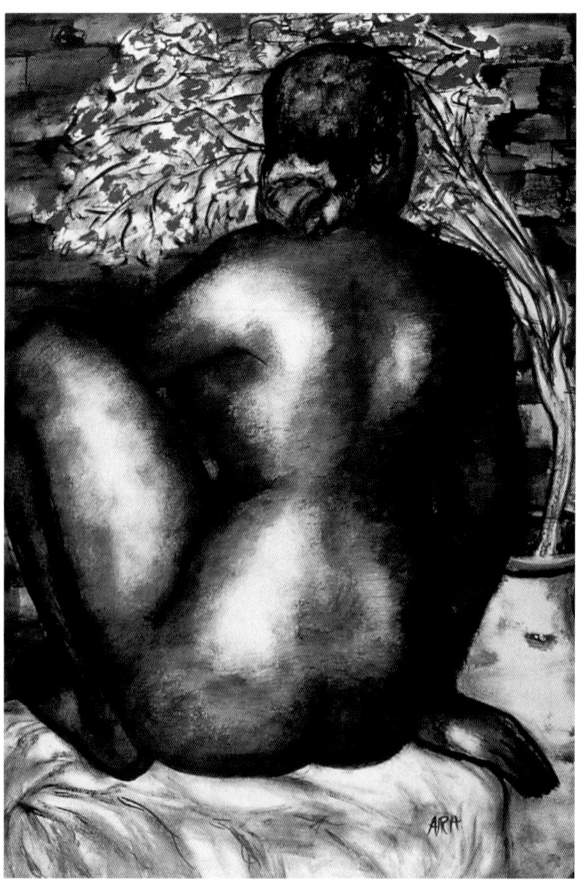

Ara, Krishnaji Howlaji: "Woman & Flowers", *Oil* on *Paper*, 1963, 76.5x56 cm.

the sensuous world of appearances in which he saw the manifestations of divinity. Refer *PAG*.

Arabesque Literally meaning like the Arabs, pertaining to the Islamic *style* of *ornament*, with its geometric *patterns*. Usually arabesque refers to long, sweeping curves based on floral *forms*, to describe curvilinear *pattern*. Mainly influencing *architecture* seen in provinces such as Jaunpur, Bengal, Bijapur and Delhi and in the *Mughal minatures*. Refer *Islamic Art*.

Arakkal, Yusuf (1945–) b. Chowghat, Kerala. Education: Dip. in *art CKP*, *Printmaking GAC*. Solos: Over 40 in Bangalore, Chennai, Hyderabad, Thiruvananthapuram, Kolkata, Mumbai, New Delhi; International: France, Nepal, Hong Kong, Dubai, London, New York. Group participations: *Triennale* New Delhi, Asian *Art*; International: Singapore, Canada, South Africa, Hong Kong, Geneva, Munich, Fukuoka Japan, *Biennales* France, Bangladesh, Sao Paulo Brazil & Cairo, Indian Artists New York. Awards: KAR *LKA*, National Award; International: *Biennale* Bangladesh. Member: Jury of Kalidas Sanman for *Art*. Commissions: *murals* & *sculptures* in *granite*, *metal*, *terracotta* & *fibreglass* in Bangalore, Kozhikode, recently 10ft and 21ft in stainless *steel* in Bangalore. Publications: Interviews on TV; Published articles on *art* in English newspapers. Collections: Godrej Mumbai, *CYAG*, pvt., national & international: USA, Japan, UAE, South Korea, Brazil, France, Germany, Australia.

Yusuf Arakkal's early works were *abstract*, following the fashion of the day, but he soon moved towards *figuration*, being inspired mostly by the people around him. He has done a series on pavement dwellers, paraplegics, street urchins and the downtrodden and the less fortunate sections of society. His *palette* is usually high *key* with intense *chiaroscuro*. Yusuf Arakkal is a versatile *artist*, exploring many *mediums* including *printmaking* and *sculpture* in addition to *painting*. Lately, he painted a series of *canvases*, when he was inspired by computer generated *images*.

He lives and works in Bangalore.

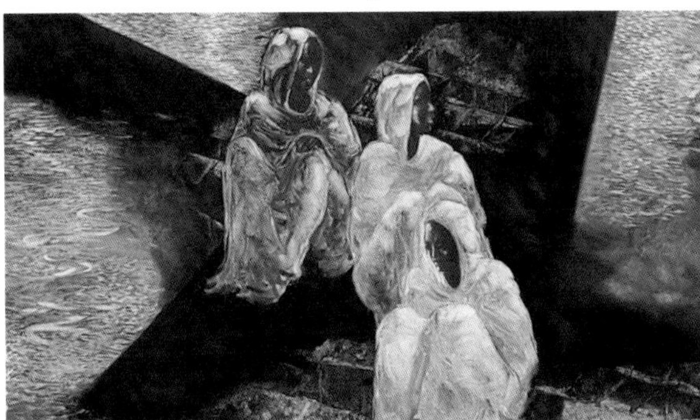

Arakkal, Yusuf: "Ganga", *Oils*, 1994, 210x120 cm.

Archaeological Museum (*Khajuraho*, MP). The *museum*, which is situated near the *Khajuraho* group of temples, displays a collection of *sculptures* salvaged from the temples. The displays have been arranged thematically, with a Vaishnava gallery, a SHIVA gallery and a *Jain* gallery. In the entrance hall there is a huge dancing GANESHA, with six arms, each holding an *attribute*. There is also a unique seated BUDDHA, the only one of its kind to be found in *Khajuraho*. He is seated in the PADMASANA with his right hand in the Bhumisparsha MUDRA. The Vaishnava gallery has a sensuous *fragment* of LAKSHMI Narayana in which the divine couple are lovingly entwined, while the *Jain* gallery houses a few *sculptures* of *Jain* Tirthankaras.

Archaeological Museum (Sanchi, MP). This site *museum* was set up at Sanchi to store and preserve the remnants of the scattered *sculptures* from the *stupas*; the collection includes sections on tools, implements, *pottery*, coins, caskets and containers found within the *stupas* and Hinayana, Mahayana and Hindu *sculptures*.

An important example is the lion capital of an Ashokan pillar, remarkably similar to the famous one found at Sarnath in UP. There are the sensuous SHALEBHANJIKAS as also various figures belonging to the Buddhist *pantheon*.

The *museum* issues publications, including a *museum* guide.

Archaeological Museum (Sarnath, UP). This is the oldest site-*museum* in India. It houses several Buddhist *sculptures* dating between the 3rd century BC and the AD 13th century. The lion capital (the *emblem* of the Indian republic) may be seen there along with two seated BUDDHAS. There is also a BODHISATTVA of the 1st century and several BUDDHAS, mostly belonging to the *Gupta* age.

Also on display are fragmented bits of Hindu *sculpture*, tools and implements and *terracottas* from the site. The sales counter has some publications by the Archaeological Survey of India.

Archer Art Gallery (Ahmedabad, GUJ). The Gallery is part of the Archer Group, of which Anil Relia, Hon. Dir. is the Founder & Chairman. The Archer Design Studio was originally set up in 1978, later it expanded to include the fields of *painting*, publication and *art* promotion. The *commercial art* gallery is the latest venture of the group. The collection includes works by the *old masters*, like *Raja Ravi Varma*, a large *oil painting* by *S. Fyzee-Rahamin*, and several *contemporary artists* like *Maqbool Fida Husain*, *Haku Shah*, *Ravishankar R. Raval* and Vasudeo Smart. Refer *Mass*.

Architecture The science/*art* of designing and constructing buildings both for public and private use. With the beginning of civilization came the need for constructing dwelling places as well as places of worship, congregation and granaries for storing food. Architecture has evolved through the ages, constantly adapting to the climatic conditions, the availability of local material and constant innovation in the technological sense. The invention of the arch was a seminal moment in the field of architecture as was the introduction of *concrete*.

In ancient India, much of the secular construction, i.e. palaces and dwelling places of the common man were made of *wood* and hence have not survived. Religious architecture in India has always been heavily embellished with *sculpture*. The Indian artisan has always been versatile, creating the lustrous Mauryan polish for the Ashokan Stambhas as aesthetically as *carving* the intricate JALI *work* of the Abu-Dilwara temples over a 1000 years later. The Mughal Emperors brought in Persian influence with Akbar preferring the dignity of red sandstone interlaced with *white inlay*, while Shahjahan opted for the pristine glory of white *marble* in his *Taj Mahal*.

The British introduced a touch of the West into the streets of India, with colonial *architecture*. *Contemporary* Indian architects are among the best in the world, designing ecological buildings, fusing the best of what technology can offer with the wisdom of ancient *tradition*. Refer *Abu-Dilwara Group of Temples*, *Altarpiece*, *Basohli*, *Bronze*, *Brass*, *Buddhist Art*, *Cave Art*, *Cement*, *Copper*, CHOLA, *Creation*, *Design*, *Granite*, *Gupta*, *Hinduism*, *Hoysala*, *Indus Valley Civilization*, *Iron*, *Islamic Art*, *Khajuraho*, *Metal*, *Marble*, *Mathura Art*, *Maurya Dynasty*, *Mughal Dynasty*, *Nagara Style*, *Neolithic Art*, *Persian Art*, *Rajasthan School of Art Jaipur*, *Rock-cut*, *Stone*, *Sunga Dynasty*, *Temple Architecture*, *Terracotta*, *Thanjavur (Tanjore) Painting*, *Wood*, *Muhammed Abdur Rehman Chughtai*, *Satish Gujral*, *Rathin Mitra*, *Ratan Parimoo*, *Dashrath Patel*, *Nachiket Patwardhan*.

Ardha-mandapa ardha=half, mandapa=hall. A *term* used in mediaeval Indian *architecture*, it refers to the front porch in the temples of north India. The ardha-mandapa functions as an entrance hall and is usually supported by decorative pillars.

Armature The initial rigid framework used by a *sculptor* to fashion his *sculpture*. The armature could be of flexible *metal* wire, pipe, or even coconut fibre. This internal skeleton is usually employed to fashion *images* of *clay*, *plaster of Paris* or *wax* objects. However, an armature cannot be used for a *terracotta* piece which has to be fired hard, or during the lost *wax casting* process. Refer *Air Vents*, *Somnath Hore*.

Arora, Sudha (1926–) b. Bareilly, UP. Education: Dip. in *sculpture* GCAC Lucknow. Solos: PUJ KB Chandigarh, State *LKA* Lucknow, *JAG*, other towns New Delhi, Hyderabad. Group participations: Kunika Chemould Art Centre & Rashtriya *LKA* Kendra New Delhi; International: New Zealand, Europe. Participated & organized *art* camps & workshops. Awards: UP, State *LKA* New Delhi, *AIFACS* Award & Title Kala Shree. Senior Fellowship: HRD Ministry 1988–90 New Delhi & UP Govt. Dept. of Cultural Affairs. Member: General Council UP State *LKA*. Publications: Modern Indian Sculpture by *Jaya Appasamy*, *LKA* "Contemporary Art and Ceramics". Collections: *LKA* & *NGMA* New Delhi, Govt. Museum of Modern Art & PUJ University Chandigarh, *BB*.

Sudha Arora has experimented with *wood*, *stone carving*, *terracotta*, *welding*, *cement* and *plaster sculpture*. Lately she has been working with *ceramics* using simple ochre *slips* and tin glazes. Her *themes* include *masks*, faces, GANESHAS and trees.

She lives and works in Lucknow, UP. Refer *Casting*, *Clay Water*; Illustration—*Terracotta*.

Art Art is skill in making or creating. There is a great difference in the intrinsic qualities of Indian *art* when compared to its Western counterpart. Indian *art* is influenced by its *culture* rather than the narrow confines of *fine art*. Though more recently, a several Western *"Isms"* have influenced Indian art, it has retained its basic traditional and *aesthetic* values.

In Indian art there is no distinction between *fine arts* and *decorative arts*. This is reflected in the *architecture*, *sculpture*, ornamentation, illustrated manuscripts, *painting*, miniatures, embroidered textiles *weaving*, music, literature, performing arts, photography and *installation* works. Today, *Modernism* has emerged as a potent force in Indian art. Visually this has ranged from use of different materials, *creation* and *form*-investigation to psychic exploration; from expressionistic *social realism*, the magical *imagery* to *symbolism* adopted from *classical folk* and *tribal arts*, *and* TANTRIC art.

Indian *artists* have changed their artistic *styles* rapidly. In *painting*, *sculpture* and *graphics* which includes *installation* e.g. by *Navjot Altaf*, *Atul Dodiya*, *Avtarjeet S. Dhanjal*, *Maqbool Fida Husain*, *Ved Nayar*, *Saroj Gogi Pal*, *Vivan Sundaram*, and several younger *artists* of today.

Art Brut French *term* for raw, brutal *art*. Brutal in this sense does not refer to the subject, but rather to the method of working both in *painting* and *sculpture*. The *images* appear to have been roughly cut or crudely painted using various materials including sand, glass-powder, etc. J. Dubuffet was the main *artist* associated with Art Brut. Refer *Colour*, *Mixed Media*, *Sand Blasting*, *Sand Moulding*, *Sand Painting*, *Glass Mosaic*, *Concrete*, *Metal*, *Iron*, *Casting*, *Aluminium*, *Form*, *Motif*, *Mosaic*, *Piraji Sagara*, *Rabin Mondal*.

Art Criticism The study of critiques, writings and theories of earlier *critics*, aestheticians and philosophers like Kant, Hegel and Worringer. Art Criticism in India is a relatively new phenomenon, with *critics* appearing on the scene only in the *post-Independence* era. Aestheticians and philosophers like BHARATA, Abhinavagupta and Bhatta Lollatta wrote on dramatics rather than *art*; however *art* historians today have adapted traditional theories i.e. RASA and Dhvani to the study of *art*.

Art Deco The predominant *style* in the *decorative arts* between 1920–30. Art Deco, a *term* coined after an *exhibition* in Paris late in 1925, "Exposition Internationale des Arts Decoratifs et Industriels Modernes" was the direct successor of *Art Nouveau*. It followed the trend towards geometricization that was apparent in the works of *modern* masters like P. Picasso, P. Mondrian and V. Kandinsky. The same severe straight *lines* and limited *colour palette* are found in furniture, textile, and jewellery *designs* as well as in *ceramics* and *architecture*.

O.C. Ganguly, an *art critic* of the 90s, first described *Ajanta frescoes* as *decorative art*. Thereafter, works of *Abanindranath Tagore* used Indian idealism as a basis of decoration. Decorative *style* in India was flat unlike the solid representations of the visual world as seen in the *Mughal miniature paintings*. Refer *Vajubhai D. Bhagat, Jyoti Bhatt, Nachiket Patwardhan, Ravinder G. Reddy, A. Ramachandran*.

Art Education In the West, as in the Far East, *artists* of earlier generations generally trained under a master running a workshop where they were trained in all aspects of grinding and correct mixing of *colours* with *oil* and other binders, finally graduating to working on the master's *paintings*, *priming* the *canvas*. One hears of Leonardo da Vinci bettering his master A. Verrochio at a young age. P.P. Rubens had upto 20 assistants working on his large *canvases*. In India, however, *art* (Chitrakala, Shilpkala and Vaastukala) was a hereditary business, with fathers initiating sons into the secret ritualistic and religious aspects of *art* as well as its practice. With the advent of *Modernism* and *Modern* educational institutions, however, everything changed. In India, this system of art education was introduced by the British in the 19th century. Though initially the *art* schools at Mumbai, Chennai, Kolkata, Lahore, etc., were set up to train the local craftsmen for the British market, a slow change of heart took place, and the British introduced the Western method of art education to Indian students. This included *drawings* from the *nude* and from the *antique* (*plaster copies* of Greek statues), *oil painting* in the *realistic* Western academic *manner* and later the introduction of *watercolours*. *Sculpture* followed a similar trend. At the same time, the British exhorted the Indians not to forget their roots. This resulted in the strange blending of Western academicism and Indian subject matter that is apparent in the works of *Ganpatrao K. Mhatre, Pestonjee Bomanjee, Vinayak Pandurang Karmarkar*. Although *Raja Ravi Varma* was not really educated in an *art* school, his *art* epitomizes all these qualities. Today *art* schools in India *JJSA, KB Santiniketan*, GSA Chennai, *CKP, RBU* and others are run on similar lines, but with a wider choice of subjects.

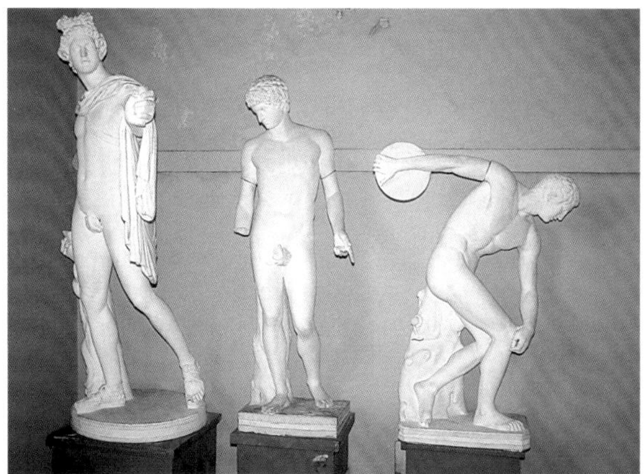

Art Education: Plaster copies of Greek sculpture, *JJSA*.

Art for Art's Sake A phrase commonly used to describe *Modern* and *post-Modern art*. First employed by C. Baudelaire and T. Gautier to explain that *contemporary art* needed no social, magical or religious crutch, an *artist* could express his inner feelings or sense of *aesthetics* without having to justify them in *terms* of subject matter or *style*.

Nandalal Bose at *Santiniketan KB* pioneered a range of bold experiments on an enlarged and open scale represented chiefly in his *murals*. Refer *Art, Aesthetic Movement, Modern, Nandalal Bose, Abanindranath Tagore*.

Art Heritage (New Delhi). Art Heritage was founded in 1977 by Roshen Alkazi. It curates some 20 *exhibitions* each year. Amongst the earliest galleries to show young *artists* of the day, properly documented and impeccably presented, its annual catalogue forms part of its permanent record of Indian *art* and its library and archives house firsthand material, invaluable to the scholar of *art*. *Artists* who exhibited here include *Chandranath K. Achrekar, Jivan Adalja, K.M. Adimoolam, Navjot Altaf, Ambadas, Dattatrey D. Apte, Gobardhan Ash, Meenakshi Bharati (Kasliwal), Veena Bhargava, R.B. Bhaskaran, Jyoti Bhatt, Jyotsna Bhatt, Nikhil Biswas*, among many others.

Art Konsult (New Delhi). The gallery which is situated in the Hauz Khas Village was inaugurated in June 1995. It is owned and managed by Siddhartha Tagore, who has been an *art* consultant since 1980. The gallery specializes in Indian *contemporary art*, especially of the period 1890–1960. Some of the *artists* whose works have been exhibited are *Shobha Broota, V. Vishwanadhan*, Gopi Gajwani, Suhas Nimbalkar among many others. They also publish the quarterly magazine "Art & Deal".

Art Nouveau (French)=new *art*. The *term* is used to describe the *style* of decoration, especially architectural and interior decoration in the late 1890s and early 1900s. It flourished in Britain and Europe, later spreading to the United States. It was known as "Stile Liberty" in Italy and "Jugendstil" in Germany. The *style* is characterized by long flowing, asymmetrical *lines* based on plant and elegant animal and bird *forms*, popular *themes* being the tulip, the peacock and the vine. The main exponents of the *styles* were designers H. Guimard (Paris Metro Station), A. Beardsley (British Illustrator), A. Gaudi (Architect and Furniture Designer in Spain). Though it was an offshoot of *Symbolism* on one hand and the *Arts and Crafts Movement* on the other, Art Nouveau relied solely on being surface *ornament* rather than following a *style*.

The *Bengal School* adapted the Nouveau movement to India's past. Refer *Art Deco, Modern Style, Bengal School, Muhammed Abdur Rehman Chughtai, Bhabani Charan Gue, Abanindranath Tagore, Sarada Charan Ukil*.

Art Society of India (ASI) (Mumbai). The Society was established in 1918 by *Haldankar Savlaram L.* with its office in Mumbai and has been holding annual *exhibitions* since then. An annual grant (towards its *exhibition* and library) is received both from the *LKA* and the Govt. of MAHA. The *study* circle regularly screens films, arranges lectures and demonstrations by some eminent *artists* who are members also.

Art Today Gallery (ATG) (New Delhi). The gallery which was part of the "India Today" group of publications was founded in 1995. It served as a platform for *contemporary* Indian *art*, hosting shows by established *artists* as well as final year *art* students. Art Today also exhibited *art* works not in the mainstream, including works by the followers of the *miniature tradition* and the Osho Communes. Art Today has also collaborated with galleries abroad in order to bring international *art* to Indian viewers. It has produced limited editions of individually signed *prints* in addition to the usual catalogues which accompanied each show. Some of the *artists* among them were *Gautam Basu, Manjit Bawa, Ashok Bhowmik, Rini Dhumal, Satish Gujral, Katayun Saklat, Amrut Patel, A. Ramachandran.*

Arte Povera (Italian)="poor" (in the sense of materials) *art*. This was a *term* coined to describe Minimal *art*, specifically *art* produced by using local, commonly found material, such as sand, junk, *wood, stones* and used newspaper.

This method started to be used by Indian *artists* after 1950 in *mixed media*. Refer *Installation, Post-Modern, Balbir Singh Katt, Harkrishan Lall, Piraji Sagara, Vasudha Thozhur, K. Vasant Wankhede.*

Artefact A handcrafted work of *art*, which could be either decorative or utilitarian in *nature*. These include the *terracotta* art of WB, *brass filigree* work from UP and *stone* and *bronze* statues from the south. Local *crafts* have been legendary and have had considerable impact on the Indian *art* scene. Even some of the materials used, such as *chalk paste*, red sand (Geru) and *wood* chips have found their way into *modern* works. Refer *Bidri, Carving, Cire Perdue, Decorative Art, Enamelling, Glass Painting, Kalamkari, Papier Mache, Thanjavur (Tanjore) Painting, Tie and Dyed Fabrics, Weaving, Folk Art, Santiniketan, Nandalal Bose, Jamini Roy, Ganga Devi, C. Jagdish, Mrinalini Mukherjee.*

Artist A person who practises a *form* of *art*, be it *sculpture, painting, graphic*, music, dance etc. The artist blends his inner feelings with creative energies and *art techniques* to express and communicate with viewers, essentially making a *visual* statement. This lends an individuality to his/her work of *art*; the *creation* lives long after the creator is dead and gone. In the Indian context, *art* (KALA) was a more complete discipline than book-learning (Vidya) (learning through books). Formerly artists worked as a group under one master artists. Artist Shaik Muhammad Amir of Karaya of *Company School/Company Painting* was one of the first Indians to work as an individual, later the individualized *styles* and *techniques* were introduced by *Raja Ravi Varma*, and the Tagore family.

Artist Groups Usually refers initially to a small number of people, sometimes including writers, as well as *artists*, with common aims and objectives. Subsequently develops into an *art movement* under its influence. With the advent of the *modern movement, artists* with a common objective often formulated a set of theories, popularly known as manifestos with common aims and objectives, e.g., the Futurists in Italy were interested in creating an *art* of the future. Their manifesto was anarchic in *nature* suggesting the wholescale destruction of *tradition*. Other groups include the Pre-Raphaelites and the Bloomsbury Group.

Modern India has also witnessed the formation of many artist groups, from the Bengal Revivalist Group formed with the nationalistic fervour of the freedom fighters to the post-Independent *PAG* in Mumbai, *Calcutta Group 43, Young Turks, Arts Acre* and Cholamandal Artists' Group. Refer *PAG, Baroda School of Arts, Cholamandal Artists' Village.*

Artist's Proof It means **1.** Originally a testified *print* by number. **2.** Also a first *impression* of the *print*, usually kept by the *artist*. **3.** In *printmaking* the series of *prints* of edition taken from one *plate* are marked thus Artist's Proof—AP/1, AP/6 or AP/10, the number showing, e.g., that it is the 1st, 6th or the 10th print, taken particularly from that *plate*. Refer *Copy, Dipak Banerjee, Naina Dalal, Rini Dhumal, Shobha Ghare, Somnath Hore, Paul A. Koli, Ajit S. Patel, Anupam Sud, Gaganendranath Tagore.*

Artists' Centre (Mumbai). This Gallery in Mumbai was established initially as Artists' Aid Centre, in 1950 under the influence of six core *artists* of the *PAG* especially *Krishnaji Howlaji Ara*. The founder members of the institution, which functions as a Trust, were A.R. Leyden and Rudi Von Leyden who were patrons of *art*, as well as *artists* themselves. The precincts of Artists' Centre were earlier known as Bombay Art Society Salon. The Centre has also organized music and dance recitals, poetry readings, film screenings, library activities, *art* camps and annual *art* shows, besides serving as a meeting place for *artists* and *art* lovers, and holding *exhibitions* and seminars for the benefit of young *artists*. Several *artists* are members of the centre. Among the *artists* who have held solos at the gallery are *Krishnaji Howlaji Ara, Suresh Awari, Pralhad A. Dhond, Anjolie Ela Menon*, Pratima Sheth.

Arts Acre In WB an *artists* village-cum-centre of *visual arts*. It was formed in 1984, the land having been donated to the trust by the nine founding *artist* members including *Shuvaprasanna*. Among the many young *artists* who have worked in this village are Gautam Das, Somenath Maity, Biswajit Saha, *Malay Chandan Saha*, Parthapratim Saha, *Jaspal Singh*. The inaugural show was held in 1987. Arts Acre receives an annual developmental grant from *LKA*. Besides offering study and lodging facilities to young *artists*, Arts Acre also holds *exhibitions* both on its premises and in other galleries throughout the country. It also holds weekend classes in *art*.

Arts and Crafts Movement Originating in Britain in the 19th century, the Arts and Crafts Movement basically countered industrialization, exhorting a return to *tradition*, in order to create a craft-based society. W. Morris, one of the leaders of the movement refers to "art made by the people and for the people, as a happiness to the maker and the user." It was J. Ruskin, however, who was to become the most influential exponent of the opinions which led to the movement. His theories were adopted as the spirit of the "Art and Crafts" beliefs. Ruskin spoke of hand-crafted as opposed to the machine-made. Many guilds were set up by *artists* and architects for providing "craftwork" for discerning clients. In India too, *art education* at *Santiniketan* stressed on the useful, i.e. craft-based activities, such as toy-making and *leather* work rather than *FA*. of *painting*, *sculpture* and *calligraphy*. Refer *Art Deco*, *Art Nouveau*, *Decorative Art*, *Tribal Art*, *GCAC* Kolkata & Chennai, *Rasaja Foundation* New Delhi, *SJM*, *Mrinalini Mukherjee*, *Haku Shah*, *Nita Thakore*.

Arya, Chetan (1925–) b. Porbunder, GUJ. Trained under his father (who painted the interiors of *Jain* temples). With his brother, Kumar, migrated to Mumbai in 1940, where they worked for the film industry, producing *posters* and *hoardings* in the pre-Independence era. They also designed film sets and costumes for films like "Chandragupta Chanakya" (1942), ballets "Ashok Medhaveen" (1946), Sachin Shankar's "Ramlila" and "Hans-Bala" (1951). Exhibited *portraits* at *JAG* "Homage to Heroes". Collections: National Defence Academy Khadakvasla, pvt. and international.

Soli Batliwala gifted the Terrace Art Gallery on the rooftop of the *JAG* in Mumbai to Chetan Arya. He and his brother have been *painting* in *oils* and exhibiting their romantic and picturesque *landscapes* of temples, village women, storm scenes and bullock carts. He also holds free *art* classes for *art* lovers.

Aryan, K.C. (1919–2002) b. Amritsar. No formal *Art Education*, from a family of traditional-style *painters*. Solos: Kumar Gallery & *LKA* New Delhi, Govt. Museum Chandigarh, SC, *AIFACS*, *JJSA*; International: Kabul, Baghabad, Beirut. Industrial show: Lahore. Group participations: National Exhibition *LKA* New Delhi, PUJ University Museum Patiala, SC, *AIFACS*. *Auction*: Osian's Mumbai. Awards: IAFA Amritsar, National *LKA* New Delhi, Kala Vibhushan *AIFACS*. Publications: "Folk Bronzes of India", "Punjab Paintings", "Punjab Murals", "Hanuman in Art", "Birds & Animals", "Cultural Heritage of Punjab", "Basis of Decorative Elements in Indian Art", "Rekha", "Little Goddesses" (MATRIKAS). In 1984, established "Home of Folk Art" Museum in Gurgaon, Haryana. Collected: Folk Objects; Collections: *LKA* New Delhi, PUJ Museum & University Chandigarh.

K.C. Aryan was a *painter*, *sculptor* and art historian. He travelled all over the country, sketching and *painting* everyday scenes. At the same time he had also painted historical subjects in the *realistic manner*, in *tempera*. Travelling brought him in contact with the rich folk *tradition* of the country which led to him discovering Amritsar. He began documenting and collecting various folk objects, including *bronzes*, jewellery and *embroideries*. The folk element also influenced his *painting style* of using simplified and decorative *forms*. As a *sculptor*, he had experimented with *assemblage*, using scrap *metal* and mesh wire.

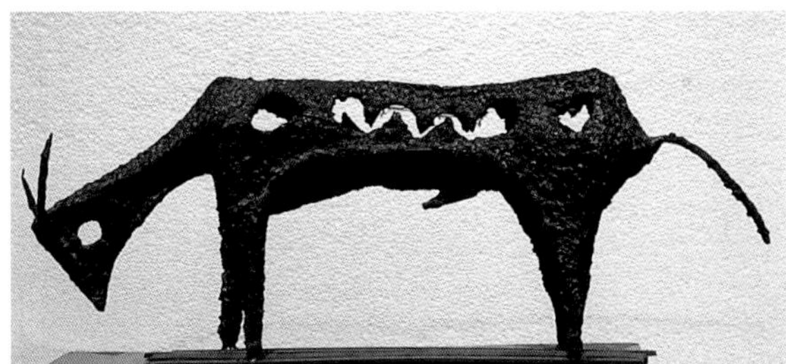

Aryan, K.C.: "Bull", Wrought *Iron*, 1957.

Asanas Postures, **1.** The set of postures and exercises adopted in YOGA for self-control and to strengthen the body and mind. These different postures influenced *sculpture* and *painting* through various *artistic styles*, where each Asana had its own significance. **2.** The seated/standing postures in which the *gods*, goddesses, minor deities and kings are depicted. Refer *Ajanta*, BUDDHA, *Ellora*, MAHAVIRA, PADMASANA, VISHNU, *Gandharan Art*, *Mathura Art*.

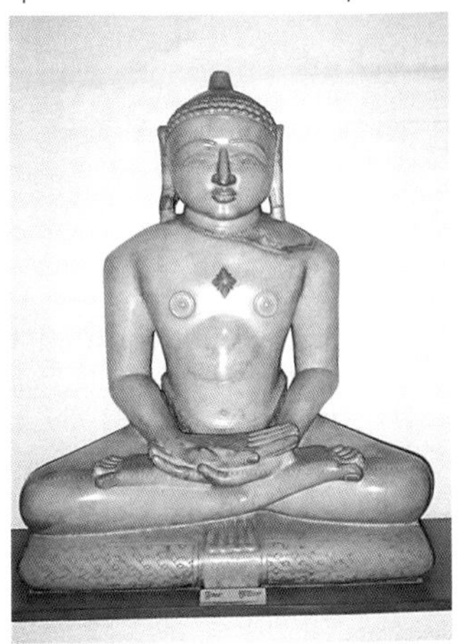

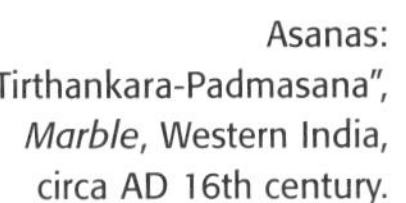

Asanas: "Tirthankara-Padmasana", *Marble*, Western India, circa AD 16th century.

Ascription Refer *Attribution*.

Ash, Gobardhan (1907–1996) b. Begumpur, WB. Education: Dip. in *FA*. GSA Kolkata, GSAC Chennai. Solos: *Santiniketan*, *BAAC* & *AFA* Kolkata, FA. Mission Begumpur, *Art Heritage* New Delhi. Retrospective: *BAAC* Kolkata. Group participations: *AFA* Kolkata, FA. Society Chennai, *AIFACS*; Internation- al: Indian Exhibition Singapore. *Auction*: Osian's Mumbai. Awards: Abanindra Award from Govt. of WB, *Art Heritage* & Felicitation by Rashtriya *LKA* 1996 New Delhi, *AIFACS* Veteran *Artist*. Member: Founder member—Young Artist's Union, Art Rebel Centre & Calcutta Group Kolkata, Founder Secretary FA. Mission Begumpur. Publications: Several articles on *art* in journals; Documentary film "Bleeding in the Sun" made on his *art*.

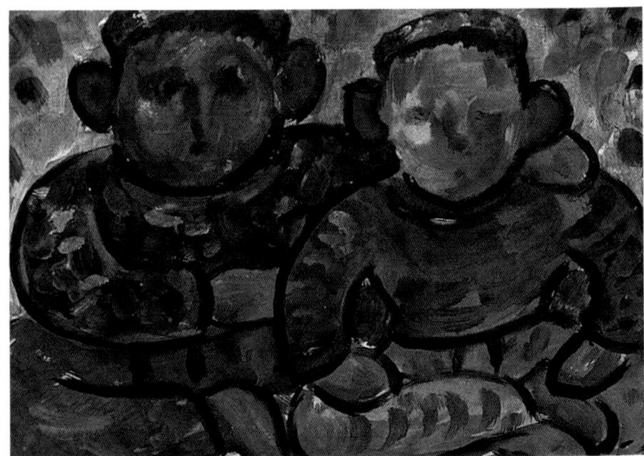

Ash, Gobardhan: "Hobu Gobu", *Gouache*, 1948, 28x38 cm.

Gobardhan Ash experimented with different *styles* while rendering the human *form* and *landscapes*. Western *Realism* and folk elements coexist in the works of the 50s. He painted in several *media*, including *watercolours*, *oils*, *pen*, *ink*; *charcoal*, *crayons* and *pencils* on *paper*; board and *canvas*. While his training in the *Calcutta School* was obvious in the early works, his later works show an expressionist use of *colours* and *brushwork*. His *landscapes* reflect the moods of *nature* with *figuration* being the rural environment.

He lived and worked in Hoogly with his *artist* sons.

Ashtanayika The classification of the eight types of NAYIKAS as mentioned in *classical* literature, RASAMANJARI of Bhanudatta and Rasikapriya of Keshvadasa. Refer ABHISARIKA, KHANDITA, KALAHAMTARITA, PROSITAPATIKA, SWADHINAPATIKA, VASAKASAJJA, VIPRALABDHA, UTKANTHITA.

Ashutosh Museum of Indian Art (Kolkata, WB). Named after Sir Ashutosh Mukherjee, an educationist, the *museum* was set up in 1937. It was relocated in its present building in 1961. It has a collection of *sculptures* from the Pala and Sena dynasties, which is characterized by the use of a hard, grey-black basalt *stone*, which when polished, acquires a glossy surface shine.

The *museum* also has a large collection of *terracotta relief* panels from Bengal's unique *terracotta* temples at Vishnupur, near Kolkata (about 200 km west).

Assemblage The three-dimensional version of *collage*. Though *collage* was a Cubist innovation, assemblage was a Dada favourite. It involved the juxtapositioning of *found objects*, frequently unrelated to each other, to create a type of *art*-object that often bordered on the fantastic or the surreal. A fine example of assemblage, also known as *junk art*, is Man Ray's "Gift" an assemblage of an *iron* with two neat rows of nails stuck to the flat underside; Picasso's "Bull's Head" made of a bicycle seat and handle bar. Refer *Installation*, *New Realism*, *Ready-Made*, *Sculpture*, *Aku*, *K.C. Aryan*, *Krishnamachari Bose*, *Partha Pratim Deb*, *Ajit R. Desai*, *Mahendra Pandya*, *G. Reghu*, *Mohan Samant*.

Asura=demon. In Indian *mythology*, a *demon*, anti-God or denizen of Naraka (the nether world) as opposed to the Devas (*gods*) who dwell in Swarga (heaven). Refer *Demons*; Illustration–DURGA.

Atelier Libre (French)=free studio. A studio where students of *art* or *artists* pay for *space* to paint and often for a *model* as well. However there is usually no teaching. The difference between an atelier libre and an *art academy* is that applicants are almost never rejected. In India, we have the *LKA* studios, e.g., *GAC*.

Atma/Atman=Soul or Spirit. The soul is the essence of the human being, and is eternal. The body (Sharir) may be destroyed, but the Atma lives on forever. *Hinduism* interprets the Atma or the individual soul as being distinct from Parmatma/Brahman or Universal Soul. Atma merges with the cosmic Parmatma (the spirit of the world) becoming the essence of life of the universe itself. Atma thus means "Universal spirit". This is useful in understanding the process of reincarnation or the concept of rebirth, in that, the soul of a dying person merges with the universal Atma and yet remains an individual, ready for reincarnation. The soul (Atma) has been of special interest to Indian *artists* since ancient *times*, from TANTRIC to *contemporary* period *artists* have constantly attempted to explore the subject both on the *spiritual* and *abstract* planes. Refer AVATARA, *Buddhism*, KARMA, UPANISHAD, JATAKA.

Atmosphere/Atmospheric Effects Not to be confused with the geographic *term*. In *art* it generally refers to: **1.** The mood of the work is the *art* language and the effect in the *paintings*, and other *art* subjects. **2.** The depiction of *space* in a *realistic* work of *art* with the use of atmospheric effect, endowing it with *perspective* i.e., the *foreground* in sharp focus against a loss of clarity in the *background*. Refer *Ramkinkar Baij*, *Sakti Burman*, *M.J. Enas*, *K.B. Kulkarni*, *Raja Ravi Varma*.

Attribute 1. Attributes are known as AYUDHAS in *Hinduism*. Though some of them are *weapons*, they are meant primarily as instruments for maintaining peace and harmony. As most of the Hindu *pantheon* has more than two attributes, there is an arm for each AYUDHA. At *times*, more than one deity carries the same AYUDHA; the placement of the object leading to the identification of the *god*, e.g., the flute and the peacock feather in the *crown* are all *symbolic* of young KRISHNA. GANESHA's attributes include the Akshamala Rudraksha (rosary), and a bowl of Modaks (a type of sweet). Refer *Weapons*, SHANKHA, CHAKRA, GADA, KHADGA, Parasu, AGNI, SHULA, TRISHULA, SHAKTI and MUDRA. **2.** A *symbolic* object which is conventionally used to identify a particular saint or *god*, e.g., the key of St. Peter, the *clay* tablets containing the 10 commandments carried by Moses in *Christian art*. These attributes have been extensively used both in *paintings* and *sculptures*, for *symbolic* effect. Refer *Nandalal Bose*, *Kanu Desai*, *Raja Ravi Varma*.

Attribution Also means ascription. The word refers to an unsigned work of *art*, wherein the *artist* is identified by referring to the similarity in *style* etc., to other works known to be by him or her. Accordingly a *painting*, *sculpture* or *graphic* is "attributed to XYZ". "Ascribed to XYZ or *studio of...XYZ*". *Artists* who worked in groups in India did not sign their works. Here, *miniature paintings* were produced by a group of *artists* working under one master. Whenever the work was unsigned, it has often been attributed by *art historians* as being predominantly in the *style* of a particular *artist*, hence it is ascribed to him. This is true of Mughal *miniature paintings*, *Company School*, *Bazaar Painting* and other indigenous *artists* before *Raja Ravi Varma*.

Auction A sale involving a series of bids by a group of buyers. The price of the object is not fixed, as is the case of the sale of works at an *exhibition*. Instead, a reserve price is set, below which the works cannot be sold and the work is offered to the highest bidder. An auction is generally conducted by an auctioneer associated with an auction house. The auction house takes a percentage of the price fetched by the object. The buyer usually indicates that he is bidding by raising his paddle (an object with his number on it). Some well-known International auction houses are Asprey's, Christie's, Bonham's, Sotheby's and Bowring's; In India, we have Saffron, Heart and Osian's among others.

Aureole The *halo* encircling the head of a person to indicate divinity. It is also known as the *nimbus*, and the MANDORLA. In India, to indicate divinity, it is usually depicted as rays of *light* emerging from the head of the sacred personage and it is known as PRABHAVALI or Tejas (variously known flames, fire, glow), e.g. the *halo* around the head of the BUDDHA in Mahayana *art*. Later, Jehangir, the Mughal Emperor invested his own *portraits* with *haloes* inspired by *Christian art*, thus conferring on himself a divine status.

Aurobindo Institute of Culture (AIC) (Kolkata, WB). The institute established in 1975 in Kolkata offers various courses in *art*, including *drawing*, *painting*, dance, music, dramatics and linguistics. The Galerie La Mere is the *art* gallery affiliated to the institute. It holds exhibitions of *arts* and *crafts* every year, among the *artists* who participated in their shows are *Shanu Lahiri*, *Veena Bhargava*, *Uma Siddhanta*, *Sohini Dhar*.

Aurodhan Art Gallery (Pondicherry). The Aurodhan Art Gallery started by Lalit and Shernaz Verma promotes *contemporary* Indian *art* through regular shows held during the year in association with the *SAI*. *Ramlal Dhar*, *Babu Xavier*, *Rabin Mondal*, *Thotha Vaikuntham* among others have participated in the *exhibitions* held by the gallery. Aurodhan endeavours to contribute towards the expansion of *art* consciousness. The gallery also offers pvt. and corporate *art* consultancy.

Auto-Destructive Art A *style* of *art* designed to bring about its own disintegration as in Process *Art*. This is possible because the use of materials in the work aid the process of decay i.e. leaves, seeds, pods, junk material etc. Refer *Piraji Sagara*, *Satish Gujral*, *Vivan Sundaram*, *Sheela Gowda* and *Ved Nayar*.

Automatism To do with free-hand expression or doodling, letting the *pencil* or *brush* wander across the surface of the *paper* or *canvas*, without conscious control, thus allowing the subconscious to rule over the *image* formed. This process was popular among the Dadaists and the Surrealists, who coined the *term*, J. Pollock and other *Abstract* Expressionists of Automatism. The Surrealists stressed and emphasized connection between *painting* and psychology by using automatism. *Rabindranath Tagore* also employed a variation of automation in his works of *art*. Refer *Action Painting*.

Avant-Garde (French)=avant=ahead, garde=time. The *term* is usually applied to *art* or an *artist* who pioneers and experiments with new elements that shake off *tradition* and embrace *Modernism*, and are bold enough to shock the viewer but not fully rooted in the *ideal*. Indian *artists* were exposed to European Avant-garde since 1920. *Bengal Revivalism* was considered to be Avant-garde at its inception, as were the progressives in all the fields of *art* and idea. Refer *Abstract*, *Assemblage*, *Body Art*, *Happening*, *Installation*, *Junk Art*, *Post-Modern*.

Avatara, Avtaar, Avatar=Descent. An incarnation as distinguished from re-incarnation. In *Hinduism*, it literally means the incarnation of a divinity who takes birth in the world in order to destroy negative forces, e.g., the 10 Avtaars of VISHNU include the Kurma (tortoise), Matsya (fish), Varaha (the bear), KRISHNA (the Blue *God*) and RAMA. VISHNU was said to have descended on earth as KRISHNA, to get rid of Kansa (uncle of Lord KRISHNA) and as RAMA to destroy RAVANA (King of Sri Lanka). Refer KURMAVATARA, MATSYA-AVATARA, PARASURAMA, VAMANA-TRIVIKRAMA; Illustration–BUDDHA, NARASIMHA, KALKI, KRISHNA, RAMA, VARAHAVATARA.

Awari, Suresh (1952–) b. Induri, MAHA. Education: GDA in *painting*, *mural JJSA*. Solos: *JAG*, BAG. Group participations: *NGMA*, Alliance Francaise & *Artists' Centre* Mumbai, MAHA Mahotsav Exhibition New Delhi, *JAG*, *BAS*. *Art* camps: KAR, AP, *Artists' Centre* Mumbai, *Nag Foundation* & *LKA* Pune. Awards: *Artists' Centre* Mumbai, National Award New Delhi, *JJSA*, *BAS*. Publication: *Sketches* published "Roop-Bheda", Annual Magazine *JJSA* and cover of "Illustrated Weekly of India". Collections: pvt, corporates, national & international.

Suresh Awari presently practises an idealized version of *figuration*, with romanticized versions of urban reality, the everyday life of the city where he lives. The children on the streets in action, people at the station longing to return home after a day's hard work and the crowd of cars which makes city-life so busy, all bursting with endless spirals of movement in the *composition*.

He lives in Mumbai where he works as a designer at the *WSC*.

Ayudha Refer *Attribute*, *Weapons*.

Ayudha-Purusha Ayudha=peace-loving, Purusha=man. The personification of an *attribute*, e.g. the personification of VISHNU's *weapon*, the Sudarshan-Chakra, is known as the CHAKRA Purush. The personification is usually shown holding the *attribute* and hovering near the *God* to whom it belongs. Other e.g. Gadadevi and Shankhadevi. Refer AYUDHA, *Attribute*, *Weapons*; Illustration–CHAKRA, *Ellora*, SHANKHA.

B

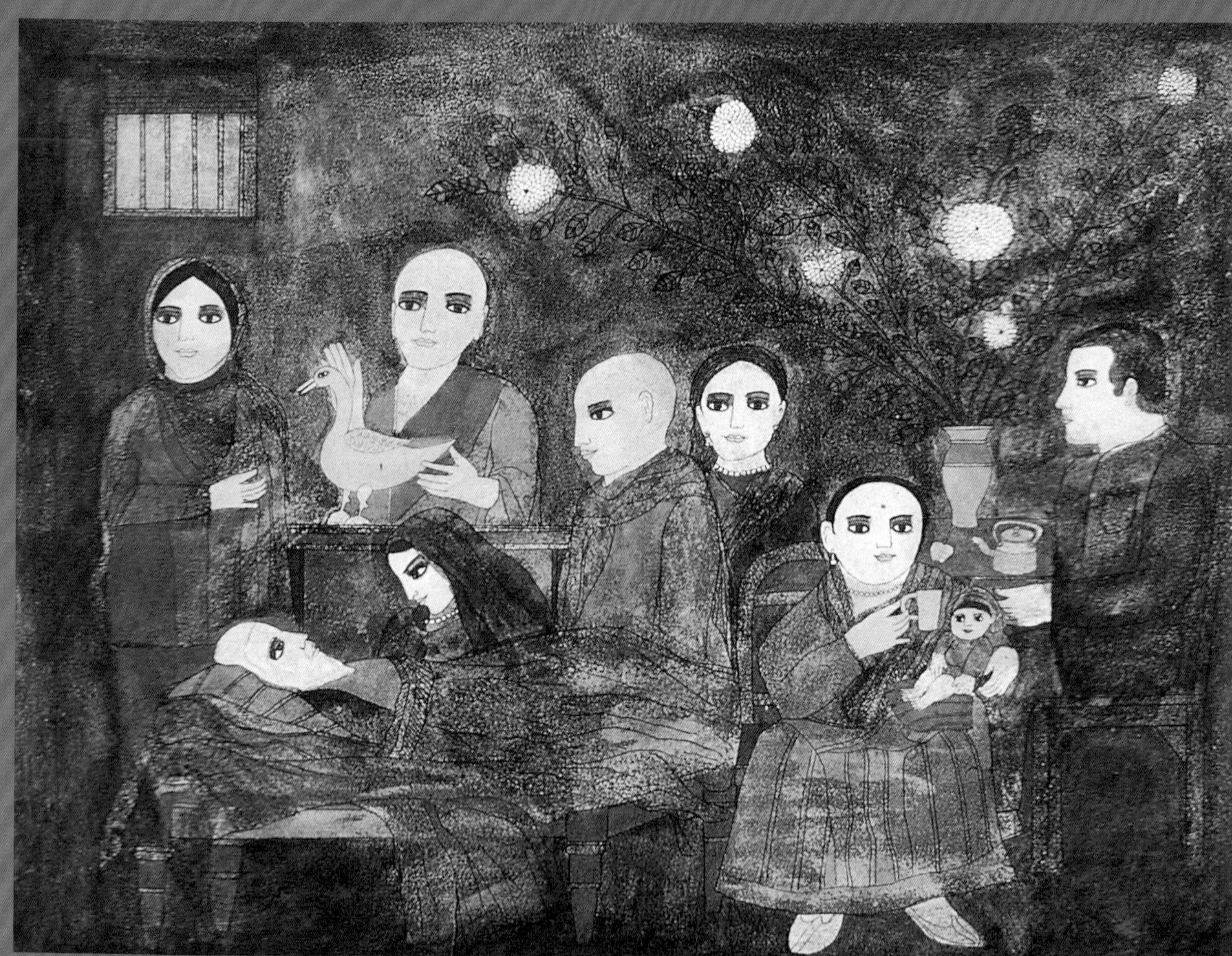

Badri Narayan: "The Vision of the Maha-Hamsa", *Watercolour* on *Paper*, 70x90 cm. (See notes on page 48)

B. Prabha (1931–2001) b. Nagpur, MAHA. Education: *Art* at Nagpur, *JJSA*, GDA in *painting*, *mural painting* in 1954–55. Over 50 Solos & five *exhibitions* with her husband, *sculptor* and *painter B. Vithal*. Group participations: Marvel Art Gallery Ahmedabad, All India Exhibitions, *BAS AIFACS*. Awards: *BAS*, *AIFACS*. Collections: *LKA* & *NGMA* New Delhi, pvt. & corporates.

Her early works were inspired by the *paintings* of P. Klee. After experimenting with various *media styles* and subjects including *landscapes*, *still life* and social events, she evolved her own formal *vocabulary* involving slim, elongated women with long graceful necks, Indian in demeanour, yet part of the universal womanhood with their embodiment of fragile strength. While working in Mumbai, B. Prabha's women stand (or sit) silhouetted against near non-existent *backdrops*, with the low *horizon* carrying an indication of their occupation or social standing. She endowed all these women, be they fisherwomen, singers or drought stricken victims, with an ageless charm that had become her signature.

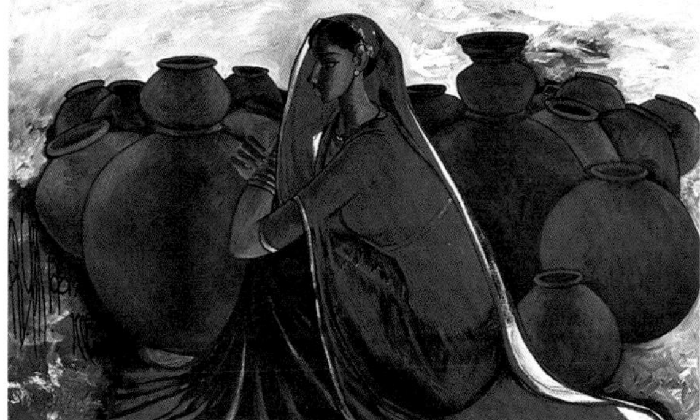

B. Prabha: "Rajasthani Pot Seller", *Oil* on *Canvas*, 1994, 75x125 cm.

B. Vithal (1933–1992) b. Wardha, MAHA. Education: GDA in *sculpture* & *modelling JJSA*. Over 40 solos & five group shows along with his wife *B. Prabha*. Collector: young *artists* work. Collections: *NGMA* New Delhi, TIFR.

B. Vithal experimented constantly with varied materials, using *aluminium*, *bronze*, welded *iron*, *wood*, *cement* and glass, for his *sculptures*. He was also a *painter*, with a *style* similar to the elongated *figurative style* works of his wife. But it is his *sculptures*, with their *monumental* massiveness that accurately portray the grandeur of his subjects. Be it the bull (a favourite *theme*), a man, a woman or any one of his many subjects, there is a majestic air in their Rodinesque sketchiness of finish. The heavy organic quality of Henry Moore, another *sculptor* he admired was prevalent in most of the works. He lived and worked in Mumbai. Refer *House of B. Vithal*, *B. Prabha*.

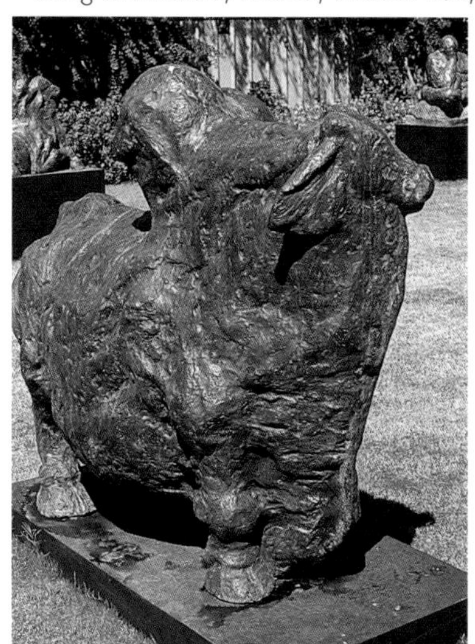

B. Vithal: "The Bull", *Bronze,* approx. 152x183 cm.

Babar-Namah The memoirs of the Mughul Emperor Babar, which were profusely illustrated during Emperor Akbar's reign. The miniatures show various incidents from the life of Babar and demonstrate his love of gardens and beautiful objects.

Backdrops The curtain or dropcloth used as the *background* of action set on stage. Many *painters* have been associated with the stage, e.g., Picasso designed costumes for Russian ballets, David Hockney designed the entire stage set for "The Rake's Progress".

In India, *painters* doing such curtain backdrops became known to the public as *painters* of repute. *Baburao Painter* not only did backdrops for the Marathi stage, but was also a producer and Dir. of films. Some *painters* employed tricks of *perspective* (the *vanishing point*, *realistic painting*) to create an *illusion* of *space* beyond the limited confines of the stage or film set. *Contemporary* backdrops are however completely individualistic and depend on the interaction between the designer and the director. This idea of backdrops was later used by some *artists* as a *background* in their *art* works e.g. *Pestonjee Bomanjee*. Refer *Crafts*, *Kanu Desai*, *Shiavax Chavda*; Illustrations: *Cityscape*, *Crafts*, *Landscape*, *Realistic*, *Studio of...*, *Visual*, *Indian Film Industry*, *Ramkinkar Baij*, *Sudhir Patwardhan*, *Sheshagiri K. Rao*, *Mohan Samant.*

Back-Glass Painting is *underpainting* on glass, i.e. *painting* on the reverse side of *transparent* glass; now also done on *acrylic plastic* (sheet) in *oils* or *tempera* or *waterproof ink*. The finished subject which one sees through the glass is painted first–either the main *outline* of the basic *paintings*, painted with a *brush* or *Chinese ink* stick, and its decorations, then with the use of various coats of *colours* for *background*. A very old *technique*, oldest of the medieval period. Refer *Cloisonnism*, *Technique*, *Glass Painting*, *Madhu Champaneria*, *P.L. NarasimhaMurti*, *Vijayalakshmi P.*, *Nalini Malani.*

Background 1. The *space* behind the main characters in a *landscape*, *figurative painting* and *sculpture*. **2.** The *negative* area against which the main *forms* are placed in an *abstract* work.

In India the background has evolved historically, starting with a flat background on wall and ceiling *frescoes* (*Ajanta*), to the clever use of shaded *colour* to blend with the *composition* (*Raja Ravi Varma*). In *contemporary* times, stage *style backdrops* were prepared by *Pestonjee Bomanjee*. It affected *sculpture* as well, where *relief* was provided to *highlight* the *form*. Thus, background evolved, more in the sense of *perspective*, among Academic *painters*. Whereas background in *installation art* is executed by using *colour*, material and not as *perspective* in the whole work. Refer *Atmosphere/*

Atmosphere Effect, Cityscape, Foreground, Malwa, Space, Baburao Painter, Manjit Bawa, Somnath Hore.

Badri Narayan (1929–) b. Secunderabad, AP. No formal *Art Education*, self-taught *painter* and writer, has worked with *mosaic, ceramic*, tiles and *printmaking*. Over 51 solos: New Delhi, Kolkata, Pune, Bangalore, Chennai, Hyderabad, *PUAG*, & at different venues in India; International: Frenshiem, Germany, USA. Group Participations: In most National *Exhibitions*, *BB* Bhopal, Art for Cry–Mumbai, Kolkata, New Delhi & Bangalore, *GC* Mumbai, Jehangir Nicholson Collection *NGMA* New Delhi, "Legacy of Art" 50 years of *JAG*, HAS, *BAS*; International: Indian Graphic Art–Warsaw & Paris, *Biennale* Tokyo, National Museum Prague, Festival of India Moscow, Indian Art Exhibition in Tokyo, Sao Paulo, Glenbarra Museum–Japanese collection in New Delhi, Kolkata, Bangalore & Mumbai. *Art* camps & workshops: Conducted for children, for TV shows. *Auctions*: Heart Mumbai. Awards: National Exhibition New Delhi, *LKA* AP, Padma Shri, MAHA Gaurav Purashkar, *BAS*, HAS. Appointments: Storyteller for 16 years–school in Mumbai; Stories & articles–"Illustrated Weekly of India" and "The Statesman". Publications: Several articles on *art*, folklore, *mythology* and short stories for children; A short TV film "Call it a Day" based on his work was produced in 1975; Also illustrated several books. Collections: *NGMA* & *LKA* New Delhi, Thiruvananthapuram Museum, *Chandigarh Museum*, *SJM*, BARC, *CYAG*, *JJSA*, TIFR; International: National Museum at Prague, Glenbarra Art Museum Japan.

Badri Narayan works mostly in *watercolour*. His *paintings* are rooted in Indian *culture* and *mythology*. The folk *idiom forms* the basis of his near illustrational *paintings* with a generous nod to various other sources, including *Ajanta paintings* and Byzantine formalism. They are suffused with RASA or emotion, the apparent serenity of the work being subtly underscored by tell-tale *symbols* and *signs*. His *allegories* bridge the gap between the ancient and the *modern* with effortless ease.

In "The Vision of the Maha-Hamsa" the juxtaposition of the swan in a semi-rural setting, seen against the middle-class ritual of tea-drinking does not set a jarring note. Badri Narayan's *colours* in these later works seem imbued with an evanescent *luminosity* as against more solid application of *colours* in the earlier works.

Badri Narayan lives and works in Mumbai. (See illustration on page 46)

Bagai, Vijaya (1941–) b. Mumbai. Education: M.A. (History) Bombay University. Trained in *drawing* & *painting NKM*, TKS. Solos: New Delhi; International: USA. Group participations: *NGMA* & *LKA* New Delhi, *AIFACS*, SKP, *BB*, *JAG*; International: USA, Bulgaria, Poland, Singapore, France. *Art* camps & workshops: *LKA* & Gallery Aurobindo New Delhi, *Artists* camp Mussoorie & *AIFACS*, Silk-screen workshop, SKP. Awards: President of India's Silver Plaque by *AIFACS*. Dept. of Culture Fellowships: 1991–94, 1996–98. Collec-tions: *NGMA* New Delhi, PUJ University Museum Chandigarh, Kerala History Museum, CCMB, *BB*; International: Japan, UK, USA.

She initially painted *figurative landscapes*. After joining TKS, she switched to portraying the human condition. Most of her works of this period have architectural ruins prominently depicted. The representation is *realistic* with carefully rendered *shadows*, dusty cobwebs and crumbling brickwork. A surrealist touch is imparted, in the portrayal of shaded *white* bricks hovering over the actual structure. This, she says is the "soul" of the city. Her *paintings*, usually rendered in *oils*, have a melancholy air.

She lives and works in Gurgaon, Haryana.

Bahulkar, Suhas (1954–) b. Pune, MAHA. Education: GDA in *painting JJSA*. Solos: *JAG*, *JJSA*, *AIFACS*, others in Pune, Ratnagiri; International: Paris. Group participations: RB New Delhi, *LKA* Chennai, *Nag Foundation* Pune, *DG*, *JAG*, *JJSA*; International: Berlin, London. Awards: Golden Trophy for the Republic Day floats designed by him for the Govt. of MAHA. Member: Was a faculty member of the *JJSA* & *JJIAA*. Commissions: *Portraits* of Dr. Zakir Hussain then President of India, Lokmanya Tilak & Veer Savarkar and *murals NCAG*, Jawahar Bal Bhavan Mumbai, Raja Kelkar Museum Pune. Appointments: Seminars and lectures, and demonstrations in *portraits* in colleges and institutions in India. Curated "Master Strokes IV" at *JAG* with *Prafulla Dahanukar*. Collections: *NGMA* & *LKA* New Delhi.

Suhas Bahulkar is primarily a portraitist and a *figurative painter*. His *paintings* reflect his childhood memories in the old *sepia* photographic *style*; The *mannerism* of the old buildings, their ornamental windows with fading *murals* on the walls, are in *harmony* with the traditional and cultural on the one side and the *art* of today on the other.

He lives and works in Mumbai.

Baij, Ramkinkar (1906–1980) b. Bankura WB. Education: National School Bankura; Aptitude for *pottery*, carpentry, *painting*, *screen painting* and stage sets; Dip. *FA*. *VBU*; Active interest in theatre for direction, stage *craft* and designing *backdrops*. Solos: First in New Delhi 1942, *Santiniketan* & Kolkata. Retrospective: *NGMA* New Delhi. Group participations: 1960 organized by *VBU* Union at *Santiniketan* & Kolkata, "Genesis of Ramkinkar" *BAAC* Kolkata, *ISOA*, National Exhibition of Art; International: Paris, Tokyo. *Auctions:* Heart Mumbai & New Delhi, Osian's Mumbai. Awards: Padma Bhushan 1970. Fellowship: *LKA* 1976. Member: Indian Sculptor's Association (Bombay) Mumbai. Appointments: HoD *Sculpture* Dept. *VBU*. Collections: *Delhi Art Gallery*, *LKA* & *NGMA* New Delhi, *BAAC* Kolkata, pvt. & public.

In 1925 he was introduced to *Rabindranath Tagore* at *Santiniketan* and a *plein-air painter*, met other *artists* of the *Bengal School*, chiefly *Nandalal Bose*. Although he began his career as a *painter* in the "Oriental" *style* of the *Bengal School*, he soon developed an interest in the *modern movements* taking place in the West. In the 40s and the 50s he became preoccupied with the principles of *Cubism* and *Surrealism*, capturing a sense of *volume* and structured *space* with his bold use of *line* and *colour*.

However it was his *sculpture*, chiefly his in-situ works that portray his creative capacities. He taught *sculpture* at

Santiniketan where he spent the rest of his life. His *sculptures* have always had a marked "outdoor" quality. The materials he used were hardly traditional: *cement, plaster* and *stone* to create works that would compose themselves in whatever *style* he preferred to use, some being *abstract* and stylized, others being representational. The *sculptures* seem to surge out of the earth with an energy that is at once rugged and *monumental*. "The Santhal Family" is one of his important pieces. It blends perfectly with its environment, its rough, primitive *texture* carrying a sense of movement and suggesting the basic character of the tribals. Ramkinkar Baij enjoyed working amongst the Santhals who were a major source of inspiration for him. His "Sujata" with her frail attenuation is placed perfectly in the tall eucalyptus grove near *Santiniketan*. His *portraits*, e.g., "Madhura Singh", are not mere likenesses but attempts to capture the psyche of the sitter as well.

His *oil paintings* verge on the unconventional (for his times) and *landscapes* in particular display a broad structural organization, a spaciousness and sense of *atmosphere* with lively brushstrokes. *Watercolours* on the other hand, are more staid, but they too are spontaneous. All his *paintings* show that his works were based on tonal and *plastic* variations. *Masses*, planes and *volumes* rather than *line* became his *key motif*. Both in his *paintings* and *sculptures*, he defined receding and advancing planes by dividing his *masses* and marking the dividing planes by etched, furrowed, or ridged *lines*; a method derived from *classical* Indian *sculpture*.

Baij, Ramkinkar: "Santhal Family", *Concrete*, 1938–39, ht 305xbth 609 cm.

Baisakh, Vaishakh One of the spring months in the Hindu calender year, conforming to April-May in the English calender. The spring full moon falls in Baisakh, a harvest time and different ways the festival is celebrated across India. One of the main subjects of the BARAMASA, in *miniature painting*. Refer HOLI.

Bajaj, Sujata (1958–) b. Jaipur, RAJ. Education: Ph.D. in *FA*. Pune, MAHA; ENSBA Scholarship—French Govt. 1988–89. Solos: Chennai, *BAAC* Kolkata, *GC* Mumbai, *JAG*, TKS, *CKP*; International: Commonwealth Art Gallery Edinburgh UK, other towns Washington, Oslo, Paris. Group participations: *LKA* New Delhi & Bangalore, *Gallery 7* Mumbai, *BAS*, HAS; International: Paris, New York, Norway, Germany, Hong Kong. Awards: MAHA State Art, *BAS*. Appointments: Talk on *tribal art* Washington, London, Edinburgh & ENSBA. Collections: *LKA* New Delhi, World Bank India, *Sayed Haider Raza*; International: Mexico, Germany, France, Norway, Holland, USA, Japan, pvt. & public.

Sujata Bajaj has worked with different *art forms* and *media*, e.g., *etching, wood cut, sculpture, murals*, cold *ceramics, fibreglass* and *metal, mixed media* and *acrylics*. After her meeting with Claude Viseux, a Prof. in Paris who worked with the *monotype*, she became fascinated with the *medium*, which involved inking a *metal plate*, working on the *black*, placing a leaf underneath and setting the press in motion.

Over the past 10 years, she has worked with this *medium*, slowly evolving a *style* that involves the use of *paper* paste, *chalk*, charred *paper* and a variety of *calligraphic scripts*, with the word OM recurring incessantly. A great gestural freedom animates these works which are now articulated with an exuberant use of creases and tears, roughened edges and bold slippages. Each frame is a variation on past *traditions*, in the ochres and warm reds she suggests the collective heritage of Indian *culture*.

Sujata Bajaj lives and works both in Norway and India.

Bakre, Sadanandji (1920–) b. Ratnagiri, MAHA. Education: GDA in *sculpture* & *painting JJSA*, taught by *Bhagwant K. Goregaoker*. Self-taught *clay modelling, plaster* work & *stone carving*, The writings of E. Lantri (Italian *sculptor*) being a major influence on his self-education. Solos: *GC* Mumbai, *BAS*, TAG, *PUAG, JAG*; International: Commonwealth Institute & other galleries in London & USA. Group participations: *BAS, PAG* in Mumbai, Vadodara & Ahmedabad; International: Zurich, Rome, Paris, London. *Auctions*: Osian's Mumbai, Sotheby's London. Awards/Certificate: Kolhapur Art Society MAHA, HAS, Scholarship Cash & Silver Medal *BAS*, Lord Mayo Gold Medal *JJSA*; Certificate in *sculpture BAS*. Founder member: *PAG*. Commissions: Worked for film studio Bombay, 1952 did photographic work for the Indian High Commission, 1954 designed costume jewellery and worked at restoring *brass* musical instruments. Collections: Dr. Mulk Raj Anand, K. Gandhy, R. Alkazi in India; International: UK, Texas, USA, Switzerland, France, Italy, Germany, Canada & other countries.

Sadanandji Bakre was one of the six founding members of the *PAG*. His intention, along with the rest of the group, was to get away from a reliance on what was considered "traditional" and forge a new path,

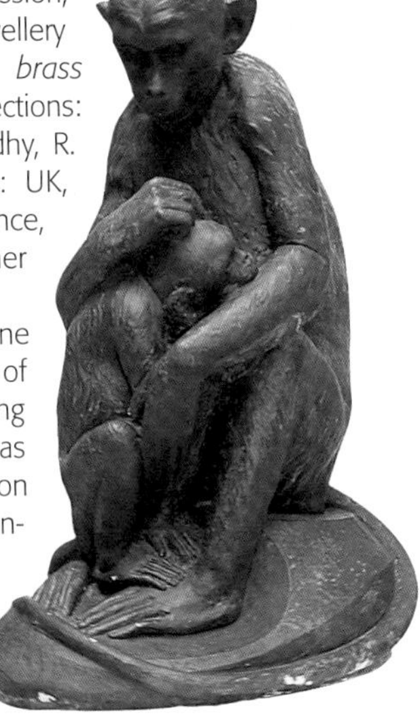

Bakre, Sadanandji: "Monkeys", *Plaster of Paris*, 81x37.5 cm.

merging the *modern* with a real understanding of Indian *culture*. The *PAG* members were experimentalists, affected by the human conditions around them.

Though he lost many of his works when he returned from abroad and also later in India, his passion for *art* stayed alive. He is a *painter* and a *sculptor*, traditionally trained and capable of *realistic* work. For him, nothing is ancient or *modern*, round or oblong in *art*: it is neither good nor bad. Admiring the *Realism* of *Ganpatrao K. Mhatre, Vinayak Pandurang Karmarkar* and other *artists*, he developed his own individualistic *style*. His *portraits*, among them the outstanding *busts* of Cowasji Jehangir and Rudy Von Leyden, reveal the inner intracasies of these personalities. His *paintings* stand comparison with any of his *contemporaries*, as do his *sculptures*. His *paintings* are an *eclectic* amalgmation of all *styles*, though cubist and impressionist elements tend to dominate.

Sadanandji Bakre lives and works in a small village in Ratnagiri MAHA. His 1997 retrospective in Mumbai came after a long hiatus of nearly 25 years after exhibiting in the Nichols Freadwell Gallery London in 1971. Refer *Krishnaji Howlaji Ara, Francis Newton Souza, Sayed Haider Raza, H.A. Gade.*

Balance The impression of stability given to a *composition*, both *pictorial* and sculptural and in a musical or dance performance. Balance in the *visual arts* means *visual harmony* and equilibrium of *form*, *colour* and *texture* in the *composition*. It also depends on psychological and *aesthetic* factors.

The *Ajanta frescoes* and *miniature paintings* are classic examples of balance in the early works of *art*. In early 20th century, *Raja Ravi Varma* brought in the balance of *perspective* in his *compositions*. *Gaganendranath Tagore* practiced balance in *tonal values* and *colours* in essentially a cubist *manner.* Refer *All-over, Closed form, Colour Wheel, Minimalism, Surendra Pal Joshi, L. Munuswamy, Ramesh Rao, Jehangir Sabavala, Abanindranath Tagore.*

Banasthali Vidyapith (RAJ). The *drawing* and *painting* dept. of the Vidyapith was started by Prof. *Deokinandan Sharma* in 1937. Possibly the only institution providing professional training in the Jaipur process of *fresco paintings*, the dept. encouraged experimentation in both Indian and Italian *styles* and other *tempera techniques* of *wall painting*. With important contributions from masters like Prof. *Benode Behari Mukherjee*, and Kala Guru *Sailendranath Dey*, the training camps in *fresco painting* were attended by many renowned *artists* from the *contemporary art* world; including were Prof *Narayan S. Bendre, Shanti Dave, Jyoti Bhatt* and *P. Vinay Trivedi*, all from Vadodara and Pradyumna Tanna, *K. Sheshagiri Rao, K.V. Haridasan, R.B. Bhaskaran, K.M. Adimoolam, Bikash Bhattacharjee, Ganesh Haloi*, Dinesh Shah and *Sukhamoy Mitra*. Refer *Santiniketan.*

Bandhani Refer *Tie and Dyed Fabrics.*

Bandhopadhyay, Sudhangsu (1949–) b. India. Education: Grad. in Western *style painting* & *sculpture GCAC* Kolkata. Degree in History of Art & Art Appreciation Calcutta University. Since, the mid-70s working in both *oils* and *watercolours*. Solos: Centre Art Gallery & *AFA* Kolkata, *AIFACS*, TKS, *JAG*; International: Germany. Group participations: *BAAC, AFA*, WB State Academy & Rabindra Bharati Kolkata, People for Animals New Delhi, "Bengal Art Today" Hyderabad, *BB Biennale*; International: Berlin. *Art* workshops: *Painting*–Govt. of Bengal, EZCC & *Art Acre* Kolkata, *ABC*; International: Artist Exchange Programme Stuttgart Germany. Awards: Lithoprint Govt. College of Arts, *watercolours* & *oil painting AFA* & WB State Kolkata. Appointments: Visited Germany on an exchange programme, visiting more than 300 galleries and was drawn towards the *landscape* in the villages there.

Over the years, Sudhangsu Bandhopadhyay's *landscapes* have evolved from the *realistic* to the *abstract*. His *colour* sense was always bright and fauvist, but earlier, one could sense the relationship between *colour* and *image*. He transforms the *landscape* into an interaction of deft brushstrokes and *colour*, infusing his *canvases* with *light* and *atmosphere*. The earlier reds and blues have given way to soft subtle grays, *white* dominates the *composition*, being applied rather lavishly with thin *black lines* showing through with exuberant patches of red and chrome applied in a gestural *manner*.

He lives and works in Kolkata. Refer *Abstraction Lyrical*.

Bandhyopadhyay, Satyendranath (1896–1978) b. Chnamosina, Bankura, WB. Bandhyopadhyay, name shortened to Banerjee by the British. Education: 1921 joined KB *Santiniketan*, under the guidance of *Nandalal Bose*; 1926 studied Western *art* under Andre Karpeles & Stella Kramrisch. Solos: In its hundred year *ISOA* held his solo show at *BAAC* Kolkata. Awards: Delhi, Kolkata, Patna. Appointments: *Art* teacher for several years in Vrindavan, UP & Karachi; HoD of Indian *painting* GCA Kolkata until retiring at 55 in 1951. Collections: KB *Santiniketan*, Patna Museum, Trivandrum Museum, *NGMA* New Delhi; International: Moscow Art Gallery.

Satyendranath Bandhyopadhyay mastered the *wash technique* of the *Bengal School*, using both *watercolour* and *tempera*, in the *style* of *Abanindranath Tagore*. His *tones* were rather subdued with a *broad handling* of *colour*. His *landscapes* have a poetic sense of *atmosphere* and delicate realistic touches are added to his mythological *paintings*. His *portraits* show his keen study of physiognomy with a subtle use of *colour* and brushstrokes. He had settled in *Santiniketan*. Refer *Portrait*.

Bandyopadhyay, Ramananda (1936–) b. *Birbhum*, WB. Education: Grad. in *FA*. *VBU* in 1957 under *Nandalal Bose*. Solos: *Santiniketan*, *BAAC* & Galerie La Mere Kolkata, *CYAG*, *AIFACS*, TKS. Retrospective: *BAAC* & *AFA* Kolkata. Group participations: All India Exhibitions; International: Moscow. Awards: Four Academy Awards 1961, 72, 78 & 80. Member: Birla Museum & Asiatic Society Kolkata. Commissions: *Murals* Ramakrishna Mission Mumbai & Purulia & an insurance building Kolkata. Appointments: Taught *art* at the Purulia Ramakrishna Mission School & Dir. Museum & Art Gallery Ramakrishna Mission Institute of

Culture Kolkata. Publications: Books on Swami Vivekananda and his ashram, C. Sarada Devi and Ramakrishna Mission, Translated "Lord Krishna" into Japanese. Collections: *NGMA* & *LKA* New Delhi, *BAAC, AFA* & State *LKA* Kolkata.

The strength of Ramananda Bandyopadhyay's works lie in the ease of their communication with the viewer. His *art* draws its inspiration from man and *nature, paintings*, which are predominantly linear with a rhythmic use of *line*, principally with *wash technique* and folk-like *form*. He has used *mythology*, with skilful *handling* of *colour* and a keen sense of the *aesthetic*. His *sculptures* are complementary to his *paintings*.

He lives and works in Kolkata.

Banerjea, Shanti (1917–2000) b. Bengal. Education: Grad. in GCA Kolkata. Solos: *Indian Museum* & *AFA* Kolkata; International: Thailand, Malaysia, Indonesia, Bali, Java, Australia, Switzerland, France, Italy. Retrospective: Stream of Time *AFA* Kolkata. Group participations: *BAAC* & *AFA* Kolkata; International: Scandinavia, France, ENSBA. Founder member: Academic Art Club, a workshop for young *artists* belonging to other professions. Appointments: Travelled South East Asia & Europe working & exhibiting on-the-spot *sketches* & *drawings*, Art Dir. of an advertizing firm, retired in 1986. Collections: India, Japan, Thailand, Scandinavia, Germany, France, England, USA & other countries.

Although Shanti Banerjea was an *artist* with a strong academic base, he did not allow it to restrain his creativity. He was a landscapist, who moved from mellow *colours* to bright *pigments* in *mixed media*. He worked with *brushes*, blades, *ink* droppers, sand and almost with every object, even with his bare hands. His earlier works show the mastery of *colour* transparency.

He lived and worked in Kolkata.

Banerjee, Amitabha (1929–) b. Barisal (now in Bangladesh). Education: *FA*. GSA Kolkata. Solos & group shows: Kolkata, Chennai, Bangalore, Thiruvananthapuram, *LKA* New Delhi, *CYAG*; International: Waterloo, Toronto, Canada, North Dakota, New York. Group participations: *Triennale LKA* New Delhi, *BAAC* Kolkata, 50 Years of Indian Independence Mumbai, others in *Santiniketan*, *VBU*; International: *Biennale* UK & Australia, *Printmaking* Festival of India USA. *Art* workshops: *Graphic LKA* New Delhi; International: Bangladesh, USA, Indian Prints Amsterdam. Awards & Hon.: All India Awards & National *LKA* New Delhi, *BAAC* Kolkata, for *etching* Chandigarh, *AIFACS*; Honorary Advisor of the State Centres of *LKA* Bhubaneshwar & Kolkata. Member: *SCA*; Responsible for building Regional Centre of Rastraiya *LKA* Kolkata. Appointments: Chief Audio-visual dept. USIS 1952 & 80 Kolkata; Freelance *artist* for four years. Publications: Articles on *Krishna N. Reddy*, Paul Lingren, *Bikash Bhattacharjee*. Collections: *NGMA* New Delhi, *LKA*, *BAAC* Kolkata, *Chandigarh Museum*; International: Washington DC, New York, London, & pvt. Bangladesh, Australia & USA.

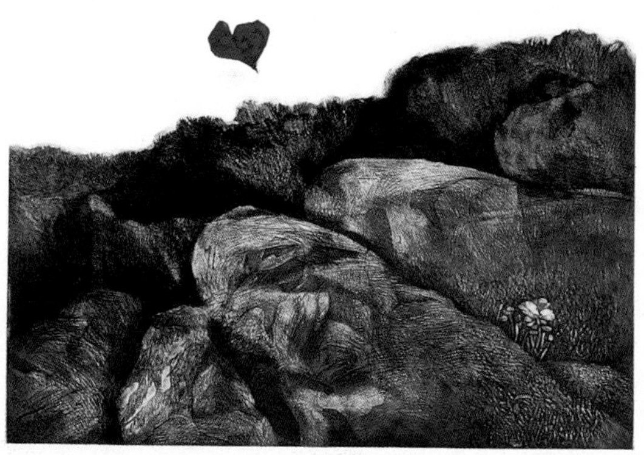

Banerjee, Amitabha: "Farm I", *Etching*, 1989, 50x36 cm.

Amitabha Banerjee, during his long career, worked with several *media*. *Printmaking* and its *forms* being his preferred *mediums* of expression. He expresses "the tools of cognition of the *artist* are through structures, structures conceived in *light, colour, texture*—a formal identity—there is a feeling, a mood, a sense of involvement and compulsion, in the end, love." His *paintings* too carry some of these feelings, the *warm colours* slowly revealing *forms* which melt back into the *shadows*.

He lives and works in Kolkata.

Banerjee, Dipak (1936–) b. Barisal (now in Bangladesh). Education: Dip. in *FA*. *GCAC* Kolkata. Solos: Held 20 solos national & international including New Delhi, Kolkata, Mumbai, Varanasi; International: Kathmandu, Paris, Oslo, Bergen, Fredrikstad, Oxford & Hamburg. Group participations: *Triennale* New Delhi, *LKA* Kolkata, Sanskriti by TATA Steel Jamshedpur, *Graphic art BB*, *CYAG*; International: *Biennale* in Tokyo, Sao Paulo, Grenchen, Norway, London & Dhaka, Festival of India USA, Contemporary Indian paintings & *graphic* in Poland & Russia 1993. *Art* camps & workshops: All India Graphic camp *Roopankar*, "Painters" organized by Sanskriti in Jamshepur. Member: *SCA*. Appointments: Worked at ENSBA & Atelier 17 Paris on a French Govt. Scholarship; A year in Oslo on a Norwegian Govt. Scholarship, Later Prof. Faculty of Visual Art Varanasi. Collections: *NGMA* & *LKA* New Delhi, TIFR; International: Bergen Art Society Norway, National Museum of Modern Art Baghdad.

Dipak Banerjee's first reaction to *printmaking* was to explore the technical possibilities of the *genre*. Initially, his *forms* were greatly influenced by Western *Art*. Soon however, he came back to his roots picking up *visual* elements from the rich Indian cultural heritage. At times, he picks up *motifs* and *symbolic* concepts from TANTRA, though at times he felt the need to be a neo-tantric *painter*. His *colours* have run the gamut of bright striking primaries, to the subtle *shades* and *transparent tints* in his recent *prints* and *canvases*.

Dipak Banerjee being a Reader in the Dept. of *Painting*, Faculty of Visual Art BHU, lives in Varanasi.

Baramasa The twelve months as described in the illustrated *classical* sets of 12 *miniature paintings*. The 12 months are:

Chaitra (March–April)
BAISAKHA (April–May)
Jyestha (May–June)
Ashada (June–July)
Shravana (July–August)
Bhadra-Pada (August–September)
Asuja (September–October)
Karttika (October–November)
Mang-asara (November–December)
Poosa (December–January)
Magha (January–February)
Phalguna (Febuary–March)

They are poetically captured in sets of 12 in *Rajasthani* and *Pahari miniature paintings*. It is usually Kesavadasa's 16th century literary work that is illustrated. This Baramasa gives an account of the life of the people, the various *rituals*, ceremonies and festivals associated with the 12 months. This was given life by *painters*, with references to the seasons, by means of *landscape* elements, costumes and festivals. Refer HOLI.

Barbhaiya, Biharilal C. (1927–) b. Ahmedabad. Education: Dip. in FAC *VBU*, a student of *Nandalal Bose*, sponsored to the USA, specialized in *fresco*, *mural*, *ink* & *batik painting*. Solos: *Santiniketan* in 1951, about 15 in Mumbai, Ahmedabad; International: USA, Japan. Group participations: *LKA* Ahmedabad, Kolkata, & Bhopal, *AIFACS*, *BAS*; International: Moscow, Japan, USA. Awards: *Painting* National Award New Delhi, *Kumar Magazine* Ahmedabad. Commissions: *Murals Santiniketan*, Parliament House, Palampur & *Fresco painting* depicting the life of Mahatma Gandhi at the Birla House New Delhi. Appointments: Lecturer in *applied art MSU*; Given lectures, radio talk shows & TV demonstrations, all on *Batik*. Publications: Specialized in *batik painting* & a book on the same subject, national & international.

His *style* is essentially *figurative* with a folk *imagery*. His subjects are exotic in the late *Narayan S. Bendre manner*, with groups of adivasis or village people in patterned costumes.

He lives and works in Vadodara, GUJ. Refer *Batik*.

Bark Painting *Painting* on prepared tree bark. The material is subjected to a variety of processes until the surface becomes smooth enough for *painting*. It is popularly used by Australian aboriginal *artists*.

Other than *palm leaf*, the second most important writing material in Ancient India was the inner bark of the Himalayan Birch tree. The famous poet Kalidasa referred to it as "Spotted like the skin of an elephant & written upon with solution of metal". Most popular in North India especially in Kashmir where it was easily available. Refer *Manuscript Painting*, *Illuminated Manuscripts*.

Baroda School of Arts (Kala Bhavan) Refer *Maharaja Fatesingh Museum*.

Baroque The *term* is possibly from the Portuguese "Barocco" meaning an irregularly shaped pearl. Baroque describes the *style* in European *architecture*, *painting* and *sculpture* between *Mannerism* and Rococo, from about 1600 to 1750. At its peak, High Baroque–all three branches of *art*, *architecture*, *painting* and *sculpture*, were usually combined. The building plan was frequently based on a series of circles or ellipses, creating *rhythms* of convex and concave curves. Baroque essentially included decorative schemes, especially internally using illusionistic effects in *painting*, with *sculpture* as part of the setting. In the theatrical spatial effects thus created, the spectator also becomes part of the action. Every *artist* had his identifying idiosyncrasies. They worked both for the church in Italy and the court in France, Spain and Flanders. The leading masters include G. Bernini in Italy, B. Neumann in Germany, and Fischer von Erlach in Austria. The *term* applies to European *artists* of the time.

Influences of this *style* are seen in the architectural models of the churches, due to the European settlements. Also in the villas & palaces of the wealthy landowners (late 19th century) in Bengal. Refer *Altarpiece*, *Closed Form*, *Iconography*, *Iconology*, *Mannerism*, *Neo-Classicism*, *Rhythm*, *Transition*, *Antonio X. Trindade*.

Barua, Atasi (1921–) b. *Santiniketan* Ashram, WB. Daughter & pupil of *Asit K. Haldar*. Solos: In 1958, 1971 in Artistry House & Birla Mandir Kolkata. Group participations: Maha Bodhi Society & *AFA* Kolkata, Lucknow University; International: SriLanka. Appointments: Gave radio talks on *art*, Lectured on her father's *paintings* at *AFA* & *VMM* Kolkata. Publications: In magazines, Bengali journals *AFA* Bulletin; International: Ceylon Times in 1950, Slides & lectures on her *paintings* in Germany; Photo & slides taken by Buddhist Harvard Scholar of Japan. Collections: Jain Temple Kolkata, Bengal Buddhist Association; International: USA, Middle East, SriLanka, Burma, Japan.

Being a staunch Buddhist, the *theme* that regularly surfaces in her works is the life of the BUDDHA. The Maha Bodhi Society of Kolkata has also published 12 postcards depicting incidents in the life of the BUDDHA, designed by her. She was also commissioned by the *Jain* DIGAMBARA Temple of Belgarhia Kolkata to *design* a series of *marble relief* works based on the life of Parsvanatha–the 23rd Tirthankara.

Atasi Barua's work, though based on the linear *wash style* of the *Bengal School* appears to veer a naive *distortion* of *form* and overworked *drapery* with heavily worked *outlines* demarcating the attenuated *figures*.

She lives and works in Kolkata. Refer *Jainism*, *Buddhism*.

Barun, Simlai (1947–) b. Kolkata, WB. Self-taught *painter WBAF* Kolkata. Has worked on a research paper on Indian *mythology*. Solos: Kolkata, Orissa, Bangladesh, his own "Simlai Cafe" Kalighat Kolkata; International: Bangladesh. Group participations: *WBAF*, *AFA* & *BAAC* Kolkata, Haryana Art Emporium New Delhi, Exhibited till 94. Fellowship: Govt. of India for *art* 1987–89. Member: *WBAF*. Publications: Statesman, Hindustan Standard in English & Anand Bazar Patrika, Desh in Bengali; AIR Kolkata & Orissa. Collections: *LKA* New Delhi, Ananda Bazar Patrika Kolkata; International: London, pvt.

Simlai Barun is basically a *figurative painter*, using a heavily *loaded brush* to cut out distorted and fragmented *forms* that are imbued with a scarcely subdued violence. There is also a heavy-handed use of *symbolism* relating to philosophy, *mythology* and social commentary.

He lives and works in Kolkata.

Barwe, Prabhakar (1936–1995) b. Nagaon, MAHA. Education: Dip. in *FA*. *JJSA*. Solos: *GC* & Sophia Art Gallery Mumbai, *JAG*, TAG, *PUAG*; International: Book Bay Gallery USA. Group participations: National Exhibitions & *LKA Triennale* New Delhi, *GC* Mumbai, *BB*, *JAG*; International: Japan, Switzerland, Germany, France, Istanbul, New York & Washington DC USA, *Biennale* in France, Yugoslavia & Chile. *Auctions*: Helpage India, Heart & Osian's Mumbai. Awards: *LKA* National award; International: Tokyo. Fellowships: International Residency Fellowship Grant "Yaddo" *Artist* Colony, New York & USA. Appointments: An *art* designer *WSC* Mumbai. Publications: 1990 "Kora Canvas" in Marathi, a book collating his thoughts & ideas on *art* & *art*-making, *BAS Art* journal & read by *Bharati Kapadia NGMA* Mumbai. Collections: *LKA* & *NGMA* New Delhi, *Roopankar*, *BB*; International: Ben & Abbey Grey Foundation USA.

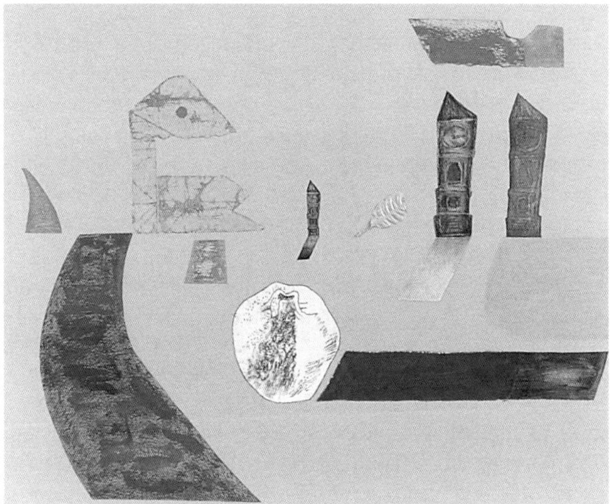

Barwe, Prabhakar: "Untitled", *Mixed Media* on *Canvas*.

Prabhakar Barwe moved from an expressionist use of *symbolic forms* in the 70s to his serene *compositions* of the 80s and 90s by suppressing the urge for textural and *symbolic* excess. As he puts it, "Initially *form* gets itself transformed into object, after which the object gets itself settled in the *painting space* as an abstract-sign. And *colour* moving towards colourlessness…merges with the *colour atmosphere* of the *painting* in its entirety."

His final works are more like annotated cryptograms becoming signs of the object rather than representations of them. Relationship between these "characters" comes across as quotes rather than as direct conversations. He lived in Mumbai. Refer Illustration—*Computer Art*.

Basak, Aditya (1953–) b. WB. Education: Dip. *GCAC* Kolkata. Group artists *AFA* Kolkata. Group participations: Over 65 in Kolkata including *BAAC*, 16 in Mumbai including *CYAG* & TG; International *art* camps: Germany, Hong Kong, Kalimpong, London, New York, Singapore, Canada. *Auctions*: Heart Mumbai & New Delhi. Awards & Hon.: SZCC Hyderabad, WB State Award, National Award *Painting*. Fellowship: Senior HRD Ministry. Member: *SCA*. Collections: Godrej Mumbai, *NGMA* & *LKA* New Delhi, *BAAC* Kolkata, *CYAG*, *Roopankar*, *BB*; International: Japan, New York & other pvt.

Aditya Basak's work blends the Indian *tradition* and *modern* Western *style*. His is primarily a linear *style* with a limited use of *colour*. He prefers using *waterproof inks*, *earth colours* and *crayons* and works on Nepalese *hand-made paper* and in *mixed media* on *canvas*. His work is predominantly *figurative*, blending *Realism* with *Surrealism* to come up with a stylized *distortion* of *form* and *pattern*.

Aditya Basak lives and works in Kolkata.

Base In referring to works of *art* this word has several different meanings. **a)** The *vehicle* used for *painting*, e.g., *canvas* for *oil painting*, *paper* for *watercolour* and *gouache*, the wall for *fresco* and *mural*. **b)** The pedestal of a *sculpture*. **c)** The lowest level of a building or a temple immediately above the platform or ground. **d)** The actual space occupied and its surrounding in the case of *installation* or *performance art*. Refer *Living sculpture*, *Mask*, RASA, *Video Art*, *Visual*, *Shakuntala Kulkarni*, *Nalini Malani*, *Mahirwan Mamtani*, *Vivan Sundaram*, *Nita Thakore*.

Basohli, Basohli Kalam, Basohli School, Basohli Miniatures Basohli Kalam literally meaning the Basohli *style* or the *style* of Indian *miniature painting* associated with the erstwhile state-kingdom of Basohli in the present-day Indian State of HP. The Basohli *style* was characterized by the use of bright, glowing, chrome-yellows, oranges and reds. The story of KRISHNA was the favourite *theme* of the *artists*. The *figures* are tall, erect and slender with flattened heads and alert expressions. Women wearing a long skirt (Ghagra) with short blouses (Choli) and a *transparent* veil (Odhani). The men wear the dress of cowherds, carrying a folded blanket over one shoulder. KRISHNA is characterized by the use of his long silk Pitambara Vastra (golden-yellow Dhoti), his blue skin and the peacock feather in his hair. Animals also find their place in Basohli miniatures, with KRISHNA's adoring cows appearing like high-stepping deer. *Perspective* is not used at all. The *background* is absolutely flat and is a perfect foil to the action taking place in the *foreground*.

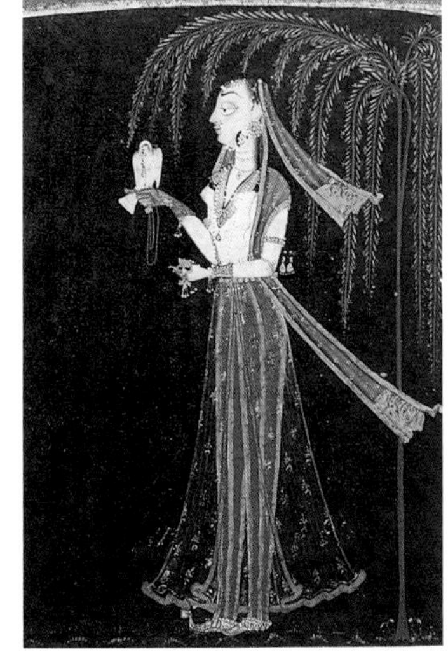

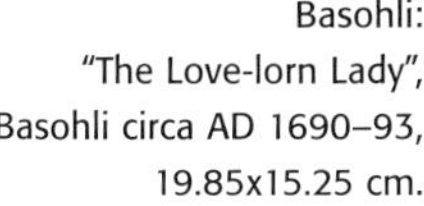

Basohli: "The Love-lorn Lady", Basohli circa AD 1690–93, 19.85x15.25 cm.

Architecture is limited to single-roomed pavilions, where lovers meet or shelter from the rains. Refer *Pahari Miniature Painting*.

Bas-Relief A panel *sculpture* in which the design projects very low from the surface used in *wood* and *stone carving*. This *style* has been seen right from the early period particularly in the *Gupta* period where the story of BUDDHA is narrated e.g. Vessantara JATAKA of circa first century BC. Also seen in the early Hindu temples. Refer *Abu-Dilwara Group of Temples, Ajanta, Ellora, Mahabalipuram, Relief, Stupa, Thanjavur (Tanjore) Painting.*

Basu, Baren (1943–) b. Dacca, Bangladesh. Education: Dip. *GCAC* Kolkata 1967. Scholarship *AFA* Kolkata, National Cultural Scholarship *Painting*, worked under *Satyen Ghosal*. Solos: Over 25 solos Nainital, UP, *LKA* New Delhi, & Chennai, *AFA* & *BAAC* Kolkata, *JAG*, TAG; International: Taiwan, China. Group participations: *AFA*, Oriental Society of Arts & *BAAC* Kolkata, *LKA* New Delhi & Kerala, MKKP Raipur, All India Art Exhibition Orissa. Awards: State Lalit Kala 1983, *AFA* Kolkata 1984. Founder member: Canvas Artist Circle Kolkata.

Baren Basu has evolved from an academic *figurative style* to a near *abstract* symbology of *space* division and textural variation in his recent thickly brushed *oils*. A constant *theme* over the years (other than his *landscapes*) is his preoccupation with the problems afflicting womanhood and the underprivileged people of India. "Mother & Child" portrays the age-old *theme* with a twist, the protagonists belonging to the animal world. His *figures* display a raw spontaneity of expression and *colour* that is almost primitive in its *nature*.

He lives and works in Kolkata.

Basu, Gautam (1950–) b. WB. No formal *Art Education*, Studied under *Atul Bose* and *Ganesh Haloi*. Solos: *AFA* Kolkata, *ATG* & with other *artists at BAAC* Mumbai, *GK*, BAG, *CYAG*. Group participations: *AFA, BAAC*, WB State Academy & Govt. of WB Kolkata, National Exhibition New Delhi, *AIFACS*. Awards: State Academy, WB Govt. & Indra Dugar's Award Kolkata. Founder member: "Five Painters" Kolkata. Collections: *BAAC* Kolkata, *Roopankar, BB*, Tata India & pvt. abroad.

Gautam Basu is an intuitive *painter* using the visual world as a basis for his *imagery*. He tries to capture the dichotomy between the representative and the essence of an object. This introversion, which tends rather to evade comprehension has been projected through his use of *tempera*. In "Her Portrait" one notices a cubist sensibility at work, along with a subtle use of near *tertiary colours*.

Gautam Basu lives and works in Kolkata.

Basu, Samhita (1954–) b. Kolkata, Self-taught. Took to *painting* after B.A. in Economics. Studied in *figurative art* & *portraits*. Solos: ANZ Grindlay Art Gallery, Sun-et-Rumiere Gallery in Mumbai, TAJ, *JJAG*. Group Shows: *AFA, BAAC* Kolkata, "Art with a Heart" and "Ideas and Images"—*NGMA*, Harmony, IOC in Mumbai, *ASI, BAS*. Publications: Magazines & newspapers. Collections: Bharat Petrolum, Quest India, Indian Oil Corporation (IOC) and Ramada Inn.

A self-taught *artist*, Samita Basu tries to bring out her preoccupation with the diverse aspects of womanhood, especially her anguish, loneliness and repression. Her *paintings* have evolved constantly, veering between the naturalistic and the expressionistic. Her *compositions* show a fine understanding of *anatomy*.

Batik A method of dyeing textiles by using the *wax* resist process. While the type of *wax* differs regionally, the basic idea is that the portion of the cloth painted with *wax* will resist the *colour* and retain the original *colour* of the fabric. The process is well-known throughout Asia, especially in Indonesia, Japan and India. The country of origin can be identified by the *motifs* used by the dyers.

In India, Batik has also been a *technique* exploited by some fine *artists*. *Santiniketan*, in WB was the first institution to offer the course. Refer *Arnawaz Vasudev, Biharilal C. Barbhaiya.*

Bauhaus A *school of architecture* and *design* which became the intellectual centre and source of inspiration for modernization throughout the world. Here *artists* such as P. Klee, M. Nagy and V. Kandinsky, designers and architects such as W. Gropius and technicians in textiles, *ceramics* and *metal craft* worked together at coordinating all the *arts* into a unified desire for *modern designs*. The teachers tried to do away with the dichotomy between the *arts* and the *crafts*, working in close collaboration with their students. Experimentation was encouraged, utilitarian and functional values were stressed upon. Though the school originated in Weimar, Germany, in 1925 it moved to Dessau and later to Berlin, where it was closed by the National Socialists in 1933. M. Nagy however opened a new branch at Chicago in 1937.

Rabindranath Tagore and *Gaganendranath Tagore* initiated the first *exhibition* in Calcutta in 1922 of the German Bauhaus Group artists. This opened the door for a new wave of international influence on Indian *Art* typified by outright rejection of confining *models* existing then of "Indian" *art* as well as combining *modern* sensibilities with nationalist fervour. Refer *Nandalal Bose, KB Santiniketan*.

Bawa, Manjit (1941–) b. Dhoori, Puj. Education: Dip. in *FA*. *College of Art* New Delhi, London School of Printing UK. Solos: Over 12 including Taj Krishna Hyderabad, *SG* Mumbai, *AIFACS, Dhoomimal, CYAG*; International: Terrace London, San-Sebastain Spain, GBP. Group participations: National *LKA* New Delhi, *ATG, JAG, BB, Computer Art* & *VAG* at *JAG*; International: *Biennale* in Tokyo, Anokava Turkey, Havana & Cuba, Fukuoka Museum Japan, Festival of India London & New York, Contemporary Indian Art USA. *Art* camps: CMC, *Graphic* camp & *LKA* New Delhi, *GAC*. *Auctions*: Heart Mumbai, Christie's. Awards: National Award *Roopankar Biennale BB*. Advisory member: *NGMA* New Delhi, *BB*, Dir. *BB*. Appointments: Visiting Lecturer *College of Art* New Delhi. Collections: *NGMA* & *LKA* New Delhi, PUJ University Chandigarh & pvt. national & international.

Three distinct phases mark Manjit Bawa's works: The first phase was of creative *landscapes*, as well as animal and human *forms* in an expressionist *style*. His second phase was when he concentrated on pure *forms* with loosely brushed *colours* like mauve, pink and green. Later he combined the two and greatly simplified his *form*. Now *form* is the main factor in his *paintings*, avoiding *texture* as it disturbs the *composition*. He needs a flat *background* to *support* the *volume* of the *forms*. He is also a fine colourist, using *colours* with a verve and intensity that is unmatched outside *Basohli paintings* that he is obviously inspired by. Unlike *Basohli painting*, however, his *forms* and *figures* float pneumatically in *space* without touching the *ground*. On the other hand, like *Basohli painting*, a favourite *theme* of Bawa's is KRISHNA and the GOPIS. We see the Blue *God* cavorting with his cows, or dancing and playing his flute. Bawa also identifies KRISHNA with Ranjha because of his penchant for Sufi poetry and Indian *mythology*.

Manjit Bawa lives and works in New Delhi.

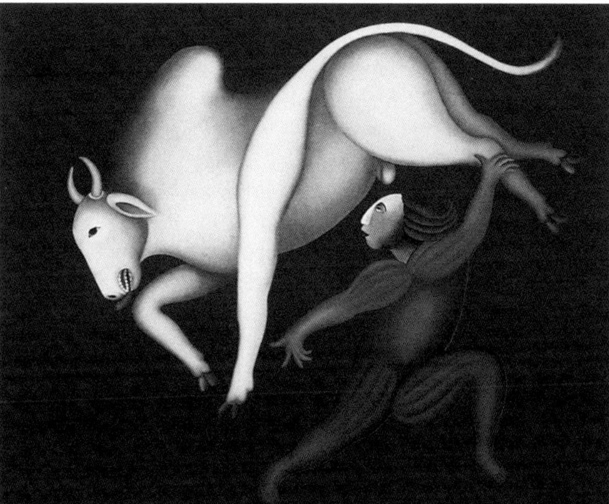

Bawa, Manjit: "Krishna Series", *Oil* on *Canvas*, 1996, 180x206 cm.

Bazaar Painting *Paintings* were sold at the foot of KALI temple (built in 1809) in Calcutta. With the Western influences, the poor *painters* migrated from the village Patuas, whose *paintings* were bought as auspicious souvenirs by pilgrims. These *artists* painted and engraved to cater to the fast and growing demand and to earn enough for the day and tried to sell the works at a very low price. They modified their materials and *techniques* by using cheap unglued mill-made *paper* and chemical *paints* with home-ground *colours*. They also adopted pure *water-colours* in place of the time-consuming *gouache* and *tempera colours*. There were two classes of *artists* and artisans who painted subjects of the KALI temple in simplified and stylized *forms* which derived from the *folk art* of the Pata *paintings* of rural Bengal. They used *light washes*, emphasizing the edges of the *forms*. The traditional flat and linear *technique* was used with the bold and sweeping *lines* of the *Kalighat Pats*, as they were known later. Refer *Jamini Roy*, *Company School* and *Kalighat Pat*, *Kalighat Folk Painting*.

Beig, Nisar A. (1933–) b. Srinagar. Education: Studied *drawing* & *painting* Sir Amar Singh Technical Institute Srinagar. Solos: Srinagar, Kolkata, *LKA* New Delhi, TAG, *JAG*. Group participations: Kashmir Week Exhibition in Mumbai, New Delhi, Chennai, Kolkata by J&K Cultural Academy. *Art* camps: All India *artist's* camp Kashmir. Awards: J&K Cultural Academy. Appointments: Secretary Kashmir Foundation & Funkar Culture Organization Srinagar, Worked as an *art* teacher, commercial *artist* & at Census Dept. & Field Survey Organization of J&K State as an *artist*. Collections: J&K Cultural Academy Srinagar, *NGMA* & *LKA* New Delhi.

His *paintings* are essentially *abstract* with a hint of the *figure* emerging through the hazy, overlying layers of *paint*. Though he paints life in general, a number of his *paintings* show the impact of life lived in the cultural and political hiatus of Kashmir.

He lives and worked as a lecturer in the Gandhi Memorial College in Srinagar.

Bendre, Narayan S. (1910–1992) b. Indore, MP. Education: GDA *Bombay School Painter*; Guidance of *Y.D. Deolalikar*, State School of Art, Holkar College Indore; Trained *Graphic Arts*, *Art* Student's League & *Ceramic* YWCA New York USA. Solos: TAG from 1943–1989, *Drawing* Exhibition Bhopal. Retrospective: 1974. Family artists group show: TAG 1999; International: USA, Czechoslovakia, Yugoslavia, Poland. Group participations: *NGMA* New Delhi, Marvel Art Gallery Ahmedabad, All India Exhibition; International: New York, Toronto. *Auctions*: Heart & Osian's Mumbai. Awards: Padma Shri 1969, MP University, *BAS* Gold Medal, *VBU*. Member: 1st Indian Cultural Delegation to China & Japan. Appoint- ments: Ex. Vice-Chairman *LKA* & National Academi of Art New Delhi, Prof. of *painting* & HoD *MSU*, Chairman International Jury 2nd *Triennale* Exhibition India. Publications: "Illustrated Weekly", "The Critical Vision"—A.S. Raman & *LKA Contemporary* Indian artists & "Profile of A Pioneer N.S. Bendre" by *Ratan Parimoo*. Collections: *NGMA* & *LKA* New Delhi, *BKB* Varanasi, *AFA* & *BAAC* Kolkata, *Museum* in Vadodara, Chennai & Bangalore, *LKA* Mysore, *SJM*, TIFR; International: Woodmare Gallery Philadelphia, Asia Institute New York.

Narayan S. Bendre's career spans more than half a century with three distinct phases. His work in the earliest phase, in the 30s and 40s, largely aligns itself with the picturesque *paintings* of 19th-century British *artists* in India. This required widespread travelling and Bendre travelled all over India, including the famous cities of Banaras and Hardwar (river banks), Kashmir, Indore, etc., for his *"plein-air" landscapes*, where he successfully attempted a merger of French *Impressionism* with German *Expressionism*. Such *landscapes* could be executed on coloured or toned *paper* with the *colour*, *space* and brushstrokes effectively capturing various parts of the *figure* "in movement", since *gouache* was used.

Simultaneously, Narayan S. Bendre also painted an extensive series of one-*figure studies* depicting different Indian ethnic types in picturesque costumes without suggesting the *backdrop*. Many of these *paintings* depicted old men from RAJ, village belles from GUJ and MAHA.

Another series of *tempera paintings* were done around 1945, after a trip to *Santiniketan*, where his use of *line* and fine stylized *draughtsmanship* was to pave the way for his cubist phase of the 50s. Among these works were two distinct groups: one comprising human *figures* and the other, *still lifes*. However Narayan S. Bendre was more interested in spatial tensions rather than cubist *distortions*. His "Sunflower" (1955) was quite well-known, with geometrical wheel-like petals against green leaves.

By the 50s Narayan S. Bendre had already established himself as a fine colourist. He started teaching at the fledgling *MSU* around this time, where his explorations in the field of *art education* won him great acclaim and also laid the foundation for the Baroda Group of Artists.

He left Vadodara after 16 years, for Mumbai. Here his early preoccupation with the picturesque returned, although his *handling* changed, from the broad brushstroke to the measured *stippling* of *Pointillism*. However he did not follow the pointillistic rules set down by Seurat, instead employing the dots to achieve *tone*, *colour* and *texture*.

His personal development ranged from his early academic *style* of the 30s to the *Abstract Expressionism* of the 60s to the *figurative New Realism* of the last 30 years. It is difficult to straightjacket him into any known *"Ism"* for his works are identified through *form*, organization and above all *colour* orchestration, which is strong and autonomous. He lived and worked in Mumbai with his *artist* wife and son. Refer *Pointillism*, *Neo-Impressionism*.

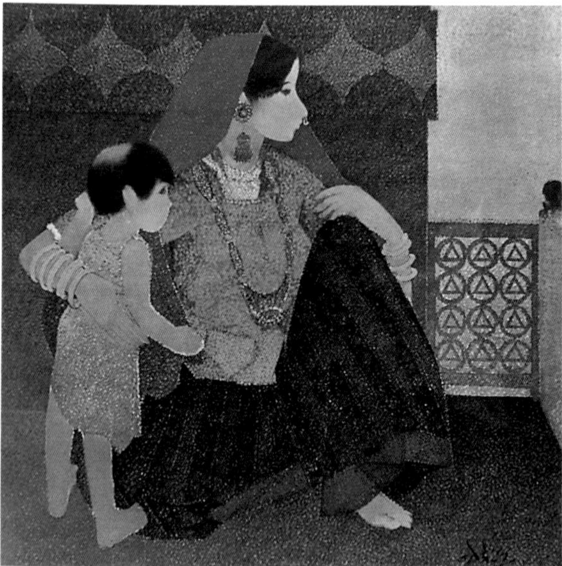

Bendre, Narayan S.: "Pratiksha", *Oil* on *Canvas*, 1982, 91.5x91.5 cm.

Bengal Oil Painting Even before *Raja Ravi Varma*, around 18th & 19th century little known *painters* in Bengal were experimenting with *oils*, executing medium-sized *paintings* of the Hindu *pantheon*, *paintings* with *narrative themes*, and stories from Hindu *mythology* depicting DURGA, KALI and Annapurna. Though using largely indigenous subjects & *iconography*, these *paintings* were traditionally described as "Dutch Bengal School" because the *medium* they used may have been learnt from the Dutch. However, they were clearly a part of the Bengali heritage.

Bengal Revivalism The word "Revivalism" meant the rebrith or return to traditional Indian *culture*. The movement took place in Bengal between 1895–1910 because of several factors, among which the primary causes were the rebellion against Western influence as epitomized by the success of *Raja Ravi Varma*, and the discovery of the *Ajanta frescoes*. A strong, nationalist spirit and the flowering of the Bengali literary field (with novels by Ishwar Chandra Vidyasagar, *Rabindranath Tagore*, Bankim Chandra Chatterjee and Madhusudan Dutt) added to the revolutionary spirit of the age.

The movement was largely moulded by *Abanindranath Tagore's* personal *style*. He in turn was encouraged by the English head of the *Calcutta School*, E.B. Havell, to "go back" to his (Indian) roots and *culture*. Other *artists* associated with the movement–*Kshitendranath Majumdar*, *K. Venkatappa*, *Benode Behari Mukherjee*, *Asit K. Haldar* and others. This group was generally identified as the *artists* of the *Bengal School*. Due to the growing wave of Nationalism, the *Swadeshi Movement* also found expression in the revivalist fervour. Refer *Bengal School*, *Mughal Dynasty*, *Abanindranath Tagore*, *Nandalal Bose*.

Bengal School (The) The *term* is associated with the *style* of *painting* prevalent between 1895–1910 rather than with a certain area or region. Though the *style* originated in Bengal, with the contribution of *Abanindranath Tagore*, it soon spread to most parts of India through the students of *Santiniketan* and the School of Art in Kolkata. It began as a rebellion against Western, especially British influence in the political, social and cultural fields. *Abanindranath Tagore* led the rebellion against the academism in *Raja Ravi Varma's paintings* preferring instead to go back to what he considered was traditional to India, namely the *Ajanta fresco paintings* with their graceful *linearity* and *Mughal miniature painting* with their sophisticated *colour* sense. The Bengal School was largely moulded by the personal *style* that *Abanindranath Tagore* evolved from his convictions.

It was characterized by slim graceful *figures*, taken chiefly from literary sources, such as Omar Khayyam's "Rubaiyat", Kabi Kankan and Indian *classical* literature. The colouring was pale and hazy, basically due to the *wash technique*, which involved the dipping and washing of the entire work (executed on *paper* with *watercolour* and *gouache*) in water, several times, in between the laying on of coats of *colour*. This resulted in the feeling of *depth*, even in the absence of Western *perspective*. Later, *contour* shading, *highlights* and touches of *gold* were added as finishing touches. The miniature format was adhered to, in the scale of the works in the inclusion of the decorative borders and *calligraphic details*, and the absence of cast *shadow*. Some of the later *artists* used *tempera*, while *Abanindranath Tagore* also painted in the Japanese *style* using spontaneous and sparse brushstrokes. The Bengal School thus stood for Revivalism Art on the one hand and the *Swadeshi movement* on the other and became known as the *Renaissance* period of Indian *Art*. Refer *Bengal Revivalism*, *Nandalal Bose*, *Benode Behari Mukherjee*, *Kshitendranath Mazumdar*, *K. Venkatappa*.

Benjamin, Siona (1960–) b. Mumbai. Education: GDA in *painting* & *metal craft*, also had photographic training *JJSA*, M.FA. Southern Illinois University Carbondale (SIUC) USA with *painting* & *metal craft*, later on theatre set *designs*, M.FA. Thesis: SIUC Museum. Solos: *JAG*, *Dhoomimal*; International: Jersey, Indiana & Chicago USA, France. Group participations: Colours of India Australia, SIUC paperworks 87, *enamel*, *gold leaf* in Kentucky, Wisconsin, Illinois, Missouri & "Waalsh Gallery" Chicago USA. Awards/ Grants: Illinois Art Council. Member: Enamelist Society USA. Appointments: Muralist Mumbai; International: Taught Art Appreciation, Assisting the curator of *art*, Lectures and demonstrations in *painting*, *enamelling* and theatre scenography to school students, Course coordinator for Introduction to Art and Graduate Assistant School of Art & Museum and Assistant in SIUC Carbondale.

She is inspired by the *images* of many *cultures*, including the *colour* in Indian miniatures. The *gold leaf* and stark staring *figures* of *Byzantine Art*, fuse well with a blend of both Western and Indian music. After fluctuating between *enamelling* and traditional *painting*, she has finally merged the two *techniques* building up the *pigment* layer by layer with intermediary stages of *firing*. Her *forms* too have changed from simple distorted *figures* to box shaped receptacles housing the human body on one side and the soul on the other.

She lives and works in Illinois, USA. Refer Illustration—*Gold*.

Betala, Pushp (1937– approx. 2000) b. Jodhpur. Self-taught *painter* & *sculptor*. Over 30 solos: Delhi, Mumbai, Ahmedabad & other towns. Group participations: *AIFACS* for *portrait* & traditional *art*. Awards: Over 12 awards National *LKA* New Delhi, *AIFACS*, *BAS*. Fellowship: Senior HRD Ministry. Member: Founder chairman who organized four International *art* workshops from *IAPC*; President of Group Art. Collections: IAFA Amritsar, *Museum* in RAJ; International: Texas, Washington.

Pushp Betala's works were generally experimental in *nature*, with a reliance on *Surrealism* and *distortion*. His *sculptures* were created in different combinations of *marble*, *stone*, *wood* and *metal*. His *paintings* depended on the use of such exotic *media* as bromide *paper* and photo chemicals to create swirling, *abstract images*, full of movement. Pushp Betala lived in New Delhi.

Bhagat, Dhanraj (1917–1988) b. Lahore, Pakistan. Education: Dip. in *sculpture* Mayo College of Art Lahore, HoD *Sculpture College of Art* New Delhi. Solos: *LKA* New Delhi, Govt. Museum Chandigarh, SC, *AIFACS*. Retrospective: *LKA* New Delhi. Group paticipations: *NGMA*, *LKA* & *Triennales* New Delhi, *AFA* Kolkata, *AIFACS*, *BAS*; International: Belgium, Paris, USA, Sao Paulo Brazil, Nairobi Kenya, PUJ Art Society Lahore, Commonwealth Exhibition London. *Auctions*: Heart Mumbai. Awards: National *LKA* New Delhi, *AFA* Kolkata, Padma Shri 1997, *AIFACS*; International: PUJ Society Lahore, Ford & Rockfeller Foundation Scholarship USA. Fellowship: *LKA* New Delhi. Member: Founder member SC, *LKA* General Council New Delhi, *LKA* & Hindu University Board of Studies Varanasi, National Committee International Assocation of Plastic Art Paris. Commissions: for *Triennale* India. Appointments: One of the judges International Women's Exhibition. Collections: *NGMA* & *LKA* New Delhi, PUJ University Chandigarh & Patiala, *AIFACS*, SKP.

As a *sculptor* he was always experimenting with new *media* including *wood*, creating *forms* out of timber that were dictated by its inherent shape. The surface *texture* too was influenced by the *nature* of forms, at times being highly polished and at others being chipped and flaked from *wood* that melted into one another with soft, undulating *lines*. After the violence of the partition, Dhanraj Bhagat's *wood carvings* acquired a rough edge, with *chisel* marks still visible.

In Delhi, Dhanraj Bhagat started his search for simplification with the elimination of extraneous detail. He started experimenting with new materials i.e. *cement*, combining them with *iron* filings, at times working with *papier mache*, *aluminium* or *copper*. After his visit to several European countries and the USA on Ford and Rockefeller Scholarships, he became obsessed with elongation. In the 1956 "Flautist" (made in *plaster*) the elongation is not as obvious because of the flow of the limbs and the flute. These musical pieces become increasingly *abstract*, as the performers and the instruments become one.

His later *sculptures* were *monumental* and powerful works mostly in *cement concrete*, based on his *composition* for the underprivileged and the downtrodden. His religious fervour came out in a series of *sculptures* that showed his ancestral heritage. His best *sculptures* were of SHIVA NATARAJA. Unlike the traditional NATARAJA, however, Dhanraj Bhagat's *sculptures* are an abstraction of dance itself, rather than the dancer.

The 60s and the 70s saw a further development of the *abstract* in his works. "Man and Cosmic Man" showed a strange being depicted with large, devouring eyes and clenched teeth, with the bodies metamorphosing into protective shields.

During the last eight years of his life, when he was too weak to sculpt, he produced thousands of *line drawings* of characteristic flying *figures* and mythological interpretations.

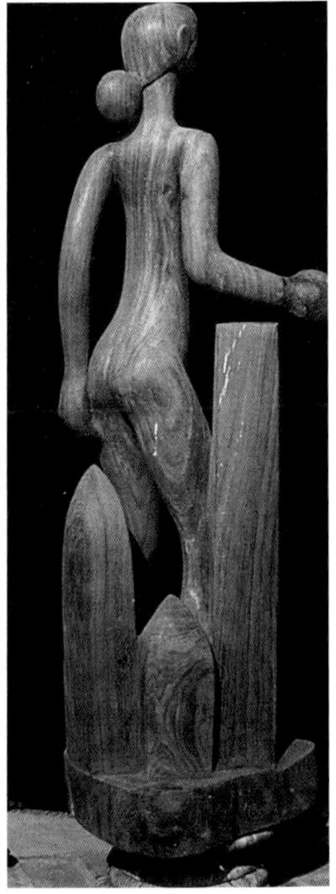

Bhagat, Dhanraj: "Figure with symbol", *Wood*, 1977 ht 120 cm.

Bhagat, Vajubhai D. (1915–1992) b. Lathi, Saurashtra. Education: Dip. in *FA*. & *mural* decoration *JJSA*. Later taught at evening *art* classes conducted by his alma-mater, before becoming a fullfledged *painter* & muralist. Solos & group participations: Mumbai, Ahmedabad, New Delhi; International: London, USA, RAA London. Awards: The book "Bhagat" with the text written by Karl Khandalavala won the National Award in 1981. Fellowship: Emeritus Fellowship 1989–90. Member: *ASI*, Treasurer &

Secretary *BAS*, Member & Advisor for All India Handicrafts Board's Design Centre & *MPCVA*, Selection Committee *JAG*, Selection & Judging Committees *BAS* & *ASI*, Founder member Museum Society Mumbai and Samkalpana. Commissions: *Murals* Parliament House New Delhi. Appointments: Supervisor Govt. of India, Ministry of Education for Young Painters.

His *paintings* are an interesting blend of traditional *style* and *modern subjects*. His love for *Jain miniature painting* is apparent in his use of flat, two-dimensional *figures* with the different *colour* areas being tightly bound within *black outlines*. He used rudimentary miniature *style perspective*, with *figures* and *forms* in the *background* appearing higher than the ones in the *foreground*. There is also interesting use of *pattern* to delineate different *masses* in his works. He lived in Mumbai.

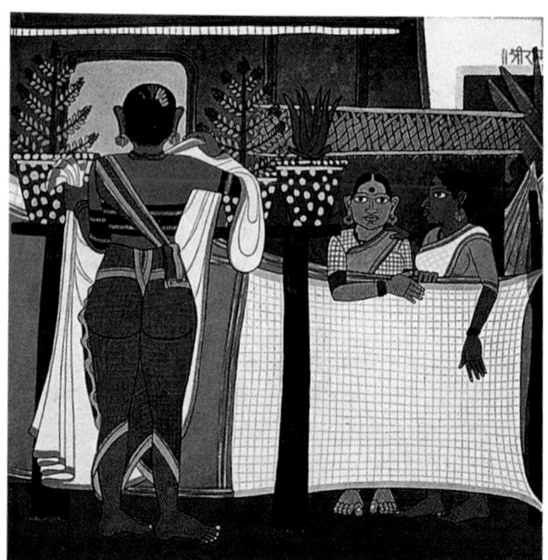

Bhagat, Vajubhai D.: "Fisherwomen drying clothes", *Watercolour*, 1947.

Bhagavad Gita=The song of the Lord. The Bhagavad Gita is an episode of 18 chapters taken from the MAHABHARATA, which tells the story of the confrontation between the warring cousins, the Pandavas and the Kauravas. It is a dialogue between Lord KRISHNA and his kinsman and friend Arjuna (one of the Pandavas), as he prepares to do battle. KRISHNA also appears in his true cosmic *form* to Arjuna, during the discourse. Many *paintings* have been based on this, especially KRISHNA as VISHNU Viswaroopa. It is also known as the Srimad Bhagavad Gita.

Bhagavan=*God*; *Spiritual* Being. Refers to any *god* in the Hindu *pantheon*. These innumerable *gods* were represented with different faces and *figures* of impeccable grace and beauty in *sculptures* of CHOLA and PALLAVA *Dynasties*; and VISHNU and KRISHNA in *Rajput miniature paintings*, *Raja Ravi Varma* in his *paintings* created the westernized *form* of LAKSHMI and SARASVATI; Later *Kanu Desai's drawing* of SHIVA, and *Reddeppa M. Naidu's painting* of (Pancha Mukh) "Five Heads" of GANESHA. Refer *Miniature Painting*; (see illustrations on pages 329, 243).

Bhagavata-Purana=the Old Book of Divinity. One of the *epics* of Hindu religious literature, dedicated to VISHNU and his AVATARAS. The 10th PURANA (book), is devoted to the exploits of KRISHNA, the most popular incarnation of VISHNU. Refer *Aesthetics*, BRAHMA-PURANA, CHITRASUTRA, *Devanagari Script*, *Illuminated Manuscripts*, *Illumination*, *Kangra*, KRISHNA, MAHABHARATA, *Manuscript Paintings*, MATRIKAS, *Picture Space*, RADHA, RAMAYANA, SANSKRIT, SHIVA, *Size*, *Spiritual*, *Visual*, *Nathu Lal Verma*.

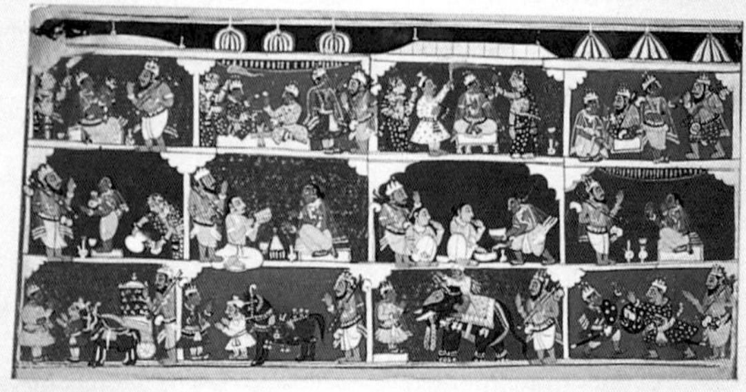

Bhagavata-Purana: "Foil", from the Malwa manuscript (Central India). Perhaps from the dated series of AD 1689, 36.5x19.5 cm. Foil 66.

Bhagwat, Nalini G. (1937–) b. Pune, MAHA. Education: M.A. in history Pune University, GDA in *painting*, *Art* Masters MAHA, Ph.D. in *art* history *MSU*, Govt. Recognition Bombay University to teach Post-Grad. Solos & group shows: on Kashmir Landscape & MAHA *Visual Art* Mumbai, *JJSA* 'FAIM-MAHA', *JAG*. Group participations: Kolhapur, *JAG*. *Art* camps & workshops: Arranged *terracotta* camps Kolhapur & Mumbai; Attended WZCC MAHA, *Enamelling* workshop & LKK New Delhi, *LKA* Lucknow, SZCC. Member: Committee *LKA*. Commissions: *Portraits*. Appointments: Lecturer in history of *art JJSA*; Entrusted the work of *NGMA* Mumbai and Documentation of the *contemporary art* MAHA. Publications: "Aalpa MAHA" State press, Reports on *art* history & seminars "Art of Ajanta and its significance in Asian Art" *MSU*, "Tribal Art" in Bhubaneshwar, Newspapers publications & *art* critiques; Special articles written on *Narayan S. Bendre*, *Francis Newton Souza*, *Madhav Satwalekar* & other *artists*; Lectures on *art* all over India. Collections: Pune, Mumbai, KAR Health Institute, *LKA* New Delhi.

Her *oil paintings* are mostly stylized *figurations* of social issues with a sense of stillness and a spatial visualization of Indian *colours*. They depend upon geometric configurations and marked *outlines* emphasizing with stillness. Other works emphasize on portraiture and *watercolour*.

She lives and works in Mumbai and Kolhapur since her retirement from college.

Bhakti=**1.** devotion, **2.** love. The word Bhakti refers to the Bhakti Cult, which is the most popular form of worship in *Hinduism*. KRISHNA is the main deity associated with Bhakti. SHIVA Bhakti is popular in South India. Bhakti scores over the cult of Dharma (religion) and that of KARMA (fate; duty), because here devotees do not have to rigorously pursue their religious duties but only love *God* with selfless devotion. The Bhakti cult inspired Vaishnavite poetry and *painting*. Most of the *Rajput miniature paintings* and the *South Indian bronzes* are based on Bhakti.

Bhalla, Pravin (1949–) b. Srigobindpur, India. Education: Grad. Chelsea School of Art. Scholarship RAA London; Fellow *sculpture* & *drawing MSU*. Solos: *JAG*, *PG*; International: Central School & Royal Contemporary Art

Gallery London. Group participations: Sculptor's Forum of India Chandigarh & New Delhi, PUJ University Chandigarh, All India Graphic Hyderabad, *PG*, *JAG*, *Biennale*; International: London. Grant/Fellowship: Scholarship *MSU* specializing in *sculpture* & *drawing*; Govt. of India; International: British Council London. Appointments: Made the documentary film "Temples of Orissa" for London University in 1980; Research on village *arts* & *crafts* of India; International Talk on BBC TV & Radio, Scottish & Bradford Radio. Collections: *NGMA* New Delhi, MMB Mumbai; International: London & pvt.

Pravin Bhalla's *sculptures* are inspired by *contemporary*, urban and social problems. He works in a variety of *styles*, combining the *classical*, *figurative* and the *abstract*. His inspiration may be found in any "object trouve", a honey-comb, a feather, horseshoe or dead bird. Accidental effects such as cracks, warps and blobs become an integral part of his *art*.

At present Pravin Bhalla lives and works in Mumbai/ London.

Bharat Bhavan (BB) (Bhopal). Established in the early 80s, this cultural complex houses a *museum*, library, theatre and music centre with special programmes, *exhibitions* and *happenings* arranged throughout the year. The *museum*, known as *Roopankar*, specializes in *contemporary art* from all over India as well as *tribal arts* and *crafts* from MP. The buildings that make up the BB were designed innovatively by the well-known Indian architect, Charles Correa.

Bharat Kala Bhavan (BKB) (Varanasi). The *museum* is located within the BHU complex. It contains collections of Indian *sculpture*, *painting* and textiles, originally belonging to Rai Krishnadas.

The *museum* was transferred to the University in 1950, *KB (Kala Bhavan)* is a part of *art* section. The collection includes *terracottas* from the Mauryan, Sunga and *Gupta periods*, Buddhist manuscripts, Mughal *paintings* of the *Hamza-Namah*, *Rajasthani* and *Pahari miniature paintings*. It also has a *modern* Indian *art* section, including works by *Maqbool Fida Husain*, *Narayan S. Bendre*, *K.S. Kulkarni*, *K.K. Hebbar*, *Dinkar Kowshik*, *Akbar Padamsee* and *Jaganath M. Ahivasi*.

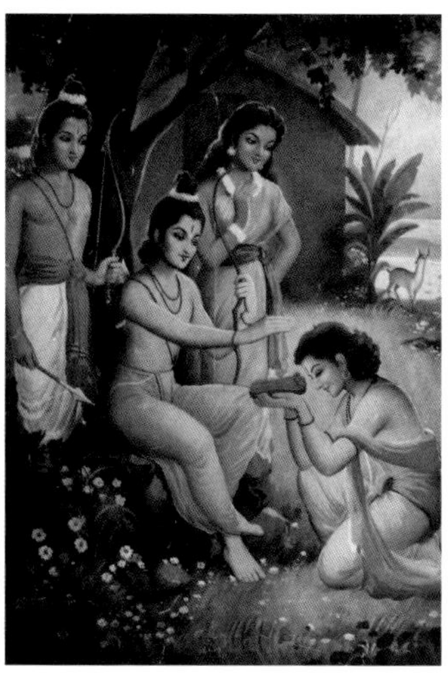

Bharata: "Bharatji-ka Tyag", Artists Mulgaokar, *Half-tone* print, circa 1930.

Bharata=fulfills all requests. A common name in *mythology* and history. **1.** A king of ancient India. **2.** The son of Dushyanta and Shakuntala in the *epic* poem Meghadoot by Kalidasa. **3.** The son of Kaikeyi: second wife of King Dashratha and the brother of RAMA and Lakshmana in the *epic* RAMAYANA. **4.** The sage (rishi) who compiled the Natyashastra. **5.** The SANSKRIT/Hindi name for India, also known as Bharatvarsha and Hindustan.

Bharati, Meenakshi (Kasliwal) (1954–) b. Jaipur, RAJ. Education: M.A. in *drawing* & *painting* University of Agra. Solos & Group participations: *GC* Mumbai, Srishti Art Gallery & Kala Mela Jaipur, National fair & *Art Heritage* New Delhi, CAG Ahmedabad, *JAG*, TKS, *VAG*; International: *Biennale* Bangladesh. *Art* camps & workshops: *terracotta* in Udaipur, *fresco* & *graphics* in Jaipur, Artists' camp by NZCC in Patiala & Allahabad, WZCC Udaipur, *LKA* New Delhi & RAJ, J&K & Akademi, *Drawing* workshop Chandigarh, Senior Artists *AIFACS*. Awards: *LKA* Jaipur, All India Amritsar. National Scholarship 1971–76. Member: "Solids" a Chandigarh based group of *contemporary artists* who organize workshops, camps & *exhibitions*. Appointments: Senior Lecturer *FA*. Kanoria Women's P.G. College Jaipur RAJ. Publications: Written articles for several publications. Collections: *Art Heritage*, *LKA* & *NGMA* New Delhi, Gallery of Modern Art & Jawahar Kala Kendra Jaipur, *Chandigarh Museum*.

Meenakshi Bharati has a predilection for textural variations using them to denote both *landscape*, mysterious deserts and abandoned *figures* with the same intensity. There is a sense of the decorative in the arrangement of windows, the drapes or simply the fish-scale grillworks. From her early *watercolour landscapes* of the mid-70s, she has evolved a quasi–abstract *vocabulary* of stylized *forms*, included wood grain *texture* in *acrylics* on *canvas*.

She works in Jaipur, RAJ.

Bhardwaj, Surinder K. (1938–) b. Lahore, Pakistan. Education: Dip. in *drawing* & *painting* PUJ School of Arts Shimla. Over 13 solos: PUJ University Museum Chandigarh, *JAG*, TAG, *AIFACS*. Group participations: Haryana State Exhibition, *LKA* Chandigarh, *NGMA* New Delhi, *AIFACS*, *BAS*; Group shows: Mumbai, Chandigarh, Chennai & New Delhi. *Art* camps: Several All India Artists Camps Srinagar, Patna, Bangalore, Gwalior, NZCC Lucknow, *LKA* Chandigarh. Awards: National Award, Creators Award (Ambala), PUJ *LKA*, Haryana State, All India Exhibitions Amritsar & Chandigarh. Member: Founder member & HoD Dept. FA. Institute J&K, General Council *LKA* New Delhi, Member of selection & judging committee for National Exhibition 1992, Life Member *AIFACS*. Appointments: Lecturer in *FA*. & HoD Adarsh Mahila Mahavidyalaya Bhiwani. Collections: *LKA* PUJ & National Academy New Delhi, Academy of Art Culture & Languages Jammu, PUJ University Museum & pvt. national & international.

His works have developed from a stylized *figuration* to heavily outlined and mystically coloured magical *landscape*. He lives and works in Bhiwani, Harayana.

Bhargava, Prithvi Nath (1913–d.) b. Agra. Education: Fellow Lucknow School of Arts under the guidance of *Asit K. Haldar* & other *artists*. Solos: New Delhi, Mysore, Kolkata, Mussorie Art Gallery, RB New Delhi, MKKP Raipur. Group participations: National & International Art New Delhi, All India Exhibition Mysore & Kolkata, Graphic show Korba MP. Awards/Hon.: Swastik Samman 1985. Appointments:

President of Bhargava Lalit Kala Sansthan, *Art* teacher at the K.R.P.G College Mathura, later became HoD of *Painting* Dept. Collections: Allahabad University, Nawab of Bhopal, Maharaja of Kashmir.

His *style* was *eclectic*, the first works being a blend of *wash* and *tone painting* in the Revivalist *manner*. His later works had a *spiritual* undertone, being full of didactic symbols and semi-traditional effects. He was also interested in handicrafts, making *designs* from waste products and porcelain. He lived and worked in Mathura.

Bhargava, Veena (1938–) b. Shimla, HP. Education: *Art* Students League of New York, Dip. in *FA*. GCA Kolkata. Solos: *GC* Mumbai, *BAAC* Kolkata, *Art Heritage* New Delhi, HCVA, *JAG*, *G88*. Group participations: 25 years *LKA* & *GC* at *JAG*, *Triennale* & *NGMA* New Delhi, *BAAC* & *CIMA* Kolkata, *G88*, *CKAG*, *GK*, *JAG*; International: Contemporary Indian Art ICCR in Bulgaria, Yugoslavia, Poland & Belgium, Festival of Painting France. *Auctions*: Helpage India Auction, Christie's & Timeless Art Sotheby's Mumbai. Awards: *BAAC* Kolkata, National Award *LKA* New Delhi. Collections: *NGMA* New Delhi, *GC* Mumbai, *BAAC* Kolkata, TIFR, *CKP*; pvt. India; International: pvt. UK, Holland, Germany, Italy, USA, Canada & Japan.

Veena Bhargava's *style* is laced with wit and irony, rich with complex, many-layered *images*. There is a play of contrasts of *forms*, *colours*, sensibilities, *shades* and *tones* which merge together in the shaping of a strong and vibrant *iconography*. The inspiration for her *paintings* has always been the *contemporary* world, each of her series of *cityscapes*, the lithe *forms*, the seated *figures*, the pavement series, the couple series, the bull series, the angst series, the goat and the performer series have been culled from her personal vision. In the earlier series she was interested merely in the formal aspect of *masses* and *volumes* and the shifting planes of *colour* and *shade*. Later, the personal element of tragedy creeps in with despair as one of the underlying emotions. One sees the jagged edges and breaks of *form* in the 1993 Performer series (1) along with the use of violent reds and *black*, greys and blue, while cities, ideas and *icons* were her subject in her 2001 series.

Veena Bhargava lives and works in Kolkata.

Bhaskaran, R.B. (1942–) b. Pallavaram, Chennai. Education: Advanced *painting GCAC* Chennai, *Fresco techniques Banasthali Vidyapith* RAJ, Post-Grad. in *printmaking* at Portsmouth Polytechnic England on a British Council Scholarship, Studied in *intaglio printmaking*, *lithography* & *ceramics* on Israel UNESCO Scholarship. Solos: Over 20 solos Pondicherry, Chennai, Kolkata, New Delhi, Mumbai & *SAI*, *JAG*, *Dhoomimal*; International: Israel, UK, Holland. Group participations: *LKA*, Mumbai, Chennai & New Delhi, *Graphic* & *drawing* Chandigarh, National Exhibition New Delhi, Printmakers *SG* Chennai, *BAAC* Kolkata, *GAC*, VG, *JAG*, *CYAG*, *SAI*, *G88*, *Triennales*; International: *Biennale* Havana Festival of India USA. Group shows: *Art Heritage* New Delhi, *Dhoomimal*. *Auctions*: Heart Mumbai & New Delhi, Osian's Mumbai. *Art* camps & workshops: *LKA* in most of the States, *GAC* New Delhi, College of FA. & USIS Kerala, *MSU*, *BB*, *GAC*. Member & Chairman: Association of Young Painters & Sculptors, Association of British Council Scholars & Life member South Indian Society of Painters Chennai. Appointments: Worked with *graphic artist* Paul Lingren & jointly organized *graphic art* workshops in Chennai; Seminars on *Art LKA* New Delhi & Chennai, *Art Education* Bangalore. National Policy on Culture Thiruvananthapuram. Collections: *LKA* & Govt. *Museum* Chennai, *Art Heritage* & *NGMA*, *LKA* New Delhi, Godrej & *SG* Mumbai, Tamil University Thanjavur, *BB*, *CKP*, *CRAR*, *SAI*, VG, *Dhoomimal*, *G88*, *CKAG*, *DG*, others in Chandigarh, Orissa; International: London, Israel & USA.

R.B. Bhaskaran has experimented with many *media*, including *painting*, *printmaking* and *relief sculpture*. Though he is basically a *figurative painter*, he is not pictographically *realistic* but instead manipulates *space* in a texturally decorative *manner*. His basic concern is not *content*, but *form* with a tangible feel for *volume* with clearly outlined *silhouettes*. He relies on known *forms* but converts them into a language of his own. The Cat series, Man-Woman series, *still life* and *landscapes* all show his spontaneous *brushwork* and love of decorative *patterns*. The *colours* have varied over the years from sophisticated *pastel shades* to a bright and *discordant palette*.

R.B. Bhaskaran lives and works in Chennai.

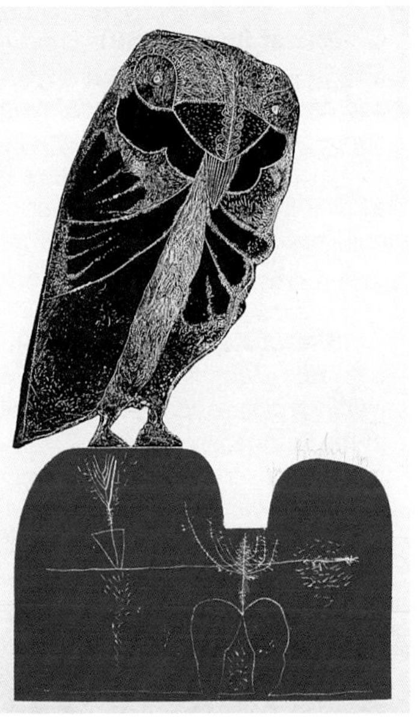

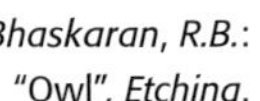

Bhaskaran, R.B.: "Owl", *Etching*.

Bhat, Madhukar B. (1935–) b. Jalgaon, MAHA. Education: Degree in *applied arts JJIAA*; *Graphic Art* experience Mumbai & Ahmedabad. Solos: *GC* Mumbai, CAG & *LKA* Ahmedabad, *LKA* & RB New Delhi, *JAG*; International: Chicago, USA. Group participations: GUJ *LKA*, MPKP Hyderabad, National Exhibition New Delhi, *BAS*, HAS, *AIFACS*; International: USA. Awards: Eminent *Artist AIFACS*, Gold Medal Bharat Kalidas Parishad Hyderabad; International: Travel to USA Scholarship Vincennes University; Hon.: Vincennes Indiana USA. Collections: *NGMA* Mumbai, *SJM* & Archaeology Museum Hyderabad, other cities Ahmedabad, Kolkata; International: USA, Canada, Hong Kong.

Madhukar B. Bhat calls himself a neo-tantric *painter* "who seeks the inner peace, joy and happiness for which contemporary restless man aspires." His *paintings* are thoughtfully worked out and infused with *spiritual* and philosophical significance. He explains "Divine Light" thus:

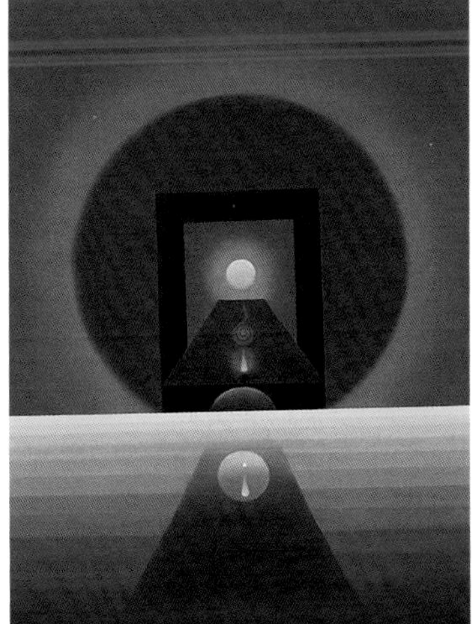

"In the darkness of our soul a divine flame emerges. This *light* has no *form*, no shape and no symbol. To get a glimpse of this *light*, man will have to ascend steep mountains and descend deep valleys."

Madhukar B. Bhat lives and works in Ahmedabad, GUJ.

Bhat, Madhukar B.: "Divine Light", *Oil* on *Canvas*, 75x100 cm.

Bhatnagar, Madan (1931–) b. Gwalior, MP. Education: Dip. in FAC *Santiniketan*. Solos: MPKP Bhopal, *KB Santiniketan*, *AIFACS*, TAG, *JAG*. Group participations: National *LKA* New Delhi, MPKP Bhopal, *AFA* Kolkata, *AFA* Amritsar, SZCC Nagpur, *AIFACS*, *BAS*. *Art* camps: *Sculptors* camps at *Mahabalipuram*, Gwalior, Kashmir, New Delhi. Awards: Shikhar Samman for excellence in *sculpture* & MPKP Bhopal, National Award *LKA* New Delhi, *AFA* Kolkata, Academy Award Amritsar, *BAS*, *AIFACS*. Member: Life Member *AIFACS*, MP Kala Parishad Bhopal, Advisory Committee in Rastriya LKK Lucknow. Appointments: Ex-Principal of Govt. Institute of FA. Gwalior. Collections: K.R.G. College & B.S.F. Academy Gwalior, *LKA* & *NGMA* New Delhi, IAFA Amritsar, *Santiniketan*, *VBU*, *BB*; International: Nepal, Germany, Italy, Canada, USA, Australia.

Madan Bhatnagar has worked with *metal* and *marble*, producing elegant pieces of abstraction reminiscent of H. Moore and B. Hepworth. This sense of the *abstract* is apparent even in the underlying *figuration* of the Flautist series. There is also an element of Bastar *folk art* in the naive rendering of certain *sculptures*.

He lives and works in Gwalior.

Bhatt, Girish C. (1931–) b. Chhatral, Vadodara. Education: Post-Dip. in *sculpture*, Specialization in *bronze casting FFA* (*MSU*). Solos: TAG, *JAG*. Group participations: All India Sculptors Forum & FFA in Mumbai & New Delhi, *MSU*; International: Japan, Nepal, Australia, Malaysia, *Biennale* Venice. *Art* camps: GUJ *LKA*, All India Sculptors Jammu. Awards: National Award New Delhi, *AIFACS*, *BAS*, for Indian *sculptors*; Scholarship Govt. of India Cultural Scholar worked under Prof. *Sankho Chaudhuri*. Member: GUJ *LKA*, All India Sculptors Forum of India Executive Member; Purchase Committee–National *LKA* New Delhi; jury member–National *LKA Exhibition* of *Contemporary Art*, Ministry of Culture and Ministry of Tourism and Culture Govt. of India New Delhi; Judge for the Art Exhibition of Baroda District 5th Youth Festival GUJ. Appointments: Gave demonstrations & lectures for *Art* schools in Jammu & *bronze casting* in *MSU*; Senior Fellow HRD Ministry New Delhi. Publications: *Kumar Magazine*, *LKA* informations, Modern Indian Sculpture (by *Jaya Appaswamy*), *BAS* journal. Collections: Modern Art Gallery, *NGMA* New Delhi, *LKA* GUJ, Goa & New Delhi, *BAAC* Kolkata, Godrej, TATA, TIFR & pvt.

Girish C. Bhatt's *forms* are essentially *figurative* though they have grown progressively *abstract* over the years. He prefers a polished surface, *texture* appearing through the grain of the *wood* or *marble*. His *figures* are slim with elongated *torsoes*, veer towards abstraction in a *manner* similar to *Somnath Hore's sculptures*. His 2003 works are concerned with capturing physical movement.

He retired from the post of Reader in the Dept. of *Sculpture*, *MSU* and works in Vadodara.

Bhatt, Jyoti (1934–) b. Bhavnagar, GUJ. Education: Post-Dip. in *painting MSU* under *Narayan S. Bendre* & *K.G. Subramanyan*; Received Govt. of Italy Scholarship in *printmaking*; Pratt Institute New York on a Fulbright Scholarship & J.D.R Award. Solos: For *painting* & *printmaking* at Ahmedabad, New Delhi & *CYAG*, photography at NCPA (*MPCVA*) Mumbai, *Art Heritage* New Delhi, *BB*; Restrospective at Graphic Art *CYAG 1998* & ABS Bayer Gallery Vadodara 2004; International: USA. Group participations: *LKA* New Delhi, "Baroda Group", "Painters as Photographers" NCPA Mumbai, National Exhibitions, *CYAG*, *BAS*; International: Print *Biennale* Italy, France, Poland, Japan, Yugoslavia & Germany, *Triennale* Sao Paulo "Chamatkar" Exhibition of *painting* London by *CIMA*, "Tryst with Destiny" Singapore Museum, on photography UK, Japan, Germany & USA. *Art* camps & workshops on *printmaking*. *Auctions*: Heart Mumbai & New Delhi. Awards: President's Gold Plaque National *LKA* Exhibition Delhi; Postal Stamp Design 25th Anniversary of Independence, Received Cultural Scholarship Ministry of Education, *BAS*. International: Gold Medal International Print *Biennale* Florence Italy. Founder member: Secretary Vadodara Group of Artists, Group 1980, Camera Pictorialist of Baroda, Graphic corporates. Appointments: Participated in Seminars, Organized Photography *Exhibition*, Taught at FFA 1959–61 and continued after 1966, and prepared documents of *murals* and *paintings* including *Nandalal Bose*, *Benode Behari Mukherjee* & *Ramkinkar Baij*; Commissioner of Indian *Triennale* of International Art *BB* and International Exhibition of Indian Prints Cuba. Publications: Indian Floor Decoration, articles on *painting*, photography, *graphic techniques* in Marg,

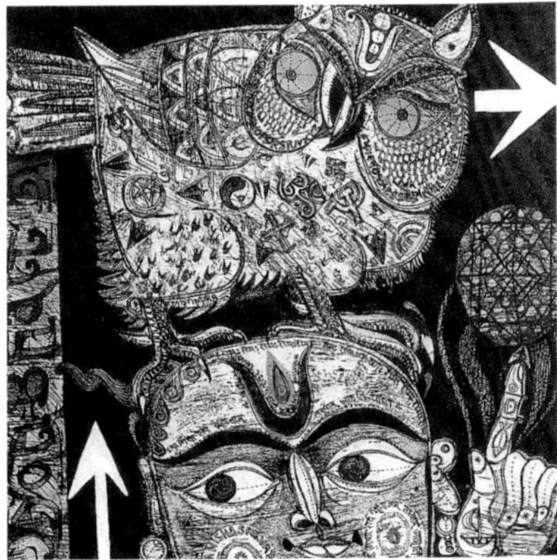

Bhatt, Jyoti: "Lost-Pundit", Mixed *intaglio*, 1966, 45x45 cm.

Fulbright Bulletin & the *LKA contemporary* among others. Collections: *NGMA* & *LKA* New Delhi, Hyderabad Museum, Baroda Museum, *CIMA* Kolkata; International: British Museum London, Museum of Modern Art New York, Uffizi Print Gallery Florence, Smithsonian Institute USA; pvt–Godrej.

Jyoti Bhatt is a versatile *artist*, working extensively with different *media* including *printmaking, etching, screen printing, serigraphy*, photography, holography, *painting* and *mural design*. He has been photo-documenting *folk* and *tribal art* in India. Jyoti Bhatt's *style* is *eclectic*, moving briefly through Revivalism, *Cubism* and various *shades* of *abstraction* and *folk art*. Today he is seen as a *modern* traditionalist, with *motifs* and *forms* culled from the *tribal* and *folk arts* that he has documented and from *contemporary* Indian society as well. His *prints* have evolved from a simple reliance of linear *forms* through a near *abstract* textural exercise to *photo-etching*, creating iconic *motifs* by juxtaposing the real with the contrived.

Underlying the decorative ornateness is a disciplined and cohesive structural awareness that holds each *composition* together. Certain *motifs* recurr, e.g., YANTRA and TANTRA diagrams in the 70s, *contemporary* symbols in the 80s and intricate wide eyed *figures* later. He has also used signs and written words in some works in the *graffiti*-like symbology of folk wall decoration.

Jyoti Bhatt lives in Vadodara with his ceramist-sculptor wife *Jyotsna Bhatt*.

Bhatt, Jyotsna (1940–) b. Mandvi, Kutch (GUJ). Education: Dip. & Post-Dip. in *sculpture MSU*; Working students scholarship Brooklyn Museum Art School. Solos: *Art Heritage* New Delhi, Vithi Art Gallery Vadodara, *CYAG*; International: New Jersey, New York, USA. Group participations: *LKA* Kolkata & New Delhi, GUJ *LKA*, *BB*, *AIFACS*, *BAS*, TAG, *JAG*, *CYAG*, *GAC*; International: *BB's* show in Europe, Inspirations in Clay Singapore. *Art* workshops: For *ceramics* organized by Art Dir. MAHA State Mumbai, *LKA* & Sanskriti Pratisthan New Delhi, *MSU* 1971 to 2000; *Terracotta* by *LKA* in Bandkura WB. Appointments: *Ceramics* Prof. *MSU*. Commissions: *Ceramic murals* R&D building & IPCL Vadodara.

Jyotsna Bhatt is chiefly a ceramist, working with *clay*, infusing it with her brand of gentle humour. Her animal *sculptures* in *clay* are especially appealing, with a simplistic yet wholesome approach that has some element of *caricature* in it. Her pots and containers again are aesthetically appealing but the utilitarian aspect is never forgotten. Her 'flower-pots' for instance have lids that can be taken off and the pots can be used. Coming from a family of chemists has stood her in good stead for the exciting *craft* of *ceramic design*.

She lives and works in Vadodara.

Bhattacharjee, Bikash (1940–) b. Kolkata. Education: Dip. in FAC ICA&D Kolkata. Solos: *CIMA* Kolkata, *GC* Mumbai, *JAG*, *G88*, others in Chennai, Jamshedpur, New Delhi, Bangalore, Hyderabad, Kuala Lampur; International: London. Group participations: National Exhibition, *Triennale* "25 years of Indian Art" & "Miniature Format" *LKA* New Delhi, *AFA* & *BAAC* Kolkata, "Four Contemporary Artists of West Bengal" & "Indian Paintings Today" Mumbai, "Highlights" at *JAG* by *CIMA* Kolkata, *AIFACS*, *ATG*; International: Festival of India London, *Triennale* Paris, *Exhibition* in Yugoslavia, Romania, Czechoslovakia, Hungary, New York, Boston, Geneva, Moscow & Germany. *Auctions*: Heart & Osian's–Mumbai & New Delhi, Sotheby's–New Delhi, New York & London, Christie's–London & Hong Kong, Bonham's London. Awards: National Award & *LKA* New Delhi, *AFA* & *BAAC* Kolkata, Received Padma Shri & Shiromoni Puraskar. Member: General Council *LKA*, New Delhi, *SCA*. Commissions: *Portraits*–President of India N. Sanjeeva Reddy & Vithalbhai Patel for HP Vidhan Sabha. Appointments: Lecturer *FA*. ICA&D & GCA&D Kolkata. Collections: Chandigarh University Museum, *NGMA* & *LKA* New Delhi, *BB*. International: Chester & David Hertwitz Boston, Masanori Fukuoka & Glenbarra Art Museum Hemeji Japan.

Bikash Bhattacharjee has evolved greatly over the years. Most of his *oil paintings* focus on a single *figure* or two at the most. Several *compositions* depict a derelict doll as the heroine of stage scenes put across as *cityscapes*. They depict timelessness, *light* and tragedy all at once. In the early phase he used a gamut of *colours* and brushstrokes to create a vision of palpable reality. However, lately, he has been limiting the range of *pigments* in order to create living reality. However, his attention to *light, texture* and *detail* is undiminished. He also experimented with new materials and *media* including Nepalese *handmade paper*, *mixed media* works using *pastels*, *conte pencils*, *watercolours*, *tempera* etc. In these experimentations, Bikash Bhattacharjee has moved from detailing to mere hints of the *figures*. Thus, dwelling in *Surrealism* and absolute *Realism*, Bikash Bhattacharjee has created his own distinctive *style* and *idiom* which is based on a continuous exploration in his quest to rediscover his roots.

He lives and works in Kolkata.

Bhattacharjee, Chandra (1960–) b. Patuli, WB. Education: Dip. ICA&D, attended *art*-appreciation course at Calcutta University. Solos: *Art Heritage* New Delhi, Centre Art Gallery Kolkata. Group participations: *AFA* Kolkata, *Art Heritage* New Delhi, *G88*, *JAG*, BAG, *SJM* by *NGMA*, *CKAG*; International: Art World Hongkong & Singapore Art Fair. *Art* camps & workshops: Reflections of Another Day (RAD) Poetry and Painting, World Enviroment Day and EZCC in Kolkata. Awards: Gold Medal *RBU*. Appointments: An *artist* for *LKA* and later *painter* of *hoardings*, A senior design officer in The Economic Times Kolkata. Collections: *PUAG*, *VAG*; International: New York.

Chandra Bhattacharjee is unabashedly *figurative* in his approach. The smudged grainy *texture* recalls the works of *Suhas Roy* and *Sunil Das*. However Chandra Bhattacharjee's *figures* are not set against empty *backdrops*. They are portrayed as people with dreams and possessions. Certain *colours* are used to *highlight* emotions and cryptic symbols emerge faintly through the layers of *paint*.

He lives and works in Kolkata.

Bhattacharjee, Madhab (1933–) b. Kolkata. Education: *GCAC* Kolkata, under senior *sculptor* Prof. Prodosh Das Gupta, Govt. Scholarship for pursuing Post-

Grad. under the guidance of Prof. *Sankho Chaudhuri MSU*. Group participations: National *Exhibitions LKA* New Delhi, Indo-American Society & *BAAC* Kolkata, *AIFACS*; International: Fukuoka Art Museum Japan, Commonwealth Institute London. *Art* camps: *Sculptors* work camps for *marble carving* Jaipur & Makrana *LKA*. Awards: *LKA* New Delhi, Gold Medal *AFA* & Merit Certificate *BAAC* Kolkata, Memorial Medal *ISOA*; Hon. Veteran Artist by *AIFACS*. Collections: *NGMA* & *LKA* New Delhi, & pvt.

His *sculptures* show an *eclectic* spirit, at times catching the spirit of traditional Indian *sculptures* (in an *abstract manner*) and at others being strictly *modern* (with constructivist principles at play).

He lives and works in his studio at Kolkata.

Bhattacharjee, Sukumar (1948–) b. Kolkata. Education: Degree in *FA*. *KB Santiniketan*, Degree in *commercial art* Indian Art College *RBU*. Solos and Group show: *AFA* & *BAAC* Kolkata. Group participations: *AFA*, *BAAC*, National Exhibition *LKA* & *Triennale* Kolkata, B.K. College of Arts and Crafts Bhubaneshwar. *Art* camps: Kolkata, Chennai, Ranchi. Awards: *BAS*, *VBU*, others in *Santiniketan*. Scholarship: Merit Scholarship *VBU*. Publications: Written & directed two telefilms, two audio cassettes for children in 1990–92. Collections: *LKA* & pvt. in India & abroad.

Sukumar Bhattacharjee's *compositions* are crowded with exotic trivia, animal and bird *forms* culled from tribal and folk *motifs*, rolls and fraying sheets of *paper*, *masks* and scarecrows in a medley of *colour* and *detail*. His "Monkey God" depicts HANUMAN as a monkey with a human face with his *attribute* the GADA (mace) lying suggestively at the bottom of the *painting*.

He lives and works in Kolkata.

Bhattacharya, Alok (1942–) b. Jharia, Bihar. Education: Dip. *GCAC* Kolkata, later *art* appreciation course Calcutta University. Solos: Kolkata 1972; Group participations: Canvas Artist's Circle, Calcutta Information Centre, *BAAC* & MMB Kolkata, *BAAC* Mumbai, National Exhibition *LKA* New Delhi, *G88*, *CKAG*, GAG; International: Munich, Commonwealth Institute London, Cairo *Biennale*. Group shows: 1982 and Central Art Gallery Kolkata. *Art* camps: All India Artists *LKA* Bhubaneshwar & Patna, Painter's camp by *LKA* & Tripura Muncipal Agartala. Awards: Youth Festival, *BAAC* & *GCAC* Kolkata. Founder Member: Canvas Artist's Circle, Rupadaksha experimental theatre group Kolkata in which he acts, *designs* costumes & sets, Gen. Council Member *LKA* New Delhi. Collections: *BAAC* Kolkata, pvt. & public.

Alok Bhattacharya is essentially a *figurative painter* making a sensuous use of *form* and *colour*. There is more than a hint of *Surrealism* in the liquid flow of skin and muscles in his works. There is also a use of *abstract* gesture in the violent whiplashed brushstrokes that hold the *composition* together.

Alok Bhattacharya lives and works in Kolkata.

Bhava=emotion, mood. It is a state of mind, which is projected to the spectator, with the use of gesture, posture and *colour* in the work of *art*. Refer *Aesthetics*, RASA, SHADANGA.

Bhavsar, Natvar (1934–) b. Gothava, GUJ. Education: *Art* Masters Certificate & GDA Mumbai, M.FA. Grad. School FA. University of Pennsylvania. Solos: *GC* Mumbai, CAG Ahmedabad, *PUAG*; International: Florida, Texas, New York, Houston, Miami, Pittsburgh, Philadelphia, Boston & Max Hutchinson Gallery New York. Group participations: *Triennale* & *LKA* New Delhi, Progressive Painters Ahmedabad GUJ, *BAS*; International: USA, California, Pennsylvania, Australia, Rockland Center for the Arts, University of Rochester, School of Vishal Arts, Art Gallery, Whitney Museum of American Art, American Society for Eastern Art & *Biennale* Print Exhibition Brooklyn Museum all in New York. Awards: Vishva Gurjari Award. Fellowships: John D. Rockefeller Fund Fellowship, John Simon Guggenheim Memorial Fellowship. Appointments: Prof. & *Art* Instructor University of Rhode Island Kingston. Publications: Art News, New York Times, Sunday Herald, Art in America. Collections: National & International: Australian National Gallery, Boston Museum of FA., Solomon R. Guggenheim Museum, The Metropolitan Museum New York, Philadelphia Museum of Art.

Natvar Bhavsar's works are indicative of a masterful draughtsman but his preferred *medium* of expression is *colour*. Though he has done *figurative* works in the past and has also gone through the cubist phase, he has been steadily de-emphasizing *drawing* and concentrating on *colour* in an *abstract* expressionist *manner*.

Natvar Bhavsar's mode of *painting* has been greatly influenced by his knowledge of Rangoli, a type of decorative floor-*painting* in India. He strains powder *pigment* on to the *paper* or *canvas* which has been dampened with an *acrylic* binder. Repeated applications later, the desired *tones* and *textures* appear in glowing *colour* fields. *Forms* seem to float gently on a surface of shimmering *colours* that, at close range, melt to display an amazing range of warmth and coolness.

Natvar Bhavsar lives in New York.

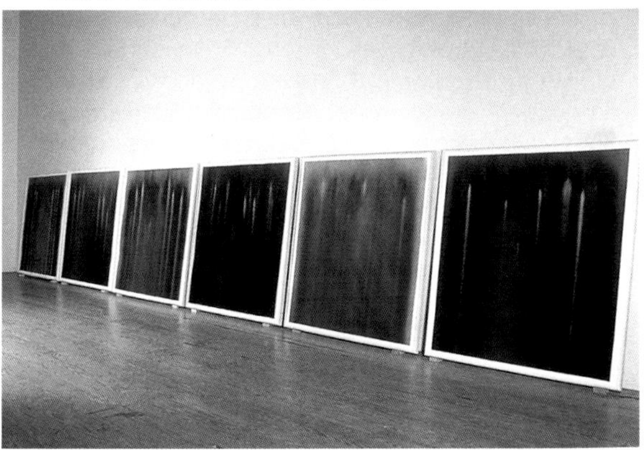

Bhavsar, Natvar: "Anjaar and Marwar series", *Paintings* on *Paper*, 1984, 115x105 cm.

Bhavsar, Ramnik (1936–) b. Pethapur, GUJ. Education: Dip. in *FA*. CNCFA. 14 Solos & group participations: Mumbai, Delhi, Kolkata, *Ravishankar M. Raval* KB GUJ, *LKA* Ahmedabad, HCVA, *JAG*. Awards: *AFA* New Delhi, GUJ State Art Exhibition & Ahmedabad Municipal Corporation Ahmedabad, MPKP Bhopal, *AIFACS*, *BAS*. Appointments: Textile *artist* at several Ahmedabad mills. Collections: *LKA* Ahmedabad & Lucknow, National Academi of Art New Delhi, PUJ Art Gallery, & pvt. Mumbai; International: USA, Australia.

Basically a *figurative painter*, Ramnik Bhavsar is inclined to work on stylized *landscapes* influenced by miniature *tradition*, *still life* and *abstracts*. He has used sand on *wood* as a base for his *calligraphic* scribbles. He has also experimented with TANTRIC *forms*, with a series of *painting* in *impasto* in *oils*.

He is a freelance *artist* in Ahmedabad.

Bhavsar, Veerbala (1941–) b. Ahmedabad, GUJ. Education: Dip. in *FA*., *Art* master in FA. College Ahmedabad, M.A. in *drawing* & *painting* Vikram University Ujjain and awarded Ph.D in *Tribal Art Motifs* RAJ University Jaipur. Over 19 Solos: New Delhi, Ahmedabad, Jaipur, Kolkata, Bhopal, *TAG*, *JAG*. Group participations: National & State *LKA* Ahmedabad, New Delhi & Jaipur. Awards: RAJ *LKA*, AIKS Ujjain. Appointments: Prof. *drawing* & *painting* RAJ University Jaipur. Publications: Several articles on *art* and *aesthetics* & books on "Tribal Art" & "Adivasi Kala". Collections: Gandhi Darshan pradarshani New Delhi, pvt. & govt.

She paints with river sand sometimes mixed with rangoli or *marble* powder and dust. She achieves tonal variations and *relief* with thin material. She has also painted *portraits* using sand. However, creative *painting* reminiscent of P. Klee's *landscape motifs* are her forte.

She lives and works in Jaipur, RAJ.

Bhitti-Chitra=*wall painting*. The Indian *term* for *mural painting*, it refers to the *fresco* or the *tempera technique* on walls. Refer *Ajanta*.

Bhoir, Dharmraj (1941–2001) b. MAHA. Education: GDA in *Art*, *Art* Master Certificate, M.A. in history. Solos: Surat, Nanded, Aurangabad, TAG, *JAG*. Awards & Hon.: for his book Vermilion & is also a poet; Honoured as Eminent Artist by the Chief Minister of MAHA Member: State Board of MAHA Secondary & Higher Secondary & Higher Secondary Board of Studies. President of Marathwada Art Society. Appointments: Taught at different *art* schools in MAHA, Abhinav Chitrakala in Nanded; Prof., HoD of *Painting* & Dean GSA in Aurangabad & *JJSA*, Faculty Marathwada University. Collections: pvt. & corporates, in Mumbai & Aurangabad; International: USA, Burma.

Dharmraj Bhoir was largely an *abstract painter* using gestural strokes and *textures* to create *forms* of surreal beauty. He was constantly experimenting with complete command of *form* and *colour*. He lived and worked in Aurangabad.

Bhowmick, Saroma (1917–) b. Barda, Kolkata. No formal training in *art*, tutored by *Gopal Ghose*. Solos: First exhibition in 1952, Academy Salon, Indian Museum, *AFA* over five solos & *ISOA* Kolkata. Retrospective: 60 years of *art* life in Kolkata, *ISOA*. Group participations: *AFA* & Women's Art Exhibition Kolkata, *ISOA*. Publications: "Anand Bazaar Patrika" & "Desh Kolkata".

Saroma Bhowmick was greatly inspired by the *folk art* of Bengal Pat *paintings*, the *Bengal School*, later also by the *arts* and *crafts* of the village she lived in, including the Alpana, floral decorations, the *clay* and pith *sculptures*. Her *paintings* are marked by their simplicity and serene *romanticism*. The *figures* are elongated with long necks and supple limbs. Most of her *paintings* are based on the love story of RADHA and KRISHNA. Her *sketches* too have a vibrant quality, freezing movement and transient emotions with a snapshot quality.

She lives and works in Kolkata.

Bhowmik, Ashok (1953–) b. Allahabad. Education: Grad. *GCAC* Kolkata. Solos: *AFA* Kolkata, Artists' Centre Mumbai, Kumar Gallery New Delhi, Senate Hall–Allahabad University Allahabad, *JAG*, *GK*, *ATG*, *G88*; International: New York, Holland, Germany. Group participations: *LKA*–UP, Chennai, Trivandrum & Ahmedabad, 4th National Art Fair New Delhi, Harmony Bombay, RGP Mumbai, *Biennale BB*, *BAAC*, Centre Art Gallery, MMB Kolkata. *Art* camps & workshops: All India Artist & Writer Camp by Dept. of Cultural Affairs UP, Directed Poster workshops at Bhopal, Azamgarh and Allahabad. Member: Council Member State *LKA* AP. Publications: Articles on *paintings* & theatre in many newspapers stories & short stories published in Hindu magazines. Collections: *LKA* & Modern Art Gallery New Delhi, RPG collections; International: San Francisco, Holland, Germany.

Ashok Bhowmik juxtaposes his flattened and abbreviated human *figures* against a dark, brooding *background*. There is no peace and *harmony* in these *pen* and *ink drawings* touched with the slightest nuances of *acrylic colour*. Instead these *allegories* veer between reality and *fantasy* with the *figures* containing references to *folk art*, especially *Warli paintings*.

His recent works are suffused with *warm colours*, especially bright yellows and deep reds, though the *background* remains dark. The *figures* are decorated with tribal jewellery and appear tattooed and impassive, staring blandly at the viewer.

He lives and works in Kolkata. Refer *Tribal Art*.

Bhowmik, Samar N. (1937–) b. Chandpur, WB. Education: Dip. in *FA*. *GCAC* Kolkata. Post-Grad. degree in Museology Calcutta University, Smithmount Fellow USA UGC scholarship 1960–62. Over 26 solos & over 200 group participations: National Exhibition *AFA* Kolkata, *BAS*, other in Hyderabad, Bangalore, Darjeeling; International: Germany, USA. *Auctions*: Osian's Mumbai. Member: Secretary *AFA* Executive Committee and *AFA* & Governing Body *GCAC* and International Committee Member Kolkata. Appointments: Curator in *RBM*, Worked to shape the Tagore House *Jorasanko* to Museum Kolkata; Commissioner for Tagore Exhibitions by ICCR & EZCC New Delhi, China, Cairo, Alexandra, Abudhabhi; International: Seminars & conferences on *art* at Germany, Denmark, Sweden, UK, France, USA, Russia, Holland, Finland & Hungary. Publications: Essays, catalogues & books on *FA*., literature & museology;

Organized 1st Asian Conference of literary, biographical and memorial *museum* in *Santiniketan* & Kolkata. Collections: *AFA* Kolkata, State Museum Venkattappa, *RBM*; International: American Museums.

Samar N. Bhowmik's *style* has evolved from the early *Bengal School style* of Chinese-inspired linear *landscapes* in the *wash technique* to a folk-like fragmentation of boldly painted *forms* and decorative *detail*. His later *paintings* are inspired by *Rabindranath Tagore's* philosophy and writings.

He lives and works in Kolkata.

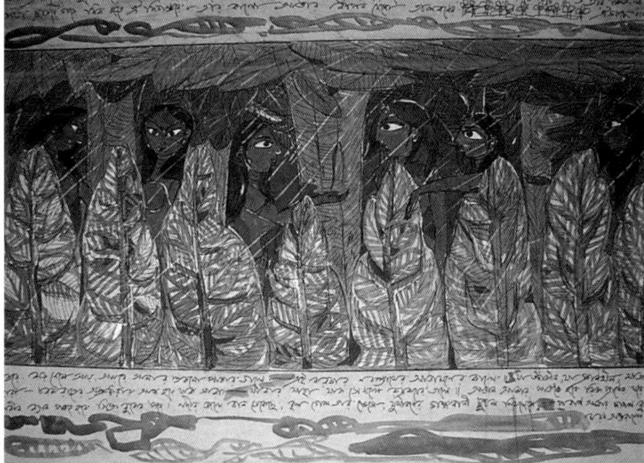

Bhowmik, Samar N.: "Rains and Women", *Oils*, 61x122 cm.

Bhudevi Bhu=earth, devi=Goddess. Bhudevi is the personification of the Earth, variously called Bhudevi, Prithvi and Bhumi. She never appears alone, but with either VISHNU or Sri LAKSHMI. She is depicted variously in *art*; one of the most interesting depictions show her clinging precariously to the tusks of Varaha, the boar incarnation of VISHNU who dived into the ocean to rescue her. Refer AVATARA; Illustration—VARAHAVATARA.

Bhujanga-Valaya Refer *Ornaments*.

Bhullar A.S. (1939–) b. Amritsar. Self taught. Solos: Over 23 solos in New Delhi, Mumbai, Chandigarh, including *JAG*, *AIFACS*; Group participations: Over 41 Group Shows in New Delhi, Mumbai, Chennai, Ahmedabad, Chandigarh, Jalandhar and Patiala, participated in all major *exhibitions* including *LKA* New Delhi, Chandigarh, Jaipur, SKP, *AIFACS*, *JAG*, *NCAG*, *Biennales*; International: Kala Kumbh Russian Centre New Delhi; Mexico, Mauritius Art Festival Sharjah. *Art* camps: Kala Vastu Academy New Delhi, IAFA & DAV College Amritsar, Kala Vrat Ujjain & Mauritius, *AIFACS*, SKP. Awards: *LKA* Chandigarh & New Delhi, IAFA Amritsar, Kala Math & Kala Shree New Delhi, *AIFACS*, Hons.: Ludhiana, Amritsar, *AIFACS* Veteran Artist 1999. Fellowship: 1992–94 Junior HRD Ministry New Delhi. Member: Council member *AIFACS*. Collections: Tata Chemicals Mumbai, Rashtrapati Bhavan, *GCA*, *LKA*, New Delhi, *LKA* Chandigarh, *Dhoomimal*, TAG; International: UK, USA, Abu Dhabi, Switzerland, Argentina, Italy, France, Germany & Czechoslovakia.

The *landscape* was central to A.S. Bhullar's pointillist *drawings* and early *oils*. He was endlessly fascinated by the three elements of *nature*, i.e. wind, water and earth as well as a surreal view of life at the bottom of sea in a surrealistic *manner*. They are interrelated with motion, thus creating new imaginative movements in the whole *composition*. Earlier attempted *Cubism* in *oils*, a series—"Temptation" was based on the relationship between men and women.

Bhushan, Vidya (1923–1996) b. Udgir, MAHA. Education: *JJSA*, AFA Yugoslavia. Retired as Vice Principal College of FA. & Architecture Hyderabad. Solos: New Delhi, L.V. Prasad Gallery Hyderabad, *JAG*, TAG, TKS; International: Belgrade Yugoslavia, Los Angeles USA. Retrospective: CMC Gallery New Delhi. Group Participations: Hyderabad, Mumbai, National Exhibition New Delhi; International: Germany, Italy & other European countries for two decades. Awards: National Gold Plaque 1957; International: Art Exhibition Moscow. Commissions: *Portraits* of Gandhiji, Nehru, Sardar Patel, Abdul Kalam Azad, Rajiv Gandhi. Appointments: HoD CFA and Architecture Hyderabad. Collections: *NGMA* New Delhi, Museum of Art Hyderabad; International: *Museum* in Germany, Moscow, USA, pvt. national & international.

Vidya Bhushan worked with a variety of materials including *oils*, *egg-tempera*, *watercolour*, *printmaking* and *murals* in *mosaic fresco technique*. He made original *copies* of the *Ajanta* cave *paintings* and executed commissioned *portraits* of several political leaders. In the 40s there was a marked academic *Realism* in his works. After his visit to Yugoslavia in the mid-50s his *brushwork* became more controlled and he started using layers of *transparent colour* in the *egg-tempera technique*. He also started using ribbon-like *abstract forms* in conjunction with jaw-like dentated shapes. His work from the 80s displays a mastery of *technique* and a simplicity of *form*.

Bidri A *craft* practised mostly in Bidar, KAR in South India. The *technique* was imported from Damascus in Syria by way of Persia. It reached its apex in India under Islamic rule between 16th and 17th centuries. It is also known as damascening and is a *form* of inlaying as surface decoration on bell-metal. An *alloy* of *copper* and tin. *Silver* wire or *silver* pieces are beaten into the grooves and *patterns* cut into the bell-metal. The whole object is immersed into an *acid bath*, then cut and polished. The *silver* glows against the blackened surface. Bidri is now used to decorate Surahis (water-jugs), snuff boxes, Pandans (betel-nut boxes) and other decorative objects. Refer *Dokra*.

Biennale An exhibition of *art*, usually at the international level which is held every two years, the Sao Paulo Biennale in Brazil, the Havana Biennale at Cuba, the Paris Biennale on the Menton Biennale.

They were also held in India in Mumbai by *CIMA* at *JAG*, *GC* and *BAS*; in New Delhi by *LKA*; in Bhopal by *BB*; in Chandigarh by *GMAG* PUJ University, in Lucknow by *LKA* and other towns Hyderabad, Nasik, Mysore, Jaipur, Cochin; International: Bangladesh, Lahore now Pakistan, Chile—South America, Sao Paulo—Brazil, Tokyo—Japan, UK, Germany, France, Italy and Switzerland.

Bindu=seed, germ, drop and zero. Today associated mostly with the works of *Sayed Haider Raza*, the France-based Indian *painter*, becoming in his words "the very genesis of creation", flowing outwards from *light* and moving into *forms* and *colours* as well as *vibrations*, energy, sound, *space* and *time*. Refer *Mahadeo Bhanaji Ingle*, *Balkrishna M. Patel*, Illustration–*Mohanti Prafulla*.

Biomorphic A *term* used in *abstract art* referring to irregular *forms* based on *nature*. These shapes evoke a feeling of organic reality, without being identifiable. Usually seen in surrealist *art*, as in the works of J. Miro, Y. Tanguy and H. Arp. In India *Setlur Gopal Vasudev's* and *P. Gopinath's forms* can be termed biomorphic. Refer *Surrealism*, *K. Damodaran*.

Birbhum A district in WB, which is famous for its many small temples profusely decorated with *terracotta* plaques. These temples were erected by all classes of people, as an act of piety. They varied in *size* from 6 to 18m. in bth and 9.2 to 21.5m. in ht. The *style* is *eclectic*, some *images* being sophisticated in the Western *manner*, while some temples have been decorated exclusively in a crude, though lively folk *style*. The subject matter, though mostly religious, is divergent; Vaisnavism, Shaivism and the SHAKTI cult are all represented. There are also scenes of *contemporary* local life, erotic scenes, *figures* of foreigners–sahibs and memsahibs with their pet dogs, dressed in the height of fashion. Refer *Santiniketan*.

Birla Academy of Art and Craft (BAAC) (Kolkata, WB). The BAAC was established in 1967, with the principal object of helping the growth of *art* and *culture*, with an emphasis on the *visual* and *performing arts*. The *Academy* has consolidated its position as a centre of cultural, artistic and educational activities, through the past three decades. This representative *museum* and *art* gallery has spacious display halls, *exhibition* areas and stage facilities. The main activities of the *Academy* consist of collecting, preserving and displaying *museum* objects, holding *exhibitions* of Indian and international *art* and educational programmes. The *museum* displays Indian *art* objects ranging from the 1st century BC to the *modern* age. One of the important *exhibitions* held by the gallery is "Genesis of Ramkinkar Baij" in which *artists* of the calibre of *Janak Jhankar Narzary*, *A. Ramachandran*, *A.S. Panwar* have also participated.

Since 1995 BAAC has branched out with an *art* gallery in the Century Bhavan premises Mumbai, exhibiting *artists'* works, with seminars, classes for young children, an open centre for *art* and *culture* and reviving Indian *craft*.

Bisht, Ranvir Singh (1928–1998) b. Garhwal. Education: *Art* Masters, Dip. in *FA*. & One year specialization course *FA*. GCAC Lucknow. Solos: *LKA*, RB & Gallery Aurobindo New Delhi, *AIFACS*, *Dhoomimal*; other solos in Lucknow, Mussoorie, Shimla, Jhansi, Kanpur, Allahabad, Mumbai. Retrospective: 1948–1985 by UP State *LKA* Lucknow; International: New York. Group participations: Kanpur, *NGMA*, National *LKA* & RB New Delhi, *LKA* Lucknow, *JAG*; International: Germany, Japan, Sao Paulo Brazil. Participated in seminars & *artist* camps. Awards/Fellowhip: UNESCO Fellowship for *Visual Art*, and from State Galleries, Museum, National Award, Fellowship *LKA* & Padma Shri New Delhi, Gold Medal UP, Kalaratha *AIFACS*; International: USA, France. Member: Board/Council of several institutions all over India and acting Chairman UP *LKA* Lucknow. Commissions: *Murals* for public places, *portraits* Indira Gandhi and other political social leaders. Appointments: Participated in seminars; Taught *FA*. 1956–89; Principal of GCAC Lucknow; Dean of Faculty of *FA*. Lucknow University; International: UNESCO to visit Art Centers, State Galleries, Universities and Art Colleges USA and France. Publications: *LKA* Monograph New Delhi & Pustak Kendra *monograph* "R.S. Bisht in Search of Self" Rooplekha *AIFACS*, All India Radio & TV. Collections: State Museum Lucknow, *LKA* Ministry of Education Govt. of India New Delhi and others.

The Himalayas, where he was born, dominated the work of Ranvir Singh Bisht. *Nature* was the centre of his consciousness, at its most colourful yet sublime. His works of the 50s show a gay world full of flowers, trees, clouds, villages and mountains. He had mastered both *watercolour* and *oils*. Like many of his *contemporaries*, he was influenced both by the linear grace of the *Bengal School* and impressionist *landscapes* of the *Bombay School*. In the 60s he cultivated a *style* that was *abstract* to the point of non-objectivity. However the glowing patches and *washes* of *colour* evoked a feeling of mountain *landscapes*.

He had also painted female *nudes* and practised *ceramics*. However he was best known as a colourist for his evocative *colour passages* of lush and vibrant *pigment*. He lived and worked in Lucknow.

Biswas, Nikhil (1930–1966). Education: *GCAC* Kolkata, also Dip. in *sculpture*. Solos: Over eight in Kolkata including *AFA* Kolkata, *Art Heritage* New Delhi. Retrospective: 1967 & 1976 *JAG*, 1994–95 *CKAG*; International: Staatliche Galarie Moritzburg, Dresten & Halle Germany. Group participations: At major *art* centres in India, including *CKAG*. *Auctions*: Heart & Osian's–Mumbai, New Delhi, Bowring's Mumbai, Bonham's London. Awards: Gold Medal–*sculpture* *AFA* Kolkata & in *painting LKA* New Delhi. Founder member: Chitrangshu *SCA* & Calcutta Painters. Appointments: *Art* Lecturer Mitra Institute Kolkata. Collections: *NGMA*, *Delhi Art Gallery* & Ebrahim Alkazi New Delhi, *AFA* Kolkata; International: Collectors in Germany including Staatliche Galarie Moritzburg, pvt. & public national & international.

Nikhil Biswas was fascinated with *black*. His *drawings* and *paintings* speak and interact effusively with each other and always move with energy. Some *compositions* deal with owls or some kind of personal *imagery* which possibly symbolizes anxiety and fear.

These *monochrome paintings* have certain *themes* dealing with suffering and anguish portrayed in *terms* of ancient *myths*, e.g., the fight between horse and bull. Other *themes* are Christ as a symbol of humanity, scenes of human struggle, the exodus of East Bengali refugees, clowns, bulls, tortured male *figures* and children. He lived and worked in Kolkata.

Bite, Biting in The action of the *acid* on a *copper* or *zinc plate* during the process of *etching* in *printmaking*. The bite varies with the length of the *time* and the strength of the *acid* solution prepared. Ramchand Roy learnt this *technique* of *printmaking*. The *artist* used *metal plates* for *intaglio printing* among which *etching* was easier with *acid resist ground* and its application on the *metal* surface, the biting stage in the *acid bath*. Refer *Aquatint, Gum Arabic, Varnish, Amitabha Banerjee, Jyoti Bhatt, Jogen Chowdhury, Krishna N. Reddy.*

Black 1. Black is a *pigment* i.e. colourless, as it absorbs *light* completely. Theoretically black is formed by mixing the *primary colours*, red, blue and yellow. **2.** *Ivory black* is a *transparent* organic *pigment*, used since *prehistoric times*. It is an amorphous carbon produced from charred or burned animal bones (formerly *ivory* tusks were used). It turns to ash at high temperatures. It is a slow drying *pigment*. **3.** *Lamp black* is a *pigment* used for all *techniques* consisting of finely divided, almost pure carbon, made from soot of burning *oil* or gas. *Lamp black* is a *pigment* that has been used since the Vedic period. **4.** Black when mixed in any *colour* creates a *shade*. Refer *Sujata Bajaj, Vajubhai D. Bhagat, Nikhil Biswas, Devraj Dakoji, Amitava Das, Phalguni DasGupta, C. Douglas, Ganga Devi, Gunen Ganguli, Ranjitsingh Gaekwad.*

Block Printing A method of *relief printing* from a block of material either *wood* or linoleum which are commonly used.

In India wooden block printing on cloth or *paper* is an *art* traced back to the 4th century AD. *Stone* and burnt *clay* were other elements used besides *wood*. *Portraits* of the BUDDHA were block printed on the pages of manuscripts. Indian manuscripts were illustrated after the 10th century AD though early history has no such evidence. Refer *Collage, Institution, Kalamkari, Mutli Block Colour Printing, Persian Art, SJM* (Hyderabad), *Wood Block Printing, K. Madhav Menon, Somnath Hore, Reddeppa M. Naidu, Roshan M. Mullan, Kailash Chandra Sharma.*

Blocking In A *technique* used by some *artists* in the initial stages of a *painting*, when they roughly fill in the *composition* with *colour*.

Traditional *artists* used layers of *transparent colours* especially in *egg-tempera technique*; they also used *colours* with *shades* and *tones*: e.g. *Jaganath M. Ahivasi, Nandalal Bose, Narayan S. Bendre*. Refer *Bengal School, Wash (Technique).*

Blot Drawing A *technique* described by the English watercolourist of the 18th century, A. Cozens in his book "A New Method for assisting the invention in Drawing Original Compositions of Landscapes", 1786. In an extension of Leonardo da Vinci's advice to *artists* to study stains on walls and other accidental effects, A. Cozens advocated the *technique* of letting blots of *colour* or *ink* fall randomly on a sheet of *paper*, sometimes folding it to create extra *patterns* and later developing a *composition* based on it. This method was later taken up by both the Surrealists (*Automatism*) and the Action *Painters*. Refer *Action Painting, Decalcomania, Abanindranath Tagore* and *Rabindranath Tagore*.

Bodhisattva Bodhi=supreme knowledge, sattva= essence. A Bodhisattva is a Buddha-to-be in *Buddhism*, a person who has striven to attain complete Bodhi and thus could achieve a state of NIRVANA, yet decides to postpone it in order to guide lesser humans who have not yet achieved the state. During the Mahayana phase of *Buddhism*, the belief arose that there were several Bodhisattvas of whom the principal five were, Samantabhadra, Vajrapani, Ratnapani, Padmapani and Viswapani. Refer *Ajanta*, BUDDHA, *Ellora, Gandharan Art, Gupta, Mathura Art, Pala Miniature, Archaeological Museum* (*Sarnath UP*). Illustration: *Ajanta*–"Bodhisattva Vajrapani".

Body Art *Art* which involves the *artist's* body. At first it was also used as a synonym for *action painting*, where the *artist's* movements dictated the *composition*. Today, the *artist's* body itself could be the instrument of *art*, with both the video camera and the still-camera recording certain actions of the *artist*, such as spitting, biting, jumping and flying. *Artists* also subjected their bodies to a variety of painful actions. Conceptually, Indian *artists* have used the *medium* to explore multiple identities through mind, body and soul. The storytelling, humour and horror, *fantasy* and reality all personified by the *artist's* intense presence has made this a popular *medium* in India. It also resonates with traditional Indian cultural events that blend fine and *performance arts*. Young Indian *artists* have broken the barriers of the merely *visual* in body art–in addition to their undoubted skill in *drawing, modeling, sculpting* and *casting*, they have incorporated the modes and *movement* of traditional and *modern* Indian dance forms, cinema and slide-projections into a buoyant *amalgam* of sculpture and Kathak and Kathakali, two *traditional* Indian dance *forms*, Ratnabali Kant has formed possibilities to build narrations of *contemporary* life, *Nalini Malani* has collaborated with Alakananda Samarth to bring a German play to *visual* as well as dramatic life. Refer *Happening, Living Sculpture, Mahirwan Mamtani, N. Pushpamala, Sheela Gowda*; Illustration–*Painting*.

Bomanjee, Pestonjee (1851–1938) b. Mumbai. Education: *sculpture & modelling JJSA* under Lockwood Kipling, *Drawing & painting* under John Griffiths. Retrospective: *NCAG*. Group participations: Simla FA. Exhibition, Annual

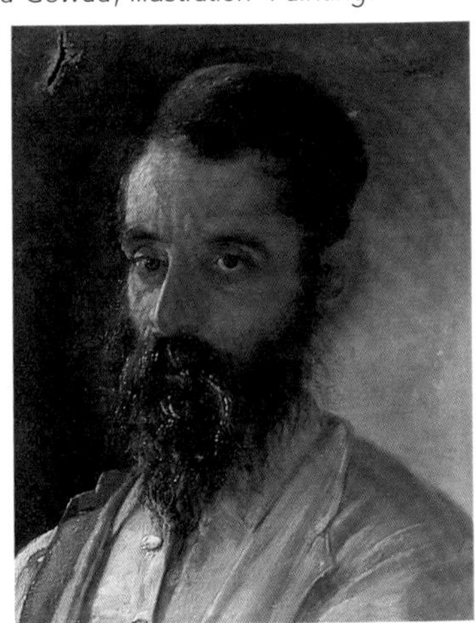

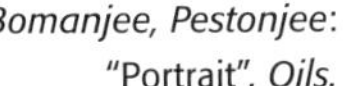

Bomanjee, Pestonjee: "Portrait", *Oils.*

Exhibition 1879 & The International 1883–84 Kolkata, *GC* Mumbai, *BAS*, Kolkata, Chennai. *Auctions:* Heart New Delhi, Osian's Mumbai. Awards: International Exhibition Kolkata, Viceroy's Prize Shimla, Madras Govt. Gold Medal, *BAS*. Collections: *NGMA* New Delhi, TATA, *CSMVS* (*PWM*), *JJSA*, pvt. & public.

Pestonjee Bomanjee was a fine portraitist and styled his *compositions* in the *manner* of the European masters. He trained first in *sculpture* and later in *painting* at the then newly established *JJSA*. He was the leader of the group of students who spent twelve years in copying the *frescoes* at *Ajanta*. Most of these laboriously worked *copies* in *oils* were destroyed in a fire when they were being exhibited in Britain. He was the first appointed Vice-Principal of the *JJSA* working under John Griffiths for a short period of time.

Pestonjee Bomanjee's *paintings* show his meticulous attention to *detail* of costume, jewellery, *background* and the objects around his *models*. His family, including brothers, sisters, wife and children were the subject of many of the works. "The Leisure Hour" of 1883 is a depiction of his wife sewing, dressed in traditional Parsee attire, while "Feeding the Parrot" shows his wife with his infant son. Almost all of his works have been rendered in *oils*, leading to the use of *colours* and *chiaroscuro* akin to the *old masters*.

Bombay Art Society (BAS) (Mumbai, MAHA). The oldest *art* society in India, established in 1888, with the objective of encouraging *art* and *artists*, promoting artistic awareness in the general public. It organizes lectures, *exhibitions* and discussions in addition to its annual *exhibition*. Over a 100 annual BAS *exhibitions* have been held, the participating *artists* including *Amrita Sher-Gil*, *Mahadev V. Dhurandhar*, *K.K. Hebbar* and *Krishnaji Howlaji Ara* all having won the coveted Gold Medal. The *exhibitions* have been held at various venues over the years, including the Town Hall, the *JJSA*, the Cawasji Jehangir Hall (presently *NGMA* Mumbai) and the *JAG*. The Journal was first published in 1910, titled as "A Brief Historical Sketch of the Bombay Art Society, with special reference to the period—1906–1910". However, its publication was discontinued for long periods of time, due to the lack of funds. The society "Salon" was founded in 1939 in Rampart Row. Here small discussions, exhibitions and lectures were held. Today, film shows and *art* demonstrations have become a regular feature at the Salon. The prestigious Bendre-Husain scholarship was instituted in 1989–90, to encourage promising young *artists*. The society is now in the process of raising funds for erecting its own *Art* Complex, through *auctions* and donations.

Bombay School The *Revivalist Movement* initiated by the *Bengal School* affected *artists* in Mumbai too. Centred around the *JJSA* the Bombay School *painters* were soon caught upwith the Nationalist fervour unleashed by the *Swadeshi Movement*. The strong textile industry of Western India with headquarters in Mumbai, soon became the *focal point* of the *Swadeshi Movement* which had influenced *Abanindranath Tagore* to found the *Bengal School* in the first place. The gradual decline of Kolkata as the political and industrial centre of India and the simultaneous rise of Mumbai as an industrial and economic powerhouse, brought about rich and powerful patrons from industrial families and the film Industry. It was not merely the Nationalist sentiment that was the essence of the Bombay School, but the cosmopolitan *nature* of the Metropolis, which contributed to its development and growth as also the influence of post-impressionist, and fauvist *art*. *Artists* like *Ravishankar M. Raval*, *Jagannath M. Ahivasi*, G.H. Nagarkar, Raghuvir Chimulkar, R.D. Dhopeshvarkar, *Rasik Durgashankar Raval*, *Abdul Rahim Appabhai Almelkar*, *Vajubhai D. Bhagat* and *Rasiklal Parikh* became well known for their *paintings*.

Bose, Arun (1934–) b. India. Education: Dip. in *FA*. *GCAC* Kolkata, Studied Italian *frescoes*, *art* & *graphic art* ENSBA & Atelier 17 Paris under the guidance of S.W. Hayter, Pratt Graphic Centre New York. Solos: *CYAG*, *CKAG*, SC; International: Colorado, New Jersey, Belgium, Paris, Arizona, Weintraub Gallery New York, GBP. Group participations: National Exhibition *NGMA* & *Triennale* New Delhi, Govt. Museum Chandigarh, *AIFACS*, *SCA*, *CKAG*, *CYAG*; International: *Triennale* Berlin, *Biennale* Italy, New York, Sao Paulo Brazil, Switzerland, Yugoslavia & Australia, Commonwealth Exhibition London Contemporary Art of India Exhibitions New York, International Art Fair—Dusseldorf, Basel & Ljubljana. *Auctions*: Heart & Osian's Mumbai. Award/Fellowship: French Govt. Scholarship, John D. Rockefeller III Fund Fellowship. Founder Member: *SCA*. Member: The Screening Committees in New York & New Hamshire. Appointments: Lecturer at the Indian CFA & Draftsmanship & *GCAC* Kolkata, Assistant Prof. New York University and Prof. at Herbert H. Lehman College of the City University of New York. Publications: *Prints* published by JMB publishers, HMK FA. John Szoke publishers New York. Collections: *LKA* & *NGMA* New Delhi; International: Bibliotheque Nationale Paris, Israel Museum, Bagdael Museum, pvt. & corporates.

Arun Bose's *paintings* have a contemplative stillness in their negation of the *background*. There is almost a surreal feeling of solitude, with shrines and windows beckoning the viewer with their empty gaze. Today Arun Bose is also known for his *colour* viscosity *prints*. His Indian roots are clearly visible in his polychromatic *colour palette*, religious and iconic *forms*.

Arun Bose works in New York.

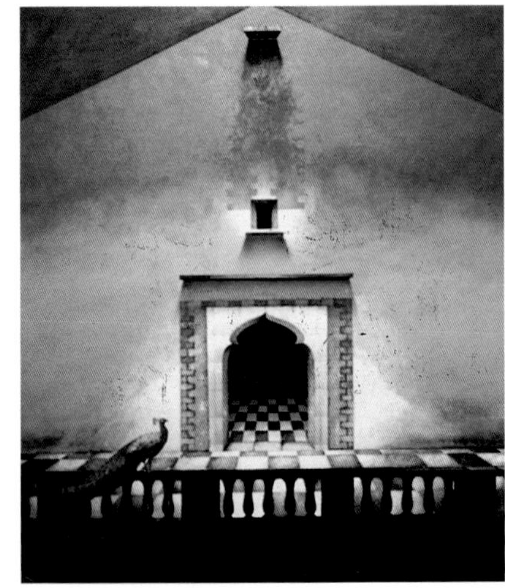

Bose, Arun: "Royal Entrance" *Acrylic*.

Bose, Atul (1898–1977) b. East Bengal (now Bangladesh). Education: Dip. in *FA*. GSA Kolkata; RAA London. Solo: *AFA* Kolkata. Group participation: *GC* Mumbai. *Auction*: Osian's Mumbai. Awards: From Calcutta University Guru Prasanna Ghosh Scholarship, D.Litt. *RBU*; International: Ivory Award RAA. Founder Member: Indian Academy of Art, *AFA* & Society of FA. Kolkata. Commissions: By Govt. of India to *paint portraits* of Edward VII & Queen Mary; International: Copied Royal *portraits* at Windsor Castle & Buckingham Palace; *Portrait Rabindranath Tagore* 1920. Appointments: Principal GSA Kolkata. Publications: Book in his name by *ISOA* and Verified Perspective Kolkata, SC; A collection of writing on *art* in Bengali. Collections: Asiatic Society Kolkata, Rashtrapati Bhavan & Parliament House New Delhi, A large number of *paintings* and *drawings* donated to *AFA* Kolkata, *Santiniketan*, *VMM*, pvt. & corporates.

The identifying features of Atul Bose's *portraits* and *figure studies* were his mastery over *illusion* and *trompe l'oeil* effects. He stressed *colour*, *line* and *tone* to translate the *visual* onto the *canvas*. While his *drawings* of the human *figure*, *highlight* his firm *line* and *handling* of *mass* and *volume*; his *paintings* are impressionistic in their use of *brushwork* and placement *manner* of later Bengal revivalists. He lived in Kolkata.

Bose, Krishnamachari (1962–) b. Angamaly, Kerala. Education: Degree in *FA*. *JJSA*. Solos: Chennai, Cochin, New Delhi, British Council Division & *NGMA* Mumbai, *JAG*, *YBCAG*, *LCAG*, *JJSA*. Group participations: Gurgaon Haryana, *GC*, *Artists' Centre*, 50 Years India, "Cutting Edge Contemporary" *NGMA*, Kala Ghoda Fair, *BAAC* & *SG* Mumbai, *CIMA* Kolkata, *JAG*, *LCAG*, *VAG*. International: San Francisco USA, Hong Kong. *Art* workshops: Organized by *NGMA* Mumbai, *MPCVA*, *BB*. Awards: *LKA* Kerala, *BAS*, *JJSA*; International: USA, UK, Mid-American Affairs Award, British Council.

Krishnamachari Bose is currently an exponent of total *art*, expanding his parameters beyond the scope of *oil*, *acrylic* and *watercolours* on *canvas* and *paper*, to the realm of the environment. He is constantly experimenting, with materials, *forms* and *themes*. His "Amuseum Memoirs" *exhibition* used books, piled together, stitched, perforated, burnt, signed, etc., presenting an argument against traditional values and knowledge. Later he incorporated the idea of *design* into *art*, making a foray into furniture making and attempting to bridge the conflict between *applied* and *fine arts*.

He works in Mumbai. Refer *Assemblage*, *Environment Art*.

Bose, Nandalal (1882–1966) b. Kharagpur, Bihar. He studied *art* at the GSA Kolkata, under the tutelage of *Abanindranath Tagore*. During this period he visited *Ajanta* & made *copies* of the *frescoes*, travelled North & South of India; Made *illustrations* for *Rabindranath Tagore's* poems & also won a prize at the first exhibition mounted by the *ISOA*.

He taught *art* for sometime at the *ISOA*, before moving to *KB Santiniketan* in 1919, by 1922 he became the Adhyaksha (president) of the institute, retiring only in 1951. In his years at *Santiniketan* he instituted a method of teaching that was prevalent at the *Bauhaus* during the same period. *Craft* was given the same level of importance as *painting* and *sculpture*. He invited *craft* and *fresco* experts from all over the country to visit *Santiniketan* and teach their traditional *techniques* to the students. He himself learnt Japanese *style ink drawing* and Rajasthani *fresco techniques*. Besides forming an *Artists* Cooperative, and exhibiting the works of his students at different venues, he published many articles contributing his views on *art*, besides illustrating many of *Rabindranath Tagore's* books. He was commissioned by the Maharaja of Vadodara to decorate the Kirti Mandir. He also painted the famous Haripura *posters* for the 1938 Congress session in GUJ. Later his works on *auctions*—Osian's & Heart Mumbai. He was honoured with the degree of D.Litt (Hons.) by the BHU, Calcutta University at *RBU*, the title of Desikottana by *VBU*, the Padma Vibhushana and the Silver Jubilee Medal of the *AFA* Kolkata. His collections are in Marvel Art Gallery Ahmedabad, *NGMA New Delhi*, Indian Museum Kolkata, *RBM*, RB VBU; International in University of Sussex England and trustees of V&A.

Nandalal Bose stood apart from the rest of *Abanindranath Tagore's* students because of his *eclectic* approach. To begin with, he adopted *Abanindranath Tagore's wash technique*, but his visit to *Ajanta* breathed a different sort of life into these works. A second linear *style* is discernible in his graceful *line drawings* as in Veena (a string instrument) Player. He also used *tempera*, the limitations of the *medium*, leading to a spontaneous quick-brushed *style* of whip-lash strokes and half stated *outlines*. The Haripura panels, which were painted in this *manner* owe something to the *Kalighat folk paintings*. The subject matter was mostly *genre*, the rural people of India depicted in a bold and decorative *manner*.

There is also a link with the Far East, in his *ink* and *brush paintings*, the firm *calligraphic* brushstrokes and diffused *masses* of *ink* showing his receptivity to *Japanese art*.

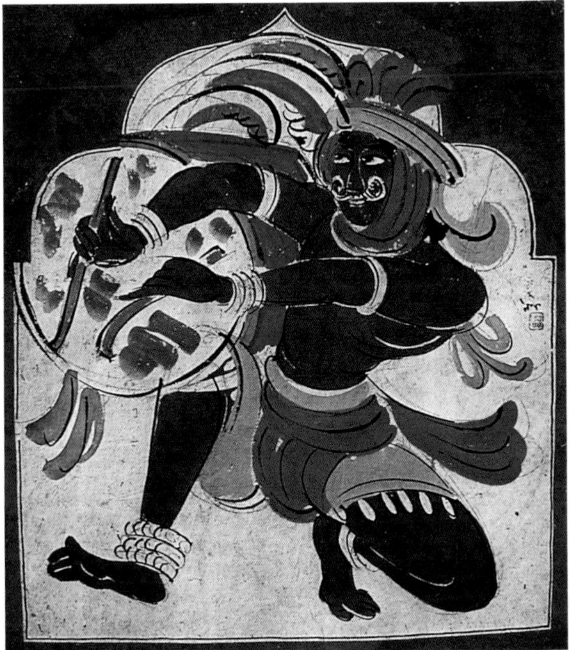

Bose, Nandalal: "Drummer", *Tempera* on *Handmade Paper*, 62.5x55.5 cm.

Boucharde Synonym of bushhammer. A multipointed hammer with the striking ends dividing into rows of metallic *points* or teeth, used in *stone carving*. Refer *Sadanandji Bakre, Sankho Chaudhuri, Satish Gujral, C. Dakshinamoorthy*.

Bowen, Eric (1929–) b. Allahabad. Education: Dip. in *Art* Delhi Polytechnic. Scholarship/Grants: Went to Rome on an Italian Govt. Scholarship for *painting*; Norwegian State Scholarship for travel/study; Two Grants from Royal Ministry Foreign Affairs 1984, 1991. Over 35 solos & group shows: Kunika Chemould, Kumar Gallery & *Art Heritage* New Delhi, *GC* Mumbai, *Dhoomimal, AIFACS*, SC; International: Galleries in Oslo, Rome, New York, Geneva, Philadelphia, Norway. Group participations: National Exhibitions in India, *AIFACS*; International: Norway, USA, Italy. Award: Hopper Art Centre New York. Founder member: "The Unknown" & *"Group 1890"* New Delhi. Commissions: Several *murals* including International Industries Fair New Delhi; International: Indian pavilion in Moscow. Collections: *NGMA* New Delhi, *Roopankar*; International: Stockholm, New York, Rome, Switzerland, National Gallery & State Gallery Norway, Henie-Onstad Museum Oslo.

Eric Bowen is primarily concerned with *form*, in the process of stripping his work of all extraneous *detail* and concentrating on *volume*, shape, *colour* and *texture*. He has used a wide range of *media, acrylic, encaustic, oil*, low *relief* and three-dimensional construction. His strongly constructed geometric *forms* are the product of his strong *spiritual background*. His earlier use of subtle *colour* groups have now been confidently replaced by brilliant primaries and *golds*.

He lives and works in New York, USA. Refer *Encaustic*.

Bowlekar, Anant M. (1941–) b. Vengurla, MAHA. Education: Dip. in *FA. MSU* under *Narayan S. Bendre* and *K.G. Subramanyan*, Drawing Teacher's Certificate *JJSA, Art* Master & photography. Solos & 19 group *exhibitions*: Nagpur, Pradarshak Mumbai, *JAG, BAG* & other places in India. Awards: Silver Medal Udaipur, MAHA State Art Award. Commissions: *Murals* Central Railway Engineering Institute Nasik. Appointments: Prof. & HoD of *painting JJSA*, Lectures & demonstrations and talk on radio Aurangabad; Paper on Common Factors in Art Application at Film and Television Institution Pune. Collections: *NGMA* New Delhi, KAR *LKA*, Govt. of MAHA Marathwada University, pvt. & corporates.

Though Anant M. Bowlekar also paints *abstracts* and *genre paintings*, he is better known as a portraitist. His *portraits* are generally of people he is familiar with, as he can then better express out the subtle nuances of character, making the *canvas* reflect the inner personality of the sitter, rather than the outward appearance.

Anant M. Bowlekar lives and works in Mumbai. Refer Illustration—*Highlight*.

Brahma=creator. The First Holy Trinity in *Hinduism*, the others being VISHNU and SHIVA. As the creator, Brahma is called Prajapati. His consort, SARASVATI, the goddess of learning and music, also called Vach or speech, is also his daughter. Brahma causes life to exist by the mere action of awakening from his sleep. He remains awake for a day (which corresponds to two billion human years. When he sleeps, life dies out).

In *art*, Brahma is represented with four faces, each one pointing to one of the four cardinal directions. His VAHANA (vehicle) is Hamsa, (a goose or a swan). He is dressed in the skin of a *black* antelope. He is seated in the yogic position in a chariot drawn by seven swans (representing the seven LOKAS—worlds). The lotus flower on which he either sits or stands, represents the earth. He carries a Kamandalu (water jar) and an Akshamala (rosary) representing *time*, and a book in his hands.

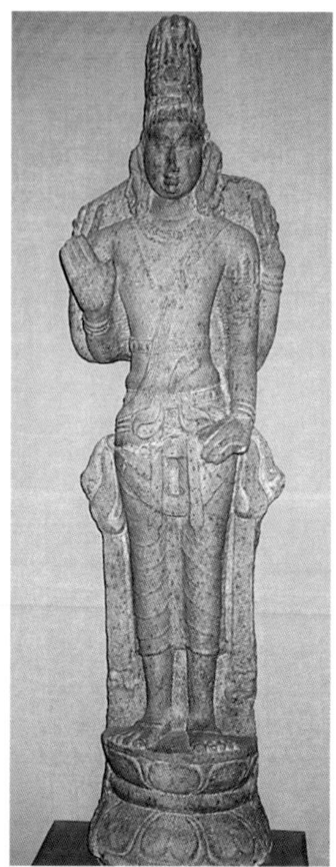

Brahma: "Standing Brahma", *Granite, Chola dynasty*, South India, AD 9th century, PALLAVA, *Chola transition*.

Brahma-Purana=the "Old Book of Brahma". It is also called Adipurana or the 1st PURANA. It is believed that BRAHMA himself dictated the 7000 verses long poem to the sage Marichi. It begins with an account of the *creation* of the world and includes a description of the universe.

Brass A metallic yellow *alloy* often used in *sculpture*. A compound of *copper* and *zinc*, it is rich golden yellow in *colour*. It is harder than *copper* and wears better. It may be protected from the atmosphere by a layer of *wax* or *lacquer* and in recent times powder coating. It can be *cast*, or wrought and is also available in sheet *form* for *relief sculpture*. Brass can also be welded, thus making it a versatile material to work with. In India brass was known in GUJ, UP and Bengal. Refer *Metal, Pala Miniatures, Meera Mukherjee, Sadanandji Bakre, Janak J. Narzary, Shankar Nandagopal, Piraji Sagara*.

Broad Handling A *term* referring to the individual *style* of the *artist*, in which *detailed work* is dispensed with. Instead the *artist* uses thick brushstrokes or the strokes of a palette knife and no *outlines* to suggest the subject. Example may be seen in Rembrandt's final *self portraits*, L. Freud's *portraits* and *nudes* of the 1980s, and *Ram Kumar's landscapes*. Refer *Distortion, Satyendranath Bandhyopadhyay*.

Bronze An *alloy* of *copper* and tin, bronze has been one of the most popular brown *metals* for *sculpture* through the ages. Since it was discovered in the Bronze Age between Stone Age and Iron Age, humans have used it extensively for making *weapons*, and other *artefacts*. Popularity is due to its many advantages; e.g., it offers a high structural strength, great physical permanence, ease of *casting*, and attractive appearance.

It has been *cast* in the *lost wax process* throughout the world. The Shang Chinese referred to it as the noblest of all materials and used it to make their *ritual* vessels; the ancient Greeks *cast* bronze for their *metal sculpture*, body-material armour and mirrors.

In India bronze was the *medium* used for the dancing girl found at *Mohenjo Daro*, though it has a high percentage of *copper*. Later bronze was used in South India during the *Pallava* and the *Chola dynasty* to *cast* both solid and hollow religious statuettes. Refer *Abstract Sculpture, Air Vents, Aluminium, Architecture, Artefact,* BHAKTI, *Casing, Cast, Chasing, Cire Perdue, Copper, Electroplating, Fibreglass, Filler, Fume Patination, Ink, Life-Size, Media, Patina, Realistic, Sand Moulding, Steel, Tensile Strength, Texture, Undercut, Wrought Metal, South Indian Bronze, S.C. Ahuja, K.C. Aryan, B. Vithal, Girish C. Bhatt, Chiru Chakravarty, Sankho Chaudhuri, Biman B. Das, Sadiq Dehlvi, M.J. Enas, Bhagwant K. Goregaoker, Usha Rani Hooja, Saroj Jain, Raghav Kaneria, Kantibhai B. Kapadia, Vinayak Pandurang Karmarkar, Latika Katt, Nilkanth P. Khanvilkar, Kanayi Kunhiraman, Leela Mukherjee, Meera Mukherjee, Nilkanth P. Khanvilkar, P.S. Nandhan, Janak J. Narzary, Mahendra Pandya, Choudhary Satyanarayan Patnaik, Sunil Kumar Paul, Niranjan Pradhan, Aekka Yadagiri Rao, Bhaskar Rao, Sarbari RoyChowdhury, N.B. Sabannavar, Sharma M.K. Sumahendra, Bayaji Vasantrao Talim, Brahman Vinayakrao Wagh, Vinayakrao Venkatrao Wagh*; Illustration—DIGAMBARA, *Somnath Hore, Ratilal Kansodaria, Chintamoni Kar, Ganpatrao K. Mhatre, Debi Prasad RoyChowdhury, Prabhas Sen*.

Bronzing A process in which a *plaster cast* or other non-metallic *sculptures* are coloured to imitate *bronze*.

This is done when an object is dipped in the *colour* of *brass*, gold, silver or any metallic *alloy* to give the look of this *metal/alloy*. Refer *South Indian Bronze, Janak J. Narzary, Shankar Nandagopal*.

Broota, Shobha (1943–) b. Delhi. Education: Dip. in *FA*. *College of* Art New Delhi. Solos: Chandigarh, Gallery 42 New Delhi, *SRAG, PUAG*; International: Chicago, London, "Origin" Schoo's Gallery Amsterdam & Netherland. Group participations: Goa, *NGMA* New Delhi, Woman Artists SKP, *Biennale* BB; International: Germany, Italy, London, Malaysia, Japan, *Biennale* Cuba, Bangladesh & Turkey, Women Artists by *NGMA* New Delhi in Bulgaria & Poland. Worked with different *media* & has exhibited her *Portraits* & *prints* in New Delhi, *BB*; International: Amsterdam. Award/Fellowship: Junior & Senior Fellowship by Ministry of Education, Award in *painting AIFACS*. Commissions: *portraits* of leading personalities. Appointments: Teaching *art* in TKS, invited for photographic workshop by MMB & *LKA* New Delhi. Publications: Works published in various catalogues, magazines. Collections: *NGMA* & *LKA* New Delhi, *Chandigarh Museum*; International: National Art Gallery Malaysia.

Her earlier works, especially in the *graphic medium* speak of her interest in *tones* and *textures*. Loosely scribbled *forms* are scratched over the plane in an *all-over pattern*. Her recent works however show a shift away from *pattern* to serene concentration on energy values. *Forms* tend to be centralized appearing to solidify out of the Rothko-like fields of stained *colour*. In the "Origins" series, *colour* and *light* play a crucial role of eternal opposites, the Purusha and Prakriti, the Yin-Yang, their juxtaposing leading to subtly pulsating *visuals* of *rhythm* and energy.

She lives and works in New Delhi. Refer *Abstraction Geometric, Hard-Edged Painting*.

Brush The tool of the *painter*, the brush is invariably made of animal hair. It has been used since ancient *times*. *Prehistoric artists* and primitive tribes used chewed twigs as brushes. The Indian miniature *painter* used the finest soft hair of kittens and squirrels besides. They were graded according to *size* and quality and pushed through the hollow part of a quill (bird's feather) and sealed with a drop of *lacquer*. The *artist* depends on the ready-made brush of hog hair used for the denser *medium* of *oil painting*, while squirrel-and *sable-hair* brushes are used for *watercolours*. They are in a variety of shapes, including rounded, flat, filbert or fan. Modern brushes are made of synthetic hair. Refer *Madhubani, Paresh Maity*.

Brush Drawing A *drawing* or *sketch* executed entirely with the *paint* or an *ink*-loaded *brush*. It has a smooth, flowing character similar to *calligraphy*. Refer *Nandalal Bose, Kalighat Pat, Jaganath M. Ahivasi, Rabindranath Tagore*.

Brushwork Refers to the *style* and *handling* of the *artist*. Brushwork is more easily visible and thus identifiable in the case of *painting*. The *viscous medium* and the soft and hard hair *brush* leave visible imprints of the *artists'* movements. As a result the *painters* exploited this effect personalizing their strokes until it became a sort of signature, or handwriting. As a result, the *impasto*, the dots and dabs, the frenzied whirligigs, the luscious sheen of silks and satins, all point to the personal brushwork, to identify the *artist* of a particular *painting*. There are differences though; In Indian miniatures and *Company painting styles, artists* created a smooth and flat finish, submerging their individual imprints. Refer *Company School, Ambadas, K.M. Adimoolam, Narayan S. Bendre, Maqbool Fiba Husain, Setlur Gopal Vasudev, Rabindranath Tagore, Gobardhan Ash*.

Buddha=The Enlightened One. (circa 563–483 BC). Siddhartha Gautama, of the Gotra family (Sakya/clan), son of Shudhodhana, king of the Sakyas, was born in the village Lumbini near Kapilavastu. Numerous myths are woven around his human life. His mother Queen Maya gave birth to Siddhartha in the midst of a groove of Sal trees; the child emerged with seven steps and was robed by INDRA, the king of the *gods*.

At the age of 29, he came to the conclusion that there was no lasting pleasure in this life and decided to live the austere life of a mendicant. Despite many obstacles he achieved "Bodhi" meaning Enlightenment. Then, in his life came the period of preaching and performing miracles, which changed the attitudes of the people towards life to achieve Parinirvana, the highest state of absolute bliss. Buddha then established *Buddhism*. The story of his life has also been the subject of *contemporary art*. Buddha is represented in early Indian *sculpture* in a *symbolic manner*. This is known as the Hinayana (little vehicle) phase, where a Chattri (umbrella), a Simhasan (empty throne), Paduka (sandals) and other assorted symbols of royalty point to his presence.

In the Mahayana (large vehicle) phase, Buddha is represented anthropomorphically with the 32 Mahapurusha Lakshanas such as the elongated earlobes, the Srivatsa mark the third eye. Stylistically the representations evolved—from the crude and the vigourous Mathura Buddha to the elegant and effete *Gupta* Buddha. Refer ABHUSHANA, *Ajanta, Archaeological Museum (Khajuraho, MP), Archaeological Museum (Sarnath, UP)*, ASANAS, *Aureole, Bas-Relief, Block Printing, Buddhism, Buddhist Art*, CHADDANTA, CHAITYA, DASAVATARA, DHYANI-BUDDHA, *Drapery, Ellora*, GAJA, *Gandharan Art, Arpana Caur, Rani Chanda, Alphonso A. Doss, Nirmal Dutta, Li Gotami, Gupta, Icon, Indian Museum* (Kolkata, WB), JATAKA, *Kushana Dynasty, Mathura Art*, PADMA (Lotus), SANSKRIT, *Stupa, Atasi Barua, Nandalal Bose, Arpana Caur, Alphonso A. Doss, Nirmal Dutta, Laxman Pai, Ratan Parimoo, Abanindranath Tagore*.

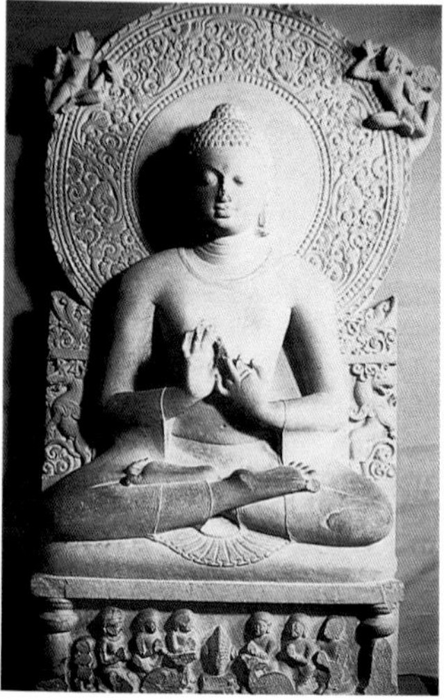

Buddha: "Preaching", AD 5th century.

Buddhism A religious system founded in South-east India in the 6th century BC. Variously called **1.** A religion, **2.** A philosophy, **3.** A way of life.

It was the BUDDHA who taught the Eightfold path–the Ashtanigikamarga. By following them, one could hope to attain salvation and liberation from the endless cycle of births and rebirths. The eightfold path was the ultimate aim of life which was NIRVANA. After the BUDDHA achieved NIRVANA, his followers organized themselves into a Sangha (community). It underwent different phases of developments like the Hinayana, the Mahayana and Vajrayana. It flourished as a main religion in the Far East and in South-east Asia, monks having spread the message to China, Japan and Sri Lanka.

In India it has had influences on *art* right from the early *Gupta period*, with *stupas* of Sanchi circa first century BC. *Ajanta* and *Ellora* caves became a subject of deep study for *artists* from 1890. *Arpana Caur's painting* series talks of BUDDHA "The Great", His journey to enlightenment. Refer *Ajanta*, ATMA, *Ellora*, KARMA, *Mahayana Buddhism, Manuscript Paintings, Kushana Dynasty, Maurya Dyanasty*, SANSKRIT, YAKSHA, *Jaganath M. Ahivasi, Atasi Barua, Li Gotami*.

Buddhist Art *Art* that developed among the followers and worshippers of the BUDDHA and his life. From the Maurya period onwards, when Ashoka decided to embrace *Buddhism*, to the *Gupta* period AD 400 to 600 one constantly sees architectural monuments and *sculptures* and *paintings* depicting the BUDDHA and his miracles. His previous births as described in the JATAKAS are the main *theme* in Buddhist *sculpture* and *painting*. The BUDDHA was represented symbolically in the early phase of Hinayana Buddhism i.e. by means of a royal throne, a set of Padukas (sandals), an open Chhattra (parasol) and the Bodhi tree (Pipal/Fig/Ficus tree) under which he achieved Bodhi or enlightenment. Later in the Mahayana phase, he was represented anthropomorphically. The *style* of execution evolved over a period of *time*, but the *iconography* however remained the same, with all the Mahapurusha Lakshmanas being represented. Thus the BUDDHA is always represented with a serene expression with half-closed eyes, the hair twisted (USHNISHA) over the protruding skull, the earlobes elongated, the smooth, broad shoulders, the hands in a variety of MUDRAS, including Varada (bestowing), ABHAYA, Dharmachakra Pravartana (the BUDDHA's discourses are known as the turning of the wheel). The palms and the soles of the feet are marked with auspicious symbols. Refer *Ajanta, Chaitya, Mathura Art, Maurya Dynasty, Stupa, Sunga Dynasty*, VIHARA.

Bundi, Bundi Kalam, Bundi School, Bundi Miniatures Bundi and *Kotah*, which are now part of the state of RAJ were originally a unified kingdom, until the mid. 17th century, when Shahjahan endowed Madhav Singh, the brother of the then ruler Satrusal, with *Kotah*. The *style* of *painting* in both these city/states are similar, with influences from the Mughal and the Maratha courts making their presence felt. The Bundi School attained perfection in the following century, being especially distinguished in its depiction of lush *landscapes* with banana and other trees bordering the high *horizon* and ponds and other water bodies teeming with pink and *white* lotus, fish and brahmini ducks. The plantation is enlivened with the spiky growth of red, *white* and yellow flowering trees, while couples cavort in stark *white* pavilions and palaces with fountains and Jharokhas. The *Mewar* influence is seen in the placing of KRISHNA and his companions against red accents. The female *figures* in Bundi *painting* have small, round faces with sharp noses and a receding double chin. Shading is used to *model* the face, which has a distinct reddish tinge. The dress is clearly Mughal, with coloured pyjamas (loose trousers) and Choli (blouses), over which a long, *transparent* gown or Ghagra (skirt) is worn. The Orhani (long scarf) is tucked into the waist or into the decorative sash and is pulled over the head. The male costume too is similar to the Mughal *style* of the Shahjahan period. Armpit shading is also present as in the Mughal *painting*.

Towards the later half of the 18th century the *style* deteriorated. What is noticeable is the use of harsher, brighter *colour* and streaky brushstrokes. The sky is now coloured with marbled patches of red, blue and *gold*. The face is also bordered by a dark patch of *colour* to *highlight* it against the *background*.

The *Kotah* School, while generally showing the same features as the Bundi, show a preponderance of hunting scenes set in the lush overgrown forests.

Burin Synonym of engraver, it is a cutting tool made of *steel* set in a wooden handle. It is used for *engraving lines* on wooden blocks or *metal plates*.

The *engraving* or scratching tool whose cutting edge is formed at an angle permitting the removal of metal with each stroke. The *depth* can be controlled by the direction of holding the burin while scratching off *metal* from the surface. Refer *Block Printing, Copper, Wood Engraving, Satish Gujral, Somnath Hore, Dashrath Patel, Krishna N. Reddy, Anupam Sub, Ali J. Sultan*.

Burman, Sakti (1935–) b. Kolkata. Education: Dip. *GCAC* Kolkata, ENSBA. Over 40 solos: *Art* & Industry & *BAAC* Kolkata, Kunika Chemould New Delhi, *CKAG, AIFACS, PUAG*; International: London, California, Milan, Geneva, Zurich, Bruxelles, Perpignain, Grand Palais Paris, ENSBA. Group participations: *BAAC* Kolkata, Helpage Auction, Heart Mumbai, *Triennale* New Delhi; International: Yokohama, Iran, London, Leningrad & Belfort, *Biennale* & Indian Artists in Paris Galerie du Cygne Paris & Museum of Moscow. Awards: Grand Palais, ENSBA & Gold Medal Salon des artists Francais Paris, Silver Medal Salon de Montmorency; Invited Hon. to Colombes, Douai, Sainte Maxime, Enghien-Les-Bains. Publications & Illustrations: Album of 12 limited edition lithographs; Illustration—A poem of Mallarme, "Gitanjali" of *Rabindranath Tagore*, album of 18 limited edition lithographs. Collections: *NGMA* New Delhi, *BAAC* Kolkata, Air India Mumbai, PUJ Museum, *Chandigarh Museum*, Allahabad Museum, *AIFACS*, BARC; International: National Gallery New Zealand, Musee de la Ville & Ministry of Culture Paris, Leicestershire & Hull Education Committee.

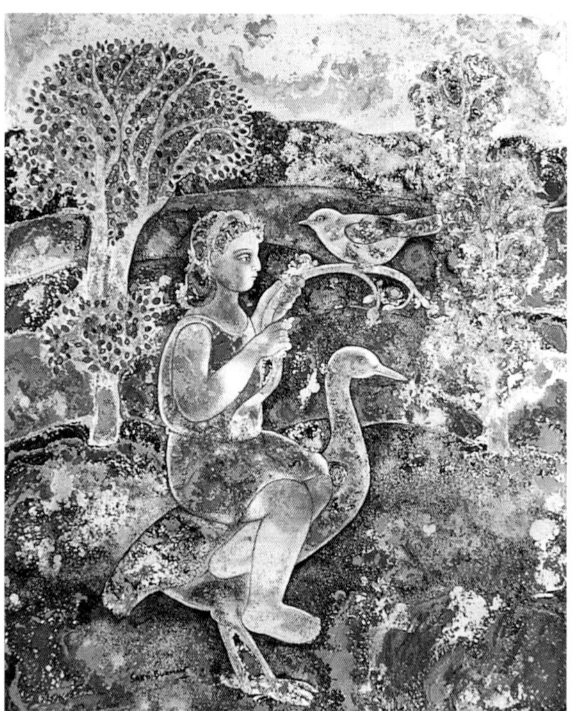

Burman, Sakti: "Maya Holding a Bird", *Oil* on *Canvas*, 55x46 cm.

Sakti Burman's *technique* is highly distinctive and unique with its gently stippled *colours* creating a dreamy *atmosphere* of sensual *Romanticism*. His characters are suspended in an Arca-dian environment, the women either stretching languorously on a couch, the uplifted arms suggesting the seductress, or swaying gently on a flower bedecked swing. A painted "Hashiya" (border) appears in several works though it is hardly distinguishable from the *painting*. "Maya Holding a Bird" has its origin in the iconic *figures* of Hindu Goddesses and the RAGINIS of the RAGAMALA series. His travels through Europe and Africa have manifested themselves in his works in an *eclectic* fashion, with Graeco-Roman *figures* and borrowings from the *old masters* co-existing harmoniously along with his native *forms*.

Sakti Burman lives and works in Paris.

Burr Scratching action with a *burin* does the process of *engraving*. This action results in to development of metallic burrs on either side of the etched surface. These burrs are then removed using burnishing tool or a *steel* scraper. Refer *Dry-Point, Printmaking, Mezzotint, Hatching, Mukul Chandra Dey, Laxma Goud, Somnath Hore, Shyamal Dutta Ray*.

Bust A *portrait painting* or *sculpture* of the sitter portraying just the head and shoulders, not the whole body. Bust *portraits* have been popular in India from the early Stone age busts of *Gods* and Goddesses. They are also prevalent at *Ajanta, Ellora, Elephanta* and were later popularized by *Company paintings* and were a frequented *art form* in *contemporary art* too. Refer *Company School, Sadanandji Bakre, Pestonjee Bomanjee, Dhiraj Choudhury, Biman B. Das, Vinayak Pandurang Karmarkar, Bhagwant K. Goregaoker, C. Jagdish, Jyotirindranath Tagore, Hitendranath Tagore, Antonio X. Trindade, Bayaji Vasantrao Talim*.

Byzantine Art A *style* that flourished especially in the eastern part of the Roman Empire after Byzantium, renamed Constantinople, became the Empire's capital in AD 330. It survived until the Turkish conquest in 1453. Though typically oriental in *nature* in its use of *frontality* and *hieratic scaling*, the subject of Byzantine Art was almost exclusively Christian. Churches were built and decorated with gorgeous *mosaics*, including *gold* leafed tessarae. The pillars were carved with a minute *designs* to resemble lace work. The Church epitomized the difference between earthly life and heavenly rewards. The plain outside surface represented daily life and the richly embellished interiors symbolized heaven. The Dome of the Church was usually decorated with the *figures* of Christ. *Artists* also produced beautifully painted manuscripts enamelled and jewelled reliquaries, candlesticks and carved *ivory* panels.

Similar phenomena can be seen in the Pahari temples and folk *styles* of Beas & Sutlej valleys. Lion door-knockers, reef knots, interlacings & confronting birds typified the *motifs*. To some extent it did influence the Indian *artist's* break from oriental art. Refer *Christian Art, Frontality, Greek Art* and *Siona Benjamin*.

C

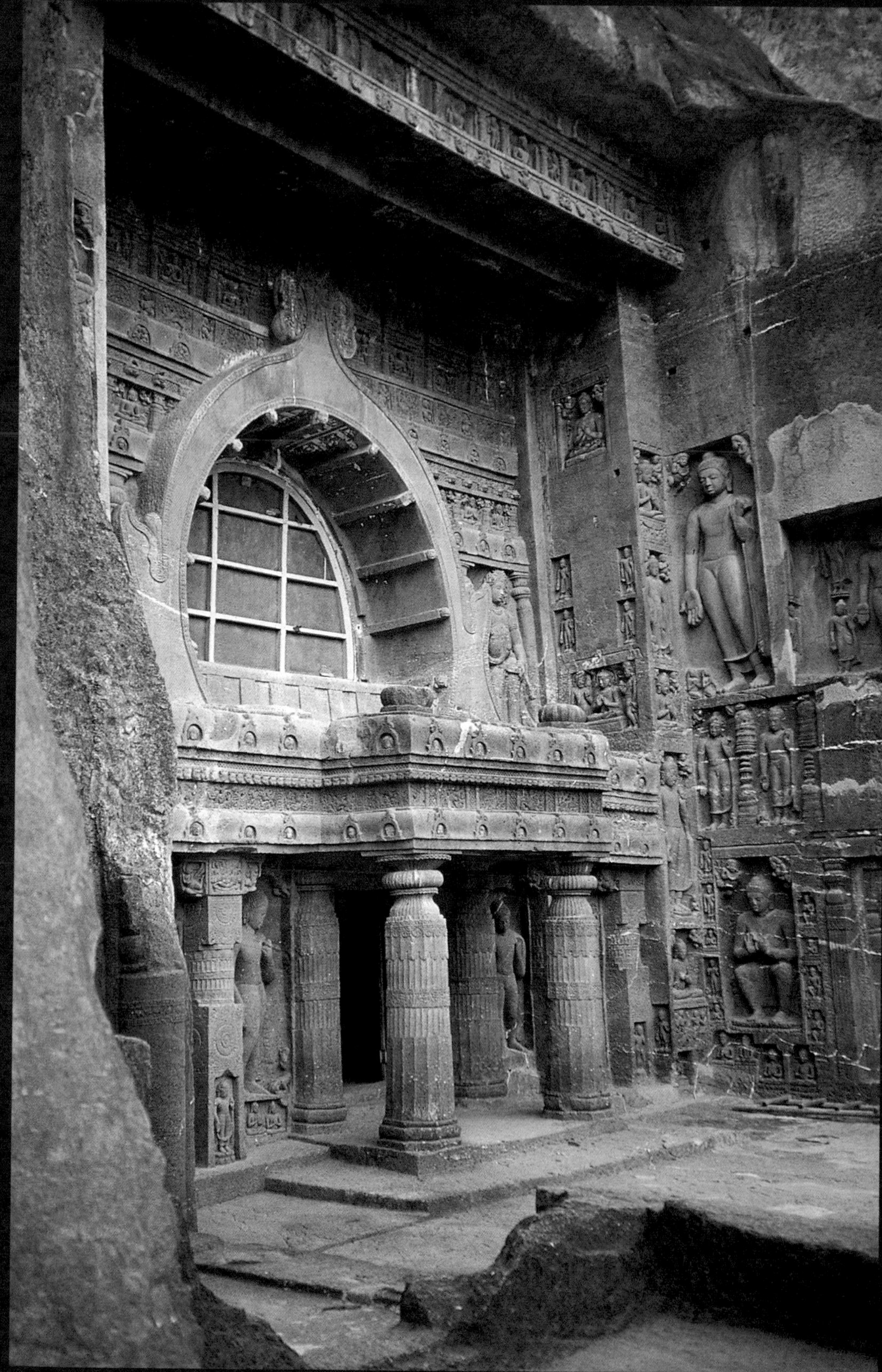

Chaitya: Ajanta Cave 26, Chaitya Arch-Facade and Court, circa AD 500–550. (See notes on page 78)

Calcutta Group 43 Formed in 1943 in Kolkata around the same time as the *Young Turks*, senior *artist Gobardhan Ash* noted its main slogan as "Man is supreme". Other slogans included their guiding motto, "Art should be international and interdependent". Humanism was the group's subject–not the idealized, Indian beauty, but rather its ugly and sordid aspect. The *artists* of this group were interested in the study of *traditions*, both foreign and Indian, and were especially interested in the development in *form* and *technique* in the Westeren world. Group members included *Hemanta Misra*, Rathin Maitra, Prodosh Das Gupta, *Nirode Mazumdar*, *Paritosh Sen* and others. Refer *Calcutta School*.

Calcutta School During the colonial period, Bengal played a leading role in the realignment of *art* and *culture*. The Bengal Revivalist School (*Bengal School*) led by *Abanindranath Tagore*, along with the *Bombay School* had influenced the entire early 20th-century *art* and *artists* in India. When *Abanindranath Tagore's style* became confining, the other members of the Tagore family pointed the way towards *Modernism*. *Gaganendranath Tagore's* cubist exercise and *Rabindranath Tagore's* surreal and expressionist works exposed India to international *Modernism*. The Calcutta *art* school and *Santiniketan* brought forth the ideas and works of a whole generation of senior *artists* like *Nandalal Bose*, *Debi Prasad RoyChowdhury*, *Ramkinkar Baij* and *Benode Behari Mukherjee*. While *Jamini Roy* was to influence a whole host of young Indian *artists* by opening the doors to an indigenous influence, namely Indian *folk art*, *Ramkinkar Baij*, worked towards a near-abstraction in *sculpture*, using new non-traditional materials such as *cement concrete*. The 1943 founded Calcutta Group too, influenced *contemporary* Indian *art* for a short time, as did the *ISOA*; founded by *sculptors* Prodosh and Kamala DasGupta and *painters*, *Subhogendra Tagore*, *Nirode Mazumdar*, Prankrishna Pal, *Rathin Mitra* and *Paritosh Sen*. The Group tried to create a new *art* language combining Indian *traditions* with the influences of French art.

Over the years, many new groups such as the Calcutta Painters and *SCA* and *art* villages such as *Arts Acre* have appeared on the scene producing several *artists* of merit. Kolkata has produced *sculptors* like *Meera Mukherjee*, *Chintamoni Kar* and *Somnath Hore* and *painters* like *Bikash Bhattacharjee*, *Ganesh Pyne*, *Jogen Chowdhury* and *Sunil Das* among others. Though there are quaint storytellers like *Paritosh Sen* and superrealists like Wasim Kapoor, the overriding mood in present-day Kolkata *art* is one of pessimism and an attitude of sad despair is prevalent in the works of several *artists*.

Calligraphic Pertaining to the spirit of *calligraphy*, it means any *pattern* or *design* that is based on calligraphic strokes. It can also be applied to the *line* or *brushwork* of an *artist*. *Rabindranath Tagore's* earliest *paintings* were based on *calligraphy*. Refer *Abstraction Lyrical*, *Bengal Revivalism*, *Bengal School*, *Calligraphic Painting*, *Jain Miniature*, *Jain Manuscript Illumination*, *Lettrism*, *Lettrisme*, *Mat*, *Primitivism*, *Thumb Impression*, *Vasant R. Amberkar*, *Ramnik Bhavsar*, *Nandalal Bose*, *Shanti Dave*, *Benode Behari Mukherjee*, *Shankar Palsikar*, *Lalu Prasad Shaw*, *Rameshwar Singh*, *V.P. Singh*, *Nathu Lal Verma*.

Calligraphic Painting A *term* where the methods of *calligraphy* are applied to *painting*. A few of the *Abstract* Expressionists, especially French *painter* Michaux and American Mark Tobey have a *calligraphic style*. In India, *Shanti Dave* works with *calligraphic* symbols and signs. *Shankar Palsikar* created a neo-tantric *painting* based on the DEVANAGARI *Script*. Refer *Abstraction Lyrical*, KALPASUTRA, *Miniature Painting*, *Vishnu Chinchalkar*, *Rabindranath Tagore*.

Calligraphy The *art* of fine free-hand handwriting, using a variety of tools including the *brush* and *pens* with shaped nibs and the crowquill. Calligraphy is an ancient *art* that has been practiced all over the world, since the invention of the written script. Indian scripts originate from Brahmi (circa 3000 BC). This widely spread to different parts of India which developed their own *styles* and scripts. The Chinese especially considered it to be one of the main accomplishments of the perfect connoisseur. The characters formed by the sweep of the *brush* and the flow of the *ink* had to be perfect in their execution and spontaneity. Any breaks in the *rhythm* of writing was immediately evident to the expert eye. Refer *Calligraphic*, *Computer Art*, *Miniature Painting*, *Poster*, *Rhythm*, *Muhammed Abdur Rehman Chugtai*, *Jalendu Dave*, *Amina Ahmed Kar*, *Asit Mukherjee*, *M.K. Muthusamy*, *Durgashanker K. Pandya*, *Gopal G. Subhedar*, *Kanhaiya Lal Verma*; Illustration–*Sujata Bajaj*, *Shanti Dave*, *K.C.S. Paniker*.

Canon of Proportion A *term* used in anthropomorphic *art*. The canon differs in different *traditions*. e.g., the Egyptian canon was different from the Greek, the *Rennaisance* and the Indian. The Greeks were the first to observe live *models* as basis for their canon, which gradually developed into what is known as the *classical* period. Even in the *classical* period there were certain *sculptors*, notably Lysippus who preferred elongating the body for greater elegance. In Egypt, the law of *frontality* dictated the character of the statues and their rigid symmetry. In India the *term* "Pramana" describes the set of *proportions*. As explained in the SHADANGA, Indian *proportions* have less to do with reality and actual perception and more to do with conceptualization.

Canvas The *term* applies to any stretched fabric. The actual material could be linen, cotton, unbleached calico, twill or duck. It is the stretched fabric on which the *artist* paints, after treating it with a special *ground* (today zinc *white* is popular) to render it capable of holding the *pigment*. *Oil paint*, *casein* and *acrylic* are some of the *media* used in *painting* on canvas. The *artist* can exploit the *texture* of the canvas weave. The Indian canvas was specially prepared in Orissa by pasting together layers of cloth called "Pati" used for Patachitra (Pata=cloth; chitra=*painting*). Refer *Abstract Painting*, *Action Painting*, *Anti-Cerne*, *Art Education*,

Automatism, Collage, Combine Painting, Distortion, Oil Painting, Soft-sculpture, Underpainting, Priming, White, Ambadas, Akhilesh, Yusuf Arakkal, Gobardhan Ash, Sudhangsu Bandhopadhyay, Atul Bose, Alphonso A. Doss, Vivan Sundaram, J. Swaminathan, Prabhakar Barwe, Yusuf; Illustration–*Abstract Landscape, Abstraction Lyrical, Action Painting, K.M. Adimoolam, Altaf, Ambadas, B. Prabha, Prabhakar Barwe.*

Canvas Board Thin *canvas* stretched on *hardboard*, creating a rigid *support* instead of the flexible stretched *canvas* on a *frame* or stretchers. Refer *Canvas, Gobardhan Ash, Manishi Dey, Rini Dhumal.*

Canvas Test A process to assess whether the *canvas* is fully prepared for *painting*. It involves the following tests: **1.** *Turpentine* (a drying *medium*) should dry slowly and not soak into the *canvas*. **2.** *Canvas* is usually stored in roll *form* and never folded. If folded, it will make linear striations, which are difficult to disguise. Even if folded, it should not develop cracks. Refer *Canvas*; Presentation of Art Objects by O.P. Agrawal, page 383.

Caricature It refers strictly to the representation of a person or an object by exaggerating certain *key* physiognomical characters to produce a humorous or satirical effect. The word comes from its popular use by the Caracci family. Today it is most often used in newspapers to lampoon politicians and other *contemporary figures*. In France in the 19th century, caricaturist, H. Daumier, was imprisoned for daring to criticise the king through his caricatures. Indian cartoonists include *Gaganendranath Tagore*, R.K. Laxman, Abu Abraham and Sudhir Das.

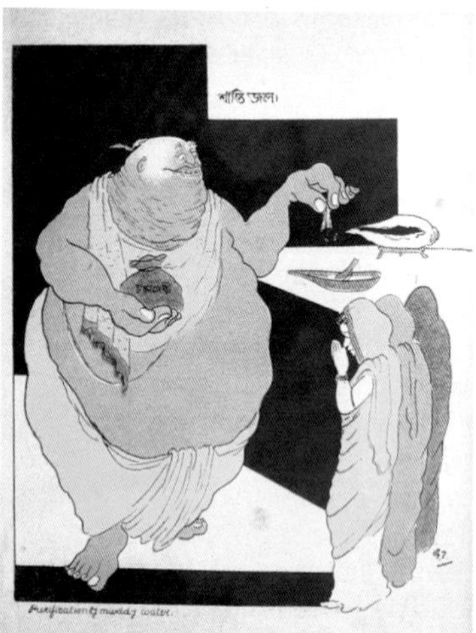

Caricature: *Tagore, Gaganendranath*, "Purification By Muddy Water", Lithograph.

Cartoon **1.** The *term* as used today refers mainly to political and satirical scenes or individuals caricaturized to create a humorous effect, especially in newspapers and periodicals. **2.** "Cartoon" was derived from the Italian "Cartone" meaning a big sheet of *paper*. It denotes a full-scale *drawing* worked in *detail* for transferring onto the wall, in the case of a *fresco*, or onto the *canvas* or panel, in the case of an *oil painting* or tapestry. The transfer was often made, in the *manner* of *modern* carbon paper, covered with powdered *chalk*, and the *lines* drawn over with a sharp instrument, thus leaving a mark on the wall, *canvas* or panel. At other times, the main *lines* of the *drawing* were pricked with a sharp instrument and fine *charcoal* dust was "pounced" through the holes until a dotted *contour* was visible on the wall. This guide *line* was redrawn and the *painting* was completed.

A similar *technique* was used for Indian miniatures, only a fine inner lining of gazelle skin was used instead of *paper*. Refer *Miniature Paintings, Mughal Miniatures*.

Carving (glyptic process). A *term* generally used in *sculpture* or any *craft* which involves the *art* of cutting and carving into *wax, wood, stone, marble* or any hard material to create *forms* based on the *sculptor's* conception or a *design* in the case of *craft*. The process is a subtractive one, with hard instruments (including *chisel, gouge*, hammers, files and for carving *wax*, ordinary pocket knives and linoleum cutting tools) cutting out extraneous *matter* to reveal the final *form*. India has a fine *tradition* in the *art* of carving with entire temples along with inner *sculptures* being carved out of living rock. *Sculptors* like *Sankho Chaudhuri, Balbir Singh Katt* and *Latika Katt* have used *marble* in this fashion. In the case of *crafts*, there is sandalwood carving in Mysore, and in places like GUJ and RAJ, and Saharanpur in New Delhi, other types of *wood* carved intricately to create functional objects of great *aesthetic* beauty like tables, chairs, beds, doors and windows. Refer *Architecture, Artefact, Bas-Relief, Dimension, Direct Carving, Indirect Carving, Ellora, Embossing, Filigree, GCAC* Chennai, *Granite*, HANUMAN, *Hoysala, Ivory, Linocut, Maurya Dynasty, Modelling, Realistic, Relief Sculpture, Visual, Wetting Down, Wood Carving, Madhab Bhattacharjee, Ajit Chakravarti, Adi M. Davierwala, Bhagwant K. Goregaokar, Satish Gujral, Ratilal Kansodaria, D.G. Kulkarni, Balwant Singh Kushawaha, Leela Mukherjee, Mahendra Pandya, Goverdhan S. Panwar, Raj Kumar Panwar, C. Ponnappa Rajaram, Bhanu Shah, Brahman Vinayakrao Wagh;* Illustration–*Abu-Dilwara Group of Temples, Sudha Arora, Sadanandji Bakre, Dhanraj Bhagat, Latika Katt, Nagji Patel, Ravinder G. Reddy, Reghu G., Vinayakrao Venkatrao Wagh.*

Casein An adhesive or *medium*, made from powdered cottage cheese (Paneer). The cottage cheese is obtained by curdling skimmed milk with acetic *acid* or vinegar.

The powder is then dissolved in hot water. Later, lime water or ammonium hydroxide is added, to make a syrupy solution that can be used either as a binder or an adhesive. Refer *Canvas, Nilima G. Sheikh*; Illustration–*V. Viswanadhan.*

Casing Meaning an outer covering or reinforcing shell. In *sculpture*, it is generally composed of *clay* or *plaster* to *support negative masses* and *moulds* made of flexible materials like rubber. Refer *Air Vent, Cire Perdue, South Indian Bronzes, Somnath Hore, Balan Nambiar.*

Cast The object produced by moulding. There can be a one-off cast in which only one object can be produced as the *negative* is destroyed in revealing it. More popularly the *negative* can produce dozens or even hundreds of identical casts. There are also many piece-casts, where a single object has to be assembled from many small *negative moulds*, which are joined together, with final touches given, by smoothening out the rough edges. *Metal casting* was the *technique* used as early as *Mohenjo Daro* and *Harappa* times. Refer *Air Vents, Casting, Brass, Bronze, Cire Perdue, Paper-Pulp Casting, South Indian Bronzes*, CHOLA, *Somnath Hore, Raghav Kaneria, Shankar Nandagopal, Debi Prasad RoyChowdhury, Sarbari RoyChowdhury*.

Cast Stone A highly refined variety of *concrete*, which is a mixture of Portland cement, *aggregate* and water. In *sculpture*, special *aggregates* are used for their *colour* and *texture*. When this material is mixed with water, it can be *cast* or poured into any shape. When it becomes hard, it is durable enough to be carved, polished or filed. It is an economical way of producing large sized three-dimensional *sculpture* that is durable even when placed out doors. *Ramkinkar Baij* was one of the first Indian *sculptors* to realize the versatility of this material.

Casting 1. The process of making a *cast* object (of *metal* or *plaster*) from an original (usually of *clay* or *wax*) by making a *negative mould* and pouring the liquid material into it to obtain dozens of similar objects. This act of pouring (called *cire perdue* in the case of *bronze casting*) is called casting. Both hollow and solid casting are practised. Refer *Bronze, South Indian Bronzes*. **2.** *Slip* Casting (plastic) is a *term* used in *ceramic* or *pottery*-making where a *slip* (heavy creamy liquid *form* of *clay*) of a different *colour* is used to coat the pot or object. The process is used to join parts of pots or objects together. Often it is also used as a decoration, the outer layer being cut away or incised to reveal the body-material underneath in the graffito method. Refer *Aggregate, Air Vents, Alloy, Armature, Bronze, Chasing, Cire Perdue, Clay Water, Concrete, Embossing, Fibreglass, Filler, Life-Mask, Lost Wax Process, Metal, Mould, Negative, Paper-Pulp Casting, Papier Mache, Parting Agent, Patina, Plaster, Reproduction, Sculptor, Sculpture, Sudha Arora, Girish C. Bhatt, Dattatrey Apte, Sankho Chaudhuri, Adi M. Davierwala, Raghav Kaneria, Ravindra Mestry, Leela Mukherjee, Janak J. Narzary, Choudhary Satyanarayan Patnaik, Niranjan Pradhan, Sarbari RoyChowdhury, N.B. Sabannavar, Prabhas Sen, Himmat Shah, Brahman Vinayakrao Wagh*; Illustration—NATARAJA, *Sadiq Dehlvi, Somnath Hore, Ratilal Kansodaria, Chintamoni Kar, Ganpatrao K. Mhatre, Meera Mukherjee, Debi Prasad RoyChowdhury*.

Caur, Arpana (1954–) b. Delhi. Received *LKA* grant for research in *painting*. Solos: RB & *Art Heritage* New Delhi, *AFA Kolkata, SG* Chennai, SRAG, *JAG, CYAG, CIMA*; International: London, Ottawa, Cardiff, Glasgow, Ethnographic Museum Stockholm, National Museum Copenhagen. Group participations: Women *artists NGMA* & *Biennale* curated by German Embassy New Delhi, *SG* & *Tao Art Gallery* Mumbai, Marvel Art Gallery Ahmedabad, *Triennale* India, SRAG, *CYAG, CIMA*; International: Fukuoka Museum, Glenbarra Museum, Saytama Museum & Yokohama Museum Japan, *Biennale* in Cuba, Baghdad & Bristol, other in Stuttgart & Frankfurt; Travelling *exhibition* UK & Paris. *Art* camps & workshops: Goa, Hyderabad & Women's camp New Delhi, PUJ University Museum Chandigarh, *GAC. Auctions*: Heart & Osian's Mumbai, Christie's & Sotheby's London, Sotheby's New York. Awards: *AIFACS*, Eminent *Artist LKA* New Delhi, Gold Medal *Triennale* India; International: Commendation certificate *Biennale* in Algiers & invited to USA as International visitor of the year. Commissions: Two large *murals*—India International Trade Fair New Delhi 1981. Appointments: Jury for Republic Day Pageants, National *LKA* & for Purchasing Committee *NGMA* New Delhi. Collections: Godrej Mumbai, *NGMA* New Delhi, *Chandigarh Museum, CYAG*; International: Stockholm, Singapore, Japan, Bradford Museum Dusseldoef and V&A.

The *image* is of chief importance in her work as is the *colour* and *composition*. Reference to *contemporary* life and events are given a timeless quality through inspiration culled from *miniature painting* and other traditional *art forms*. Her recent *diptychs* and *triptychs* show a chronological progression rather than a continuity of *images* and *imagery*. There is also a steady movement towards *abstract symbolism* in some works. The "body is just a garment" series has been inspired by the words of the poet Saint Kabir, in which the body has been described thus "here today, in tatters tomorrow," followed by a new one. In yet another poem, a 14th-century poetess describes her journey from being a cotton flower to a piece of cloth, created at the loom to being washed by the washerman and cut with great care by the tailor. One sees a variation of this *imagery* in "Threat", where a woman is embroidering flowers into a shawl while sharp knives hover threateningly over her.

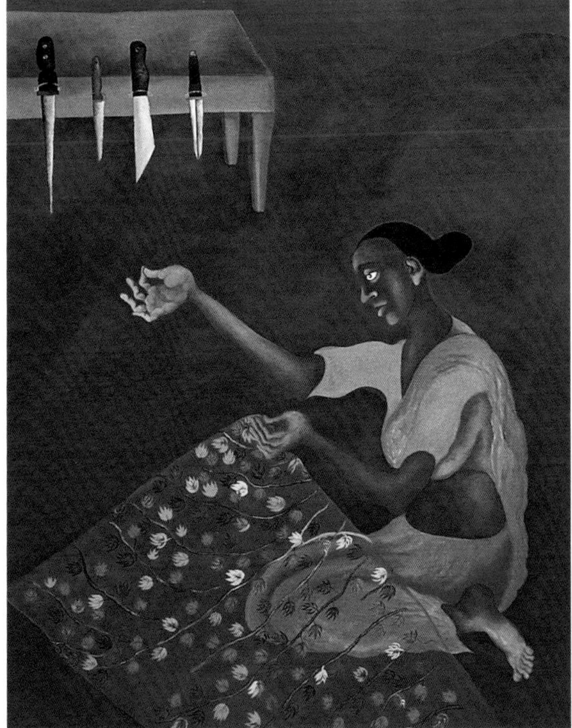

Caur, Arpana: "Threat", *Oil* on *Canvas*, 183x152 cm.

Arpana Caur has always been concerned with the plight of women, be it the widows of Brindavan or the universal mother who suffers her lot uncomplainingly, they have all found place in her works. Later, even BUDDHA found a place on her canvas.

She lives and works in New Delhi.

Cave Art The *painting*, *relief* and *drawings* belonging to the old Stone Age. Cave art has been discovered throughout the world, with Altamira in Spain and Lascaux in France having beautiful examples of *prehistoric painting*. In India, some *drawings* of this era, have been found in Bhimbetka in MP. The *art* of the cave men is characterized by its *magic symbolism* and simplicity of *form* and movement. *Colours* were organic, taken from the site itself as were the chewed *brushes* and twigs that were used for *painting*.

Cement It is a mixture of lime and earth-clay or impure calcium *aluminium* silicate ground to a fine powder and calcinated in a furnace. This is further pulverized and about two percent of *gypsum* is added. This is then mixed with water to *form* a paste that remains plastic for sometime before setting into a hardened *mass*. Though cement is mostly used in *architecture*, *sculptors* are utilizing its possibilities, especially after colouring it. Portland cement is considered to be the finest cement for sculptural use, because of its great strength and uniformity in hardening in water. Refer *Abstract Sculpture, Architecture, Clay, Concrete, Ecological Art, Form, Media, Mural, Polychromatic Sculpture, Sculpture, Treatment, Sudha Arora, B. Vithal, Dhanraj Bhagat, Jalendu Dave, Shanti Dave, M. Dharmani Somnath Hore, Mahendra Pandya, Goverdhan S. Panwar, Jayant Parikh, Sunil Kumar Paul, Himmat Shah, Uma Siddhanta*; Illustration–*Mosaic*, SHANKHA, *Ramkinkar Baij, Vinayak Pandurang Karmarkar, Kanayi Kunhiraman, Pilloo Pochkhanawalla*.

Ceramics A general *term* used for objects made of different types of *clay*, covered with *slips* or glazes and then fired. Also used to mean porcelain and *terracotta*. It is also used as a sculptural *medium*. *Satish Gujral* has made ceramic *murals*. Refer *Antique, Decorative Art, Facing, Firing, Glazing, Mural, Polychromatic sculpture, Pottery, Reproduction, Wetting Down, Jyotsna Bhatt, Jalendu Dave, Latika Katt, Mrinalini Mukherjee, Saroj Gogi Pal, Raj Kumar Panwar, S.L. Parasher, Jayant Parikh, Dashrath Patel, M.K. Puri, Vimoo Sanghvi, Sardar Gurcharan Singh, Pratima Devi Tagore, Radhika Vaidaynathan, Umesh Varma*; Illustration–*Sukhen Ganguly*.

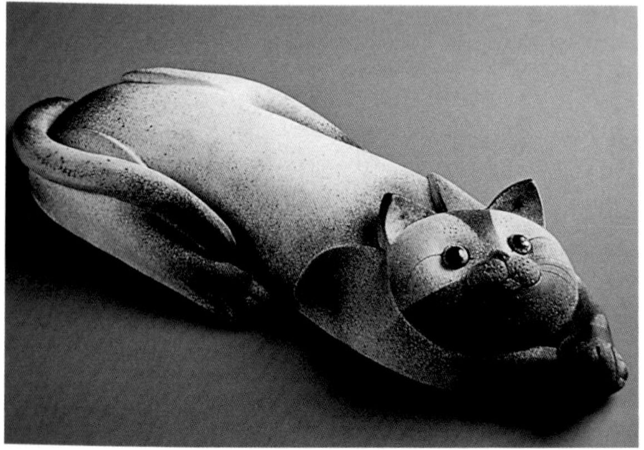
Ceramics: *Jyotsna Bhatt*, "Stone ware Cat", Slab built, 1994.

Cerography Refer *Encaustic*.

Chaddanta A SANSKRIT *term* meaning "one with six teeth or tusks". The *term* is referred to in the Buddhist JATAKA's. Chaddanta was BUDDHA in a previous life a six tusked *white* elephant, with two wives. The younger wife Chulla-Subbada was jealous of the older one Malla-Subbada. After a series of accelerating events, she committed suicide after praying that she be reborn as the queen of nearby Varanasi. As the queen, she remembered her old jealousy and sent the royal hunter, Sonuttara to kill Chaddanta and procure the six tusks for her. Chaddanta, being the all-knowing BODDHISATTVA, helped Sonuttara saw off his tusks before collapsing and dying in a pool of his own blood. The queen also died in remorse after being told of the incident. The Chaddanta JATAKA was popularly illustrated in many Buddhist monuments, being represented twice at *Ajanta*. The *illustration* was not in a continuous *narrative form*, with all the scenes involving the elephants in the forest being on one side and the palace and city scenes on the other. Little *vignettes* like Chaddanta spraying his head with the pollen from a blossom before giving it to Malla-Subbada is beautifully portrayed as are the ants and bare twigs falling on Chulla-Subbada. Refer *Continuous Representation*.

Chadha, Amarjit (1931–) b. Gujarkhan, now Pakistan. Education: Dip. in *FA. JJSA* & Scholarship in *mural*. Solos: *AIFACS*, SRAG. Group participations: National *LKA*, Sahitya Kala Academy & Kala Mela New Delhi, *AIFACS, JAG*; International: Paris, Dubai. Attended camps. Collections: *NGMA* & *LKA* New Delhi; International: Germany, Canada, France, UK, USA & pvt.

Amarjit Chadha prefers working with *oils*, dipping a rope in the *colour* which she drags over the surface of the *canvas*. The *form* thus is submerged in the resultant spread of the *pigment*. Her *paintings* show faintly outlined *silhouettes* of *forms* and animals on bright luminous *backgrounds* with predomonance of *texture*.

Amarjit Chadha lives and works in New Delhi.

Chaitya A *term* used in Indian and especially Buddhist *architecture*, generally meaning a a Cita (mound), *stupa* (a hall or temple), for religious purposes. Above the entrance is a horseshoe-shaped window through which *light* penetrates inside and on to the *stupa* at the other end. The entrance is narrow and there are pillars with carved capitals running the length of the Chaitya on both sides thus creating aisles. The worshipper walks down the aisle created by the pillars and the side wall, thus making an ambulation (Pradakshina) around the *stupa*. Sometimes the *stupa* has an anthropomorphic representation of the BUDDHA carved onto its front. The ceiling is barrel vaulted with horseshoe ribs of *wood* or *stone*. The earliest prototypes of the

Chaityas were built by Ashoka circa 268 BC. They were the Lomas–Rishi, Sudama in Barabal hills and the Sita Marhi caves in Nagarjuni hill. Later, Chaityas were both structural, as at Guntapalle in AP and *rock-cut* as at Bhaja, Pitalkhora, *Ajanta*, Kondane and other sites in the Deccan. Refer *Ellora*, *Gupta*, *Maurya Dynasty*, *Relief*, VIHARA. (See illustration on page 74)

Chakladar, A.N. (Amol) (1936–) b. Bangladesh. Education: Dip. in *art GCAC* Kolkata. Solos: Galierie La-Mere, *AFA* & Gallery A Kolkata. Group participations: Calcutta Painters' at Information Centre & *BAAC*, Ashutosh Centenary Hall Indian Museum, Calcutta Metropolitan Art Festival, National Exhibition & *AFA* Kolkata, "Bengal Art Today" Hyderabad, *AIFACS*, *JAG*. Awards: *ISOA*, *AFA* & *BAAC* Kolkata. Founder/Organizer: Calcutta Art Fair. Collections: *BAAC* Kolkata, *Delhi Art Gallery*, pvt. Kolkata, Hyderabad, Mumbai, New Delhi; International: Washington DC, Vienna, Singapore.

Amol Chakladar is a *contemporary* practitioner of the *Bengal School style*. However his subjects are not derived from *classical* literature and *mythology*; instead he makes a fine observation of *nature* and natural elements in his muted *linear composition*.

He is a faculty member of the *GCAC* Kolkata.

Chakra 1. (SANSKRIT) It is an *attribute/weapon* of the Hindu *God* VISHNU, his AVATARS and of the Goddess DURGA. Known as Sudarshana, it appears in the *form* of a disc or wheel with spokes like the rays of the sun. When hurled by VISHNU it never misses its mark. It is represented as rotating around his upraised finger. **2.** Chakra also denotes the six centres of energy in the human body according to the *traditions* of TANTRA. Refer *Abstract*, *Abstract Art*, *Attribute*, AYUDHA-PURUSHA, CHATUR BHUJA, *Gupta*, MATRIKAS, KAAL, KRISHNA, *Nagara Style*, RAVANA, SARASVATI, SHIVA, VISHNU, *Weapons*.

CHAKRA.

Chakrabarti, Matilal (1934–) b. Tripura. No formal training, studied under *Nirode Mazumdar*, *Dhirendrakrishna Deb Barman* Kolkata. Solos: Over 5 shows, *AFA* & Metro Art Gallery Metro Railway Station Kolkata, *Art Heritage* New Delhi. Group participations: *AFA*, *BAAC* & RB Kolkata, *ISOA*, *CKAG*; Participated in set *designs* for Utpal Dutt's plays. Awards: *ISOA* 1983 & 1986. Publications: Illustrated books & decorated rooms with Alpana (Rangoli), *patterns* drawn & painted on the floor. Collections: Pvt. in India & abroad I.K. Kejriwal Kolkata, *CKAG*; International: USA, Paris.

His Indian *style* of *painting* in *watercolours* are both on *paper* and silk cloth. Some of his *paintings* are in *wash techniques*. His *landscapes* are simple reminders of life, with narrow pathways or fencing, distant huts or lines of trees. His *colour* sense is illustrational and naive.

Matilal Chakrabarti lives and works in 24 Parganas, WB.

Chakraborty, Mrityunjoy (1934–2001) b. Bengal. Education: Grad. *GCAC* Kolkata 1955. A disciple of Late Dilip Das Gupta. Solos: Over 14 solos in Kolkata & others in New Delhi, Dehradun. Group participations: *LKA* New Delhi, Calcutta Artists Group Kolkata, *AIFACS*, *ISOA*. Member: *ISOA*. Appointments: Vice-President, President & Honorary Dean *ISOA–FA*. Other interests: Everest base camp Nepal, & Zongri Pass; Trekking & travel writing. Publications: Magazine "Land of Passes". Collections: *NGMA* New Delhi & pvt. in India; International: Germany, East European countries, Russia, USA.

Mrityunjoy Chakraborty practised a variation of the *watercolour wash technique* in his works, in which the *composition* was built up from dark to *light* instead of the traditional *light* to dark *shades*. By immersing the *paper*, on which dark *shades* have already been applied and allowed to dry, he managed to scrape off *pigment* in the desired areas by using soft *brushes*. *Forms* were built up in this *manner*, with the *paper* being immersed several times to get the desired result. The *figures* were iconic in their still watchfulness. An element of the macabre, in the inclusion of skulls, grotesque *masks* and heads, added to the drama, being in sharp contrast to the calm, implacable faces of his protagonists. He lived in Kolkata.

Chakraborty, Sadhan (1952–) b. Assam. Education: Dip. in *FA*. Indian Art College Kolkata. Over 70 group participations: Mumbai, Bangalore, Chennai, other organized by Govt. of WB & *LKA* Kolkata, National Exhibition New Delhi, *Biennale BB*; International: Berlin, Hamburg, Singapore, Indian Festival USA. *Art* workshops: *Printmaking* workshops by *BAAC* & Sanskriti Art Gallery Kolkata, *Painting* workshop Jamshedpur. Awards: Govt. of WB. Member: *SCA*. Collections: *NGMA* & *LKA* New Delhi, *BAAC* Kolkata.

Sadhan Chakraborty started his career as a printmaker but has later switched to *painting* with *acrylics* and *watercolour*. Both his *etching* and his *paintings* portray the dichotomies apparent in *nature*, the coexistence of joys and sorrows, youth and old-age, victory and defeat, through the use of *colour* and *light*.

He lives and works in Kolkata.

Chakravarti, Ajit (1930–2005) b. Chittagong, now in Bangladesh. Education: Dip. *GCAC* Kolkata, Scholar exchange programme Prague Czechoslovakia. Solos: USIS Gallery Kolkata, *Santiniketan*, *GK*, *AIFACS*, *SCA*, TKS; International: Prague. Group participations: *LKA Contemporary Sculpture* Mumbai, *MSU*, *Triennale BB*, 25 years of Indian Art *LKA* New Delhi, *SCA*; International: *Biennale* Sao Paulo Brazil & Budapest Hungary, Commonwealth Art Today London, Fukuoka Art Museum Japan, Modern Asian Art China, *Plastic arts* Vienna, European *sculptors* Austria. *Sculpture* camps: J&K, *Cholamandal*, *BB* & abroad. Awards: *AIFACS* 1962. Appointments: Participated in Conferences; Lectures in sculpture *MSU*; HoD–*Plastic art* CFA, BHU; Principal, Vice-Chancellor *KB VBU*. Collections: *NGMA* & *LKA* New Delhi; International: National Gallery of Art Prague.

Ajit Chakravarti had worked with various materials including *wood*, *stone* and *terrocotta*. His formal *vocabulary* has been derived from temple *carvings* and *tribal art*.

Nature had been the inspiration behind his almost unrecognizable *distortions* of the animal and human *forms*. The works are rich in *texture* though simplistic in *form*. He lived and worked at *Santiniketan*.

Chakravarty, Chiru (1936–) b. Faridpur, now in Bangladesh. Studied briefly at Indian School of Art Kolkata, before working as a draugtsman. Solos: *Artists' Centre*, *GC* Mumbai, *AFA* & *BAAC* Kolkata, BAG, *JAG*, TAG, *AIFACS*. Group participations: *GC* Mumbai; International: Melbourne, London. Commissions: *Murals* & *sculptures* in mild *steel*, *bronze* & welded *brass casting* Mumbai, Goa, Kolkata, New Delhi; International: Abu-Dhabi Airport, Oman. Appointments: Worked as a draftsman under Govt. of WB; Later joining the Mumbai Film Industry as cinematographer. Collections: Pvt. national & international.

He has worked with different *media* including *ceramic*, *metal*, *mosaic*, *acrylic* and photography. Chiru Chakravarty's *forms* are basically *figurative*, simplified to a degree of abstraction. These fragmented and muted body shapes float or dance in slow motion on the surface of the *canvas*, with the textural brushstrokes plainly visible in an abstraction that is almost gestural. His *colours* are at once ponderous and sumptuous.

He lives and works in Mumbai.

Chalk **1.** Chalk, made of calcium carbonate mixed with gum or by moulding calcium sulphate (*plaster of Paris*) into a stick form. A small amount of *clay* or petroleum jelly is sometimes added to make dustless chalk. Chalk was used since *prehistoric time* in India for cave and *wall paintings*. The famous *Ajanta frescoes* too had a base made of calcium carbonate in order to hold the natural *pigments* together *colours* used. **2.** Conte *crayon* is sometimes called chalk. It is slightly greasy and is made with carbon *black*, earth reds and browns, and titanium *white* as the main colorants. The marks are difficult to erase. Refer *Artefact*, *Cartoon*, *Conte Pencil*, *Crayons*, *Distemper*, *Drawing*, *Fixative*, *Gesso*, *Gouache*, *Life-Drawing*, *Papier Mache*, *Pouncing*, *Oil Pastels*, *Synthetic*, *Tempera*, *Thanjavur (Tanjore) Painting*, *Abalal Rahiman*, *Jamini Roy*, *Samarendranath Tagore*.

Chalk Drawing A drawing made using coloured *chalks*, *pastels* or *crayons*. Dark red *drawings* made with *chalk* are found in India, used by primitive men of the Indus Valley and Vedic civilizations. Refer *Life-Drawing*, *Jamini Roy*, *C. Douglas*, *Abalal Rahiman*, *Samarendranath Tagore*.

Champaneria, Madhu (1943–) b. Surat, GUJ. Education: Drawing Teacher's Certificate & *Art* Masters Dip. in *FA*. *JJSA*. 45 years experience in *back glass painting* inherited from his grandfather & father Ghanshyam. Solos: Gallerie Leela, *Artists' Centre* & Jasabhai Art Gallery Mumbai, *JAG*. Group participations: *NGMA* & *Artists' Centre* Mumbai, *JAG*, *ASI*, *AIFACS*. Awards: *ASI*. Collections: Mumbai, Surat, Ahmedabad; International: London, California, Chicago, Canada, Thailand, Hong Kong, pvt. & public.

Madhu Champaneria does *oils* on *transparent* glass and *acrylic* sheets. Using mainly emotional and environmental *themes* from the Indian ethos and his later works reflect the folk life. He displays the patience, practice and perception that are required to paint on the back of *transparent* materials, where the true *image* or *composition* is only visible on the reverse side.

He lives and works in Mumbai. Refer *Glass Painting*.

Champleve Refer *Enamel*.

Chamunda, Chandi, Chandika Synonyms of the Goddess SHAKTI in her terrible or malevolent aspect. The *term* is bestowed on her as a slayer of the *demons*, Chanda and Munda. She is usually represented as dark-skinned, with blood-red eyes and emaciated breasts hanging on her rib-cage with her blood-dripping tongue hanging out between sharp canine teeth. She is armed with many *attributes* like a sword, mace, and noose and is clad in an elephant skin. Refer MATRIKAS.

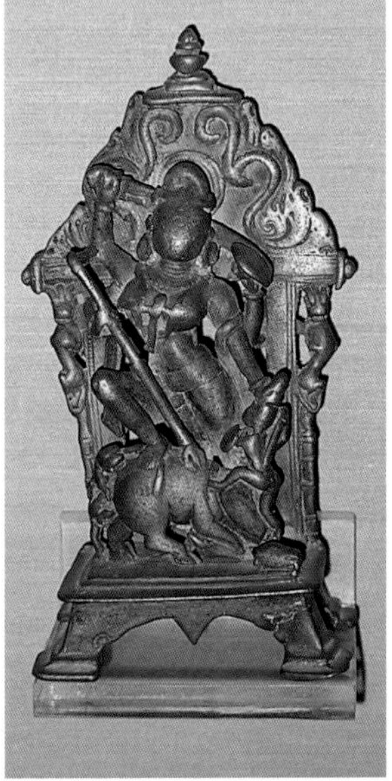

Chamunda, Chandi, Chandika: Chamundi Mahisasramardini, Brass, GUJ, circa 12th century AD 17x9x6 cm.

Chand, Roop (1936–) b. Dhundahera, Gurgaon, Haryana. Education: M.A. (*Art* & Museology) & *Art* Masters Certificate *JJSA*, Ph.D. Denmark. Solos: PUJ University & Govt. Museum Chandigarh, Govt. Museum Chennai, TKS, *JAG*, other towns Ludhiana, Kolkata & Jaipur; International: Nepal, France, Bahrain, Denmark. Group participations: New Delhi, Haryana, PUJ Artist Exhibition & *LKA* Chandigarh, *AIFACS*, National Exhibitions. Member: Upsurge Group of Artists Chandigarh, *LKA* Haryana, *INTACH* New Delhi. Appointments: Founder Chairman National Art Centre Gurgaon. Publications: Writes prose & poetry. Collections: PUJ University Museum, Govt. Museum Chandigarh, National Gallery of Art Chennai & pvt.

Roop Chand's early *figurative compositions* were painted in deep, dark browns and dull *blacks* picked out with fine *highlights*. The *paintings* have a psychoanalytic edge in his interpretation of human character and frailties. He soon turned to abstraction, using *colour* in conjunction with *form*. His later *oils* are formed organically in the process of their making. They possess a new "reality" of their own, rather than representing worldly reality. In 1992, he painted a series of works in *monochrome* which were basically studies in *texture*. A departure from his usual *style* was apparent in several *ink drawings* in the late seventies. Both TANTRIC and geometric *hard-edge painting* made their presence felt in these works.

He lives and works in Gurgaon, Haryana.

Chanda, Rani (1912–) b. India. Youngest sister of *Mukul Chandra Dey*. She was educated at *KB Santiniketan*, under the guidance of *Nandalal Bose*. Her first solo *art exhibition* was sponsored by *AIFACS* and some of her original *paintings* are in Rashtrapati Bhavan, 1949–50. She also took part in the 1956 BUDDHA Jayanti exhibition in New Delhi. *Mukul Chandra Dey* published a portfolio of her *prints*—"Linocut Prints" after her grad. from *KB*. She has written the history of the Tagore family. Among her better known *paintings* are "Kacha and Debjani".

Chander, Kanchan (1957–) b. New Delhi. Education: Degree in *FA*. *College of Art* New Delhi, Student in *printmaking*, CFA Santiago; Scholarship: French Govt. to *study printmaking* in Paris. Solos: British Council Division New Delhi, IIC, *GG*, TKS, *JAG*; International: Miyasika Gallery Tokyo. Group shows: Two *artists* in *GAC* & *TKS*, *JAG*, *VAG*, *GE*; International: Paris, Bristol, Hamburg, Schoo's Gallery Amsterdam, Indian Printmakers Kathmandu, Fukuoka Art Museum Japan. Group participations: National Exhibition Chennai, All India Women *AIFACS*, Mini Prints Show *GE*, *LTG*, Husain Ki Sarai Faridabad New Delhi, All India Exhibition Prints Chandigarh, *Biennale BB*, *SKP* & *AIFACS*, *JAG*, *CYAG*, *CKP*; International: *Biennale* in Yugoslavia, Japan, France & UK. *Art* camps & workshops: Udaipur, Bangalore, New Delhi, *BB*; International: Fukuoka Art Museum Japan. Awards: Yuva Mahotsav by SKP, *AIFACS*; International: Print *Biennale* UK, Japan, France & Holland. Fellowship/Grants: Won Research Fellowship CFA & Grants by *LKA* New Delhi. Appointments: Lecturer *College of Art* New Delhi. Collections: *NGMA*, *College of Art* & *LKA* New Delhi, *Chandigarh Museum*; International: Fukuoka Art Museum Japan, ENSBA, British Museum.

Kanchan Chander started out as a printmaker, making stark *black* and *white images* of despair and desolation. Soon, she started using tribal *forms* from KAR, Nagaland and Molela, evolving her own metaphorical interpretation. In the *triptych* "The Eternal Race", the sinuous "Waqwag" tree in the centre sprouts unicorn heads. On the right is the fecund fertility of the female *image*, on the left a slender male is portrayed.

Kanchan Chander's *paintings* do not change radically in spirit from her *prints*. Her works have always verged on the autobiographical, with complex *imagery* and use of *space*. She uses luminous *colours* which are sensual rather than overtly feminine.

Kanchan Chander lives and works in New Delhi.

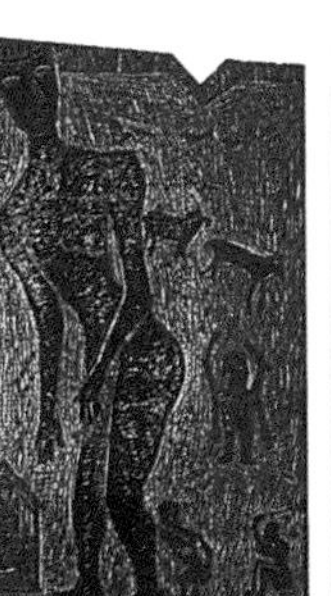
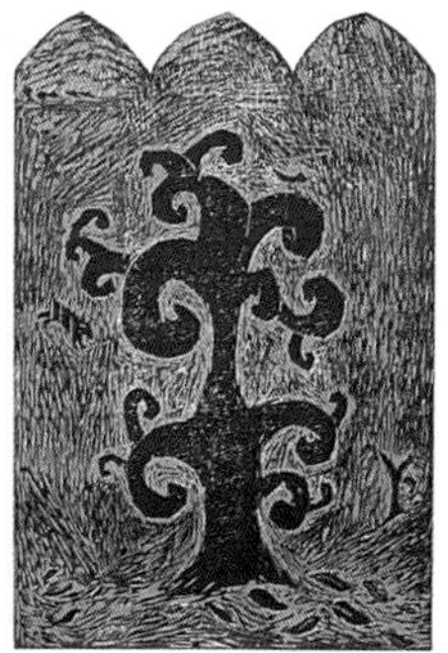
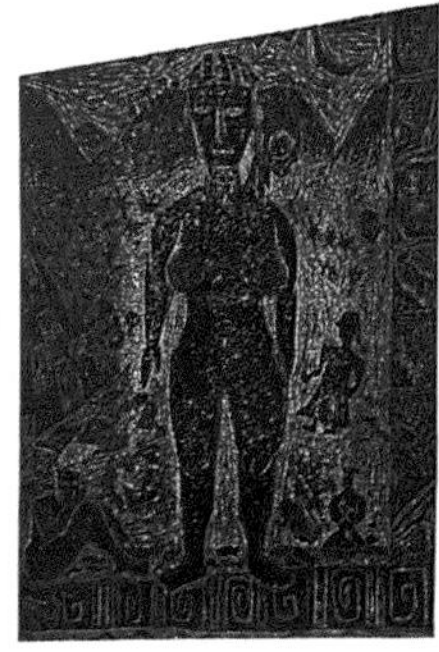

Chander, Kanchan: "The Eternal Race", *Triptych*, *Wood Cut*, 1994, 90x180 cm.

ChanderSheker, P.S. (1940–1997) b. India. Education: Dip. with Hon. *drawing* & *painting* Hyderabad. Solos: Hyderabad, *Art Heritage* New Delhi, The Heritage Chennai, *JAG*, *SAI*. Group participations: Mumbai, *Biennale* Hyderabad, *Triennale* New Delhi. *Artists* camps: *Graphic* camps New Delhi, Chennai, *Santiniketan*, KAR. Awards: National Award New Delhi, *Graphic*, *Portrait* & Gold Medal Hyderabad, *Artists' Centre* Mumbai. Collections: *NGMA* & *LKA* New Delhi, *LKA* Hyderabad, *SJM*; International: Malaysia.

P.S. ChanderSheker's works were either in *oil* or *pastels* with ape-like men, women, and animals placed in *landscapes*. A shepherd with his flock or just a person under a tree, an unruly horse, all in the skeletal formal in addition to elongated or distorted limbs. He had also worked on *pen* and *ink*, *drawings* with tonal variations.

Chandigarh Museum (Government Museum & Art Gallery). The *GMAG*, is the most prominent landmark of Chandigarh, a *modern* city, and houses several sections. The main *museum* contains historical antiquities and documents, an *art* gallery to promote awareness about *contemporary* Indian *art*, a science *museum* depicting the story of man and his scientific achievements, a photography workshop, and a library are the multiple facets of the *museum*. A unique feature is its very *modern* arrangement for stacking of *paintings*, making for great ease in referencing. The *art* gallery organizes *exhibitions* and other *art* events.

Chandra The moon *god*, a male deity also called Soma. The second day of the week, Somawara (Monday) is named after him. His symbol is a *silver* crescent. At *times* he is depicted as being caught up in the matted locks (Jata) of SHIVA. He is represented as riding a chariot drawn by ten horses and bearing the mark of an antelope or hare.

The phases of the moon became the determinants of the Hindu calendar and were used for climatic forecasts, and became the popular subject of *miniature paintings* and *mythology*. Refer ABHISARIKA, BAISAKH, VAISHAKH, *Ritual*, *Silver*, MATRIKAS, SHIVA, *Ganga Devi*, *Bharati Kapadia*, *Baburao Sadwelkar*, *Mohan Samant*, *Setlur Gopal Vasudev*, *Harkrishan Lall*.

Chandra, Satish (1941–) b. Gaziabad, UP. Education: Post-Dip. in *landscapes* & *watercolour painting* GCAC Lucknow. Solos: Over 27 shows Mussoorie, Kanpur, *LKA* Lucknow & Roorkee University UP, TAG, *GG*; International: New York. Group participations: National Exhibitions & *Triennale* New Delhi, *AFA* Kolkata, *LKA* State UP, *AIFACS*, *Dhoomimal*; International: *Biennale* Bangladesh & Japan. *Art* camps: *Painter's* camp Dehradun by UP *LKA*, International camp Regional Art Centre by *LKA* New Delhi NZCC Lucknow. Awards: *AFA* Kolkata *LKA* State UP, Gold Medal UP Govt., National Award New Delhi. Member: Secretary Visual Art Society Lucknow, Nominated Member Executive Council Lucknow University, NZCC India, Chairman & General Council *LKA* UP. Appointments: He has been an *artist* at the Dept. of Architecture Roorkee University UP, Lecturer & HoD GCAC Lucknow. Commissions: *Murals* in *ceramic* & *wood* in Lucknow & Kanpur. Collections: *LKA* UP, *NGMA* & British

High Commission New Delhi, BARC, TAG; International: Toronto University Canada, California University USA.

Satish Chandra is primarily landscapist, *painting* hazy near-impressionistic vistas of trees in wildy swaying lush meadows. The *colours* are naturalistic with grey blues, cadmium yellows, mauves and greens. He has used *water-colours, oil paint* and *pastels* among other *media*.

He lives and works in Lucknow.

Charcoal Sticks of charred *wood*, usually willow. It can be used for *drawing* on *paper, canvas* or walls. Thin *black* powdery *lines* are obtained by rubbing the sticks against these surfaces. The powdery *lines* can be easily rubbed away and hence charcoal is often used as a *medium* for a preliminary study on *canvas*. In the case of charcoal *drawings*, they can be preserved by spraying them with a *fixative*. Charcoal is also available in *pencil form. Jogen Chowdhury* has made extensive use of the charcoal *medium*. Refer *Cartoon, Drawing, Fixative, Frottage, India Ink, Ink, Life-Drawing, Line, Line and Wash, Gobardhan Ash, Sohini Dhar, Sheela Gowda, Akbar Padamsee, Mona Rai, Rajen, Piraji Sagara, Laxman Shreshtha, V.P. Singh, Swaminathan J., Vasudha Thozhur*; Illustration–*Shuvaprasanna, Still Life*, Pratima Sheth.

Charcoal Pencil Refer *Charcoal*.

Chasing A *technique* employed in finishing *metal* work, and in the case of delicate detailing on jewellery. Chasing is used to correct the imperfections left by *casting metal*, and smoothening out the rough edges and joints especially *bronze*. The striking edge of the tool is held against the surface to be chased and lightly hammered.

This process has been used by, the PALLAVA and CHOLA *sculptors* to *cast* their *bronze images*. Refer *Cire Perdue, Cold Working, Embossing, Sculpture, C. Dakshinamoorthy, Adi M. Davierwala, Shankar Nandagopal*.

Chasis A method used for enlarging small *models* or maquettes. It involves the use of a calibrated framework, and two stands, one for the small *model* and the larger one for the proposed enlargement. *Ramkinkar Baij* executed *sketches* of a Santhal family in Delhi in concrete as an illustration in *clay*, but the final work was executed in *Santiniketan*. Similarly *Kanayi Kunhiraman* worked with earth, *C. Jagdish* worked with *papier mache*, *Chintamoni Kar* worked in *clay* and other *media*, while *Vinayak Pandurang Karmarkar* created a *museum* in his house of all small-scale *models* of his works.

Chatterjee, Sukumar (1937–) b. Darbhanga, Bihar. Education: Dip. College of Art Patna. Solos: Gallery 42 & *LKA* New Delhi, Jamaat Art Gallery Mumbai, *CYAG, JAG, ABC, CKAG*. Group participations: People for Animals at *JAG, Triennale* & *LKA* New Delhi. Awards: National Awards, *LKA Triennale* New Delhi, Gold Medal Shilpa Kala Parishad Patna. Fellowship: A Senior Fellowship by Minister of Culture Govt. of India 2002–2004. Commissions: Arranged *exhibition* for *NGMA* abroad. Appointments: Joined the *NGMA* as a Technical Officer, Joined the Hindustan Times group of publications as Chief *Artist* & took to *illustration* & designing. Collections: *NGMA* & *LKA* New Delhi, PUJ University Chandigarh, *BB, ABC*, & pvt.

Sukumar Chatterjee paints faces: stoic, pensive-eyed survivors of tragedy, victims of *nature* watching the world with bleak eyes. He achieves his corrosive *texture* by using *white acrylic* overlaid with uneven patches of *paint* and *pastel*. Some of his works also arouse feelings of nostalgia through a *visual* juxtaposition of natural growth and singular *form* of existence.

He lives and works in New Delhi/Mumbai.

Chatterjee, Sunirmal (1929–) b. Patna, Bihar. Education: Dip. in *applied arts GSAC* Kolkata. Specialized in *printmaking* Academy of Applied Art Belgrade Yugoslavia. Over 50 Solos: Shimla, *LKA* New Delhi. Retrospective: PUJ, KB sponsored by *LKA* Chandigarh; International: Represented India at Liepzig, Lugano Warsaw. At least 25 group participations. Awards: Scholarship under Govt. of Yugoslavia in 1962. Hon.: by Chandigarh Administration for meritorious service in *Art Education*, by *AIFACS* as Senior Citizen Artist. Appointments: Taught GSAC Shimla, GSAC and College of Architecture Chandigarh. Collections: *NGMA* New Delhi, RAJ State Museum, PUJ University Chandigarh.

Sunirmal Chatterjee has worked in diverse *media* such as *wood, stone, metal, clay, paper, plaster* and *fibreglass*. His *forms* too could be *figurative*, stylized or *abstract*. He is self-expressive and free from any *illusions*.

Sunirmal Chatterjee is now practising as a freelance *artist*, interior designer, muralist, *sculptor* and commercial *artist* in Chandigarh/Shimla.

Chattopadhyay, Sunayani Devi (1875–1962) (Also known as Chatterjee or Chatterji) b. Kolkata, WB. Self-taught *painter*, belonging to the Tagore family. Solos: *AFA, BAAC* & Alliance Francaise Kolkata; International: London, *ISOA* exhibited her works in Europe. Retrospective: exhibition in Kolkata after her death. Group participations: Thiruvananthapuram. Awards: *ISOA* sponsored a number of *exhibitions* in India & Europe. Founder Member: *LKA* New Delhi. Publications: *Paintings* & articles on her work published in several periodicals. Collections: *NGMA* New Delhi, National Art Gallery Chennai, Jaganmohan Palace (Mysore Art Gallery) Mysore, *AFA* Kolkata, *CTAG, RBM*, pvt.

Though she was the younger sister of *Abanindranath Tagore* and *Gaganendranath Tagore*, her works bear no resemblance to the delicate *wash drawings* of the former or the cubist and satirical works of the latter. Instead, it is the religious *folk art* that she was exposed to as a housewife, that appears in her works. She has been termed as "primitive", for her spontaneous use of *line* and *wash*. There is little use of *detail* or ornamentation. The *colour washes* define certain areas but do not indicate *modelling* or *tones*. While she painted *Gods* like KRISHNA, SHIVA and also used elements like the *Halo*, she did not treat them iconically. It was the *narrative* aspect that interested her; therefore she painted subjects like, "Krishna leaving Gokul" and "Shiva carrying the body of Sati". The simply drawn eyes are the defining feature of her works along with the *flat application* of *colour* and delicate fluttering *figures*.

Chatur Bhuja=four-armed. Indian *gods* and goddesses are frequently depicted with multiple limbs and heads. VISHNU is depicted at *times* with four arms, each holding one *attribute* or AYUDHA namely, SHANKHA, GADA, CHAKRA and PADMA, also known as conch, mace, wheel and lotus respectively. Refer MUDRA, BRAHMA, SARASVATI, LAKSHMI; Illustration–SHIVA, GANESHA, GANJIFA.

Chaudhuri, Sankho (1916–) b. Santhal Parganas, Bihar. Education: Bachelor of Arts & Dip. in *FA*. in *sculpture KB Santiniketan*, Studied Nepalese system of *metal casting* to assist *Ramkinkar Baij* 1945–1950. Solos: Kolkata, First solo Bombay Art Society solon *Artists' Centre NGMA* New Delhi, *LTG*, *CYAG*. Retrospective: *NGMA* in New Delhi. Group participations: *LKA* New Delhi, *VBU*, presented in National & International *Exhibitions*. *Auctions*: Osian's Mumbai. Awards & Hon.: 1st Hon. Joint Secretary Indian Sculptors Association Mumbai, Hon. Secretary *LKA*, National Award & Fellow *LKA* New Delhi, Padma Shri, Aban-Gohan Award *VBU*; International: D.Litt. Center Escolor University Phillipines. Member: Chairman & Member *LKA*, Delhi Urban Art Commission, International Jury 5th *Triennale* India & President Rashtriya Manav Sangrahalaya New Delhi. Appointments: Study tour of Europe; Worked in Paris & England; Reader, HoD of *Sculpture* & later Dean of *FFA* (*MSU*); Visiting Prof. at BHU, Visiting Fellow at *VBU*; Organized Artist's Studio *GAC* by *LKA* 1976–77, organized & exhibited on *Folk* and *Tribal Images* of India *LKA* New Delhi; International: Prof. of *FA*. University of Dar-e-Salam Tanzania; Lecture tour to Polland; Invited to International Art Festival Baghdad; Represented International Conference India at UNESCO Paris & *Venice*; Participated in seminar on Tagore in Dartington England. Commissions: *Brass sculpture* World Bank, in *Marble* UNICFF & *NGMA* New Delhi, Mahatma Gandhi for Copenhagen.

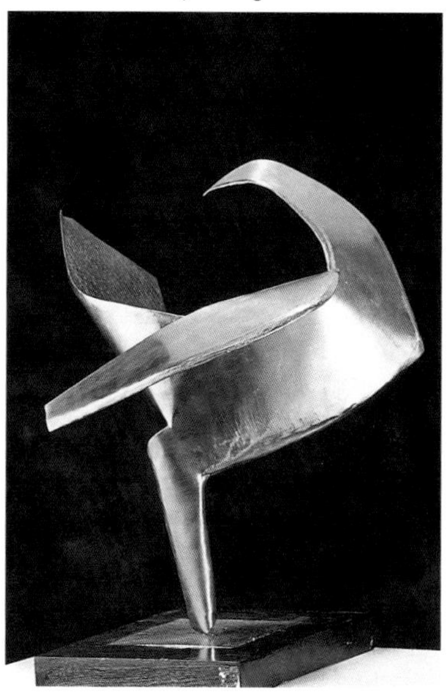

Chaudhuri, Sankho: "Bird", Stainless *Steel*.

Among his commissioned works is a *bronze* statue of Mahatma Gandhi for Rio de Janeiro and a 5ft *marble sculpture* for UNICEF New Delhi. Sankho Chaudhuri has been one of the formative influences in the history of *modern* Indian *sculpture*. He is both a *monumental sculptor* and a portraitist. His *portraits* are depersonalized and almost iconic in a mannered *Romanticism*. His early works were cubist in sensibility but over the years, his *forms* have grown simpler, yet fragile with a delicate linear pulsation. He has experimented with most *mediums* including *wood*, *stone*, *bronze*, welded *metal* and *plaster*. His recent works are organic cutouts and foldouts of birds and animals.

Chauduri, Anju (1944–) b. Kolkata. Education: Dip. in *painting GCAC* Kolkata; Commonwealth Scholarship to study at St. Martins School of Art London, French Govt. Scholarship ENSBA. Solos: *Art Heritage* New Delhi, *BAAC* Kolkata, *GE*, *CKAG*, *PUAG*; International: London, Paris, Zurich, Amsterdam, Vienna, Germany. Group participations: National & International *LKA Biennale* New Delhi, *GC* Mumbai, *BB*; International: Commonwealth Institute London, & other *exhibitions* in Paris, Finland & Japan. Awards: "Realistic Painting" *GCAC* Kolkata; International: Stamp Designing RAA London; *Illustrations* of the Book of Praise of Krishna with original *linocuts* published by Doubleday New York and Mini *prints Biennale* Candaces & Spain. Collections: *NGMA* New Delhi, *BAAC* Kolkata; International: New York, France, V&A.

For the past several decades she has lived and worked in Europe. For her, the abstraction inherent in her work is merely a gesture. Her freely worked *images* breathe vitality and vigour. She depicts *nature* and all its myriad elements–plants, roots, leaves, barks and vegetation. Her *paintings* are a positive blend of both oriental and occidental.

She lives and works in Paris.

Chauhan, Dayhalal K. (1931–) b. Bhiloda, GUJ. Education: GDA in *art mural* decoration *JJSA*. Solos: TAG, *JAG*. Group participations: GUJ State, Nasik Kalaniketan, *LKA* Gwalior & New Delhi, MPKP. Awards: Silver Medal Nasik Kalaniketan, Merit certificate Gwalior, *BAS*. Appointments: Lecturer Indian Art Institute Mumbai, Senior textile *artist* Standard Mill Company Ltd. Commissions: An *eclectic artist*, having been commissioned for interior designing & *murals paintings* in different *styles*. Collections: *NCAG*, *mural paintings* Srinagar; International: London.

An *eclectic artist* who created his *compositions* that developed changes in *rhythm* with *time*. His works on *canvas*, *paper* or *metal* show an interesting use of different *styles* including *Raja Ravi Varma's form* of *Realism*, traditional Hindu *iconography* and Chinese *Romanticism*.

He lives and works in Mumbai.

Chauhan, Nagjibhai V. (1938–) b. Jamnagar, GUJ. Education: Dip. in *painting* & *sculpture* CNCFA GUJ. Solos & other group shows: Jamnagar, *LKA* KB Ahmedabad, *JAG*. *Art* camps & workshops: Jamnagar, Mount Abu, GUJ *LKA*, *Graphic* Ahmedabad & *JAG*, *AIFACS*, MPKP; "Workshop for Illustrators of Childrens Books" held by National Book Trust of India. Awards: *LKA* Silver & Bronze Medals GUJ, *AIFACS*, All India Exhibitions. Commissions: *Portraits* of Sardar Vallabhbhai Patel (of the Indian National Congress). Appointments: Lecturer & HoD of *Painting* CNCFA. Publications: Several illustrated books. Collections: Central & State *LKA*, pvt. national & international.

Nagjibhai V. Chauhan is both a *painter* and *sculptor*. His *paintings* are usually untitled and painted with vibrant *colours* depicting emotional values. He has experimented with *watercolours*, with Chinese and Japanese *brushwork* and several *styles* over the years before evolving his present *abstract style*. His sculptural *forms* echo the *paintings* with the shapes seeming to emerge from the two-dimensionality of the *canvas* and freezing into real *space*.

At present he is in Ahmedabad.

Chaura Panchasika An 11th-century poem of 50 verses written by Bilhana, a Kashmiri robber-poet on his great love for the Princess Champavati. It translates as the "love story of the thief." It has been illustrated in the Sultanate *style* of *miniature painting*, which is a development on the stiff and angular *Jain Style*. Refer *Mewar*.

Chavan, Bhagwan (1958–) b. Kurduwadi, MAHA. Education: Dip. in *FA*. *JJSA*, advanced ENSBA, French Govt. Scholarship. Solos: British Council & *SG* Chennai, *PUAG*, *JAG*, *GE*, *BB*. Group participations: *CIMA* Kolkata, *Biennale* Bhopal, RAGM; International: Galerie Siene Paris, ENSBA. *Art* camps: Hyderabad, *LKA* Chennai, *WSC* camp Tarara Calicute by MMB. Awards: Research Grant *LKA* National Award New Delhi, Regional Centre *LKA* Chennai, *BB Biennale*.

Bhagwan Chavan is basically a *painter* who works on *abstract themes*, layering *oils* and *acrylics* and sometimes *distemper* with *brushes*, rags, rollers and *palette knife*. He tries to create surface areas of varying *depth* with *colour* and *space illusion*. Lately, his *compositions* have become tighter as he slashes diagonally or erects triangles over a heavily impastoed surface of reds, blues and purples.

Bhagwan Chavan lives and works in *Cholamandal*.

Chavda, Shiavax (1914–1990) b. Navsari, GUJ. Education: GDA *JJSA*, Dip. in *FA*. Slade School of Art London, Studied AGC. Over 40 solos: Ahmedabad, *PUAG*, *JAG*, TAG; International: Djakarta, Singapore, London, Paris, Zurich, New York. Group participations: Marvel Art Gallery Ahmedabad, 25 years of Indian Art *LKA* New Delhi; International: UNESCO Exhibition & Salon de Mai Paris, *Biennale* in Sao Paulo & Venice, Non-Abstract Painting Tokyo, *Contemporary* Indian Art Japan, *Graphic* Switzerland, others in Burlington, Essen London, USA, Mexico. *Auctions*: Osian's & Sotheby's Mumbai, Christie's London, Sotheby's New York. Awards: MAHA State Govt. Award. Fellowship: Elected Fellowship of *LKA* New Delhi & Felicitated by GUJ *LKA* 1986. Member: Elected eminent *artist LKA*. Commissions: *Murals* Air India, Parliament House, Tata Theatre NCPA Mumbai. Appointments: In 1955 worked under Helmut Ruhemanan the former chief restorer of the National Gallery London & Vladimir Polunin the first to introduce *modern* stage decor to Britain. Collections: *LKA* & *NGMA* New Delhi, *Maharaja Fatesingh Museum*, Nagpur Museum, J&K Academy; International: Singapore, Europe, Canada, USA, Australia, Budapest Museum, Late President Sukarno Indonesia, V&A.

Shiavax Chavda travelled all over India & the South East Asian subcontinent making lightning *sketches* & *painting* exotic dancers. He also toured Britain, France & Switzerland between 1946–65. He had a deep knowledge of dance and music, both Indian and Western. Like *K.K. Hebbar*, he made sinuous and energetic *line drawings* of dancers, capturing them mid-movement. His *pastel sketches* too were much appreciated by the cognoscenti.

His *images* of Indian and foreign dancers are captured with a minimum use of *line*, *tone* and *colour*. With all its simplifications, the *line* manages to capture the characteristic *form*, pose and expression entirely. He has painted many subjects on serpents in *oils* explaining that in addition to the religious significance of the reptile, it was also a symbol of a lightning release of linear energy.

His main *theme* was always human beings, though he has painted a few *landscapes* in Kulu and Kashmir. Good *draughtsmanship*, *pattern*, textural and *tonal values* were of prime importance to him, which he brought to completion in his *abstract compositions*. Here, he emphasized solely on *colour* or sometimes on the linear, to be attuned to the *harmony* of *hues*. Refer Illustration–*Form* and *Line*.

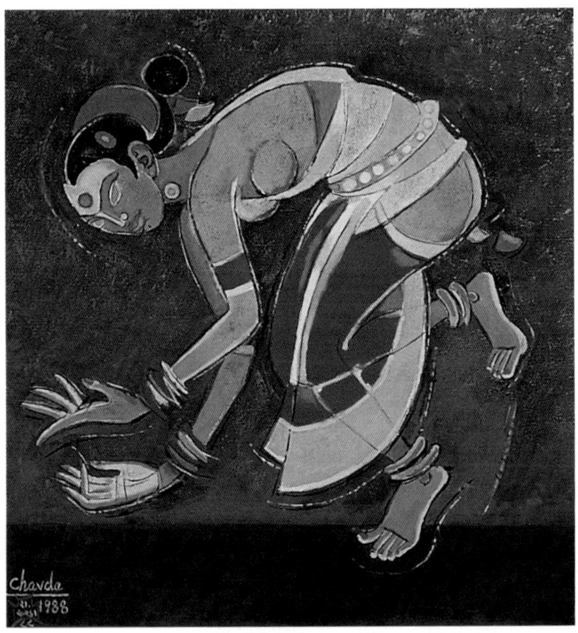

Chavda, Shiavax: "Bharatnatyam IV", *Oil* on *Canvas*, 1988, 100x100 cm.

Chaze Centre for the Arts & Crafts (CCACM) (Margao, Goa). The Chaze Centre, which was opened in 1989 by Thomas Chaze, consists of around 200 sq.m. spread over two floors containing a gallery for the *exhibition* of works of *art*, and areas marked for studios where visiting *artists* can work. The Centre intends holding workshops and short courses on *art* and *crafts* throughout the year. The gallery's collection include works by *Prabhakar Barwe* and *Jatin Das*.

Chequering A *pattern* of alternating squares or lozenges of contrasting *colours* or *textures* generally seen as *ceramic* decoration. *Lalitha Lajmi* often uses the chequer *motif* in the *form* of alternating tiles in her *prints* and *paintings*. Refer *Shail Choyal*.

Chetty, Adiveppa Murigeppa (1907–) b. Athani, Belgaum. Education: GDA in *drawing* & *painting JJSA*. Solos: In Bangalore. Group participations: Oudh, *BAS*. Awards: Mysore DAE, KAR *LKA*, *CKP* Honour, All India Art Exhibition Oudh, *BAS*. Fellowship & Scholarship: 1931, 32, 33. Member: *LKA* Mysore, KAR for several years. Appointments: Vice-Principal & Principal Vijaya Art Institute Gadag for 30 years. Publications: Illustrated books on religious history & social subjects, mathematics, magazines & religious tracts, including 10,000 books on *art*. Collections: Mysore Museum, Vidhana Soudha Bangalore, Institute in Gadag, *ACB*, others in Dharwad, Sholapur, Akalkot, Mumbai, pvt. & public.

Adiveppa Murigeppa Chetty has worked in *oils*, *watercolours* and *pencil*. His output includes *portraits*, *landscapes*, *line drawings* as well as *compositions*. His subjects ranged from *gods* and goddesses on the one hand to beggars, poverty-stricken children and village beauties on the other. While 'Shiva and Parvati', painted in *tempera* shows a romanticized blend of *Ajanta*-like *lines* and *Raja Ravi Varma* Kitsch, "Kittur Rani Chennamma" has an illustrational feel to it.

He has been a resident of Gadag since 1944. Refer *Vijaya FA Society*.

Chhabda, Bal (1923–) b. PUJ, India. Self-taught *painter*, Started *painting* in 1958 after a stint at runningan *art* gallery Gallery 59 Mumbai. Solo: *JAG*. Group participations: National Exhibition & *LKA* New Delhi, *Triennale* India, Modern Indian Paintings *BB*, *JAG*; International: Tokyo *Biennale*, Contemporary Art Dialogues between East & West & Festival of India Japan, Commonwealth Art Exhibition, Newcastle & Festival of India London. Attended *Art* camps. Awards: Gaurav Puraskar Govt. of MAHA 1990, *LKA* & National Exhibition New Delhi; International: *Biennale* Tokyo. Fellowships: JDR Fund USA. Member: Advisory panel of *Roopankar* & *BB*. Earlier he had intended being a filmmaker; After a stint in Hollywood for a year and a half years, he made a film "Do Rahee" (Two Travellers) about a young female *artist*.

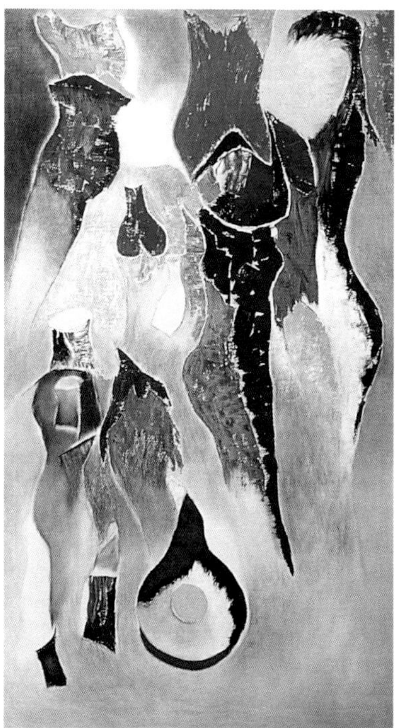

Chhabda, Bal: "Cocktail Party".

Bal Chhabda has evolved a free flowing, gestural *abstract style*, with thickly encrusted *pigment* growing out of luminous *washes* of *colour*. He works in a semi-automatist *manner*, letting the *brush* dictate the *form* against the whiteness of his primed *canvas*. There is an almost surrealist will at work with *anatomy*, bird and animal *forms* being united in the half-formed *images*.

Bal Chhabda lives and works in Mumbai. Refer *Gestural Abstraction*.

Chhannavira Refer *Ornaments*.

Chhara, Mansing L. (1931–1997) b. Ahmedabad. Education: Dip. in *FA*. *MSU*, *Art* Masters Certificate GUJ State University, Studied in *art* under *Ravishankar M. Raval*. Solos: Ahmedabad, Mumbai, New Delhi. Group participations: By National *LKA* Veteran Artists' of India at Bhubaneshwar & Bangalore, *AFA* Kolkata, Municipal Corporation Ahmedabad, *BAS*. Awards: Ahmedabad, *AFA* Kolkata, *BAS*. Junior & Senior Fellowship: Dept. of Culture Govt. of India. Member: GUJ State *LKA*; Founder Member Progressive Painters & Founder Secretary Practising Painters Ahmedabad. Appointments: Several talks on Child Art to *art* teachers & young *artists*. Collections: GUJ State *LKA*, *LKA* New Delhi & pvt. national & international.

His *paintings* do not reveal a constant evolution of *imagery* or *style* as he loved to experiment with a variety of impulses. He was an *eclectic artist*, the highlight of his *figurative* works being the highly expressive faces.

In the works of the early 80s one notices a P. Klee-like nativity of *forms* through the use of tribal *motifs*. He had painted *landscapes* and group *studies*, at times using violent *colour* contrast and at others a gentle *cross-hatching* of *pencil lines*. He lived in Ahmedabad.

Chhatrapati Shivaji Maharaj Vastu Sanghralaya (CSMVS) (formerly Prince of Wales Museum of Western India [PWM]) (Mumbai, MAHA) The *museum* was named after Prince George (later King George V) who laid the foundation stone of the building. The architect George Witter has synthesized the Mughal architectural *style* with British sensibility in its *construction*.

The central hall is dominated by a staircase, which leads to the upper floors, all of which have galleries stretching out on either side. The *ground* floor hall gives one a synoptic view of Indian *art* through the ages while the *sculpture* gallery on the first floor has excellent examples of *Gandharan* and Chalukyan *art* among others.

The landing has a well-labelled display of the Indus Valley *artefacts*. These include reconstructed *models* of the towns, along with items of domestic use, such as storage jars and vessels, seals and jewellery. The central balcony on the first floor displays decorative objects in *ivory*, *silver* and wood belonging to the late 18th and 19th century.

The pride of the *museum* is the Indian *miniature painting* gallery on the first floor. One gets to see miniatures of almost every school here. The "Portrait of a Black Buck", the "Lapwing" and the "Woodcock" all show the Mughal love for natural history. There is also an illustrated manuscript of the

KALPA-SUTRA and the "Kalakacharyakatha" (*Jain style*) belonging to the late 15th century there are also some outstanding examples of *Pahari miniature painting* on display here. In a *Bundi painting* "Lady Looking in a Mirror" one sees the ever-present *Bundi* characteristic of a lotus pond filled with fish, ducks and lotuses in the *foreground*. The Nepal and Tibet gallery facing the *painting* gallery on the first floor houses a collection of *art* that has been donated by the Tata industrialist family. They include Thankas–cloth *paintings* of Buddhist origin as well as *metal images* of Buddhist and Hindu *gods* and goddesses.

The second floor houses a miscellaneous collection of objects made in glass, jade and porcelain. There is *ivory* work from Japan and porcelain from China.

The European *painting* galleries, also on the second floor, exhibit a large number of *copies* in addition to some small *landscapes* by J. Constable.

There is also a natural history section on the *ground* floor. The Coomaraswamy Hall is used only for special *exhibitions*. Postcards and publications are available at the sales counter and The Museum Gallery at Kala Ghoda.

Chhillar, J.K. (1945–) b. Bamnoli, Haryana. Education: Dip. in *Arts* and *Crafts* JMI, Post-Dip. in *sculpture MSU*. Solos & Two Artists shows: *BAG*, TAG, *JAG*. Group participations: All India Exhibitions, National Exhibition of Art & *Triennale* New Delhi. *Art* camps & workshops: Jammu, All India Sculptor Amritsar, Hyderabad *LKA*, *BB*. Awards: GUJ State *LKA*, MAHA Gaurav Puraskar, Govt. of Haryana, All India Exhibition Bihar, National Exhibition *LKA* New Delhi, *BAS*, *ASI*. Scholarships/Junior & Senior Fellowship: Govt. of India. Member: Jury National Exhibition of Art New Delhi, All India Exhibition Lucknow, MAHA State Art Exhibition. Appointments: Instructor in the Dept. of Museology *MSU* 1971–73. Collections: *LKA* & *NGMA* New Delhi, *BB*.

J.K. Chhillar is basically a *figurative painter* and *sculptor* using animal and human *forms* in a highly stylized *manner*. He prefers working with the intense polished surface of *marble*.

He lives and works in Mumbai with his *artist* wife *Prayag Jha Chhillar*.

Chhillar, Prayag Jha (1945–) b. Agra, UP. Education: NDFA *College of* Art New Delhi, Post-Dip. in *printmaking MSU*. Over 14 solos: *JAG*, TAG. Group participations: National Exhibitions, Art Festival in India, Graphic Art *AIFACS*, *Biennale BB*; International: Hawana, Cuba, Mexico, Art Festival in Japan & USA. *Art* camps & workshops: *Triennale LKA* New Delhi, *LKA* Lucknow, *GAC*, *BB*. Awards/Certificates: *College of Art* & National *LKA Triennale* New Delhi, GUJ *LKA*, *Artists' Centre* & MAHA Gaurav Puraskar Mumbai, *Graphic BAS*, Bronze Medal International Women's year & Vijoo Sadwelkar Award *JAG*, *AIFACS*, *CYAG*. Fellowship: HRD for a project in etching 1995–97. Founder Member: MAHA Visual Art, FAIM. Collections: *NGMA* & *LKA* New Delhi, *AFA* Kolkata, *Artists' Centre* Mumbai, *Chandigarh Museum*, *FFA* (*MSU*), pvt. & public.

She has worked in *terracotta*, *oil painting* and *printmaking*. Her *etchings* are meticulously detailed interiors and *landscapes* with crows. Her painted *landscapes* show an impressionistic sense of speed and *colour* application.

She lives with her *artist* husband *J.K. Chhillar* in Mumbai and teaches *art*.

Chiaroscuro (Italian)=light-dark. The *term* was first used to describe the depiction of *light* and *shade* and the *handling* of *shadows* by *Renaissance artists*, especially Leonardo da Vinci. *Artists* B. Caravaggio (Tenebrism–the *technique* of extreme chiaroscuro used by the mannerist and Baroque artists in the 17th century) and H.V.R. Rembrandt also used chiaroscuro. The effect was more easily obtained with the slower *drying oil* paint, and hence is associated with the rise and popularity of *oil painting*. *Raja Ravi Varma* was among the first Indian *painters* to use chiaroscuro, and ever since, many Indian *artists* have used chiaroscuro. Refer *Bengal School*, *Engraving*, *Fine Arts*, *Modelling*, *Painterly*, *Yusuf Arakkal*, *Pestonjee Bomanjee*, *Shaibal Ghosh*, *Jyotish Dutta Gupta*, *Savlaram L. Haldankar*, *Somnath Hore*, *Durgashanker K. Pandya*, *Mahendra Pandya*, *Kartick Chandra Pyne*, *A. Ramachandran*, *Debi Prasad RoyChowdhury*, *Anilbaran Saha*, *Yagneshwar Kalyanji Shukla*, *Shuvaprasanna*, *Vrindavan Solanki*, *Laxman Narayan Taskar*, *Raja Ravi Varma*.

Chidambarakrishnan, K.P. (1947–) b. Madurai. Education: Studied in *FA. painting* GCAC Kumbakonam TN. Solos: Mumbai, Regional Centre Chennai & Madurai, *JAG*. Group participations: South Indian Society of Painters Madras in Mumbai, New Delhi, Bangalore & Chennai, *LKA* in Mysore State Bangalore, Kerala State Trichur, Regional Centre Chennai & New Delhi, TN in Mumbai, *WSC* Artists Group in Mumbai, Kolkata, Chennai & New Delhi, *Biennale* Chandigarh, 50 Years of Indian Art New Delhi, Bharat Kala Parishad & Summer show in Hyderabad, *AIFACS*, *BAS*; International: *Drawings* Yugoslavia. Awards: TN *LKA*, *AIFACS*. Member: *AIFACS*, *BAS*. Appointments: Designer *WSC* Hyderabad. Collections: Central & State *LKA*, British Council Chennai, Chennai Museum, Govt. Art Gallery Mysore.

He has worked with various *media*, including *collage*, *mixed media*, *ink* and *wash*, experimenting with a meandering *line* and detailed *passages* of *form* and *colour*. His *forms* are based on the *figurative*, though they are highly distorted and fragmented.

He lives in Hyderabad.

China Clay Synonym of Kaolin, it is the purest of natural white *clay* and when hardened by *firing* becomes fine China. It is also used as an extender or *filler* in the making of *paints* and coloured *pencils*. Refer *Sukhen Ganguly*.

Chinchalkar, Vishnu (1917–2000) b. Aaloth, MP. Education: GDA *JJSA*, Studied under D.D. Deolalikar, the principal of the Indore School of Art; Taught at the same school 1955–67. Solos: *AFA* Kolkata, *JAG*, *AIFACS*, *BB*. Group participations: Kolkata, Patna, National Exhibition New Delhi 1945–55, *AIFACS*. Attended camps. Fellowship: *FA* College Indore. Awards: Gold medal *FA*. Kolkata, Govt. MP Felicitated in Utsav 73, Foundation MAHA Puraskar 1979, *Biennale AIFACS* for *portraits*. Founder Member: Friday Group 1960 Indore. Member: Indore University, Children's Film Society of India & NZCC Indore, *Roopankar BB*. Appointments: Worked for "Illustrated Weekly of India" Mumbai; Affiliated with "Daily Naidunia" Indore for 50 years. Collections: *NGMA* & Gandhi Smarak Nidhi New Delhi, Raj Bhavan Bhopal, *SJM*, *BB*. Almost gave up *painting* in favour of *wood collages*, bark-sculptures 50s & 60s.

Making *art* objects from waste and scrap material was Vishnu Chinchalkar's *style*. At first he painted *portraits*, *landscapes* and *abstracts*; later he turned to *found objects* for inspiration, using twigs and leaves. He also experimented with the DEVANAGARI *script* in the *calligraphic* shapes, finding them in all these ephemera of *nature*. He lived in Indore.

Chinese Art The *art* of China, refers generally to *painting* on rice *paper* and screens with a type of *black ink*. The favourite *theme* of Chinese *painting* was *landscape*, usually with large mountains, trees, streams and waterfalls, dwarfing the humans with typical Chinese straw hats with donkeys and water buffaloes. The hallmark of Chinese *painting* was the brushstroke, which was of various types and which had to be firm and spontaneous. Chinese art also refers to the *casting* of *bronze ritual* vessels and other *crafts*, including *metal*, *lacquer* and bamboo work. Indian *artists* especially those of the *Bengal School* were influenced by Chinese *wash painting*. It was first adopted by *Abanindranath Tagore*, and later by *Nandalal Bose*, *Benode Behari Mukherjee*, *Gopal Ghose*, *Gaganendranath Tagore* and others. Refer *Japanese Art*, *Mughal Dynasty*, *Yagneshwar Kalyanji Shukla*.

Chinese Ink Refer *India Ink*, *Back-Glass Painting*, *Drawing Ink*, *Ink*, *Waterproof*, *Pen*, *Sailoz Mookerjea*, *Maqbool Fida Husain*, *Abanindranath Tagore*.

Chipping Mould The process of releasing waste or one-off *mould* from a *positive cast* by lightly hammering with a mallet and *chisel*. Refer *Brass*, *Bronze*, *Cast*, *Cast Stone*, *Cire Perdue*, *Copper*, CHOLA, PALLAVA, *C. Ponnappa Rajaram*, *Ramkinkar Baij*, *Satish Gujral*, *Vinayak Pandurang Karmarkar*, *Nagji Patel*.

Chisel Instrument, usually made of *metal* with a wooden handle, used for *carving wood*, *marble*, *stone* or any other hard material. One end is used as the cutting edge, while the other receives the blow from the hammer or mallet.

Flat chisel is used for working on softer varieties of *stones* especially for *carving* low *reliefs*. Claw chisel, with a row of teeth has been used since ancient times tool for *stone carving* and *sculpture*. Bush chisel unlike other chisels was used to block out or mark/define the surface. Refer *Boucharde*, *Carving*, *Chipping Mould*, *Texture*, *Wood*, *Dhanraj Bhagat*, *C. Dakshinamoorthy*, *Leela Mukherjee*, *Mahendra Pandya*.

Chitra=picture, finished *drawing* or *painting*. According to the myths, the first picture was a *portrait* drawn using the juice of a mango.

Chitrakathi=picture-narrators. The CHITRA (picture) Kathi (narrators) *tradition* of story-telling with the aid of painted pictures, is still existent in the village of Pinguli in MAHA. The narrators belong to the Thakar community, a nomadic tribe which now lives in Gudhiwadi in Pinguli village. Though they were basically craftsmen, their primary occupation was to move from village to village, entertaining people with their primitive audio-*visual* performances with the Chitrakathi, string puppets and *leather shadow* puppetry.

A team of five to six performers are required for each performance–one asking questions (the Nacha or player), the storyteller (NAYAK) and the musicians, who provide the background-music and chanting. The language used is Marathi.

Some of the pictures are nearly 250 years old. They are painted in loose-leaf *manuscript form* known as Pothis using mineral *colours* mixed with glue. Each episode (from various religious *epics*) is sequentially arranged and wrapped in a coloured cloth, known as Rumal (handkerchief). The first page of each Pothi has an *image* of Lord GANESHA painted on it. Some of the Pothis are Yuddha-Kanda, Lav-Kush Akhyan, Indrajit-Vadha, Sita Shuddhi, Karna Parna, and Vikramasara Hans Dwaja.

Each Pothi has between 30–50 leaves, with pictures painted back to back. Each picture is displayed for approximately 1.5 minute as the storytelling goes on, therefore the narration of each Pothi takes between 2–2.5 hours.

These Pothis can be divided into three *styles*: in the first the *drawing* is firm and the *figures* are crisply rendered with ornamented *drapery* and jewellery. In the second, the *figures* are simple, but the *composition* is skilful and imaginative. The third *style* developed by local *artists* called Chitaris is highly expressive, with the flora and fauna of the Konkan region predominating. The *colour* is greatly simplified and limited in range. Refer *Flora & Fauna Painting*, RAMAYANA and MAHABHARATA.

Chitrakoot Art Gallery (CKAG) (Kolkata). Established in 1984, by Dr. Prakash Kejariwal and Sumitra Kejariwal, as an outlet for the *contemporary artists* in WB to display their works. The gallery has one of the largest collections of Bengal *art*, especially the works of *Jamini Roy*, *Ganesh Pyne* and the early *Bengal School artists* like *Jogen Chowdhury*, *Chintamoni Kar*, *Amitabha Banerjee*, *Lalu Prasad Shaw* and *Veena Bhargava*.

Situated in the heart of Kolkata, CKAG has been holding *exhibitions* of major *artists* around the country since the past 20 years.

Chitrala Art Gallery (Sri) (CTAG) (Thiruvananthapuram). Originally known as the Sri Chitralayam Thiruvananthapuram, it was opened to the people of Travancore by H.H. the Maharaja of Travancore in 1935. The gallery is divided into several sections, such as one devoted to the *Bengal School*, another the works of *Raja Ravi Varma*, and their *contem-*

poraries. In addition to *Abanindranath Tagore* and *Nandalal Bose*, the works of *Sunayani Devi Chattopadhyay*, *Kshitendranath Mazumdar*, the *Ukils*, and *Muhammed Abdur Rehman Chughtai* are also displayed. Certain *artists* from GUJ including *Kanu Desai* and *Chhaganlal R. Jadav* are on view here too. The works of Mangala Bai Tampuratli and C. Raja Raja Varma, brother of *Raja Ravi Varma* are also displayed. In the traditional section, Rajput, *Mughal* and Persian *miniatures* are displayed, as are *copies* of the *murals* at *Ajanta*, Bagh, Travancore and Cochin. *Chinese* and *Japanese art* can also be seen here.

Chitraniketan Art Gallery Earlier known as Chitram Art Gallery in Cochin now in Thiruvananthapuram.

The first private *art* gallery of its kind in Kerala, it opened in 1992 and promotes *contemporary art* and *artists*. The gallery also keeps works on consignment basis in addition to hosting one-man and group shows. *Artists* including *K.V. Haridasan*, *C.N. Karunakaran*, *K.C. Murukeson*, *K. Damodaran*, *Prem Raval*.

Chitrasutra The oldest standard text on *art* taken from the Vishnudharmottara PURANA dated 4th century AD. It covers several topics including the classifications of pictures, the materials and *techniques* used in *painting*, the merits and defects in *painting* and the right attitude to be adopted by a good *artist*/artisan. Refer *Aesthetics*, *Ajanta*, *Colour*, *Ideal*, *Proportion*, SHADANGA.

Chittaprasad (1915–1978) b. Naihati, 24 Parganas, WB. No formal training in *art*, but inspired by the village *sculptors* and the puppet players. Education: Studied in Govt. College Chittagong Bangladesh; In the 60s learnt puppet making from Mr. Frantisek Salaba a Czech in Mumbai. Solos: Shilpayan, Calcutta Information Centre by Chittaprosad Art Archive–Govt. of WB, 77th Birthday–The Centre Art Gallery Kolkata, Alliance Francaise de Delhi & Galerie Romain Rolland New Delhi, *CKAG*; International: His 1st *Exhibition* in Prague Czechoslovakia, others in Denmark, Holland, Germany; Retrospective in Czechoslovakia. Awards and Hons: After his death in Kolkata, and a tribute printed in "Daily" Hyderabad. *Auctions*: Heart New Delhi, Osian's Mumbai & Sotheby's London. Appointments: Served–made a series of *linocuts*–under the title "Angels Without Fairy Tales"; Started working on Hindu epic RAMAYANA and MAHABHARATA all in *illustrations*. Publications: His *drawings* on famine in Bengal pubished in communist Journals and a book "Hungry Bengal" with his *illustration*, "Chittaprosad" Asst. Editor Amit Mukhopadhyay *LKA*; Information published in journals, essays magazines, and *auction* and *exhibition* catalogues. Collections: Lagest public collection in Kolkata by his sister Gouri Chatterjee, Goodricke Group Ltd. Kolkata, *Delhi Art Gallery*, *Art Heritage* & *NGMA* New Delhi; International: National Gallery & Prague Museum of Art Czechoslovakia, UNICEF Committee Denmark, Wolfson Initiative Miami USA.

Chittaprasad was first noticed for his powerful and sensitive *drawings* of the tragic victims of the 1943 Bengal Famine. These *pencil sketches* were later finished in *brush* and *ink*. He also painted large *hoardings* in *oils* for the communist party of India. However, he is mostly known for his *linocuts–printmaking*. These powerful *black* and *white* works almost always depict the plight of the downtrodden. Several were published as a series by the Danish UNICEF committee in 1969. Chittaprasad also published two books on poetry and illustrated a set of Bengali folk-tales, retold by himself. After several experiments he also started a puppet-theatre–Khelaghan–for slum children in Mumbai, in the 60s. He made the puppets himself, out of *wood*, coconut shells, ropes, strings and cotton. He also designed the stage, wrote the plays and worked on the performances himself.

Chola, Chola Dynasty A dynasty of kings who ruled in South India after the fall of the PALLAVAS. They ruled between the 9th and 12th century AD. Since they were mainly Shaivites, the majority of temples built by them were dedicated to SHIVA. Two of the most magnificent temples were the Brihadisvara at Thanjavur built by Raja and the Brihadisvara built by his son Rajendra I at Gangaikonda-cholapuram. The Thanjavur temple was constructed out of large blocks of *granite*, with a Vimana rising upto a ht. of 66 mtrs. and standing on a base of 30 mt. The temple is Chatur-Mukha, having openings on all four sides, with 16 successive storeys. Though Chola *art* evolved out of PALLAVA and Pandyan *art*, it generally shows greater movement and rhythmic freedom, with a clear differentiation between the representation of *Gods* and humans. The *gods* are idealized types while the humans show greater individuality and character. Chola *sculptures* are in *light relief* and mostly face forward. The SHIVA NATARAJA on the southern wall of the Garbhagriha of the earlier mentioned Thanjavur Brihadisvara temple is both massive and dynamic. Also some of the finest *bronzes* were *cast* during the Chola period. The Chola *bronzes* contained a higher than usual percentage of *copper*. Refer DRAVIDA, *Dravidian Style*, *South Indian Bronzes*, *Architecture*, *Bronze*, *Chasing*, *Chipping Mould*, *Cire Perdue*, *Lost Wax Process*, *Mural*, NATARAJA, *Relief Sculpture*, *Wax*, *Subrayalu Dhanapal*, *K.S. Kulkarni*; Illustration–BRAHMA.

Cholamandal Art Gallery (COAG) (Chennai) Refer *Cholamandal Artists' Village* Chennai.

Cholamandal Artists' Village (Cholamandal) (Chennai) Cholamandal was set up in 1966 by *K.C.S. Paniker* on 8.5 acres of land, about 6 miles south of Adyar along the new *Mahabalipuram* road. It consists of *artists*, studios, a permanent *art* gallery, a workshop for *batik* and *metal* work, guest houses, the office of the *artists*, Handicrafts Association and the residences of *artists* living and working there. The village grew out of the need felt by *artists* graduating from *Madras School of Arts* to live a fuller life as creative *artists*. In order to earn an independent living, they employ themselves part-time in creative handicrafts which are then sold. They manage to support themselves with their income which enables them to work on their respective artistic disciplines. *Artists* currently associated with the COAG are *Shankar Nandagopal*, *P.S. Nandhan*, *K.V. Haridasan* and others. Refer *GCAC* Chennai.

Choudhary, Suresh (1943–) b. Indore, MP. Education: GDA Dip. *JJSA*, Post-Dip. in *painting*, *applied arts* FA. College Indore. Solos: *Dhoomimal*, TKS, SRAG, *JAG*, GAG, *CKAG*. Group participations: *LKA* Bhubaneshwar, National Exhibition & Trade Fair New Delhi, *Roopankar BB*, *AIFACS*, GAG, *CKAG*, *BAS*, All India Art Exhibition Kolkata. *Art* camps: organized by *LKA* New Delhi, Kalidas Academy Ujjain MP, *BB*. Awards & Fellowship: Amrita Sher-Gil Govt. of MP, Creative Painting Govt. of India. Member: Ex-member General Council *LKA* New Delhi, SZCC Nagpur, Advisory Committee for Rashtriya *LKA* Lucknow, Jury National Exhibition *LKA* New Delhi. Collections: *NGMA* & *LKA* New Delhi, *BB*, Air India Mumbai; International: USA, England, France, Japan, Germany, Switzerland, Canada, Norway, pvt. & corporates.

Suresh Choudhary practises an abstraction based on the use of the *palette knife*. His *forms* are in the *landscape* format, the strokes recollecting lost cities and the souls of storm-tossed ships.

He lives and works in Bhopal where he was an assistant Dir. of Agriculture.

Choudhury, Dhiraj (1936–) b. East Bengal, now Bangladesh. Education: Dip. in *FA*. GCA Kolkata; Studied in Delhi Polytechnic. Over 64 solos: Exhibited in India; 20 abroad including France, Switzerland, UK, USA, Singapore since 1957. Group participations: National & International with Miro & Dali in 1979, including France, Switzerland, UK, USA, Singapore. *Art* camps: Prime Minister's at Raj Bhavan Delhi. Awards: *LKA* & *NGMA* New Delhi, *BAAC* Kolkata & other National Awards. Founder Member: Quartet Artists, Artists' Forum, Gallery 26 & The Line New Delhi. Appointments: Was a lecturer & HoD at the *College of Art* New Delhi; Associated with Calcutta Painters. Publications: A portfolio of *prints* by 19 *artists*, also two books of *drawings* & edited an *art* magazine titled "Impression". Collections: *NGMA*, *LKA* & Raj Bhavan New Delhi, *BAAC* Kolkata; International: V&A, pvt. & corporates.

Dhiraj Choudhury's works are the reflection of his thoughts. At first he was inspired by the Brahmaputra river and the smell of its banks. Later in Kolkata, he became fascinated with the kinetic nature of *line*, experimented with changes in *tactile* pressure to get thick or thin, frail or robust sweeps and curves. His *paintings* are motivated by several social *themes*, including bride-burning, widowhood and the general plight of womanhood. There is also a sense of the *abstract* and the Indian miniature in his use of coloured, painted borders.

He lives and works in New Delhi.

Chowdhury, Jogen (1939–) b. Faridpur, Bengal. Education: Dip. in *FA*. *GCAC* Kolkata. Awarded French Govt. Scholarship Post-Grad. study in *painting* at the ENSBA learnt Italian *mosaic* & *fresco*; Later studied *etching* at Atelier 17 Paris. Solos: Kolkata, New Delhi, Chennai, Vadodara, Ahmedabad, Mumbai, *Santiniketan*; International: 1st solo ENSBA & later in 1976 Paris. Retrospective of the *drawings* in Kolkata, New Delhi & Mumbai in 1994. Group participations: National Exhibition, *Triennale* & *LKA* New Delhi, *BAAC* Kolkata, *CIMA* in Kolkata & New Delhi, Galliera, *GC* & *Gallery 7* Mumbai, Indian Artists at Raj Bhavan, *AIFACS*, *BAS*, *PUAG*, *Roopankar BB*; International: Cannes-Sur-Mer Festival France, *Biennale* in Sao Paulo Brazil, Cuba & Turkey, Asian Art Fukuoka Japan, Hirshhorn Museum Washington & Indian Art Exhibition New York USA, Contemporary Indian Painters in London, Oxford, Tokyo, Switzerland & Seoul. *Art* camps: Hudco New Delhi, Indo-French Kolkata; International: Bangladesh. *Auction*: Christie's Helpage India, Heart & Osian's Mumbai, Heart New Delhi. Awards: Chandigarh, *AFA*, University, College of Arts and Crafts & *BAAC* Kolkata, *AIFACS*. Member: Calcutta Painters a group representing Kolkata reality; Founder Member: Gallery 26, Artists' Forum. Appointments: Has been a designer at the *WSC* Chennai, *Curator* of *paintings* at the Rashtrapati Bhavan New Delhi; In 1987, he left New Delhi & joined *KB* at *Santiniketan* where he was the Principal. Collections: *NGMA* New Delhi, *BAAC* Kolkata, *Chandigarh Museum* & University, *Roopankar*, *CYAG*, *CKP*; International: Masanori Fukuoka & Glenbarra Museum Japan, Chester & Davida Hertwitz Boston, V&A.

Sinuous *outlines* and flaccid flesh draped in thick cotton appeared in Jogen Chowdhury's works for the first time after his return from France. He worked with *drawings* in *charcoal* and *ink* rather than *oil-painting* for several years, using people and objects from everyday life and experience. These objects are juxtaposed on a flat plane; the *handling* is at once personal and whimsical. These organic shapes

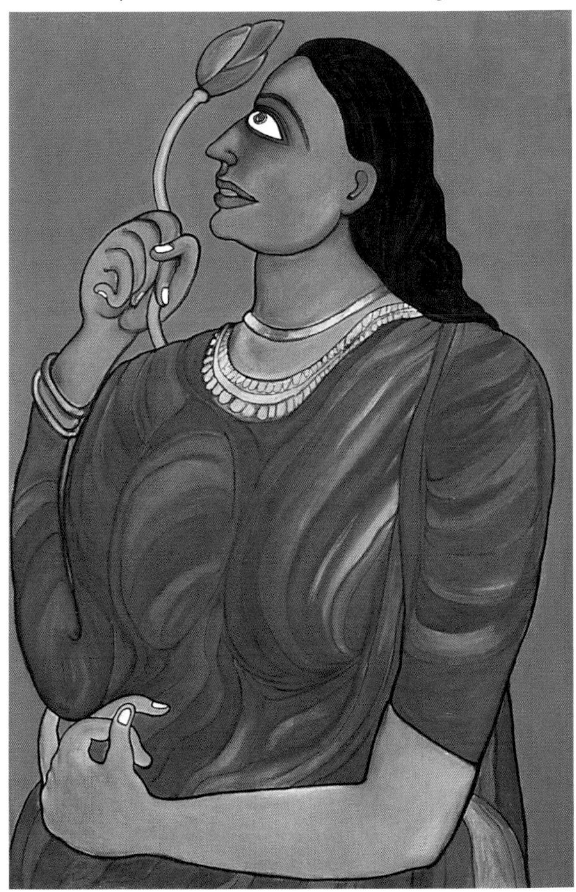

Chowdhury, Jogen: "Lotus Lover", *Oil* on *Canvas*, 1990–94, 61x92 cm.

and fecund females have a certain amount of *fantasy* invested in them as well. Strange leaping tigers, lush foliage and over ripe fruits and vegetables are all part of the Jogen Chowdhury *vocabulary*. There is more than a hint of the *Kalighat Pat style painting* in his use of soft *outlines* and *distortions*. His *oil paintings* too display the same features with the *colour* merely adding another interesting aspect to his works.

He lives in *Santiniketan*.

Choyal, P.N. (1924–) b. Kota, RAJ. Education: Dip. in *FA*. & DTT (Diploma in *tempera technique*) School of Arts & Crafts Jaipur; Govt. Dip. in *painting JJSA*; Attended Slade College of Art London. Solos & Group shows: Jaipur, Kota, Udaipur RAJ, *BAAC* Kolkata, *AIFACS*, *Dhoomimal*, TKS, *ISOA*, *JAG*, *SAI*; International: Japan. Group participations: *LKA*, National & International *Biennales* & *Triennales* Bhopal, *BAAC* Kolkata; International: Exhibition Brazil Sao Paulo, Kyoto Japan, Singapore, Germany. *Art* camps, seminars & workshops: Mumbai, Udaipur, Agra, Mandav MP, KAR Academy; Attended *fresco* & *mural* camp *Banasthali Vidyapith*; Veteran *Artist AIFACS*. Awards: National Award *LKA* New Delhi, IAFA Amritsar, *AIFACS*. Appointments: Fellow of the RAJ *LKA*. Collections: *NGMA* & *LKA* New Delhi, *Chandigarh Museum*; International: Yamaso Bijitsu Art Gallery Japan.

P.N. Choyal learnt the traditional *techniques* of *wash painting*, *tempera* and *miniature painting* under the tutelage of *Sailendranath Dey* and *Ram Gopal Vijaivargiya* of the Jaipur School of Art. He was also acquainted with Western academics. His subjects were always from the real world, the women of RAJ, the picturesque countryside, windows and walls. His works offer fragmented *collage* of *forms*, both human and otherwise, suggesting the violence of *contemporary* life. He uses *abstract* expressionist gestural slashes of *paint* to *outline* the human *form*. His later series titled "Dissolving Ruins", clearly expresses the architectural ruins without myths, *legend* or narratives.

He lives and works in Udaipur, RAJ.

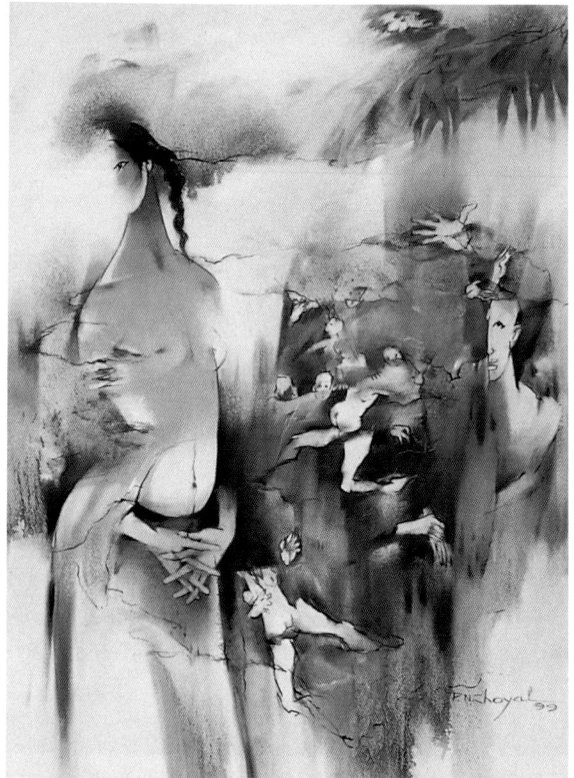

Choyal, P.N.: "Life as Such", *Oil* on *Canvas*, 122x92 cm.

Choyal, Shail (1945–) b. Kota, RAJ. Education: Dip. in *art RSA*, M.A. in *painting* University of Udaipur, Ph.D. Nathdwara School of Painting; Specialized in *printmaking* Slade School London. Solos: New Delhi, Jaipur, Kota, Mumbai; International: UK, Paris, Spain, Latvia, Bali, Japan. Group participations: Chennai, Bangalore, Lucknow, Jaipur, Chandigarh, *LKA Triennales* New Delhi, *AFA* Kolkata, *AIFACS*, *CYAG*, *JAG*; International: UK, Tokyo, Japan, Cuba, Switzerland, Holland, Spain, France, Germany, USA, Austria, Belgium, Italy, Indonesia. *Art* camps & workshops: Several in India; International: Indonesia, Russia. Awards: *AFA* Kolkata, *BAS*, *AIFACS*, AIKS, National Scholarship Ministry of Culture. Fellowship: British Council. Member: *AAJ* Udaipur. Appointments: Was a Prof. in the Dept. of FA. Sukhadia University Udaipur.

Shail Choyal is both a *painter* and printmaker, using *oils* and *mixed media* with equal facility. His *style* marks him as a follower of the traditional miniature *style painting* in RAJ—especially in his space-division and choice of brilliant *colours*. The use of certain *motifs* like the architectural *details* of cusped *arches* and pillars, chequered tiles and ladies peeping through Jharokhas (balcony) evoke a nostalgic feeling, both for the *art* and the life of the past.

Shail Choyal lives in Udaipur.

Choyal, Surjeet Kaur (1948–) b. Jaipur. Education: M.A. in *painting* University of Udaipur, studied in *art FFA* (*MSU*). Solos: RB Jaipur, *JAG*, *Dhoomimal*. Group participations: Chennai, Bangalore, Jaipur, Udaipur, Chandigarh, *Triennales LKA* & Kala Mela New Delhi, *AIFACS*, *CYAG*, *JAG*, *BAS*; International: *Biennale* Fukuoka Japan. Group show: Frankfurt. Awards: RAJ *LKA*, AFA Amritsar, National Exhibition New Delhi, *AIFACS*. Senior Fellowship: Govt. of India. Member: *AAJ* Udaipur. Collections: *NGMA* & *LKA* New Delhi, SKP; International: Fukuoka Museum Japan.

Surjeet Kaur Choyal uses the *painterly techniques* of *photo-realism* to create a surreal world of *images* and objects. There is an undercurrent of fear in her meticulously rendered *paintings* of people standing against architectural features like doors and windows. She has also been interested in Social Commentary, especially concentrating on the subjugation of women. Her later works show the use of photography, in this case, of ancient royalty. She paints them in *sepia tones*, placing them against an ambiguous *background* of *colour* stains and patches.

She lives and works in Udaipur, RAJ.

Christian Art The *art* that propagates Christianity. Early Christian art in the West was limited to the use of certain representative symbols such as the anchor, lamb, fish and orante in dark catacombs during the period of persecution in the Roman Empire. It was only after Emperor Constantine converted to Christianity and made it the state religion, that churches were built and embellished with *mosaics*, *stained glass* and *icons*. The *style* developed over the centuries, from the formal *frontality* of *Byzantine Art* to the graceful attenuation of the *Gothic* period. It was the *Renaissance* which saw a further flowering of Christian art, e.g., "The Last Supper" of Leonardo da Vinci and the Sistine Chapel of Michelangelo. Christian art has continued to be a source of inspiration in the West and in Latin American countries to this day. In India, Christian art began with the imitation of Biblical pictures by Akbar's *artists* at the Mughal court. Certain *artists* of the 20th century have also depicted Christian stories and symbols in their work. *Jamini Roy* was one of the first to use the iconic *forms* of the Crucifixion, the Last Supper and *portraits* of Jesus Christ. *Francis Newton Souza*, also painted series of works based on Christian subjects. Other *artists* to have painted on similar *themes* include *Maqbool Fida Husain*, *Krishen Khanna* and *Alphonso A. Doss*.

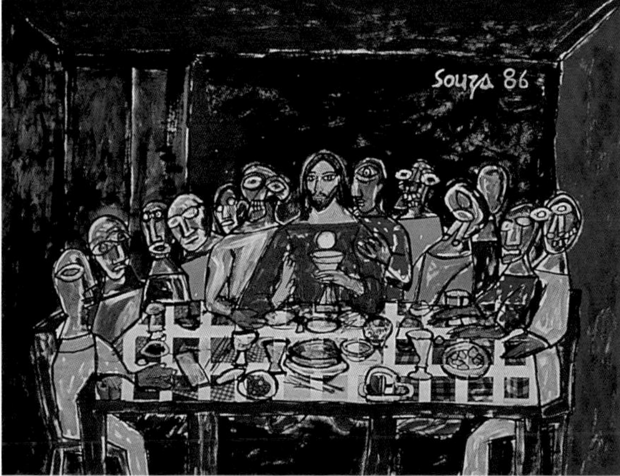

Christian Art: *Francis Newton Souza*, "Last Supper", *Oils*.

Chughtai, Muhammed Abdur Rehman (1897–1975) Also known as Rahman, b. Lahore now Pakistan. Education: Mayo School of Art Lahore—Dip. photo lithography, later a student of *printmaking* in London; Trained under *Abanindranath Tagore* in Kolkata. Solos: *ISOA*; International: London, Paris Punjab FA. Society Lahore his home town. Group participations: Hyderabad, *AFA* Kolkata, *NGMA* New Delhi, & National Art Galleries. International: Royal Academy England. *Auctions*: Heart Mumbai & New Delhi. Awards: Title of Khan-Bahadur by the British Govt. of India; Appointments: Lecturer in Chromolithography Mayo School of Art Lahore; Appreciation in Europe as an Indian *artist* with traditional *style* before Independence. Publications: Several volumes of *reproductions*. Collections: *NGMA* New Delhi, *SJM* Hyderabad, National Art Gallery Chennai, Central Museum & Mayo School of Art Lahore.

Muhammed Abdur Rehman Chughtai was a photographer and a *drawing* teacher early in his life, after the untimely demise of his father. In the beginning his *art* was known for its linear *line sketches* and later his *style* blended the *Lyricism* of the *Bengal School* with the fastidious attention to *detail* that one notices in *Mughal miniatures*. Many of the *paintings* show his minute study of Islamic *architecture* with its geometricity and delicate cusped arches, while his *draughtsmanship* is comparable to the sinuous *outlines* of Islamic *calligraphy*. Chughtai also did some *etchings*, which are similar in *style* to his *linear paintings*. Some of his works carry echoes of *Abanindranath Tagore's wash style* and literary subject matter; yet his figural *contours* and sophisticated colouring owe more to *Art Nouveau* and *Persian art* than to the *Bengal School*.

An *artist* of undivided India, Muhammed Abdur Rehman Chughtai's *themes* were both literary and historical, with Pan-Islamic and erotic subjects being a favourite. He also painted Hindu subjects, including a *watercolour* "Radha and Krishna". Though he drew delicate *pen* and *ink drawings* based on oriental fantasies, his *paintings* were usually rendered in *transparent* and harmonious *colour washes* with a touch of *tempera* to capture luminosity. Muhammed Abdur Rehman Chugtai emigrated to Pakistan after the partition.

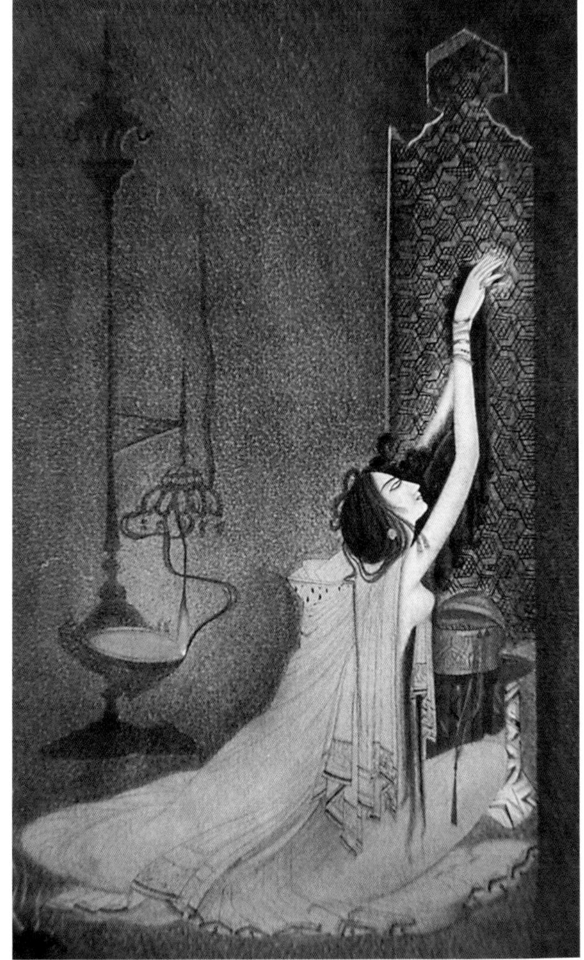

Chughtai, Muhammed Abdur Rehman: "Untitled", *Watercolours Wash*, early 20th century, 30x18 cm.

CIMA Gallery (Kolkata). The Centre of International Modern Art (CIMA) was set up in 1993 in Kolkata under the auspices of the Ananda Bazar group of publishing. It was conceptualized to be a vital link between *artists, critics* and collectors. It is a complete resource and documentation centre with *restoration* and evaluation facilities. CIMA maintains an extensive library of archival materials, films, slides and tapes besides exhibition *space* spread over 11,000 sq.ft. with strict temperature and humidity control. CIMA also publishes books and catalogues on *art* besides organizing lectures by eminent *art historians* and *critics*, both Indian and International. The gallery represents *Manjit Bawa, Atul Dodiya, Anjolie Ela Menon* and *Thotha Vaikuntham* among others.

Cinema When applied to *arts*, it is a relatively new *medium* of *visual* expression. It relies on still pictures moving at a certain pace to give the *illusion* of continuous movement and thus narration. The history of cinema in India begn in 1899 when H.S. Bhatavadekar produced short films & documentaries. This was almost parallel to the development of this *medium* in France & USA. However the first full-length silent feature film was produced by Dada Saheb Phalke followed by the first talkie "Alam Ara" by Ardeshir Irani in 1931. Today, the Mumbai Film Industry (Bollywood) is the largest producer of feature films in the world.

It is also used as a means of expression by several *artists* especially those in the performance, environmental or *happening* category. Several *happenings* in fact, rely solely on cinematic or videographic technology, as a means of recording split second actions. Also, cinema has been exploited as a *medium* to record the lives or working methods of certain *artists*. The film on Jackson Pollock's studio methods for example led to the coining of the *term action painting* as also the understanding of the *technique*. In India several films have been made for and by *painters*, one of the most famous being "Through the eyes of a Painter" by *Maqbool Fida Husain* who also went on to experiment with this *medium* to emphasise importance of *treatment* over subject. His films "Gaja-Gamini" and "Meenaxi" have also been released commercially. Several *painters* including *Kanu Desai, Shiavax Chavda, Baburao Painter* designed sets and worked as *Art* Dir. for films. Refer *Graphic Design, Indian Film Industry, Atul Dodiya, Shamkant Jadhav, P. Krishnamurthy, Vivan Sundaram*.

Cipher Symbols, initials or signs in the *form* of a monogram used in the work of *art*, often used by *artists* in place of a full signature. *Abanindranath Tagore* and his followers tried the Japanese method of signing works in a vertical format. Refer *Brushwork, Ideal Art, Tribal Art, Thumb Impression, Sudhakar K. Lawate, Shiavax Chavda, Shankar Palsikar, K.C.S. Paniker, B. Prabha, Ganesh Haloi*.

Cire Perdue=*lost wax process*. It is an ancient *technique* used in *casting metal*, especially *bronze* objects. The *sculptor* or craftsman first makes a *piece mould* of the *sculpture* in *plaster*, over which he applies a layer of *wax*, and *fills* with *plaster* core (a mixture of *plaster* and brick powder), then nails it to hold the core and outer shell after opening the piece mould. He attaches *wax* and resin rods for runners/*air vents*. Liquid *plaster* mixed with brick powder, is again applied over this *wax* work and left to harden. The *wax* is later removed by dewaxing, by baking the *mould*, which is put into a sandpit, and rammed. Hot molten *metal* (*bronze*) is poured into one of the risers/runners, the channel made for *casting*. Air and gas is thrown out through the *air vent*. As soon as the *bronze* comes in contact with the outer air, it hardens. The *model* is now allowed to cool down before the outer *mould* is chipped off to reveal the *metal* object within. The object will have long rod adhering to it, which are filed off and a neat finishing and polishing process is followed.The cire perdue process is a 4700 years old method. It was used in India from the time of *Mohenjo Daro* and *Harappa* civilizations using the *clay*, cowdung and paddy husk instead of *plaster*. This process was also used then to *cast* their *ritual bronzes* while the PALLAVA and CHOLA *sculptors* used the same process to *cast* their *bronze images* of SHIVA and VISHNU. The Eastern *technique* involved the use of Dhuna i.e. resin plus mustard oil; while Southern *technique* used *wax* on *clay* core *model*. Refer *South Indian Bronzes*.

The process and it's applications generally run as follows:

A.	Piece *mould* from *sculpture*	a ready *sculpture*, piece *mould*, mother *mould*.
Aa.	*Wax model cast* from piece *mould*	a. *wax* layer (outer surface modelled). b. heat proof core (mixture of *plaster* and brick dust). c. *metal* pins.
C.	Heat proof mould surrounding *wax model*	d. *wax* cone shape *mass*. e. thick *wax* rods or runners. f. thin *wax* rods or runners.
D.	Reversed *mould*	g. *air vents*.

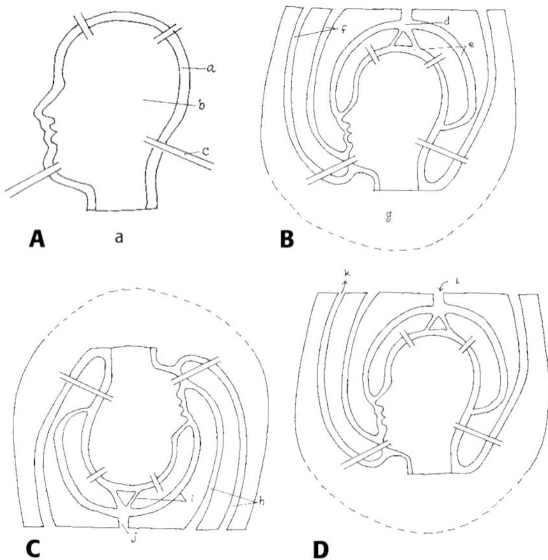

Cire Perdue: Diagram A, Aa, B, C, and D.

with *wax* pouring out.	h. *wax* runners (channel).
	i. cone shaped funnel from which melting *wax* escapes.
E. Molten *bronze* being poured in the *runner*.	j. air escapes.
	k. molten *bronze*.

Cityscape Cityscapes serve as a *backdrop* to *figures*, which are mostly painted in *watercolours*, *tempera* and *oils*. Stylized *figures* and the city *landscape backgrounds* are the *key* note of *Company painting* in India. Everyday life in the city/town became one of the *motifs* of the *artist's* experience with painted streets that also documented the important events of India's struggle for freedom. Later on *artists* experimented with the Eclecticism of *Cubism* and *Impressionism* to create cityscapes in *tempera*, *gouache* and *oil*. Refer *Suresh Awari*, *Veena Bhargava*, *Bikash Bhattacharjee*, *Bhupen Khakhar*, *Sudhir Patwardhan*, *Ram Kumar*, *Piraji Sagara*.

Classical **1.** A period in Greek history (circa 5th centry BC–4th century BC) when, *art*, philosophy and society achieved the pinnacle of excellence. *Art* especially was based on the *ideal* rather than the real. **2.** Refers to the established excellence in a *form* of *art*. Classicism derived from the classical *style*. **3.** Classical also means *style*, simple, serene, proportionate & finished or *art* of a later *period* that revived the classical *ideals*, e.g., *Renaissance*, *neo-Classicism*. **4.** Also means enduring, perfection. In India, the *Gupta* period is usually referred to as the Classical or Golden period of *art*. Refer *Ajanta*, *JJSA*, *KB Santiniketan*, *Academy*, *Anatomy*, BARAMASA, *Renaissance*, *Madras School of Art*, *Bengal School*, *Ramkinkar Baij*, *Raja Ravi Varma*, *P. Vijyalakshmi*, *P.L. NarasimhaMurti*.

Clay A fine-grained earth deposit composed chiefly of *aluminium* silicate, or plastic earth, which holds its shape when wet and becomes hard when dried or when baked at a high temperature. Used for making *pottery* and *sculpture* and other objects. The object will *form* a solid *mass*, which is hard to destroy, and the *colour* of the final object depends on the *composition* of the soil. During the time of the *Indus Valley Civilization*, clay was the material, which was widely used for building towns and paved a path as a continuing *tradition* in Punjab and Sindh. *Ramkinkar Baij*, *Debi Prasad RoyChowdhury* were the first *artist* of the *contemporary* period to make *models* in clay, *cement* and other materials. Refer *Abstract Sculpture*, *Casting*, *Ceramics*, *China Clay*, *Clay Water*, *Terracotta*, *Treatment*, *Wetting Down*, *Sadanandji Bakre*, *Jyotsna Bhatt*, *Sudhir R. Khastgir*, *Mahendra Pandya*, *Rajendar Tiku*, *Ravinder G. Reddy*, *Himmat Shah*.

Clay Water Known as *slip*, this is *clay* mixed with water to a milky consistency. It can be used to hold different *clay* shapes together or to coat a *clay* object with another *colour*. Also used as a *parting agent* in making *plaster moulds*. Refer *Abstract Sculpture*, *Casting*, *Sadanandji Bakre*, *Debi Prasad RoyChowdhury*, *Himmat Shah*, *Vinayakrao Venkatrao Wagh*.

Cloison=partition, it is used to describe the thin wires soldered (joined to) on to a *metal* backing so as to form small cells to be filled with coloured *enamel* powder in the process of *enamelling*. This is known as *Cloisonnism*. The *technique* has been in use since ancient *times*, especially in the Byzantine period for making jewellery and book-covers. In Indian *sculpture*, e.g. *Shankar Nandagopal* employs this *technique* to make *copper* and *steel reliefs*.

Cloisonnism Cloisonnism also refers to a *technique* in *painting*. The *outline* is boldly drawn and the *colours* are flatly filled in as seen in *miniature paintings*, *Thanjavur (Tanjore) Painting* and much of *folk art*. *Jamini Roy* also used heavy *outlines* while *Tyeb Mehta* created the *outline* by leaving the *canvas* bare. Refer *Cloison*, *Back-Glass Painting*, *Atasi Barua*, *Vajubhai D. Bhagat*, *Surinder K. Bhardwaj*, *R.B. Bhaskaran*, *Nandalal Bose*, *Jogen Chowdhury*, *Muhammed Abdur Rehman Chughtai*.

Closed Form The opposite of *open form*. In *sculpture* it means self-contained and balanced and does not reach out into the surrounding *space*. In *painting* it refers to the compositional *balance*. *Renaissance paintings* are usually referred to as having a closed form, e.g., certain *paintings* by *Raja Ravi Varma*, *Pestonjee Bomanjee*, while *Baroque* and mannerist *paintings* are open formed.

Codex Ancient *term* meaning a book made up of separate leaves or pages, as opposed to a scroll. This *form* was first used in the 1st century AD. In India it was written on *palm leaves* either with *black*, *gold* or *silver colours*. The earliest manuscript still surviving date to the 9th century AD and are in the PALA *style*. Refer GANJIFA, *Pala Miniatures*, *Jain Illuminated Manuscripts*, *Ganga Devi*, *Santokba Dudhat*.

Cold Working The process of working on *metal* (hammering and *chasing*) without first heating it. TANTRIC *forms* were usually embossed on *metal* in this *manner* with one of these processes to create the *symbolic forms*. Refer *Repousse*, *Chipping Mould*, *Embossing*, *Ram Kishore Yadav*, *Pilton Kothawalla*.

Collage The word is derived from the French 'Coller' meaning 'to stick'. This *technique* involves pasting *paper*, cloth, sand and other assorted objects on to a *paper*, *canvas* or *wood ground*. It was used by P. Picasso and G. Braque during their analytical cubist phase and later by the

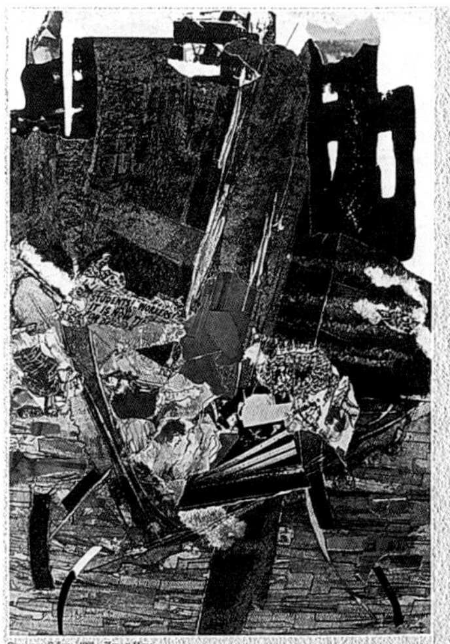

Collage: *B.R. Panesar*: "Cityscape Collage", 1988, 75x55 cm.

dadaists and surrealists. Today, collage forms a regular part of *mixed media painting*. e.g., *Shakila, C. Douglas, Vishwanath M. Sholapurkar*. Refer *Abstract Painting, Assemblage, Combine Painting, Constructivism, Cubism, De'collage, Decoupage, Facing, Found Object, Frottage, High Relief, Junk Art, Media, Mixed Media, New Realism, Painter, Paper-Pulp Casting, Photo-montage, Relief Painting, Surrealism, Vignette, Wood, Vasant D. Agashe, Krishnaji Howlaji Ara, K.P. Chidambarakrishnan, Vishnu Chinchalkar, P.N. Choyal, Partha Pratim Deb, Avinash S. Deo, R.S. Dhir, Vasant Ghodke, Paresh C. Hazra, Reba Hore, C. Jagdish, Pilton Kothawalla, Anjolie Ela Menon, Brinda C. Miller, M.K. Muthusamy, Vamona A. Navelcar, B.R. Panesar, Bhanwar Singh Panwar, Dashrath Patel, Janak Patel, L. Anand Patole, Sagara Piraji, Katayun Saklat, Kashinath Salve, Sumant V. Shah, Vinod Shah, Shakila, Gulam Mohammed Sheikh, Vishwanath M. Sholapurkar, Rameshwar Singh, Gopal G. Subhedar, Anupam Sud, Amrit Lal Vegad, K. Vasant Wankhede*.

College of Art The College of Art New Delhi was founded in 1942 by the Ministry of Education. It was first known as the Dept. of Art and was under the aegis of the Delhi Polytechnic. It first functioned from the old St. Stephen's Library Building. Later it moved to the Birla Pavilion and Promila College, from there it moved to its present premises. From the earlier dip. course the college, has now advanced to offering degree courses at the under-graduate and post-grad. levels. The three dept. in the college are the Dept. of *Painting, Sculpture* and *Applied Art*. There are places to set up an *art* gallery and offer post-dip. courses in *photography, printmaking* and *art* history. There are various extra curricular activities being held including dance, music and drama competition besides the college magazine, "Impressions" which was launched in 1994.

College of Fine Arts (CFA) (Thiruvananthapuram) The college was founded in 1935, by the then Maharaja of Travancore, H.H.V.T. Rama Varma. It was first known as The Maharaja's School of Arts, which offered coaching classes in *arts* and *crafts*. It was later transferred to the control of the University of Travancore. In 1957 it was brought under the control of the Dept. of Technical Education, Govt. of Kerala. In 1975 it was upgraded as The CFA and now provides instruction and training in *painting, sculpture* and *applied Arts*. The degree course of four years duration was implemented in 1979–80.

Collography This is a process in *printmaking* by which the *design* to be printed is built on the surface of the *plate* (either by block or a piece of cardboard) by pasting or glueing. The block is then inked and the *print* is taken. Both the *intaglio* and the *relief print* is possible in this *technique*.

The technique started in India only in the 19th century, when some missionaries in Bengal commissioned the first press. In 1816, the first *lithography* book "Oonoodah Mongul" (book on poem) was released by Jairam Das (who ran the *lithography* firm). Towards the end of the century, it took firm roots. Refere *Krishnan Ahuja, Naina Dalal, Relief Printing*.

Collotype An early photomechanical printing process in which the *images* are transferred from a raised *gelatine film* surface on a glass *support*. The *print* is almost continuous in *tone*, with no *half-tone* screen effects. Refer *Jyotirindranath Tagore*.

Colour 1. A *paint* or *pigment*. Its major property is the colour sensation it emits, which is what defines it's use. **2.** A wavelength of *light* reflected from an object or surface that creates a *visual* sensation. Colour plays a major role in Indian *art* right from *Ajanta* and *miniature painting*. In Indian Art colours speak of emotion, sentiment and RASA. India has a centuries old *tradition* of using colours made of plant substances, vegetable, *oils* and gem *stones* that have had a long-lasting effect. Meticulously prepared, these colours posses a distinctively Indian *hue*. Colour, its prepration and application are the subject of various treatises in the CHITRASUTRA and other antient Indian texts. Refer BHAVA, *Malwa, Natural Colours, Tint and Tone, Value, Shade, Jamini Roy, Abanindranath Tagore, Gaganendranath Tagore*.

Colour-Field Painting The *term* is primarily used to denote the type of American *Abstract Expressionism*, that differs from *gestural* or *action painting*. Instead of multi-coloured strokes or splashes of *colour*, colour-field *painters* stain large *canvases* with *tones* of unvarying *hues*, suggesting large fields of *colour* that suggest an infinity beyond the *canvas*. *Artists* included M. Rothko, A. Reinhardt, R. Motherwell and B. Newman. Refer *Shobha Broota*.

Colour-Grey The *hue* that results from mixing *complementary colours* (i.e. red and green; blue and orange; and yellow and violet). The *colour* is not a true grey. Refer *Grisaille, Ram Kumar*.

Colour Printing & Four Colour Process Printing by any process involving more than one *colour*, known as *multi block colour printing*. The standard *colours* used are cyan (blue), yellow, magenta and *black*. Earlier it was known as chromolithography or four colour process. Refer *Lithography, Collography, Single Block Colour Printing, Key Block, Serigraphy, Krishna N. Reddy, Rini Dhumal*.

Colour Wheel, Colour Circle The colour wheel is necessary to understand *colour* theory. The three *primary colours* red, yellow and blue are placed at equidistant *points* around a circle. The *secondary colours* and other intermediary *hues* are placed in-between.

Colour Wheel.

This colour wheel indicates the *complementary colours*, adjacent or *analogous colours*. By adding *white* to any of these *colours* hues or tints are obtained while *tones* are achieved by adding *black*. *Manuscript paintings*, *Tribal art and folk art* were mostly executed in *primary colours*, and later in the *secondary colours*. Refer *Nandalal Bose*, *Jamini Roy*, *Jaganath M. Ahivasi*, *Narayan S. Bendre*.

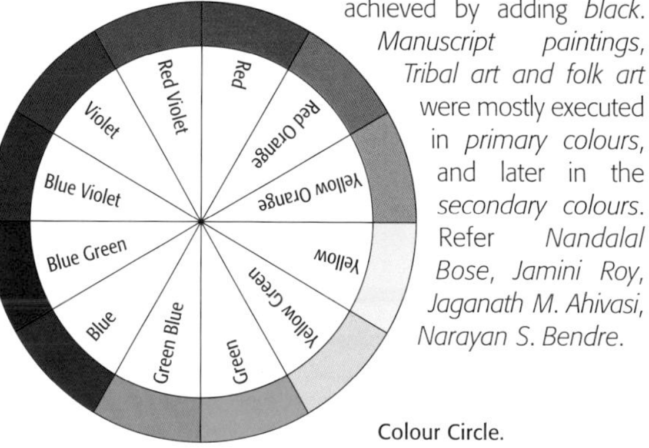

Colour Circle.

Coloured Ground A *painting ground* that has been treated with a final layer of *colour*. Usually *white* is normally used as a *ground colour*. Refer *Bal Chhabda*, *Ram Kumar*, *Laxman Shreshtha*.

Combine Painting A three-dimensional *collage*. The *term* was coined by R. Rauschenberg, the American Pop *artist* who used stuffed goats, tyres and mattresses in his *painting* by attaching them to the surface of the *canvas* and *painting* over them. *Vivan Sundaram*, *Navjot Altaf* and *Shakuntala Kulkarni* have worked on similar lines.

Combing A *texture* created by *dragging* the teeth of a comb over a freshly applied coat of *pigment* resulting in thin parallel *lines* of *colour*. Refer *Rekha Krishnan*, *P. Srinivasan*, *K.G. Subramanyan*, *Setlur Gopal Vasudev*.

Commercial Art Synonym for *applied art*. It refers to *design* and decoration especially in the field of advertising, *illustration* and photography, along with *craft* and jewellery designing. However, the distinguishing *line* between the two fields was increasingly difficult to draw in India with *artists* and designers both influenced by the rich traditional *arts* and *crafts* of India. *Jamini Roy* was influenced by *Kalighat pat painting*, while *Maqbool Fida Husain* brought the large sweeping *style* of *film poster design* into his *art*.

Company School/Company Painting Named after the British East India Company, company painting was the attempt of the English patrons to alter the *aesthetic* sense of indigenous *artists*, by introducing him to Western *techniques* and *style*. The local *artists* in British settlements like Calcutta, Patna, Varanasi, Lucknow, Delhi and Tanjore learnt by observing travelling Western (mostly British) *artists* like the Daniells,Tilly Kettle and William Hodges.

As a genre, Company painting was interspersed with elements of the *picturesque landscape art* of Romanticist England. Local *artists* like Sheikh Muhammed Amir used *perspective* and lush *backgrounds* in the European *manner*. The *technique* changed with the use of new *media* like *watercolour* and mica (Sanskrit–Abhraka), rather than *gouache*. They no longer used bright, *primary colours* as in *miniature painting*; instead they used stark, sombre *hues* that the British appreciated.

The subjects appear to be painted snap-shots, essentially capturing *vignettes* of Indo-British life that would appear *picturesque* to the viewer back home. They include Indian Ayahs (maid servants) and servants taking care of their pony-riding wards, houses, market-places, and quaint temple-scenes. *Flora & fauna painting*, Indian occupations, festivals, and *portraits* of 'natives' (British term for the local people) were popular. A gentle *modelling* and shading was used instead of the flat decorativeness of Indian *miniature painting*. Company paintings are also known as Patna *painting* or *Bazaar paintings*. Refer *Artist*, *Attribution*, *Brushwork*, *Bust*, *Folk Art*, *Kalighat Pat*, *Kalighat Folk Painting*, *Landscape Format*, *Modern Style*, *Modernism*, *Modern Movement*, *Oil Paint*, *One-Point Perspective*, *Orthogonal*, *Painter*, *Painting*, *Shade*, *Style*, *Wood Block Printing*, *Wood Engraving*.

Complementary Colours These are the contrast *colours* that lie directly opposite each other on the *colour wheel*. Therefore, green is the complementary of red, whereas orange is the complementary of blue. These and other principles of *colour* were the study of *Raja Ravi Varma* with mysteries of *perspective* and *chiaroscuro*. Refer *Colour*, *Colour Wheel*, *Mixed Contrast*, *Op* or *Optical Art*, *Tonal Values*, *Thanjavur (Tanjore) Paintings*, *Chhaganlal D. Mistry*; Illustration–*Colour Wheel*.

Composition The *art* of combining various elements in *painting* or *sculpture*, in both *realistic* and *abstract* works, so that they may appear complete or satisfactory to the *artist*. The *term* only defines a concept, which is governed purely by the choice of the individual *artist*. This is true for all *artistic* expression through the ages from Prehistory to the present times, which including *Bengal Revivalism*, *Symbolic Art* and TANTRA *Art*. Refer *Abstract*, *All-over*, *Balance*, *Manjit Bawa*, *Laxman Shreshtha*, *K.C.S. Paniker*, *Raja Ravi Varma*.

Computer Art *Art*, mostly *drawings*, *paintings* and *graphics*, especially *calligraphy* and *commercial art*, produced with the aid of computers. The first such use of the computer dates back to the 1950s. In 1991, the computer-produced works of nine leading Indian *artists* including *Maqbool Fida Husain*, *Sayed Haider Raza* and

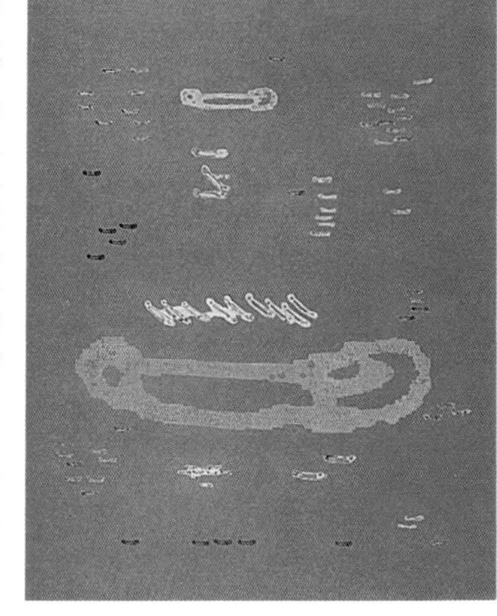
Computer Art: *Barwe Prabhakar*, "Eighty-Five Safety Pins", 1990, 150x120 cm.

Atul Dodiya were exhibited at the *JAG*. The computer is thus an addition to the vast array of tools available to the *contemporary artist*. Apart from the simulated traditional implements of *paintings* like the *brush*, the *pen*, *charcoal*, *crayons*, the *pencil*, and an infinite *palette* of *colours*, the computer also provides access to a variety of special *techniques* like instant enlargements, reductions, distortions, rotations, diffusion and multiplications as seen in the work of *Prabhakar Barwe* where he had replicated the humble safety pin several times. Refer *Half-tone*, *Modernism*, *Modern Movement*, *Akbar Padamsee*.

Conceptual Art, Concept Art According to conceptualists, an *abstract* idea or concept is of prime importance in a conceptual work of *art*, with the actual execution itself being perfunctory.

Language is an important tool of the conceptualist, who considered a work of *art* complete, by just stating or writing or advertising the concept of the work. Conceptual art, which means–having to do with *abstract* ideas, invites the active participation of the viewer by asking him to analyse and imagine the work. Here the *forms*, *colours* etc. used in *art* are more *symbolic* or expressive, rather than *realistic*. *Vivan Sundaram's* later works border on the conceptual. Refer *Abstract Art*, *Abstract Movement*, ATMA, *Composition*, *Critic*, *Fantasy*, *Figurative Art*, *Ideal*, *Ideal Art*, *Image*, *Installation*, KARMA, *Living Sculpture*, *Matter*, *Modern Style*, *Monumental*, *New Realism*, *Open Form*, *Sculpture*, *Serial Imagery*, *Theme*, *Tradition*, *Avtarjeet S. Dhanjal*, *Somnath Hore*, *Kanayi Kunhiraman*, *Nalini Malani*, *Anjolie Ela Menon*, *Dashrath Patel*, *Pushpamala N.*, *Ghulam Rasool Santosh*; Illustration–*Aku*, *Vivan Sundaram*.

Concrete A mixture of Portland *cement*, *aggregate* and water, concrete is commercially used for building purposes. However *artists* like *Ramkinkar Baij* have used it in making their outdoor *sculptures*. The *cement* mixture is rendered plastic and pliable by the addition of water. While it is in this state, it can be shaped by means of *casting* or *modelling*. After it hardens into a solid *mass*, it can be carved, polished or otherwise finished. Refer *Abstract Sculpture*, *Acrylics*, *Architecture*, *Cast Stone*, *Cement*, *Chasis*, *Dimension*, *Matter*, *Plein-air*, *Polychromatic Sculpture*, *Sand Blasting*, *Tensile Strength*, *White*; Illustration–*Ramkinkar Baij*, *Latika Katt*, *Pilloo Pochkhanawalla*, *Earth Art* & SHANKHA–*Kanayi Kunhiraman*.

Conservation International statutes describe conservation as any action (a) to determine the *nature* or properties of materials used (b) to understand and control causes of deterioration (c) to better the condition... of cultured holdings. Conservation has assumed great significance with rise in awareness about mankind's global heritage. Pioneering conservation work has been done in India indude the Sanchi STUPAS, the famed *frescoes* of *Ajanta*, the KAILASH temple at *Ellora* and many other works of *arts* and *architecture*. Institutions such as *INTACH* and *National Museum* in Delhi are focusing great public attention to the *art* and science of conservation and preservation; especially their work is dedicated to *Ellora*. Refer article "Preservation of Art Objects" page 383; INTACH.

Conservation Board Also known as *museum* board, used for framing and mounting. These mounts are made of high quality cotton rag fibres (with low *acid* content). *Prints*, *drawings* or *paintings* can be directly attached to the mounts by fabric strips or separately with fabric hinges and gummed *paper*. Even the backboard should be similar in order to protect the *art* work. Refer *Mat*, *Mughal Dynasty*, *Khodidas Parmar*, *K. Vasant Wankhede*.

Construction Refer *Architecture*, *Abstraction Geometric*, *Anti-Art*, *Creation*, *Constructivism*, *Dadaism*, *Environment Art*, *Mobile*, *Ready-Made*, *Vesara Style*, *Eric Bowen*, *Balbir Singh Katt*, *Shakuntala Kulkarni*, *Mohan Sharma*, *Vivan Sundaram*.

Constructivism *Art* movement, inspired by the machine culture. A Russian artists, Vladimir Tatlin developed *collage* into *relief constructions* using a variety of materials including wire, glass, and sheet *metal* between1913–17. Constructivism was first the expression of a deep conviction that the *artist* could contribute to society by entering directly into a rapport with machine production and architectural engineering and thus pave the way for the socialization of *art*. *Painting* and *sculpture* became part of the process through which *architecture* or industrial products were fully realized. Technically, all the essential elements of *form*, *mass*, the flat plane, *space*, *proportion*, *rhythm*, the natural *proportion* of the material used plus the function of the object were brought together in the final product. The other *artists* associated with this movement included A. Pevsner and N. Gabo. Refer *Cubism*, *Installation*, *Isms*, *Modernism*, *Modern Movement*, *Adi M. Davierwala*, *Ajit R. Desai*.

Conte Pencil A non-greasy carbon *pencil* in red, *black* or brown, for preparatory work not meant to be printed on a lithographic *plate* or *stone*. Refer *Chalk*, *Bikash Bhattacharjee*, *Jatin Das*.

Contemporary Pertaining to the present time. In *art*, it refers to the *art* scene, *graphic art*, *painters* and *sculptors* of the past decade. Making a distinctive dividing line between traditional Indian *art* and *sculpture* and *contemporary art forms* was the cultural conflict India went through with 250 years of western rule and influence in all aspects of political and social life. The period of *Company painting*, introduction of the Western academic system and the influence of European *Isms*, during which period the *artist* began experimentation that led to the current phase of personal self-expression. Cultural ethos and *tradition* thoughts still maintain their important position in Indian contemporary *style*. Most of the contemporary *artists* are from these schools–*Bengal School*, *Santiniketan*, *Bombay School*, *Madras School of Art*, *Calcutta School*, *Bansthali Vidyapith* RAJ. Refer *Academy*.

Content In *art terms* content refers to the subject matter or *theme* of the work. Later it came to refer to only material, when it was an *installation* or *conceptual art*. Content also represents the *artist* experience of *visual* reality. Both *form* and content co-exist harmoniously in the work of *art*. The *colour* study is also important.

In India, the *theme* or content has always been important, often being overwhelmingly religious in character. With the advent of *Modernism* content becomes increasingly the individual choice of the *artist*. *Raja Ravi Varma* chose to *paint* mythological *compositions*, while *Nandalal Bose* and *Jamini Roy* preferred to illustrate rural life. Social commentary became an intregral part of the work of the *artists* of the *Post-Independent* era. Refer *Expressionism, Image, Form, Adi Davierwala, Manoj Dutta, Rasik Durgashankar Raval, Shekhar Roy, Ghulam Rasool Santosh*.

Continuous Representation A *technique* used in *painting* or *relief sculpture* showing several successive incidents in a *narrative* against an apparently continuous *background*. This *technique* has been employed in depicting the JATAKA stories at *Ajanta*. Also known as continuous narration. Refer CHADDANTA, *Miniature Painting, Relief, Relief Sculpture, Space*.

Contour It is the *outline* which forms the border of a *composition* defining it in relation to another. By just changing the *texture* of the contour *line*, a good *artist* is able to suggest many things, e.g. a thick soft *line* would suggest fleshiness, while a blurred *line* with short strokes could depict hair. Refer *Nandalal Bose, G.A. Dandekar, Subrayalu Dhanapal, Raghav Kaneria, Prokash Karmarkar, Sudhir R. Khastgir Dinanath Pathy, L. Anand Patole, Lalu Prasad Shaw, Abanindranath Tagore, Kanhaiya Lal Verma*; Illustration–*Cartoon, Jatin Das*.

Contour Shading As against regular *modelling* with observation of the *light* and *shade*, contour shading means either lightening or darkening the edges of the *forms*. In the *Ajanta murals*, e.g., such *shading* is concentrated on the palms, hands, lips, etc. Refer *Bengal School, Shade, Muhammed Abdur Rehman Chughtai, Jahar DasGupta, Kavita Deuskar, Paramjeet Singh, Ram Gopal Vijaivargiya*.

Contrapposto Italian *term* meaning a pose in which the upper part of the human *torso* is twisted in the opposite direction to that of the lower half. It was developed by Greek *sculptors* and carried to extremes in the 16th century mannerist period. Similar poses are essence in TRIBHANGA. Refer *Mannerism*; Illustration–*Muhammed Abdur Rehman Chughtai*.

Cool Colour This refers to the family of blues, greens and violets. Cool colours appear to recede from the surface of the *painting* and create a cool feeling. Also known as retreating *colour* that seems to recede from picture plane. Some of *Narayan S. Bendre's, paintings* in *style* of *Pointillism* achieve the *tonal value* of cool colours. Refer *Colour*; Illustration–*Colour Wheel*, Seascape.

Copper A red-brown *metal*, believed to have been used by the primitive man. In North India copper replaced *stone* for tools and *weapons* in the *Indus Valley Civilization*. Copper being *cast* as *sculpture* as well as used in the *form* of thin sheets for *relief* and *intaglio* work. The addition of tin to copper resulted in *bronze alloy*, which is largely used in making instruments of war.

Pure copper is quite soft, and can be shaped by hammering. Copper sheets in various gauges (indication of thickness) are also used by printmakers for *etching* and *repousse* work. Refer *Bidri, Bite, Biting in, Brass, Bronze*, CHOLA, *Printmaking, Dhanraj Bhagat, Bishamber Khanna, Balan Nambiar, Ram Kishore Yadav, Janak J. Narzary, Shankar Nandaqopal*.

Copy A duplicate or imitation of an existing work of *art* either in *painting, graphics* or *sculpture*, the *artist* of the 1st decade of 20th century copied the *Ajanta, Ellora paintings* and from the sculptural *images* from all over India in the academic study, *artist Jaganath M. Ahivasi, Pestonjee Bomanjee, Nandalal Bose, Vidya Bhushan, Asit K. Haldar*. Refer *Replica, Artist's Proof, Pouncing, Reproduction, Variant*.

Court Artists/Court Painters/Court Paintings Refer *Bundi, Flora & Fauna Painting, Miniature Painting, Mughal Dynasty, Pahari Miniature Painting, Painter, Portrait*, RAGAMALA, *Ved Pal Sharma, K. Venkatappa*.

Crafts A *term* in *fine art* that refers to manual work from various materials, handicraft, involving the use of workmanship skills in the *creation* of utilitarian objects, e.g., in *backdrops, pottery*, textile, *leather, wood, metal* and *mixed media*. The first craft school was started at *Santiniketan* in WB. Refer *Fine Arts, Iron, Installation, Jagdish & Kamla Mittal Museum of Indian Art* (*Hyderabad*), *National Handicrafts and Handlooms Museum New Delhi, Santiniketan, K.C. Aryan, K.G. Subramanyan, Dhirendrakrishna Deb Barman*; Illustration–*Aku, Nita Thakore*.

Crayon Similar process to *oil pastels*, the powdered *pigments* are mixed in *wax* and sticks are moulded for *drawing* and colouring, e.g. *Rabindranath Tagore* experimented with crayons in 1932. Refer *Chalk, Chalk Drawing, Conte Pencil, Frottage, Lithography, Oil Crayons, Screen Printing, Silk Screen Printing, Repousse, Gobardhan Ash, C. Douglas, Ram Kishore Yadav*.

Crayon Manner A *technique* to reproduce any work of *art* giving it the effect of *chalk* or *crayon style*, either in *drawing, painting* and *lithography* where the *texture* is a result of the artists' *technique* e.g. *Narayan S. Bendre* and *Krishna N. Reddy*. Refer *Gouache, Malwa, Lithography, Anis Farooqi*.

Creation The act or process of producing or bringing into existence. Creation also means the original work of an individual. Creativity is the faculty of an *artist* that produces original and innovative work. Creativity is the general measurement of the originality of an *artist*. In India groups of *artists* from different areas with varied *culture, styles* and *technique* come together to *form* a common creative path. *Bengal School*, the *Kalighat Pat*, *Kalighat Folk Paintings* are examples. So are works of *Raja Ravi Varma*, *Abanindranath Tagore*, *Gaganendranath Tagore* and *Rabindranath Tagore*. Thus, common *content* in creative processes established completely new vistas while still retaining the individual creative spirit of the *artists*.

Crimson–The Art Resource (CRAR) (Bangalore). CRAR an *art* gallery situated in a commercial shopping complex in Bangalore. It was opened in 1989 by Silloo Daruwalla and has since then had a number of group shows of *artists* together *with P.N. Choyal*, *Rekha Rao*, *Bhaskar Rao*, *Yusuf*, and one man shows of upcoming *artists*. This *art* resource has a branch in Mumbai.

Critic The *term* refers to a person who analyzes *style* and originality of a work of *art* or *artist*, and also its context with reference to historical, social and political *background*. With the beginning of *Bengal School*, *Modernism* was a new found need for a person, not necessarily the *artist*, to analyze the *modern* works, speak to the *artist* and critique him/her and the works, while at the same time demystifying the process of making *art* and interpreting it to the *art* loving layman. In earlier generations, the *art* historians, chronologically record *art* works; the critic however speaks mostly of *art* of the present. In India *art criticism* is a relatively *modern* concept. Refer *Art Criticism*, *Art Deco*, *Dhoomimal*, *Jaya Appaswamy*, *Bhupen Khakhar*, *Dinkar Kowshik*, *Ratan Parimoo*, *Shantilal Shah*, *Prem Chandra Goswami*, *Natu J. Parikh*, *Prem Singh*, *Umesh Varma*.

Cross-Hatching A *technique* for creating tonal variations usually in *pencil* or *pen*, by laying a series of parallel, crisscross strokes, first, in one direction and then in the opposite direction. Also used by printmakers mostly in *dry-point* process.The printmakers of the 19th century in Bengal had noticed that the European *artists* resorted to cross-hatching to make their *drawings* volumetric, and employed the same *technique* in their *prints*. Refer *Hatching*, *Line Engraving*, *Mansing L. Chhara*, *Dhruva Mistry*, *Natver Mistry*, *Anupam Sud*, *Murlidhar Nangare*; Illustration–*Laxma Goud*.

Crown Refer MUKUTA.

Cubism Originally the *term* applied to the distorted works of P. Cézanne, P. Picasso and G. Braque when it was shown at Kahnweilars Gallery; the first truly cubist works are the *landscapes* and *still life* of these *artists* in which a geometrization of *form* is seen along with multiple point *perspective*. The next phase known as Analytic Cubism, saw the cubic *forms* become even smaller, merging into an over all *pattern* with the use of a limited *colour palette* until it became almost impossible to decipher the subject. *Colour* was once again introduced in the final phase of Cubism, which is known as Synthetic Cubism, from its combination of *painting* with real material, i.e. collage. Cubism was to influence a whole lot of *modern movements* including *Futurism*, Suprematism, *neo-Plasticism*, *Constructivism* and later Post World War II movements. In India, the first cubist *artist Gaganendranath Tagore* had also opted for a similar geometricisation of *form* in some of his works in *wash* and *tempera*. *Post-Independence artists* were very much influenced by cubist theories and *style*. These included *Jehangir Sabavala*, *Sankho Chaudhuri* and *K.G. Subramanyan*.

Culture An intellectual and artistic expression or the refind appreciation of the *arts*. It could also mean the customs and *arts* related to particular civilizations at different times. In India, culture is highly diversified, varying from region to region and from period to period. Indian culture during the *Gupta* or Maurya period, for example would be entirely different from the culture and customs of the Mughals or the Marathas. For that matter, culture in the urban areas would differ from the tribal or rural belt in the same age.

Culture is an integral part of the traditional ethos of the people and the land. Culture has been influenced by many facters, including religion, lifestyle, languages, etc. *Art* especially has always been steeped in culture. This is particularly true of India, with the *artists* never forgetting their traditional roots even in *contemporary* times. It is clearly visible in the works of *Jamini Roy*, *K.G. Subramanyan* and *Badri Narayan* among others. Refer *Folk Art*, *Maurya Dynasty*, *Mughal Dynasty*, *Mythology*, *Bengal Revivalism*, *Erotic Art*, *Sculpture*, *Tribal Art*, TANTRA, *Gupta*, *Amal Ghosh*, *Badri Narayan*, *Sakti Burman*, *Shail Choyal*, *Shanti Dave*, *K.V. Haridasan*, *Ramananda Bandyopadhyay*, *Ram Kishore Yadav*, *Kanayi Kunhiraman*, *Narayan R. Sardesai*, *Shankar Nandagopal*, *Ravinder G. Reddy*, *Raja Ravi Varma*.

Curator Literally means one who takes care of works of *art*. A *museum* curator is responsible for the management and care of its collections.

Cymroza Art Gallery (CYAG) (Mumbai). The gallery was established in 1971 and functions as a centre for interdisciplinary education in *art*. It celebrated its silver jubilee in 1996. The exhibitions sponsored by the gallery cut across the barriers of different *media*, including the works of ceramists and potters, photographers, printmakers and *sculptors* in addition to *painters*. Computer-generated *images* and *folk* and *tribal arts* such as Khovar Setrai and Santhal pats, *Picchwais* and *Jain paintings* from GUJ and RAJ have also been exhibited. It presents lectures and discussions on the *arts* covering a wide range of subjects such as *mythology*, history, *architecture* and *paper conservation*. It also provides gallery *space* for charitable organizations and NGOs in addition to stocking a wide variety of *paintings*, *sculptures* and *prints*. It has exhibited the works of various *artists* and has a vast collection of works including that of *Arpana Caur*, *Sankho Chaudhari*, *Haku Shah*, *Vrindavan Solanki*, *Latika Katt*, *Balbir Singh Katt*, *Dakoji Devraj*, *Saroj Gogi Pal*, *Ved Nayar*, *Thotha Vaikuntham*, *K.G. Subramanyan* and Pratima Sheth.

D

Das, Sunil: "Bombay Blast", *Oil* on *Canvas*, 1996, 183x152.5 cm. (See notes on page 103)

Dadaism The anti-art movement which derived its name from "Dada" a nonsensical *term* taken from artless fashion, meaning "hobby-horse" occurred during the First World War. In India, *Rabindranath Tagore's* non-figurative experiments comes close to this. Later, Dadaism represented rejection of all religious and moral principles with an attempt against establishment *art*. With its incongruous works, incoherent performances, poetry readings and the use of the *ready-made* and as a manifestation of the reaction to over-materialistic values of society, the movement was primarily meant to shock and scandalize the erstwhile *art*-lover. The development of *Pop art* was influenced by Dadaism with *mixed media assemblages*, using sandstone, *terracotta*, *acrylic* sheet, *steel*, mirrors and *metal* chiefly in conjunction with *wood* and *ready-made* objects, to introduce the creative possibilities of working with *leather* and other materials in making elaborate *constructions*. Refer *Automatism, Collage, Fantasy, Found Object, Krishnamachari Bose, N. Pushpamala, Vivan Sundaram*.

Daguerreotype/Daguerrotype An early photographic process patented by a Frenchman, Louis Jacques Mande Daguere, in 1839. The method, which transferred the *image* on to silvered *copper plates* sensitized with iodine and bromine, resulted in a direct *positive* and became popular during the 1840s. The first daguerreotype studio in India was probably that of Augustus G. Roussac in Meadow Street, Mumbai, established in 1850. Refer *Photograph*.

Dahanukar, Prafulla b. Goa. Education: Dip. in *art JJSA* 1955, Govt. of France Scholarship to *study graphic art* ENSBA, had an *exhibition* of her *paintings*, Regular *exhibitions* since 1956. Solos: New Delhi, *AFA* & *BAAC* Kolkata, TAG, *JAG, SAI*; International: Paris, London. Group participations: *BAAC* Kolkata, *LKA* New Delhi, *Biennale BB*; International: Hungary, Switzerland, Germany, Australia, Japan, France; Attended *art* camps. Awards: *BAS*, Veteran Artist *LKA* New Delhi; Member: President of *BAS* & *ASI*, Vice Chairman of *Artists' Centre* Mumbai, Committee member of Kala Akademi Goa & *LKA* New Delhi 1974–79. Collections: *NGMA* & *LKA* New Delhi, Central Museum Nagpur, TATA & J.J. Bhabha Mumbai, *BAAC* Kolkata, *JJSA, JJIAA*; International: pvt. collection Germany, France, USA, Japan.

Dahanukar, Prafulla: "Untitled", *Oil* on *Canvas*, 1996, 90x90 cm.

At first, her *paintings* were based on *nature*, depicting serene *landscapes* with trees, mountains, villages and fields. Later, however, individual *forms* began to blur and dissolve into a near *monochrome* haze more akin to mindscapes rather than *landscapes*. Lately, however, portraiture incorporated with everyday reality seems to form the basis of her *painting*. She has executed several *murals*. With such diverse material as *wood, glass, aluminium, metal* scrap, *fibreglass* and *ceramic*, she arranges and combines these pieces into variegated *compositions*. Her *murals* adorn the facades of theatres in Muscat and Jodhpur besides several buildings in Mumbai where she has been living and working.

Dakoji, Devraj (1944–) b. Hyderabad. Education: Dip. in applied & *FA*. College of FA. & Architecture Hyderabad, Studied *printmaking MSU*, Post-Grad. in *printmaking* Chelsea School of Art London, Professional Printers Training Programme at Tamarind Institute Albuquerque. Solos: *Paintings* & *prints–Art Heritage* New Delhi, USIS & KB Hyderabad, *CYAG, JAG, PG, SAI*; International: Germany, UK. Group participations: *LKA, Triennale* & *Biennale* New Delhi, *ATG, BB Biennale, CYAG*; International: *Graphic arts Biennale*–Cuba, Norway, Yugoslavia, Germany, Amsterdam, Italy, Spain, Iraq & UK. *Art* camps & workshops: *LKA* New Delhi, *BB, MSU*; Supervized workshop *LKA* Bhubaneshwar, Lucknow & New Delhi, HAS by *LKA* Hyderabad, *Triennale*, organized by *LKA* New Delhi, *GAC*; International: UK, Germany. *Auctions*: Heart New Delhi. Awards: National *LKA* New Delhi & AP, *AFA* Kolkata, *Biennale BB*, HAS. Fellowship: Dept. of Culture HRD Ministry; International: Travel Grant USIS. Appointments: External examiner in *VBU, MSU*, RAJ College of Education Jaipur; An instructor in *printmaking* in several New York colleges. Collections: Godrej Mumbai, *NGMA, LKA, Art Heritage* & *College of Art* New Delhi, Jaipur Museum of Modern Art, *Chandigarh Museum*, TIFR, *SAI, BB, FFA* (*MSU*), *SJM*; International: British Museum UK, Grafilkunst Hamburg, New York City Library.

Switching back and forth between *black* and *white drawings* to *graphics*, Devraj Dakoji emphasized simple *forms* by the use of *technique, black* and *white* contrast, subtleness and mystic qualities. He has also worked on a combination of *serigraphy* and *lithography, mixed media* in *acquatint* and *etching*. His fascination with all *forms* of *nature* comes out in his works, be it his suspended stones (inspired by the rocks that dot his native Hyderabadi *landscapes*) or his recent preoccupation, the animal world. In his *paintings*, Dakoji Devraj wishes to break away from the accepted central forces and goes in for a centrifugal *composition* almost in the mannerist *style*. His subtle *gradation* of *colour* is an outcome of studying *mezzotint* at the Chelsea School.

He lives and works in Delhi.

Dakoji, Pratibha (1954–) b. Nairobi, Kenya. Education: Degree in *graphic design MSU*; *Printmaking* course Chelsea School of Art London. Solos: *GC* Mumbai, *Art Heritage* & Kala Mela New Delhi, *FFA* (*MSU*), *SAI*. Group participations: Vadodara, Bangalore, Ahmedabad, *NGMA*, *LKA* New Delhi, *Biennale BB*; International: London, Asian Women Artists, Indian Council General New York, *Biennale* Bangladesh & Germany. Group shows: Kanoria Art Gallery Ahmedabad, *CYAG*, *HCVA*. Awards: *LKA* New Delhi, *AIFACS*, *GAC*. Fellowship: 1987 Dept. of Culture Ministry of HRD. Collections: *NGMA*, *LKA* & *Art Heritage* New Delhi, *Chandigarh Museum*, *GC* Mumbai, Kanoria Art Centre Ahmedabad, *SAI*; International: Kansas State University USA.

Her work ranges from the representational to the *abstract* and back to plain representation again. Signs and *doodles* float on the surface of her *paintings* offering a coded language to the interested. She has worked with a variety of media, including *watercolours*, *acrylic* and *mixed media* on *canvas* and *paper*. She has also dabbled in *printmaking*.

Pratibha Dakoji lives and works with her *artist* husband *Devraj Dakoji* in New Delhi.

Dakshinamoorthy, C. (1943–) b. Gudiyattam, TN. Education: Dip. in *FA*. *GCAC* Chennai, Advanced *printmaking* Groydon College of Design & Technology under British Council Scholarship. Solos: Anamika Art Gallery New Delhi, *DG*, others in Chennai, Bangalore; International: Groydon UK, Budapest. Group participations: National Exhibition of Art, *Triennales* & *Art Heritage* New Delhi, *BAAC* Kolkata, *JAG*, *CRAR*, others in Chennai; International: Hungary, Australia, Buenos Aires Argentina, Morley Gallery UK. *Art* camps: Over 25 camps Udagamangalam, Chennai, *LKA* New Delhi, All India Painters Kanpur, International Stone Sculptors by *LKA* New Delhi & National Stone Sculptors by SZCC Thanjavur in Mahabalipuram, *BB*, *COAG*. Awards: *CKP*, Mysore DAE, State & National *LKA*. Junior & Senior Fellowship: Dept of Culture New Delhi. Member: Executive Board *LKA* New Delhi, Jury Member for Telugu University, Annual Arts show by AP Govt. 1997 & *BAS* Annual Exhibition 1998. Commissions: *Murals* in *terracotta*, *fibreglass* & *ceramic* in Chennai, Fountain *sculpture* in Chennai, *metal* garden *sculpture* in Coimbatore. Collections: *NGMA*, *Art Heritage* & *LKA* New Delhi, SZCC Thanjavur, National Art Gallery Chennai, *BAAC* Kolkata, *Chandigarh Museum*, Hyderabad Museum; International: Asian Sculptures Museum Hiroshima Japan.

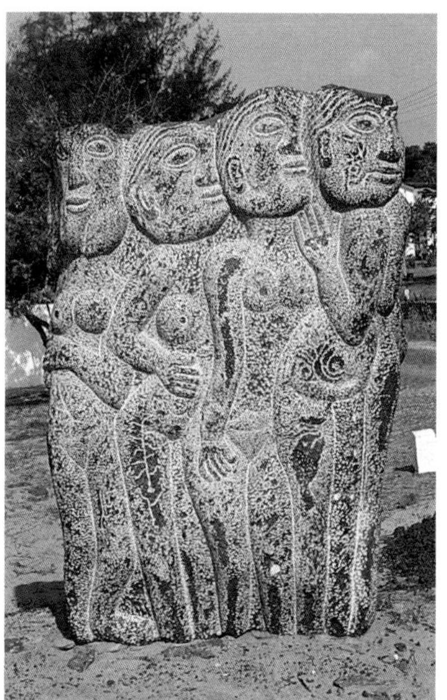

Dakshinamoorthy, C.: "Group", Granite, 152.5x122.61 cm.

From *painting* and *drawing* in *oils*, *pencil* and *pastels*, C. Dakshinamoorthy has changed focus to *sculpture*. He uses materials such as *stone*, *marble*, and *granite* to sculpt the human being in tight-knit groups, with the *lines*, curves and *chisel* marks suggesting both facial expressions and bodily movements. He avoids the use of extraneous detail, preferring instead to bring out the quality of the material that he carves into or the *terracotta* that he *moulds*.

He lives and works in Chennai.

Dalal, Naina (1935–) b. Vadodara, GUJ. Education: B.A. (Fine) & M.A. (Fine) *MSU*, Lithography Polytechnic London, *Etching* Pratt Graphic Centre New York. Solos: Ahmedabad, New Delhi, Kolkata, *CYAG*; International: Singapore—Retrospective Graphics & Drawings 1960–2003. Group participations: Women Artists Mumbai, CMC, *NGMA*, *Biennale* & *LKA* New Delhi, *BAAC* & *CIMA* Kolkata, *Biennale BB*, *FFA* (*MSU*), *VAG*; International: Senefelder Group of Artist Lithographers & Young Commonwealth Artists Show London, Festival of India USA; International: Graphic Exhibition in British Columbia & Canada organized by *CIMA* Kolkata, Contemporary Women Artists of India California, others in New York, Singapore. *Art* camps: Pavagarh, Goa, Kashmir; Lecture-demonstration workshop *LKA* New Delhi. Awards: *Painting* & *printmaking BAS*, GUJ State, Veteran Award *AIFACS* for *graphics*. Fellowships: For Research in Alternative Printing Techniques & Recipient of Fellowship Dept. of Culture Govt. of India for *printmaking*. Appointments: Taught *arts* and *crafts*, *FFA* (*MSU*). Collections: *LKA* & *NGMA* New Delhi, *BKB* Varanasi; International: New York, Museum of Oriental Art Durham.

Naina Dalal prefers *handling* alternative *techniques* like *collography* in addition to the known ones. Her *imagery* is based upon her experiences as an Indian woman. Her environment, her agonies, her position in the social hierarchy and how she relates to the world. There is an element of the surreal and the nihilistic in her *handling* of *form* and *colour*.

She lives and works with her *art*-historian husband, *Ratan Parimoo* in Vadodara.

Damodaran, K. (1934–) b. Tellicherry, Kerala. Education: Dip. in *FA*. *GCAC* Chennai. Solos: Mumbai, Ernakulam Kerala, *SAI*, *Dhoomimal*. Group participations: Chennai, *LKA* all over India, Fine Arts Society Kolkata, *BAS*; International: Through cultural exchange programmes Govt. of India in cooperation with its foreign counterparts Mexico, Yugoslavia, USA, Expo 70 Tokyo, *Biennale* Ljublijana. *Art* camps & workshops: *LKA* Kerala & New Delhi, *LKA* International Graphic Camp Bhubaneshwar. Awards: *LKA* Chennai & New Delhi, SKP; Junior Fellowship: Govt. of Culture India. Collections: *LKA* Kerala, TN & AP, *NGMA* New Delhi, *Chandigarh Museum* PUJ, SKP.

His *watercolour* and *mixed media paintings* on *paper* and *canvas* are suffused with memories of his native Kerala *landscape*, transformed into a glimmering *fantasy* world of P. Klee-like *light* and *colour* and *biomorphic* shapes. Tranquillity is the *key* to his *paintings*.

He lives and works in New Delhi.

Dandekar, G.A. (1949–) b. Bilhashi, MAHA. Education: Dip. in *art* teachers training, GDA & Art Masters Teaching *JJIAA*. Solos: *JAG*, *NCAG*, *SAI*. Group participations: Goa, National Exhibition New Delhi, Rashtriya Kala Mela Chennai, *NCAG*, *BAS*, *ASI*, *Dhoomimal*; International: Jakarta, London. *Auction*: Sotheby's London. Awards: MAHA State Art Exhibition. Commissions: Mumbai & Mauritius including *murals*. Appointments: Given lectures & demonstrations. Collections: *LKA* New Delhi, *JAG*; International: Japan, CitiBank New York, & pvt. collections.

His preferred choice of subject fluctuates between the *landscape* and the human *figure*. His *style* has evolved from a near-realistic approach to an impressionist one with short jerky *lines* indicating the *contour* of the *form*. He makes a sketchy application of *colours*, *acrylics* and *mixed media* being his preferred *medium*.

Das, Amitava (1947–) b. Delhi. Education: Grad. in *FA*. *College of Art* New Delhi. Solos: *Art Heritage* New Delhi, *SG* Mumbai, *Dhoomimal*. Group participations: Chennai, Bangalore, National Exhibition, Kunika Chemould & "The Pictorial Space" *LKA* New Delhi, *BAAC* Kolkata, *Triennales* & *Biennales BB*, *AIFACS*, *ATG*, *JAG*; International: Norway, Contemporary Indian Painting–Germany & New South Wales Museum Sydney Australia. *Auctions*: Heart Mumbai. Awards: National Award SKP; International: Bonn, Munich, Bremen Germany. Fellowship: Federal Republic of Germany for advanced exposure to *exhibition* & *graphic design*. Member: Founder member New Group a Delhi based *Artists* Group. Appointments: Lecturer Art Institute JMI, Visiting lecturer *College of Art* & the Women's Polytechnic in New Delhi. Collections: *LKA* New Delhi, PUJ University & *Chandigarh Museum*; International: London.

Since the late 80s Amitava Das has evolved a *technique* based on *drawing*, with macabre *images* of broken limbs, animals and the inhumanity of mankind. The *paintings* though richly coloured with oranges and reds, crimsons and *blacks*, contribute towards a chilling effect especially because of the fragmentary *nature* of the drawn *images*. He has worked in all *mediums*, including *acrylics*, *oils* and *watercolour*.

He works as a *graphic* designer in New Delhi, where he lives with his *artist* wife *Mona Rai*.

Das, Arup (1956–) b. WB. Education: *Painting* CVA Kolkata. Solos: *AFA* Kolkata, *CKAG*, *JAG*, *LTG*. Group participations: *AFA*, *BAAC*, State Academy & *LKA* Kolkata, 'Bombay' show by RPG 1965, *ISOA*, *GK*, *CKAG*, *JAG*. Group shows: Pune, Haryana. *Art* camps: *Arts Acre* Kolkata. Awards: *ISOA*. Collections: *LKA* New Delhi; International: Holland, Germany, Glenbarra Art Museum Japan.

Arup Das uses *overlapping colours* and *transparent washes* in addition to interweaving *lines* to come up with *abstract images* that seem to owe a lot to *action painting* and *gestural abstraction*. Lately, the human *figure* has also found its way into his *painting*, though in a disembodied *manner*.

He lives in 24 Parganas WB.

Das, Biman B. (1943–) b. Tamluk, WB. Education: Dip. in plastic art *GCAC* Kolkata. Solos: *LKA* New Delhi, *AIFACS*, TKS, *JAG*, TAG, *G88*; International: New Jersey USA, Belgium, Seoul. Group participations: *LKA Biennale*, *Triennale* in India & abroad; International: Fukuoka Art Gallery Japan, India Festival Moscow, *Biennale* Belgium & *Art* show Seoul. *Art* camps: Kashmir, *LKA sculptors* Amritsar, *AIFACS*. Awards: National Cultural Scholar 1967–69 & British Council Scholar UK 1973–74, National Award *LKA*, *BAAC* Kolkata, PUJ *LKA*, *Debi Prasad RoyChowdhury* Memorial Medal *AIFACS*. Fellowship: Fulbright Fellow USA. Commissions: *Bronze* & *marble busts* of the seniors in India; *Art* project installed in Brazil, San Marino Italy, Spain, Mauritius. Appointments: Lecturer of *sculpture* at the *College of Art* New Delhi for 25 years (1969–94); Later principal *GCAC* Kolkata. Collections: *NGMA*, *LKA*, *College of Art* & Rashtrapati Bhavan New Delhi, Museum Jaipur, Chandigarh, *AIFACS*, TKS, & pvt in India & abroad installed in Brazil, Italy, Spain & Mauritius.

Like H. Moore, Biman B. Das has based his *sculptures* on organic *forms*, suggesting humans and animals in a fragmented and highly stylized state. He has experimented with various sculptural and *painting media*, including painted *bronzes*. *Tradition* and modernity have fused in his works.

He lives and works in Kolkata & New Delhi.

Das, Jatin (1941–) b. Mayurbhanj, Orissa. Education: Dip. *JJSA*. Over 50 solos: *GC* & *BAAC* Kolkata, Kumar Art Gallery & RB New Delhi, *NGMA* Mumbai, SRAG, *AIFACS*, *JJSA*, *JAG*, TAG, *PUAG*, *CYAG*, others in Orissa & Goa. Retrospectives: *NGMA* 2001, RB & *LKA* New Delhi, Govt. of Chandigarh Museum; International: Commonwealth Institute Art Gallery London, City Museum Birmingham, others in Finland, Germany, Amsterdam. Group participations: *LKA* & *NGMA* New Delhi, MAHA State Art Mumbai, *Triennale* India, *Biennale BB*, *Dhoomimal*, *LTG*, *AIFACS*, *JAG*, *BAS*, other groups in Kerala, Chennai, Ahmedabad, J&K, Chandigarh, Orissa; International: *NGMA* in Yokohama & other *museums* & countries Japan, Berlin, Russia, Cuba, Bangladesh, UK, France & Germany, *Biennale*, Cuba, Bangladesh, Tokyo, Bradford, Venice & Paris, India *Triennale* documenter Kassel. *Art* camps: Kashmir, Mussoorie, Kolkata, *LKA* camps in Udagamangalam, New Delhi, Bhubaneshwar & Shimla; Workshops: New Delhi; International: Germany. *Auctions*: Bombay Asprey's UK–Helpage Auction, Heart New Delhi, Osian's Mumbai, Sotheby's & Bowring's New Delhi, Christie's & Sotheby's London. Awards: MAHA State Mumbai, *Biennale BB*, *AIFACS*, *BAS*. Senior Fellowship: Dept. of Culture Govt. of India 1989–90. Appointments: Lectured extensively at several important *art* & *design* institute in India; International: V&A, Cambridge University, Van Gogh Museum Amsterdam. Publications: Research on Folk Art & Handicrafts of Eastern India; Writes poetry in English; Documentary film made on him by Doordarshan. Collections: *NGMA* New Delhi, *JJSA*; International: Abbej Grey Foundation, Illinois Dalhen Museum Berlin, Washington DC.

Jatin Das has always been preoccupied with the human *figure*. In the mid 70s his main *theme* was based on social injustice. His later *paintings* became sensual with semi-erotic rendering of the female *form*. Man is sometimes present as the other half of a couple. Jatin Das' *nudes* are voluptuous in the *manner* of the ancient YAKSHIs and SHALEBHANJIKAs. He plays with textural variations, the glistening bodies having the smooth *texture* of wet *clay* with short, jerky brushstrokes complementing the long undulating body *contour*. *Drawing* with *ink* and *conte pencil*, is a *matter* of creating positive and *negative spaces*, according to him.

He lives and works in New Delhi.

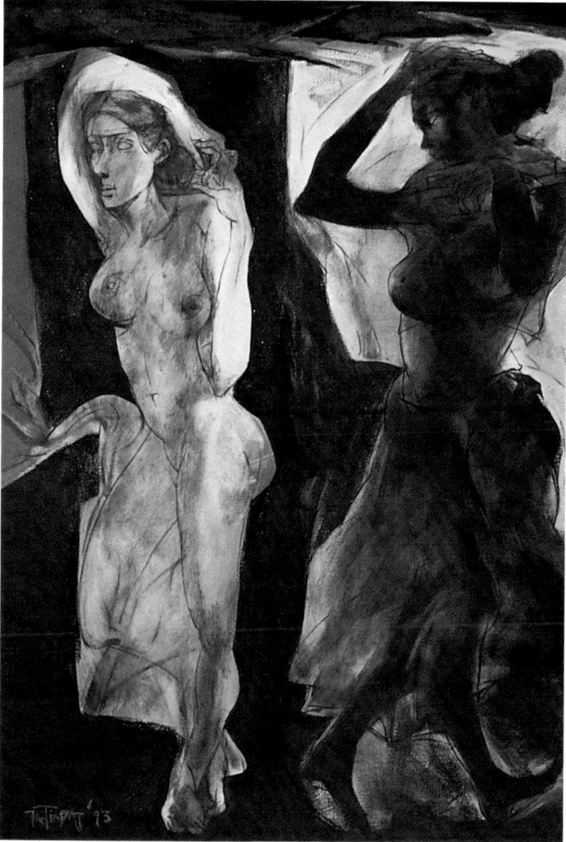

Das, Jatin: "2 Amayakataruni", *Oils*, 1993, 160x110 cm.

Das, Sukumar (1923–1990) b. Pabna, Bangladesh. No formal *art education*. Experimented with a variety of *mediums*, including *oil painting*, *watercolour*, *pastels* & *printmaking*. Solos: Over 5 solos at *AFA* Kolkata. Group participations: National Exhibitions, *AFA* 40 years regularly from 1952–1990 & *BAAC* working *artist* Kolkata, *BAS*, *AIFACS*, HAS; Exhibited: *BB Biennales*; International *Graphic* Exhibition Zambia. Awards: Gold Medal *AFA*, WB State & WB Govt. Exhibition Kolkata. Founder member: Society of Working Artists Kolkata. Collections: Raj Bhavan & *LKA* New Delhi; International: pvt. collection America, England, France, Germany, Japan, Australia.

Sukumar Das was *eclectic* both in his choice of *media* and his *imagery*. He was one of the first *artists* to use an artificial *stained glass* process in addition to his *watercolours*. His *forms* were at times, soft, sensual and other times, hard-edged and naive, his chronological study evaluated his contribution to Indian *modern style*. He lived in Kolkata.

Das, Sunil (1939–) b. Kolkata. Education: Grad. *GCAC* Kolkata, Studied ENSBA, Research in *painting* Atelier 17 & Atelier Julian Paris on a French Govt. Scholarship; Research in *fresco* & *mosaic* with Monsieur Shapple Midie & Aujum and *graphic art* with W. Hayter and *Krishna N. Reddy*. Over 43 solos: *GC* Mumbai, *BAAC* & *CIMA* Kolkata, *Dhoomimal*, *AIFACS*, *GG*, *CYAG*, *ABC*, *RG*, *JAG*; International: United States, France, Germany, Switzerland. Retrospective: *BAAC* & Sonar Bangla Art Gallery Kolkata; International: Kuala Lumpur, Basle, New York. Group participations: Over 50 during 1959–99, *NGMA*, *LKA*, Habitat Centre & *Triennale* New Delhi, *BAAC* & *CIMA* Kolkata, *AIFACS*, VG, *VAG*, *G88*, *GK*, *CKAG*, *PUAG*, *CYAG*, *SUG*; International: Germany, Polland, Hong Kong, London, Glenbarra Art Museum Japan, National Museum Singapore, *Biennale* in Havana & Sao Paulo, GBP, other *exhibitions* organized by Apparao Gallery in India & abroad. *Auctions*: Heart New Delhi, Osian's & Bowrings Mumbai, Christie's & Sotheby's London. Awards & Hon.: *LKA* National 1959 & 1978, *GCAC*, *AFA* & Calcutta University Kolkata, Shiromani Puraskar 1991, HAS, *BAS*, *AIFACS*; International: Sao Paulo *Biennale* Brazil. Founder member: *SCA*. Collections: *BAAC* & Deutsche Bank Kolkata, TATA Jamshedpur, *LKA*, *NGMA* & *Delhi Art Gallery* New Delhi; International: Kuala Lumpur, Singapore, New York, Paris, Masanori Fukuoka & Glenbarra Museum Hemeji Japan, seven works at Goludwig Cologne.

Sunil Das began his academic career by *painting* horses and bulls, trying to capture their dynamism and restlessness. His current works still retain some of that energy and *rhythm*; however he himself has moved to *painting* women, dark-eyed magnetic women with full, seductive lips. His *paintings* have been termed as "feminist" protests against a male dominated society. They are the *artist's* personal prayers for the equality of the sexes. The large bare areas in the *canvas* add to the drama behind the main protagonists, with certain recurring leitmotifs, like arrows emphasizing them. Certain *colours* too, like *black*, red and *gold* are repeated. They have a *symbolic* value for Sunil Das–*black* signifying darkness and evil, red the *colour* of blood, thus standing for warmth and *gold* standing for purity.

He lives and works in Kolkata. (See illustration on page 99)

Das, Swapan Kumar (1955–) b. Kolkata, WB. Education: Dip. in *FA*. *GCAC* Kolkata. Post-Dip. *printmaking Santiniketan*, Studied in *printmaking* Japan. Solos: *AFA* Kolkata, *GC* Mumbai, *G88*, *CKAG*; International: Japan, Norway. Group participations: National Exhibition *LKA* & Kala Mela New Delhi, *AFA*, *BAAC* & State Govt. Art Exhibition Kolkata, UP State Academy, MKKP MP, Govt. Museum Chandigarh, *AIFACS*; International: Nagoya, Bangladesh, Cuba, including Festival of India USA. *Art* camps: International

India Contemporary Printmaking San Diago State University. Awards: For *Graphic* prints *AFA*, WB State Akademi, *BAAC* Kolkata, *AIFACS*, National Scholarship 1980–82; International: Monbusho Scholarship by Govt. of Japan, Norwegian Print *Triennale*, Taipei *Biennale* Taiwan. Collections: India & abroad.

Fantasy with a fusion of reality, forms the *theme* of his *prints* and *paintings*. His *style* fluctuates between the naive to the illustrational and the semi-*abstract* and back. He prefers the manual method of *printmaking* made by pressing with the back of a spoon over the *paper* to the machine pressed *technique* used by most *artists*. This enables him to treat the works almost like *paintings*, inking and printing only one part at a time.

He lives and works in Kolkata.

Dasavatara=ten incarnations. The ten incarnations of VISHNU declared to have been assumed by him on 10 different occasions, with a view to destroy certain ASURAS, *demons* and setting right the havoc created by them in the world. These 10 AVATARAs are Matsya (fish), Kurma (tortoise), Varaha (boar), NARASIMHA (man-lion), VAMANA-TRIVIKRAMA (dwarf), PARASURAMA, RAMA, KRISHNA, BUDDHA and KALKI. At times BUDDHA was replaced by Jaina (victorious) or Balarama (abode of strength). It was from the *Gupta* period that the Hindu Dasavatara temples were built e.g. Deogarh Orissa. Illustration–GANJIFA, KALKI; Refer *Jainism*, *Hinduism*, *Iconography*.

DasGupta, Bimal (1917–1995) b. Bengal. Education: *GCAC* Kolkata. Over 55 solos: New Delhi, Kolkata & other towns; International: Poland, Berlin, Chicago, New York. Group participations: *Triennale*, *Biennale*, National Exhibition, All India Exhibition & *NGMA* New Delhi, *AIFACS*, others in Chandigarh, Hyderabad, Chennai; International: Sao Paulo Brazil, Tokyo & Osaka Japan, Australia, Travelling Exhibitions at China, Japan, Moscow, Germany & other countries. Awards: National Awards *LKA* & *College of Art* New Delhi, *AFA* Kolkata, Hyderabad Museum, *AIFACS*. Appointments: Prof. at *College of Art* New Delhi. Collections: *NGMA* & *Delhi Art Gallery* New Delhi, & others in Chandigarh, Hyderabad & Chennai Museum & pvt. in India & abroad.

Bimal Dasgupta's *paintings* have always been based on *nature* right from the very beginning. His roots in the riverine *landscape* of Bengal have contributed to his *imagery*. While he started *painting* with *realistic landscapes* after his 1961 tour of Europe, he took to abstraction, but always with *visual* clues pointing to identify the *painting* as a *landscape*. Even his short-*term* use of TANTRIC *imagery* points to his roots in *nature*.

He started off with *watercolour landscapes*, but his *abstract* works were mostly in *oils*, the *nature* of the *medium* contributing to the *impasto* swirls and drips that characterize them. Towards the end of his life in New Delhi, he had come full circle, once again turning to *watercolour* on *paper*.

DasGupta, Dharmanarayan (1939–1997) b. Tripura. Education: Dip. in FAC *VBU*. Solos: Kala Yatra Chennai, *Dhoomimal*, *G88*, *VAG*, *JAG*, *CKAG*. Retrospective: *BAAC* Kolkata. Over 50 *Artists Group Shows* & group participations: National Exhibition New Delhi, *AFA* & *BAAC* Kolkata, Indian

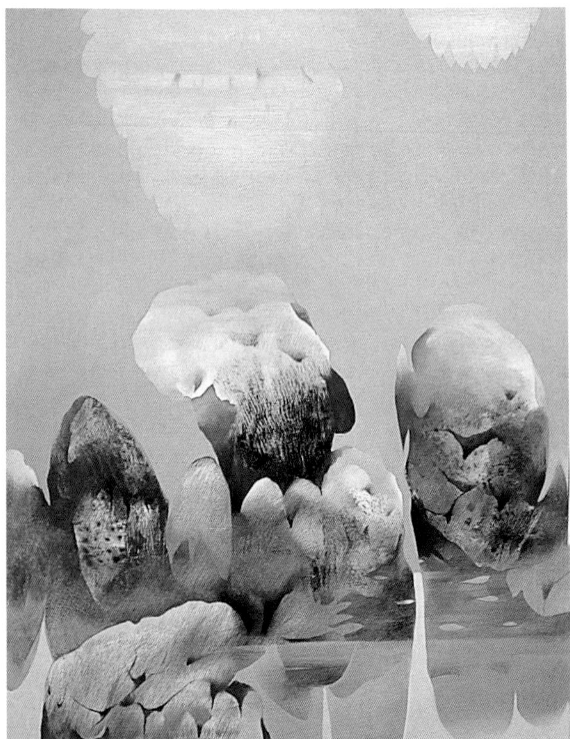

DasGupta, Bimal: "Untitled", *Acrylic* on *Canvas*, 1990, 112.5x90 cm.

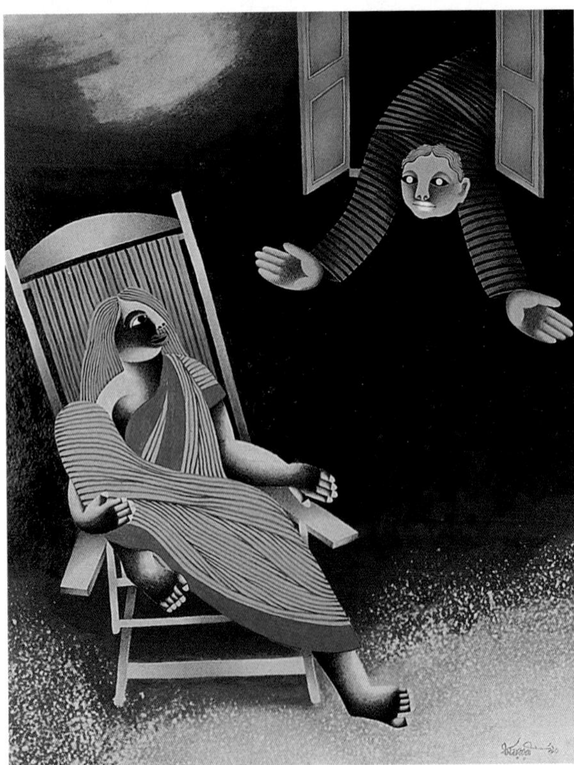

DasGupta, Dharmanarayan: "Midday Affair", *Acrylics*, 1990, 71x56 cm.

Paintings Today *JAG*, *AIFACS*, *BAS*; International: Kala Yatra London, others in Paris, Manchester, Sao Paulo *Biennale*, Festival of India Havana, Book Fair Poland. *Auctions*: Heart Mumbai & New Delhi, Christie's London, Sotheby's New York. Awards: *BAAC* Kolkata. Member: *SCA* Kolkata since 1961. Collections: *NGMA* & *LKA* New Delhi, *BAAC* Kolkata; International: Masanori Fukuoka & Glenbarra Museum Hemeji Japan, V&A.

Dharmanarayan DasGupta's *style* was achieved from combining traditional Indian *art* with Western thought. *Gouache*, *oil*, *tempera* being his *medium*. The protagonists in his *paintings* stand against a flattened *backdrop* with no indication of conventional *perspective*, indicating a preference for Basohli like *composition* without the use of bright *colours*. The subjects are M. Chagall-like, with flying *figures*, animals and *landscape* elements floating in a dream *space* punctuated with minor details, such as the *pattern* on a dress on the wings of the flying creatures. Dharmanarayan DasGupta lived in Howrah, WB.

DasGupta, Dilip (1914–1989) b. Shillong. Studied GSA Kolkata, later Paris School of Art. Physically handicapped at a young age, Dilip DasGupta moved, first to Malaya, then to Shanghai and finally to Paris. Preparing a prolific portfolio while in Malaya, he toured and exhibited in cities like Tokyo, Singapore, Hong Kong, Shanghai, Java and Sumatra. Thereafter, he moved to Paris returning back to India in 1952. Set his own studio in Kolkata. Won Hon. for his *portrait* of *Rabindranath Tagore*. Later a Retrospective Exhibition at *CKAG*.

Dilip DasGupta pioneered the use of *transparent watercolours*, a *style* that was neither a fully oriental e.g. Japanese *wash technique* nor the romantist Western type. His use of basic *colours* later blended harmoniously with darker *shades* combined to make his *paintings* portray the soothing and self-explicit display of a multi-layered experience, both in *form* and *content*.

DasGupta, Dilip (1931–) b. Shimla, HP. Education: Dip. in *arts* New Delhi Polytechnic; Certificate Academia Della Belle Arte Naples Italy. Italian Govt. Scholarship 1963–64. Over 45 solos: *LKA* New Delhi, *BAAC* Kolkata, *AIFACS*, *Dhoomimal*, *JAG*, TAG, others in Jamshedpur, Hyderabad; International: Germany, Malta (Europe), Copenhagen Denmark. Group participations: *LKA* & *Triennale* New Delhi, *BAAC* Kolkata, *AIFACS*; International: Italy, Bangladesh, London, South Korea, Australia, *Biennale* Bangladesh & *Contemporary Art* Exhibition Melbourne Australia. *Art* camps: Attended All India Painters' Camp in Lucknow, *LKA* New Delhi, *AIFACS*. Awards: Presidents *Plaque AIFACS*, National *LKA* New Delhi, Merit Certificate Kanpur & UP State Artists Association Lucknow. Member: General Council & Jury UP State *LKA* Lucknow, *BAAC* Kolkata, GUJ *LKA* Ahmedabad. Appointments: Taught *art BHU* for the last 25 years. Collections: national & international.

His *paintings* are *nature*-oriented with rocks, trees, rivers, the sea merging together to create a semi-*abstract* wear *monochrome landscapes* resembling those of his better known *artist* brother *Bimal DasGupta*.

He lives and works in Varanasi/New Delhi.

DasGupta, Jahar (1942–) b. Jamshedpur, Bihar. Education: Dip. in FAC *KB Santiniketan*. Solos: *AFA* & *BAAC* Kolkata. Over 33 "Painters Orchestra" group shows all over India. Group participations: *LKA* New Delhi, *Contemporary artist* by Centre Art Gallery, *BAAC* & *AFA* Kolkata, *Santiniketan*, *JAG*, *NCAG*, *AIFACS*; International: South Korea. Attended workshops of *paintings* in WB. Founder member: Painters Orchestra & Vice President *AFA* Kolkata. Publications: Album "Poetry on drawings", postcard portfolio of *paintings*.

His *painterly style* is based on a naive *figuration*, with distorted objects and *contour shading*. He has a predilection for soft *colours*. With a juxtaposition of imagination and experience gathered from rude reality, his *images* are neither *realistic* nor *abstract*, but stylized.

He lives and works in Kolkata.

DasGupta, Phalguni (1934–) b. Bengal. Education: Grad. in *applied arts GCAC* Kolkata. Solos: Approximately 36 in New Delhi, Kolkata, Mumbai, Chennai, Kalimpong. Group participations: *AFA* Kolkata, Graphic Exhibition Hyderabad, *AIFACS*, *BAS*; International: Italy, England. *Art* camps: Stamp Designer–Nasik, *Graphic art* organized by USIS, *LKA* Chandigarh, Silk Screen camp New Delhi. Member of Jury–All India *AFA* Society & for All India Childern's Painting, Children Book Trust in illustration exhibition; International Book Fair Italy. Awards: *AFA* Kolkata for *painting* & *graphic*; Hon.: Veteran Artist by *AIFACS*; International: USA. Member: Calcutta Painters. Appointments: Lecturer *College of Art* New Delhi, finally retiring as HoD of *applied art*. Publications: *Illustrations* National Book Trust New Delhi. Collections: New Delhi, Kolkata, pvt. & public.

Phalguni DasGupta's *style*, in keeping with his study of *applied arts*, is rather illustrational, be it *landscapes* or mythological *figures*. His favourite *medium* is *watercolour* and while he exploits the transparency of the *medium* in the Western *manner*, he also incorporates Indian folk *style* by the simple addition of *black outlines* and frontal postures. This is especially seen in his recent series on Indian *gods* and goddesses.

He lives and paints in Dehradun, UP.

Dasha-bhahu, Dasha-bhuja Dasha-bhahu=ten armed SHIVA and Dasha-bhuja=ten armed DURGA. An epithet generally applied to Lord SHIVA and Goddess DURGA respectively. Dasha meaning 10 and Bhahu/Bhuja meaning arms. Refer Illustration–DURGA.

Datta, Ranen (1933–) b. Narayanganj, Bangladesh. Education: Dip. in *sculpture GCAC* Kolkata, Dip. in *FA*. *GCAC* Chennai, Dip. in *sculpture* Akademie der Bildenden Kunst Munich with scholarship. Solos & group participations: Varanasi, Bangalore, *GCAC*, *AFA*, MMB & *BAAC* Kolkata, *LKA* & Progressive Painters Association Chennai, Rashtriya Kala Mela *LKA* New Delhi; International: Munich, Kolin. Member: Vice-President Association of Young Painters & Sculptors Chennai, later Prakriti Bhawan Gallery *Santiniketan*. Appointments: Prof. of *sculpture CFA* Thiruvananthapuram Kerala, retiring from the post in 1988; Freelance *sculptor* Rashtriya LKK Kolkata. Commissions: including *portraits* Thiruvanathapuram, *sculp-*

tures at Raj Bhavan and garden *sculptures AFA* Kolkata. Collections: *Santiniketan*, Thiruvananthapuram, Raj Bhavan & *AFA* Kolkata, *NGMA* & *LKA* New Delhi.

He has a liking for *monumental sculpture*, often preparing *terracotta* maquettes for various projects. His *style* is rather *eclectic*, impressionist at times and naive or *symbolic* at others.

He lives in Kolkata.

Dave, Jalendu (1940–) b. Vadodara, GUJ. Education: Dip. in *painting* & Art Masters Certificate GUJ University. Over 27 solos: Palace & *Maharaja Fatesingh Museum* Vadodara, *JAG*; International: London. Group participations: GUJ *LKA*, National Exhibition, *LKA* New Delhi, Kolkata, Chandigarh, Chennai, Bangalore & Lucknow, Artist Association Vadodara, HAS, *BAS*, *AIFACS*. *Art* camps: *LKA*, also for educational purpose by *LKA* & Vadodara Art Teachers. Awards: GUJ *LKA*, HAS. Commissions: Over 15 *murals* in *cement*, *wood*, *ceramics*, glazed tiles, *oils* & *watercolours*. Appointments: *Art* teacher at the Shree Narayan High School Vadodara since 1962. Collections: GUJ *LKA*, *Maharaja Fatesingh Museum* Vadodara, *LKA* New Delhi & Lucknow, Hyderabad Museum; International: USA, Germany, Oshica Art Gallery Singapore, British Council London.

His *painting style* is based on TANTRIC *imagery* and *calligraphy* using *watercolour*, *oils* and *mixed media* arranged in a geometricized *pattern*. He has also used GANESHA, SHAKTI and other *gods* and goddesses in his *composition*.

Dave, Shanti (1931–) b. Ahmedabad. Education: Post-Grad. Dip. in *painting MSU*, *Graphic arts* Indian Govt. Culture Scholarship. Over 43 solos: *GC* Mumbai, *JAG*, *PUAG*, TAG, *Dhoomimal*, *ABC*, others in Ahmedabad, Chennai, *CRAR*, *CKAG*; International: Grabowski Gallery London, Frankfurt Kunstkabinett Germany, others in Rome, Tel Aviv, New Orleans. Group participations: 25 years of Indian *Art LKA*, *Triennale* & Contemporary World Art New Delhi, *Dhoomimal*, *JAG*; International: Modern Indian Art Switzerland, Germany, Washington, Egypt & South America, Commonwealth Exhibition London, Asia Society New York, *Biennales* at Sao Paulo, Tokyo & Cannesuimarie France, Indian Contemporary Art Sofia at Prague, Tehran, Warsaw & Damascus, Asian Artist Fukuoka Art Museum Japan; Represented Indian Festivals & Seminars. *Auctions*: Osian's & Heart Mumbai, Christie's London. Awards: *AFA* Kolkata, Padma Shri, Cultural Scholarship Govt. of India New Delhi, *Triennale* India Gold Medal, *BAS*, National Awards; International: Tokyo *Biennale*. Founder member: Baroda Group of Artist. Commissions: Several *murals* including two in the Parliament House New Delhi, Air India & NCPA Mumbai; International: Tokyo & Japan. Collections: *NGMA* & *LKA* New Delhi, *Maharaja Fatesingh Museum* Vadodara; pvt. national & international.

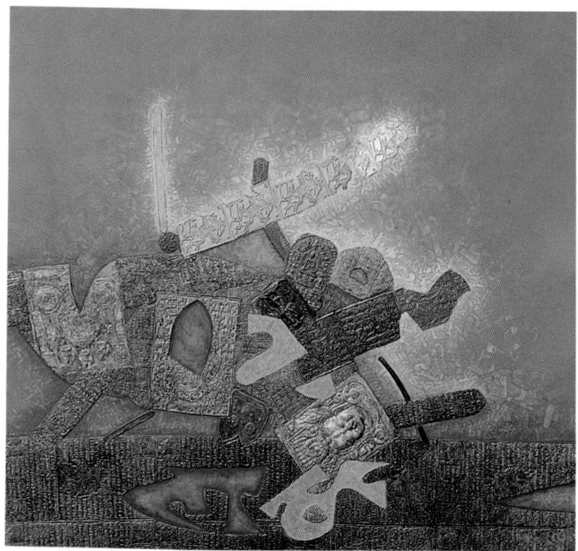
Dave, Shanti: "Title No. 59", *Medium* Intoxic, 1989.

Shanti Dave made striking large-sized *linocuts* in the mid-fifties before going on to doing *oil paintings* and *murals*. He soon evolved a personal *imagery* based on the decorative *forms* and *colour* in his native GUJ. He also used Tibetan *calligraphic* wooden blocks as well as blocks with *Gods* and ritualistic *forms*, with *mixed media*. The *high relief* and textural variations in his *paintings* recur in the *graphic medium* to which he returned. He achieved the *relief* and *embossing* effects by employing *wax* and *cement moulds* and *paper* pulp and later by means of *etching*.

However it was the *wood cut* that most suited his temperament. He uses plywood sheets which he cuts into desired shapes and applies *colour* with a roller. At times he uses as many as eight different sheets of plywood in order to get the desired effect.

He lives and works in New Delhi. Refer *Paper*.

Davierwala, Adi M. (1922–1975) b. Mumbai. Self-taught as a *sculptor*. Solos: Over 6 to 8 in Mumbai, New Delhi 1956–65; Retrospective in Mumbai 1979; International: Represented India at Commonwealth Art Today London & Edinburgh by Berthe Schaefer Gallery New York. Group participations: State Exhibition Mumbai, *LKA* New Delhi, *PUAG* 1986, *BAS* & other participation with All India Sculptors' Association; International: Zurich, USA, Venice & Sao Paulo *Biennales*, Commonwealth Art Today London & Edinburgh, Exhibition of the Institute of International Education USA. *Auctions*: Heart Mumbai. Awards: *BAS* Bronze & Silver Medal, *LKA* New Delhi, All India Sculptors' Associations, *LKA* 1965. Fellowship: One year USA on a John D. Rockefeller III. Collections: In Institutions, Galleries, Atomic Energy Co.op. & TATA Mumbai, *JAG*, pvt. national & international.

Adi M. Davierwala was a chemist by profession, mastering the elements of *sculpture* largely on his own, with a little guidance from N.G. Pansare. He worked with several *media*, including *wood*, *stone* and *marble carving*, *metal casting*, *welding* and working with plastic.

His *images* evolved from the simplified organic *forms* in the H. Moore and J. Epstein *style* in the 40s and 50s to a near *abstract* play with scrap *metal* in the 60s and 70s. His subjects ranged from *mythology*, both Indian and Western to simple portraiture and cosmology. However, the works are not illustrative, but instead *form* a fusion between the literary *content* and the *tactile*, resulting in a highly personalized realization. He was fascinated by the *transparent nature* of perspex, using it in the constructivist *manner* of N. Gabo.

De, Biren (1926–) b. Bengal. Education: Studied in *art GCAC* Kolkata; left Kolkata college & settled in New Delhi with his career. Solos: Kunika Art Centre, Kumar Art Gallery & Gallery Chanakya New Delhi, *GC* & The Window Mumbai, *AIFACS*; Retrospective *Dhoomimal* 1950–77; International: Atelier Galerie Hamburg; Invited solo: Pittsburgh USA, Stockholm & Goteborg. Group participations: *Triennales*, *Symbolism* & Geometry in Indian *Art NGMA* New Delhi, *AIFACS*; International: Los Angles USA, Salon de Mai Paris, *Biennales* all in Mainichi, Sao Paulo, Venice, Sydney; Museum of Art Fukuoka Japan, RAA London, Eight Contemporary Indian Artists Sweden, other towns Greece, Belgium, Poland, Bulgaria, Yugoslavia. *Auctions*: Heart Mumbai & New Delhi, Osian's Mumbai. Awards: National Award New Delhi. Member: Visiting Faculty of the School of Planning & Architecture New Delhi. Appointments: Taught senior students at School of Art New Delhi; International: Worked in New York on Fulbright Grant; Lived & worked in Germany & Australia; Seminars "Concepts of Space" with 81 slides of his works from 1950–1980, on "Time" organized by IGNCA, "Tradition: A Continual Renewal" organized by ICCR. Collections: *NGMA*, *LKA*, Rashtrapati Bhavan & New Delhi University New Delhi, TATA Mumbai; International: Museum of Modern Art New York, Museum of Art Himeji Japan, National Gallery of Czechoslovakia Prague.

Though Biren De's present works point to an influence of TANTRA, he himself professes no such label. Instead it is energy, the eternal struggle between the opposites, the Purusha-Prakriti that results in his unusual *pictorial imagery*. The *figurative* works of the 50s were progressively simplified until they became a codified language, a curved U-shape representing the feminine principle and the straight, edge-shape representing the male, other fundamental shapes like the circle and square, cylinder and the parabola were arranged with the main symbols to achieve that final burst of energy that *forms* the core of his *paintings*. The eroticism in this union of *forms* is overt rather than obvious. The emphasis being more on the relationship of man and woman and their transcendental journey through life together. In the final analysis, it is *light* that *forms* the nucleus of his *painting*. He would call his works as representing "Symbolic-*Abstract Expressionism*" or seeking a path towards ultimate realization of Man and his relationship with the Universe.

Biren De lives and works in New Delhi.

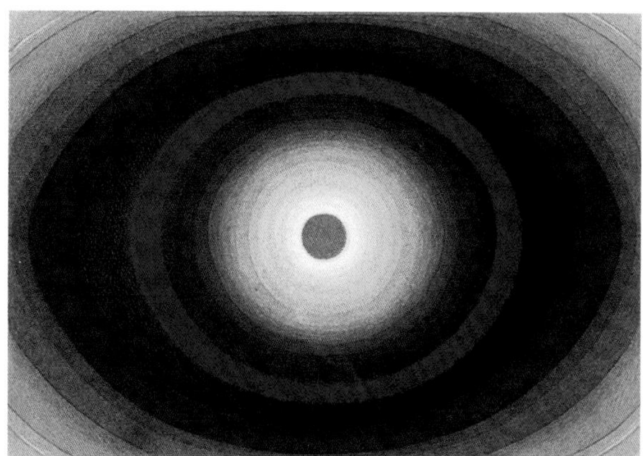

De, Biren: "Untitled", *Watercolours*.

De Stijl (Dutch)=*style*. The *art* and *architecture* group was founded by Teo Van Doesburg in Holland in 1917 (taking its name from his magazine of the same *title*), and lasted until his death in 1931. De Stijl advocated the use of purely *abstract forms* based on the mathematical theories of Dr. Schoenmakers and the architectural concepts of Frank Lloyd Wright, which stressed the importance of horizontal and the vertical, and the use of *primary colours*. The Neoplastic *paintings* of Piet Mondrian, who dominated the movement, and the furniture of Gerrit Rietveld, form the epitome of De Stijl in these fields. Refer *Neo-Plasticism*.

Dead Colour A *neutral colour*, usually dull brown, green or grey used especially as *underpainting*, often applied in varying *tones* to indicate *light* and dark. The *lay-in technique* was used earlier in *tempera*. Refer *Ajanta*, *Fresco*, *Bengal School*, *Company School*.

Deb Barman, Dhirendrakrishna (1902–1995) b. Agartala, Tripura. Education: *Santiniketan* in 1911, Was among the first pupils of *KB Santiniketan*, under *Nandalal Bose* & *Asit K. Haldar*; International: RCA. Solos: Mumbai. Group show: *AIFACS*; International: London, America, Paris, Russia, Mexico. Awards: *VBU*, WB Govt. Abanindra Award & 'Nivedita Puraskar' Howrah; Hon.: D.Litt award *RBU*. Commissions: *Murals* in Kolkata, Madurai, Tripura Castle Shillong; International: Mural Indian House London. Appointments: Accompanied *Rabindranath Tagore* on his visit to Bali & Java in 1927; Visited major galleries & *art*; Travelled all over the Far East, participated in seminars—UNESCO, Tokyo on *Arts & Crafts*; Joined *KB Santiniketan* 1951 & HoD 1954–60 Dept. of *painting*. Collections: All over Britain & Europe.

Dhirendrakrishna Deb Barman's early *paintings* exuded an *atmosphere* of *Romanticism* in the *Bengal School manner*. Like his tutors, he worked with *tempera*, *wash* and *watercolour*, achieving a spontaneity of expression and a delicacy of *tone* in his *paintings* and *drawings*. He had also contributed greatly to the revival of local *arts* and *crafts* in Tripura and also in increasing the level of *art*-consciousness in the State. He died in *Santiniketan*.

Deb Partha, Pratim (1943–) b. Kolkata. Education: *VBU*, Post-Dip. in *painting MSU*. Solos: *BAAC* Kolkata. Group shows: Every year since 1968. Group participations: National Exhibition *AFA* & *BAAC* Kolkata. *Art* workshops: Organized by *RBU*, Painters' Orchestra & British Division Kolkata. Member: Painters' Orchestra Kolkata. Appointments: Joined *Santiniketan* as an *art* teacher & the Dean of the Institute; Dean of the *FFA RBU*. Collections: Tripura Govt. Museum & pvt. national & international.

His works of the 90s are mainly inspired by Pop *imagery* with *collages* and junk, *assemblages* in a fusion of *painting* and *sculpture*. He uses bizarre *forms* and *colours*, juxtaposing materials as diverse as *leather*, *terracotta*, *metal* and *paper* to portray the humanistic condition.

Decadent Art The *term* relates especially to the artistic and literary movement of the late 19th century when

European society and cultural activities were considered to be on a decline. The *term* refers to perverse and *erotic art*, associated with *Symbolism* and the *themes* that shock conventional morality. Aubrey Beardsley's *drawings* and Oscar Wilde's writings are examples of decadent art. In India, the *term* could be applied, though not in a pejorative sense, to some works of certain *artists*, including *Bhupen Khakhar*, *Laxma Goud*, *Maqbool Fida Husain* and *Manu Parekh*. Refer Illustration–*Erotic Art*, *Laxma Goud*.

Decalcomania A surrealistic *technique* for creating spontaneous *images*. The *artist* puts a blot of *ink* or blob of *paint* on a sheet of a *paper* or *canvas*, then either folds it in half or presses another sheet of *paper* over it to create a mirror *image*. The *artist* then develops the *painting* further as in *blot drawing* or subsequently as required. Refer *Ink Drawing*, *Surrealism*, *Blot Drawing*.

Deccani Miniature Painting Deccani (meaning of the South) miniature painting flourished in the Sultanates of Ahmednagar, Bijapur and Golconda. The *paintings*, often executed by Hindu *artists*, combined Persian elements with Indianized *figures* and setting. There is also a marked influence of the *murals* at Hampi and Lepakshi, in the decorativeness of the *figures* while the *landscape* details are typically Deccani. The *calligraphy* was also derivative of Persian miniatures. Deccani *portraits* show traces of Mughal influence with a certain European *Naturalism* and three-dimensional effect. Refer *Miniature Painting*.

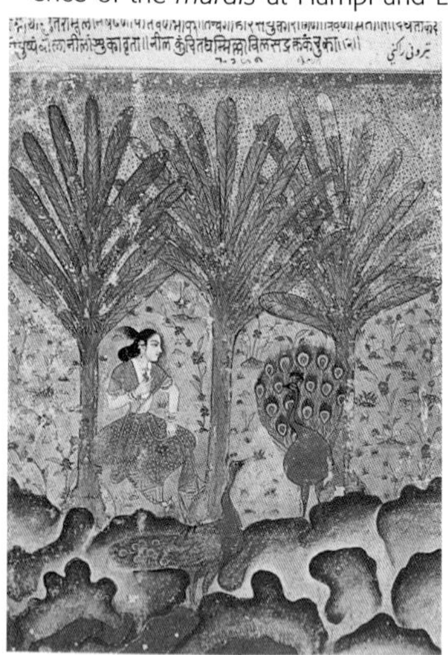

Deccani Miniature Painting: "Deccani School", end of 16th century.

De'collage (French)=unsticking. Exact opposite of *collage*. It is *technique* of creating a *composition* which is made by peeling away layers, usually of found *images*, like *posters* and other materials, which are partially torn away, resulting in new *texture*-based *images*. This *technique* is used mainly in *installation*. Refer *Vivan Sundaram*, *N. Pushpamala*, *Bharati Kapadia*, *Manu Parekh*.

Decorative Art **1.** The works of *art* or *craft* such as *applied arts*, *ceramics*, *metal craft*, textiles and furniture, which were made in attractive *patterns*. **2.** Can also refer to pleasing, repetitive *patterns* in *art* work i.e. the decorative Hashiyas (mount) in *Mughal miniatures*, the decorative *compositions* of *Jamini Roy*, *Jaganath M. Ahivasi*, *Shail Choyal*, *Ghulam Rasool Santosh*, *Laxman Pai* and *modern* miniaturists. *Modern* Indian Art, though Western in outlook, may still carry traces of its cultural past in the decorative *motifs* used. Much of TANTRA *painting* is also decorative in appearance. Refer *Applied Art*, *Art*, *Art Deco*, *Indus Valley Civilization*, *Miniature Painting*, *Terracotta*, *Tribal Art*, *Enamel*, *Folk Art*, *Temple Architecture*, *National Museum* (New Delhi), *Indian Museum* (Kolkata, WB), *Maharaja Fatesingh Museum* (Vadodara), MUKUTA, *GCAC* (Kolkata, WB), *BHU*, *MSU*, *CSMVS* (*PWM*), *Nandalal Bose*, *Jyotirindranath Tagore*, *Kanu Desai*, *Abdul Rahim Appabhai Almelkar*, *Baburao Painter*, *K.C. Aryan*, *P.L. NarasimhaMurti*, *Vijyalakshmi P.*, *Nathu Lal Verma*, *J. Swaminathan*.

Decoupage (French)=cutting out. The *term* usually refers to the cutting of *paper* in various *patterns*, the pieces of which can then be applied to a surface to *form* a *composition* in *collage* format, e.g., the last works of Henri Matisse. In India, rather like the ageing Henri Matisse, *Benode Behari Mukherjee* turned to making *paper* cuts, *drawings* and lithographs.

Degenerate Art The *term* has political overtones, with *avant-garde art* and *artists* usually being vilified as being degenerate by new regimes, as they were nonconformist to the *art* of the day. The Nazis called most of the *modern* masters by this epithet, as did the Russians. In India, the *term* "obscene" or "obscenity" is prevalent. In the 1950s it was *Akbar Padamsee* who was nearly put in jail for producing Degenerate art, while in the 1990s it is *Maqbool Fida Husain* who became the target.

Dehlvi, Sadiq (1950–) b. Delhi. Education: B.FA. *College of Art* New Delhi. Solos: USA and New Art Centre London. Group show: Beaux Arts, Delfina Studio Trust Shows & New Art Centre London. Group paticipations: Mumbai; International: UK, USA, Salisbury, Chicago, London. Scholarships: National Culture by HoD 1975–77 guidance of *Dhanraj Bhagat*, British Council Scholarship Slade School of Art London UK, Delfina Studios Trust London, Greater London Art Grant. Collections: *NGMA* New Delhi; International: Edinburgh, Sweden.

Sadiq Dehlvi's *sculptures* have a *spiritual* quality, the animal *sculptures* especially having the charm of indigenous folk toys. These animals usually stand as metaphors for his emotions and are *cast* in *bronze*. He delineates precise areas for *textures* and posture, polishing some

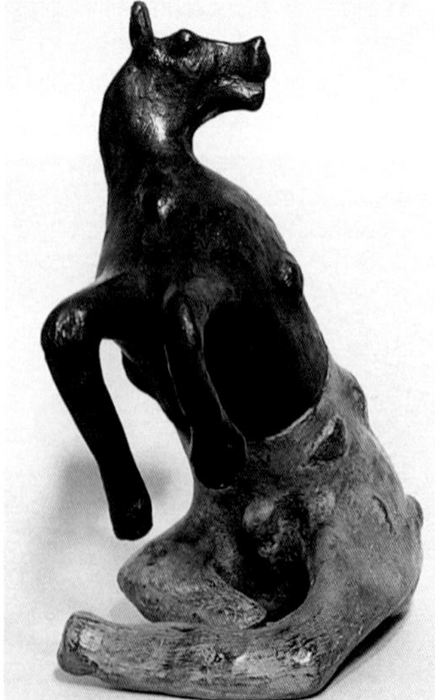

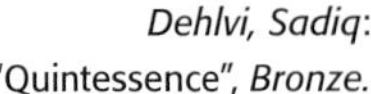

Dehlvi, Sadiq: "Quintessence", *Bronze*.

areas to a high gloss while colouring others. He has lately been using the human *figure* to great effect in his works, working towards sculpturing a family group.

He works in his studio, UK.

Delhi Art Gallery (New Delhi). The gallery was opened in 1993 by Rama Anand. The present Dir., Ashish Anand has been looking after the gallery since 1996. It specializes in the works of the old and *contemporary* masters of the 20th century, especially those belonging to the earlier half—*Nandalal Bose*, *Manishi Dey*, *Mukul Chandra Dey*, *Jamini P. Gangooly*, *Gopal Ghose*, *Asit K. Haldar*, *Kshitendranath Mazumdar*, *Abanindranath Tagore*, *Rabindranath Tagore*, and young *artists* of the present generation. The in-house collection includes *contemporary paintings*, *prints* and *sculptures*. They source material for international *auction* houses such as Sotheby's and Christie's. There is also an *art* consultancy dept. to provide service for the corporate, pvt. & public buyers. They recently held a group show of 100 artists at their own gallery & RB New Delhi, *JAG* and *NCAG*.

Demons In Indian *art* and *sculpture*, they are the subject of many *miniature paintings*. In Hindu, Buddhist and *Jain mythology*, one finds varieties of *demons*, from the vicious ASURAs and Rakshasas to the sexually voracious GANDHARVAs and APSARAs, who at *times* mate with lonely travellers in forests, producing offspring of dubious character. Demons are an integral part of work of *art* in most *cultures* around the world.

Deo, Avinash S. (1935–1995) b. Wardha, MAHA. Education: GDA in *painting* & Post-Grad. Dip. in *mural painting JJSA*. Group participations: Goa National Exhibitions & *LKA* New Delhi, State MAHA Exhibition, *Triennale* India, *BAS*. Organized & attended camps: Goa, Pune, Mumbai, *LKA* New Delhi & many other towns all over India. Fellowship: *JJSA* 1967. Member: General Council & Executive member *LKA* New Delhi. Commissions: *Mural* for Govt. of MAHA 1969 & Goa 1977. Appointments: Lecturer in *painting JJSA* 1968–73, later Principal College of Art Panaji Goa.

Avinash S. Deo began working with *collage*, being highly influenced by the works of P. Picasso. His mature *paintings* reflect a subtle use of geometry and *colour*. His rather *abstract images* float on the surface of the *canvas* in the *form* of diagonals and intersecting planes. The *painting* takes shape in a semi-automatic *style*, the act of *creation* being apparent in the final work.

Deolalikar, Y.D. (1931–) b. Indore, MP. Learnt *painting* under his father, D.D. Deolalikar, Participated in Venice *Biennale*, before securing Dip. in *drawing* & *painting JJSA*. Over 11 solos: *BAAC* Kolkata, *JAG*, TAG, BAG; International: Sponsored at Commonwealth Institute London. Group participations: in Venice *Biennale* & Germany. *Art* camps: *LKA* Orissa. Awards: MAHA State Art Exhibition Mumbai, Govt. MP National Awards, *BAS*. Fellowship *JJSA*. Appointments: Joined the *WSC* Mumbai, designing several wall hangings & *screen printings* before being invited to Tokyo by the International known fashion designer Hanac Mori to create Indian Fabric *Designs*. Collections: *NGMA* New Delhi, Gwalior Art Gallery, *LKA* Orissa, *BB*; International: Modern Art Gallery Rome, pvt. USA, Switzerland, Czechoslovakia, West Indies.

He has been inspired by *folk* and *tribal art* and *design*, incorporating elements of *Basohli painting* and Indian textile *design* into his *paintings*. His rhythmical *figures* blend in the shadows or stand out in contrast to the *background*.

He lives and works in Mumbai.

Depth A *term* used in *art*, as pertaining to the *perspective* used with an acute recession showing an *illusion* of more *space*. In Indian sculptural *relief*, height and width have been used to create depth and three-dimensional effects, e.g. *Ellora*. In miniatures, especially in *Mughal miniatures*, depth is represented by the *figures* moving to the upper part of the *picture*, while those in the lower part represent the *foreground*. In *modern* times it has been seen in the works *Raja Ravi Varma*, *Ramkinkar Baij*, *Pestonjee Bomanjee* and *Hemendranath Mazumdar* among others, and the earlier works of *Jamini Roy* and *Jamini P. Gangooly* with the depiction of *space* in a *realistic manner*, with the use of *atmospheric effect*. Depth has also been conveyed in Indian *sculpture*, with both high and low *relief* being used. Refer *Bengal School*, *Dimension*, *Drapery*, *Sculpture*, *Landscape*, *Frontality*, *Gupta*, *Bhagwan Chavan*, *Vinod Dube*, *Gajanan S. Haldankar*, *K.B. Kulkarni*, *Kanayi Kunhiraman*, *Anjolie Ela Menon*, *Bhanwar Singh Panwar*, *Ravinder G. Reddy*, *M. Sanathanan*.

Desai, Ajit R. (1943–1994) b. Pipaldhara, GUJ. Education: Dip. in *applied arts MSU*. GDA *sculpture*, *fresco* & *mural* Banasthali. Solos: Mumbai, Ahmedabad, Surat. Group participations: Mumbai, Ahmedabad, New Delhi, *Biennale BB*; International: Houston USA. Awards: GUJ State *LKA*, *AIFACS BAS*. Senior Fellowships: HRD 1993–94. Appointments: Was Principal CNCFA. Collections: *NGMA* & *LKA* New Delhi, GUJ *LKA*, Air India Mumbai; His *drawings* & *graphics* collection in Mumbai, Ahmedabad & Germany.

Ajit R. Desai had explored many *mediums* including *drawing*, *printmaking*, *sculpture* and *painting*. From the strict horizontal and vertical division of *space* with minutely detailed *forms* in the late 60s, to subtly graded floating *forms* and *J. Swaminathan* inspired *minimalism* in the 70s and then on to the gestual floating *forms* in the 90s, he had exploited each *technique* to the fullest. His *mixed media sculptures* show his interest in *Constructivism* and *Assemblage*. Here too he preferred to use contrasting *textures*, like juxtaposing the polished, shining surface of *brass* against grained *marble* or *wood*.

Desai, Bhupendra (1932–) b. Piphalgabhan, GUJ. Education: Post-Grad. Dip. in creative *painting MSU*. Over 16 solos: *LKA* Ahmedabad, TAG, *JAG*. Group shows: Baroda Group of Artists in New Delhi & Mumbai. Group participations: National Exhibition & *Triennale* New Delhi, GUJ State Exhibition, *AIFACS*, *BAS*. Awards: GUJ *LKA*, *BAS*, *AIFACS*. Commissions: *Murals* Parliament House New Delhi also including Kennedy Airport USA. Appointments: Lecturer for *painting MSU*; Joined *WSC* Mumbai & worked for nearly 30 years. Collections: *LKA* & *NGMA* New Delhi, TIFR; International: Air India, USA pvt. & public national & international.

His work as a designer has served as a source of inspiration for his *painting*, which has a wall-hanging-like effect to it. In the earlier works, there is a restraint both in the application and in the use of straight *lines* of *colours* against a pale, sober *background*. Since the beginning of the 90s, he began *painting* with the *palette knife*, applying thick, bright patches of *paint* for a frenzied, sculptural look.

He lives and works in Valsad, GUJ.

Desai, Kanu (1907–1980) b. Bharuch, GUJ. Education: *Santiniketan*, under the tutelage of *Nandalal Bose* with the encouragement of *Ravishankar M. Raval*. Solos: Including *JAG*; International: USA. Received awards. Appointments: *Art* Dir. in the film industry for several years. Publications: several albums of *drawings* & *watercolours* few entitled "Rup-Lekha", "Nritya-Rekha", "Mangalashtaka"—works of love life & marriage. Collections: pvt.

Kanu Desai's two years at *Santiniketan* served to infuse his *drawings* with a delicate and linguistic grace of *line* and *colour*. He not only designed the stage *backdrops* for the films of which he was Art Dir., but also designed the costumes, jewellery and other decorative objects used as stage props. While he first joined Prakash Pictures he also worked with the *art* Studio of Dir. V. Shantaram. His *compositions* in *painting* and subjects were at once religious, literary and romantic. While most of the *gods* and goddesses were romanticized and depicted in semi-contemporaneous attire, his metaphorical *compositions* show the amalgamation of the traditional with the faux *modern* in his negation of the *background* to stylized *lines* and *forms*. Most of his albums were produced with a view of bringing *art* within the reach of the common man. Refer Illustration–SHIVA.

Design In *contemporary art*, the *term* means the building up of general compositional work or a detail thereof. Design in India have been inspired by traditional, *sculpture*, *folk* and *tribal art*, incorporating elements as diverse as *motifs* from of *miniature painting* and textile *design* ancient *pottery* and *metal craft*. YANTRA & TANTRA *motifs* are also commonly found. Refer. *Art Deco*, *Art Nouveu*, *Backdrop*, *Craft*, *Ceramic*, *Calligraphic*, *Flora & Fauna Painting*, *Printmaking*, *Jyoti Bhatt*, *Jyotsna Bhatt*, *Kanu Desai*, *Shaibal Ghosh*, *K.V. Haridasan*, *Ganga Devi*, *Baburao Painter*, *J. Swaminathan*, *Raja Ravi Varma*.

Designscape Gallerie (DG) (Mumbai, MAHA). DG was set up in 1985 in response to the widely felt need of opening an *art* gallery in the suburbs of Mumbai. Since then, the gallery has held shows of *paintings*, *sculptures*, *ceramics*, *metal craft* and *stained glass*. *Narayan S. Bendre*, *K.K. Hebbar*, *Sunil Das*, *Shanti Dave*, *Ram Kumar*, *Akbar Padamsee*, Micky Patel, *Gopal S. Adivrekar*, *K.M. Adimoolam*, *Vinod Shah*, *Vrindavan Solanki*, *B. Prabha*, *B. Vithal*, Mani Narayan, Sigrun Srivastav, *Jyotsna Bhatt*, Primula Pandit, Pratima Vaidya, *Chhaganlal D. Mistry* are among some of the artists who have exhibited here. It has been situated at Dadar T.T. since 2000.

Detailed Work It is the opposite of the broad *manner*; detailed work involves the use of many *motifs* or intricate *patterns*, usually on a miniature scale. Certain *styles* evolved based on the amalgamation of *colour*, *theme* and *pictorial* quality of Indian and Persian miniatures emphasizing minute *designs* elements, especially in the *patterns* on costumes and carpets. Refer *Ajanta*, *Ellora*, *Broad Handling*, *Folk Art*, *Sculpture*, *Papier Mache*, *Technique*, *Bengal School*, *Bombay School*, *Madras School of Art*, *Pestonjee Bomanjee*, *Nandalal Bose*, *Hemendranath Mazumdar*; *Raja Ravi Varma*; Illustration–*Ajanta*, APSARA.

Deuskar, Gopal Damodar (1911–1994) b. Ahmednagar. Education: Dip. in *painting JJSA*, Nizam Govt. Grant, Scholarship for 5 years study in Europe, specialized in *painting*, Art Academies London, Paris, Vienna, Madrid, Berlin. Group participations: *LKA* New Delhi, Simla Art Exhibition, *BAS*; International: Exhibition at Burlington House, Exhibition of Modern Indian Art New Burlington Gallery, Contemporary Indian Art Royal Institute Piccadilly, RAA. Awards: Viceroy's Medal at Simla Art Exhibition, Hon. *LKA* New Delhi, Gold Medal *JJSA*, *BAS*; Represented India International Conference on Plastic Art Vienna. Appointments: Deputy Dir. *JJSA*; Worked in *LKA* New Delhi for 6 years. Collections: *Murals* Bal Bhavan Mumbai, Tilak Smarak Mandir Pune, *Paintings* Parliament House, Supreme Court & Rashtrapati Bhavan New Delhi, Vidhan Bhavan & High Court Mumbai, *Maharaja Fatesingh Museum* Vadodara, Bal Gandharva Theatre & Tilak Smarak Mandir Pune, *VMM*; International: India House London, pvt. & public in national & international.

Gopal Damodar Deuskar's field of specialization was portraiture. He was commissioned by the Indian Parliament to paint the *portrait* of Jawaharlal Nehru. *Portraits* of many other national leaders and eminent industrialists adorn the walls of august buildings and royal houses such as those of the Gaekwads of Vadodara. Two of his *drawings* from an exhibition of works of students of *JJSA* were selected by Her Majesty Queen Mary.

His *style* of portraiture was different. Not only did he capture the physical likeness of his subjects but created a *visual* impact by the life-like vividness of the personality. This was mainly due to the fact that he did not use *photographs* of his subject but preferred live sittings and in the case of deceased persons he used similar looking live *models*. Details of clothes and accessories underline his artistic sense and sensibility. His works show sensitivity in *colour* and *composition* which combine Indian and Western influences.

Deuskar, Kavita b. Hyderabad. Education: Dip. in *painting* & *sculpture* College of FA. & Architecture Hyderabad, Specialized in *mural design MSU*. Solos: Hyderabad, New Delhi, Mumbai, Kolkata, Mysore, Vadodara; International: Germany. Group participations: Hyderabad, Galleria Mumbai, *GG*, *JAG*; International: Germany, Hongkong, Singapore, London. *Art* camps & workshops: MMB Kolkata, others in Chennai, Hyderabad & Jamshedpur. Awards: Gold Medal 1971 All India Art Exhibition & Stree Mela Hyderabad, AP *LKA*. Appointments: HoD of *painting* JNTU. Collections: AP *LKA* Hyderabad, *NGMA* New Delhi, *SJM*; International: UK, USA, UAE & pvt.

Kavita Deuskar comes from a family of well known *artists* like the late R.W. Deuskar, Sukumar Deuskar, *Gopal Damodar Deuskar* and Shashi Hesh. She has explored several *mediums* in *drawing*, *painting* and *mural* designing using *fresco*, *egg tempera*, *terracotta*, *mosaic*, sand and *cast cement*, *wood* and *stained glass*. However, her preferred mode of expression is *pencil drawing*, both in *black* and *white* and *colour*. Her subjects are culled from her immediate environment. There is an element of satire in her minutely observed portrayals of the colourful Telengana and Hyderabadi people that she comes across in the poorer quarters of that city. There is no decorative approach to her *themes*. Kavita Deuskar is more *realistic* and uses few *colours*, with a subtle use of *contour shading*.

She lives in Hyderabad.

Devanagari Script The Brahmi script of the Mauryan period was one among some sixty-four scripts then known in India. It was a highly developed writing system with simple geometric *forms* of minute accuracy. It was to provide the base for the development of various scripts all over India. Although they differ in signlist and depiction of letters, most of them inherit a common feature–a specific sign for a specific sound and phonetic, rather than syllabic or ideographic.

A non-decorative Brahmi descended from the North to the West, eventually becoming Devanagari. Derived its name from the Nagar Brahmins of GUJ who originally practised it, it is easily the most widely used of the scripts.

The most scientific of all languages, it can be classified into two groups according to *size*, i.e. full-size letters and extra-sized letters, which go over or under the *line*, and two groups according to simplicity i.e. single stroke letters or letters with more than one stroke, seven groups according to motion, stroke and angles, six groups according to endings and flourishes. Refer Illustration–KARMA.

Devanagari Script: "Adi Purana Paper", circa AD 1425–1450, Delhi Gwalior.

Dey, Gopal (1929–) b. Dacca, Bangladesh. Education: *GCAC* Kolkata. Solos: Kolkata, Varanasi, *AIFACS*. Retrospective: *AFA* Kolkata. Group participations: Varanasi, Allahabad, with his little friends (children) *AIFACS*. Awards: *AFA* Kolkata. Member: Anand Bazar Patrika Manimela Kolkata. Appointments: Once held a visual publicity for the film "Kabuliwala"; radio talks relating to children. Publications: poems, short stories "Chitrakares Dairy, i.e. Path Chalty". Collections: national & international also from children's *exhibitions*.

He joined the Botanical Survey of India in 1957 which brought him in close contact with *nature* which in turn was reflected in his *painting*. His preferred *medium* is *watercolour* which he approached with a spontaneity and naivety only seen in child *art*. He has a rich sense of *colour* with subtle and powerful brushstrokes. His later series of *paintings* are titled "Man is the only animal to fear". Gopal Dey tries to make a statement on behalf of the poor and the downtrodden.

He lives and works in Kolkata.

Dey, Jagadish (1942–) b. Bengal. Education: *College of Art* New Delhi. Solos: Gallery Sanskriti Kolkata, TKS, *Dhoomimal*, TAG, *JAG*. Group participations: Hyderabad, *LKA*, *NGMA*, Group 8, RB & People of Animals New Delhi, *Harmony* Mumbai, *BAAC* Kolkata, *Chandigarh Museum*, *Biennale BB*, *AIFACS*, SKP, *JAG*; International: Washington DC, Bangladesh, *AIFACS* shows in London, Sharjah & Mexico, *Biennale* Tokyo & Bangladesh. *Art* camps: *LKA* New Delhi, SKP, *Graphic GAC*; Workshops: *LKA* New Delhi, *AIFACS*; International: American Centre Washington DC. Awards: *AIFACS*, SKP. Member: Founder member Group 8, The Six & Gallery 26 New Delhi. Commissions: *Mural* National Book Trust New Delhi. Collections: Rashtrapati Bhawan, *NGMA* & *LKA* New Delhi, *Roopankar BB*; International: Smithsonian Institute Washington DC.

The subject of Jagadish Dey's *painting* has varied from the strong vertical *lines* of *drapery* to the use of vases and mushroom *motifs* with petal like delineations. He later concentrated on the human *figure*, predominantly pensive female *figures* with dark shadowed eyes holding *attributes* like peacocks and phallic blossoms, in the *manner* of NAYIKAs in the RAGAMALA *paintings*. His *colours* are luminous, in the *manner* of M. Chagall. His *paintings* do not convey any political or day-to-day messages, but the dreamy quietness is still full of meanings.

Jagadish Dey lives in New Delhi where he is a lecturer at the *College of Art*.

Dey, Manishi (1912–1967) b. WB. Studied *art* under *Abanindranath Tagore* & *Nandalal Bose*. Collections: Pusa Research Institute Library & pvt.

The younger brother of *Mukul Chandra Dey*, Manishi Dey was well known as a commercial *artist*, in addition to his occa-

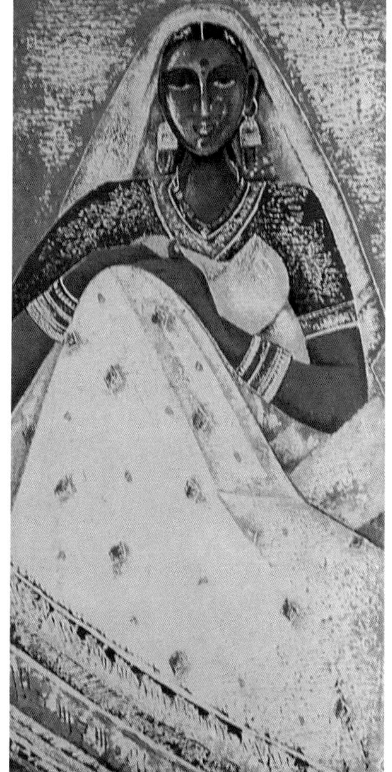

Dey, Manishi: "Untitled", *Tempera* on Board, 1965, 60x30 cm.

sional creative works. Though he studied at *Santiniketan*, he did not adhere to the *Bengal School style*. He was proficient in *watercolour*, *wash* and *tempera*, producing more *figure studies* than *landscapes*. He travelled the length of the country, living mostly in Mumbai and Bangalore. In Mumbai, he designed several *posters* for the TATAs, the railways, textile mills and factories. In the South, he experimented in *tempera* and *watercolour* sketching Indian women dressed in colourful costumes, playing with *form* and *colour*. In Mumbai, he worked on a variety of *themes*, concentrating chiefly on *tempera* and *line drawings*. In Gwalior, he produced some of his most *modern* works, without recourse to repulsiveness or *distortion*. The works of Manishi Dey are not rooted in any one *style* or *technique*. From his early decorative phase to his later austere stark *Realism* (Gwalior), his output represents a kaleidoscopic convergence of feeling and moods. He was meticulous painstakingly, achieving pieces of elaborate refinement, such as his elusive *paintings* of Indian maidenhood.

Dey, Mukul Chandra (1895–1989) Education: ARCA, FRSA (London), MCSE (USA), IES, Grade 1 (Retd.) Rabindranath Tagore School *Santiniketan*, *Art* with *Abanindranath Tagore* 1911–15; Slade School of Art, University College, RCA South Kensington & King Alfred School London, Fulbright Scholar USA, Dip. in *mural painting* 1920–21 copied cave *frescoes* of *Ajanta* & Bagh. Solos: Nagpur, Varanasi, Suri Birbhum Kolkata, *Visva Bharati*, *VBU*, *ISOA*; International: Royal Academy, British Museum London, Walker Art Gallery Liverpool, V&A. Group show: with T. Sugimoto Kolkata. Group participations: Kolkata; International: Paris, Holland, London, Tokyo, San Francisco, Art Institute Chicago, Walker Art Gallery Liverpool, London, Royal Academy & British Museum V&A. *Auctions*: Heart Mumbai & New Delhi, Osian's Mumbai. Awards: Receiver of their Majesties' Royal Command and forwarded *paintings* & *etchings* for their Majesties inspection at Buckingham Palace 1927, Received their Majesties King George V & Queen Mary's Jubilee Medal & Coronation Medal, Won scholarship RCA; Received WB Govt. "Abanindra Puraskar" & Conferred with Hon. D.Litt. by *RBU*. Member: Advisory Committee for *murals* New Delhi, Founder of Suri Birbhum Kolkata & Kalika Art Gallery *Santiniketan*; International: India House London, Life member Chicago Society of Etchers. Commissions: Indian *murals* at Wembley Exhibition. Appointments: *Art* teacher *Santiniketan*, first Indian Principal of the GSA, Trustee & Curator in art section of *Indian Museum* & elected a Fellow of *LKA* Kolkata; International: *Art* teacher King Alfred School London, Lecturer London County Council & Art Workers Guild London, Bedeles School Birmingham & at various pvt. gatherings in England; Prof. at College of Idaho Caldwell, Hollins College, Virgin Alabama, Montevallo USA. Publications: "My pilgrimages to Ajanta & Bagh", "My Reminiscences", "Fifteen dry-points", "Twenty portraits", "Portraits from life of Mahatma Gandhi", "Temple terracotta of Birbhum" & several articles on Indian *art* & travels.

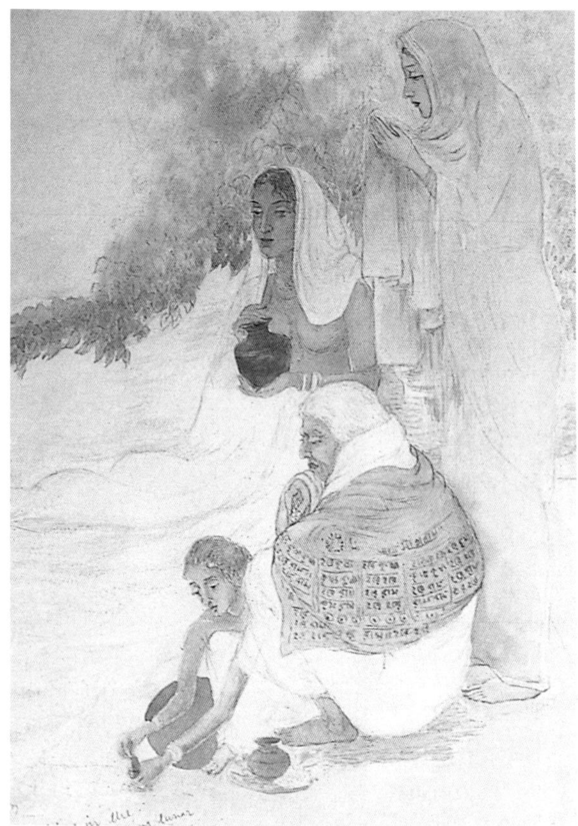

Dey, Mukul Chandra: "Lunar Eclipse", *Watercolours*.

He studied *etching* and mastered the *technique* of *dry-points*, which he was to use to great effect, merging the *linearity* of that *technique* with the *Bengal School style*. This can be seen in the "Boat on the river Ganga".

Mukul Chandra Dey had an indigenous and native outlook on life and *arts* and was an accomplished *artist* before he toured Europe. He could therefore master Western *techniques* without losing any of his traditional *background*. His *etchings* display the skilful manipulation of *lines* and strokes, suggesting *space*, *tone* and *volume* with minimal effort. He used both decorative detailing and bold *brushwork* with equal ease. His head studies of Einstein, Sven Hedin, Annie Besant and others show his fine understanding of characterization. His *sketches*, too were bought by discriminating collectors, pointing to his skill in that *art form* as well.

Dey, Sailendranath (d. 1971) b. Allahabad, UP. Education: Calcutta School of Arts, *BKB* Varanasi, Patna School; Studied under *Abanindranath Tagore* and *Rabindranath Tagore*, Studied Patra Kalam under Ishwari Prasad. Solos & group participations: *BKB* Varanasi; International: London. Publications: Book on Indian *painting* (about 1959) describing the *painting manners*, primitive *style* of making *colours*. Set up an institute to impart *art education* along with *art* historian Rai Krishnadas. Collections: *BKB* Varanasi, *Banasthali Vidyapith* RAJ & other museums; pvt. *Deokinandan Sharma*.

A forerunner of the *Bengal School*, Sailendranath Dey tried to approach *painting* in the *manner* of *Abanindranath Tagore*, especially in the *matter* of compositional elements.

However, his *style* was basically decorative and had its roots in traditional Indian *art*. The 'Meghdoot' (Rain God) series, based on Kalidasa's work of the same name shows a more naturalistic approach. Here *landscape* is highly simplified, and stylized into mere *form*. The use of unmodulated planes of *colour* too signals this simplistic and delicate approach, which is in total contrast to his earlier works.

Dhanapal, Ravi (1956–) b. Chennai, TN. Son of *sculptor Subrayalu Dhanapal*. Education: Dip. & Post-Dip. *GCAC* Chennai. Solos & group shows: State Academy & Values Art Foundation Chennai, *CKP, JAG*. Group participations: National Exhibition & *WSC* New Delhi, Mumbai, Chennai & Kolkata, All India Exhibition Bangalore, *AFA* & *BAAC* Kolkata, *LKA* New Delhi, Art World Gallery Chennai, *CKP, ABC. Art* camps: Kodaikannal by State Academy Chennai, *LKA* Chennai at Amarvati. Awards: TN State Academy Annual Scholarship, *SAI*. Collections: *LKA* New Delhi, Govt. Museum Chennai.

Dhanapal Ravi's *paintings* are *landscapes* of diffused *colour*, each one of his "Crystal World" series being a near *monochrome* approach towards abstraction with dark *tones* submerged into thin *washes* at the edges of the *canvas*.

He lives and works in Chennai.

Dhanapal, Subrayalu (1919–2000) b. Mylapore, Chennai. Education: Madras School of Arts & Crafts under *Debi Prasad RoyChowdhury*. Group participations: All India Exhibition 1985, National *LKA* Exhibition 1962, *Art Heritage* New Delhi, "The Madras Metaphor" *exhibition* Mumbai & Chennai; International: Art Exhibition Germany, Commonwealth Exhibition London & others. *Art* camps: Srinagar, Jammu and Kashmir, for *Sculptors* Regional Center *LKA* Chennai, Tamil University Thanjaur. *Auctions*: Heart & Osian's Mumbai. Awards: National Award *LKA* New Delhi. Fellowship: TN Chennai & HRD for two years. Founder member: *Cholamandal* along with *K.C.S. Paniker*. Appointments: *Art* Instructor Madras School of Arts & Crafts Chennai, Principal of *GCAC* and retired in 1977.

He worked with the *graphic medium* in the early days, executing delicate *brush drawings* of CHOLA and PALLAVA *bronzes*. Later he switched to *sculpture*. He was one of the first *sculptors* in the country to break away from academic *Realism*. From the simplified heads and Rodinesque *portraits* in the 50s he experimented with various *media*, including *concrete, plaster, lead, stone, terracotta* and *metal*. He explored constructivist methods in the 60s, creating *sculptures* out of hollows and pierced *forms*. However his preference for linear *form* had always surfaced in most of his *creations* either as decorative patterning or in the *contour* shapes of his *sculpture*. He lived in Chennai.

Dhanjal, Avtarjeet S. (1939–) b. Dalla, PUJ. Education: Dip. in *sculpture* School of Art Chandigarh; Advanced *sculpture* St. Martin's School London, *Artist* in residence Alcan Aluminium UK. Solos: Dudlet Castle & Gallery 27 UK, Spring Museum Germany. Group participations: "Forma Viva" Yugoslavia, Galton Valley & Aston University Birmingham UK, South of the world show Sicily Italy. Commissions: *sculptures* including Bodicote House Oxen, British Gas Training College Leeds, Dunstall Henge at Peace Green Wolverhampton, Senneley's Park Birmingham UK; Environmental *sculpture* Chandigarh India; Worked on *installations* at the St. Louis *Arts* Festival in USA & the Museu de Arte Contemoranea Sao Paolo Brazil & co-designed a 10 acre park at Cardiff Bay–making a conceptual piece of *sculpture* that weaves through the whole park, UK and other *sculptures* in Yugoslavia & Wales. Publications: Report Folk Arts & Crafts PUJ, Delivered series of 10 lectures at the University of Sao Paolo Brazil; Interviewed on British TV & Radio & a channel for documentary film *sculptures* in Yugoslavia & Wales. Collections: National *LKA* New Delhi, PUJ University Patiala, Govt. Museum Chandigarh; International: Cortwright Hall Bradford, Dominion Centre Southall London, Museu de Arte Contemporanea Sao Paolo Brazil, Town Parks Telford & Warwick University.

Highly polished *metal* structures, buttress or imprison large pieces hunks of rock in some of his works. He has also used fire, incorporating candles into small holes drilled into the rock surface. He also uses photography as a means of making *images*, delicately observing natural phenomena, helping to release his idea of material into its broader meaning of the native and of the elements. From this he went on to make outdoor *sculptures* where the *image* is modified by its relationship to the surrounding *space* and heightened by the play of *shadows*. His work at Cardiff park is a conceptual *sculpture* that weaves through the whole park. The work titled "Contribution" is approached by a defined pathway which starts at the low seat placed in a direct *line* with the main orientation of the piece.

He lives and works in Shropshire UK.

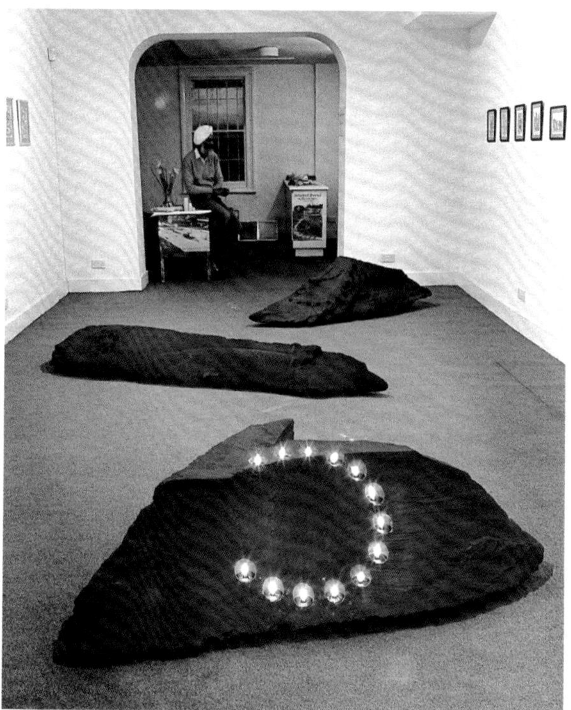

Dhanjal, Avtarjeet S.: "Contribution", Horton *Stone* & *Aluminium*, 1981, 9.7x5.8x3.5 mt.

Dhar, Ramlal (1953–) b. Karimganj, Assam. Education: Dip. in Indian *style* of *painting GCAC* Kolkata, under *Atul Bose*; Ecole National des Arts Decoratifs de Nice France. Solos & group shows: *Santiniketan*, Guwahati, Kolkata, New Delhi, Chennai; International: Nice, Cannes, Marseilles, Vichy, St. Paul de Vence all in France, Milan Italy, Singapore. Group participations: National Exhibition *LKA* New Delhi, MMB 300 years of Kolkata & Silver Jubilee *BAAC* Kolkata, WB Govt. & *ISOA, G88, JAG, Biennale BB*; International: *Biennale* France. *Art* camps & workshops: SZCC Gwalior, *BAAC* Kolkata, *LKA* New Delhi. Awards: National Scholarship in *mural* & *GCAC* Kolkata, *ISOA*; French Scholarship in *mural* & *mosaic* 1978–80. Commissions: *Mural painting*, *frescoes* & *mosaic* works in India; International: in Nice France 1978–84. Appointments: Prof. at *GCAC* Kolkata.

The *highlight* of his *paintings* is a simplicity of expression, emotive qualities and a brilliant almost fauvist use of *colours*. Though he has experimented with *encaustic*, *fresco*, *mosaic*, *ceramic*, *watercolour*, *pastels*, *acrylic* and *mixed media*, his preferred *medium* is *gouache*. His *landscapes* open up a world of enchantment, pointing to his close communion with *nature*.

He works in Kolkata.

Dhar, Sohini (1963–) b. Kolkata. Education: B.FA., M.FA., Ph.D. with *landscape VBU*. Joint shows: Alliance Francaise Chennai, *Art Heritage* New Delhi, *SAI*. Group participations: *BAAC*, *AFA* & WBSA Kolkata, National Exhibition *LKA* New Delhi, *BB*. Awards: *VBU*; UGC Junior Research Fellowship.

Sohini Dhar has explored several *mediums* including *mixed media* with conte, *charcoal*, *pastel* and *ink*, in addition to *painting* with *oils* on *canvas*. Since the past few years, she has worked exclusively on the *theme* of *landscape*. Her *drawings* in conte and *pastel* have a degree of *Realism* that is greatly subdued in her feminist *paintings*. These arbitrarily coloured works veer towards abstraction with their *aerial perspective* and simplified shapes.

Sohini Dhar lives and works in Kolkata along with her *artist* husband *Ramlal Dhar*.

Dharmani, M. (1931–) b. Bhiria, Sind. Education: M.A. in history PUJ, Dip. in *FA*. *VBU*. Specialized *sculpture* under *Ramkinkar Baij* 1952. Solos: RB & Rashtriya Kala Mela New Delhi, *AIFACS*, TKS; International: USA, Germany. Group participations: RB New Delhi, *Chandigarh Museum*, *LKA* Lucknow, *AIFACS*, *Dhoomimal*, TKS, *JAG*; International: Portorz Yugoslavia, Antwerp Belgium, South Korea, *Biennale* Sao Paulo Brazil. *Art* camps & workshops: *LKA Mahabalipuram* & Srinagar, *Art Education* workshop for teachers New Delhi, SKP in Haryana, *AIFACS*. Member: Jury—All India Education *LKA* UP, Patna & *AIFACS*. Commissions: Mussoorie, New Delhi. Appointments: Graduate & Post Graduate examinerships in *sculpture*—College of Art Gwalior, Jabalpur & Lucknow, BHU, JMI, *VBU*. Publications: "Marg" magazine Mumbai, "Art News" *AIFACS*, *Jaya Appasamy's* "Modern Indian Sculpture". Collections: *NGMA* & *LKA* New Delhi, *Chandigarh Museum*, J&K Academy Srinagar; International: Open Air Sculpture Museum Portroz Yugoslavia & pvt. USA, Russia, Germany.

M. Dharmani has experimented with various *media* including *wood*, *stone*, *bronze*, *cement*, polyester and sheet *metal*. His early works were geometric. His *figurative* works are Indian showing simplification of structure and *colour*. He has also worked on *aluminium* sheet painted with *oil colours*.

He lives and works in New Delhi.

Dhawan, Rajendra (1936–) b. New Delhi. Education: Dip. *College of Art* New Delhi. Studied Belgrade Yugoslavia. Solos: *GC* Mumbai, *PUAG*, *VAG*, *Dhoomimal*; International: Galerie Francois Mitaine & Gallery du Haut-Pave Paris, Gallery Horn Luxeumberg. Group participations: National Exhibition & *Triennale* New Delhi, *Gallery 7* Mumbai; International: *Biennale* Ten Painters 1971, Indian Artists Galerie du Cygne & City International in Paris. Founded group: The Unknown. Collections: *NGMA* & *LKA* New Delhi, PUJ University Museum Chandigarh, *BB*; International: Paris, Museum Rigand Perpignan.

Rajendra Dhawan's *paintings* are essentially non-objective in *nature*, made up of elements which if taken in isolation would appear absurd. They are diffused together in a *harmony* of *colour* and non-*colour form* and formlessness. In the early 70s he employed patches of pure *colour*, which though seductive by themselves, did not integrate with the rest of the *composition*. He has overcome this in his latest works where, beyond the use of detail, he establishes the relationship of *forms*.

Dhir, R.S. (1937–) b. India. Education: M.FA. in *painting* BHU & HoD of *painting*. Solos: KB (*BKB*) Varanasi, Information Centre & *LKA* Lucknow, *BAAC* Kolkata, Birla Museum & MPKP Bhopal, BHU, others Ujjain, Agra; International: Nepal. Group shows & participations: National Exhibition New Delhi, *AFA* & *BAAC* Kolkata, All India Exhibitions, *BAS*, HAS, *AIFACS*; Participated: Teachers' Organization by Indian Society for Technical Education Board New Delhi at *JJIAA*. *Art* camps: State *LKA* UP, Central *LKA* Lucknow, HRD Education Dept. New Delhi & demonstrations in Bareilly & Agra University. Awards: Including IAFA Amritsar, Gold Plaque MKKP Raipur MP, State *LKA* Lucknow, *AFA* Kolkata.

He started working with the *watercolour medium* using the *wash* process later adding *collage* and knife *painting* to his repertoire of *techniques*. He prefers *figuration*, with *landscapes* and *still lifes* being his favourite subjects.

He lives in Varanasi.

Dhond, Pralhad A. (1908–2001) b. Ratnagiri, MAHA. Education: Dip. in *drawing* & *painting* & Art Masters *JJSA*, Arts & Crafts Teacher's certificate *Santiniketan*, Prof. & Dean of the *JJSA* for a period of 10 years 1937–1968, Art Dir. MAHA State 1968. Solos: *Santiniketan* 1949, *Artists' Centre* & Son-et-Lumiere Mumbai, Kala Academy Goa, *JAG*. Group participations: *LKA* & National Exhibition New Delhi, *AIFACS*, *BAS*; International: Kabul, Ankara, China, Russia through *AIFACS*; Participated: In seminars on *Art Education*. Awards: *BAS* in Pune & Mumbai; National Exhibition & Medals in India. Publications: "Rapan" in Marathi to his credit. Collections: Including National Museum *LKA* New Delhi,

Bhau Daji Museum Mumbai, Nagpur Museum, *Maharaja Fatesingh Museum* Vadodara; International: Moscow Art Museum, Pvt. London, USA, San Francisco, Russia, Germany, Durban.

He has specialized in *watercolour seascapes*, producing spontaneous impression of water, boats and sky in a broad *harmony* of *brushwork* and *colour*. His main *colours* are *transparent* blue, bluegreen. He painted fast without any kind of retouching.

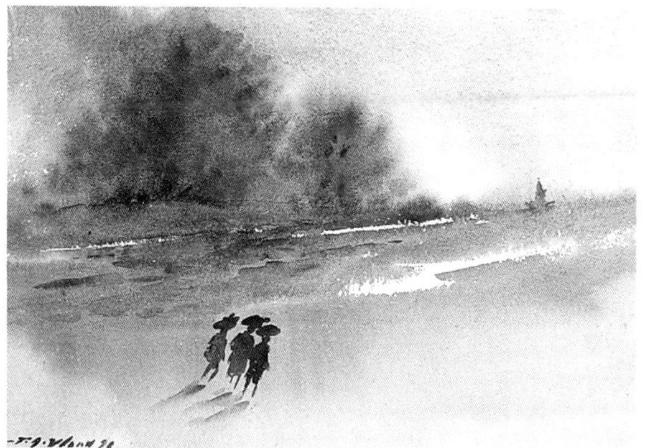

Dhond, Pralhad A.: "Landscape", *Watercolours*, 1996, 37x54 cm.

Dhoomimal Art Centre (Dhoomimal) (New Delhi). Situated in Connaught Place in New Delhi, was originally part of the Dhoomimal founded in 1936 by R.C. Jain. After the passing away of the father and his two sons, Ravi and Mohinder, the gallery was divided into two sections. This *Art Centre* is devoted to the cause of promoting *art* awareness and is run by Sushma Jain (wife of Mohinder) and her son Mohit Jain since 1984. Solo shows of senior and junior *artists* are held here including *Laxman Pai*. Refer *Dhoomimal Art Gallery*.

Dhoomimal Art Gallery (Dhoomimal) (New Delhi) It was founded in 1936 by Ram Chand Jain, is the oldest *art* gallery in India. Later Ram Babu's (as R.C. Jain was affectionately known) two sons, Mohinder and Ravi Jain looked after the gallery. In 1989, Ravi Jain extended the activities of the gallery by creating two new wings: Open Air Sculpture Garden and Collector's Gallery. Since his demise in 1991, his wife (Uma) set up the Ravi Jain Memorial Foundation to promote young *artists* by offering three fellowships each year–two for *painters* and one for a *sculptor*. An additional scholarship for *art critics* has also been instituted. The foundation also promotes *art* activities by organizing *exhibitions* on an All India level arranging seminars and interaction between *artists*, *critics* and *art* lovers. *Artists* whose works have been exhibited here include *Jaya Appaswamy*, *Biren De*, *Gopal Ghose*, *Satish Gujral*, *K.K. Hebbar*, *Sailoz Mookerjea*, *P.T. Reddy*, *Jamini Roy*, and *Abanindranath Tagore*.

Dhuliya, Dwarika P. (1923–1991) b. Garhwal, UP. Education: Dip. in *FA*. GCAC Lucknow, HoD *FA*. & Music at the Gora-khpur University UP. Solos & group participations: Allaha-bad, Varanasi, Lucknow, Chennai, Goa, New Delhi, *LKA* Kolkata. Member: Executive Council, General Council UP State *LKA*. Hon.: Eminent *Artist* in 1979 UP *LKA* Lucknow & Silver Plaque & Shawl *AIFACS*. Publications: Several articles on *art*, Book "Chitra Darshan" (Glimpses of the Paintings of the Ajanta Caves) in Hindi, which was awarded a prize by the UP Govt. Collections: State Museum, UP State *LKA* & Vadhan Bhavan Lucknow, Allahabad Museum, Gorakhpur University UP, LKA Goa, *College of Art* New Delhi & SKP; International: Japan.

Being a student of *Asit K. Haldar* resulted in Dwarika P. Dhuliya's *style* being an *eclectic* amalgamation of certain elements of the *Bengal School* with a touch of academic *Realism*. He practised both the *wash technique* of *watercolour* and the modelled *form* possible in *oil painting*. His subjects were mostly *landscapes* and the inhabitants of his native Garhwal (village) with a predominance of hills and rocky terrain. The *style* is illustrational even in the *portrait compositions*.

Dhumal, Rini (1948–) b. Bengal. Education: M.A. in *painting MSU*. Solos: *Gallery 7* Mumbai, *SG* Chennai & Bangalore, *CYAG*, *Dhoomimal*, CCAG, *ATG*; International: Paris, Chile, Spain. Group participations: *LKA* Chennai, *CIMA* Kolkata, Art for Cry Mumbai & New Delhi, *CYAG*, *JAG*, *BB*; International: Greece, USA, UK, Holland, Germany, Cuba, Turkey, Taiwan. *Art* camps & workshops: *Graphic* camp Bhubaneshwar, *Painting* Workshop Hyderabad & Kolkata, Lithographic Workshop USIS, *Graphics* WZCC Udaipur, Chamarajendra Academy of Visual Art Mysore, *LKA* New

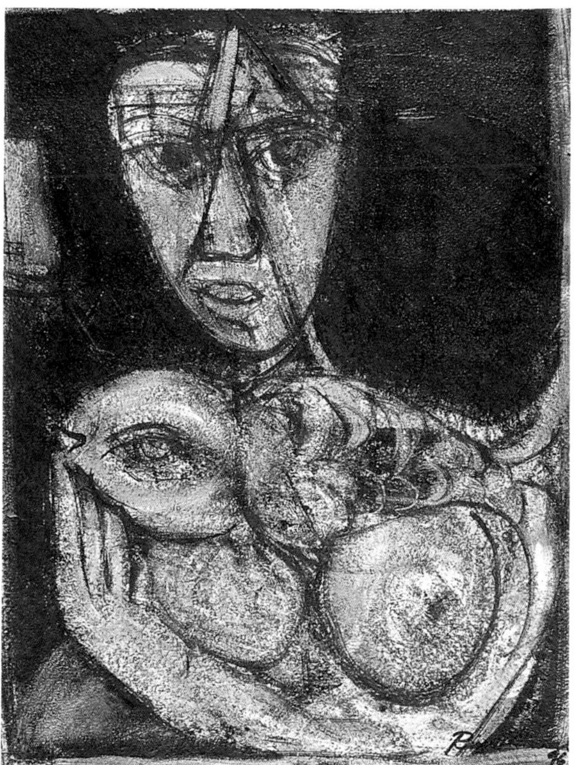

Dhumal, Rini: "Untitled", *Mixed media* on *Paper*, 1997.

Delhi, Alembic Vadodara, *MSU*, NID; International: *Graphic* workshop San Diego USA. Awards/Grants: *AIFACS*, *LKA*, Govt. of India Scholarship New Delhi, Governor's Gold Medal Kolkata, Group 8-Award, French Govt. Chancellor's Gold Medal Vadodara. Fellowship: Senior Fellowship HRD & Research Fellowship HRD New Delhi. Collections: Godrej Mumbai, *LKA* & *NGMA* New Delhi, *CYAG*, *BB*; International: Museum of Modern Art Baghdad, Bibliotheque Nationale Paris, Bronx Museum New York & pvt.

Rini Dhumal is both a *painter* and printmaker. She has explored several *mediums* and *techniques* including *linocut*, *lithography* and viscosity. *Colour printing* in *printmaking* and *painting* on *ceramic* tiles, board *canvas*, glass and *paper* using mostly *acrylic colours*. She has also worked with *pastels* exploiting the diffused malleability of that *medium* to the fullest. In most of her works, including the 'Bull' and the 'Head' series, one notices an iconic stillness of *form*, with her use of *frontality* coupled with primary areas of *colour*. The *opaque* resilience of board allows her to build up *form* in thick *overlapping* layers of *pigment* while glass brings a *luminosity* and unpredictability to her *composition*. The organic interplay between her heads and the surrounding vegetal and animal life in her recent works is a departure from the earlier isolated *figures*. Her *pictorial vocabulary* deals with the mythic and dream world, being punctuated with *images* both from the real and the subconscious. The female *form* predominates, vibrating with a latent yet vital energy.

She lives in Vadodara.

Dhurandhar, Ambika M. (1912–) b. Mumbai. Daughter of *artist Mahadev V. Dhurandhar*. Education: GDA *JJSA*. Besides arranging solos of her late father's works, she has regularly participated in several *exhibitions* all over India. Group participations: Women's *FA*. Kolkata, Shimla Fine Art Society, DAE Mysore, others in Nagpur, Chennai, Kolhapur, *BAS*. Her works are in several collections & she has also held a solo *exhibition* in Palanpur in 1946 at the invitation of the then Maharaja of the State. Collections: Patiala, Palanpur, Chhota Udaipur, Aundh, Miraj, Kolhapur, Mysore, Vadodara & Nagpur Museum.

Her works propagate the illustrational *style* of her father's, with historical and semi-mythological, literary subjects, serving as the main *themes*.

The *artist* is from Mumbai.

Dhurandhar, Mahadev V. (1867–1944) b. Kolhapur, MAHA. Rao Bahadur Mahadev V. Dhurandhar was a younger *contemporary* of *Raja Ravi Varma*, achieving recognition even when the *old master* was still alive. After studying at the British-run *JJSA*, he was appointed a teacher there. No solo during his lifetime but solos were held after his death by his daughter. Group participations: Shimla, Nagpur, Pune, Mysore, *BAS* & other. *Auctions*: Osian's & Heart Mumbai, Heart & Bowring's New Delhi, Bonham's, Christie's & Sotheby's London. Awards: He won several awards while still a student, winning a total of 19 gold, silver & bronze medals in his lifetime; Besides being honoured with the title of Rao Bahadur & being the first Indian to officiate as the Dir. of *Art* MAHA even though he never held a single solo *exhibition* of his works, his works were displayed at several prestigious *exhibitions* throughout the country. Publications: A book on his long association of over forty years with *JJSA* 1890–1951; He illustrated several books by various authors, mythological tales in several magazines & textbooks for children. Collections: His works are in the permanent collections of Imperial Secretariat New Delhi, Chota Udaipur Palace & Laxmi Vilas Palace GUJ (where *Raja Ravi Varma's* works are also displayed); International: Buckingham Palace, South Kensington Museum London.

Mahadev V. Dhurandhar belonged to the *Bombay School*, his *style* being more oriented towards *heroic illustration* in the neo-classical *manner*, though without the corresponding weight of the neo-classical use of *oils*. His *portraits* and *genre paintings* offer us a slice of life, with his minutely observed details of costume and custom. He basically painted female *models* of his native MAHA, wearing the typical nine-yard Saree and jasmine garlands in their hair. He also painted several mythological and historical *paintings*, displaying the bravery of the Maratha King, Shivaji. He used both the *watercolour* and *oil painting mediums*.

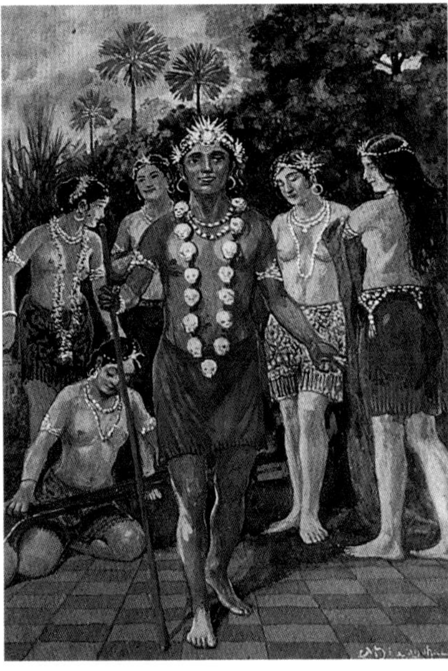

Dhurandhar, Mahadev V.: "Indian Music, Raga Marakash", *Watercolours*, 1943, 37.5x30 cm.

Dhyani-Buddha Dhyana=meditation, therefore the Dhyani-Buddhas are usually represented in *sculpture* as being absorbed in profound contemplation. They are supposed to have emanated from the Adi-Buddha (the first BUDDHA, again purely conceptual). They number five in all representing the five cosmic elements, *form*, sensation, name, conformation and consciousness. The conception of the five BUDDHAS was already known by AD 300. They are named Vairochana, Ratnasambhava, Amitabha, Amoghasiddhi and Akshobhya. Apart from meditation, they represent the attitude of beneficence, instruction and protection. They are represented in the PADMASANA position with the hands in the Dhyana MUDRA, with or without a cup resting on the opened palms, signifying receptivity. They are usually accompanied by their consorts thus representing the union of the opposites. Refer BODHISATTVA.

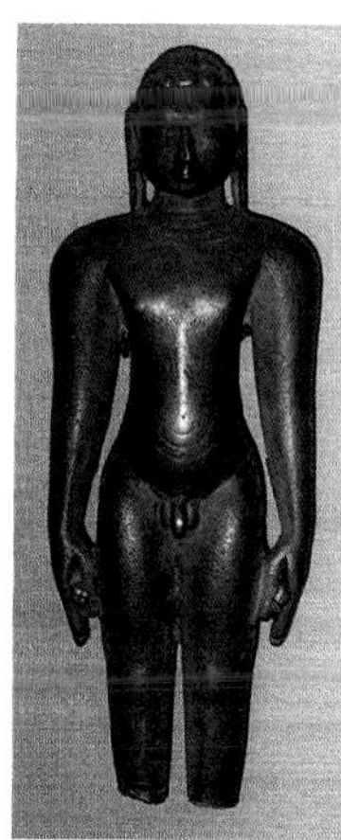

Digambara One of the two main sects in *Jainism*, Digambara literally means sky-clad. Therefore, monks of this sect usually do not wear any clothes at all. Sravanabelagola of the 10th century, the colossal 17 metre high statue of Gomateshwara, representing Bahubali the son of the Tirthankara Rishabadeva is representative of the Digambara sect. Refer *Ellora*, *Heroic*, SVETHAMBARA.

Digambara: "Standing Jina", *Bronze*, Karnataka, circa 13th century AD.

Dikhole, Namdeo B. (1923–) b. Yaoli, MAHA. Education: GDA in *painting* & Art Master Maha Kala Vidyalaya Nagpur. Solos: CAG Ahmedabad, WZCC Udaipur, *JAG*, *AIFACS*, *CYAG*, BHU & other towns Kolkata, Hyderabad, Jamshedpur, Pune; International: Windser Australia, Nepal Kathmandu. Group participations: Rashtriya Kala Mela *LKA* New Delhi, *AIFACS*, *BAS*. Workshops: UP *LKA* Lucknow. Awards: All India Exhibition HAS; Hon.: Veteran Artist by *AIFACS*. Member: *INTACH* New Delhi, Aurobindo Society Pondicherry, *BAS*, *AIFACS*. Founder Principal MAHA Kala Vidyalaya Nagpur. Collections: *BAAC* Kolkata, *LKA* New Delhi & Hyderabad, TATA-TELCO Jamshedpur, Museum Nagpur; International: Australia, England, USA, Canada, pvt. & corporates.

Namdeo B. Dikhole practised a *form* of academic impressionistic *landscape* in the 50s and 60s before simplifying the *landscape* elements. His *colours* changed from the natural to a gay *Fauvism* in the 80s. The setting of his *landscape* is always rural, a fact which is emphasized by the addition of a female *figure* either balancing a pot on her head or carrying a Puja Thali.

He lives and works in Nagpur. Refer Illustration–*Fauvism*.

Dimension The overall measurement of a work of *art*. In the case of *paintings*, height is given before width. In the case of *free-standing sculpture*, only its height, usually without the base or pedestal is given; in *bas-relief carvings*, height, width and sometimes *depth* used are stated. *Ramkinkar Baij* was one of the first Indian *sculptors* to realize the versatility of three-dimension effects in *modern sculpture* e.g. "Santhal Family", *Concrete*, 1938–39 ht 305 x bth 609 cm. Other examples–*Sculpture Aku*–"M-3", *leather*, *wood*, *alum*, 1997, 7.5 x 67 x 55 cm.; *Painting K.M. Adimoolam* "Red, Orange, Grey" *oil* on *canvas* 110 x 110 cm.; *Sculpture Navjot Altaf* "Across the Crossing", painted on *wood*, 110 x 42.5 x 45 cm. Refer Illustrations–*Installation*, *Seascape*.

Diptych A pair of panels made of *wood*, *ivory*, etc., hinged together, usually with scenes painted or carved on each. As with the *triptych*, the diptych was commonly used for religious *art* in mediaeval Europe. In India, *Akbar Padamsee*, *Laxman Shreshtha* and a few other *artists* have used this format for some of their works.

Direct Carving A method used in *sculpture*, when the *sculptor* directly works on the block of *stone* or *wood* or *marble*, without making any preliminary maquettes or *sketches*; this *technique* has been in use from the Stone age. Refer *Boucharde*, *Carving*, *Chisel*, *Sculpture*, *Ivory*, *Abu-Dilwara Temples*, *Ellora*, *Sadanandji Bakre*, *Dhanraj Bhagat*, *Adi Dawierwalla*, *Bhagwant K. Goregaoker*, *Debi Prasad RoyChowdhury*.

Discordant Synonymous with jarring or clashing in *painting*, discordant usually refers to the choice or application of *colour* not in *harmony*. The fauvists used discordant *colours* in their *compositions*. *Arpana Caur's* "The Body is just a garment" is a series that reflects this characteristic. Refer *Mannerism*, *Oil Pastels*, *Oil Crayons/Pastels*; Illustration–*Fauvism*, *R.B. Bhaskaran*, *Harkrishan Lall*, *Shantanu Ukil*.

Distemper A *painting medium* consisting of a mixture of water, *glue* as the binder, and powdered *colour* or *chalk*, generally used in *wall painting* or wallpaper printing. *Bhagwan Chavan* and *Manu Parekh* are among those who use *oils* and *acrylics*, sometimes distemper in *mixed media compositions*. *Manu Parekh* also uses *cement* and distemper. Refer *Gelatine*, *Pigment*, *Size*, *Tempera*, *Vehicle*.

Distortion It means out of shape or *proportion*. In a work of *art*, distortion of an *image* is sometimes used by an *artist* to reflect his ideas and sensitivities about a subject. Every *artist* has his own unique *style* of distortion; *Maqbool Fida Husain* preferring to use short, choppy strokes and *broad handling* in delineating the human *form*, while *B. Prabha*, elongated her *figures* endowing them with a timeless elegance. *Manjit Bawa* on the other hand, distorts his *figures* by endowing them with a curious boneless quality, that makes them appear to float on the surface of the *canvas*.

Divisionism Refer *Pointillism*, *Narayan S. Bendre*.

Diwali/Dipavali Also known as the festival of *lights*, Diwali marks the day when RAMA, one of the main AVATARs of VISHNU returned to his kingdom after an exile of fourteen years. The

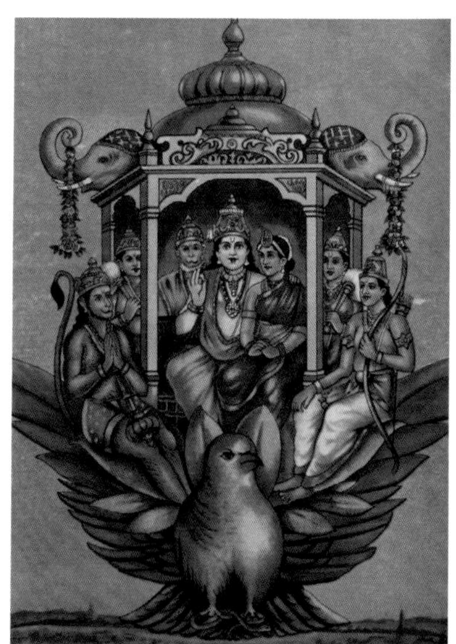

Diwali/Dipavali: "Ramchandraji" (Pushpkavimana), Litho stone with manual *colour* separations, circa 1920.

people greeted him by lighting rows of Diyas or Deepas (earthern lamps) outside their homes. This event is commemorated to this day on the New Moon night in the dark fortnight of the Hindu month of Kartik (October–November) by the lighting of lamps and then bursting of crackers. This is a popular subject for *painting*, especially because of the charm of small pinpricks of bright *colour* against the dark sky. The Goddess LAKSHMI is also worshipped during Diwali.

Dodiya, Atul (1959–) b. Mumbai. Education: Dip. in *FA. JJSA*. Solos: MMB, *GC* Mumbai, *CIMA* Mumbai & Kolkata; International: Gallery Apunto Amsterdam, GBP. Group participations: *Gallery 7*, *GC*, Cinemascape—100 years of Cinema *LCAG*, 50 years of Freedom *JAG*, *JNAG's* collections *NGMA*, State-of-the-Art Computer-aided *paintings JAG*, *GE*, *CIMA*, Academy of Art & Literature, *Triennale LKA*, *NGMA*, *VAG* & "Husain ki Sarai" Inaugural Exhibition New Delhi, *CIMA* Kolkata, other shows in Chennai, Bangalore & Ahmedabad; International: Kuwait, Paris, London, Berlin, New York, World Trade Centre Amsterdam, Singapore Art Museum. *Auctions*: Heart Mumbai. Awards: MAHA State Art Exhibition at *JJSA*, *ASI*, *BAS*; International: French Govt. Scholarship. Collections: Anand Bazaar Group Kolkata, Times of India, *GC* & RPG Mumbai; International: Chester and Davida Herwitz family collection Massachusetts, pvt. & public.

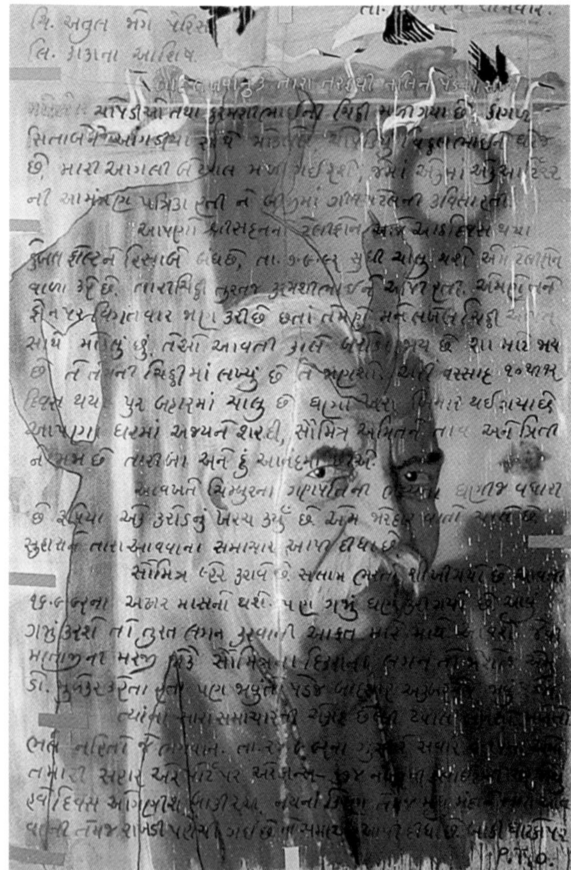

Dodiya, Atul: "Letter from a Father", *Oil* & *Acrylic* on *Canvas*, 1994, 190x90 cm.

Though Atul Dodiya briefly worked with abstraction, his preferred mode of expression is *figurative*. His early works were basically photo-realistic renderings of places and people he was familiar with. Later on an element of Pop *imagery*, especially in the use of D. Hockney-like pretension made its appearance in his *paintings*. The setting however remained autobiographical in nature, relying more on metaphor rather than on reportage, with interludes of pure textural *paint* appearing amidst *narrative* sequences. Atul Dodiya is also inspired by *cinema*, not only by the *hoardings*, but also by the filmmaker's mode of *handling* human element. His recent *assemblages* include wall mounted *still lifes* complete with pelmet, curtain and wall mounted radio. The group of framed *photographs* all point towards his quest of personal identities.

He lives and works in Mumbai.

Dokra, Dhokar Casting The word refers to the small *figures* of tribal *gods*, godesses and animals *cast* by the tribals of Bastar, MP. The *technique* used is the *lost wax process* with the *linear* decorations also done in *wax*. The *metal* used is bell-metal, which is an *alloy* of approximately 13 parts of *copper* 4 parts of tin-bell-metal originally found in Kerala and Thanjavur. Some of the modern *sculptors* influenced by Dokra include *Meera Mukherjee*. *Nandalal Bose* brought the artisans to demonstrate *metal casting* in Dokra process at *KB Santiniketan*. Refer *Bidri*, *Tribal Art*.

Donor, Donor Couple Applied to *art*, these *terms* refer to the person or persons who commissioned a particular work. They are sometimes represented in the *painting* or *sculpture* as donor *portraits*, a practice common both in Europe e.g. in a mediaeval *altarpiece*, and in India e.g. the Dampati (donor couple) among the *sculptures* at the Karla Caves, MAHA at the side of the entrance to the caves. These were to later develop into full-fledged MITHUNA *sculpture*.

Doodle To scribble aimlessly. Sometimes found in the surrealist automatist works, which were loaded with Freudian connotations. In India, it was *Rabindranath Tagore* who used the doodle, along with erasures and cancellations in his early (relatively speaking) *drawings*. More recently *Pratibha Dakoji* has used this *technique*. Refer *Surrealism*, *C. Douglas*, *V.P. Singh*.

Doss, Alphonso A. (1939–) b. Bangalore, KAR. Education: Degree in *FA. GCAC* Chennai. Solos: Coimbatore, CAG Ahmedabad, TAG, *JAG*, *SAI*, *VEAG*, *CRAR*, *RAG*; International: Holland, Japan, Festival of India USA. Group participations: SZCC TN 1984, *Triennale* New Delhi; International: Commonwealth Art Festival UK, *Biennale* Dhaka, Exhibition Cuba, Mexico, Malaysia & Singapore. *Art* camps: SZCC Chennai, Tanjore (Thanjavur) University, COAG. Awards: HRD ministry, National *LKA* & International Cultural Centre New Delhi, *LKA* Chennai, Gold Medal Gwalior, National Scholarship Govt. of India; International: Culture Doctorate Award by world University USA 1995. Appointments: Principal of *GCAC* Chennai; International: Visiting Prof. Brigham Young University & Eastern Menonite

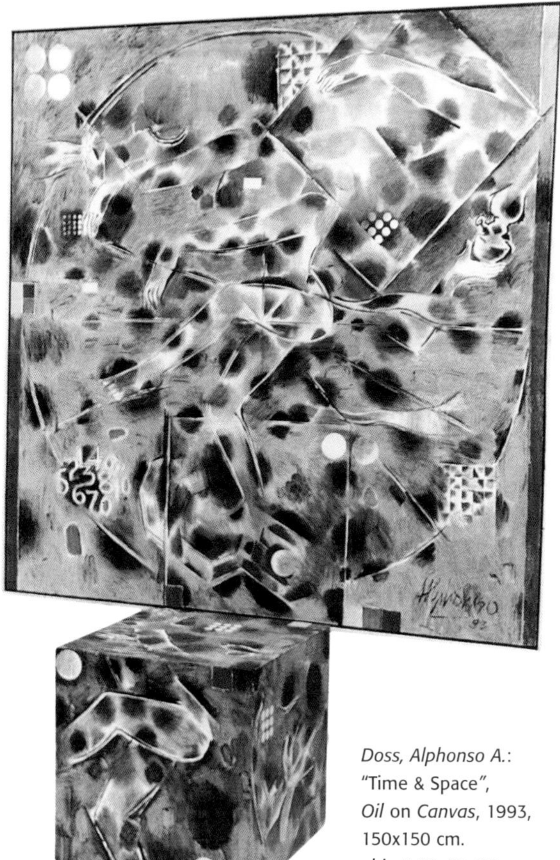

Doss, Alphonso A.: "Time & Space", *Oil* on *Canvas*, 1993, 150x150 cm. object 60x60x60 cm.

University USA. Collections: National Gallery Chennai, *LKA* & *NGMA* New Delhi, *LKA* TN & KAR; International: Singapore & other pvt. in national & international.

His *paintings* are stylized depictions of various *Gods* including Christ, SHIVA, KRISHNA and BUDDHA, using the conventional postures and *attributes*. The rather sketchy art-lines hold together his gestural applications of brilliant *colours* toned down by the bare areas of the *canvas*. He has also worked down to the bare areas of the *canvas* and three-dimensional *paintings*, creating a cube-shaped canvas, *painting* it and placing it below another conventional square *canvas*.

He lives in Chennai.

Douglas, C. (1951–) b. Kerala. Education; Dip. in *painting GCAC* Chennai. Solos: *SG* Bangalore, Mumbai, Chennai; International: Munich, Amsterdam. Group participations: National Exhibition *Triennale* & *NGMA* New Delhi, *SG* Bangalore, *Biennale BB*, *VAG*, *JAG*; International: Delfina Gallery England, Gallery School Amsterdam, Groningen Holland, Munich. *Auction*: Heart Mumbai. Awards/Grant: Charles Wallace (India) Trust Award, National Award New Delhi, *LKA* Chennai, *BB*; *LKA* Research Grant, Govt. of India Cultural Fellowship Junior & Senior; International: Invitation European Ceramic Centre & UNESCO Grant Netherlands. Collections: *NGMA*, *LKA* & Ministry of External Affairs New Delhi, TATA Mumbai, Art Gallery Ernakulam, Deutsche Bank Mumbai & Bangalore, *BB*; International: Netherlands, Japan.

C. Douglas moved to *Cholamandal* at the end of his student days, where he was highly influenced by the exotic *doodles* and *drawings* of *K. Ramanujam*. C. Douglas's *drawings* of this period, metaphorically represented the foetus, the prenatal condition in which there is neither separation nor participation. Soon his *form* became geometricized into triangles, squares and *lines* of *colour*, *tint* and *tone*. His *colour* was never intense or bright; instead he used murky *monochromes* to render a dense *opacity* of *form*. After he returned from Europe, a vague *figure* started materializing in his works. As is visible in the new expressionistic tendencies abroad, C. Douglas's world is a chaotic one, with *figures* appearing to be tortured by scratched *lines* and inflicted with wounds, spurting blood.

C. Douglas prefers working with *chalks* and *crayons* on crumpled and muddied *paper* glued and at times stitched on cloth. His *colours* are unobtrusive, grays, browns and *blacks* which are applied in *overlapping* layers. He has also worked on sculptural *installations*, in which the painted heads in his *drawings* metamorphose into the three-dimensional, being fleshed out using *ceramics*. The same air of whimsy pervades these *installations* as well.

He lives and works in *Cholamandal*.

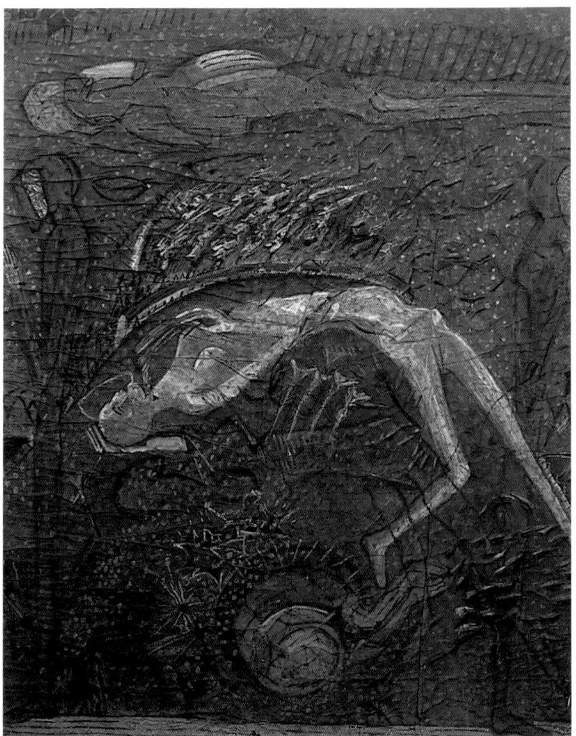

Douglas, C.: "Untitled", *Mixed Media* on *Paper* mounted on *Canvas*, 1996, 120x120 cm.

Dragging A *technique* used mainly in *oil painting*, in which a *brush* loaded with almost dry *pigment* is drawn over a wet undercoat, producing textural effects of broken *colour*. Refer *Dry Brush Painting*, *Combing*, *Painting Knife*, *P. Srinivasan*, *K.G. Subramanyan*, *Setlur Gopal Vasudev*.

Drapery The word refers to the "fall" of fabric, as represented in *painting* and *sculpture*. *Key art* elements in drapery are the feeling of *depth*, the three-dimensional vision of the folds and intricate/*detailed work* on *designs* and *colours*. The *style* of rendering drapery is distinctive in each period and *art historians* have classified *sculpture*, using the reference of drapery and also identified the *artist* from his rendering of drapery. To take a simple example, the *treatment* of the BUDDHA's Sanghati (robe) in the contemporaneous Mathura and Gandharan phase of Kushana period is entirely different. Refer CHITRAKATHI, *Gold*, *Thanjavur (Tanjore) Painting*, *Atasi Barua*, *Jagadish Dey*, *Savlaram L. Haldankar*, *G.Y. Hublikar*, *Kshitendranath Mazumdar*, *Ravindra Mestry*, *Roshan M. Mullan*, *Manchershaw F. Pithawalla*, *Amrita Sher-Gil*, *Shantanu Ukil*, *Raja Ravi Varma*.

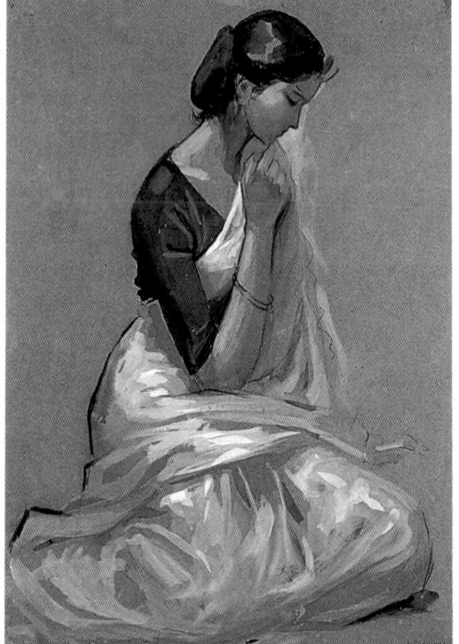

Drapery: *Kulkarni K.B.* "Reverie", *Mixed media* on Tinted *Paper*, 47.5x32.5 cm.

Draughtsmanship Refers to *drawing* and other skills such as *painting* or *printmaking*, of an *artist* to show the *form* of his work. It also refers to *pattern*, *texture* and *tonal values* as of prime importance to some *artists*, from which they complete their *compositions*. The *Ajanta style* of draughtsmanship indicates elements of romanticized *form* and *colour*. The draughtsmanship course school was elevated in 1951 *GCAC* Kolkata, WB and later that school was converted into Dept. of Decorative Arts and Crafts. Refer *Narayan S. Bendre*, *Shiavax Chavda*, *Muhammed Abdur Rehman Chughtai*, *Shuvaprasanna*, *Anupam Sud*, *Sarada Charan Ukil*.

Dravida=of the South. Dravida, the word, used to describe people, *culture*, *art* and *architecture*; being one of the two major traditions of the India, the other being Aryan. Refer *Dravidian Style*, CHOLA, PALLAVA, *Elephanta*, *Ellora*, *Mahabalipuram*.

Dravidian Style This refers to the South Indian *style* of building temples. The Garbhagriha or the sanctum sanctorum is housed in the Vimana which is sometimes extended to contain the MANDAPA and an ARDHA-MANDAPA as well. Many of the Dravidian style temples were hewn out of living rock, rather than being structural temples as is more common with the *Nagara style*. This results in an *eclectic* exterior appearance, compared to the nearly uniform exteriors of the *Nagara* temples. In addition to the usual platform, base, walls, pillars, entablature, the Beki (neck) and SHIKHARA of the temples, Dravidian temples at *times* have extra storeys inserted between the entablature and the neck. Each of the floors is called a HARA as it is made up of an alternating series of domical and wagon-vaulted shrines (Kutas and Salas respectively). Each Kuta and Sala is further connected by interrelated path called Harantara.

A single storeyed temple is termed Ektale, with each extra floor—Dvitale, Tritale. Some important examples of the Dravidian style would be the Rathas (chariots) of Mamallapuram, the KAILASH temple at *Ellora*, the *Elephanta cave* temples off the coast of Mumbai. The Dravidian society of South India also created megalithic tombs, primitive burial cists of pit covered with *stones*. However, these tombs have never been accurately dated nor properly documented. These could be the earliest relics probably going way back to the Iron age. Refer DRAVIDA, CHOLA, PALLAVA, *Elephanta*, *Ellora*, *Mahabalipuram*.

Drawing A *form*, either *figurative* or *abstract*, created by means of *lines* in *pen* and *ink*, *pencil*, *charcoal* or *chalk* usually applied to two-dimensional subjects on *paper*. Drawings also refer to preparatory *studies* for *compositions*, *portraits* or *still lifes*, a finished work in itself. There is an interlink in the process of *drawing* and *painting*. Refer *Abstract Expressionism*, *Brush Drawing*, *Chalk Drawing*, *Charcoal*, CHITRA, CHITRAKATHI, *Computer Art*, *Conservation Board*, *Crayon*, *Crayon Manner*, *Decadent Art*, *Decalcomania*, *Etching*, *Fixative*, *Flat Colour*, *Graffitti*, *Graphic Art*, *Graphite*, *Half-tone*, *History Painting*, *Illustration*, *India Ink*, *Ink*, *Landscape Format*, *Lay-In*, *Line and Wash*, *Line Engraving*, *Mewar*, *Modelling*, *Monocular Vision*, *Monograph*, *Mughal Dynasty*, *Neo-Tantricism*, *Oeuvre*, *Outline*, *Relief*, *Scraperboard*, *Scratchboard*, *Sepia*; Illustration—*Erotic Art*, *Folk Art*, *Jain Miniature*, *Jain Manuscript Illumination*, SHIVA, *Ranjitsingh Gaekwad*, *Rathin Mitra*, *Mohan Samant*, *Ved Pal Sharma (Bannu)*, *Vrindavan Solanki*, *Rabindranath Tagore*, AGNI & MAKARA—*Nagesh Bhimrao Sabannavar*, *Hatching*—*Laxma Goud*, *Life-Drawing*—*Muralidhar R. Achrekar*, *Line*—*Shiavax Chavda*.

Drawing Inks *Inks* used in *drawing pens* or with *brushes* are generally available in dye based or *pigment* based *forms*. Dye based *inks form* clear, *transparent films* suitable for *glazing* whereas pigmented *inks* look similar to *watercolour paints* as they use water as the binding agent. Refer *Dyestuff*, *Muhammed Abdur Rehman Chughtai*, *Ganga Devi*, *P.T. Reddy*, *Vrindavan Solanki*, *Abanindranath Tagore*, *D. Venkatpathy*. Refer Illustration—*Hatching*, *Line*, *Ratin Mitra*.

Drip Painting A synonym for *action painting*, a method involving the splattering or dripping of *paint* on a *canvas* by *painting* in the *wash manner* and allowing the *colour* to flow down. The *artist* creates his *composition* based on the *colour* flow i.e. *Bimal DasGupta's style* of work contributes to the *impasto* swirls and drips of the *medium*. Refer *Abstract Expressionism*, *Blot Drawing*, *Wash* (*technique*), *Mansimran Singh*, *Sardar Gurcharan Singh*; Illustration–*Action Painting*, *Seascape*.

Dry Brush Painting A *painting technique* used to create a characteristic *texture* by the use of almost dry *pigment*. The *paint* adheres only to the raised surface of the *ground* i.e. *handmade paper* in case of *watercolour* and grained *canvas* in the case of *oil painting*. *Ramkinkar Baij*, *Bikash Bhattacharjee*, *Seltur Gopal Vasudev*. Refer *Abstract Impressionism*; Illustration–*Narayan S. Bendre*, *Chhaganlal D. Mistry*.

Dry-Point A simple *engraving technique* involving the use of a sharp needle to carve or scratch directly into the *metal plates*, without a prepared *ground*. This action throws up a *burr* on either side of the groove, which holds the *ink* during printing. This produces a characteristic fuzzy, rather than sharp, *line* when printed; the *plate* itself wears quickly when using this *technique*. *Mukul Chandra Dey* studied *etching* and mastered the *technique* of dry-points, which he used to a great effect, merging the *linearity* of this *technique* with the *Bengal School style*. Refer *Hatching*, *Printmaking*, *Amitabha Banerjee*, *Shyamal Dutta Ray*, *Anupam Sud*.

Drying Oils A synonym of fixed oils. This denotes fatty *oils* of vegetable origin like linseed, walnut and poppy, which are used as binders in *oil painting*, because they harden into a solid, *transparent* substance on exposure to air, without affecting the *colour* or purity of the *pigment* they bind. *Raja Ravi Varma* who learnt by observing Theodore Jensen (Dutch origin artist) was one of the first Indian *artists* to use this *technique*. Other *artists* from Bengal, who started *painting* in *oils* around the same time as *Raja Ravi Varma*, learnt the *technique* by observing foreign *artists* like William Hodges and the Daniells.

Dube, Vinod (1942–) b. Narsinghpur, MP. Education: GDA, Dip. in *painting* & Art Masters *JJSA*. Over 20 solos & group participations: *Artists' Centre* Mumbai, *JJSA*, TAG, *JAG*, *YBCAG*.

Vinod Dube's preferred mode of expression is the *landscape*, in both *realistic* and semi-*abstract styles* with an element of stillness and melancholy. In the late 80s his *style* resembled that of Fernand Leger a French *artist* with a cubistic *distortion* of fragmented *forms*. He also reflected conflicts, of speed and stillness, of energy and tepidity, of *rhythm*, grace and *distortion*, etc.

He lives and works in Mumbai.

Dudhat, Bhanu (1949–) b. Junagarh, GUJ. Education: Dip. *FFA* (*MSU*), under Prof. *K.G. Subramanyan*; Studied in *fresco painting* under *Deokinandan Sharma–Banashali Vidyapith* RAJ. Solos: New Delhi, Ahmedabad, *JAG*, *FFA* (*MSU*); International: Germany, Australia. Group shows: *Santokba Dudhat* (his mother) & his wife in Vadodara, Mumbai, New Delhi, Bhopal, Udaipur; International: Germany, Australia. Participated in seminars. Awards: State *LKA*, All India Fine Arts Academy Amritsar, *Biennale* Chandigarh, WZCC *exhibition* Nagpur; International: RAA UK, Japan Stamp Contest certificate. Appointments: Lecturer *Painting* Dept. Kala Kendra, CFA Vallabh Vidyanagar. Publications: Including MAHABHARATA, Children's book published by Bal Bhawan Society New Delhi; TV programmes; prepared a documentary film on *Santokba Dudhat*. Commissions: *Fresco paintings*, *terracotta murals* with *Santokba Dudhat* & his wife. Collections: India & abroad working with his mother & wife.

Bhanu Dudhat son of the noted folk *artist*; his work is based on *folk art*, his subjects being mostly mythological with a touch of *Surrealism*. His *colours* are from *nature* as are his women and animals. Because the *lines* and the *forms* are not definitive, they come alive in their movement because of choice of *colours* and *gradation*. His works are executed jointly with his family. Refer *Santokba Dudhat*.

Dudhat, Santokba (1910 approx) b. GUJ. Self-taught *artist*, *painting* in the traditional *manner*. Solos: *MSU*, later in Mumbai. Group participations: Ahmedabad, Udaipur, Bal Bhavan New Delhi, *GC* Mumbai, IGNCA, TKS, *JAG*; International: Germany, UK. Participated seminars: *Folk Art* Vadodara. Collections: Air India, Rashtrapati Bhavan & Bal Bhavan New Delhi, IGNCA & pvt.

Santokba Dudhat began *painting* at an advanced age after seeing the *paintings* executed by her son, *Bhanu Dudhat*. She preferred using indigenous materials like ash and matchsticks to the *ink* and *colours* used by her son. She added gum to the carbon collected from *oil* lamps and created *images* of *Gods* by using a matchstick. These were displayed for the first time at the *FFA* (*MSU*). After 1978, the Dudhat family comprising Santokba, Bhanu and his wife Prabha, started working jointly on *paintings* which were executed in the naive *style* of *folk art*. In 1985 the family painted incidents from the RAMAYANA on a 35ft. long scroll made of *handmade paper*. The *drawing* was executed in *ink*, but natural *pigments*, made by Santokba Dudhat herself which were used for the colouring. Between 1987–1992 family painted the MAHABHARATA on a long cotton-scroll measuring 1200 mt. This collaborative work is said to be the largest in the history of Indian *art*.

Durga = impenetrable. Durga has different names each one representing SHAKTI. One of the many names for this Goddess KALI or PARVATI, of the 15th century AD. Durga means impenetrable like a mountain fortress. She

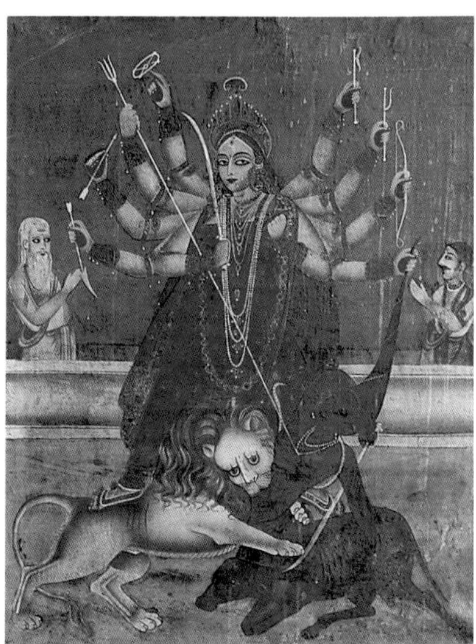

Durga: "Anonymous", Tempera on Cloth, Mid-19th century, 77x61 cm.

may have four, eight or more arms holding various *attributes* like the trident conch, spear, sword, wheel and lotus. She wears a KARANDA-MUKUTA and stands erect on a lotus throne or on a buffalo or a lion. As Mahishasura Mardini, she is shown spearing, Mahisha, the buffalo-headed *demon* to death. In Bengal *sculpture*, she is represented with long fish-shaped eyes, a Paan (heart-shaped) face and protruding tongue. Refer DASHA-BHUJA, DURGA-PUJA, *Bengal Oil* Painting, *Calcutta School*, CHAKRA, DASHA-BAHU, *Ellora*, *Gupta*, *Installation*, KALI, *Metal*, PALLAVAS, *Pallava Dynasty*, SHAKTI, SHIVA, *Terracotta*, *Wood Block Printing*, *Maqbool Fida Husain*.

Durga-Puja The festival symbolizes the triumph of good over evil as epitomized in the slaying of the buffalo-*demon* Mahisha, by the Goddess DURGA. It is celebrated in autumn, the Hindu month of Kartik (October–November). Though the festival is celebrated in most parts of the country, it is especially popular in East India WB and the grand celebrations are popular subjects with *artists* from the area. Refer DURGA.

Dutta, Manoj (1956–) b. Kolkata. Self-taught. Solos: *BAAC* Kolkata, *GE*, *JAG*. Group shows: *AFA* Kolkata, TKS. Group participations: *LKA* 1980–84, RB & India Today New Delhi, WBSA, *BAAC* & *AFA* Kolkata, *CKAG*, *JAG*; International: Holland, Boulder City USA, *Biennale* Korea. Attended camps: All India Contemporary Art New Delhi. Won Awards. Appointments: Elected Commissioner International *Biennale* Korea 1992. Collections: *BAAC* Kolkata, *LKA* WB, *NGMA* New Delhi, pvt. & international.

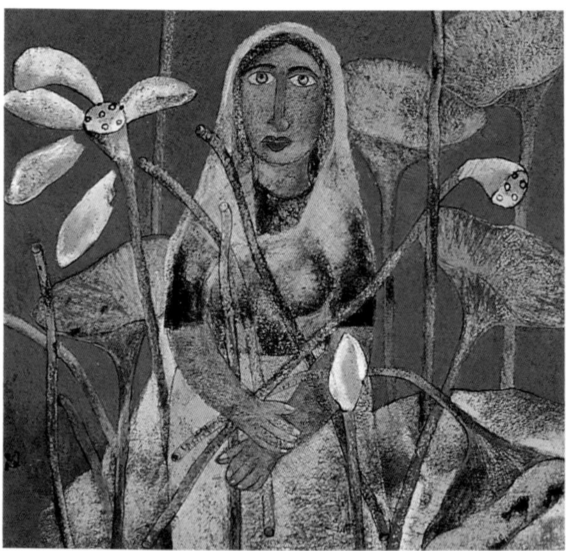

Dutta, Manoj: "Autumnal Night", *Pastel* on *Paper*, 1992, 100x100 cm.

His *style* stands out because of its simplicity and ethnic innocence. This simplicity of *content* however does not clash with his sophisticated *palette* and *aesthetic* sensibility. His *painting* draws its strength from city life without forego-ing the spontaneity of *folk art*. "Autumnal Night" is both *contemporary* and traditional in its use of *distortion* and *colour*.

Manoj Dutta lives and works as a freelance *artist* in Kolkata.

Dutta, Nirmal (1926–) b. Kolkata. Education: Dip. *GCAC* Kolkata 1950. Solos: *AFA* Kolkata, *LKA* New Delhi, *ABC*. Group participations & awards: *GCAC*, *AFA*, *LKA* & WB State Govt. Kolkata. Commissions: A 1000 ft long *mural* depicting the life of the BUDDHA in Buddha Bihar, Dharamakur Sabha at Buddhist Temple Street Kolkata, 1950–55 & part of the work in Burma. Appointments: Worked for Dept. of Education Kolkata Municipal Corporation. Collections: *NGMA* New Delhi, *BAAC* Kolkata, *RBU*.

His *style* of *painting* is both lyrical and romantic based on elements of *nature*. His early works show the blurred and hazy effect of impressionistic strokes, a stylistic trend that still crops up in his recent works. Rural subjects with *pastoral* scenes and village women seem to be his personal favourite, though he has also rendered *portraits* and *nudes*.

He lives and works in Kolkata.

Dyestuff They are coloured compounds or *pigments*, which are soluble in the *vehicle* or solvent. They give transparency and purity to a *colour*. Sometimes they are used to *tone blacks*, resulting in blue-blacks, green-blacks or slate-blacks.

In India dye was used in the textile printing industry in Gujarat, and through the *wax* resist process in South India. Refer *Batik*, *Block printing*, *Picchwais*, *Tie and Dyed Fabrics*, *Transparent*, *GCAG* Kolkata, *Cholamandal* Chennai, *Biharilal C. Barbhaiya*; Illustration–*Sohan Qadri*, *Pratima Devi Tagore*.

E

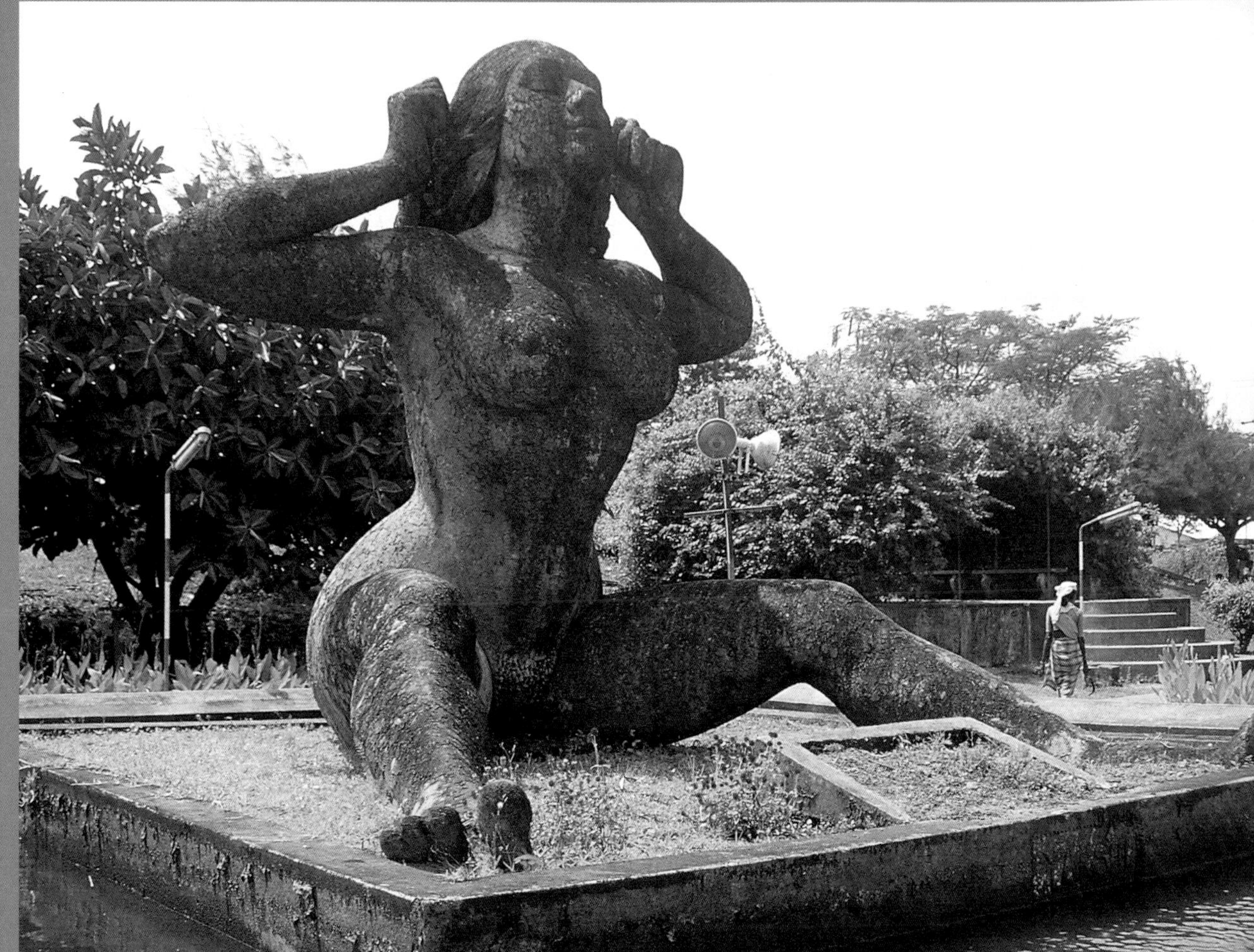

Earth Art, Earth Works, Land Art: *Kanayi Kunhiraman*, "Yakshi", *Concrete*, 1969. (See notes on page 124)

Earth Art, Earth Works, Land Art Earth art can be visualized as an extension of *landscape painting*. Instead of being content with fixing *landscape* elements on the surface of the *canvas*, *artists* in the 1960s and 1970s increasingly worked with or in the actual *landscape*. The British *artist* Richard Long's *art* is ephemeral in *nature* with *photographs* and films serving as reminders of the *art* experience while the American Robert Smithson's Spiral Jetty, an extravagant exercise involving the creation of an artificial spiral, 1500 ft long, out of *black* rock, salt-crystal and earth, in the great Salt Lake, Utah has lasted from 1969.

This *art form* is still in its infancy in India, a notable exception being the sculptural garden created by *Kanayi Kunhiraman* at Thiruvananthapuram. The younger generation of *artists* have been experimenting lately with the *medium*. The works are necessarily large in scale and sculptural, instead of maintaining the illusionistic two-dimensionality of *landscape painting*. It has been called "sculpture in the expanded field" by *Kanayi Kunhiraman*. Earth Art is characteristically larger than life in scale, Indian Earth art involves the use of much less *space*. Refer *Ecological Art*, *Concrete*, *Nature*, *Space*, YAKSHI, YAKSHINI. (See illustration on page 123.)

Earth Colour Organic *pigments* found in their natural state in the earth. Earth colours are chiefly ochres, reds, red-browns and *blacks*. They are *ground* in running water (or any other solvent) purified and used in *painting*. Earth colours have been used by *prehistoric* man in conjunction with animal fat to produce the exquisite examples of cave *art*.

In India, traditional *painters* have used earth colour in addition to *gold*, *silver* and ground precious gems in the *painting* of miniatures, *glass paintings* and *frescoes*. In *Ajanta*, for example the *pigments* were extracted from the rock excavated during the creation of caves.

In *miniature painting*, orpiment was one of the minerals from which the yellow *colour* was extracted. When mixed with deep brown, orpiment yielded the *colour* of parrot feathers.

Earth colours are among the most permanent and least expensive of *pigments*. They are still used by *modern* practitioners of traditional *painting* in India especially in Banasthali RAJ, as well as by *artists* of the younger generation. Refer *Clay*, *Chalk*, *Fresco*, *Ground*, *Natural Colours*, *Painter*, *Pigment*, *Aditya Basak*, *Samir Ghosh*, *Krishen Khanna*, *Benode Behari Mukherjee*, *Raju A. Paidi*, *Sita Ray*, *Jamini Roy*, *Premalatha H. Seshadri*, *Haku Shah*, *Ved Pal Sharma* (Bannu), *Vasudha Thozhur*, *Nathu Lal Verma*.

Eclectic, Eclecticism Eclecticism refers to an amalgamation of different *styles* and *techniques* into a successful whole by the *artist*. The *term* originated in Greek philosophy where it was applied to the works of philosophers who combined the best theories from several different schools of thought. In *art*, it refers to the assimilation of existing or primitive modes of expression by *artists*. A famous example would be P. Picasso's "Les Demoiselles d' Avignon" wherein he combines the theories of P. Cezanne with Iberian and African *sculpture*. This is observed in the works of *Rabin Mondal*.

Jamini Roy's folk *idiom* was actually the amalgamation of several pre-existing *craft* expressions, including *Kalighat folk painting*, Kanthas (embroidered textiles from Bengal) and Rangoli/Alpana (floor decoration). *F.N. Souza's* works on the other hand owe their eclectic character to primitive and *tribal art*. Refer *Post-Independence*, *Sadanandji Bakre*, *Gunen Ganguli*, *Nand Katyal*, *K.S. Rao*, *Sita Ray*, *Yagneshwar Kalyanji Shukla*; Illustration—*Jyoti Bhatt*, *Sakti Burman*, *Rabin Mondal*, *Roshan M. Mullan*, *Gulam Mohammed Sheikh*, *Francis Newton Souza*, *Abanindranath Tagore*, *Sanat Thaker*, *Kanhiyalal R. Yadav*.

Ecological Art The *term* has been used since 1960s, and this deals largely with *earth art*, without the displacement of natural resources. The *artist* involved with this *art form* interacts with *nature* in a *manner* designed to conserve it, not destroy it. In India *Kanayi Kunhiraman* created an erotic squatting female *nude figure*—the 18 ft "YAKSHI" in *cement concrete* in 1969–70 at Malampuzha, Kerala, and "Landscaping & Environmental *Sculptures*" at the Veli Tourist Village, Thiruvananthapuram. Refer *Latika Katt*, *Vivan Sundaram*; Illustration—*Earth Art, Earth Works, Land Art*; *Avtarjeet S. Dhanjal*, *Dhruva Mistry*.

Egg-oil emulsion A *painting medium*, which can be considered an intermediate step between *egg-tempera* and pure linseed *oil painting*. One part of the whole egg or yolk mixture is added to crude vegetable *oil* and mineral dyes, which were and are still made by some *artists* themselves. Water is added to this mixture, which has to be shaken vigorously to be emulsified. This is the *vehicle*, which has to be mixed with the *pigment*. The subjects were mostly *portraits* of *gods* and goddesses executed on the walls of temples and palaces and on glass, *ivory* or *paper*. The *technique* is still being use by group of *artists* belonging to the *Banasthali Vidyapith* RAJ. Refer *Bengal Oil Painting*, *Bazaar Painting*, *Bengal Revivalism*, *Glass Painting*, *Medium*, *Miniature Paintings*, *Mixed Media*, *Oil*, *Tempera*, *Vidya Bhushan*, *Samir Ghosh*, *Paresh C. Hazra*, *Deokinandan Sharma*, *Ved Pal Sharma*, *Nathu Lal Verma*, *Sarada Charan Ukil*.

Egg-Tempera Refer *Tempera*, *Miniature Paintings*.

Egyptian Art The *art* and *architecture* of ancient Egypt flourished in varying degrees from about 3000 BC to about 30 BC, originating in the Nile valley. Since Egyptian art was governed by the belief in life after death, it was inspired by the needs of the dead rather than the living. Pyramids and Mastabas (simple tombs) were built during the Old and Middle Kingdoms, for the burial of Pharaohs, Queens and Nobles, e.g., Saqqara and Gizeh. The sarcophagus was often richly decorated while the *stone* walls of the burial chamber were at first carved in *relief* and painted, and were later painted in *tempera* with scenes showing everyday life of the Egyptians. During the New Kingdom, instead of pyramids, temples were built to the *gods*. Egyptian *sculpture*, followed the law of *frontality*, being blocks, rigidly symmetrical, *facing* forward with both arms by the side and one foot slightly in front of the other. Several Indian *artists* have been influenced by the formal *nature* of Egyptian art. These include a series of *concrete sculptures* by *Kanayi Kunhiraman* and a series of *painting* circa 1966, "An Egypt Reverie" by *Jehangir Sabavala*.

Electroplating A method by which a metallic sculptural or ornamental object can be coated with a thin layer of another metallic salt solution, by means of an electric current. *Graphite* and *silver* are also used for plating. Electro-plating was first used circa 1800. Indian *artists* learnt the *technique* from the jewellers. *Shankar Nandagopal's* rich repertoire of *folk*-inspired *sculptures* have been electroplated partially with *copper* and/or *silver*. Some of these *murals* are approximately 20–25 ft high. Refer *Bronze, Gold, Metal*.

Elephanta The *rock-cut* cave temple at Elephanta, a small island six miles from Mumbai, was built by the Rashtrakutas during the 8th century. It is renowned for its huge triple-headed *bust* of SHIVA as Maheshmurti. This 18 ft high *sculpture* represents the supreme aspect of SHIVA as the Creator, Preserver and Destroyer. To the right is Vamadeva—the Creator, with a soft feminine visage, with pearls and flowers decorating the hair and a PADMA—lotus bud, held in the hand. On the left is the complementary aspect, that of the Destroyer–SHIVA as Bhairava with a cruel fanged mouth covered with a moustache, the head ornamented with a NAGA (cobra-snake) and KAPALA (skull). The central, serene *image* of the Preserver-Mahadeva represents SHIVA in his Tatpurusha aspect–i.e. the supreme and beneficent one.

There are other *rock-cut* shrines on the island, but the main one housing the Maheshmurti (SHIVA MURTI), has about 16,000 sq. ft. of excavated floor *space*. It opens to the East, while on the Western side is a courtyard. There is a massive *free-standing* Garbhagrha—the inner housing the LINGAM, with huge Dvarapalas (guardian *figures*) flanking the entrances to the shrine. Twenty restored pillars with rounded shaft and fluted cushion capitals *support* the Mahamandapa (great hall). The Mahamandapa has a projection on the northern side, which has been divided into the Mukha and ARDHA-MANDAPA. On the two side-walls of this porch and at seven other locations within the hall are *relief* panels depicting SHIVA in various manifestations, such as NATARAJA, Ardhanarishwara (the dual male-female aspect), Gangadhara (SHIVA helping the Descent of GANGA, the river Goddess) and Kalyana Sundaramurti (the marriage of SHIVA and PARVATI). The *figures* in these sculptural panels seem about to move in the changing *light* of the day, the dramatic effect being enhanced by the *images* emerging from the dark *background*. The Elephanta *figures* have broad faces and foreheads, with long Dhanush (bow) shaped eyebrows, thick lips, fleshy jaws and chins.

Ellora A set of 34 cave temples and monasteries excavated out of the vertical face of an encarpment extending in a linear arrangement (as different from the horseshoe formation of *Ajanta* caves), they contain CHAITYAs (halls of worship) and VIHARAs (monasteries). A unique feature is the blend of Buddhist (caves 1 to 12) Hindu (caves 13 to 29) and *Jain* (caves 30 to 34) temples excavated between AD 5 and AD 11.

Cave 10 dedicated to Vishvakarma, the architect of the *gods*, exemplifies the CHAITYA *architecture* in India. The cave is a complete representation of the spirit of Ellora—containing a *stupa*, a seated *figure* of lord BUDDHA, CHAITYA window *motifs* and BODHISATTVAs with female attendants.

The most impressive structure of the complex is undoubtedly the majestic KAILASH temple (cave 16). The largest single monolithic structure in the world, it is dedicated to Hindu *god* SHIVA and makes a comprehensive statement on *Hinduism* through intricately carved scenes of Hindu mythological *epics* such as RAMAYANA and MAHABHARATA. The carved statuettes of goddesses DURGA and LAKSHMI and that of lord SHIVA's son GANESHA are exquisite. Carved out of a single piece of giant *stone* formation and carved out from top to bottom, its geometrical accuracy speaks *volumes* for the advanced architectural practices prevailing centuries ago.

Cave 32 is the finest excavation of all *Jain* caves. *Jain* Tirthankaras are all depicted with particularly impressive panels of lord MAHAVIRA, Gomateshwara, the son of Adinatha—the 1st Tirthankara and Parshwanatha with rows of Lions and elephants. It is a monolithic Shrine, double-storeyed, with an open court in front and a MANDAPA at the lower level which are incomplete.

The Ellora caves were never rediscovered (as *Ajanta* caves were). They have continuously attracted pilgrims through the centuries. Whereas *Ajanta* is most impressive for its *paintings* and *frescoes*, Ellora is more pronouncedly brilliant in *architecture*, *carving* and *sculptures*. Ellora caves are located 26 kms from the city of Aurangabad. Refer KAILASH, KAILASA.

Emblem Symbol, logo; a composite *image* usually with a specific meaning. A familiar concept usually of religious or political nature. An example would be the emblem of the Indian Republic, the Sarnath Lions or the Ashoka Chakra in the Indian flag. *Images* were usually drawn from the Indian *culture*. Refer CHAKRA, *Mauryan Dynasty*, *Tantra Art*, *Neo-Tantricism*, *Biren De*, *K. Jayapala Panicker and K.V. Haridasan*, *Shankar Palsikar*, *K.C.S. Paniker*, *Sohan Qadri*, *P.T. Reddy*, *Ghulam Rasool Santosh*, *J. Srividya*.

Embossing A synonym of *repousse*, it means any process, including *casting*, *chasing* and *carving*, used to make a *relief*, usually in *metal*, *leather* or *paper*. e.g. *Shanti Dave* achieved the *relief* and embossing effects by employing *wax*, *cement moulds*, *paper* pulp and later by means of *etching*. Refer *Aku*, *Pilton Kothawalla*, *Prabha Panwar*, *Ashit Paul*, *Ram Kishore Yadav*.

Embroidery The *technique* originally refers to a method of decorating textiles with *patterns*, it is the *art* of embellishing textiles with ornamental stitchery. This is done by means of handwork, with the help of a needle and thread, or, as is more usual in *contemporary* times, with a machine. The needle can be of different shapes and *sizes*, i.e. with an eye or with a hook. Other than threads, sequins, beads and buttons may be used. Materials on which embroidery can be done include linen, silk, cotton, velvet, *leather*, cambric, muslin and satin and man-made fibres such as nylon, chiffon, organza and dacron. The threads can be of silk, cotton, wool or even metals like *gold*, *silver* and *copper* and are used in various thicknesseses.

Some of the embroidery *styles* native to India:

1. Kashidakari from Kashmir, using chain stitch.

2. Chikankarigiri, i.e. *Shadow* work, from Lucknow in UP.

3. Phulkari, i.e. Flower work, from PUJ.

4. Kantha, from Bengal, using simple darning stitch and waste cloth.

5. Sujani, appliqued quilts from Bihar.

6. Kasuti, from KAR, using simple directional stitches.

7. RAJ and GUJ are an embroiderer's delight, with several types of embroidery. Abhla work (with mirrors) and Badla work (using tiny *metal* pieces).

8. Zardozi, i.e. Zari work or embroidery with *gold* and *silver* threads, sequins and stars is done all over India, for weddings and auspicious occasions.

9. Lace, as it is known in colloquial parlance, is also being used as edgings for veils, eg., crochet from Jamnagar in GUJ.

10. The Parsis use all the *techniques* of Chinese embroidery, to make their beautiful Garas (sarees).

Contemporary artists, especially women are now using embroidery as an added *technique* in creating *mixed media* works, principally *installations* and conceptual work. Refer RASA LILA, *Shakuntala Kulkarni*, *Nita Thakore*, *Bhanu Shah and C. Douglas*.

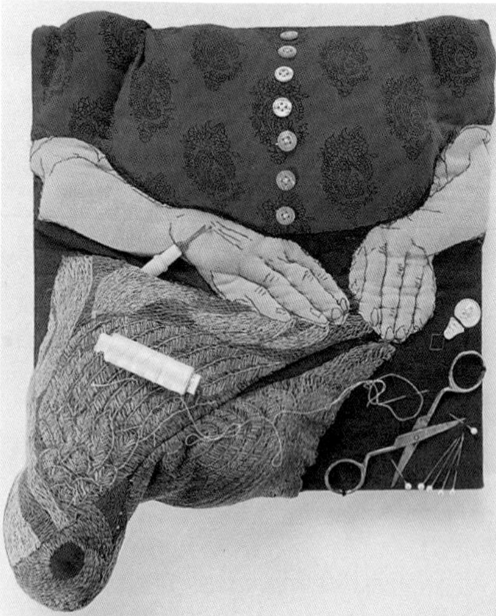

Embroidery: *Thakore Nita*, "Homage to the Embroider", 38x38 cm, 2D *Relief*.

Empaquetage (French)=wrapping, empaquetage specifically refers to certain works by the Bulgarian *artist* Christo Javacheff which involve the temporary wrapping, in 1958 of large scale objects, including trees, buildings, airplanes, palaces, even coastlines by tarpaulins and other packaging materials. Refer *Installation*, *N. Pushpamala*, *Vivan Sundaram*.

Empathy A word used by psychologists and aestheticians alike to describe a feeling akin to sympathy; in the field of *art* it denotes a similar feeling for an *art* object by both *artist* and spectator. It is similar to the feeling of RASA experienced by *artist* and evoked in the mind of the viewer. Refer *Dattatray B. Pardeshi*, *Amrut Patel*, *Jamini Roy*.

Emulsion A combination of two liquids which do not ordinarily mix, one being suspended in the other in the *form* of minute droplets. Refer *Casein*, *Egg-oil emulsion*, *Gel*, *Screen Printing*, *Silk Screen Printing*, *Tempera*, *Waterproof*, *Reba Hore*.

Enamel (Meenakari) was originally a *craft form*, mostly used in the making of jewellery and precious objects. It has been used as an *inlay* work on *gold*, *silver*, or *copper*.

Enamels can be *transparent*, *translucent* or *opaque*. They derive their *colour* from the addition of various metallic oxides to the flux. Coloured glass which is powdered and sometimes mixed with *oil* is bonded or fused on to *metal* surface by *firing* in a *kiln*. The *techniques* employed in the making of enamelled objects include the *champleve*, in which grooves are cut into the surface of a thick *metal* plaque, filled with powdered *enamel colour* and then fired, the cloisonne, in which the various *colours* are separated by *metal* wires soldered to the *plate* surface and painted with layers of enamel of different *colours*. Some *artists* dust the *plate* with finely sieved powder before *firing* to achieve certain effects.

Indian *artists* have been using the *technique* to create colourful *sculptures* and *paintings*. *Balan Nambiar* uses both *copper* and *silver plates* baking them several times to achieve his glowing *colours* and organic *forms*, while *Bishamber Khanna* often used the accidental *image* caused by the heating process. *Shankar Nandagopal* uses the *technique* in his large-scale decorative *sculptures* which can withstand the elements. Refer *Artefact*, *Cloison*, *Decorative Art*, *Lay-In*, *Matter*, *Outline*, *Bhanwar Singh Panwar*, *Himmat Shah*, *Setlur Gopal Vasudev*; Illustration—*Siona Benjamin*, *Chandrakant N. Mhatre*.

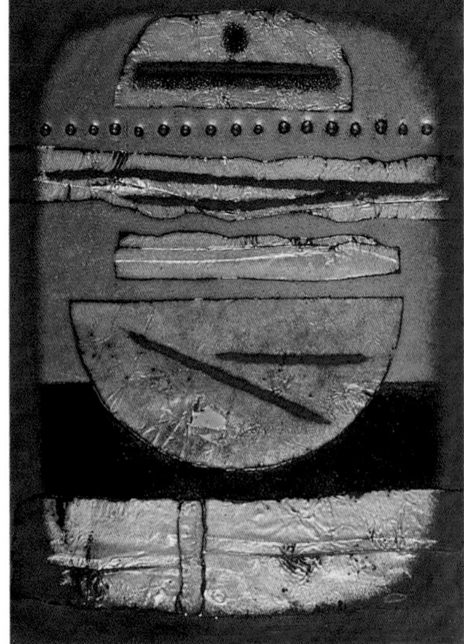

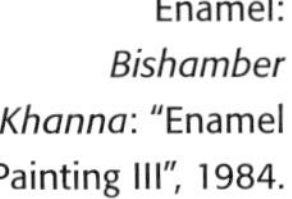

Enamel: *Bishamber Khanna*: "Enamel Painting III", 1984.

Enamel Colours Refer *Enamel*.

Enamelling Refer *Enamel*.

Enas, M.J. (1962–) b. Kanichar, Kerala. Education: B.FA. in *sculpture CFA* Thiruvananthapuram, M.FA. in *sculpture College of Art* New Delhi. Solos: *Art Heritage* New Delhi, *JAG*. Group shows: National *LKA*, *College of Art* New Delhi, *GE*, All India Art Exhibition Kochi (Cochin), *Triennale* New Delhi, CHAG. Commissions: *Monumental* statue of Rao Tulla Ram a freedom fighter at Mahendragarh Haryana and a large *terracotta mural* at the Centre for Management Development UP. Appointments: *Sculpture art* teacher New Delhi School. Collections: *NGMA* New Delhi, pvt. & corporates.

Having undergone religious training in the Jesuit order for nearly nine years. M.J. Enas's *sculptures* have an inherent spirituality that manifests itself in his *life-size figures*. He has worked with *stone*, *wood*, *terracotta*, *bronze* and *fibreglass*. *Lead* is another material he uses because "it has connotations with death and *magic*".

He has been influenced by the cinematic, specifically the films of Andrei Tarkovsky. He usually combines different objects to create a stage link *atmosphere*. This is seen in the *life-size fibreglass sculpture*. M.J. Enas's *art* is thus intuitive of the human condition and sense of being.

He lives and works in New Delhi.

Encaustic=burning in. A *painting technique* practised in antiquity, involving the use of *wax* as a binder. The *pigments* were mixed with *wax* and painted onto the surface, being fixed by heating with hot *irons* or similar methods, which would serve to permanently bond the *colour* to the surface. It was used for making posthumous *portraits*, at Fayum near Egypt in the AD 1st century, Encaustic has been used in the *modern* period by *Ramlal Dhar* and *Eric Bowen* who experimented to create a thickly laid *impasto* surface or used it to create smooth or glossy surfaces. Refer *Tempera*, *Fresco*, *Banasthali Vidyapith* RAJ.

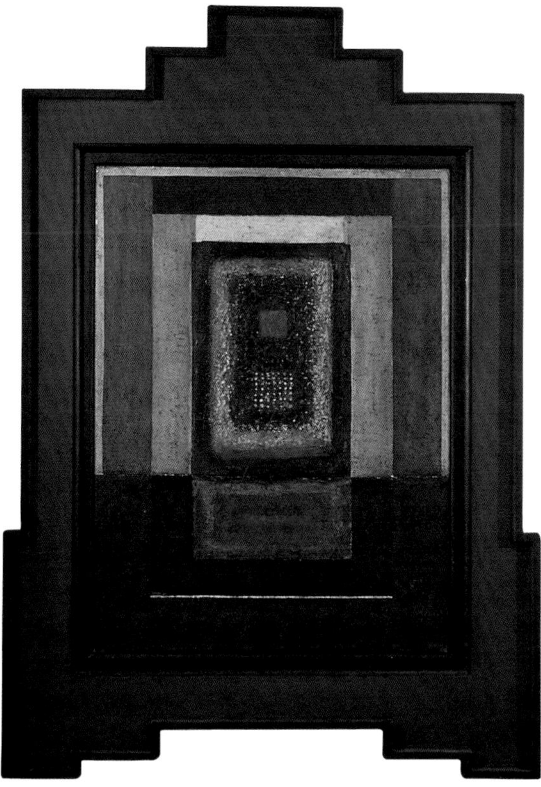

Encaustic: *Eric Bowen*, "From the World of the Ascetic", *Oil/Encaustic* on *Canvas*, 1991, 162.5x125 cm.

End-Grain Sectioning of the end piece of the *wood* across the grain or direction of its fibres. It is used in *wood* marquetry as shown in the works of *Vishwanath M. Sholapurkar*. (See illustration on page 330.)

Engraving A method of cutting grooves in *metal plates* or wooden blocks by means of the needle and other push cutting tools. A *design* or *image* is carved upon the surface. *Ink* is then "pushed" into these grooves and a *print* is taken on *paper*. *Wood engraving* was introduced in India early 19th century by Company *painters*. These *artists* were later employed to produce creative *block printing* on textiles. This process was established in Kolkata, Mumbai and Chennai. The *technique* of cutting and engraving produced to create a rich *chiaroscuro* of *black* and *white*. This *term* is also used to cover all processes of *intaglio* method of *printmaking*. In the 20th century, *artists* began engraving on *steel plates*, as *copper* was too soft to allow a large number of reprints. Refer *Company School/Company Painting*, *Etching*, *Mezzotint*, *Dry-Point*, *Line Engraving*, *Photo-engraving*, *Creation*, *Jyoti Bhatt*, *Krishna N. Reddy*, *Yagneshwar Kalyanji Shukla*, *Anupam Sud*, *Ali J. Sultan*.

Environment Art An extension of *sculpture*, a *term* since 1950, *art* involves the use of many *sculptures* or *creations* into which one can walk. Often these works are of a temporary *nature*. It was introduced by American *artists*. In India, *Vivan Sundaram's* later works which can be reassembled at different venues and involve the use of three-dimensional *constructions*, tube *lights*, coloured water, bricks and photographic material. Refer *Cinema*, *Ecological Art*, *Funk Art*, *Photograph*, *Navjot Altaf*, *Dattatrey D. Apte*, *Ramkinkar Baij*, *Krishnamachari Bose*, *Madhu Champaneria*, *Avtarjeet S. Dhanjal*, *Balbir Singh Katt*, *Kanayi Kunhiraman*, *Rm. Palaniappan*, *Nagji Patel*, *Vivan Sundaram*.

Epic A description or *narrative* of *heroic* achievements of important personages in history generally in poetic form. In India Sage Valmiki narrated *heroic* deeds of lord RAMA in RAMAYANA and Sage Vyasa those of the Pandava brothers in MAHABHARATA. These have often been used as subject matter for *miniature painting*, *glass painting* and *fresco painting* in India. The epics still continue to be a source of inspiration for *modern* and *contemporary artists* of today.

Erotic Art Erotic *term* refers to expression of love or sexual desire and excitement derived from Eros, the *god* of love in Greek *mythology*. There are references to such joyous expressions right from the RIG-VEDA to *modern* times. The quest for fulfillment has been endless. Urvashi-Pururavas and Nala-Damayanti are early love stories that inspired eroticism. One can see their depiction in the KAILASH Temple at *Ellora*, in *Khajuraho* and Konarak temples as well as in Belur-Halebid in the south (almost exclusively from the period AD 950–1250). Even earlier, eroticism was entwined in TANTRIC *culture*. Erotic *sculptures* are popularly considered to be illustrative of the TANTRIC *spiritual* goal of non-duality. However, the singular influence on Indian eroticism has been that of KAMA-SUTRA. A treatise on sex, it is described variously, both as *art* and science, to be practised in conjunction with Dharma (practise of religion) and Artha (practice of profession). Erotic art has influenced almost all *forms* of *art* in India. The *Mughal* and *Rajasthani miniature paintings*, the *Basohli paintings* of KRISHNA and RADHA, all had a generous sprinkling of erotic art. Indian erotic miniatures were influenced by GITA-GOVINDA and other erotic poetry. Among more *contemporary artists*, *Francis Newton Souza*, *Akbar Padamsee*, *Satish Gujral*, *Jatin Das*, *Laxma Goud*, *Laxman Pai* have all worked on erotic themes. Refer *Bhupen Khakhar* and *Tyeb Mehta*.

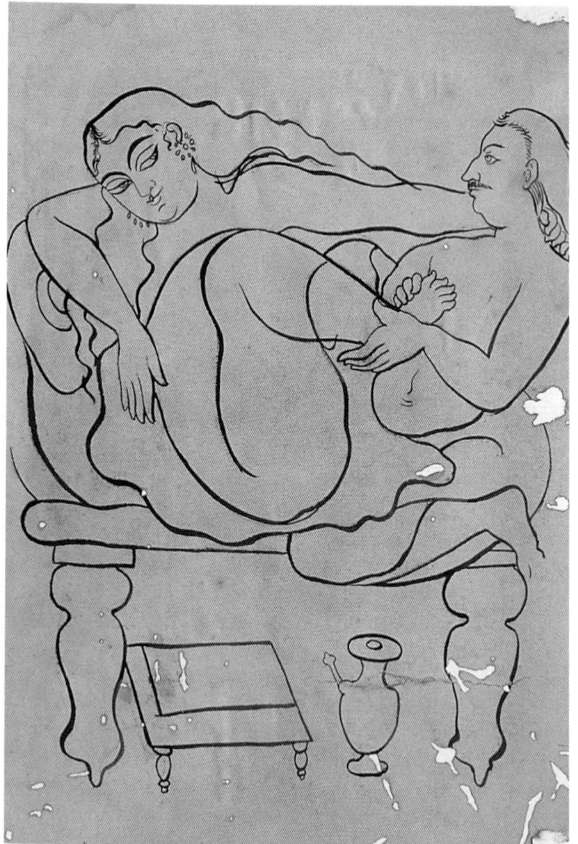

Erotic Art: "Kalighat", *Drawing*.

Etching A mode of *printmaking* involving the etching of a *metal plate* with *acid biting in* into the *plate*. A *drawing* or a *design* is made with an etching needle, a sharp pointed *steel* tool, used for incising *lines* on a *metal plate* previously coated with a *wax* and resin mixture. The *plate* is immersed into *acid bath*, which corrodes the parts laid bare by the needle. The strength of the *acid* solution and the length of the *plate* is submerged in it, determines the *depth* of the *bite*. Different *tonal values* are obtained by open *bite* or *aquatint* layers. *Ground* and *varnish* coating are then cleaned with white spirit. The *print* is taken from the *plate* thus prepared and *copies* are then taken as required. This was first taught at *Santiniketan* (WB) with *Mukul Chandra Dey* and *Nandalal Bose*. *Muhammed Abdur Rehman Chugtai*, Ramendranath Chakravarty, Samanendranath Gupta and *Benode Behari Mukherjee* all experimented with etching. Refer *Company School*, *Intaglio*, *Printmaking*, *Jyoti Bhatt*, *Naina Dalal*; Illustration–*Amitabha Banerjee*, *Anupam Sud*, *Somnath Hore*, *Krishna N. Reddy*.

Exhibition (Art) The display of works of *art* to the general public, the connoisseur and the *art critic* at an *art* gallery, *museum*, institution, or the *artist's* studio. The exhibited works may consist of work done over a period of time, or it may constitute works of several *artists*, perhaps working on a common *theme*. Such exhibitions are generally curated. *Raja Ravi Varma* first exhibited his two *paintings* in 1873 at *Fine Arts* Exhibition in Madras. *Rabindranath Tagore* and *Gaganendranath Tagore's* first exhibition was held in Calcutta in 1922 with the German Bauhaus Group *artists*. In 1930 *Rabindranath Tagore's* first exhibition was held at Gallerie Pigalle, Paris.

Expressionism is a term that is applied to that quality in most works of Indian *art* today, which are based on emotional values—a deliberate *distortion* of the rational and traditional methods of representing the subject. This trend towards *distortion* refers in particular to the outburst of *art* in the early 20th century in Germany.

The *artists'* works contained powerful elements of *colour*, *line* and *content* that heightened the emotional impact on spectators.

Expressionism in India is almost a movement in itself. It has, since the time of *Ramkinkar Baij*, become a part of the *modern style*, surfacing time and again in *contemporary* works. Refer *Abstract Expression*, *Abstract Sculpture*, *Action painting*, *Modern*, *Neo-Expressionism*, *Narayan S. Bendre*, *Dhanraj Bhagat*, *Biren De*, *Rabindranath Tagore*, *Gaganendranath Tagore*.

Eye-Level It is an imaginary or actual *line* horizontally running across a *painting* or two-dimensional *composition* which corresponds to the *artist's* vision level. The laws of *perspective* are then applied to the object in the *painting* with some of them rendered as being above eye-level and others below.

In India, *Academic art* brought in *perspective* and the use of the eye-level, with *painters* mainly expressing themselves in the traditional *style* set by *Raja Ravi Varma*, i.e., a group of *figures* set in a *landscape background*. Refer *Jaganath M. Ahivasi*, *Baburao Painter*, *Vajubhai Bhagat*.

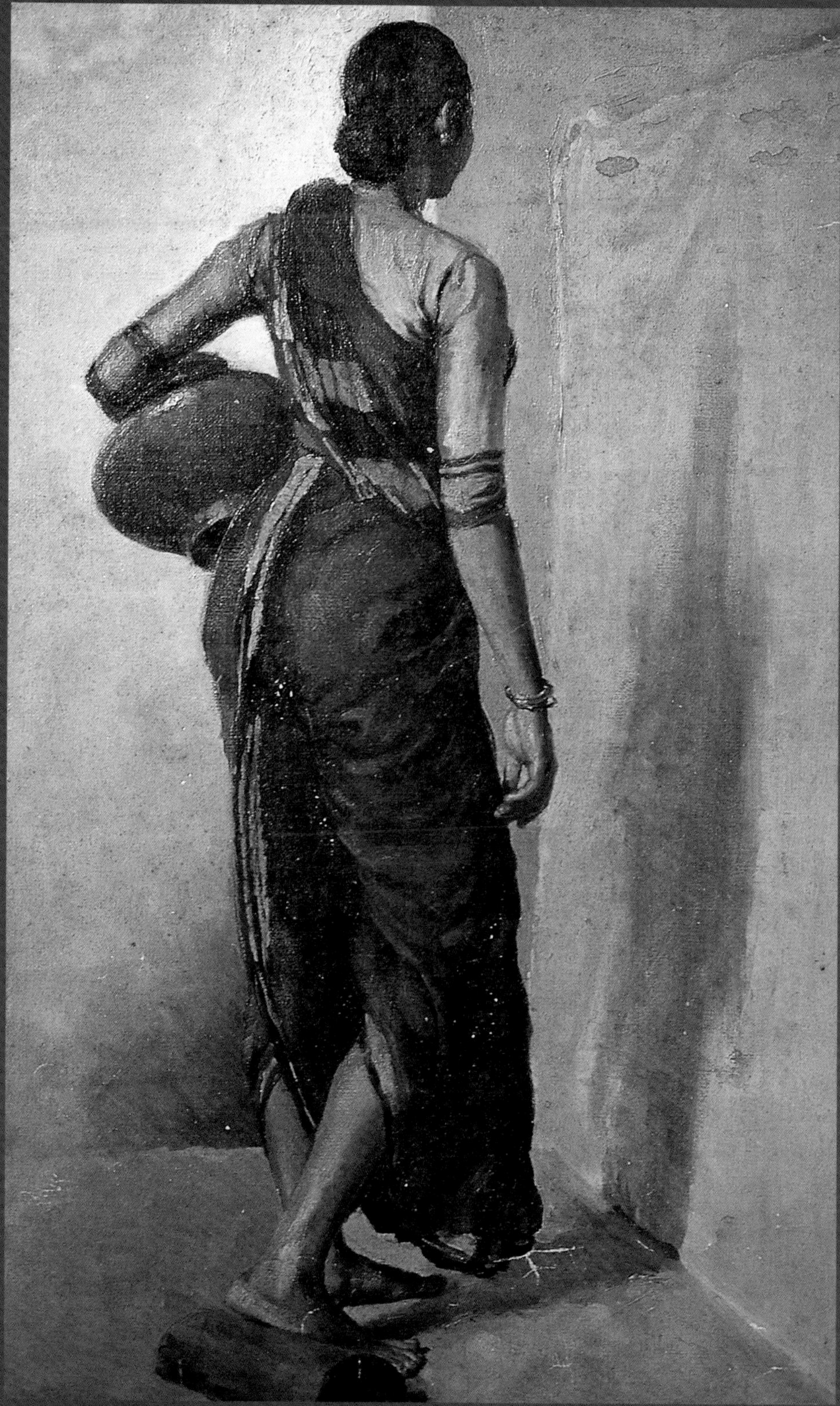

Figure Painting: *Vinayak Pandurang Karmarkar*, "Untitled", *Oils*. (See notes on page 132)

Facing Coating of different materials or *colours* in its layers to *support* the lower layer especially in the work of *art*. **1.** In *sculpture*, the first layer of the *negative* moulding material which comes into direct contact with the object to be *cast*. It is thin bodied and made from the finest sieve mesh. **2.** Also refers to a method of *conservation* where the main elements of *composition* are covered with tissue, while rest of the *painting* is being restored or transferred to a fresh support after the *painting* is complete. **3.** In *tempera*, *paintings* were usually burnished with a final coat of either olive or coconut *oil*. Refer *Acrylics*, *Bengal School*, *Ceramics*, *Collage*, CHITRAKATHI, *Etching*, *Fibreglass*, *Metal*, *Miniature Painting*, *Mixed Media*, *Murals*, *Watercolour*, *Wash (Technique)*, *Wood Cut*, *Nandalal Bose*, *Benode Behari Mukherjee*, *Hemendranath Mazumdar*, *Abanindranath Tagore*, *Raja Ravi Varma*.

Faculty of Fine Arts (FFA) (Vadodara) The FFA is part of the *Maharaja Sayajirao University* (*MSU*) of Vadodara which was founded in 1950. It was the first institute in the country to offer degree and post-grad. courses in various branches of *FA*. It is divided into six major depts. of *painting*; *sculpture*; *applied arts*; *graphic arts*; *art* history; *art* criticism and *aesthetics* and museology. There are also associate sections attached to these dept. The *painting* dept. provides large studios for the study of traditional and *modern media*, offering specializations in creative *painting* and portraiture. The section on *mural design* offers training in *fresco*, *tempera* and other indigenious *mural media*.

The *sculpture* dept. has a foundry, a carving shed, forging and *welding* facilities. The *pottery* and *ceramics* section is part of this dept., photography is an essential subject in the *applied arts* section, where typography is supplemented with printing, the process and *engraving* section.

The *graphics* dept. too has associate sections for photography, *wood*, *lithography* and printing in addition to the facilities for *printmaking* by *lithography*, *wood cut*, *intaglio*, *serigraphy* and letter press printing.

The dept. of *art* history and *aesthetics* covers both oriental and Western *Art* history together with an insight into *aesthetics*. It houses a growing archive of *visual* documentation, including original works of *art*, both traditional and *contemporary*, *prints*, *photographs*, slides and film-strips.

The museology dept. offers both fulltime and short *term* courses in *museum* and *conservation techniques*.

The FFA also has its own library specializing in books on all areas of *FA*, as well as an auditorium for viewing slide-demonstrations and films. Students can also avail of the facilities of the Smt. Hansa Mehta Library, which forms part of the University.

Faculty of Visual Arts Rabindra Bharati University Refer *Rabindra Bharati University* (Kolkata).

Fakir The Arabic word for ascetic or mendicant, literally meaning a "poor man". Such characters often feature in Mughal-Basawan *miniature paintings*. Refer *Mughal Dynasty*.

Fantasy The world of make-believe, of impossible things, fantasy could be an offshoot of *Surrealism*. In the West, fantasy fascinated *artists* like H. Bosch and P. Bruegel. In the 20th century, Freudian theories like *Automatism* and dream *imagery* were incorporated by *artists*, *Dadaism*, *Surrealism*, and the works of *artists* like Bacon captivated *art* lovers.

In India, however, fantasy has always played an important part of folklore. The concept of 6-, 8- or 10-armed *gods* and goddesses did not seem strange even to the common man. It was the foreigners who labelled them monsters along with the GANDHARVAS, Kinnaras and APSARAS who appear in Indian *painting* and *sculpture*. The same is the case with *contemporary* Indian *artists*—fantasy rules here, be it in the traditional sense or in the Western sense. *Laxma Goud's* safety-pinned and darned women co-exist with *Gulam Mohammed Sheikh's* intersecting interiors and *Arpita Singh's* flying *figures*. Refer *Body Art*, *Found Object*, *Legend*, *Swapan Kumar Das*, *Satyen Ghosal*, *K. Ramanujam*, *H.R. Kambli*, *Hiralal Khatri*, *Ram Nath Pasricha*, *Ghanshyam Ranjan*, *Ananda Gopal Roy*, *Gopen Roy*, *Hitendranath Tagore*, *Arnawaz Vasudev*; Illustrations—*Jogen Chowdhury*, *Satish Gujral*, *Tyeb Mehta*, *Ved Nayar*, *Saroj Gogi Pal*, *B.P. Paliwal*, *Ratan Parimoo*, *Shekhar Roy*, *Suhas Roy*, *Sarbari RoyChowdhury*, *Rameshwar Singh*, *Gaganendranath Tagore—Abstraction Geometric*, *Rabindranath Tagore—Surrealism*, *Jai Zharotia*.

Farooqi, Anis (1938–1994) b. Dist. Sultanpur, UP. Education: Dip. in *drawing* & *painting* Mumbai, M.A. & Ph.D. in *drawing* & *painting* & History of Indian *arts* under the guidance of the Late Prof. Niharranjan Ray, Agra University; Museum technique & History of *art* Institute of FA. New York University. Solos: Dehradun, New Delhi, Aligarh. Group participations: National Exhibition *LKA*, *Triennale* & *NGMA* New Delhi, others in Lucknow, UP, Hyderabad, SKP, *AIFACS*; International: Prague Czechoslovakia, *Biennale* Bangladesh. Organized *exhibitions*: Contemporary Indian Art Australia, Indonesia, Japan, South Korea, Mangolia, China, Russia, Yugoslavia, Bulgaria, England, France, Portugal, USA; Exhibition programmes of foreign *artists* in India—Including those of H. Moore, P. Picasso, Russian Museum, Kinetic Sculptures Germany & others; Computerization of 13,000 *paintings/art* objects to make *art* easily accessible to people at *NGMA* New Delhi. *Art* camp: Kashmir. *Auctions*: Heart Mumbai. Awards: All India Exhibition PUJ, Gold Medal UP, National Award *LKA* New Delhi & others. Member: Central Academy of Art, Decoration Committee—Parliament House, Museum President Palace, Vigyan Bhavan. Publications: Including contributed articles in Indian Research & *Art* Journals; Two books—"Art of India & Persia"—1979 & "Hindustani Musawiri-Ek Khaka" (Urdu) 1981; International: Book on Indian contemporary paintings—Syria, Egypt, Israel, Ghana & Japan. Appointments: Was Museologist, *Art* historian, Dir. *NGMA* New Delhi 1985–1994; Organized Seminars & *Art* Conferences: Fukuoka Art Museum Japan; Secretary, Advisory, *Art* Purchaser at *NGMA* New Delhi. Collections: *LKA*, *NGMA* & Doordarshan New Delhi, PUJ Govt. & University Chandigarh.

Anis Farooqi's *paintings* range from portraiture to creative *landscapes* and *figurative compositions*; *oil* being his main *medium*. His *figures*, though in *oil*, are painted with subdued *colours* and generally carry a core message e.g. 'Peace and Beauty', etc. "Configuration!"—with three female *figures* in a pensive mood. "Dream" and "Patronage" show female *figures* enveloped by floating bits of *drapery*, creating a feeling of disquiet.

Fat over lean *Term* used when a thick layer of *paint* mixed with *oil* is applied over a thin (*lean*) layer of quick drying *paint* mixed with *turpentine*. Refer *Impasto, Lean, Scumbling, Bal Chhabda, Brinda C. Miller, Dinanath Pathy*, Pratima Sheth.

Fauvism A *style* of *painting*, in which *discordant* and bright striking *colours* were sketchily applied on distorted *forms* with boldly decorative effects. The word derived from the French *critic* Louis Vanxcelles' *term*, Les Fauves meaning wild animals. This owed its origins to the post-Impressionists especially P. Gaugin and V. Van Gogh. H. Matisse continued to use bright *colours* but his application and *forms* varied after a period of *time*; other *artists* later became enamoured of *Expressionism*. Fauvism, had influenced many later 20th-century *artists*. Refer *Isms, Modern, Oil Paint, Post-Impressionism, Sayed Haider Raza, Maqbool Fida Husain, Bhupen Khakhar*.

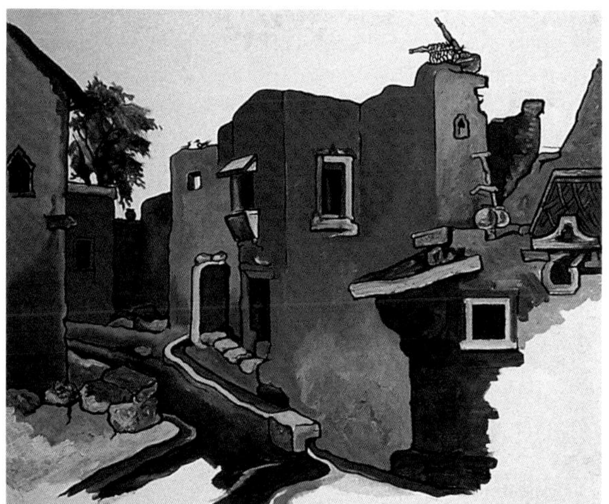

Fauvism: *Namdeo B. Dikhole*, "A Dwelling in Jaisalmer Fort (RAJ)", *Oil* on *Canvas*, 66x96 cm.

Fernandes, John (1951–) b. Belgaum, MAHA. Education: Studied *art* in Chitra Mandir in Belgaum for nine years under the guidance of *K.B. Kulkarni*. Solos: *JAG* in 1991, 1993, 1996 & 2003, Indian art Gallery Pune. Group participations: MAHA State Art Mumbai, *BAS* & other towns of MAHA. Appointments: Worked as illustrator in Mumbai for nine years, a portraitist. Collections: pvt. Mumbai, Agra; International: USA, Germany, Spain.

His works generally centre around the human *figure*, especially the young female *figure*, viewed either in isolation, or in groups of two or more or as part of crowd in a *landscape*. The women are young, mostly half clad, in a romanticized mood. He is equally at ease with all *media*.

His *style* can be termed as impressionist, with quick, spontaneous brushstrokes full of *light* where *oils* give the effect of *watercolours*.

He also *paints* commissioned *portraits* and works as a freelance *artist* in Mumbai. Refer *K.B. Kulkarni*.

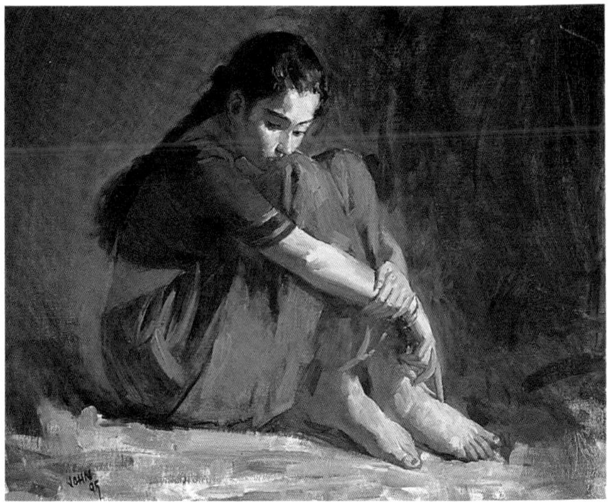

Fernandes, John: "Day Dreaming", *Oil* on *Canvas*, 1995, 75x90 cm.

Fibreglass A material now used in the making of lightweight but extremely durable *sculpture*. The basic materials are thin filaments of glass combined with a *synthetic* resin. The objects are slowly built up in thin, brushed layers, with fibreglass sheets layered in after one or two coats of resin. The glass can be woven into thin sheets of fabric-like consistency and used in *casting*. It can be textured or coated to imitate other more traditional materials like *bronze*. *Ravinder G. Reddy* uses gilded fibreglass polished to a high gloss, while *MJ. Enas* exploits its sensitivity to create *tactile* surfaces resembling *wood* and *cast cement*. Refer *Bronze, Casting, Inorganic, Kinetic Art, Media, Mobile, Mural, Polychromatic sculpture, Synthetic, Texture, Yusuf Arakkal, Krishnamachari Bose, C. Dakshinamoorthy, Usha Rani Hooja, Nilkanth P. Khanvilkar, Balan Nambiar, Mahendra Pandya, Raj Kumar Panwar, Ankit Patel, Niranjan Pradhan, Vivan Sundaram*.

Figuration, Figurative The *term*, which determinates a certain *form* which is represented by a *figure* or *emblem*, has come into wide use. Subsequently it was intensely used in defining abstraction. *Art* has always been based on the figurative, though *figure styles* varied regionally and from period to period. It was only in the 20th century when *art* became increasingly non-representational that representational i.e. *figurative art* was debated upon. In the *contemporary* scene, most *figurative art* has been tinged with a certain degree of abstraction and stylization; *Amrita Sher-Gil's figures* are less *abstract* than *Maqbool Fida Husain's* while *B. Prabha's* women are more stylized than *Anjolie Ela Menon's*. Refer *Aerial Perspective, Background, Drawing, Form, Imagery, Impressionism, Modern Style, Monochrome,*

Post-Independence, Realism, Realistic, Space, Watercolours; Illustration–*Altaf, Navjot Altaf, Yusuf Arakkal, Gobardhan Ash, B. Prabha, Ramkinkar Baij, Narayan S. Bendre, Atul Dodiya, Gajanan S. Haldankar, Savlaram L. Haldankar, C. Jagdish, Surendra Pal Joshi, B.P. Kamboj, Kanayi Kunhiraman, Krishen Khanna, P. Khemraj, K. Khosa, Veer Munshi, Shankar Palsikar, Sudhir Patwardhan, Shyamal Dutta Ray, Jehangir Sabavala, Bhabesh Chandra Sanyal, Narayan R. Sardesai, Prabhas Sen, Raja Ravi Varma, Academic Art–Muralidhar R. Achrekar, Accidental Light–Savlaram L. Haldankar, Action Painting–Pratima Sheth, Relief–Piraji Sagara.*

Figurative Art Synonym for representational art, meaning any subject however distorted but inspired by things in the visible world.

Ramkinkar Baij was one of the first *modern sculptors* at *Santiniketan*, who used the *figurative composition* in a conceptual *manner*. Even the material used was replete with *symbolic* meaning. Refer *Conceptual Art, Distortion, Figuration, Figurative;* Illustration–*Ramkinkar Baij, Dhanraj Bhagat, Kanayi Kunhiraman, Meera Mukherjee, Ashoke Mullick, Arpita Singh, K. Khosa.*

Figure The depiction of a human figure in *painting* or *sculpture* in a definite external *form*, either in *torso* or in full figure. The *style* ranges from the classically academic as in *Mahadev V. Dhurandhar's painting*, to folk-inspired in *Jamini Roy*, to the heavily distorted in *Francis Newton Souza's* works. Refer *Academic Art, Altarpiece, Basholi, Classical, Folk Art, Nude, Temple Architecture, Narayan S. Bendre, Dhanraj Bhagat, Vajubhai D. Bhagat, Sakti Burman, C. Jagdish, John Fernandes, Gajanan Narayan Jadhav, Kanayi Kunhiraman, Vinayak Pandurang Karmarkar, Sailoz Mookerjea, Benode Behari Mukherjee, Shankar Palshikar.*

Figure Painting *Paintings* in which the *realistic form* with the study of the human *anatomy* is the principal subject. This could vary in *style* and *technique among* different *artists*, e.g. *figure paintings* of *Savlaram L. Haldankar, Murlidhar R. Achrekar*. In "fictive sculpture" the *figures* and *forms* are painted to imitate *sculptural* effect. (See illustration on page 129)

Figure-Ground Relationship This means the way in which an object or *motif* in a *painting* is related to its *background*. It is of equal importance both in *resentational* and non-representational *art*, e.g., in *Manjit Bawa's paintings* the subtly shaded *figures* stand out against the flat, coloured *background*, while in *Vasudeo Santu Gaitonde's compositions*, the *foreground* merges into the *background* in *terms* of *colour* and *tonal value*. Refer *Abstract Art, Abstract Sculpture, Figurative Art, Imagery, Narrative, Pattern, Significant Form.*

Filigree This means delicate *open work patterns*, mainly made from precious *metals*, by soldering (joining) together fine wires and minute spheres, usually used for making jewellery. The *technique* is also incorporated into *sculpture* and temples. The *Abu-Dilwara Group of Jain Temples* incorporated the filigree *technique* of delicate *carving in marble*. Refer *Jali Work, Fretwork, Abu-Dilwara Group of Temples.*

Filler A semi-solid or liquid material used to fill or stuff a hole or a gap. An ingredient that is added to the *paint* to increase its *opacity*, or used to fill the porous *ground* in *printmaking, painting*, or cracks in *stone* or *wood*. etc. This is the method also used in *casting*, moulding etc. Refer *China Clay, Gouache, Screen Printing, Cloison, Enamel, Kalamkari, Cire Perdue, Soft-Sculpture, South Indian Bronze, Bishamber Khanna, Somnath Hore, Meera Mukherjee.*

Film A thin layer of *paint, varnish* or any other *transparent medium* that is applied on the surface of a *canvas, sculpture* or *graphic* print, normally for protection. Refer *Ajanta, Drawing Ink, Oil, Screen Printing, Silk Screen Printing, Tempera, Wash (Technique), Abanindranath Tagore, Gaganendranath Tagore, Deokinandan Sharma, Banasthali Vidyapith* (RAJ).

Fine Arts *Architecture, sculpture, painting*, music, and the performing *arts* are considered to be the *fine arts*, as opposed to applied, decorative or commercial *art*. This distinction has only been made since the mid-19th century, to distinguish its *aesthetics* and theoretical *values*. It is not stratified or explicitly named nor distinctly recognized as a separate class. The school of *art*, which in 1850 was known as School of Industry was organized by Dr. G. Buist, editor of the "Bombay Times". A similar School of Arts and Crafts had been founded in Madras by Dr. Hunter. But earlier in India there was no distinction between *miniature paintings, arts* and *crafts* and creative fine arts. Later, Indian *artists* were eager to learn new *art* in the *form* of adopting the *realistic* approach, its *technique* of linear *perspective* and *chiaroscuro* in addition to keeping the spirit of individualistic culture of the Indian subcontinent. Refer *Academy, GCAC & Madras School of Art* Chennai, *GCAC & Madras School of Art* Kolkata, *JJSA (Bombay School), KB* in *Santiniketan, Ajanta, Bauhaus, Bengal Revivalism, Bengal School, Benode Behari Mukherjee, Nandalal Bose, Ramkinkar Baij.*

Finish **1.** A protective coating applied to the surface of the work of *art*, including both *painting* and *sculpture*. **2.** The actual final surface of the completed work. **3.** The use of minute *detail* in a work of *art*.

This *term* also refers to the spreading capacity of a *pigment* covering an underlying surface of the work. e.g. the *technique* in *tempera* where the *paint film* dries very quickly and the finishing of the final touch is given sometimes by applying *oil* for *glazing*. In *sculpture* it is characterized either by a smooth and sensual, or rough and earthy, or a glossy shining polished surface. Refer *Illuminated Manuscripts, Bengal School, Naive art, Opacity, Sketch, Stone Carving, Texture, Varnish, C. Ponnappa Rajaram, Nagji Patel, Kahini (Arte) Merchant, Rabin Mondal, Rabindranath Tagore, Raja Ravi Varma, Sarada Charan Ukil.*

Firing The heating or baking of an object in a *kiln* in order to harden it, e.g. in the case of *sculpture*, and *ceramics* or to fuse the components as in *enamelling*. This process has been in use since the earliest times, when man accidentally learnt to bake *clay* pots. The same principle is used even in *modern* gas or *oil*-fired or electric ovens. Refer *China Clay, Enamel, Balan Nambiar, Bishamber Khanna, G. Reghu, Siona Benjamin.*

Fixative A thin *varnish* either natural or *synthetic*, that is sprayed on to *charcoal, chalk* and *pastel drawings* to protect them against being rubbed or accidently smudged. Refer Illustration—*Portrait, Still Life; Satyendranath Bandhyopadhyay, Samarendranath Tagore, Jogen Chowdhury, Ram Kishore Yadav, Piraji Sagara, Rajen, Akbar Padamsee, Mona Rai, Nita Thakore.*

Flat Application It refers to a plain, untextured surface in the work of *art*; in *painting*, this is achieved with the use of a flat *brush*, roller or air brush etc. *Jaganath M. Ahivasi's* interpretations *of modern* Indian miniature *style* had bright *colours* with a flat application. Refer *Air Brushing, Bazaar painting, Sunayani Devi Chattopadhyay, Shankar Palshikar.*

Flat Colour An even *opaque* layer of *colour* applied over a large surface in a *composition*. There are no textural or tonal variations. The *folk art style* with its bold linear *drawings*, bright, flat colour application and decorative rhythmic repititions is a perfect example of this *style*. Refer *Tonal Value, Manjit Bawa, Tyeb Mehta.*

Flora & Fauna Paintings Natural history *paintings* with flowers and plants; birds and animals, etc., as the main subject. In India, these subjects were popular during the Mughal period, especially during the time of Jehangir who was fond of exotic flora and fauna and his court *artists*, especially Mansur, painted them. Later, between about 1780 and 1860, natural history subjects were commissioned from Indian *artists* by East India Company officers, some for official reasons, others for pvt. collections. Refer *Arabesque*, CHITRAKATHI, *Company School/Company Painting, Design, Miniature Painting, Mughal Dynasty, Pattern, Persian Art, K.V. Haridasan, C.N. Karunakaran, Prabha Shah, Saroj Kumar R.K. Singh, K. Venkatappa, Bal Wad.*

Folio **1.** One leaf (sheet of a book). **2.** A complete (small or large) book composed of sheets folded once to make two leaves of four pages. **3.** *Illuminated manuscripts* in which leaves are numbered as folios and not pages. Refer *Akbar-Namah, Hamza-Namah, Miniature Painting, Mughal Dynasty, National Museums.*

Folk Art The *term* refers to the indigenous *art* of a particular community; the signs, symbols and *style* being the result of a collective consciousness rather than one individual's vision and repeated with minor variations through the ages. The *style* is usually simple with bold linear *drawings*, bright, *flat colour* application (if *colour* is used) and decorative rhythmic repetitions. Folk art survived centuries of external influences due to the prevailing social structure based on the village or tribal community. Refer *Kalighat Folk Paintings, Warli Paintings, Madhubani (Mithila), Company School.*

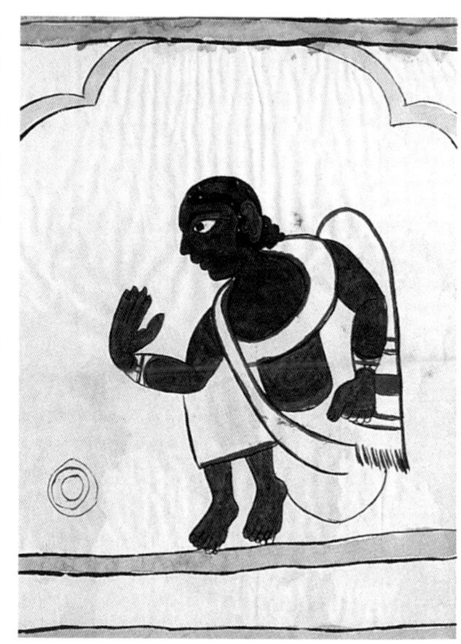

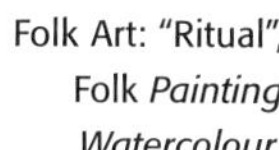

Folk Art: "Ritual", Folk *Painting* *Watercolour.*

Folk Decoration An offshoot of *folk art*, the *term* refers to the decoration created from the daily life of the people; e.g. Rangoli and Alpana floor decoration, traditional and tribal *weaving*, textiles, *embroidery, ceramic*, etc., in which the symbols and *motifs* have a specific, often auspicious, meaning. Many *contemporary artists* have been using folk *motifs* and materials in their *paintings, sculptures* and *installations*. Refer *Sheela Gowda, Shakuntala Kulkarni, Madhvi Parekh, Nita Thakore, Bhanu Shah.*

Folk Inspiration In the search for a truly Indian *"Modern"* vision as against a servile imitation of the West, *artists* turned to *folk art* for inspiration. Panels in *tempera* show the spontaneous application of *line* and *colour* that can be seen in *Kalighat folk paintings*. While most *artists* practised an *eclectic form* of folk *painting*, this *Eclecticism* has been carried forward by *contemporary* Indian *artists* by mixing elements of *naive art* with folk *rhythms*, folk myths and *legends* into their *compositions*. Refer *Jamini Roy, Nandalal Bose, Madhvi Parekh, Badri Narayan.*

Folklore Museum (Mysore, KAR) Established in 1968, the Folklore Museum forms part of the Kuvempu Institute of Kannada Studies, of the University of Mysore. It is housed in the Royal Vijayalakshmi Mansion in the Manasa Gangotri campus and has a priceless collection of over 7000 folk *artefacts* and *art* objects from KAR. The *museum* has twenty-one sections including those on puppetry, temple *carvings*, Yakshagana headgear and costumes, toys, musical instruments, agricultural implements, tools, basketry, wooden and *metal images*. Some of these objects have also been exhibited abroad.

Foreground The *images* or *figures* that seem nearest to the viewer on the picture plane. The *term* is generally used when describing the *composition*.

In miniature *style*, generally *forms* in the *background* appear higher than the *figures* in the foreground. In *Basohli* miniatures the *background* of the *paintings* are absolutely flat and are a perfect foil to the action-taking place in the foreground. *Raja Ravi Varma's* is *realistic figurative landscapes* were termed academic, with the detailed foreground in sharp focus against a perspectival rendering of *landscapes*. Refer *Academic Art, Ajanta, Savlaram L. Haldankar, Muralidhar R. Achrekar, M.T.V. Acharya, Jaganath M. Ahivasi, Kshitendranath Mazumdar, Nathu Lal Verma.*

Foreshortening The *term* that describes the recession within a picture plane of a particular object by means of *perspectival* devices. This is applied to the reduction in *size* and *colour* as the object recedes to create the *illusion* of a three-dimensional object in a two-dimensional plane, which the spectator automatically recognizes. Foreshortening is treated differently in *miniature painting* and in *Academic Art*. In some of the *miniature paintings* e.g. 'HOLI'. Refer Illustrations—DURGA, *Life-Drawing, Seascape, Sakti Burman, Pralhad Dhond, Mahadev V. Dhurandhar, Balvant Joshi, B.P. Kamboj, Bhupen Khakhar, Paresh Maity, Amrut Patel, Sudhir Patwardhan, Ramesh Rao, Raja Ravi Varma.*

Form Classification of substance—*creation*, arrangement or *volume* in the work of *art*, and also its components and their relationship within an outer appearance of the work. The *composition* in the same degree, is distinct from its *contents*. Even as in method, *installation* and *sculpture*, the *term* refers to its tangible *mass* rather than the *space* around it.

In Indian *art* the form, which is termed 'Rupa' conveys the relationship of the *artist* with his or his/her work. e.g. the female figurative forms of *Raja Ravi Varma, Rabindranath Tagore's sketches* in *ink*, *Ramkinkar Baij's cement* forms in *sculpture*. The geometric character and *abstract* forms in some works could refer to certain symbols with specific meaning as in *Tantra Art* and the neo-Tantric works of *Biren De* and *Ghulam Rasool Santosh*. Refer SHADANGA.

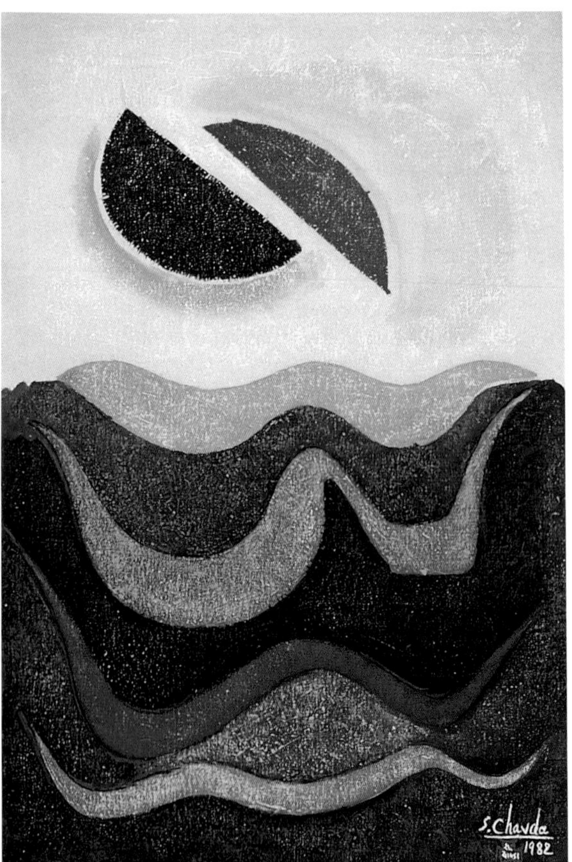

Form: *Shiavax Chavda*, "Seascape–I", *Oil* on *Canvas*, 1982, 115x80 cm.

Found Object Literally translated from the French term for object trouve, it refers to any object or *ready-made* or unconventional material in the work of *art*. These include both animate and inanimate objects, like dried leaves, pods, *stones* or even kitchen ware and machine-made objects, *paper* and junk. Indian *artists* have used found objects in *collages* and *installations* in addition to *sculptures*. With the use of found objects, the distinction between *painting* and *sculpture* has become progressively finer, with *painting*, sporting a heavy *relief*-like appearance.

Since the 1980s and 1990s Indian *artists* have worked with *mixed media assemblages* using sandstone, *terracotta, acrylic* sheets, *steel, leather*, mirrors, *fibreglass* and *metal* in conjunction with *wood* and *ready-made* objects. *Artists* like Rummana Hussain have also used photographic documents. *Artists* in India today are more radical in their approach towards experimention with new ideas. Refer *Automatism, Collage, Fantasy, Junk Art, Sculpture, K. Vasant Wankhede, Vishnu Chinchalkar, Anjolie Ela Menon, N. Pushpamala, Vivan Sundaram, Nalini Malani, Navjot Altaf, Krishnamachari Bose*, and many other younger *artists*.

Frame A case or border—a structural *design* to enclose works on *paper, paintings* on *canvas*, panel or other *media*, either with or without a glass covering it. These are either traditional, made of cardboard, *paper, wood, metal*, or similar material. Generally used for decoration, protection and display of the works.

The framing varies from past *traditions*, features including the addition of decorative borders similar to that on of the *miniature paintings. Handmade paper*, and silk are often used as *mounts*. Refer *Screen Printing, Silk Screen Printing, C. Douglas, Anjolie Ela Menon.*

Free-Standing *Sculpture or decorative object* which is not attached to a *background* in the *form* of *relief*, and can be viewed from all sides. Refer *Dimension, Elephanta, Gandharan Art, Installation, High Relief, Ganpatrao K. Mhatre, Laxma Goud, Vivan Sundaram, Ravinder G. Reddy, Shankar Nandagopal.*

Fresco (Italian)=fresh. The method of *painting* on wet, fresh laid lime *plaster* on the wall or ceiling with powdered earth *pigments* mixed with water, (not vegetable *pigments* which react adversely with lime). Also known as "true fresco". This is distinguished from fresco secco [dry fresco]—

which is painted on dry *plaster*. The *painting* becomes part of the wall when dry and the *pigments* bond with the *plaster*, thus forming a permanent layer of *colour*. This was used by Renaissance artists in Italy.

Banasthali Vidyapith (RAJ) the only institution providing professional training in the Jaipur process of fresco *paintings*, experimented with both Indian and Italian *styles* and other *tempera techniques* of *wall painting*. Refer *Ajanta, Art Deco, Background, Balance, Base, Bengal Revivalism, Bengal School*, BHITTI-CHITRA, *Cartoon, Chalk, Conservation, Ellora, Encaustic, Epic, Ground, Landscape, Linearity, Linear Composition, Linearly, Mosaic, Mural, Oil Painting, Overlapping, Pigment, Priming, Pala Miniatures, Plaster, Reproduction, Rock-Cut, Stone Carving*, VIHARA, *Wall Painting, Banasthali Vidyapith, Indian Society of Oriental Art, Jaganath M. Ahivasi, Biharilal C. Barbhaiya, Vidya Bhushan, Pestonjee Bomanjee, Arun Bose, Nandalal Bose, P.N. Choyal, Sunil Das, Ajit R. Desai, Mukul Chandra Dey, Ramlal Dhar, Bhanu Dudhat, S. Fyzee-Rahamin, Li Gotami, Asit K. Haldar, K.V. Haridasan, Santosh Jadia, P. Krishnamurthy, V. Nagdas, Amrut Patel, Sharad Patel, Choudhary Satyanarayan Patnaik, Kartick Chandra Pyne, A.A. Raiba, A. Ramachandran, K. Sheshagiri Rao, Avijit Roy, Jagu Bhai Shah, Sumant V. Shah, Bhawani S. Sharma, Deokinandan Sharma, Kailash Chandra Sharma, Yagneshwar Kalyanji Shukla, P. Srinivasan, Sharma M.K. Sumahendra, Abanindranath Tagore, Alokendranath Tagore, Pratima Devi, (Thakur) Tagore, Shantanu Ukil, D. Venkatapathy, K. Venkatappa, Nathu Lal Verma*; Illustrations—APSARA, *Ajanta*, CHITRA, GANDHARVAS, JATAKA.

Fretwork, Fret Pattern Synonym for Greek *key pattern*. A geometric ornamental *pattern* made up of vertical and horizontal *lines* repeated to *form* a decorative band, found originally in *Greek art* and *architecture*. Also means a decorative angular *relief* or *open work pattern* carved in *wood* panels or *metal* sheets. Refer *Filigree, Gandharan Art, Jali Work, Mughal Dynasty, Pattern, Relief, Wood.*

Frontality The *term* refers to the front view of the human *figure* without emphasis on *depth* or *perspective*. It is a characteristic example of *Egyptian* and *Byzantine art*; and mostly seen in *folk art*. Samabhanga is the *term* used in India to denote the front view of a *figure* without flexions. Refer *Maurya Dynasty, Christian Art, Depth*; Illustrations—*Rini Dhumal, Balvant A. Joshi, Ravinder G. Reddy, Jamini Roy.*

Frottage=rubbing. A *technique* introduced by surrealist Max Ernst, of reproducing a particular *relief design, motif* or *texture* by placing a sheet of *paper* on top and taking an *impression* by rubbing with *crayon, charcoal, pencil* etc. The same process is used in brass-rubbing. *Collages* of these rubbed *textures* and *patterns* also *form* part of large *compositions*. This *technique* was first followed by *artists* of *Santiniketan* and Kolkata such as *Nandalal Bose, Mukul Chandra Dey.*

Fume Patination A green or brown *film* on a *metal* surface, especially *bronze* acquired by the exposure to the fumes of concentrated acetic *acid* and ammonia. Hydrochloric *acid* and calcium carbonate can also be used. Refer *Cloison, Somnath Hore, Pilton Kothawalla, Shankar Nandagopal.*

Funk Art *Term* coined to describe certain types of *art* in the USA originally around San Francisco, in the 50s and 60s. Funk art usually borders on the bizarre with its *contents* or *imagery* usually pornographic in nature ie. lying somewhere between *painting* and *sculpture*. Funk art used materials deliberately to shock the public, e.g., works of E. Kienholz. *Artists* such as *Krishnamachari Bose, N. Pushpamala, Jaideep D. Mehrotra, Sheela Gowda* and many others attempted funk art. Refer *Environment Art, Content.*

Futurism An *art* movement founded in 1909, by the Italian writer, Filippo Marinetti. It was anarchist in theory, aiming to break off from all *tradition* and making industrialization and technology, namely "speed", the inspiration of all *art*. There were written manifestoes on futurist *paintings* and *sculptures*, all aiming to the portrayal of dynamism. However, the *style* remained nihilistic only in theory with the actual *imagery* being inspired by *Impressionism* and *Cubism*. *Artists* include U. Boccioni, G. Balla, C. Carra and G. Severini. It was represented in India by *Modernism*, focussing on issues of cosmopolitanism, revolutionary innovations and influence of European developments. Refer *Abstraction Geometric, Gaganendranath Tagore, Raghav Kaneria, K. Vasant Wankhede.*

Fyzee-Rahamin S. (1880-1964) b Pune. Also known as S. Rahamin Samuel. Studied at Bombay *art* school, and Royal Academy School London, under John S. Sargent and Solomon J. Soloman. Exhibited at the Royal Academy in 1906. First International solo at Galerie Georges Petit Paris, and Goupil Galleries London in 1914, Tate Gallery & Arthur Tooths in London. Later at *BAS*.

Initally *painting portraits* in *oils*, he changed over to the Mughal *style* upon his return to India, but preferred Hindu *themes*. Became Art Advisor and court *painter* to the State of Baroda. Painted *frescoes* at the Imperial Secetaraiat in New Delhi and assisted the Victoria and Albert, and Metropolitan Museum in reorganizing their oriental sections. His works generally were of extremely large size, specializing as he did in *Mass paintings*. Also a poet and a playwright, he spent his last years in Karachi, Pakistan after Independence. Collections: Five accomplished *oil portraits* of the Gaekwad Royal Family of Baroda; Anil Relia's 'Archer House' Ahmedabad; International: Tate Gallery Sothebys'. Refer *Image, Ranjitsingh Gaekwad, Company School, Mughal Dynasty, Mughal Miniatures*; Illustration—*Mass.*

G

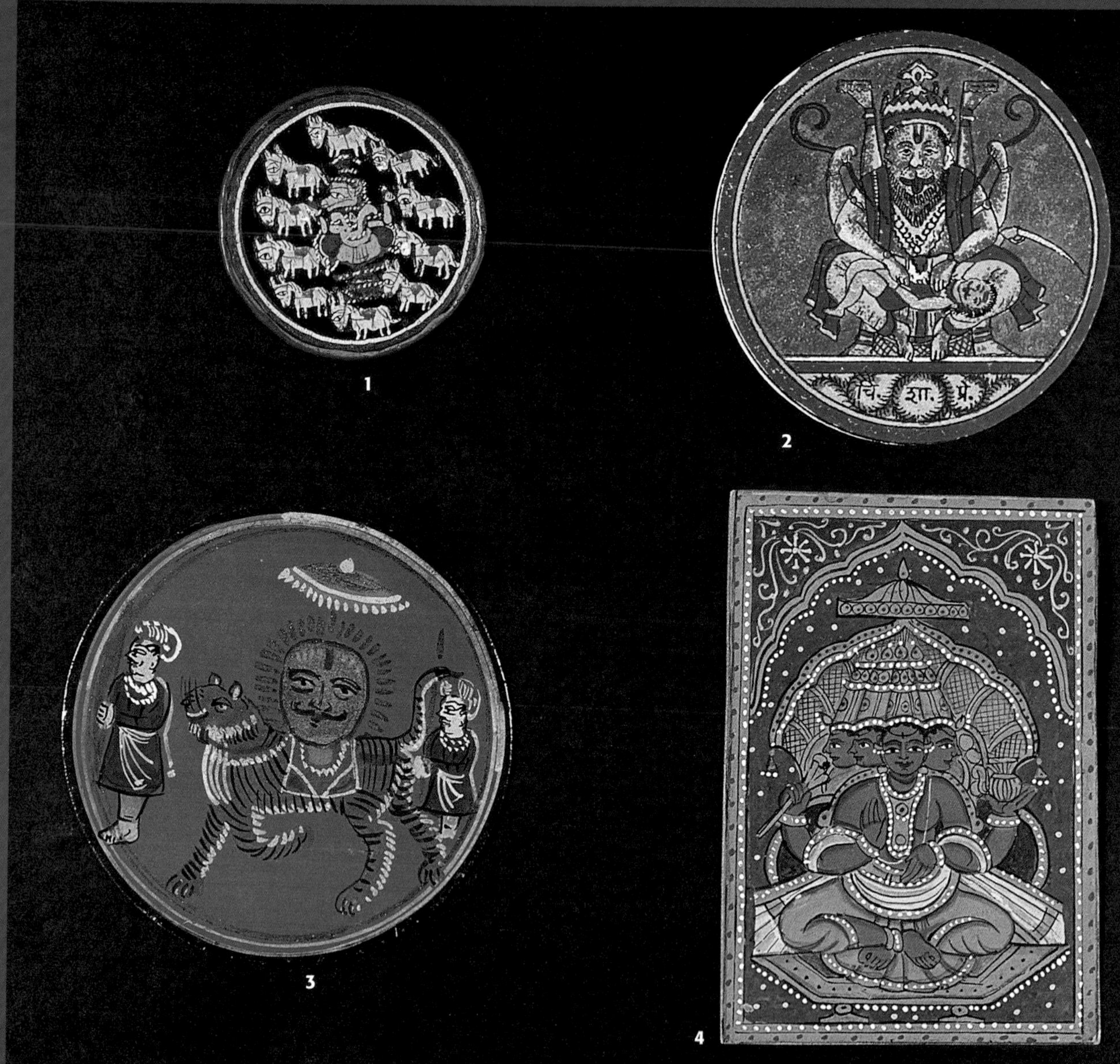

1) DASAVATARA from 120 cards Darachitritype, KALKI (KALKIN) AVATARA, ten of KALKI, Kurnol, Deccan hand-painted, AD 1840, diameter 4.6 cm.
2) DASAVATARA, Ganjifa from 120 cards, Raja of NARASIMHA, Printed in Pune, 1940, diameter 7 cm.
3) Mughal Ganjifa, Surkh Raja from 96 cards hand-painted of Rajasthan *style* by Sawantwadi *artist* 1999, diameter 7.6 cm.
4) BRAHMA, Raja card from 72 cards of Krishnaraj Chad of 19th century hand-painted in Mysore—1992, 6.3x9.3 cm.
(See notes on page 142)

Gada The ordinary Indian club or mace, held by VISHNU and various other *gods*, and heroes, e.g. Bhima. It is usually shown held in the hand or rested on the floor with the hand placed on it. The sculptural representation could be a plain *weapon* with a tapering top and stout bottom or in rare cases the club would be decorated elaborately. In certain *sculptures* it was represented in anthropomorphic *form*, as a lady holding a club, e.g. Gadadevi. Refer *Attribute*, AYUDHAPURUSHA, CHATUR BHUJA, *Gupta*, MATRIKAS, SARASVATI, SHANKHA, *M.T.V. Acharya*, *Sukumar Bhattacharjee*.

Gade, H. A. (1917–2001) b. Telegaon, MAHA. Education: GDA Art Master's certificate *JJSA*. Solos: Over 25 shows in India—Mumbai, Hyderabad, Nagpur, *Dhoomimal*. Retrospective: Mumbai, *Art Heritage* New Delhi; International: Budapest, Bucharest. Group participations: *PAG* Mumbai, Vadodara, Ahmedabad & Kolkata; All India shows at Nagpur, Mumbai, Kolkata, New Delhi, Chennai, Hyderabad, MAHA State Art & *NGMA* Mumbai, *BAS*; International: Salon de wai, Paris, Stanford University USA, *Biennale* in Saigon, Sao Paulo & Venice, Indian Art Exhibition Czechoslovakia, Hungary, Russia, Rumania, Poland, USA, Indonesia, Japan, Australia & Switzerland. *Auctions*: Osian's Mumbai, Bonham's, Christie's, & Sotheby's London, Christie's & Sotheby's New York. Awards: Several awards at All India Exhibition including *BAS* Gold Medal, *AIFACS*; International: Saigon *Biennale*. Founder member: *PAG* Mumbai, *BAS*. Collections: *NGMA*, Ministry of Culture Govt. of India & *LKA* New Delhi, State *LKA* Imphal, State Museum Nagpur, Vadodara, Hyderabad TIFR, *JJSA*; International: Budapest, Bucharest, Venice & pvt.

H.A. Gade, a contemporaneous *artist*, began by *painting* naturalistic *landscapes*. He worked mostly with *watercolour*, *tempera* and *gouache*. It was his *handling* of *colours* that was striking for his time, with *nature* transformed by the use of vivid imaginative *colours* into a *visual* delight referred to as the "resplendent splendour of his *colours*" and "dramatic compositions" in his 1949 series of works.

Later, his *landscapes* veered towards abstraction though his choice of *colours* remained intact, while the *composition* gained virility and precision. Like the Fauvists, H.A. Gade articulated that the juxtaposition of *colours* with its emotive functions were his primary concern. In his later works, he drove towards emotion and its equivalence in *pictorial terms* through a system of interacting shapes. While he simultaneously defused or eliminated non-art elements and structures, his *visual* statements lent credence to primacy of *paint*. He lived and worked in Mumbai.

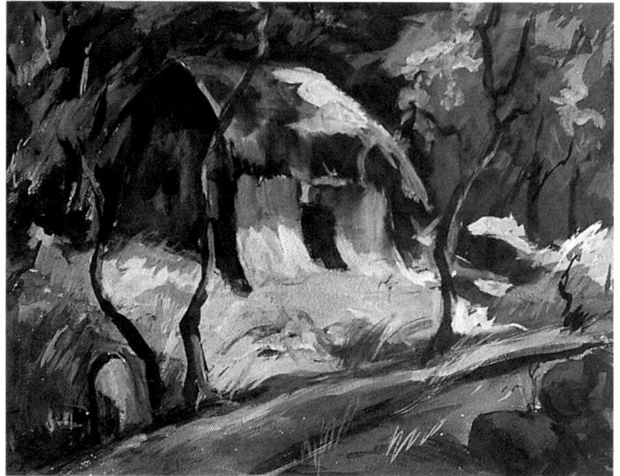

Gade, H.A.: "Landscape" Horizontal, 11.25 cm.

Gaekwad, Ranjitsingh (1938–) b. Vadodara. Education: Dip. in *art* RAA UK, *FA*. M.A. *MSU*. Also a classical singer. Solos: *JAG*, TAG, SRAG, *CKP*; International: Majhlis Gallery Dubai. Group participations: *LKA* GUJ, *AIFACS*; International: London. Awards: Academic Painting Arts & Crafts Society of India, *LKA* GUJ for *drawing*; International: David Murray Scholarship for *landscape painting* London. Member: Former Royal family of the State of Baroda. Collector: Royal Gaekwad family collection—paintings of *Raja Ravi Varma* at *Maharaja Fatesingh Museum* Vadodara which was exhibited at *NGMA* New Delhi & Mumbai.

His *pictorial images* are *eclectic* in spirit, with a combination of academicism, *Realism* and stylization. It is the linear quality which appeals to him in both *drawing* and *painting*. His early works were mostly *portraits* in the RAA *manner*. Later, he resumed *painting* after a hiatus of nearly 30 years, working on four-sided *canvases*, that are not meant to be displayed on the wall.

He lives and works in Vadodara, GUJ.

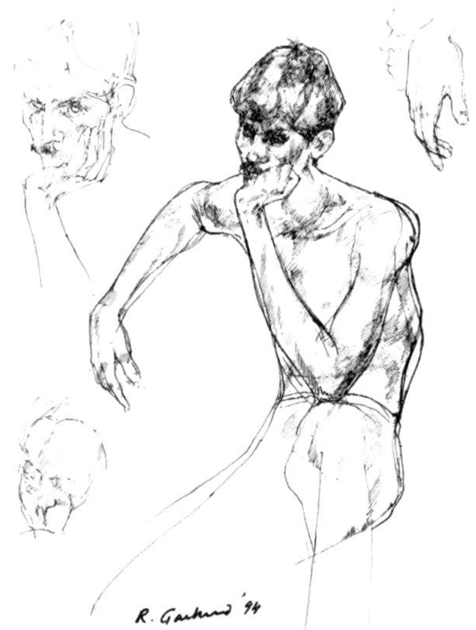

Gaekwad, Ranjitsingh: "Drawing", *Pencil*, 1994.

Gahlot, Virendra Pratap Singh (1938–) b. Meerut, UP. Education: Dip. & Post-Dip. in *sculpture* GCAC Lucknow; Worked under *Sankho Chaudhuri* for two years. Group participations: Rashtriya Kala Mela, national & international, *LKA* New Delhi, *AFA* Kolkata, *AIFACS*. *Art* camps: Participated in *sculpture* camps in different states, International *sculptors* & Painters' camps in *Mahabalipuram* Chennai. Award: *LKA* New Delhi. Collections: Chennai, Lucknow, PUJ, *NGMA* & *LKA* New Delhi. Commissions: Among his many commissions are an 8ft. bust of Mahatma Gandhi.

Organic shapes with a geometric simplicity seem to be the hallmarks of Virendra Pratap Singh Gahlot's *style*. The *sculptures* appear weighty and thus seem to be rooted to the ground, in terra firma, hence perhaps his favourite *theme* is "Terrigenous". His *sculptures* reflect intense familiarity with *prehistoric* animals and a deeply religious fervour.

He lives and works in New Delhi.

Gaitonde, Vasudeo Santu (1924–2001) b. Nagpur, MAHA. Education: Dip. *JJSA*. Over 10 solos: Gallery Chanakya Delhi, *PUAG* Mumbai; International: New York. Group participations: National Exhibitions New Delhi, *GC* Mumbai, *JAG*, *BAS*; International: Indian Art Exhibition Eastern Europe, Festival of India RAA & *Triennales* London, Hirschhorm Museum Washington DC USA, Graham Gallery New York, 5000 years of Indian Art Essen, Young Asian Artists Tokyo. *Auctions*: Osian's Mumbai, Heart Mumbai & New Delhi. Awards: *BAS* Medal, Padma Shri; International: Young Asian Artistic Award Tokyo. Fellowship: J.D. Rockefeller III Fund Travelling Fellowship USA. Collections: *NGMA* & *LKA* New Delhi, *PUAG*, TIFR; International: Museum of Modern Art New York; pvt. *Bal Chhabda*, *Ram Kumar* & institutional.

Vasudeo Santu Gaitonde (also known as V.S. Gaitonde) was one of the fringe members of the *PAG* Mumbai. He also exhibited with the Bombay Group. Though he was known as an abstractionist, his first works were basically *figurative*, being inspired by the angularity of *Jain* and *Basohli* miniatures. By the mid-fifties, an increasingly cubistic vision saw these *figures* being heavily geometricized. His *line* followed the wiry and witty *outlines* of P. Klee's *drawings*. *Colour* and *texture* played an increasingly important role in these *paintings*, which were to serve as a bridge to the world of abstraction and Zen. He began dispensing with titles at this stage, preferring to work with the *palette knife*, capturing *light* in broad horizontal swathes of *colour*, with small *forms* floating in between. The most important phase of his career came after he won the Rockefeller Fellowship. These final works were like *translucent* fields of *colour*, executed meticulously with the roller, with tiny Zen-inspired *motifs* interspersed in between, in an interplay of *light*, *texture* and *space*. Vasudeo Santu Gaitonde lived in New Delhi.

Gaja=an elephant. Gaja is one of the eight elements of the regions. The word could stand for Gajapati=lord or keeper of elephants, e.g. GANESHA, or Gajapatti=the frieze of elephants on the lower most *register* of the Adisthana (base) of a Vesara temple, denoting strength and stability. The elephant itself is a symbol of strength and royalty. It is one of the four animals representing the cardinal directions on the Ashoka pillar. A *white* elephant is especially auspicious, denoting the birth of an important personage, e.g. BUDDHA and MAHAVIRA, in addition to being the mount of the chief of the *gods*, INDRA. It is often represented in many schools of Indian *miniature painting*, e.g., *Bundi*, Pahari and Mughal. Refer GANESHA, LAKSHMI, *Vesara Style*.

Gaja-Hasta A MUDRA or hand position (as graceful as the motion of an elephant movement, with the right or left arm crossing the body diagonally, with hand relaxed and fingers pointing down, usually to be found in SHIVA NATARAJA. Refer NATARAJA.

Gaja Prsthakara It literally means the back of an elephant but denotes a shrine with a rounded end resembling the elephant's back as in the Nakula-Sahadeva RATHA at Mamallapuram (*Mahabalipuram*).

Gajalakshmi An iconographic *form* of LAKSHMI, the graceful goddess of wealth being honoured by two *white* elephants standing on either side of her. They hold garlands or pots of milk and honey in their upraised trunks. The *image* is usually found at the entrance of temples or on the doors of household shrines.

Galerie' 88 (G88) (Kolkata, WB). G88 was set up in 1988 by Supriya Banerjee in the heart of Kolkata's commercial centre, for the purpose of exhibiting works by *contemporary* Indian *painters* and *sculptors*. The gallery also holds exhibitions of its collection in other cities including the *artists Paritosh Sen*, *Ganesh Pyne*, *Ghulam Rasool Santosh* and *Badri Narayan* as well as the younger generation *artists* such as *Shekhar Roy*, *Ashoke Mullick* and others.

Gallery 7 (Mumbai, MAHA). The gallery was founded in 1984 by Arun Sachdev. It deals with *contemporary art*, displaying the works of both older established *artists* including *Ram Kumar*, *Prabhakar Barwe*, *Krishen Khanna* and *Sohan Qadri*, as well as several younger *artists*.

Gallery Art A gallery is a place where *art* is displayed for commercial purposes. In old times, there were picture galleries in which *paintings* and *sculptures* were displayed. These works were usually collected or commissioned by the kings or clergy of that particular region. An *art* gallery became popular increasingly in the late 19th century in Europe. The gallery owners' practice is followed worldwide and some galleries assist the *artists in* selling their works in return for a percentage of the sale. In India includes *SG* Mumbai, *Dhoomimal* (the oldest gallery) & *Art Heritage* New Delhi, *BAAC* & *CIMA*, Kolkata, *JAG*, *CYAG*, *AIFACS*, TKS, *ATG*, *SAI*, *CKAG*.

Gallery Chemould GC (Mumbai, MAHA). Situated on the first floor of the *JAG*, GC opened in 1963 for the promotion of *contemporary art*. The gallery was set up by Kekoo Gandhy whose interest in *art* extended from his shop "Chemould Frames". The word "Chemould" was made of two words Chemical Moulding. He set up in the 1940s for the purpose of framing *art* works. Kekoo Gandhy participated in modern art movement for 20 years before starting GC and also contributed to the rise of Progressive Artists Group (PAG) Mumbai. GC spread its activities in New Delhi & Kolkata. Later organized exhibitions in Ahmedabad, Rourkela, Cochin, Jamshedpur and abroad. The gallery regularly exhibits works by *Bhupen Khakhar*, *Nalini Malini*, *Vivan Sundaram*, *Amit Ambalal*, *Shakuntala Kulkarni*, *Maqbool Fida Husain*, *Anjoli Ela Menon*. The gallery celebrated its 40th anniversary at *NGMA* Mumbai by an exhibition of *art* spanning four generations.

Gallery Espace (GE) (New Delhi). The gallery was set up in 1989 by Renu Modi to promote the works of both young and established *artists*. They also take works on consignment and have a collection of works ranging from *paintings* to *sculptures* including *Manoj Dutta*, *Sakti Burman*, *Laxma Goud* and *Shyamal Dutta Ray*.

Gallery Ganesha (GG) (New Delhi) The gallery was founded in October 1989 with the objectives of promoting *art* in an emerging society, identifying and promoting young talents, resurrecting old and unknown masters and encouraging international *art* exchanges. GG stocks over 1000 works of *art* by *old masters* like *Jamini Roy*, *Nandalal Bose* and *Asit K. Haldar* and younger *artists Paresh Maity*, *Babu Xavier*, *Sisir Sahana* and others.

Gallery Katayun (GK) (Kolkata). Inaugurated in 1989, GK named after the owner who is also a practising *artist*, holds one-to-two shows a month. Besides promoting and exhibiting *artists* like *Paresh Hazra* and the late *Shaibal Ghosh*, the gallery also hosts talks and discussions on *art*.

Gana Also known as Bhuta-ganas they are the minor deities or demon-spirits who hover around SHIVA-PARVATI. They are presided over by his elephant headed son GANESHA, also called Ganapati—Lord of the Ganas. They are usually depicted as dwarfs or ugly creatures. Refer *Kailash*, *Kailasa*, NANDI.

Ganapatye, Pramod (1953–) b. Dewas, MP. Education: Dip. in *FA*. MP Technical Board Bhopal, M.A. in Ancient History Culture & Archaeology Vikram University Ujjain, M.A. in Museology *FFA* (*MSU*). Solos: Ujjain, Indore, TKS, *Dhoomimal*, TAG; International: Finland. Group participations: National Exhibition New Delhi, MPKP Bhopal, *SKP*, *AIFACS*. Group shows: State Museum Indore, MPKP Bhopal, *JAG*; International: Berun. *Art* camps & workshops: Bhopal, New Delhi, State Academy Bhubneshwar. Fellowship: by Dept. of Culture Govt. of India New Delhi. Commissions: *Murals* New Delhi, Vadodara & Ahmedabad. Appointments: A curator of the Rashtrapati Bhavan. Collections: *Chandigarh Museum*, Bhubaneshwar State Academy, MPKP Bhopal, SKP, pvt. & public.

At one point, Pramod Ganapatye studied and painted the chromatic character of astrological signs and was totally into abstraction. He was an ardent admirer of *modern* Hindi poetry, in particular the poems of Sarveshwar Dayal Saxena. Later he switched over to figuration. In this, he is influenced by the colourful simplicity of *Malwa* miniatures. He uses *colour* accents and *patterns* to enliven his *composition*. His *backgrounds* are lushly brushed in, with thick drapes fluttering in a stage set for human drama.

Pramod Ganapatye lives in Delhi.

Gandharan Art This *art* developed from the 1st century BC under the patronage of the Kushanas and continued upto the AD 5th century. Gandhara included the west bank of the Indus (now in Pakistan). This area was continuously under various foreign rulers, including the Persians and Greeks followed by Chandragupta Maurya, the Sakas, the Parthians and later the Kushanas. This led to a cosmopolitan feeling in Gandharan art.

Gandhara was one of the provinces that Ashoka had converted to *Buddhism*. Many Buddhist *sculptures* have been found there and they have greatly influenced Far Eastern *Buddhist art*. Being cosmopolitan in nature, Gandharan art is not homogenous. The most striking feature of Gandharan art is the obvious Greek influence. Certain *reliefs* found in Takht-i-Bahai show men and women wearing Hellenistic costumes. This soon became Indianized as the *artists* tried to interlink Greek and local ideas to create new *images*. The most important contribution of this school was the *creation* of the anthropomorphic BUDDHA *image*. With the change from the Hinayana to the Mahayana phase, the BUDDHA appeared almost simultaneously in Gandhara and Mathura, but while the Mathura *artist* drew his inspiration from the folk-like YAKSHA *figures* of earlier *periods*, the Gandhara *artist* turned to Greece.

The head of these BUDDHA *images* are usually *classical*, being oval in shape with even features, the eyes half-closed to indicate meditation, arched eyebrows with a sharp browline, a straight nose and wavy hair in a tuft, closely imitating the Krobylos of the Greek Apollo. Almost all the 32 Lakshanas (the marks of a great man) are seen, including the USHNISHA the elongated ears and the Urna (the 3rd eye). The serene face has a benevolent look.

The standing BUDDHAS display the s-curve rather than the TRIBHANGA. The Sanghati (robe) looks like the Roman toga, covering the whole body with deep, heavy folds. The *halo* or Prabhavati is again Hellenistic in appearance.

The seated BUDDHAS are shown in the PADMASANA with the hands in the ABHAYA, Dhyana or Dharmachakra MUDRA.

The Gandharan School is also credited with creating the BODHISATTVA *image*. These princely *figures*, gorgeously attired with jewellery and expensive clothes are usually depicted as standing or sitting and follow the same Hellenistic type.

A variety of materials, including fine grained local *stone*, *terracotta*, lime-stucco, grey schist, steatite, slate and *metal* were used. The two most important examples of *metal sculpture* are Kanishka's relic box and the Bimaran reliquary. Both are small cylindrical boxes with *reliefs* worked all around the sides. The lid of the first box is topped by three *free-standing* statuettes, the BUDDHA in the centre being flanked by a worshipful INDRA and BRAHMA. Refer ASANAS, BODHISATTVA, *Fretwork*, *Fret Pattern*, INDRA, *Kushana Dynasty*, *Mathura Art*, MUDRAS/HASTAS, *Relief*, YOGA.

Gandharvas They are semi-divine beings usually depicted along with Kinnaras (dancers) in the celestial world. Together they are the musicians of the *gods*, and form the retinue of Kubera (also *god* of the richest treasures), who is also the Lord of APSARAS, the divine dancers and the Rakshakas (protectors). Refer APSARA, *Demons*, *Fantasy*, *Murals*, *Muralidhar R. Achrekar*.

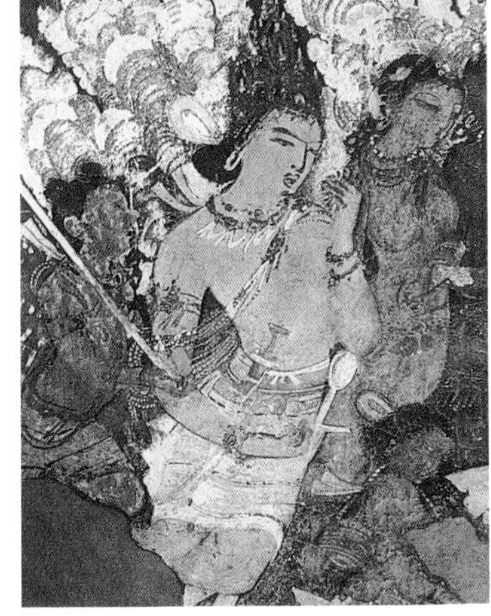

Gandharvas: "Flying Gandharvas', *Ajanta* Cave 17, *Tempera*.

Ganesha The son of SHIVA and PARVATI, is one of the most popular and lovable of all Indian *Gods* and is invoked at the beginning of every venture as he is the bestower of success. He is depicted as being elephant-headed and pot-bellied. His vehicle is the mouse, Mushaka. There are various reasons for the zoomorphic head. One *legend* states that after PARVATI created him as a guardian of her modesty, SHIVA became enraged with him and cut off his head when denied entry into PARVATI'S quarters. Later, to pacify a tearful PARVATI, he cut off the head of the first creature he saw (an elephant) and stuck its head on to Ganesha's body. He has two wives, Siddhi (achievement) and Riddhi (intelligence). He is not only Ganapati, the lord of the GANAS, but also the Lord of all scribes, sciences and skills. Ganesha has been depicted in both *sculpture* and *painting*. The *style* of depiction varies with the region. He is also the most popular *god* to be painted and sculpted by *modern artists* including *Satish Gujral, Maqbool Fida Husain, Manjit Bawa, Jogen Chowdhury, B. Vithal, Sudha Arora* and others. His *form* lends itself easily to the fantastic distortions and abstractions practised by *modern artists*. Refer *Attribute*, CHATUR BHUJA, CHITRAKATHI, *Ellora*, GAJA, LAKSHMI, *Mask*, MATRIKAS, MURTI, *Spiritual*, *Jalendu Dave*, *Hinduism*, *Vinayak Pandurang Karmarkar*, *Nilkanth P. Khanvilkar*, *Dulal Mondal*, *Rajen*; Illustration—*Reddeppa M. Naidu*.

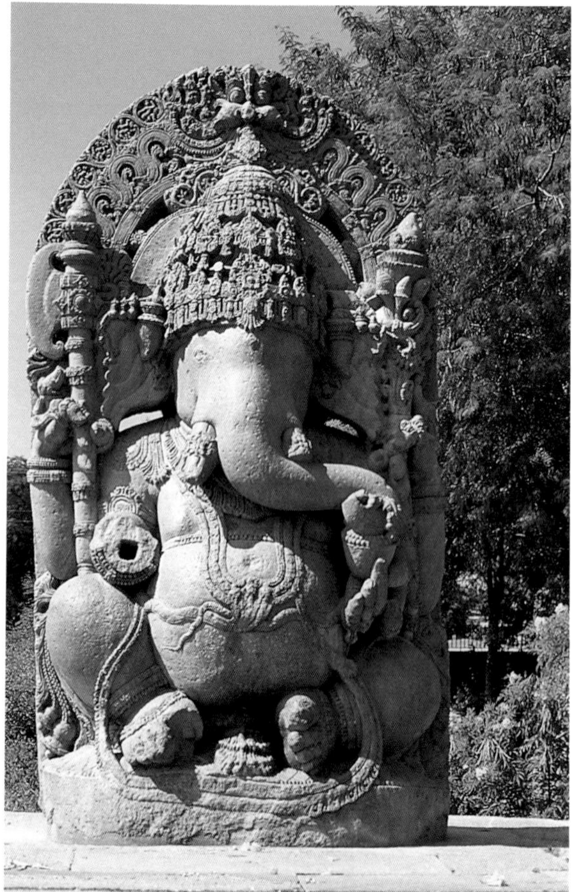

Ganga The personification of the holy river Ganga, running through the northern and eastern part of India. According to Hindu *mythology*, Ganga was brought down to earth from the celestial world by Bhagiratha's penance, in order to liberate the ashes of his ancestors. She is therefore called Tripathaga, which means traversing the three worlds and depicted with three heads in early *sculptures*. To save the earth from cleaving into two by the force of her fall, Bhagiratha prayed, to SHIVA who caught the Ganga in his mighty locks and let her flow gently on to earth. Ganga is thus depicted as struggling in SHIVA'S Jata (matted hair) before flowing downwards. This is depicted at *Elephanta* as Gangadhara—SHIVA. Refer *National Museum*, *Elephanta*, *Ghats*, JATA MUKUTA, NATARAJA, *Orthogonal*, PALLAVAS, PALLAVA DYNASTY, SHIVA, *Yusuf Arakkal*, *Mukul Chandra Dey*.

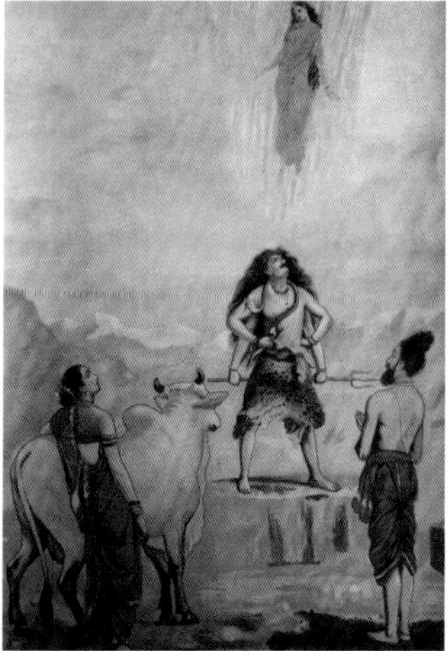

Ganga: *Raja Ravi Varma's* "Gangavataran", *Half-Tone*.

Ganga Devi (1928–1991) b. Chatara, Bihar. Self-taught, traditional *artist*. Awards: National Award, Padma Shri. Commissioned: *murals* for the Development Commissioner for Handicrafts. Collections: *National Handicrafts & Handlooms Museum* & Craft Museum New Delhi; International: Mithila Museum collection Japan.

Ganga Devi was born in the *Madhubani* region of Bihar; the *tradition* of folk *painting* was thus inborn in her, being commonly pursued by the women of the area. Originally, these *murals* were executed on the walls and floor of the house, the aripana being painted on the floor and the Kohbar (lotus plant) being painted on the walls of the nuptial chamber. Since 1960 however, the women started executing *paintings* on *paper*, which was introduced to the area by the members of the All India Handicraft Board in order to develop *Madhubani paintings* as a handicraft. *Paper* had been used earlier only as the painted wrapper of sindoor (red powder symbolizing the married woman).

Ganga Devi's *paintings* received an additional impetus from her chaotic, unordered life. The upheavals in her marital life (her husband remarried) led her to pursue *painting* as a panacea, slowly leading to the formation of a personal vision, rather than imitating the works of her ancestors. While the symbology and *motifs* remained the same, personal overtones began to appear in the *paintings*. Thus, she chose to illustrate scenes from the RAMAYANA, due to her total identification with the fate of Sita (another unaccepted woman). Three types of *pictorial narrative* can be isolated in the work: **1.** Illustration of a single episode, **2.** Selected episodes with the intermediary incidents omitted, **3.** An entire chapter of the RAMAYANA.

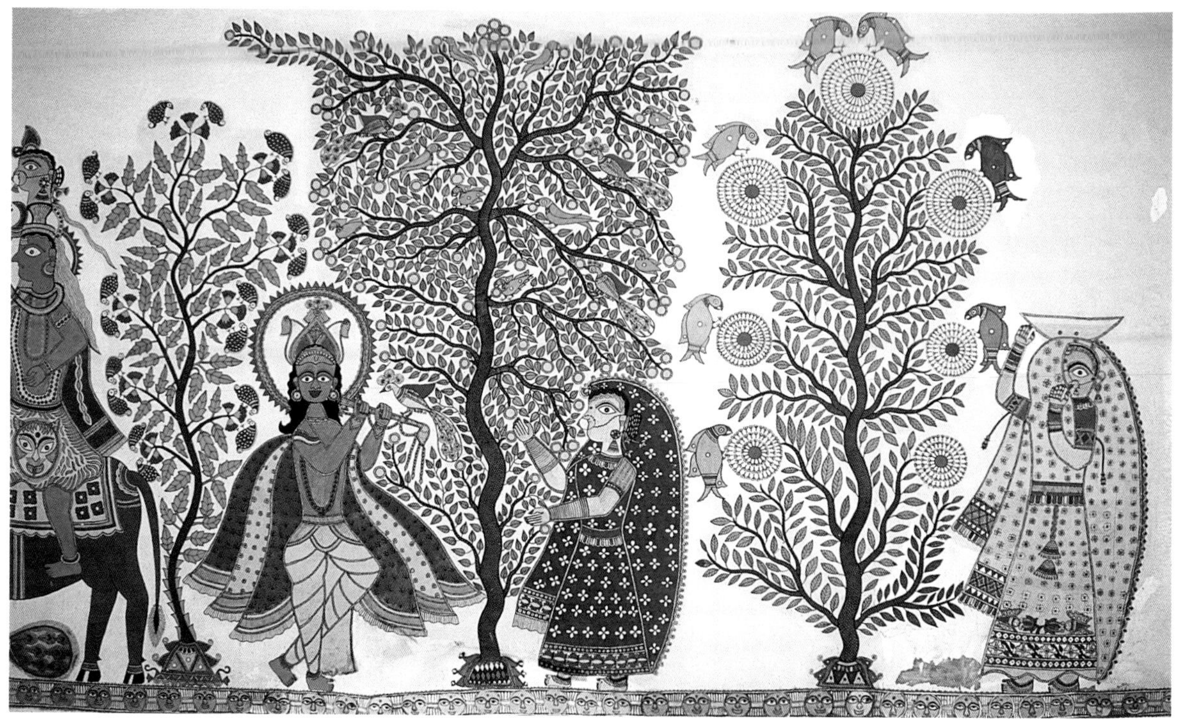

Ganga Devi: Central Wall of Kohbar Ghar. Left to right Lord SHIVA; KRISHNA playing his flute under the Kadamba tree & RADHA, 1989.

The *imagery* includes anthropomorphic representations of the sun and moon. *Gods* are indicated as denizens of the celestial world, and therefore represented floating in *space*. Vegetation indicates the earth, the abode of sages and other men. The borders of individual incidents are decorated with rows of Paan-shaped leaves, flowers and scrolls.

Towards the end of her life she painted a series of autobiographical works, including the "American series", "Pilgrimage to Badrinath" and the "Cancer series". The cancer series is a moving account of her experience of contracting the disease and the futile attempts at treating it. These autobiographical works mark her as a *contemporary artist* and not merely a practitioner of traditional *art form*. The inclusion of such mundane *motifs* as the electric bulb and the fan represented in her personalized version of *Madhubani art* places her on par with the *artist* of today.

Ganga Devi was initially promoted by the "Madhubani Office", which gave grants of Rs.1500/- to selected *artists*. Yves Vequand, a Frenchman appreciated her works and started promoting her. He recommended her to Pupul Jayakar, and the then Prime Minister of India, Indira Gandhi. She worked on "The Cycle of life" at the Crafts Museum. She also painted a Kohbar-ghar (nuptial chamber) at the *museum*. It is one of her rare works in *colour*, most of her other works being in *black* and red *pen* and *ink*. Refer *Kraft Paper*.

Gangooly, Ino (1930–) b. Kolkata. Self-taught, inherited from his ancestors the Tagore family & uncle *Jamini P. Gangooly*. Solos: *AFA* & *BAAC* Kolkata, *CKAG*, *GK*, *JAG*, IIC. Collections: *BAAC* Kolkata, *CKAG*, pvt. & public in Kolkata, New Delhi, Mumbai.

He is inspired by the *Impressionism* of J.W.M. Turner like his uncle, *Jamini P. Gangooly*. In "*Seascape* Vyzak", he has delineated the human *figure* in the spontaneous *manner* of the impressionist. His mountain scapes in bright *colours* are among the more prominent of his work.

In 1990, Doordarshan made a documentary film on him, titled "Landscape Paintings".

He lives and works in Kolkata.

Gangooly, Jamini P. (1876–1953) b. WB. A nephew of *Abanindranath Tagore*, he received pvt. tuitions in *art* from Gangadhar Dey, a local Indian *artist* & Charles Palmer an English *artist* for *oil painting*, before studying at the Calcutta School Art *(GCAC)* Kolkata. Exhibited at several exhibitions organized by the *ISOA* & in the exhibition of Indian *Art* during the 1900 session of the Indian National Congress in Kolkata. Solos, group participations & awards at Shimla Art Society, *ISOA*, *BAS* a Gold Medal in 1910. *Auctions*: Heart & Bowring's New Dehi, Osian's Mumbai, Bowring's Kolkata, Bonham's & Sotheby's London. Member: Bhagiya Kala Samsad founded by E.B. Havell, other members including *Abanindranath Tagore*, Bamapada Banerjee, O.C. Gangooly & Ananda Prasad Bagchi. Appointment: Deputy Principal *GCAC* Kolkata. Publications: in various periodicals and articles on his works appeared in the *Prabasi*, *Modern Review*, Sahitya, Bharati & Pradip; In books by Partha Mitter. Collections: The Maharaja Jatindra Mohan Tagore collections, Indian Museum Kolkata, Royal Families of Bhopal, Indore, Jodhpur, Tripura.

Though Jamini P. Gangooly was quite proficient in the *Bengal School style*, he was primarily an exponent of the academic *oil painting* in the *manner* of J.F. Millet and G. Courbet. Known as the "Corot of India" for his fine *landscapes*, was also a fine portraitist and combined his atmospheric riverscapes and *pastoral* scenes with *illustrations* of SANSKRIT drama, specifically Banabhatta's "Kadambari". His *landscapes* were often described as a perfect marriage of East and West. He replaced *Abanindranath Tagore* as Vice-Principal of the GSA Kolkata.

Ganguli, Gunen (1924–) b. Hizuli, WB. Education: Dip. in *art* Delhi Polytechnic, *Graphic Art* Govt. Institute of Art Florence Italy. Solos: *AIFACS* 1954, 1962; International: Italy 1960. Group participations: National Exhibition, *Triennale* & Kunika New Delhi, *BAAC* Kolkata, SC, *JAG*, others in Amritsar, Hyderabad; International: UNESCO Paris, Geneva & London, Contemporary Indian *Art* & *Graphics* Bulgaria, Poland, Leipzig, East Africa, Switzerland & Zambia. *Art* workshop: *printmaking* art USIS by Smithsonian Institute California. Awards: Art Industry Hyderabad, AFA Amritsar, *AIFACS*, National Award for silk screen; International: Scholarship Research in *Graphic Art* Italy. Nominated member & selecting Judging Committee: State *LKA* RAJ, *AIFACS*, SKP. Commissions: *Murals* in New Delhi. Appointments: Examiner Technical Education New Delhi, Taught Child Art and organized exhibitions in India. Publications: *LKA* New Delhi, Roop-Lekha *AIFACS*. International: 'The Artist' Magazine London. Collections: Represented in the collections of *NGMA*, *LKA*, *College of Arts* New Delhi, PUJ University Chandigarh.

Basically Gunen Ganguli was a *landscape painter* with a love for *nature*, his focus being the Northern part of India including Kashmir and Ladakh Valley. Later developing a strong inclination for *graphic art* his *designs* became *eclectic*, being based on simplified and geometricized *forms*.

He prefers working on *black* and *white* and now is living in New Delhi.

Ganguly, Sukhen (1929–) b. WB. Education: Dip. in *FA.*, Post-Dip. in *mural design VBU*; Specialized Research Sumi-e (*art term* for *monochrome ink painting– Japanese art)* Japanese Contemporary Art Kyoto University; Research under Japanese scholars & *artists*; Studied under *Nandalal Bose*, *Ramkinkar Baij*, *Benode Behari Mukherjee* & Japanese Prof.; Over 33 *murals* designed at Santiniketan, Jabalpur, Kolkata, Mumbai, Ranchi, Renusagar UP. Gandhi Bhavan Beleghara WB. *WSC* Maldha. Group participations: Kolkata, New Delhi, Mumbai, Hyderabad, Lucknow, Chandi-garh & others. Award: *Mural design* Govt. of India. Hon.: *AIFACS* 1993. Appointments: Was the Principal, Vice-Principal & Head of the Faculty, *Painting VBU.* Publications: His documentary film prepared in 1998 with Japanese *classical* artist the theme being Traditional/Classical Art in Japan.

Though he paints in *watercolour*, *acrylic* and *mixed media*, Sukhen Ganguly is basically a muralist, having executed a *mural* almost every year in India as well as abroad from 1952 onwards. Some of them are at Mahayati Sadan in Kolkata, the Baroda Maharajah's temple, and the ISKCON temple. After using *mosaic* as his main *medium*, he has also executed *murals* with brick, *tempera*, *stone inlay* and kaolin (*China clay*). "Come to life" is a huge 12'x50' *mural* in *mosaic* and *ceramic* in *colours* with its source in life science. He has managed to contain the brilliance of the tessarae in *forms* of great clarity.

He lives and is working in *Santiniketan*, WB.

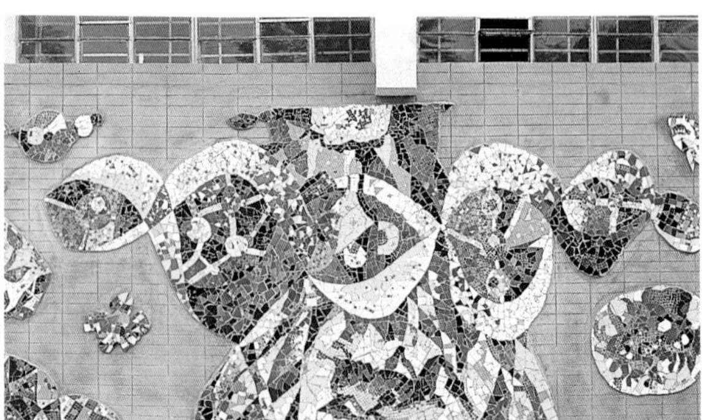

Ganguly, Sukhen: "Come to Life", *Mosaic mural & ceramics* 360x1500 cm.

Ganjifa (Indian playing cards) Ganj=treasure, treasury/ minted money (Persian). First introduced by the Moghul/ Mughal ruler Babar in 1527, by the 16th century several different types of games were developed in India. The two basic types of Indian Ganjifa are: **1.** Mughal Ganjifa of 96 cards: eight suits of 12 cards each. **2.** DASAVATARA Ganjifa of 120 or 144 cards:10 or 12 suits of 12 cards each.

Either type has only two court cards–Raja and Pradhan and ten numerals.

Handmade and hand-painted, these cards are usually circular in shape, with square or rectangular cards coming from the Deccan States particularly Sawantwadi in MAHA. Hindu themes adapted to the Mughal Ganjifa cards contributed greatly to the spread and popularity of the game. RAMA Pattabhishekha or the enthronement of Shri RAMA, the stories of KRISHNA/Balaram and Eight Malls, and the depiction of the ten "AVATARAS" of VISHNU were some of the *themes* painted on the Ganjifa cards. Later animal/bird versions of both Mughal and DASAVATARA Ganjifa sets were developed in RAJ, Deccan, Orissa & Sawantwadi. Artist Prakashchandra Mahapatro of Parlakhemundi, Orissa has recently made a facsimile of the 125-year-old RAMAYANA set of DASAVATARA Ganjifa on which the *narrative* is in comic-book format on the 80 numeral cards.

Variations of Ganjifa card games and their symbols used were the Nava-graha or the Nine Planets; the Ashta-dikapala showing the Eight Regents/ Guardians of the Quarters of the World, with animal vehicles

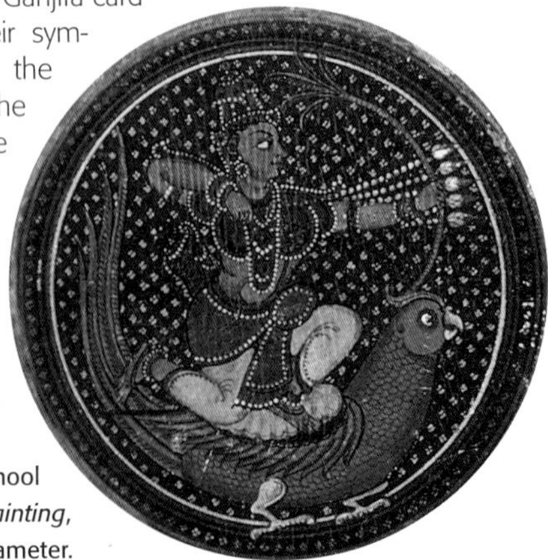

Ganjifa: Patna School Kama, *Tempera Painting*, 8.5 cm diameter.

and *weapons* and *attributes* of the *gods* as suit symbols. Two inches diameter round painted RAMAYANA Ganjappa cards from Sonepur in Subarnapur district of Orissa have the first six suits of 72 cards of RAMA, his brother and allies and the last six suits of 72 cards having RAVANA, his brothers, sons and followers. These are known as Putalabandi Ganjappa and come in their own painted box. Chad–originated in Mysore in early 19th century under the patronage of Krishnaraj III Wodeyar, having 13 different Chads with the largest having 360 cards and the smallest with 36 cards. The games were played with numerous suits and all have six court cards instead of the normal two as in Mughal & DASAVATARA.

Naqsh–played during the festival season between Dasera and DIWALI in Northern, Central and Eastern India. The well known cards are made in Bishnupur in WB, consisting of 48 cards in four suits of 12 cards each and suit signs taken from traditional Mughal & DASAVATARA Ganjifa. The materials used for these cards range from *ivory*, tortoise-shell and mother-of-pearl for the royals to *paper*, fabric, Patachitra (scroll *painting*), *palm leaf*, etc., for the common man.

Currently varieties of Ganjifa cards are being made at Sawantwadi in MAHA; Puri District, Parlakhemundi, Raghurajpur, Chikiti & Sonepur in Orissa; Bishnupur in WB and Nirmal in AP.

Well-researched catalogues on collections of Indian Ganjifa cards compiled by Austrian collector late Dr. Rudolf Von Leyden exist in *museums* in Germany, Austria and England. Historian and collector Kishor N. Gordhandas of Mumbai is also an expert on Indian Ganjifa cards. Refer KALKI (KALKIN). (See illustrations on page 136)

Garhi Artist's Complex (GAC) (New Delhi) GAC was set up in 1976, when several *artists* affected by the lack of studio *space* in the city of Delhi, got together to persuade the Delhi Development Authority to release some land for them. The complex which was handed over to the *LKA* for administration had seven individual studios and three common ones, one each for *ceramics*, *graphics* and *printmaking* and *painting*. Today there are some 20 studios more to enable the *artists* to work. Some of the artists who have worked here include *Sankho Chaudhuri*, *Haku Shah*, *Krishen Khanna*, *Aparna Caur*.

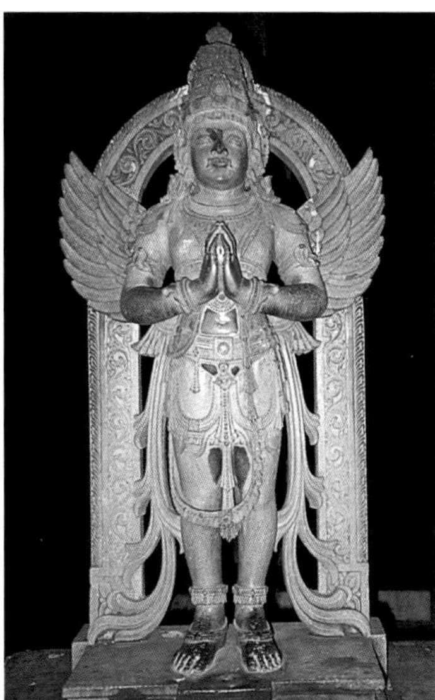

Garuda A hybridized version of the eagle, a mythical bird, it is the mount (VAHANA) of VISHNU. e.g. *K. Venkatappa "RAVANA and Jatayu* (Garuda)". Refer MATRIKAS, PURANA, RAVANA; Illustration–DIWALI.

Garuda: Eagle, Belur.

Gel Thick and normally *transparent emulsion*. Also known as binder or gum. When added to *paints*, *oils* or *acrylics*, it gives glaze effect as seen in *impasto* but with greater textural possibilities and heavy consistency. Gels are also excellent adhesives but take longer to dry. When applied to *synthetic* resin used in *sculpture*–it is the first phase of the curing process. Refer *Chalk*, *Fibreglass*, *Gum Arabic*, *Egg-oil emulsion*, *Litho-graphy*, *Mixed Media*, *Medium*, *Size*, *Varnish*, *Watercolour*, *Wax*, *Santokba Dudhat*.

Gelatine A type of jelly glue, binder or *size* made by boiling organic *matter* in water, it is available as granules, in sheet *form* and as powder. It is amorphous, *transparent* and *white* to amber in *colour*. It is brittle and soluble in hot water. It has been used in the making of flexible *moulds* since the late 19th century. Refer *Collotype*, *Glue Size*, *Distemper*, *Gesso*, *Mould*, *Cast*, *Pigment*, *Jyotirindranath Tagore*, *Natvar Bhavsar*.

Genre (French)=kind; type. A collective *term* for *paintings* which depict scenes and subjects from everyday life, including *still life*, *portraits*, *history paintings*. It was first seen in 17th century. Dutch *art* and popularized by Frans Hals and Vernieer.

Such genre works have been rather popular with *contemporary* Indian *artists* due to their proximity to ordinary people. Genre *art* is not necessarily influenced by religion nor can it be identified with specific persons nor do they narrate a story. They generally depict a "way of life". In *contemporary* Indian *Art*, the works of K.T. Shivaprasad, *Sudhir Patwardhan*, *Ramesh Rao*, some of the earlier works of *Vivan Sundaram* and *Bhupen Khakhar* to name a few, conform to this subject. Refer *Company School/Company Painting*, *Naturalism*, *Vignette*, *Dipak Banerjee*, *Anant M. Bowleker*; Illustration–*Chintamoni Kar*, *Nandalal Bose*, *Mahadev V. Dhurandhar*, *Naina Kanodia–Naive Art*.

Gesso A mixture of finely ground *chalk* or *gypsum*, mixed with a pliable glue. It is dense and brilliantly *white* with a high degree of absorbency. Several coats are layered over a wooden panel to cover the grain before the actual *painting* is done. This is also used in *tempera painting*. At times, gesso was used in the making of ornamental mouldings for picture *frames*. *Vrindavan Solanki* prepares his *canvases* with rabbit glue and gesso to achieve a smooth working surface for his *monochromatic* work. Refer *Ground*, *Scraperboard*, *Scratchboard*, *White*.

Gestural Abstraction Refer *Gestural Painting*, *Abstract Expressionism*, *Action Painting*, *Colour-Field Painting* and *Maqbool Fida Husain*.

Gestural Painting A *style* of *painting* in which brush marks are directly representative of the *artist's* own physical gestures and indeed of his personality. Usually long, broad and vigorous *brush* strokes are used. It is also the *term* used to describe the works of American and European *abstract* expressionists. Several Post-Independence *artists* adopted this rather fluid *manner* of using *brush* and *pigment*.

Ambadas, Homi Patel and *Santu Gaitonde Vasudeo* are two such examples. Of the younger generation, *Ravi Mandlik* uses a similar mode of application in rendering his naturescapes. Refer *Abstract Expressionism, Action Painting, Gestural Abstraction, Installation, Ambadas, Setlur Gopal Vasudev, Mahirwan Mamtani, Krishna N. Reddy, Vivan Sundaram, J. Swaminathan*; Illustration—*Homi Patel*.

Ghare, Shobha (1951–) b. Guna, MP. Education: GDA in *applied art* & Art Masters *JJSA*. Solos: Bhopal, Indore, Chennai, *GC* Mumbai, *JAG*. Group participations: *BB Biennales, BAS*, Delhi Festival of India, All India Women's Exhibition; International: Poland, Festival of India USA. Participated: several *artist* camps *printmaking, metal-casting, ceramics*. Awards: *LKA's* Research Scholarship, *BAS*. Fellowships: *Amrita Sher-Gil* Fellowship for Creative Art MP, *Graphics* Fellowship from Govt. of India. Appointments: Visiting Prof. in video photography Govt. Polytechnic Bhopal. Collections: *LKA* & *NGMA* New Delhi, Raj Bhavan Bhopal, *BB, JJSA*, pvt. & public.

Shobha Ghare, working as a *painter* and printmaker specialized in rather *abstract images* of *landscapes* applying her own *style* to express ideas & emotions in an elegant and *tactile manner*. In her earlier works she brings a wealth of detail to her *prints*, building them up with a filigree of intricate stories and myths, creating a *visual* representation of the felt moment. Her works are soft with predominantly cool *tones* and feathery planes of *colour*, with *form* reduced to simple *lines* and geometric shapes.

She lives and works in Bhopal.

Ghats (Hindi) The chain of Eastern and Western mountains (Ghats) in South India. It also refers to the steps leading to the banks of a river, especially the banks of the GANGA at Hardwar. It had become a highly popular theme with many *painters* in the 1970s and early 1980s, the elements of the *landscape* adding to the romanticized feeling. *Laxman Narayan Taskar's* (1870–1937) *paintings* of the Ghats (mountain slopes) of Nasik, are well known. Refer GANGA, *Shivananda P. Akki, Dulal Mondal, Satyasewak Mukherjee, Siddhartha Sengupta, Yashawant Shirwadkar.*

Ghodke, Vasant (1934–) b. MAHA. Education: Dip. *JJSA*. Solos: Varanasi, *Artists' Centre* Mumbai, *LKA* New Delhi TAG, *JAG*; International: Italy, Amsterdam, New York, Washington. Group participations: Varanasi, *LKA* New Delhi, *JAG*; Participated: In Hyderabad, *WSC* Mumbai, *LKA* UP & MP, SZCC Nagpur & Pune *BAS, JAG, AIFAC*. Awards: Lucknow, Haryana, SZCC Nagpur, MAHA Pune, *JJSA, AIFACS*. Collections: *LKA* New Delhi & Lucknow, Air India, Godrej & *Prafulla Dahanukar* Mumbai, *GE, Dhoomimal*; International: London, Vienna, Austria, California, Amsterdam, Holland, Germany.

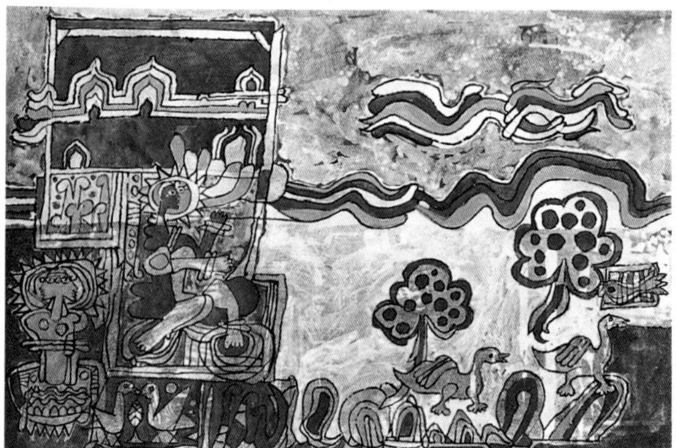

Ghodke, Vasant: "Untitled", *Acrylic* on *Paper*, 37.5x55 cm.

Vasant Ghodke's inspiration lies in *folk art*, from the mythical *figures* seen on temple walls to traditional manuscripts and other sources. His *paintings* are marked by an element of patterned *design* and naive colouring. However the *paintings* are not *narratives* in the traditional sense. Instead, the individual elements such as the winged snake, the archer, the horseman, the mother Goddess and the tiger *God* are collaged together because of their *visual* appeal.

Vasant Ghodke lives and works in Barsi, Sholapur.

Ghosal, Satyen (1921–) b. Patna, Bihar. Education: Dip. *GCAC* Kolkata; Certificate Slade School of Fine Art London. Solos: Mumbai, New Delhi, Kolkata; International: Tokyo, London. Award: Govt. of WB Abanindra Award; Asian Exhibition Tokyo, Manila, Hong Kong & Bangkok 1965. Member: *Artists* Committee Lok Sabha Secretariat New Delhi, Academy Council *VBU*, University Council *RBU*, Vice President *AIFACS* & later President & Member of various groups, Art-Purchase & Selection committees. Commissions: *Painting* Rashtrapati Bhavan 1947. Appointments: Prof. Delhi Polytechnic, Prof. & HoD *GCAC* Kolkata. Publications: Newspapers in New Delhi, Kolkata; International: London, Tokyo. Collections: *NGMA* & *LKA* New Delhi, *AFA* Kolkata, PUJ, MP, *RBM*; International: Europe, America & Far-East, pvt. & public.

The first few years that Satyen Ghosal spent in New Delhi were years of intense research, study and experiment, when he was still working to evolve a personal *style*. The result was a broad *Realism*, with bold patches of *paint* with which he built up the organic *mass* of trees and rock, seen in *perspective*.

Between 1948–55, he shifted towards a post-Impressionist approach, softening the bright areas of *colour* with a Far Eastern imprint. *Line* is especially of great interest to Satyen Ghosal. He gathered fresh ideas and inspiration from his sojourn in Europe, synthesizing Indian mannerisms with a Western outlook.

His works are near *abstract* flights of *fantasy* showing his progress from the materialistic to the subtly *spiritual*, as he weaves a magical web of strange visionary *compositions*, surreal, *patterns* and amoeboid shapes.

Satyen Ghosal lives and works in Kolkata.

Ghose, Gopal (1913–1980) b. Kolkata. Education: Training in art Maharaja's School of Arts & Crafts Jaipur under *Shailendranath Dey*; Sculptor in *Madras School of Art* under *Debi Prasad RoyChowdhury*. Solos: 46 solos throughout India including Mumbai, *BAAC* Kolkata, Indian Museum New Delhi, *CKAG, GG* 1940 held by Late Prime Minister Pandit Jawaharlal Nehru; Retrospective: *Art Heritage* New Delhi as homage 1986–87, pvt in 1995 & *BAAC* Kolkata; International: New York, Washington DC. *Auctions*: Heart & Osian's Mumbai, Heart & Bowring's New Delhi, Bonham's

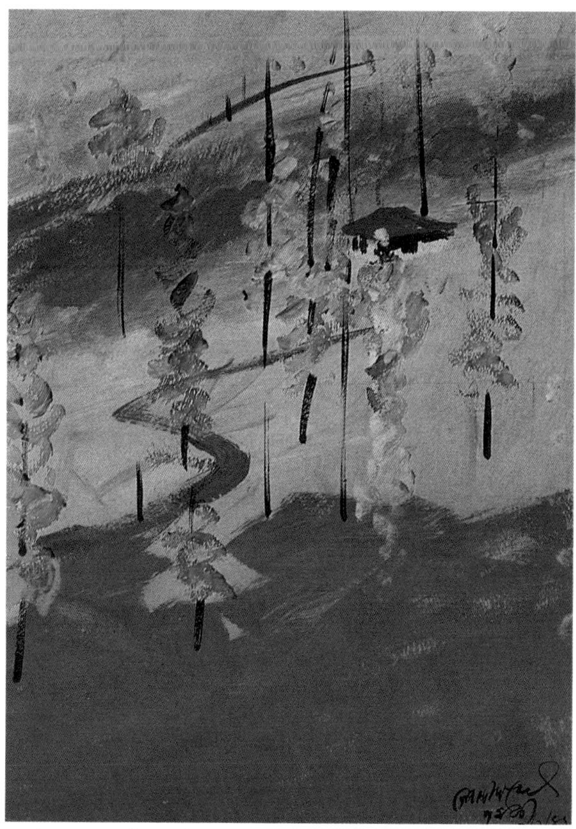

Ghose, Gopal: "Landscape II", 1945.

London, Christie's New York. Member: Calcutta Group, Joint Secretary *AFA* Kolkata with Ratin Maitra till 1980. Appointments: Taught *painting* at the ISOAS & Architectural *Design* Bengal Engineering College; 1950 taught at *GCAC* Kolkata, introduced the traditional *wash manner* of Bengal *watercolours*, showed how to control and apply *water-colours* with a spontaneity that was lacking in the *wash technique*. With swift and sure brushstrokes he captured the strutting vanity of a peacock, the curve of a cooing pigeon, the craftiness of crows and the feline grace of prowling cats. Collections: *AFA* & *BAAC* Kolkata, *NGMA* & *Delhi Art Gallery* New Delhi, *CKAG*, *CKP*.

His *drawings* appeal to the senses in their vitality and simplicity. He also drew delicate *pencil sketches* of temples and *landscapes*, as well as a number of *brush drawings* of *nature's* vagaries, the brevity of his brushstroke recalling the gracefulness of Far Eastern *landscapes*.

He is revered today as the originator of *modern landscape painting* in India; having led it away from its traditional role of *backdrop* to the *figures* and making it the mainstay of *composition*.

Ghosh, Amal (1933–) b. Kolkata. Education: Dip. in *painting GCAC* Kolkata; Post-Grad. in *mural* Central School of Art & Design London; Post-Grad. Hertfordshire College of Arts St. Alban's England. Solos: New Delhi, *BAAC* & British Council Kolkata, *CKAG*; International: Leinster FA., Horizon Gallery & Meghraj Gallery London, Nottingham Play House England, others in Lancashire, Leicester, Norway, Sweden. Retrospective: Mermaid Theatre Gallery London. Group shows: London, Denmark, England. Group participations: RAA, Whitechapel Gallery, Camden Art Center, Indian Art Mermaid Theatre & Indian *Artist* London UK, *Biennale* France, other towns California, Germany, Tokyo, Spain. Commissions: *Murals* Kolkata; International: House of Lords, Palace of Westminister Manchester Cathedral UK. Appointments: Visiting Prof. *GCAC* Kolkata; International: Prof. Central School of Art & Design, St. Martin School of Art, Central London Institute; Lecture on philosophy of Indian *drawing* V&A. Collections: *BAAC* & British Council Kolkata; International: Art Council of Great Britain, Leicester University, Birmingham Museum, Bradford Gallery, Museum England & V&A and others in Sweden, France, Lithuania, Italy, Bangladesh.

Amal Ghosh's *paintings* display a fusion of his Indian roots with the simplification of the British *modern*. Since his arrival in England, his *imagery* has undergone a sea-change from the surreal and the bizarre to the suave and the iconic. He uses the transcultural language of the myth and symbol to weave complex and subtle commentaries. *Images* drawn from different *cultures* are sometimes used to signify philosophical or *spiritual* indicators. His *forms* are *symbolic*, *narrative* and poetic in *nature* and at the same time appear to be mysterious as well. Clarity and simplicity of *form* bely the complexity of their internal structures. They are imbued with hidden meaning, an indicator of which can generally be found in the way he *titles* his works.

He lives in London.

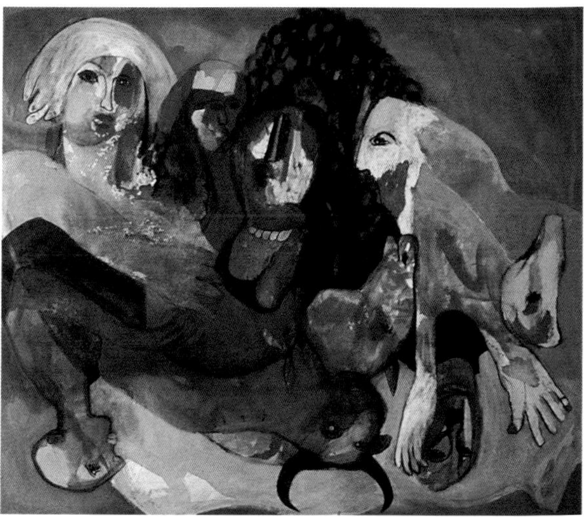

Ghosh, Amal: "Mirage", *Oil* on *Canvas*, 1994, 153x183 cm.

Ghosh, Prateep (1959–) b. Kolkata. Education: Studied in *FA*. College of Visual Art Kolkata. Solos: *AFA* & Gallery Tagore Kolkata, Gallery Shrishti Lucknow, BAG. Group participations: College of Visual Art & Culture Dept. Govt. WB, *BAAC*, Kala Mela, *AFA*, *Terracotta GC* & MMB Kolkata, All India Exhibition, RB, *LKA* & Kala Mela New Delhi, Indian Oil Limited Bandra Mumbai, *Roopankar Biennale* by *BB* for MAHA earthquake, *ISOA*. *Art* camps & workshops: Govt. of WB, Young Artist's workshop at Kolkata Airport organized by IAAI Conservation, Preservation & Restoration by *BAAC* Kolkata & *INTACH*

Lucknow. Awards: AAI, Certificate College of Visual Art Kolkata. Member: *BAS*. Collections: *LKA* New Delhi, Anand Agarwal Kolkata, *BB*, *ABC*; International: Australia, USA, Bangkok, Sweden.

It is the innocence of childhood or rather the loss of it in our complex urban structure that *forms* the basis of Prateep Ghosh's *paintings*. The rudimentary patches of pure *colour* depict the simple joys of flying a kite, chasing a butterfly or just running about in lush green fields, activities that the children of this generation have probably lost out on, due to increasing mechanization of our lives.

Prateep Ghosh lives and works in Kolkata.

Ghosh, Samir (1937–) b. Kolkata. Education: Dip. in *FA*. ICA&D Kolkata. Solos: *WBAF* Kolkata. Participated: Hyderabad, *AFA*, *BAAC* & *WBAF* Kolkata, *BAS*, *AIFACS*, over 30 group participations. Member: *WBAF* Secretary, Calcutta Art Fair & Press. Collection: *AFA* Kolkata.

Several *styles* can be discerned in his *paintings* although *figuration* remains his strong point. He distorts the *figures* in accordance with the context of the subject. *Earth colours* dominate his *palette*, though he also uses bright turquoises, yellows, reds and blues. He prefers to draw and *paint* in *egg-tempera* on cloth pasted on masonite or ply board.

He lives and works in Kolkata.

Ghosh, Shaibal (1951–2000) b. Kolkata. Education: Grad. *GCAC* Kolkata. Solos: *KB Santiniketan*, *CKAG*, *GK*, *AIFACS*, *CYAG*; International: Coopersburg P.A., USA. Group participations: *BAAC* Kolkata, *LKA* Bangalore, *CYAG* Silver Jubilee, *JAG*, *GK*, *G88*, TKS. Awards: *GCAC* WB Gold Medal & *AFA* Kolkata, All India Educational Conference Medal. Commissions: *Murals* Kolkata & Varanasi, Designed Grand Prix International Children Film Festival Kolkata. Appointments: Participated in English & Hindi Films. Collections: Godrej Mumbai, *GCAC*, *BAAC* & *LKA* Kolkata, pvt. & public.

Shaibal Ghosh had concentrated on the *medium* of *watercolour* ever since he grad. from *art* college. His obsession was to evolve the same solidity of *mass* and *volume* i.e. possible with the dense *medium* of *oil painting*, in *watercolour*. He first experimented with *tone* limiting himself to the use of *black* and *white*. He later went on to reproduce the lush tactility of the Dutch masters using *watercolour*. Here he was successful in building up the *chiaroscuro* of these masters with remarkable dexterity using *overlapping tints* of *watercolour*.

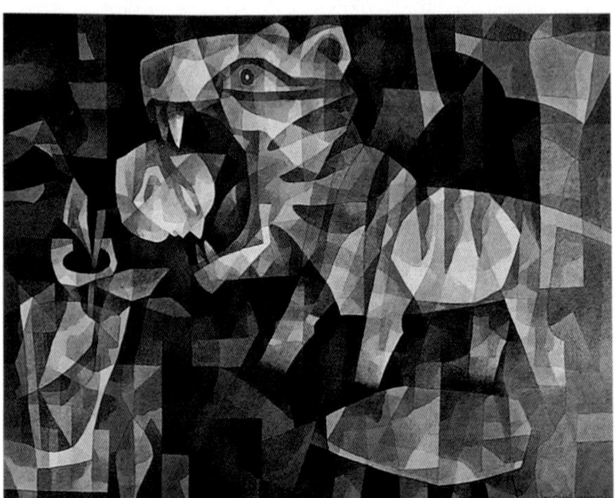

Ghosh, Shaibal: "The Show", *Watercolour*, 1993, 55x70 cm.

Gradually, he developed an identity of his own by creating prismatic *allegories* of life and death, in which an obsession with the autobiographical is immediately apparent. The *motif* of the *self portrait* is still visible in his later works, his *style* becoming economical and spare, eliminating much of the heavy handed *allegory* and philosophy. He had also simplified his *manner* of applying *paint*. Instead of breaking up the *pictorial space* into innumerable splinters as is apparent in the 1993 "The Make-Up", the surfaces of his *paintings* composed of solid areas of *colours* which create the *impression* of *mass*. *Colours* are rich without being sumptuous, as if to prove that there is no substitute for simplicity.

Ghosh, Tapan (1943–) b. Kolkata. Education: Dip. *GCAC* Kolkata. Over 19 solos: Kolkata, New Delhi, Mumbai; International: Paris, Norway. Group participations: National, *Triennale* & *LKA* New Delhi, MKKP Raipur, *AIFACS*, *CYAG*; International: *Biennale* Seoul, Paris, Madrid, Indian Festival USA. Workshops: *Graphic LKA* Kolkata, Multimedia *artists* camp Shimla. Awards: *AIFACS*, HAS; International: Paris. Member: Kolkata Painters' Group. Collections: Hyderabad, *NGMA* New Delhi.

Though he started off as a printmaker after training at Hayters Atelier in Paris, he turned more and more towards *drawing* in the late 70s when he was teaching *graphic design* to the students of the Film and TV Institute at Pune. His *style* has also evolved over the years from an *abstract* expression to a *figurative* one.

Most of his *drawings* especially those of human visage have an air of severe *Romanticism* about them, the faces appearing to materialize out of thin air, in a blur of one directional strokes, recalling the *images* of *Bikash Bhattacharjee* and the *style* of *Suhas Roy*.

Tapan Ghosh lives and works in Kolkata.

Ghurayya, Seema (1963–) b. Gwalior. Education: Dip. in *FA*. Govt. Institute of FA. & M.A. in *painting* Gwalior. Solos: Bhopal, The Gallery Chennai, Kala Vithika Gwalior, *GC* & *Tao Art Gallery* Mumbai, TAG, *GE*. Group participations: *FA*. from MP, Indo-Russian International Exhibition & National Exhibition in New Delhi, *FA*. from MP & *Graphic* in Bhopal, *GC* Mumbai, *BB* Biennale, *JAG*; International: Japan, *Biennale* Egypt. *Art* camps & workshops: *Graphic*, *Painters* NZCC Bhopal, *INTACH* Gwalior, *Painting* & *sculpture* workshop & seminar. Awards & Fellowship: All India Kalidas Ujjain, SZCC Nagpur, MP State Exhibition Gwalior, *AIFACS*; National Scholarship & Junior Fellowship Govt. of India, National Research Grant *LKA* New Delhi. Collections: MP Vidhan Sabha Bhavan Bhopal, *NGMA* & *LKA* New Delhi, *INTACH* Gwalior, State *LKA* Lucknow, SZCC Nagpur, *Roopankar BB*.

Seema Ghurayya uses the *colour* viscosity *technique* of *printmaking* to obtain the subtle variations of *hue* in her *prints*. Her *images* of thin sheets of *paper* strung together offer her endless possibilities to experiment with *tone* and density. She obtains similar effects in her *drawings* and *paintings* with the use of *stencils* and thin diluted *washes* of grainy *oil* and *colour pencils* to portray *light*. Worked under the guidance of *J. Swaminathan*.

Seema Ghurayya lives and works in her studio at Bhopal.

Gita-Govinda A 12th century poem on the love-trysts of KRISHNA and RADHA written by Jayadeva. Most of the Rajput miniatures are based on these verses. Refer *Erotic Art, Kangra Kalam, Kangra School, Kangra Miniatures, Manuscript Paintings*, RADHA, *Laxman Pai, Nathu Lal Verma*.

Glass Mosaic Refer *Mosaic, Back-Glass Paintings, Stained Glass—Katayun Saklat*.

Glass Painting The era of glass paintings in India began in the 18th century, gaining momentum in the early 19th century. Several centres emerged, e.g., Kutch and Saurashtra in GUJ and the Peshwa kingdom in MAHA registering its early presence, influenced most probably by Chinese *artists* who migrated there after the fall of Srirangapatnam. However, with the *passage* of time local *artists* developed their own *style* based on local *craft* and *traditions*. In Bihar and Bengal, glass paintings were mainly used in prayer rooms and therefore carried devotional *themes*. However, the most significant characteristic is *Thanjavur (Tanjore) paintings*, the Thanjavur (Tanjore) *style* is influenced by the Thanjavur *icon paintings* on *wood*. Extensive use of *gold* and *metal* foil used to simulate *ornaments* and gems set them apart distinctly in a class of their own. Refer *Thanjavur (Tanjore) Painting on Glass, Back-Glass Painting, Epic, Stained Glass, Madhu Champaneria, Shanu Lahiri, P.L. NarasimhaMurti, D.L.N. Reddy, Sisir Sahana, Gopal G. Subhedar.*

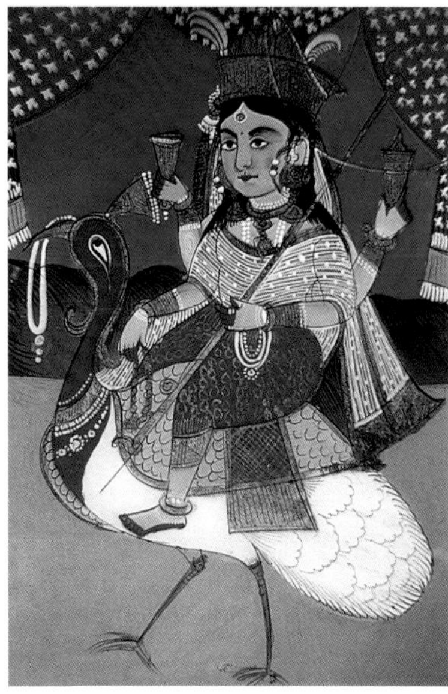

Glass Painting: "Deity Seated on a Swan", Anonymous, early 19th century 30.5x23 cm.

Glazing Opposite of *scumbling*. Glazing is the *term* applied to the process of applying *transparent* layers of paint over a solid one so that the *colour* of the first layer is modified. Thus a thin layer of yellow over a solid blue, will give the effect of various *shades* of green. An *illusion* of *depth* is created due to the reflection of *light* and its passing through the layers. It also makes for a glossy *finish*. The *technique* was used mostly by the *old masters*. Today it is used to achieve certain *tones* and *textures*. The *term* is also used in *ceramics* and *glass painting*. So also in *tempera* where the final touches are applied in *oil* for *glazing*. Refer *Drawing Inks, Sable Hair, White*.

Glue Size A glue or binder made from boiled hide and bones. Buffalo hide was frequently used in the making of Indian miniatures. Refer *Size*.

God=Deva, a Deity, a Creator; Heavenly divine, Ishwara, the gods as the heavenly or shining ones—(Visva deva), all the gods of RIG-VEDA; the one universal super natural power. The representation of gods in *art form* was replete with the use of *symbolic* poses, gestures, *weapons* and attendant *figures*. The *style* of depiction varied through the elegant elongation of PALLAVA *art* to the robust earthiness of Rashtrakuta *art*. *Raja Ravi Varma* introduced the Western element of cloying *neo-Classicism* into his gods and Goddesses, making for a whole new range of popular *images*, including cherubic pink-cheeked KRISHNAS and Aphrodite (Greek goddess of love and beauty) like—LAKSHMIS, with Indian facial characteristic and costumes. More recently, Anjolie Ela Menon's 2004 *installation* at *JAG*, in collaboration with a billboard *painter* shows large iconic *images* of many gods. Refer *Government Museum*, AGNI, BHARATA, BRAHMA, GANESHA, HANUMAN, *Hinduism, Iconography, Iconology, Ideal, Idol*, INDRA, KAILASH, LAKSHMI, PARVATI, SHIVA, *Thanjavur (Tanjore) Paintings, Reddeppa M. Naidu, Kanu Desai, Shantanu Ukil*.

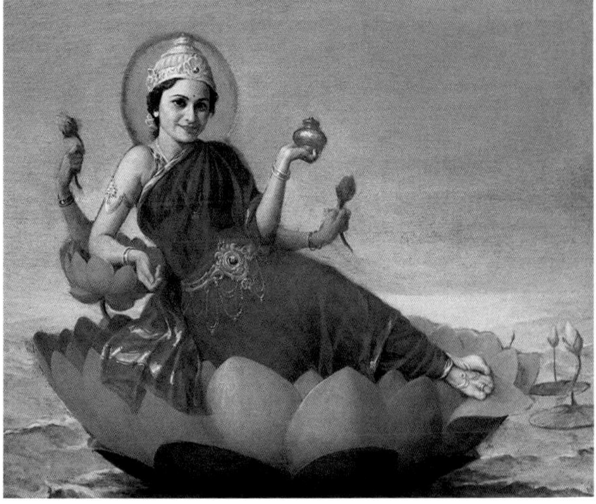

God: *Baburao Painter*, "Laxmi", *Oil painting*, 68.5x93 cm.

Gold A precious yellow *colour metal* capable of being beaten into extremely thin sheets. It has been used throughout the ages both as a *medium* and to decorate *sculpture, paintings*, manuscripts *artefacts*, etc. In the West including Greece, it was one of the materials used in the making of chryselephantine statues, others being *ivory* and *wood*, the *drapery* was made of gold sheets on a *wooden core*, while the skin was of *Ivory*.

As a colouring agent, gold was extensively used in India since ancient *times*. *Gold leaf* was reduced to small pieces and levigated in a smooth *stone* mortar along with sand and water. After the gold powder was free from impurities it was mixed with glue and applied on to the *painting* or *sculpture*. Later the gold was burnished with a boar's tusk to impart gloss. This gold powder was used to indicate gold *ornaments*, zari work on costumes and *Haloes* of divinities and kings. *Silver* was also used in a similar fashion. *Contemporary* artist-like *Satish Gujral*, *K.K. Hebbar* and *Siona Benjamin* have also used *gold leaf* in a less traditional *style*. Refer *Basohli, Bengal School, Bronzing, Bundi, Codex, Earth Colour, Electroplating, Embroidery, Enamel, Glass Painting, Harappa, Illuminated Manuscripts, Jain Miniature, Jain Manuscript Illumination, Kangra Kalam, Kangra School, Kangra Miniatures, Marbles, Metal Cut, Mohenjo Daro, Mughal Dynasty, Pala Miniatures, Picchwais,* SURYA, *Tree of Life, Trompe L'Oeil, Wrought Metal, Eric Bowen, Balan Nambiar, Mona Rai, Sunil Das, V. Viswanadhan,* Illustration—*Ravinder G. Reddy, Thanjavur (Tanjore) Paintings.*

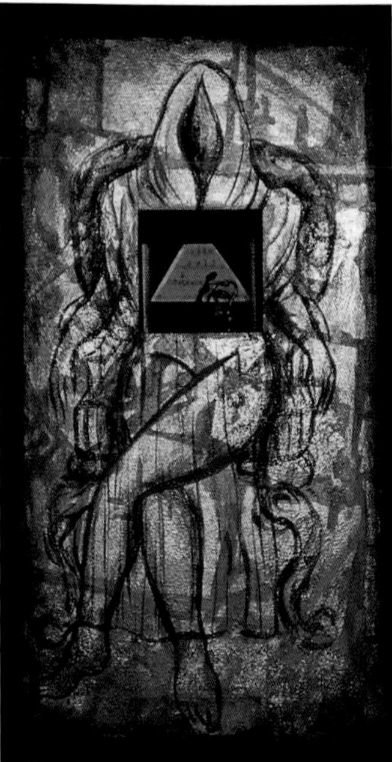

Gold: *Siona Benjamin* "Giant Steps" *Gold leaf* on *Canvas* & *Mixed media* 78.75x46.25x15.75 cm.

Gold Leaf Refer *Byzantine Art, Gold, Illumination, Leather, Matter, Miniature Painting, Mosaic, Mural, Thanjavur (Tanjore) Paintings, Thanjavur (Tanjore) Paintings on Glass, Siona Benjamin, Satish Gujral, Ved Pal Sharma.*

Gopa A cowherder, who along with their female counterparts, GOPIS, tended cows in Gokula, the birthplace of Lord KRISHNA. They are depicted as the playmates of KRISHNA in *miniature paintings*. Refer *Kangra*; Illustration—*Pastoral*, HOLI, RASA LILA.

Gopi, Gopika=A female who tends cattle in the land of Gokula. GOPIS are popularly represented in *miniature paintings*. They are the symbols of BHAKTI usually represented as adoring KRISHNA or dancing with him (RASA LILA). They also stand for the physical body, while KRISHNA stands for the soul, especially in the episode of chiraharana, the stealing of clothes. Refer *Kangra Kalam, Kangra School, Kangra Miniature, Picchwais,* RADHA; Illustration—*Pastoral*, HOLI, RASA LILA, KRISHNA, *Manjit Bawa, Nathu Lal Verma*.

Gopuram The multi-storeyed gateways to the Dravidian temple complex. It originally referred to the village gates of the Vedic age, through which the cows were let out to graze. The Gopuram was similar in appearance to the South Indian Vimana temple, with an oblong plan and a long barrel vault crowned with a row of stupis (finials). Refer PALLAVAS, *Pallava Dynasty.*

Goregaoker, Bhagwant K. (1901–1977) b. MAHA. Education: GDA in *modelling JJSA, Carving, stone, metal* work, Academy in Paris; Training at *art* classes conducted by Narayan Govindji Mantri; Visited the studio of *sculptor Ganpatrao K. Mhatre*. Group participations: *BAS*. Awards: Merit certificate, Bronze Medal & Silver Medal *BAS*; International: Medal in Rome. Commissions: Busts, statues, equestrian statues in *marble* & *bronze*, including *sculptures* for Vadodara's Kirti Mandir; Some of his works are installed in public places, e.g., earlier the police commissioner's statue at Crawford Market Mumbai, Raniof Jhansi at the Jhansiwale Smarak Smriti Pune. Collections: public places, & pvt.

Bhagwant K. Goregaokar evolved a sculptural *vocabulary* in *stone, plaster of Paris* and *metal*, that was near neo-classical in its perfection and elegance of *form*. His "Newspaper Boy" in *plaster of Paris* captures the youth in the act of hurling the *paper*. This *sculpture* demonstrates his keen sense of observation, the detail of the bundled *papers*, the clothes of the boy, and his posture. His public commissions also display the same nobility of visage and *classical* calmness of expression.

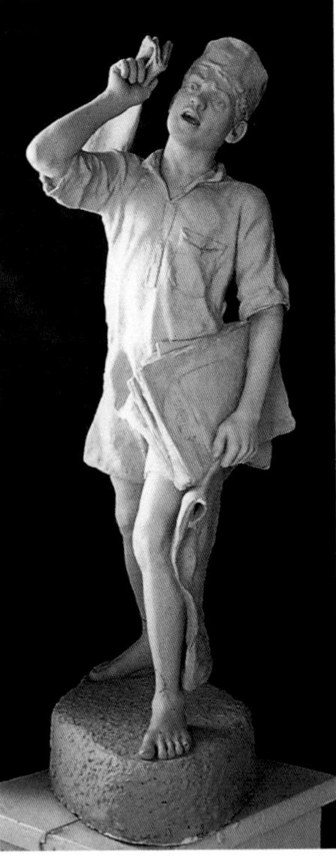

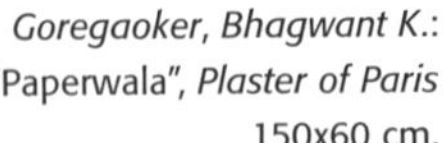

Goregaoker, Bhagwant K.: "Paperwala", *Plaster of Paris* 150x60 cm.

Goswami, Prem Chandra (1936–) b. Bikaner. Education: Dip. in *FA. painting*, B.A. in *drawing* Govt. College Jaipur. Solos: Bikaner, Alwar, Kota, Mumbai, New Delhi, Jawahar Kala Kendra Jaipur. Group participations: National Exhibition & *LKA* New Delhi, *LKA* & Kala Academy Jaipur, Art Exhibition of RAJ Painters Mumbai. Awards & Felicitations: *LKA* RAJ, Ratna Fellowship Certificate & Hon. with shawl, Bikaner community honoured, RAJ Govt. Honoured Literature, RAJ Sahitya Academy Udaipur Literature, RAJ Hindi Academy Granth Literature; Recognized as *art critic* in RAJ State. Member: Working committee *LKA* RAJ for several years, *PAG* & Art Research Organization Jaipur, Young Artists

Bikaner. Publications: *Monographs* published *LKA* RAJ, author of *Art* book, poems, children's literature & about 1000 *art* related articles in magazines; Talks, interviews, plays, music etc. Akashwani Radio & Doordarshan TV Jaipur. Collections: Central & State *LKA*, British Council, RAJ House New Delhi, *LKA* RAJ, national & international pvt. *museums*.

Prem Chandra Goswami's *paintings* show his experiments with different *colours*, moods and pathos. The delicate choice and *handling* of *colours* and *tonal value* with ease, has always been in his imaginative works. For him *colours* are *forms*, *lines* and words that talk.

His *style* is based on the *abstract handling* of *colours* applied thickly with a *palette knife*, the effect being that of heavily impasted dabs of *paint* swirling in open fields of flat *pigment*.

He lives and works in Jaipur.

Gotami, Li (1906–1988) b. as Rati Petit in an aristocratic Parsee family in Mumbai, she adopted the name Li Gotami when she formally embraced *Buddhism* in 1947, after which she married Lama Anagarika Govinda, a Bolivian German Prof. of Philosophy at the *VBU*. Studied *art* under the tutelage of the Bengal Master's, *Abanindranath Tagore*, *Nandalal Bose* & *Manishi Dey*. She was also a founder member of "Camera Pictorialists of Bombay", winning world-wide acclaim for her *photographs* with a Kodak Box camera. She was also a dancer, winning the prestigious award of the Astrova Academy of Russian Dance Arts. She spent 12 years at *Santiniketan*, obtaining degrees in both *arts* and music. After her marriage, she and her husband travelled to Western and Central Tibet where she photographed, traced and made free-hand *sketches* of Tibetan *frescoes*, and the sight of Tsaparang the ancient capital, thus tracing the evolution of *Buddhist art* from the cave *paintings* at *Ajanta* and *Ellora* to the 11th century works at these places. The "Illustrated Weekly of India" and some other journals published part of this work. Three of her *frescoes*, forming part of her "Life of Buddha" set of 31 scenes, are now at *PWM*. The *photographs* and notes were also published in two volumes titled "Tibet, In Pictures, A Journey Into The Past".

Li Gotami's individual *style* is also Tibetan in *nature*, with the same *pastel colours* and caricaturized *figures* and *landscape* scenes.

After her husband's death, she settled down in Pune where she died two years later in 1988.

Gothic A word now used to describe European Mediaeval *art*, from the end of the Romanesque—12th century to 16th century, the birth of the *Renaissance*. It is in particular used to describe *architecture* and its related *arts* of the period. Gothic *architecture* is characterized by the use of the pointed *arch*, flying buttresses, elaborate vaults, soaring clustered columns and the extensive use of *stained glass* & tracery. There was a strong emphasis on the vertical, even in *sculpture* and *painting*, leading to an extreme elongation of the human body. The *style* spread from France to England and Germany. In the 19th century where there were frequent Gothic revivals. Many churches in India built during the colonial period were designed in the Gothic *style*. Refer *Neo-Classicism*, *Christian Art*.

Gouache It is a water based *paint*. Unlike *transparent watercolours* it is possible to work from dark to *light* and the *pigment* is made thicker and *opaque* by the addition of gum and *white filler* (*clay* or barite). However it dries much lighter in *tone* than it seems when wet and thus has a typical "chalky" look. Gouache used by mediaeval manuscript *painters* also known as body colour.

This *style* was first practised in India in 1790s by *painters* of murshidabad. Also known as poster paints or poster *colours*, it was used in company *paintings* by *artists* in Kolkata, Lucknow, Delhi and Agra. Refer *Abstract Painting*, *Base*, *Bazaar Painting*, *Bengal School*, *Cityscape*, *Company School/Company Painting*, *Gum Arabic*, *Illumination*, *Miniature Painting*, *Mixed Media*, *Miniature Painting*, *Opacity*, *Opaque*, *Paint*, *Painter*, *Painting*, *Pigment*, *Realistic*, *Tint*, *Tempera*, *Wash (Technique)*, *Watercolours*, *White*, *Narayan S. Bendre*, *Dharmanarayan DasGupta*, *Ramlal Dhar*, *H.A. Gade*, *Mrugank G. Joshi*, *Ganesh Pyne*, *K. Seshagiri Rao*, *Sayed Haider Raza*, *Lalu Prasad Shaw*, *Gulam Mohammed Sheikh*, *Prem Singh*, *Laxman Narayan Taskar*, *Vasudha Thozhur*, *Zahoor Zargar; Illustration—Gobardhan Ash*, *Ganesh Haloi*, *Bharati Kapadia*, *Dinkar Kowshik*, *Ved Nayar*, *Saroj Gogi Pal*, *Rabindranath Tagore*, *Shantanu Ukil*.

Goud, Laxma (1940–) b. Nizampur, Hyderabad. Education: Dip. in *drawing* & *painting* Govt. College of FA. & Architecture Hyderabad; Trained in *mural painting MSU* under a scholarship; Specialized in *printmaking*. Solos & Group shows: since 1965 Hyderabad, New Delhi, Bangalore, Marvel Art Gallery Ahmedabad, Jamaat Gallery, The Window & The Museum Gallery Mumbai; International: London, Europe, Japan; Participated: National & international Exhibition, *Biennale* Tokyo, Sao Paulo & Warsaw. *Auctions*: Heart, Osian's & Bowrings Mumbai, Heart & Bowrings New

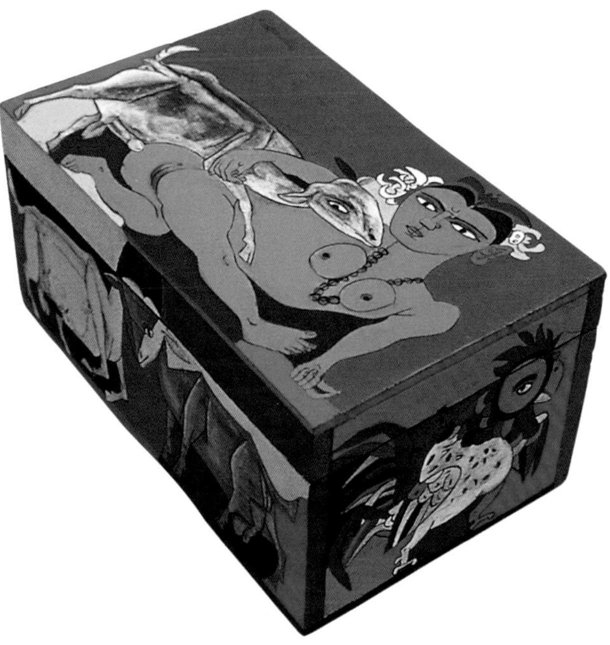

Goud, Laxma: "Box of Teakwood", *Acrylic*, 1998

Delhi, Christie's & Sothebys London, Sothebys New York. Awards: AP *LKA*, Silver Medal & Gold Medal HAS. Member: HoD *SNSPA, FA. & Communication* Hyderabad. Appointments: Graphic Designer for 15 years with Doordarshan National TV. Collections: *Art Heritage, LKA & NGMA* New Delhi, *SJM*; International: Masanori Fukuoka & Glenbarra Museum Hemeji Japan, Chester & David Herwitz Boston.

Laxma Goud began printing in *black* and *white* adding *colour* only after 15–20 years. His *iconography* is earthy, sensuous, erotic and demonic at the same time. He is influenced by his roots in rural India, with its frank and open attitude towards sex and eroticism unhindered by the guise of hypocritical *Symbolism*. His animals and humans copulate unrestrainedly and openly in the village *landscape* of trees and bushes. The element of *fantasy* comes in the surreal *imagery* of hybrid animals and sexual genitalia pierced with *ornaments* and objects like safety pins and staples. Through all this *imagery* it is his delicate use of *line* that stands out, adding *tones* out of crisp *patterns*.

In his "untitled" *etching*, one sees him exploring the relationship between the sexes in the dark interplay of physical and psychological *forms* as well as his interests in both folk and *modern imagery*.

He lives and works in Hyderabad. Refer *Hatching*.

Gouge A hand tool used to scrape out large areas of unwanted surface material in the preparation of a *wood cut* or a *linocut*. The gouge chisel has a strong wooden handle so that a mallet can strike it in order to make deep cuts in the *wood*. It has either curved or V-shaped cutting edge. Large curved gouges are used for soft *stone*. Refer *Printmaking, V Tools, Carving*; Illustration–*Wood Cut, Wood Cut Printing*: *Sudhir R. Khastgir*.

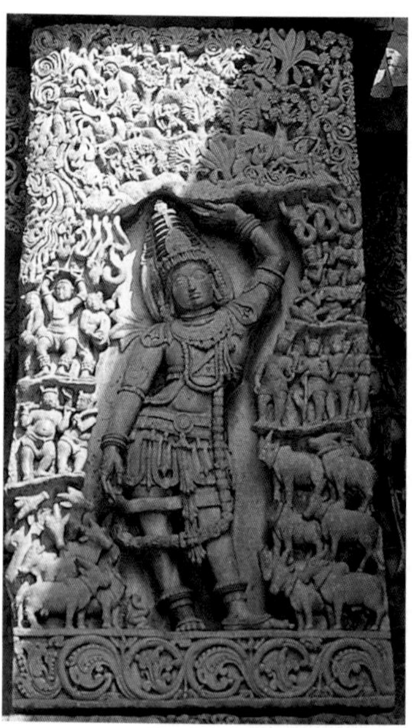

Govardhan, Govardhanadhara Or Giri Govardhan. A synonym of KRISHNA pertaining to his miraculous feat of lifting up the mountain Govardhan and balancing it overhead on the tip of one finger to protect the people of Brindaban from the rainstorm sent by INDRA. It is a popular subject in *Rajasthani miniature painting*.

Govardhan, Govardhanadhara: "Krishna lifting Govardhana", Helebid, AD 13th century.

Government College of Arts & Crafts (GCAC) (Kolkata WB) The *Industrial Art Society* founded in 1854 in Kolkata, ran a school of Industrial *art* which was later converted into the GSAC Kolkata during the Governor Generalship of Lord Northbrook who added an *art* gallery to it. It has a collection of works of *Atul Bose, Nandalal Bose, Mukul Chandra Dey, Somnath Hore, Ganesh Pyne, Rabindranath Tagore* among others. The college is an important part of the history of *modern art*, starting from the period when the Indophile, E.B. Havell became principal. He was to appoint *Abanindranath Tagore* as the vice-principal of the school in order to promote a return to the *aesthetic values* and *traditions* of India by the Indian *artists*.

The school was elevated into a full-fledged college in 1951. The *draughtsmanship* course was abolished and the Dept. of Decorative Arts and Craft was introduced. Courses conducted by the college include a foundation course, dip. courses in *applied art, decorative art* and *craft, drawing* and *painting* (Indian *style* and *murals*) and (life, *nature* and *murals*) *sculpture* of *modelling* and certificate courses in *Batik*, decorative *wood* work, *leather craft* and *weaving*.

Government College of Arts & Crafts (GCAC) Chennai TN). *Madras School of Art* was founded by Dr. Alexander Hunter in 1850. However when he discovered that the students were becoming more adept at imitation rather than originality, he decided to convert the school into the *Government School of Industrial Art* consisting of two dept.–the Artistic and the Industrial (meaning *fine* and *applied Arts*). Photography was also included as a subject. By 1868, about 3,500 students had graduated from the college, some of them becoming teachers in the other *art* school, others travelling abroad. In 1884, the new principal, E.B. Havell made a great impact on the Indian *art* scene by his promotion of Indian *ideals* and *aesthetics*. He was responsible for the introduction of *wood carving*, carpentry and *metal* work units in the school Rao Bahadur N.R. Balakrishna Mudaliar become its first Indian superintendent in 1927, though his connection with the school went back to the year 1889.

Debi Prasad RoyChowdhury became the first Indian principal of the *Madras School of Art* in 1929. Under his guidance, the school stopped being an institute for training teachers and turned into a school of *artists*. *K.C.S. Paniker*, succeeded him as Principal in 1957.

K.C.S. Paniker was the person around whom the movement in South developed, to be popularly known as the *Madras School of Art K.C.S. Paniker* broke with the authority of Western and academic masters. Unlike conceiving *form* as *mass* disciplined into a *body*, he rendered it as a continuous and linear movement, rhythmic and whole. Following *K.C.S. Paniker*'s success with this *art form*, many *artists* began to follow such as Santhanaraj, Antony Doss, Rajavelu, *Reddeppa M. Naidu* and *K.M. Adimoolam*. Later *artists* like *V. Viswanadhan, Narayanan Akkitham, Setlur Gopal Vasudev* as well embraced the style. The *Madras School of Art* had thus carved a niche for itself in the general uncertainty created by the "modernistic" *ideology* and the sundry idealistic reaction that had broken out with it in the country.

Madras School of Art was upgraded into a college in 1961. In 1979, the Dept. of Technical Education upgraded the various courses of study upto the degree level. In 1994, the college became an autonomous institute. In 1997, the college set up a *Museum of Contemporary Art* in its premises. Refer *Calcutta School*, *Bombay School*, *Banasthali Vidyapith* and *Santiniketan*.

Government Museum (Alwar, RAJ) This *museum* is housed in a portion of the old city palace of Alwar. It has a collection of *sculptures*, *paintings*, manuscripts and a number of articles belonging to the royal family. The *museum* has a copy of the famous "Gulistan" written in 1258, and an illustrated scroll, near, 80 yards long. In addition to the *paintings* from the Alwar School, there are some late *Mughal miniatures* as well.

Government Museum (Mathura, UP) This *museum* was set up in 1874, to function primarily as a storehouse for *art*; the *sculptures* here, being constantly removed to more important *museum* in Kolkata and Lucknow. The present *museum* was built during the 1930s. The headless *figure* of Vima Kadphises seated on a lion throne belonging to the Kushana *style* is placed in the reception. Opposite to this, is the standing *figure* of his successor, Kanishka. They both wear boots, indicating their foreign origin.

A section of the gallery exhibited *sculptures* with specimens belonging to all the early periods of Indian history. There is also a small room containing *terracotta figures* from Mathura.

The *sculpture* gallery continues on the left side as well, with the remnants of *stupas* being displayed along with Hindu *Gods* such as SURYA.

Government Museum (Thiruvananthapuram, Kerala) The *art* collection in this *museum*, founded in 1857 showcases the rich cultural heritage of the state. The gallery of *bronzes* shows that the Kerala *bronzes* differ markedly in appearance from the CHOLA and PALLAVA ones. There are *sculptures* and chariots in *wood* from the old temples in the state. There is also a natural history section along with a zoological garden. Refer *CTAG*.

Government Museum & Art Gallery (GMAG) (Chandigarh) The *museum* is a combination of the *art* gallery, *museum* and science wings. The *museum* documents *art* objects and also provides facilities to scholars for studying them, and makes available *black* and *white photographs* of the same. There is a well-equipped library and reference section. The *art* gallery hosts exhibitions on a regular basis. The *museum* also publishes books and sells slides and post-cards of *miniature paintings*.

Government School of Industrial Art Refer *GCAC* Chennai.

Government State Museum & National Art Gallery (Chennai, TN) The *museum* complex includes the *museum* itself, a theatre and the National Art Gallery. The *museum* has innumerable sections on Geology, zoology, botany, mineralogy, philately, and a gallery of musical instruments. The most important galleries are the ones housing the Amravati collection and the *bronze* gallery. The former contains the remnants of the Amravati (in AP) *stupa*, of which a few pieces are also seen in the *National Museum* New Delhi, the *Indian Museum* Kolkata and the British Museum London. These *sculptures* carved out of milk-white *marble* extend over both the Hinayana and the Mahayana phases of *Buddhist art*. They depict various stories from the JATAKAS; including "The Taming of Nalagiri".

Some of the best examples of *South Indian bronzes* are found at the *bronze* gallery, these *sculptures* are *cast* in the *cire perdue technique*, and were meant to be taken out in temple processions. The best of these belong to the PALLAVA and CHOLA *periods*. SHIVA NATARAJA, Somaskanda and the group of RAMA, Lakshmana and Sita are among the best of the works on *display*.

Gowda, Sheela (1957–) b. India. Education: Dip. Ken School of Art Bangalore, Post-Dip. *VBU*, M.A. RCA, *MSU* studied under *K.G. Subramanyan*. Solos & group participations: Bangalore, Mysore, *Gallery 7* Mumbai, National New Delhi, *Biennale* Bhopal, "Timeless Art" Mumbai, *JAG*; International: Switzerland. Awards: Inlaks Foundation Scholarship & Burston Award RAA London. Member: *Gallery 7*. Appointments: Lecturer in *painting* Mysore for 11 months.

Sheela Gowda's earlier work show a predilection for a subtle interplay of emotional states between the portrayed characters. Her *drawing* has always been important, appearing as a female means of structuring *figures* and objects, imbuing them with vitality and life without weighing them onto a flat *ground*.

She has moved towards a new language of representation, seeking new options of expressing her urge for authencity and immediacy in *terms* of the material she uses. However the formal element of representational feminist objects which still dominate in the end, the cowdung, fragments of fabrics, *charcoal* and wooden sticks serving to enhance the *image* rather than submerge it. Sheela Gowda presents a feminist stance by using these materials which are all fraught with religious and socio-cultural overtones.

Sheela Gowda lives and works in Bangalore.

Gradation A subtle *transition* between *colours* or *tones* without any abrupt or sharply defined boundaries. e.g. *K.V. Haridasan's paintings* in *abstract*, have gradations of *colours*, yellow, red, blue and green. Refer *Shade*, *Value*, *Watercolours*.

Graffitti (Italian)=scratched *drawing*. It usually means words or *drawings* (usually obscene) scrawled or scratched on walls and public places. Graffitti was raised to an *art form* by artists like Kleith Haring. Today it has been incorporated into *painting*, introducing obscure messages and anagrams into their large *compositions* on *canvas* and board. In the 1980s, graffitti especially in the USA, became an *art form* in itself by the works of J. Michel Basquiat and K. Haring. Refer *Rabindranath Tagore*, *Satish Gujral*, *Jyoti Bhatt*, *Siona Benjamin*, *Manu Parekh*.

Granite An igneous or volcanic rock-like stone. At Mamallapuram (*Mahabalipuram*) in TN, large blocks of granite have been used to construct the Thanjavur temple. The CHOLA temples have *sculptures* in *light relief* and mostly face forward. A granite *carving* school was set up in 1957–*GCAC* Chennai. Refer *Stone, Mural, Medium, Pallavas, Pallava Dynasty, Satish Gujral, Nagji Patel, Aekka Yadagiri Rao;* Illustration–BRAHMA, *P.S. Nandhan, C. Dakshinamoorthy.*

Graphic A synonym for *printmaking*, which was introduced to Indian *artists* by visiting European *artists* in the 19th century. In the 20th century Indians studied *printmaking* abroad and popularized in India after the 1950's. The *technique* became popular especially among the younger generation of *artists.* Refer *Graphic Art, J.R. Yadava, Bhawani S. Sharma, Janak Patel;* Illustration–*Krishna N. Reddy, Anupam Sud, Rm. Palaniappan.*

Graphic Art Any *art* work i.e. essentially a *drawing* rather than a *painting*. The *term* includes everything from the simple *sketch*, to all types of *printmaking* and typography. Refer *Drawing, Contemporary, Graphic Design, Lithography, White Line Engraving, Benode Behari Mukherjee, Chittaprasad, Somnath Hore, Amina Ahmed, Gunen Ganguli, Kar, Paul A. Koli, J.R. Yadava.*

Graphic Design The *art* work associated with *applied art* for commercial purposes as in *designs* for brochures and packaging, *cinema*, *posters* and publishing. *Bharati Kapadia* and *Amitava Das*, are some *graphic* designers who have branched into *fine arts* while *Tapan Ghosh* has taught graphic design to the students of the Film and TV Institute at Pune.

Graphic Prints Refer *Graphic, Half-Tone, Lithography, Printmaking, Jivan Adalja, Krishan Ahuja, Swapan Kumar Das, Saroj Gopi Pal, Paul A. Koli, Raja Ravi Varma, Vivan Sundaram.* Illustration–DIWALI, INDRA, PARAVATI, *Rm. Palaniappan, Krishna N. Reddy, Anupam Sud.*

Graphite A natural from of crystalline carbon powder. **1.** It is used in stick *form (lead pencil)* in *drawings*, either as it is or mixed with *clay*. Hardness of *lead* depends upon *proportion* of graphite to *clay*. When used in *art* works, it shows *blacks* and greys with a *tonal value* and surface shine. **2.** Graphite is also used during the process of *electroplating* sculptural objects. The coating of fine graphite gives a metallic effect and shine to the object. This has been used by *sculptor Shankar Nandagopal.* Refer *Pouncing.*

Greek Art Greek also known as Hellenic *art* developed in the Greek islands. It is broadly divided into Pre-Hellenic, the Cretan and Mycenaean period at about 3000 to 1100 BC.

Greek art is generally illustrative of scenes from the lives of anthropomorphic deities–*gods* and the *epics* of Homer. Thus, Greek art specialized in representing *anatomy*, motion and *perspective*. The greatest influence was in *architecture* and *sculptures*. It proliferated far and wide, influencing even *Roman* and *Byzantine art*. Lack of evidence of authentic Aryan or Indian architectural *style*, till after the rule of king Ashoka, lent credence to the influence of Hellenic *art* on the ancient Indo-Aryan civilization. However, this premise has been disputed strongly by various research scholars basing their treatises on old narrative texts accompanied by *illustrations* of cornices, columns, plinths and pedestals. Coomaraswamy was one of the strongest defenders of the concept of originality of 'Indian Ideal' in *art*.

Grisaille A *painting* executed entirely in grey, *white* or *black monochrome*, frequently giving effect of bas-relief. This is executed as a *composition* by itself, or as a *model* for an engraver. Refer *Roop Chand, Nikhil Biswas, C. Douglas.*

Ground 1. The prepared surface on which the *painting* is executed, it could be zinc *oxide* or *white oil paint* in the case of *canvas painting; gesso* in *fresco painting*. The ground heightens the brilliance of *colours* and retards chemical interaction between the *paint* and the *support*. **2.** In *printmaking*, ground refers to the *acid* resistant coating given to the *plate* before a *pattern* is scratched through and the *plate* immersed in *acid* for *etching*. There are two types of ground, i.e. *soft ground*, which is *wax* and grease based and gives a softer effect and *hard ground*, which is a mixture of beeswax, bitumen (asphaltum *varnish*) and resin resulting into a sharp, clear-cut *pattern*. Refer *Aquatint, Acid Bath, Acid Resist, Collage, Bite, Biting in, Coloured Ground, Etching, Dry Brush Painting, Dry-Point, Earth Colour, Paper-Pulp Casting, Raja Ravi Varma, Pestonjee Bomanjee, Kanu Desai, Ramkinkar Baij, Bikash Bhattacharjee, Jyoti Bhatt, Krishna N. Reddy, Rm. Palaniappan, Vrindavan Solanki.*

Group 1890 (GUJ). The Group, which derived its name from the number of the house where the members held their meeting and formulated their manifesto, was a single event rather than a group in the proper sense. It was formed in 1962 in Bhavnagar, GUJ by *J. Swaminathan* and other like-minded *artists*, including *Jeram Patel* who was the secretary, Rajesh Mehra, *Gulam Mohammed Sheikh, Raghav Kaneria, Himmat Shah, Jyoti Bhatt, Ambadas, Reddeppa M. Naidu, Eric Bowen* and others. Though the Group had no shared *ideology*, nor a common regional or geographical affiliation, it was bound together as a voice against the "established" *artists* and *art* of that time and generally against the increasing influence of European *art*.

Gue, Bhabani Charan (1910–d) b. Varanasi. Education: Dip. in *FA*. GSA Lucknow, Studied Slade School of Art, Central School Art & Fellow & Royal Society of Arts London. Solos: Allahabad, Jaipur, Mount Abu, Mussorie, Shimla, Mumbai; Retrospective Exhibition 1933–90 organized by *LKA* RAJ 1990; International: Cambridge University UK. Awards & Hons.: PUJ Govt. Silver Medal, Fine Art Society Lahore, Silk painting & H.H. Maharaja Mysore, *AFA* Kolkata, *Landscape painting* Hyderabad. Member: *LKA* New Delhi, Elected Vice-President & Fellow *LKA* RAJ; International: Royal Drawing Society, National Art Society & Royal Society of Art London. Publications: *Portfolios* of six *painting, monograph* & a short film in 1995 *LKA* RAJ. Collections: Museums of Modern Art Mysore, Allahabad & Thiruvananthapuram, Raj

Bhawan & Gallery of Modern Art Jaipur; International: Lahore, Japan, USA, Australia, UK, Singapore, Russia, Canada, Germany, Switzerland.

Bhabani Charan Gue painted *landscapes* and mythological *paintings* in a highly romanticized *style*. He adopted the linear softness of the *Bengal School* with the detailed rendering of *Chinese art*. There is also an *art nouveau* use of sinuous curves and decorations.

The Himalayas held particular a fascination for him and therefore he strived hard to bring majestic beauty on *canvas* to delight the viewers.

He lived in Ajmer, RAJ.

Guild (The) (TG) (Mumbai, MAHA). The gallery deals with *contemporary* Indian *art*, bringing quality works for the discernment of the *art* connoisseur and promoting works by younger promising *artists*. The owner, Shalini Sawhney places great emphasis on documentation as well. *Laxma Goud*, *Thotha Vaikuntham*, *Jogen Chowdhury* and *Akbar Padamsee* have exhibited here.

Gujral, Satish (1925–) b. Jhelum now Pakistan. Education: Dip. in *arts*, *drawing* & *painting*, *sculpture*, object *design*, *graphic design* & *engraving* Mayo School of Arts Lahore, *JJSA*, *Painting*, *composition* & *stone carving* Placio National de Bellas Artes Mexico; Imperial Services College Windsor UK. Solos: Bhopal, Kolkata, *Painting*, *Drawing* & *Sculpture ATG* & *JAG*; Retrospective RB New Delhi; International: Mexico City, New York, London, Montreal, Rome, Chicago & Stockholm, Vesile University USA. Group participations: *Triennale* India & other group shows; International: *Biennale* Venice, Tokyo & Sao Paulo, Commonwealth Art London. *Auctions*: Heart Mumbai. Awards: Scholarship Govt. of Mexico, National Award for *painting* on Rudyard Kipling & other National Awards *LKA* New Delhi, Aga Khan Award *Architecture*, Order of the Crown Belgium & received Hons. & Fellowships, including Rockfeller Council of Economic & Cultural Affairs New York. Member: *LKA's* Council New Delhi, Art Executive PUJ Govt. Publicity Division; Commissions: *Portraits* for National & Parliament House; *Murals* & *Designs*: Apprenticeship with Diego Rivera & David Alfaro Sequiros Mexico, Oman & Muscat; India: Hyderabad, New Delhi, Mumbai, & other towns. Publications: Portfolios *LKA*—An Autobiography. Collections: *NGMA* & *LKA* New Delhi, PUJ Museum Chandigarh, other pvt. & public; International: Including Museum of Modern Art, World Trade Centre, New York Hartford Museum Connecticut.

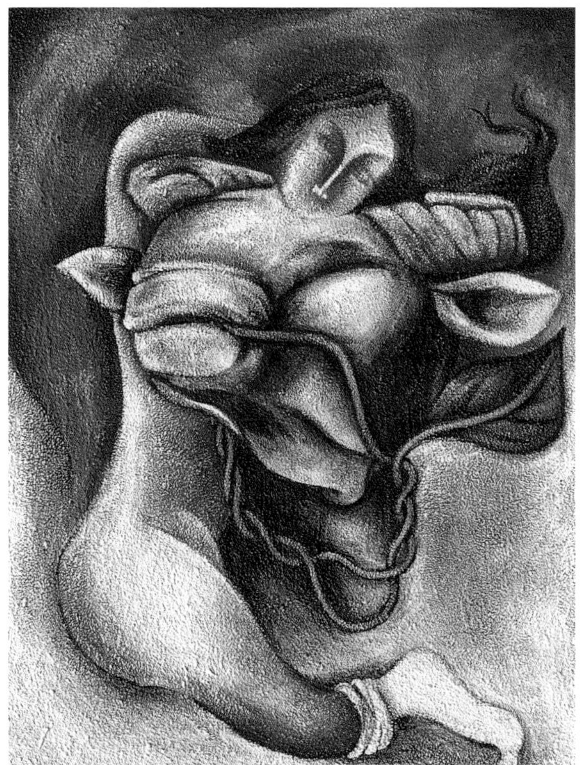

Gujral, Satish: "Fantasy", *Mixed media*, 91.5x122 cm.

Satish Gujral has been endlessly inventive, exploring such diverse *mediums* of expression as *murals*, *architecture*, *painting*, *drawing* and *sculpture*. His *themes* have also evolved with the times, being at first sociological and political, then iconic with *themes* such as GANESHA, whom he visualized as burnt *wood reliefs* embellished with *leather* cards, *ceramic* beads, crushed *leather* sheets, glowing vermilion powder mixed and patented with *gold leaf*.

Still later he moved on to overt sexual *images* of woman hybridized with birds and animals. The *colours* are now aggressive with lurid reds, hot pinks and parrot greens. Satish Gujral's *sculptures* are similar to his *paintings*, his *imagery* being conceived first in paint and later replicated in *sculpture*. The women, who could have been born out of Indian *mythology* are depicted in smooth whiteness of *marble* as well as *granite*.

He lives and works in New Delhi.

Gum Arabic A natural soluble gum which is obtained from the acacia plant. It varies in *colour* from pale yellow to reddish brown and is used as the binding agent in *watercolours*, *gouache* and *pastel pigments*. In *printmaking* it is used as a *translucent* solution in the preparation of lithographic *stones* and *metal plates*. Refer *Lithography*, *Medium*, *Gaganendranath Tagore*, *Raja Ravi Varma*, *Satyendranath Bandhyopadhyay*, *Manoj Datta*.

Gupta The rise of the Gupta dynasty in the 4th century marked the end of a period dominated by foreign rulers like the Yavanas, Sakas and the Kushanas and the return of a unified India under the Mauryas. It is often referred to as the golden age of Indian *art* and *culture* and was marked by a highly developed intellectual *culture* which survived the dynasty and in fact became the high point of Indian civilization.

The Gupta age has been termed as the Indian *Renaissance* with remarkable works being produced in all fields of *art* literature, with several treatises on *Mahayana Buddhism* and the Vedanta (ancient Indian scripture) being written as also the works of Kalidasa. Several temples and *Chaitya* halls were built, indeed the genesis of the Hindu temple is to be found at the DASAVATARA temple at Deogarh, built during this period. The *paintings* at *Ajanta* too were executed during the reign of the Gupta-Vakatakas (Kings). However, it is Gupta *sculpture*, in particular, the Gupta version of BUDDHA that has left a lasting impression through the ages. All Gupta *sculpture*, regardless of its place of origin displays masterly *style* of execution and a serenity of expression. The Hindu *Gods* and Goddesses were now executed with a systemic use of *symbolic* poses, gestures, *weapons* and attendant *figures*. The *figure* of VISHNU, one of the more popular *Gods* with the Guptas was identifiable by the four *attributes* of SHANKHA, GADA, CHAKRA and PADMA. SHIVA, DURGA, the BUDDHA and the BODHISATTVA were the other deities venerated by the Guptas. The *proportion* for both the Hindu and Buddhist *Gods* was identical—nine thalams.

One of the more important Buddhist *sculptures* is that of the seated BUDDHA from Sarnath. The *figure* was greatly stylized, seated in the PADMASANA posture with upturned soles. The hands were held with Dharmachakra-mudra (MUDRA). The robe was suggested only by fine grooves around the neck, wrists and ankles. The head was oval shaped, with small tight curls and all the features of the mahapursha lakshana (sign of a great man). The *halo forms* the back of the throne and is decorated with MAKARAS.

The *relief sculptures* found at the Deogarh temple are theatrical with an *illusion* of *depth* and *space*. The central *image* of VISHNU always appears calm and collected. With the decline of the Gupta dynasty, much of this serenity of expression disappears, to be replaced by stylized modes of expression.

Gupta, Jyotish Dutta (1935–) b. Feni Bangladesh. After the 1947 partition he arrived in Kolkata where he later studied at the *GCAC*. Solos: *AIFACS*, TKS, SRAG, TAG. Group participation: *AIFACS*. Appointments: Worked & designed books in 14 languages at the National Book Trust.

His works of the 90s were *figurative*, though *form* has dissolved somewhat into a haze of *watercolour washes*. The *paintings* however are still about people, watching them, listening to them, observing the play of *chiaroscuro* throughout the day and through the changing seasons. It is the melancholic, the morose sadness of life, that appeals to him. The *paintings* have evolved from the earlier polychromicity to a near sombre *palette* of *colours* that evoke the atmospheric quality of anguish.

Jyotish Dutta Gupta lives and works in New Delhi.

Gypsum Hydrated calcium sulphate a natural crystalline form, from which *plaster of Paris* is made. It is appropriate for use in the fashioning of *sculptures* or statuettes. The substance is found in sedimentary rocks and *clays*, is colourless or *white*, *opaque* or *transparent*. Refer *Plaster of Paris, Chalk, Mould, Sadanandji Bakre, Bhagwant K. Goregaokar, Vinayak Pandurang Karmakar, Ganpatrao K. Mhatre, Mahendra Pandya.*

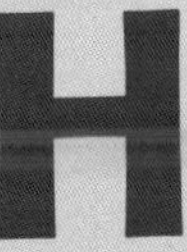

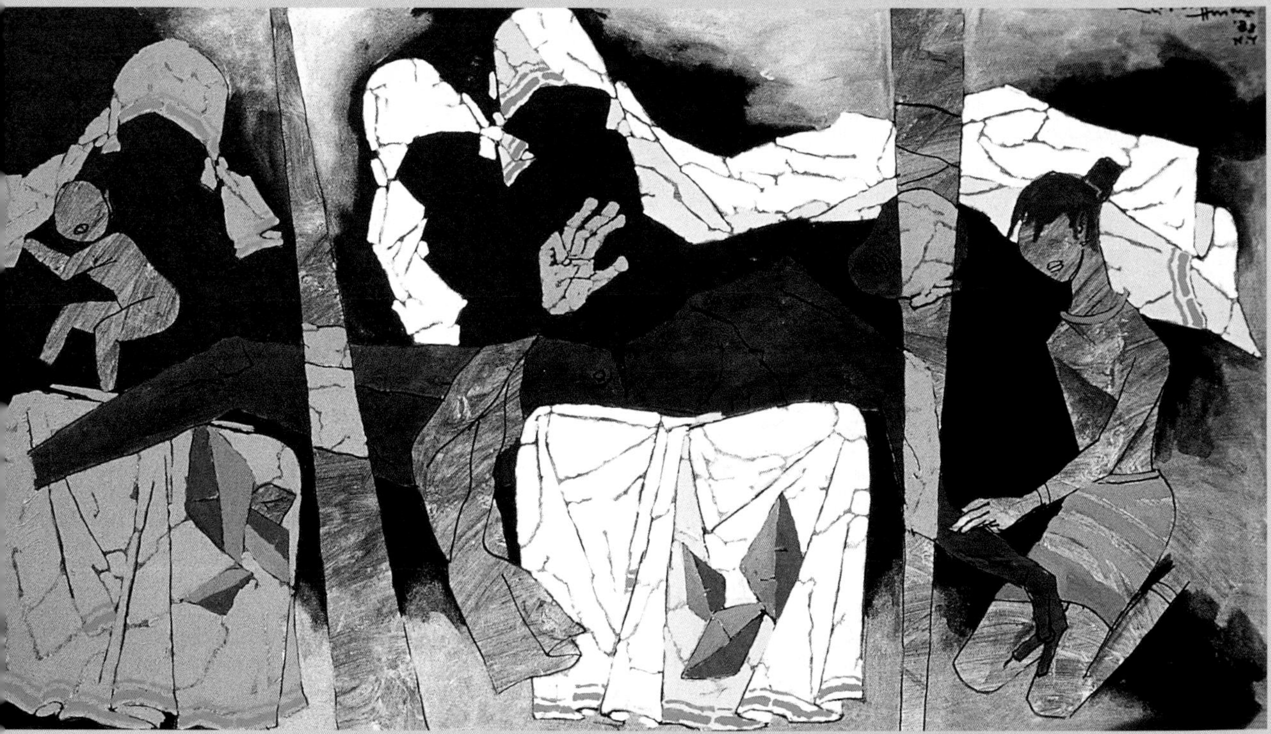

Husain, Maqbool Fida: "Mother Teresa", *Oil* on *Canvas*, 1988, 128x233 cm. (See notes on page 164)

Halatol (Indore, MP). Halatol, meaning "Creative restlessness" is a group of 22 *artists* based in Malwa (Indore) in MP. The group was formed when these *artists* decided to fight communalism by making social concern a *theme* of their *art*. *Ishwari Rawal*, *Vishnu Chinchalkar*, Vishwa Bhatnagar, Ranesh Kher, *Akhilesh*, Anis Niyazi, Safdar Shamee, Devilal Patider and others are the members of the group.

Haldankar, Gajanan S. (1912–1981) b. MAHA. Studied *art* under his father, *Savlaram L. Haldankar*. *Auctions*: Christie's London. Awards: Gold Medal *AFA* Kolkata, Silver Indian Industries Fair Mumbai, Gold & Silver Medals *BAS*. Member: Was the secretary & later Chairman of *ASI*. Commissions: *Portraits* including those of Mahatma Gandhi, Field Marshal Maneckshaw & Attorney General. Appointments: Taught *art* for nearly 60 years at Haldankar's FA. Institute, which was founded by his father in 1908. Collections: Dir. of Art Govt. of MAHA and pvt. *Hema Joshi*, Vijay Haldankar, Shrikrishna Haldankar.

Gajanan S. Haldankar was basically a *portrait painter* though he had painted *figurative* and group *compositions* as well. His *portrait* of his father shows a subtle use of *wash* and *drawing* done in a semi-impressionistic *style* to suggest both *mass* and *depth*.

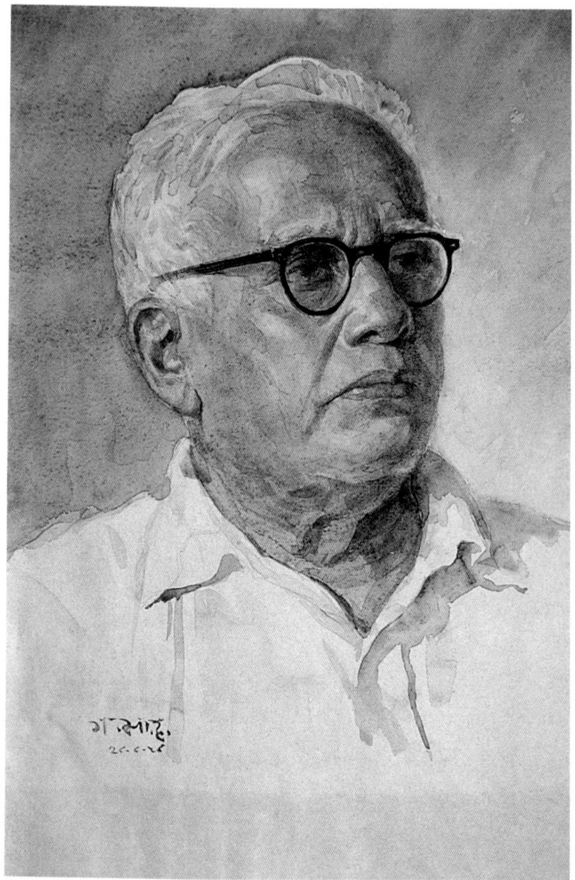

Haldankar, Gajanan S.: "Portrait of Savlaram Haldankar", *Watercolours.*

Haldankar, Savlaram L. (1882–1968) b. Savantwadi, Mumbai MAHA. Education: Dip. *JJSA* 1903. Established Haldankar's FA. Institute Mumbai in 1907 & set *Art Society of India (ASI)* in 1918. Solos & Group shows: *NCAG*, *BAS*, *JAG*; International: 1915 exhibited at the Royal British Society of Arts London. *Auctions*: Osian's Mumbai, Bonham's, Christie's & Sotheby's London. Awards: All Major *exhibitions* including Madras Fine Art Society, Shimla Fine Art Society & DAE, Gold Medal *BAS*. Fellowship: *LKA* New Delhi. Member: Hansa Mehta committee for reorganizing of *art education* MAHA; President MAHA Chitrakar Mandal. Commissions: Several *portraits* including Pandit Madan Mohan Malviya at Rashtrapati Jagannath Sunkersett, Sir Leslie and Lady Wilson & Rajasaheb of Savantwadi. Collections: In *museums* & galleries, pvt. & *JJSA*, "Divine flame" in the *NGMA* New Delhi, "Niranjan" in Nagpur Museum, "Swatmananlal" in Academy of Art Moscow, "A Mohamedan pilgrim" in *PWM*, "Glow of Hope" in Jaganmohan Palace Mysore.

These *paintings* reveal his mastery over *chiaroscuro* and his fine study of *anatomy*. His love of textural details results in the authentic feeling for *drapery*, the hat and staff carried by the pilgrim, and the lamp carried by the lady. He was consummate in using *watercolours* as his principal *medium* in his *figurative* and *landscape paintings*, and known as a master *painter* of *portraits* with the source of *light* effect in his works. Refer Illustration–*Accidental Light*.

Haldar, Asit K. (1890–1964) b. Kolkata. This pioneer of the Bengal Renaissance was not only a grandnephew of the Tagore family but was also one of the earliest disciples of *Abanindranath Tagore*. At an early age, he displayed interest in the "Pat" *painting* practised by village craftsmen and hence was sent to the Kolkata GSA. While still a student *Nandalal Bose* and *K. Venkatappa*, decorated the Shamiana (large tent) erected in Kolkata to welcome King George V. Most of his large *paintings* during this period were like *murals*, done in the *fresco technique*; he later formed the nucleus of *KB Santiniketan* and became its Principal; During his 12 years there, he both designed the sets and acted in most of Tagore's plays; he introduced Alpana, a traditional floor decoration in the curriculum; Later he was the Principal at the Maharaja's School of Arts Jaipur and was the first Indian to be appointed Principal of the GSA Lucknow; he also illustrated a limited addition of "Gitanjali" and other works by *Rabindranath Tagore*.

He was influenced to a great degree by ancient literature, *mythology* and history. The exacting *copies* of the *frescoes* at *Ajanta*, Bagh and Jogimara that he executed for the Archaeological Dept. fascinated him, though he was already working in a similar *style* well before he saw these *paintings*. "APSARA" is a suitable example of this similarity in *style*. His European sojourn in 1923, merely served to entrench his *style* firmly as an *artist* of the East. He did not favour *drawing images* just from *visual* observance nor did he like meaningless *forms* and *abstract sketches*. His *paintings* are drawn from his rich, creative imagination. While illustrating Omar Khayyam's verses, Asit K. Haldar realized the spirit of the poet and translated this into a *pictorial* expression with great clarity of vision and intuition. His *art* is based on the *narrative*, albeit with a greater "inner" meaning. *Rabindranath Tagore* himself was inspired to compose his poems by Asit K. Haldar's sensitive *brush drawings* of village life, in which he immortalized the Santhals, their vibrant dances and simple beauty. Asit K. Haldar had experienced with various *mediums* including *oil*, *tempera*, *watercolours*, and lacquer *painting* on *wood*. He had also studied *sculpture*, making a *portrait* plaque of *Rabindranath Tagore* in 1927.

Apart from this, he was also a composer of songs, poetry, playlets and essays on *art* and philosophy. He had translated several SANSKRIT *classics* into Bengali. He was also the first Indian *artist* to be elected Fellow of the Royal Society of Arts London, and his *paintings* are represented in Rothenstein London and V&A, many other *museums*, galleries and pvt. collections in India and abroad. Several of his works have been recently auctioned at Heart New Delhi and Osian's Mumbai. A "Haldar Hall" containing a large collection of his *paintings* was opened at the Allahabad Museum in 1938. In 1958, an auditorium was newly built and dedicated to him at the GCAC Lucknow.

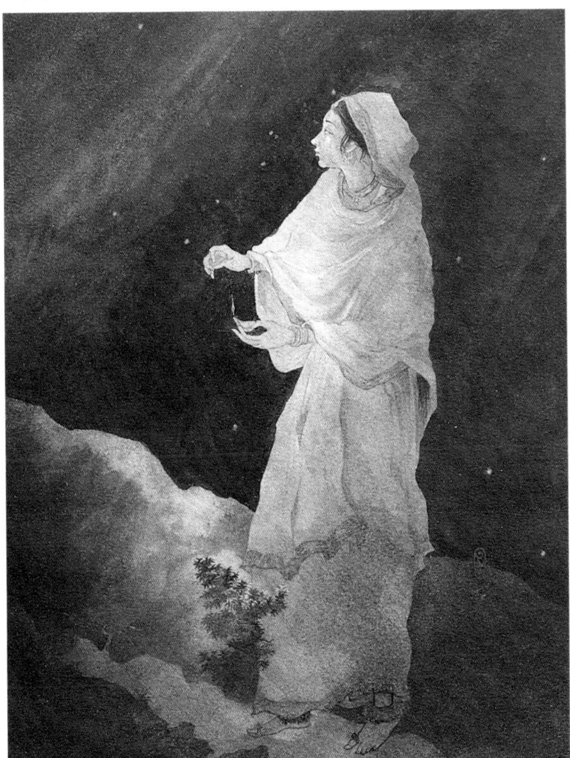

Haldar, Asit K.: "Lipika", *Watercolour* & *wash* on *paper*, 32.2x18 cm.

Half-tone The word refers to all the intermediary *tones* between the lightest and the darkest shades in *colour* without a visible break. It is used in reference to printing, *painting*, *drawing*, *computer art* and photography. Refer *Collotype*, *Modern Review*, *Prabasi*, *Tonal Values*; Illustration–GANGA.

Halo Refer *Aureole*, MANDORLA.

Haloi, Ganesh (1936–) b. Jamalpur, Bangladesh. Education: Dip. GCAC Kolkata; Archaeological Survey of India at *Ajanta* Caves. Solos: *AFA* & *CIMA* Kolkata, *JAG*, *GE*, *CKAG*. Group participations: *BAAC* & *CIMA* Kolkata, *NGMA* New Delhi, *G88*, *SCA*, *GG*, *AIFACS*, *CHAG*; International: Melbourne, Dhaka, Hong Kong, Japan, GBP. *Auctions*: Heart Mumbai & New Delhi. Awards: Seven Silver Medals Calcutta University Institute, 7 Gold Medals *AFA* Kolkata, 1991 Shriromani Prashashar, 1996 Children Best Choice Award for his book "Frogs & Snakes" New Delhi. Member: *SCA*. Commissions: Two *mosaic murals* Jamshedpur, Tripura. Appointments: Later became lecturer; Reader at Alma Mater Kolkata & visiting Prof. at *KB Santiniketan*. Publications: *Paintings* reproduced in "Landmarks of Western Art, Oriental Word" published by Paul Hamlyn London; Souvenir of the 13th Asian Advertising Congress New Delhi; Research & published on "Ajanta, its Technique & Execution" Journal; Two documentary films have been on him, for Kolkata Doordarshan & Govt. of WB for State Archives. Collections: *LKA* & *BAAC* Kolkata, *NGMA* New Delhi, *Roopankar*; International: Singapore, Japan, pvt. & public.

Ganesh Haloi creates a *pictorial space* in which the plastic *content* represents his experience of *visual* reality. The elements in his earlier *landscapes* were rivers, paddy fields, villages next to lush dark forests. His abstraction is strongly charged with *Realism*. There are two specific *styles* of abstraction in Ganesh Haloi's work. In some, it is the sharp-edged geometric *forms* and shapes and in others it is *paint* in graded *shades* and *tones* and textured *passages* of *abstract* or semantic *content*.

In both cases the surface is strategically strewn with marks or tiny dashes of *colour*, broad or bristly *brush* marks, coloured dots or triangles or rectangles, serrated shapes and curly or spiral streaks. At times he scatters his signature all over the *canvas* in the *manner* of musical notes. These marks function as Ganesh Haloi's system of hieroglyphs signifying movement, sound, sensation and emotion. His *palatte* includes *shades* of vibrant greens, cool blues, grays and warm yellow ochres and oranges. His preference for *gouache* is well known.

He lives and works in Kolkata.

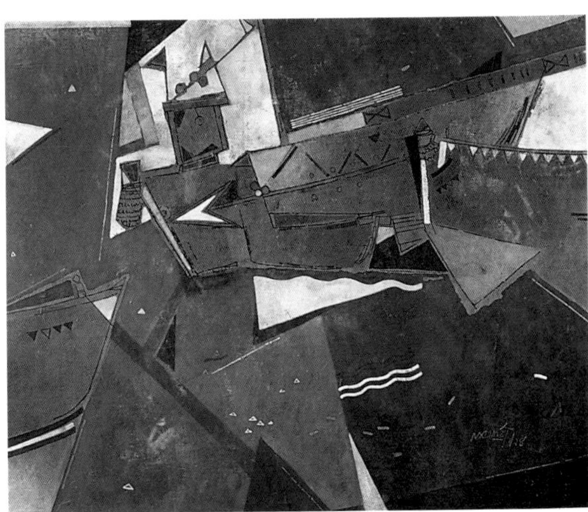

Haloi, Ganesh: "Untitled", *Gouache*, 1994, 75x65 cm.

Hamza-Namah (Or the Dastaan-E-Amir Hamza) relating the adventures of Prince Hamza, an uncle of the Prophet Muhammed, in *epic* form. It was one of the first books to be illustrated at the court of Humayun and was completed during Akbar's reign. It took over 15 years to complete and comprised over 1400 *paintings* bound together in *folios* of 100 each. The *paintings* were large, when compared to the rest of the *Mughal miniatures*, being 22 x 28" in *size*. They were painted on cotton rather than *paper* and have a strong Persian flavour, being painted by Mir Sayyid Ali and Abd-us-Samad along with their Indian assistants. The *compositions* are intricate and full of mosaic-like *colour* and movement. Refer *Mughal miniatures*.

Hand Gestures Refer MUDRAS.

Handmade Paper *Paper*, which is made by hand, as opposed to machine-made *paper*. True *paper* was invented by the Chinese in the early part of the 1st millennium. It was a thin felted material formed on flat, porous *moulds* made up of a mixture of vegetable fibres, rags and textiles. In India, *paper* making was common by the 11th century, *paper* replacing *palm leaf* (Talipot) as the material used for *manuscripts*. By the 16th century, *paper* was being extensively produced in India, each quality being identified by its place of manufacture. Thus Daulatabadi came from Daulatabad and Nizamshahi from Nizamabad. It was also classified according to the material from which it was made, that is, Sanni from flax, Mahajal from old fishing nets and Nukhayyar meaning watered *paper*. Other materials from which *paper* was made were bamboo, jute, rice, straw and silk waste. To make the smooth surface, *paper* was burnished by being dipped into a solution of *alum* and allowed to become partly dry, after which it was rubbed with an agate burnisher. Another variation is *oil paper* which is translucent and *waterproof* as it is prepared by soaking *paper* in *oil*.

Today, handmade paper is the artistic option to machine produced *paper*. It is identifiable by its "Deckle Edge"–the uneven natural edge of *paper* when it is lifted from the deckle or *frame*. The *texture* of handmade paper can vary with the type of materials used as also the net stretched over the *frame*. Refer *Paper-Pulp*, *Casting*, *Dry Brush Painting*, *Waterproof*, *Watercolours*, *Aditya Basak*, *Ved Pal Sharma*, *V. Viswanadhan*, *Yusuf*.

Handling The synonym of facture, it refers to the actual execution of the work. The characteristic in the work of *art* is highly personal with the expressionistic brushstrokes or use of knotted hemp fibres or any technical skill or method used by the *artist*. Refer *Distortion*, *Broad Handling*, *Detailed Work*, *Muralidhar R. Achrekar*, *K.M. Adimoolam*, *Narayan S. Bendre*, *Jogen Chowdhury*; Illustrations–*Atul Dodiya*, *Gajanan Narayan Jadhav*, *Madhav Satwalekar*, *Narayan R. Sardesai*, *Debi Prasad RoyChowdhury*, *Manchershaw F. Pithawalla*, *Laxman Pai*, *Mrinalini Mukherjee*, *Sailoz Mookerjea*.

Hansa, Hamsa=swan, goose. In Hindu *mythology*, the bird is BRAHMA's and SARASVATI's VAHANA. It also appears in *temple architecture* and *painting*. The Hansa-Patti is the top-most band on the Vesara temple (Halebid-Belur), platforms, *symbolic* of the poetic mind, soaring high in the sky. The birds appear in pairs in several Kangra *paintings* marked by the Shringara RASA. In *modern* times *artists* like *Badri Narayan* and *Mrinalini Mukherjee* have often used the swan in their works.

Hanuman The monkey *god*, son of Pavana–the wind *god*, Hanuman was one of RAMA's most faithful devotees. He possessed the faculty of flight and could assume a gigantic *form*, with yellow fur and a red face. His tail was long and his voice was as loud as thunder. RAVANA's Rakshashas (*demons*) set his tail alight but Hanuman used it to set fire to the entire city of Lanka. He is a celibate *god* and a master of all the Shastras, sacred books including the *fine arts*, sciences, philosophy and grammar. He has inspired *artists* not only from India, but from other Asian countries as well, being pictorially depicted in *painting*, *stone*, *bronze*, *wood carving*, *masks* and *leather* puppets. He is worshipped by most cults, Vedic, TANTRIC, Shaivite, Vaishnavite and Shakta. Refer *Mask*, *Sukumar Bhattacharjee*.

Happening An apparently impromptu performance, action or series of events, sometimes including the spectator as well. The Happening was developed in the 1950s and 1960s as an *avant-garde art form*. At times it does not include an actual work of *art*, but is considered to be an *art* work by itself. Later, happenings could be repeated, but the only record of these works are through still *photographs* and video. The Dadaists were the first to exploit this *technique*, but the *term* "happening" only came to be used in the USA in the post-World War II period; in India, this *art form* began to be experimented with in the 1990s. Refer *Krishnamachari Bose*, *Vivan Sundaram*.

HARA Refer ABHUSHANA, *Dravidan Style*, *Ornaments*.

Harappa An ancient Indian city which flourished in the 3rd millennium BC. It was discovered along with *Mohenjo Daro* along the banks of the Indus River in PUJ in 1924. It was excavated by Madho Sarup Vats, who discovered that several cities lay buried one beneath the other, pointing to countless rebuilding, after the havoc caused by the annual flooding of the Indus. Several *artefacts* unearthed at both sites point to an advanced civilization with trade and communication flourishing with the contemporaneous civilization in Mesopotamia. The most striking feature of the excavated site is the perfection of town planning. The houses, the roads and all public buildings appeared to have been constructed according to a master plan; the sanitation facilities were also extraordinary for that era.

At present, Harappa is a small village near the old bed of the river Ravi (in *modern* Pakistan); the excavations so far have exposed the citadel and areas of the upper city. To the north of the citadel ran a double row of workmen's dwellings with 16 furnaces (probably used for *metal* working). Further north lay 18 brick platforms probably used for pounding grain from the nearby granaries. This granary complex reinforces the view that these people were primarily agriculturists. Sculptural remains include a few statues made of steatite, alabaster and limestone as also *terracotta*. Numerous seals were also found. Jewellery was found in abundance; *gold*, *silver*, jade and faience beads, necklaces, earrings and pendants were very common. *Pottery* was an advanced *art* in *Indus Valley Civilization* with beautiful *motifs* adorning pots made in a variety of shapes. Refer *Cast*, *Cire Perdue*, *Sand Moulding*, *Visual*.

Hardboard A thin, dense board made from shredded *wood* fibres, compressed under heat. Slightly flexible, hardboard is smooth on one side and textured on the other, it is more resistant to warping due to dampness. It is often used by *modern artists* working in *oil* or *acrylic* as a substitute for *canvas*. Refer *Canvas Board*; Illustration–*Manishi Dey*.

Hard-Edge Painting A *term* coined in the 1950s to describe certain *abstract* works in *painting*, having razor-sharp edges and flat colouring defining clear cut *forms*. American *artist* Ellsworth Kelly was called the "father" of hard-edge painting. *V. Viswanadhan*, whose works are similar to this *style* and certain neo-tantric works by *Ghulam Rasool Santosh*, *K.V. Haridasan* and *Biren De* share similar characteristics. Refer *Op or Optical Art*, *Tantra Art*, *Shobha Broota*, *Roop Chand*; Illustration–*K.V. Haridasan*.

Hard Ground Refer *Printmaking*, *Ground*, *Soft Ground*.

Haridasan, K.V. (1937–) b. Cannanore Dist., Kerala. Education: Grad. Madras University, Dip. in *painting GCAC* Chennai, National Culture Scholarhip Govt of India, Trained in *fresco painting Banasthali Vidyapith* RAJ. Solos: FA. Society Kolkata, *LKA* New Delhi, British Council Chennai, "Brahma-sutra" Series Kala Peetom Cochin, *JAG*, TKS. Group participations: *LKA* New Delhi, Cholamandal Artists Group; International: Paris *Biennale*, New Tantra Exhibition Germany, Neo-Tantra Exhibition Festival of India California, Asian *Biennale* at Bangladesh, Festival of India Exhibition Moscow. *Art* camps: *LKA* New Delhi & Chennai, Tamil University Thanjavur, *Nag Foundation* Pune, Academi's of Kerala, Kashmir & Chennai, International Tapestry weaving camp Kozhikode (Calicut) & Chennai. *Auctions*: Osian's Mumbai. Awards: *LKA* Chennai, Gold Medal *LKA* Kerala. Fellowship: Senior Fellowship Dept. of Culture HRD Ministry. Member & Jury: *LKA* New Delhi. Appointments: Prof. & HoD of *painting* & later Principal of the *CFA* Thiruvananthapuram. Publications: A book "Intimations" on *art* since three decades from 1967 to his 1997 "Yantra" & "Brahma-sutra" series in Mumbai; Edited "Art Trends" the *art* magazine of the Progressive Painters Association, Cholamandal; Produced a telefilm on "Modern Art" Hyderabad. Collections: *NGMA* New Delhi, *LKA* New Delhi, Hyderabad & Bangalore, *Nag Foundation* Pune, *CTAG*.

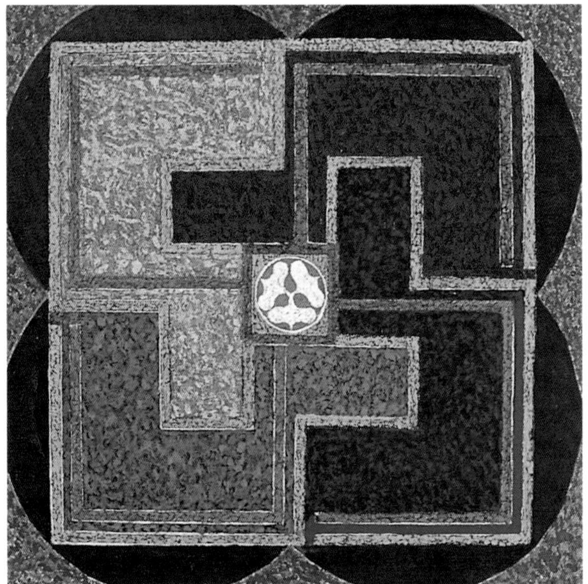

Haridasan, K.V.: "Brahma-sutra", *Hard-Edge Painting*, *Oil Colour*, 1994, 60x60 cm.

K.V. Haridasan is the pioneer of neo-Tantric *art* in India. His early *paintings* were *figurative landscapes* with predominantly linear characteristics. In 1967, he began practising YOGA, which was to influence him in his later work; including the "YANTRA" and the "Bija Yantra" series. The "Brahma-sutra" series on which he has been working for the past 20 years, seem inspired by the Advaitic vision of Shankaracharya and the Saiva-Shakti cult. His *paintings*, though *abstract*, have *colours*, *gradations* of yellow, red, blue and green. Some of his geometric *motifs* are inspired by Kolam (a type of *flora & fauna painting*) and his metaphors are drawn from the psyche of Indian theology. The *motifs* are usually symmetric with concentric ovals and floral *motifs*.

K.V. Haridasan lives and works in Chennai.

Hariram, V. (1948–) b. Alwaye, India. Education: Grad. University of Mysore, Dip. in *FA*. Kalamandir School of Art Bangalore, Studied in *printmaking graphic* workshop *LKA* Chennai. Solos: *LKA* Chennai, *GK*, *VEAG*, *AIFACS*, *JAG*; International: Botswana, UK. Group participations: National Exhibition New Delhi, Regional Centre *LKA* Chennai, Progressive Painters *COAG*, *CKP*, *CYAG*; International: Royal Institute London, others in USA, Germany, Spain; Travelling shows in Japan, France. *Art* camps: South Region Graphic *LKA* Chennai; International: Tapestry Weaving Germany. Awards: International *Biennale* China, *Triennale* small *prints* Romania. Member: *Cholamandal*. Commissions: *Paintings* Visakhapatnam, Cochin. Collections: *LKA* Chennai, KAR *LKA* Bangalore, *NGMA* New Delhi, *VEAG*, *COAG*; International: Turkey, Italy, Botswana, USA, UK.

His early works were intensely cerebral being based at times on *classical* literature with a bright *palette* of *colours* and a natural tendency toward textural effects. He rarely made use of *perspective* and preserved the planes of flat decorative surface with the *rhythm* of *colour* and *line* suggesting both *space* and movement. V. Hariram has been inspired by *nature*, especially by the effect of *light* on the broad *masses* of trees and branches. In "Untitled 94", the feeling is of near anthropomorphic *forms* dutifully worshipping the tree with its forked branches itself resembling the upraised arms of some tribal deity. His recent works have undergone a drastic change, being overwhelmingly geometric in structure. Houses and windows are still recognizable but the *images* are subdued in the context of a larger reality.

V. Hariram resides and works at *Cholamandal*.

Hari-vamsa, Harivansa An *epic* poem an addition to the MAHABHARATA, about the life and *times* of KRISHNA and his family, the eight incarnations of VISHNU. Incidents from the poem have been illustrated in *Rajasthani miniature paintings*.

Harmony A *term* used in *art* to refer to harmony of *colours*, harmony of *forms*–the usual meaning being a *balance* or equilibrium of *forms*, shapes, *textures* and *colours* to produce a visually pleasing work of *art*. Refer *All-over, Analogous Colours, Tone, Value, Rajendra Dhawan, Benode Behari Mukherjee, L. Munuswamy, Bhawani S. Sharma, Abanindranath Tagore*; Illustrations–*Nandalal Bose, Shiavax Chavda, Hemendranath Mazumdar, Nagesh Bhimrao Sabannavar, Jehangir Sabavala*.

Hatching A method to create *tones* or *shades* by means of *drawing* or incising a series of parallel *lines* or crisscrossed *lines*. It is commonly used in *pencil drawings* or in *printmaking*, notably *dry-point, etching, lithography*. e.g., *Laxma Goud*. Refer *All-over, Burr, Cross-Hatching, Drawing Inks, Line Engraving, Lithography, Metal Cut, Metal Block, Shade, Sketch, Mansing L. Chhara, Dhruva Mistry, Natver Mistry, Ashit Paul, Yagneshwar Kalyanji Shukla, Anupam Sud*.

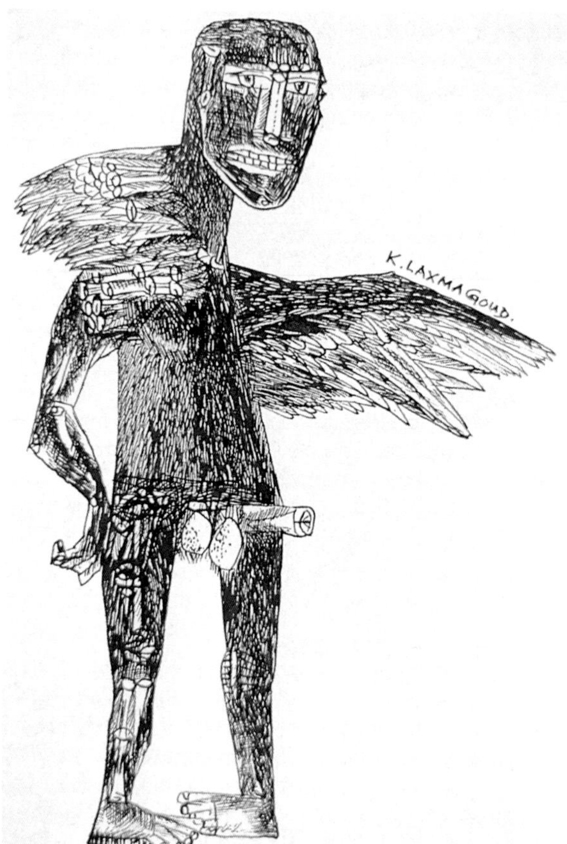

Hatching: *Laxma Goud, Pen & India Ink Drawing* on *Handmade paper*, 1983, 10x15 cm.

Hazra, Paresh C. (1952–) b. Midnapore, WB. Education: Dip. GCA Kolkata, Post-Grad. Dip. Teacher of *Art*. Solos: *CKP, CKAG, GK, JAG*, IIC. Group participations: *LKA* New Delhi, *AFA, BAAC, LKA* & Calcutta Art Fair Kolkata, *ISOA*; International: Hongkong, Nepal, London, Gallery Asiana New York, Indian Heritage Washington DC. *Art* workshop: Krishnamurthy Foundation Brooke Wood UK. Awards: *BAAC &* Silver Medal GCA Kolkata, *ISOA*. Appointments: *Art* teacher Military School Bangalore. Collections: Central *LKA* & *NGMA* New Delhi, Archaeological Museum of KAR.

Paresh C. Hazra began as a *painter* in the *tradition* of the *Bengal School* with his works of the early 80s clearly revealing the seminal influences of *Nandalal Bose* and *Abanindranath Tagore*. He evolved from the fine delicate *lines* of these works to the *wash technique* of the late 80s by adopting a new sturdiness of approach. He began working with *terracotta*, which experience drew him towards the folk *idiom*. He later began using *egg-tempera*, a *medium* that was to add to the rustic, tribal feeling. His *motifs* and using *collage, texture* and *tactile* sensations thus play an important role in his works.

Paresh C. Hazra lives and works in Bangalore.

Hebbar, K.K. (1912–1996) b. Kattingeri, KAR. Education: Formal training in *art NKM*, Dip. in *drawing* & *painting JJSA*; Study tour of Europe & course in *painting* at

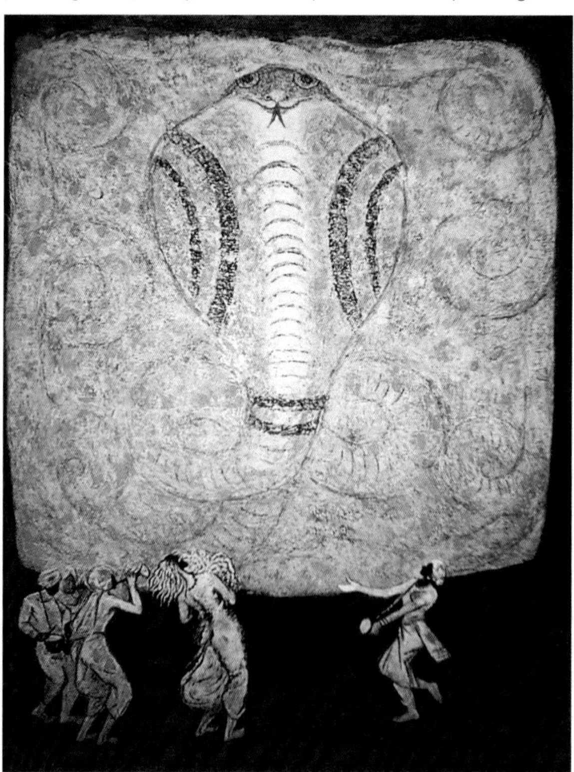

Hebbar, K.K.: "Naga Mandala", *Oil* on *Canvas*, 1986, 102x122 cm.

the Academy Julien Paris. Solos: Sponsored to Kolkata, New Delhi, Hyderabad & Bangalore, *AIFACS*; International: London, Berlin, Basel, Paris, New York, Sydney. Retrospective: by *LKA* Mysore 1969; "A Tribute" *JAG* 1997, A camp in his name at *VEAG* 1997. Group participations: *AFA* Kolkata, National Exhibition & *LKA* New Delhi, *Triennale* India, *BAS*, *ASI*; International: Salon de May Paris, *Biennale* Sao Paulo Brazil, Venice & Tokyo. *Auctions*: Asprey's, HelpAge Mumbai, *JAG*; Chester & Davida Herwitz's Collection & Sotheby's New York. Awards: Accolades, Padma Shri, Padma Bhushan 1989, MAHA Gaurav Puraskar 1990, Soviet Land Nehru Award, Gold Medal *BAS*, *LKA* KAR. Member, Chairman & President: *Artists' Centre* Mumbai, KAR *LKA*, Central LKA New Delhi, *ASI*, *BAS*. Appointments: *Art* teacher *JJSA*. Publications: Several books & articles published on him are the "Voyage in Images", the Singing Line, An "Artist's Quest" & Lalit Kala Monograph "Hebbar". Collections: *NGMA* & *LKA* New Delhi, *BAAC* & *AFA* Kolkata, TIFR, *PWM*, *BB*; International: Dresden Gallery Germany, Masanori Taluvoka collection in Japan, Museum of Modern Art Paris, Govt. Museum Poland, Commonwealth collection Australia & pvt.

K.K. Hebbar, aimed to freely express his emotional state by means of *line* and *colour*. Although he was sometimes termed a *painter* of social *themes*, K.K. Hebbar's *colours* uplift even the most morbid of subjects. Both *form* and *content* coexist harmoniously in his works. Earlier, he used to paint *landscapes* and *figure compositions* in the accepted academic *style*. After coming into contact with *miniature paintings*, traditional *murals* and seeing their effect on *Amrita Sher-Gil*, K.K. Hebbar's *style* evolved from the academic to a bold stylization, especially after a tour of South India. One of the most famous *paintings* of this period is the "Cattle Mart" now in the collection of the *JJSA*. Here the flat *figures* are simplified, outlined and arranged in planar *perspective*.

After his return from Europe, he studied Kathak (an Indian dance *form*) in order to understand *rhythm* and portray it with grace in his *drawings* and *paintings*. Indian music also had a great influence on him. His *drawings*, earning the sobriquet "Singing Lines" were drawn freely with his *pen*, eliminating detail and stressing *rhythm* aspect. His subjects were diverse, temple *sculptures*, the Yakshagana (women) performers, musicians and dancers as well as his favourite social *themes*. However, it is *colour*, bright or diffused, definite or *polychromatic*, which plays the main role in his *paintings*.

The textural quality is broken with *overlapping* strokes. His later *paintings* veered towards the *abstract*, with just that touch of *Realism* and a *"spiritual"* quality.

Heroic Any *figure* in *painting* or *sculpture*, who is depicted as a hero; over-dramatic, and larger than *life-size* is termed to be heroic in scale. According to Indian *mythology*, VISHNU Viswarappa is usually shown in this scale as is Bahubali or Gomateswara (minor deities) Sravanabelagola. Refer *Epic*, *History Painting*, *Monumental*, *Neo-Classicism*, RASA, *Mahadev V. Dhurandhar*, *Dhruva Mistry*, *Brahman Vinayakrao Wagh*.

Hieratic Scaling The word is used in reference to the mismatched *proportion* or scale of some *forms* in relation to others, especially in *paintings* or *sculptures* of the earlier period. The BODHISATTVA Padmapani for example in cave 1 at *Ajanta* is massive in *composition* with the diminutive lady and young boy next to him. This serves to show his importance in relation to them. At times skin *colour* (yellow as against brown) is used to differentiate between primary and secondary characters. This is known as hieratic scaling. Refer *Byzantine Art*, *Mass*.

Highlight The most prominent part of a *composition* to which the *artist* intends to draw viewer's attention. e.g., the glint of *light* in the eye or the sheen on the tip of the nose in case of *portraits* and the reflected light on *still life* objects, which normally represents lightest *colour* in the work. Refer *Background*, *Bengal Revivalism*, *Bengal School*, *Bundi*, *Mewar*, *Mewar Kalam*, *Mewar School*, *Mewar Miniatures*, *Mezzotint*, *Nude*, *Still Life*, *Wash (Technique)*, *Watercolours*, *Atul Bose*, *Roop Chand*, *Rekha Krishnan*, *S. Krishnappa*, *G. Reghu*, *Shekhar Roy*, *S.K. Sahni*, *Subhogendra Tagore*. Illustrations–*Portrait*, *Dinanath Pathy*, *Manchershaw F. Pithawalla*, *Jehangir Sabavala*, *Paramjit Singh*, *Rameshwar Singh*.

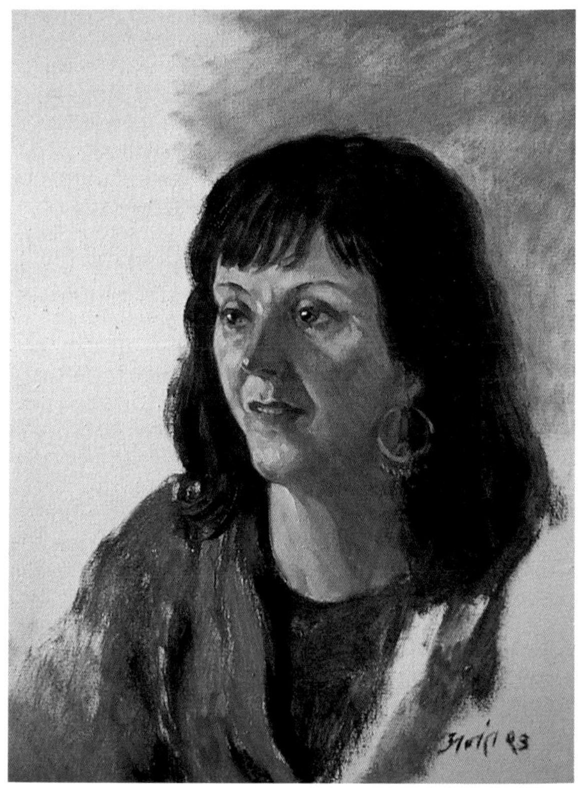

Highlight: *Anant M. Bowlekar*, "Portrait", 1993.

High Relief It is full *relief* where the *forms* are often modeled in the full round but remain attached to the *background*, though some portions may be entirely free from the *background* and the base. Wall *sculptures* of *Ajanta*,

Ellora, *Mahabalipuram*, *Khajuraho* and other ancient temples are classic examples of high relief. In contemporary times *Satish Gujral* has used high-relief in his burnt *wood* and *mixed media collages*. Refer *Depth*, *Dimension*, *Elephanta*, *Ellora*, *Figuration*, *Figurative*, *Found Object*, *Fretwork*, *Gandharan Art*, *Gupta*; Illustration–*Shanti Dave*, *Piraji Sagara*.

Hinduism The traditional religious faith and practice of the majority of the Indian sub-continent. Hinduism is based on the four VEDAS: the Rig, Sama, Yajur and the Atharva; the UPANISHADS and the Brahmanas (they are a series of books containing commentaries on the ancient VEDAS and Upanishadic texts). Hinduism, known for its holy trinity, BRAHMA (the Creator), VISHNU (the Preserver) and SHIVA (the Destroyer), developed from the earlier Vedic religion with *gods* merging and losing their fixed identity. It is a pantheistic religion with several *gods* and goddesses associated with various aspects, e.g. GANESHA, the elephant-headed *god* is considered to be the bestower of success. The *gods* of contemporary Hinduism are principally VISHNU and SHIVA and their followers are called Vaishnavites and Shaivites respectively. VISHNU is benevolent and reappears on earth in successive incarnations or AVATARS. SHIVA variously signifies *creation* and destruction. He is also the epitome of sexuality and is associated with KALI.

Several literary works and *epics* are devoted to these *gods* and these stories and myths have been illustrated in several *murals* and miniatures. Hindu worship is centred in temples–various temples being dedicated to different *gods* and identified by the AYUDHAS above the SHIKHARA. Hinduism, especially from the *time* of the Brahmanas also preaches the distinction of exclusive casteism. Refer AVATARA, AHIMSA, *Architecture*, ATMA, *Attribute*, BHAKTI, BRAHMA, DASAVATARA, *Ellora*, *Icon*, KARMA, MATRIKAS, MOKSHA, RIGVEDA, *Thanjavur (Tanjore) Paintings*, YAKSHI, YAKSHINI.

History Painting As a subject, history painting was considered by 17th- and 18th-century European theorists, to be the highest and noblest *art form*. In India history painting included scenes from ancient *classical* history and *mythology*. The people, historical costumes, e.g. in battle or attending an *heroic* event, would be easily recognizable to the spectator and were represented in an grand Indian *manner* often on a grand scale. Even *paintings* depicting more recent events invariably showed people wearing *classical* dress. This was accepted as a viable *art form* particularly by the *academies*. These *paintings* were painted in the traditional, *classical* or romantic *style*, especially in *terms* of the *composition*, thus conforming to the fashion and taste of the *times*. The following *painters* have painted historical paintings subjects in their earlier works, e.g. *Baburao Painter*, *Mahadev V. Dhurandhar*, *Ksihtendranath Mazumdar*. Several *wood cuts* and oleography works of the 19th and 20th century were also based on this subject. Refer "Glimpses of Evolution of Indian Art", page 14.

Hoarding Also known as bill-boards or sign-boards, hoardings are advertising instruments strategically placed to attract maximum attention. The *art* of *painting* hoardings is a commercial one with the message being short and simple. *Cinema* hoardings, especially in the South of India with massive cut-outs of stars and actors are especially popular as are cut-outs of politicians during election time. *Maqbool Fida Husain* developed his freehand *style* of *painting monumental canvases* from his earlier foray into *painting* hoardings. Refer *Mass*, *Poster*, *Chetan Arya*, *Chandra Bhattacharjee*, *Chittaprasad*, *Ishwari Rawal*.

Holi Holi is a popular Indian festival dedicated to KRISHNA and GOPIS associated with the burning of Holika Rakshasi, Prahlad's tormenter and Hiranyakashipu's (*demon*) sister. It is celebrated in the month of Phalgun (February–March). Bonfires are lit in the evening on the eve of Holi of the previous day (celebrating both the burning of Holika and the liberation of the world from Hiranyakashipu's tyranny by NARASIMHA, one of the AVATARS of VISHNU). The next day, people celebrate by spraying vermilion-coloured powder (Gulal) and water on each other. It is also *symbolic* of love-play and thus associated with the Shringara RASA. Holi is depicted in certain *Pahari* and *Rajasthani miniature paintings* as part of the BARAMASA (the 12 months) as it clearly denotes Phalgun. Refer BAISAKH, VAISHAKH, RITU, *Foreshortening*, GOPA, GOPI, GOPIKA, *Spiritual*, *Warm Colours*.

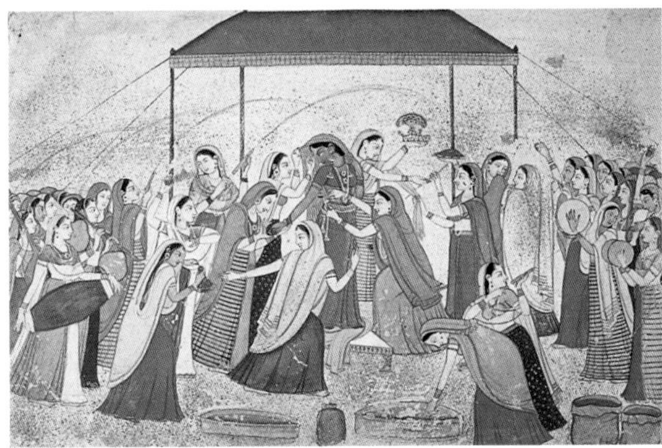

Holi: "Krishna playing Holi", Guler-Kangra.

Hooja, Usha Rani (1923–) b. Delhi. Education: Studied *sculpture* Polytechnic London. Solos: Jaipur, New Delhi. Group participations: National Exhibition *LKA*, *Sculptors* Forum & International Exhibition of Women Artists New Delhi. Awards: *Sculptors Forum* New Delhi, RAJ *LKA*, RAJ Shree Award, Maharana Sajjan Singh Award *Mewar*, *AIFACS*. Member: Fellow of *LKA* RAJ. Commissions: Public commissions in New Delhi, Jaipur, Udaipur; International: Washington. Publications: New Delhi TV, Jaipur Doordarshan; Newspapers & Magazines. Collections: Udaipur, Jaipur, *NGMA* New Delhi, Tata Mumbai & pvt.

Usha Rani Hooja has explored several *mediums* in *sculpture* over the past 50 years. Her early *sculptures* have the organic and undulating character of H. Moore, understandable because she was trained in England. Her *reliefs* of the same period however reveal her Indian roots, in the use of simple yet decorative *outlines* and the indigenous *nature* of the subject. The next decade saw her adopting a *realistic* yet stylized approach. These solid *bronze* and *wood sculptures* gave way to the airy *outlines* of "Chetak" made of scrap *metal*. This drawing-like *sculpture* is placed in a park in Washington. The later works show an *eclectic* amalgamation of *styles*, from the decorative "Puppet" in *fibreglass* to the *abstract* and scattered shapes in the *bronze* "Structure in Space". She has dabbled in poetry as well.

Usha Rani Hooja lives in Jaipur.

Hore, Reba (1926–) b. India. Education: Grad. in *FA*. *GCAC* Kolkata. Solos: Over 15 Kolkata, *Santiniketan*, Mumbai 2001 *Art Heritage* New Delhi. Group shows with her husband *Somnath Hore*. Group participations: National & International 25 years of Indian Art, Commonwealth Art Today London, *Biennale*, Sao Paulo. Awards: National *LKA* New Delhi for *painting*. Appointments: Taught *art* to children in Kolkata. Collections: *LKA* & *Art Heritage* New Delhi, *BAAC* & *CIMA* Kolkata, PUJ Museum, pvt. national & international.

Reba Hore started *painting* in *oils*, did resist *drawing* and *collages* while in Delhi with her husband. However, she really came into her own upon returning to *Santiniketan*. Reflecting strong political and social influence, she also developed a sensitivity towards children, animals and people. This reflected strongly in her *oils*, works in *wax* and egg *emulsions* and in the sensitively executed faces of her *terracotta* works. Refer *Egg-oil emulsion*.

Hore, Somnath (1921–) b. Chittagong, Bangladesh. Education: Dip. in *FA*. *GSAC* Kolkata. Solos: New Delhi, Kolkata. Retrospective: *Art Heritage* New Delhi. Group shows: Poland, Yugoslavia & Bulgaria. Group participations: National & International *Triennale*, *NGMA*, Kunika Chemould & National *LKA* New Delhi, *CIMA* Kolkata, The Window Mumbai; International: *Graphic Biennale* in Lugano, Venice, Sao Paulo & Poland, Contemporary Indian Painting from Chester David Herwitz USA. *Auctions*: Sotheby's, Heart & Osian's India. Awards: National Exhibition. Member: *SCA*, General Council of *LKA* Kolkata. Appointments: HoD—*Graphic Art VBU*, Incharge *Graphic* section—*College of Art* New Delhi, Lecturer GCA&D Kolkata, Visiting Prof. *MSU*, *KB Santiniketan*. Collections: *NGMA*, *LKA*, Art Heritage, Ministry of Education & Bahai Museum New Delhi.

His Bengal famine *sketches* of skeletal human beings and animals became Somnath Hore's leitmotif, recurring constantly, either in *abstract* or realist *form*, throughout his career. He constantly experimented with *printmaking*, trying out new *techniques* and textural qualities. His early *prints* were *portraits* and group studies of peasant women, children and resistance fighters. Here he used the *technique* of cutting and *engraving* to create a rich *chiaroscuro* of *black* and *white* in his *prints*. He also achieved mastery over, the *wood cut*, *wood engraving*, *linocut* and multi-*colour wood cut*. Later, he learnt the *intaglio technique* in the *etching* and *dry-point media*. After seeing *Krishna N. Reddy's colour* viscosity *prints*, he took to experimenting in this direction. At the same time, he was also devoting his time to *painting*.

He then turned to *lithography*, using such striking *colours* as scarlet and *black*, to indicate flat silhouette-like *figure masses* against a severely minimalistic *background*.

At *Santiniketan*, Somnath Hore concentrated on an ongoing series of near *abstract prints* entitled "Wounds" taken from moulded *cement* matrices. These blind *prints* made out of uncoloured *paper* pulp are made of a few, scattered organic shapes and scars. They suggest suffering and mourning without actually representing it. They are more *tactile* than *visual*, beginning to give sensations of skin and flesh pierced by bullets and knives, and oozing gangrene and pus.

In his 50s, he enlarged the scope of his works by turning to *sculpture*, using the difficult *lost wax process* to *cast* objects in the round. He has used the *technique* of *bronze casting* with its *armatures*, *air vents* and escape pipes to create the skeletal structure of humans and animals with bones and veins covered with sheets of *metal* stretched like skin over them. Most of these *sculptures* were dedicated to freedom fighters of Vietnam. Since then, he has worked on

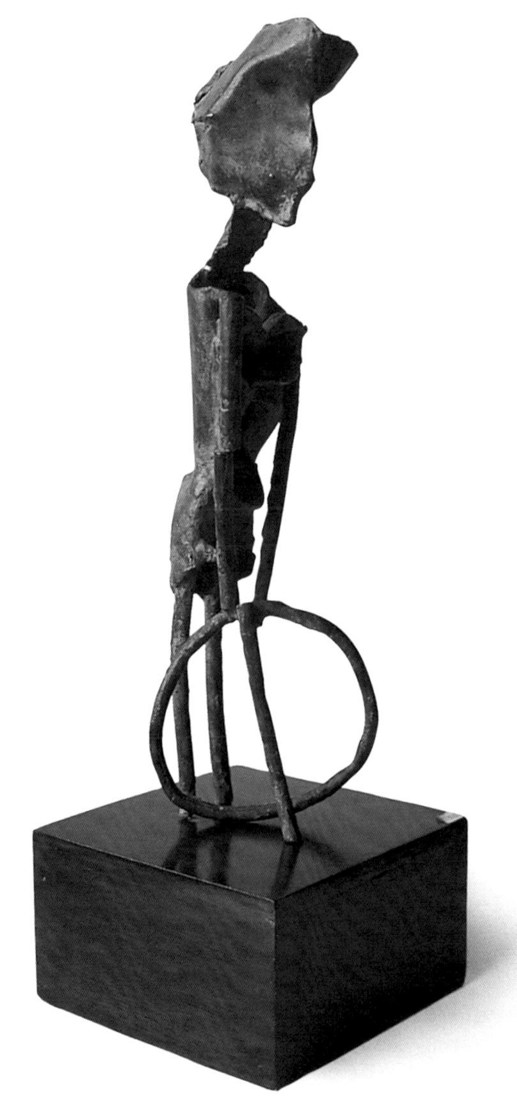

Hore, Somnath: "Boy playing", *Bronze*, 1990, 42x10 cm.

printmaking, *drawing* and *sculpture*, giving objective *form* to conceptual *themes*.

He lives and works at *Santiniketan*.

Horizon The imaginary *line* where the earth and sky appear to meet. This is usually represented pictorially by using linear *perspective* and identifying the *vanishing point*, which is the position on this *line* towards which all parallel *lines* appear to converge. Refer *Abstraction Organic*, *Bundi*, *Landscape*, *Baburao Sadwelkar*, *Laxman Narayan Taskar*; Illustration–*Seascape*.

House of B. Vithal (Mumbai, MAHA). Founded in 1988, with the intention of promoting works by other *artists*. *Laxman Shreshta*, *Sunil Das*, *Maqbool Fida Husain* and *Gopal S. Adivrekar* had displayed their works here. This was in the care of *artists B. Prabha*, *B. Vithal*.

Hoysala (1027–1342). The Hoysalas formed an independent kingdom in Mysore for nearly 250 years, after defeating the Chalukyas in the 11th century. During this short period, they erected over 100 finely decorated temples in the Halebid, Belur area. These temples were carved out of soft greenish-grey soapstone which later hardened on exposure to air. This resulted in temples with elaborately carved *sculptures* and pillars, adopted from *forms* in *metal* work, sandalwood and *ivory carving*. The Chenna-Kesava, Hoysalesvara and the Kesava temples are the best known of these temples built in the *Vesara style*. Refer *Architecture*, *Palm Leaf*.

Hublikar, G.Y. (1941–) b. Hubli, KAR. Education: *NKM*, Dip. in *FA.*, *JJSA*. Solos: Dharwar, Badami, Hubli, Bangalore, Mumbai, Bijapur; International: Berlin, Paris. Group shows: Ravindra Kala-Shetra Bangalore, *VEAG*. Group participations: Mumbai, Hyderabad, Mysore, Vadodara, Chennai; International: Texas. *Art* camps: at Jagmohan Palace by *LKA* Mysore. Member: Committee Member for Selection & Purchase of Art Objects for Govt. Museum in the KAR; Founder President of the Mysore Art Council has exhibited regularly under the aegis of "We Four". Appointments: Worked for the Mumbai Film Industry; Principal of Bijapur School of Art; *Artist* for the Deccan Herald group of newspapers in Bangalore. Collections: Mangalore, Gulbarga, other state *museums* & abroad.

Earlier, his *paintings* were *abstract* in *nature*, but subsequently he veered towards *figuration*. His figural *composition* could be termed semi-realistic with the use of *drapery* to conceal facial features to avoid, as he puts it "being called illustrational." The early *figurative compositions* were inclined to be both sentimental and folk-like, but the later ones are thickly brushed ones with patches of high *key colour*.

He lives and works in Bangalore.

Hue The variety of *colours* in the spectrum or *colour* scale from violet through indigo, blue, green, yellow, orange and red (VIBGYOR) with many hues between them. At least 150 separate hues are discernable to the eye. *K.G. Subramanyan's* work tilts towards earthy hues while *Manjit Bawa's* works are associated with psychedelic hues and *tints*. Refer *Colour Wheel*, *Colour Circle*, *Tempering*, *Tint*, *Shade*, *Shiavax Chavda*, *Seema Ghurayya*, *Jamini Roy*, *Amrita Sher-Gil*, *K.S. Viswambhara*; Illustrations–*Madhukar B. Bhat*, *Tyeb Mehta*, *Surya Prakash*, *Syed Haider Raza*, *Jehangir Sabavala*, *Gulam Mohammed Sheikh*.

Husain, Maqbool Fida (1915–) Pandharpur, MAHA. Education: Studied briefly at Indore School of Art, moved to Mumbai 1937 & joined *JJSA*. Solos: First solo 1950, *Art Heritage* New Delhi, *Tao Art Gallery* Mumbai, *Dhoomimal*, *JAG*, *PUAG*, *ATG*, *GE*, *VAG*, then Kolkata, Ahmedabad, Bangalore & other towns; International: Zurich, Prague, Frankfurt, Tokyo, Rome, Baghdad, Kabul, Sao Paulo, New York, Poland, Czechoslovakia, Geneva, Paris, Boston, Moscow, London, Beirut. Retrospective: Mumbai, New Delhi 1973, *BAAC* Kolkata. Group participations: National *LKA* & *NGMA* New Delhi, *JAG*, *NCAG*, *BB*, later Bangalore, Marvel Art Gallery Ahmedabad; International: *Biennale* Tokyo, Venice & Sao Paulo, 1971 Exhibition as a special invitee along with P. Picasso–Sao Paulo, Indian *Art* Museum of Modern Art Oxford, Hirchhorn Museum & Festival of India Washington DC USA, Gallery Arts Indian Watercolours & Drawing–Chester & David Herwitz Collection in New York. *Auctions*: Heart, Osian's & Bowring's Mumbai, Sotheby's, Heart & Bowring's New Delhi, Bonham's, Christie's & Sotheby's London, Christie's & Sotheby's New York, Christie's Singapore, Hong Kong, South Kensington. Awards: Gold Medal Indore, Fellow *LKA*, National & *LKA* Award New Delhi, Padma Shri, Padma Bhushan & Padma Vibhushan. Member: Founder member *PAG* 1947 Mumbai; Hon. Doctorate BHU & Mysore University; International: Tokyo *Biennale*, International Exhibition Japan, Berlin Film Festival; Nominated Member of Parliament; His own museums–Hyderabad, Husain Sankalana Bangalore, Husain-Doshi Gufa Ahmedabad, Husain ki Sarai Faridabad New Delhi & others. Commissions: *Murals* in major cities in India & abroad. Appointments: Worked on the computer for *Computer Art*; Designed & painted *cinema hoardings*, toys, furniture for children 1937–45. Publications: *Art* & *Cinema* on "Husain" by *LKA* New Delhi, Vakils Mumbai & Harry N. Abrams Incorporated New York, "Story of a Brush" *PUAG*, others in New York & Geneva & articles in newspapers, magazines, newsletters & *art* journals; Film: made over 12 films since 1967 including "Through the Eyes of a Painter"–won Golden Bear Award & "Gaja-gamini". Collections: *NGMA*, *Art Heritage* & *LKA* New Delhi, *NGMA* Mumbai, Kejriwal Gallery Bangalore, TIFR, BARC, *CKP*; International: Masanori Fukuoka & Glenbarra Museum Hemji Japan, Chester & David Herwitez Collection USA, others national and international.

Maqbool Fida Husain migrated to Mumbai in 1937 and began *painting cinema hoardings* to support himself. It was the *monumental* scale and urgency of execution of these *hoardings* that was to influence his subsequent works. Maqbool Fida Husain's *style* is an amalgam of Western *style* and Indian *imagery*, his *brushwork* is spontaneous with a forceful, expressionistic *line* that enlivens the simplified, apparently accidental *motifs*, such as the horse and the *landscape*. He also has a flair for using evocative *colour passages* that "run" in interrupted spurts throughout the *painting*. His *images* are typically Indian, relying on the sensuous grace of traditional Indian *sculpture*, the vibrancy of *folk art* and the *colours* of Indian *miniature painting*. His *themes* range from the village and *pastoral* life and Indian *mythology* in the early days to personalities like Mother Teresa, film actress Madhuri Dixit and goddesses like DURGA, KALI and SARASVATI. Later he began *painting* several *epic*-scale subjects, including the "Theorama" based on the religions of the world, the RAMAYANA and the MAHABHARATA. He has worked with post-modernistic *techniques*, using the computer to create *paintings* and done an *installation* "Svetambari" at the *JAG*. He has also painted large *canvases* in a "Jugalbandi" (duet) with Indian classical musicians. Some of his works have been in the *form* of serigraphs. Maqbool Fida Husain has worked on a wide range of *media*, including *oil* on *canvas*, silk screening, mylar (polyester) paper, *watercolours drawings* using *Chinese ink* and other material. (See illustration on page 155)

Husain, Shamshad (1946–) b. Mumbai, India. Education: Dip. in *painting MSU*; Post-Grad. RCA national & international. Solos: Bangalore, Chennai, Hyderabad, Mumbai, New Delhi, Varanasi; International: Copenhagen, Denmark, London, Geneva. Group shows: Geneva, Hong Kong, USA, *Biennales* Tokyo & Bangladesh. Group participations: National Exhibition *LKA* & *Triennale* New Delhi, GUJ State Exhibition, Marvel Art Gallery Ahmedabad, *AIFACS*, *ATG*, *BB*, others in Chandigarh, Bangalore, Chennai; International: Perth Festival Australia, Fukuoka Museum Japan, Husain, Husain & Husain Cairo & Egypt. *Art* camps: Haryana, New Delhi, Hyderabad. *Auctions*: Sotheby's New York. Awards: National Award *LKA*. Fellowship: Govt. of India 1983–85. Commissions: *Mosaic murals* in Delhi & Jaipur, *Sculptures* in Hyderabad, *Fiberglass sculpture* New Delhi & Mussorie, *portraits* for the British Council Division. Collections: *NGMA* & *LKA* New Delhi, *Chandigarh Museum*.

Shamshad Husain primarily paints human beings, going about the business of living out their very ordinary lives. It is the mundane, the commonplace that he observes and puts down, transforming them into *patterns* of *line*, *colour* and *texture*. His *colour* verges on the *monochrome*, with sudden interesting *passages* of blood reds, mustards and pinks.

He lives and works in New Delhi.

Hyper-Realism A type of ultra *realistic art*, popular in the USA in the 1970s. e.g., in *painting*, copies of *photographs* were sometimes used, and in *sculpture*, direct *casts* were used to brighten the verisimilitude of the human *figure* in each *medium*. It was somewhat less common in Europe. The *style* is also known as hyper-realism.

Indian *artists* like *Jaideep Mehrotra* and *Bikash Bhattacharya* have used *passages* of Hyper-realism to enliven their surreal *compositions*. Refer *Super Realism*.

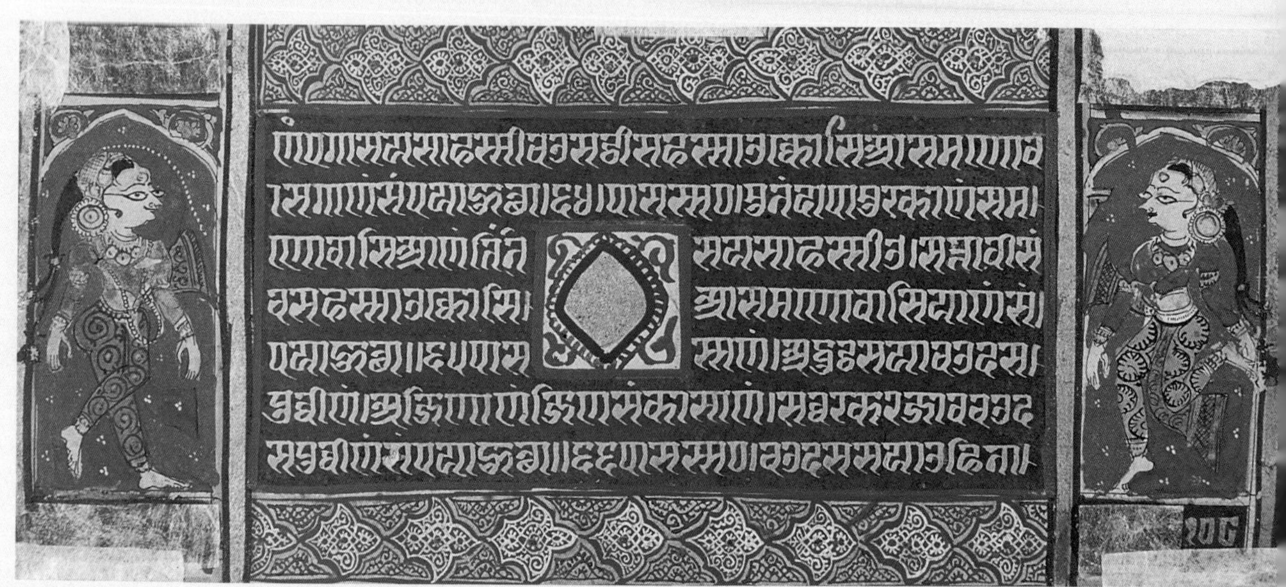

Illuminated Manuscripts: "Jain Miniature Painting". (See notes on page 168)

Icon (Greek)=*image*. The *term* refers to *images* or sacred statues or *symbolic figures* in the *form* of *art*, used for worship in temples, churches and in homes. They usually depict mythological and religious *legends*; as in the Virgin and Child, Christ or as saints and sages. The BUDDHA was the first iconic *image* found in India; the earliest *form* appearing in the Gandharan and Mathuran regions, with all its iconographic appendages, i.e. the protruberance on the head, USHNISHA, the elongated earlobes, the robe, the ASANAS and the MUDRAS. Though this *image* evolved stylistically, the basic idea remained the same. With the advent of *Jainism* and *Hinduism*, icons of *Jain* Tirthankaras and Hindu *gods* and goddesses were created. Today, artisans continue producing icons in the traditional *manner*, whereas *artists* use the *images*, *distorted*, at times in the *modern manner* to make personal statements. Christ is also a popular choice for Indian *artists* since *Jamini Roy* was captivated by his dignity and monumentality. *Maqbool Fida Husain* has also introduced Christ into the great Indian *pantheon* of deities. MURTIS are *icons* of *gods* or goddesses meant primarily as an object of worship. Kerala and Bengal are centres for icon *images* and objects, the *style* and subject remain largely unchanged throughout India. *L. Munuswamy* belonged to a family of artisans that made icons. Today the *term* has a wider connotation. *Anjolie Ela Menon* brought two world famous icons i.e. Mother Teresa and Christ together on a single *canvas* and Badri Narayan uses his own vision depicting Christ as a Yogi. Refer *Ajanta*, *Ellora*, *Christian Art*, *Distortion*, GANDHARVAS, *Gupta*, KRISHNA, *Idol*, *Iconology*, *Iconography*, *Mahabalipuram*, *Maurya Dynasty*, NATARAJA, LINGAM, *Stupa*, *Nagara Style*, *Thanjavur (Tanjore) Painting*.

Iconography, Iconology *Art* historical *term* with similar meanings, i.e. the study of symbols in a work of *art*, and the investigation of their meanings in the social and historical context, e.g. mediaeval Christian iconography differs from *Baroque* iconography, each requiring a different approach and knowledge of the subject. Similarly, Indian *art* presents wide-ranging symbols that relate to the numerous Hindu *gods*: KRISHNA, VISHNU, etc. Iconology is helpful in dating works of *art*. Refer KRISHNA, VISHNU, DASAVATARAS, MATSYA-AVATARA, KURMAVATARA, VARAHAVATARA, NARASIMHA, VAMANA-TRIVIKRAMA, PARASURAMA, *Attribute*, *Buddhist Art*, *Bengal Oil Painting*, *Mannerism*, *Mathura Art*, *Mythology*; *Akbar Padamsee*, *Dayhalal K. Chauhan*, Illustrations—*Reddeppa M. Naidu*, *P. Krishnamurthy*, *P.T. Reddy*.

Ideal That which is perfect in every sense, generally beyond the scope of the *realistic* or naturalistic. The concept is not based purely on the observation of *nature* but rather on a synthesis of perfect parts, based on *aesthetic* values, making an ideal whole, e.g. the perfect human body. Thus the Greek *classical figure* and many High *Renaissance figures* are classified as ideal, their *form* and *proportions* being based on *contemporary* philosophical notions of beauty. The Ideal *forms* an essential part of Indian *art*, with the CHITRASUTRA specifically providing the scale of *proportions* to be followed in the depiction for man, woman and child, *gods* and goddesses, *demons*, etc.; it states that, unless noted otherwise in a text, the human *figure* should be neither too thin, nor too fat; it should not have a hairy body, nor be ugly. Indian *mythology* proclaims Adarsa/Adris which is the act of perceiving by the eye or perfection in appearance. Refer RASA, *Aesthetics*, *Anatomy*, CHITRASUTRA, CHOLA, *Chola Dynasty*, *Classical*, *Kishangarh*, *Mathura Art*, *Nagari Das*, *RAMA*, *Proportion*, *Realistic*, *Vinayak Pandurang Karmarkar*, *Ganpatrao K. Mhatre*, *Raja Ravi Varma*.

Ideal Art A synonym for *conceptual art*. Dating from the 1960s the *term* means the representation of an idea as distinct from an object. It formed a logical development from minimal *art*. Documents, charts, photographs, maps, films, language etc. replaced traditional *media*, which in themselves convey ideas. Instead today the *forms* are unintangible, which are mostly seen as relationships between abstract, *patterns*, symbolically reduced to *ciphers*. Refer *Installation*, *Minimalism*, *Ready-Made*.

Ideal Fine Art Society (IFAS) (Gulbarga). The society was conceived and set up by J. Khanderao in 1965, offering Dip. in *painting*, *V.G. Andani* took over the reins of the institute in 1972. In 1980, the KAR Govt. leased land to build an *art* complex to house the society. There are many dept. including an *Art* gallery, a *Folklore Museum*, Theatre, Studio, Workshop and Seminar Hall. The complex itself comprises the Ideal Fine Art Institute and CVA. The society conducts seminars on *art* and allied topics, organizes *painting* and *sculpture* workshops, camps, and arranges *exhibitions* on an all India basis. It also publishes *art* journals and magazines. *Artists* who exhibited here are *Sisir Sahana*, *V.G. Andani*. Their collection includes the works of *Anil Kumar*, *Goverdhan S. Panwar*, *Bairu Raghuram* and other senior *artists*.

Ideology The science of ideas which, in relation to *art*, means a set of beliefs which may be shared by a particular group of *artists* at any point of time. Pre-Modern India had no particular ideology, being affiliated to the court and was more or less overwhelmingly religious.

After the advent of the British in India, the School of Art as *Industrial Art* had carved a niche for itself in the general uncertainty created by the "modernistic" ideology and invited sundry idealistic reactions against it within the country.

The *contemporary art* scene was, thus, besieged by opposing ideologies. India's is a society based on struggle and strong belief in fate, whereas Western influence gave it a sense of history and reinforcement of individualism. However the awareness that came with self-determination caused coexistence of traditional Indian ideology with modern and even *abstract art*.

Artists who lent dynamism in evolving this new ideology included, from *Raja Ravi Varma*, *Rabindranath Tagore*, *Nandalal Bose*, *Jamini Roy*, belonging to the pre-Independence era and others, to *Maqbool Fida Husain* and *Jogen Chowdhury* among others in the present era. Refer *Industrial Art Society*.

Idiom This refers to the overall *style* and expression used by *artists*. In India, this could span the traditional, the religious and secular *themes*, in a combination of traditional *folk* and *tribal art*. Refer *Eclectic, Mahayana Buddhism, Badri Narayan, Bikash Bhattacharjee, P. Gopinath, Bhagwan Kapoor, P. Khemraj, Meera Mukherjee, P.L. NarasimhaMurti, Raju A. Paidi, Rasiklal Parikh, Vinod Parul, Sunil Kumar Paul, Amrita Sher-Gil, Abanindranath Tagore*.

Idol A *figure* or *image*, often a statuette of *god* i.e. the object of worship found in both temples and private shrines. Idols usually installed conform to certain canons of scale and appearance. Refer MURTI, *Icon, Iconology, Metal, Nude, Proportion*, SHIVA, *South Indian Bronzes, Thanjavur (Tanjore) Paintings, Tradition, Vinayak Pandurang Karmarkar*.

Illuminated Manuscripts Ancient texts usually written on *palm leaves* sometimes in *gold* and *silver colours* giving a highly reflective finish, and illustrated with either geometric *motifs* or *figures*, as in *Jain illuminated manuscripts* or Pala *manuscript painting*. Refer *Folio, Illumination, Jain Miniatures, Pala Miniatures, Palm Leaf* and *Manuscript Painting*. (See illustration on page 166)

Illumination Latin word illuminare=to adorn. The decoration, including the lettering, and *illustration* of manuscripts, which were often in book *form*. The pages were usually minutely painted in *gouache* or *tempera* and enriched with *gold leaf*. Many religious and secular illustrated manuscripts date from the Medieval period in Europe. In India, the most celebrated *illuminated manuscripts* include the *Jain* and *Pala miniatures*. Refer *Illuminated Manuscripts, Jain Miniatures* and *Pala Miniatures, Calligraphic, Gold Leaf, Gouache*, MAHAVIRA, *Narrative*, PURANA, SVETHAMBARA.

Illusion, Illusionism Different *pictorial* devices used by *painters* throughout the ages to deceive the eye in order to persuade the spectator that the *figure* or object in the picture is real. Refer *Backdrop, Cinema, Perspective, Depth, Foreshortening, Glazing, Gupta, Mixed Contrast, Relief, Space, Tactile, Trompe-L'Oeil, Atul Bose, Bhagwan Chavan, Kanayi Kunhiraman, Jaideep D. Mehrotra, M. Sanathanan*.

Illustration A pictorial or *drawing form* used to emphasize the accompanying text or writing. Due to frequent usage it came to be known as illustration–*printing*. Illustrations were usually engraved on *wood* and later on *metal* for *printing*. Indian deities and religious *symbols* were also used to illustrate book texts or articles. The earliest example was "The Asiatick Researches printed in 1789".

Image A *form* used in work of *art*, it means an imitation or visualization of subjects and objects. It is also a mental picture, idea or concept, e.g. the image of KRISHNA, is ingrained in one's consciousness as being blue skinned. Image can vary in *style* and *content*. Refer *Icon After Image, Architecture, Birbhum, Cast, Chasing, CHATUR BHUJA, Cire Perdue, Collotype*, CHITRAKATHI, *Decalcomania*; Illustrations–*Ajanta, Gold, Amit Ambalal, K.M. Adimoolam, Arpana Caur, Sankho Chaudhuri, Bal Chhabda, Avtarjeet S. Dhanjal*.

Imagery The *visual* elements in a work of *art*, often derived from the imagination, e.g., symbols, *motifs, figures*, objects etc., and their relationship to one another within the picture. *J. Swaminathan* had a compact set of imagery based on his tiny, precisely-delineated birds, hills, and trees, while *Manjit Bawa* popularly used floating cows and cowherds. The *self portrait* dominated in most of *Bhupen Khakhar's* works, while *Prabhakar Barwe's* work was laced with the impersonal, even the mundane. Refer *Partha Pratim Deb*; Illustrations–TANTRA, *Figurative, Amit Ambalal, Navjot Altaf, Nikhil Biswas, Bimal DasGupta, Shanti Dave, Francis Newton Souza, Syed Haider Raza*.

Images Art Gallery (Bangalore/Mumbai) The gallery opened its first branch in the suburbs of Bangalore in 1996. The second gallery, which was inaugurated in 1997 at Infantry Road is one of the largest private *art* galleries in Bangalore, with a total carpet area of 2200 sq.ft., and wall *space* of 225 running ft. It can be partitioned into two separate exhibiting areas with the help of movable screens. Prakash Revankar is the Dir. while *artist* M.G. Doddamani is the gallery in charge. The gallery also houses a collection of the works of several *Contemporary artists* including *Akbar Padamsee, Chandranath K. Achrekar, Shakuntala Kulkarni*, Anjana Mehra, K.T. Shivaprasad, Dilip Ranade, *G. Reghu, Deepak Shinde*.

Impasto The thick application of *oil paint* on the surface of the *canvas*, using a *brush, palette knife* or roller, with the result that the *paint* appears in *relief*. Use of impasto *medium* in *watercolours* achieves the same results. Pratima Sheth began using a heavy impasto, with the *palette knife* and later the roller to create textural variations in her works. Refer *Brushwork, Drip Painting, Dry Brush Painting, Encaustic, Fat over lean, Gel, Loaded Brush, Painting Knife, Gopal S. Adivrekar, Ramnik Bhavsar, Krishen Khanna, Brinda C. Miller, Natver Mistry, Dinanath Pathy, Bhanwar Singh Panwar*.

Impression **1.** Impressions are sketch-like effects, which are produced by ideas, feelings or opinions of an *artist*. Illustrations–*Ramkinkar Baij, Nandalal Bose, Shiavax Chavda*. **2.** The *term* refers specifically to the *image* on the individual sheet of *paper* taken, or impressed, during *printmaking*, the *print* from a block or *plate*. Illustrations–*Jyoti Bhatt, Sudhir R. Khastgir, Anupam Sud*. **3.** In *sculpture* it is an impression of the object created in the *mould* to obtain its proper shape. The phase of personal self-expression and ideas dominating the *composition* which began with *Ramkinkar Baij*, and his experiments with several *media*. Illustrations–*Art Education*, NATARAJA, *Sadanandji Bakre, Bhagwant K. Goregaoker, Somnath Hore, Ratilal Kansodaria, Chintamoni Kar, Sudhir R. Khastagir, Ganpatrao K. Mhatre, Meera Mukherjee, Debi Prasad RoyChowdhury, Prabhas Sen, Himmat Shah, Bayaji Vasantrao Talim*. Refer *Abstract Impressionism, Artist's Proof, Frottage, White Line Engraving, Atul Bose, Pralhad A. Dhond, Shaibal Ghosh, Paresh Maity, Gaganendranath Tagore*.

Impressionism The 19th-century *art* movement in France, the name of which derived from a *painting* entitled "Impression Soleil levant" ("Impression—Sunrise", 1872) by C. Monet, exhibited in Paris in 1874 with C. Pissarro, C. Renoir, E. Degas, A. Sisley and P. Cezanne. Impressionism is classified as being the first of the *modern art* movements. The main aim of the group was to achieve greater naturalistic and *atmospheric effects* by *painting* out of doors rather than in the studio. The *artists* were also aware of the *contemporary* scientific research into the physics of small strokes, pure *colours* rather than the traditional blended *colours* of the Salon *painters*. By analyzing these *colours* and their *colour* complementaries, they aimed to represent the play of *light* on the surface of objects, including those in *shadow*. The peak of the Impressionist Movement was between 1870 and 1880. Impressionism was introduced into India by the British, e.g. through the *JJSA* by W.E. Gladstone Solomon. *Debi Prasad RoyChowdhury* introduced the Western idea of *sculpture* to *art* schools. This included the Impressionism handling of Auguste Rodin. Refer *Abstraction Figurative*, *Expressionism*, *Hue*, *Isms*, *Landscape*, *Modern*, *Neo-Impressionism*, *Optical Mixing*, *Pointillism*, *Post-Impressionism*, *Narayan S. Bendre*, *Ino Gangooly*, *Chintamoni Kar*, *P.T. Reddy*, *Jehangir Sabavala*, *Sayed Haider Raza*, *Vasantrao A. Mali*.

India Ink *Chinese Ink*. The *ink* was actually manufactured in China, but the carbon *pigment* was from India, as most of the Indian *inks* were made from *charcoal* i.e. *lamp black* hence the name, India Ink. The *ink* is produced by grinding one part of either carbon, *lamp black pigment* with two-three parts solution of hide glue. The mixture is ground until smooth and allowed to dry in a *ceramic* dish. It is brushed with water until its surface liquefies and then used in *ink* and *brush painting*. India ink gives *transparent* glazes of *colour*, which *Sailoz Mookerjea* preferred in *drawing*. It can also be moulded into a stick *form* and rubbed in water on a slate slab and used. Sometimes a little shellac or any other water dispersed resin is added in the manufacturing stage to make the *ink* water-resistant. This *ink* is permanent. Refer *Glazing*, *Abdul Rahim Appabhai Almelkar*, *V. Viswanadhan*, *K. Sheshagiri Rao*; Illustration—*Laxma Goud*.

Indian Film Industry The largest producer of cinematic films in the world with the Mumbai Film Centre being the largest, popularly known as "Bollywood"—a pseudonym joining the words Bombay (Mumbai) and Hollywood. The Indian Film Industry encouraged many fine *artists* to move into *commercial art form* in order to make a viable career with *backdrop paintings*, e.g. *Pestonjee Bomanjee*, *Ramkinkar Baij*, *Kanu Desai*, *Shiavax Chavda*. *Artists* like *Maqbool Fida Husain* started their careers by *painting* film *posters* and sets. The Indian Film actress Madhuri Dixit inspired *Maqbool Fida Husain* to do a series of *paintings* called "Gaja-gamini". D.G. Phalke, the pioneer of Indian *cinema*, was in fact a student of *JJSA* and *KB* Vadodara. The Indian Film Industry promoted many *artists* particularly in the fields of blockmaking, *enamelling*, printing in addition to *paintings*. Refer *Cinema*, *P. Krishnamurthy*, *Vivan Sundaram*.

Indian Museum (Kolkata, WB). This is the oldest museum in India, the building having been completed in 1875 by Walter L.B. Granville. The archaeological section is to the right of the main entrance. The first room in this section is known as the Bharhut Room contains the 2nd century BC *stone* railings and *sculptures* from the Buddhist *stupa*, Bharhut in MP, which survived the vandalism of the neighbouring villages. The railings stand nearly 9ft. high, with *sculptures* carved all over in low *relief*. Bharhut, belonging to the Hinayana phase of *Buddhism* has only *symbolic* representations of the BUDDHA, in the *form* of an empty throne or the Bodhi tree (Pipal/Fig/Ficus tree) under which he attained enlightenment.

The Gandhara *sculptures* in the next gallery belong to the Mahayana phase of *Buddhism*. Therefore, one gets to see the BUDDHA depicted in anthropomorphic *form*. The next gallery has been divided into small niches housing *sculptures* from different *periods* and regions.

In addition, there is a numismatic gallery, a mineralogy gallery and a zoological section, along with a fine collection of Indian textiles and *decorative art* objects in *wood* and *metal*.

Indian National Trust for Art & Cultural Heritage (INTACH) (New Delhi). INTACH is a non govt., non-profit, voluntary organization that seeks to conserve and promote the Indian traditional and cultural heritage. It was founded in 1984 and has over 140 chapters spread throughout India. The members of INTACH focus on a wide variety of issues, including preservation of environment and cultural and architectural heritage. The inputs from the various chapters are backed up by technically equipped personnel who constitute their support system. These have emerged into four functional areas: Material Heritage Division, Architectural Heritage Division, Natural Heritage Division and Legal Cell. Material Heritage Division is now known as the Indian Council of Conservation Institute, (ICCI) functioning under the direction of Dr O.P. Agrawal, an international authority in *conservation* of Cultural Property. ICCI has started its own *conservation* centres in various cities including the first one at Lucknow in 1985; the ICCI is also equipped with a photography cell, a research and analysis wing and a growing library. They organize regular workshops and short-*term* training programmes on *conservation techniques*. They also bring out a newsletter and publish manuals and brochures on *conservation*. Training is the main thrust area of the Indian Council of Conservation Institute.

ICCI has also been active for the development of *museums*, in India and has under it a Museum Development Cell. A large number of *museums* have been surveyed and action plans prepared for them. (Refer page 343.)

Indian Society of Oriental Art (ISOA) (Kolkata) ISOA was founded in 1907, and its office was, at first, in the GSA. It counted amongst its members, both Indians and foreigners, judges, merchants and Maharajas alike with Lord Kitchener as its first President. *Abanindranath Tagore* was one of its secretaries. The society had organized various programmes including deputing *Nandalal Bose* and *Asit K. Haldar* to *copy* the *Ajanta frescoes*.

The main objective of the society was to free Indian *art* from the influence of *academic* Western *art*. The society has thus been encouraging the study of traditional Indian and oriental *art* by its members, creating the same awareness amongst the general public by means of *exhibitions*, lectures and discussions on *art*, maintaining a well-stocked library and publishing books and journals on *art*, which were once edited by the likes of *Abanindranath Tagore* and Stella Kramrisch. *Artists* associated with the society included *Debi Prasad RoyChowdhury*, *Sailendranath Dey* and Surendranath Kar.

Indirect Carving A method of *carving* in which the approach is indirect and involves the use of three-dimensional *sketches* or maquettes, as in the case of preparing a *clay model*, before *carving marble*. Refer *Wetting Down*, *Sadanandji Bakre*, *Bhagwant K. Goregaokar*, *Goverdhanlal Joshi*, *Sudhir R. Khastgir*, *S.L. Parasher*, *Sunil Kumar Paul*.

Indra=the deity who fights the *demons*. The supreme *god* of the *atmosphere* and sky of Vedic *times*. Indra also rides a *white* elephant called Airavata and his *weapon* of choice is the Vajra or thunder-bolt. He is usually depicted with white skin and bejewelled body. Refer APSARA, BRAHMA, BUDDHA, *Gandharan Art*, *God*, MAHAVIRA, MATRIKAS, RAVANA, RUDRA, SHIVA, SURYA, VAHANA, VISHNU.

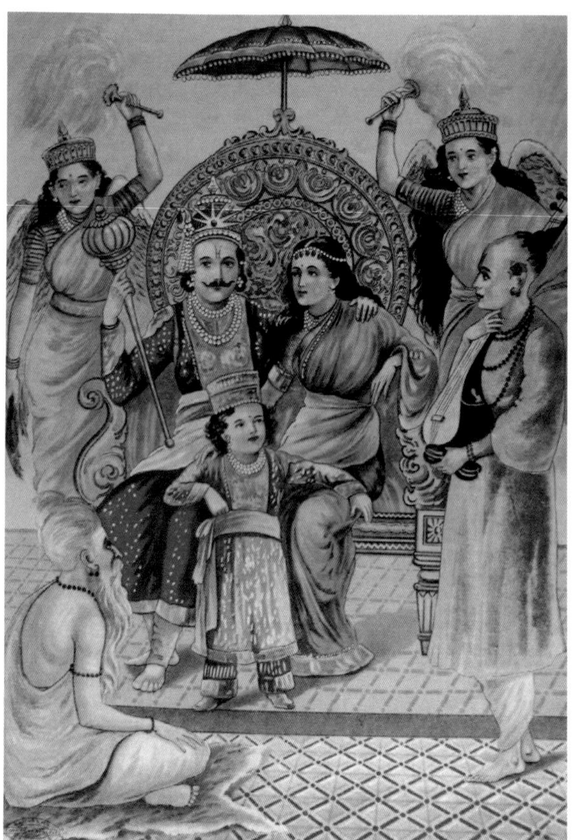

Indra: *Raja Ravi Varma*, "Indra Kacheri" (Court of Indra), Ravi Varma Press, Malavli, circa 1920.

Indus Valley Civilization An ancient Indian civilization, which flourished in circa 2500–1500 BC around the banks of the river Indus and its five tributaries (in *modern*-day Pakistan). Many highly advanced cities were discovered, including *Harappa*, *Mohenjo Daro*, Kot-Diji, Chanhu-Daro and Lothal. These cities were well constructed, with advanced town planning and a proliferation of *decorative arts*. *Sculptures*, toys, seals and jewellery were found in almost all the towns. Refer *National Museum* (New Delhi), TANTRA.

Industrial Art Society The society was founded in 1854 in Kolkata by Rajendralal Mitra, Jatindra Mohan Tagore and Justice Pratt. *Gunendranath Tagore* and *Jyotirindranath Tagore* were admitted to the School of Industrial Art run by the society. The school was later converted into a GSA, during the governor generalship of Lord Northbrook who added an *Art* gallery to it. Refer *GCAC* Kolkata, *Ideology*

Industrial Design The successful combining of *fine arts* and *applied arts*, as in the application of *aesthetic* sensibility to utilitarian objects as in making grillwork, designing girders, windows, lights etc. The British-operated *art* schools in India were originally founded with a view to teaching native craftsmen the methods of Industrial design. Refer *JJSA*, *GSAC* Kolkata.

Ingle, Mahadeo Bhanaji (1946–) b. Panora, MAHA. Education: *Art* Nagpur School of Art Nagpur, GDA *JJSA*, M.FA by research Bombay University 2000. Solos: *JAG*, TAG. Group participations: MAHA State Mumbai, *Triennale LKA* New Delhi, *Biennale LKA* Lucknow UP, *DG*, *JAG*, *BAS*, *JJSA*. Awards: Gold Medal *JJSA*, International Exhibition for Yoga Art & *Biennale* New Delhi. Appointments: Prof. & Dean *JJSA* & Dir. of Art MAHA. Delivered radio talks on *art*. Collections: *LKA* & *NGMA* New Delhi, Jawahar Kala Kendra Jaipur, pvt. national & international.

Mahadeo Bhanaji Ingle is an abstractionist, in the tight, yet *painterly style* of Barnett Newman. The BINDU *forms* a recurring *motif* in his works, serving to express the dichotomy between different *textures*. It is usually set in *matte backgrounds* of dull browns, *white* or glowing oranges and crimsons, standing at times for the sun in the *abstract landscape* and at other times being eclipsed by a *black* hole. He makes extensive use of *stencils* and rollers in creating his *texture* based *paintings*.

He lives and works in Mumbai.

Ink **1.** Different coloured inks and *India inks* used in *pen* and *wash drawings*. In India, the reed *pen* was made in such a way that ink could flow from it for writing, *painting*. Such ink was made from *lamp black* or *charcoal*. **2.** *Opaque* inks used in *printmaking*. Inks are both water-based, *oil* based and metallic. Water-based inks are *transparent* and thin *washes* of this ink may be overlapped to great effect; printing inks are generally *opaque* and do not allow *light* to be transmitted from the inks underneath. Metallic inks are composed of *aluminium*, *bronze* and *copper* powders to give a lustrous and brilliant finish to the printed surface. Lithographic inks are more *viscous* and greasy. Refer *Blot Drawing, Brush Drawing, Calligraphy, Chinese Art, Decalcomania, Drawings, Form, India Ink, Japanese Art, Life-Drawing, Line and Wash, Pigment, Scraperboard, Scratchboard, Thumb Impression, Transparent, Wash (Technique), Waterproof, Abdul Rahim Appabhai Almelkar, Jaya Appasamy, Gobardhan Ash, Nandalal Bose, Roop Chand, Chittaprosad, Jogen Chowdhury, Muhammed Abdur Chughtai, Jatin Das, Yagneshwar Kalyanji Shukla, Rabindranath Tagore, Arnawaz Vasudev, Setlur Gopal Vasudev, D. Venkatapathy, V. Viswanadhan, K. Vasant Wankhede, Babu Xavier*; Illustrations–*Line–Shiavax Chavda, Hatching, Wood Cut, Wood Cut Printing, Ganga Devi, Santokba Dudhat, Rathin Mitra, Vrindavan Solanki, Rabindranath Tagore, Yusuf.*

Inlaid Refer *Inlay*.

Inlay Any process by which small pieces of material, e.g. *wood, ivory, marble, metal*, semi-precious *stones* etc. are inserted into a cut-out portion of the main object to create a *pattern* or *design*. Known as marquetry in *wood* work. In India, the *inlaid marble* at the *Taj Mahal* Agra, the *ivory* inlay of PUJ form some of the finest examples of such workmanship. Refer *Architecture, Enamel, Mughal Dynasty, Pattern, Sukhen Ganguly, Wood*; Illustration–*Vishwanath M. Sholapurkar*.

Inorganic 1. It means a *pigment* derived from chemical or *synthetic materials*. **2.** In *terms* of *form* in *art*, inorganic points to the 20th-century phenomenon of using cold, clinical shapes rather than organic, lively ones. This can be seen in the limited *colours* and grid-like *forms* of Piet Mondrian, *Dashrath Patel* and *Om Prakash Sharma* as against the amoeboid, wriggling organisms of Joan Miro and *P. Gopinath* and the impersonal, metallic shapes of Anthony Caro or the organic shapes of Henry Moore, *Adi M. Davierwala* and *Sankho Chaudhuri*. Here the identity of *metal* as *metal* is not lost nor submerged in the transformation of *metal* into human *figure*. **3.** It could also refer to *modern* materials such as synthetic latex, *fibreglass, acrylic*, PVC (poly vinyl chloride).

Installation In the West, the installation was an *art form* that grew quite naturally out of *sculpture* in the 20th century. It has borrowed elements from the theatre, photography, performance and *happening* on the one hand and from *Assemblage* and *Constructivism* on the other. It can be fragile and momentary and may exist for posterity only through the means of still or video photography. It has embraced elements of *earth art, conceptual art, Minimalism* and sometimes exists either as a propagation or negation of *art* history. It can variously be a religious and aesthetically satisfying experience, or an offensive showpiece.

In India, several *artists* have adopted this *form* of expression over the last two decades. Also, the *happening art* had it's roots in traditional, rural and *tribal art* as seen at events like Muharram, the Tazias & the DURGA-PUJA. However, *Vivan Sundaram's* installations of 1991 whose global perspective created a new political *art* in the *technique* of installation. But it became popular only after it gained ascendancy in the West and *artists* such as *Satish Gujral, Manjit Bawa, Maqbool Fida Husain, Shamshad Husain*, Late R-Umanna Hussain, *Saroj Gogi Pal, Ved Nayar* and Kapuria Naresh all started practising Installation *art* as a part of their repertoire. Refer *Acrylic Plastic, Arte Povera, Background, Base, Content, Crafts, De'collage, Dimension, Empaquetage, Free-Standing, Ideal Art, Kinetic Art, Leather, Mixed Media, Modernism, Modern Movement, Monotype, Op or Optical Art, Performance Art, Photograph, Plaster of Paris, Ready-Made, Space, Stone, Term, Tradition, Treatment, Video Art, Maqbool Fida Husain, Hema Joshi, Nalini Malani, Saroj Gogi Pal*; Illustrations–*Navjot Altaf, Yashwant Mali, Vivan Sundaram.*

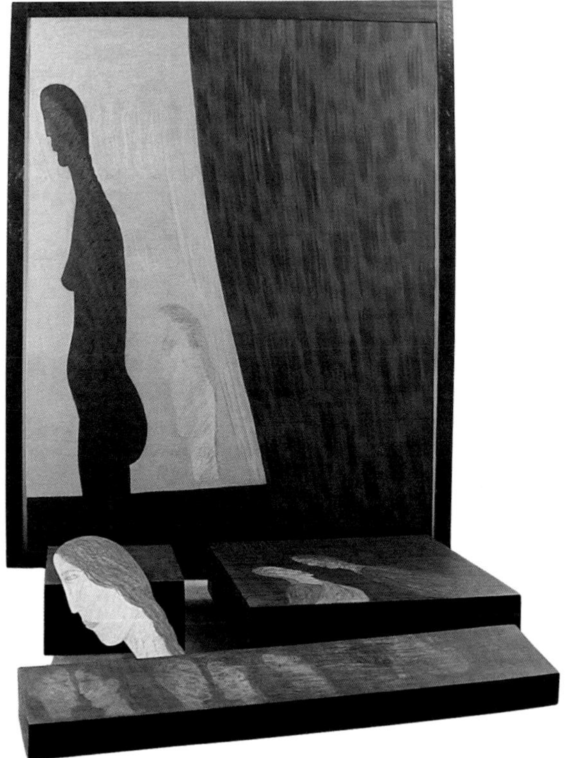

Installation: *Shakuntala Kulkarni*, "The brown *nude*", *Acrylic*, 1994.

Intaglio The *term* is derived from the Italian "intaglione" ("tagliare"), the process in which the *design* is engraved or cut into, the block of *wood, metal plate*, or *copper*, as opposed to *relief*. Various *techniques* are combined in the preparation of a *plate*. Refer *Bite, Biting in, Collography, Copper, Engraving, Lithography, Photogravure, Printmaking, Zinc, Somnath Hore, Krishna N. Reddy, K.S. Viswambhara*; Illustrations–*Jyoti Bhatt, Sanat Kar*.

Intaglio Printing Refer *Intaglio, Etching, Print* and *Printmaking*.

International Art Promotion Centre (New Delhi). The IAPC is purely a non-commercial body of *artists* and *art* lovers, without any grant or financial aid from any govt. body. The IAPC organizes workshops for the duration of a month or two during which *artists* from India and abroad interact with one another and produce works that are later exhibited. Founded in 1986 by *Pushp Betala*.

Iron=Lohaa in Sanskrit. It is a grey *metal* with a high melting point (reddish in colour) and low fluidity when in a molten state. When it is used in *sculpture*, it is invariably wrought and not *cast*. Sheet iron of different guages can be cut, hammered and bent in making *relief sculpture* and *murals*. Iron denotes the antiquity; the Iron Age relics probably going way back to the *Dravidian Style*.

The AD 5th century Qutub Minar south of Delhi stands with the great towering iron pillar inside. Iron was also a durable *metal* for religious *images*, ritualistic items and objects of utility. It was used in the making of arrow heads, spears, knives etc. In India, iron *craft* was the domain of the Lohaar tribe and such craftsmen stated to be called "Lohaars" or ironcraftsmen. Refer *Assemblage, Cire Perdue, Sand Blasting, Medium, Oxide, Pala Miniatures, B. Vithal, Dhanraj Bhagat.*

Islamic Art This is understood to be *art*, which reflects the Islamic faith in most middle Eastern countries. Since *figuration* was taboo according to Islam, decoration, especially geometric and floral decoration became the hallmark of Islamic art. *Arabesques*, rosettes, squares, checks and such other *patterns* were used to great effect in the decorating of *pottery*, carpets, *architecture* and *paintings*. In India, Islamic art included *Mughal miniatures* and architecture and Deccani *art*. Refer *Bidri*.

Isms A suffix used in *art* to denote various *styles* since the *term* identifies a distinctive theory, doctrine or practice e.g. *neo-Classicism, Romanticism, Impressionism, Expressionism, Cubism, Fauvism, Constructivism*, etc. In India, *artists* of the post-Independent era have constantly been influenced by different Isms at different stages of their careers. i.e. *Jehangir Sabavala* and *Gaganendranath Tagore* by *Cubism*, *Maqbool Fida Husain* by *Expressionism*, *Sayed Haider Raza* by *Impressionism*, *Gaganendranath Tagore* in particular, was one of the first *artists* in India to be influenced by *Cubism*. Refer Illustrations—*Cubism, Narayan S. Bendre, Shiavax Chavda, Biren De, Namdeo B. Dikhole, K.V. Haridasan, Mahirwan Mamtani, Prafulla Mohanti, Shankar Palsikar, Sohan Qadri, Sayed Haider Raza* and *Om Prakash Sharma*.

Italic A *form* of *calligraphy* with slanting letter-forms first used by the Italian humanists in the 15th century.

Ivory Strictly speaking, the tusk of an elephant, though its dentine properties are identical with organic material of tusk of animals such as walrus, narwhal, hippopotamus, wild pigs, etc. Ivory is hard, *white*, grained (dense) substance is more brittle then bone and can be finely polished to give an aesthetically beautiful surface. These properties have made ivory an important material for intricate *carving* and sculpting. Small sheets of ivory can also be painted or engraved. These are very precious and delicate works of *art*. During the Mughal period, this *art form* reached the zenith of finesse and elegance. Generally very small, can be worn as an *ornament*, they were called "Shast", a Persian *term* used for miniature *portraits*. Used for centuries, particularly in China and India.

Ivory Black Refer *Black*.

Ivory Painting Refer *Ivory*.

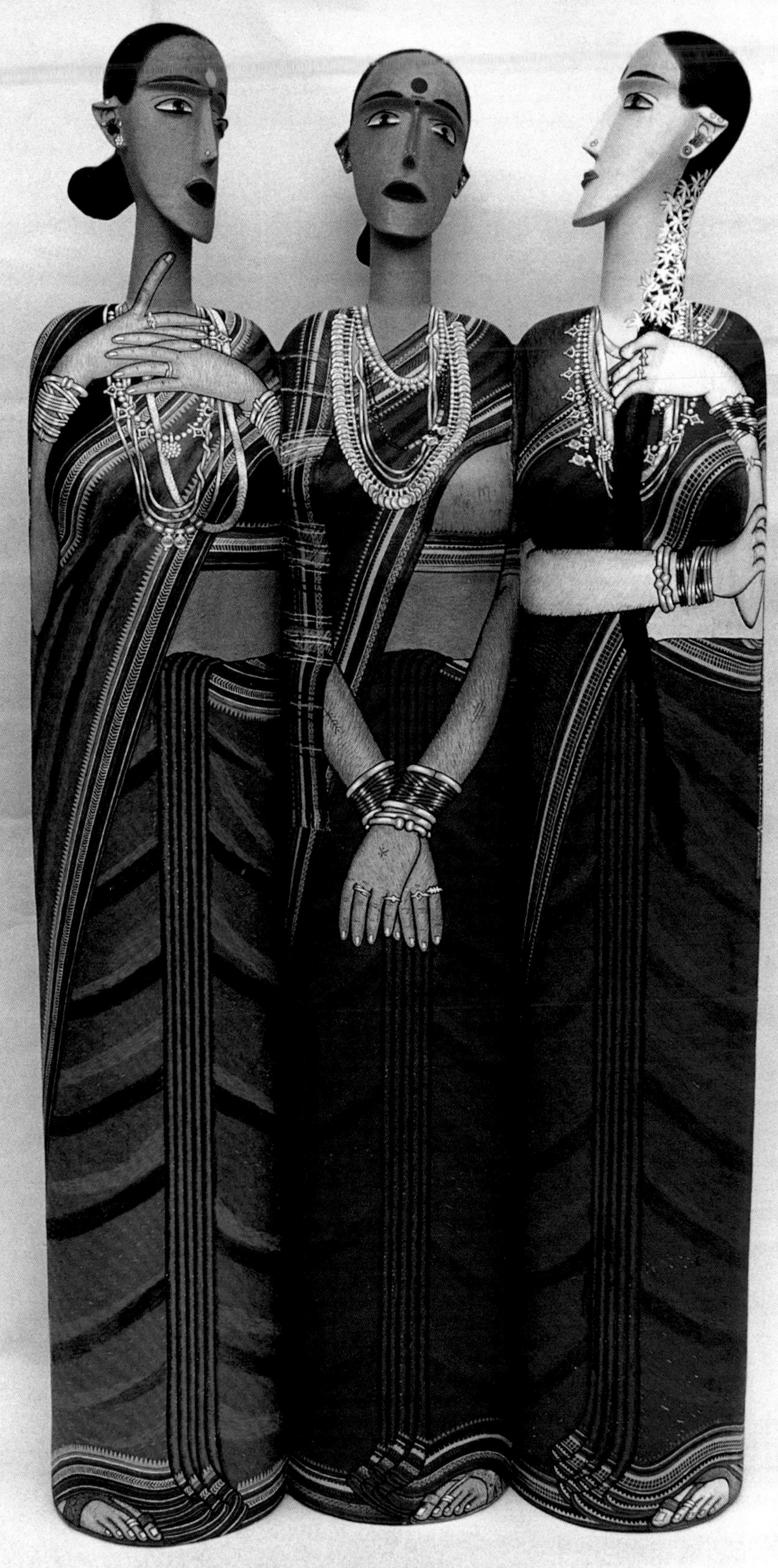

Jagdish, C.: "Rich Women", *Paper sculpture*, 150cm ht. (See notes on page 176)

J.J. Institute of Applied Arts (Sir) (JJIAA) (Mumbai). The *commercial art* course was first offered in *JJSA*, in 1935 by Charles Gerrard. In 1958, the JJIAA was formed as an independent body, housed in a building on the same campus. The institute now offers training exclusively in the *applied arts*. Advertising, Photography and other *mediums* of communication are some of the subjects taught in the institute. There is also a library of reference books on communication design.

J.J. School of Art (Sir) (JJSA) (Mumbai). JJSA was founded in 1857 with a generous endowment of Rs. 100,000 by the philanthopist and businessman Sir Jamshedjee Jeejeebhoy. At first, *art* classes were conducted at the Elphinstone Institute by Prof. William Jerry. When the *design* & *engraving* classes were added the school moved to a building on Abdul Rehman Street. The school relocated to its present premises in 1878. At this time, the subject of *drawing* was added to the existing courses which by then included decorative *painting*, *modelling* and ornamental wrought *iron* work. The Lord Reay Art Workshops (now the Dept. of *Arts & Crafts*) was established in 1891. The dept. for training *art* teachers was initiated in 1910. By 1900, the English Art School *pattern* was adopted. The *architecture* course (then part of the school) was reorganized in 1914. Charles Gerrard who came to assist the Dir., Capt. W.E. Gladstone Solomon, was instrumental in starting the section for *commercial art* (now a separate institute, known as the *JJIAA*).

In the *post-Independence* era, *Vasudeo Adurkar* became the first Indian Dir. The MAHA Directorate of Art was formed in 1965. The school became affiliated to the Bombay University from June 1981, with degree courses being offered in *painting* (1981) *sculpture* (1983) and *arts* and *crafts* (1990). The school has a large *exhibition* hall, an extensive library and *visual* aids, and a large collection of *miniature paintings* and *contemporary art*. Refer *Bombay School*, *Monocular Vision.*

Jadav, Chhaganlal R. (1903–1987) b. Nava Vadaj, Ahmedabad GUJ. Education: Studied *art* under *Kanu Desai*, *Ravishankar M. Raval*, attended classes Indore School of Art and Lucknow School of Art, several scholarships from private charitable trusts, in a career, interrupted by his stint as a freedom fighter also. Solos: Ahmedabad, Pondicherry, New Delhi, Vadodara, "Gandhi Series" Exhibit at Jawaharlal Nehru's residence. Group participations: National *LKA* New Delhi, *BAS*, & later Mysore, Shimla, Ahmedabad. Received scholarship: GUJ Gold Medal, DAE Mysore & Shimla, *BAS*. Received Scholarship in Ahmedabad & New Delhi. Member: Progressive Painters Ahmedabad. Commissioned: *Portraits* while in jail in Surat & Nasik after "Dandi March". Collections: *NGMA* & *LKA* New Delhi, Vadodara Museum, Trivandrum Art Gallery, Mysore Art Gallery, Gandhi Smriti Bhavnagar, Gandhi Smarak Nidhi New Delhi; International: Cairo, Moscow, Baghdad, England, Switzerland, France, USA & pvt.

Chhaganlal R. Jadav held several *exhibitions* of his *paintings* inspired by the many moods of *nature*. Unlike several of his *contemporaries*, his was a straight forward approach towards *landscape* without any misty *Romanticism* or folk-like stylization. His use of the impressionistic *technique* did not preclude him from introducing delightful details. His *paintings* between 1935–45 were inspired by the *Social Realism*, being full of scenes of domestic bliss. His visits to Kashmir & Kulu brought out an inherent love of *landscape*. Between 1945–60 he turned towards *Impressionism*, cultivating a heightened *colour* sense. Like Van Gogh, the *colour* yellow predominates his *compositions* at this stage. The assassination of Mahatma Gandhi gave birth to the Gandhi series, which were full of confused emotion heightened by the use of a near *abstract* expressionist *technique*.

His later *paintings* were homages, in a sense, to the *images* of J. Miro, P. Klee, V. Kandinsky and P. Mondrian, with their subtle interplay of the inner mind & outward appearances.

Jadhav, Gajanan Narayan (1917–2004) b. Kolhapur. Education: GDA *drawing* & *painting JJSA*. Solos: New Delhi. Awards: MAHA State Award, for portraits Kolhapur & Belgaum. Commissions: several *portraits*. Collections: Rashtrapati Bhawan New Delhi, Vidhan Bhavan Mumbai, Pune, Vidyapath and pvt. Kirloskar Press.

Gajanan Narayan Jadhav's early education in the *fine arts* was under *artists* like *Baburao Painter*, Babasaheb Gajbar and G.R. Wadangekar, all of whom were also involved in designing film sets. He joined the Kirloskar press as a staff *artist* in 1938, producing various *illustrations* for three monthly magazines "Kirloskar", "Stree" and "Manohar". In a *manner* typical of this generation of *artists*, Gajanan Narayan Jadhav became adept at not only doing *illustrations* but also at *handling landscapes* and *portraits* in the academic *manner*. His *compositions* were creative in decorative-folk-inspired *manner*.

He lived in Pune, MAHA.

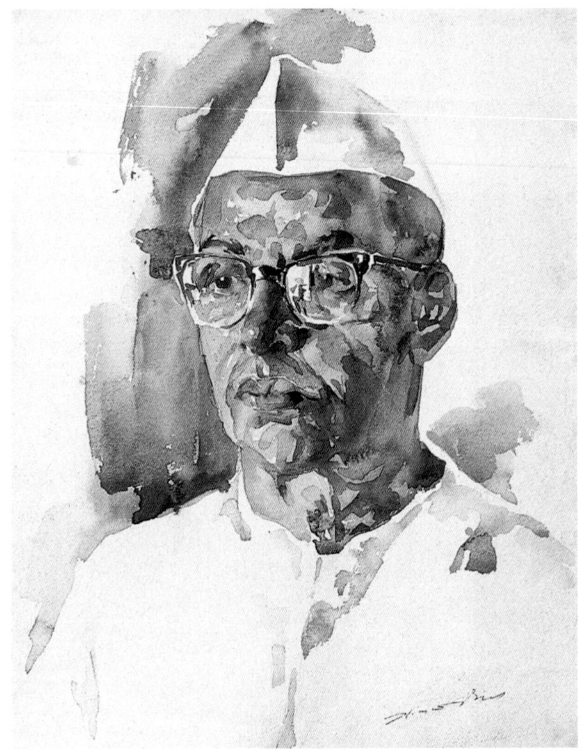

Jadhav, Gajanan Narayan: "Portrait", Watercolours.

Jadhav, Shamkant (1932–) b. Kolhapur, MAHA. Education: GDA *Art* Master Kalaniketan Mahavidyalaya in Kolhapur, Child Art Education & Research Mumbai. Solos: Nasik, Kolhapur Museum, *JAG*. Group participations: MAHA State Art Exhibition Mumbai, *LKA* New Delhi, Kolhapur Museum, *BAS, ASI*. Participated several seminars: *Cinema, Sculpture*, Literature & Music. Founder member: President of Rangabar an institution founded in Kolhapur 1978, held *art* camps, seminars & demonstrations. Collections: Kolhapur & Nagpur Museum; International: USA, Germany.

Shamkant Jadhav is basically a *landscape painter* taking inspiration from *nature*. From a simplified *Realism* in the 60s he has now moved to an impressionist grouping of *landscape* elements like trees or mountains against an impersonal *background* of sky or land.

He has always lived and worked at Kolhapur.

Jadhav, Shrikant G. (1950–) b. Kirloskarwadi, MAHA. Education: GDA *painting, Graphic*, Post-Dip. *mural painting* & *Art* Master's Certificate *JJSA*, Drawing Teacher's Certificate Abhinava Kala Mahavidyalaya Pune MAHA. Solos: *JAG*. Group participations: *Artists' Centre* and Son-et-lumiere Mumbai, *BAAC* & *AFA* Kolkata, *LKA* Chennai, *JAG, NCAG, AIFACS*, TKS. *Art* camps and workshops: *Artist's Centre* Mumbai, *LKA* Chennai, SZCC Nagpur, *Colour etching* organized by British Council Diarama; Designed Float for Republic Day celebrations, and drama "Ramayana" in the Discovery of India *NCAG*. *Auctions*: A charity *auction* for Concern India Mumbai. Awards: MAHA State Art Award & Govt. of MAHA Agricultural *Mural Design* Mumbai, Artist Guild Pune, Assam Gold Medal, *BAS, ASI*. Commissions: *Murals JJSA*, Nagpur; International: Dubai. Appointments: Lecturer *JJSA*. Collections: Directorate of Art, Govt. of MAHA; College of Arts & Crafts San Francisco, & pvt.

Shrikant Gajanan Jadhav works in the accepted academic *manner*, executing *portraits* and *landscapes*, in *oils* & *watercolours*. His creative *compositions* show his interest in romanticized views of architectural edifices and flowering trees painted in warm, golden *tones*.

He lives and works in Mumbai.

Jadhav, Tuka (1957–) b. Roulashgaon, MAHA. Education: GDA, Dip., Certificate *mural painting*, B.FA. & M.FA. *painting JJSA*; Dip. in Journalism Mumbai. Solos: *JAG*. Group participations: Pune, Lucknow, *NGMA* New Delhi & Mumbai, National *LKA* New Delhi, *Biennale BB, BAAC* Kolkata, SZCC Nagpur, *BAS*; International: *Biennale* Bangladesh, India Art Network Jakarta. *Art* camps: *Biennale* Bangladesh, Malshej Camp arranged by *Artists' Centre* Mumbai. *Auctions*: "Art for Concern" Concern India Foundation—Christie's Mumbai. Awards: MAHA State Art, *LKA* RAJ, Bendre-Husain Award *BAS, ASI*. Appointments: Prof. & HoD Dept. of *Arts & Painting* SNDT Women's University Mumbai. Collections: *NGMA* & *LKA* New Delhi, SZCC Nagpur; International: Singapore, USA, Japan, Germany, pvt. national & international.

Tuka Jadhav, though inspired by *K.K. Hebbar's* glittering brush-strokes and broken *colour*, veers away from representation. The subject is always apparent, in the *form* of a brooding *figure* or omniscient animal, but it has undergone a series of changes, due to the gestural application of web-like skeins of *colour*. The dark dancing *lines, forms*, colourful patches and *abstract images* all contribute to the intense play of human relationships and free application of *colours*.

Tuka Jadhav lives and works in Mumbai.

Jadia, Santosh (1943–) b. Neemuch, MP. Education: Dip. *FA. sculpture* & *painting*. Over 13 solos: New Delhi, Indore, Gwalior, MPKP Bhopal, *JAG*. Group participations: Ahmedabad, Lucknow, *LKA* New Delhi, *BAS, BB*; International: America, Russia, Japan, England, Germany, Cuba, Singapore, Canada. Awards: National Award, Gold Medal for Philosophy & Literature of *Jain* Religion. Publications: A film on his work has been produced by Rinki Bhattacharya, National Radio & TV network. Though basically a *sculptor*, he has also illustrated books and executed *frescoes*. Collections: *Art* galleries & *museums* in India; International: USA, UK, Japan, Cuba and Singapore.

Santosh Jadia's main quality is his simplicity of *form*. He combines *realistic* appearance with a degree of abstraction reflecting a patterned relationship between two shapes echoing each other's impulses. The relatively small sized "After Union" executed in *wood*, displays a monumentality of scale due to the cutting off of extraneous detail and the fine understanding of the *grain* of the *wood*.

Santosh Jadia lives and works in Indore.

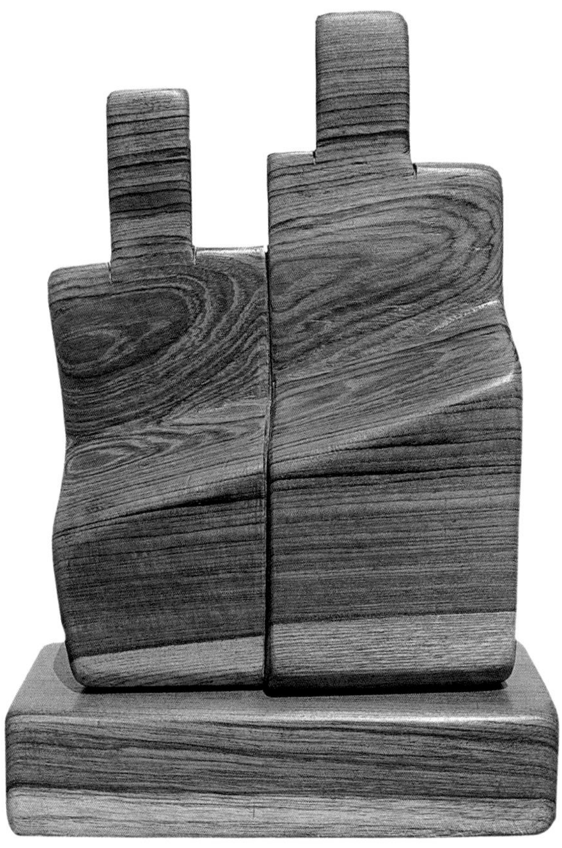

Jadia, Santosh: "After Union", *Wood,* 25 cm ht.

Jagdish & Kamla Mittal Museum of Indian Art (Hyderabad). The *museum* was formed in 1976 as an irrevocable Public Charitable Trust. It owes its birth to the collection of *art* objects and *paintings* assembled over the period of 40 years by the *artist* couple, Jagdish & Kamla Mittal. It specializes in the traditional *arts* & *crafts* of the Indian subcontinent upto the beginning of the 20th century, and consists of over 2000 objects which include *miniature paintings* representative of the *Jain*, Rajasthani, Deccani, Mughal, Bengal and Pahari *styles*; *drawings*, manuscripts, folk and *classical bronzes*, *terracottas*, *ivory* figurines, jade objects, metalware, textiles and *weapons*. There are also selected examples of Nepali and Tibetan Thanakas (painted cloth roll) and *metal images* on view here. Several miniatures and *drawings* have been reproduced in prestigious publications by reputed *art* historians and writers. The *museum* has also lent *art* objects for *exhibitions* elsewhere, both nationally and internationally, and organizes illustrated lectures by eminent scholars of *art*.

Jagdish, C. (1956–) b. Hyderabad. Education: Dip. in *drawing* & *painting* JNTU CFA, Studied *fresco*, *graphics* & stucco *painting MSU*. Solos: *SG* Chennai & Bangalore, L.V. Prasad Eye Institute Hyderabad, *SUG*; International: Chicago, Saugatuck USA, London & Castle Gate House Gallery UK, Schwer Punt Gallery Stuttgart Germany, Blue Court Gallery Liverpool. Group participations: India *Triennale* New Delhi, *Biennale BB*, *PUAG*; International: Stuttgart, Chicago, UK. *Art* camps & workshops: *LKA* AP, Regional Art Center Chennai, All India Artists Hyderabad, *NGMA* New Delhi; International: UK, USA, Artist-in-Residence status by Lakeside Studios in Chicago and later in Sangatank, Wolverhampston Museum in England. Awards: Hyderabad; International: British Council Charles Wallace Travelling Grant in UK, Pollock-Krasner Foundation USA.

Encouraged by *K.G. Subramanyam* to try new *forms* and *media*, C. Jagdish works mostly with *paper*, a material which is not only cost-effective but also versatile. His first works were the "Door" series which were three-dimensional re-creations in cardboard of artistic doorways in India. Today, he sculpts human *figures* in *paper*, creating *masks*, *collages* and cutouts inspired both by his early life in the rural Telangana region and his contemporary life in the West. They represent men and women with painted bodies detailing spectacle cases, umbrellas, jewellery and ethnic costumes. Taken as a group, these *figures* are *vignettes* of small town life in semi-rural India. His work in America includes interesting *busts* in *papier mache*, with a series called "American Friends" and a series of *paper* animals with corresponding Aztec-like urns.

His *paper collages* are *landscapes* created of poster *paper*. Panoramic views of morning and evening skies, banana plantations, rainbows, hillocks and clouds floating behind them are captured in animated detail.

C. Jagdish lives and works in Hyderabad India and Michigan USA. (See illustration on page 173)

Jain, Jainism Jainism, one of India's ancient religions comes from the word Jaina, which means conquerer. The Jainas are those superior beings who have achieved NIRVANA (enlightenment). Jains are the followers of the Jainas. The Jains believe that their religion is timeless. To them the cosmic cycle is like a pendulum with upward and downward swings. Each swing of the pendulum produces 24 Tirthankaras or teachers, of whom MAHAVIRA is the 24th. He advocated much the same principles as Parshvanatha, the 23rd Tirthankara, with the addition of Brahmacharya (celibacy), the other four principles being AHIMSA (non-violence), Asteya (taking only what is given), Satya (truthfulness) and Aparigraha (detachment from worldly possessions).

The early Jains spread from Bihar to GUJ and South India. At a later stage they split into two sects, the SVETHAMBARA and the DIGAMBARA. Their holy scripture is laid down in 12 books in the Prakrit language. Their cosmology teaches that the world is eternal and space immense. Above the earthly place, there are *gods* who themselves are subject to the laws of KARMA. Higher than the abode of *gods*, lay the realm of those who have attained NIRVANA, and therefore exempt from the pains of rebirth. The Jains thus aspire to attain this state, meanwhile following vegetarianism and complete non-violence. Refer *Ellora*, *Icon*, KALPA, *Khajuraho*, *Malwa*, *Manuscript Paintings*, *Miniature Painting*, MOKSHA, *Mural*, *Painting*, *Palm Leaf*, *Picture Space*, *Proportion*, *Space*, *Wood Carving*, *Chetan Arya*, *Atasi Barua*; Illustrations—*Abu-Dilwara Group of Temples*, *Illuminated Manuscripts*, KALPA-SUTRA, MAHAVIRA, MANDAPA.

Jain Miniature, Jain Manuscript Illumination To help preserve the teachings of MAHAVIRA and the other Tirthankaras, the canons were recorded on several *palm leaf* manuscripts from around the AD 5th century. These manuscripts were later illuminated with the addition of small decorations and *figure drawings*. The leaf of the fan-tail palm (the Talipot) was prepared by boiling, drying and burnishing to a smooth and flexible, *light* brown surface. A pile of these leaves were neatly cut to a pre-arranged *size*, strung together on a cord and protected on either side by a pair of wooden covers. From the 13th century onward *paper* was generally used, but the *size* and the format remained the same (3.5x100 cm).

Columns were marked out and the text was written in a decorative *calligraphic* script known as *Jain* Nagari. The *illustrations* were in small square panels inserted between the columns. The subject was generally the life of MAHAVIRA, and other *Jain* stories like the KALPA-SUTRA, Kalakacharyakatha, depictions of *gods* and goddesses, decorative roundels etc.

The *style* of *drawing* was decidedly linear, with wiry, taut *outlines*, exaggerated angular *body proportions* and the most characteristic feature, the protruding farther eye, with the face in profile, a sharp nose, slight double chin, a distended chest tapering to a slim waist. Male *figures* were usually bare-chested with a shawl and a Dhoti, while females wore a short bodice, decorative skirt wound tightly around both legs and an Odhni (head covering) standing stiffly with a *halo* behind the head. Foreigners however,

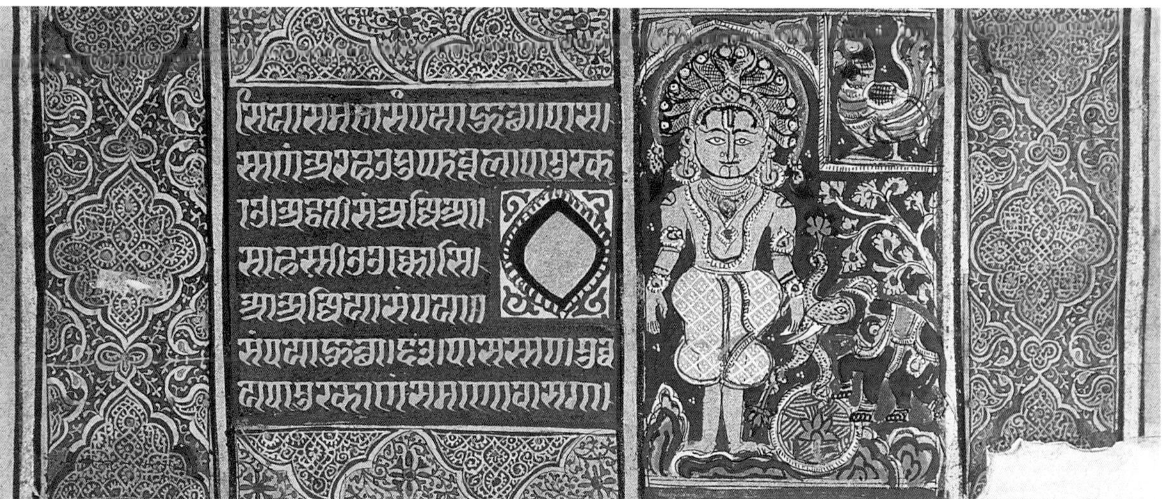

Jain Miniature, Jain Manuscript Illumination.

were depicted in three-quarter face and were usually portrayed wearing heavy boots and stitched garments. Animals, trees and other *landscape* elements were greatly stylized. Early miniatures were characterized by a red *background* while later, ultramarine blue and *gold* was increasingly used. Refer *Calligraphic*, *Codex*, *Gold Leaf*, *Illumination*, KALPASUTRA, *Landscape*, MAHAVIRA, *Manner*, *Manuscript Paintings*, *Miniature Painting*, *Narrative*, *Painting*, *Palm Leaf*, *Picture Space*, *Proportion*, *Space*, *Vignette*, *Chaura Panchasika*, *Vajubhai D. Bhagat*, *Kailash Chandra Sharma*; Illustration—*Illuminated Manuscripts*.

Jain, Saroj (1945–) b. India. No formal education. Studied *sculpture* at TKS. Solos: For the past two decades. Group participations: *LKA's* annual *exhibition* & Kala Mela's group shows RB New Delhi, *AIFACS*, *Dhoomimal*, SRAG, *JAG*. Awards: *AIFACS*. Collections: *NGMA* & *LKA* New Delhi, pvt. in Montreal, Chicago.

Initially Saroj Jain adopted a constructivist attitude towards *sculpture*, starting with the sphere, slicing segments out of it, to create *form* with linear movement. Since the beginning of the 90s, however, she has moved on to using other geometric *forms*, such as cubes and rectangles, at times creating a distinctly anthropomorphic *image* in *marble*, *bronze* and *aluminium*. Sculpturally speaking, her works are a complex interplay of curves and straight *lines*, sculptural *space* moving within and without, in tune with an inherent *rhythm*.

She lives and works in New Delhi.

Jain, Shrenik (1933–) b. Barnagar, MP. Education: GDA & Post-Dip. *mural design JJSA*. Studied under D.D. Deolalikar. Solos: Hyderabad, Jabalpur, *JJSA*, *JAG*, *BB*. Group shows: Mumbai. Group participations: State & All India Exhibition New Delhi, Mumbai, Amritsar, Hyderabad, Lucknow. Awards: Shikhar Samman MP, Gold Medal *AFA* Kolkata & Amritsar, Kalidas Award Ujjain, *JJSA*, *BAS*. *Art* camps & seminars: MPKP in Bhopal, Gwalior SZCC, *BB*. Commissions: *Murals* Indore School of Art, State Festival Bhopal MP, Gokuldas Tejpal Auditorium Mumbai. Appointments: Worked as freelance *artist* in Mumbai, A lecturer at Kalaniketan in Jabalpur, Principal of the Govt. Institute of FA. Indore. Collections: *AFA* Kolkata, *LKA* New Delhi, Air-India Mumbai, Nehru Kala Kendra Indore, *BB*; International: pvt. Canada, Australia, Poland, Holland, Denmark, England, America & Japan.

Shrenik Jain is basically a *painter* of dreamy romanticized *landscapes* full of lush trees and poetic architectural *sketches* of minars and temple domes. Though he has used *oil paints* in the 70s, he is presently drawn to the *transparent washes* of *acrylic* and *watercolours*.

He lives and works at Indore, MP.

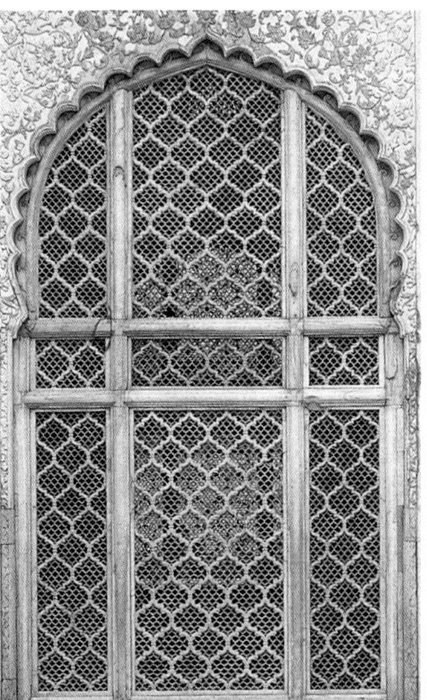

Jali Work, "Bibi-ka-Maqbara", Aurangabad.

Jali Work A synonym for *fretwork* or *open work*. It means carved decoration in *stone*, *wood*, *marble* or *metal*, which is pierced through from one side to the other. Jali work is commonly found in the *stone* screens and windows in temples and certain types of Islamic *architecture*. Refer *Mughal Dynasty*.

Jamod, Jiwan (1935–2003) b. Zezara, GUJ. Education: Studied *Painting* at Govt. KB Ahmedabad under a senior *Art* Prof. Babubhai Gajjar & *NKM*. Exhibiting regularly in National

Exhibitions & group shows since 1956. Won awards for *graphic design* since the 60s. Collections: Pvt. Chennai, Bangalore, New Delhi & Ahmedabad; International: London, Austin, Nairobi, Canada, Ghana, Chicago.

He had worked in both *oil* and *watercolours*, employing a wide variety of *styles*, including a constructivist abstraction and a naive *figuration*. His *abstract landscapes* were dominated by one or more sun-like discs against an explosion of straight and diagonal *lines*. His *colours* verge on the *monochrome* with shrill oranges and yellows standing out against the dusty olive and mustard *backgrounds*. He lived in Ahmedabad, GUJ.

Japanese Art Japanese art traces its origins to the influence of *Buddhism* (6th century) and *Chinese art* (7th–9th centuries). Later, these were joined by the colourful Japanese *style*, Yamato-e and Yoseki-Tsukuri. However, the most striking impact on Japanese art was from Zen *Buddhism* notably in the *monochrome ink paintings* (Sumi-e). Japanese *landscapes* and *narratives* can usually be seen on room screens, sliding panels and scrolls.

The Japanese *style* of *Painting* was adopted by many *artists* at *Jorasanko*, in Kolkata, where the Japanese *artists* Okakara Kakuzo, Hishida and Y. Taikan were frequent visitors. Here *Abanindranath Tagore* got the inspiration to develop the famous *Bengal School "wash style"*, but his *wash technique*, unlike the Japanese, involved both *watercolour* and *tempera*. Refer *Bengal Revivalism*, *Bengal School*, *Nandalal Bose*, *Sukhen Ganguly*, *Sita Ray*, *K. Madhava Menon*, *Abanindranath Tagore*, *Hemendranath Mazumbar*.

Jaspal, S. (1958–) b. Patiala, PUJ. Education: M.FA. *Drawing* & *Painting*, M.FA. in History of *Arts* PUJ University PUJ. Solos: Hoshiarpur, Jalandhar, NZCC Patiala, *LKA* PUJ & Vishakhapatanam. Group shows: *Santiniketan*, Chandigarh. Group participations: National Exhibition, Kala Mela & *LKA* New Delhi, *Biennale* Chandigarh, *AIFACS*, *BB*; Travelling Exhibition SZCC Nagpur, Mumbai, Indore & Pune. *Art* camps: Hoshiarpur, Patiala, Jalandhar, Kurukshetra, Chennai, Chandigarh, *LKA*, Art Heritage & NZCC PUJ, Mount Abu RAJ. Awards: Over 25 awards PUJ University Gold Medal, All India Exhibition Award Raipur MP, SZCC Nagpur, Silver Medal Guntur, *ISOA*; International: Honourable Mention in USA. Member: Founder President of TIAS (Thoughts in Arts) in Hoshiarpur exhibited regularly with them. Appointments: Was a lecturer Govt. College for Women Patiala; Research on Terracota Archeological Finding in PUJ. Collections: SZCC Nagpur, *LKA* Vishakhapatanam & New Delhi, *BB*, also pvt.; International: Mauritius, Switzerland, England, Italy.

His *paintings* have a semi-surreal quality reminiscent of Marc Chagall. His *sketches* in pen and *ink* have been executed with a "Nadi Qalam" (a young bamboo shoot). The quality of *line* produced by it varies from a mere scratch to a full, lush *brush* stroke. These *sketches* depict bare *landscapes* with clown, bicycles and solitary human beings with an everpresent undertone of violence. His later *paintings* were heavily impastoed with *shades* of blue, involving floating objects.

He is presently in Hoshiarpur PUJ.

Jataka A story or parable about one of the incarnations of the BUDDHA prior to his birth as Prince Siddhartha, son of King Suddhodhana and Queen Maya. Jatakas were extensively used to proclaim the message of BUDDHA to the pilgrims. The monks employed *artists* who turned bare *stone* walls into *frescoes* to narrate the life and teachings of BUDDHA, as in CHHADANTA Jataka, Ruru Jataka, Mriga Jataka or Kapi Jataka. Refer *Ajanta*, ATMA, *Bas-Relief*, BUDDHA, *Buddhist Art*, CHADDANTA, *Continuous Representation*, *Narrative*, *Outline*, *Pala Miniatures*, *Spiritual*, *Stone Carving*, *Theme*.

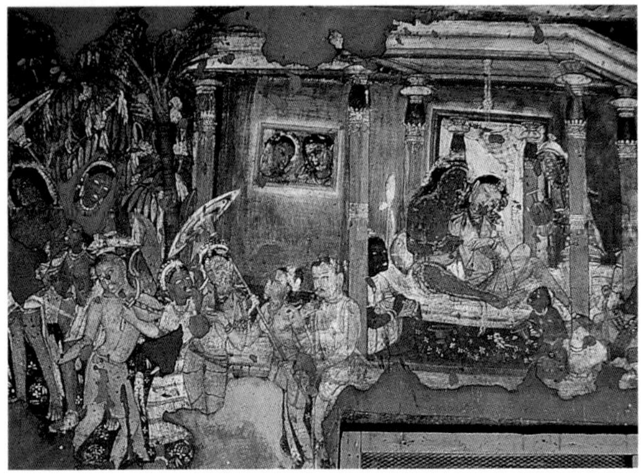

Jataka: "Ajanta Cave 17", Aurangabad, Verandah *Fresco*.

Jayachamarajendra Art Gallery (Sri) (KAR). The Jaganmohan Palace in Mysore was converted into a Museum of Indian Arts & Crafts in 1924. *K. Venkatappa* later further extended the scope of the gallery. The then Maharaja of Mysore, Sri Jayachamaraja Wodeyar bequeathed the entire art gallery along with its extensive grounds to the nation. This was constituted as a Public Trust in 1955, the same year in which the gallery became popularly known as the Sri Jayachamarajendra Art Gallery. Many important examples of *modern* Indian *art* are to be found in its collection. Among these are several *oil paintings* by *Raja Ravi Varma*, the "Glow of Hope" by *Savlaram L. Haldankar* and works by *Nandalal Bose* and *K. Venkatappa*. The *crafts* section has sandalwood and *ivory carvings*, jewellery boxes, old coins, *paintings* and *carvings* on rice *grains*, *brass* and *bronze* articles and Thanjavur (Tanjore) *metal* trays on display. There are several *portraits* and *photographs* of the Royal Family on display, as well as a Western Art Gallery with an original *painting* by Peter Paul Rubens and *copies* of Rembrandt. The New Building at the rear contains other *craft* items such as rosewood panels and Japanese *ivory* and mother-of-pearl *inlay* in addition to the usual *portraits* and *models* of the Mysore Palace and palace officials. There is an entire gallery devoted to the works of Mysore *artists*. The Ranga Mahal section contains *copies* of *Ajanta* and Sittanivasal *murals*.

Jehangir Art Gallery (JAG) (Mumbai). An important landmark in Mumbai, the JAG came into being with the munificence of three parties: Sir Cowasji Jehangir who provided the funds, the trustees of the *PWM*, in the compound of which the gallery stands, and the state govt. who agreed to make a regular grant towards the upkeep of the building. The Gallery was formally inaugurated on the 21st of January 1952 and celebrated its golden jubilee in 2002. In 1990 the gallery was renovated and brought upto International standards. It now has two halls: The Auditorium Hall and the Exhibition Gallery. The former has about 2700 sq.ft. of floor *space* and a wall display area of about 180 running ft. The latter has a climate control and security system with floor *space* of about 3700 sq.ft. and the display area of 370 running ft. This gallery is normally divided into three sections namely no.1, no.2 and no.3. The gallery also houses the Dr. Homi Bhabha Art Reference Library, a lending library of original works of *art* and a sales room of its *art* collections, *prints* and publications. It also organizes *art* appreciation and other courses dealing with the *visual arts* from time to time. Jehangir has its "Monsoon Sale" every year. The Golden Jubilee "Master Strokes" *exhibition* displayed several works from its collection–*A.A. Almelkar*, *K.A. Ara*, *M.R. Achrekar*, M.S. Joshi, Lalkaka, *Hemendranath Mazumdar*, A.H. Muller, S.M. Pandit, *Y.K. Shukla*, *L.N. Taskar*, *A.X. Trinidade* with the other seniors *artists*.

Jehangir Nicholson Art Gallery (JNAG) (at NCPA Mumbai). The JNAG, housed in the premises of the NCPA was inaugurated in 1976. It was donated by *art* patron, Jehangir Nicholson, and displays over 58 *paintings both Indian and International* from his pvt. collection. Several *exhibitions* have been held in the gallery. These include *graphics* by Emilio Greco, *prints* by P. Picasso and *caricatures* by Jose C. Orozco, the Mexican muralist. Jehangir Nicholson an *art* collector encouraged *artists* by collecting their works. Some of these works were later exhibited at "The Museum Gallery" Mumbai near *JAG*.

Jnana-Mudra Jnana=knowledge. Refer MUDRAS.

Jorasanko The Tagore family home, a mansion situated in a large estate with parklands, Kolkata, where the family members were exposed to the cultural soirees and receptions hosted for a galaxy of scholars, *artists* and musicians, both Indian and foreign. *Abanindranath Tagore* was said to have painted some or most his important works and written his books in the southern verandah of the house.

Joshi, Balvant A. (1928–) b. Chotila, GUJ. Education: Dip. *Painting JJSA*, *Art* Master's Certificate CNCFA. Solos: Rajkot, *LKA* Bhavan Ahmedabad, *JAG*. Group participations: Chandigarh, *LKA* New Delhi & Ahmedabad, Kalidas Academy Ujjain, *AFA* Kolkata, *AIFACS*. Awards: Art Teacher Education Dept. & State Art Exhibition GUJ, National Exhibition New Delhi, Veteran Artist Award AIKS, *AIFACS*. Hon.: By President of India organized by Mahatma Gandhi Charitable Trust 2003. Collections: National Museum, *NGMA* & *LKA* New Delhi, Vikram Vishwa Vidyalaya Ujjain, pvt. Ahmedabad, Kolkata, Mumbai; International: USA, England, Canada.

Balvant A. Joshi's *art form* is based on the traditional with folk-like *frontality* and simplicity, though with a near *monochrome* use of *colours* as against the bright *colours* of true *folk art*. His *paintings* have the appearance of *murals* due to the almost complete absence of *background* which is suggested through the use of single elements like a tuft of grass or a gateway. His subjects are taken from rural life, with the Krishna Lila being especially popular.

He lives and works in Rajkot, GUJ.

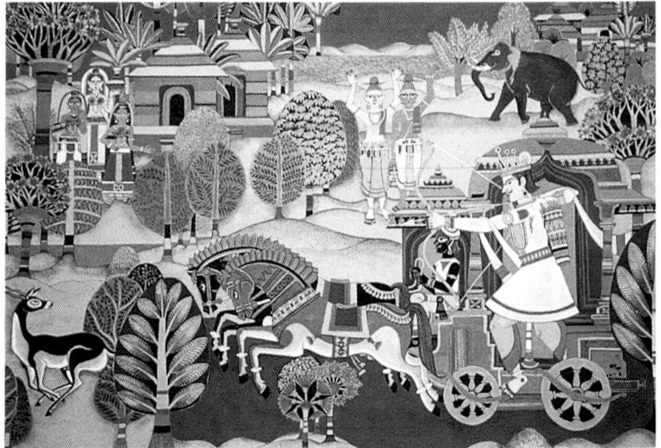

Joshi, Balvant A.: "Hunting", *Watercolour*, 28x36 cm.

Joshi, Goverdhanlal (1914–1998) b. Kandaroli, RAJ. Education: Before joining *Santiniketan* & studying under *Nandalal Bose*; Studied *drawing* from an *artist* of the traditional Nathadwara School; Later learnt *clay modelling* from *Sudhir R. Khastgir* Dehradun. Solos: Amritsar, Thiruvananthapuram, Jaipur, Udaipur; International: Egypt. Group participations: National Exhibition *LKA* New Delhi, IAFA Amritsar, *AIFACS*, also Jaipur, Udaipur, Kolkata, Mumbai, Mysore. Attended camps. Awards: Govt. Industrial Educational Dept. National Award New Delhi, Gold Medal Thiruvananthapuram, *LKA* RAJ. Fellowship: by the *LKA* New Delhi to study the life of Bhil tribes RAJ & GUJ. Member: National & Regional *LKA* New Delhi & Jaipur, *AIFACS*. Founder member: Tulika Kalakar Parishad Udaipur & the group was interested in tribal life–a fact that is endorsed by Goverdhanlal Joshi's *manner* of *painting*. Publications: Newspapers & Magazines; Radio talks on "Beginning of Mewar Paintings", "Rajasthan Painting & the Language". Collections: Trivandrum Art Gallery, Amritsar Art Gallery, Udaipur Museum.

He had worked both on *paper* and on fine cotton cloth, with *tempera* and *watercolour* respectively. His *paintings* were full of *colour* and a folk-like vigour of *line* and *form*. His favourite subject was the Bhil dances and the rhythmic movement of the Bhil women engrossed in their daily chores. He lived in Udaipur and Jaipur.

Joshi, Hema (1934–) b. Mumbai, MAHA. Education: GDA *JJSA*, Guided by *Savlaram L. Haldankar* & *Gajanan S. Haldankar*. Solos: New Delhi, Bangalore, *JAG*, TAG; International: UK, New York. Group participations: National *LKA*, *NGMA Triennale* & New Delhi, *GC* & RPG Mumbai, Several shows in India–"50 years of India's Independence"; International: New York, New Jersey, Germany, France, Visual Art Gallery UK. Collections: *NGMA* & *LKA* New Delhi, *CYAG*, Air India & abroad.

Hema Joshi is primarily a *painter*, but she has dabbled with *sculpture* and has created an *installation* "The Bombay Seat" for a specially curated show. Her *forms* in *painting* veer from large *abstract*, introspective *canvases* to smaller, *figurative* works on *paper* which represent aspects of day-to-day *impressions*.

Joshi, Mrugank G. (1940–) b. MAHA. Education: Govt. Dip. *JJSA, FFA* (*MSU*). Over 8 solos: *JAG*. Group participations: Alliance Francaise & MAHA State Art Exhibition Mumbai, National Exhibition New Delhi, *BAS, JAG, DG*. Awards: Govt. of India Cultural Scholarship, *BAS*. Member: *LKA* & WZCC Goa. Appointments: Prof. at *JJSA*, Principal & later Dean of FFA Goa University. Commissions & studies: *Mural designs, Art Conservation* at *National Museum* New Delhi. Publications: Author article on *Jain* KALPA-SUTRA in Roop-Bheda, Marathi Vishwakosh (Encyclopaedia). Collections: "Panorama of Mars"—large *painting* done for *NCAG*.

Mrugank G. Joshi shows an affinity for exploration & experimentation with *themes* as well as materials. He has worked with *pencil drawings, oil paintings* and *gouaches* in rendering subjects both from historical study and *contemporary* experience. He shows a proclivity for the *figurative*, with various *styles* including the oriental and the expressionistic making themselves felt.

He lives and works in Mumbai.

Joshi, Surendra Pal (1958–) b. Dehradun, UP. Education: B.FA. GCAC Lucknow. Solos: State *LKA* Lucknow, AFA New Delhi, RAJ *LKA* Jaipur, *JAG*, TAG, SRAG, *ABC*; International: Wales, UK. Group participations: National Exhibition *LKA* all over India, Habitat Center New Delhi, SZCC Nagpur, *Biennale* Jaipur, *BB, JAG, Dhoomimal*; International: Indian Festival USA, Kobe Japan. *Art* camps & workshops: *LKA* & *NGMA* New Delhi, State Resource Centre Jaipur, Exhibited & mural workshop Art Folio Chandigarh, others in Udaipur, Kota. Awards: Scholarship UP State *LKA* Lucknow, Several RAJ *LKA* Awards; International: Asian Cultural Centre UNESCO Japan. Fellowship: *Mural Design* British Council Arts Council and Charles Wallace Trust Wales Cardiff UK. Commisions: *Murals* Jaipur, New Delhi, Mumbai; International: Wales, UK. Collections: *NGMA*, National *LKA* & Ministry of Education New Delhi, SZCC Nagpur, Allahabad University, Art Folio Chandigarh, State Resource Centre & RAJ *LKA* Jaipur, *ABC, GE*; International: Holland, Wales, UK, UNESCO Japan.

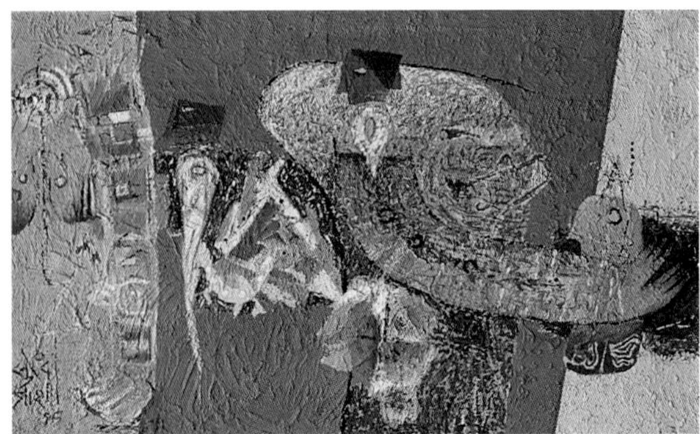

Joshi, Surendra Pal: "Coming of Krishna", *Oil* on *Canvas*, 1996 91.5x152.5 cm.

His *forms* though appearing *figurative* are heavily *symbolic* with cryptic signs and marks balanced against the plethora of heavily pigmented brushstrokes.

Striking a delicate *balance* between *murals* and *paintings*, he gives his work a quality of substance through certain touches and glimpses, *texture* and *colour* and the three and two-dimensional exploration. He has also specialized in the warp and weft as patchwork *texture* on raw *canvas* and *murals*. It is the work of *visual art* which fascinates to understand the quality of the surface of the *composition*.

He works in Jaipur.

Junk Art *Art* produced by using local, commonly found material, such as sand, junk, *wood, stones*, used newspaper and objects like dried leaves, pods, *stones* or even kitchen ware and machinery parts, *metal, fibreglass* and any scrap. In India since 1990s many *artists* have been inspired by Pop *imagery* with *collages* and junk *assemblages* in a fusion of *painting* and *sculpture*. *Pilloo Pochkhanawalla* began incorporating junk and scrap material into her works of the later *period*, when exploration of *space* and *texture* became her overriding concern. Refer *Assemblage, Found Object, Krishnamachari Bose, N. Pushpamala.*

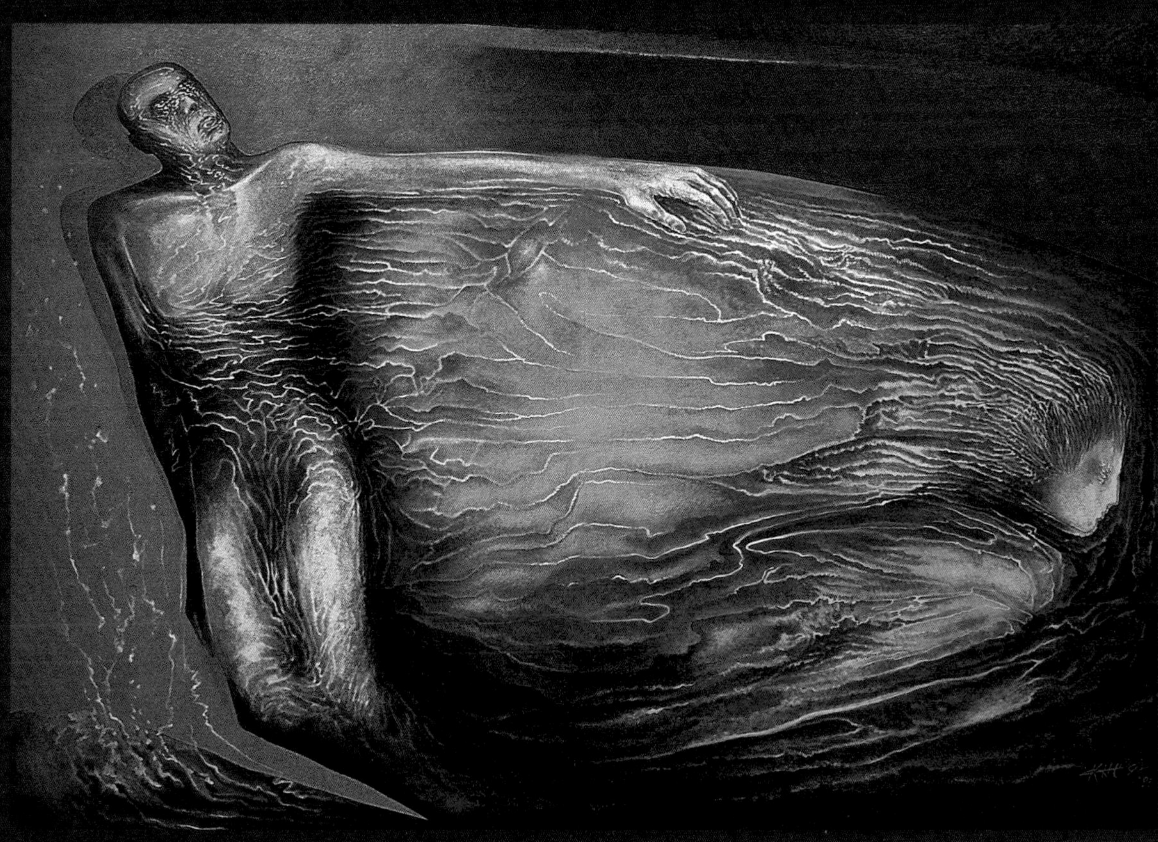

Khosa, K.: "Air, Earth & Water", *Oil* on *Canvas*, 1993, 150x200 cm. (See notes on page 195)

K. Ramanujam (1941–1973) b. Chennai. Education: Dip. College of Art Chennai; Physically handicapped later worked in *Cholamandal* under *K.C.S Paniker*. Group shows: Mumbai, Chennai, New Delhi. Group participations: National Exhibition *LKA*; International: Commonwealth Arts Festival London. *Auctions*: Heart Mumbai. Commissions: Three *murals* in Chennai. Collections: *NGMA*, *GC* Mumbai, State *LKA* Chennai.

K. Ramanujam's *style* was basically linear, the wiry *lines* twisting and *turning* to form sprites and goblins propelling a fantasy-filled world of chimeras in anxiety filled in his works. There was a child-like naiveté in his *themes* and *images*. His *paintings* are small sized with subtle effects of *shade* and *light* enhancing the palaces, boats and monsters, that he loved.

Kailash, Kailasa The legendary, *silver* mountain in the Himalaya range on which SHIVA resides along with PARVATI and his host of GANAS. It has been majestically depicted at *Ellora* as Kailash temple in cave No. 16, in the *relief sculpture*. "Ravana Shaking Mount Kailash", which is also of the 7th century in Cave 14. Refer *Conservation*, *Dravidian style*, *Ellora*, *Erotic Art*, GANA, *God*, *Relief*, *Relief Sculpture*, SHIKHARA, *Spiritual*; Illustration—RAMAYANA, *Sarada Charan Ukil*.

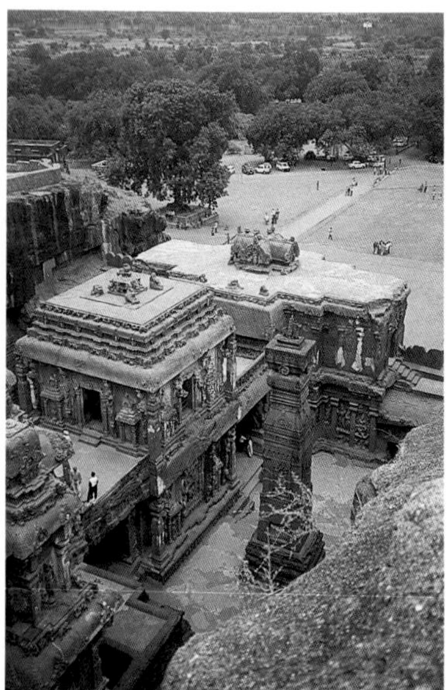

Kailash, Kailasa: "Ellora Cave 14", 8th to 10th century AD.

Kala/Kaal Also known as *time*; Kaal, according to many Indian myths is endlessly cyclical, with *creation* leading to destruction and vice-versa, with good *times* following bad and so on. This is different from the Christian and Islamic belief that *time* moves in a straight path starting from the day of Creation and ending once and for all on the day of Judgement.

According to the Hindu religion, the holy trinity of BRAHMA, VISHNU and SHIVA are responsible for *time* Cycles (Kaal Chakra). According to one such version, SHIVA dances his terrifying dance, the Tandava-Nritya as NATARAJA when he is destroying the world. At the same *time* the world is regenerated from the ashes of the previous world and this regeneration is represented in *sculpture* in the *form* of the *halo*-like *aureole* around NATARAJA (with the flames licking it representing destruction). Refer *South Indian bronzes*; Illustration—NATARAJA.

Kala Bhavana (KB) (*Santiniketan*). In 1919, *Rabindranath Tagore* invited *Nandalal Bose*, a pupil of *Abanindranath Tagore* to take charge of KB a newly-formed *art* school at *Santiniketan*. For some time, *Nandalal Bose* vacillated between teaching at KB and at the Oriental Society of Art in Kolkata. In 1920 he chose to move to *Santiniketan* for good. KB sought to bring together the past and the present, the East and the West. *Rabindranath Tagore* donated a sizable *art* library which included books on *modern art*. By the mid- 20s KB was beginning to resemble the *Bauhaus* with a steady stream of visiting teachers in addition to *artists* and artisans. Today, along with *Visva Bharati*, KB is well-known as a centre for the study of the *visual arts*. The syllabus includes studio courses in "Indian style" and "Western style" *art*, *art* history and *aesthetics*. Lectures, *art* discussions, debates and *exhibitions* are regularly held.

KB at present offers five major streams of studies: *painting*, *sculpture*, *design*, *graphic art* and *art* history with both degrees and diplomas at the undergraduate and post-graduate levels, as well as a Ph.D. programme. There is a library and the Nandan Museum. The Bhavan also publishes books and journals on *art*, *art* history and *aesthetics*, including the annual journal "Nandan".

Kalahamtarita (Abhisandhita) One of the eight specific types of NAYIKAS mentioned by ancient Indian writers and poets. She is the bad-tempered heroine, who alienates her lover due to her own lack of consideration. The NAYAK is usually depicted walking away from her. Refer ASHTANAYIKA.

Kalamkari Kalam=*pen* or stylus, Kari=work or *craft*. A fabric, generally coarse handwoven cotton, patterned through the *medium* of dye rather than the loom. *Artists* draw *motifs* using the Kalam, a slim bamboo stick with a piece of rag tied to its tip, then fill them with *colours* made from vegetable dyes. Earlier *designs* were drawn by hand, but later *block printing* became more economically viable. The process generally starts with a series of well-coordinated strokes and slashes, applied with a *charcoal pencil*, which

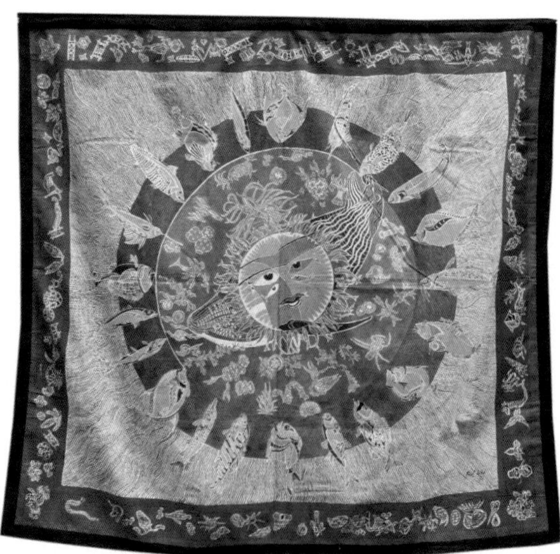

Kalamkari: *Bal Wad*, "Surya", 8'x8'.

demarcated the *outlines* of *figures*. The Kalam dipped in *black* dye is used to accentuate the *outlines*. Finally, intricate detailing is done producing *aesthetic* work, that is unsurpassed in its vigour of *design* and richness of *colours*. Starting from temple hangings and canopies, Kalamkari *art* spread its popularity to household usage as well. Popular Kalamkari centres are Srikalahasti and Masulipatam in South India. Vibrant examples can be found in the Calico Museum of Textile Ahmedabad, GUJ, AP and TN. Refer *Artefact*, *WSC*, *Salar Jung Museum* Hyderabad, *K. Madhava Menon*, *Roshan M. Mullan*, *Kailash Chandra Sharma*; Illustration–*Bal Wad*.

Kali=blackness, destroyer of *time*. Kali is DURGA in her fearsome *form* representing *time*, both giving life and taking it. She is adored and worshipped as the main deity of Bengal. She has *black* skin, sharp protruding fangs, a protruding tongue and the third eye in the forehead. She generally depicted with hands raized, or bestowing a blessing (for the faithful), the other forbidding fear (for the evil doer). Generations of *artists* have found awesome beauty in the symbolization of Kali. Also known as CHANDI, Bhairavi or Mahakali (names of the chief of SHIVA's hosts). Kali became a popular subject in 19th-century Bengal–the Pata *painters* constantly depicting her as a bloodthirsty figure with tongue hanging out and ghoulish necklace adorning her. Refer *Bazaar Painting*, *Bengal Oil Painting*, DURGA, *Hinduism*, *Kalighat Pat*, *Kalighat Folk Painting*, MATRIKAS, *Oil Paint*, SHAKTI, *Spiritual*, TANTRA, *Tantra Art*, TANTRIC, *Maqbool Fida Husain*, *Jamini Roy*, *Shakila*; Illustration–*Tyeb Mehta*.

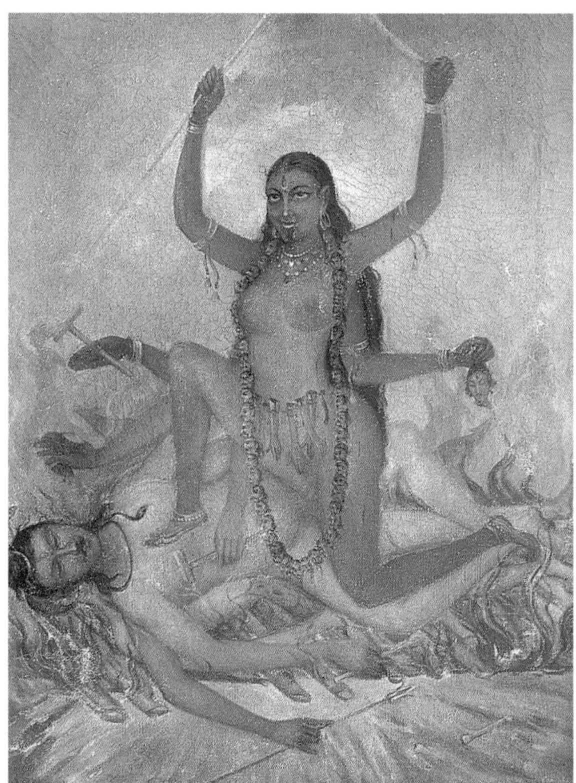

Kali: "Anonymous", *Oil* on *Canvas*, early 20th century, 48.26x33 cm.

Kalighat Pat, Kalighat Folk Painting Kalighat=an area in Kolkata WB, Pat=scroll. An Indian school of popular or folk *style painting* which originated near the KALI temple at Kolkata around 1820 from the village Patuas who migrated to Kolkata. The *paintings* were executed in *watercolour* (*oils* were rarely used) in imitation of the English *watercolour* and were mass-produced on *paper* as souvenirs and objects of devotion for the poorer pilgrims. The *paintings* were rapidly executed with a few, bold, sweeping strokes of the *brush*, *modelling figures* in near *monochromatic colours*. The subject was religious at first, mythical and *legends*, but later *contemporary* subjects crept in, often being treated with more than a touch of satire. A famous subject is on the murder story of "Elokeshi & the Mahant". The more elaborate *paintings* show details of costume & jewellery. These Pats have continued to serve as inspiration to many *modern painters* in particular *Jamini Roy*. Refer *Bazaar Paintings*, *Brush Drawing*, *Cloisonnism*, *Commercial Art*, *Company School/Company Painting*, *Creation*, *Eclectic*, *Eclecticism*, *Folk Art*, *Folk Inspiration*, KALI, *Line and Wash*, *Media*, *Monochrome*, *Monochromatic*, *Outline*, *Painter*, *Painting*, *Print*, *Synthetism*, *White Line Engraving*, *Nandalal Bose*, *Jogen Chowdhury*, *Jamini Roy*; Illustration–*Erotic Art*.

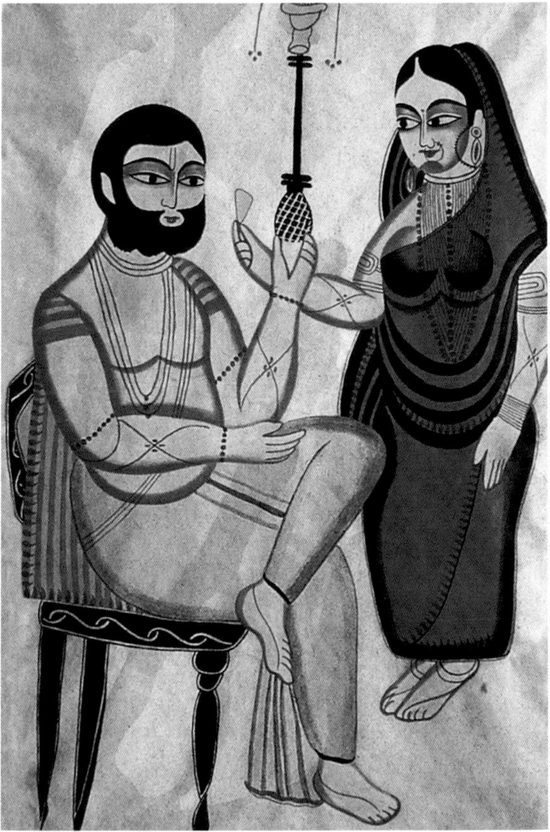

Kalighat Pat, Kalighat Folk Painting: Mahanta & Elokeshi-I
"Anonymous", *Watercolour* on *Paper*, early 20th century, 43x27 cm.

Kaliyadamana, Kaliyamardana The vanquishing of Kaliya, the hydra-headed snake by KRISHNA. One of the many titles of KRISHNA. This adventure has been the subject of countless *miniature paintings* of diverse schools & of *sculpture* as well. In almost all of them, KRISHNA is depicted dancing on the snake's hood, gripping its tail firmly in one hand. In a few *paintings* there is a huge lotus bed beneath KRISHNA's feet, pertaining to the use of the *term* "lotus feet of Krishna."

Kalki, Kalkin=destroyer of sins. The future, 10th incarnation of VISHNU will supposedly descend upon the earth at the end of the present age–Kaliyuga, the last & worst of the four ages, when human life-span is at its shortest. Also known as the Age of Darkness. He will come with a drawn sword and riding a *white* horse, destroy all evil, dispel darkness & again usher the Golden Age of peace, purity & righteousness. Refer AVATARA, AVTAAR, AVATAR, DASAVATARA, YUGA, GANJIFA, KALA/KAAL.

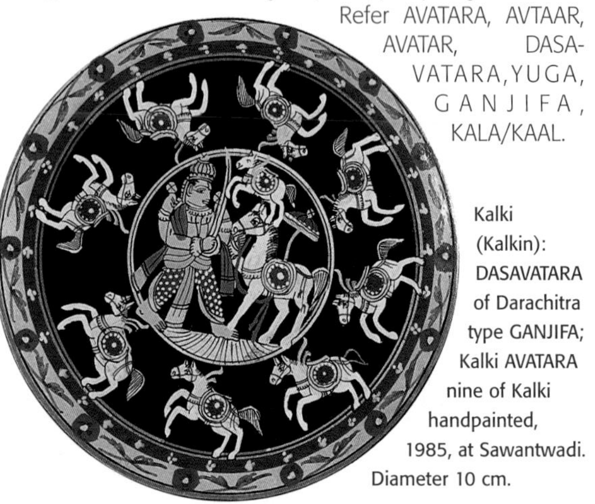

Kalki (Kalkin): DASAVATARA of Darachitra type GANJIFA; Kalki AVATARA nine of Kalki handpainted, 1985, at Sawantwadi. Diameter 10 cm.

Kalpa 1. A single day of the *God* BRAHMA, equivalent to 4.32 billion human years. **2.** The uppermost level of the universe according to *Jain* cosmology, divided into 16 Devalokas or heavens, each one with a name & its own inhabitants. Refer *Jain, Jainism,* LOKA.

Kalpa-Sutra One of the most revered books of the SVETHAMBARA *Jains* as well as one of the most ancient, it is attributed to Acharya Bhadrabahu who lived in the 4th century BC. The text represents a section of the *Jain* canons. It is a treatise concerned with the correct forgiving conduct i.e. to be followed by the ordained during the rainy season, a period of rest for both *Jain* & Buddhist monks, nuns & acolytes. It has 1200 Shlokas (verses) & three parts of prose, Jaina Charita, Sthaviranali & Sadhu Samachari. According to *Jain tradition*, all monks recited the Kalpa-sutra on the 15th night after the commencement of their rest for the rainy season. This necessitated the ready availability of the text & as a result, the Kalpa-sutra became one of the most widely reproduced manuscripts. Refer *Jainism*.

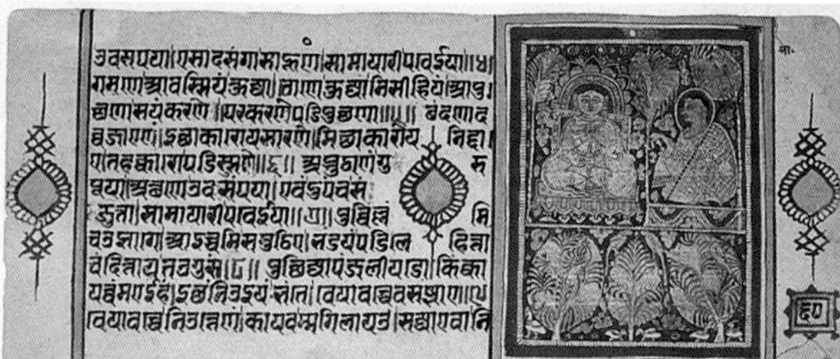

Kalpa-Sutra: Jain Manuscript–Jain School, 17th century.

Kamarpatta Refer ABHUSHANA, *Ornaments*.

Kama-Sutra An ancient Indian text on the *art* of making love and other erotica by Vatsayana. Kama means wish, desire, longing. Sutra means to string or put together. Kama is also *god* of love. The profusion of erotic *sculptures* in Hindu temples, the most famous examples being at *Khajuraho*, were probably inspired by the Kama-Sutra. Refer *Erotic Art, Khajuraho, Relief Sculpture*.

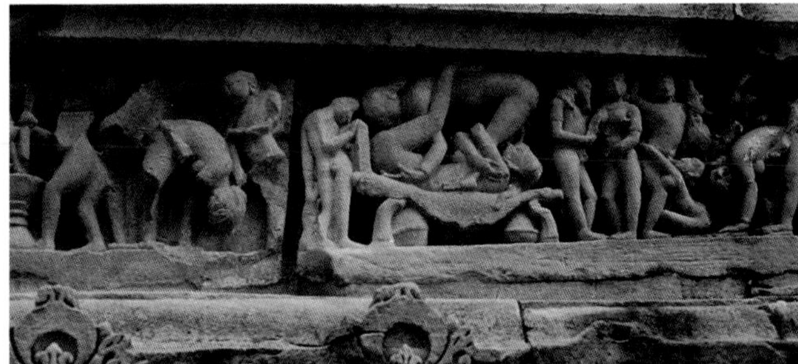

Kama-Sutra: *Khajuraho*, MP.

Kambli, H.R. (1956–) b. Goa. Education: B.FA. Goa College of Art, M.FA. *Printmaking KB Santiniketan*. Solos: Goa, *Art Heritage* New Delhi, *JAG*; International: London. Group participations: National Exhibition & *LKA* New Delhi, *BAAC* Kolkata, *INTACH* Exhibition Goa, *Biennale BB*, *CHAG*, *AIFACS*; International: *Biennale* Cuba, Taipei & Taiwan, *Printmaking* USA, Japan, Spain, Egypt & Norway, *Triennale* Japan & Sao Paulo Brazil. *Art* camps & workshops: *Printmaking/Graphic LKA* New Delhi, *KB Santiniketan*, *Triennale* Goa, *GAC*. Awards: Fellowship College of Art Goa; Honoured All India Exhibition *Prints* Chandigarh; Grant *LKA* New Delhi. Founder member: Goan Art Forum. Appointments: Head of *Printmaking* Goa College of Art. Collections: *LKA* New Delhi; International: USA, Poland & Wimbledon School of Art UK, pvt.

H.R. Kambli's *paintings* have their roots in the gestural *figurative* with scratched and incised *lines* dominating a deeply expressionistic people-scape. His "Head" series is reminiscent of F. Bacon's *style*, with motion and movement captured in a blur of *fantasy*. His *prints* and *drawings* are more intricate with a fine understanding of *line* and *texture*. The series he did in London displays his roots in Indian *mythology* and *tradition* juxtaposed against *contemporary* Indian urbanization; an added element is the exposure to a new, yet strangely familiar *culture*. He has exploited almost all the finer qualities of *etching* during this sojourn.

H.R. Kambli is presently in Goa.

Kamboj, B.P. (1928–) b. Dehradun, Uttaranchal. Education: M.A. *Painting* Agra University, earlier studied under S. Pooran Singh in Lahore School, later studied under *Sudhir Khastgir* and Ranvir Saxena. Solos: Dehradun, Varanasi,

Mumbai, Agra, *AIFACS*. Group participations: *LKA* Lucknow, All India Art Exhibition Kolkata, National Exhibition *LKA* & "50 years of India" *NGMA* New Delhi, *JAG*; International: Srilanka, London, Prague. *Art* camps, workshops & seminar: Meerut, Agra, Jaipur, Udaipur, New Delhi; International: Represented India at Asian Art Conference Fukuoka Japan. Awards: Veteran Artists Award *AIFACS*, Doon Ratan Award Dehradun, State *LKA* UP. Member: Academic & Executive Council Agra University, General Council National *LKA* New Delhi, Executive Board Member of the National and UP State *LKA* 1998–2001; Founder member Doon Kala Chakra Dehradun & TRIA Artist Association Agra. Appointments: Taught *art* from 1949 to 1989 Agra & later Dehradun. Publications: Author of "History of European Art", "Wall Paintings of Garhwal". Collections: *NGMA* & *LKA* New Delhi.

A *landscape* with a *theme* is how one can describe B.P. Kamboj's *paintings*. Dehradun where he was born was once a beautiful green area, subsequently deforested due to rampant urbanization. This destruction of Mother Earth features constantly in B.P. Kamboj's works, which lies beyond the *illusion* of *Realism*, and often with a quasi-naive illustrational *style* executed in flat rich *colours* of Indian miniatures.

B.P. Kamboj lives in Dehradun, after his retirement as Dean & HoD *FA*. Agra College.

Kamboj, B.P.: "Yakshi pray for survival", *Oils*, 1995, 125x100 cm.

Kaneria, Raghav (1936–) b. Anida, GUJ. Education: Dip. *Sculpture FFA* (*MSU*), M.A. *FA*. RCA. Solos: *CYAG*. Group participations: Ahmedabad, *Art Heritage* & *Triennale* New Delhi, *BAAC* Kolkata, The Bombay Art Festival, *JAG*; International: Festival of India Exhibition, Germany, *Biennale* Paris, Antwerp, Travelling Exhibition Moscow, Warsaw, Prague, Budapest, Exhibitions in USA, Japan, London. Awards: National Awards *LKA* New Delhi, Silver Plaque *AIFACS*, *BAS*. Scholarship & Fellowships: Including Commonwealth Scholarship RCA, Visiting Artist Fellowship to teach *sculpture* Hull College of Art England, Cultural Scholarship Govt. of India. Appointments: HoD of *Sculpture MSU*. Collections: *NGMA* & *LKA* New Delhi, *SJM*, *Roopankar*; International: London, Cambridge UK.

Raghav Kaneria can be called a Futurist as his *sculptures* usually have sleek and gleaming *contours*. Movement seems to be the hallmark of the works whether *abstract* or semi-figurative. One also finds the beauty of the machine in several of his works. He has used various *techniques*, including *casting*, *welding* different *metals* and *alloys* including *bronze* and *steel*. He has also worked with *terracotta*. His later works became increasingly surreal incorporating junk, found objects with their rusty, decomposed surfaces imparting a primordial air to his light and airy *creations*.

At present he is in Vadodara. Refer *Junk Art*, *Found Objects*.

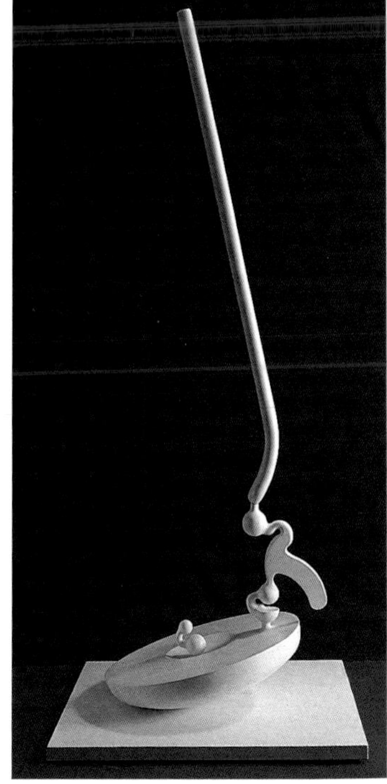

Kaneria, Raghav: "Untitled", *Steel*, 1991, 305 cm. ht.

Kangra, Kangra Kalam, Kangra School, Kangra Miniatures *Rajput miniature paintings* from Pahari (mountainous) region of Kangra valley in the Punjab in North-western India. There is influence of *Mughal miniature style* in both *Pahari* and *Rajasthani miniatures paintings*, due to interaction between the Hindu Rajput Rajas (rulers) and courts of Islamic Mughal Emperors; and possibly also due to migration of many master *artists* at the decline of the Mughal Empire. The Kangra *style* evolved from the nearby tiny State of Guler whose Rajas were ardent supporters of poetry, music and *art*, based on their Hindu-Vaishnavite faith devoted to KRISHNA worship or BHAKTI, as were most Rajput rulers of Rajasthan and North India. The most refined of the Kangra miniatures were made in prolific numbers from late 18th to first quarter of 19th century, during the reign of Raja Sansar Chand.

These works therefore are *pictorial* depictions of love poetry (Sat Sai), nature (BARAMASA) music (RAGAMALA) and love and devotion to *god* (GITA-GOVINDA and BHAGAVATA-PURANA), as shown in RADHA-KRISHNA cult which combines the sensuous with the mystic and devotional feelings. Other major *themes* of Kangra works are records of royal activities and court scenes. Also seen are *portraits* or *miniature paintings* of girls playing games or musical instruments or bathing.

Kangra *style* is based on extremely fine and refined *lines* (like most Indian *miniature paintings*) to depict natural and human details, jewellery, clothing etc.; though the complexities of *perspective* were not mastered. There is a harmonious blending of bold *colours*, graceful *forms*, gracious poses and gestures giving eloquent expression to the Rajput ideas of feminine beauty, romance and religion.

The Kangra female face is distinguished by a straight nose, long curved eyes and a dreamy, romantic look. The hair is carefully delineated flowing down the back under a softly draped, *transparent* Odhni (veil). She wears a short, fitting Choli (blouse) and Ghagra (long flowing skirt). The men are dressed mostly in Mughal fashion with jewelled *ornaments* placed on Pagdi (turban). GOPAS (cowherds) wear the Dhoti (loosely knotted sarong) for the bottom and Chadar (top sheet) to cover the *torso*. The Pagdi is a pointed cap with decorated tassels.

The Kangra *landscape* is nearly naturalistic; sylvan vistas of mountains and fertile grazing lands, large heavy bodied cattle, caves, snakes, deer, clouds, sunsets and lightning are all favourite Kangra devices. Yellow, orange, green, pink, mauve, grey and *white* with *gold* and *silver* were some of the *colours* used by Kangra *artists*. The borders of miniatures were both plain or decorated with floral and other *motifs*. The oval format with corner spandrels was especially popular in the 19th century. Refer HANSA, HAMSA, *Mughal Dynasty*, *Pahari Miniature Painting*, PURANA, RADHA, *Laxman Pai*, *R. Abdul Rahim*; Illustration–HOLI.

Kankana Refer ABHUSHANA.

Kanodia, Naina (1950–) b. India. Self-taught *artist*. Solos: TAG, *CYAG*, *JAG*, *LTG*. Group participations: Mumbai; International: New York. *Auctions*: Osian's Mumbai. Awards: Women Artist of the year 2002 Vijoo Sadwelkar Award–*JAG*. Collections: International: Switzerland, Germany, London, USA & pvt.

Naina Kanodia's works exploit the *genre* of naive *painting* to depict the world that she is familiar with, that of the urban Indian. Different cultural types, the Goans, Parsis and Maharashtrians are all dwelt upon with a degree of understanding not only of their picturesqueness but also their idiosyncrasies. "The Chowdhury Family" is a *portrait* of a typical Bengali family, the bunch of *keys* dangling from the sari end of the mother the bespectacled and jacket-clad father and the docile daughter.

Naina Kanodia lives and works in Mumbai. Refer *Naive Art*.

Kansodaria, Ratilal (1961–) b. Saurashtra, GUJ. Education: B.A & M.A. in *Sculpture MSU*. Solos: *Art Heritage* New Delhi, *LKA* Ahmedabad, *JAG*. Group shows: Vadodara, HCVA, SRAG. Group participations: All India Exhibition Chandigarh, GUJ *LKA*, National Exhibition New Delhi, *BAS*, *BB*, *NCAG*, *AIFACS*; International: *Biennale* Dhaka. *Art* camps: WZCC at Goa, *Wood Carving* National *LKA* New Delhi, "Non Violence through Art" by Darpana Academy Ahmedabad. Awards: GUJ *LKA*, SZCC Nagpur, Rashtriya Kalidas Academy Ujjain MP, *BAS*, *AIFACS*; International: Art Horizon New York. Appointments: Assistant lecturer *MSU* three years, Lecturer Dept. of Sculpture *CNCFA*; Organized sculptors' camp National *LKA* New Delhi, Given slide talks in Australia, Ghana & Zambia. Collections: *LKA* Goa & Lucknow, National *LKA* New Delhi, SZCC Nagpur, *BB*; International: New York, Washington DC.

Ratilal Kansodaria's *sculptures* present *vignettes* of small-town reality merging a fine degree of observation with gentle wit. The making of his groups suggest his ability to deal with spatial relationship. He has worked with *wood* as well as *metal*. His animal *forms* as seen in "The Last Attempt" are often elongated and assume characteristic postures.

He lives in Ahmedabad.

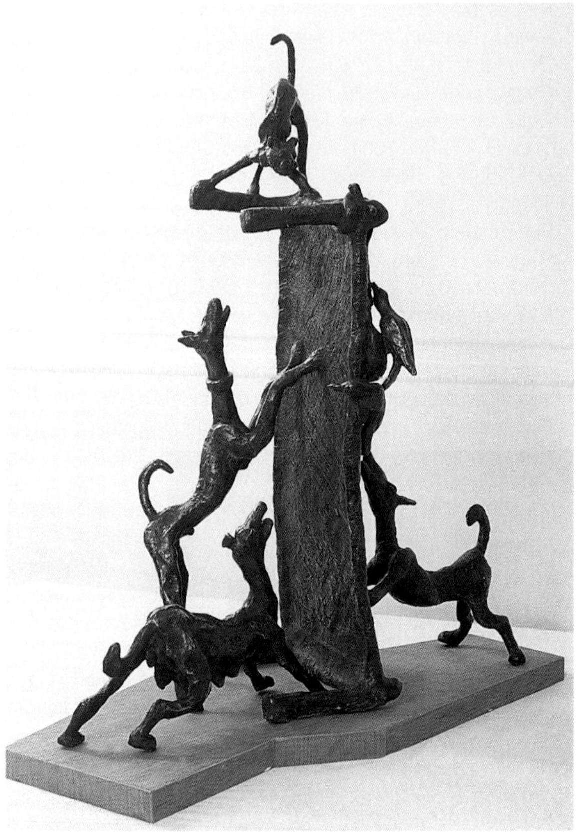

Kansodaria, Ratilal: "The Last Attempt", *Bronze*, 1994, 67.5x42.5x55 cm.

Kapadia, Bharati (1946–) b. Mumbai. Education: Dip. *Applied Art JJIAA*, *Serigraphy GAC*, Studied *painting* at Kanoria Centre for Arts Ahmedabad. Solos: *GC* Mumbai, *JAG*. Group participations: Chennai, *Artists' Centre* & Army & Navy Building Gallery 2003 Mumbai, All India Women Hyderabad, Kanoria Art Centre Ahmedabad, *LCAG*, *JAG*. *Art* workshops: Hyderabad, WZCC Udaipur. Appointments: Curated, designed & presented *art* collections' *exhibitions* in Mumbai; Slide lecture of five Contemporary Indian Artists Seattle Museum USA & RCA.

She is a *graphic* designer who has now branched into the *FA*. Her 1997 *exhibition* in Mumbai show her using *handmade paper*, sculpting it into various hanging *forms*, crushing, twisting and tying it into textural surfaces reminiscent of the surface of the moon and emptied river beds. She uses nylon fabric instead of *canvas* and splashes *acrylic colours* and threads to achieve a structural quality depicting intermingling of lives. Using *mixed media* she demonstrates emotional turbulence by splashing dyes, soil and *poster colours* on *paper*.

She lives and works in Mumbai. Refer *Gouache*.

Kapadia, Kantibhai B. (1911–2002) b. Valsad, GUJ. Education: GDA *JJSA*; Scholarship to USA. Awards: Vadodara, GUJ *LKA*, *JJSA*, *BAS*, *AIFACS*. Commissions: Several monuments for public places, *portraits*, memorials, trophies, medals, including seven Mahatma Gandhi memorials sculptural *portraits* of Jawaharlal Nehru & Dr. Radhakrishnan, *relief* panels based on mythological *themes*. Appointments: *Sculptor artist* at Bombay Talkies & Bombay Pottery; Worked as *artist*, press *artist*, ceramicists *sculptor* finally retiring as HoD of *Sculpture MSU*. Publications: Articles on *art* & *culture* for *Kumar magazines*, Navachetan & Hindustan Newspapers. Collections: *PWM*, *MSU*; International: Paris, Holland, Denmark & others.

Kantibhai B. Kapadia's works were basically *figurative* with portraiture being his forte. Having worked in *stone*, *wood*, *bronze*, *terracotta* and other *media*, he believed in naturalistic and *classical forms* with minute details and simplified human *figures*. He also has a few *abstract* works to his credit. His mythological panels were stylized in a highly romanticized *manner*. He lived in Vadodara.

Kapoor, Bhagwan (1935–) b. India. Education: GDA *JJSA*; Studied ENSBA & Atelier 17 under a French Govt. Scholarship; Bob Blackburn Printshop New York. Solos: Kolkata, *JAG*, TAG, *AIFACS*; International: ENSBA, India House London, other galleries in New York. Awards: National Exhibition New Delhi, Calcutta Art Society, Gold Medal *JJSA*, *BAS*, HAS, *AIFACS*. Fellowship: *JJSA*; Dip. d'honneur International Art Exhibition in France. Collections: *NGMA* & *LKA* New Delhi, *AIFACS*, *SJM*; International: Museum of Modern Art Paris.

Bhagwan Kapoor's *style* is based on the decorative & folk *idiom* with a *background* in Indian kitsch. Wide-eyed damsels and Choli (blouse) clad ladies holding lamps emerge out of pink lotuses against cerulean clouds.

He lives and works in New York.

Kar, Amina Ahmed (1930–1994) b. Kolkata. Education: *GCAC* Kolkata, Delhi Polytechnic; Academy Julien, AGC, graphic art Haytor's Studio worked under P. Picasso Paris. Solos: Delhi, Kolkata; International: Paris; Group participations: *LKA*, *NGMA* & Alliance Francaise New Delhi, *AFA* & *CIMA* Kolkata, *AIFACS*. Awards: French Govt. Scholarship. Publications: Magazine Art Deal New Delhi, Her Book "The Angkorian Records" Kolkata. Collections: *NGMA* New Delhi & international.

Amina Ahmed Kar's development as an *artist* was greatly influenced by her stint in the Paris studio of M. Cesar Domela, a *De Stijl artist*. She was an abstractionist–her *paintings*, *graphic arts* and *murals* being synthesis of European *Modernism* and Indian *aesthetic* and philosophical sensibilities. On one hand is the linear and introspective approach of the East and on the other the intellectual and experimental attitude of 20th-century Western *art*. Certain *paintings* of the 50s show a fluidity of *line* and cadences comparable to Islamic *calligraphy*. By the 70s, the gentle *Lyricism* of the 50s had developed into a sure expressionist touch with bold, *black lines* offsetting planes of red, brown, *white* and *black*.

Kar, Chintamoni (1915–2005) b. Kharagpur, WB. Education: *FA*. *ISOAS*, *Sculpture* AGC. Solos: New Delhi, Kolkata; International: Paris, London, Romania; Group participations: National Exhibition Chandigarh; International: Paris, London, Sao Paulo *Biennale*, *Triennale*. *Auctions*: Heart & Osian's Mumbai. Awards: Padma Bhushan, Desikottam *VBU*. Member: Royal Society of British Sculptors, Inter-national Institute for Conservation of Historic & Artistic Work, London. Appointments: Before settling down, in London as a practising *artist*, taught *art* at Calcutta University & Delhi Polytechnic; Principal of *GCAC* Kolkata. Publications: Several books in English & Bengali; Two documentary films "The Graven Image" & "The Sculptor Speaks" made on his works. Collections: *NGMA* New Delhi, *Chandigarh Museum*, Parliament House, *CKAG*; His own *museum* in Kolkata is at his residence.

Chintamoni Kar was a *painter* as well as *sculptor*. His *style* spans many *genres*, including picturesque Indian *figures* and an impressionistic *style*. His early works show his intuitive *handling* of *oils* and his understanding of *modern sculpture*. There is the movement of C. Brancusi and the simplification of A. Bourdelle in his *sculptures*. His later works show a return to his Indian roots with the delicate stance of Mathura and Gandhara *sculpture* appearing in a stylized *manner* in works like "Vasantasena". He lived and worked in Kolkata.

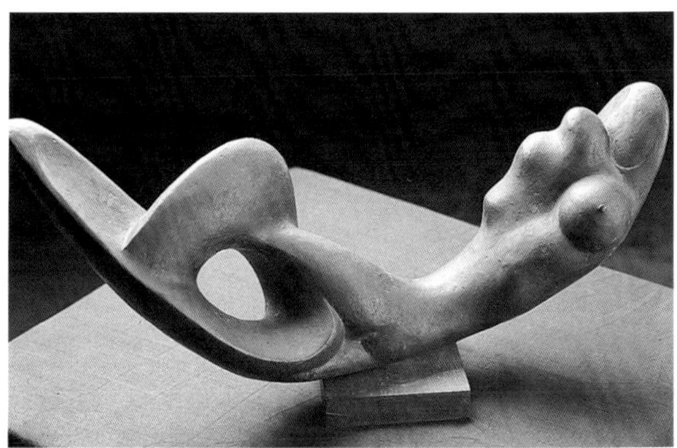

Kar, Chintamoni: "Ondine", *Bronze*, 1972.

Kar, Sanat (1935–) b. WB. Education: Dip. *GCAC* Kolkata. Solos: Kolkata, *Santiniketan*, Bangalore, Goa, *Art Heritage* New Delhi, *CYAG*, *PUAG*, *SAI*, *VAG*, *CKAG*, *G88*. Group participations: *LKA* New Delhi, *BAAC* Kolkata, *CYAG*; International: *Biennales* Europe, USA, Russia, Japan. *Art* camps & workshops: Smithsonian *printmaking* workshop & *LKA*, *GAC*, New Delhi, All India Printmaking workshop held by *BB*. *Auctions*: Heart & Osian's Mumbai, Christie's, London. Awards: All India *FA*. Exhibition New Delhi, WB, *LKA*, Kolkata, AI*FACS*. Member: National Exhibition *LKA* New Delhi, *BAAC* Kolkata; Founder member & secretary: Artists' Circle Kolkata, *SCA*. Presented papers in seminar: Art Education by *LKA* Kolkata, All India Seminar on *Art Education* & Evolution of Printmaking in India *VBU*. Appointments: Teacher, Prof., Principal at *VBU*, also HoD of Dept of *Graphic Arts*. Collections: *NGMA*, *LKA* & *Delhi Art Gallery* New Delhi, *BAAC* Kolkata; International: Pratt Graphic Art Centre New York.

Sanat Kar is primarily a printmaker, using similar *images* in both his *paintings* and *prints*. A dream-like reality crystallizes into nebulously shaped faces; with hands reaching out, gesturing or clasping a flower. The *background* is textured, blending into the face with a smoothness that shows off his technical expertise. He showed an inclination toward *Impressionism* in the 1950s and 60s, when he painted with *oil colours*. He has also used *tempera* and dabbled with *sculpture*.

Sanat Kar lives in *Santiniketan* where he was principal of *KB* until 1991.

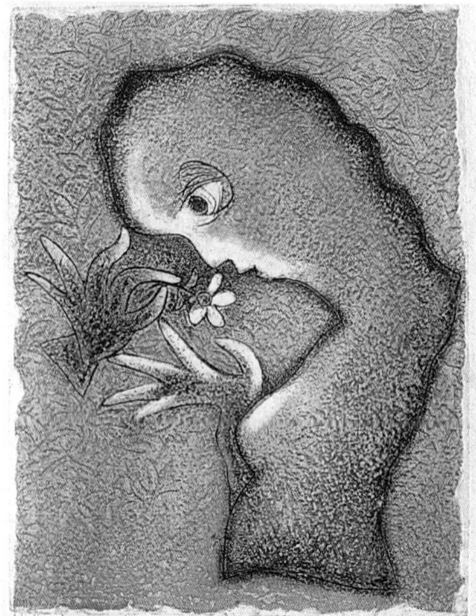

Kar, Sanat: "Face", *Intaglio*.

Karanda-Mukuta Refer MUKUTA.

Karma=fate. The doctrine of Karma, the law of cause and effect is one of the basic concepts of the three religions in India, i.e. *Hinduism*, *Jainism* and *Buddhism*. It presupposes that, all human actions, mental or physical, are motivated by desires, and one has to face the consequences in this or the next world resulting in the Samsara (transmigration) of the ATMA (soul or principal of life). The four principal steps of psychological development that influence the Karma of a mortal being, are Kama (lust), Krodha (anger), Moha (attachment) and MOKSHA (detchment). The ability of a human being to control the first three, and achieve detachment is a sign of good Karma. Refer BHAKTI, *Jain*, *Jainism*.

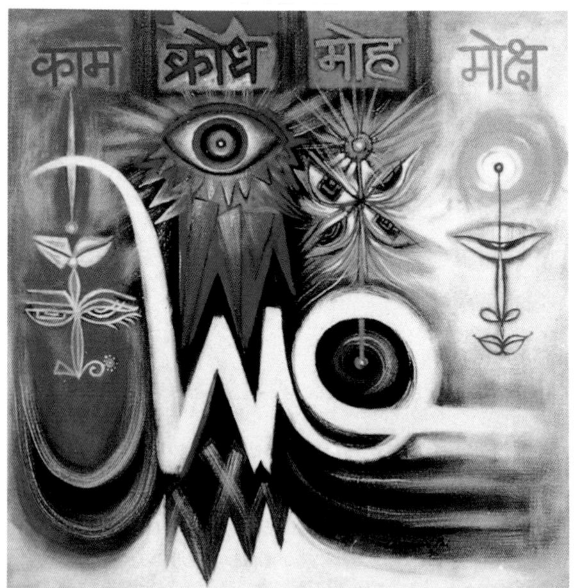

Karma: *Laxman Pai*, "*Kaarma* Series", 1996, Acrylic.

Karmarkar, Prokash (1935–) b. Kolkata. Education: Studied *GCAC* Kolkata. Solos: New Delhi, Kolkata, Mumbai. Retrospective: UP *LKA* Lucknow. Group shows: *LKA* New Delhi, *AIFACS*, TKS, *LTG*. Participations: *Triennale* New Delhi, *BAAC* & *CIMA* Kolkata, UP *LKA*, *SCA*; International: *Biennales* in Sao Paulo, Havana & Dhaka, Commonwealth Art Exhibition London. *Auctions*: Osian's Mumbai, Bonham's London. Awards: National *LKA* New Delhi, RB & *BAAC* Kolkata. Fellowships: To study Museums of Art France. Collections: *NGMA*, *Art Heritage* & *LKA* New Delhi, *BAAC* Kolkata, Allahabad Museum, *BB*.

Prokash Karmarkar's *paintings* usually centre around the female, who is variously a victim and a temptress. She is the ultimate female, hedonistically caressing or admiring herself, looking out at the spectator either with wide-eyed simulated innocence or with wanton smoky-eyed lust. His textural application has varied over the years, from a bristly, thorny *tactile* surface to smooth, glossy contoured *forms*.

He lives and works in Howrah, WB.

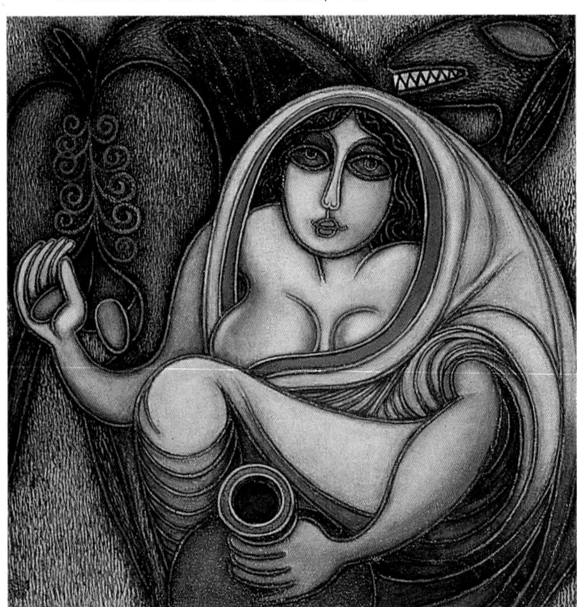

Karmarkar, Prokash: "Untitled", *Oils*, 90x92.5 cm.

Karmarkar, Vinayak Pandurang (1891–1966) b. Sasavane, MAHA. Education: Dip. *Sculpture* & *modelling JJSA*; also learnt sculpture-making from his father, a well-known maker of GANESHA *idols*; Later Surendranath Tagore, nephew of *Rabindranath Tagore*, set him up in a studio in Kolkata in 1916; In 1920, he went to UK for further studies, visiting many *sculptors* and *painters*; In 1923, returned to Kolkata, finally arriving back in Mumbai in 1925. Exhibited in several *art* centres including RAA London. Awards: *BAS*, *ASI* Medals. Commissions: 13ft. equestrian statue of Shivaji Maharaj and Lokmanya Tilak statue Pune, two Jamshedji Tata statues Mumbai & Jamshedpur; *NCAG* organized a posthumous solo show 1997.

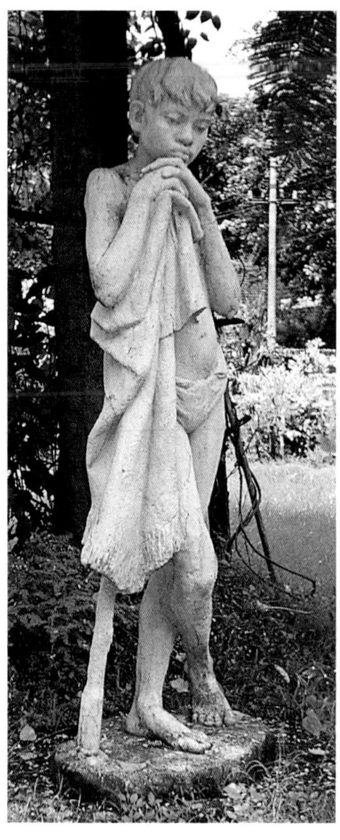

Among his creative *sculptures* are the neo-classically graceful "Blow-ing the Conch", "Fisher Girl", the startlingly *realistic* "Buffalo" and "Chipliwali". He idealized his *models*, who were mostly his domestic help, acquaintances or villagers, smoothening away wrinkles and rough features in pursuit of academic reality. His favourite materials were *cement* and *plaster of Paris*, though the public statues were mostly *cast* in *bronze*.

His *sculptures* can be viewed at the Vinayak Pandurang Karmakar Sculpture Museum in his bungalow at Sasavane, MAHA.

Karmarkar, Vinayak Pandurang: "Cow-herd", *Cement*, 1960, *Life-Size*.

Karnataka Chitrakala Parishad (CKP) (Bangalore). The Chitrakala Parishad (CKP) was established in 1960 for the promotion of the *visual arts*. In 1964, the Chitrakala Vidyalaya, an *art* school was launched to ensure the spreading of *art education* in the state. In 1983, the school was upgraded as the CFA, affiliated to the Bangalore University awarding a degree in the *FA*. In addition to organizing *art* exhibitions in the city, the CKP also encourages research in the *visual arts* besides housing large collections of *leather* puppets and traditional Mysore *paintings*. The *art* complex houses the works of the well-known Russian *painter* S. Roerich, H.K. Kejriwal's collection of *modern* Indian *art*, and *Krishna N. Reddy's prints*. The CKP also has a publishing wing. In addition to the CFA, the CKP runs the Roerich Institute of FA. and the Chitrakala Institute of Advanced Studies. It also runs summer *art* classes and weekend hobby classes for children.

Karunakaran, C.N. (1940–) b. Brahmakulan, Kerala. Education: Dip. *Design GCAC* Chennai. Solos: Chennai, Cochin, Kozhikode, Thiruvananthapuram, *JAG*, TAG, *ABC*. Group shows: In India & abroad. *Art* camps: Organized by the *LKA* at Bhoothathankettu & *terracotta* at Perumbavoor. Awards: Govt. of Chennai Gold Medal, *LKA* Chennai & Kerala, P.T. Bhaskara Paniker Award in 2000 Kerala. Member: Founded "Chitrakoodam" first pvt. *art* gallery Kerala. Appointments: Worked as designer with Madras Design Demonstration Centre–a Govt. unit for Research and Improvement of Handicraft; *Art* instructor at Kalapeetom Cochin; Vice-Chairman Kerala State *LKA*; *Art* direction for several films. Publications: *Illustrations* in several Malayali publications. Collections: *Murals* commissioned all over Kerala, *Govt. Museum* Thiruvananthapuram, others in Cochin, Ernakulam & Chennai, pvt. national & international.

The female *form* is central to C.N. Karunakaran's highly schematized perception of folk-inspired *space*. They are voluptuous yet contained within the predictability of their postures amongst lush *flora* and *fauna paintings*. The *colours* are equally inviting, blue and green complexioned damsels cavorting in semi-Thanjavur & semi-Mattanchery *mural style*. He has employed a geometricized overall *pattern* in his recent works *overlapping* the rectangle and squares over his usual *motif*, the female Form.

He lives and works in Cochin, Kerala.

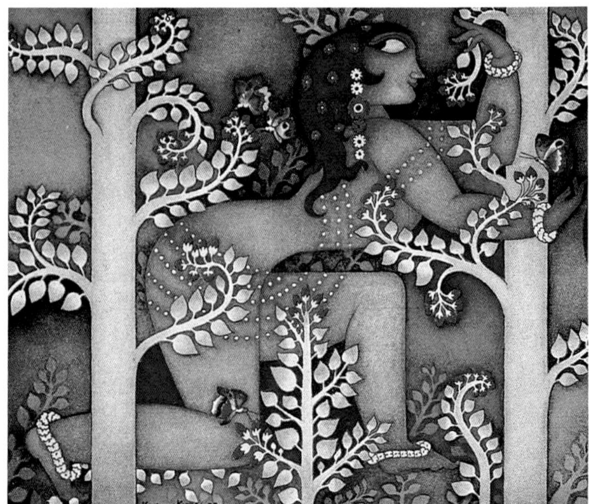

Karunakaran, C.N.: "Woman in Garden", *Oil* on *Canvas*, 1995, 97.5x112.5 cm.

Kataka Refer MUDRAS.

Katchhi, Musa G. (1943–) b. Jamnagar, GUJ. Education: Post-Dip. Creative *painting MSU*. Solos: pvt. *exhibition* for Sonia and late Prime Minister Rajiv Gandhi, *Maharaja Fatesingh Museum* Vadodara, Musa Gallery Katchhi (*artist's* own studio), FA. Gallery Vadodara, CAG Ahmedabad, TAG; International: Berkeley San Francisco USA. Collections: pvt. R.P. Gaekwad Vadodara, S.P. Gaekwad Mumbai, Teen Murti Bhawan Museum New Delhi; International: Germany, San Francisco USA, Preston England.

His works show his fascination for *Surrealism*; he explores the psychological and subconscious "enigma of pain and sexuality and life after death," through the use of surreal *imagery*. He has also painted *portraits*. His favourite *medium* is *oil* on *canvas*, though he also uses *pencil* on *paper*.

He lives and works in Vadodara.

Katt, Balbir Singh (1939–) b. Rawalpindi. Education: Dip. *FA. Santiniketan*; National Cultural Scholar *FFA* (*MSU*), *Santiniketan* and British Council Scholar–*Sculpture* RCA. Solos: *CYAG*, *JAG*. Group participations: *BB Biennale*, *Arts Acre* WB, *BAS*, National Academi of FA. Silver Jubilee show, *LKA Triennales* New Delhi, IAFA Amritsar, *AFA* Kolkata, *CKP*, *AIFACS*; International: Belgium, Moscow, Japan, Canada,

Yugoslavia, Turkey, Israel, Finland, Egypt. Participated/convened camps: BHU, BVB, *GAC*. Awards: *LKA* National Award, HAS Silver Plaque, *AFA* Gold Medal Kolkata, *AIFACS* Silver Plaque, *BAS*. Fellowship: Senior Fellowship Govt. of India. Member: Founder & First Secretary Sculptors Forum of India. Appointments: Convener seminars/symposium at Srinagar, Jammu, Gwalior, Guwahati, Kerala, Udaipur, Jaipur, Ahmedabad, Hyderabad, Vishakhapatnam, New Delhi; Delivered lectures at UGC National seminars in several universities. Collections: Mumbai, *NGMA*, National Academi of FA. & Govt. Museum New Delhi, Govt. Museum Bangalore, Kanoria Arts Centre Ahmedabad, *Arts Acre* WB, *CYAG*, SKP, *CKP*; International: Canada, Yugoslavia, Sweden, Israel, Finland.

Balbir Singh Katt had always worked on a *monumental* scale, *handling* large blocks of *stone* from the very beginning of his career. *Clay*, *plaster*, *cement* and *wood* were the *mediums* favoured by *sculptors* at *Santiniketan*. Balbir Singh Katt's work at this stage was reminiscent of his teachers, mentors especially *Ramkinkar Baij*. He soon realized his fondness for direct carving as opposed to *modelling*. Again, while his *imagery* was basically *abstract*, there is an element of the organic and the figural that serves to anchor his work to the real world. This aspect also serves to soften the overwhelming geometric feeling of his *sculptures*. The horizontal character of certain commissioned works displayed in Delhi's parks and squares brings the *landscape* element to the fore in its penetration of the environment. After his sojourn in England, he started experimenting again with geometric *constructions*. His works at a later stage retain the block-like character of the *stone*, while *carving* out the interior. At times the *stone* or the *marble* seems to have melted from within, the liquid slowly eating away part of the exterior as well. Balbir Singh Katt has used a wide range of materials from pink Chunar sandstone, Jaisalmer *stone*, *cement*, Baijnath *stone* to *wood*, *black marble* and Orissa Tapang *stone*.

He was the Dean of the Faculty of *Visual Art*, BHU (*BKB*).

Katt, Latika (1948–) b. Ghaziabad, UP. Education: B.FA. BHU, M.FA. *MSU*. Scholarships: National Cultural Scholarship *MSU*, UGC New Delhi; International: British Council Scholarship Slade School of Art London. Solos: *Art Heritage*, MMB & Kala Mela Lawns in New Delhi, Calcutta Art Gallery Kolkata, *Sculptures*, *Drawings* & *Prints JAG*, *CYAG*; International: Woodstock Art Gallery London UK, Tingsryd Sweden. Group participations: *Triennale*, *LKA* & *Art Heritage* New Delhi, *Dhoomimal*, *AIFACS*, *NCAG*, *JAG*; International: *Biennale* Paris, Festival of India RAA London, Fukuoka Museum Japan. *Art* camps: All over India & abroad. Member: Examination Board *FFA* & BHU; Jury *LKA* New Delhi, GUJ *LKA*, *AIFACS*; International: Member of Jury Commonwealth Scholarship London, Australian & Chinese by Ministry of Culture; Invited to curate & advisory member *NGMA* New Delhi. Appointments: *Art* Prof. BHU, *Sculpture* Dept. JMI. Collections: *NGMA* New Delhi & Mumbai, *LKA* New Delhi & Lucknow, FA. Museum & Govt. Museum Chandigarh, Late Rajiv Gandhi—12" statue TN, *CYAG*, *BB*; International: Pandit Nehru's *bust* commissioned for Australia, Zambia, Yugoslavia, Mauritius & pvt. UK.

Latika Katt has always been fascinated by the continual changes in the organic world. The scale of her experiences ranges from the minute to the *monumental*. She includes the human, vegetable and animal world within the scope of organic *form*, and incorporates the intricately knotted trunk of the banyan tree, the mud nests of wasps, the geometric order of a bee-hive, the waves of the sea and the growth of other roots of trees within the earth (to name a few examples) into her *sculpture*.

She has used various materials like *bronze*, *marble*, *stone*, plastic, bamboo, *ceramics*, *terracotta*, *papier mache* and cowdung.

She lives in Delhi.

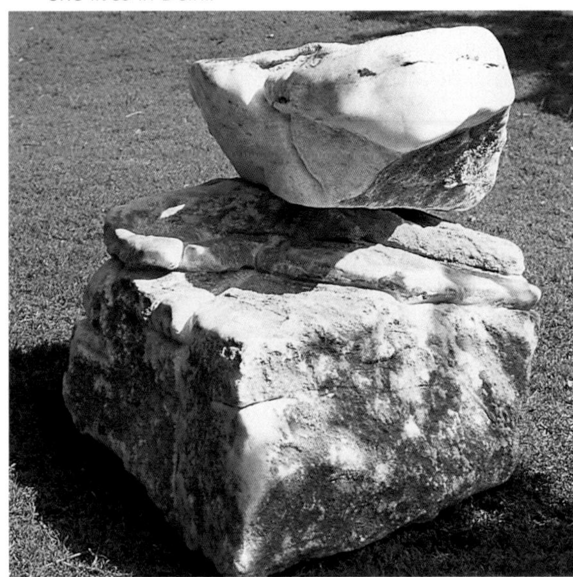

Katt, Latika: "Decay", *Marble carving,* 1995.

Kattur, G. Narayana Pillai (1946–) b. Mavelikara, Kerala. Education: Dip. *FA*. *GCAC* Chennai, Dip. & Post-Dip. in *painting* Ravi Varma School of Painting. Solos: Thiruvananthapuram. Group participations: National Exhibition New Delhi & Regional Centre *LKA* Chennai, *BB Biennales*, Trivandrum Art Group, Art & Literary Academy & Kerala Kala Peetom, Thapasya Kerala. *Art* camps & workshops: Kala Niketan Jabalpur, *LKA* Regional Centre Chennai, *LKA* Thiruvananthapuram. Fellowship: Central Cultural Dept. Govt. of India for Research of Traditional Kerala Paintings. Appointments: Prof. & HoD of *Painting* in the *CFA* Thiruvananthapuram. Publications: Articles published on *painting* in major periodicals & seminars subjects—"Modern Indian Painting", "Mural Paintings of Kerala & Raja Ravi Varma" & "Portrait Painting" in Thiruvananthapuram & Thrissur. Collections: Central & Kerala *LKA*, Chithra Art Gallery Thiruvananthapuram, *GC* Mumbai.

G. Narayana Pillai Kattur fills his *pictorial space* with semi-figurative *forms* and pleasant *colours*, representing a dream-like state in *terms* of *colour*, *line*, *mass* and *texture*. There is an understanding of the principles of pattern-making and repetitiveness which give his *paintings* a tapestry-like appearance.

He lives and works in Thiruvananthapuram.

Katyal, Nand (1935–) b. Lahore (Pakistan). Education: Dip. *FA*. Delhi Polytechnic. Solos: SRAG, *Dhoomimal*, *CYAG*. Group participations: National Exhibition & All India Exhibition New Delhi & International. Attended *artists* camps. Won 1995 National Award. Member: "Unknown" a group founded in 1960; SC 1962–67. Collections: *NGMA* & *LKA* New Delhi, PUJ Museum, *BB*.

Nand Katyal is an intuitive *artist*, letting his inner self take over the *painting*, which starts as an *image* that appeals to him. In the conscious level there could be a degree of studied *Eclecticism*, or influence from various sources, but finally it is the joy of RASA that emerges.

He lives and works in Delhi.

Kaul, Kishori (1939–) b. Srinagar, Kashmir. Education: Post-Grad. Degree in *FA*. *MSU*; Studied under Narayan S. Bendre, *K.G. Subramanyan* & *Sankho Chaudhuri*. Solos: Academy of Art Kolkata, Kumar Art Gallery, *LKA*, *Art Heritage* New Delhi, *JAG*; International: Cambridge UK. Retrospective: *LKA* New Delhi. Group participations: International Women's Art New Delhi; International: Prague, Belgrade, Budapest, Bucharest, Frankfurt, *Biennale* Japan. Awards: Ahmedabad, Vadodara, National *LKA* New Delhi, Govt. of India Scholarship for Post-Graduate. Fellowship: Senior Fellowship the Dept. of Culture Govt. of India. Appointments: Artist-in-Residence at the Hood College in Maryland, USA.

Kishori Kaul is inspired by the *colour* and floral beauty of her native Kashmir. Like C. Monet, she strives to capture the grace, shimmering *light* of the Dal Lake, the waterlilies and other multihued flowers growing in or near it. The same im-pressionist *technique* of broken, flecked strokes vibrates across her *canvas*, submerging *form* within its larger surface *pattern*.

She lives and works in New Delhi.

Kaul, Manohar (1925–1999) b. Srinagar, Kashmir. Education: Studied *Art* Sir A.S. Technical Institute Srinagar, London University *painting* examination (correspondence). Solos: SRAG & Retrospective three decades of work *AIFACS*. Group participations: *LKA* New Delhi, *AIFACS*. Participated seminars: *LKA* New Delhi, *AIFACS*. Awards & Hon.: Honoured as a Veteran Artist by *AIFACS* and awarded the title of Kala Vibhushan. Member: INTACR, Chairman *AIFACS*. Publications: Editor of several publications including "Art News", "Roop Lekha", "Kala Darshan"; Authored books "Trends In Indian Painting–Ancient, Medieval, Modern" & "Kashmir: Hindu Buddhist and Muslim Architecture". Collections: *NGMA* & *LKA* New Delhi, PUJ Museum, *AIFACS*, & pvt.

Manohar Kaul was a landscapist, *painting* the fleeting moods of *nature* in *oils* and *watercolours*. His rendering was fresh and spontaneous at times capturing the surreal aspects of dreamscapes, at other times creating a rich romantic *atmosphere* of diffused *colour* and *light*. The Himalayas and his native Kashmir are constantly recurring *themes* in his works.

Kaur, Narula P. (1920–) b. Amritsar, PUJ. Education: Dip. *FA*. Delhi Polytechnic; Merit Scholar Art Education State League N.Y. Over 20 solos: *AIFACS*, *SC*, SRAG; International: New York. Group participations: National level representing India in *exhibitions*; International: Australia, Russia, Africa, America. Awards: IAFA Amritsar, All India Women Artists 1956, *AIFACS*. Member: *AIFACS*. Appointments: Taught at State University Teachers College New York. Publications: Articles in Roop Lekha *AIFACS*. Collections: *NGMA* & *LKA* New Delhi, *AIFACS*; International: NGMA in Yugoslavia.

Narula P. Kaur had designed several *murals* in *mixed media*. Her *paintings* are largely *abstract*, with "*form* being its own *content*", helping in both manifesting man's union with *nature* and discovering a symmetry that is unknown in *nature*.

She lives and works in New Delhi.

Kazi, Sayed A.G.M. (1922–2000) b. Kolhapur, MAHA. Education: Dip. *FA*. *JJSA*. Over 21 solos: Srinagar, Kolhapur, Mumbai, Delhi, Lucknow; 50 demonstrations of *landscape painting* all over India. Awards: Gold Medal Raja Ram Art Society Kolhapur 1949. Collections: *SJM* & pvt. collections in Egypt, Japan & UK.

Sayed A.G.M. Kazi specialized in *landscapes*, especially country scenes with their colourful festivities. His *images* of the Himalayas capture the beauty of snowcapped mountain peaks as well as the lush green forest in the lower plains. He worked with a variety of *media*, including *watercolours*, *oils*, *pastels* and *acrylics*. He lived in Mumbai.

Keote, Ram (1932–) b. Yeotmal, MAHA. Education: GDA *FA*. & GDA Applied *JJSA*; Received U.N. Fellowship to study fabric design, *graphics, ceramics* & photography at the Philadelphia College of Art USA. Solos: TAG, *JAG*, *PUAG*; International: Philadelphia. Group participations: Mysore, Pune, *LKA* Chennai, *BAAC* Kolkata, *SAI*. Awards: MAHA State Mumbai, Mysore DAE, *BAS*, *CKP*, HAS. Member: MAHA State Art Council, *BAS*. Appointments: Fellow 1956–57 *JJSA*, Dir. of *WSC* Mumbai worked for 31 years. Collections: Bangalore, Mumbai, *LKA* New Delhi, *SAI*; International: USA & pvt.

Ram Keote has worked with different *media* and materials through the course of his 30-year career. He experimented with *figuration* briefly before moving on to abstraction in 1966, when he started working on *wood*. There is an exhilarating approach to *colour* and formlessness in his recent works, which witness a festive explosion of reds, greens, blues and *whites*.

Ram Keote lives and works in Mumbai since his retirement as Dir. of the WSC Mumbai.

Kerkar Art Complex (Goa). Founded by *Subodh Kerkar*, the Kerkar Art Complex attempts at incorporating *contemporary art*, handicraft and classical Indian music and dance under one roof. Kerkar Art Gallery, a part of the complex, exhibits *contemporary art* from all over the country, besides organising workshops and initiating dialogues between *artists*. Another part of the complex, the Nirmiti Craft Gallery has its own workshop where one can watch artisans work with *clay*, *wood* and *metal*. There is also an open air auditorium called Abhivyakti. The inaugural *exhibition* featured *artists* like *B. Prabha*, *Prabhakar Barwe*, *Narayan S. Bendre*, *Bikash Bhattacharjee*, *Krishen Khanna*, *Nalini Malani*, *Sayed Haider Raza*, *Mrugank G. Joshi*, *Subodh Kerkar*, along with several promising younger *artists*.

Kerkar, Subodh (1959–) b. India. Self-taught *painter*. Solos: Kala Academy & *Kerkar Art Complex* Goa, Organized by Alliance Francaise in Pune, Pondicherry, Thiruvananthapuram, Bangalore, Chennai, Ahmedabad, Bhopal & Vadodara, India Habitat Center New Delhi, *CYAG*, *JAG*, TAG; International: Germany. Group participations: Art Folio & *LKA* New Delhi, *GC* Mumbai, Kala Mela Bangalore, *AIFACS*. Awards: State Awards Goa, *AIFACS*. Appointments: Political & Social Cartoonist for "Illustrated Weekly of India". Collections: *NGMA* New Delhi, *LKA* & Kala Academy Goa & pvt.

Subodh Kerkar was initiated into the *art* of *painting* by his father, Chandrakant Kerkar. He paints *landscapes* in *watercolour*, capturing the sunny vistas of Goa, with its ancient churches and boat-filled beaches. He achieves a "picturesque" look with his use of *transparent wash* and broken strokes of *colour*. He has designed *murals* in different *mediums*. He owns an *art* gallery, the *Kerkar Art Complex* Goa.

He lives and works in Calangute, Goa, where he also practises medicine and illustrates children's books.

Key The predominal *tonal value* of a *painting*. A high key *painting* is closer to *white* in *tone*, while a low key *painting* is dark in *tone* and closer to *black*. It also it means vital/important. Refer *Amit Ambalal*, *Yusuf Arakkal*, *Ramkinkar Baij*, *K. Damodaran*, *G.Y. Hublikar*, *Isha Mahammad*, *Rabin Mondal*, *Sailoz Mookerjea*, *M.K. Muthusamy*, *Shankar Nandagopal*, *Nareen Nath*, *Shankar Palsikar*, *K. Jayapala Panicker*, *Nagji Patel*, *Sharad Patel*, *Ram Kumar*.

Key Block The printing *plate* or block (usually *black* or another dark *colour*) which determines the position (registration) of the succeeding printing *plates* or blocks in multi *colour* printing. The first *colour* to be printed is usually referred to as the key *image*. Refer *Artist's Proof*, *Collography*, KALAMKARI, *Modern Review*, *Prabasi*, *Block Printing*, *Multi Block Colour Printing*, *Print- making*, *Single Block Colour Printing*; Illustrations–*Wood Cut Printing*, *Krishna N. Reddy*, *Gaganendranath Tagore*.

Keyura Refer ABHUSHANA.

Khadga The word denotes a sword which is used along with a Khetaka or shield made of *wood* or skin. The Khadga can be single or double-edged, with a decorative handle. Khetaka can be circular or square-shaped with a strap on cross band at the back, by which it is grasped. The face of the shield is usually decorated.

Khajuraho Khajuraho is located in MP or Central India. It was the capital of the Chandella dynasty which ruled from 10th to the 12th centuries. The Chandellas built many temples of which Khajuraho is the most *monumental*. The temples fall into three main groups i.e. the western group consisting of temples to SHIVA and VISHNU, the northern group with Vaishnava temples and the south-eastern group with *Jain* temples. Built from fine grained sandstone, only 22 temples remain of the original complex comprising 80 temples. Most are Shaivite and some are from the Vaishnava and the *Jain* sects, though architecturally, there is little distinction between them. The temples built on high platforms are tall (31mt. above ground) beautifully and artistically carved. *Sculptures* of deities, female *figures* in various poses, flying APSARAS, heavenly dancers, musical instruments and garlands are exquisitely sculpted. Apart from the architectural importance, the Khajuraho temples are also well known for their erotic *sculptures* that depict the joyous expression of love as espoused in the earliest RIG-VEDA. Though love was abstract in the thoughts of sages, in TANTRIC expressions it was a natural process of life. It is said, the man should practise Dharma, Artha and Kama in a *manner* that they harmonize well together. Kama is the enjoyment by all of five senses i.e. hearing, feeling, seeing, tasting and smelling. This contact between the organ of sense and its object and the consciousness of pleasure that results, is known as the *art* of Kama. The *relief sculptures* at Khajuraho on the outer platform walls are intricately carved where passion is poetry. Subsequently, it is possible that the invasion of Central Asian and West Asian influences drove men and women behind closed walls. Refer *Erotic Art*, KAMA-SUTRA and *Tantra Art*.

Khakhar, Bhupen (1934–2003) b. Mumbai, MAHA. Education: Attended evening *art* classes before M.A. in *Art Criticism MSU*. Solos: Kunika Chemould New Delhi, *GC* Mumbai, CAG Ahmedabad, *PG*; International: London, Pompidou Paris, Den Haag. Group participations: *Biennale*, National *LKA* & Kumar Art Gallery New Delhi, *SG* Mumbai, Marvel Art Gallery Ahmedabad, *VAG*, *JAG*; International: *Biennale* Sao Paulo Brazil, "Six Indian Painters" at Tate Gallery & "Festival of India" RAA London, "The Other Self" Sedeljik Museum Amsterdam, On paper GBP, "Indian Songs" Perth. *Auctions*: Heart, Osian's, Bowring's–Mumbai, Bowring's & Heart New Delhi, Christie's, Sotheby's–London & New York. Awards: GUJ *LKA*, Padma Shri Govt. of India

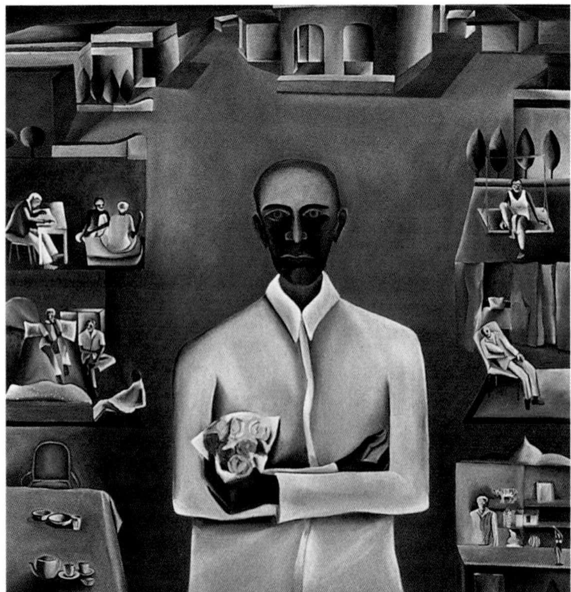

Khakhar, Bhupen: "Man With a Bouquet of Plastic Flowers", *Oil* on *Canvas*, 1975, 140x145 cm.

New Delhi. Publications: First of his short stories in Gujarati, "Bhupen Khakha" by Timothy Hyman. Collections: *NGMA* New Delhi; International: British Museum, Chester & Davida Herwitz Trust Boston, Museum of Modern Art Sydney Australia, V&A.

The human being by himself and in relation to another had always been the main *theme* in Bhupen Khakhar's work. People in ordinary, everyday situations, a man combing his hair, wearing a shirt, cleaning fish, watching a crowd from the safety of his balcony, were a few of the subjects he painted, mostly with his trademark "crude" blues, greens and pinks. However, these seemingly mundane subjects had an undertone of irony, wit and homosexuality. He had also painted a few fables commenting on people and society in general. The *term* "Narrative Painting" had been used for his many-layered *allegories* of *contemporary* life. The *landscape*, the *foreground*, the *background*, the people and places in his works are invested with his brand of energy and mystery.

His *watercolours* did not have the solid structures of his *oils*; instead a diaphanous and semi-dissolved brushstroke delineates *figures* and groups of animals and objects that appear randomly chosen. He lived in Vadodara.

Khan, Anwar (1964–) b. Ambah, MP. Education: National Dip. *FA*. Gwalior. Solos: Bhopal, Gwalior, *JAG*, *CRAR*, *GE*. Group participations: Indore, Bhopal, Gwalior, *GC* & *Tao Art Gallery* Mumbai, *GE*, *Dhoomimal*, *JAG*; International: USA, Japan. *Art* camps: For *Graphic BB*, *INTACH* Gwalior. Awards: MP State Exhibition, SZCC Nagpur, *BB*, *AIFACS*, Govt. of India Scholarship; Hons.: National *LKA* New Delhi, Govt. of India Senior Fellowship. Collections: *NGMA*, *LKA*, *INTACH* Gwalior, *BB*; International: CMC London & pvt.

The *line* is of utmost importance, especially in Anwar Khan's early *drawings* and *prints*. *Tints* which were sparingly used in his lithographs and *etchings* slowly developed a strength of their own leading him into *painting*. There is a *visual harmony* in his *paintings*, with their sophisticated *light* shards and embryonic *forms*, and other in *monochrome* of blues in dry *pastel* on *paper* with the power of energy.

He lives and works in New Delhi.

Khandita One of the eight specific types of NAYIKAS mentioned by ancient Indian writers and poets. She is angry at her lover's unfaithfulness and is usually depicted as reproaching him for his laxity. Refer ASHTANAYIKA.

Khanna, Bishamber (1930–) b. Peshawar, now Pakistan. Education: Dip. *FA*. Delhi Polytechnic, Post-Dip. *Graphics AFA* Kolkata; Prague on Govt. of India Scholarship. Solos: Gallery Chanakya New Delhi, SC, *LTG*, *PUAG*; International: Hollar Gallery Prague, Czechoslovakia. Group participations: National Exhibition, All India Graphics, *Triennale* & *LKA* Silver Jubilee New Delhi. Awards: National *LKA* New Delhi; International: Designation "Honorary Academician" Florence Italy; Honoured Padma Shri 1990. Member: Member of Jury for Short Films Committee for National Award, others in Printing & Designing Books & Publications; Advisory Committee for New Delhi TV & Broad casting. Publications: In magazines & journals, designed books & published. Collections: *NGMA* & *LKA* New Delhi, PUJ Museum; International: Smithsonian Institute Washington DC, Indian Embassy Moscow & Islamabad.

Bishamber Khanna had been working with *copper enamelling* since the mid-60s. He was guided by Oppi Untracht's book "Enamelling on Metal" making several large outdoor *murals*. He normally used a small-sized *plate*, taking care to degrease it and also remove the "firescales" (flakes of *copper* produced by *firing*) before dusting the *plates* with *colour*. Several applications of different *colours* are necessary to get the final result. Bishamber Khanna's *forms* were generally *abstract* with circles and other geometric shapes predominating in a flurry of reds, *blacks* and yellows. He worked in Delhi having retired from Delhi Modern School, where he taught *art* for several years. Refer *Enamel*.

Khanna, Krishen (1925–) b. Lyallpur, (now Pakistan). No formal *art* education; Studied as Rudyard Kipling Scholar at Imperial Services College, Windsor UK & at Govt. College Lahore (now Pakistan). Solos: Over 40 & group shows Kumar Art Gallery New Delhi, *SG*, *Gallery 7*, Gallery 59 & Saffron Art Gallery Mumbai, USIS Chennai, with *Maqbool Fida Husain AIFACS*, *Dhoomimal*, CCAG, *VAG*, TAG, *PUAG*, *JAG*; International: Leicester Galleries, New Art Centre London, Watkins Gallery Washington DC, Egan Gallery New York; *Biennales* Tokyo & Sao Paulo, Contemporary Indian Art Essen, Dortmund & Zurich, Modern Indian Art Cairo, *Contemporary painters* from India Gallery 63 Modern Indian Painters New York, National Museum of Modern Art & Fukuoka Museum Tokyo. *Auctions*: Helpage by Christie's & Timeless Art by Sotheby's Mumbai, Heart & Osian's Mumbai. Awards: Padma Shri, National *LKA* & Gold Medal *Triennale* New Delhi, SKP, *BAS*; Gold Medal *Biennale* Lahore. Fellowship: Rockefeller Council New York, *Artist*-in-residence American University Washington DC. Member: *PAG*, for General Council, Executive Board & Finance Committee *LKA*

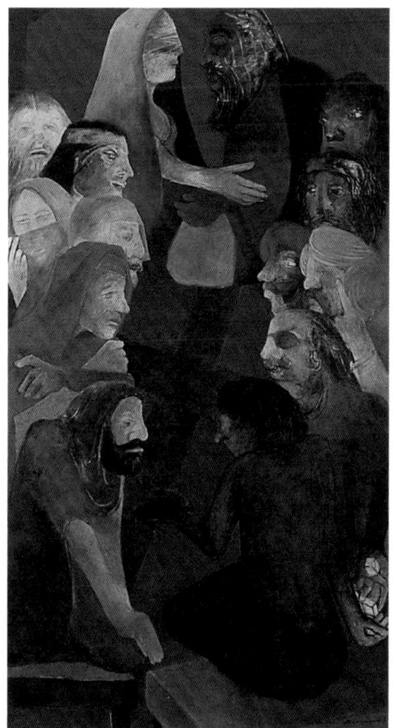

Khanna, Krishen: "The Game of Dice", *Oil* on *Canvas*, 1999, 180x90 cm.

New Delhi; Trustee *BB*, Advisory Committee *Roopankar*; Chairman Purchase Committee *NGMA* New Delhi; Sole Juror *AIFACS*. Commissions: *Murals* in New Delhi, Chennai; Osaka, Zagreb. Appointments: Contemporary Art–Dialogue between East & West National Museum of Modern Art Tokyo. Publications: In Marg Magazine Mumbai, Roop Lekha & *LKA* Journal New Delhi. International: Art News New York, Review London. Collections: *NGMA*, *LKA* & Ford Foundation New Delhi, TIFR, *JNAG*; International: Museum of Modern Art New York, Museum of Indian Art Berlin Germany, Ben & Abbey Grey Foundation Minnesota USA, American University Washington DC USA.

Krishen Khanna is basically a *figurative painter*, being one of the few *painters* to have exhibited in the short lived Gallery 59. His early works show simplified *figures*, *form* and *content* having equal importance. The early emphasis on *drawing* has now given way to a looser structure with the process of *painting*, especially the application of *pigment*, either *acrylic* or *oils*, with the *palette knife*. However, instead of the usual thick *impasto*, Krishen Khanna's *handling* of the knife has a streaky, polychromatic delicacy, through which his *figures* have to be discovered gradually. There has always been an element of satire in his portrayal of humanity, be it his reminiscences of his childhood or the corrupt and inhuman byproducts of the present age. The early *earth colours* have also given way to a polychrome medley of *hues*, that are subdued by the many *overlapping* and undercutting strokes.

He lives and works in Shimla and New Delhi.

Khanvilkar, Nilkanth P. (1932–2004) b. Mumbai, MAHA. Education: B.A. with Philosophy & Psychology & GDA *Sculpture* & *Modelling JJSA*; Nilkanth P. Khanvilkar an *artist* of the third generation who created the statues of GANESHA for the festival of Ganesh Chaturti at Girgam Mumbai; Studied under Prof. V.V. Manjrekar for *stone sculpture*, and later under his father & also *sculptor* Ram Sutar. Group participations: MAHA State Art. Awards: MAHA State Awards in 1962 & 1974. Member: Board of studies in *FA*. of Bombay University Mumbai. Commissions: Several *portraits* & statues all over India; Also executed the Sarnath *emblem* of the Ashokan Stambha, in *bronze*–this 18ft. *sculpture* has been installed on the dome of the New Council Hall of the MAHA Legislative Assembly Mumbai; also executed the 11ft. statue of the Maratha Admiral Kanoji Angre at Alibagh & that of Shivaji Maharaj as Chhatrapati. Appointments: Prof. then Head of the *Sculpture* & *Modelling* dept. & later the Dean of *JJIAA*, retired in 1990. Collections: *JJSA*, Museums, in Govt. premises, pvt. & public.

Nilkanth P. Khanvilkar had worked with several traditional sculptural *media*, including *stone*, *clay*, *bronze*, *marble* and later in *fibreglass*, though *bronze* was his passion. His *portraits* of eminent personalities were not mere likenesses; they reflected on aura of their power and grandeur in their monumentality of scale and vision. The 1977 project of the Sarnath *emblem* was difficult to execute, the *image* being in two sections. It was *cast* in 34 different sections at the *JJSA* foundry and was later welded together. He lived and worked with his son in Thane, MAHA.

Khastgir, Sudhir R. (1907–1974) b. Kolkata, WB. Education: Studied *KB Santiniketan* under *Nandalal Bose*; Studied *bronze casting* in England at various *art* galleries & studios. Solos: Nainital, Shillong, Shimla, Mussorie, *AFA* Kolkata, *Dhoomimal*. Group participations: *Santiniketan*, Kolkata, *BAS*, *AIFACS*; International: Lahore, London. *Auctions*: Osian's Mumbai. Awards: Padma Shri. Fellowship: Royal Society of Arts London. Appointments: Joined the Scindia School as an *art* teacher immediately after leaving *Santiniketan*; In 1936 he left Gwalior for Dehradun teaching *art* at the famous Doon School; In 1956 Principal GCAC Lucknow. Publications: Articles in "Orient Illustrated Weekly" & "Illustrated Weekly". Collections: Allahabad Municipal Museum, *NGMA* New Delhi, *CKP*.

Sudhir R. Khastgir's subjects ranged from *portraits*, head *studies*, *landscapes*, musicians and dancers to fisherwomen and *nudes*. While his Indian *images*, more specifically form his *Bengal School* training is apparent in his rhythmic *lines* and subjects his understanding of the *modern* masters like Van Gogh and J. Augustine comes through in his use of *texture*, most often a *wood cut* like hacking brushstroke fills in the *background*, while the *figures* are modelled within strict *contour lines*.

"The Flutist" shows the influence of both Van Gogh and *Santiniketan*. As a teacher, he was instrumental in bringing in the *Santiniketan* method of incorporating *craft* teaching rather than strictly adhering to Western academicism. Refer *Wood Cut*.

Khatau, Abhay L. (1927–d.) b. Mumbai. Trained informally under Pulin Behari Dutt. Solos: Over 30 including Mumbai, New Delhi, Kolkata, Hyderabad, Bangalore, Ahmedabad; International: Rome, Colombo, Tokyo, Jerusalem, Munich, Basel, New York, San Francisco, Berlin; Represented India at the International Exhibition of Indian Art in Europe; 1968 Research on *Japanese* & *Chinese art*. Publications: Author of booklet "Some thoughts on Asian Art".

In the 40s, his *theme* was predominantly Indian. The opera singers of the 50s gave way to muscular, African dancers in the 60s. His favourite *theme* however was the graceful dances of Bali (Indonesia) & Bastar (India); a *theme* which he began in the 70s & is continuing with even today. The same rhythmic *lines* that one observes in the *drawings* of *K.K. Hebbar* and *Shiavax Chavda* are also apparent in Abhay L. Khatau's work. His response to movement in all its manifestations made some writers to *term* these as the dancing *lines* of Abhay L. Khatau. Added to this was vibrancy in the use of *colour* which was uncharacteristic of the times. This combination representing inner richness of mind full of eternal optimism is the hallmark of Abhay L. Khatau's *art*.

Abhay L. Khatau lives in Mumbai where he was the *Art* Dir. of Khatau Mills.

Khatri, Girish H. (1945–) b. Ahmedabad, GUJ. Education: GDA *Painting* CNCFA GUJ. Solo & group shows: Ahmedabad, Piramal Art Gallery Mumbai, Vadodara *Painters* Goa, *Paintings* & photography *JAG*; International: Houston. Group participations: Mysore DAE, National Exhibition New

Delhi, All India Exhibitions Amritsar, *AIFACS*. Workshops: *Graphic FFA* (*MSU*), National seminars & symposium on *printmaking FFA* (*MSU*). Awards: in *painting* GUJ State *LKA*, Mysore DAE, MPKP; Also for photography including GUJ *LKA*; International: UNESCO Japan. Appointments: Lecturer in photography *MSU*. Collections: *LKA* New Delhi & GUJ State, & in other *artists* collections.

His early works were filled with dark *colours* that were offset by tiny human *figures*. Some of his works show the repetitive *motif* of the Tekra (hillock), suffused with rich glowing *colours*. The sheer repetitiveness of the *motif* transforms the work into an abstraction of *form* and *colour*. The *texture* is *painterly* with the brushstroke being very apparent to the naked eye.

Girish H. Khatri lives in Vadodara.

Khatri, Hiralal (1906–1991) b. India. Self-taught *painter*. Group participations: Major *art exhibitions* in India. Awards: Ludhiyana, MAHA Art Association Pune, *AFA* Kolkata, Nagpur School of Arts Society, GUJ *LKA*, Mysore DAE, IAFA Amritsar, *BAS*; Honoured by *AIFACS*, GUJ State *LKA*, Ahmedabad Municipal Corporation. Collections: Gandhi Ashram Ahmedabad, GUJ Raj Bhavan, Rashtrapati Bhavan New Delhi, AP; International: Akshar Purushottam Mandir Trusts, Organizations & pvt. in India, UK, USA, & other countries.

Hiralal Khatri was primarily a *portrait painter* in *oils*, having painted many religious and political *figures*. His uncanny ability to depict the emotions and feelings felt by his subjects into his *portraits* and *compositions* brought him acclaim. Mahatma Gandhi's *portrait* leading the Dandi March vividly brings out the innocent defiance, his 1948 prayer scene shows up the anguish of the Partition & riots. The steely resolve on the face of a Sardar V. Patel's *portrait* reflecting his strong personality too is a manifestation of the *artist's* ability to penetrate the subject's very psyche. Hiralal Khatri also did some creative works reflecting religious and spiritual thoughts through *form* and *colour* of *fantasy*.

Khemraj, P. (1934–2000) b. Mumbai. Education: GDA *Painting JJSA*; ENSBA on a French Govt. Scholarship;

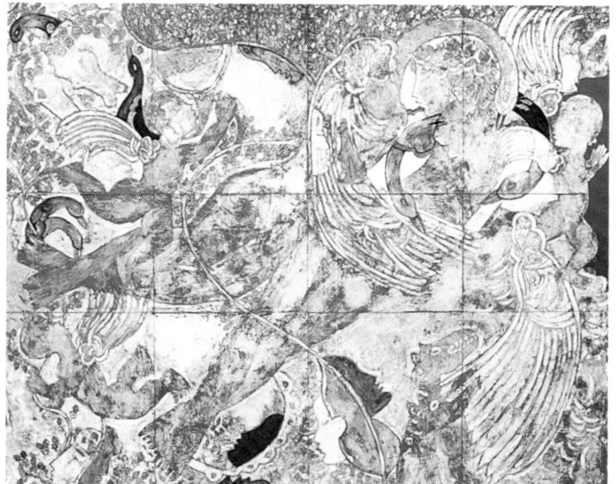

Khemraj, P.: "Birth of a Sailing Poem", *Mixed media*, 213.5x259.25 cm.

French Fellowship for research in *stained glass* in 1987. Solos: *AIFACS*, *NCAG*, International: Paris, South of France, Germany, Beirut, Ankara, Nigeria, Hong Kong, Switzerland, South Korea, Seoul. Group participations: National Exhibition & International Art Festival New Delhi, *AIFACS*; International: *Biennale* Paris, *Watercolours* Seoul, South Korea, Tokyo. *Art* camps: Kolkata. Commissions: *murals*, *stained glass murals* & *stone sculpture* in New Delhi and Dusseldorf Germany. Awards: *LKA* New Delhi, Gold Medal President of India Award Amritsar, Academy AIR Silver Plaque. Appointments: Lecturer in Delhi Polytechnic, TKS; Also a musician, played Violin & Sarod. Collections: *NGMA*, *LKA* New Delhi, SKP; International: Museum of Modern Art Paris.

There is a delicate fairy-tale-like quality to his large works. The *drawing* with its minute detailing is ephemeral in its non-*colour*. Tinges of yellow, pink, green & blue enliven the *canvas* in small bursts. His *painting* is peopled with graceful men and women, birds and winged cupids in full flow. Like the works of G. Klimt, a sense of *pattern* overpowers the use of the *figurative idiom*. He lived and worked in New Delhi.

Khosa, K. (1940–) b. India. Education: Dip. *FA*. Delhi Polytechnic (*College of Art*) New Delhi. Solos: MMB, New Delhi, *Gallery 7* Mumbai, SC, TKS, *ATG*, *JAG*, Projected his *paintings* for 20 years at Sriram Centre Experimental theatre New Delhi. Group participations: CRY Mumbai, Bangalore, State *LKA* UP, SC, *Triennales* India, SC, *AIFACS*; International: Belgium, Poland, Yugoslavia & Bulgaria, Washington DC Hirshhorn Museum, Tokyo Japan, Copenhagen, UK, Dubai, Hungary. *Auctions*: Support of "Helpage India" India. Awards: National Awards & President of India's Silver Plaque New Delhi. Senior Fellowship: Dept. of Culture Govt. of India 1979–82. Publications: *Paintings* reproduced in India & International magazines. Collections: *NGMA*, New Delhi, SKP, pvt. India; International: Switzerland, America, Hongkong, London.

K. Khosa *terms* his work as *metaphysical*, as beyond physical appearance. However, this *metaphysical Realism* does not approach the realm of the fantastic as in surrealistic *painting*. Rather, the *figures* appear as if sculpted rather than painted. The spectral, hallucinogenic quality of the *colour* shaded *images*, *figures* add to the metaphysicality of the works. A cosmic silence, a slight stirring of the body surrounded by an calm and quiet, though pushed forward by gentle ripples of flowing movement.

He lives and works in New Delhi. (See illustration on page 181)

Kiln A kiln is known as a Bhatti in India. A special oven used for *firing pottery* or *enamel*. The kiln ranges from the primitive baking holes hollowed in hillsides by potters belonging to ancient civilizations (*Mohenjo Daro*) to the *modern* gas or *oil* fired or electric furnaces. Refer *Firing*, *Paresh Hazra*, *Balan Nambiar*, *G. Reghu*.

Kinetic Art *Art*, usually *sculpture*, involving movement, either real or apparent. The movement was first proposed by the futurist U. Boccioni, but it was the *mobiles* of A. Calder, N. Gabo and A. Pevsner that really incorporated movement into the work of *art*. In India, *artists* were fascinated with the kinetic *nature* of *line* and experimented with changes in *tactile* pressure to get thick or thin, frail or robust sweeps and curves. Certain experimental *sculptures* by *Navjot Altaf*, *Dashrath Patel* and *Vivan Sundaram* incorporated actual movement into the work of *art*. *Ankit Patel's* early *mobile* works were in *wood* and *fibreglass*. They were organic *abstracts* delicately poised on pedestals moving with the help of machines. Refer *Installation*, *Found Objects*, *Mask*, *Op* or *Optical Art*, *Post-Independence*, *Anis Farooqi*.

Kirita Mukuta Refer MUKUTA.

Kishangarh, Kishangarh Kalam, Kishangarh School, Kishangarh Miniatures The city-state of Kishangarh was founded in 1609 by Kishan Singh, who worshipped KRISHNA fervently and was a follower of the BHAKTI cult. His descendents especially Savant Singh were also to follow the cult, which was to influence *art*, literature and music. Devotion to KRISHNA was an integral part of his life, which was nurtured by the love poetry of the KRISHNA *legend* sung by Bani Thani, a young, beautiful madin.

Kishangarh *painting* is distinguished by an elegant elongation of the *figure* with the elaborate costumes of the Mughal court. It was the face of Bani Thani that was to inspire the Kishangarh's *artist's* quest for the *ideal* female face. The eyes were elongated, almost like pink lotus buds and heavy-lidded, the eyebrows arched over the half-closed eyes, the nose pointed and the long neck caressed by long curly tendrils of dark hair. All the Kishangarh ladies appear the same, Bani Thani and Savant Singh always appearing in the centre of the *composition* dressed as RADHA and KRISHNA.

The Kishangarh *style* always sported riotous *colours*, not always representing the palace, but an idealized assumption of KRISHNA's kingdom at Dwarka. The lake features in several *paintings* and is usually portrayed as teeming with marine and avian life. Refer *Nagari Das*, *Rajasthani Miniature Painting*, *Ved Pal Sharma*.

Koli, Paul A. (1945–) b. Mumbai. Education: GDA *Drawing* & *painting* and studied *printmaking JJSA*, Certificate *Commercial art JJIAA*, M.FA. Research Bombay University; Invited two months to study Japanese traditional *wood cut technique* for printing Kyota. Solos: Pune, Regional Centre Chennai, *JAG*, TKS, *SAI*; International: Indian Cultural Centre Nepal. Group participations: MMB, YMCA & Sophia Art Gallery Mumbai, Regional Centre Chennai, *CYAG*, *JAG*, *JJSA*, BAG; International: Algeria. Workshops: *Printmaking* workshop conducted by Paul Lingrea USIS & by *Vivan Sundaram LKA* New Delhi, *LKA* Kerala, Carol Summers Chennai, WZCC & Takman group of *artists* Udaipur; Also conducted workshops & gave demonstrations on *printmaking* both national & international. Awards: For *Graphic art* MAHA State & AP; Honourable mention *Biennale BB*. Commissions: *Murals* for International Tourist Fair Mumbai, along with *Murlidhar R. Achrekar*; Copied *murals* at *Ajanta* with students of *JJSA*. Appointments: Lecturer & HoD of *Printmaking JJSA*; Seminar & workshops in Bali, Indonesia, Sheffield England. Collections: Bangalore, Hyderabad, *NGMA* & *LKA* New Delhi; International: Japan, pvt. & corporates, UK, USA & France.

Paul A. Koli began by exploring the *techniques* of *linocut* and *wood cut* while attending evening classes in *printmaking*. The *colour* viscosity *prints* of *Krishna N. Reddy* fascinated him and he began exploring various avenues to achieve the same results. Many of his works have a religious undertone, with flying angels and surrealistically placed thorny crowns hovering above the *horizon*. At times his love of *texture* comes through in his arbitrarily placed *forms* and polished spheres hurtling towards each other.

He lives and works in Mumbai.

Kolte, Prabhakar (1946–) b. MAHA. Education: GDA *JJSA* 1968 and Prof. for *FFA* Mumbai. Solos: Indo-German Culture Society & *GC* Mumbai, *SG* Chennai & Bangalore, *Art Heritage* New Delhi, *JJSA*, *VAG*; International: Amsterdam. Group participations: National Exhibition *LKA* & MAHA State group show New Delhi, Alliance Francaise 20 *artists*, MAHA State Art Exhibition, *GC* and for its 25 years in 1987 & Cry Mumbai, "Contemporary Artists" Kolkata 1992, 100 years *BAS*, TAG, *JAG*, *BB*. *Auctions*: Heart Mumbai. Awards: Gold Medal *BAS*, MAHA State award and Prof. Langhammer award. Appointments: Prof. *JJSA*. Collections: Aurangabad, *NGMA*, *LKA* & *Art Heritage* New Delhi, J&K Academy of Art & Culture Jammu, KAR *LKA* Mysore, Kerala *LKA* Thrissur, Air India, Godrej, *GC* & *SG* Mumbai, *Roopankar BB*, TAG, *JJSA*, pvt. & public national & international.

Prabhakar Kolte's works in *watercolour* and *acrylic*, with layered *pictorial spaces*, materialize as epiphanies. He uses an inner geometry centering on academics and cultural orientation, the *form* and *colour* do not represent, convey or narrate anything. The *compositions* are spontaneous and intuitive using sensibility and initial impetus. The *lines*, dots, strokes and parallel strokes wipe off recognizable *forms* revealing narrow recesses of underlying strata, thus achieving tonal uniformity with unconventional dexterous *handling* of thoroughly explored *watercolours*.

He lives and works in Mumbai.

Kotah, Kotah Kalam, Kotah School, Kotah Miniature Paintings Kotah is one of the hilly tracts of RAJ and was ruled by a Raja Ummed Singh, who always spent his time in hunting expeditions. Kotah School *paintings* of this period reflect subjects of hunting in the 8th century. The *theme* of Kotah is the jungle with its wild life, with hunters playing only a minor role. The *style* is represented by boldly simplified *forms*. Refer *Bundi*, *Rajasthani Miniature Painting*.

Kothawalla, Pilton (1948–) b. Jodhpur, RAJ. Education: Dip. in GDA *JJSA*. Solos: Defense Service Associations all over India including New Delhi, *JAG*, *AIFACS*. Group participations: *JAG*, Association with defence services *murals* & *collages* displayed at various centres New Delhi, Mhow, Pune, Jamnagar, Bareilly Nasik, Hyderabad & Deolali. Collections: At major Army centres varying *size* from 30x60 cm. to 1500x1020 cm. & pvt. national & international.

Pilton Kothawalla is mainly a *mural* and *collage artist*,

with over 500 works to his credit. Known as "Army Artist", Pilton Kothawalla has been repeatedly commissioned by the Defence services to provide them with *murals*, *collages* and *sculptures*. His *technique* of *wood* singeing with *metal embossing* in various heavy *forms* and shapes working with glass, *copper*, *alluminium* and other materials as *mixed media* with special emphasis on cut-outs. His *compositions* mainly reflect nationalist and marshal spirit on the one hand and scenes from Indian *mythology*, RAMAYANA, MAHABHARATA on the other. Chariots, Golconda Fort and horses often get depicted.

Pilton Kothawalla lives and works in Deolali.

Koul, Rakesh K. (1960–) b. Srinagar, Kashmir. Education: BAF Institute of Music & FA. Srinagar. Solos: *LKA* Lucknow, MPKP Bhopal, *BAAC* Kolkata, *JAG*, TAG, TKS. Group participations: Jammu, Srinagar, Chandigarh, Mumbai, New Delhi, Kolkata, IAFA Amritsar, National Exhibitions; International: Jan Heestershuis Museum Netherlands. *Art* camps: All India Artist camp Srinagar & Ootacamund, Print Makers Bhopal. Awards: Rashtriya *LKA* Research Scholarship New Delhi, IAFA Amritsar. Fellowship: Junior—Govt. of India Dept. of Culture. Collections: *NGMA* New Delhi, J&K Academy Art Culture, *LKA* TN, *BB*.

Rakesh K. Koul's preferred *medium* is *oil painting*, though he also works with *watercolour* and *ink*. He uses floating *forms* filled with a subtle use of *texture* to indicate elements of *nature*. These *textures*, emphasized by the use of short, sharp, arbitrary *lines* have the naive quality of P. Klee's works.

He lives and works in Rewa.

Kowshik, Dinkar (1918–) b. Dharwar, KAR. Education: Grad. Bombay University; Dip. *FA. Santiniketan*; Belle *art* Rome. Solos: *KB Santiniketan*, Center Art Gallery Kolkata, SC, SRAG; International: Rome, Zagreb Yugoslavia, Paris. Group participations: *LKA* New Delhi, National Exhibitions; International: Venice *Biennale*, International Centre Tokyo. Publications: "Age & Image", Written books—*Nandulul Bose*, "Blossoms of Light" Okakuro Kakuzo. Collections: *Santiniketan*, Delhi, pvt. & international.

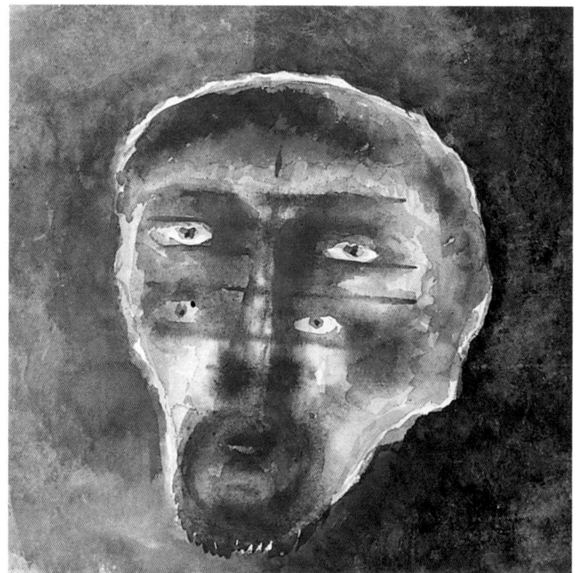

Kowshik, Dinkar: "Mask", *Gouache Watercolours.*

Dinkar Kowshik being an *artist*, *art* teacher and *art critic*, has taught at the *College of Art* New Delhi and the GCA Lucknow, before retiring as principal of *KB VBU Santiniketan*. He constantly spoke about the merits of oriental *art* as against that of occidental *art* and theory. His recent works in different *mediums*, including *gouache* and *oil painting*, show a naive and spontaneous application of *colour* to broken *forms* suggesting a lost magical world of wonder, epitomized by the use of *masks*.

He lives and works in *Santiniketan*.

Kraft Paper A strong grade of wrapping *paper*, made from unbleached soda pulp, usually brown or buff in *colour*, with a coat of polythene applied on one or both sides to make it *waterproof*. Refer *Empaquetage*, *Embossing*, *Wetting Down*, *Ganga Devi*, *Somnath Hore*, *C. Jagdish*.

Krishna=*black*, dark blue. The eighth and the most popular AVATARA of VISHNU. He is considered by his devotees to be the lord himself and not just a mere incarnation. The son of Vasudeva and Devaki of the Yadava clan, he was born on the Ashtami day in the month of Sinha (Leo—the Lion) and was fostered by a herdsman called Nanda and his wife Yashoda in Gokula and Vrindavana, to escape the clutches of his evil uncle Kansa, the king of Mathura. He was to eventually fulfill his destiny (as an incarnation of VISHNU) by killing Kansa. Krishna's exploits are detailed in several PURANAS including the BHAGAVATA-PURANA, HARIVAMSA, Srimad BHAGAVAD GITA, the MAHABHARATA and the VISHNU PURANA. Krishna is the supreme statesman, warrior, hero, philosopher and teacher. He is the great expounder of the BHAGAVAD GITA, holy book of the Hindus. He has been the subject of several *sculptures* and *paintings*. He is usually represented as wearing Pitambara Vastra (yellow silk garments), KIRITA MUKUTA with peacock feathers adorning it, garlands and jewellery. He is always painted a dark blue, representing his victory over Kaliya the snake whose poison turned his skin blue. It is the early stage of his life, his youth in Gokula, playing pranks on the GOPIS, stealing butter and clothes, his numerous dalliances with RADHA and the GOPIS that are popularly represented in *miniature paintings*.

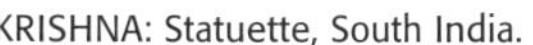

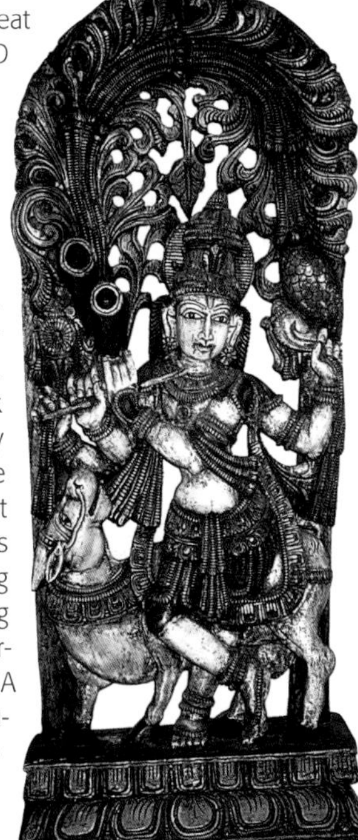

KRISHNA: Statuette, South India.

As *icons* in temples, however, he is represented as having both hands playing the flute, resting his weight on one leg, while the other is bent at the knee and crossed at the ankles. Although Krishna had two wives, Rukmini and Satyabhama, RADHA is represented on left side, at other *times* a cow is represented as gazing enraptured at him, listening to the music of his flute. Refer ABHISARIKA, *Attribute*, *Basohli*, BHAGAVAN, BHAKTI, *Bundi*, CHAKRA, DASAVATARA, *Erotic Art*, GANJIFA, GITA-GOVINDA, *God*, GOPA, *Iconography*, *Iconology*, *Image*, KALIYADAMANA, KALIYAMARDANA, *Kangra*, *Kishangarh*, *Madhubani*, *Manuscript Paintings*, *Mathura Art*, *Murti*, NAYAK-NAYAKA, NAYIKA, *Pastoral*, *Picchwais*, *Ritu*, *Spiritual*, *Theme*, *Amit Ambalal*, *Saroma Bhowmick*, *Chattopadhyay*, *Muhammed Abdur Rehman Chughtai*, *Alphonso A. Doss*, *Sunayani Devi*, *Jamini Roy*, *Abanindranath Tagore*, *P. Vinay Trivedi*, *Sarada Charan Ukil*, *Raja Ravi Varma*. Illustrations—GOVARDHAN, GOVARDHANADHARA, HOLI, *Mewar*, RASA LILA, *Thanjavur (Tanjore) Paintings*, *Manjit Bawa*, *Ganga Devi*, *Surendra Pal Joshi*.

Krishnamurthy, P. (1948–) b. Kaveripoomttnam, Thanjavur, TN. Education: Dip. *FA*. *GCAC* Chennai, *Fresco Banasthali Vidyapith* RAJ. Solos: Mumbai, Govt. Museum & *LKA* Chennai, Tamil University Thanjavur, Tamil Sangam New Delhi, *SAI*. Group participations: National *LKA* Exhibition New Delhi, *AFA* Kolkata, Progressive Painters Association Chennai, *CKP*, *AIFACS*; International: Paris, Sweden, Denmark, Washington, Brussels, Amsterdam, Vienna, Copenhagen, Sydney, Canberra. Participated: In *artists'* camps, workshops, seminars, on *art* & *cinema*. Awards: Chennai *LKA*, Wallace Fox Prize, Young Painters' Association & South Indian Society of Painters Chennai. Scholarship Ministry of Cultural Govt. of India, Junior Fellowship for *tribal art*. Member: *Cholamandal* & Koothupattari. Collections: National Gallery, Govt. Museum & *LKA* Chennai, *LKA* New Delhi, *Chandigarh Museum*, Manipur Museum.

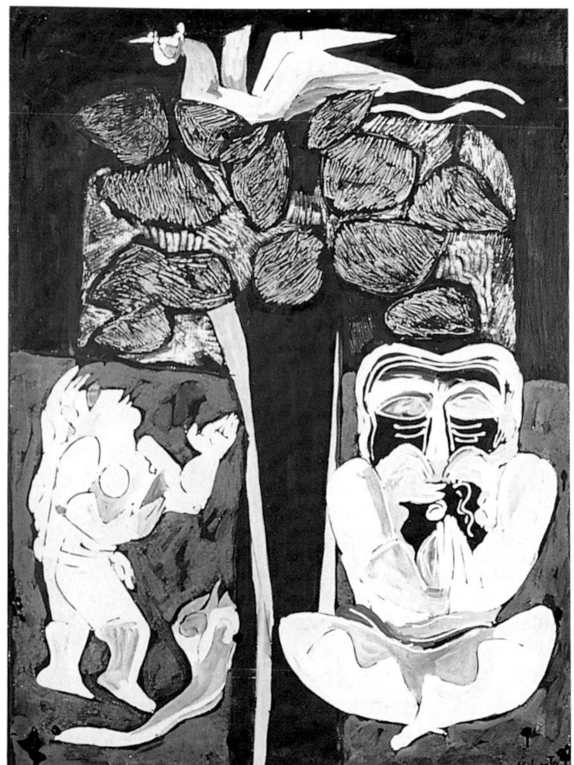

Krishnamurthy, P.: "Under the Tree".

Wiry *lines*, expressionistic *colours* and *graphic images* abound in P. Krishnamurthy's works. His subjects are rooted in the complex social structure of India, with obvious references to traditional *imagery* and religious mythological *iconography*. He has also won several awards for his *art* direction for regional *cinema*.

He lives and works in Chennai.

Krishnan, Rekha (1954–) b. Hyderabad, AP. Education: GDA *Drawing & painting JJSA*. Solos: Gallery Durga Mumbai, Alliance Francaise Bangalore, *LKA* & KB Hyderabad, Vinyasa Art Gallery Chennai, *JAG*. Group participations: New Delhi, *Artists' Centre* & Indian Oil Art Exhibition Mumbai, *JAG*; International: Indian Fairs Switzerland. Awards: Govt. of Indian Cultural Scholarship. Commissions: *Murals* Indian Railways, *portraits*. Collections: Rashtrapati Bhavan & pvt.

Rekha Krishnan's *paintings* reflect the world around her. From her "windows" series to the works inspired by music, Reiki and Energy manifestations, the use of bright, vibrant *colours* is a common *theme*, as is a highly simplified use of figural *imagery*. *Light* is also an integral element in her *compositions*, which sometimes uses the geometricity of a frame-like *motif* to *highlight* issues and *images*. *Texture*, achieved both through the brushstrokes, as well as the *combing technique* are inherent in her works.

She lives and works in Mumbai. Refer YANTRA. (See Illustration on page 379.)

Krishnappa, S. (1945–) b. Sarjapur, KAR. Education: Dip. *FA*. Kala Mandir Bangalore; *NKM*. Solos: Bangalore, Galleria Mumbai, *JAG*. Group participations: Jaipur, Shimla, Guntur, *LKA* annuals New Delhi, Southern States Regional Academy Chennai, *WSC* Chennai, Mumbai, Kolkata & New Delhi. *Art* camps: KAR *LKA* Dharwad; *Artists* & Writers Guild Bangalore, SZCC Vijyawada. Awards: KAR *LKA*, Andhra Academy of Art. Appointments: Working at *WSC* as Art Designer Chennai. Collections: KAR *LKA* & Govt. Museum Bangalore, Regional Centre & MMB Chennai, School of Arts and Crafts Davangere; International: Eastern Modern Art Gallery Japan.

S. Krishnappa is basically a colourist, using flowing *colour washes*, belonging to either cool or warm families, with faint *outlines* and subtle *highlights* indicating the shape of the *figures*. His subjects are mostly *genre* based, with musicians appearing in his later works, owing a debt to *K.K. Hebbar*. He has also painted *landscapes*.

He lives in Bangalore.

Kulkarni, D.G. (1921–1992) b. Shedbal, KAR. Education: GDA *Drawing & painting JJSA*. Solos: Over 12 of *paintings* & 6 of *stone carvings*—New Delhi, Kolkata, Hyderabad, Artist's Aid Centre Mumbai, *JAG*. Group participations: National Exhibition *LKA* New Delhi, MAHA State Art, *BAS*. Awards: *LKA* New Delhi, MAHA State Award, MAHA Gaurav Puraskar. Appointments: Made a brief attempt at initiating a School of Art (as Dir.) near Halebid in KAR; Joined "Quit India" Movement as a student; Joined "Indian Express", "Illustrated Weekly", "Free Press Journal" as a cartoonist. Collections: Two *paintings* on display adjacent to *painting* by P. Picasso at the U.N. building in New York.

He was primarily a cartoonist, working with several prestigious newspapers and magazines in Mumbai. Some of his political *cartoons* were reproduced in the "New York Times" and other major newspapers abroad. His *paintings* have the simplification of *form* and brilliance of *colour* associated with Indian miniatures. But it is his *sculptures* in *stone* that display his understanding of *texture* and his use of mythic *imagery*. The voluptuous simplicity of his linear *drawings* find fruition in his *tactile stone* works. Refer *Cartoon*.

Kulkarni, K.B. (1920–) b. Hindalga, Belgaum. Education: *Drawing* Teacher's Certificate & *Art* Master *JJSA*. Solos: Belgaum, Bangalore, Kolhapur, Pune, Mumbai. Group participations: *Nag Foundation* Pune. Member: Ex-member of the Advisory Board of *Art Education* & member at KAR *LKA*. Appointments: *Art* teacher & Principal at Chitramandir Belgaum; Principal of J.N. Bhandari School of Art Shinoli Dist. Kolhapur. Collections: Kolhapur, Mumbai, Abhinav Kala Mahavidyalaya Pune, pvt. & public.

K.B. Kulkarni is one of the early practitioners of the romantic *realistic style* in the *manner* of the *Bombay School*. His poetic feminine *figures* are placed against dream *landscapes*, textured by his versatile *handling* of the *medium* of *oils* and *watercolours*, but *watercolours* are his favourite. He has also painted *landscapes*, with highly simplified elements and *colours*.

He lives and works in Belgaum. Refer *Figure*; Illustration–*Drapery*.

Kulkarni, K.S. (1918–1994) b. Belgaum, KAR. Education: GDA *JJSA*, Research Scholar of Sir Tata Trust for Indian *Painting*. Solos: Over 71 show including Kumar Gallery, *Dhoomimal*, SC, *AIFACS*, TKS, SRAG, TAG, *JAG*, *SJM*; International: Germany, UK, USA, Japan, Egypt. Group participations: National *LKA* New Delhi, *JAG*; International: Russia, USA, Japan, *Biennale* Sao Paulo Brazil & UK. Participated: Seminars, workshops & discussions on *art* in India & abroad. Awards: Rockefeller Foundation Scholarship USA, *LKA* annual awards, Awards for *murals* & *concrete sculptures* in India & for Indian Trade Fairs abroad; Elected Fellow of *LKA*, "Kala Samman" New Delhi, SKP; Hon.: "Emeritus Professor" HRD Dept. of Culture New Delhi. Member: Founder member TKS, SC. Commissions: *portraits* of political *figures*, including Motilal Nehru, Dr. Radhakrishnan & Dr. Sanjeeva Reddy. Publications: "Human form in Indian Art" & articles on *art* in newspapers, periodicals and magazines. Collections: *NGMA*, *LKA* & *National Museum* New Delhi, *Maharaja Fatesingh Museum* Vadodara, *Chandigarh Museum*, *BKB* Varanasi, *SJM* & also abroad.

K.S. Kulkarni also being a *mural painter*, started his artistic career by *painting* signboards and billboards in the early 30s. He was inspired by Western *landscape painting* and film *posters*. His years at the *art* school introduced him to *wash painting* as well as the Western academic *style*. He became known as a fine portraitist as well as a muralist. He did a series of 200 *pen* and *ink drawings*, inspired by the erotic *sculptures* at *Khajuraho* and primitive *art*, *CHOLA bronzes*, Mayan and Etruscan *art* including the *art* of Africa, as well as the works of the *modern* masters, including P. Picasso and *Rabindranath Tagore*. In his *compositions*, creativity of *forms* are linked with and without. He himself had been the source of inspiration for a great many *artists* of the younger generation, being a Prof. at various *art* schools including Delhi Polytechnic, BHU, (where he later became Dean), Skidmore College New York where he lectured on Indian *art* and the New Delhi *College of Art* as a visiting Prof. for Post-Grad. students.

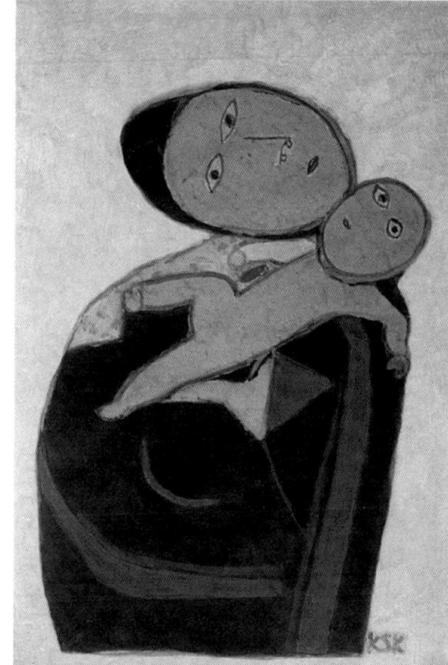

Kulkarni, K.S.: "Mother & Child", *Acrylic* on *Paper*.

Kulkarni, Shakuntala (1950–) b. Dharwar, KAR. Education: Dip. *Painting* & Post-Dip. *Mural Design JJSA*, *Graphics MSU*. Solos: *Gallery 7*, *GC* & NCPA Mumbai, *Image Art Gallery* Bangalore, *JAG*, *PG*, SRAG. Group participations: MMB, *GC*, *Artists' Centre*, *BAAC* & *Gallery 7* Mumbai, *LKA* Exhibitions New Delhi, Group 8 Chandigarh, *CYAG*, *JAG*, *NCAG*, *PUAG*, *LCAG*, *PG*. *Graphic* & theatre workshops: Vadodara, *Santiniketan*, NCPA Mumbai, *FFA* Vadodara organized by *Vivan Sundaram* & supervized by *Somnath Hore*, *GAC*. Awards: Govt. of Indian Culture Scholarship, Residency at the Brewery Arts Centre Kendal UK.

Shakuntala Kulkarni is one of the *artists* to have broken away from the two-dimensional surface of *watercolour painting*. Since the mid-90s she had began exploring the possibilities of *installation*, with "Beyond Proscenium" being an extension of her earlier trysts with theatre. From designing *spaces* and sets for theatre, "Beyond Proscenium" became painted theatre itself, with *canvases* placed three-dimensionally, *figures* and stage-like props, continuing across the divisions. She has also constructed plyboard pillars and incorporated the *craft* of quilt-making in her later works. These works have a definite slant towards feminity, with the *nude* female *figure* being a constant *motif* in her *drawings* and *constructions*.

She lives and works in Mumbai. Refer *Installation*.

Kulkarni, Uday (1952–) b. India. No formal education in *Arts*. Solos: *LKA* New Delhi, *AFA* Kolkata, *JAG*, TAG, *AIFACS*, SRAG, IIC. Group participations: *LKA* Exhibitions New Delhi, MAHA State Art Exhibitions, Gallery Genesis Kolkata, *BAS* Exhibitions, *Biennale BB*, HG, *VAG*. *Art* camps: New Delhi. Awards: Nagpur University. Member: Indian Society of Art Appreciation Mumbai, *BAS*. Collections: *NGMA* New Delhi, Gallery Genesis Kolkata, HG, pvt. & corporates in India & International: USA, UK.

Though Uday Kulkarni initially began *painting* as a hobby, he became associated with *art* organizations in Mumbai and was included in group shows of young *artists*. He has painted *abstract* naturescapes, with the emphasis on bright, *translucent colours*. Brushstrokes are his main *technique* with *mediums*, including *oils* and *acrylics*, but *watercolour* remains his favourite.

He lives and works in New Delhi.

Kumar, Anil (1961–) b. Gwalior, India. Education: NDA *Sculpture* Govt. Institute of FA. Gwalior. Solos: *JAG*, TAG. Group participations: National Exhibition, *Triennale LKA* New Delhi, *JAG*, TAG, *CYAG*, *ATG*, SAG, *Biennale BB*; International: Havana *Biennale* Cuba. *Sculpture* camps: IAFA Amritsar, J&K Academy Jammu, *BB*, BHU, IFAS. Awards: National *LKA* New Delhi, MP State Raza Award, *BAS*, *BB*; *Amrita Sher-Gil* Fellowship, Govt. of India Fellowship. Collections: *NGMA*, *LKA* & Sanskriti Pratishthan New Delhi, *Roopankar BB*, pvt. & corporates national & international.

Anil Kumar works with *marble* and *stone*, using certain favourite animal and insect morphology to create simplified *forms* enhanced by the use of subtle *texture* or polish. Though his *form* is basically inert, with tortoises lying upside down or retreating within their shells, its inherent organic *nature* still stands out.

He lives and works in Gwalior MP.

Kumar Magazine A magazine in the Gujarati language set up in 1924 by *Ravishankar M. Raval* an *artist* and Bachu-bhai Rawal, based on the *Modern Review* prototype. There are articles on science, *art* and literature along with *illustrations* aimed at educating the taste of a reader.

Kumar, Sanjay (1961–) b. Allahabad, UP. Education: M.A. *Drawing* & *painting* University Agra & Research Scholarship Philosophy of colours in Modern Painting. Solos: Kanpur, *NCAG*, SRAG, *JAG*. Group participations: Allahabad University UP, State *LKA* Lucknow, Agra Artist Association Allahabad, *YBCAG*. Awards: Inter University Competition, Association of Indian University New Delhi, Silver Medal at National Competition Chennai.

Sanjay Kumar distorts and texturizes the human *form*, breaking it and placing it against contrasting diagonals of *colour* and *form* to come up with *compositions* exuding pathos as the primary emotion. In several of his surrealistic mental works his careful arrangement of contrasting *figures* and *forms* and their vigour are barely contained in the *space* thus exuding the emotion of restlessness.

He lives and works in Mumbai.

Kundala Refer ABHUSHANA.

Kundu, Bimal (1954–) b. Kolkata. Education: Dip. *FA*. Dip. *Sculpture GCAC* Kolkata. Solos: *VAG*. Group participations: *AFA*, *BAAC*, State *LKA*, R.K. Mission Institute of Culture & *CIMA* Kolkata, Sanskriti, *CYAG*, *JAG*, *LTG*, *ISOA*, *G88*, GAG, *CKAG*, *BAG*. Workshops: Kolkata, Bankura WB. *Art* camps: "Art in Industry" Jamshedpur, *Sculpture* camps *Santiniketan*. Awards: Rajaram Scholarship Govt. of KAR, H.C. Ghosh Award, Gaganendranath Memorial Medal, *AFA* & *BAAC* Kolkata. Member: *SCA*. Commissions: *sculptures* in Kolkata. Collections: *NGMA* New Delhi, *BAAC* Kolkata, Vivekananda Art Gallery KAR.

Bimal Kundu, a *sculptor* has a preference for *wood* and different *metals*, primarily for the play of *textures* possible within these *mediums*. His *form* is cubistically simplified and based on *forms* and *figures* found in *nature*, though *masses* and planes, *light* and *shade* seem to be the main *theme*. He is especially interested in open-air *sculptures*, for their large scale.

He lives and works in Kolkata.

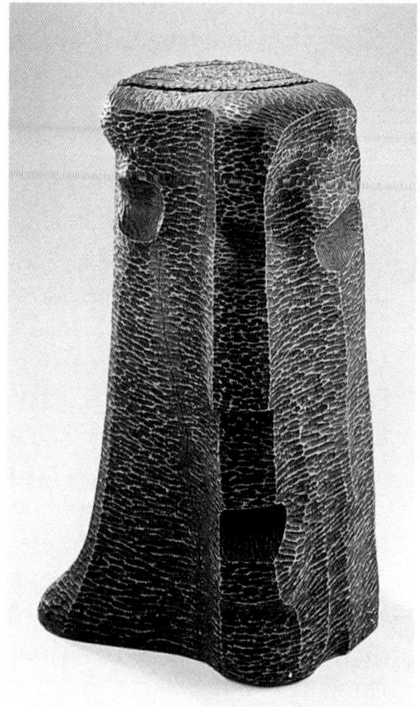

Kundu, Bimal: "Head", *Wood*, 1985, 55x35x29 cm.

Kundu, Subrata (1970s–) b. WB. B.FA. Education: *GCAC* Kolkata, M.FA. *College of Art* New Delhi. Solos: Over 18 including *BAAC* Kolkata, *GG*, SRAG, *VAG*, TAG, *CKAG*. Group participations: *LKA* New Delhi, *AFA* Kolkata, HG, *LTG*, *GE*, *JAG*. *Art* camps: All India Artist camp New Delhi, Meyo College Ajmer, *RBU*. Awards: *ISOA*, *AIFACS*, SKP. Appointments: Visiting lecturer at the *College of Art* New Delhi. Collections: *NGMA*, *LKA* & *College of Art* New Delhi, Governor's House Kolkata, pvt., corporates & institution; International: Germany.

Subrata Kundu uses *colours* in an *abstract* expressionist *manner*, exploring *line*, *texture* and *tone* rather than *form*. Leaving behind a very visible brushmark, he juxtaposes broad patches with slapdash *lines* and fluid *spaces* of a contrasting *hue*, in the improvisory *manner* of early V. Kandinsky, using both *figures* and *abstract forms* with equal ardour.

He lives and works in New Delhi.

Kunhiraman, Kanayi (1937–) b. Kuttamathu, Kerala. Education: Dip. *FA*. GSAC Chennai; Studied *sculpture* Slade School of FA. London under Commonwealth Scholarship; Grant enabled him to visit London & Italy. Solos: Progressive Painters Association & South Indian Painters Association

Chennai, Kerala *LKA* Exhibition, *Triennales* & *LKA* in New Delhi, "New Trends" in South India organized by Central *LKA*; International: *Triennale* & Festival of India Exhibition London. Awards: Progressive Painters Association & *LKA* Chennai, Kerala *LKA*. Member: Chairman *LKA* Kerala, *LKA* New Delhi, Dir. of Board & Dir. of Kerala Handicrafts Association. Appointments: Has held various posts, including the portfolio of the Principal of the *CFA* Thiruvananthapuram. Collections: Open-air *sculptures* & *bronze* statues—Kalayatra, *NGMA* New Delhi, *LKA* Chennai, Cochin, Thrissur, Patiala, Quilon, *CKP*, *bust* of *Rabindranath Tagore*, Thiruvananthapuram, Landscaping & Environmental Sculptures at Veli Tourist Village Veli Thiruvananthapuram.

The bulk of his works are magnanimous *monumental* outdoor & environmental *sculptures*.

Kanayi Kunhiraman tries to represent the vastness of the universe in his works. Starting with the *figurative* "YAKSHI" of 1970, through the "Mother" & "Fertility" *sculptures* to the outdoor *sculpture* at Veli, Kanayi Kunhiraman has been inspired by *Pop art* at times and by Teyyam, a ritualistic performance native to Kerala. The "mother-figure" also recurs time and again in his works. "Mukkola Perumal" symbolizes the past, present and the future carrying on a dialogue on the stage-pedestal. The vertical and horizontal *lines* in *white* add to the *illusion* of *depth* against the pitch *black figures*. The work is an amalgamation of Indian concept and Western *technique*. In Veli, a tourist village constructed by the Kerala Govt., Kanayi Kunhiraman has taken certain familar *images*, like conch shells, lotus pads, the female *figure* and given them an Oldenburg-like scale to fit them into the environs of the seaside site. The onlooker is free to interact with the work, indeed he is invited to sit on one & walk on another in a true amalgamation of *art* with *nature*.

At present, he is working as a project consultant for the Govt. of Kerala Dept. of Tourism. (See illustration on page 123 also.) Refer *Aggregrates*, *Bronze*, *Chasis*, *Conceptual Art*, *Concrete*, *Depth*, *Ecological Art*, *Egyptian Art*, *Environment Art*, *Figurative Art*, *Illusion*, *Mass*, *Monumental*, *Nature*, *Open Form*, *Performance Art*, *Plein-air*, *Pop Art*, *Primitivism*, *Space*, YAKSHI, YAKSHINI; Illustrations—*Earth Art*, *Earth Work*, *Land Art*, SHANKHA.

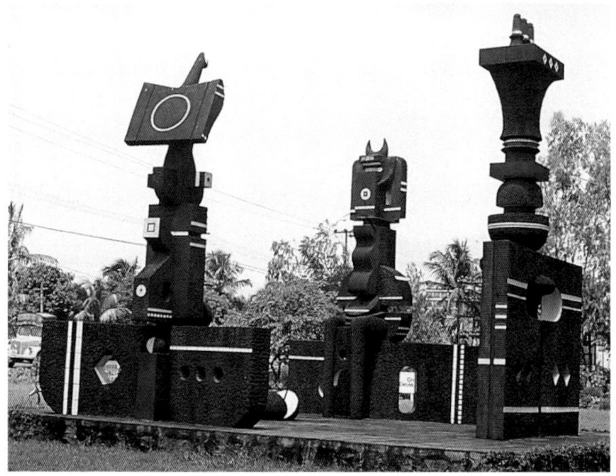

Kuntala Refer MUKUTA.

Kurmavatara Refer *Iconography*, *Iconology*, VISHNU.

Kushana Dynasty The Kushanas (AD 1st–3rd century) were a branch of the Yueh-Chi tribe of China. They settled near Bactria and divided the land into several regions including Kushan. A century later, one of the Kushan rulers Kujula (Kadphises) overthrew the other chiefs and declared himself king. His son Vima Kadphises brought several parts of Northern India under Kushan rule. Kanishka was the greatest of all Kushan kings ruling a empire stretching from Khotan in the North to Bihar in the East and *Malwa* in the South. He was a great patron of all the *arts* and literature. One phase of Kushan *art* centred at Gandhara while the other grew around *Mathura*. Important works of *sculpture* and *architecture* were found at both centres. Indian *art* is indebted to the Kushans for patronising both these flourishing schools where the first mature *images* of BUDDHA were developed. Refer *Gandharan Art*, *Mathura*, BHAGAVAN, *Drapery*, *Mahayana Buddhism*, *Mathura Art*, *Amrita Sher-Gil*.

Kushawaha, Balwant Singh (1932–) b. Ujjain, MP. Education: Dip. *FA*. & *Applied Art* Indore School of Art Indore MP; Specialization in *Visual Arts—wood carving* & *sculpture*. Solos: New Delhi, Ujjain, Nagoda, Jabalpur, Raipur, *JAG*. Group participations: *LKA* New Delhi, Indore School of Art Indore, Bhopal. Workshops: Demonstations in wooden blockmaking Sanchi & All India Handicrafts Bhopal & New Delhi, *Wood carving* BKB Ujjain. Awards: Over seven awards in MP State, others in Vijaiward AP, Amritsar PUJ, Bombay FA and Craft Pune, All India Handicrafts Board, National Award & *LKA* in *Nude* 1965 New Delhi. Hon.: Title of Shrestha Kala Acharya Bhopal Govt. of MP; International: Vatican Museum Award Italy. Member: *LKA* & All India Handicrafts Board New Delhi; Founder: Rethyam Art Society Bhopal. Appointments: Arranged various handicrafts fairs & tribal Melas, Conducted research & survey on Harijan & tribal *craft*; Gave technical demonstrations on handicrafts; Established Lalit Kala & Hastashilp Co-op. Society Bhopal. Publications: A book on *wood engraving* for rural artisans in Hindi. Collections: *Wood carving LKA* & All India Handicrafts Board New Delhi, Maharaja Sahib Kota RAJ, State Academi Bhopal & pvt.; International: *Wood carvings*—UNESCO, Thailand, Canada, USA, Yugoslavia, Japan, Vatican Museum Rome and pvt. Berlin.

Balwant Singh Kushawaha's works with the tribal & folk artisans have influenced him in making of his own *sculptures*, mostly in the Saag *wood carving technique*. The *eclectic imagery* includes references to myths, *legends* & *epics*. His academic *studies* also play a role in his assimilation of *images* with references to *Jamini Roy*, and also *abstract* simplification appearing in some of the works. Finally, he settled on the *figurative style creating nudes* with the grain of the wood brought out prominently.

He has held a variety of posts pertaining to tribal welfare. At present, he lives and works in Bhopal MP.

L

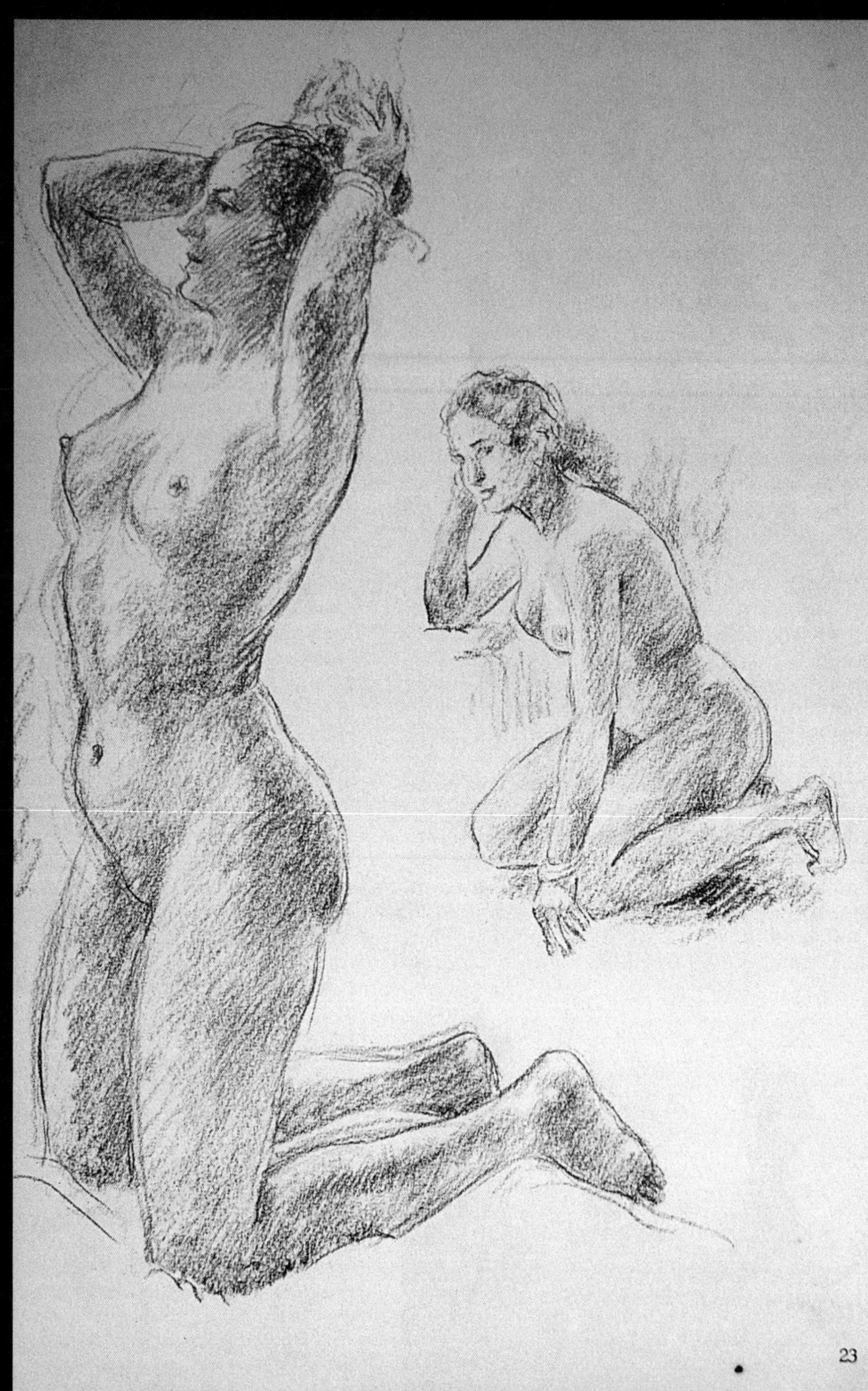

Life-Drawing: *Muralidhar R. Achrekar*, "Nude", *Pencil.* (See notes on page 206)

L.S. Raheja School of Art (LSRSA) (Mumbai, MAHA) The Institute was established in 1953 under the name "Bandra School of Art" by S.K. Patkar and D.R. Parulekar. In 1980, it was renamed as the L.S. Raheja School of Art (LSRSA). The School offers several dip. and certificate courses in both *FA* and *applied arts*. These include a one-year Foundation Dip., four years Govt. Dip. in *drawing* and *painting/applied art*. There is also one-year certificate course in photography. The Institute is run by the Bombay Suburban Art & Craft Education Society. Refer *Ravi Mandlik, Dattaprasanna S. Rane*.

Lacquer A *film* forming material derived both naturally and synthetically for giving finishing coats to *metal*, furniture and decorative articles. Lacquer is a *varnish* used since ancient *times* in China and Japan. There are two kinds of lacquer. One from the sap of the plant Rhus Vernicifera and the other known as shellac, made from the insect Laccifer Lacca.

The rapid drying time of lacquer and shellac makes them useful in high speed works. However, unless they are applied under controlled conditions, their durability may get considerably affected. They can then crack, darken, yellow or lose adhesion. Lacquering was most widely used in China, Korea, Japan, and India. Layers and layers of lacquer were used in creating objects such as bracelets, ornamental boxes, toys and screens etc. Refer *Palm Leaf, Screen Printing, Varnish, Asit K. Haldar*.

Lahiri, Shanu (1928–) b. Kolkata. India. Education: Dip. in *FA*. *GCAC* Kolkata, Studied Academy Julien & Art Appreciation course Ecole de Louvre Paris. Solos: Over 31 shows, *AFA* & *BAAC* Kolkata, others in New Delhi, Guwahati, Ahmedabad, *JAG*; International: Toronto Canada, San Francisco, New York, Washington DC, Philadelphia, Texas USA. Group participations: *BAAC* Kolkata, "The Group" *exhibitions* New Delhi & Kolkata; International: Washington DC, USA, Montreal Canada. Participated: *Exhibition* of 125th birth anniversary *Rabindranath Tagore* sponsored by WB Govt. & *RBU*, another at *BAAC* Kolkata. Awards: *AFA* Kolkata; President of India New Delhi, Governor of WB at *AFA* Kolkata. Commissions: *Sculptures* & *murals*, created 40 *mural* panels approximately 1500 ft. with graduated students Kolkata; *Mural* 3500 ft. sponsored by Philips Company Kolkata; Designed stage sets & costumes for Tagore's dance, dramas & Sircar's ballets Kolkata. Appointments: Lectures & talks on radio & TV Kolkata, Guwahati, Canada, France, USA, UK; Reader of *Painting*, Prof. & Dean of the Faculty of Visual Arts *RBU*. Publications: Articles on Art, Journal on Picasso for the Indian Museum, *Prabasi*, Jugantar, Shiladitya. Collections: *NGMA* New Delhi, *SJM*; International: Berlin Gallery Germany; pvt., institutional & corporates.

The *narrative*, be it based on *mythology* or on the lives of great men is always present in Shanu Lahiri's *paintings*. Other subjects include the musical modes, social *themes* and Bengali folk tales, especially the Thakurmar Jhuli series.

Her visit to Paris and subsequent exposure to the works of the *modern* masters brought a marked *eclecticism* in her works, with *form* and *colour* gaining in importance. *Images* become greatly simplified and *figures* are suggested with large spontaneous sweeps of the *brush* to the exclusion of detail. Her *murals*, especially those worked on as community projects are large in scale and innovative in *nature*. She has worked with a variety of *media*, including tapestries, *glass painting* and X-ray films.

She lives and works in Kolkata.

Lahoti, Murli (1945–) b. Marathwada, MAHA. N.T.C. *Painter* & decorator. Education: GDA in *painting* & *commercial art* Abhinav Kala Mahavidyalaya Pune. Solos: Over 105 in Mumbai, Pune, New Delhi, Kolkata, Chennai, Hyderabad, Bangalore, Aurangabad & abroad. Group participations: *AFA* Kolkata, *LKA* New Delhi, IAFA Amritsar, *BAS*, *ASI*, HAS. *Art* camps: Dehradun, Udaipur, New Delhi, Bangalore, Pune. Awards: *LKA* New Delhi, MAHA State, F.I.E. Foundation National Award 1991. Commissions: *Murals* in *media* like *metal*, scrap *metal*, *fibreglass*, *wood*, *mosaic*, *ceramics*, *steel* & waste material Mumbai, Pune, Nagpur, Nasik; International: Beirut, USA. Collections: Mumbai, *LKA* & *NGMA* New Delhi, *BAAC* Kolkata, *Maharaja Fatesingh Museum* Vadodara; pvt., corporates & institutional.

Murli Lahoti's early works were filled with *pastoral* scenes and mythological *themes*. His *figures* were greatly stylized and marked by rhythmic flowing *lines*. He has also experimented with the *form* of the bull and with TANTRA. His recent works show his preoccupation with textural *masses* and drippings, with the three-dimensional quality of *relief* being an interesting innovation.

He lives and works in Pune, MAHA.

Lajmi, Lalitha (1932–) b. Kolkata, WB. Education: *JJSA*. Solos: Vadodara, *Gallery 7*, *Tao Art Gallery* & *GC* Mumbai, *Art Heritage* New Delhi, HCVA, *PUAG*, *PG*; International: Seattle, Boston & Los Angeles USA, Hegen & Hale Germany, Rome Italy. Group participations: USIS Mumbai, *LKA Exhibitions*

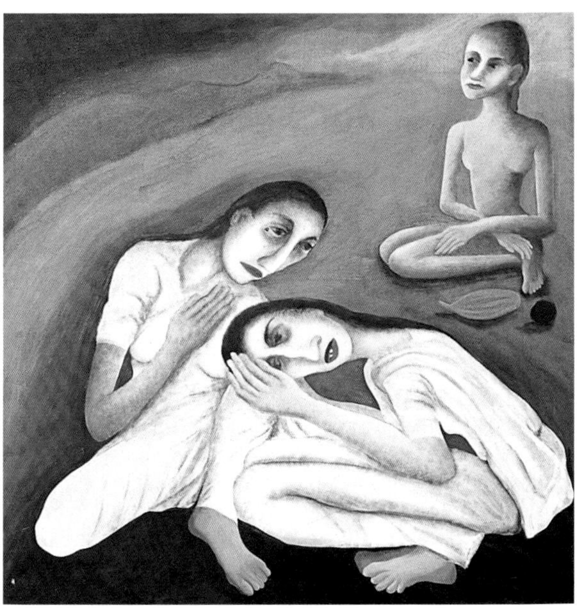

Lajmi, Lalitha: "Untitled", *Oil Painting*, 1998, 105x105 cm.

New Delhi, International *printmaking Biennale BB, PUAG, CYAG, SAI*; International: Berlin, Kanegawa, Yugoslavia, London. *Graphic* workshops: Vadodara, *JJSA*; *Painting* workshop Goa. *Auction*: Sotheby's. Awards: MAHA State Mumbai, *BAS*; International: Germany & California India Women's Art Exhibition. Fellowship: Govt. of India Ministry of Education & Culture New Delhi. Collections: Godrej Mumbai, *NGMA* & *LKA* New Delhi, *Chandigarh Museum, CYAG*, TIFR; British Museum London, Bradford Museum England, pvt. & corporates.

Lalitha Lajmi has evolved a distinctive *imagery* over the years, comprising highly personalized and evocative statements of her inner psyche. She employs *masks* as symbols of subterfuge, using them either in isolation or as part of a greater *narrative*, with *figures* camouflaged with them or dressed as clowns and jokers. Though she concentrated on small-sized, *sepia* toned *etchings* at the start of her career, she has, over the past decade, used similar *imagery* in her colourful *oils* and *watercolours*.

After teaching *art* in schools for over 20 years, she now lives and paints in Mumbai.

Lakeeren–The Contemporary Art Gallery (LCAG) (Mumbai), was inaugurated by *Maqbool Fida Husain* in 1995. The intention of the owner, Arshiya Lokhandwala was to bring *art* to the suburbs of Mumbai. Though the gallery has featured *theme* shows such as "Cinemascape" on the centenary of *cinema* and had also displayed works by established *artists* such as *Laxman Shreshtha, Akbar Padamsee, Krishen Khanna, Vivan Sundaram* and *Atul Dodiya*, it mainly served the cause of upcoming talents.

Lakshmi=good future, prosperity. Senior of the two wives of VISHNU (other being Bhu), Lakshmi is the goddess of wealth, good fortune and prosperity. She is generally depicted sitting with her leg crossed, carrying a lotus in her left hand, with the right resting on the PADMA (lotus). She is associated with wealth and beauty and is one of the most popular of Hindu female deities. Probably because of the latent desire in all humans for wealth and beauty, she has evoked a large number of folk elements during her evolution into a widely accepted member of the Hindu *pantheon*. Lakshmi may have four arms when worshipped on her own but is usually shown with two when with VISHNU. Hindus normally start all new ventures after paying obeisance to goddess Lakshmi and GANESHA. Refer BHUDEVI, DIWALI/DIPAVALI, GAJALAKSHMI, MUKUTA, PADMASANA, PADMA-ASANA, RADHA, VAHANA, *Raja Ravi Varma*; Illustration–*God*.

Lalit Kala Akademi (LKA) (New Delhi). The Akademi/Academi was established in 1954 by Maulana Azad as the National Apex Body for the promotion of the *visual arts* in the country. The main branch is in New Delhi. It was registered as a society in 1957. It is an autonomous body, fully financed by the Govt. of India through the Dept. of Culture, in the Ministry of HRD. It has established its institutional personality through the yearly awards (10 National Akademi Awards for the National Exhibitions) and commendations it confers on *artists*. Every three years the LKA organizes its International Exhibition of Art called *Triennale* India. The Akademi also organizes the Rashtriya Kala Mela, which is an *exhibition* on the lines of the village fair, where *artists* can exhibit without restriction. It also organizes workshops, *exhibitions* and seminars on *art*, apart from its various publications on *art* which include *monographs* on *artists* like *K.K. Hebbar, Debi Prasad RoyChowdhury, Jamini Roy* and others; picture postcards of *paintings* and *sculptures, print* portfolios, folders and journals. The Akademi also publishes its own journal called Kala Samvad in addition to its two periodicals, "Lalit Kala" and "Lalit Kala Contemporary". In addition, the Akademi offers five cash research grants per monthly every year to practising *artists* in the field of *paintings* and endows eminent *artists* with emeritus fellowships. The Akademi also has a guesthouse for *artists* visiting the capital. The regional centres are at Chennai, Lucknow, Kolkata, Bangalore and Bhubaneshwar to name a few. Lalit Kala celebrated its golden jubilee in 2004.

Lall, Harkrishan (1921–2001) b. Ludhiana, PUJ. Education: Dip. in *FA. JJSA*; Govt. of India Cultural Scholarship. Solos: Srinagar, Kolkata, Govt. Museum Jaipur, *Artists' Centre* & Gallery Rampat Mumbai, Patiala PUJ University, Chandigarh University Museum, *JAG*, TAG, *Dhoomimal*; International: Paris, San Jose. Group participations: National Exhibition Mumbai, *BAS*; International: Venice, Sao Paulo, Tokyo *Biennales*, besides exhibiting in UK, Afghanistan, USA, Canada, Egypt, Turkey, Japan & China

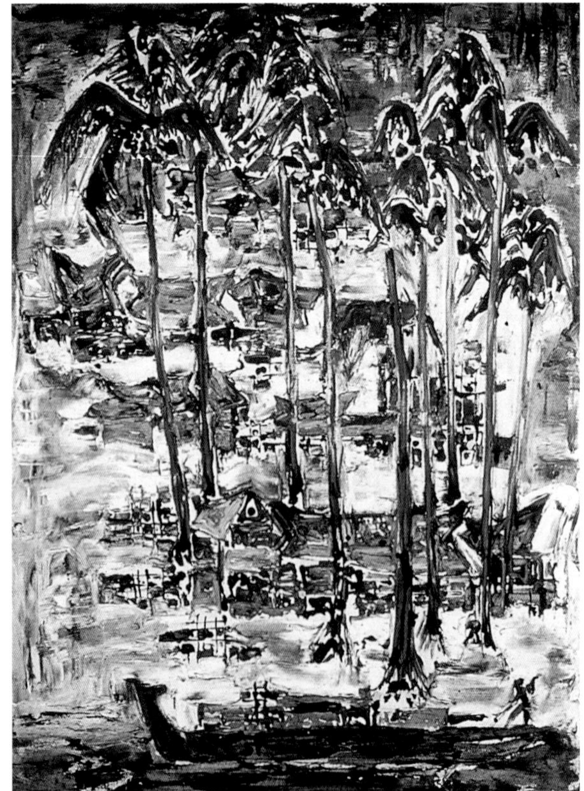

Lall, Harkrishan: "Kerala White Sand Village", *Oils*, 1963, 118x88 cm.

over the years. Appointments: At first an *art* teacher at the Delhi Polytechnic & later became the Deputy Dir. *Designs* in the Ministry of Commerce & Industries New Delhi. Collections: *NGMA* & *LKA* New Delhi, *PWM* & pvt.

Harkrishan Lall was basically a landscapist, first in the *Jaganath M. Ahivasi manner*, being influenced by the *Ajanta frescoes* and Rajput miniatures. Slowly, *Realism* took a back seat and later he began concentrating on *brushwork* and application of *colours*. The *colours*, though *discordant*, managed to accurately convey the harshness of Indian summer and the coolness of moonlit nights. The works of the 60s are nearly *abstract*, being geometrically simplified rather than *figurative*. However he was best known for his expressionist *landscapes*, integrating *texture*, *tone* and *technique* in a harmonious whole, full of both warm and cool *colour passages*.

Lamp Black Refer *Black*.

Landscape A *painting* in which elements of *nature*, rather than human *figures* and animals predominate. Landscape elements such as the sky, trees, rivers and streams do appear regularly in traditional *painting*, both in India and in the West. While in Indian *miniature painting*, the NAYAKA and NAYIKA were always the main focus of the works, landscape served as a *background* in the *Ajanta frescoes* and *Jain manuscript paintings* and heightened the emotions of the hero-heroine in *Rajasthani miniature paintings*. It was in the *Mughal miniatures* that landscapes were given equal importance.

With the emergence of the English Romantics, i.e. J.M.W. Turner and J. Constable, landscape was given respectability in the West. Soon with the arrival of W. Daniells and other landscape *painters* in India, the subject gained recognition as *portrait*, *figurative* landscape and landscape *backdrops*. *Raja Ravi Varma* was among the first Indian *artists* to use naturalistic landscape *backdrops* in his mythological works. *Abanindranath Tagore* popularized Oriental *style ink* and *wash* landscapes, a *technique* that was followed by many practitioners of the *Bengal School*. The British Principals of the *JJSA* brought *Impressionism* to the *artists* of the *Bombay School*. Landscape *painting* in the open air soon became an accepted part of the curriculum. *Artists* like *Pralhad A. Dhond* specialized in *painting* landscapes, especially *seascapes*, while others like *Gopal Ghose*, *Harkrishan Lall* and *Narayan S. Bendre* returned to it time and again, exploring the subjects using different *media* and *styles*. *Narayan S. Bendre* finally started *painting* pointillistic landscapes with a group of *figures* enlivening the painted *space*, while *Harkrishan Lall's* landscapes became increasingly *abstract*. Most *artists* have used landscape at sometime or the other; these include *Bimal DasGupta*, *Francis Newton Souza*, *Laxman Shreshtha*, *Gopal S. Adivrekar* and *Ambadas*. In each case it is the *artist's* personalized *vocabulary* of *forms* and *colours* that predominates over traditional expectations of landscapes as the sum total of trees, sky, the *horizon*, the sea and other such mundane elements. Refer *Abstract Landscape, Abstraction Organic, Academic Art, Background, Backdrop, Bundi, Company School/Company Painting, Depth, Dimension, Drawing, Earth Art, Earth Work, Land Art, Eye-Level, Foreground, Ghats, Jain Miniature, Jain Manuscript, Illumination, Impressionism, Kangra, Landscape Format, Local Colour, Mixed Contrast, Mughal Miniatures, Nature, One-Point Perspective, Proportion, Realistic, Romanticism, Space, Townscape, Trompe L'Oeil, Vanishing Point, Vignette*; Illustrations—*Abstract Landscape, Cubism, Deccani Miniature Painting, Prafulla Dahanukar, Bimal DasGupta, Pralhad A. Dhond, H.A. Gade, Gopal Ghose, Balvant A. Joshi—Folk Art, B.P. Kamboj, Bhupen Khakhar, Harkrishan Lall, Paresh Maity, K. Madhava Menon, Sudhir Patwardhan, A.A. Raiba, Baburao Sadwelkar, Narayan R. Sardesai, Deokinandan Sharma, G.S. Shenoy, Vishwanath M. Sholapurkar, Laxman Shreshtha, Paramjit Singh, J. Swaminathan, Abanindranath Tagore, Sanat Thaker, K. Venkatappa, Kanhiyalal R. Yadav; Abstraction Geometric—Gaganendranath Tagore; Broad Handling—Ram Kumar; Horizon—Seascape; Pastoral—Nathu Lal Verma; Pointillism—Narayan S. Bendre*.

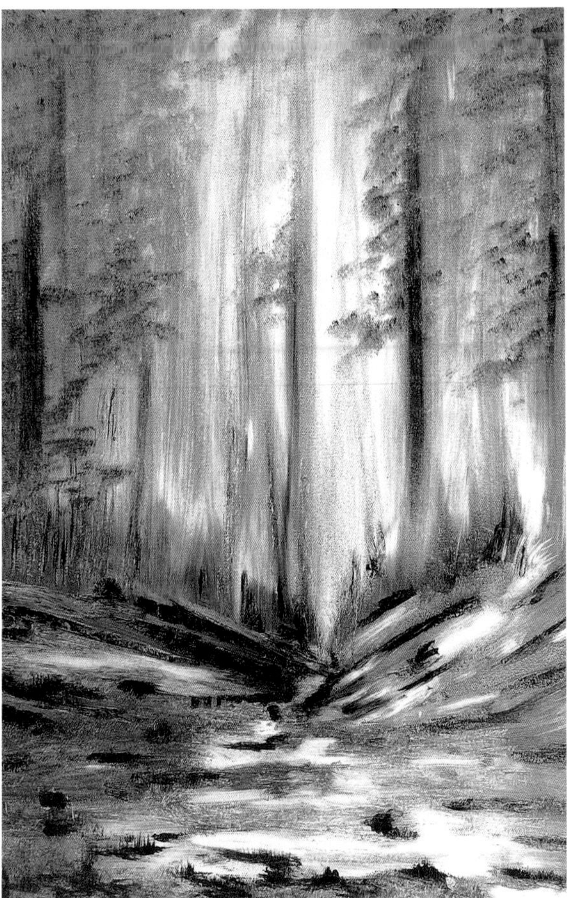

Landscape: Pratima Sheth, "Path of light", *Oil* on *Canvas*, 2004, 61x92 cm.

Landscape Format It is the shape and *size* of a *painting* or *drawing* that is wider than it is in height, opposite of portrait format. The *handling* of *paint* and *texture* are woven into the format of the *painting*, with both *colour* and *compositions* playing an important role. *Landscapes* were used principally as *background* by the *Company School* and earlier in *miniature painting*. Initially practiced by *Jamini P. Gangooly*, several *artists* of the *post-Independence* era however chose to make *landscape painting* their forte. These included *Sayed Haider Raza*, *Ram Kumar* and *K.C. Murukeson* among others. Refer *Suresh Choudhary*, *Harkrishan Lall*, *Gurudas Shenoy*, *Shiv Dutt Shukla*.

Lawate, Sudhakar K. (1937–) b. Jalgaon, MAHA. Education: GDA in *painting* & *Art* Master *JJSA*. Solos: *JAG*, TAG, *CKP*, *RSA*. Group participations: Mumbai, Aurangabad, Pune, New Delhi, Chennai, Bangalore, Hyderabad, Kolkata, Ahmednagar; International: Germany, UK, France, Switzerland, USA. *Auction*: Sotheby's 1995. Awards: Assam Gold Medal, Amritsar Silver Medal, *BAS*, MAHA State Award. Founder member: FAIM. Appointments: Hon. Joint Secretary *BAS*; Lectures & Demonstrations at Art Institute India. Collections: *NGMA* & *LKA* New Delhi, Govt. of MAHA Mumbai, KAR *LKA* Bangalore, *JJSA*, *CKP*; pvt. & corporate collections.

The human *figure* is both the means and the end in Sudhakar K. Lawate's *oil painting*. He believes that *art* has to communicate with and exist in society. Though *figurative*, his *paintings* are a combination of the concrete and the *abstract*. The human being acquires the status and *nature* of a *symbolic cipher*, while *texture* and *colour* control the *composition*.

Since his retirement as Prof. in the *JJSA*, he has been living and working in Mumbai.

Lay-In One of the traditional *techniques* used in *painting*. The *painter* often began by making an exact *drawing* or *sketch* on the *canvas*. Later filled in or "layed-on" the *tones* in *monochrome*, so that the tonal effect was visible in *terms* of *masses* and *volumes*. Refer *Dead Colour*, *Enamel*, *Enamelling*, *Kalamkari*, *Miniature Painting*.

Lead (in SANSKRIT Sisaka) The softest of many *metals*, it is silvery-grey in *colour*, with a surface that easily tarnishes. It is extremely plastic and can be *cast* or hammered into shape. It has a fairly low melting point, but contracts considerably on cooling. It is used in making garden *sculpture* or architectural *reliefs*. It is also used in manufacturing *paints*, both in the ancient and *modern* period. Refer *Graphite*, *Medium*, *Metal Cut*, *Miniature Painting*, *Sculpture*, *Stained Glass*, *White*, *Sabrayalu Dhanpal*, *M.J. Enas*, *Pilloo Pochkhanawalla*.

Lean A *term* used in *oil painting* to describe *paint* to which little or no *oil* has been added. Instead a different dilutant such as *turpentine* is mixed with the *paint* in order to make it dry quickly. Opposite to *fat paint*. Refer *Broad Handling*, *Canvas Test*, *Dry Brush Painting*, *Fat over lean*, *Oil*, *D.B. "Deven" Seth*; Illustrations—*Narayan S. Bendre*, *Bal Chhabda*, *Chhaganlal D. Mistry*.

Leather Animal skin, cured by tanning or similar processes, using several chemicals. The process renders leather impervious to moisture yet preserves its flexibility. Traditionally, Indian leather is mostly used for manufacturing general footwear. Embroidered foot-wear (Mojdis) are made in RAJ, while garments are produced in Kashmir and puppets in AP and KAR.

Contemporary artists use leather in their work specially in the field of *sculpture* and *installation*. *Satish Gujral's* burnt *wood reliefs* are embellished with leather cards, *ceramic* beads, crushed *leather* sheets, glowing vermilion powder mixed and patinaed with *gold leaf*. *Aku* worked in leather making *mixed media assemblages* with *wood* and *metal*. Refer *Arts and Crafts Movement*, *CKP* Bangalore, *GCAC* Kolkata WB, HANUMAN, CHITRAKATHI, *Embossing*, *Embroidery*, *Found Object*, *Soft-Sculptures*, *Partha Pratim Deb*, *Prabha Panwar*, *Pratima Devi Tagore*, *Rabindranath Tagore*.

Legend Myths/Ancient Stories/Fantasy Fables or Akhyana. The oldest surviving ancient stories from the RIG-VEDA verse are narrated in the dramatic dialogues written by a class of Akhyana writers known as Akhyana Vilas. These date frequently to antiquity, as opposed to historical or *contemporary* subjects. They are frequently religious or mythological in *nature* and are often the subject of *paintings* and *sculptures*. Refer *Artefact*, *Folk Inspiration*, *Icon*, *Kangra*, *Kishangarh*, *Mewar*, *Rajput Miniature Painting*, *Rhythm*, RIG-VEDA, *Sufism*, *P.N. Choyal*, *Balwant*, *Singh Kushawaha*, *Nilima G. Sheikh*, *P. Vinay Trivedi*, *Vijyalakshmi P.*, *Setlur Gopal Vasudev*; Illustrations—GANESHA, KAILASH, KAILASA, *Kalighat Pat*, *Kalighat Folk Painting*.

Lettrism, Lettrisme A *term* is used since the 1950s to describe *paintings* which comprised of words, letters, signs and sentences, mostly for their *visual* appeal as opposed to *graffiti*, where the meaning is more important. *Calligraphic* signs and letters have always been used in the works of *art* in India. Refer *Calligraphy*, *Calligraphic Painting*, *Conceptual Art*, *Jainism*, *Miniature Paintings*, *Visual*, *Shankar Palsikar*, *Shanti Dave* and *Sujata Bajaj*.

Life-Drawing A *pencil*, *chalk*, *charcoal* or *ink* study *drawing* directly from a live male or female *model* in the studio. The *figure* was either draped or *nude*. This was introduced by the British in the government run *art* schools in the late 19th century—e.g. *Raja Ravi Varma* (1846–1906). *Debi Prasad RoyChowdhury* studied under *Abanindranath Tagore* and an Italian *painter* taught him life-drawing and portraiture. *Life-size figures* which were conventional earlier, are now increasingly being used in conjunction with *abstracts*, *installations* and *found objects*. Refer *Academy*; Illustration—*Ranjitsingh Gaekwad*. (See illustration on page 202)

Life-Mask A *casting* made from a *mould* taken from a live *model*. It is sometimes used as an aid in making *portrait* heads. It has been used by several pop *artists* including J. Johns. The *mask* is also worn for various performances, which is then photographed, filmed or video filmed. Refer *Body Art*, *Pop Art*, *C. Jagdish*, *Mahirwan Mamtani*.

Life-Size The *term* refers more to sculptural works than *painting*. It describes the scale of the *portrait* heads or *busts* or at times even full *figure portraits*, as being the same as the *models'*. In India, the *Academy style*, life-size *figures* especially of politicians or famous people are popularly commissioned even today. This trend began around 1850. Materials, however have evolved from the traditional *bronze* and *marble*, *plaster of Paris* to *fibreglass* and even *paper* and *papier mache*. Refer *Ramkinkar Baij*, *M.J. Enas*, *Bhagwant K. Goregaoker*, *C. Jagdish*, *Ganpatrao K. Mhatre*, *Dhruva Mistry*, *K. Sheshagiri Rao*, *Bayaji Vasantrao Talim*, *Vinayak Pandurang Karmarkar*, *Raja Ravi Varma*.

Light In *painting*, there are various meanings of the word light. Light reveals *colour*. It also refers to light and heavy strokes, to the source of light in *painting* which can be either be artificial, for example, candle light, fire light and electric light; or natural light such as sunlight or moonlight, e.g. "Accidental Light" by *Savlaram L. Haldankar*. A picture may contain direct or indirect lighting, or both. Another *form* of light is that which emanates from *colours* themselves for without light there can be no effect of *colour* as is evident when they are in complete darkness. *Manchershaw F. Pithawalla's portraits* show a fine understanding of light and *shade*. Refer *Aureole*, *Background*, BINDU, *Bengal Revivalism*, *Bengal School*, *Chiaroscuro*, *Foreshortening*, *Glazing*, *Halo*, *Image*, *Impressionism*, *Maniere Noire*, *Neo-Tantricism*, *Nude*, *Translucent*, *Transparent*, *Value*, *Dinkar V. Wadangekar*, *K. Vasant Wankhede*; Illustrations—*Stained Glass*, *Amitabha Banerjee*, *Madhukar B. Bhat*, *John Fernandes*, *K. Ramanujam*, *Paresh Maity*, *Chittrovanu Mazumdar*, *K. Jayapala Panicker*, *Manchershaw F. Pithawalla*, *Jehangir Sabavala*, *Ghulam Rasool Santosh*, *V. Viswanadhan*, *Jai Zharotia*. Refer article "Preservation of Art Objects", page 343.

Line The line is the most essential and basic element in *drawing*, it has been in use since the dawn of *pictorial art*. Lines vary enormously in *terms* of *style* and expression. They are used to convey both the visual world, such as the human *figure* represented for example in *outline*, and *abstract* concepts such as a straight line representing the shortest distance between two *points*, or a curved line representing movement. The various *media* e.g. *pencil*, *charcoal*, *paint* produce different linear *textures*, a hard or soft line. Indian *artists* have long exploited the power of the line in *painting*; certain *modern* Indian *artists* are known particularly for their innovative use of line, i.e. *K.K. Hebbar* for his rhythmic "singing lines", *Shiavax Chavda* for the spontaneous movement in his *drawings* of dancers, and the delicate *prints* and *drawings* of *Laxma Goud* that contrast with the bold use of line by *Jogen Chowdhury* in his coloured *drawings*. Refer *Cartoon*, *Commercial Art*, *Combing*, *Contour*, *Cross-Hatching*, *Drawing*, *Drawing Inks*, *Dry-Point*, *Engraving*, *Etching*, *Expressionism*, *Eye-Level*, *Folk Art*, *Fret Pattern*, *Horizon*, *Ink*, *Kinetic Art*, *Line and Wash*, *Line Engraving*, *Linearity*, *Linear Composition*, *Linearly*, *Lyricism*, *Mass*, *Metal Cut*, *Metal Block*, *Multi block colour printing*, *Neo-Plasticism*, *One-Point Perspective*, *Orthogonal*, *Outline*, *Perspective*, *Rhythm*, *Scraperboard*, *Scratchboard*, *Sketch*, *Stone Carving*, *Synthetism*, *Vanishing Point*; Illustrations—*Ajanta*, APSARA, *Devanagari Script*, *Mewar*, *Miniature Painting*, MUDRAS/HASTAS, *Thanjavur (Tanjore) Painting*, *Undercut*, *Vocabulary*, *Wash (Technique)*, *White Line Engraving*, *Wood Engraving*, *Dhanraj Bhagat*, *Nandalal Bose*, *Manishi Dey*, *Ranjitsingh Gaekwad*, *Maqbool Fida Husain*, *Tyeb Mehta*, *Reddeppa M. Naidu*, *Laxman Pai*, *Saroj Gogi Pal*, *Rm. Palaniappan*, *Ramachandran A.*, *Shyamal Dutta Ray*, *Jamini Roy*, *Haku Shah*, *Lalu Prasad Shaw*, *Abanindranath Tagore*, *Rabindranath Tagore*, *Vasudha Thozhur*, *Sarada Charan Ukil*, *Shantanu Ukil*, *Thotha Vaikuntham*, *K. Venkatappa*, *Kanhiyalal R. Yadav*, *Yusuf*, AGNI & MAKARA—*Nagesh Bhimrao Sabannavar*; *Caricature*—*Gaganendranath Tagore*, *Hatching*—*Laxma Goud*; *Pastoral*—*Nathu Lal Verma*; SHIVA—*Kanu Desai*.

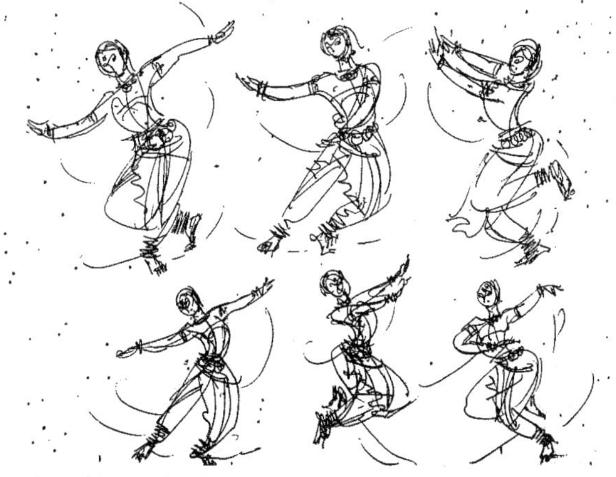
Line: *Shiavax Chavda*, "Pen & Ink Drawing".

Line and Wash Using *pen* and *ink*, linear *images* are first drawn, then brought alive by application of dilute *washes* of *watercolour* or *ink*. This method of *line* and *wash drawing* can also be reversed where *line drawings* are done over dried *washes* and can also be adapted to other linear *drawing media* such as *pencil* or *charcoal*. *Kalighat Pat Paintings* are in the *nature* of wash *drawings* being spontaneous yet succinct. Refer *Bazaar Painting*, *Bengal School*, *Tempera*, *Wash (Technique)*, *V.G. Andani*, *Jaganath M. Ahivasi*, *Ramananda Bandyopadhyay*, *Nandalal Bose*, *Sukhamoy Mitra*, *Sailoz Mookerjea*, *Sachida Nagdev*, *Ravishankar M. Raval*, *Abanindranath Tagore*, *Sarada Charan Ukil*, *Shantanu Ukil*, *Arnawaz Vasudev*, *K. Venkatappa*.

Line Engraving A type of *engraving* in which the *design* is made directly on the *metal* (usually *copper*) *plate*, with the *burin* or sharp needle. This line engraving and *cross-hatching* has been used since 18th century in conjunction with other *techniques*. The *ground* is not used in this *technique*. The resulting *burr* or spiral of *metal* is removed with the help of a scraper so that the mark, when inked, will *print* as a sharp *line*. Though this *technique* is now used to produce mostly two-dimensional *drawings*, *artists* in the past have used *cross-hatching* to indicate *tones*. Refer *Arabesque*, *Art Deco*, *Block Printing*, *Copper*, *Engraving*, *Printmaking*, *White Line Engraving*, *Wood Engraving*, *Ramkinkar Baij*, *Dhanraj Bhagat*, *Satish Gujral*, *Somnath Hore*, *Dashrath Patel*, *Krishna N. Reddy*, *Anupam Sud*, *Ali J. Sultan*.

Linearity, Linear Composition, Linearly The predominance of *line* rather than *colour*, *texture* or *tone* in any *composition*, as in the *wash paintings* of the *Bengal School* and the *frescoes* at *Ajanta*. Refer *Bengal School*, *Calligraphic*, *Dry-Point*, MUDRAS, *Painterly*, *Abdul Rahim Appabhai Almelkar*, *Amol Chakladar*, *N. Chandrasekhar Rao*, *G. Rajendran*; Illustrations–*Mukul Chandra Dey*, *Reddeppa M. Naidu*, *Abanindranath Tagore*.

Linga, Lingam=Phallus. The phallic symbol of SHIVA. It is represented as a cylindrical object with a rounded top, in *marble* or *stone*. The Lingam is worshipped as an *icon* in the Shaivite temple. The Lingam sometimes had a niche hollowed in front, in which the *figure* or head of SHIVA may be represented. There were twelve great Lingams in India, of which several have been destroyed over the centuries. The Jyotirlingam at Varanasi (Banaras) is one of the few to have survived and is being worshipped even today. Refer *Elephanta*, PURANA, SHIVA, *Tantra Art*, YONI.

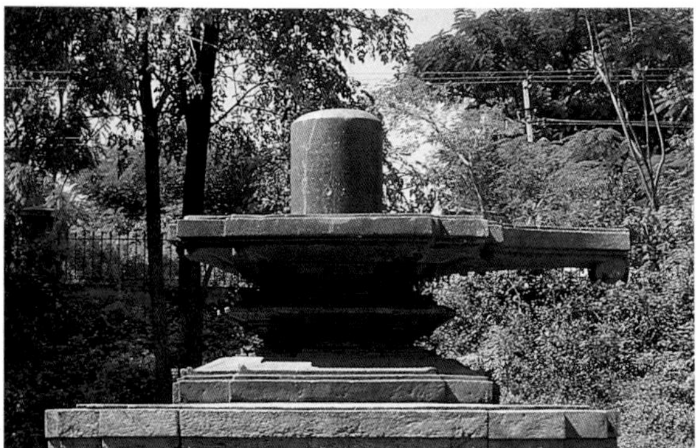

Linga, Lingam: Halebid-Belur, South India.

Lino The shortform of linoleum. This material is made by impregnating a fabric, which *forms* the *base*, with a mixture of oxidised linseed *oil*, resins, and *fillers* such as cork. *Nandalal Bose* used linoleum circa 1930 to make stark and simple *linocut prints*, which were used as *illustrations* in *Rabindranath Tagore's* book "Sahajpath". *Chittaprosad* was one of the best exponents of the lino *print* in India. His stark *black* and *white images* of the hungry famine stricken people of Bengal were perfectly suited for the *medium*. Refer *Linocut*, *Printmaking*, *White Line Engraving*, *Mukul Chandra Dey*.

Linocut A *form* of *relief printmaking*, the linocut is a softer material to work with. Linoleum can be carved into and incised quite easily by V-shaped tools, knives and *gouges*, thus creating different *textures*. After the block is designed and prepared with the help of the tools, *ink* is applied with the roller, and the *print* is taken, either by passing the block and a sheet of *paper* on it, through the press, or by placing the *paper* over the inked block and gently rubbing on it with the back of a spoon or any rounded object. Multi coloured *lino prints* are possible with the use of several blocks of differently inked *lino*. Refer *Block Printing*, *Carving*, *Multiple Tool*, *Relief*, *Relief Printing*, *V Tools*, *Nandalal Bose*, *Mukul Chandra Dey*, *Somnath Hore*, *Paul A. Koli*, *Sukhamoy Mitra*, *Ashit Paul*, *P. Perumal*, *Gurudas Shenoy*.

Lithography 1. This is a planographic process of *printmaking* where the *print* is taken from a flat surface. Unlike *relief* and *intaglio printing*, both the *image* to be printed and the *negative* area lie on the same plane. The process depends much on the antipathy of grease to water. The block is first prepared, on which the *design* is traced. This could either be a heavy and thick limestone block known as levegator, which has to be *ground* and grained (or, as is more usual in recent times, a *zinc* or *aluminium plate*), and wiped clean with a *gum arabic* solution. The *image* is then drawn or painted on this surface, with special grease-based lithographic *pencils crayons* or similar materials, including *wax* or *oil pastels*, candles, shoe polish or *chinagraph pencils*. The block is then damped. The grease-based *image* will repel the water, which soaks into the non-printing area. Lithographic *ink* is *viscous*, but is basically *transparent* in comparison to other *inks*; it adheres to the greasy *image*, and is then rolled on to the block. *Paper* is then placed on the block and both are run through the press, transferring the *image* on to the *paper*. Effects close to *painting* are possible with this process.The photolithography *technique*, which was also used in lithography, was the *image* on the *stone* that was created by photographic or electronic means for *printing*. Refer *Print*, *Offset Printing*, *Oleography*, *FFA* (Vadodara), *R.B. Bhaskaran*. **2.** Chromolithography is the *technique* of producing picture *prints* in four colour process. In this process each *colour print* prepared on a separate *stone* or *plate* for printing, a *technique* no longer in use.

In India lithography was introduced by two French artists, M. Belnos and M. de Savignhac, who worked in Calcutta. The British used lithography in the 1820s on a strictly functional basis to reproduce maps and charts. Asiatic Lithographic Press was established in 1825 in Calcutta. Later, *Raja Ravi Varma* set up a lithographic press in 1894 in Bombay with German staff. Refer *Collography*, *Colour Printing & Four Colour Process*, *Hatching*, *Devraj Dakoji*, *Naina Dalal*, *Rini Dhumal*, *Somnath Hore*, *Kavita Nayar*, *Rm. Palaniappan*, *Lalu Prasad Shaw*, *Gaganendranath Tagore*, *Hitendranath Tagore*, *K.S. Viswambhara*.

Little Theatre Group Art Gallery (LTG) (New Delhi). This *art* gallery is a relatively new addition to the already existing Little Theatre Group in New Delhi. Having opened in February 1990, the gallery functions on a sponsoring/commercial basis to promote *contemporary*, especially young and relatively unknown *artists*. The duration of their *exhibitions* is normally a fortnight; the gallery looks after the invitations, catalogues and press and *media* coverage. The gallery also accepts works on a consignment basis. Some of the *artists* who have exhibited here include *Balbhadra Agarwalla*, *Kanchan Chander*, *Arup Das*, *Naina Kanodia*, *Bishamber Khanna*, *Bimal Kundu*, *Subrata Kundu*, *Saroj Gogi Pal*, *Rabin Mondal*, *Babu K. Namboodiri*, *Kavita Nayar*, *Ved Nayar*, *Avijit Roy*, *Bulbul Sharma*, *Francis Newton Souza*, *Vasudha Thozhur*, *Zahoor Zargar*.

Living Sculpture A synonym of *body art*, it refers to the use of the *artist's* own body, or that of living, posed *models* in making *sculpture*. It is usually a part of temporary display or what is known as *performance art* or *conceptual art*, as in the works of *Mahirwan Mamtani*, *N. Pushpmala*, *Sheela Gowda*.

Loaded Brush A *brush* dipped into thick *paint*, to create *relief*-like strokes of *colour* as in *Chittrovanu Mazumdar's* or *Bal Chhabda's oils* on *canvas* or *Paresh Maity's* monumental *watercolours* with broad *brush* strokes. Refer *Brush Drawing*, *Dragging*, *Impasto*; Illustration–*Paresh Maity*.

Local Colour This refers to the actual *colour* of an object, without considering the effect of *light* on it. The natural *colour* of grass is green, though it may appear grey at night and yellow in the afternoon. Until the impressionists arrived on the scene, *painters* always used local colours. The impressionists were among the first to use optical colours, based on their observation of *nature* and its effects on different objects. Refer *Impressionism*, *Landscape*, *Natural Colour*, *Tempera*, *Narayan S. Bendre*, *Ganga Devi*, *P.T. Reddy*.

Loka SANSKRIT for "world", or a part of the cosmos or universe. According to Hindu *mythology*, there are either three or seven worlds in the universe. The first, the Tri-loka comprises of heaven, earth and the underworld, viz. Swarga, Bhu-loka and Patala respectively. The Tri-loka is often depicted in *sculptures* and *paintings*, e.g., Gangavataran in Mamallapuram.

The Sapta-loka (seven worlds) are classified as follows: Bhu-loka or the earth, Bhuvar-loka or the sky where the holy men, i.e. Munis and Siddhas dwell, Swarga-loka meaning the heaven of INDRA and the other *gods*, Mara-loka, where Bhrigu, the great sage resided with the other saints. Above this is the Jana-loka where BRAHMA's sons lived, and the Tapa-loka where the deities called Vairagis (ascetics) lived. Last is the Satya-loka where BRAHMA himself resided along with such exalted beings who were exempted from further rebirth, i.e. had gained MOKSHA. The first three worlds were destroyed at the end of each Kalpa, or day in the life of BRAHMA, the last three at the end of his life. The fourth or the Mara-loka was always uninhabitable at the *time* of destruction of the first three worlds, hence, at that particular period of time, Bhrigu and the other saints ascended to Jana-loka. Refer Illustrations–BRAHMA, DURGA, GANGA, GANESH, GOVARDHAN, GOVARDHANDHARA, GARUDA, INDRA, KAILASH, KAILASA, NANDI, NARASIMHA, NATARAJ, PARVATI, RAMAYANA, RASA, RASA LILA, RAVANA, SHANKHA, SWASTIKA, VISHU, *Ganga Devi*, *Sarada Charan Ukil*, *K. Venkatappa*.

Lost Wax Process The synonym for *cire perdue technique*. The sculptural *form* was created in *wax*, which was overlaid with *clay* or *plaster of Paris* with tube like outlets. When hot molten *metal*, usually *bronze* was poured into one of these channels, it melted the *wax*, which ran out of the lower outlets, resulting in *bronze casting*. This was known in India since the *Indus Valley Civilization*, as can be seen in the "Dancing Girl". The process became popular in the CHOLA Age, several *bronze gods* and goddesses being *cast*. Tribals in Bastar MP also used similar *technique*, which became known as *Dokra casting*. Refer *Air Vents*, *Carving*, *South Indian Bronzes*, *Somnath Hore*, *Meera Mukherjee*, *Pilloo Pochkhanawalla*.

Luminosity The degree, or the *saturation* of *light* found in a *painting*. Refer *Colour*, *Light*, *Badri Narayan*, *Muhammed Abdur Rehman Chughtai*, *Rini Dhumal*.

Lyricism The *word* as used in describing works of *art*, refers to the poetic or the *aesthetic* sensibility, awakened by certain *painterly* or sculptural *passages*; e.g., the "Lyricism" implicit in *K.K. Hebbar's* singing *line*, the hazy *washes* of *Abanindranath Tagore's paintings* and *Vinayak Pandurang Karmarkar's sculptures*. Refer *Motif*, *Amina Ahmed Kar*, Illustration–*Muhammed Abdur Rehman Chughtai*.

M

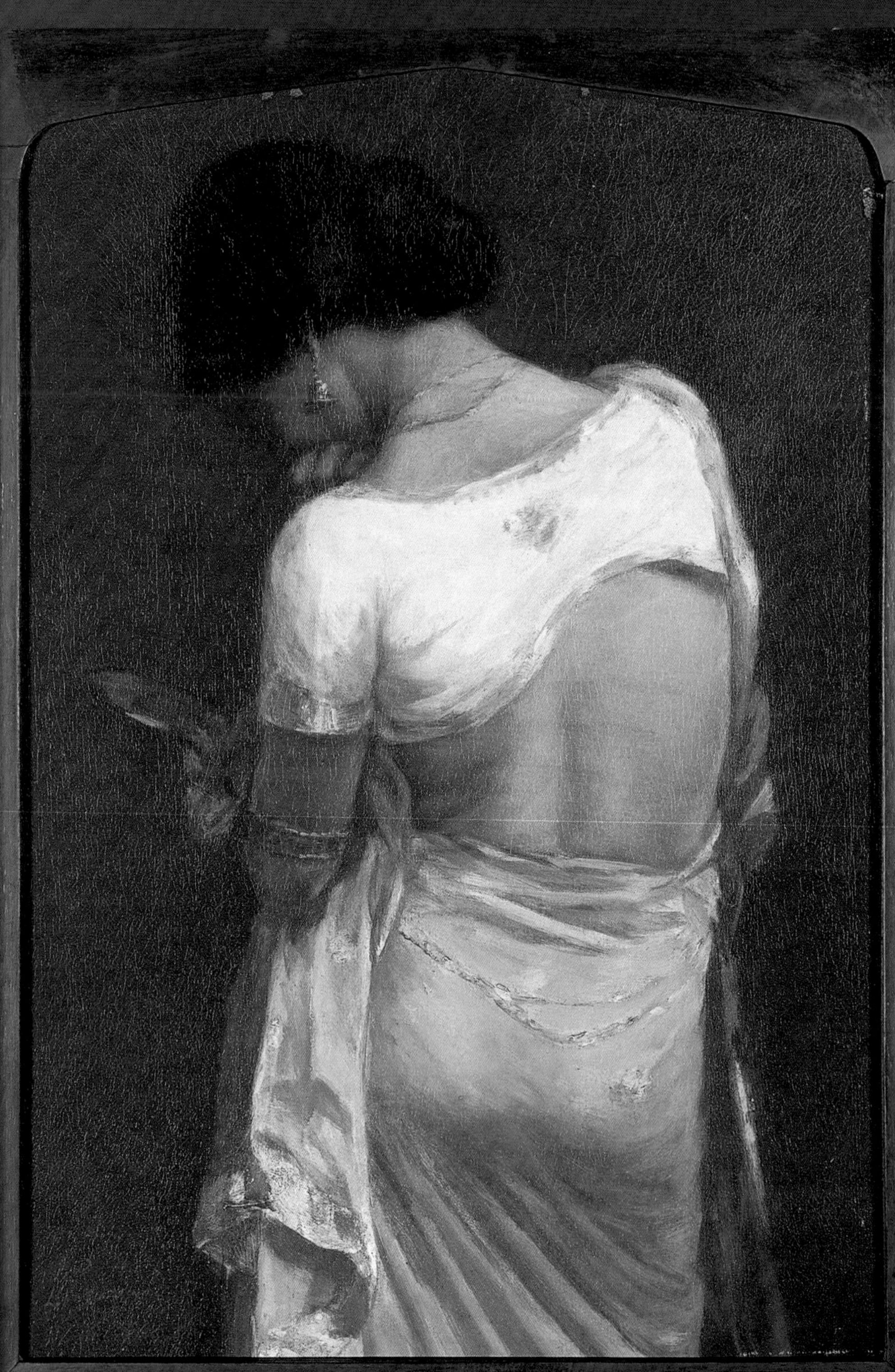

Mazumdar, Hemendranath: "Harmony", *Oil* on *Canvas*, 1926, 50x36.5 cm. (See notes on page 219)

Madhavan Nayar Foundation (Museum, Gallery, Library) (Edapally, Kerala). The Madhavan Nayar Found-ation, as the name suggests, was set up by Madhavan Nayar in Edapally, Kerala. The Foundation is a tripartite complex with one building housing the *museum* of Kerala history with its son-et-lumiere show, another four-storey, climate-controlled building known as the gallery of *paintings* and *sculptures* and a third two-floor edifice known as the Centre for Visual Arts.

The gallery with a floor *space* of 9300 sq.ft. contains about 250 original works of Indian masters both *modern* and *contemporary*. The Centre for Visual Arts has an area of 10,000 sq.ft. with the ground floor housing high quality *reproductions* of *old masters* and the architects of *modern* Western *art*, ranging from Leonardo da Vinci and R.S. Raphael on the one hand to P. Picasso, V. Van Gogh and P. Cezanne on the other. There is also an *art* library which students and scholars alike will find invaluable.

There are plans to set up an archive in the Centre for Visual Arts, with slides and photo-documentation of *contemporary artists*. Refer *Rabin Mondal.*

Madhubani A type of folk *painting* practised by the women of Mithila (a region in the state of Bihar) replete with religious fervour and *symbolism*. The *paintings* were originally confined to the nuptial chambers and conveyed the wish for a fertile married life. Several amorous incidents from the Krishna Lila and scenes from the marriage of RAMA and Sita were painted along with various other symbols. There are two visibly different *styles*; one being a rendering of stylized *forms* as practised by the educated Kayastha women and the other, a naive, earthy *style* with brilliant *colours* preferred by the others. *Natural colours* were used with home-made *brushes*. Refer *Folk Art, Folk Decoration, Folk Inspiration,* KRISHNA, *Mithila Painting, National Handicrafts & Handlooms Museum, WSCs* New Delhi, *Ganga Devi*.

Madras School of Art Refer *GCAC* & *Museum of Contemporary Art* Chennai; *Academy, Style, Classical, Contemporary, Detailed Work, Fine Arts, Modern Style, Watercolours, Cholamandal Artists' Village, Museum of Contemporary Art* (Chennai), *Subrayalu Dhanapal, Gopal Ghose, Shankar Nandagopal, Raju A. Paidi, K.C.S. Paniker, Rasiklal Parikh, P.T. Reddy, Debi Prasad RoyChowdhury, Shantilal M. Shah, Abanindranath Tagore, GCAC* Chennai.

Mahabalipuram Also known as Mamallapuram after the PALLAVA Kings Mahendravarman I and Narasimhavarman I who built the coastal town 51km south of Chennai in AD 688. He introduced the method of hewing entire temples out of living rock. Among the many examples of *Dravidian architecture* are the famous Rathas (chariots) named after the Pandavas. Refer *Bas-Relief, Cholamandal Artists' Village*, GAJA PRSTHAKARA, *Granite, High Relief, Icon, Mask, Pallavas, Pallava Dynasty, Rock-Cut, Stone Carving, Nagji Patel, Manickam Senathipathi.*

Mahabharata One of the greatest *epics* ever compiled; Vyasa is the semi-mythical editor of the 220,000 line-long Mahabharata. It narrates the saga of war between the Pandavas and the Kauravas. Traditionally, Mahabharata is history (Itihasa), whereas RAMAYANA, the *epic* by Valmiki is taken to be poetic composition or a literary piece. Refer BHAGAVAD GITA, CHITRAKATHI, *Ellora, Epic,* KRISHNA, *Mughal Dynasty,* NAGA, *Pattern,* PURANA, RAMAYANA, *M.T.V. Acharya, Santokba Dudhat, Pilton Kothawalla, Reddeppa M. Naidu, Vamona A. Navelcar, Ganesh Pyne, Gopal G. Subhedar, Raja Ravi Varma, Nathu Lal Verma.*

Mahammad, Isha (1933–) b. Konnagar, Kolkata. Education: Dip. in *drawing* & *painting GCAC* Kolkata; Teachers training in *art* appreciation certificate Calcutta University, *Graphic art* training Dusseldorf Academy Germany. Solos: Indo American Society Kolkata, GAG, *AIFACS, VAG, JAG*; International: Germany, London. Retrospective: *BAAC* Kolkata. Group participations: *CKAG, AFA* & *BAAC* Kolkata. *Art* camp: *Painters* camp Kashmir. *Auctions*: Osian's Mumbai, Bowring's New Delhi. Awards: For *graphic art* Calcutta University, *BAAC* Kolkata. Member: Calcutta Painters. Commissions: Portraits of eminent personalities including Jawaharlal Nehru, *Rabindranath Tagore* & Maulana Abdul Kalam Azad Kolkata; International: Harrow School England. Collections: *NGMA* New Delhi, *BAAC* Kolkata, Academy of Art & Cuture J&K, State Academy of Art Manipur; International: Museum of Indian Art Berlin.

He is basically a *figurative painter*, using *themes* based on social commentary and upliftment. Pathos, passion, protest and pain are the key notes of his lavishly executed *compositions* and *still lifes*. There is also a hint of *surrealism* in some of the works, with *symbolic* references to certain objects.

He has been living and working in Kolkata since his retirement as principal of the *GCAC* from 1980 to 1994.

Maharaja Fatesingh Museum (Vadodara). The Maharaja Fatesingh Museum, Vadodara was established by the late Maharaja Fatesinghrao Gaekwad with the aim of bringing under one roof some of the best and rarest *artefacts* collected by the late Maharaja Sayajirao–III (1875–1939), his great-grandfather, the founder of Vadodara city and Baroda State as a whole. The collection consists of objets d'art which were displayed in various palaces of the Gaekwads in India and abroad.

The late Maharaja Fatesinghrao decided to open the collection to the public in the form of a *museum* which was inaugurated in 1961 by the then Governor of GUJ. The collection has been arranged in two main groups; the *portraits* of the Royal Family and Western and *Modern* Indian *Art*. There is also a section on Far Eastern *art* and European *applied art*.

The *museum* houses an exclusive collection of *Raja Ravi Varma's paintings* consisting of several family *portraits* and *paintings* on mythological *themes*. A. Felici, the Italian *sculptor/painter*, produced a number of works of *art* for the Gaekwads. Some of them are displayed in the galleries of the *museum*. *S. Fyzee Rahamin, Muhammed Abdur Rehman Chughtai, Gopal Damodar Deuskar, Antonio X.*

Trindade and *sculptor* Phanindranath Bose are some of the noted *artists* whose works adorn the walls of the *museum*.

The European section has *paintings* of the 19th and 20th centuries as well as *copies* of some *old masters*. European *Renaissance* and post-Renaissance works, *copies* of famous Greco-Roman *sculptures* as well as original European *sculptures* belonging to the 19th century are also presented here.

The *Chinese* and *Japanese art* works, though small in number, are representative of the *art* of those *cultures*. *Decorative arts* include *enamel* and *lacquer* ware, small *bronzes*, porcelain and *pottery* of significant workmanship.

The *applied art* section has fine examples of French furniture of Rococo and the Empire *style* as well as glass and porcelain *artefacts* of famous workshops in Europe. It is one of the few non-governmental *museums* in our country. Refer *Ranjitsingh Gaekwad*.

Maharaja Sayajirao University (Vadodara). Refer *Faculty of Fine Arts/FFA* (Maharaja Sayajirao University= MSU), *Maharaja Fatesingh Museum* (Vadodara).

Mahavira The 24th Tirankara of this era according to *Jainism*. He was originally conceived in the womb of Devananda, wife of a Brahmin, Rishabhadatta. He was transferred, in the embryo state to the womb of the Kshatriya queen, Trishala, wife of King Siddhartha. The event was ordered by Shakra (INDRA) king of the *gods*. This was preordained, since a Tirthankara could only be born in a Kshatriya clan, as he would be a leader, albeit a *spiritual* one.

Mahavira was named Vardhamana (increasing in prosperity) because the family fortunes increased markedly after his birth. He lived the life of a householder until he was 30, when he renounced the world and took to the life of a mendicant. For 12 years, Mahavira wandered from place to place practising meditation and severe austerities, including fasting even without water, for several days. It was only after this that he reached the omniscient stage, becoming a Tirthankara. This act of renunciation is a celebrated event among *Jains*. There are two principal sects that differ as to the question of nudity for monks, the DIGAMBARA stating that it was mandatory and the SVETHAMBARA making it optional, each of whom influenced *Jain sculptures* from their differing view of *Jainism*. *Jain manuscript paintings* represent him with a golden body (sometimes bejewelled). The Tirthankara is also represented with eight *attributes*: a throne, a three-tiered parasol, a *halo*, an Ashoka (Saraca indica) tree, 64 attendants with Chauris (yak-tail fan), celestial music, the beating of kettle drums and cascades of flowers. Mahavira also added a fifth vow–of celibacy–to the *original* four of AHIMSA, Asteya, Satya and Aparigraha propounded by the Tirthankaras preceding him.

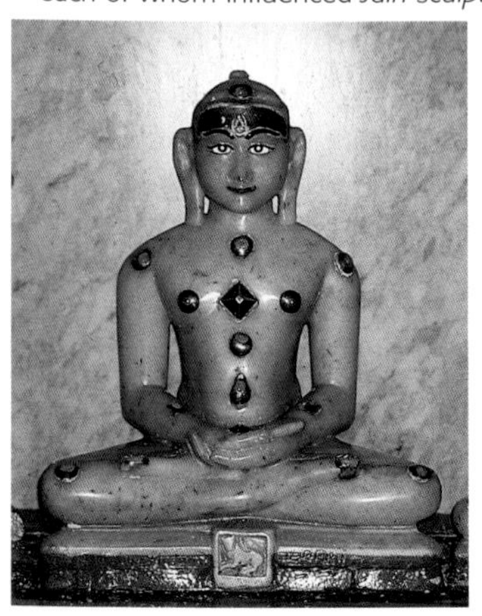

Mahavira: "24th Tirthankara", *Marble*.

He attained MOKSHA, that is liberation from earthly life at the age of 72 circa 527 BC. Refer *Jain Miniature*, *Jain Manuscript Illumination*, ASANA, *Ajanta*, *Ellora*, GAJA, *Sumant V. Shah*.

Mahayana Buddhism="Great Vehicle". Known earlier as the Mahasanghikas which broke away its traditional *Buddhism* into new Mahayana School. Here BUDDHA was increasingly deified and represented anthropomorphically. This dates from the Kushana period with the BUDDHA being depicted in both the Gandhara and the Mathura *idiom*. Refer *Kushana Dynasty*.

Mahurkar, Ambadas (1933–) b. Chandrapur, MAHA. Self-taught *painting*. Solo and Group shows: Chandrapur, Gallery Aurobindo & Kala Mela New Delhi, Sponsored by–USIS, Progressive Group of Artists, Giants International & MMB Hyderabad, Koratkar Art Gallery Nampelly, RAJ *LKA* Jaipur, *AIFACS*, HAS; International: Munich Germany. Group participations: Hyderabad, *AIFACS*. Awards: HAS All India Contemporary Miniatures, Chitrakala Kaushal by Yoga Vedant Forest University Rishikesh Himalaya, Honoured as Veteran Artist by *AIFACS* 1993. Member: Kala Mandir Hyderabad. Collections: *LKA* RAJ & AP CAG Hyderabad & pvt.

Ambadas Mahurkar is a senior *artist* and *art* teacher who has painted *landscape* as his speciality. Using either *watercolours* or *acrylics*, he captures *nature's* vibrant moods in soft, pleasing *colours*, emphasizing, in particular, mountains and clouds. *Pastoral* and picturesque ruins are another favourite *theme*.

He lives in Hyderabad, where he runs Kalamandir, his personal studio, *art* gallery and institute. He is also the Dir. of Koratkar Art Gallery Nampally.

Maity, Paresh (1965–) b. Tamluk, WB. Education: B. FA. *GCAC* Kolkata, M.FA. *College of Art* New Delhi. Solos: Bangalore, *CIMA*, British Council, *BAAC* & *AFA* Kolkata, Hungarian Information & Cultural Centre New Delhi, The Gallery Chennai, *JAG*, *CYAG*, *GK*, SRAG, TKS, *GG*, *AIFACS*; International: Germany, Kathmandu, ARKS Gallery London. Group participations: *BAAC* & *AFA* Kolkata *CYAG*, *G88*; International: Toronto, Cleveland, Tokyo. *Auctions*: Heart & Osian's Mumbai. Awards: British Council Visitorship, National Scholarship, Pt. Jawaharlal Nehru Award New Delhi, Governor's Gold Medal *AFA* & *Jamini Roy* birth centenary award Kolkata, *AIFACS*, *ISOA*, Gold Medal USSR. Collections: Godrej Mumbai, *NGMA* New Delhi, *BAAC* Kolkata, *CYAG*; International: British Museum London, pvt. & corporates.

Paresh Maity is an *eclectic artist*, working with and exploring different *themes* and *media* in a constantly evolving *style*. During the past decade, he has worked with both *figuration* and abstraction, seeking all the while, for a simplification and a minimisation of *form* and *colour*. His *landscapes* are worked in scales varying from the miniature to the *monumental*, however the broad *washes* of *colour*

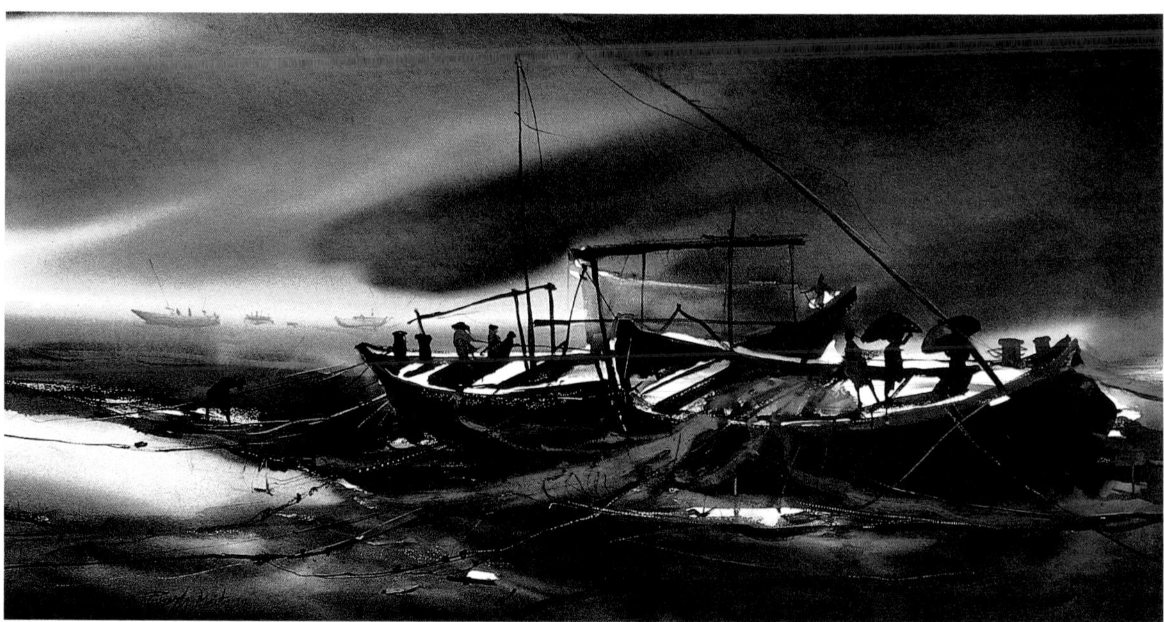

Maity, Paresh: "Cloudy Coastline", *Watercolour* on *Paper*, 112x230 cm.

and the abbreviated, jerky brushstrokes appear as annotated *forms* in both *sizes*. His conte *drawings* show his keen sense of observation and simplification of commonplace objects and animals. In a radical change of both *style* and *idiom*, his *oils* are a riot of brilliant *colour*, with *lines* appearing only intermittently in a pseudo-naive *manner*. However, the unifying factor in all these works is the study of how *light* plays on *colour* and vice-versa. His recent works are large, vibrant and colourful with the simplified *figures* carved out in great swathes of *pigment*.

Paresh Maity travels all over the world, these travels being an integral part of his *style*. In India he lives between New Delhi and Kolkata.

Makara 1. A chimaera or hybrid animal, it is found in temple *sculptures* and platforms. It is usually represented as having the tail of a crocodile or fish, the head of an elephant and it holds a pearl in its mouth. It is also the VAHANA of Varuna, the *god* of the ocean and gives the water of life to the good and death to the wicked. **2.** Makara is also the tenth Rashi or sign of zodiac according to Hindu astrology, corresponding to Capricorn of Western astrology. Refer GARUDA, *Gupta, Vesara Style, Laxma Goud, Satish Gujral, Rabindranath Tagore.*

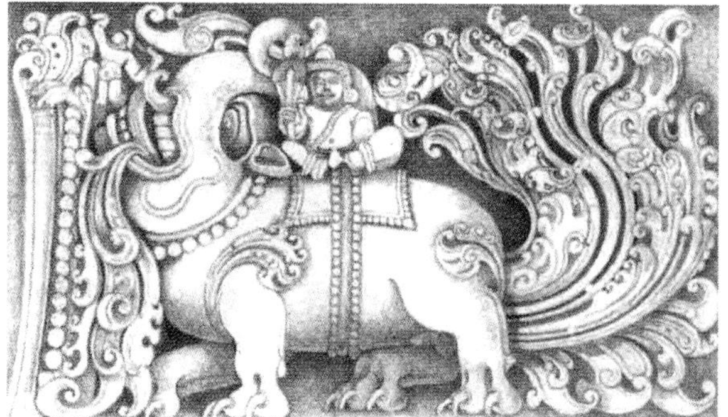

Makara: Nagesh B. Sabannavar, Pencil Drawing on *paper.*

Makara-Sankranti This festival is celebrated throughout India. It falls on 14th January usually in the month of Magh of Hindu calender and is considered to fall on the day that the Sun, the King of all the planets, enters the Rashi (sign) of Makara (Capricorn), considered to be the most beneficial Rashi of the sun. It is celebrated by the flying of kites and the exchange of sesame seed sweets (Til Ladoos). It is sometimes used in the BARAMASA to represent the month of Magh. The *artist Bhanu Shah,* for almost four decades, has researched the field of kite-making and kite-flying. Refer BARAMASA.

Malani, Nalini (1946–) b. Karachi, Pakistan. Education: Dip. in *FA. JJSA*. Solos: Chennai, Bangalore, *GC* & MMB Mumbai, *Art Heritage* New Delhi, CAG Ahmedabad, *PUAG*, *JAG*, *LTG*. Group participations: *SG*, *GC* & Times of India Mumbai, Kala Yatra Bangalore, RB & *LKA* New Delhi, *JAG*, *BB*, SRAG; International: Camden Arts Centre & RAA London, Museum of Modern Art Oxford & other galleries in UK, New South Wales Gallery, Festival of India Paris, Havana *Biennale*, Switzerland, Germany. Workshops: Kasauli Art Centre HP, *MSU*; International: Germany. *Auctions*: Heart Mumbai. Awards: French Govt. Scholarship FA. Paris. Fellowships: Junior & Senior Govt. of India; International: Residency Fellowship FA. work Centre USA. Commissions: *Mural* with *Bhupen Khakhar* & *Vivan Sundaram*. Publications: Articles & two films, "Figures of Thought" & "One World Art" made on Nalini Malani's work; Also directed two video films, "City of Desires" & "Medeamaterial" a collaborative work with a theatre person. Collections: *NGMA* & *LKA* New Delhi, *JNM*, TIFR, *Roopankar BB*, pvt. & corporates.

Over the years, Nalini Malani has evolved considerably as a *painter*, moving through various stages of *figuration*—from hard-edged, well-defined *colour* areas to fluid, organic fusion with the *background* to *installation* and interaction with theatrical performances. Her concerns have varied from the fate of traditional *painting*, as in "City of Desires", to *modern* versions of Greek *mythology* to general concern for the ways of the universe. She has also been influenced by *contemporary* literature, including feminist writing, and has experimented with non-traditional *media*, including *glass painting,* bookmaking, *performance art* and video films.

She lives and works in Mumbai.

Mali, Vasantrao A. (1911–) b. Kolhapur, MAHA. Education: Dip. in *FA*. *JJSA*. Group participations: MAHA State Art Exhibition Mumbai, *AFA* Kolkata, *BAS*. Awards: "Sanman Chinha" MAHA State Art Exhibition, *Artists' Centre* Mumbai, *AFA* Kolkata, *BAS*, *ASI*, *JAG*, *AIFACS*. Commissions: *portraits* of several personalities, including Mumbai Mayor Bohman Behram & Industrialists G.D. Birla, S.L. Kirloskar & M.R. Ruia. Collections: Victoria Museum Kolkata, Bombay High Court Mumbai, *Maharaja Fatesingh Museum* Vadodara, *PWM*; International: India House London, Chinese Govt.

Vasantrao A. Mali is a *painter* of the *Bombay School*, *painting* romanticized versions of young maidens, sometimes attired in the traditional Maharashtrian Sari, set in a dreamy *Raja Ravi Varma*-like *landscape* of rocks and shrubs. His *painting* of a young, dark-skinned Adivasi girl selling peacocks won him several accolades including a gold medal.

At present Vasantrao A. Mali, the son of Anantrao Mali also an *artist* (*contemporary* to *Mahadev V. Dhurandhar*), lives in Mumbai.

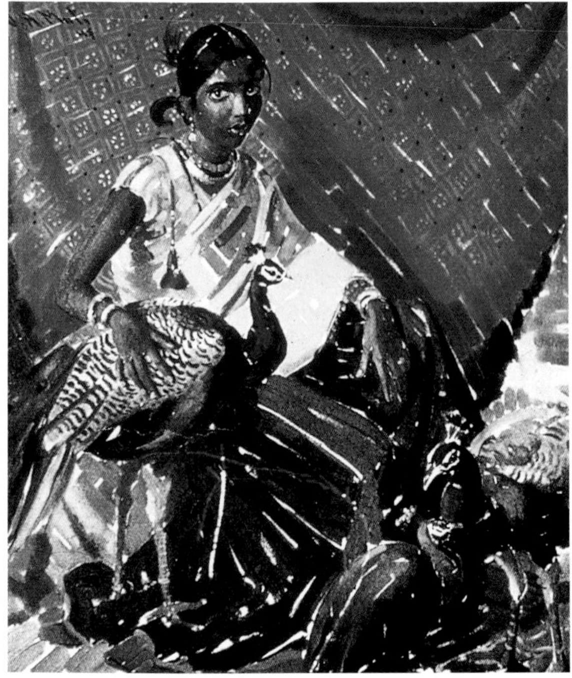

Mali, Vasantrao A.: "Beauties", *Oils*, 1945.

Mali, Yashwant (1934–) b. India. GDA in *FA*. Education: *JJSA*. Solos: *LKA* New Delhi, *JAG*, TAG, SRAG; International: UK, London, Surrey, Oxford, Mayfair, Brighton, Manchester University Gallery, Galerie de Universite Paris. Group participations: *CYAG*; International: Over 19 in UK, Six Indian Painters, Commonwealth Institute, Four leading Indian artists India House & William Morris Gallery London, Commonwealth Artists Manchester, Oxford Art week Festival, Contemporary Art Milan Italy. Member: Commonwealth Institute, Waterman Art Centre, Museum of Modern Art Oxford, RAA London. Publications: Catalogues & press reviews of his work in "The Observer" Mumbai & "The Times" UK. Collections: India & International.

Yashwant Mali works with conceptualism, presently using video covers in conjunction with other materials to represent books, i.e. knowledge. However Yashwant Mali's *creations* cannot be read or leafed through, as they are frozen representations of fables and surreal thoughts. Hence his "Brain-wave" from JJ shows an open book *form*, with a bust cradled by two bent forks, in a semi-lewd reference to groping fingers.

He has been working in UK for several years.

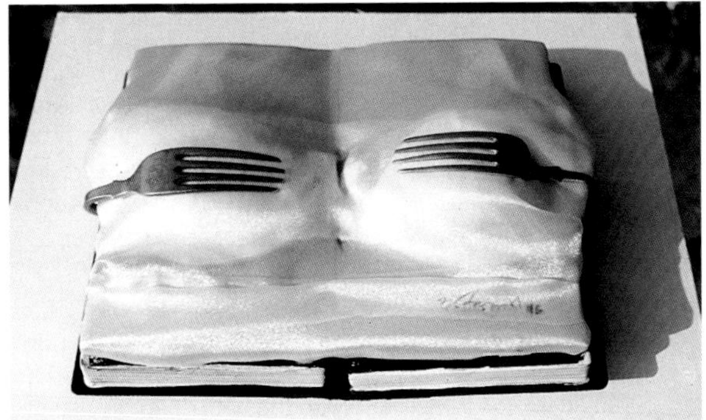

Mali, Yashwant: "Brain-Wave", *Installation-Mixed media*, 1986.

Malwa, Malwa Kalam, Malwa School, Malwa Miniature The court of Malwa, located in Central India, provided great patronage of the *arts*. Being Muslims, the Persian influence is quite strong with the Mongolian features, Persian costumes and formalized vegetation in early Malwa miniatures. By 1540, the Indian elements became dominant, though the Persian *background* still existed. The *Jain* element appeared in the *draperies* and in the alert, vital urgency of the work. The story of Baz Bahadur and Rupmati, RAGAS and RAGINIS were the favourite topics of the Malwa *artist*. The female *figures* are represented as having sturdy, well-formed bodies, with arms tapering to fine wrists with strong hands. The forehead is broad and low, the eyes long and wide open with a slightly uptilted nose. The hair is braided into a long plait, twisted and tied with ornamental tassels, and hangs stiffly to the hips. A fine, gauzy scarf covers the head and flares out stiffly at the ends. *Figures* are usually represented against a *background* of solid *colour.* The earlier *paintings* were coloured with the primaries, reds, greens, blues, and yellows but later *pastel shades* are used. The trees are stylized with foliage in fixed *patterns*. Refer *Kushana*

Dynasty, Miniature Painting, Picture Space, Rajasthani Miniature Painting, Pramod Ganapatye, Nareen Nath.

Mamtani, Mahirwan (1935–) b. Sind. Education: NDA Delhi Polytechnic. Solos: Gallery Chanakya New Delhi, *AIFACS*, *Dhoomimal*; International: Galerie Stenzel, Kunstverein, Art Galerie Schwabylon, Taufkirchner Kunstlerkreis, Galerie Transart, Galerie Rozmarin, VHS Galerie all in Munich, Galerie Winfried Gurlitt Mainz Frankfurt, Commonwealth Art Gallery London, Grenchen Switzerland. Group participations: National *LKA* Exhibitions, *Triennales* & *Graphic* Exhibitions New Delhi; International: Surya Galerie Mannheim, Inter-national Art Fair Dusseldorf, *Biennale* Italy, Ibiza & France, Salon de Mai Paris, Bochum Museum Germany, Kunsthalle Aarau & Stadttheatre St. Gallen Switzerland. Awards: National *LKA*, Graphics India; Tokyo *Biennale*, Scholarship German Academic exchange service. Member: Neo-Tantra Group (1980–86). Appointments: Group of *artists* working on "Spiritual Content in Art" in Italy & Switzerland. Collections: National & International.

The MANDALA is the central *theme* in Mahirwan Mamtani's works, symbolizing the four elements, the four seasons and the four cardinal directions, when so divided. Mahirwan Mamtani uses four circles at times, *overlapping* and meeting at a central point, where the "self" was said to be located. This was the "Centrovision" series, which the *artist* describes as the path to the centre. The circle in these works represents soul, square–body, triangles–male and female principle, according to the *artist*. The later series "I am" sees the emergence of the MANDALA in a *mask* format. Mahirwan Mamtani wore the *mask* for various performances which he then photographed, filmed and video-taped. He also repainted some of the *photographs* and exhibited them.

He lives and works in Munich Germany.

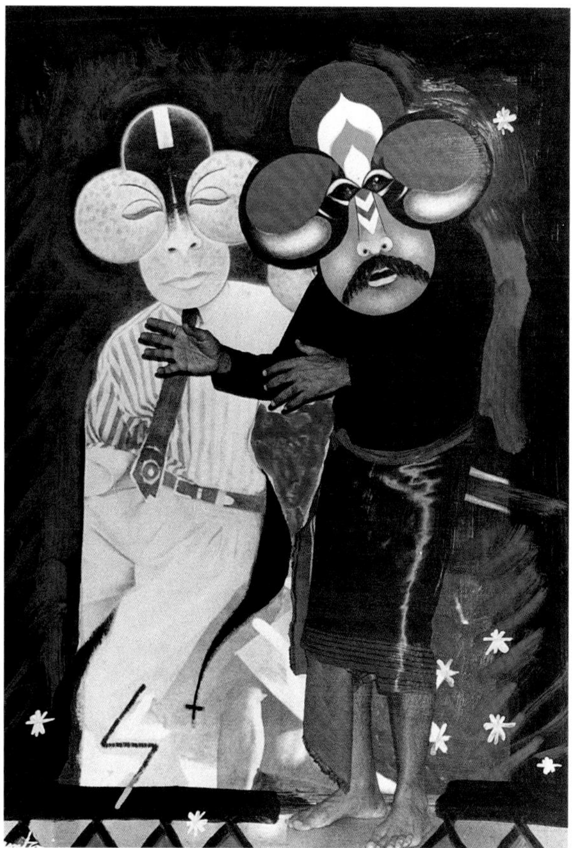

Mamtani, Mahirwan: "Story-Teller", Mixed *Technique,* 1992.

Manchanda, Santosh (1927–) b. Srinagar, Kashmir. Education: *FA*. PUJ University Lahore. Solos: RB New Delhi, RAJ *LKA* Jaipur, Arts Group Patiala, SRAG, *AIFACS, GMAG*; International: London. Group participations: National *Exhibitions*, All India & International Women Artist's Exhibition, Indo-German Artist's Exhibition, Veteran Artist's Exhibition all in New Delhi. *Art* camps: In Ganderbal (Kashmir), organized by *LKA*. Collections: *Chandigarh Museum*, Jaipur Museum, PUJ University Museum.

Though she studied *FA.* for two years, she is basically a self-taught *artist*, learning through experimentation and experience. She has handled a versatile range of *media*, including *pen* and *ink*, *oil painting* and *acrylics*. She has also not limited herself to *figuration*, having worked with *abstract forms* and *textures* with equal ease. Among her favourite *themes* are "Mother and Child", "Seated Figures" and "Village Scenes". She has worked in *monochromes* as well as polychromes. Her travels in Italy led to a series of heavily impasted *oils*, capturing the spirit of the country's magnificent churches and *art* works.

She lives and works in New Delhi. She also sings in Hindi under the pseudonym Tosh.

Mandala=a disk, or a sacred circle. A sacred *form* of the cosmos, as seen in Indian *sculpture*, *painting* and *architecture*. It was a *metaphysical* manifestation of the *symbolic* ground plan which determines the architectural *proportion*. It can also be applied in any square or triangular unit which also appears in TANTRIC and neo-Tantric *art*. Refer *Neo-Tantricism, Proportion,* TANTRIC, YANTRA, *Mahirwan Mamtani, Om Prakash Sharma, V. Viswanadhan.*

Mandapa=hall. It refers to the large, pillared hall, standing in front of the sanctum sanctorum (Garbhagriha) in the temple complex. It is usually connected to the Garbhagriha by means of a vestibule, although at times it opens directly from it. It is

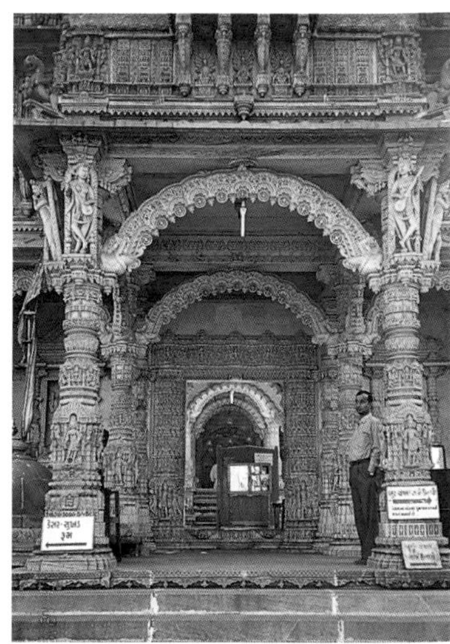

Mandapa: Mukhmandapa, lower storey, Hutheesing Jain Temple, Ahmedabad.

in the Mandapa that the people congregate to offer worship. It differs from region to region, with the Orissan temple complex terming it as the Jagamohana. The Mandapas in the temple structures at Madurai are renowned for their many rows of elaborately carved *stone* columns. Refer *Dravidian Style, Ellora, Nagara Style, Pallavas, Pallava Dynasty, Vesara Style,* VIHARA.

Mandlik, Ravi (1960–) b. Achalpur, MAHA. Education: GDA in *painting JJSA*. Solos: *Tao Art Gallery* Mumbai, *JAG,* TAG, *DG, YBCAG, Dhoomimal*. Group participations: RB & *NGMA* New Delhi, *Artists' Centre* & 50 years of India's Independence *NGMA* Mumbai, *JAG, DG,* BAG, *NCAG, CRAR*; International: Japan, Nairobi, Seychelles. Invited *artist* camp: *BAS*. *Auction*: by Heart *JAG*. Awards: Nasik Kala Niketan for *portraits ASI*; International: Seychelles Visual Art *Biennale*, Fell Winsor & Newton worldwide millennium *exhibition* in London, Brussels, Stockroom & New York. Fellowships: *JJSA*, Junior Fellowship from Cultural Dept. Govt. of India. Member: Elected Hon. Secretary *BAS,* Jury *LKA* New Delhi. Appointments: Lecturer *LSRSA, JJSA*. Collections: *NGMA* Mumbai, *LKA* New Delhi, pvt. & corporates.

Though *nature* is the central *theme* of Ravi Mandlik's *paintings*, it is *texture* that clearly predominates. His *abstract* renderings of waterworn rocks, clouds and the sea have a sensuous tactility that is almost palpable. His later works show the adoption of a looser, serene *handling* of paint. These *painterly* works are interspersed with patches of stained *canvas* against which the slightly raised crumpled ridges of thickened paint stand out. His *colour* ranges widely from warm earthy *hues* to pale electric blues and leaf greens.

He lives and works in Mumbai.

Mandorla The *nimbus* or *halo* of *light*, enclosing the entire *figure*, instead of just the head, usually of Christ or the Virgin. Similar to the PRABHAVALI or the Tejas (variously understood as flames, fire, glow) in Indian *sculpture*. Refer *Aureole.*

Maniere Noire A *technique* used by some lithographers whereby the *stone* or sheet is covered with *ink* and then scraped through to expose the *stone* surface when printed, this produces a *white negative image*, e.g., G. Rouault, used this *technique* to great effect.

Calcutta *artists* used this lithostone *technique* to perfection to acheive subtler *tonal values* and greater effect of *light* and *shade* in their *portraits*. These *prints* were circulated by the Calcutta Art Studio in 1878–79. Refer *Metal Cut, Metal Block.*

Manner A synonym for *style*. The *term* generally describes the stylistic elements of the work of known, unknown or anonymous *artists.* Manner could be used in the general sense to refer to the works of a group of *artists,* i.e. *Kishangarh* manner or *Bundi style* where the overall characteristics define the school. In recent times, manner has been used to refer to certain predominant traits in the works of certain *artists* i.e. the manner of *Raja Ravi Varma* usually referring to an academic *narrative style*, the manner of *Maqbool Fida Husain* referring to his trademark brush-strokes and so on. Students of *art* or young *artists* imitating these various *styles* would be said to be working in the *manner* of...whichever *artists'* works they are imitating. Refer *Basohli, Bundi, Folk Art, Jain Miniatures, Khajuraho, Madhubani* (Mithila), *Malwa, Mewar, Mughal Dynasty, Palm Leaf, Pala Miniatures, Tempera, Manuscript Painting, Warli Paintings.*

Mannerism French "manier"=a way and *manner*; Italian "maniera"=a personal *style*. The *term* is now used to describe *pictorial* and sculptural works of certain European, and especially Italian, *artists* of the period from about 1520 to 1620. High *Renaissance artists* had attained perfection and the period was followed by experimentation and a disregard for *classical* rules. Mannerist *compositions* tended to be asymmetrical and unbalanced, *figures* were frequently elongated or portrayed in *contrapposto* (i.e. contradictory or twisted) poses, and *colours* were often harsh and discordantly theatrical. As a result, the expressive and emotional qualities of the work of *art* were heightened, as compared with the harmonious calm and *ideal forms* of the High *Renaissance*. The most important mannerist *artists* include Jacopo da Pontormo, F. Parmigianino, Giovanni Rosso and El Greco; the last works of Michelangelo and certain works by Jacopo Tintoretto have been described as mannerist.

This *art* first came to India during the reign of Mughal emperor Akbar who was greatly intrigued by it. Subsequently, *artists* incorporated it disregarding Christian *iconography*. Made famous by *Raja Ravi Varma*. Refer *Baroque, Renaissance, Transition.*

Manuscript Paintings Manuscripts were narrations of various *gods* and goddesses of the Mahayana *pantheon* of *Buddhism* where extensive coloured *illustrations* were used depicting Buddhist scenes. Mostly executed in *primary colours* (red, *white* and *black*) in the later *periods* even *secondary colours* were used (green, violet, pink and grey). Some of these manuscript *illustrations* also show a marked TANTRIC influence. Some of the famous *styles* were Orissa *Palm leaf, Jain* manuscripts, Pala manuscripts. Manuscripts of *epics* such as RAMAYANA, BHAGAVATA-PURANA, GITA GOVINDA, "Chaitanya Charitra" (by Krishnadasa) are some of the famous ones. These manuscript paintings form part of the oldest artistic heritage of Indian *art*. Refer *Bark Painting, Colour Wheel, Colour Circle, Jain, Jainism, Jain Miniature, Illuminated Manuscripts, Illumination, Land-scape,* MAHAVIRA, *Miniature Painting, Orissa State Museum, Pala Miniatures, Space.*

Marble Marbles are limestones formed by various natural forces, in crystalline or granulated *forms.* They are softer, easier to carve and polish and therefore used for *sculpture*. Marble is a close grained, compact *stone* capable of taking a high smooth polish. This characteristic, derived from the Greek word meaning "shining *stone"* gives it the name Marble. There are three main varieties of marble i.e. calcite, dolomite and mixed *forms*. In India different qualities of marble are found in GUJ, Bihar, UP, WB, AP, MP, KAR and particularly in RAJ, which is the main source of producing marbles.

Mughal architecture saw extensive use of *white* marble embellished with *gold* and semi-precious *stones* and JALI *work*. The greatness of the *Taj Mahal* as a monument lies in its subtlety—the delicacy of the *white* Makrana marble.

The delicate marble *carvings* and *sculptures* are also the hallmark of the *Abu-Dilwara Temples.* Marble *relief* principally depicting religious *figures* and *episodes* adorn many temples. Early 20th-century Indian *sculptors* worked on marble using grace of neo-classical *style* on typically Indian subjects. *Contemporary* Indian *sculptors* have used different combinations of marble, *stone*, *wood* and *metal*. Marble powder too was frequently used to impart lustre to *paintings*. In *sculptures*, use of marble dust enables Indian *artists* to create unique *textures*. Refer *Classical, Atasi Barua, Pushp Betala, Madan Bhatnagar, Girish C. Bhatt, Veerbala Bhavsar, Mahendra Pandya, Nagji Patel, Pilloo Pochkhanawalla, Sand Painting, Himmat Shah, Sharma M.K. Sumahendra, Bayaji Vasantrao Talim, Vinayakrao Venkatrao Wagh;* Illustrations—ASANAS, MAHAVIRA, *Latika Katt.*

Marothia, Lal Chand (1949–) b. Jaipur, RAJ. Education: GDA *RSA*. Solos: Jodhpur, Kota, Nathdwara, Jawahar Kala Kendra Jaipur. Group participations: Jaipur, Udaipur, Varanasi, Patna, Bhopal, Kala Mela & *LKA* New Delhi, Regional Centre Chennai, *AFA* Kolkata, *AIFACS*, *JAG*. *Art* camps: *PAG* & *LKA* Jaipur, Jaisalmer. Awards: RAJ *LKA*, RAJ Artist Association, *AIFACS*. Member: *PAG* Jaipur. Appointments: Senior *artist* in the Agricultural Dept. Collections: Gallery of Modern Art Jaipur, Govt. Museum Manipur, *LKA* RAJ, pvt. & institutional.

Lal Chand Marothia has worked with a wide range of materials, including *oils*, *watercolours* and *ink*, using the various elements of *nature* in his naive *landscapes* and *vignettes* of knotted tree trunks. There is a hint of *surrealism* in his stylized arrangements of trees against desolate *backgrounds* of other-worldly skies and sand dunes.

He lives in Jaipur.

Mask 1. A *replica* of the face made by taking a *cast*; mask making is also a *ritual* at times as the individual who wears it conceals his/her own identity and identifies himself/herself with the character he/she personifies as seen on the mask. This may be from either a living person, or dead person i.e. a death mask. Masks can be made from a variety of materials such as carved *wood*, *papier mache*, cloth and even pumpkin shells, which are then richly painted and decorated. **2.** Masks can be used as puppets in "Ramlila", theatre, dance, masquerade etc. **3.** A painted or carved facial representation of a person or animal symbolizing an ancestor during *ritual* performances. **4.** A painted or carved mask found as architectural *ornament* representing comedy and tragedy—*Mahirwan Mamtani, C. Jagdish.* Refer *Life-Mask, Pallavas, Pallava Dynasty,* MATRIKAS, HANUMAN; Illustrations—GANESHA, NARASIMHA, VARAHAVATARA, *K. Venkatappa.*

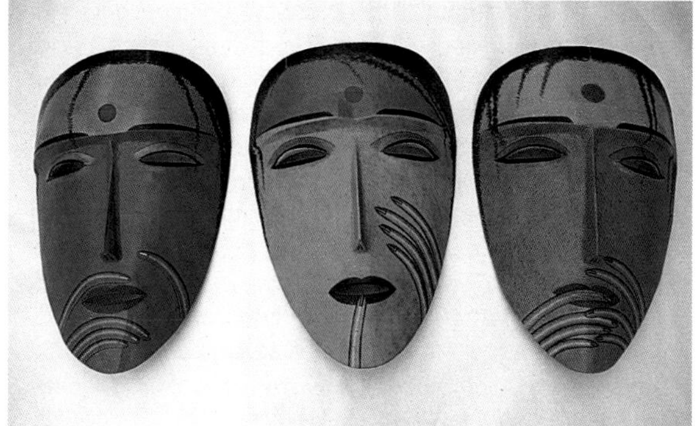

Mask: *C. Jagdish*, "Working Girls", *Paper Sculptures*, 91.5x183x30 cm.

Mass In *art*, the word refers to the largest and most simplified shapes in a particular work of *art*. The *composition* of the work is also judged by its mass, in addition to other elements such as *line*, *tone*, *colour*, *texture* and subject. The use of detail usually distracts from concentration upon mass. *Ramkinkar Baij's* works emphasized masses, planes and *volumes* rather than *line* which became his *key motif*, both in his *paintings* and *sculptures*. *Kanayi Kunhiraman's sculptures* represent vastness of the universe. *S. Fyzee-Rahamin's* works were extremely large in *size* specializing as he did in mass *paintings. Painting* and *portraits* were created by groups of *court painters* e.g. *S. Fyzee-Rahamin*. Refer *Hieratic Scaling, Hoarding, Lay-In, Painterly, Ready-Made, Volume, B. Vithal, Damodar Deuskar, Gajanan S. Haldankar, Balbir Singh Katt, Latika Katt, Somnath Hore*; Illustrations—*Ramkinkar Baij, Nagji Patel, Meera Mukerjee.*

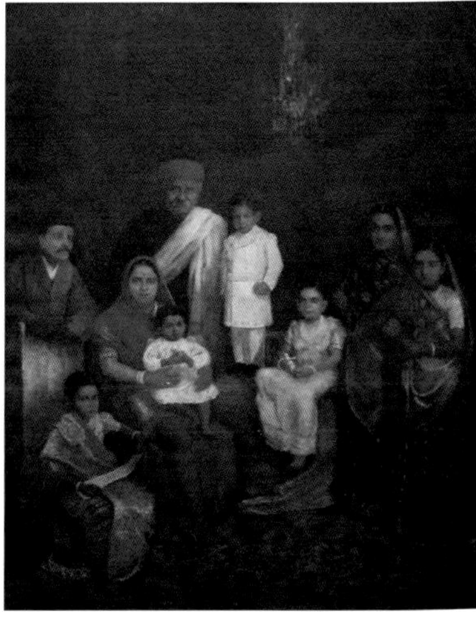

Mass: *S. Fyzee-Rahamin*, "Family", 1910, *Oil* on *Canvas*, 274.5 x 213.5 cm.

Masterpiece Originally the *term* meant any piece of work worthy of a master, in particular under the guild system whereby an apprentice, having produced a masterpiece, qualified as a master of his *craft*.

Since then, it has come to mean any work of pre-eminent achievement e.g. an outstanding work of a particular *artist*, *sculptor*, architect, etc., that is also often considered to be a masterpiece of *art* or architectural history. It is the seminal work of an *artist's* career and is characteristic of his or her *style*, capable of holding its own position in *art* history. e.g. The "Santhal Family" of *Ramkinkar Baij*, "The Horses" of *Maqbool Fida Husain*, the *portraits* of *Raja Ravi Varma*, and the "Bindu" of *Sayed Haider Raza*, "Mother and Child" of *Jamini Roy*, "Death of Shahjahan" by *Abanindranath Tagore*, and many others.

Mat A thick piece of material used for protective or decorative purpose, yet forming an *aesthetic* surround within the picture *frame*, through which the *painting* or *print* is visible. The mounts or mats are made of *paper* or board. The best types are coloured or colourless. *Colour* mats are also the *colours* that are dyed into the board and are not coloured *papers* stuck to an inner core of cardboard.

Mughal miniatures had some of the most beautiful decorated mounts, or Hashiyas (colourful edges) as they were known. *Designs* ranging from the floral to the geometric to the *calligraphic* were used to embellish these borders. As many as five to ten Hashiyas sometimes were used to mount a single work.

Mathura Art The *art* of the *Kushana dynasty* crystallized in two separate areas. Gandhara towards the North and Mathura, 85 miles south of Delhi. Mathura, however, was known as a centre of *Jainism* even before the arrival of the Kushans and their activity continued during the Buddhist phase in the Kushana and the *Gupta* eras. Later Mathura was also to be associated with KRISHNA and Vaishnavite activities. However, Mathura is best known for its contemporaneous development (along with the Gandharas) of the anthropomorphic *image* of the BUDDHA. This was the Mahayana phase, when the symbols of the Hinayana period were slowly giving way. Unlike the foreign influence apparent in Gandharan *sculpture*, Mathura *sculpture* is totally indigenous. It is the YAKSHA *figure*, with its pneumatic, folk quality, which has been transformed with the use of Buddhist *iconography* into the BUDDHA and BODHISATTVA *figures*. The *sculptures* are usually carved from the local red sandstone, dressed in *transparent* muslin that covers the left shoulder and gathers in small folds along the upper left arm. This rendering of *transparent* fabric, as against the sculptural folds of the all-enveloping Gandharan Sanghati (BUDDHA's robe) is a typical Mathuran characteristic. Instead of the feminine grace of the Gandharan BUDDHA, the Mathura BUDDHA has a full, rounded face with a slight smile, the stylized scalloped curls of the hair (USHNISHA) having given way to a more naturalistic top-knot. The belly too is full of Prana (life-breath) in the correct *manner* as prescribed in the SHADANGAS. The *figure* is much more vigorous than the idealized Gandharan type. Some of the important examples of Mathuran art, during this period, include fragmentary *portraits* of Vima Kadphises and Kanishka, the main Kushana rulers, along with several pieces depicting Kushana princes and YAKSHA and YAKSHI *figures*. Refer *Gandharan Art, Mahayana Buddhism, Amrita Sher-Gil, Chintamoni Kar.*

Matrikas Literally meaning mothers, the word refers to a set of goddesses, whose number varies from seven (as in Sapta-Matrikas) to over 190 in various treatises. In all early references, they are considered to be inauspicious though this quality changes in medieval references, albeit subject to their being propitiated in the prescribed *manner*. The most popular belief is that all the goddesses are, in effect, facets of one female principle, the energizing force that stimulates the masculine principle, i.e. male godhead. The Devi Mahatmya is one of the texts to discuss the Sapta-Matrikas. These seven SHAKTIS closely resemble the *gods* from whom they have been created. Brahmani, created from BRAHMA, thus holds a rosary (Akshamala) and water-pot (Kamandalu); Mahesh-vari created from Mahesh/SHIVA is seated on a bull, holds a trident (TRISHULA) wears serpent bracelets and is adorned with the crescent moon (CHANDRA); Kaumari created from Karttikeya rides a peacock and holds a spear; Vaishnavi created from VISHNU is seated on an eagle (GARUDA) and holds a conch (SHANKHA), disc (CHAKRA), mace (GADA), bow (Dhanush) and sword (KHADGA); Varahi created from Varaha has the face of a boar; Narasimhi created from NARASIMHA has the *form* of a woman-lion and Aindri created from INDRA holds a thunderbolt (Vajra) and is seated on an elephant (Airavata).

The Vamana Purana however states that the Matrikas, though described and named after the male *gods*, actually arise from different parts of the Devi's (supreme goddesses) body. The chief characteristic of these Matrikas is that they act as a group and fight ferociously. Most *sculptures* especially after the medieval period, depict them collectively in a panel, flanked by SHIVA at one end and GANESHA on the other. Refer *Attribute,* CHANDRA, CHAKRA, *Ellora, Fantasy, Gupta, Hinduism, Icon, Manuscript Paintings,* VAMANA-TRIVIKRAMA, *K.C. Aryan, Meera Mukherjee, Reddeppa M. Naidu, Raja Ravi Varma*; Illustrations—CHAMUNDA, CHANDI, CHANDIKA, DURGA, KALI, SHAKTI.

Matsya-Avatara Refer VISHNU.

Matte=dull, not glossy. The word refers to the surface finish of a *painting* or *photograph*; a matte finish is flat and absorbs *light*, while a glossy finish has a shine that reflects *light*.

In *oil painting*, glossy can appear matte by the addition of drying agents, while *acrylic* gives a matte finish, but tends to shine considerably when layers of *light colours* are overlaid. Refer *Tempera, Varnish, Roop Chand, Mahadeo Bhanaji Ingle, Papri B. Mehta, Ram Kumar, Jamini Roy, Nilima G. Sheikh.*

Matter Is the physical substance in the work of *art* i.e. the materials that are used in creating the *form* in *sculpture*, *painting*, *manuscript* and *graphic prints* etc. In ancient times, materials used for creating *pigments* were obtained from minerals and vegetable matter. *Black* was obtained from carbon, the most popular being soot. *Silver* and *gold leaf* were also used. Various *shades* of red were obtained from red *lead*, red ochre and shellac dye. Today, *colours* are mostly chemical based, *sculptures* vary from traditional material like *marble, stone, clay* and *metal* to *fibreglass*, *paper*, and at the extreme end to conceptual material rather than the tangible. Matter thus has changed with the times and the theme. Refer *Aluminium, Bidri, Carving, Casting, Cire Perdue, Colour, Concrete, Decorative Art, Enamelling, Folk Art, Form, Glass Mosaic, Glass Painting, Installation, Iron, Kalamkari, Mixed Media, Motif, Mosaic, Papier Mache, Sand Blasting, Sand Moulding, Sand Painting, Metal, Thanjavur (Tanjore) Painting, Tie and Dyed Fabrics, Weaving, Aku, C. Douglas, Nalini Malani, Janak Jhankar Narzary, Vivan Sundaram.*

Maurya Dynasty The first great imperial dynasty, lasting circa 322–185 BC. It was founded by Chandragupta Maurya.

The greatest Mauryan Emperor was Chandragupta's grandson Ashoka. The eighth year of his reign was an important one for *Buddhism*, for it was after the bloody battle at Kalinga, where over 100,000 people died, that Ashoka decided to shun violence and convert to *Buddhism*. He sent preachers (among them his son and daughter) all over the world and erected several STUPAS, Stambhas and *rock-cut* chambers to propagate the tenets of *Buddhism*. The Stambhas had edicts, expounding the virtues of Dharma, cut into them. These *stone* columns were erected at places associated with the major events in the life of BUDDHA or along pilgrim routes. The best preserved of these columns, with the shaft and capital intact is the lion capital *stone* column at Lauriya Nandangarh in present-day Bihar. However the best known of the capitals is the Sarnath capital, which has been adopted as the *emblem* of the *modern* republic of India. Its high surface polish, known as "Mauryan polish" also appears on other Mauryan *sculpture*, including the YAKSHI found at Didarganj and the YAKSHAS from Patna and Parkham. One of the earliest examples of the statue of a Tirthankar also is dated to the Mauryan period because of the polish. A common trait of Mauryan *sculpture* is its monumentality and *frontality*, even though the *carving* is sensuously *realistic*.

Of the noteworthy *rock-cut architecture* of this period are the Lomas Rishi and the Sudama caves, both of which have barrel-vaulted interiors. The Lomas Rishi cave is the forerunner of the later CHAITYAS.

The Mauryan Empire eroded soon after Ashoka's death. In 185 BC the last Mauryan emperor was killed by one of his generals who then founded the *Sunga dynasty*.

Mazumdar, Chittrovanu (1956–) b. Paris, France. Education: Dip. in *FA*. *GCAC* Kolkata. Solos: Chennai, *AFA*, *BAAC* & VMM Durbar Hall Kolkata, *LKA* New Delhi, *JAG*, *PG*; International: GBP. Group participations: Fonds Regional d'Art & Art Contemporain Pays de la Loire workshops France, Salon d'Automne & Salon d'Artistes Francaise Paris. *Auction:* Heart New Delhi. Publications: Book & Magazine cover *design*; *Illustration* for short fiction. Collections: *NGMA* New Delhi, *BAAC* & Seagull Kolkata & pvt.

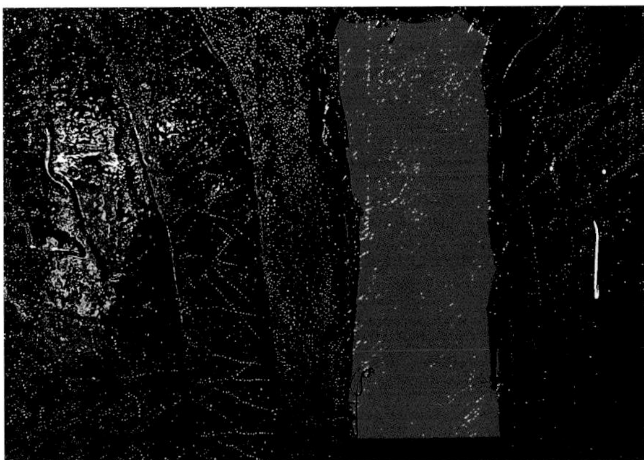

Mazumdar, Chittrovanu: Untitled", Tar & *Acrylic*, 1997.

Chittrovanu Mazumdar straddles two vastly different *cultures*—Indian and French, not merely juxtaposing them but fusing them into a unique and personal *vocabulary* of *form* and *texture*. The layers of *colour* are palpable, having been applied in thick, mason-like strokes, the *blacks* absorbing *light*, while brilliant reds and yellows shine through. In the early 90s he painted a series of works inspired by the *wood cuts* of Kolkata, subtly altering the *imagery* using an expressionist brushstroke and unstructured blobs and patches of *colour*. He has incorporated soil, mixing it with *acrylic* resin and using it along with the other *colours* in his works and also using *natural colours* in his *paper* works. He prefers working on *monumental* scale, his *canvases* having at times measured 30x20 ft.

At present he lives and works in Kolkata.

Mazumdar, Hemendranath (1894–1948) (also known as Majumadar Hemen) b. Mymensingh, now in Bangladesh. Education: Graduated *GSAC* Kolkata, Joined Jubilee Art Academy & later Indian Academy of Art Kolkata. Works exhibited at *VMM* & All India Exhibition Kolkata. *Auctions:* Heart Mumbai & New Delhi, Osian's Mumbai. Publications: "Shilpi" Journal Kolkata, Art Deal New Delhi, Indian Express. Collections: *NGMA* New Delhi, Calcutta Bikaner Palace, *BAAC* & *AFA* Kolkata, Maharaja of Jaipur, Maharaja of Jodhpur Palace, Maharaja of Patiala, M.K. Kejriwal *CKP*; International: Aziz Khan USA.

Hemen specialized in *painting* Indian subjects in a predominantly Western academic *style*. Female *portraits* was his forte although he was also an accomplished *landscape painter*. His works can be classified in three broad categories: allegorical, religious and romantic, of which allegorical *paintings* are the ones for which he is most known along with the *nudes* and semi-nudes, the sensational, the magnificent and the sublime, all receiving equal *treatment*. The expression and body language of the woman standing and waiting for her lover, with a wet *transparent* Sari draped over her body is the *style* used in almost all his *paintings*. He had acquired mastery over *oils*, *watercolours* and *pastel mediums*. (See illustration on page 210)

Mazumdar, Kshitendranath (1891–1975) b. Bengal. Education: Studied under *Abanindranath Tagore*; Later HoD of *Art* Allahabad University UP. Solos: *ISOA*; International: Festival of Empire Crystal Palace England, Athena Gallery Geneva. Group participations: Young Men's Indian Association Chennai, National Exhibition & RB *LKA* New Delhi, *GG*. *Auctions*: Heart New Delhi, Osian's Mumbai. Publications: Including written by O.C. Ganguly, *Benode Behari Mukherjee* LKC 1962 & *Jaya Appasamy* in *LKA* New Delhi 1967. Collections: Govt. of India & *NGMA* New Delhi, *BKB* Varanasi.

An extremely shy, silent, sensitive, intensely emotional and religious Kshitendranath Mazumdar evolved his *style* of *painting* from *Abanindranath Tagore*. While he used the *wash technique*, his natural *style* was related to *tempera* in its clarity of *form* and vision. His *drawings* are precise, his *figures* tall and elegant, *lines* long and flowing with rhythmic repetitions. His distinctive *style* is clearly visible in the "Sri Chaitanya" series. The *figure* is placed in the *foreground* in a stage-like setting. The *background* may comprise of other *figures* or trees with twisted trunks and textured bark. The angularity of these trees and the balustrades in the *foreground* are offset by the soft flowing lives of the *drapery* and the branches of the tree, as in Indian miniatures, the *background* seen as an emotional accompaniment to the main *figure*. His *colours* too are subtle and suffused with RASA.

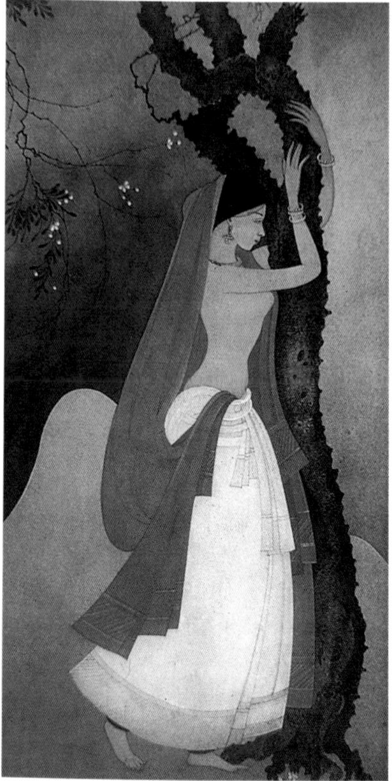

Mazumdar, Kshitendranath: "Untitled", *Watercolours*, Early 20th century, 45.5x32 cm.

Mazumdar, Nirode (1916–1982) b. Kolkata, WB. Educated under *Abanindranath Tagore* at ISOAS, Ecole du Louvre & Studied general history of *art* & *painting*, 19th & 20th century Paris; Research on Medieval art in Europe. Solos: "Images Ecloses", "Wing of No End", Ten years of Painting in Kolkata, "Nine Variations on Symbolic Nine", "Final Spring", "Nityakola", "Boitoroni" all in Kolkata & mostly at *AFA*, *Santiniketan*; International: Galerie Barbizen, His own studio Exhibited series "Images Ecloses", Galerie Transposition & Lyons Paris. Retrospective: in New Delhi 1968 & Kolkata 1981. Group participations: Kolkata; International: Paris, London. Awards: French Govt. Scholarship. Founder member: "Calcutta group". Appointments: Incharge of the *art* gallery India House London. Publications: "Punashcha Paree" (Paris revisited) in Bengali weekly magazine, last published in a form of a book—1983, several articles on *art* & *artists* in various magazines & periodicals. Collections: In galleries & *museums* in India & abroad.

Nirode Mazumdar was trained in the *Abanindranath Tagore style* of *wash painting*, but he soon turned to a more modernistic *style*, with bold *lines* enclosing flat areas and brilliant *colours*. His study of the *modern* Western masters in France and his research into Medieval *art* was to influence his *form* and *technique* to a great extent. He based his *paintings* on "constructive symbolism", trying to fuse the cultural and *symbolic* values of ancient *art* with the *aesthetic* norms of the present age. Some of the works posses the iconic grandeur of *stained glass*.

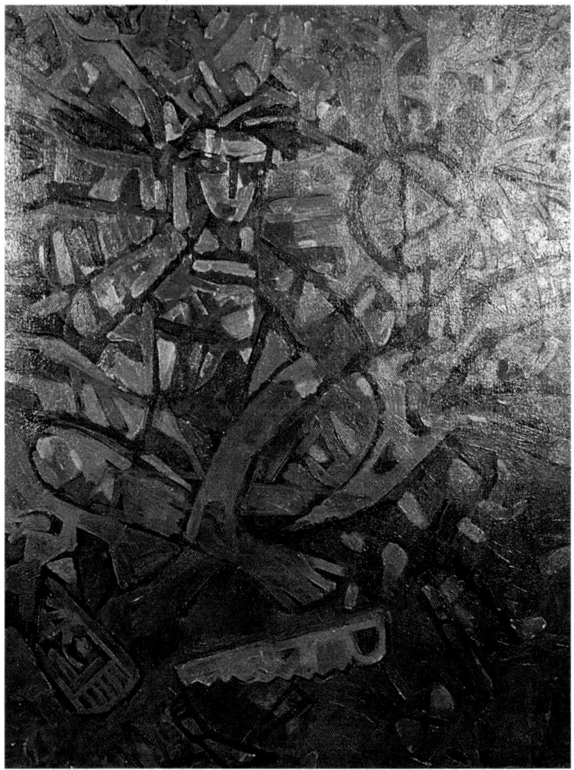

Mazumdar, Nirode: "The First Watch".

Media In *art*, the word refers to the plural of *medium*. **1.** The *form* or material or physical substance i.e. media used by the *artist* as his or her means of expression e.g. *tempera*, *watercolour*, *collage*, *oil painting*, *acrylics*, and *mixed media* are some of the options available to the *painter*, while *stone* of various kinds, including *terracotta*, *marble*, *granite*, sandstone, portland stone and varieties of *metal* and metallic *alloys*, including *bronze*, *copper*, *aluminium*, *lead*, *steel* and *iron*, *cement*, *fibreglass*, and *plaster* are all suitable *mediums* for the *sculptor*. **2.** *Medium* also refers to the liquid (binding agent) in which *paint pigment* is mixed traditionally—raw rice paste mixed in water was and is still one of the *mediums* in *Warli paintings*; whole egg or egg-yolk for *tempera painting*, *gum arabic* for *watercolour* and *pastel*, linseed *oil* for *oil painting*, etc. **3.** *Medium* also means a *size* in the work of *art*. *Artists* have now started exploring many media including *printmaking* and *sculpture* in addition to *painting*, with *Junk Art/Found Objects*. Refer *Acrylic, Ajanta, Ellora, Egg tempera, Erotic Art, Kalighat Pat, Printing, Olegraphy, Relief Printing, Screen Printing, Silk Screen Printing, Tempera, Tanjore Painting, Watercolour, Muralidhar R. Achrekar, K.M. Adimoolam, Ambadas, Jyotsna Bhatt, Nandalal Bose, C. Dakshinamoorthy, Manishi Dey, Avtarjeet S. Dhanjal, Vasudeo Santu Gaitonde, P.S. Nandhan, Nagji Patel, Manchershaw F.*

Pithawalla, Jamini Roy, Ali J. Sultan, Gaganendranath Tagore, Abinindranath Tagore, Sarada Charan Ukil, Raja Ravi Varma.

Medium Refer *Media.*

Mehrotra, Jaideep D. (1954–) b. India. Self-taught *painter* & *sculptor*. Solos: Chetana, MMB Mumbai, The Gallery Chennai, *CYAG*, TAG, *JAG, GE, CKAG*. Group participations: 50 years of India *Nehru Centre* & *NGMA* Mumbai, *JAG, YBCAG*; International: Amsterdam, Hong Kong, Germany. Workshops: Mumbai; International: New York. Lecture/ Demonstrations: NCPA Mumbai; Museum of Art & Chinese University Hong Kong. Collections: pvt. & corporates India; International: USA, UK, France, Germany, UAE, Nigeria, Taiwan.

Jaideep D. Mehrotra has explored a wide range of materials and *media*, including *painting* with *oils*, *oil* sticks, *acrylics*, *watercolours*, *chalk pastels*, *pen* and *ink*, and *sculptures* using fabric and resin and making computer-generated digital *prints*. His *images* are basically surreal, being reactions to all sorts of stimuli and displaying an over-riding concern for the various problems besetting humanity. His *style* is *narrative*, with the story tightly woven into the many layers of *images* graphically represented in them. It is his use of *illusion* that is his forte, with *textures* and *colours* adding to the near photographic appearance of the works.

He lives and works in Mumbai.

Mehta, Papri B. (1954–) b. India. Education: Dip. in *applied art* Sophia Polytechnique Mumbai; *Fresco painting* RAJ; *Icon painting* Volk Kunst Schule Vienna. Solos: *GC* Mumbai, *CYAG*, *JAG*, TAG. Group participations: Indian Oil Bhavan, Concern India, World Wildlife. *Art* camp: Concern India & Art Trust Mumbai. Collections: Daya's collection Mumbai.

Papri B. Mehta is a *figurative painter*, using the human face and *torso* to mirror her state of mind, dredging *images* that are rooted deep within her psyche. There is an organic looseness of structure, that makes her work *painterly*, rather than appearing as coloured *drawings*. Her preferred *palette* is rich browns, yellows and dull greens. She has also been influenced by Taoism. She juxtaposes *modern images* of aeroplanes and chairs with more primordial ones like animal and algae formations evoking both a temporal and spatial timelessness.

She lives and works in Mumbai.

Mehta, Tyeb (1925–) b. Kapadvanj, GUJ. Education: Dip. in *FA. JJSA*. Solos: The Window, Gallery 59 & *GC* Mumbai, Kumar Art Gallery, Kunika Chemould, Black Partridge Art & *Art Heritage* New Delhi, Nandan, *KB Santiniketan* & *BAAC* Kolkata, TAG, *BB*; International: Oxford, Commonwealth Institute Art Gallery London. Group participations: National Exhibitions, *Triennale* & "Pictorial space" *LKA* Exhibitions New Delhi, "Focus" *GC* & "Timeless Art" Mumbai, *CIMA* Kolkata, *VAG, JAG*, CCMB; International: Northampton Museum, New Jersey State Museum, *Biennale* Menton, Hirschhorn Museum Washington DC USA, Museum of Modern Art Oxford, Coups-de-Course Geneva, Tate Gallery London. *Auctions*: Heart Mumbai & New Delhi, Osian's Mumbai; International: Conducted by Christie's in 2002 & Sotheby's. Awards: *LKA* National Award, *Triennale* Gold Medal New Delhi, Filmfare Critics Award, Kalidas Sanman Govt. of MP, Artist-in-Residence *VBU, BAS*. Fellowship: J.D. Rockefeller III Fellowship New York. Hon.: MAHA State Art Mumbai. Collections: *NGMA* New Delhi, TIFR, *Roopankar BB*, pvt. & corporates.

"The Trussed Bull" was his first major *painting*, painted after his visit to Paris and London. This was to be the first in the series of blocked energy leading to his second major *image*: "the rickshaw puller". The falling *figure* appeared in his works in the mid 60s after a five-year sojourn in London and Europe. The heavy *texture* of these *paintings* and their emotional overtones are reminiscent of the fantasy-oriented works of Francis Bacon. He discarded *texture* and tonalities, in favour of starkly outlined *figures* and flat areas of almost pure *hue* bisected by a thick, jagged diagonal in the late 60s. Since then, he has created many memorable *images*, including that of KALI. His large *mural*-sized *painting* for Times Bank in Mumbai which was auctioned, shows his *style*, with a dozen splintered, almost cubistically distorted *figures* prancing in an ambiguous *space* along with a young goat. It is derived from his earlier series on the Charak festival celebrated during the spring by the Santhals. The brilliant yellows and *whites* of the *figures* are carefully orchestrated against the pale blue and browns of the *background*.

Tyeb Mehta lives and works in Mumbai.

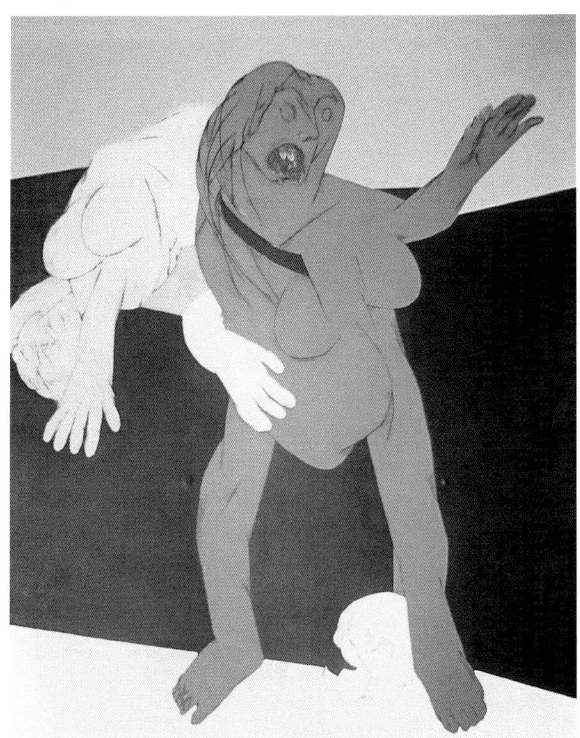

Mehta, Tyeb: "Kali", 1986, 170x137.5 cm.

Menon, Anjolie Ela (1940–) b. Burnpur, WB. Education: WB. Studied briefly *JJSA*. Studied *Fresco Painting* ENSBA. Over 34 solos: Chennai, Kolkata, *Artists' Centre* & Bhulabhai Institute of Art Mumbai, SRAG, *VAG*, *JAG*; International: Gallery Winston, Gallery Radicke Bonn, Blackheath Gallery London. Retrospective: *NGMA* Mumbai 2001, SRAG, *JAG*. Group participations: *NGMA* & *LKA* New Delhi, Timeless Art & RPG Mumbai; International: *Biennale* Sao Paolo, Aliers, Frankfurt Book Fair, Festival of India Moscow, Saffronart Los Angeles. *Auctions*: Timeless Art Sotheby's, Heart & Bowring's Mumbai, Sotheby's New Delhi, Christie's, Sotheby's—London & New York. Awards: Has won awards including the *Biennale* of Algiers award & the Bronze Award *JJSA*. Scholarship: From French Govt. ENSBA. Commissions: Several *murals* both indoors and outdoors. Appointments: In Advisory & Purchase Committee and a co-curator for a French Contemporary Art at *NGMA* New Delhi. Publications: "Anjolie Ela Menon" published by Times of India; A film by *Doordarshan* on her. Collections: *NGMA* & *LKA* New Delhi, *BAAC* Kolkata, *Chandigarh Museum*, *CYAG*; International: Fukuoka Museum Japan, Benjamin Grey Museum New York, pvt. & corporates.

Anjolie Ela Menon has been *painting* over five decades, evolving a *technique* reminiscent of the *old masters* in its sheer feeling for *depth* and *space*. She has constantly experimented with *media* as diverse as *oils*, *acrylics*, *inks*, computers, photography and *collage*. She has also used *found objects* with *styles* verging on *Pop* and *Op art* and also with *imagery* culled from her own works. She had already been using window *frames* and *glass painting*, both real and simulated, as frames for her glowing dusky *nudes* and surreal *figures* with deep-set haunted eyes. Her *portrait* of "Karteni-amma" showcases her versatility, being deliberately arranged in the *manner* of traditional portraiture, especially of the aristocratic Keralite families. We see the matriarch seated on a luxuriant padded chair, next to an open window through which the green Kerala *landscape* is clearly visible. Anjolie Ela Menon's *palette* is discernible in this work. The brilliant *white* of the set, Sari gleaming against the jewel red of the chair which in turn is heightened by the lush green of the outdoors.

She lives and works in New Delhi.

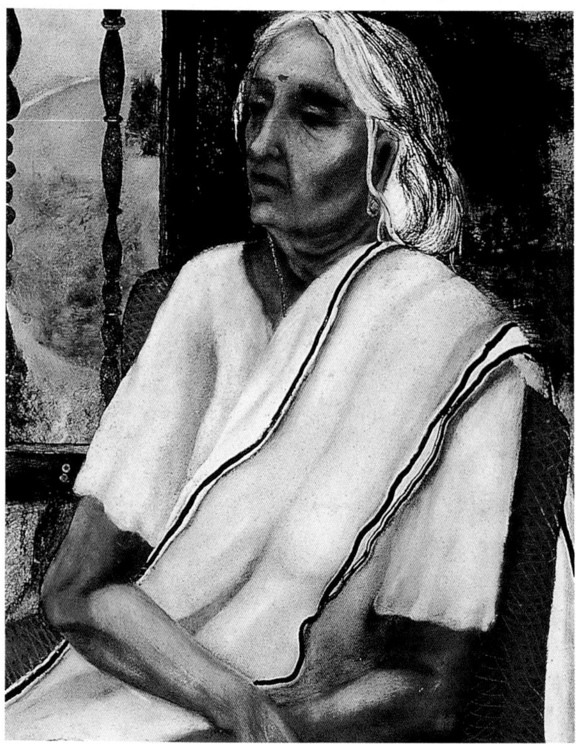

Menon, Anjolie Ela: "Karteni-Amma", *Oil* on Masonite, 1996, 72.5x10 cm.

Menon, K. Madhava (1907–d.) b. Pullot, Kerala. Education: Studied *painting* under Ramendranath Chakravarty, Andra Jateeya Kalasala Masulipatam AP, *Santiniketan*, Final year studies *GCAC* Chennai. Solos: Gallery Aurobindo New Delhi. Group participations: *LKA* & *NGMA* New Delhi, Govt. Museum Chennai, *CTAG*. Appointments: HoD Annamalai University, Advisory Committee on Art Govt. of India Chennai, Dir. *CTAG*. Collections: Mysore, Vadodara, *NGMA*, *LKA* & Gallery Aurobindo New Delhi, Govt. Museum Chennai, SZCC Thanjavur, *CTAG*, *SJM*.

K. Madhava Menon was an *artist* of the old school. His early training at various centres, including Masulipatam (famous for its *Kalamkari*), *Santiniketan* (where he studied under *Nandalal Bose* and *Abanindranath Tagore*) and the *art* school at Chennai, was visible in his works, which were based on the real world, though stylized to a certain extent. K. Madhava Menon's subjects comprise the lush Kerala countryside, in the *form* of *landscape* or elements from *nature* like birds or floral studies. There is also a subtle influence of Japanese *painting*, in the use of flowing, decorative *outlines* and oriental *colour*.

K. Madhava Menon retired to the ancient village of Thiru-vanjikulam in Kerala where he lived and painted not only on *paper*, but also on *canvas*, silk, chiffon, masonite and plain cloth.

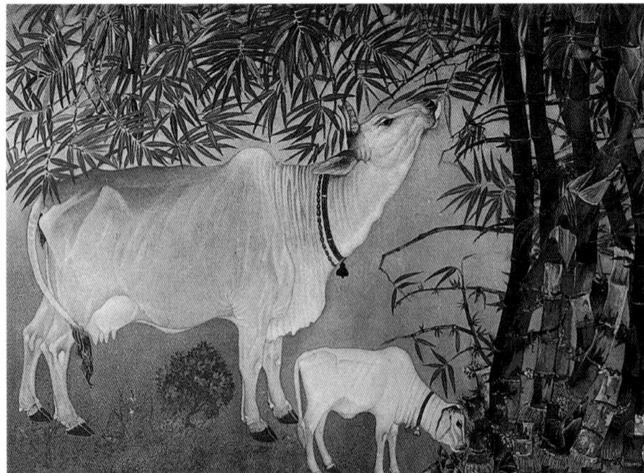

Menon, K. Madhava: "The Last Meal of The Day", *Watercolour* on *Paper*, 1936, 43.7x52 cm.

Merchant, Kahini (Arte) (1960–) b. New Delhi. Education: Dip. in international *design JJSA*. Solos: *JAG*, TAG. Group participations: *NGMA*, "CRY" & Kala Ghoda Fair

Mumbai, Indian Habitat Centre New Delhi, Harmony at *NCAG, BAS, RPG, CYAG, ATG, CKP*; International: Intex Universal Dubai, Apparao Galleries Singapore. *Auction*: Sotheby's. Commissions: Worked on *murals* Mumbai.

Kahini (Arte) Merchant usually paints *portraits* of perfectly similar women staring passively out of the painted *space*, usually in their personalized interiors. Men do make an appearance in her works, but usually as secondary characters or mere adjuncts of the female. *Texture* is almost non-existent in these works, as she prefers the sleek almost photographic finish possible in *oil painting*. There is also an element of the surreal in these still, timeless interiors filled with details of floor tiles, fruit, pillars, barred windows and broken-down shutters.

She lives and works in Mumbai.

Mesopotamian Art Mesopotamian art and *architecture* (in present day Iraq) was contemporaneous with the *art* of the *Indus Valley Civilization* and *Egyptian art*. Unlike Egyptian and Indus Valley *art* however, Mesopotamian art is the sum total of the *art* of various tribes, including the Sumerians, Chaldeans, Assyrians and the Babylonians who lived along the banks of the Tigris and the Euphrates and vied for supremacy at any given *time* between the fourth and the first millemnium BC. The ziggurats that were used as temples and storehouses were built during this period. Unfortunately, Mesopotamian art and *architecture* did not survive, mainly because of the material used i.e. sun-dried mud bricks for the buildings and *wood* for the *sculptures*. However, much of the *craft* has survived, including the jewellery and wall decorations, which comprises the *clay* cone *mosaic* and brilliantly coloured glazed tiles, and some votive *sculptures* as well. Relics of Mesopotamian art and Indus valley *artefacts* show great resemblance indicating close *content* between the two. *Saroj Gogi Pal's* installation "Red Sarayu has eyes" is influenced by the inner sanctum of the ziggurat. Refer *Mural, Tree of Life.*

Mestry, Ravindra (1928–1995) b. Kolhapur, MAHA. Education: GDA in *painting JJSA*. Solos: *NCAG*. Group participations: MAHA Chitrakala Pradarshan, MAHA State *Exhibition, BAS*. Awards: *BAS* Silver Medal for *portrait*, MAHA Chitrakala Pradarshan. Commissions: Several *portraits, sculptures* & *paintings*, including public commissioned statues of Maharani Tarabai, a seated *sculpture* of Shivaji Maharaj, *portraits* of Dr. Ambedkar, Lokmanya Tilak & Shahu Maharaj. Publications: He also painted cover *illustrations* for various vernacular magazines. Collections: Dalvi's Art Institute, Kolhapur Museum & Bhavani Museum Aundh Satara MAHA.

Ravindra Mestry was the son of the gifted *Baburao Painter*. He followed in the footsteps of his father by assisting him in the *casting* of several *monumental sculptures*. He also studied *oil painting* under him. However, unlike his father who went in for detailed *realism* by paying meticulous attention to details of *drapery* and *background*, Ravindra Mestry practised an impressionistic *style*, looking for the overall effect rather than detail. A *portrait painter*, he also painted *landscapes* in the *style* of *Abalal Rahiman*, which show an understanding of *atmosphere* and *colour*. His *sculptures* were impressionistically handled.

Metal In Latin "metallum"=metal, or mine. Metal is an *opaque* substance with a particular lustre that, in its elementary *form*, is mined in various parts of the world. Any mixture of metals is known as an *alloy* e.g. *bronze* which is a mixture of *copper* and tin. Metals have been in use since *prehistoric* man made simple utilitarian instruments for particular use. In *fine art*, metals e.g. *bronze* and *gold* have been used for *sculpture* throughout the ages; many *printmaking techniques* also use various metals for *engraving* the *plates*, in *copper, steel*, etc.

In India since the times of the RIG-VEDA two *casting* processes were followed i.e. Ghana (solid) and Sushira (hollow). The later examples of antiquity and durability of *iron* works could be divided into religious *images*, ritualistic items and objects of utility.

Copper and *iron* were among the earliest metals to be discovered and used; *iron* being used in arrow heads, spears, knives etc. *Bronze* was used for *image casting* from in the Christian Era. Bell-metal is found in Kerala and Thanjavur and used in *Dokra casting* by the Bastar tribe. *Brass* and *copper* items are known in GUJ and UP, while Bengal for its *brass* and RAJ for *zinc*.

Kerala and Bengal are centres for *icon images* and objects, e.g. temple lamps, Kumbh lamps and hanging lamps. The most important *images* being the NATARAJA in the Tandava-Nritya pose and DURGA shown with spear seated on a buffalo or a lion.

The early artisans worked with different *styles* and *techniques* in India. Mirrors were earlier made from essentially an *alloy* of *copper* and tin in Aranmula (Kerala). They were used for the *crowns* of the local deity known as the *idol* of the mirror.

Today metal has been put to artistic use by artisans with *techniques* such as applique, inlaying and *enamelling* and also used as coatings. Presently a mixture of welded joint scrap is used in the making of *junk art* and *assemblage*. Refer *Metal Cut, Metal Block, Mobile, Mohenjo Daro, Monograph, Mould, Mural*, MURTI, *New Realism, Outline, Overlapping, Pala Miniatures, Patina, Photo-engraving, Pigment, Plate, Polychromatic Sculpture, Priming, Printmaking, Relief printing, Reproduction, Rhythm, Rajasthan School of Arts (RSA)* (Jaipur), *Wax, Welding, White, Wood, Wrought Metal*, YANTRA, *Zinc, Meera Mukherjee, Naren Panchal, K. Jayapala Panicker, Goverdhan S. Panwar, Raj Kumar Panwar, Ankit Patel, Jeram Patel, Abalal Rahiman, Aekka Yadagiri Rao, Radhika Vaidyanathan;* Illustrations—NATARAJA, *Shankar Nandagopal, P.S. Nandhan, V. Viswanadhan, Repousse—Ram Kishore Yadav, Yusuf.*

Metal Cut, Metal Block This *technique* is akin to the *wood cut*. The *metal plate* is cut and printed in *relief*, i.e. from its surface, as opposed to the *intaglio* method. It was popular from the 15th century especially for book *illustration* and decoration, and was often combined with "maniere criblee" (sieved *manner*) the dotted *technique* used in *engraving* on *metal*. It was used in 18th century in conjunction with other *techniques*, such as *line engraving* and *cross-hatching*. *Copper* and *zinc* are some of the *metals* that are used. This *technique* was earlier used by blacksmiths and goldsmiths from whom our Indian *artists* acquired the requisite knowledge. Refer *Acid Bath, Acid Resist, Dry-Point, Printmaking, Laxma Goud, Krishna N. Reddy, Anupam Sud.*

Metaphysical A term that is used in *art* to mean that which is beyond mere physical appearance. It usually denotes work of *art* that are based on dreams and dream *imagery*. Used by Italian *painters* in about 1910 to 1920; also used by *K. Khosa* in the metaphysical *paintings* where the realm of the fantastic figures appear rather sculpted than painted. Refer MANDALA, *Spiritual,* TANTRA, *Radhika Vidyanathan.*

Mewar, Mewar Kalam, Mewar School, Mewar Miniatures The historical *Chaura Panchasika* series (AD 1550 to 1600) represented the pre-Mughal and earliest the phase of *Rajasthani miniature paintings*. The school presented the traditional *themes* from SANSKRIT or Brajbhasha texts like RAGAMALA, Krishna Lila, Nayika Bheda. The earliest RAGAMALA series were made in Chawand, which was the capital of Mewar. From the beginning of the 17th century, brilliant *colour* areas of red, yellow and blue combined with the angular *lines* of *drawing*, remained the outstanding characteristics of Mewar *painting*. The crimson base of the *paintings* was taken from the Mewar flag. *Backgrounds* are patches of bright *colour* against which incidents were set, highlighting the *figures* and separating each group of incidents from the next. The *background* was stylized and the *perspective* elementary. However the trees were naturalistically rendered with sprays of flowers, water been depicted by wavy *lines* and horses and elephants usually treated in a *realistic manner*. *Architecture* was limited to simple domed pavilions and turreted parapets.

The *figures* were strong and sturdy with sharp noses and fish-shaped eyes. Women were rendered with angular *lines*, they wore plain or flowered shirts, blouses and scarves and their wrists were decorated with *black* pompoms. The men wore the Jama with full skirt, a long Sash decorated with geometric *motifs*. The turban was loosely wound and the armpit shaded.

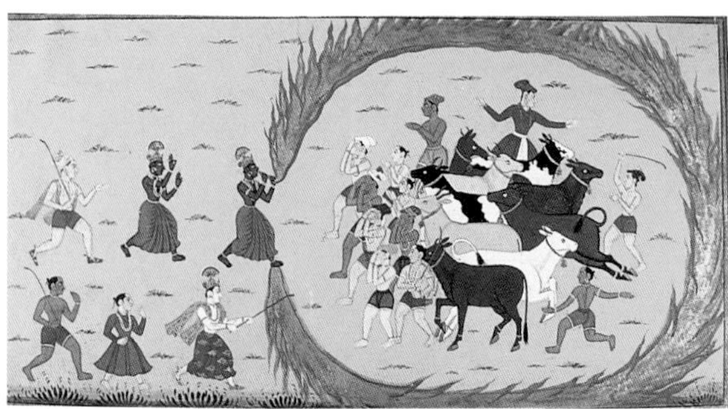

Mewar, Mewar Kalam, Mewar School, Mewar Miniature: "Krishna Drinks The Forest Fire", circa 1770, *Painting*.

The KRISHNA *legend* and other mythological or historical subjects formed the main *themes* of Mewari *paintings*. Refer AAJ, *Miniature Painting,* NAYIKA, *Bundi, Picture Space,* RAGA, *Space, Kanhaiya Lal Verma, Nathu Lal Verma.*

Mezzotint (Italian)=half-tint. The *technique* was invented by the German, Ludwig von Siegen, in 1624, although it did not become a fully developed process until the late 1650s. Mezzotint requires a rocker which is used for grounding the entire surface of the *copper plate*. To achieve this, the rocker has to be worked across the *plate* in different directions. If the *plate* was to be printed at this stage, the *print* would be completely *black*. Mezzotint is the only *engraving* process in which the printmaker works from dark to *light*, rather than from *light* to dark. The rocking process throws up a *burr* which holds the *ink*; in order to create the *design*, the *burr* is then gradually smoothed out with a burnisher or scraped with a *steel* scraper to produce *highlights* and graduated *tones* which, when printed, have a rich velvety quality. Mezzotint was very popular in the 18th century especially for portraiture. Practiced voluminously by *Raja Ravi Varma* in his lithographs, it later spread to the *art* schools of Pune, Vadodara, Kolkata, etc. Refer *Printmaking, Lithography, Devraj Dakoji.*

Mhatre, Chandrakant N. (1923–) b. India. Education: Studied *JJSA*; Dip. in *murals* Escuela de San Fernando Madrid; Studied in *copper enamelling* Escuela Massana Barcelona. Solos: *JAG*, TAG; International: Madrid, Barcelona & La Coruna Spain. Commissions: Several *murals* & *copper* enamelled works for corporate offices in Mumbai, Pune, Agra, Goa, Abu Dhabi, Muscat, Dubai, Bahrain & Madrid Spain; A *copper repousse* plaque depicting Himalayan goat for Hanover Fair. Appointments: Visiting lecturer at *JJSA*. Collections: NCPA Mumbai, corporates & pvt.

Chandrakant N. Mhatre uses *copper enamelling* to create his commissioned *murals* and *sculptures*. He is

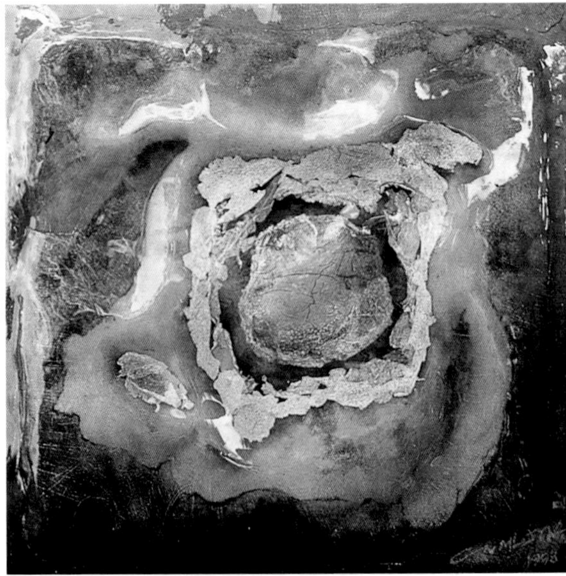

Mhatre, Chandrakant N.: "Composition", *Enamel*, 27.5x27.5 cm.

stylistically versatile, changing from abstraction to *figuration* according to the demands of the client. He has also painted *murals* in *oils*, using medieval *imagery* to great effect.

At present he lives and works in Mumbai.

Mhatre, Ganpatrao K. (1876–1947) b. Pune, MAHA. Education: Dip. *JJSA*. Group participations: New Delhi, *BAS*; International: Paris. Awards: *BAS* Silver Medal, Imperial Durbar Award New Delhi; International: Bronze Medal Dip. Honour Paris. Commissions: *Sculptures*, including over *life-size* memorial statue of Queen Victoria installed in Ahmedabad. Collections: *JJSA*, public & royal.

Ganpatrao K. Mhatre's most memorable work was his first known *sculpture* of a young, Maharashtrian lady, carrying a "Pooja Thali" (plate of offerings for prayer) and a small bell, on her way to a place of worship. This piece, entitled "To the Temple", was executed in *plaster of Paris* when he was a student of *fine arts* at *JJSA*. It has a neo-classical grace and elegance of *form* and expression, pointing to the Graeco-Roman *ideals* of *art* taught at British-run *art* schools. His later works attempted to adapt Western *Symbolism* to Indian *themes*, thus, his SARASVATI, exhibited in the Paris *exhibition* poses in the typical S-curve of the West, rather than the TRIBHANGA (triple flexion) of Indian *art*. She also wears a British crown, rather than the Indian MUKUTA, her sari being *contemporary* rather than traditional. Later, he set up his own practice and established a foundry, receiving several commissions from the princely states of Kolhapur, Gwalior and Mysore.

Mhatre, Ganpatrao K.: "To the Temple", *Bronze*, 142.5x45 cm.

Miller, Brinda C. (1960–) b. India. Education: Dip. in textile *design JJSA*; Studied *painting* Parsons School of Design New York. Solos: Grindlays Bank & Museum Art Gallery Mumbai, Urja Art Gallery Vadodara, *JAG*, TAG, SRAG, TKS. Group participations: Harmony, *Tao Art Gallery, BAAC* & Kala Ghoda Art Festival Mumbai, International Women's Day Chennai, *CYAG* by RPG, *JAG*. *Art* camps & workshops: "Concern India Foundation" at *Artists' Centre* & *BAAC* Mumbai, Monsoon Magic Goa, Ceramic Centre Vadodara. *Auctions*: Christie's. Commissions: For Calendars by "Jindal" & CRY. Appointments: Collaborator Kala Ghoda Art Festivals Mumbai.

Her early works can be termed naturescapes, with birds, the sea and skies appearing as semi-abstract elements against a geometric *background*. Her recent works incorporate the human *figure* as an elusive, wraith-like two-dimensional swirl of *white* against an *abstract* medley of stained *colours*, variously evoking the myriad faces of *nature*. She has explored several *media*, including *oil*, *acrylic* and *collage*, in the *impasto technique* with several layers describing human *figures* and their moods.

She lives and works in Mumbai.

Miniature Painting A small-sized *painting*, usually executed in *watercolour*, *gouache* or *tempera*. In India, however, the word miniature refers to *paintings* other than *murals*, executed in a portable *size*. In the larger sense, painted manuscripts belonging to the Pala period of Bengal, depicting the Buddhist religion, and the *Jain manuscript paintings* of GUJ were also sometimes categorized as miniatures. These were earlier painted on the leaves of the Talipot (*palm leaf*). By the 14th century however, *paper* was being used as the *vehicle* of *painting* all over India. The *Mughal miniature* was first painted on cloth, later *paper* came into use, being painted, mounted and bound elaborately into *folios*. It is the miniatures produced in RAJ, the Pahari hill states and in the Deccan, which are most popularly known as Indian miniatures.

The *technique* of *painting*, the preparation of the *paper*, *colours* and *brushes* was the same, with only the subject matter, the costumes and the *style* helping in differentiating the various schools. *Paper* was dipped in a solution of *alum* and then polished with an agate burnisher, to have a smooth enough surface for *painting*. *Brushes* were made from the hair of squirrels, kittens and calves, drawn through one end of a feathered quill. *Pencils* were made from a mixture of cowdung, powdered slag and water. *Pigments* were obtained from minerals and vegetable *matter*. *Black* was obtained from carbon, the most popular being soot. *Silver* and *gold* leaf were also used. Various *shades* of red were obtained from red *lead*, red ochre and shellac dye. The process was laborious, with *white lead* being roasted in an open fire until it turned a deep *colour*. It was then ground under water for 12 hours, the process being repeated for 24 hours after five days. The *pigment* was then filtered and gum from the Neem (Azadirachta indica) tree added to it as a binder.

Other *colours* were also prepared in a similar fashion from ingredients ranging from indigo, lapis lazuli, orpiment and even from the urine of a cow that had been fed on mango leaves for a few days. The *colours* were mixed according to set formulae, written in ancient treatises, with exact *proportions* being followed. The usual method for *painting* was burnishing of the *paper* followed by a rough *sketch*, the details and corrections being done by the master *painter* with in a mixture of *black* and carmine. Then began the actual process of filling in the *colours*, usually by experts. The *background* and the *foreground* were filled in first, body *colours* next, even under the clothing, the costumes and the other minor objects and finally the *silver* and *gold leaf*. The final *outline* was given, the dots of pearls painted and the hands and lips reddened. Between each stage of colouring, the *painting* was burnished, being placed face down on a smooth *marble* surface. This ensured a smooth surface, with a mellow glow. The *painting* was then mounted and the borders painted, elaborately in the case of *Mughal miniatures* and more simply in the *Rajasthani* and *Deccani miniature painting*. The *calligraphy* was then filled in, the *painting* trimmed and bound together in *folios*.

Subject matter differed, from the court *paintings* of the Mughals, with their biographies and *flora and fauna paintings*, to the predominantly Vaishnavite *themes* of the Rajasthani and *Pahari miniatures*. Refer *Basohli*, BHAGAVAD GITA, *Bengal School, Bundi, Design, Flat Application, Jain Miniatures, Kishangarh, Malwa, Manuscript Painting, Mewar, Mughal Dynasty, Pahari Miniature Painting, Pala Miniatures, Palm Leaf, Pattern, Picture Space, Rajasthani Miniature Painting, Rajput Miniature Painting*, RAMA, *CSMVS/PWM* Mumbai, *SJM* Hyderabad, *Tempera*, VISHNU, *Jaganath M. Ahivasi, Vajubhai D. Bhagat, Arpana Caur, P.N. Choyal, Ved Pal Sharma (Bannu), Kanhaiya Lal Verma, Nathu Lal Verma.*

Minimalism A movement of the 60s, which totally rejected the notion that *art* was self-expression; subjectivity and emotionalism were also vetoed, as was the question of personal *style*. To the minimalists, *art* has to be rational, ordered and precise, with a *visual* symmetry and perfect *balance* of *form*. *Sculpture*, more than *painting*, was chosen as the perfect minimalist *medium* suited for the mathematically precise rectangular and cubic *forms* that are not only repetitive and equal in *size*, in most cases being machine-made and coloured and consequently purged of all differing interpretations. In India, few *artists* associated with the Minimalist *style*, one of them being *Nasreen Mohamedi*. Refer *Ideal Art, Installation, Bauhaus, Dashrath Patel.*

Misra, Hemanta (1917–) b. Sibsagar, Assam. Privately tutored in *art* by John Hassal England. Solos: New Delhi, Mumbai, Guwahati, *AFA* Kolkata; International: Moscow, Bangkok. Retrospective: *AFA* Kolkata 1983 & 88. Group participations: Mumbai, *LKA* Orissa, National *LKA & Triennale* New Delhi, *AFA* & WB Painter's Exhibition Kolkata, Calcutta Group of *Artists, AIFACS*; Workshops: Conducted *LKA* workshops in Manipur. Appointments: Delivered lectures at Kolkata, Dibrugarh, Moscow. Collections: *NGMA* New Delhi, *AFA* Kolkata, State Museum Guwahati, State Art Gallery; International Museum of Oriental Culture Moscow.

Hemanta Misra's early works were impressionistic in *nature*. Later he attempted a synthesis of Eastern and Western *art*. Since then he has been interested in *surrealism*, filling his *canvas* with *images* from the subconscious in *form* of dreams and fantasies. There is also his poetical imagination at work, as he has also published his poems in two different languages. *Colour* also plays an important role in the formation of his *images*.

He lives and works in Kolkata.

Mistry, Chhaganlal D. (1933–) b. Bulsar, GUJ. Education: GDA in *painting* & *Art* Master's CNCFA. Solos: Sanskar Kendra Museum, GUJ Vidyapith, CAG & Archer Art Gallery Ahmedabad, Gallery Aurobindo New Delhi, *JAG, DG*, TKS; International: Commonwealth Institute London. Group participations: National Exhibition, *Triennale* & LKA New Delhi, Harmony Mumbai, *JAG, AIFACS, FFA, ATG, DG*, TKS; International: *Biennale* Tokyo Japan & Havana Cuba. *Art* camps: Goa, Udaipur, Bangalore, All India Artists Kulu Manali, GUJ *LKA*, HCVA. Awards: Gwalior, Kalidas Samaroh Ujjain, GUJ *LKA*, National *LKA*, HAS, *BAS, AIFACS*. Senior Fellowship: Dept. of Culture & Human Resources, GUJ State *LKA* 2001. Member: *BAS*, Jury—National *LKA* New Delhi, SZCC Nagpur & GUJ State *LKA*. Appointments: Lecture & HoD in *FA* at CNCFA. Collections: *NGMA* & *LKA* New Delhi, GUJ *LKA* & KAR, *CKP*, AP HAS, pvt. & corporates; International: Fukuoka Art Museum Japan, pvt. USA.

Chhaganlal D. Mistry tries to achieve a textile-like *texture* in his *paintings*, by using the dry *brush* process and local powder *colours*. His is a primitive *technique*, the brilliance of the *colour* contrasts being achieved by not mixing the *colours*, in the *manner* of making Rangoli (floor design). There is no *light* and *shade* in the *realistic manner*. Rather *light* emanates from the *colours* he has used. His subjects are mostly mythological and his *images* are characterized by a folk-like naiveté and simplicity. Later some of his *drawings* are in *mixed media* on *paper* show the influence of P. Picasso.

He lives in Ahmedabad.

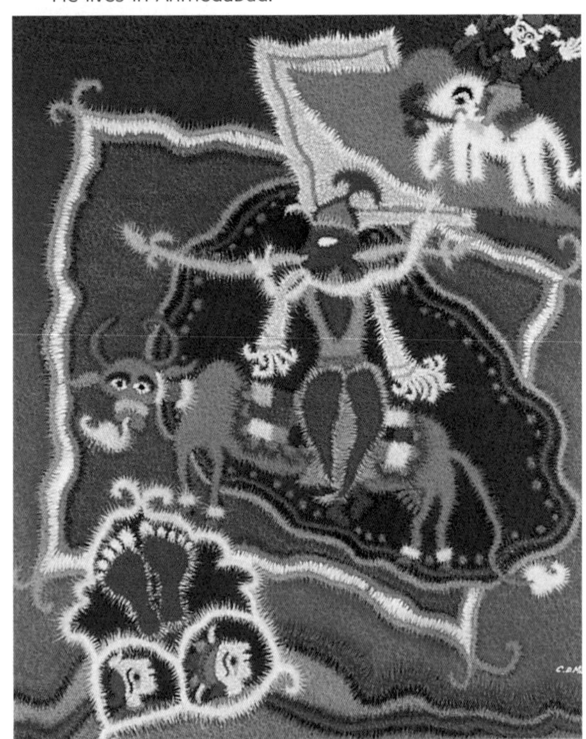

Mistry, Chhaganlal D.: "Govardhandhari", Folk *style painting*, 122x91.5 cm.

Mistry, Dhruva (1957–) b. Kanjari, GUJ. Education: B.A. in *FA. sculpture* & M.A. in *sculpture FFA MSU*; M.A. in *sculpture* RCA. Solos: *Art Heritage* & *LKA* New Delhi, CAG Ahmedabad, Nazar Gallery of Contemporary Art Vadodara, *SG* Mumbai, *GE, JAG*; International: Cambridge, Bradford, Bristol, Llandudno, Liverpool, Bath, Middlesborough, Glasgow,

St. Andrews, Newcastle-upon-Tyne, West Bretton Great Britain, Ireland, Fukuoka Asia Art Museum Japan, RAA London. Group participations: National & International since 1978 to 2004. Fellowship: *Artist*-in-Residence Kettles Yard Gallery at Churchill College Cambridge Great Britain. Member: RAA Great Britain. Fellow: Royal Society of British Sculptors. Public commissions: London, Liverpool, Cambridge, Glasgow, Cardiff, Birmingham, Japan. Collections: Dept. of *FA*. PUJ University, *LKA* New Delhi, WZCC Udaipur, *GMAG*, *Roopankar*; International: Arts Council, Contemporary Art Society, RAA, Tate Gallery, British Council, British Library & British Museum London, Birmingham Museum & Art Gallery Birmingham, Glym Vivien Art Gallery Swansea, National Museum of Wales Cardiff, Walker Art Gallery Liverpool, Fukuoka Art Museum & Asian Art Gallery, Jiguo-Chuo-Koen Park, Hakone Open Air Museum Japan, RCA, V&A.

Dhruva Mistry lived and worked in Great Britain for over 20 years, leaving Vadodara in 1981 when he won the British Council Scholarship. His works have an International appeal, because of his choice of *imagery* and subject matter, which cut across the barrier of traditional roots. Influences as diverse as Egyptian, Greek and Western, constantly show up in his *monumental sculptures*, especially in the "Victoria Square Guardians" which are installed in the square of the same name. Since 1990, the RASAS which form the essence of Indian *art* and *aesthetics*, have been his primary concern. Dhruva Mistry however combines two of the RASAS, Raudra (furious) and Vira (*heroic*) to make room for Shanta (calm, quiescent) in his set of 8 RASAS. For the *images*, he drew upon the *styles* and *imagery* that had marked his career. Dhruva Mistry has also done a series of *etchings* which recall P. Picasso's "Minotaurmachy" series, in their classically majestic but distorted *nudes*. His *drawings* here are marked by a restless *line* and *cross-hatching* for the tonalities. His prints "Thought about Things: Leaves from Ire" exposed his ideas gathered from his visit to the coast of Southern Ireland.

He lives in Vadodara where he was the Prof. of *Sculpture* and Dean of the *FFA* (*MSU*).

Mistry, Natver (1928–) b. Amreli, GUJ. Education: Studied evening classes *JJSA*. Solos: Jamaat Mumbai, *JAG*, TAG. Group participations: National Exhibitions New Delhi & Kolkata, MAHA State *Art Exhibition* & Kala Gurjari Art Exhibition Mumbai, *BAS*. Awards: *BAS*. Commissions: *Murals* for corporate offices. Collections: Maharaja of Porbunder, Air India pvt. & corporates.

Natver Mistry uses bright, decorative *colours* to create his mountainscapes and *cross-hatching landscape compositions*. He has also sometimes opted for the geometric approach, similar to TANTRIC *paintings*. His *handling* of *oil paint* also varies from the *impasto* to liquid *washes* of *colour*.

He lives and works in Mumbai.

Mithila Painting Refer *Folk Art, Madhubani, Manner, Ganga Devi*.

Mithuna 1.=twin, couple. The word refers to the loving couples, found entwined on temple *sculpture*, especially in Orissa and *Khajuraho*. They symbolize the *ideal* marriage, being man and wife. In a more *spiritual* sense, they could symbolize the union between the divine and the human. Mithuna means sexual intercourse. Refer *Erotic Art*. **2.** The third sign of the zodiac—Gemini—according to Western astrology. Refer *Donor, Donor Couple, Ghulam Rasool Santosh, Francis Newton Souza, Setlur Gopal Vasudev.*

Mitra, Rathin (1926–) b. Howrah, WB. Education: GDA Kolkata. Over 30 solos: Kolkata, Musoorie, Dehradun, Darjeeling, RB New Delhi, IAFA Amritsar, SRAG; International: Kuala Lumpur, Singapore, Tokyo, Bath Academy England. Group participations: With Calcutta Group, National *LKA* Exhibitions New Delhi, *PAG* Mumbai. Senior Fellowship: Ministry of Education & Culture & UGC New Delhi. Appointments: Documented several buildings in cities for various boards & govt. offices. Publications: Several books including "Gandhi—An Artist's Impression", "Ghats of Calcutta", "Colonial Architecture of Calcutta", "Institutions of Calcutta" & "Calcutta Then & Now". Collections: *NGMA* New Delhi, Allahabad Museum, *LKA* UP.

Rathin Mitra taught *art* at several schools in India and England, finally joining the famous Doon School as HoD of *Art*. He is known for his meticulous *black*-and-*white*, *pen* and *ink drawings* of various monuments, especially of the better known edifices in Kolkata. He acts as an *artist*-cum-historian recording the grandeur of the bygone era and preserving the cultural heritage of the country.

He lives and works in Kolkata.

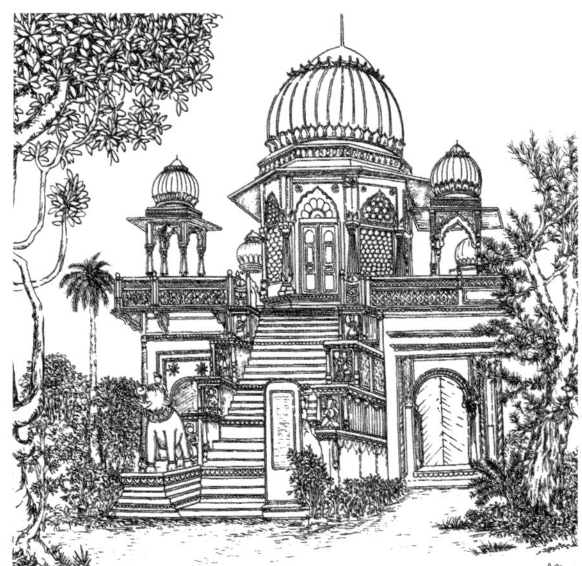

Mitra, Rathin: "Sati temple", *Pen drawing.*

Mitra, Sukhamoy (1921–2004) b. Noakhali, now Bangladesh. Education: Dip. in *FA*. *VBU*. Solos: Mumbai, Patna, Ahmedabad, Agartala, Varanasi, *KB Santiniketan* & *AFA* Kolkata. Conducted *fresco* camps: Bhubaneshwar *LKA*, Patna Art College, Assisted *Nandalal Bose* with Kirtimandir *murals* & Haripura panels, *Benode Behari Mukherjee* with his *mural* at *KB Santiniketan*. Member: Academic Council, also of Samsad (court) & also a sitting member. Commissions: *Santiniketan*, *Murals* in Mandanapalle Theosophical Society South India, Jabalpur Town Hall, Maha Jati Sadan Kolkata, Patna Art College & pvt. houses Kolkata. Appointments: Served in *Santiniketan* as Adhyapaka (teacher), Acting Proctor, HoD of *Painting* & *Design VBU* & a Reader in *Painting*. Publications: Works published in *"Modern Review"*, *"Prabasi"*, *"VBU* News", "Taruner Swapna". Collections: *Santiniketan*, Thiruvananthapuram, Maha Jati Sadan & pvt.

Like many of his *contemporaries* at *Santiniketan*, Sukhamoy Mitra took great delight in experimenting with different *media* and *materials*, including masonite, *hardboard*, *handmade paper*, earthen *plates* and with *oils*, *tempera*, *wash painting* and *linocuts*. His love and keen sense of observation are apparent in his *nature* studies and *landscapes*. Like *Nandalal Bose*, his *style* depended on his versatile *handling* of the *medium*, hence the detailed lined *drawings*, flowing *watercolour washes* and spontaneous *tempera paintings*. He lived and worked in Bolpur, WB.

Mitra, Tapan (1947–) b. Howrah, WB. Education: B.FA. in *painting Santiniketan*, Studied *serigraphy Santiniketan* under the guidance of Biswarup Bose. Solos: *Santiniketan* & *AFA* Kolkata, Art World Chennai, *GK*; International: Gallery Tone Dhaka. Group participations: *Santiniketan*, Kolkata, New Delhi, Mumbai, Chennai; International: Festival of India in USA. *Art* workshops & seminars: Ranchi, Siliguri, *Graphic* workshop USIS, Werner Reister & Peter Foeller MMB, British Deputy High Commission & *GCAC* Kolkata. Conducted *serigraphy* workshops *KB Santiniketan*, *RBU* Kolkata, Agartala Govt. Art College Tripura. Awards: State Academy WB & *AFA* Kolkata. Collections: *LKA* & *NGMA* New Delhi, pvt. & corporates.

He began his artistic career as a serigrapher, using surreal *images* like empty bottles, chairs and sofas and also billowing garments to suggest the loneliness or hollowness of our social norms. He transferred similar *images* to his *acrylics*, adding expressive faces to his repertoire. Later, however he diverted his attention towards reproducing barren *landscapes* on *canvas*, the vastness of the twilight sky, with its atmospheric haze adding to the quiet unease of the *composition*.

He lives and works in Kolkata.

Mixed Contrast The *illusion* of another *colour* by the *optical mixing* of an *after image* with a *hue*; e.g. yellow is the *after image* produced by violet; when this yellow is superimposed (visually) on a blue field, the optical colour produced will be green. Refer *Op Art, Narayan S. Bendre.*

Mixed Media The word refers to the type of *art* that results, when two or more different *mediums* are used in the execution of a single work, i.e. when a *painting* is not exclusively a *watercolour*, *oil painting*, *gouache* or *acrylic*, but is made of two or more of these different *mediums*. The rule is applicable in *sculpture* too. The *media* used must be compatible with each other, in the sense that while it is not possible to use *watercolour* and *oil painting* in a single work, *pastels*, *pencils*, *gouache*, *acrylic* and *collage* can all be used to enhance a *watercolour*. *Egg-tempera* can be used to accentuate certain details on *oil paintings*, and can even be used as fast drying *underpainting* material. In addition, foreign material such as sawdust, *wood* scraps, glass powder and thick adhesives may also be added to a mixed media work. Refer *Assemblages, Distemper, Found Object, Installation, Ready-Made, Krishnamachari Bose, Pilton Kothawalla, N. Pushpamala, Dashrath Patel, Kashinath Salve, J. Srividya;* Illustrations—*Embroidery, Mask, Shanti Dave, C. Douglas, Somnath Hore, Bharati Kapadia, Meera Mukherjee, Rm. Palaniappan, Manickam Senathipathi, Vishwanath M. Sholapurkar, Vivan Sundaram and Thotha Vaikuntham*

Mobile A synonym for kinetic *sculpture*. The mobile as a sculptural *form* was invented by Alexander Calder, and consists primarily of lightweight shapes cut from sheet *metal* or *wood* and interconnected with flexible wires or *metal* rods, so as to cause the whole *construction* to move and interchange places three-dimensionally with the slightest breeze or the lightest of touches. The shapes were usually brilliantly coloured. *Vivan Sundaram* incorporated movement into the work of *art* and *Ankit Patel's* early mobile works were in *wood* and *fibreglass*. Refer *Kinetic Art, Op or Optical Art, Post-Independence, Anis Farooqi, Bharati Kapadia, Ved Nayar.*

Model A synonym of maquette—a small three-dimensional model, usually in *clay* or *wax*, for a larger *sculpture* or *mural*. In the work of *art*, a person who poses as an *artist's* model is the subject. A small or full scale version of the final *sculpture*, used by the *sculptor* as a *visual* aid or *sketch*. Refer *All'antica, Anatomy, Canon of Proportion, Chasis, Cire Perdue, Indirect Carving, Life-Drawing, Life-Mask, Living Sculpture, Life-Size, Pestonjee Bomanjee, Ramkinkar Baij, Gopal Damodar Deuskar, Dwarika P. Dhuliya, C. Jagdish, Kanayi Kunhiraman, Chintamoni Kar, Vinayak Pandurang Karmarkar, Niranjan Pradhan.*

Modelling **1.** The process of depicting three-dimensional objects in *chiaroscuro*. **2.** So as to achieve a three-dimensional effect in primary *sketch* for *painting* or *drawing* with *tonal value* on a *flat surface*. **3.** An additive process in *sculpture*, consisting of the building up of the *sculpture* by using *clay*, *wax*, *plaster* or any such material. It is the opposite of *carving*. **4.** Use of live *models* in the *art* schools of Mumbai, Chennai, Kolkata and Lahore first introduced by the British government in early 19th century. This *form* of learning typified *nude painting and sculpture* using live *models* and *sculptures*, using *plaster copies* of old Greek statues. Refer *Model, Nilkanth P. Khanvilkar;* Illustrations—Academic Art, *Art Education, Cire Perdue, Concrete, Kalighat Pat, B. Vithal, Sadanandji Bakre, Pestonjee Bomanjee, Bhagwant K. Goregaoker, Debi Prasad RoyChowdhury, Savlaram L. Haldankar, Brahman Vinayakrao Wagh.*

Modern In general *art terms*, modern refers to *contemporary art* or *art* of the present day, and usually implies innovation and initiative on the part of the *artist*. In particular, modern also refers to *art* produced since the beginning of the 20th century and the *styles* of movements that followed *Impressionism*. These included *post-Impressionism, Fauvism, Expressionism, Cubism, Surrealism,* etc., and the entire range of *abstract art*. In India, modern refers to the *art* produced since about 1880 and the rise of individualism among *artists* e.g. *Raja Ravi Varma,* to distinguish it from earlier schools or *styles* e.g. Mughal, Deccani, Pahari, Company. Refer *Abstraction Lyrical, Acid, All-over, Aquatint, Art Deco, Artefact, Artist Groups, Avant-Garde, Body Art, Brush, Company School/Company Painting, Contemporary, Post-Modern, Post-Independence, Jaganath M. Ahivasi, Jaya Appasamy, Aditya Basak, Madhab Bhattacharjee;* Illustrations–*K.M. Adimoolam, Badri Narayan, Ramkinkar Baij, Sadanandji Bakre, Manjit Bawa, Vajubhai D. Bhagat, Jyoti Bhatt, Sankho Chaudhuri, Vivan Sundaram, Janak Jhankar Narzary, Dhruva Mistry, Tyeb Mehta, Computer Art– Prabhakar Barwe.*

Modern Review An illustrated monthly magazine, published in English since 1907, by Ramananda Chatterjee to carry his messages of reform and nationalism to English-speaking Indians nationwide. Chatterjee replaced the poor quality lithographic and *wood* block *illustrations* in earlier journals with the naturalistic *illustrations* made possible by *half-tone* blocks. The softer *tones* of *oil painting* were revealed to the public by this process. *Raja Ravi Varma's* and *Mahadev V. Dhurandhar's* works were regularly featured in the *Prabasi* and the Modern Review. Coloured *reproductions* were first used in 1903, when *Raja Ravi Varma's* "AJA's LAMENT" was reproduced in three *colours*. Refer *Prabasi* and *Kumar Magazine*.

Modern Style Synonym for French *Art Nouveau*. The *style* refers to the present period, which has broken away from the *forms* of *tradition* and the past. *Bengal School's* association with a *style* made it the first *aesthetic* development that occurred in India at the turn of the century. *Santiniketan*, Jaipur School (which taught *tempera*), *JJSA* and the *artists* of *Madras School of Art* were known for changes in the modern style of Indian *art*. Today, *modernism* in India ranges from the purely *figurative* to *figurative-abstract* from the naive and childlike to the sophisticated *installations* and *conceptual art,* and from folk and tribal *imagery* to TANTRA. Refer *Art Deco, Company School, Folk Art, Naive Art, Primitivism, Tribal Art, Muhammed Abdur Rehman Chughtai, Bhabani Charan Gue, Abanindranath Tagore, Sarada Charan Ukil*.

Modernism, Modern Movement The *modern* usage of expression, each time referring to the latest experiments and innovation in the field of *art*. Modernism in the Indian context started in 1895–1910 in Bengal. Rebellion against Western influence on *art*, the impact of Nationalism arising out of colonial rule, the revivalist fervour and then abstraction in *art form*, all evolved from this movement. *Artists* started to get identified with groups which epitomized such movements e.g. *Bengal School, Company School, Bombay school* Revivalist Group or *Progressive Artist's Groups.* In India, several *artists* have adopted to the expression of modernism through *Isms, installation, assemblage, Constructivism,* photography, xerox, *found objects* and *junk art, computer art* and *video art.* Refer *Aesthetic Movement, Arts and Crafts Movement, Banasthali Vidyapith* RAJ, *Contemporary, Young Turks, Narayan S. Bendre, Amina Ahmed Kar, K.C.S. Paniker, Amrita Sher-Gil.*

Mohamedi, Nasreen (1937–1990) b. Karachi, now Pakistan. Education: Studied *painting* in St. Martin's School of Art London. Solos: Gallery 59 & *GC* Mumbai, Kunika Chemould & *Art Heritage* New Delhi, TAG, *JAG, PG,* SRAG; International: Bahrain. Retrospective: after her death, in 1991 *JAG*. Group participations: *Triennale* & *LKA* Exhibitions New Delhi, All India Exhibition of *drawing* at Atul GUJ, *GC* Mumbai, *ATG*; International: Festival of India London, Artistes Indiens en France Paris. *Auctions:* Heart Mumbai. Awards: Atul GUJ, National *LKA* for *drawing*, French Govt. Scholarship to study *Graphic* Paris. Appointments: Lecturer *MSU* 1972–1988.

Nasreen Mohamedi, the sister of *artist Altaf*, was one of the youngest *painters* to have worked at the Bhulabhai Desai community studios, where many other senior *artists* of today started working.

She was interested in the long undulating *patterns*, the ever-changing *colours* of the sea and the shore, incorporating them into her work, both as *photographs* and as *drawings*. *Nature* was her primary source with its optical *illusion* of organic *forms*. It was only later that she branched out into her own brand of stark *minimalism*, with her *black* and *white* works on *paper*. Unlike the lack of emotion seen in most minimalist works, a sense of poetry infused her repetitive *lines*, dots and graced arrows. Later an interest in *primary colour* manifested itself as also an interest in architectural *drawings*.

Primarily, however, she was interested in *form* as *design* and functional *design* at that.

Mohanti, Prafulla (1930s) b. Nanpur, Orissa. Education: Dip. in *architecture* J.J. College of Architecture Mumbai, Post-Dip. Town Planning Leeds England. Solos: New Delhi, Mumbai, Chennai, Kolkata, Bhubaneshwar; International: London, Leeds, Germany, Milan, Manila, Paris, Tokyo, UK. Group participations: National Exhibition *LKA* New Delhi, &

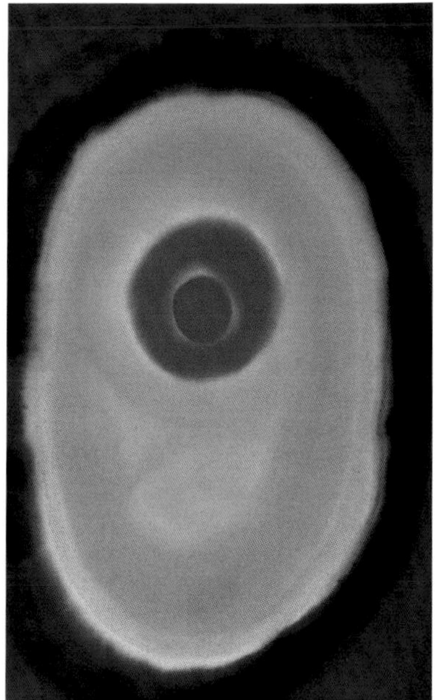

Mohanti, Prafulla: "Shakti", *Watercolour* on *Paper*, 1996.

Triennale; International: Montreal, Zurich, Commonwealth Art Festival London. Member: Associate member at Town Planning Institute London. Appointments: Taught YOGA & Indian dancing; Arranged *exhibitions* of Oriya *crafts* in UK. Publications: Autobiography "My Village, My life" in London. Collections: *NGMA* & *LKA* New Delhi, *AFA* Kolkata; International: Leeds City Gallery, Wakefield City Gallery, Brighton Gallery, University of Leeds, University of Sussex, University of Kent & Museum of Modern Art Berkeley all in UK and pvt. USA.

Prafulla Mohanti's *paintings* are rooted in the life and *culture* of his native village in Orissa. It is the religious and the meditative aspect of the Indian way of life which suffuses his *art* with its complex yet direct *Symbolism* and *imagery*. As with certain other *paintings*, it is the BINDU, variously called the circle or the dot from which his creativity begins. This BINDU dissolves into a void, absolute nothingness in total abstraction or it can expand to embrace the entire cosmos within itself. These perfect circles could represent BRAHMA, VISHNU and SHIVA; a *stone* smeared with Sindoor (red powder symbolizing the married woman) is transformed into *god*; these are the *images* along with brilliant *colours* and depiction of *light* that form the central *theme* in his *paintings*.

He lives and works in London, England.

Mohenjo Daro The name refers to the "hill of the dead". Mohenjo Daro is one of the *prehistoric* cities on the Indus river (Sind province of Indian subcontinent) which was discovered in 1922 by Sir John Marshall. It is nearly 400 miles further south of *Harappa*, and displays an astonishing similarity of development and *culture*. Both these two major ancient cities are models of urban planning, being built mostly of fired brick. Mohenjo Daro's buildings were further massed into blocks, intersected by grid-like streets and lanes, interspersed with some of the most advanced sewage and sanitation systems known to mankind. The citadel contained most of the important buildings which included the great bath and a sophisticated granary complex. *Sculptures* ranging from tiny steatite seals to larger *metal*, limestone and *terracotta representations* of dancers, mother goddesses and priest-like men have also been found in Mohenjo Daro in addition to *gold* and bead jewellery and toys. Refer *Indus Valley Civilization*, *Harappa*, *National Museum* (New Delhi), *Cast, Cire Perdue, Relief Sculpture, Visual.*

Mohile-Parikh Centre For The Visual Arts (MPCVA) (Mumbai) The National Centre for the Performing Arts (NCPA), a premier institution devoted to the development and preservation of *classical*, traditional and *contemporary* music, dance and theatre, established the MPCVA in 1990. The MPCVA perceives the *visual arts* as a *vehicle* for personal and social renewal and has worked towards developing and sustaining a significant discourse in this field, through international conferences and seminars, workshops, lectures, audio-visual presentations and publications. Several *monographs*, books and *posters* have already been published. In 1997, the centre initiated the *Architecture* Forum, in addition to its commitment to *painting*, *sculpture*, the *graphic arts*, *installation* and *video art*. It is committed to providing a platform for new work, ideas and debate and fostering cross-cultural exchanges internationally. It maintains an updated and comprehensive library and archives of books, slides, *photographs*, videotapes and films on *art*.

Moksha=emancipation, liberation, freeing, salvation, deliverance and release from the worldly existence. It is the goal of every follower of *Hinduism*, and is also followed in the Buddhist and the *Jain* way of life. It is the release of the soul from the endless cycle of birth and rebirth and can only be achieved through the total annihilation of KARMA (deeds). This is achieved through meditation, obtaining the right knowledge of the self and right conduct. This helps the soul to revert to its original state of pure perfection i.e. Moksha. Refer LOKA, MAHAVIRA, NIRVANA; Illustration—KARMA by *Laxman Pai*.

Mondal, Dulal (1939–) b. New Delhi. Education: NDA *College of Art* New Delhi. Solos: Delhi College & *LKA* New Delhi, *AFA* & *BAAC* Kolkata, Gallery Pradarshak Mumbai, *AIFACS*, TKS; International: British Council Kaduna Nigeria. Group participations: Varanasi, Lucknow, CKP Dehradun, *AIFACS*, SKP. *Art* camp: Hudco Habitat New Delhi, *AIFACS*. Awards: Rajiv Gandhi Award New Delhi; International Govt. of India for research in *painting* at AFA Istanbul. Hon.: *LKA* New Delhi. Fellowship: Senior Fellowship Dept. of Cultured Govt. of India 2000–02. Member: *AIFACS*. Appointments: HoD Sokoto Teachers Training College Nigeria. Collections: *College of Art* New Delhi, Istanbul State Gallery & pvt.

Dulal Mondal is a skilled draughtsman, adept in *handling* of *pastels, pen* and *ink*. The granular *texture* that he achieves with these two *mediums* is comparable to the best of *aquatints*. The brilliance of *light* achieved in these works is mainly by using *translucent colours*. His favourite *themes* include the Varanasi *ghats* and GANESHA.

He lives and works in New Delhi.

Mondal, Rabin (1932–) b. Howrah, WB. Education: Indian College of FA. Kolkata, *Ashutosh Museum of Indian Art* Calcutta University. Solos: *AFA*, Arts & Prints Gallery, Artistry House, *GC* & *BAAC* Kolkata, *Delhi Art Gallery,* MMB Mumbai, *JAG* & *Art Heritage* New Delhi, GAG, TKS, SRAG, *LTG,* TAG, *CYAG* Group participations: Bangalore, Kolkata, National *LKA* Exhibitions, *Triennales*, Miniature Format Exhibition *LKA* & Safdar Hashmi Memorial Trust New Delhi, CRY Art Exhibition Mumbai; International: Bangladesh. *Art* camps: CMC *artists* & MMB Kolkata, Hudco camp New Delhi. *Auctions*: Heart & Osian's Mumbai. Member: Founder member Calcutta Painters, Calcutta Art Fair. Publications: In books, *Drawings* 1970–1988; *Drawings* by 14 Contemporary Artists of Bengal & represented in films, "Contemporary Indian Painters", "Destination Art". Collections: *NGMA* & *College of Art* New Delhi, *BAAC* Kolkata, Godrej Mumbai, *Madhavan Nayar Foundation* Kerala, *CYAG*.

Over the years, Rabin Mondal has evolved a personal *eclectic style* full of throbbing vitality, with thick impasted applications of painted and scribbled, incised *lines*. He uses rich, saturated *colours*, his *palette* mostly verging on low *key* browns, *blacks* and deep dense blues and greens. One encounters mask-like heads and *portraits* in dominantly tribal and folk *style form*, replete with jewellery. There is also a sense of deep foreboding in these *compositions* of impassive males and females, staring dispassionately past the viewer.

He lives and works in Howrah.

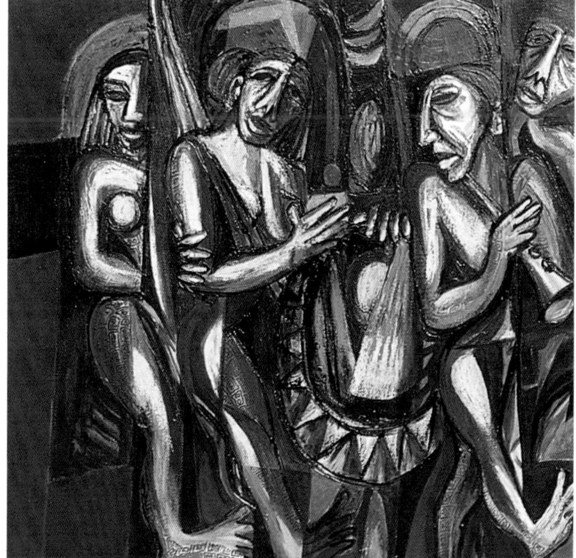

Mondal, Rabin: "Festivity", *Acrylic* with *Oil* finish, 1989, 107x107 cm.

Monochrome, Monochromatic A single *colour.* The word refers to a *painting* executed in one *colour*, though with its accompanying *shades* and *tints*. Monochromatic refers to the varying of *tints*, tones and *shades* of one *colour*. *Kalighat pat paintings* were rapidly executed with a few bold, sweeping strokes of the *brush* in near monochromatic *colours*. *Vrindavan Solanki's figurative* works are monochromatic, capturing men and women from his native Saurashtra. Refer *Grisaille, Kalighat Pat, Still Life, Mahadev V. Dhurandhar, Nareen Nath, Vasudha Thozhur, Nita Thakore;* Illustration—*Seascape.*

Monocular Vision As opposed to normal vision when a person observes with both eyes to "obtain" a three-dimensional effect, monocular vision refers to observation through only one eye. This is a common practice among *artists* especially when *drawing* objects by reducing the *image* to a two-dimensional format; it thus avoids perceiving double *images*. This system of viewing is frequently adopted in *life-drawing*, portraiture and *still life*.

The British influence brought it to Indian *art* schools under the tutelage of English teachers in Chennai, Mumbai, Kolkata and Lahore (now Pakistan). Refer *Academic Art, Academy, JJSA*.

Monograph A *print* or *wash drawing*, which is executed in one *colour* only. *Printmaking technique* started in monograph in *wood cut, metal engraving* and *lithography* in the 19th century in Goa, Calcutta and Bombay.

Monograph is also a short essay or critique on an *artist* published in book or catalogue *form* (especially for *auctions*) along with a few *illustrations* of his/her *art* work.

LKA publicationed monographs on *artists* like *K.K. Hebbar, Debi Prasad RoyChowdhury, Jamini Roy, while AIFACS* publicationed several portfolios in monograph. Refer *Block Printing, Grisaille, Roop Chand, Nikhil Biswas, C. Douglas, Gaganendranath Tagore.*

Monotype Similar to the monoprint, in that only one *print* is possible, the monotype involves *painting* on a *copper plate* or a similar hard surface, such as perspex, glass, porcelain or *stone*, with *oil paints* or *printer's ink* and pulling a *print* on *paper*, either in the press or by burnishing. The only advantage of this *technique*, over *painting* directly on *paper* or base used, is the characteristic *texture* that is achieved. It has been practised by *Sujata Bajaj, Shanti Dave, Atul Dodiya, Seema Ghurayya, Mahadeo Bhanaji Ingle* and many other young *artists* of today. Refer *Assemblage, Constructivism, Happening, Installation, Photography, Stencil.*

Monumental Refers to the *heroic* scale or *size* of a work. It can be applied equally to the huge pyramids of Egypt, the *Taj Mahal* in India or the *prehistoric* Venuses found in Europe. In India monumental *art* was principally seen in temples and other structures around it. *Artists* in India created large *paintings* and *sculptures. Avtarjeet S. Dhanjal* and *Dhruva Mistry's compositions* are monumental and brutal in scale and conception leading it towards the *open form*. Refer *Ramkinkar Baij, Dhanraj Bhagat, Santokba Dudhat, Maqbool Fida Husain, Kanayi Kunhiraman, Meera Mukherjee, Amrita Sher-Gil.*

Mookerjea, Sailoz (1907–1960) (also spelled Mukerjea) b. Kolkata. Education: Studied GSA Kolkata. Solos: Posthumous solos *AFA* Kolkata, *LKA* & Kunika Art Centre New Delhi. Three Retrospective shows: 1960–62. Group participations: Kolkata, New Delhi; International: Salon de Mai Paris. Received several awards. *Auctions*: Heart & Osian's Mumbai, Bowring's & Heart New Delhi, Sotheby's London & New York. Member: Judging panel Rashtriya Kala Pradarshini New Delhi. Appointments: Was Art Dir. Designer Imperial Tobacco Co. India; Prof. at *SUSA* & later Govt. Polytechnic School (*College of Art*) New Delhi. Collections: *NGMA* New Delhi, *AFA* Kolkata, *AIFACS*.

Sailoz Mookerjea can be considered to be a transitional *painter*, bridging the gap between the early *moderns* and the post-Sher-gil phase with ease. His thematic concerns were the same as that of the *Bengal School artists*, with a preponderance of artistic subjects: women idling and gossiping, drawing water from the village well, *pastoral* scenes and *landscapes*. It is his *handling* of *line* and *colour*, however that marks him as a modernist; it is spontaneous, with a *painterly*, almost sketchy *treatment*. The *line* does not confine the *figure* as in the *Bengal School*; instead, patches of *colour* mingle freely with the broken, exuberant *outlines*. His main *medium* was *oil painting*, but he also did *drawings* in *India ink* and coloured *inks*. He preferred using thin, *transparent* glazes of *colour* rather than using thick impasted patches of *pigment*. His choice of *colours* bordered on the adventurous, while his *figures* added the requisite touch of *rhythm* to his works. Another characteristic was the use of short *black* or *white lines* accentuating the *key* notes of the *composition*. In his final works, Sailoz Mookerjea goes beyond subject matter, using *colour* and movement, *texture*, *space*, *line* and *mass* to create near *abstract* works.

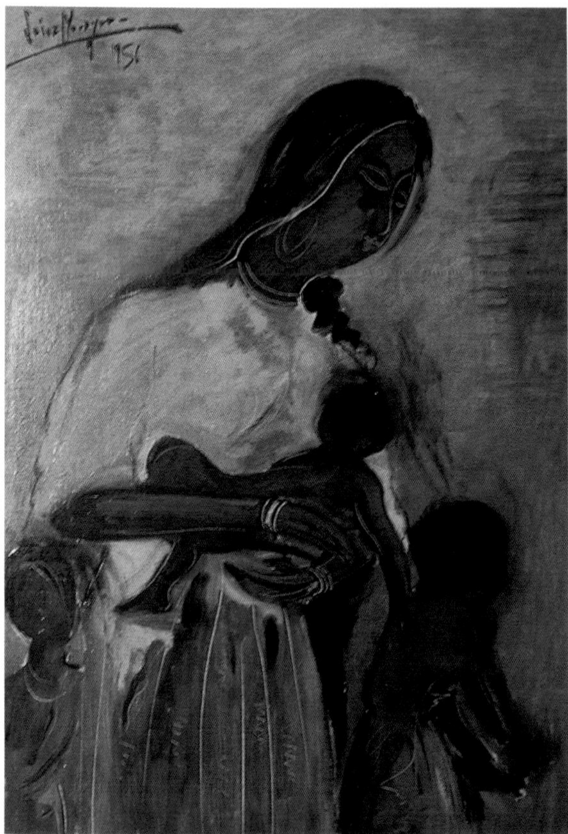

Mookerjea, Sailoz: "Village on Canvas", *Oil* on *Canvas,* 1956, 54.6x75 cm.

Mosaic One of the ancient *forms* of wall and floor decoration. Mosaics are highly durable, because of the hardness of the material used in their making. From the crude *stones* of the early pavements to the machine-cut squares of *ceramic* tiles favoured by *contemporary* muralists, mosaics are one of the most colourful means of decoration. The *technique* is simple–the subject is drawn on the relevant area, which is then covered with *cement*. The Tessarae (pieces of mosaic) are then embedded into this area, keeping in mind the various *colours* and effects that are needed. Floor mosaic has to be flat and level with the ground, so as to be comfortable to walk on. However, wall mosaic, especially when pieces of coloured glass are used, were placed at slightly varying angles so as to catch and reflect *light*. Some of the materials used in mosaic-making include limestone, basalt, *marble*, glass, *ceramic*. In the Byzantine period, thin *gold leaf* was sandwiched between two layers of clear glass which was then fused. The vast areas of *gold leaf* inspired a feeling of awe, as it indicated divine *light* streaming from the head of Christ in the skylit Byzantine churches. The most intricate mosaics were executed by the Roman Emperors, especially in the grand baths and in their villas. The degree of *modelling* was so intricate, so as to pass for *fresco painting*. In India, though *inlay* work was practised, mosaic as a *technique* has been mostly used by muralists in the *post-Independence* era. Refer *Byzantine Art, Cement, Christian Art, Glass Mosaic, Matter, Mesopotamian Art, Mural, Spiritual, Still Life, Stone Carving, Vidya Bhushan, Chiru Chakravarty, Kavita Deuskar, Ramlal Dhar, Shantilal M. Shah, Bal Wad*; Illustration–*Sukhen Ganguly*.

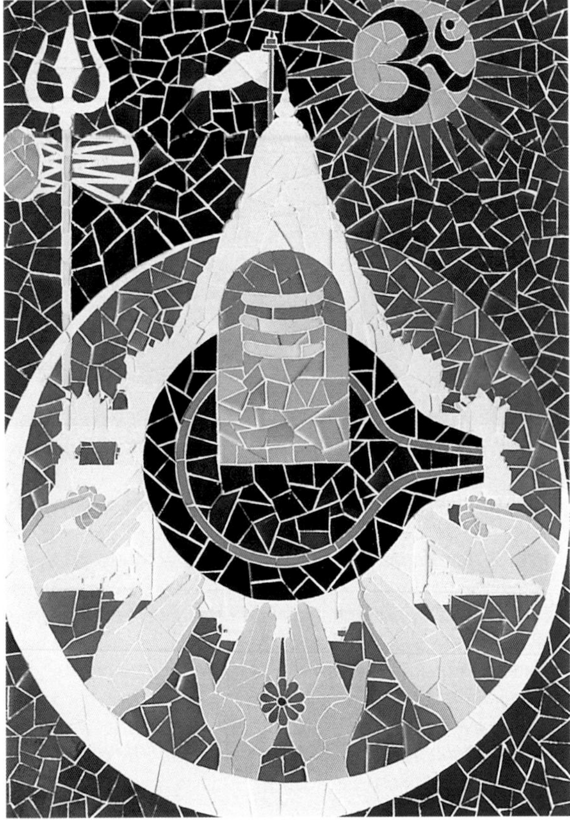

Mosaic: "Shah Shanti", *Mural* at Ambaji.

Motif 1. A distinct, identifiable element (usually the predominant one) in a work of *art*, i.e. *arches* in a building, horses in *Maqbool Fida Husain's painting*, the *colour* application in *K.K. Hebbar's* or *Manjit Bawa's paintings*, the sentimental *Lyricism* in *Vinayak Pandurang Karmarkar's* and G.D. Mhatre's *sculptures*. **2.** The word also refers to the *theme* of an individual work, i.e. the Santhals in *Ramkinker Baij's* "Santhal Family" or the erotic *sculptures* at *Khajuraho*. Refer *Aesthetic Movement, Batik, Byzantine Art, Chequering, Design, Detailed Work, Ellora, Figure-Ground Relationship, Folk Decoration, Frottage, Imagery, Kalamkari, Kangra, Mewar, Mughal Dynasty, Neolithic Art, Pattern, Pouncing, Rhythm, Sand Painting, Tree of Life, Tribal Art, V Tool*, YONI, *WSC, Dipak Banerjee, Sukumar Bhattacharjee, Mansing L. Chhara, Shail Choyal, Jagadish Dey, Paresh C.*

Hazra, Mahadeo Bhanaji Ingle, Girish H. Khatri, Shakuntala Kulkarni, Animesh Nandi, Prabha Panwar, Ashit Paul, Gopal Sanyal, Rangaswamy Sarangan, Nilima G. Sheikh, G.S. Shenoy, K.S. Sherigar, Subhogendra Tagore, P. Vinay Trivedi; Illustrations—*Illuminated Manuscripts, Altaf, Amit Ambalal, Ramkinkar Baij, Jyoti Bhatt, Veerbala Bhavsar, Vasudeo Santu Gaitonde, Ganga Devi, Shaibal Ghosh, K.V. Haridasan, Maqbool Fida Husain, Rekha Krishnan*—YANTRA, *Reddeppa M. Naidu,* Balan *Nambiar, Shankar Nandagopal, K.C.S. Paniker, Ganesh Pyne, Jamini Roy, Katayun Saklat, Bhabesh Chandra Sanyal, Manickam Senathipathi, Himmat Shah, Om Prakash Sharma, Lalu Prasad Shaw, Ali J. Sultan, Nathu Lal Verma.*

Mould Mould is a shaped hollow container in which *wax*, plastic or other liquefied material is *cast* or shaped. It is the *negative form*.

A piece mould is made of two or more sections which are joined together to make a *casting*. Later the pieces are carefully dismantled and the object is removed. The piece mould can be reused several times. However, the *cast* object will have several fine seams at places of joints of the piece mould. These are then to be filled, cut or polished away for the final product. Refer *Cire Perdue, Clay, Facing, Filler, Frame, Handmade Paper, Impression, Mask, Paper-Pulp Casting, Papier Mache, Parting Agent, Plaster, Positive, Pottery, Sand Moulding, Waste-Mould, Wax, Wrought Metal, C. Dakshinamoorthy, Shanti Dave, Somnath Hore, Meera Mukherjee;* Illustrations—*Himmat Shah, C. Jagdish.*

Mudras/Hastas=hand gestures. Denotes various positions that the hand is held in *sculpture*, *painting* and live dance. Period *sculptures* in various temples, particularly, at Mount Abu, *Ajanta, Ellora* and also found in the *icons* of the BUDDHA, MAHAVIRA and Hindu *gods* and goddesses. Refer *Abu-Dilwara Temples;* Illustrations—*Line,* NATARAJA. Some of the main positions are:

Abhaya—The "fearless" gesture of protection. Refer BUDDHA.

Anjali—Refer ANJALI.

Bhumisparsha—"Touching the earth". Refer *Archaeological Museum* (*Khajuraho*, MP).

Dharmachakra-mudra="Turning of the wheel of Law". Refer *Buddhist Art, Gandharan Art, Gupta.*

Gaja-hasta or Danda-hasta—Refer GAJA-HASTA.

Jnana-mudra—"Imparting knowledge".

Kartari-hasta—Palms held like the horns of a deer.

Katyavalambita-mudra—"At ease" pose.

Kataka-hasta or Simhakarna-mudra—Fingers *form* a ring, into which a fresh flower is inserted everyday.

Varada-mudra—"Conferring a boon". Refer VISHNU.

Vismaya-mudra—"Astonishment". Refer VISHNU.

Yoga-mudra, Dhyana-mudra—"Meditation" posture. Refer ASANAS, DHYANI-BUDDHA.

Refer *Attribute, Buddhist Art,* CHATUR BHUJA, DHYANI-BUDDHA, *Icon, Line*, NAMASKARA, YOGA, *National Museum* (New Delhi), *Archaeological Museum* (Khajuraho, MP), PARVATI, *Abanindranath Tagore.*

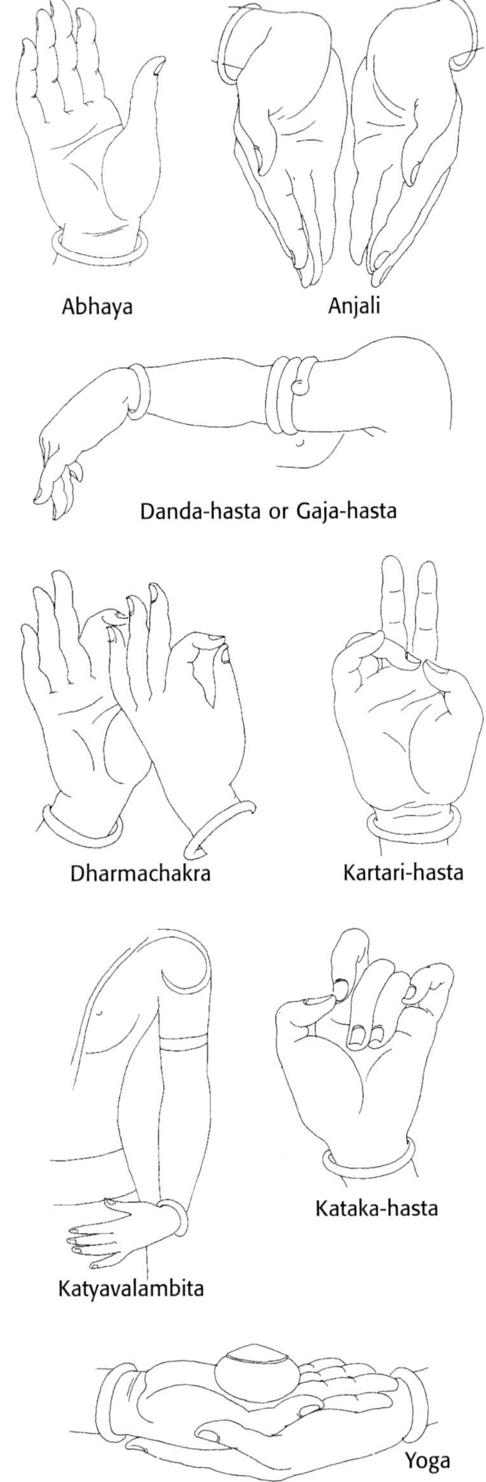

Mudras or Hastas

Mughal Dynasty The word is adapted from the word "Mongo" from Persia of whom Babur (1483–1530) was a descendant through his mother. He was the founder of the

Mughal dynasty in India. His son Humayun ruled for some years, before he was ousted for some 15 years, but it was his young grandson Akbar, the well-known Mughal Emperor, ruling between 1556–1605 who created a stable, cultured empire that spread over more than half of India, making amiable vassals of the Rajputs and spreading the Mughal *style* and *culture* throughout these areas. His son Jehangir (1605–27) and grandson Shahjehan (1628–58) continued to patronize court *painting* and build monuments. The decline set in with the rule of the fanatical Aurangzeb (1658–1707) who refused to commission *paintings* claiming that it was an un-Islamic practice.

Mughal *architecture* shows two distinct phases of development. During Akbar's reign, red sandstone was used, while later Shahjahan preferred the pristine whiteness of *marble*. The tomb of Humayun displays the one defining characteristic of Mughal *architecture,* its setting of orderly laid out gardens. Akbar built fortresses at Agra, Lahore and Allahabad—however his most ambitious achievement was the *construction* of his new capital, Fatehpur Sikri, some 36 km. West of Agra, in gratitude of the fulfillment of the prophecy of the saint Salim Chisti, of the birth of his heir, Salim (Jehangir). The Jama Masjid, the Bulund Darwaza, the tombs of Salim Chisti and Islam Khan are among the more impressive structures at Fatehpur Sikri. Like Mughal *painting*, Mughal *architecture* too is a fusion of Persian and Indian features. Here the arches and domes are typically Persian, while the cupolas and masonry are Indian in *design* and execution.

It was under Shahjehan's rule that Mughal *architecture* reached the peak of perfection. Shahjehan also shifted the imperial capital from Agra to Delhi, where he built the Red Fort, the last of the great Mughal citadels. He also built the Jama Masjid in Delhi and the *Taj Mahal* in Agra, one of the Seven Wonders of the World, erected in the 17th century in memory of his favourite wife, called Mumtaz Mahal.

Mughal *painting* was introduced by Humayun who invited two Persian *painters*, Mir Sayyid Ali and Abd-us Samad to be his *court painters*. After his unfortunate death, it was left to Akbar to nurture the *art* of *painting*. One of the first works to be illustrated in what was to become the Mughal atelier was the Dastaan-i-Amir Hamza, the story of the exploits of Amir Hamza, uncle of the prophet Muhammed. The pictures, some 1400 in *folios* of 100 each, were quite large-sized for *miniature paintings*, being 56.4x71.7 cm. and painted on cotton cloth. The *style* is typically Persian, with bright mosaic-like areas of *colour* and foliate *patterns*, pale Persian complexions and costumed *figures*. Later, *paper* was employed, the *size* immediately becoming smaller and easier to handle. By the middle of Akbar's long reign, the *colours* changed to become more Indian, with Akbar employing many Indian *artists*, some of whom were Baswan, Daswanth, Nanha and Bishan Das. Works that were illustrated in Akbar's period included several *classics*, like the "Razm Namah", the Persian translation of the "MAHABHARATA", the "Babur Namah", Babur's memoirs, the *"Akbar-Namah"*, his own biography, written by Abdul Fazl.

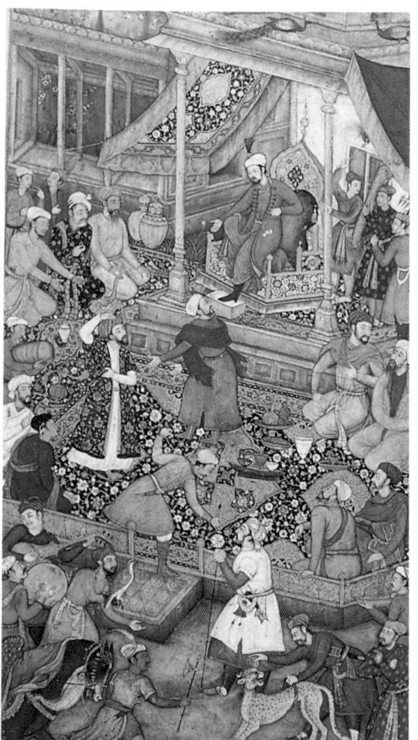

Mughal Dynasty: Anwar-e-Suhailli, AD 1596, An *illustration*.

Jehangir's favourite *paintings* were of exotic flora and fauna, with *painters* like Mansur excelling in capturing the likeness of falcons, camels and zebras. Jehangir also exhibited a fondness for state *portraits*, depicting him in an exalted *light*, as the ruler of the universe, as greater than all the other kings and emperors. The use of the *halo*, particularly the *halo* made of the sun and the crescent moon, surrounding him, became popular after he saw similar *motifs* in the Bibles that were being brought into India by Christian missionaries.

Shahjehan's miniatures were marked by an increased use of *gold* and *colour*, the lavishness of the elaborate court (Darbar) scenes being marked by the undercurrent of mysticism. Scenes of *fakirs* and *portraits* were increasingly painted with the stark profile replacing the three-quarter face. Shahjehan's taste for *architecture* was also evident in the buildings depicted in the miniatures.

As was the case with *architecture*, Aurangzeb frowned upon *painting* as well, leading to a general exodus by the *painters* towards Pahari states, thus generating a new *school of painting* there.

The identifying characteristics of *Mughal miniatures* are the use of mixed *perspective*, *figures*, buildings and trees at *eye-level*, while terraces, carpets and water bodies are seen in *aerial perspective*, the influence of *Chinese art* in the depiction of rocks, cliffs and the sky and the use of *landscape*. The early Akbari miniatures used the device of cutting off *figures* or buildings at the margins to suggest the continuation of the action. The costumes too are an indication of the period in which the miniature was painted, with the four pointed or six-pointed Jama (coat) appearing in the early Akbari *paintings*. Midway through his reign, we find the short, knee-length scalloped jama coming into vogue, the length increasing through the reign of successive emperors until the ankle-length Jama appears during the reign of Farrukhsiyar, Aurangzeb's son. The Sash too becomes longer and more elaborate from the simple tied piece of cloth of Akbari costumes to the wide and beautifully designed floral borders of Shahjehan's and Aurangzeb's time.

Mughal *drawing* is finer and more graceful than most other Indian *styles* of *painting*. The faces are oval and subtly shaded; hair is depicted with hundreds of tiny brushstrokes and the attention to minute detail results in *paintings* of timeless beauty. Refer *Miniature Painting, Flora & Fauna Paintings, Persian Art, Jali Work* and *Inlay*.

Mughal Miniatures Refer *Bengal Revivalism, Islamic Art, Landscape, Mat, Miniatures Painting, Mughal Dynasty, R. Abdul Rahim*.

Mukherjee, Asit (1933–) b. Srikshetra Puri-Dham near Pathuria Sahi-Puri. (Son of *artist* Krishna Das Mukharjee) both in the field of *visual art*–a *painter*, and performing arts actor, composer, director working with Balanga and other theatre groups at Puri and taught *craft*; Education: Dip. in *Applied Arts GCAC* Kolkata; Studio "Silparupam" at Cuttack. Solos: Cuttack, *Drawing* and *painting* entitled "Modern Graphics" at Chitra Vithi (O.T.D.C Art Gallery) and *paintings* in Utkal Charukala Parishad–Regional Art Centre Bhubaneswar. Has participated in many group shows. Workshops & Seminars: On *art* and *crafts*, *graphics art* education organized by *LKA* inside and outside Orissa. Awards: Best Pavilion Designer in Gandhi Century Celebration Fair New Delhi. Hons./Felicitations: "Uttarayani Club" Jatni Golden Jubilee, "Orissa Sahitya Akademi", "The Jiban Ranga", "The Manapaban", Silver Jubilee, "Mayadhar Mansingha Sanmana", from "The Samaya" and "Asian Age", "Prajatantra prachar Samity", 51st Visubha Sanmana–2000, "Utkala Sahitya Klala Parishad", 2002, Indian Metals Public Charitable Trust, 2004. Member: EZCC, State Art Commission 1987 to 1990, Chairman of the Commission from 2000, Orissa State Council of Culture; Founder Member: "Shilpi Samsad", "Chitram" a school of *art* & *craft* (1970) Bhubaneswar, College of Art & Craft Cuttack 1977 & Vice-Principal. Commissions: Pavilion Designer for a firm in New Delhi. Appointments: Advisor to State Govt. for Pavilion Designing for State, National & International Exhibitions, President of Shilpi Samuel Bhubaneshwar, Organized 1st Sunday Weekly Illustrated Magazine "Sambad", Vice-Principal Orissa *LKA* 1981–84 & President 1984–1991 & again 1997–2003. Publications: In journals on traditional and *contemporary art* in Orissa on *art education*; Talks & Interviews A.I.R. Cuttack, Doordarshan, T.V. Bhubaneswar, Interview on his lifestyle and experience–ETV 2002. Hobbies: Photography, Poems for children, Essays on *art* and *art*-history.

Asit Mukherjee was influenced by *folk art* right from his childhood, spent near Chitrakars Sahi, the village of traditional *sculptures* and Pata-chitrakars. After his diploma in *Applied Art*, he began working as a freelance designer of magazine and book-covers. He also painted in the *"modern" manner*; however, his forte lay in traditional and *decorative art*. He has several *pen* and *ink sketches* in the Orissan *manner* to his credit, in addition to which he also took up *graphics* to work *calligraphy* and book *illustration* in the *manner* of the illuminated Pothis (refer CHITRAKATHI). Later worked on distorted cubistically emotional *figures,* with only required *texture* and tonalities, and in favour of dismally outlined *figures*.

Mukherjee, Benode Behari (1904–1980) b. Behala, Bengal. Education: *Santiniketan*, *KB VBU* & also Prof. of *art*. Solos: National Kolkata, others in Mumbai, Mussoorie, Ahmedabad, *ISOA*; International: Tokyo. Retrospective: New Delhi. Appointments: *Curator* of Govt. Museum & Advisor to Education Dept. Nepal, Teaching Musoorie, Experience at *KB Santiniketan*, Educational Advisor Art School Patna; Worked at *Banasthali Vidyapith* RAJ. *Auctions*: Heart New Delhi, Osian's Mumbai. Collections: *NGMA*, RB, *Delhi Art Gallery*, Kumar Art Gallery & *LKA* New Delhi, *AFA* Kolkata, Hindi Bhavan & *KB Santiniketan*.

Benode Behari Mukherjee, who was taught by *Nandalal Bose*, was perhaps one of the few Bengali *artists* to stop using the sentimental *wash technique* of the *Bengal School*. Instead he experimented with a variety of *styles*, his being the *calligraphic* pictogram-like *styles* of Far Eastern *art*. *Landscape* happened to be one of his usual *themes*. Over the years, he practised a simplified language of *form* and naive *harmony* that depended on a *vocabulary* of brushstrokes and slashes of *earth colour*. He made significant contributions to the field of *printmaking*, doing several *wood* and *linocuts* between1930–50.

His memory for these *forms* stood him in good stead, as he lost his eyesight completely in 1957. He began teaching *art* history after this unfortunate event, but did not give up *painting* entirely. Rather like the ageing Henri Matisse, Benode Behari Mukherjee turned to making *paper* cuts and *drawings* and lithographs. He also executed a *mural* in 1972 consisting entirely of *figures* done in folded *paper* and made permanent in *ceramic* tiles. Naturally, he had to limit himself to the use of a few basic *colours*. The *murals* that he had executed before going completely blind can be seen in several sites in *Santiniketan*. One of the best known *murals* is at Hindi Bhavan in *Santiniketan*. The *theme* he chose to portray was the saints of medieval India. He often used the compositional devices of the Japanese screen *painter*. Though he was one of the first of the *Bengal School artists* to use *oil paint*, his *style* resembled the *tempera technique*. Parallel to the *calligraphic style*, he also worked in the expressionistic mode. His main contribution to *art* was as a teacher, first at *KB Santiniketan*, later at the short-lived "Benode Behari Mukherjee's Training Centre of Art and Craft." Refer *Decoupage, Bengal Revivalism*.

Mukherjee, Leela (1916–d.) b. Hyderabad, Sind. Education: *FA. KB Santiniketan*; Studied in *wood carving* from master craftsman Sri Kulsunder from Nepal in 1948. Solos: New Delhi, Kolkata, Mumbai. Group participations: *NGMA* & *LKA* New Delhi, *AIFACS* & served women *artists* shows. Member: *LKA* & *GAC* New Delhi. Collections: *NGMA*, *LKA* & MMB New Delhi, *AIFACS*, pvt. & public.

Materials used and learnt were *wood carving*, *casting* in *bronze*, *etching,* printing in *graphics*, while *painting* and *drawing sculptures* have a strong feeling of traditional *relief carving*, albeit with a touch of *modern primitivism*. Studied under *Nandalal Bose*, but *Ramkinkar Baij* who was her teacher also seemed to have exerted a strong influence on her. Her *wood carving* "family" has a folk-iconic feeling about it, not only in the *style* of *carving* with the strokes of the *chisel* left untouched, but also in its archetypal simplicity. Leela Mukherjee had worked with *painting* and *printmaking* and executed two large *murals* in tiles and *tempera* in Dehradun, where she had established an *art* dept.

Mukherjee, Meera (1923–1998) b. Kolkata. Education: Dip. *ISOAS*, *College of Art* New Delhi; Certificate Munich Academy Germany. Solos: Kolkata, New Delhi, Hyderabad, Mumbai. Group participations: *AFA* Kolkata, *Triennales* New Delhi; International: *Biennale* Antwerp, Japan & Germany. *Auctions*: Heart Mumbai & New Delhi, Osian's Mumbai. Awards: Padma Shri, President's Award of Master Craftsman, Abanindranath Award WB Govt.; International: German Scholarship, Commonwealth Institute London & Japan. Fellowship: Research Fellowship from Anthropological Survey of India. Publications: "Metal Craftsmen in India", "Folk Metal Artisans", "Brass workers", "Gods & Goddesses" & "Brassware in Bastar", "Gharuas of Bastar", "Gharua & their craft" in "Man in India", "Is Art Incomprehensive?" Anand Bazaar Patrika & Children's Book. Collections: Hermann Abstract Museum Frankfurt.

Meera Mukherjee initially studied *painting* (Kalipada Ghoshal) at the *ISOAS* but switched to *sculpture* at the Delhi Polytechnic. Later spent two years in Chennai and studied under Vysamsthapathi and Srinivas Achari. Her European sojourn with its diverse *art forms*, both ancient and *modern*, opened her eyes to the suitability of one's own *culture* as a personal *idiom*. It was then that she lived with the tribals in MP, in Bastar (Bihar) and *Dhokra* (WB) where she learnt the lost *wax casting technique*. With her studies of *bronze casting* in Chennai, she developed her own *technique* which is an amalgam of the folk, South Indian and the Western method. The *wax* moulding and *metal casting technique* has been elaborated to create intricate *forms*, webbed with loops of *wax* snaking around the main *figures*, creating interesting accents of *pattern*. She translated the minuscule scale of the *Dhokra* lost *wax* method to gigantic *figures* of women working. Her close contact with the rural world crystallized in her *sculptures* as women repairing fishing nets, stitching and embroidering, grading wheat and generally toiling away. Her *imagery* also includes objects from myth and folklore. Refer *Lost Wax Process, Cire Perdu, Casting.*

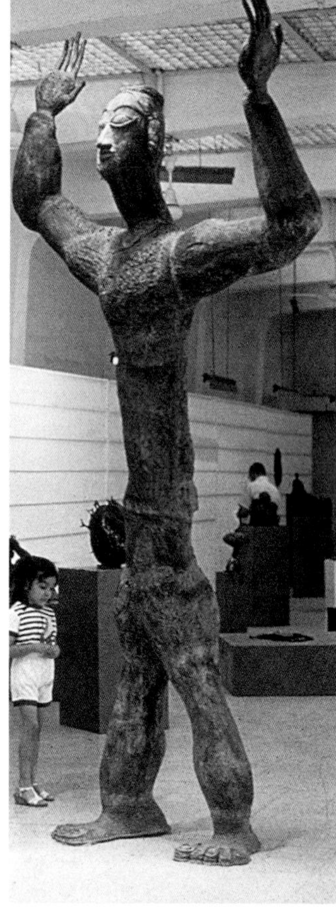

Mukherjee, Meera: "Figure".

Mukherjee, Milon (1939–) b. Kolkata. Education: Dip. in *FA*. *GCAC* Kolkata. Solos: *AFA* Kolkata, Alliance Francaise Bangalore, TAG, *JAG*, BAG; International: Dubai, Gallery Transposition Paris. Group participations: *AFA* Kolkata, Indian Oil Exhibition, World Wildlife Fund group show Mumbai, *BAS*. *Art* camp: Kashmir. Member: Life member *BAS*, *Artists' Centre* Mumbai. Commissions: *Murals* Kolkata, Mumbai. Publications: Written short stories in Bengali & translated selected ones into other Indian Languages & Russian. Collections: corporates & pvt.

Milon Mukherjee works with a wide range of *figurative vocabulary*, using an expressionist brushstroke to animate his colourful *canvases*. *Line*, *colour* and *texture form* the basic *palette* from which he carves out his stylized and lively men and animals, in a world full of angst and chaos.

He lives and works in Mumbai.

Mukherjee, Mrinalini (1949–) b. Mumbai. Daughter of *Benode Behari Mukherjee* & *Leela Mukherjee*. Education: B.A. in *FA*. *painting* & Post-Dip. in *mural design MSU*. Solos: RB & British Council New Delhi, *SG* Mumbai, SRAG, TKS, *PUAG*; International: Oxford, Yorkshire Sculpture Park, West Bretton, London, Netherlands. Group participations: National *LKA*, *Triennales* & *NGMA* New Delhi, *Print* Exhibition Chandigarh, Timeless Art Festival Mumbai, *AIFACS*, *Roopankar BB*; International: *Biennales* Paris, Cuba & Australia, Festival in Russia & Bangladesh. Symposiums/workshops & camps: With Dutch *Artist* New Delhi, Seminar Shimla; International: Oxford, Netherlands. *Auctions*: Timeless Art Sotheby's Mumbai. Awards: British Council Scholarship *Sculpture* UK. Member: Advisory member *Roopankar BB*, First *Biennale* & *NGMA* New Delhi. Commissions: Works at various hotels & institutions National & International. Publications: In *LKA* Roop-Lekha New Delhi; International: Museum of Modern Art Oxford, "London Magazine", "Women's Art Magazine" & "Audio Art Magazine" London. Collections: *NGMA* & *LKA* New Delhi, PUJ Museum Chandigarh, *Roopankar*; International: pvt. & public in Lisbon, Sara Hindon Museum Finland, Gandhi Memorial Institute Mauritius.

Mrinalini Mukherjee started working with natural fibres right from her days at *MSU*. In the beginning, there was a strong bias towards *craft* and the traditional role of woman as homemaker in the choice of *imagery* and material. The macrame-like knotting and *weaving* revealed artisanal *forms* like hanging baskets, and lamp shades. Over 25 years later, Mrinalini Mukherjee has evolved a repertoire of universal *images* based on a variety of influences, including traditional Indian *art*, primitive *art*, organic plant and animal *forms* and *folk art*. The *sculptures* are dauntingly colossal, with the heavy textural intensity being muted by the subdued dyes of the knotted hemp. Some are suspended from the ceiling, others grow out of the floor, all of them are paradoxically rigid in opposition to the soft layered feel of ordinary textile *art*. The *sculpture* "Woman on Peacock" at once evokes memories of Hindu *iconology*, first, in the use of the animistic VAHANA (vehicle) and secondly in the almost direct reference to goddess SARASVATI in the choice of the peacock as VAHANA.

Most recently she has turned to *ceramics*. Her latest *sculptures*, though showing a similarity of *form*, yet are more *abstract*, the different *medium* achieving vibrant *textures*. Refer *Handling*, *Weaving*.

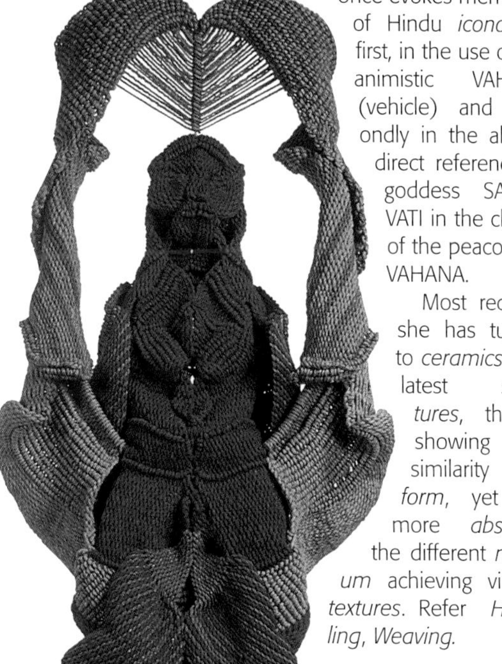

Mukherjee, Mrinalini: "Vanshri", Hemp, 1994, 250x130x90 cm.

Mukherjee, Satyasewak (1933–) b. Varanasi. Education: Dip. ICA&D Kolkata, Post-Grad. in *art* appreciation Calcutta University. Solos: New Delhi, Mumbai, Chennai, Allahabad. Group participations: Kolkata, Allahabad, Lucknow, Varanasi, Hyderabad, *LKA* Exhibitions, UP. Awards: Gold Medal–*AFA* Kolkata & National Academy of Fine Arts & Crafts UP *LKA*, National Award for *graphic* New Delhi. Member: Founder member *SCA* & Prayag Kala Samity Allahabad, Member of Judging & Purchasing Committee of *LKA* UP State. Collections: *NGMA* New Delhi, UP *LKA*, Allahabad Museum, *Ashutosh Museum of Indian Art* Kolkata, *BKB* BHU, pvt. & corporates.

Satyasewak Mukherjee can be termed a romantic realist, with his charming and direct interpretations of *nature* and the role of the human being within it. There is no esoteric *symbolism* involved in these studies of crumbling interiors, forts, *Ghats* and rural settlements. Neither is the study of the village woman with the bright red Sindoor (red powder symbolizing the married women) in the parting of her hair, meant to convey any other message–she is simply a woman caught in her own environment. His *colours* too convey the rich bounty of *nature*.

After a brief stint as lecturer in the Indian Art College in Kolkata, he was settled in New Delhi where he was Art Dir. at "The Hindustan Times"; now in Mumbai.

Mukuta=Headgear, *Crown*. Refers to the elaborate headgear were by *gods*, goddesses and heroes. Jata Mukuta sometimes worn by BRAHMA and RUDRA are made up of twists of matted hair done up in the *form* of a high *crown*, with a crescent moon on the left side in the case of SHIVA, along with a coiled hooded snake. Kirita Mukuta a conical *crown* with a central pointed knob, it is covered with jewelled discs and bands, usually worn by VISHNU Narayana and emperors. Karanda Mukuta a *crown* made in the shape of a Karanda or bowl-shaped vessel used for subordinate *gods* and most goddesses and kings of smaller kingdoms. Kuntala, not headgear but a mode of dressing the hair, usually employed for the goddess LAKSHMI and queens of emperors. These are reflected in *decorative art* and *architecture* as well as *miniature paintings* in India. Refer ABHUSHANA, DURGA, KRISHNA, NATARAJA, SURYA.

Mukuta: "Jata Mukuta".

Mullan, Roshan M. (1943–) b. Mumbai. Education: GDA *JJIAA*, *Clay modelling JJSA* (evening class), *Ceramics* Sophia Polytechnic Mumbai. Solos: *JAG*. Assisted Nelly Sethna with her *exhibitions*. Publications: Books & research into various textile *forms*, including *Kalamkari*, *weaving* & *embroidery*. Commissions: *Illustrations* for Nelly Sethna's books "Shal" & "*Kalamkari*".

Roshan M. Mullan practised being a freelance textile designer since her student days at *JJIAA*. Her meeting with Nelly Sethna was decisive in turning her into a fulltime textile *artist*. She learnt *weaving*, macrame and drawn threadwork as well,

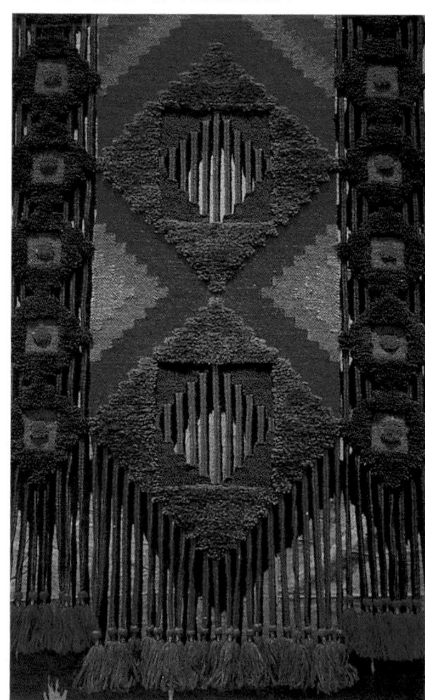

Mullan, Roshan M.: "Wall Hanging", Textile, ht. 160x90 cm.

designing wall-hangings, floor coverings, tapestries, upholstery, *drapery* room dividers with macrame or any type of *embroidery* or printed fabric. Her *style* is *eclectic* being suited to the technicalities of the particular *medium*.

She lives and works in Mumbai. Refer *Embroidery* and *Weaving*.

Mullick, Ashoke (1957–) b. Kolkata. Education: Dip. in *FA*. *GCAC* Kolkata. Solos: *AFA* & Park Hotel Kolkata, The Gallery Chennai, Display Gallery New Delhi, *G88*, *PUAG*, *JAG*, *CRAR*, *ATG*. Group participations: RB & Om Gallery New Delhi, *GC*, *BAAC* & Sanskriti Kolkata, *ATG*, *JAG*, *G88*, GAG, *SAI*, *Biennale BB*; International: Sweden, Germany, France. *Art* workshops & camps: *Painting* MMB Kolkata, HAS. Awards: Govt. of India Cultural Scholarship. Collections: *NGMA* New Delhi, Sanskriti Kolkata, *Roopankar BB*, *SAI*, *PUAG*; International: Glenbarra Art Museum Japan.

Ashoke Mullick carefully constructs his *imagery* juxtaposing the real with the imaginary, choosing objects carefully with a view to unsettling the viewer by its seeming correspondence to real life situations. His placement of the *nude* with draped *figures* and the animal or the bird with unprepossessing looking women has an element of the surreal, while his choice of *hue* refers to the darker side of humanity.

He works as a fulltime *painter* in Kolkata.

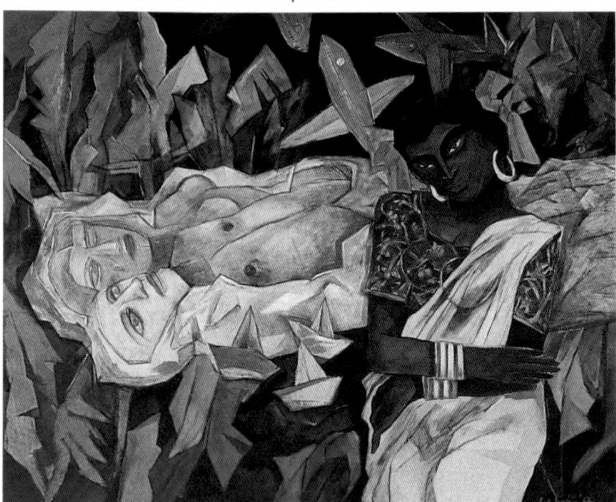

Mullick, Ashoke: "Floating Figures", *Oil* on *Canvas*, 120x150 cm.

Multi Block Colour Printing In 1930 Biswarup Bose learnt multicolour *block printing technique* in Japan and on his return he reproduced Indian *themes* under the guidance of *Nandalal Bose*. *Nandalal Bose* himself visited Japan in 1924 to master the same *technique*. This involved the use of several blocks, each *block printing* one *colour*. The *key plate*, with the *black* outlined *image* helps in the registration of each subsequent *plate* or block. A slight misplacement of any one of the *plates*, result in the *overlapping* of *colours* and thus gives an erroneous *print*. *Contemporary* printmakers sometimes exploit this. Multi block colour printing is still the method used to *print colour reproductions* in magazines and is usually referred to as the *colour printing & four colour process*. Refer *Artist's Proof, Copy, Single Block Colour Printing, Wood Cut, Wood Cut Printing, Krishan Ahuja, Dipak Banerjee, Nandalal Bose, Naina Dalal, Rani Dhumal, Somnath Hore, Paul A. Koli, Ajit Patel, Krishna N. Reddy, Anupam Sud, Gaganendranath Tagore*; Illustrations—*Sudhir R. Khastgir, Jyoti Bhatt.*

Multiple Tool A tool used in *relief printmaking*, it has two cutting edges on the head so as to make parallel incisions on the *plate*, which is also used for *Wood Cut, Wood Cut Printing* and *Linocut*. Refer *Lino, Photo-engraving, Printing, Nandalal Bose, Mukul Chandra Dey.*

Munshi, Selim (1938–) b. India. Dip. in *FA*. *KB VBU* & College of Arts and Crafts Kolkata. Solos: *Santiniketan*, Kolkata, Patna, Lucknow. Group participations: National Level Exhibitions.

Selim Munshi has worked with diverse *mediums* and in various *styles*, a fact which is clearly discernible in his *paintings* and *sculptures*. His *landscapes* are painted in the *manner* of the impressionists, with sketchy sweeps of the *palette knife*, while his *portraits* are *realistic*, with judiciously placed *highlights*. Eternal rest, a *sculpture* in *cement concrete*, shows his tentative foray into abstraction.

He lives and works in *Santiniketan*.

Munshi, Veer (1958–) b. Kashmir, India. Education: Dip. in *FA*. *painting MSU*. Solos: Vadodara, *Tao Art Gallery* Mumbai, *Art Heritage* New Delhi, *JAG*, *AIFACS*; International: United Nations Geneva, E-C-Galleria Edinburgh. Group participations: J&K, National *LKA*, ISCC, International Art Centre New Delhi, *BAAC* Kolkata, PUJ Academy of Culture Chandigarh, *VAG*, *AIFACS*, *Dhoomimal*, *Biennale BB*; International: United Nation Geneva, India–Australian Culture Perth Australia. *Art* camps: *GAC artist* camps *LKA* New Delhi. Awards: Prize for best tableau J&K Republic Day 1997. Fellowships: Research Grant Fellowship *LKA*, Junior Fellowship from Ministry of Culture, Govt. of India & Dept. of Culture New Delhi.

Veer Munshi is a *figurative painter*, *painting Social Realism*, especially of senseless violence and the viciousness of war. His works have been influenced by the situa-

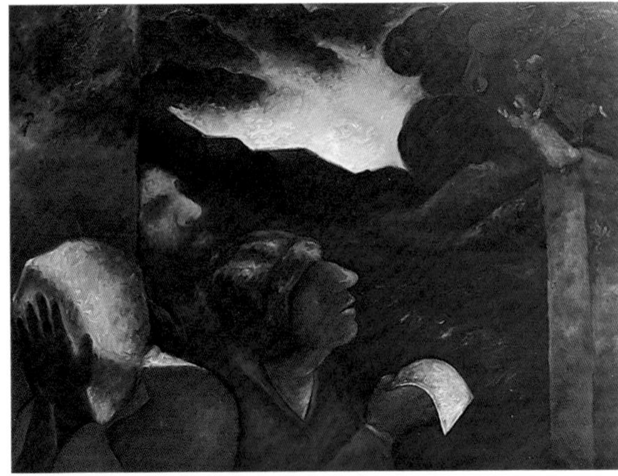

Munshi, Veer: "The Temparal Distress", *Oil* on *Canvas*, 91.5x91.25 cm.

tions in his homeland–Kashmir. His near *realistic* approach is heightened by his *symbolic* use of *colour*, with reds standing for violence and, dark blue for death, equating people with symbols of pain helplessness, terror and evil. That most of the works are meant to be taken as personal statements is brought home to the viewer by his use of the *self portrait*, making himself one of the main protagonists.

He lives and works in New Delhi.

Munuswamy, L. (1927–) b. Chennai, TN. Education: Dip. in *painting GCAC* Chennai; *Graphic design* Bournemouth England; Studied under *K.C.S. Paniker* & *Subrayalu Dhanapal*. Solos & group participations: Chennai, National Exhibitions *LKA Triennale* & *Biennale*. *Art* camps: All India Painters Camp Thrissur, Southern Region Artists Camp Thanjavur; Workshop & seminar: *BB*. Awards: Govt. of India Cultural Scholarship for research in *painting*, Colombo Plan Scholarship for study in England, National *LKA* Award, TN *LKA* Award. Collections: *NGMA* New Delhi, National Art Gallery Chennai, Tamil University Thanjavur, *BB*.

L. Munuswamy belonged to a family of artisans, that traditionally made *icons* and intricate jewellery. Therefore, he already was a trained *artist* when he joined the school of *art* where he was taught *portrait painting* in the Academic British Manner and *compositions* in the *Bengal School style* (due to the influence of the principal, *Debi Prasad RoyChowdhary*). He was also exposed to the influence of *Subrayalu Dhanapal* and *K.C.S. Paniker*. He began his academic career by favouring the *style* of the impressionists. In the 60s he turned to the human *figure*, experimenting with the idea of real as well as illusionistic, by creating a composite structure into which the *model* was placed in *terms* of *balance* and *harmony*. These works were in *oils*, while his early works were mostly in *tempera* and *watercolour*.

With the death of his wife in the mid-70s, he switched his *theme* to "Women and Mother", *painting* in *oils* and for a brief period, making *sculptures* as well in the shape of flowers and foliage. Since then, he has continued to paint women, incorporating them into near *abstract* expressionist *landscapes*, with stark, jagged *lines* fading out at the edges. In fact the *line* has been a constant feature of his works right from his earliest *compositions* and *figure* studies.

L. Munuswamy who has been the principal of the *GCAC* Chennai, continues to live and paint there.

Mural A mural is a synonym for *wall painting*, as against *miniature painting* or easel *painting*. It is directly painted on the wall, or is attached in such a *manner* so as to make removal difficult, if not impossible. It is the oldest *form* of *painting*, appearing in *prehistoric times* in the *form* of cave *paintings* of animals and hunting *rituals*. Mural *painting* or decoration as it can be more appropriately termed, can be executed with a wide variety of *media* and *techniques*. From the simple *fresco painting* of the cave man to the most sophisticated use of *metal* and *mosaic*, mural decoration is one of the most popular methods of architectural embellishment. The Romans, the Greeks and the Mesopotamians used *mosaic* decoration to great advantage, while the Christians kept their religion alive in the early days by *painting* symbols on the walls of their catacombs. The Byzantine churches had awesome *mosaics*, executed in part with *gold leaf*, to add to the overall grandeur, while murals on the ceiling of Sistine Chapel are easily known all over the world. In India, the *Ajanta frescoes* are the earliest surviving examples of mural *painting*, having been executed in the *Gupta* era. Other famous murals were executed mainly on temples and palaces. The Brihadiswara temple of CHOLA period in Thanjavur TN, Vardhamana temple in Kanchipuram depicting *Jain* murals, the Mattancheri palace in Cochin and Shekhawati murals of Rajasthan are the most famous of all. Mural making in the *contemporary* era are an altogether different phenomenon, with religion no longer being the predominant subject. In India, there are the murals of *Satish Gujral*, at first being in the social commentary class of the Mexican muralists, Orozco and Siqueros. Later he experimented with different *media*, including *ceramics*, *mosaic* and *wood* in his quest for architectural pattern-making. Sheet *metal*, especially the rich gleam of *copper*, is also a popular *medium* with muralists, though *aluminium*, *fibreglass*, different types of *cement*, both coloured and sandblasted are also used. Murals can be used to enhance the character of a building as does Howard Hodgkin's *black* and *white* tree in *granite* and *marble* for Charles Correa's *design* for the British Council Library in New Delhi, or it may merely serve as an accent as *Prafulla Dahanukar's* mural does for a residential building in Mumbai. Refer APSARA, GANDHARVAS, BHITTI-CHITRA, *Chitrala Art Gallery, Contour Shading, Deccani Miniature Painting, Electroplating, Flat Application, Hinduism,* LAKSHMI, *Miniature Painting, Model, Oeuvre, Warli Paintings, Wood, Jaganath M. Ahivasi, K.C. Aryan, Nandalal Bose, Suhas Bahulkar, Sujata Bajaj, Jyoti Bhatt, Vidya Bhushan, Shanti Dave, Kavita Deuskar, M.J. Enas, Ganga Devi, Satish Gujral, Asit K. Haldar, K.K. Hebbar, Balvant A. Joshi, Surendra Pal Joshi, Amina Ahmed Kar, Narula P. Kaur, Subodh Kerkar, Bishamber Khanna, Pilton Kothawalla, K.S. Kulkarni, Shanu Lahiri, Chandrakant N. Mhatre, Benode Behari Mukherjee, Leela Mukherjee, P.S. Nandhan, P. Vijyalakshmi., Raju A. Paidi, Naren Panchal, S.L. Parasher, Jayant Parikh, Vinod R. Parul, Sunil Kumar Paul, M.K. Puri, A. Ramachandran, Kashinath Salve, Shantilal M. Shah, Sumant V. Shah, Amrita Sher-Gil, Bal Wad;* Illustrations–*Mosaic, Sukhen Ganguly, C.N. Karunakarn; Tyeb Mehta.*

Murti An *icon, idol* of a *god* or goddess meant primarily as an object of worship and placed in the Garbhagriha (sanctum sanctorum) of a temple or in the shrine in houses. A Murti has to conform to certain iconographical rules–a slight deviation in *proportion* or in the depiction of *attributes* will result in ill-luck to both *sculptor* and the owner. Kerala and Bengal are the very well known centres for traditional *images* created in *stone, metal, terracotta, wood, ivory.* The KRISHNA Murti, as a blue-coloured Balakrishna (young) with peacock feather crown, Pitambara Vastra (dressed in yellow shining dress) and playing the flute is one of the more popular Murtis.

Nilkanth P. Khanvilkar was a traditional *sculptor* working with *stone, clay, bronze* and *marble.* He created Murties of

GANESHA for the festival. Refer *Architecture, Temple Architecture, Elephanta, Ellora, Dravidian Style,* SHIKHARA, *Ganpatrao K. Mhatre*.

Murukeson, K.C. (1944–) b. Madurai, TN. Education: Post-Dip. in *painting GCAC* Chennai. Solos: MMB, Bangalore, Govt. Museum Madurai, Vinyasa Art Gallery Chennai, *SAI, CKP, JAG, CRAR.* Group participations: *LKA* Exhibitions New Delhi, TN *LKA*, Rashtriya Kala Mela Chennai, *AIFACS* , HAS, *JAG*. *Art* camps: Chennai, Okenakkal TN, Pondicherry, Thanjavur & Goa. Awards: South Indian Society of Painters & TN *LKA*, Association of Young Painters & Sculptors Chennai, *BAAC* Kolkata, *CKP.* Collections: *LKA* New Delhi, *AFA* Kolkata,TN *LKA*, Govt. Museum Chennai, TATA Jamshedpur, *BAAC* Kolkata, HAS, *CKP,* pvt. & corporates.

K.C. Murukeson began his career as a *figurative painter*, working in the expressionistic *manner* of *Maqbool Fida Husain*. Later he shifted to *painting landscapes*, being inspired by the rocky terrain of his native Kallindiri district. However, later subject has taken a backseat to *technique* in his works. His *handling* of paint and *texture* are woven into the *landscape* format of his *painting*, with both *colour* and *composition* playing an important role. The shattered and fly-away *forms* of the early 90s gave way to a neutral *palette* with painstaking *cross-hatches* of near non-*colour*. His recent works are an amalgamatiom of both geometric and organic abstraction. Small triangles and squares of *warm* and *cool colours* are sporadinglly intersperced with tree like *motifs*.

He lives and works in Madurai TN. Refer *Abstraction Organic.*

Museum of Contemporary Art (Chennai) Established in 1996, the *museum* is located inside the 19th-century Indo-Gothic building of the *GCAC* Chennai, popularly known as the *Madras School of Art.* It houses a valuable collection of Indian miniatures, Japanese *wood cuts*, *South Indian bronzes*, carpets, *ivory carvings* as well as *prints, drawings, paintings* and *sculptures* of prominent *artists* of the *Madras School of Art.* Most of the ancient items on display were collected by its founder Sir Alexander Hunter. Refer *GCAC* Chennai–TN.

Museums A building complex where specimens and objects of historical, sociological, cultural and scientific interest are displayed in an orderly *manner*. Refer *National Museum, NGMA* & *National Handicrafts and Handlooms Museum* New Delhi, *Indian Museum* & *Victoria Memorial Museum* Kolkata, *Maharaja Fatesingh Museum* Vadodara, *CSMVS* (*PWM*), *CTAG*, *BB*, *SJM*, THAG (Refer *Thanjavur [Tanjore] Paintings*) TN, *BKB* Varanasi. Refer *GCAC* Chennai.

Muthusamy, M.K. (1932–) b. Salem, TN. Education: Dip. in *FA*. *GCAC* Chennai, Teacher's training Saidapet Chennai. Solos: TN *LKA* Chennai. Two person show: *SAI*. Group participations: National *LKA* & TN; South Indian Association, *GCAC*, Progressive Painters Association & Soviet Cultural Centre Chennai, *SAI*; Participated in all major *art exhibitions* in various states, Kala Mela New Delhi, Mumbai & Chennai. *Art* camps: Padappi, TN *LKA* Manipal & Kodaikanal. Awards: Progressive Painters Association Chennai, Mysore DAE, TN *LKA*, TN Govt. Kalaichemmal Award, Pondicherry University Award. Appointments: Lecturer & HoD *GCAC* Chennai & Secretary from 1980 to 1990. Collections: *LKA* & *NGMA* New Delhi, TN *LKA*, CAG Museum Chennai, *SAI*.

M.K. Muthusamy uses *collage* in his *mixed media compositions* of Indian peasant life and dancers. He uses newspaper, a symbol of present day's ephemeral *culture*, carefully replicating the fold of the garment here and curve of a necklace there.

There is a touch of humour in his use of appointments columns, book reviews and other newspaper articles to cover *key* areas in his *compositions*. He also incorporates *calligraphy* into the works. However, in spite of this Western *technique*, his *figures* are essentially Indian, recalling traditional Indian *sculpture* as well as the works of the Progressive Group of Painters.

He lives and works in Chennai.

Mythology (Greek) mythos= tale, history, communication. Mythology is the study of myths, i.e. stories from every corner of the world, which need not be historically or scientifically accurate, but nevertheless offers a fascinating insight into the *culture* of various people. Every civilization has its own myths, about its *creation*, its religious beliefs, about life itself. From the Greek myths about Olympus and *gods* and heroes that populate it, to the Indian belief in their *pan theon* of *Gods*, the Ocean of Milk, Mount KAILASA, the RAMAYANA and so on, myths serve the purpose of glorifying a particular *culture* that gave birth to it. The study of mythology is interesting for various reasons: *iconology* and *iconography*, which is useful in the identification of religious works of *art*, *forms* part of it. Refer ASURA, *Bengal Oil Painting,* CHANDRA, *CYAG*, *Demons*, HANSA, HAMSA, *Heroic, History Painting, Ideal,* LOKA, NAGA, *pantheon*, *Swadeshi Movement, Transition*, *Tree of Life, Ramananda Bandyopadhyay*, *Amol Chakladar, Adi M. Davierwala, Satish Gujral, Gulam Mohammed Sheikh, Maqbool Fida Husain, H.R. Kambli, Pilton Kothawalla, Shanu Lahiri, Nalini Malani, Nita Thakore, Setlur Gopal Vasudev;* Illustrations–BHARATA, *Erotic Art,* GANGA, APSARA, *Badri Narayan, Manjit Bawa, Asit K. Haldar,* RAMAYANA.

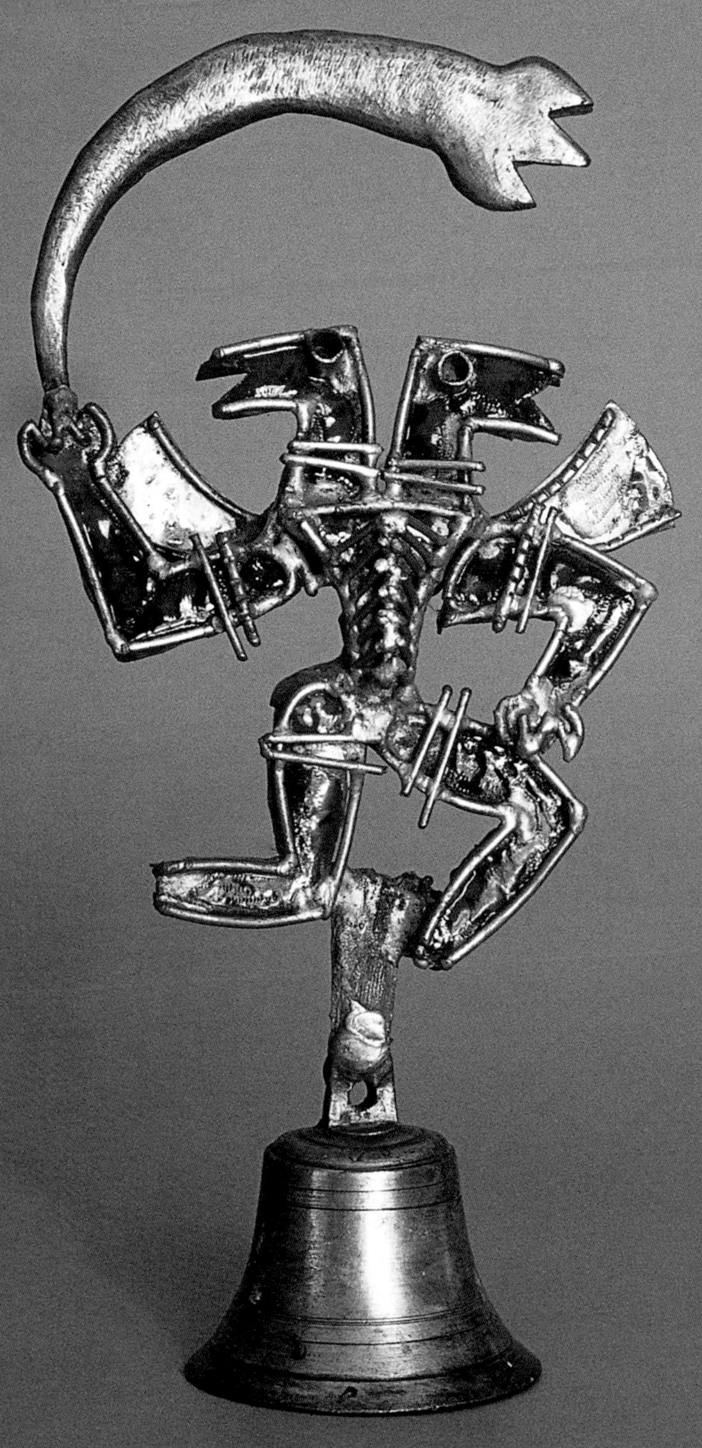

Nandagopal, Shankar: "Dancing Bird", *Copper, brass & enamels*, 1993, 60x30x15 cm. (See notes on page 244)

Nag Foundation (Pune). The Nag Foundation was established in 1989 as a trust formed by K.K. Nag Ltd. to promote *visual arts* in Pune by assisting local *artists* and arranging *art exhibitions*, seminars, workshops, camps, lectures, demonstrations and performances. It has conducted some of these in collaboration with *LKA* & *NGMA* New Delhi, *INTACH* Lucknow and *BAS*. *Avinash S. Deo*, *K.V. Haridasan*, *Murlidhar Nangare*, *N. Chandrasekhar Rao P. Gauri Shankar*, *G.S. Shenoy* and *Yusuf* are some of the *artists* who have exhibited here.

Naga=snake. In Indian *mythology*, refers to the snake or snake-spirit usually depicted as a denizen of the lower world the Hell or Patala. They are represented with a human face and the tail of a serpent. The Nagas are descendents of Kadru, wife of Kasyapa and can be very beautiful, like Ulupi associated with Arjuna, (MAHABHARATA) the Pandava hero. Also a tribe still living in North East India. Refer *Elephanta*, *Mythology*; Illustration—*K.K. Hebbar*.

Nagara=town. The 2nd major *tradition* of Northern India, mainly in the Madhyadesa: Madhya=middle; Desa=country. The region between Varanasi and the Aravallis, and foot of the Himalayas and Narmada. Refer *Nagara Style* and DRAVIDA.

Nagara Style This is the North Indian *style* of temple- building, though a few isolated examples can be found in the South as well. The identifying features of the *Nagara* temple are its curvilinear SHIKHARA crowned with a huge Amalaka (ribbed *stone* disc), the projections which rise vertically all around the temple walls, the square interior of the Garbhagriha (the sanctum sactorum) and the linear placement of its rooms, with the Bhog Mandir (offering hall) leading into the Nat Mandir (Dance Hall), which in turn led into the Jagamohana (assembly hall) and Garbhagriha. Within the Nagara style itself, there are variations as seen in the temples in Orissa and those seen in Central India. The Orissan SHIKHARA is a single one, with simple vertical projections running down the exterior, right down to the platform of the temple. It also has passages between the various rooms. In the Central Indian type, one finds that each of the various projections end in a SHIKHARA and Amalaka that is attached to the main one, and the passages are done away with, leading to rather squashed appearance on the exterior. Some of the latter type also have an interior passage running around the Garbhagriha, enabling one to make a Pradakshina (circumambulation) around it. This led to the introduction of windows/balconies on the exterior walls for the purpose of letting in *light* as also beautiful *stone sculpture* to enliven the appearance.

The temple elevation is also compared to the human body, with the Pabhaga (base) of the temple compared to the foot, the walls to the legs, the entablature to the groin *line*, the lower half of the SHIKHARA, the Gandi to the *torso*, the Beki to the neck, the Amalaka (ribbed element) to the Mastaka (head) and the Kapuri to the skull. Above this was placed the Kalasa symbolizing the pot of holy nectar, in direct *line* with the *icon* placed centrally in the Garbhagriha below. This Kalasa was placed only after the temple was consecrated. Above the Kalasa came the AYUDHA or identifying *attribute* of the deity housed within, i.e. a CHAKRA for VISHNU and a TRISHUL for SHIVA.

These temples though simple in the beginning, became more elaborately decorated over the centuries, the projections on the exterior increasing from a simple Triratha (a single projection with three RATHA) in the VISHNU temple at Deogarh, to Pancharatha, Saptaratha and Navaratha (either five or seven or nine RATHA respectively in projections) each with a sculptural *form* attached to the many corner niches that were formed. The Konark temple, the Rajarani temple and the Lingaraja temple are fine examples of Orissan Nagara style *architecture*, while the *Khajuraho* temples are the most outstanding examples of the Central Indian *style*. Refer *Dravidian Style*, MANDAPA, *Vesara Style*.

Nagari Das The pseudonym of Raja Sawant Singh of *Kishangarh* who fell in love with Bani Thani, the slave girl, his stepmother's maid, who was the inspiration for the feminine *ideal* in *Kishangarh painting*. Refer *Jain Miniature*, *Jain Manuscript Illumination*.

Nagdas, V. (1957–) b. Palghat, Kerala. Education: Dip. in *painting* Govt. College of FA. Thiruvananthapuram, Dip. in *graphic art KB Santiniketan*. Solos: Museum Auditorium Thiruvananthapuram, Nandan Gallery *Santiniketan*, *LKA* Cochin, *Art Heritage* New Delhi, *CYAG*, *JAG*, Group participations: National *LKA* & RB in *painting* & *graphics* New Delhi, *AFA* & *BAAC* Kolkata, SZCC Nagpur, *LKA* Lucknow, Chennai & Jaipur, *AIFACS*, SKP, *CYAG*, *JAG CKP Biennale BB*; International: Festival of India USA, *Biennale* Ankara Turkey. *Art* camps & workshops: For *graphic* under *Krishna N. Reddy*. Prof. Paul Linegran of USA at *VBU* & *LKA* Regional Centre Chennai; Executed Italian *fresco* at Belaghata Gandhibhavan Kolkata under *Sukhen Ganguly*. Awards: Kerala *LKA* Award, SZCC Nagpur, *CKP*, *AIFACS*. Fellowships: Cultural Scholarship HRD Ministry for practical research *KB Santiniketan*, Senior Fellowship HRD Ministry Dept. of Culture New Delhi. Collections: *NGMA* & *LKA* New Delhi, SZCC Nagpur, *BB*.

Bold, disproportionate bodies, fragmented and scattered across the *canvas*, agonized faces screaming in agony—these *form* the main leitmotifs in V. Nagdas's *paintings* and *prints*. His stated belief in humanity is not as apparent as the utter disregard by the world for human life and values. The *artist* appears in most of the works, perhaps sharing the terrible agony of the damned.

He lives and works in Kerala.

Nagdev, Sachida (1940–) b. Ujjain, MP. Education: GDA *JJSA*, M.A. (Ancient Indian History of Culture) & M.A. in *painting* Vikram University Ujjain. Solos: Kala Parishad Gallery Bhopal, School of Art Indore, *Dhoomimal*, *AIFACS*, *PUAG*, TAG, *JAG*, SAG, *SAI*; International: Osaka Japan, Dubai UAE, Germany, France. Group participations: National Exhibition & *Triennale* New Delhi, *SAI* National Exhibition Chennai & Mumbai, *BAAC* Kolkata, *Roopankar BB Biennale*,

AIFACS; International: Czechoslovakia, Tokyo. Participated: Several National level *artists* camps. Awards: All India Exhibition Indore Silver Plaque, MP State Award, State Award Bhopal; International: Osaka *Triennale* Japan. Fellowships: *Amrita Sher-Gil* MP for Creative *art* Govt. of India. Member: *LKA* New Delhi, *Roopankar BB*. Collections: *NGMA* & *LKA* New Delhi, *Roopankar BB*, *Dhoomimal*, *CTAG*, *PUAG*, *SAI*; International: Contemporary Art Museum Osaka Japan.

Sachida Nagdev's childhood experience of signboard *painting* led him to practising *figuration* for quite sometime. His *style* developed on the *lines* of the Bengal *painters*, with *wash painting*, delicate linear works and spontaneous tempera-like works in poster *colours* all being attempted. Slowly his later exposure to *Prehistoric* rock *painting* (he had assisted Dr. V.S. Wakankar in recording these *paintings*) influenced him and he has lately turned to abstraction. These works are full of *colour* and expressionistic *texture*, with cryptic signs and *outlines* delineating bird and human *form*.

He lives and works in Bhopal MP. Refer *Gouache*.

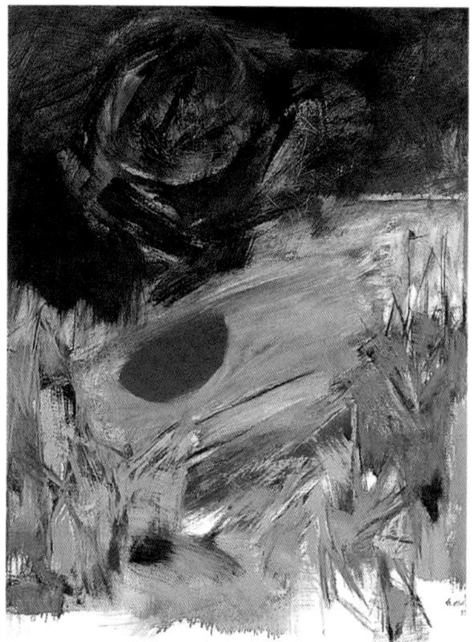

Nagdev, Sachida: "Untitled', *Oil* on *Canvas*, 1997, 102x76 cm.

Naidu, Reddeppa M. (1932–1999) b. Kapulapalem, AP. Education: Dip. in *painting GCAC* Chennai, Govt. of India Cultural Scholarship in *painting*. Over 12 solos: Hyderabad, "Deity Series" Bangalore, "Mahabharata" Gallery Ashoka New Delhi, "Paintings, Drawing & Meta Relief Sculptures" & *Apparao Galleries* Chennai, *Dhoomimal*, SAG, *NCAG*; Retrospective: The Gallery Chennai. Group participations: National Exhibition *LKA*, *Triennales* & RB New Delhi, *AFA* Kolkata, Chennai by Values Art Foundation, *Biennale BB*, *JAG*; International: *Biennales* Sao Paulo & Paris, Contemporary Indian Art London & Europe. *Art* camps: Thanjavur (Tanjore). *Auctions*: Heart Mumbai & New Delhi, Osian's Mumbai. Awards: National *LKA* Awards, *AFA* Kolkata, States AP, TN & Kerala, HAS, *BAS*; Hons.: Elected Fellow TN, *AIFACS* Award–Veteran Artists of India; Doctorate from Sri Venkateshwara University Tirupati AP 1997. Appointments: Joined *WSC* for the tradition of Karpuri sari & Retired as Deputy Dir. after 27 years. Collections: *NGMA* & *LKA* New Delhi, SZCC Thanjavur, *LKA* Hyderabad, Govt. Museum Chennai, *Dhoomimal*; International: USA, UK, Australia, France, Germany.

Reddeppa M. Naidu's works can be easily divided into several clearcut phases. In the *art* school, he used impressionistic brushstrokes to capture *vignettes* of *contemporary* life, with *colour* and *form* dominating *line*. In the early 60s he began preparing *line drawings* of churches and cathedrals, being clearly fascinated by the clean soaring *lines* and repetitive *patterns* of the *architecture*.

His most easily identifiable *style* has developed between 1963–70. Hindu *gods* and goddesses, with their easily identifiable *iconography* submerged within a KALAMKARI-like patternization emerge from his studio. This phase continued for two decades with *epics* like the RAMAYANA and the MAHABHARATA being among his chief *themes*. The scribbling between *motifs* is reminiscent of the neo-tantric works of his teacher *K.C.S. Paniker*. However his *art* does not depend entirely on the stylized folk *forms* practised by several other *painters*. He added a touch of the *modern* by incorporating *linearity*, the fragmented *forms* and the abbreviated brushstrokes of R. Dufy in his works GANESHA was the main *theme* of his last set of *paintings*. Reddeppa M. Naidu lived and worked in Chennai.

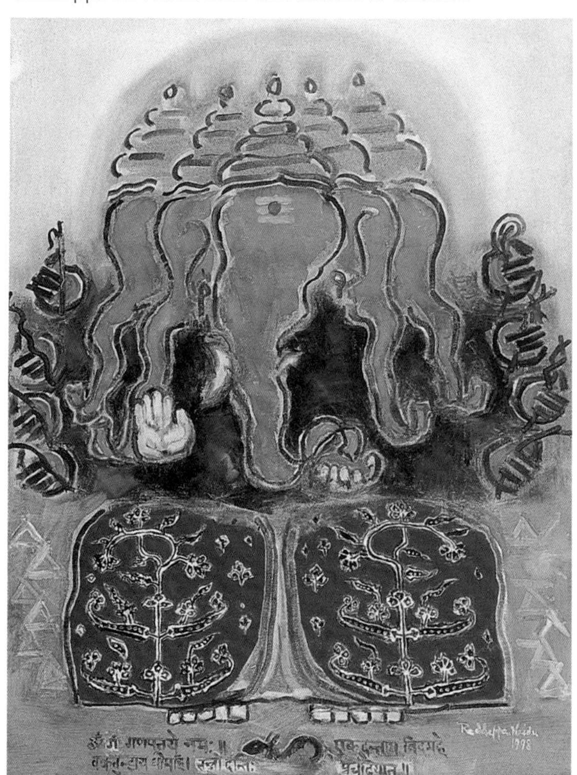

Naidu, Reddeppa M.: "Heramba Ganesh" (Five Heads) *Oil* on *Canvas*, 1998, 100x85 cm.

Naive Art Naive art is distinguished only by the basic *colour*-sense and *form*, untutored appearance and finish. It is very similar to primitive *art*, but differs from the primitive in the sense that it is produced by *artists* living in a sophisticated society. These *artists* would produce works that were unconsciously naive, simple technology similar to the works of Grandma Moses. In India, *artists* from New Delhi and GUJ made deliberate attempts at Naive art, e.g. of *Naina Dalal*, *Naina Kanodia*, *Madhavi Parekh*, *Amit Ambalal*. Refer *Finish*, *Folk Inspiration*, MADHUBANI, *Modern Style*,

Oil Paint, Primitivism, Rhythm, Rajendra Agarwal, Atasi Barua, Madan Bhatnagar, Matilal Chakrabarti, Sukumar Das, Swapan Kumar Das, Jahar DasGupta, Ranen Datta, Gopal Dey, Santokba Dudhat, Vasant Ghodke, Jiwan Jamod, K. Ramanujam, B.P. Kamboj, Naina Kanodia, Rakesh K. Koul, Lal Chand Marothia, Benode Behari Mukherjee, B.P. Paliwal, Madhvi Parekh, Abdul Qadir, A.A. Raiba, Anjani P. Reddy, Ananda Gopal Roy, Gopal Sanyal, Rangaswamy Saranagan, Kailash Chandra Sharma, Narendra Rai Srivastav, Subhogendra Tagore, Jaidev Thakore, Kanhaiya Lal Verma, Illustrations—*Dinkar Kowshik, Chhaganlal D. Mistry.*

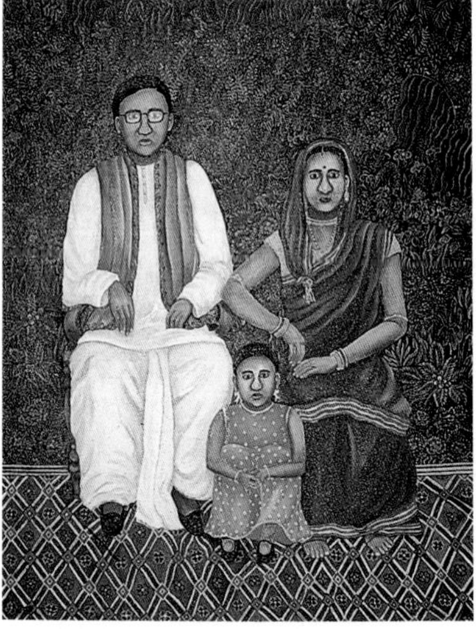

Naive Art: *Naina Kanodia,* "The Choudhary Family", *Oil* on *Canvas,* 105x90 cm.

Namaskara Refer ANJALI & MUDRAS.

Nambiar, Balan (1937–) b. Kannapuram, Kerala. Education: Dip. in *FA. GCAC* Chennai. Over 30 solos: Thiruvananthapuram, British Council Chennai, Garden Sculpture Bangalore, *JAG*; International: Germany, Italy. Group participations: *Visual Art* Mumbai, *Triennale* New Delhi; International: Industrial Fair & Tantra Indian Art Germany, Venice *Biennale* Italy. Awards: National *LKA* Awards New Delhi, State *LKA* KAR. Fellowships: Nehru Fellowships & Senior Fellowship Govt. of India New Delhi. Appointments: Research & Documentation on The *Ritual* Art Forms (including music, *drawing*) of Kerala & South KAR; Co-authored *paper* "Virali Pathu" a *Ritual* textile of Kerala; Presented several slide-lectures NCPA Mumbai; International: The "House of World Culture" Berlin. Publications: Articles photo-journalistic features in Marg magazine & India Today. Collections: *NGMA*—5 garden *sculptures* & one *enamel* New Delhi, Govt. Museum Chennai, Bangalore & Jaipur, *BAAC* Kolkata, NCPA & Air India Mumbai, Institutions, Industries & pvt.; International: USA, Norway Canada, Switzerland, Italy, France, Germany, Australia, England, Holland.

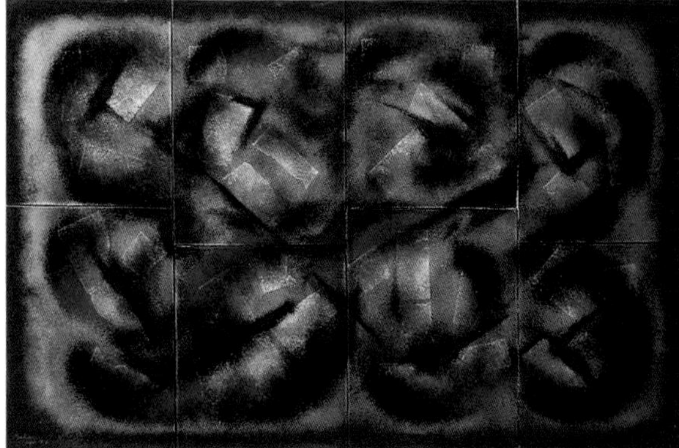

Nambiar, Balan: "Untitled", Jewellery *Enamel* on *Silver* & *Copper,* 1997.

Balan Nambiar was a *sculptor* at first, using his technical knowledge of engineering to come up with *concrete sculptures* reinforced with *fibreglass*. It was his marriage to an Italian nuclear physicist that brought him in contact with the *art* of *enamel painting*. He works on both *copper* and *silver plates* using more than 200 quality *enamel colours*, including *gold* and *silver*. Several bakings in the *kiln* are required to achieve perfect results which in Balan Nambiar's case is never dependent on the accidental effect. The small *size* of the kiln dictates the *size* of the *plate*, therefore for a larger work, he has to join several such small-sized *plates* together. The recurring *motif* in Balan Nambiar's works, be it *oil painting*, *enamel painting* or *sculpture* are *forms* and *colours* based on *nature* and South Indian *rituals* that he documents. Leaves, *landscapes*, elements and dance *forms* are seen in a highly linear *style* based on *rhythm* and *masses* of *colour*.

Balan Nambiar lives part of the time in Bangalore and spends the rest of the year in Italy. Refer *Enamel* and *Painting*.

Namboodiri, Babu K. (1964–) b. Kottavattom, Kerala. Education: B.FA. in *painting CFA* Thiruvananthapuram, M.FA. in *painting College of Art* New Delhi. Solos: *CFA* Thiruvananthapuram, *LKA* New Delhi, *JAG*, *CKP*; International: Tokyo, Korea. Group participations: *NGMA*, *Triennale*, *College of Art* & Solidarity with Cuba New Delhi, Kerala *LKA*, *JAG*, Harmony Mumbai, *LTG*; International: *Biennale* Dhaka, Group Exhibition Tokyo 2000 & 2001, Gallerie le Petite Paris. *Art* camps: Kerala & KAR *LKA*. Awards: Merit Kerala *LKA* & *College of Art* New Delhi, Research Fellowship from UGC & Japan Govt. Scholarship. Appointments: Lecturer *CFA* Thiruvananthapuram; Research on Contemporary Indian Painting—*National Museum* New Delhi under Dr. Mulk Raj Anand; International: Research studies Dept of Painting at National University of FA & Music Tokyo; Presented research papers in seminars, slide shows and talks.

Babu K. Namboodiri is basically a *figurative painter* often using simplified or surrealistically exaggerated *figures* to convey human emotions and frailties. Each *figure* has an individual existence, even while grouped together as a collective whole into a crowd. His later works are highly expressionistic and incorporate scribbles, *doodles* and picturesque signs when compared to the near folk-quality of the early works.

At present he lives and works in New Delhi.

Nandagopal, Shankar (1946–) b. Bangalore, KAR. Education: Dip. in *FA. GCAC* Chennai. Solos & *artists group* shows: Mumbai, Chennai. Group participations: *Triennale* 25 years of Indian Art *LKA* & All India Exhibition Nuclear

Disarmament Chennai; International: Japan, Travelling Exhibition *NGMA* New Delhi in Tehran, Moscow & East Europe, *Biennale* Open Air Sculpture Antwerp Belgium, Asian Art Exhibition Fukuoka Japan, Indian National Trade Fair Moscow. *Art* camps: International *Sculptors'* Camp University of Patiala, TN University Thanjavur; International: *Sculptors'* camp & seminar Yugoslavia. *Auctions*: Heart & Osian's Mumbai. Awards: National Award & Gold Medal *Triennale* New Delhi, *AFA* Kolkata, Won *LKA* TN Scholarship. Fellowships: Homi Bhabha Fellowship 1980 & Senior by Dept. of Culture Govt. of India 1984. Appointments: Secretary Progressive Painters Association *Cholamandal*; Pioneered the *Madras School of Art* for *artists* in 1966, Nomination by Govt. of India as an Advisor and served on the purchase committee *NGMA* New Delhi. Commissions: *Murals* & *sculptures* in welded *metal* Chennai, New Delhi, Khajuraho, Bangalore; A 20 ft. *sculpture* of stainless *steel* installed in Mumbai (Priyadarshini park) by NCPA. Collections: *NGMA & LKA* New Delhi, RAJ Museum Jaipur, Govt. Museum in Bangalore & Chennai, TIFR, *BB*; International: Titograd Yugoslavia.

Shankar Nandagopal's *sculpture* can be termed as frontal *metal sculpture* influenced by the works of Henry Moore and other Western *artists* with basically the *modern* traditional expression of Indian folk *style*. He prefers "*drawing* in *space*", avoiding all attempts at three dimensionality in his linear *reliefs*. The *forms* are derivations of folk *motifs*, scraps of *metals* welded together to create linear *rhythms*. He uses *copper*, *brass* and *enamels* to add *colour* to the works. Cows, snakes, lattices, AYUDHAS and *abstract* doodles are some of the *key motifs* in these *free-standing* decorative *drawings*.

He lives and works at the *Cholamandal*, an *artist's* village conceptualized by his legendary father *K.C.S. Paniker*. Refer *Welding*. (See illustration on page 241)

Nandhan, P.S. (1940–) b. Madhunatakam, TN. Education: Dip. in *painting* *GCAC* Chennai. Solos & *artists group* shows: Regional Centre Chennai, *AIFACS*, *JAG*. Group participations: British Council & Progressive Painters Association in Chennai & Mumbai, UNICEF, National *LKA* & *Triennale* New Delhi, *AFA* & *LKA* Kolkata, *LKA* Chennai *AIFACS*; International: *Biennale* Ankara in Turkey. *Art* camps & workshops: *LKA* New Delhi, Kerala *LKA*, *Sculptor's* camp *Cholamandal*, TN *LKA* & SZCC Nagpur, International *Granite* camp at *Mahabalipuram*, *GAC*; *Clay* workshops for children Chennai. Awards: TN *LKA* & National *LKA* New Delhi. Member: *Cholamandal*. Commissions: Govt. of TN British Council Chennai; International: London. Collections: *LKA* KAR & Orissa, Museum of Madras Chennai, *NGMA* New Delhi; International: United National University New York, Gallery Indira & University of Toronto Canada, pvt. Australia, Europe, Denmark.

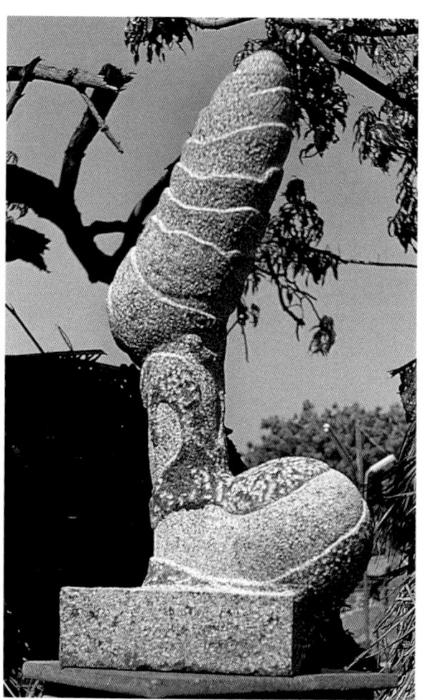

Nandhan, P.S.: "Plant", *Granite (stone)*, 1995, 65x36x24 cm.

He has experimented with many *media*, including *terracotta*, *metal*, *bronze*, *wood* and *granite*. The influence of *tribal art* is felt in most of his works including his *murals*.

He lives and works at the *Cholamandal*.

Nandi The VAHANA of SHIVA, Nandi is a *white/black* bull, the guardian of all quadrupeds. He always accompanies SHIVA and is also the chief of his GANAS. Every SHIVA temple contains a shrine or *image* of Nandi.

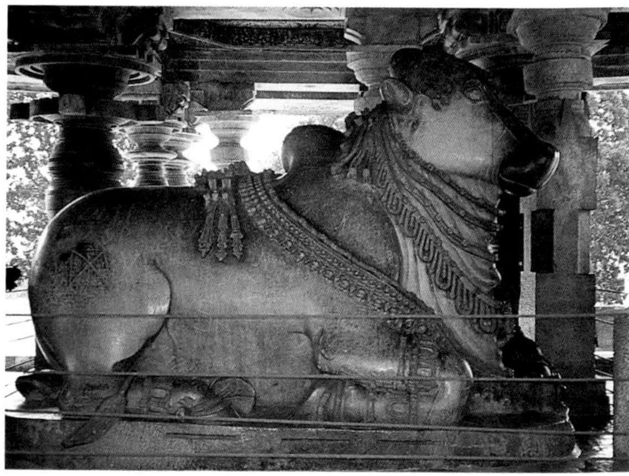

Nandi: Bull, SHIVA Temple, Halebid.

Nandi, Animesh (1940–) b. India. Education: Dip. in *FA*. *GCAC* Kolkata, M.A. in *fresco painting* & *mosaic* AFA Belgrade; Scholarship Yugoslavia. Solos: Over 28 solos New Delhi, Mumbai, Kolkata; International: Bosnia, Yugoslavia, Sweden, Belgrade, Vienna, Berlin, Germany. Group shows: Kolkata, New Delhi, Mumbai; International: Yugoslavia, Stockholm, Germany. Member: Artists Association of Belgrade. Appointments: Experience from 1969 to 1982 Freelance Artist Belgrade; Guest lecturer *RBU*. *Paintings* collections: pvt. & corporates, Mumbai, Kolkata, New Delhi; International: Germany, UK, Japan, USA.

Animesh Nandi's meticulously crafted *paintings* show the influence of surrealistic masters like R. Magritte and M. Ernst. The *paintings* usually contain the *motif* of strange, other-worldly cliffs or mountain settings, with a phantom like face emerging out of it, hovering silently over an expanse of eerie-blue coloured water.

He lives and works with "Silence" an organization of the handicapped in Kolkata.

Nangare, Murlidhar (1941–) b. Ahmedabad. Education: M.A., GDA, *Art* Master, CTC. Solos: Balagandharva Art Gallery Pune, RB Hyderabad, Kala Mela New Delhi, *JAG*. Group participations: *NGMA*, *Triennale*, RB New Delhi, National Exhibition of *LKA* New Delhi, Chandigarh, Hyderabad, Raipur & Mumbai, MAHA State Mumbai, Drawing *exhibition* Chennai, Monsoon shows *JAG*, Autumn show of Prof. *JJSA*, *BAS*, *ASI*, *VEAG*. Workshops: *Printmaking* by US Information Centre New Delhi, *Printmaking* with *Krishna Reddy* at *JJSA*. Scholarship & Awards: MAHA State Education, Nasik Kala Niketan & *NGMA* Mumbai, National Exhibition in Ahmedabad, New Delhi, Chandigarh, Hyderabad, Raipur, & Mumbai, *BAS*, *ASI*. Member: *LKA*-General Council & Education Programmed Committee New Delhi, WZCC Udaipur. Appointments: *Art* Appreciation Course *JJSA*, Orientation Programmes History of *Art* & *Aesthetics* by Directorate of Art Mumbai, Taught *art* at the Abhinava Kala Mahavidhyalaya Pune & later the Principal of the Institute, Ex-Dir. of the MAHA Directorate of Arts. Collections: *LKA* New Delhi, *NGMA* Mumbai & New Delhi, in Directorate of Art MAHA State Mumbai, TKS, *Dhoomimal*, pvt. & corporates.

Murlidhar Nangare has always preferred the vivid contrast effected by *black* and *white*, displaying his mastery over the *tone* in the use of *cross-hatching*. In the 80s he did a series of impressionist *paintings* on the "Warkari", the pilgrims of Pandharpur. His later works show a creative juxtaposition of limbs and faces in *shade* and *light*.

Murlidhar Nangare lives and works in Pune.

Narasimha/ Narasinha The man-lion *form* assumed by VISHNU (in his fourth incarnation) to fight the *demons* Hiranyaksha and Hiranyakashipu. He is represented with a lion's face, the body of a man and is depicted springing out of a pillar or placing the *demon* on his lap and ripping his chest apart. Refer AVATARA, AVTAAR, AVATAR, DASAVATARA, HOLI, *Iconography*, *Iconology*, *Mask*, MATRIKAS, *Spiritual*, *Stone Carving*, *Wetting Down*; Illustration—GANJIFA.

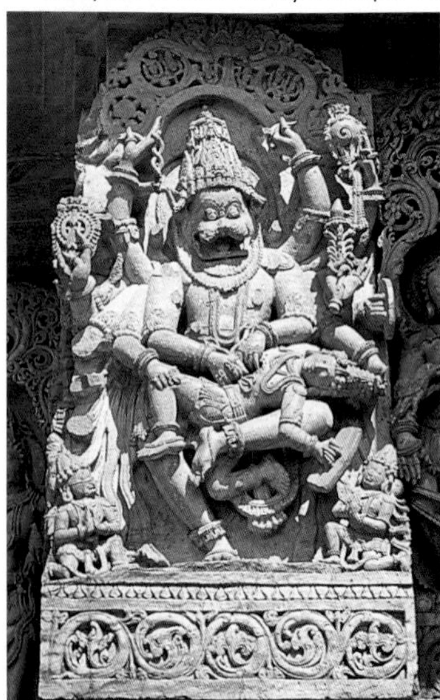

Narasimha: *Avatar*, *Stone*, Belur.

NarasimhaMurti, P.L. (1918–) b. Batalanka. GDA in *painting*, *graphic* & studied *sculpture* under *Debi Prasad RoyChowdhury*. Solos: Sponsored by *LKA* Trichy. Group participations: New Delhi, MMB Chennai & Bangalore, Madras Museum & Alliance Francaise Chennai, *CKP*; International: France. Fellowship: Ministry of Education & Culture by Govt. of India. Appointments: Treasurer Progressive Painters Association Chennai. Publications: Modern Indian Painting by P.R. Ramachandra Rao, Modern Review London; Contributed articles on Art in English & Telugu daily; Contributed around 600 *paintings* in SANSKRIT volume of RAMAYANA, along with his wife *Vijyalakshmi P*. Collections: Govt. Museum Chennai & Hyderabad, Thiruvananthapuram, KB Varanasi, *CTAG*.

P.L. NarasimhaMurti belongs to the old school of traditional *painting*, using both religious and secular *themes*, in a *manner* that is a combination of *styles* of the South Indian *Thanjavur (Tanjore) glass painting* and the *Bengal School idioms*. Hence there is a reliance on decorative *lines* and romantic colouring, along with repetitive dots and *patterns*.

He lives and works in Chennai, with his wife *Vijyalakshmi P*. Refer *Glass Painting*, *Thanjavur (Tanjore) Paintings on Glass* and *Back-Glass Painting*.

Narrative A narrative work of *art*, implies a literary *theme*; i.e. a story to be communicated to the spectator. This can be achieved in various ways—the use of the seminal moment in the story, like the use of continuous narration, i.e. two or more incidents of the story, illustrated in one picture *frame*, as seen in the JATAKAS illustrated at *Ajanta*. There is also the comic strip type of narration, which is seen in certain miniatures including *Jain manuscript Illumination*, wherein the *picture space* is divided into two or more *registers*, with different incidents being portrayed in each. Narrative *painting* is popular among groups of *artists* in the *post-Independence art* scene in India, with *Bhupen Khakhar*, *Gulam Mohammed Sheikh*, *Reddeppa M. Naidu* and *Santokba Dudhat* being among its prime exponents. Refer *Bengal Oil Painting*, CHADDANTA, *Continuous Representation*, *Epic*, *Figure-Ground Relationship*, GANJIFA, *Illumination*, *Jain Miniature*, *Significant Form*, *Space*, *Sunayani Devi Chattopadhyay*, *Ganga Devi*, *Shanu Lahiri*, *Jaideep D. Mehrotra*, *P. Vijyalakshmi*, *Dashrath Patel*, *Jagu Bhai Shah*, *Sumant Shah*, *Vinay P. Trivedi*; Illustration—GANJIFA, JATAKA, *Navjot Altaf*, *P.N. Choyal*, *Atul Dodiya*, *Ganga Devi*, *Amal Ghosh*, *Asit K. Haldar*, *Bhupen Khakhar*, *Lalitha Lajmi*, *Baburao Painter*, *Madhvi Parekh*, *Katayun Saklat*, *K.G. Subramanyan*, *Vivan Sundaram*, *J. Swaminathan*.

Narzary, Janak J. (1948–) b. Kokrajhar, Assam. Education: B.FA. & Ph.D. *VBU*, M.FA. *MSU*, Studied in *art* history Boston University USA. Worked under *Ramkinkar Baij*; Research work under *K.G. Subramanyan*. Solos: *ABC*, *JAG*; Retrospective: *BAAC* Kolkata. Group participations: *NGMA* New Delhi, Town Hall & *AFA* Kolkata, *JAG*. *Art* camps: *LKA* Kolkata, other towns Guntur, Vishakhapatnam, Varanasi; Major Artist's Exhibition, *BAAC* Kolkata. Participated: *Mural casting*. Awards & Scholarships: Govt. of Assam, Govt. of India, *AFA* Kolkata, Varanasi University, *AIFACS*; International: Awarded Fullbright & Boston University USA. Commissions: *Installations* Sea Weaves in *stone* & *steel* Vishakahapatnam. Appointment: Seminar & lectures mainly on *Ramkinkar Baij*—*AFA* & Information Centre Kolkata, *NGMA* & *National*

Museum New Delhi, *LKA* Bhubaneshwar, Dhaka Institute of FA. *RBU*, BHU; Principal *KB Santiniketan*. Collections; *NGMA* New Delhi, *LKA*, *AFA* & *BAAC* Kolkata, *VBU*, *ABC*, *CKP*.

Janak J. Narzary has work in diverse *media* since the early 70s. He mainly uses *bronze*, *brass* and *aluminium*, fusing *space* and *form*, *volumes* and voids, delivering a new experience in time and *space*.

His early phase was characterized by his belief that generating power was the essence of life. In this phase, he did *sculptures* depicting the power and force of *nature*.

In the second phase, the mystery of *space* obsessed him, thus his *sculptures* took *form* that emphasized horizontal and vertical *visual* order. Finally, he landed on his favourite *theme*: "The Essence of Woman". In the most recent phase, he has been concentrating on *"creation"* and the new cultural *form*. His recent works are in the nature of *installations* comprising of ephemeral objects like eggs, seeds, apples and earth.

He lives and works in *Santiniketan*.

Nataraja Nata=dancer, Raja=King. A synonym of SHIVA, meaning the Lord or King of Dancers. Here, he is depicted dancing the Tandava-Nritya, the cosmic dance of both destroying and recreating the universe. The universe itself is depicted as the circle or oval ring encircling the deity vertically. The destructive aspect is shown through the Prabhamandala, the row of flames licking the ring of the cosmos, and the single flame held in one of the *god's* hands. While the MUDRA and the *attributes* may vary in different examples, like the Jata Mukuta (matted hair), with the hair flying wildly with the force of the dance, the moon and the river GANGA depicted either anthropomorphically or symbolically entwined in the hair. The *imagery* differs from *icon* to *icon*. Nataraja is a popular *icon* with the CHOLA, *bronze* casters. Refer AGNI, *Elephanta*, GAJA-HASTA, *Metal*, PRABHAVALI, *South Indian Bronzes*; Illustration—*Alphonso Doss*.

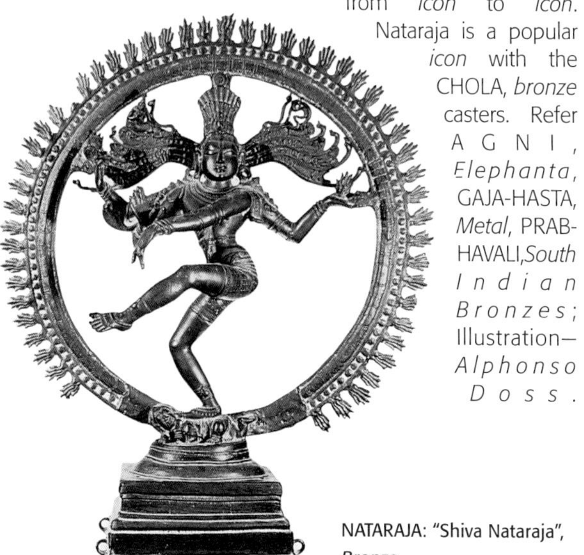

NATARAJA: "Shiva Nataraja", *Bronze*.

Nath, Nareen (1937–) b. Yeotmal, MAHA. Education: GDA in *FA. painting* CFA Indore, *JJSA*. Solos: Konark Art Gallery & Chanakya New Delhi, *PUAG*, *Dhoomimal*; International: Berlin Germany. Group participations: Kumar Art Gallery, National *LKA*, Chanakya, *NGMA LKA & Triennales* New Delhi, SKP, *PUAG*, *Roopankar BB*, also in Bangalore, Kolkata, Kanpur; International: Australia, Tokyo, Bangladesh. *Art* camps: Bhopal, Srinagar, Indore, Bangalore, Chennai, Udaipur. Awards: National Award *LKA*. Member: Advisory Committee *Roopankar BB*; Dir. *GAC*. Commissions: *Murals* in New Delhi & Kathmandu. Collections: *NGMA*, *LKA* & Chanakya New Delhi, *LKA* Jaipur Museum, *Chandigarh Museum*, J&K Academy Srinagar, *PUAG*, *Roopankar BB*; International: Ford Foundation, Rockefeller Foundation USA.

Nareen Nath is inspired by the myriad moods of music—Indian music in particular, with its highly *spiritual* and *abstract* dimensions. He associates these organized notes with past memories and more importantly with the concept of BHAKTI (*spiritual* devotion). His *paintings*, thus, are not mere arrangements of *form* and *colour* in the *abstract manner* of musical *compositions*. They are *symbolic* manifestations of the temple *landscape* and are suffused with direct allusions to *nature*. The colourful miniatures from the state of *Malwa* also inspires him, with its near musical division of *space*, and *pattern*. Nareen Nath's *palette* has veered from the *monochromatic* and near *black* in the 80s to a high *key* effusion of yellows and *whites* enlivened by small *colour* accents of red and deep grey in the 90s.

He works at the *GAC* studios in New Delhi.

National Gallery of Modern Art (NGMA) (New Delhi/Mumbai). NGMA New Delhi inaugurated on March 29,1954, is the only institution of its kind, now with a branch in Mumbai, run and administered by the Govt. of India. The main objective of NGMA is to conserve and preserve *modern* and *contemporary* Indian *art* thus charting its evolution during the period 1850 onwards. It also organizes special *exhibitions* not only in its own galleries but also in other parts of the country and abroad. There is a Reference Library and Documentation Centre with books and latest issues of magazines on *art*. Not only are the principal galleries in NGMA climate-controlled, the damaged works are also restored by experts. NGMA arranges specialized lectures, seminars and conferences on *art* and related subjects.

The collection of works centre around the works of *art* of different schools and groups such as the *Bengal School*, *Raja Ravi Varma* and followers of his *style*, *Amrita Sher-Gil* and other *contemporary* masters. NGMA Mumbai opened at the C.J. Hall in December 1995. Housed in a heritage building of historical significance (one of the 600 such monuments in Mumbai), it has a gallery at the top (below the Dome) measuring 80 ft. in diameter without any pillars/columns.

The original area of 5000 sq.ft. has been increased to 20,000 sq.ft. by astute architectural designing, which preserves the outer facade in its original shape, *form* and condition. Eight galleries enable NGMA to conduct diverse activities simultaneously. The gallery recently celebrated then golden jubilee by arranging a large *exhibition* of their collected works.

National Handicrafts & Handlooms Museum (New Delhi). Colloquially known as the *crafts museum*, the core collection here was put together to serve as reference material for craftsmen. The permanent collection of some 20,000 objects of folk and tribal *craft* is housed in a large building designed by Charles Correa, the architect. The building has been disguised to a great extent by the sloping tiled roofs supported by Ballis, with old, carved wooden (including Jharokhas) doors and windows from GUJ and RAJ. There are *bronze images*, lamps and incense burners, *Ritual* accessories, utensils, *wood* and *stone carvings*, *papier mache* objects, *ivories*, dolls, toys, puppets, *masks*, jewellery, *paintings*, Bhuta *figures* from KAR and various types of textiles including brocade, Kat, Jamdani, tie and dye, shawls and applique.

The *museum* also invites 50 traditional artisans from all over India, every month, to be in residence at the *museum*; they demonstrate their skill to lay persons, as well as conduct creative experiments and market their products. *Ganga Devi* was one such *artist*. Her *paintings* in the Mithila *style* are *contemporary* in their *imagery*, and though the *themes* may be taken from the *epics*, the stories are based on experiences from her own life.

There is also the village-complex shaped over four acres. The remnant of a temporary *exhibition* in 1972, the complex comprises 15 structures representing village dwellings, courtyards and shrines from several Indian states. The dwellings are fitted with items of daily use in order to give the viewer a true *perspective* of the cultural context of the objects, which later become objects of display in *museum*.

The *museum* has a library with more than 10,000 books and periodicals pertaining to Indian *folk* and *tribal art* and *culture*. The *museum* also commissions field research scholars to document traditional *art* and *craft*, in *monographs*. The *conservation* laboratory looks after the preservation and *conservation* of the *art* collection. There is also a shop selling books, postcards and other handicrafts. Refer *Bandhani*, *Madhubani* and *Tie and Dyed Fabrics*.

National Museum (New Delhi). The Foundation *stone* of the National Museum was laid by Pandit Jawaharlal Nehru in 1955. The *museum* was moved to the present building in 1960. It also has an Institution for Research Centre. The *museum* has a huge collection of over 150,000 works of *art*, ranging from Indian prehistory to the late medieval period. There is also a small collection of Central Asian and Pre-Columbian Art. The various galleries within the *museum* house *artefacts* belonging to different periods in Indian history. Thus we have the *Indus Valley Civilization* gallery, with its *pottery*, *sculptures* and seals followed by some excellent examples of Mauryan, Sungan and Satvahana *art*, and the *art* of Gandhara and Mathura. The Mathura *sculptures* are easily identifiable being carved out of red sandstone. There is a significant *sculpture* of a SHALEBHANJIKA holding the branch of an Ashoka tree (Asokadhana—which refers to the fertility myths), which is sacred to the Buddhists.

One of the most important examples of *Gupta art* is present in the *museum*. This is a 5th-century *sculpture* of the standing BUDDHA from Sarnath. With one hand raised in the ABHAYA MUDRA and one knee bent gracefully to create an S-curve, this is a perfect example of the golden period of Indian *art*.

The medieval *sculpture* galleries house a variety of sculptural *styles*, including *sculptures* dating to the PALLAVA, Chalukya, GANGA, Pala, Sena and *Hoysala* ages.

There is also the Indian *bronze* gallery with the famous "Dancing Girl" from *Mohenjo Daro* and the *South Indian bronzes*, all produced by the *lost wax process*.

The gallery of manuscripts and *paintings* has a varied collection of *illuminated manuscripts*, *miniature paintings* and *calligraphic* texts. There are examples of *flora fauna paintings* dating to the time of Jehangir as well as *folios* of the *"Babar-Namah"* belonging to Akbar's period. There are examples of the *Basohli* and *Kangra Schools*, with the RADHA-KRISHNA story being the predominant *theme*, as well as exquisite *paintings* belonging to the *Kishangarh style*.

Other galleries in the *museum* house Central Asian antiquities, Indian textiles, decorative *crafts* like *ivory* work, *tribal art* and *antique* jewellery.

There is a sales counter with *prints*, slides, postcards, *monographs* and such souvenir items as *plaster cast models* of *sculptures* belonging to the *museum*.

Nationalism in Art Pertaining to a Nation. In *art*, it would refer to the overwhelming character of the *art* of a particular nation or region. However, while one can safely talk of a Graeco-Roman character or Chinese or Japanese character, it is more difficult to speak of a nationalistic character in Indian *art*, be it traditional or *modern*. Refer *"Art, Nation and Identity: Colonial India—The First Phase"*. (See notes on page 19)

Natural Colours This refers to the *colours* obtained directly from *nature* as opposed to chemical *colours*. They are *earth colours*, *colours* obtained from herbs or minerals, made of plant substances, vegetables, *oils* and gem stones, which have traditionally been used for centuries in India. Before the invention of chemical *colours* in the 19th century, *artists ground* their own *colours*. e.g. In *Ajanta*, the *colours* were created out of the various rocks and soil found on the site. The Indian miniaturist refined various rocks and semi-precious stones to obtain the *colour* for his *painting*. *White* was made from burnt and powdered conch-shell, while yellow was obtained from the purified residue of the urine of a cow fed with mango leaves for a fortnight. Vegetable dyes are also natural colours. Refer *Gum Arabic*, *Madhubani*, *Miniature Painting*, *Pigment*, *Tempera*, *Warli Paintings*, *Santokba Dudhat*, *Ganga Devi*, *Ved Pal Sharma*, *J. Swaminathan*, *Nathu Lal Verma*.

Naturalism Quite similar to *Realism*. Naturalism does not mean a slavish imitation of reality, but an interest in the depiction of mundane, ordinary, everyday events not only in literature, but also in work of art. Naturalism was essentially a 19th-century phenomenon in Europe. In India *Jamini P. Gangooly* was one of the earliest practitioners of

Naturalism. Later *artists* like *Narayan S. Bendre*, *H.A. Gade* and *Hemendranath Mazumdar* popularized Naturalism.

Presently, *Sudhir Patwardhan's themes* have been based on every day life in suburbs of metropolitan cities. Refer *Art*, *Cityscape*, *Genre*, *K.C. Aryan*, *Suresh Awari*; Illustrations—*Sadanandji Bakre*, *Narayan S. Bendre*, *Pralhad A. Dhond*, *Ranjitsingh Gaekwad*, *Harkrishan Lall*, *Vinayak Pandurang Karmarkar*, *Bhupen Khakhar*, *Kshitendranath Mazumdar*, *Hemendranath Mazumdar*, *Ganpatrao K. Mhatre*, *Raja Ravi Varma*.

Nature **1.** Refers to work that is *landscape* based, and mostly *figurative* though recently even *abstract art* has turned organic and hence based in nature. e.g. the works of *Jamini P. Gangooly*, *Sayed Haider Raza*, *Ambadas*. **2.** Refers to the chief characteristic of the work, either in the *style* as in the nature of *Maqbool Fida Husain's* strokes or *Jamini Roy's* heavy *outlines*, or the material used—as in the rough quality of *cement concrete* in *Ramkinkar Baij's sculptures*, or the smooth, glossy quality of *Satish Gujral's marble sculptures*. **3.** Also refers to the studies from nature. Refer *Landscape*, *Warli Paintings*; Illustrations—*Earth Art*, *Earth Works*, *Land Art*, *Life-Drawing*, *Seascape*, *K.M Adimoolam*, *Ambadas*, *Gobardhan Ash*, *Dhanraj Bhagat*, *Prafulla Dahanukar*, *Bimal DasGupta*, *H.A. Gade*, *Amal Ghosh*, *Gopal Ghose*, *Bimal Kundu*, *Kanayi Kunhiraman*, *K. Madhava Menon*, *Balan Nambiar*, *Madhvi Parekh*, *Surya Prakash*, *Sayed Haider Raza*, *Krishna N. Reddy*, *Suhas Roy*, *Anilbaran Saha*, *Shantilal M. Shah*, *Deokinandan Sharma*, *G.S. Shenoy*, *Laxman Shreshtha*, *Ali J. Sultan*, *Sanat Thaker*.

Nava Rasa The nine RASAS. Refer *Aesthetics*, RASA.

Navelcar, Vamona A. (1929–) b. India. Education: Post-Grad. in *FA*. Escola Superior De Belas Artes in Lisbon Portugal; Gulbenkian Foundation Scholarship; Lived in Mozambique & Portugal for nearly 25 years before returning to Goa in India. Solos: Goa; International: Helsiniki Finland, Lisbon Portugal, Mozambique, Angola, London, Geneva, Nampula, Maputo. Group participations: Goa; International: Porto, Coimbro, Escola Superior De Belas Artes Lisbon; International Exhibition Monte Carlo Monaco France, Calads Da Rainha Portugal & Macau Carribean Island. Worked on *murals* in *iron* structure, & *painting* Mozambique. Publications: "Dictionary of 20th Century" Portuguese Artists London & "Encyclopaedia of Portuguese Artists" Lisbon.

His works of the 70s and the 80s reveal a stylized *figuration*, with *paint* applied in flat, *collage*-like patches against a non-descript *background*. His other series were also on "RAMAYANA", "MAHABHARATA" and "Poems of Tagore". In Mozambique he produced 70 *drawings* depicting the freedom struggle of the Mozambique people, then on the liberation of Bangladesh and on the crucifixion. His works are *collages*, with torn *paper* forming a kind of *landscape* against the *white* and sand *colour* of the *background*.

He lives and works in Goa.

Nayak-Nayaka The hero or the protagonist depicted in the *Rajput miniature paintings*. KRISHNA is the Nayaka in a large number of these Vaishnav BHAKTI-inspired miniatures. Other heroes include Laurik (Laur-Chanda), Dhola (Dhola-Marwani), RAMA, Mahiwal (Sohni-Mahiwal) and the various RAGAS, Refer NAYIKA, CHITRAKATHI, KALAHAMTARITA, KRISHNA, RAMA, *Spiritual*, SWADHINAPATIKA.

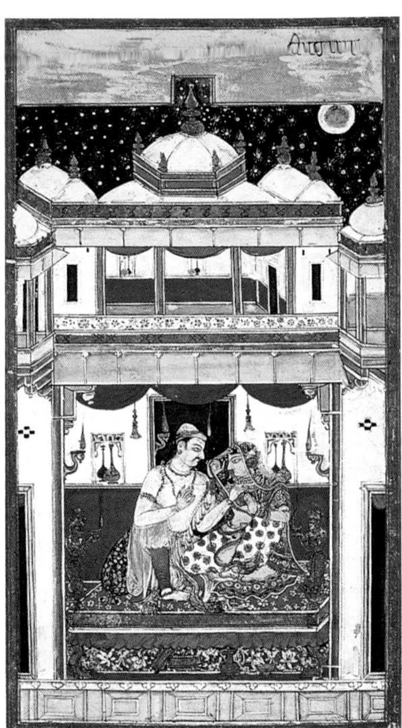

NAYAK-NAYAKA: *Bundi*, RAJ.

Nayar, Kavita (1957–) b. Amritsar, Education: PUJ. B.FA. *Santiniketan*, M.FA. *College of Art* New Delhi. Solos & group shows: *BAAC* Kolkata, *JAG*, *GG*, *LTG*; International: Luxembourg Europe. Group participations: *CIMA* Kolkata, *CYAG*, *Biennale BB*; International: Exhibition of Print Japan, *Biennale drawing* & *graphic art* Yugoslavia, Festival of India USA, Group show Paris, Indian Printmaker organized by *CIMA* in Canada, *Triennale* Switzerland. *Art* camps: for *graphic* works demonstration Mumbai & Jaipur, SZCC Jaipur, *AAJ* Group Udaipur, *BAAC* Kolkata, *GE* & *LKA* New Delhi. Awards: Charles Wallace Trust Scholarship to study at Oxford for six months, French Govt. Scholarship to study *lithography* & *etching* ENSBA Paris. Fellowships: Junior Fellowship from Ministry of Art & Culture. Appointments: Visiting lecturer at *College of Art* New Delhi, Vice-president of Indian paintmakers guild. Collections: *NGMA* & *LKA* New Delhi, *BAAC* Kolkata, *Chandigarh Museum*, *GG*, pvt. & corporates.

Kavita Nayar's work is dominated by human relationships. The human *form* is present whether floating in limbo-like *space* or intermingling with the organic *forms* of *nature*. The *theme* is common to her lithographs, *paintings* and *serigraphy* as well. There is a subtle use of the *negative space* in the *aesthetic* interplay of *colours* and *textures* in her *prints*.

Kavita Nayar lives and works in New Delhi.

Nayar, Ved (1933–) b. Lyallpur, Education: PUJ. National Diploma in *FA*. *College of Art* New Delhi. Solos: Kumar Art Gallery. Retrospective: Artist Studio Gallery New Delhi; International: Pakistan. Group participations: *Triennale*, *LKA*, CMC Art Gallery, Artist Studio Gallery, *NGMA* & 50 year India New Delhi, *GC* Mumbai, *SG* Mumbai & Chennai, *CIMA* Kolkata, Kala Yatra Bangalore, *GAC*, VG, *LTG*,

CYAG, *JAG*, *G88*; International: Budapest, Japan, London, Frankfurt, Maine, Bangladesh. *Auctions*: HelpAge India by Asprey's London. Awards: Including *LKA*, Fifth *Triennales* & Certificate by International Jury for *installation* New Delhi. Commissions: *Murals* in *copper*, *Installation* at MMB & *Triennales* New Delhi; Designed Citation Trophy of Jawaharlal Nehru & Award for International Understanding. Publications: "Contemporary Indian Art" published by Glenbarra Museum Japan. Collections: *NGMA & LKA* New Delhi, Godrej Mumbai, *CYAG*, National & International.

Ved Nayar has expressed himself through different *media*, including *painting*, *drawing*, *sculpture* and lately, through *installation*. His work has involved various stages, derivation, introspection and self-discovery. There has always been an element of *fantasy*, of dreaming about the future in his *sculptures* and *installations*. In achieving this, he employed certain leitmotifs: the Kalpavriksha, the tree of fulfillment and an elongated female *form*, that he *terms* the supermodel, an *icon* of the advertising age.

He lives and works in New Delhi.

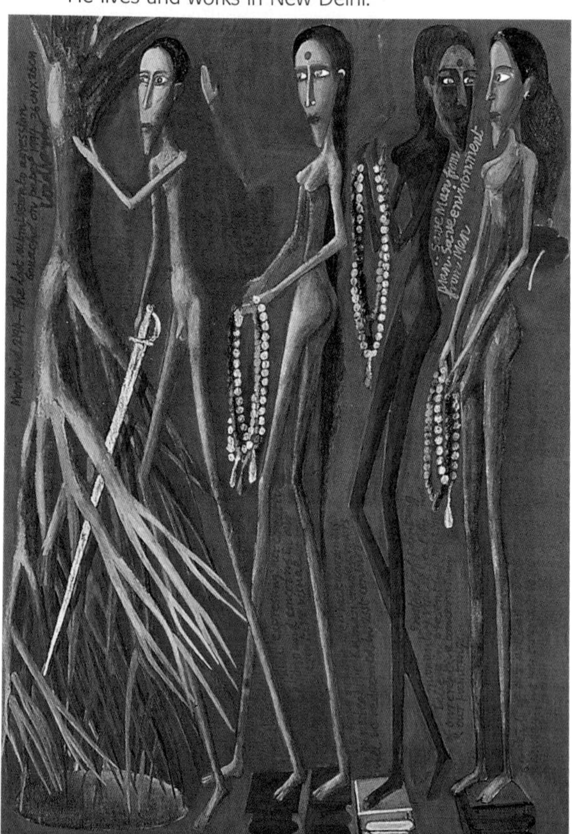

Nayar, Ved: "The Last Submission to Aggression", *Gouache* on *Paper*, 1994.

Nayika A heroine in a drama, noble lady, a mistress or even a courtesan. The ASHTANAYIKA describes the eight types of heroines. Nayika are a popular *theme* in *Rajasthani miniature paintings* illustrating the traditional stories from SANSKRIT or Brajbhasha texts like RAGAMALA, Krishna Lila, Nayika Bheda. Refer ABHISARIKA, KHANDITA, *Landscape*, PROSITAPATIKA, RASAMANJARI, SWADHINAPATIKA, UTKANTHITA, UTKA, VIPRALABDHA, VASAKASAJJA, *Saroj Gogi Pal*, *Amrita Sher-Gil*, *Francis Newton Souza*, *Narendra Rai Srivastav*; Illustrations—NAYAK-NAYAKA, *Mewar*, *Thotha Vaikuntham*.

Negative **1.** The *mould* from which the *positive* is *cast*. Refer *Casing*, *Cast*, *Casting Facing*, *Mould*, *Waste-Mould*. **2.** In photography, the *plate* or film in which the *image*, *tonal values* (in the case of *black* and *white* photography) or *colour* (in *colour* photography) is reversed. **3.** In *printmaking* the *image* to be printed and the negative area lie on the same plane. Refer *Lithography*, *Maniere Noire*, *Photo-etching*, *Print*, *Stencil*. **4.** It can also refer to the empty *space* or *volume* in *painting* or sculptural *composition*. This contributes equally to the work of *art*, the work being judged by the *balance* of the two elements. Refer *Background*, *Jatin Das*, *Somnath Hore*, *Kavita Nayar*, *Janak Patel*, *Vasudha Thozhur*, *Raja Ravi Varma*.

Nehru Centre Art Gallery (NCAG) (Mumbai, MAHA), was set up in 1992 at Worli. Since then it has featured *exhibitions* by *artists*, ranging from the well-known to the student of *art* and the amateur, all working in several *media*, including *painting*, *sculpture*, *printmaking*, *calligraphy*, *ceramics*, textile *painting* and photography. Recently, the gallery *space* was expanded and is now available in two parts: one air-conditioned and approximately 2300 sq.ft., with 150 running ft. of wall *space*, the other a circular gallery with 125 running ft. of display *space*. Both galleries are situated on the ground floor of the "Discovery of India" building. The gallery also conducts annual study camps for the *art* students from rural areas in the state. In collaboration with various groups, the gallery organizes lectures on advertising. It also arranges seminars and workshops & regularly screens films on *art* and advertising, both national and international in addition to the annual monsoon shows known as "Chatak", the gallery also holds yearly retrospectives on the *old masters*, bringing out catalogues and *prints*. *Gopal Damodar Deuskar*, *Vinayak Pandurang Karmarkar* and *Gajanan S. Haldankar* are some of the *artists* covered so far. Several new activities including summer workshops for the children are being planned.

Neo-Bengal School The Neo-Bengal School was originally known as the *Bengal School* as founded by *Abanindranath Tagore* and his followers. Later during the second half of the 19th century, *artists* both self-taught and academically trained at the Calcutta Art School were included in the Neo-Bengal School. According to Subho Tagore a poet, *artist* and an *art* collector, *Bengal School* had begun before the *art* schools came up. The European *artists* settled in Calcutta, also influenced Bengali *artists* working in *oils*. Some people were of the opinion that there was the Dutch influence on some of the works and would classify them under another category—the Chinsurah Dutch School as Chinsurah near Calcutta was under the Dutch occupation. Refer *Calcutta School*, *Nandalal Bose*, *Muhammed Abdur Rehman Chughtai*, *Sailoz Mookerjea*, *Abanindranath Tagore*.

Neo-Classical Style Referring to the use of neo-classical ideas and *manner*. In India, neo-classical tendencies are found in some of the early the works of *moderns art*, practising in the Western *manner*. This appeared in various guises i.e. the theatrical postures in *Raja Ravi Varma's painting*, the romanticized but impersonal coolness in *Ganpatrao K. Mhatre's* and *Vinayak Pandurang Karmarkar's sculptures*, similar to the works of A. Canova (1757–1822). The graceful yet artistically altered *proportions* of the ladies in *Ganpatrao K. Mhatre's* and *Vinayak Pandurang Karmarkar's* works; i.e. in "To the Temple" and "Fishergirl" also point to the neo-classical source of the works respectively. Refer *All'antica*, *Marble*, *Sculpture*; Illustrations–*Bhagwant K. Goregaokar*, *Mahadev V. Dhurandhar*, *Ganpatrao K. Mhatre*, *Baburao Painter*, *Bayaji Vasantrao Talim*, *K. Venkatappa*.

Neo-Classicism The mid-18th century excavations of the Roman cities of Herculaneum and Pompeii were some of the main reasons for the revival of *classical* tastes in Europe. People, jaded by the excessive frivolousness and frippery of the *Baroque* and Rococo period, were looking for a change, and the stability and relative *balance* of *classical* ideas provided them with an answer. In France, this revival was also echoed in the change in govt. The French Revolution ushered in changes in the *art* scene as well. However, unlike earlier revivals of *classical* taste, as during the *Renaissance*, *artists* were conscious of what they were trying to imitate. It was *sculpture* rather than *painting* that attracted them. This was to result in a bas-relief type of *composition* in the *paintings* of neo-Classicism's chief exponent, Jacques Louis David. A stage-like setting and lighting, relative unimportance given to *colour* and the choice of *heroic* subjects, posing and posturing for the edification of the spectator, were the hallmarks of David's *style*, which he imposed on most of the *artists* in France, in his role as Dir. of Academy of Art. Similar characteristics were to be observed in the works of *sculptors* like A. Canova, A.R. Mengs and B.A. Thowaldsen as well. Neo-classical ideas manifested themselves in *architecture* and its related fields like interior decoration and furniture making as well, as exemplified by absence of *colour* and curvilinear *lines*.

The *Bengal School*, and others, with their British academic grounding, also received the imprint of neo-Classicism through revivalist Indian literature. Refer *God*, *Gothic*, *History Painting*, *Isms*, *Neo-Classical Style*, *Vinayak Pandurang Karmarkar*, *Raja Ravi Varma*.

Neo-Impressionism Also known as *Pointillism* and *Divisionism*, this movement was initiated by the scientifically precise *paintings* and theories of the 19th-century *artist* G. Seurat. It was basically an off shoot of *Impressionism*, but unlike the looseness and weblike *handling* of patches of pure *colour* by the impressionists, G. Seurat applied his *colours* in dabs and dots of equal *size* at precisely the same distance from each other, arguing that this should make for an even more vividness and intensity of *colour* than the slap dash application of the impressionists. The same theories of *colour harmonies*, complementaries and importance of optical as against *local colour* were used. However, the interspersion of *white* (of the *canvas*) between each dab of pure *pigment*, effectively subdued the intenseness of effect that G. Seurat was looking for, resulting in *paintings* looking as though they were enveloped in a haze.

In India, *Narayan S. Bendre* adopted the *technique* of *Pointillism*, by using small, evenly sized and spaced dots of *balance* in his *colours*, pastoral scenes of village belles gossiping and drawing water from wells. He even used complementary *shades* of *colour* at times, but without adhering to the principles of G. Seurat. Refer *Optical Mixing*, *Stippling*.

Neo-Plasticism The theory of *art* proposed by Piet Mondrian, the Dutch *artist*. Following the 20th-century trend of abstraction, he proposed that *art* should be based chiefly on mathematical principles, with only horizontal and vertical *lines* to be used and only the primaries, i.e. red, blue and yellow in addition to *black*, *white* and grey which were the only *colours* that fit in with his theory of pure mathematics. Refer *Abstract Movement*, *Cubism*, *De Stijl*, *Line*, *Space*.

Neo-Tantricism Part of a *post-Independence* movement in *modern* Indian *art*, neo-tantric *artists* used the elements of traditional *Tantra art* and Science to come up with *paintings* with an individualistic approach. While the *visual* elements, i.e. the *drawings* of YANTRAS and MANDALAS may seem similar to true TANTRA for the most part, neo-tantric *artists* have only concentrated on certain vital elements. *Shankar Palshikar*, used the resonance of the sounds, Klim, Rhim and Shrim in his works, while *Sayed Haider Raza* used the primeval element of the BINDU, variously termed as a dot, a point or a seed, as the germinal element in his *paintings*. *Ghulam Rasool Santosh* on the other hand was fascinated by the sexual *imagery* implicit in TANTRA, while *Biren De* speaks of the evanescent *light* emanating from TANTRIC diagrams. Refer *Biren De*, *K.V. Haridasan*, *K. Jayapala Panicker* and *Balkrishna M. Patel*.

Neolithic Art Neo=New, Lithic=*Stone*. The word refers to the *art* and *architecture* of the New Stone age. Man had begun using tools by this era, having turned to agriculture, rather than depending exclusively on hunting. *Pottery* was invented, the *clay* pots being decorated with simple geometric *motifs*; rudimentary shelters were being built as well as temples to certain *gods*.

In India, one sees Neolithic *imagery* in the works of *Dattatray B. Pardeshi* among others.

Neutral Colours *Colours* that do not distinctively tilt towards a particular *hue*. Generally used to describe a range of mixed greys and beiges. Sometimes, *black* and *white* are also described thus. It is a *term* also used by *artists* to denote the middle *tone* in a *painting* that sets off the adjacent *colours*. e.g. The greys and browns, yellows and dull greens of *Ram Kumar's landscapes*, and the dull yellows and blue-greys predominating in *Mohan Sharma's* works. The neutral colours started to represent those that are pleasing, harmonious and low *key*. Refer *Harmony*, *Kashinath Salve*; Illustrations–*Laxma Goud*, *Laxman Shreshtha*.

New Realism The English translation of the French Nouveau Realisme, a *term* used by French *critic* Pierre Restany to refer to the Pop-like works of French *artists*. In India the *style* has been popular since 1980s. *Artists* created *art* objects from waste, scrap and *found objects*. They also experimented with shapes with the use of *ready-mades*, sandstone, *terracotta*, *acrylic* sheet, *steel*, *leather* mirrors, *fibreglass* and *metal*, of interrelating *assemblage* with *sculpture*, *junk art*, and *installations*. *Computer art*, *Video art*, photography, and *collage* also became popular. The manifesto of New Realism emphasized that the vision of things should be inspired by the feelings of *modern* nature, which is that of the factory, city, publicity and mass media, science and technology. This was heavily influenced by the commercialization witnessed by an industrialized world and the need to view it in a romanticized *manner*. *Pop Art*, *Minimalism*, *Op Art*, *Kinetic Art*, post-modernism photo-realist *paintings* all represented this New Realism manifesto. In India New Realism took many *forms*. With *traditions* running strong initially, it acquired the *hues* of protest *art*. Then *artists* started experimenting with Indian spirituality and philosophy, depicting it using *found object* or geometric *patterns*. Thus was born a uniquely Indian concept of New Realisms as seen in the works of *Aku*, *N. Pushpamala*, *Vivan Sundaram*, *Nalini Malani*, *Navjot Altaf*, *Krishnamachari Bose*, *G. Reghu*, *Mohan Samant*.

Nimbus The circular or oval golden disc or *halo* placed behind the head of saints or other divinities or royal personages. Refer *Aureole* and MANDORLA.

Nirvana Literally a "state of neither being nor not-being", but it is not the liberation from the endless cycle of birth and rebirth, promised by MOKSHA. It is voluntary *transition* of a BODHISATTVA, i.e. a person who has attained Bodhi, or enlightenment, by means of consciously subjugating all earthly pleasures, *illusions* and desires. Nirvana is a psychological condition rather than a physical one, in that even a living person can experience it, having become a BUDDHA himself and being in constant touch with, and having an all encompassing knowledge of all living matter, yet not being affected by it. Nirvana also speaks about total compassion for all living matter. Refer *Buddhism*, *Jain*, *Jainism*, KARMA, *Indian Museum* Kolkata, *Laxman Pai*.

Non-Figurative Art A synonym of *abstract art*, or *art* in which no *figures* appear. Western influence in Indian *art* was most profound on non-figurative *artists*, for example, even roughly-formed sculptured pillars of Indian temples exude the same spirit as of the living. Refer *Abstract*, *Abstract Expressionism*, *Abstract Landscape*, *Abstract Movement*, *Abstract Painting*, *Abstract Symbolism*, *Abstraction Geometric*, *Abstraction Lyrical*, *Abstraction Organic*, *Anti-Art*, *Dadaism*, *Ambadas*, *Bimal DasGupta*, *Vasudeo Santu Gaitonde*, *Chittrovanu Mazumdar*, *Sayed Haider Raza*.

Nootan Kala Mandir (NKM) (Mumbai, MAHA). Established in 1932 as a private enterprise in the field of *Art Education*, it was housed on the famed French Bridge of central Mumbai. NKM was founded by late G.S. Dandavathimath who was an *artist* himself, being an expert in *pastel* portraiture. After his demise, his son Shashi Dandavatimath, an architect, became the principal.

Eminent personalities like G. Badiger, V.R. Rao, D.A. Shetty, *Abdul Rahim Appabhai Almelkar*, V.V. Godkar and *Vasantrao A. Mali* were associated with it. Recognized by Govt. of Mumbai the institution had up to 150 students each year. Presently, Anand Pardesee is the principal. Prominent students of NKM were S.M. Pandit, *K.K. Hebbar*, *Sayed Haider Raza*, *Vasudeo Santu Gaitonde*, V.G. Baraskar, *Vasantrao A. Mali* and D. Nadkarni an *art critic* who studied *drawing*. Today the classes are conducted for *landscapes* and *portraits*, in the *realistic style* using live *models* and object *drawings*.

Nude The word is used in preference to "naked" to describe the undraped human *figure* as depicted in *sculpture*, *graphic* and *painting*. The study of the nude is an essential part of an *artist's* academic training. It is from the nude that the *artist* gains an insight into the structure and working of the human body, having studied the bony skeleton and the musculature earlier. The earliest nudes were the mother goddesses or "Venuses" found in the old Stone age. However it was the aspect of fertility rather than *anatomy* that are the *highlights* of these votive *figures*. The concentration on the nude *figure* as an artistic expression was seen much later in the Greek use of the male *figure*. *Artists* like B. Michelangelo and A. Rodin have exploited the nude to make memorable works of *art*, though for long periods in history, religious organizations have condemned the display of human flesh as pagan. In India, the nude or semi-nude human body was always a part of traditional Indian *sculpture* and *painting*, in as much as the *artist* was only depicting what he saw in the tropical climate of the country. For sometime however, especially after the advent of the Islamic invaders, the nude was taboo, appearing only in private semi-pornographic *miniature paintings*. In the modern period, we have certain *artists* who often depict the female nude, like *Jatin Das*, *Francis Newton Souza*, *A. Ramachandran*, *Muralidhar R. Achrekar*, *Krishnaji Howlaji Ara*, *Akbar Padamsee*, *Bhupen Khakhar*, *Anupam Sud*, *K. Shenoy*; Illustration–*Life-Drawing*.

O

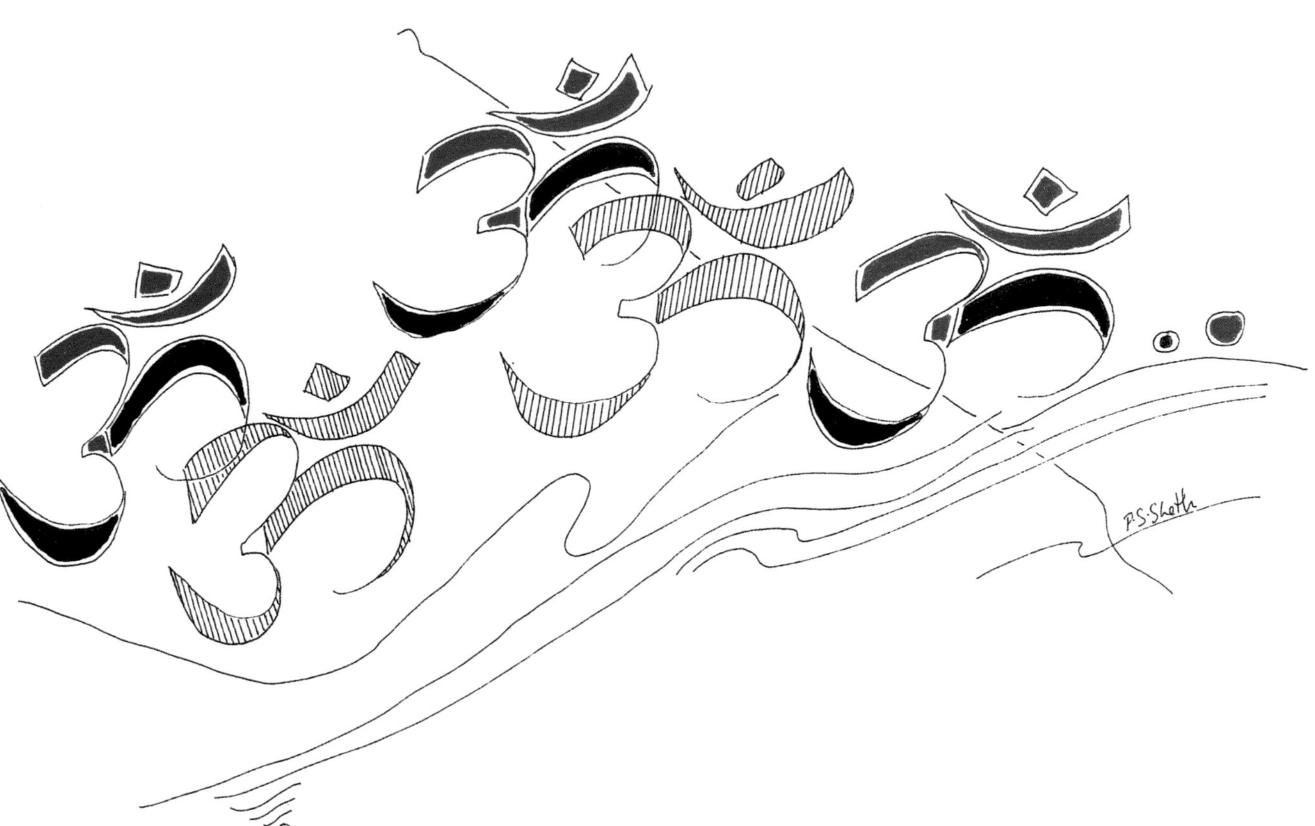

OM; Pratima Sheth, Drawing, *Pen* & *Watercolours*, 1993 (See notes on page 255)

Oeuvre (French)=work. The word refers to every single work, *painting, drawing, sketch* or *sculpture* of the *artist*; in short a documentation of his or her total output over a lifetime. E.g. *Satish Gujral's* total output as an artist would include his *paintings murals, sculptures, relief assemblages,* architectural *designs* and interior *designs*. Refer *Creation, Sheila Thadani*; Illustrations–*Akbar Padamsee, Piraji Sagara–Relief, Abanindranath Tagore, Sanat Thaker.*

Offset Printing In India this method was used approximately since the end of the 18th century. As against direct printing, offset has the advantage of printing the same *image* that is worked on a *plate*, rather than giving a mirror *image*. This process overtook *lithography* and could be operated manually or through the machine, in the printing process. A large rubber-covered blanket cylinder on an offset press first picks up the *impression* from the inked plate and transfers the imprint onto a sheet of *paper*, which has been damped and placed to receive the *print*. The plate has to be re-inked by hand. Refer *Oleography, Printmaking, Viscosity Printmaking.*

Oil Binder used in the mixing of *oil paints* and coating *paper* with oil for *oil painting*. India has a centuries-old *tradition* of using *colours* made of plant substances, vegetable oils and gem *stones* that have had a long lasting effect. The crude vegetable and oil are still used by some *artists* as one of the protective *mediums* in *egg-tempera, tempera*. In India, oil became the main *medium* in *painting* since the 19th century. It was known as Bengali *art* because *Abanindranath Tagore* was one of the first *artists* to explore the *medium* in WB, and *Raja Ravi Varma* in the South. Refer *Drying Oils, Egg-oil emulsion, Facing, Neo-Bengal School, Turpentine, Anjolie Ela Menon, Rabin Mondal.*

Oil Paint A *paint* in which dry *pigment* is suspended in *drying oil* base to hold together the particles of the *pigment* to *form paint*. Linseed oil, pressed from seeds of flax plant is the most widely used oil. It makes for tough, resilient *paint films* and is compatible with most *colours*. Poppy seed and sunflower oil have also been used. In Kerala *artists* were known to use olive oil as well. *Oil paintings* are usually executed on *canvas* or specially treated panels, masonite or *oil papers*. The slow drying *nature* of oil paint is an advantage as *paintings* can be worked and reworked until a satisfactory result is achieved. However, over a period time, oil paints tended to become yellow and brittle. *Oil painting* was first introduced to India by the Company *painters*, like Tilly Kettle, William Hodges, who were patronized by the Maharajas. The first extensive use of oil paints in India was by the artist of the *Neo-Bengal School* who used this *medium* to *paint* in the European *style*. Observing foreign *artists Raja Ravi Varma* became one of the first Indian *artists* to start with *oil painting*. Refer *Company School, Company Painting, Oil, Bengal School, Benode Behari Mukherjee, Abanindranath Tagore*; Illustrations–*Abstract Landscape, Academic Art, Christian Art, Encaustic, Fauvism, Form,* KALI, *Naive Art, Sakti Burman, Shiavax Chavda, K. V. Haridasan, Surendra Pal Joshi, C. N. Karunakaran, B.P. Kamboj, Laxman Pai, Kartick Chandra Pyne, Antonio X. Trindade, Raja Ravi Varma, Jai Zharotia.*

Oil Painting *Paintings* executed by the use of *oil paints*. It was first employed by the Italian *artists* about 500 years ago, as an alternative to *fresco* and *tempera paintings*. The surface of an oil painting, though usually glossy, can appear *matte* by the addition of drying agents. Thin, *transparent* glazes of *oil* can be used in conjunction with thick, *opaque* strokes of *paint*, which can be both flat and non-reflective or impasted and heavily textured as though in *relief*. Oil painting is thus a versatile *medium*, capable of being handled differently by different *artists*.

In India, oil painting was introduced by the British *portrait* and *landscape painters* in the 18th century. As these works were prized by Indian rulers for their novelty value as well as alien *technique*, Indian *painters* too started adopting this *technique*. *Raja Ravi Varma* was among the earliest Indian *artists* to work with the *medium*, experimenting with *pigments* for quite sometime before finally understanding the *technique*. In the present century, *artists* including *Manjit Bawa, K.K. Hebbar, Maqbool Fida Husain, Anjolie Ela Menon* and *Jehangir Sabavala* have all worked with the *medium*, exploiting it in their own *manner* to come up with *colour* application and *texture*, that is uniquely their own, above the vagaries of changing subject matter. Refer *Art Education, Bengal Oil Painting, Cartoon, Lean, Miniature Painting, Mixed Media, Modern Review, Oil, Oil Paint, Oil Pastels, Opacity, Opaque, Painting, Pigment, Portrait, Style, Tempera, Viscous, Sudhangsu Bandhopadhyay, Prayag Jha Chhillar, Mahadev V. Dhurandhar, Jamini P. Gangooly, Santosh Manchanda, Ravindra Mestry, Ramesh Pandya, K. Jayapala Panicker, Narayan R. Sardesai, Siddhartha Sengupta, Prabha Shah, Kailash Chandra Sharma, Jaspal Singh, Rameshwar Singh, Sovon Som, Shamendu N. Sonavane, Ali J. Sultan*; Illustrations–*Francis Newton Souza, Jogen Chowdhury, S. Fyzee-Rahamin, Mass.*

Oil Pastels, Oil Crayons These are small, soft *pigments* bound together in oil-impregnated sticks. *Paint* sticks are similar but larger in *size*. Oil crayons are far more malleable than *wax crayons*, they can be applied thickly, scraped thinned with spirit or *brush*. *Pastels* have varied over the years from sophisticated *pastel shades* to a bright and *discordant palette*. e.g. *Shiavax Chavda* was one *artist* who used *pastel* for its spontaneity and lightning effect. Refer *Chalk, Crayon Manner, Fixative, Medium, Mixed Media, NKM, Gobardhan Ash, Anis Farooqi, Hemendranath Mazumdar, Dulal Mondal, Milind Phadke, B.R. Panesar, Kartick Chandra Pyne, Rajen, Paramjit Singh, Abanindranath Tagore, Samarendranath Tagore, Nita Thakore, Dinkar V. Wadangekar, Babu Xavier*; Illustrations–*Manoj Dutta, Portrait–Satyendranath Bandhyopadhyay, Repousse–Ram Kishore Yadav.*

Old Master A *term* used to refer to an accomplished *artist* and his work, usually produced before the 19th century. Similar works of the 19th century and the early part of the 20th century are known as *modern* masters. In India, however the *term* Old Master is usually employed to refer to the works of certain *artists* of the pre-Independence era, including *Raja Ravi Varma*, *Rabindranath Tagore* and *Jamini Roy*. They were all offsprings of families of artistic background. Refer *Artist*, *Bengal Oil Painting*, *Bengal School*, *Company School/Company Painting*, *Flora & Fauna Paintings*, *Glass Painting*, *Glazing*, *History Painting*, *Industrial Art Society*, *JJSA*, *Kalighat Pat*, *Kalighat Folk Painting*, *Kangra*, *Oleography*, *Painter*, *Painting*, *Replica*, *School of...*, *Santiniketan* (WB), *Sculptor*, *South Indian Bronzes*.

Oleography A process used in *lithography* to reproduce multi-coloured *paintings* or *designs* in *oil*. A separate *stone* or *plate* is used to *print* each *colour* individually on to the required *paper* or *canvas*. However, oil-based *paints* rather than printer's *ink* are used to further the *illusion* of *oil painting*. In India, Bamapada Bandopadhyay in Calcutta and later *Raja Ravi Varma* in Bombay were among the first *artists* to exploit this *technique*. While the former had his *paintings* oleographed in Germany, *Raja Ravi Varma* set up a press in Mumbai in 1893. The first oleograph to be printed here was "The Birth of Shakuntala", one of his most famous works. In fact, much of *Varma's* popularity lies in the production of these *prints*, which, being cheap could easily reach almost every Indian home. However because of his ill-health, he soon sold the press in 1901, along with the right for the *reproduction* and sale of 89 of his works. Refer *History Painting*, *Lithography*, *Offset Printing Reproduction*.

OM=the *spiritual* sound-symbol sacred to the Hindus. The Vedic-*time* symbol which is *creation*, development and destruction; pronounced as "A" "U" "M" meaning VISHNU, SHIVA and BRAHMA respectively, to create *spiritual* energy. The syllable "OM" represents the deepest vibration of the cosmos. It is also said to have been recited by SHIVA when he performed Tandava Nritya (dance) to energize *creation*. It is a sacred symbol hummed at the beginning of all Mantras (Vedic hymns). Refer *Pattern*, SHIVA, *Spiritual*, *Sujata Bajaj*. (See illustration on page 253)

One-Point Perspective Refers to linear *perspective* in *painting* in which the eye is drawn towards the focal point of one single *vanishing point* in the centre of the *composition*. This type of *perspective* was popularized by the *artists* of the *Renaissance*. The *Company School* introduced one-point perspective to India. *Academic Art* in India followed the rules set by the *Company School* even in *watercolour* study. Refer *Aerial Perspective*, *Atmosphere/Atmospheric Effect*, *Backdrop*, *Orthogonal*, *Space*, *Gaganendranath Tagore*.

Op or Optical Art An *art* movement in the 60s, which sought to exploit both abstraction and *Kinetic art*. Though all *art* is basically optical in *nature*, in that it seeks to induce the spectator into believing the *illusions* of *landscape*, *portraits*, *still lifes* and other such subjects, Op *artists* concentrated on making large-scale *patterns*, that were themselves static, but appeared to move when focused upon for a period of time. For this, the *patterns* had to be absolutely geometric in *nature*, scale and also complementary (preferably *black* and *white* as they offered the highest *colour* contrast) in *colour*. The *optical colour mixing* of an *after image* with a *hue* is created in some of the works of *P. T. Reddy*, *Dashrath Patel*, and other *artists*. Refer *Abstraction Geometric*, *Colour Wheel*, *Colour Circle*, *Complementary Colours*, *Hard-Edge Painting*, *Kinetic Art*, *Mixed Contrast*.

Opacity The power to render the surface *opaque*, by means of applying thick, obscuring layers of *pigment* over the *canvas* or *paper* as in *oil painting*, *gouache*, *casein* and *acrylics*.

Artists have used relatively heavy *opaque colours* by thick application of *pigment* or by mixing *colour* with *white*. *C. Douglas* used dark *monochromes* to render opacity of *form*. Refer *Filler*, *Finish*; Illustrations–*Bal Chhabda*, *C. Douglas*, *Rini Dhumal*.

Opaque Not *transparent*. They are non-translucent or non-reflecting *colours*, mixed *white*. *Gouache*, which was first used in India by *painters* in Murshidabad in the 1790s is opaque due to the inclusion of *white*. *Oil painting* can be variously opaque or *transparent*. *Enamels* can be *transparent*, *translucent* or opaque. They derive their *colour* from the addition of various metallic oxides to the flux. Opaque *ink colours* are used for *printmaking*. Refer *Acrylics*, *Casein*, *Opacity*, *Shade*, *Tempera*, *Tint*, *Abdul Rahim Appabhai Almelkar*; Illustrations–*Enamel*, *Thanjavur (Tanjore) Painting*, *Gobardhan Ash*, *Manjit Bawa*, *Rini Dhumal*, *Ganesh Haloi*, *Dinkar Kowshik*, *Ram Kumar*, *Tyeb Mehta*, *Ved Nayar*, *Krishna N. Reddy*, *Laxman Shreshtha*, *Saroj Gogi Pal*, *Rabindranath Tagore*.

Open Form The opposite of tectonic or *closed form*, open form refers to *compositions* in *painting*, *sculpture* and even *architecture*, which are expanded, unfolded or outspread, need not be balanced, symmetrical or centralized, e.g. *K.C.S. Panikar*, the first Indian *artist* to break away from the confines of *figurative art*, preferred the exciting possibilities of open form compositions to the static stability of *art* with the elements of TANTRA. In the field of *sculpture*, *Avtarjeet S. Dhanjal*, *Kanayi Kunhiraman* and *Dhruva Mistry's* compositions are *monumental*, conceptual, and open form. Refer *Abstract*, *Figure*, *Ramkinkar Baij*, *Prabhakar Barwe*, *Balbir Singh Katt*, *Rabindranath Tagore*.

Open Work Refer *Jali Work*.

Optical Colour, Optical Mixing Optical colours are the result of various factors affecting both the eye and the object which is studied, e.g. the *local colour* of grass is green, but it may appear yellow at noontime or grey in the dawn or dusk. According to the *colour* theories of the impressionists and the neo-impressionists (G. Seurat), optical mixing of *colours* resulted in brighter secondaries than was possible by the actual mixing of the *colours*. At a distance, the eye visualized the mixing of the two patches to produce an intense third *colour*. *Narayan S. Bendre* varied the *size* of the patches of *colour* to be more scientifically accurate, using dots of precise *size* all through the *painting*. Refer *Impressionism, Neo-Impressionism, Neo-Tantricism, Op or Optical Art, Secondary Colours, Tantra Art, Biren De, K.V. Haridasan, Laxman Pai, K. Jayapala Panicker, Sayed Haider Raza.*

Orissa State Museum (Bhubaneshwar, Orissa). The collections at this *museum* have a regional bias, with almost all examples belonging to Orissa. There are several galleries devoted to *sculptures* from the Sun (SURYA) Temple at Konarak and other temples of Bhubaneshwar from 10th to 13th centuries. There is also on extensive and interesting collection of *palm leaf* manuscripts, written in the Oriya Script of rounded letters. The remarkably detailed miniature *manuscript paintings* (17th century) follow a *style* particular to Orissa and are painted in *primary colours*.

Ornaments Refer ABHUSHANA.

Orthogonal In *one-point perspective*, the *lines*, which seem to converge at the *vanishing point* in reality, would be at right angles to the picture plane. The *artists* of the High *Renaissance* perfected this use of *one-point perspective* and *vanishing point*. The *composition* would be in the *foreground* with the *landscape* in perspectivial clarity behind.

In India it started with the *Company School, Bengal School* and the *academic style* dealing with the teaching of the *arts* with sharp foreground in focus against *perspective* clarity in the *background*. In earlier works, as in some of the *miniature paintings,* one sees the *perspective* of the picture plane very clearly, but not so in the whole *composition*. Refer Illustrations–*Seascape*, DIWALI/DIPAVALI; GANGA–*Raja Ravi Varma, Madhukar B. Bhat, Pralhad A. Dhond, Balvant A. Joshi, B. P. Kamboj, Paresh Maity, Amrut Patel, Gaganendranath Tagore, Sarada Charan Ukil.*

Outline The *line(s)* enclosing the simple exterior shape of a plane, *figure*, object or *form*. **1.** A simple *line drawing* can be said to be made of outlines. The outline can be used in *enamelling* as well–the cloisonnes of *metal* keeping the area of brilliant *colour* intact. *Artists* like *Tyeb Mehta* and *Syed Haider Raza* outline their flatly coloured forms. **2.** This may be an imaginary outline, the *drawing* or *sketch*, which is used in certain *styles* of *painting* showing the basic plan in the work of *art*. In India this *technique* was used in different methods in the *artists'* works, e.g. *back-glass painting, printmaking* and *sculpture*. *Artists* like *Nandalal Bose* used spontaneous quick-brushed *style* of whip-lash strokes and half stated outlines in his *tempera paintings*. Later, *artists* such as *Shiavax Chavda, Satish Gujral, Ram Kumar, Tyeb Mehta, Maqbool Fida Husain, Sayed Haider Raza* employed it in their *composition*, where the outline was created by splitting the *painting* into two *colour* next to each other or leaving the *canvas* bare. Refer *Ajanta, Contour, Cloisonnism, Miniature Painting, Stone Carving, Thanjavur (Tanjore) Paintings, Atasi Barua, P.N. Choyal, P. Vijyalakshmi, Jamini Roy, Rabindranath Tagore*; Illustrations–*Gobardhan Ash, Nandalal Bose, Jyoti Bhatt, Jamini Roy.*

Overlapping The application of layers of *colours*, one over the other, in the *frescoes* at *Ajanta*; in *transparent* glazes or in *opaque* layers of *oil painting*, which started from, *Neo-Bengal School*, in *transparent* layers of *watercolour*, and the *wash technique* introduced by *Abanindranath Tagore*. In *acrylic painting Arun Bose* and *Bimal DasGupta* used the same overlapping *technique* to create different *tints* and *shades* or textural variations. The overlapping of *forms* and *colours* in *abstract* works as in *Chittrovanu Mazumdar's compositions*. This was also used in *mixed media composition,* by *Satish Gujral* and *Dharmanarayan DasGupta; sculpture* and *printmaking, metal* sheets by *Shankar Nandagopal; Krishna N. Reddy's* work in several *colours* in *viscosity printmaking* respectively. Refer *Multi Block Colour Printing, Photo-montage; C. Douglas, Shaibal Ghosh, K. K. Hebbar, Krishen Khanna, Mahirwan Mamtani, K. Vasant Wankhede.*

P

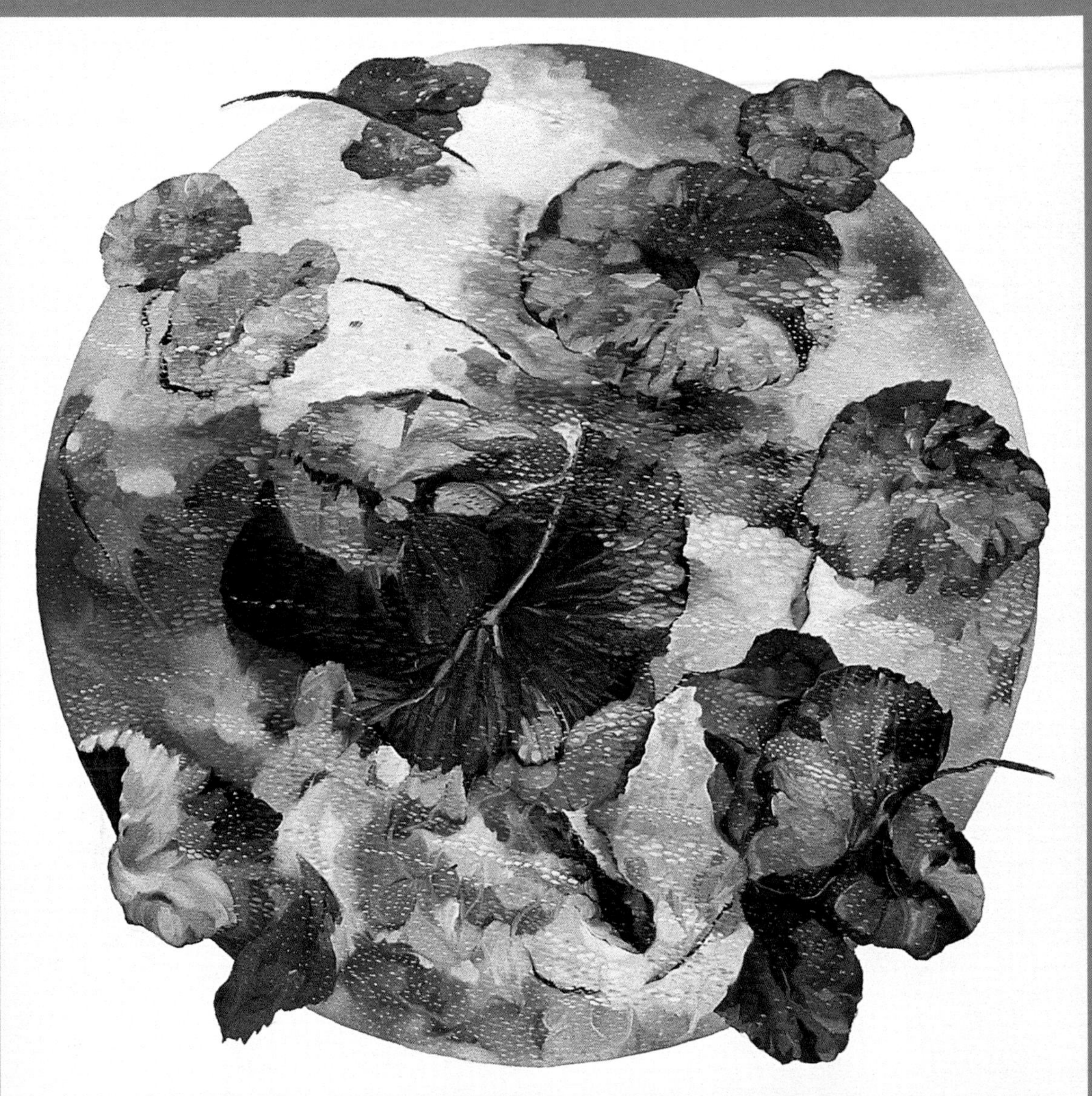

Prakash, *Surya*: "The Pool of Life", *Oil* on *Canvas*, 1995, 80x80 cm. (See notes on page 283)

P., Gopinath (1948–) b. Kerala. Education: *FA. painting GCAC* Chennai. Group shows & participations: *AFA* & *CIMA* Kolkata, TN *LKA* Galleries, 40 Artists British Council, Gallery Easel, Grand Charity Auction of Contemporary Art Tapestry & Values Art Foundation Chennai, AP Council *graphic art* Hyderabad, "Pictorial Space" & "100 years of Indian Art" curated by Geetha Kapoor, National Exhibition, Graphic Exhibition, *NGMA* & *LKA* all in New Delhi, Progressive Painters Association & Three Decades of Cholamandal by *artists* of the village at *JAG*, Kala Yatra Travelling show in India; International: Kala Yatra Malaysia, International Festival of Painting at Chatrau-Muse de Cannes-sur-Mer France, *Biennale* Valparaiso Chile, Cholamandal Artists' show Morocco. *Art* camps & workshops: by *CKP* in Kerala, All India Artists' camp show Hyderabad, Regional *graphic* camps *LKA* & *Graphic* workshop *GCAC* Chennai, *Printmaking* workshop MMB with *LKA* New Delhi also at Shimla by PUJ University; International: RCA. *Auction*: Sotheby's in Mumbai. Awards: Elected Eminent Artist by *LKA* New Delhi. Collections: *NGMA*, *LKA* & Ministry of External Affairs Govt. of India New Delhi, State *LKA* Cochin, *Govt. Museum* Thiruvananthapuram, *BB*, *CHAG*; International: Poland Chester Herwitz Collection USA.

Gopinath P. attempts to unveil the mysteries of various *forms* of *nature* through a subtle mix of *light* and *space* perceptions. This *idiom* of *forms* reveals infinite variations and imitations driven by his quest for pure plastic order, *natural forms* and *patterns* of growth.

He lives in *Cholamandal*. Refer *Biomorphic*.

P., Gouri Shanker (1936–) b. Hyderabad. Education: Dip. in *drawing* & *painting* Mumbai & Hyderabad, Post-Dip. in *portrait* Hyderabad; Specialization in *graphic art MSU*. Over 26 solos: Hyderabad, Kritika Gallery Bangalore, *JAG*, TAG, *SAI*. Group participations: Chennai, Jammu, Chandigarh, *LKA* AP, KB Hyderabad, *LKA* & National Exhibition *LKA* New Delhi, *CYAG*, SRAG, *BB*, *Triennale* & *Biennales* in India & abroad; International: USA, Turkey. *Art* camps: *Painting* & *Graphic* camps SZCC, Regional Centre Chennai, National Akademi New Delhi, Orissa Akademi, *LKA* Manipur, Srinagar & Hyderabad; Seminar: Hyderabad. Over 40 awards: including Gold Medals HAS, All India Graphics New Delhi, Mysore DAE. Fellowships: Senior and Emeritus fellowship Govt. of India. Members: HAS, General Council AP, *LKA* New Delhi, Board Studies FA. University Gulbarga. Appointments: Seminars Hyderabad, Visiting demonstrator & examiner at *CFA* University Kerala. Collections: AP Museum & *LKA* Hyderabad, *LKA* & *NGMA* New Delhi, PUJ University Museum Chandigarh, *SJM*, pvt. Chennai, Bangalore; International: Australia, USA, France, Denmark, Germany, Ford Foundation Members USA.

Gouri Shanker P. has been inspired by *nature* and the circumstances of his life which he depicts on *canvas*. *Nature* however, is distorted, using the basic academic principles of *colour* and *form*, into *abstract* shape and *patterns*. He has also painted a series of village and *pastoral* scenes, rickshaw pullers and ecological *themes* on the forest and environment. In his recent *oils* and collographs, the emphasis is on textured *abstract forms* combined with *lines* of varied modulation.

P., Vijyalakshmi (1929–) b. South India. Studied *art* privately; Specialized in *miniature painting*, also studied under *Debi Prasad RoyChowdhury*. Solos & group participations: Ujjain, Mysore, Madras Regional Centre & Madras Museum Chennai. Awards: Junior Fellowship HRD Ministry, AP Miniature *Biennale*, Golden Mudrika Thiruvananthapuram, Mysore DAE; Contributed over 600 *paintings* to the SANSKRIT volume of RAMAYANA, along with husband, *P.L. NarasimhaMurti*. Collections: Govt. Museum Chennai.

Vijyalakshmi P.'s *paintings* are influenced by traditional South Indian *murals* and *Thanjavur (Tanjore) glass painting*. Her subjects are mainly religious inspired by Lepakshi, its *tradition* and *miniature paintings*. Episodes from *legends* of RAMAYANA and MAHABHARATA in their *classical* narrative stylized mode and *colour*. There is an emphasis on decorative *outline* and intricate jewellery. Her *figures* are large-eyed and sinuous.

She lives and works with her husband *P.L. NarasimhaMurti* in Chennai.

Padamsee, Akbar (1928–) b. Mumbai. Education: GDA in *painting JJSA*. Solos: *Art Heritage* New Delhi; Sanskriti Art Gallery Kolkata, *PUAG*, *CYAG*. Retrospective: by *Art Heritage* New Delhi & Mumbai, Six decades *PUAG*; International: Montreal. Group participations: Marvel Art Gallery Ahmedabad, *CYAG*, *PUAG*, *JAG*; International: Galerie Saint-Placide, Galerie Raymond Creuse Paris, Gallery One, Museum of Modern Art & RAA England, *Biennales* Venice, Tokyo & Sao Paulo. Participated: In the first *computer art* show in India "State of the Art". Workhop: For *artists* & film-makers. *Auctions*: Christie's for Helpage India, Osian's & Heart in Mumbai. Awards: Kalidas Samman Award MP. Govt; International Artist-in-Residence Stout State University Wisconsin, French Art Journal "Art" Award. Fellowship: Jawaharlal Nehru Award; International J.D. Rockefeller Fund USA. Appointments: Visiting lecturer *JJSA*. Publications: Made short films with his set of geometrical drawings. Collections: *NGMA*, *LKA* & *Art Heritage* New Delhi, *M.F. Husain*, Godrej, Deutsche Bank Mumbai, *JNM*, *PUAG*; International: Masanori Fukuoka & Glenbarra Museum Japan; pvt. & public, National & International.

Akbar Padamsee's *oeuvre* comprises a wide range of subjects, including metascapes, *still lifes* and *figure* studies. He started with *figuration*, using the stylized yet vital, simplified *vocabulary* of the *PAG painters* in the early 50s. His study of SANSKRIT and consequent understanding of Indian philosophy had its impact on his *paintings*. His use of traditional Indian *iconography*, in the rendering of one of his *nudes*, triggered a new *style*. In the late 50s, he painted his versions of the *landscape*, entitled "metascapes". The fractured *handling* of the jewel-bright *paint* in these works was carried into his *nudes* and *portraits* as well. In the 90s, he painted a new version of these *landscapes*, calling them "Mirror Images". He has continued with his *figure* and *portrait* studies, stylizing them to the point of anonymity. The grey-black of his *charcoal drawings* strip the *figure* of its sensuality, and it is *form*, structure and *line* that excite the *artist's* sensibility. Akbar Padamsee has also prepared *compositions* using computer generated digital *forms*, which are then printed.

Akbar Padamsee lives and works in Mumbai.

Padma=lotus. **1.** In *architecture*, the Padma–lotus appears variously as the capital or base of pillars in several temples. **2.** It is the VAHANA the support of Goddess LAKSHMI, the consort of VISHNU. She is usually represented as standing or sitting on an open lotus pedestal; a number of half-opened lotuses and lotus buds float around her; she also carries a lotus in one hand. In later Hindu and *Buddhist art*, the lotus serves as a pedestal for many divinities, including BRAHMA, who is called Padmaja (born of the lotus) and BUDDHA, who sometimes has a lotus cushion on his throne. **3.** The famous BODHISATTVA Padmapani, in *Ajanta*, is depicted with a blue lotus in his hand, the graceful curve of the flower being echoed in the tilt of his head. Refer *Ajanta*. The lotus is also one of the four main *attributes* of VISHNU and his many AVATARAS, the others being the conch (SHANKHA), disc (GADA) and club (CHAKRA). **4.** *Modern artists* of the 19th-century continued to *paint images* of *gods* and goddesses, including LAKSHMI and SARASWATI on the lotus. Refer CHATUR BHUJA, *Elephanta*, *Gupta*, PURANA, *Thanjavur (Tanjore) Painting*, *Raja Ravi Varma*; Illustrations–*God*, LAKSHMI, NAYIKA, *Jogen Chowdhury*.

Padma

Padmasana, Padma-asana=Lotus-seat. Dhyanasana: seated in the Padmasana with the legs crossed and the feet resting on the thigh. Padmasana: Same as Dhyanasana; seated with legs crossed. Padmasana is also a circular seat in the shape of an open lotus, serving as the seat of certain *gods* and goddesses, e.g. LAKSHMI and BRAHMA. Refer ASANAS, DHYANI-BUDDHA, *Gandharan Art*, PADMA, YOGA, *Dinanath Pathy*.

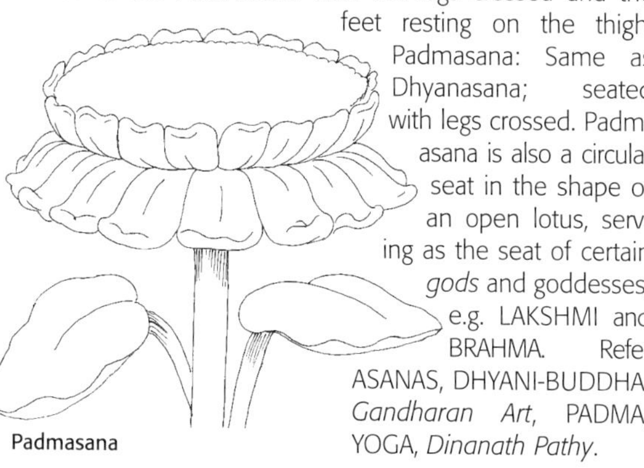

Padmasana

Pahari Miniature Painting Pahari means the hills, the generic *term* given to the *paintings* produced in the hill states in present-day PUJ and HP. The *style* varied from kingdom to kingdom, the dates being impossible to analyze, though with the exception of *Basohli*, the *court painters* practising at Kangra, Guler, Jammu and Mandi had all fled the Mughal court in search of better prospects during the reign of Aurangzeb. The original Pahari *style* includes elements of Gujarati *style* of manuscript illustration, the Mughal *style* of the Aurangzeb period and the early half of the 17th-century collection of Rajasthani School. Refer *Basohli*, *Kangra*, *Mughal Dynasty*, *Miniature Painting*, *Rajput Miniature Painting*.

Pai, Laxman (1926–) b. Margao, Goa. Education: GDA in *painting JJSA*. In Paris for 10 years 1951–1961. Over 100 solos: Kolkata, Chennai, Panaji Goa, Bangalore, *JJSA*, *Dhoomimal*. Retrospective: Goa, Mumbai, New Delhi; International: Paris on GITA-GOVINDA, London, Munich, Stuttgart, Bremen, New York, Bangkok, Kuala Lumpur, Singapore. Group participations: *Biennales* Sao Paulo Brazil & Tokyo. *Auctions*: Heart & Osian's Mumbai, Bowring's New Delhi, Sotheby's & Bonham's–London. Awards: National *LKA* Award, Padma Shri Govt. of India, Hon. Govt. of Goa, Jawaharlal Nehru Award Goa. Member: General Council *LKA*. Commissions: Two *murals* for Patradevi Memorial Goa. Appointments: Was the Principal of Goa College of Art. Publication: Book "My Search My Evolution" in 2000. Collections: *NGMA* New Delhi, PUJ, Chennai & Nagpur Museum; International: Museum of Modern Art Paris, Ben & Abbey Grey Foundation USA, New York Public Library, pvt. & corporates.

Laxman Pai was fascinated with the beauty of the Goan skyscape, capturing sunsets and palm trees in *ink* and *water-colour* on *paper*. His subjects include a series of *paintings*, inspired by Jaidev's GITA-GOVINDA, the life of Mahatma Gandhi, the life of BUDDHA, the RAMAYANA, Kalidasa's Ritu-Samhara, the RAGAMALA, Kashmir, Purush and Prakriti, Indian dance, *Kangra portraits*, RAJ, *images* of Goa, the KARMA/MOKSHA series and RASA. There is a definitive use of the folk *idiom* in his works, with linear *outlines* and *rhythms* leading to large fish-shaped eyes and curved nostrils. The "Festival of Season" series on five seasons done in 1993, has strident *colours*, with foliage occupying most of the formally structured *space* within the works. There is also a close resemblance to the works of certain neo-tantric *artists*, especially in his *handling* of fragmented human *forms* and limbs.

After ten years of being principal of Goa College of Art 1977–87, he now lives and works in New Delhi. Refer *Kangra*; Illustrations–KARMA, MOKSHA.

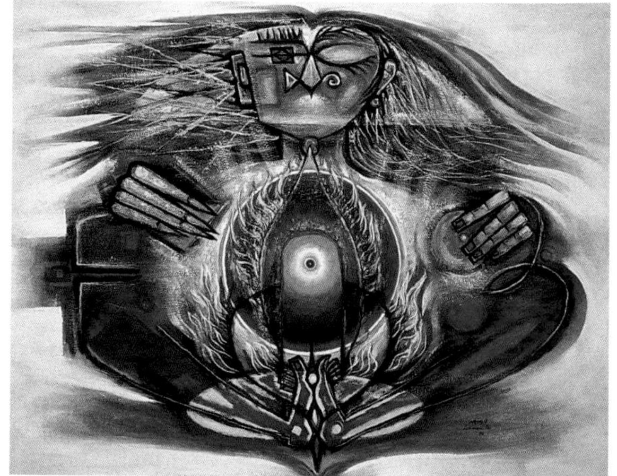

Pai, Laxman: "Purush Prakriti in Kamasutra", No.1, *Oil* on *Canvas*, 1994, 153x203 cm.

Paidi, Raju A. (1919–1997) b. Bobbili, Srikakulam, AP. Education: Joined GDFA *Madras School of Art* Chennai 1940, Started *FA*. Institute Paidi Raju School of Art & Craft Vizianagram, AP. Solos & group participations: Vizianagram,

Rajamundry, Hyderabad, Kharagpur, Visakhapatnam, Orrisa, *Santiniketan*, *AIFACS;* International: RAA London. Awards: *AIFACS*, several Gold Medals *LKA*, MP, PUJ Govt.; Also for "Rural Life". Member: Academic Council & *LKA* AP, CKP Vizianagram, HAS. Publications: "The Sunday Times", "Enlite" news magazine & AP *LKA* Catalogue. Collections: USSR national & international.

Raju A. Paidi's early works depicted the village belles of his native AP. The female *figure*, especially in the village, going about her various chores, was to be his major concern, the *images* being executed in a decorative, folk-based *idiom*, with large, staring eyes, stylized limbs and decorative panels in the *background*. His use of *colours* too, has its basis in *folk art*, with earth *tones* predominating. His larger *mural size paintings* show the influence of *Ajanta*, in the elongation of the *figures*.

Paint It is made of raw powdered *pigment* with a *vehicle* (fluid) that spreads the *colour*. *Oil*, water or any other *medium* (*vehicle*) helps to thin and spread the *pigment* thinner. There are *solvents* used to clean the paint from *brushes*, tools and the hands. Refer *Acrylic*, *Encautic*, *Gouache*, *Oil Paint*, *Oil Pastels*, *Tempera*, *Watercolours*.

Painter A person producing works of *art*, generally *original*, by means of *painting* with a variety of *media*, including *watercolour*, *oil*, *gouache*, *acrylics*, *collage* and *mixed media*.

In the early days in India, a *painter* would generally work in a guild, for the court of certain kings. *Paintings* were not individual efforts, but worked upon in a group with several Chitrakaras contributing variously to a single work. In *contemporary* times, while groups of *artists* may share common *ideologies*, works are highly individual, with the personality of the *artist* being more important than the dictates of the buyer. Refer *Blot Drawing*, *Chiaroscuro*, *Company School*, *Contemporary*, *Earth Colour*, *Engraving*, *Foreshortening*, *Kalighat Pat*, *Kalighat Folk Painting*, *Mughal Dynasty*, *Oil Paintings*, *Studio of...*, *Tantra Art*, *Thanjavur (Tanjore) Painting*, *Volume*, *Wood Block Printing*, *Wood Engraving*, *Jaya Appaswamy*, *Dipak Banerjee*, *Narayan S. Bendre*, *Madhukar B. Bhat*, *Sailoz Mookerjea*, *Benod Behari Mukherjee*, *Baburao Painter*, *Madhav Satwalekar*, *Ved Pal Sharma*, *Rabindranath Tagore*, *K. Venkatppa*, *Nathu Lal Verma*.

Painter, Baburao (Baburao Krishnarao Mestry) (1890–1954) b. Kolhapur. No formal education in *arts*. Trained under his artisan father in *ivory carving*, carpentry. Specialized in *painting backdrop* curtains for the Marathi stage, including scenic *backdrops* for Bal Gandharva's drama troupe in Pune. Constructed the box camera & established the Maharashtra Film Company & worked with his cousin brother Anandrao Painter. He wrote, produced & directed 26 films between 1920–30. He later became the head of Shalini Cinetone, the talkie movie company established by Rajaram Maharaj, the erstwhile ruler of Kolhapur. *Auctions*: Osian's Mumbai. Award: A certificate of merit Wembley Festival London. Appointments: *Sculpture* Sangali, including the famous *bust* of Shivaji Maharaj's *sketch* & *sculpture* in Kolhapur. Publications: Books & cover magazines which depicted *portraits*, Book on his Centenary 1890–1990. Collections: Kolhapur, Aundh, Nagpur, *BAAC* Kolkata.

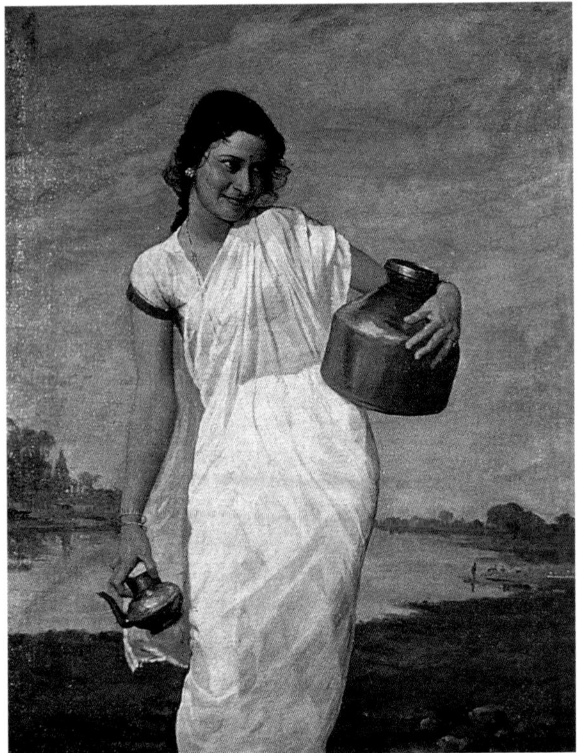

Painter, Baburao: "To the temple or Jalvahini", *Oil* on *Canvas*, 1946, 105x85 cm.

There is a neo-classical delicacy of appearance in his *oil paintings* of young women, variously fetching or drawing water from the well, dressed as goddesses or part of a larger mythological *narrative*. His choice of *colour* was subtle in the Western *manner*, rather than bright and *discordant*. His *paintings* were generally stylized, decorative and complete in *perspective* with the main *figure* in full action. He also painted the *posters* the for all his films. Refer Illustration–God.

Painterly A *term* applied to a work of *art*, where objects and *masses* are defined through the application of broad areas of *colour*, *tone*, and *chiaroscuro*, as opposed to a *linearly* work of *art*, where *line* predominates. The *term* was first coined by the German *art* historian, Heinrich Wolfflin to differentiate between the *styles* of various *painters*. In India *Raja Ravi Varma* used a painterly *style* when compared to *Abanindranath Tagore* and *Jamini Roy*. Refer *Lyricism*, *Picture Space*, *Serigraphy*, *Surjeet Kaur Choyal*, *Jahar DasGupta*, *Mahadeo Bhanaji Ingle*, *Girish H. Khatri*, *Ravi Mandlik*, *Papri B. Mehta*, *Sailoz Mookerjea*, *Niranjan Pradhan*, *Ganesh Pyne*, *Kashinath Salve*, *G.S. Shenoy*, *Akkitham Narayanan*.

Painting A work, usually consisting of two-dimensional images produced either by a group of *artists*, or a professional independent *painter*, using a variety of *techniques* and from various materials on various *supports*.

Earlier paintings in India were variously painted on *palm leaf*, cloth, walls of caves and *paper*, e.g. *Ajanta* and *miniature paintings*. Later works were created in *tempera*, *gouache* and *watercolours* i.e. *Company School*, *Bazaar painting*, where the *styles* and *techniques* changed after the 18th and 19th century (refer *history painting*). At times *ivory*, silk, Indian *canvas* (refer *canvas*), *oil* and *acrylic* on *canvas* were the materials used. After *Raja Ravi Varma*, *oil painting* became popular, while *folk art* developed in different parts of the country. Miniature *art* continues mainly in RAJ and other schools. *Art* changed considerably after 1947 in its *style*, subject and *technique*. 1930s to 1950s was the transition period, while 1950s to 1960s assimilated a language of non-objective *art* including *Tantra art*. *Acrylic paint* and its *technique/style* was brought in around 1970. Rapid changes took place every decade as *artists* tried to be independent with their ideas, style and expressions. Between the years 1980 and 1990 *paintings* expanded to include even xerox and computer material, e.g. *Navjot Altaf, Akbar Padamsee, Atul Dodiya*. *Body art* is one of the *styles* of the 20th–21st centuries, where artists like C. Krishnaswamy from Chennai combines YOGA with painting to create a symbol of human *form* in his *compositions* with earthy *colours* and *texture*. Refer *Collage, Mixed Media, Paper, Jaganath M. Ahivasi, Nandalal Bose, Maqbool Fida Husain, Hemendranat Mazumdar, Sailoz Mookwrjea, K.C.S. Paniker, Amrita Sher-Gil, K.G. Subramanyan, Vivan Sunaram, Abanindranath Tagore, Gaganendranath tagore, Ravindranath Tagore.*

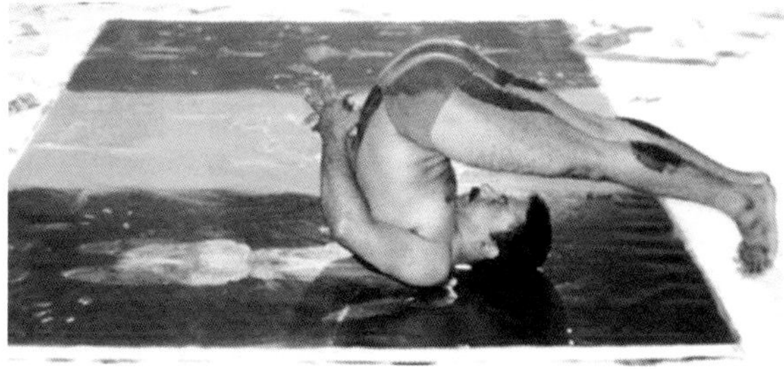

Painting: "Krishnaswamy, C.; (who himself is performing) *Yoga* (Halasana–Plough pose)", *Oil* on *Canvas* 2005, 305x183 cm.

Pal, Saroj Gogi (1945–) b. Nedi, UP. Education: Dip. in *painting GCAC* Lucknow, later *Banasthali Vidyapith* RAJ & Post-Dip. *College of Art* New Delhi. Solos: Black Partridge, *Art Heritage*, Gallery Aurobindo & Gallery Artist Studio New Delhi, Vithi Gallery, Vadodara, Jamaat & *GC* Mumbai, SC, TKS, *SAI, JAG, CYAG*, SAG; Inter-national: Mon-treal, Rawalpindi, Westmount, Germany, UK.

Group participations: *LKA* Exhi-bitions, Masanori Fukuoka's & 50 years of India's Independence at *NGMA* & Gallery Artist Studio New Delhi, *GC* Mumbai & Kolkata, *SG* Mumbai, Bangalore, Chennai, SC, *GAC*, SRAG, TKS, VG, *LTG, CYAG, JAG;* International: Karachi. *Auctions*: Heart New Delhi, Osian's Mumbai. *Art* workshops & camps: PUJ University Museum Kasauli, *Graphic* workshop *LKA* New Delhi, *Santiniketan*, *Wood cut* workshop *MSU* & Chandigarh; NZCC artist camp Srinagar, SKP & *GAC* New Delhi. Awards: Group 8 Medal *Graphic print* Chandigarh & New Delhi. International: *Biennale's* Jury Commendation Certificate, Algeria National *LKA* New Delhi. Fellowships: *LKA* Fellowship, Junior Fellowship Dept. of Culture New Delhi. Collections: Godrej Mumbai, *CYAG*, pvt. & corporates.

Saroj Gogi Pal works with several *mediums* simultaneously. These include *painting*, *sculpture*, *printmaking*, *ceramics*, jewellery making, *weaving* and *installation*. Her *installation* "Red Saryu has Eyes" was a composite of several *mediums*. Her earlier works revolved around society and her immediate world. She soon created figural types, providing them with additional *visual Symbolism* culled from myths and ritualistic and religious sources. They include women with wings—a creature hovering between the realms of the terrestrial and the celestial, flitting between reality and *fantasy*. Her NAYIKA also appears in the guise of Kamadhenu, the wish-fulfilling cow. Her *gouache colours* took on the appearance of small *paintings* on glass, with heavy *outlines* and flesh pink skin *tone*. Saroj Gogi Pal was a lecturer in *art* and *printmaking* at many Delhi colleges in the 70s.

Since then she has been working as a full-time *artist* in New Delhi.

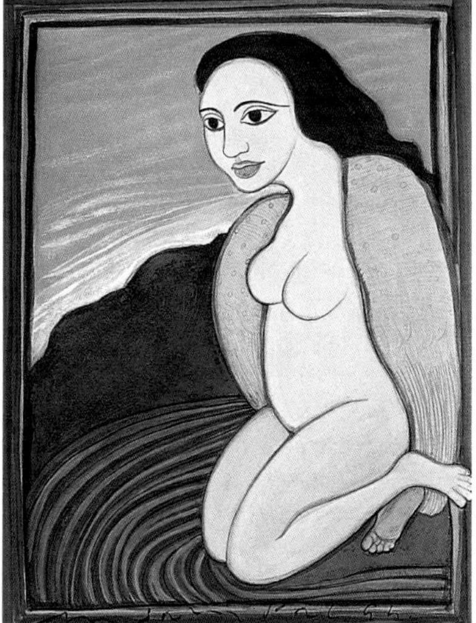

Pal, Saroj Gogi: "Kinnari", *Gouache* on *Paper*, 1994.

Pala Miniatures The Pala dynasty lasted from circa AD 8–10th century in the Eastern parts of India, specifically Bengal and Bihar, and gave a fresh lease of life to *Buddhist art* in these parts of India. Dharmapala, son of the founder of the Pala dynasty, Gopala II, was the most famous ruler. He not only rebuilt the ruined Buddhist monasteries but also founded new ones. Bengali artisans produced several BODHISATTVA *figures* in *bronze* and Ashta-Dhatu (an *alloy* of eight *metals* as *gold*, *silver*, *copper*, tin, *lead*, *brass*, *iron* and *steel*). The *masterpiece* of Pala *sculpture* is the Sanchi torso identified as the Kasarpana Avalokitesvara (lord of compassion), because of the antelope skin worn across the body like a scarf.

However, it is their exquisite *miniature paintings* on *palm leaf*, that the Palas were most known for. These *paintings*, very few of which have survived, continue the linear *tradition* of the *Ajanta frescoes*, being identical in *style*, except for the difference in *technique* and material. Like the *Jain manuscript paintings* in Western India, Pala miniatures were also executed on the treated and trimmed leaves of the talipot palm. Most of the *palm leaf* was occupied by the *calligraphy* detailing the various stories illustrated. Only a small square *space* was painted, using similar tools and *colours*, as the

Jain paintings. The difference lay in the angular uneven surface of the wiry *Jain outline* and the graceful, elegant curves of the Pala. The difference between the *Ajanta* and the Pala *paintings* lay in the choice of subject matter, with Avalokitesvaras and BODHISATTVAS predominating the Pala miniatures to the exclusion of the JATAKA stories. Refer *Ajanta, Jain Manuscript Painting*.

Palaniappan, Rm. (1957–) b. Devakottai, TN. Education: Dip. in *FA*. & Post-Dip. in *ceramic design GCAC* Chennai. Solos: *Art Heritage* New Delhi, *SG* & *LKA* Chennai, *CYAG, JAG*; International: Dayton, Cincinnati & Manhattan USA, Galleries Den Haag Netherlands, Museum of Contemporary Art Holland. Group participations: *SG* Bangalore, *LKA* Exhibitions New Delhi, *CYAG*; International: Finland, Taipei, France, USA, UK, Japan, Spain, National Exhibitions Festival of India USSR, Museum of Modern Art Mexico, Contemporary Indian Art Havana. Workshops: *LKA* workshops Regional Center *LKA* Chennai, *LKA* Bhubaneshwar, *BB*; International: *Lithography* workshop University of Mexico USA. Awards: Fulbright travel grant, USIS International Visitorship programme, Merit Award Bhopal *Biennale*, National *LKA* Award; President of India's Silver Plaque, State *LKA* Chennai; International: Taipei Biennale. Fellowship: Junior & Senior Fellowship Govt. of India. Appointments: Delivered lectures & *printmaking* demonstrations in universities & institutions. Collections: *NGMA, LKA* & *Art Heritage* New Delhi, National Museum Chennai, XAL & Praxis Foundation Mumbai, *BB, CYAG*; International: British Museum London, Cincinnati Art Museum USA, V&A & pvt.

In the past over fifteen years, Rm. Palaniappan's work has focussed on the concept of motion. This involved interaction between *space, time* and environment. This was depicted as a man with winged head in his "Flying man" series, and was then systematically reduced to culturally neutral symbols and *ciphers* in the *form* of dots, *lines* and arrows. The document series of *prints* showed his use of materials as diverse as shellac seals, rubber stamps, phrases, numbers and tape. "Planets" is a later series, where he brings out the apprehension of mankind when confronted with the unknown frontiers of *space*.

Rm. Palaniappan has been working with *mixed media printmaking* for more than 15 years, exploring the relationship between shapes and movement, trying to find himself in the existing source of both the conscious and sub-conscious. He has also ventured into the field of *drawing* since the early 90s.

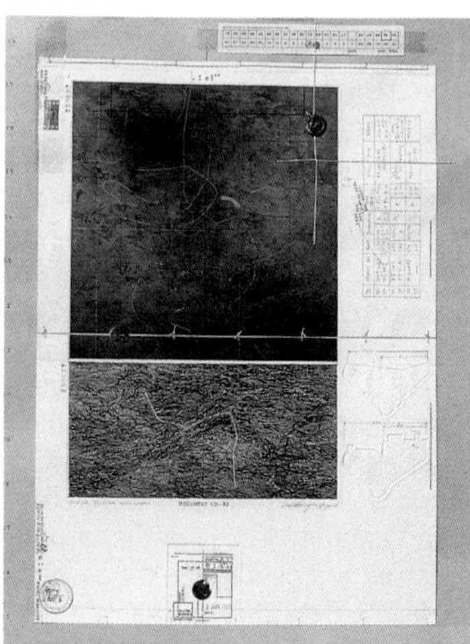

Palaniappan, Rm.: "Document x23" *Mixed Media Graphic*, 1985.

He had been in charge of the *graphic* workshop at the Regional Centre, *LKA* Chennai, was in Lucknow and now lives in Chennai.

Palette 1. The surface on which *pigments* are mixed, prior to their application in a *painting*. These can be made of *wood, plastic*, porcelain, coated *steel*, glass or disposable paper. The *watercolour* palette has a number of indentations for holding the *colours*, with large hollows for the mixing of *colours*. The traditional wooden *oil* palettes are flat with dippers attached to hold *oil* or *turpentine*. In India, conch shells were also used to *paint* in *tempera technique* e.g. *Ved Pal Sharma*. Refer *Gopal S. Adivrekar, Pratima Sheth*.

2. Also refers to the range of *colours* used by or chosen by the *artist*, which may be the characteristic of his *style*. i.e, the *warm colour* palette of *J. Swaminathan*, the yellows and overwhelming *black* of *Yusuf Arakkal* and the near *monochromes* of *Jehangir Sabavala*. Refer *Art Deco, Cubism, Opaque, Oil Pastels, Oil Crayons, Narendra Amin, Jyotish Dutta Gupta, V. Hariram, Papri B. Mehta, K.C. Murukeson, Nareen Nath, Dattatray B. Pardeshi, Premalatha H. Seshadri, Mohan Sharma;* Illustration–*Computer Art, Yusuf Arakkal, R. B. Bhaskaran, Arun Bose, Manoj Dutta, Ganesh Haloi, Anjolie Ela Menon, Rabin Mondal, Madhav Satwalekar*.

Palette Knife / Painting Knife An instrument used for applying *paint* on the *canvas*, especially for *impasto* effects. Also used for scraping *paint* off a *painting* in progress. They are available in many shapes and *sizes* and are different from the palette knife (used for cleaning the *palette*). The blade is blunt and is made of tempered *steel*. Refer *Broad Handling, Flat Application, Young Turks, Narendra Amin, Bhagwan Chavan, Suresh Choudhary, Bhupendra Desai, R.S. Dhir, Vasudeo Santu Gaitonde, Prem Chandra Goswami, Ghanshyam Ranjan, Prem Raval, Sagara Piraji, D.B. "Deven" Seth, Gurudas Shenoy, Shamendu N. Sonavane, Vasant S. Sonavani, Narendra Rai Srivastav, Harish Srivastava, Sumatimohan, Haripal Tyagi;* Illustrations–Landscape, *K.M. Adimoolam, Krishnaji Howlaji Ara, Krishen Khanna, Homi Patel, Baburao Sadwelkar, G.S. Shenoy*.

Paliwal, B.P. (1941–) b. Delhi. Education: Dip. in *art,*

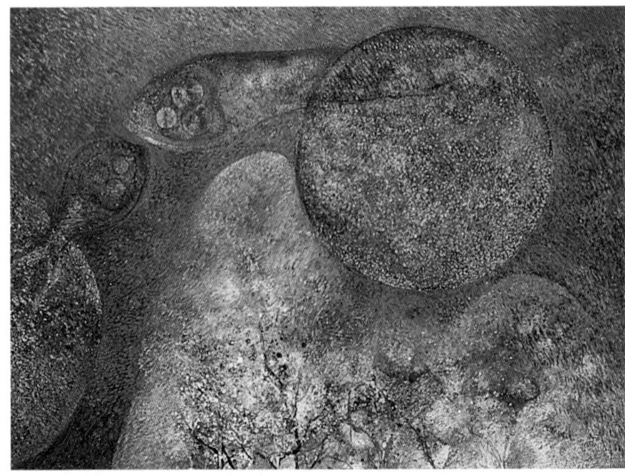

Paliwal, B.P.: "Fantasy I", *Mixed Media*, 48x65 cm.

teacher JMI & NDFA & *College of Art* New Delhi. Solos: *AIFACS*, TKS, SRAG. Over 66 group shows in India and abroad since 1966. Group participations: National *LKA* & *Triennales* New Delhi, IAFA Amritsar, All India Drawing Chandigarh & Lucknow, State Academy Patna, SKP, Over 22 annuals at *AIFACS*. *Art* camps: Dehradun, SKP Karnal, *AIFACS* Exhibition in Goa. Awards: IAFA Amritsar, Title Kala Shree *AIFACS*, SKP. Members: Life member *AIFACS*, Founder member Young Group New Delhi & Delhi Teachers Group Council member *AIFACS*. Collections: *NGMA* & *LKA* New Delhi, PUJ University Chandigarh, *AIFACS*, pvt. & corporates.

For the past 25 years, B.P. Paliwal has been fascinated with the teeming vegetal and aquatic life. There is a touch of *fantasy* in his depiction of marine creatures. Both *texture* and *colour* play an important role in his quasinaive renderings of fish and algae.

He lives in New Delhi.

Pallavas, Pallava Dynasty They succeeded the Andhras in South-east India in the 6th century, although they were known to have existed as far back as the 1st century BC. They were probably Buddhists who converted to Brahmanism around the 5th century. Their greatest contribution was the city of Mamallapuram, near Chennai (Madras). It was not only built by their greatest kings, Mahendravarman I & Narasimhavarman I, but was also named after them. They were known as Mamalla, the Great Warriors or Heros.

The most outstanding examples of Pallava *art* are the *rock-cut* temples and *reliefs* hewn out of living *granite* at Mamallapuram (*Mahabalipuram*). These include the Rathas (chariots) and the massive Gangavataran *relief*. In addition, the Pallavas also erected structural temples in Mamallapuram and their capital at Kanchipuram. Several *stones* were experimented with, including grey-white *granite*, leptinite and gneiss. Instead of the different *forms* of the Rathas, these Pallava temples were typically *Dravidian style* in plan and elevation. Of these the Shore Temple at Mamallapuram is perhaps the best known. It is constructed out of *black* leptinite and comprises of three shrines and the GOPURAM. It is similar to the Kailashnatha temple in Kanchipuram, erected by Rajasimha and his son Mahendravarman. A Pallava inscription, running to twelve verses in SANSKRIT in praise of Rajasimha, is seen outside the main shrine, which has four storeys. Pallava *sculptures* are graceful, slender and elongated. Their thin and tubular limbs make them appear ever taller. The slim female *figures* lean against their tall, broad-shouldered male counterparts. They have narrow chests and waists and wear few garments and *ornaments*. The DURGA Mahishamardini panel in the Mahishasura MANDAPA, depicts the slender, young goddess shooting arrows over the *demon's* head, as she serenely advances towards him with drawn sword and other *weapons* in her eight arms. There is no dramatic exaggeration, only a quiet but firm restraint. The Pallavas were especially skilled in depicting animals, as is evident in the many groups of animals, including elephants and monkeys in the Gangavataran panel. A few examples of Pallava *bronzes* also exist. The differentiating characteristic between Pallava and the more known CHOLA *bronzes* is the depiction of the sacred cord falling across the right forearm. Refer BRAHMA, *Chasing*, *Chipping Mould*, *Cire Perdue*, DRAVIDA, *Dravidian Style*, GANGA, *God*, *Mask*, *Subrayalu Dhanapal*.

Palm Leaf Talipot palm leaves (Talapatra) are leaves dried, smoothened, cut into strips as required, bounded with cord for *illustrations* and *painting*. This was enclosed between painted, lacquered wooden covers. The earliest palm leaf *illustration* being from Jaina manusripts, others from all important villages in Orissa, and even others from *Hoysala* and Bengal. Refer *Handmade Paper*, *Jain Miniature*, *Jain Manuscript Illumination*, *Illuminated Manuscript*, *Miniature Painting*, *Pala Miniatures*.

Palsikar, Shankar (1917–1984) b. Sakoli, MAHA. Education: GDA in *painting JJSA;* (1942–47); Studied under *Narayan S. Bendre*. Memorial Retrospective by *JAG* 1984. Group participations: All India National Exhibitions & *LKA* New Delhi, *AFA* Kolkata, *AIFACS*, *ASI*, *BAS*; International: Indian Art Exhibition Eastern Europe, Represented at various International Exhibitions including *Biennales* & *Triennale*. *Auctions:* Heart Mumbai. Awards: Mayo Medal, Gold Medal *BAS*, FA. Society Kolkata, Recipient of the First Cultural Scholarship in FA. awarded by Govt. of India, Honoured Gold Medal & later Silver & Bronze Medal by Art Academy of Italy in the field of *art* & *art education*. Member: Bombay Group of Artists; Life member of Art Academy of Italy. Appointments: International invitation by Govt. of SriLanka as an Art Educationist; Represented India Plastic Art Conference England. Collections: *NGMA* & *LKA* New Delhi, *JJSA*.

Shankar Palsikar was a versatile *artist*, equally proficient at *portraits, compositions* in the *figurative,* as well as the *abstract* mode. *Pastoral* scenes and high *key compositions* in *watercolour* are seen in the works of the early 40s. The Far Eastern use of the planar *perspective* disappears within the *space* of the decade, instead, a folk element emerges in the use of decorative *figures* placed against a flat *background*. His use of *oils*, however, is entirely different, with impasted *texture* in the *abstract* expressionist *manner* of de Kooning. His *tempera* works were spontaneous *line drawings* against broad, *flat applications* of *colour*. His *compositions* of the 70s showed his foray into *neo-Tantricism*, with the introduction of *calligraphic* symbols and words. However he is best known for his quick fire *portraits* and *portrait* demonstrations at the *JJSA* where he was first a teacher and later Dean (1968–75). They are not mere likenesses, but instead provide us with a psychological insight into the *model's* mind.

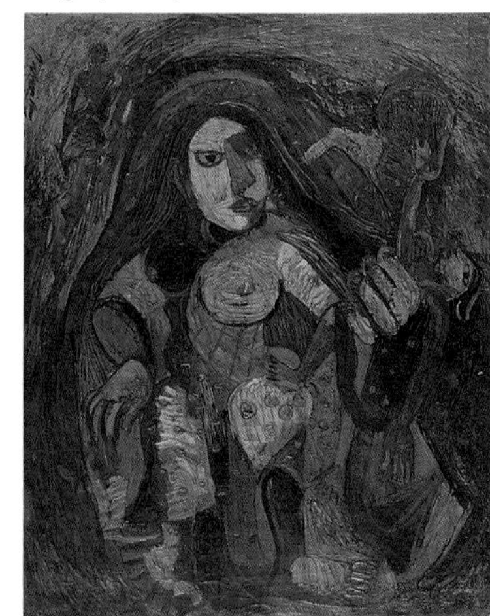

Palsikar, Shankar: "Maya", *Oils*, 61x50 cm.

Panchal, Bharat (1944–) b. Nadiad, GUJ. Education: GDA in *painting*, GDA in *commercial art*, Art Master's Certificate CNCFA & later lecturer. Solos & group shows: Ahmedabad, Mumbai, New Delhi. Group participations: *Art Heritage* New Delhi, *LKA* Ahmedabad, *JAG*. *Art* camp & workshops: GUJ *Artists* camp Mount Abu RAJ, *Graphic* workshop *LKA* Ahmedabad, *Illustration* workshops. Awards: GUJ *LKA*, *BAS*. Member: GUJ *LKA*. Collections: *LKA* GUJ Ahmedabad, *NGMA* & *LKA* New Delhi, *LKA* Lucknow, pvt. in National & International.

There is an element of the surreal in Bharat Panchal's *pen* and *ink drawings* and *oil paintings*. This is apparent in his use of winged, headless creatures, floating in free *space* along with brightly coloured chairs and *stones*. The influence of *Basohli* miniatures is seen in the flat and strident *colour* application.

Bharat Panchal lives in Ahmedabad.

Panchal, Naren (1936–) b. Umargaon, GUJ. Education: GDA in *FA*. *JJSA*. Solos: Gallery 127, Gallery Chetana Mumbai, Gallery Aurobindo New Delhi, Heritage Chennai, *ABC* TAG; International: New York. Group participations: Harmony, Gallery Chetana Mumbai, National Exhibitions & Contemporary Erotic Art-New Delhi, *Arts Acre* Kolkata, Kala Yatra Chennai, *BAS*, *VAG*; International: Geneva, Nairobi. Award: *BAS*. Commissions: *Murals* Mumbai, Ahmedabad, Bangalore, Panjim, New Delhi, Vadodara. Appointments: Has worked as a stage set & toy designer, as *Art* Dir. for short advertising films. Collections: *LKA* New Delhi, pvt., institutions & corporates, National & International.

Naren Panchal has worked with different *mediums* including *watercolour*, *acrylics* and *mixed media*. His earlier works were in traditional *metal reliefs*, textile *colours* and ancient *forms*, as being done by a craftsman, but later his forte lies in creating *murals* and *painting* on sheet *metal* and *wood*. His *forms* are culled from rural life, presented in a highly fragmented and distorted state. This originates from his vision of squares and circles influenced by *Cubism*.

He lives and works in Mumbai.

Pandya, Durgashanker K. (1907–1993) b. Gondal, GUJ. Education: GDA *JJSA*. Awards: Felicitation, bestowed title of Kalabdi (Sea of Art). Founder member: National Academi, dance, music Mumbai 1937–41. Publications: Illustrated several of Premchand's stories & various Gujarati magazines, including "Janmabhoomi" (newspaper), whose logo he designed; Other magazines include "Sharada" "Ravivar" & "Vande Mataram"; Illustrated several novels & greeting cards & invented a new typography for English magazines, incorporating the elements of *illustration* into *calligraphy*. Collections: Navneet Prakashan Mumbai.

Durgashanker K. Pandya was a *painter*, and a master draughtsman, using the *line* with great dexterity, creating *chiaroscuro* at will. His favoured *themes* were romantically entwined couples set in a mythological *background*. He also did several patriotic *illustrations* of freedom fighters. He was meticulous in his approach to minute details of costume and jewellery. This veteran journalist and illustrator worked alongside *Ravishankar M. Raval* and *Kanu Desai*.

Pandya, Mahendra (1926–) b. Bharuch, GUJ. Education: B.A. in fine, *sculpture MSU*. Solos: TAG. Group participations: *LKA* New Delhi, Indian Sculptor's Forum Chandigarh, TAG; International: Venice, Japan, Sao Paulo. *Sculptor's* camps: Makrana RAJ, Pawagadh GUJ State, at Mollela (Madalpur) by *LKA*, J&K Akademi Kashmir. Awards: National Scholarship for two years, *BAS* Prize, Tamrapatra HAS Certificate; International: British Council Scholarship England. Member: GUJ State Akademi, Jury *LKA* New Delhi & RAJ *LKA*, India sculptor's Forum Chandigarh. Commissions: Several *murals* & *sculptures* in sesame teak *wood*, *plaster of Paris*, *bronze*, *marble*, *cement*, *terracotta* and *mixed media*. Appointments: Prof. *Santiniketan* & BHU; Selection Committee AP University, HoD *FFA (MSU)*. Collections: *NGMA* & *LKA* New Delhi, *LKA* GUJ, *SJM*, TATA.

Mahendra Pandya experimented widely with sculptural *media* including new industrial *mediums* like *fibreglass*, though he preferred *marble* and *wood*. This curiosity about the material and its possibilities intruded into his teaching as well (he retired as Dean of *FFA [MSU]* Vadodara). He exposed the fine *grain* of the *marble* and *wood* through his *carving*. Since sandstone had no such *grain*, he used textural surfaces ranging from the rough to the smooth to create a subtle interplay of *chiaroscuro*. The works of the late 50s show a reliance on heavy solid *masses*.

He handled *portraits* in the *manner* of A. Rodin, with impressionistic smudges and pinches of soft *clay*. His *wood carvings* of the early period show *chisel* marks roughly following the directions. of the *wood grain*. He also did some *assemblages* in *wood*, mounting organic shapes with pegs in a strongly vertical or horizontal configuration. He also employed the blowtorch, charring the pieces to achieve a unified *block*-like look.

The "Balcony" series in *wood* and *marble* dates from the 70s. The *figures* or heads rest against or above a railing suggestive of the Indian Jharokha.

He lives and works in Vadodara.

Pandya, Ramesh (1930–) b. Vadodara. Education: B.A. & M.A. in *FA*. with *painting MSU*, Illinios State University, followed by part-time lecturer USA. Solos: CAG Ahmedabad, Indore School Art Gallery, *AIFACS*, TAG; International: Illinois, USA. Group participations: *LKA* New Delhi, GUJ *LKA*, Mysore DAE, MPKP Exhibition, PUJ University Graphics Exhibitions, *AIFACS*; International: Poland. *Painter's* camp: *LKA* GUJ. Awards: *AIFACS*. Member: GUJ *LKA*. Commissions: *Mural* for Parliament House, Worked with *K.G. Subramanyan* 1982. Publications: Has also prepared *illustrations* & *art* work for Gujarati dailies & "Span" magazine.

He simplified the *figure* studies in his *compositions* in the accepted *modern manner*, along with his impressionistic *landscapes* in *watercolour*. After his visit to United States, he adopted a slightly cubist approach in his *compositions*. He also experimented with crumpled *paper*, using both *oil painting* and *watercolours* in an *abstract manner*.

He lives in Vadodara, where he retired as a reader in *FFA (MSU)*.

Panesar, B.R. (1927–) b. Hoshiarpur. No formal education in *art*. Solos: *BAAC*, *AFA*, American Centre & Gallery Unique Kolkata, *AIFACS*, *CKAG*. Group participations: National Exhibition *LKA* & *Biennales* New Delhi, *AFA*, *BAAC* & *CIMA*, Kolkata, *AIFACS*, *GK BAS*, HAS; International: *Graphic Biennale* Germany & Australia. *Art* camps & workshops: *Painting* camp Sanskriti Art Gallery Kolkata, *Graphic* workshop *LKA* New Delhi. Awards: *Atul Bose* Award *AFA* & *BAAC* Kolkata, Govt. Museum Chandigarh, *BAS*. Member: Joined *Dilip Das Gupta's* studio for two years & *AFA* Kolkata 1965–74 and *SCA*. Collections: *LKA* New Delhi, *BAAC* Kolkata, Govt. Museum Chandigarh & pvt.

B.R. Panesar tried his hands at sketching, *pastel* studies, *watercolour* and *oil painting*, the subjects being "Beyond the poverty line" and *landscapes*, before selecting *collage* as the *medium* most suited to his temperament. The feeling of creating a work of *art* out of waste is an added incentive, as is the element of the accidental–the act of finding potential material anywhere. Abstraction naturally predominates in his subtly coloured *compositions*, as *figuration* would appear contrived and artificial.

He lives and works in Kolkata. Refer Illustration–*Collage*.

Panicker, K. Jayapala (1937–2003) b. Quilon, Kerala. Education: Dip. in *FA*. GCA Chennai. Solos: *Chitraniketan Art Gallery* Thiruvananthapuram, DC Art Gallery Kottayam. Kerala Kalapeotom, *COAG*, SAG. Group participations: Emakulam, Bangalore, National Academi Exhibition New Delhi, Kolkata, Mumbai & Chennai, *LKA* Chennai & Kerala, *AFA* Kolkata, HAS, *JAG*, *Triennale* India; International: Brussels, Amsterdam, Copenhagen, Prague, Paris, Asia Today Milan, *Biennale* Bangladesh & Chile, RCA. *Art* camps & workshops: *Graphic* workshops *LKA* New Delhi, Camps at Kerala *LKA*, Creative Weaving and Dyeing MMB Chennai & Thiruvananthapuram; International *Artists*, Camps Morocco. Awards: National Award & New Delhi, *AFA* Kolkata, Kerala *LKA*, HAS. Fellowships: Fellowship Govt. of India HRD *Painting* New Delhi. Member: *Cholamandal* group of *artists*. Collections: *LKA* New Delhi, Chennai & Kerala, *AFA* Kolkata, Air-India Mumbai, Quilon Kerala, CCMB Hyderabad, & other pvt.

The *colour white*, variously signifying *light*, purity and VISHNU, was the *key* note in K. Jayapala Panicker's *paintings*. He was a deeply religious person and the Advaitic belief is brought out through the *medium* of *painting*. *White*, he said, mixed with every other *hue* i.e. its relationship with VISHNU. The hard-edged symbols and *ciphers* in his early works were still used, but later they were diffused through multiple layers of *paint*. There was also a division of the painted *space*, in effect offering two separate areas of meditation. K. Jayapala Panicker had worked with *metal* sheets using *repousse technique* in addition to *oil painting* on *canvas*. K. Jayapala Panicker lived in Quilon.

Paniker, K.C.S. (1911–1977) Coimbatore, TN. Education: Dip. in *art Madras School of Art* and a lecturer & joined under *Debi Prasad RoyChowdhury* Chennai. Solos: Chennai, Mumbai, Kolkata, New Delhi; International: London, Paris, Lille. Retrospective of his works by *LKA* Chennai & New Delhi. Group participations: *Triennales*, of World Art India 1968–76 *LKA* Exhibitions; International: *Biennales* Sao Paolo & Venice, India Art Exhibitions Mexico, Russia & Tokyo. *Auctions:* Osian's Mumbai. Awards: Eminent *Artist LKA* New Delhi, Fellow *LKA*. Founder Member: Established the Progressive Painters Association & *Cholamandal* Chennai. Upgrading *Madras School of Art* & renaming *GCAC*. Member: Executive Board *LKA* New Delhi; International: Indian Delegation World Art Congress New York. Appointments: Vice Principal & Principal of *Madras School of Art*. Collections: *NGMA* & *LKA* New Delhi, National Art Gallery Chennai.

K.C.S. Paniker was both an influential *art* teacher, having retired as Principal of the *GCAC* Chennai, as well as an innovative *painter* heralding the birth of *Modernism* in South India. He was to influence many *artists* of the younger generation, not only through his seminal works and experimentations, but also through his conception of *Cholamandal*, as a self-sufficient *artists'* village. He was one of the first *artists* to break away from the confines of *figurative art* (his *figures* were *monumental* and brutal in their scale and conception) leading the *composition* towards *open form*. The neat scribbles and cryptic diagrams were influenced by his chance encounter with the notebook of a student of mathematics. An element of TANTRA was slowly ushered in, mainly because of the play of astrological-looking diagrams and *calligraphy*. There is also the piquancy of the folk *motif*, which crops up every now and then in his works, acting almost as catalyst or footnotes in the *composition*.

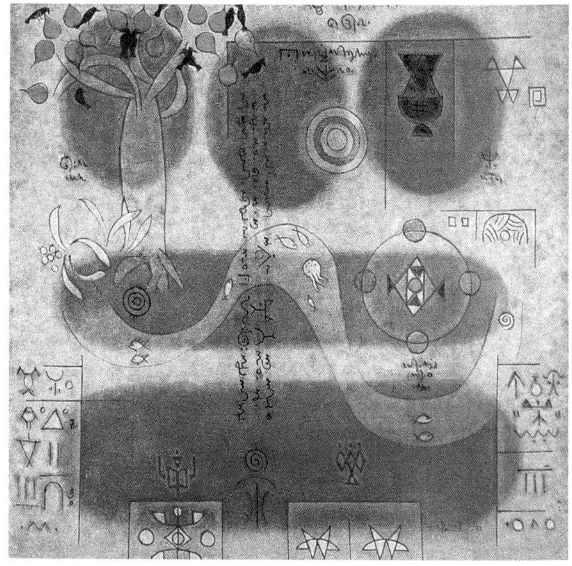

Paniker, K.C.S.: "Words & Symbols", *Oil* on *Canvas*, 1972, 90x90 cm.

Pantheon A large number of *gods*/deities belonging to one religious sect. i.e. Hindu pantheon. Refer *Archaeological Museum*, *Attribute*, *Bengal Oil Painting*, BHAGAVAN, GANESH, LAKSHMI, *Manuscript Paintings*, *Mythology*, PARVATI, *Manickam Senathipathi;* Illustrations–GANESH, LAKSHMI, PARVATI, SHIVA.

Panwar, A.S. (1929– d) b. Tehri, Garhwal. Education: Dip. in *FA*. *KB Santiniketan*, Specialization in *sculpture KB*

Santiniketan & *MSU*, studied under *Nandalal Bose*, Kripal Singh Shekhwant, *Ramkinkar Baij* & *Sankho Chaudhuri*. Solos: New Delhi, Kolkata, Lucknow, Kanpur. Group participations: *BAAC* Kolkata. *Art* camps: Various *artists* camps in *sculpture* & *painting*, seminars, & workshops. Awards: National Award, *AFA* Kolkata, Honorary degree D.Litt. conferred on him by Kanpur University. Members: *LKA*, *VBU*, BHU, *MSU* & took part in education board planning. Appointments: Delivered lectures, Seminars & gave demonstrations in *paintings* & *sculpture* Aligarh, In *sculpture* at *KB Santiniketan* assiting *Ramkinkar Baij* & taught three decades; Was HoD of *sculpture* Dept. *FFA* Lucknow University; International: Tokyo Japan, Kansas USA. Publications: Various articles in Hindi & English for various newspapers & periodicals, books–"My Encounters with my Models", "The Art of Sculpture", "Bengal School of Painting", "Vanishing Landscape of Garhwal", "Vanishing Landscape of Santiniketan", "Vanishing Landscape of Lucknow", "My Japan Visit", "The Cockfight".

A.S. Panwar has practised both *sculpture* and *painting*, besides being a writer. He has executed sculptural *portraits* of Indian personalities, including the late Mother Teresa, Jawaharlal Nehru, *Nandalal Bose*, *Ramkinkar Baij*, *Maqbool Fida Husain*, *Bhabesh Chandra Sanyal* and many others from life.

Panwar, Bhanwar Singh (1939–) b. Jarau, RAJ. Education: GDA CNCFA Ahmedabad, Art Master's Certificate Mumbai. Solos: *LKA* State Art Gallery Ahmedabad 1987, 92 *JAG*. Group shows: Mumbai & Ahmedabad. Group participations: Ahmedabad, New Delhi, Mumbai. *Art* camp: *LKA* camp Saputara, Mount Abu. Workshop: HCVA, Conducted child *art* workshops GUJ. Awards: *AFA* Kolkata, *LKA* GUJ, HAS. Collections: *AFA* Kolkata GUJ *LKA*, TIFR Mumbai, pvt. & corporates.

He started *painting* with materials as diverse as *enamel colours*, sawdust and Fevicol, creating simple *collages* with simplified *figures*. Later, he started to add detail and *depth* to the works, turning to abstraction with *impasto*. Soon he began assimilating Indian elements in the works, which were variously labelled folk, tribal and neo-tantric. His latest works show a creative use of *distortion* and simplification in his *landscapes*. He uses *oils* and *transparent washes* like *watercolour*.

At present he is an *art* teacher in Ahmedabad.

Panwar, Goverdhan S. (1938–) b. Deogarh, RAJ. Education: B.FA. in *sculpture MSU*–Studied Blue pottery & *paper machine*, Handicrafts Training Crafts Training Institute Jaipur. Solos: Panaji. Group participations: RAJ *LKA*, *LKA* New Delhi, Goa State Kala Academy Exhibition, SZCC Exhibition Nagpur, *AIFACS*. *Art* camps: *Sculpture* camp, WZCC Udaipur, *Stone carving LKA* Gulbarga & Hyderabad. Awards: Goa State Kala Academy, State Award, SZCC Award. Members: Govt. of Goa, State Handicraft, WZCC Udaipur, also in RAJ. Appointments: RAJ *LKA*, Secretary *MSU*, different sections General Council *LKA* & RB New Delhi; Designed for Floats & Tableaux for State & National pavilions for republic parades. Collections: *LKA* & *NGMA* New Delhi, SZCC Nagpur, WZCC Udaipur, *IFAS*, pvt.

Goverdhan S. Panwar has evolved a *style* of his own, often turning to *caricature* in his sculptural *portraits* of politicians and bureaucrats, using certain fruits and vegetables based on brinjals or balloon *form* (which in RAJ is associated with ambiguity) to convey his resentment. The *sculptor's* works are mainly in *terracotta*, rosewood, teak wood and *cement*. He also uses *metal* at times.

He lives and works in Goa.

Panwar, Prabha (1932–) b. Gwalior, MP. Education: Dip. *KB Santiniketan* Studied under *Nandalal Bose*, Surandranath Kar, *Ramkinkar Baij*, Kripal Singh Shekhavat. Solos: Meerut, Lucknow, New Delhi, Gwalior; International: Represented Indian Cultural Delegation with Solos Russia & Czechoslovakia. Group participations: *LKA* New Delhi, *LKA* Lucknow; International: Louisiana, USA. Workshops: Gave demonstrations in Alpana (Rangoli–floor *design*) & *Batik* in UGC workshop Agra. Awards: UP *LKA*, National Award & Research Scholarship All India Handicraft Board New Delhi, *AIFACS*. Appointments: Lecturer Lucknow Art College. Publications: Articles on *Batik*, Alpana in several magazines. Collections: *NGMA* New Delhi, UP *LKA*, Lucknow University, Gwalior Art Gallery, pvt.

Prabha Panwar has specialized in *Batik painting*. The ambience in *Santiniketan*, with its emphasis on *craft* training and the presence of Gauri Bhanja, senior Prof., helped her develop a personalized *style* in *Batik*, though she also learned *leather* work and Alpana (Rangoli). Her National Award winning piece, "Dragon" was made entirely with vegetable *colours*. Prabha Panwar also does *wash paintings* in the traditional *Santiniketan style*. Later she has also experimented with embossed *leather*. Her *motifs* show the impact of folk *imagery* in its simplicity and decorativeness.

She lives in Lucknow.

Panwar, Raj Kumar (1964–) b. Prangarh, UP. Education: M.FA. in creative *sculpture College of Art* New Delhi, Dip. in *drawing* teacher & Dip. in *commercial art SUSA*, Dip. in *art* appreciation *NGMA* New Delhi, Dip. in Indian *art* & *culture National Museum* New Delhi. Solos: New Delhi, Mumbai, Bangalore. Group participations: National *LKA* Exhibitions New Delhi, *BB Biennales*, Harmony Mumbai, other in Bangalore, Chennai, Meerut, Chandigarh; International: Japan, France. *Stone carving* camps: *LKA* & *Ceramic* camps New Delhi, SKP. Award: SKP. Collections: *NGMA* & *LKA* New Delhi, UP *LKA*, pvt. & corporates.

Raj Kumar Panwar is a *sculptor*, working with and constantly exploring new *mediums*, including *ceramics*, *stone*, *wood*, *metal*, *fibreglass* and *terracotta* to create his forceful organic works. He is inspired by his roots in the rural *culture* of India. He attempts to express the relationship between *volume*, shape and surface through his *medium*.

He lives in New Delhi, where he teaches *sculpture* at the *College of Art*.

Paper It was invented in the AD 2nd century in China. The process of paper making remains the same from the pulp process, which is made from cotton, bamboo, rice straw, or machine-made from *wood* pulp. Lignin in *wood* pulp can lead to formation of *acids*; and therefore machine made paper has a relatively shorter life than hand made paper. The Fourdrinier machine for making paper efficiently and economically had been refined in 1803. Different types of papers used in *art* are *oil* paper, rice paper, glass paper and a variety of different machine made paper and hand made paper. *Oil* paper has a *transparent* look and is *waterproof* as it is prepared by soaking paper in *oil*. Rice paper is a thin delicate sheet made from rice straw. Glass paper is paper coated with fine powdered glass also used for polishing. Refer *Handmade Paper*, *Papier Mache*; Illustrations–AGNI, BHAGAVATA-PURANA, *Caricature*, *Collage*, *Devanagari Script*, *Drapery*, *Drawing*, *Dry Brush Painting*, GANJIFA, *Hatching*, MAKARA, *Mask*, *Miniature Painting–Mughal Dynasty*, *Still Life*, *Thanjavur (Tanjore) Painting*, *Krishnaji Howlaji Ara*, *Gobardhan Ash*, *Badri Narayan*, *Natvar Bhavsar*, *Nandalal Bose*, *Shanti Dave*, *Rini Dhumal*, *C. Douglas*, *Manoj Dutta*, *Ganga Devi*, *Vasant Ghodke*, *Asit K. Haldar*, *C. Jagdish*, *Sanat Kar*, *K.S. Kulkarni*, *Paresh Maity*, *K. Madhava Menon*, *Rathin Mitra*, *Prafulla Mohanti*, *Ved Nayar*, *Saroj Gogi Pal*, *Manu Parekh*, *Sohan Qadri*, *Manickam Senathipathi*, *Bannu/Ved Pal Sharma*, *Rameshwar Singh*, *Vrindavan Solanki*, *Vivan Sundaram*, *Rabindranath Tagore*, *Thotha Vaikuntham*.

Paper-Pulp Casting A *technique* used by printmaker *Dattatreya Apte*. A large sheet of *wax* is made, which can be either carved as in *linocut*, or cut, pressed and moulded into many small shapes, varying in height. Tiny *found objects* are also incorporated into the soft and malleable *wax*.

Later, four to six successive coats of liquid latex (rubber solution) are brushed over the *wax collage*. It is then allowed to cure overnight. A *plaster mould* is prepared to *support* the sensitive latex *mould*.

Pre-soaked, coloured, *handmade paper* is torn into small pieces and *ground* along with a few drops of preservative and natural glue. The excess water is drained off and gently pressed into the latex *mould* by hand or with sticks and spoons (to reach deep crevices). Newspapers and sponges drain away excess moisture and the *cast* pulp is allowed to dry naturally in the shade. Refer *Carving*, *Glue Size*, *Paper*, *Papier Mache*, *Printmaking*.

Papier Mache (French) A synonym for mashed *paper*; it is used all over the world to make *craft* objects. India had its own distinctive method of making papier mache. Tribal *artists* mixed the pulp with starch. While each area in India had its own *technique* and *style* in preparing the pulp and creating its objects of *art*. One of the *techniques* was: pulped *paper* was first soaked in water and mixed with glue, *chalk* and sometimes sand, and later moulded and baked. It is used to make *sculptures*, boxes and other fragile articles. This *craft* was originally practised in Persia, some Asian countries, and in Kashmir in India. While *gods* and goddesses were the chief subject of papier mache artisans, Kashmir boxes sport delicate Mughal type *designs* and *colours*. At times small items of furniture such as tables were also created. Refer *Detailed Work*, *Life-Size*, *Paper-Pulp Casting*, *Dhanraj Bhagat*, *Latika Katt*, *Mask*, *National Handicrafts & Handlooms Museum*; Illustration–*C. Jagdish*.

Parab, Vasant (1928–) b. Mumbai. Education: GDA in *painting JJSA*. Solos: *JAG*. Group participations: *AFA* Kolkata, MAHA State Art Exhibitions, National *LKA* New Delhi *BAS*, *ASI*, *AIFACS*; International: Switzerland, New York, Tokyo, Poland. Awards: *BAS*, HAS. Founder member: Vidarbha Art Society Nagpur. Appointments: Prof. & Ex-Dean *JJSA*. Publications: Articles in Roop-Bheda & other journals. Collections: Rashtrapati Bhavan New Delhi, Nagpur, *ASI*, *BAS*, HAS & pvt.

Vasant Parab was trained in the Western *style* at his alma-mater. He is essentially a fine portraitist, having the *portraits* of several eminent personalities, including that of R. Venkatraman, the former president of India, to his credit. His *style* is *realistic*, with short impressionistic strokes enlivening the *portrait*. He has also introduced *printmaking* and established the *graphic* workshop at *JJSA* Mumbai.

He lives and works in Mumbai.

Parasher, S.L. (1904–1990) b. Badoki (now Pakistan). Studied under M.A. Aziz Mysore, Special course *JJSA*. Solos: New Delhi, Mumbai, Lahore; International: Frankfurt, Paris, Washington D.C. Group shows: All India Sculptors' Association Mumbai, Kolkata New Delhi & Hyderabad. Group participations: Mumbai, Kolkata, New Delhi, Hyderabad; International: Frankfurt. Appointments: Founder Principal School of Art Shimla; Dir. All India Handicrafts Board. Commissions: Several *murals* & *sculptures* including *ceramics*, *stone*, *brass*, *copper*, *aluminium*, *concrete* & steel in Amitsar, Chandigarh, New Delhi, & Kanpur. Collections: New Delhi, PUJ University and *landscape sculpture* in *concrete* Lesisure Valley Chandigarh.

S.L. Parasher was trained in *portrait* and *landscape painting* and clay modelling by M.A. Aziz; later in Mumbai, he worked in the studio of *Vinayak Pandurang Karmarkar* gaining proficiency in *sculpture*. However, his forte seemed to be *mural design*: he designed and executed several *murals*, keeping in mind the *contemporary* architectural ambience within which it is seen. His used of material was versatile; he has used pebbled surrounds in conjunction with *concrete forms*. His linear sense of *design* was strong, creating a rhythmic flow of thrust and counter-thrust i.e. essential in large outdoor works of *art*.

Parasurama Refer VISHNU, DASAVATARA.

Parchment A thin layer of animal skin, usually *translucent*, prepared for writing. Has been used instead of *paper* in mediaeval *times*. In India, animal skin was used as a tracing, in *miniature paintings*. Refer *Leather*, *Size*.

Pardeshi, Dattatray B. (1938–1992) b. Nimgaon, MAHA. Education: Art Master's Certificate, CTC & GDA in *drawing & painting JJSA*, Ph.D., Bombay University. Solos: Pune, Dhule, MAHA, *JAG*, BAG. Group participations: MAHA State Art, Mumbai, *LKA* New Delhi, *Biennale Roopankar*, *BAS*; Awards: Ph.D., FFA Bombay University. Member: *BAS*. Appointments: Lecturer *JJSA* & *JJIAA*. Publications: Press & Magazines. Collections: *NGMA* & *LKA* New Delhi; International: France, Japan, Switzerland, USA, V&A, pvt.

Dattatray B. Pardeshi who was a lecturer at *JJSA* Mumbai, was both an academician and an *artist*. His doctoral thesis was on the history and development of the school. As a *painter*, he was basically *figurative*, stylizing/distorting the human form to underline the despair of the people he depicted in *oils* as well as in *watercolours*. The faces of the people resemble those of Neolithic *creations*, their physique empathizes with emotional appeal and *tonal value*. His *colours* followed the academic *pattern* of *warm* or *cool colour palettes*.

Parekh, Madhvi (1942–) Sanjaya, GUJ. No formal education in *art*. Solos: *GC* Mumbai, *BAAC* Kolkata, Urja Art Gallery, Nazar Art Gallery, Vadodara, *PUAG*, *JAG*, *Dhoomimal*, *VAG*; International: Foundation of Indian Artists Amsterdam, IWALEWA Haus Germany, Al-Khaleeja Kuwait, GBP. Group participations: *BAAC* & *CIMA* Kolkata, Chetna Mumbai, *LKA*, Husain Ki Sarai & *NGMA* New Delhi, *JAG*, *NCAG*, *LCAG*, *Dhoomimal*, *GAC*, *LTG*, *GE*, *VAG*; International: Yugoslavia, UK, Netherlands, Hong Kong, Australia. *Art* workshops & camps: PUJ University Museum, *LKA* Chennai, *Graphic* workshop *GAC*, Vadodara & *ABC*, *FFA* (*MSU*), *CKP*, *BB*. *Auctions*: Timeless Art Sotheby's, Helpage India Asprey's Heart & Osian Mumbai, Artists Alert, New Delhi; International: Christie's, London. Publications: A documentary has been filmed on *Manu Parekh* (her husband) & her works by the Ministry of External Affairs. Collections: *NGMA* New Delhi; International: Rade Museum Hamburg, Bayreuth Museum Germany.

Madhvi Parekh's works are influenced by *folk art* as well as works of *modern* masters like P. Klee and F. Clemente. Her *imagery* has remained naive and semi-decorative, but her *vocabulary* has evolved from the dotted surface of her early *oils* to the stark yet dramatic enclosures of her recent *black* and *white* works. Most of her works are *narrative* in *nature*, with some depicting entire folk tales or religious *themes*. It is her use of accidental *images*, like the transmuting of a flower into a bird, that intrigue and delight the senses.

She lives and works in New Delhi along with her *artist* husband, *Manu Parekh*.

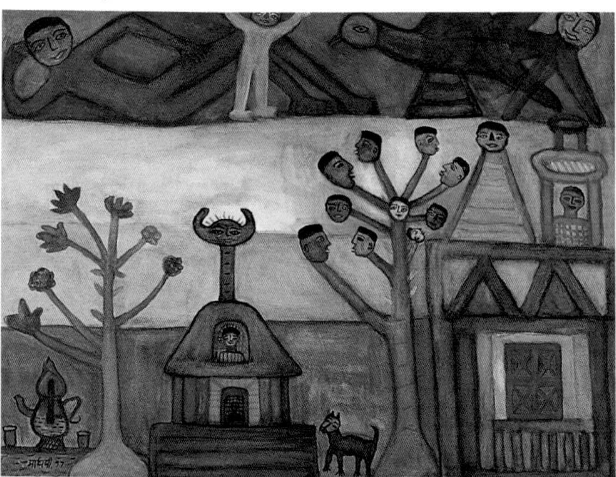

Parekh, Madhavi: "Way to Pahelgav", *Watercolours*, 1997.

Parekh, Manu (1939–) b. Ahmedabad, GUJ. Education: GDA *JJSA*. Solos: New Delhi, Ahmedabad, 10 years work *exhibition* in *BAAC* Kolkata, *CIMA* Kolkata, *Tao Art Gallery* Mumbai, TAG, *Dhoomimal*, *CKAG*, *JAG*, *VAG*, *JJSA*; International: New York London. Retrospective: By Seagull Foundation New Delhi, Kolkata & Mumbai. Group participations: National Exhibitions & *Triennales*, *CIMA* at *NGMA*, 50 years of Independence by *VAG* at *NGMA* & *LKA* New Delhi, *CIMA* Kolkata, *SG* Mumbai, Marvel Art Gallery Ahmedabad, *LCAG*, *JAG*, *CYAG*, *AIFACS;* International: Berlin, Dubai Germany, Festival of India RAA London, Hirschhorn Museum Washington DC. Workshop: Kashmir by *LKA* and J&K Govt., PUJ University Chandigarh, Vadodara by *ABC* other in Nathdwara, Ahmedabad, Mumbai & Dalhousie; International: New York & Mauritius. *Auctions*: Heart & Osian's Mumbai, Heart New Delhi. Awards: *BAAC* Kolkata, Silver Plaque *AIFACS*, National *LKA* Award New Delhi, Padma Shri Govt. of India. Members: *LKA* New Delhi, *SCA*. Collections: *LKA* & *NGMA* New Delhi, PUJ University Museum, *BAAC* Kolkata, TIFR.

Manu Parekh's work can be divided into three distinct phases: one dealing with organic eroticism, another with the *landscape* of Banaras (Varanasi) and the third with violence. The phases overlap and recur constantly, his *vocabulary* is in a constant state of flux; thus one can see both decorative *landscape* in more or less *Basohli style* along with his *abstract* references to Banaras (Varanasi). The works associated with violence fluctuate between references to real incidents of terror and carnage and the metaphorical use of the animal face with a human expressiveness. The former, as epitomized in the "Bhagalpur Blindings" are *graphic* and bordered on the literal, while the latter, as seen in "Stilled lives (with details)" are more meditative, with the textural quality of old wall *paint*, with a liberal use of *cement* and *distemper*. The "Flower-portrait" series is replete with *texture* and full of *colours*.

He lives and works in New Delhi along with his *artist* wife *Madhvi Parekh.*

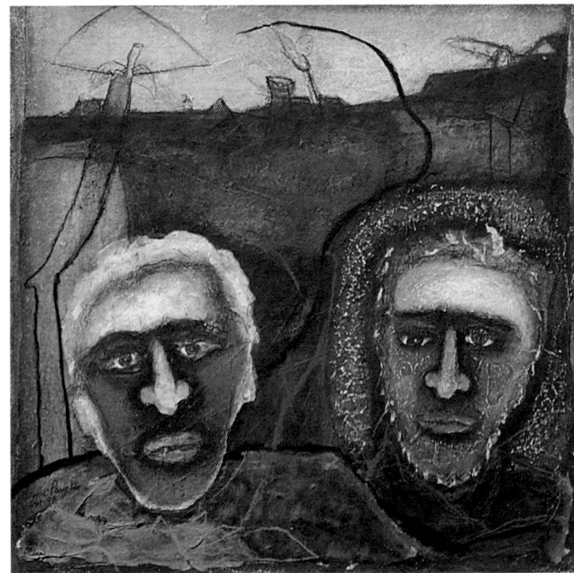

Parekh, Manu: "Two Heads", *Mixed media*, Rice *Paper*, 1997.

Parikh, Jayant (1940) b. Bandhani, GUJ. Education: Post-Dip. in *painting FFA* (*MSU*). Over 54 solos: *GC* Mumbai, CAG Ahmedabad, Form Function Art Gallery Chandigarh, Urja Art Gallery & Fine Arts Gallery Vadodara, *PUAG*, TAG, *JAG*, *RSA*. Group participations: *Triennales* New Delhi, GUJ *LKA*

Exhibitions; International: Leipzig, Saigon, Paris, Poland, Berlin, Japan, Helsinki USA. Awards: GUJ *LKA*, *BAS*, HAS, *AIFACS*. Scholoraship: Govt. of India Cultural Scholarship, Research Fellowship Govt. of India in *painting* & *graphic*. Commissions: *Murals* in *oils*, *cement*, *aluminium*, board, *ceramics* & *terracotta* in pvt. & public buildings. Publications: Works published in "Indian Printmaking Today". Collections & *murals*: *NGMA* & *LKA* New Delhi, GUJ *LKA*, Hyderabad Museum, *Chandigarh Museum*, TIFR, *JJSA*, *MSU;* International: USA, New York.

Jayant Parikh is a versatile *artist*, equally at home while *printmaking*, *painting*, sculpting and executing *murals*. A fine sense of *colour*, inherited from his tutor, *Narayan S. Bendre* runs through his works in these different *mediums*.

His sources are as varied and as diverse as plant and vegetal *forms*, ancient monuments and temples and most importantly mother *nature*. A lively sense of *pattern* and rhythmic repetition pervades his works with *tactile* vibrancy. His *watercolours* feature huge rhythmic shapes depicting the musical modes.

He lives and works in Vadodara.

Parikh, Natu J. (1931–) b. Bandhani, GUJ. Education: Art Master's Certificate Mumbai, GDA in *painting*, GUJ State, M.A. *Art Criticism FFA* (*MSU*). Solos: CAG, Archer Art Gallery & *Ravishankar M. Raval* KB Ahmedabad, Sardar Smruti Bhavanagar, *JAG*. Group participations: National Exhibition *LKA* New Delhi, *LKA* GUJ & MP Golden Jubliee *JAG*. Conducted *Landscape* workshops: Junagadh, Mount Abu. Awards: State *LKA* GUJ, Mysore DAE, *AIFACS*. Member: *LKA* GUJ. Appointments: Visiting Lecturer NID, lecturer for *painting* CNCFA, Conducted seminar: Nargol GUJ. Publications: Articles in magazines & newspapers "Kumar Magazine", "Navchetan" & "Jansatta" newpapers. Collections: *LKA* New Delhi, Governor Raj Bhavan GUJ & Chief Minister GUJ State; International: USA.

Natu J. Parikh has used both *watercolours* and *oils* in rendering his naturalistic works. His recent *landscapes* are worked in *watercolour* in *plein-air*, to capture the spontaneity of the moment. The works in *oils* are more composed and creative, having been rendered in the confines of the studio.

He lives and works in Ahmedabad.

Parikh, Rasiklal (1910–1982) b. Valia, GUJ. Education: Studied *at Madras School of Art GACA* Chennai, under *Debi Prasad RoyChowdhury*; Dip. Bombay School of Art (*JJSA*). Influence of Dr Solomon, also studied *mural paintings*. Solos: Major shows at GUJ *LKA* & City Musuem Ahmedabad. Group participations: *LKA* Ahmedabad, *BAS*, other towns Vadodara, Mysore, Thiruvananthapuram. Awards: Gold Medal *BAS* & GUJ Exhibition, *LKA* Award New Delhi. Appointments: Teacher & Principal of Vidya Vihar School (CNCFA) for 35 years. Collections: Most of his works at GUJ *LKA* Ahmed-abad, Borada Museum.

Rasiklal Parikh was essentially a *painter* in the old *manner*, being versatile enough to handle *oils*, *watercolour* and *pen* and *ink sketches*. He painted *portraits* in the Western academic *style*, with impressionistic brushstrokes, and handled *figure compositions*, both in the Western sense and in the *Jamini Roy manner*, the *line* and decorative colouring dominating to the exclusion of absolute reality. He has also attempted *wash landscapes* in the oriental *style*. He is best known for his rural scenes, with young maidens and mothers working in fields and villages in an *idiom* similar to that of his first teacher, *Ravishankar M. Raval*.

Parimoo, Ratan (1936–) b. Srinagar, Kashmir. Education: B.A. & M.A. in *FA.*, & *painting MSU*, Post-Grad. Dip. in museology *MSU*, B.A. Hons. in *art* history London University UK, Ph.D. in *art* history *MSU*. Solos: Mumbai, Ahmedabad, Srinagar, *LKA* New Delhi, *AIFACS;* International: Oxford, Durban, England. Group shows: With his wife *Naina Dalal* in New Delhi, Vadodara, *CYAG*. Retrospective: RB New Delhi 1972, *JAG* & *CYAG* 1999. Group participations: National Exhibitions *LKA* & CMC Ltd. New Delhi, Baroda Group in Mumbai, *BAAC* Kolkata; International: UK. *Auctions*: Osian's Mumbai. Awards: Govt. of India Cultural Scholarship for *painting*, Commonwealth Scholarship London, J.D. Rockefeller III Grant USA, Nehru Trust Grant Fellowship. Members: *LKA*, Advisory Board History of Science of Ancient Period-Indian National Science Academy New Delhi; Central Advisory Board of Museum HRD Ministry New Delhi. Organized National Level Art Historical seminars: "Problems of Teaching & Research in History of Art in Indian University", "Impact of Vaishnavism on Indian Art", "Ellora Caves–Sculpture & Architecture", "Henry Moore & Contemporary Sculpture", "Art of Ajanta & Its Significance in Asian Art", &

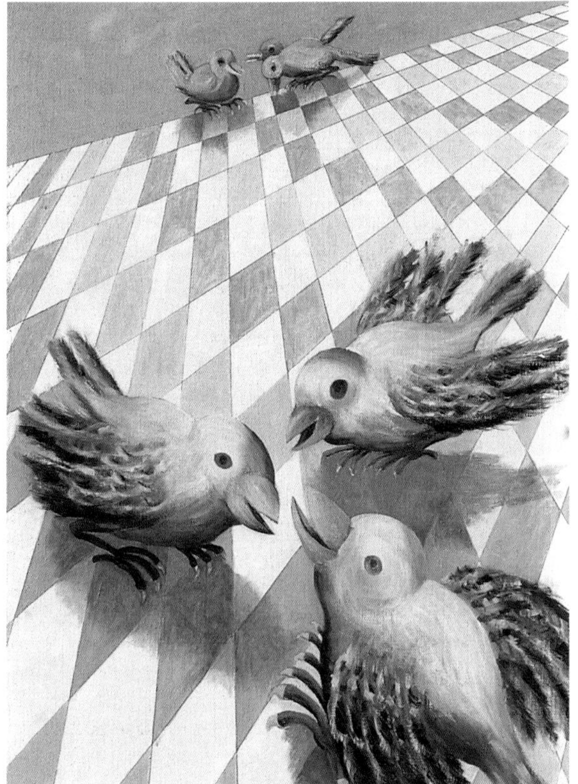

Parimoo, Ratan: "Birds", *Oils*, 1990.

"Comparative Aesthetics & The Criticism of Contemporary Arts". Appointments: Besides being Prof. & HoD of *Art* History & *Aesthetics*, Served as Dean of the *FFA* (*MSU*). Publications: Books including "Paintings of the Three Tagores- Abanindranath Tagore, Gaganendranath Tagore, Rabindranath Tagore–Chronology & Comparative Study", "Studies in Modern Indian Art", "Life of the BUDDHA in Indian Sculpture", "Sculptures of Shesasayi Vishnu" & also published several articles on *Art* History & edited books on *Art* History including, "Vaishnavism in Indian Arts & Culture" & "The Paintings of Rabindranath Tagore". Collections: PUJ University Chandigarh, GUJ *LKA*, J&K Academy & *NGMA* New Delhi; International: Hermitage Leningrad.

Ratan Parimoo is better known as an *art* historian of repute. His *paintings* of the 50s were an outcome of his training in *art*, which led him to the analysis of the *perspective* and *line* in oriental art as adapted to his *visual* experience of *contemporary* subjects and objects. His second phase concerned working primarily with *colour*, gesture and tactility. By the 70s he had developed his interest in the surreal world of *fantasy* and macabre introversion. *Themes* taken from the past as seen with a *contemporary* bias have appeared often in his *oils*, as has the use of the *self portrait* in various situations.

Ratan Parimoo lives and works in Vadodara.

Parmar, Khodidas (1930–) b. Bhavnagar, GUJ. Education: M.A. with Gujarati & SANSKRIT, Studied in *painting* under *Somalal Chunilal Shah*. Solos: Ahmedabad, Vallabh Vidyanagar, Rajkot, Bhavnagar. Group participations: Kolkata, Chennai, Hyderabad, Chandigarh, LKA & Marvel Art Gallery Ahmedabad, *AIFACS*, *BAS;* International: London, Moscow, Sharjah. Awards: National *LKA* New Delhi, Gold Medal GUJ University, *LKA* & *AFA* Kolkata, Kala Shree & Veteran Artist award. Silver Medal *BAS AIFACS*. Senior Fellowship: HRD Ministry. Member: Member & Associated with institutes including *LKA* GUJ, WZCC RAJ. Appointment: Folk *artist* in Sangeet Nritya Akademi GUJ. Lectuer on folk literature Bhavnagar university. Commissions: *Murals* Yashwantrai Natya Gruha & other pvt. homes Bhavnagar. Publications: His works have been printed in several books; Articles & research *papers* on *Folk Art*, Folk Literature & Bird in Folklore; A *monograph* published by the *LKA* GUJ. Collections: Air India Mumbai, *NGMA* New Delhi, *LKA* GUJ & Gandhinagar, Amritsar Art Gallery PUJ, Orissa Museum Bhubhaneshwar, Gandhi Smruti Museum Bhavnagar, pvt. & corporates.

Khodidas Parmar derives inspiration from the native folk *style* of Saurashtra, GUJ where he hails from. He has used the elements of this rich *tradition* to evolve a highly personal *style* of his own, replete with references to the folklore of the region. The basic features of *folk art*, including decorative outlining, rhythmically repetitive *patterns* and bright *colours* are present in these works. He executes his *paintings* in various *mediums*, including *watercolours*, *pastels*, *acrylics*, powder *paintings* and *tempera*. He has likewise painted on *paper*, *hardboard*, mount board and cloth.

He lives and works in Bhavnagar, GUJ.

Parting Agent=A release agent applied to the surfaces to prevent another material from adhering to the first, like on a *mould* in *casting*, before the *casting* is done. It helps in easy removal of the *cast* object. Substances generally used are soft soap, shellac, *wax* or similar materials. Refer *Abstract Sculpture*, *Cire Perdue*, *Clay*, *Clay Water*, *Wetting Down*, *Sudha Arora*, *Himmat Shah*.

Parul, Vinod R. (1939–) b. Ahmedabad, GUJ. Education: Art Master's Certificate CNCFA. Solos: Over 12 to 13 in Mumbai, Ahmedabad. Two men International: London, Dubai. Group participations: Ahmedabad, Mumbai, Kolkata, New Delhi, Orissa, Chennai, Vidyanagar. *Art* camps & workshops: *LKA Graphic* workshop GUJ, International Artist Group 1970 & 1975. Awards: National *LKA* New Delhi, *LKA* & University Festival Award GUJ, *LKA* PUJ, National Scholarship New Delhi; Fellowship Ministry of HRD Ministry. Member: Contemporary Painters Group Ahmedabad. Commissions: *Murals* Ahmedabad. Collections: *LKA* GUJ, Times of India, *GC* Mumbai, *LKA* New Delhi, *LKA* AP Hyderabad, *LKA* Orissa Bhubaneshwar, HCVA, GAG, pvt. & corporates. National & International Dubai, Germany, London & New York.

Vinod R. Parul works in the *figurative idiom*, using stylized *folk* and *tribal art*-inspired *forms* in addition to simple *distortions* in a semi-abstract *manner*. His subjects are varied, from the rural and the *pastoral* to animal studies to semi-surreal *landscapes* with folk *forms*. He is adept at using *oils*, *acrylics* and *watercolours* in addition to his *murals*.

He lives and works in Ahmedabad.

Parvati Daughter of the mountain. The wife of SHIVA, the reincarnation of Sati, an aspect of SHAKTI. She is the daughter of King Himavat (King of the mountains). She is usually represented along with SHIVA in the Kalyanasundaramurti, the marriage of SHIVA and Parvati, and the Somaskandamurti (SHIVA=Uma, Skanda). If she is represented with four hands, the front two hands are held in the ABHAYA and Dhyanamudra, and the back two hold a (SHULA) javelin and a (Tanke) chisel. Refer AYUDHA, DURGA, *Elephanta*, GAJA, GANESH, KAILASH, KAILASA, *Adiveppa Murigeppa Chetty*, *Jamini Roy*.

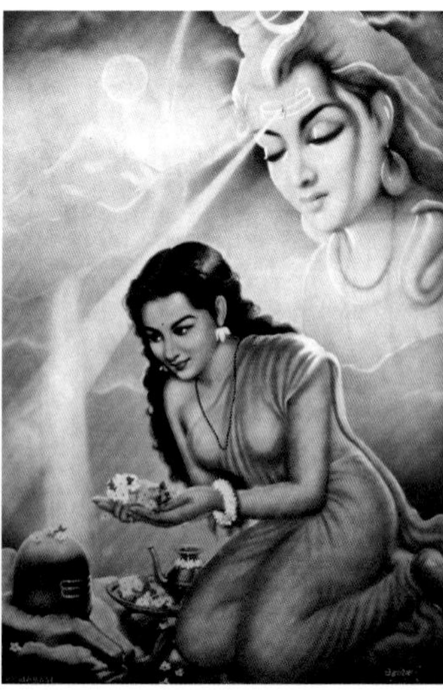

Parvati: "Parvati Aradhana", Artist Pednekar, *Half-tone* print, Circa 1930.

Pasricha, Ram Nath (1926–2001) b. Amritsar. No formal *art education*. Taught at the *College of Art* New Delhi. Over 33 solo sponsored *exhibitions*: *Art Heritage*, Alliance

Francaise, Gallery Aurobindo, Hungarian Cultural Centre & Indus Gallery New Delhi, IIC, *AIFACS*. Solos: New Delhi, Chandigarh, Varanasi, Mumbai, Chennai. Retrospective: *Art Heritage* New Delhi. Group participations: National Exhibitions, International Exhibitions. *Art* camps: J&K Govt., SKP, *AIFACS*, Awards: Honoured by *LKA* as Eminent *Artist* Awards *AIFACS*. Senior Fellowship HRD Ministry. Appointments: Taught *landscape painting* at *College of Art* New Delhi; Gave demonstrations lectures on *watercolour paintings* FFA BHU. Publications: Bibliography Samkaleen Kala *LKA*, Roop Lekha, Monograph Ram Nath Pasricha, *AIFACS* & other periodicals. Collections: *NGMA* & *LKA* New Delhi, PUJ University Museum, Govt. Museum Chandigarh, Air India Bombay, *AIFACS*, SKP & other pvt. & institutionals.

Ram Nath Pasricha began *painting landscapes* in 1947. Three years later, he travelled through the Himalayas, marking the *beginning* of a thematic concern that has continued to date. Has travelled extensively in the Himalayas and painted on the spot at high altitudes. He made quick *watercolour sketches* of the mountains and their many moods, using some as the basis of more structured and creative *paintings* in his studio. From simple *Realism*, his *art* has now converged on *fantasy*, *symbolism* and semi-abstraction.

He lived and worked in New Delhi.

Passage A synonym for merging. **1.** A section passing through or across something, or even *time*. **2.** It refers to the area in the work where one *colour* or *texture* blends into another. **3.** Empty *space* between two areas of *colours*, deliberately executed so as to bring the *composition* into sharper focus. Refer *Lyricism*, *Picture Space*, *Transition*, *Vent*, *Ranvir Singh Bisht*, *K.P. Chidambarakrishnan*, *Ganesh Haloi*, *Maqbool Fida Husain*, *Shamshad Husain*, *Harkrishan Lall*; Illustration—*Tyeb Mehta*.

Pastels Refer *Oil Pastels*.

Pastel Shades Refers to *light* sophisticated *colours* of high *tint*, the different *shades*, *colours* and softness which give a gentle romantic air to the whole *composition*. The *artists* of late 19th century and early 20th century used these *colours*. Some of the *artists* who went through phases when they used pastel shades were, among others—*Jaganath M. Ahivasi*, *R.B. Bhaskaran*, *Nandalal Bose*, *Muhammed Abdur Rehman Chughtai*, *Mukul Chandra Dey*, *Mahadev V. Dhurandhar*, *Kshitendranath Mazumdar*, *Abanindranath Tagore*, *Gaganendranath Tagore*, *Ram Gopal Vijaivargiya*. Refer *Malwa*, *Oil Pastels*, *Wash (Technique)*.

Pastoral In Western Art an idyllic *landscape* featuring the countryside as an Utopian place peopled with attractive shepherds and shepherdesses.

In Indian miniatures especially *Kangra* and *Pahari miniatures* many *paintings* feature GOPAS and GOPIS playing RASALILA with KRISHNA. *Post-Independence* pastoral scenes have village belles fetching water from wells or groups of gossiping women. Refer *Kangra*, *Neo-Impressionism*, RIG-VEDA, *Narayan S. Bendre*, *Nirmal Dutta*, *Jamini P. Gangooly*, *Maqbool Fida Husain*, *Murli Lahoti*, *Ambadas Mahurkar*, *P.Gouri Shanker*, *Shankar Palsikar*, *Vinod R Parul*; Illustrations—GOPA, *Sailoz Mookerjea*, *Ram Kishore Yadav—Repousse*.

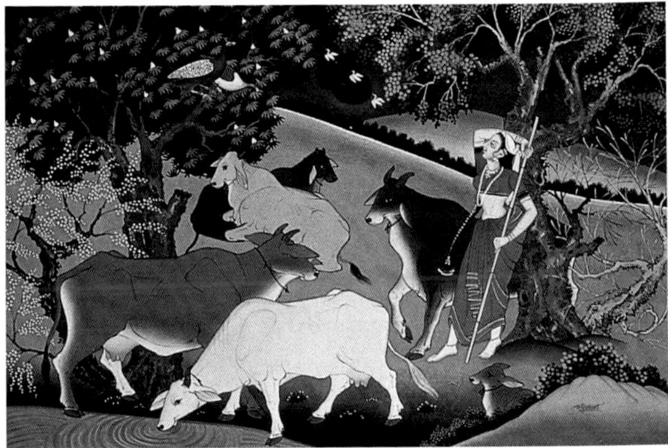

Pastoral: *Nathu Lal Verma*, "Untitled", *Tempera*.

Patel, Ajit S. (1949–) b. Anand, GUJ. Education: GDA in *painting* GUJ State, Art Master's Certificate Vallabh Vidyanagar, *Painting* & block making process *MSU*, Advance printing Mumbai. Solos: CAG Ahmedabad, Sardar Patel University GUJ; International: Mauritius. Group show: *JAG*, TAG, HCVA. Group participations: *LKA* Ahmedabad, Nationals & State *exhibitions*, *Biennale BB*; International: National Exhibition of Graphics London. Awards: GUJ *LKA*, MKKP Raipur, MP, *BAS*. Member: *BAS*. Appointments: Lecturer & Principal at Kala Kendra, CFA Vallabh Vidyanagar 1983–83; International: Seminar Koln Germany. Collections: Pvt & corporates. Ahmedabad, Anand, *B. Vithal*, *Prafulla Dahanukar*.

Ajit S. Patel is basically a serigrapher, working with silk screen *technique* to create *landscapes* with selective elements of *nature*, extolling the wonder at the *creation* of the Almighty. His *colours* are mostly bright primaries like red and yellow with other *colours* forming the textural element of the works. Ajit S. Patel has also worked on *canvas*.

He lives in Anand, GUJ.

Patel, Amrut (1947–) b. Ahmedabad. Education: Dip. in *painting* GUJ State; Trained in *fresco* & *mural technique Banasthali Vidyapith* RAJ. Solos: Gallery Chanakya, New Delhi, CAG Ahmedabad, *JAG*,

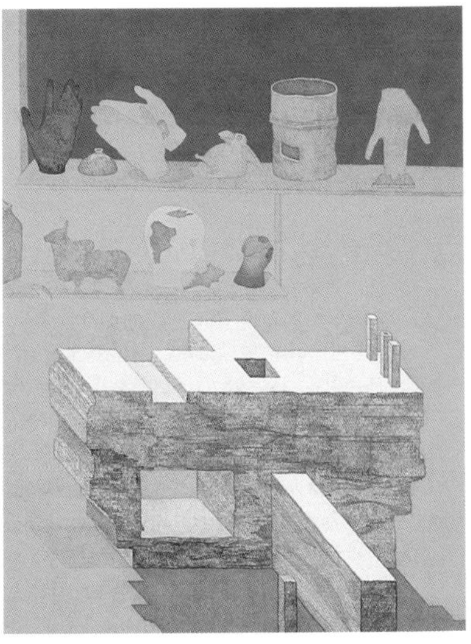

Patel, Amrut: "Sculptor's studio" *Acrylic* on *Canvas*, 1997, 142x114 cm.

BAG, IIC, *SAI*, *ATG*. Retrospetive: Germany. Group show: *JAG*, SRAG, HCVA. Group participations: Mumbai, *Triennales* & *LKA* New Delhi, *AIFACS*; International: USA, Kuwait, Germany, Paris *Biennale*. *Art* camps: GUJ *LKA*, National *LKA*. Awards: GUJ *LKA*, National *LKA* Award, *AIFACS*, SKP. Appointments: Attended seminars school of *art* Jabalpur; Lecturer FAC Ahmedabad, Vallabh Vidyanagar GUJ. Collections: GUJ *LKA*, Manipur *LKA*, UP *LKA*, *NGMA* & *LKA* New Delhi, Nehru Kala Kendra Jaipur & pvt. & corporates.

Amrut Patel began his career, *painting* with the meticulous attention to detail that a five-years study of the Indian miniature *style* was to bring about. He personalized these works by the use of non-colour rather than bright *colours* that Indian miniatures are known for. Later he made a foray into neo-tantric *art*, creating geometric *patterns* in different *colours*. The next phase saw the erasing of the constricting details of *miniature paintings*. Instead *space* itself became the mainstay of his works, holding apparently unrelated objects in tangential relationships. There was an *empathy* with the contemporaneously produced works of *Prabhakar Barwe*. He believes he was among one of the first *artists* in India to work with *acrylics*, indeed the instructions for the use of Camel's *artists acrylic colours* were written by him. He was also the first Indian *painter* to have an all-acrylic show in 1971–72, and has also been a designer at the *WSC*.

He lives and works in New Delhi.

Patel, Ankit (1957–) b. Surat, GUJ. Education: Post-Dip. in *sculpture MSU*. Over 25 solos: CAG Ahmedabad, *JAG*, TAG, *DG*, TKS, SRAG, others Vadodara & Jaipur. Group participations: Godrej Mumbai, GUJ *LKA*, RAJ *LKA*, *JAG*, BAG, *CYAG*, *BAS*, *AIFACS*, *Biennale BB*. *Art* camps: GUJ *LKA* Mount Abu, *Sculptor's* camp Jaipur, J&K, Ahmedabad, Hampi. Awards: National *LKA* New Delhi, RAJ State *LKA*. Appointments: Lecturer in the *RSA*. Collections: GUJ *LKA*, Modern Art Gallery, Jawahar Kala Kendra Jaipur, Godrej Mumbai, Surat Museum, *BAS*, *NCAG* pvt. & corporates.

Ankit Patel is a *sculptor*, working with kinetic movement, in his large scale *metal sculptures*. His *forms* though organic, are not *figurative*. Instead they can be termed as expressive *abstracts*, standing on delicately poised pedestals, that evoke comparisons with traditional Indian utensils and vases. His early *mobiles* were in *wood* and *fibreglass*. However, it is the sheen and strength of beaten *copper* and *brass* that enhance the slow, majestic movement of his *sculpture*.

He lives and works in Jaipur.

Patel, Balkrishna M. (1925–2003) b. Ahmedabad. Studied in *painting* under *Ravishankar M. Raval* Ahmedabad, *FFA* (*MSU*). Solos: *GC* Mumbai, *GC* & *Art Heritage* New Delhi, CAG Ahmedabad *JAG*, *Dhoomimal*, HCVA. Group participations: *Triennale* National Exhibition & *LKA* New Delhi, *BAS*. *Art* camps: Udaipur, Kashmir, Kolkata, GUJ. Awards: National Exhibitions & *LKA* New Delhi, *BAS*. Member: *Group 1890*; Selections Committee Doordarshan Kendra Ahmedabad. Appointments: Participated in theatre & TV plays. Collections: *NGMA* & *LKA* New Delhi, *Roopankar*, pvt.

Balkrishna M. Patel used the BINDU as a metaphor for sound in his works. He explored the meditative qualities of *transparent*, almost weightless *colours*, letting dissolving blots of *colour* emerge at will from the act of *creation*. Though *watercolour* seemed more suitable *media* for these works, he has also used *oils*. His subjects encompass *Realism*, *Impressionism*, *neo-Tantricism* and even pure abstraction. He lived in Ahmedabad.

Patel, Dashrath (1927–) b. Nadiad, GUJ. Education: Dip. in *FA*. College of Art Chennai, Post-Dip. in *FA*. ENSBA Paris, Post-Dip. in *art ceramics* School of Art Prague; Studied with William Hayter, School of Engraving & Photography with Herbert Matter New York. Solos: Ahmedabad, Delhi, Chennai, Bangalore, *NGMA*, *Tao Art Gallery* Mumbai; International: Paris, London, Prague. *Auctions*: Heart New Delhi. Workshops: 1980–95 conducted a series at several venues in India & Philippines in *design*, technology, vegetable dying, *craft*, low cost *printing*, multi media for rural & urban based voluntary organizations. Awards: Padma Shri 1981 for Design & Design Education; Rockefeller Foundation Scholarship Design & Architecture USA. Appointments: Professional career 1961–80 at NID & began for the first time in India a professional 5 years course in Exhibition Design Ahmedabad; Was a Project Dir., Chief Designer, Visualizer & Conceptualizer in *exhibitions* & other projects; Extensive photo-documentation of Indian life *style*, *crafts*, festivals & habitats for the past 40 years; Involved with *exhibitions* & other projects in *graphic* & *design* for 35 years, Book & *poster designer*, Photograph editor of visual book series for Vikas Publication House New Delhi. Collections: National & International.

Dashrath Patel's work spans several disciplines, including *painting*, *ceramics*, photography, *design* and *design* education. Also an innovator in *industrial design*, industrial *ceramics* and stadium scale *exhibitions*. His *paintings*, include *figurative*, *narrative* and impressionist work from the 40s through his apprenticeship with *Rasiklal Parikh* and *Ravishankar M. Raval*. Later he switched gradually towards

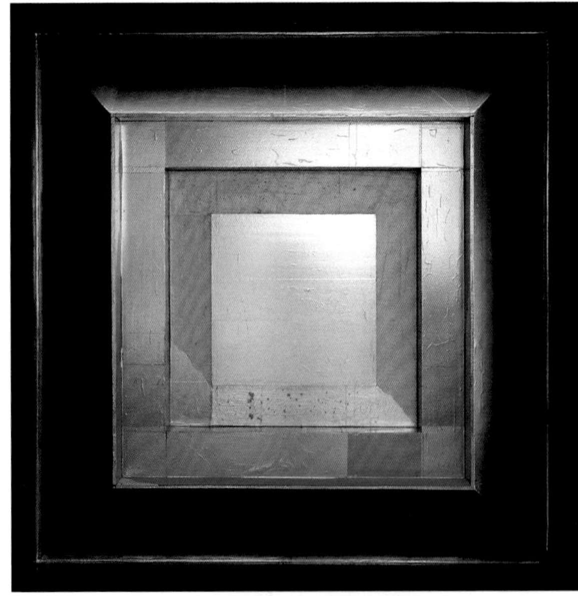

Patel, Dashrath: *Paper On Wood*, 1999, 183x183 cm.

abstraction and more recently to *mixed media paintings, collages* and *installations*. His early *watercolours* display the robust vitality of curvilinear *lines* that are present even in his latest works. His *collages* and *installations* are relief-like and geometric in their approach; his forte is his *treatment* and visualization of India's *light, colour* and sense of *space*.

He lives and works in Ahmedabad and Alibag near Mumbai.

Patel, Gieve (1940–) b. Mumbai. No formal education in *art*. Solos: New Delhi, *GC* Mumbai; International: UK, USA, Italy, Belgium. Group participations: GC Mumbai; International: "Myths & Reality" Museum of Modern Art, Oxford, Festival of India RAA London & Grey Art Gallery New York. *Auctions*: Christie's for Helpage India, Heart & Sotheby's-Timeless Art Mumbai. Publications: Poems published in Mumbai appeared in "Young Commonwealth" & "New Voices" of the Commonwealth London; Written plays: "Princes" and "Sovaksa" in Mumbai. Collections: *NGMA* New Delhi, NCPA Mumbai, *BB*, *JNAG*; International: MOMA Achim D'Avis Collections France, Chester & Davida Herwitz Trust Collection USA.

Gieve Patel is a trained medical practitioner, a poet and *painter*. His poems and plays have been published in several collections. As a *painter*, the human *figure* was central to his works. It was usually in an environmental setting, either urban or rural, enabling him to explore one of the enduring *themes* in the history of *art*, namely man in relation to his world. Birds and animals also being his source of inspiration, earlier one of his most evocative series has been "Looking into the well". The format allows for rich sensualism, in the simple depiction of organic growth and *colour* on the sides of the well, as well as the centralized focus of the well. It also allows for the introspective activity of looking at one's reflection, both physically and spiritually.

He lives and works in Mumbai.

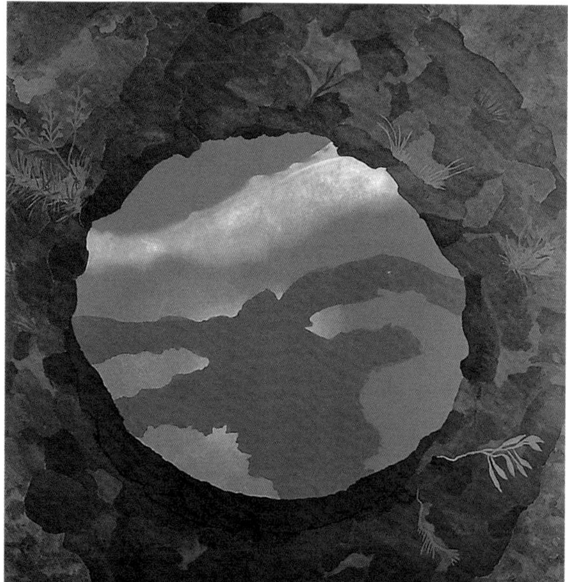

Patel, Gieve: "Looking into the Well", *Acrylics* on *Canvas* 1999, 180x180 cm.

Patel, Homi (1928–2004) b. Mumbai. Education: GDA in *painting JJSA*. Solos: Over 14 solos: *GC* Mumbai, Kunika Chemould New Delhi, *JAG, PUAG*; International: Germany. Group participations: *GC* Kolkata, National Exhibition New Delhi, *JAG, BB Biennale;* International: Italy, Switzerland, Japan, Germany, Iran, Canada, *Biennale* Venice. *Art* camps: J&K. *Auction*: Sotheby's in Mumbai. Awards: *Krishnaji Howlaji Ara* Memorial Trust Award. Fellowship: Ministry of Education & Culture. Collections: *NGMA* New Delhi, TIFR & pvt.

Colour and *composition* are the mainstay of Homi Patel's *paintings*. They may be termed *gestural paintings*, but they do not have the violence of Jackson Pollock's works. Instead a gentle, almost lyrical quality pervades the *canvas*, in spite of the tachist quality of textural variation. He applied *paint* with his hands, in addition to the traditional tools like *brushes* and *palette knives*. *Light*, through *colour*, is intrinsic to Homi Patel's works as he cultivated a subtle and sensitive understanding of *rhythm* and *harmony*.

He lived and worked in Mumbai. Refer *Action Painting*.

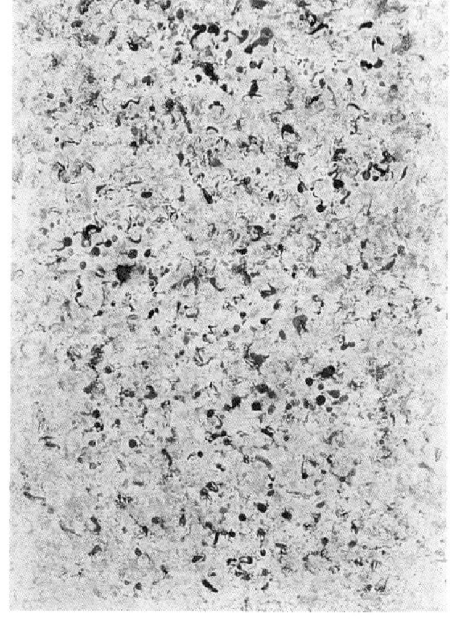

Patel, Homi: "Untitled", *Oil* on *Canvas*, 1990–91, 140x100 cm.

Patel, Janak (1935–) b. Mehsana, GUJ. Education: GDA in *painting JJSA*, Certificate in *applied art JJIAA*. Solos: Ahmedabad. Group shows: Mumbai 1975–78. Group participations: Progressive Painters group in Ahmedabad, Mumbai, New Delhi & Kolkata, Exposition 88 Kanoria Centre for Arts Ahmedabad, National *LKA* Exhibitions, *BAS* Exhibitions. Awards: GUJ State Art Exhibition, *BAS*. Member: Progressive Painters Ahmedabad. Commissions: *Murals* in *mosaic* in GUJ. Collections: GUJ *LKA*, *LKA* New Delhi & other corporates & pvt. Industries.

Janak Patel is a designer and *graphic artist*, using simplified geometric and *abstract* shapes in his creative works. He uses these shapes sparingly, letting the *negative space* dominate over them, creating magnetic relationships with *space*. He has explored almost every *medium*, including *watercolour, pencil* work and *paper collage* in pursuit of his vision of perfect *space*.

He lives and works in Ahmedabad, GUJ.

Patel, Jeram (1930–) b. Sojitra, GUJ. Education: GDA in *drawing & painting JJSA*, National Dip. in *design* typography & publicity *design* Central School of Art London. Solos: Over 30 in India including Ahmedabad, Kolkata, Mumbai,

GE; International: London. Group participations: *Triennale*, Kunika Chemould & *LKA* New Delhi, MMB Mumbai & Indian Painter Kolkata, *ATG*, *JAG*; International: *Biennales* in Tokyo, Sao Paulo & London, *Graphic Biennale* Baghdad, Ten Contemporary Painters from India in USA Hong Kong, & Singapore. *Auctions*: Heart & Osian's Mumbai. Awards: National Awards New Delhi, *BAS* Silver Medal, GUJ *LKA*, National Award (*design*) New Delhi, GUJ *Ravishankar M. Raval* Award, Govt. of India Emeritus Scholarship. Member: *Group 1890*. Appointments: Prof & Dean of *Applied Arts FFA* (*MSU*), *Design* Consultant NID, Reader in *visual design* School of Architecture Ahmedabad, Chairman, GUJ *LKA*. Collections: *NGMA* & *LKA* New Delhi, *GC* Mumbai, Chandigarh University Museum, *Dhoomimal*, *ASI*, *Roopankar BB*, Museum of Modern Art Baghdad & pvt.

Jeram Patel has worked exclusively on two different *media*: his *drawings* are executed in *ink* on *paper*, while his *reliefs* are in *wood* and *metal* sheet. His *images* are largely gestural and almost "automatist" in *nature*. They assume organic shapes almost instinctively and therefore echo certain elements seen in *nature*.

He works in Vadodara, GUJ.

Patel, Nagji (1937–) b. Juni Jidhardi, GUJ. Education: M.A. in *FA*. *sculpture MSU*. Solos: Mumbai. Group participations: Mumbai, Ahmedabad, National Exhibitions & *Triennales* New Delhi; International: *Biennale* Sao Paulo Brazil & Antwerp Belgium, Contemporary Asian Art Festival Japan, Festival of India London; International Festival Baghdad, Olympic Park Korea. *Art* workshops & camps: Vadodara, Nagothane, *LKA* New Delhi & GUJ, *BB*, *BAS*; International: Namibia, Zimbabwe. *Auctions*: Heart New Delhi. Awards: Cultural Scholarship, National *LKA*, GUJ *LKA*, & MAHA State Award. Fellowship: Cultural Ministry of Education & Culture New Delhi. Member: Jury All India Sculpture British Council India; Judging Committee at National Exhibitions New Delhi & *BAS*. Commissions: "Banyan Tree" *stone* & *Monumental sculptures* Vadodara GUJ; International: Yugoslavia, Korea, Japan. Appointments: External Examiner *FFA*, *MSU*. Collections: *LKA* & *NGMA* New Delhi, *LKA* Bangalore & Ahmedabad, Madhvan Nair Foundation Kerala, Museum of FA. Chandigarh, *Roopankar*, pvt. National & International.

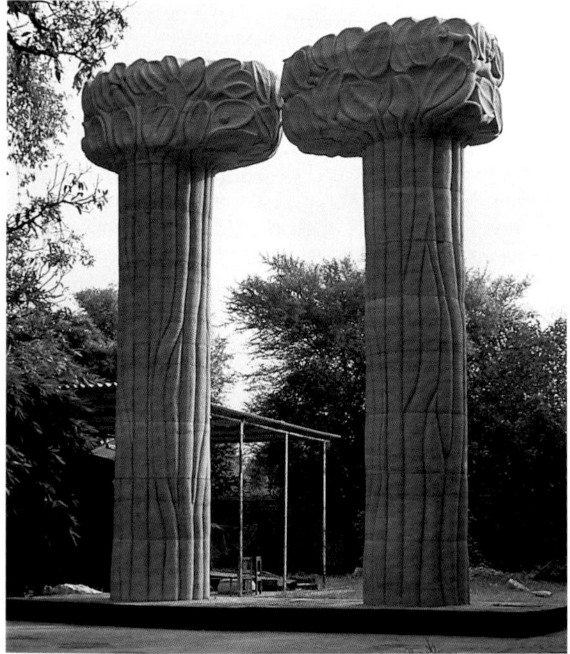

Patel, Nagji: "Banyan Tree", Sandstone, Jodhpur, 1992, 600x480x150 cm.

The act of *carving* is central to Nagji Patel's *sculptures*, therefore he works mostly with *stone* (*marble*, *granite* and sandstone) and occasionally with *wood* (Sheesham). After his initial training in the *fine arts* in Vadodara, he studied sandstone *carving* in *Mahabalipuram* under Sthapati Ganapati and *marble carving* in the *marble* quarries of Makrana in RAJ. His *forms* are essentially organic, with bird and animal *forms* appearing quite frequently. Simplifications and contrast of *textures* (the smooth and polished as against the grainy and unfinished) are the *key* notes of his works. He has executed a few *monumental* environmental *sculptures* in addition to his smaller works. The simple cuboid structures of his early works became rounded and feminine in the 70s. The massive "Banyan Tree" of the early 90s recall the organic sensuality of the gateways at Sanchi.

He lives and works in Vadodara, GUJ.

Patel, Sharad (1934–) b. Ahmedabad, GUJ. Studied CNCFA under *Rasiklal Parikh*, Art Master *JJSA*, GDA (applied) GUJ State; *Fresco painting Banasthali Vidyapith* RAJ. Solos: *Ravishankar M. Raval LKA* Ahmedabad, HCVA *JAG*. Group participations: Ahmedabad, GUJ *LKA* Exhibitions, *JAG*. *Art* camps: Mandu, Dakor. Workshops: *Graphics* GUJ *LKA*, *Wood cut* workshop Kanoria Art Centre Ahmedabad, *Screen printing* HCVA *Painting* workshop Pansar GUJ. Awards: GUJ *LKA*, Mysore DAE, Shawl & Silver Plaque *AIFACS*, *BAS*. Commissions: *Murals* for pvt. & corporates collections. Publications: Illustrated story books for children & Atlas in Gujrathi. Collections: Air India & TATA Mumbai, GUJ *LKA*.

Sharad Patel, who was a lecturer at the CNCFA uses an academic *style* of geometric divisions of *space* in his series of *still lifes*. He uses elements from *nature* and *architecture*, *overlapping* simplified shapes, integrating them into forming pleasing decorative *patterns* with the use of straight and curvilinear *lines*. He uses different types of *paper*, for creating variations in *pattern* and *texture*. His *colours* too are pleasing and harmonious, with low *key*, cool blues and greys predominating over bright primaries.

He lives and works in Ahmedabad.

Pathy, Dinanath (1942–) b. Digapahandi, Orissa. Education: Dip. in *FA*. GSAC Khallikote, M.A., Ph.D. in history Utkal University, Ph.D. in *art* history *VBU*, *Curator* Bhubaneshwar, Training in *visual media* & *museum* method & display Zurich Switzerland. Solos: RB & British Council New Delhi, Kalamanda Bhubaneshwar, IIC, *JAG*, TAG. Retrospective: RB New Delhi; International: Switzerland, Japan, Indonesia. Group participations: Chennai, Bangalore, Chandigarh, RB New Delhi, *JAG*. Seminars & workshops: PUJ University Chandigarh, *LKA* New Delhi, *KB Santiniketan*,

Triennale New Delhi; International: Cairo *Biennale* Egypt, Bali. Awards: President of India Silver Plaque *AIFACS*, *AFA* Kolkata, *LKA* Orissa, Prof. A.L. Basham Memorial Award, Surya Samman Govt. of Orissa; International: China Art Exhibition. Fellowship: Jawaharlal Nehru Fellowship, Japan Foundation Fellowship, Nehru Trust Research Fellowship V&A, British Council Visiting Fellowship London. Member: Of several boards & panels for *exhibitions*, Educational research and *National Museum* Purchase Committee *NGMA*, Jury *LKA* Exhibition & National Council for Education Research & Training New Delhi. Commissions: New Delhi, Bhubaneshwar; International: Sweden, Cairo, Egypt, Bali. Appointment: Secretary of National Academy of Art New Delhi; Dir. Survey of Contemporary Art & Artist Orissa; Founder Principal Govt. B.K. College of Art & Crafts Bhubaneshwar. Publications: In different languages (Oriya, English, German), including "Mural for Gods & Goddesses", "The Painted Icons", "Traditional Paintings of Orissa" & "Avanti". Collections: *NGMA*, *LKA*, MMB, *College of Art* & British Council New Delhi, *Orissa State Museum*, *LKA* Bhubneshwar; International: Korea, Sweden, Bali, Switzerland, London, Beijing.

Dinanath Pathy is a writer and a scholar of repute. His *paintings* show his love of bright, *primary colours* and his fascination for *icons*, both religious and *contemporary*. While his "Homage to Bali" series, show his close study of *gods* and goddesses, being frontal studies of anonymous deities seated in the PADMASANA pose, with esoteric symbols scattered at the edges in a decorative *manner*. His recent series "The Moving Arrow" *highlights* the car as a *modern* day deity. He depicts himself, his wife as lovers draped alongside their car, capturing the moment of proud possession with a decorative clarity of *form* and *colour*. He has experimented with various *techniques*, including *transparent watercolour* and heavy *impasto* during his early years to a flowing use of coloured *inks* and smooth well-modulated *contours* in his latest *oil paintings*.

He lives and works in Bhubaneshwar.

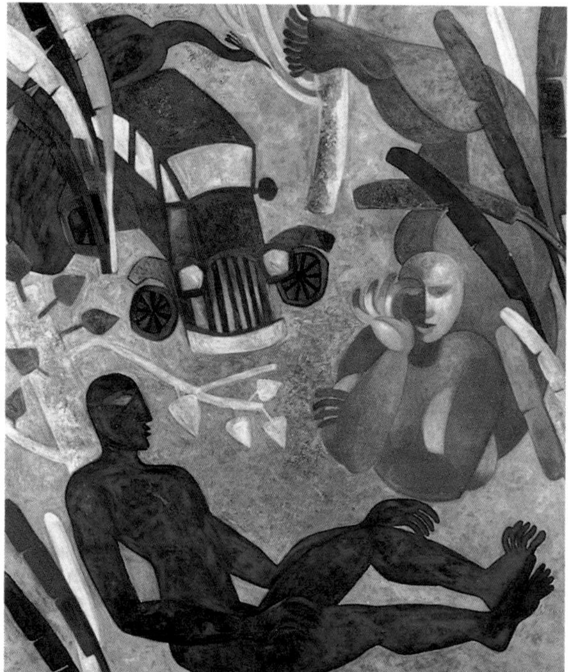

Pathy, Dinanath: "Lovers relaxing in Park with Car", *Oil Painting*, 92x107 cm.

Patil, Shankar (1947–) b. Garag. Education: GDA in *Applied Arts JJIAA*, Apprentice courses in *lithography*, block making, interior decoration. Solos: Hubli, Panjim, Davangere, MMB Bangalore, *LKA* Hyderabad, TAG, *CKP*; International: USA. Group participations: Davanagere, Chennai, Hyderabad, MMB & Kala Mela, Bangalore *VEAG*. Member: KAR Painters Group, President Creative Art Council, Secretary Art Guild Davangere, *BAS*. Appointments: HoD of *Commercial Art* at the Kuvempu University CFA.

Shankar Patil's *paintings* are an effort to express in *visuals*, that which is purely inexpressible. It is the sense of *aesthetics*, both on his part and that of the viewers that he strives to capture in his mostly *figurative* works in *oils* and other *media*. His *styles* also vary with his *themes*, at times being linear and folk inspired and at others being both impressionistic and expressionistic. He has also experimented with TANTRA, and inspired division of *space*.

He lives in Davanagere, KAR.

Patina The green or greenish-brown coloured incrustation of *bronze* caused by oxidation; The pleasing alteration of surface *colour* or *texture* due to age, use or exposure. Patina can also be induced artificially by the application of certain chemicals. The traditional Indian *sculptures* allowed colouring more naturally, to cause coagulation i.e. by *casting* one liquid into another or coating over the *original metal*. *Metal* either covered by *palm leaves* or soaked in different wet mud/sawdust, cotton and cloth covering the *metal* and applying the chemical, or chemically boiling the object and cooling it until in the chemical for the *colour* required. Refer *Art*, *Design*, *Lost Wax Process*, *Tribal Art*, *Sankho Chaudhuri*, *Somnath Hore*, *Meera Mukherjee*, *Pilloo Pochkhanawalla*.

Patnaik, Choudhary Satyanarayan (1925–) b. Badam, AP. Education: Dip. in *FA*. *GSAC* Chennai, Specialized *fresco* & *mural painting Banasthali Vidyapith* RAJ, Training in *arts* & *crafts* National Institute of Basic Education New Delhi. Solos: Govt. Museum Chennai, *LKA*, & ICCR Hyderabad, The Gallery Chennai, BVB Guntur *GG*, *AIFACS*, HAS, *SUG*. Retrospective: 1950–80 ICCR. Group participations: AP *LKA*, *AIFACS*, *Dhoomimal;* International: Poland, West Germany, Japan, Australia, Mungary, Romania, Bulgaria, USA, *LKA* New Delhi & *AIFACS* in USSR. *Art* camps: *GAC* & *Triennale* New Delhi. Awards: *AIFACS*, Prasamsapatram Govt. of AP, AP *LKA*, Mysore DAE. Appointments: Seminars *Art & Craft* Education New Delhi & Mysore, *Art* New Delhi by AP *LKA* Hyderabad in Lepakshi & Warangal. Was a lecturer in *sculpture* at the Govt. College for Women Guntur, Vice-President of AP *LKA*. Publications: Interviewed on radio & TV, reviewed in newspapers & *art* journals; A *monograph* has been published on his works by the AP *LKA*, His book on "C.S.N Patnaik Bronze Sculptures". Collections: National Art Gallery & Govt. Museum Chennai, AP *LKA* Hyderabad, *NGMA* New Delhi.

Choudhary Satyanarayan Patnaik is a *sculptor* who has experimented with most *mediums*, including *terracotta*, *wood*, *stone* and *bronze* in addition to *painting* with *oil colours*. Most of his creative work has been *cast* in *bronze* as he has the equipment for *casting* in his studio in Guntur. He prefers to use *themes* based on rural and folk life and lifestyles, often exhibiting a keen sense of observation in his *vignettes* of rural musicians and the poor, and in his succinct *portraits*. His *paintings* show the same application of roughly applied impasted *colour*, revealing his love of tactility.

He lives in Guntur, AP.

Patole, L. Anand (–) b. Sholapur, MAHA. Education: Dip. *JJSA*, School of Visual Art New York USA. Solos: Technical College Jabalpur, TAG; International: New York Michigan, Holland & over 25 shows for University, Clubs & Churches USA 1971–75. Group participations: Gallery at 678 & JM Gallery New York, Indian Consulate & USA cities.

Also a musician L. Anand Patole's *style* blends the elements of his Indian *background* with those of the *modern* Western world. His works of the early 60s, while he was still in India are representational with *watercolour* studies of monuments and *sculptures*. Abstraction and simplification of *form*, through the disintegration of *contour* and surface appear in the mid-60s, this is seen in his *oil paintings* as well as his *collages* and *etchings*. He uses *mixed media* with an *acrylic* and metallic *paint* combination, painted in the *style* of temple-stone rubbings on *stone*-like *painting* surface.

His *paintings* basically communicate heritage of Indian philosophy and spirituality in a Western *abstract* guise.

He lives and works in New York.

Pattern A rhythmic usually repetitive use of certain *motifs*, to create a *design*, in *painting*, *sculpture*, *architecture* and most of the *minor arts*. It is usually decorative and pleasing to the eye. The *Abu-Dilwara Temples* are decorated with repeated patterns of elephants, lotus flowers and dancers (APSARAS). *Miniature painting* is full of rhythmic pattern in the use of architectural *motifs*, carpet and pavilion *designs* and decorative borders. Jewellery traditionally has always followed a repetitive pattern of certain *motifs* like mangoes, suns, moons and traditional/religious symbols like "OM". Historically Indian *sculpture* and *miniature paintings* vary in pattern from region to region and also from period to period. Later, in *abstract* and TANTRA *art forms* are *abstract*, *symbolic* and theoretical and are mostly expressive in relationships with patterns, which represents the *artist's* interest in the work of *art* with his/her own *technique* and *style*, yet with a free-flowing sense of *lines*, *forms*, movement in the *composition*. Refer. *Detailed Work, Flora & Fauna Painting, Fretwork, Fret Pattern, Inlay, Rhythm, Akhilesh, Vasudev Arnawaz, Aditya Basak, Vajubhai D. Bhagat, P. Khemraj, Jayant Parikh, Amrita Sher-Gil, Rabindranath Tagore*.

Patwardhan, Nachiket (1948–) b. MAHA. Education: B.A. *Architecture MSU*, no formal training in *arts*; Influenced by the works of *Sankho Chaudhuri* & *K.G. Subramanyan* in Vadodara. Solos: Vadodara, Pune, *JAG*, *CYAG*. Group participations: *Nag Foundation* Pune, *CYAG*. Participated in variety of projects; even designing a residential campus & a feature film. Collections: pvt. & corporates.

Nachiket Patwardhan is an architect, a filmmaker, an *Art* Dir., a costume and set designer, whose *art* has evolved from *abstract landscape* in *oil* in the 70s to *pen*, *pastel* and *watercolour drawings* based on his *impressions* of cities and their *art* and *architecture*. His training as an architect, comes to the fore in these linear elevations of cities he has visited, the *modern* touch appearing in the introduction of personal anecdotes in a highly stylized *manner*. There is a use of both the *Art Nouveau* and the *art deco* type of *representation* in the use of decorative and sinuous *lines*.

He lives and works in Pune.

Patwardhan, Sudhir (1949–) b. Pune, MAHA. No formal education in *arts*. Solos: *Art Heritage*, New Delhi, *GC* Mumbai *VAG*, *JAG*. Group participations: Fine Art Company, *Gallery 7*, *GC*, *SG* & *BAAC* Mumbai, RB & *LKA* New Delhi, *BAAC* & *CIMA* Kolkata, *BAS*, *JAG*, *GE*, *VG*, *VAG*, *BB*, *CHAG*; International: Oxford, London, Germany, Paris, Geneva, Kuwait, New York, Houston. *Art* camps: HP, Kerala, *MPCVA;* International: Germany, Century City, Tate Modern London. *Auctions:* Heart, Osian's, Timeless Art Sotheby's Mumbai, Herwitz Collection New York, Christie's London. Awards: Eminent *Artist LKA* National Exhibition New Delhi. Appointments: Seminars and films on a *painter* & a city Mumbai. Collections: *Roopankar BB*, *NGMA*, *LKA* & *Art Heritage* New Delhi, *GC*, NCPA & Deutsche Bank Mumbai, PUJ University Museum Chandigarh; International: Peabody Essex Museum & Hewitz Collection USA.

Sudhir Patwardhan's *themes* are basically depictions of "everyday life" as witnessed in the suburbs of a major metropolis. Though largely objective, the *artist* shares his inner views on his experiences by the simple means of distorting and texturing his largely *figurative* works. His aim is to *paint figures* that "can become self-images for the people who are the subjects" of the works. At times the *figure* is painted as a mere *representation*, and at others as a projection of the *artists* emotions. The *landscape* (especial-

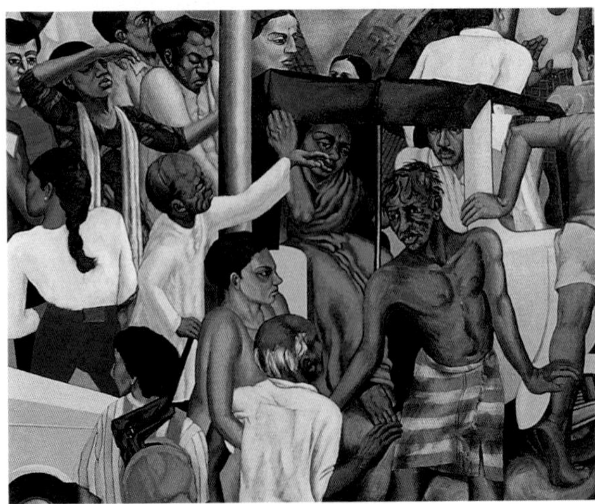

Patwardhan, Sudhir: "Station Road", *Acrylic* on *Canvas*, 1996, 100x120 cm.

ly the claustrophobic *cityscape*) serves as a *backdrop* to his *figures* which are mostly painted in *oils*. His *drawings* are synoptic, while the *paintings* are measured statements, made after much consideration.

He lives and works in Mumbai.

Paul, Ashit (1945–) b. Kolkata, WB. Education: Dip. in *FA*. *GCAC* Kolkata. Solos: *AFA*, *GC* & Centre Art Gallery Kolkata, Agartala Museum Tripura; International: Melbourne, Australia. Group participations: *BAAC*, *AFA* & Centre Art Gallery Kolkata, *Triennale*, National Exhibition & *LKA* New Delhi, UP *LKA* Lucknow, *BAAC* Mumbai, BAC; International: Australia. *Art* camps: National *art* camps Jammu, *Sculpture* from waste product, CMC Festival of Art Kolkata. Member: Established Dhritee Art Centre & Vice-President *AFA* Kolkata. Publications: Albums of serigraph, Three Albums *"Linocuts"*, *drawing* & *painting*, *drawing* & *graphics*. Edited 'Artist' (Periodical), "Woodcut Prints of Nineteenth Century Calcutta" (book). Collection: Agartala Museum Tripura.

Ashit Paul has explored most *mediums* and *styles* in the course of his career. He has also used *aluminium* sheets for *embossing* decorative folk-like *motifs*. His *watercolours* and *pastels* are quite *realistic*, with *themes* taken from the village. His strokes are restless, with a reliance on *hatching*, yet the *texture* remains delicate and subtle.

He lives and works in Kolkata.

Paul, Sunil Kumar (1920–) b. India. Education: Dip. in *clay modelling GSAC* Kolkata. Solos: *Sculpture* & *painting* of Ramakrishna Mission & Lake Town Kolkata. Group participations: *AFA* Kolkata, *AIFACS*. Awards: Governor's Gold Medal for *sculpture AFA* Kolkata, *AIFACS* Award, Silpa Kala Parishad Patna, WB *RBU*, Abanindranath Puraskar WB Govt. Commissions: *Sculptures* & *murals* at several venues including the *AFA* building in Kolkata. Collections: *AFA* Kolkata, pvt. & public.

Sunil Kumar Paul is a *sculptor* of the old school, having worked with various *mediums* including *bronze*, *stone*, *cement* and *clay* in the *figurative idiom*. His *portraits* are Rodinesque, with the finger marks of the *artist* clearly visible even in the final product. His award-winning *portrait* of *Abanindranath Tagore* is a case in point. His *murals* and *relief compositions* revel in stylization i.e. at times decorative and at other times folk-like in character. He has also attempted a *modern* simplification of *outline* and subjugation of detail in some of his creative work, as in the 1988 *plaster sculpture* of "SARASVATI".

He lives and works in Kolkata.

Paul, Sushil (1917–) b. Faridpur. Education: Dip. in *FA*., Western *painting GSAC* now *GCAC* Kolkata, Dip. in *FA*. Indian *painting* ISOAS, *art* appreciation course Calcutta University. Solos: Kolkata, Bhopal, Kathmandu, Panchmarhi, Shimla, Mumbai. Retrospective: *JAG*. Group participations: National & State Exhibitions Kolkata, New Delhi, Patna, Hyderabad, Gwalior & Bhopal. *Art* camps: Panchmarhi by NZCC Allahabad. Awards: *AFA* Kolkata, Hon. Silver Plague by *AIFACS*. Members: Rhythm Art Society Bhopal, Board of studies of *FA*. Vikaram University Ujjain, Bhopal Indore University and Ex-member MPKP Text Book corporates. Publications: Biography published in India & International. Collections: *Ashutosh Museum of Indian Art* Kolkata, State Art Gallery Gwalior & pvt.

Sushil Paul is essentially an impressionist, executing serene *landscapes* and *portraits*, with only a brief *brush* with abstraction in the early 80s. He uses both *oil* and *water-colours* for his *impressions* of the lush Indian countryside. His *tempera landscapes* have a spontaneity of execution and a solidity of *form* that is difficult to achieve.

He lives and works in Bhopal.

Pen A writing and *drawing* instrument, including steel-pens, crow-quill steel-pens, lettering pens, bamboo pens, reed and natural quill pens. Each type of pen gives a different characteristic *line*. They are used with *inks*. An ordinary fountain pen with interchangeable nibs and 'cut-nibs' is a useful *drawing* instrument.

A bamboo pen can be cut at various angles, shaped and then dipped into the *ink* reservoir and brushed on to the *paper* for spontaneous marks as in Japanese and Chinese *brush paintings*. Markers are felt-tipped pens, available in coloured and *black ink*, that dry very quickly by the evaporation of the solvent that carries the colourant. They are usually toxic. Refer *Chinese Ink*, *Computer Art*, *Cross-Hatching*, *Drawing*, *Hatching*, *Ink*, *Kalamkari*, *Line*, *Line and Wash*, *Oil Pastels*, *Oil Crayons*, *Realistic*, *Thumb Impression*, *Gobardhan Ash*, *Jogen Chowdhury*, *P.S. ChanderSheker*, *Muhammed Abdur Chughtai*, *Ganga Devi*, *K.K. Hebbar*, *S. Jaspal*, *K.S. Kulkarni*, *Santosh Manchanda*, *Jaideep D. Mehrotra*, *Rathin Mitra*, *Dulal Mondal*, *Bharat Panchal*, *Rasiklal Parikh*, *Nachiket Patwardhan*, *Ghanshyam Ranjan*, *P.T. Reddy*, *Anilbaran Saha*, *Gopal Sanyal*, *Manickam Senathipathi*, *Somalal Chunilal Shah*, *Pratima Sheth*, *Rohini Sinha*, *Vrindavan Solanki*, *Rabindranath Tagore*, *Arnawaz Vasudev*, *Setlur Gopal Vasudev*, D. *Venkatapathy*; Illustrations–*Rathin Mitra,Solanki Vrindavan*, *Rabindranath Tagore*, *Yusuf*, *Hatching–Laxma Goud*, *Line–Shiavax Chavda*.

Pencil Refers to drawing and writing implement which is usually made by encasing *clay* and *graphite* mix in a wooden sleeve. It was invented first in late 18th-century by N.J. Coute. Nowadays the *casing* is made of plastic, metal or a combination. In *miniature paintings* pencils were made from a mixture of cowdung, powdered slag and water. *Drawing* pencils are now available in hardnesses ranging from 6H (hardest) to 6B (softest). They can be sharpened to a fine point.

Coloured pencils are *leads* composed of *pigments*, toners or metallic flakes and *clay* for binding and hardness.

Pastel pencils are *pastels*, usually encased, and are softer than coloured pencils.

Watercolour pencils are pigmented *leads*, and are bound in a water-gum binder, water soluble dispersion of *oil*, soluble soaps, or fatty *acids*. They are used like regular pencils, then brushed with water to create *washes*. Refer *Automatism*, *Charcoal*, *China-graph Pencil*, *Conte Pencil*, *Crayon Manner*, *Cross-Hatching*, *Drawing*, *Frottage*,

Graphite, Kalamkari, Lead, Line, Line and Wash, Pouncing, Realistic, Muralidhar R. Achrekar, Vasudeo Adurkar, Murigeppa Adiveppa Chetty, Mansing L. Chhara, Jatin Das, Kavita Deuskar, Gopal Ghose, Mrugank G. Joshi, Musa G. Katchhi, Janak Patel, Sagara Piraji, M.K. Puri, Laxman Narayan Taskar; Illustrations–*Life-Drawing–M.R. Achrekar, Ranjitsingh Gaekwad.*

Performance Art Crossing over from the *visual arts* to the field of theatre performance art became popular in the second half of the 20th century. It has three characteristics viz. **1.** It is live. **2.** It takes place in front of an audience, emerging from dance, music, poetry and other subjects. **3.** It sometimes involves the audience and/or performing *artists*, and reflects in *modern art* movement as well. Performance art is used psychologically and aesthetically to describe a feeling in the field of *art*, it denotes a similar feeling for an *art* object as to the feelings of RASA experienced by the *artist* and evoked in the mind of the viewer. At times, actual *art* work is used along with live performing *artists*, to showcase a *theme* or new ideas, along with *photographs*, films and video films. Refer ANJALI, *Backdrop, Balance, Body Art,* CHITRAKATHI, *Cinema, Dadaism, Happening, Installation, Living Sculpture, Life-Mask, Mask,* YOGA, *Kanayi Kunhiraman, Nalini Malani, Bhanu Shah*; Illustration–*Painting, Mahirwan Mamtani.*

Persian Art Refers to *arts, architecture* and *culture* of ancient Iran. Persian art is colourful, and is characterized by intricate floral and geometric *pattern*, mainly of Arabic influence. Mughal *painting*, Indian textiles and carpets of that period were a fusion of Persian and Indian *art* elements. Refer *Flora & Fauna Paintings, Kalamkari, Mughal Dynasty, Muhammed Abdur Rehman Chughtai.*

Perspective 1. A *technique* used in *art* whereby a three-dimensional effect is obtained on a flat surface. In linear perspective, the sensation of *depth* is obtained by using converging *lines* and *vanishing points*, which may be either one or multiple. This makes the object in the distance appear smaller than the object in the *foreground*. This was one of the salient features of high *Renaissance Art.* Perspective was introduced to India by European painters like Tilly Kettle and William Hodges. *Artist* like *Raja Ravi Varma* and *Mahadev V. Dhurandhar* started using Western perspective in their *compositions*. **2.** In India, traditional and *Miniature paintings* did not see the use of proper perspective, e.g. *Ajanta, Miniature paintings–Basohli* and Mughal *paintings*. Here perspective was used only now and then in the depiction of lakes, rivers, fountains, terraces and floor *spaces*, including carpets. Most importantly mixed perspective was used, i.e. *Mughal miniatures. Contemporary* expression changed the *art* after 18th and 19th century with *Academic art.* Refer *Aerial Perspective, Atmosphere/Atmospheric Effects, Backdrop, Background, Balance, Bengal School, Company School/Company Painting, Complemen-tary Colours, Depth, Eye-Level, Fine Arts, Foreground, Fore-shortening, Frontality, Horizon, Mughal Dynasty, One-Point Perspective, Orthogonal, Overlapping, Picture Space, Space, Two-Point Perspective, Vanishing Point, Volume, Satyen Ghosal, Ishwari Rawal, Anjani P. Reddy, Kailash Chandra Sharma, Gurudas Shenoy, Rohini Sinha, Surinder (Kaur), Laxman Narayan Taskar;* Illustrations–*Academic art, Cubism–Gaganendranath Tagore, Installation, Landscape, Line, Mewar, Mughal Dynasty, Vajubhai D. Bhagat, Dharmanarayan DasGupta, K.K. Hebbar,* PARVATI-*Raja Ravi Varma, Baburao Painter, Ratan Parimoo, Kartick Chandra Pyne, Jaidev Thakore, Kanhiyalal R.Yadav.*

Perumal, P. (1935–) b. Kamraj, TN. Education: B.A. Old history, Dip in *painting GCAC* Chennai, Govt. Technical Teachers Certificate *oil painting*, Education Dept. Chennai. Solos: *LKA* Regional Centre Chennai, *SAI*. Group shows: Govt. Museum Chennai, *SAI*. Group participations: Govt. Museum, Regional Centre Chennai, *LKA* National Exhibitions New Delhi, *AFA* Kolkata, RAJ *LKA* Jaipur, *SAI*, HAS, *CKP, JAG, BAS*, other towns Chandigarh, Thiruvananthapuram & Cochin. *Art* workshops & camps: Amravati, Regional Centre Chennai, Painters camp Kodaikanal. Awards: National *LKA* New Delhi, *LKA* Chennai, TN. Fellowship: Senior Fellowship Dept. of Culture Govt. of India. Member: Executive Board South India Society of Painters Chennai. Appointments: Drawing master, Art Instructor & a lecturer in Chennai; President of Teaching Staff Association *GCAC* 1976–91. Collections: *NGMA* New Delhi, *LKA*, National Art Gallery & Govt. Museum Chennai, *SAI, VEAG* & pvt. in India; International: Italy, Germany, USA, Canada.

Having come from a small village in TN, the rural *theme* predominates in P. Perumal's *paintings*. He has worked with *oils, watercolour* and *copper reliefs*, in addition to his works with *linocut*. His early works, being influenced by his teachers moulded by the *Bengal School*, were in *tempera*. The *themes*, though still rural have evolved into an optimistic look at the colourful village life, from the nostalgia and melancholia of the early works.

Since his retirement from the *GCAC*, he has been residing in Chennai.

Phadke, Milind (1951–) b. Pune, MAHA. Education: GDA Applied Abhinava Kala Mahavidyalaya Pune. Solos: RB Hyderabad, *JAG, CKP*, Balgandharva Art Gallery & Sushoban Art Gallery Pune. Group Shows: Pune, Satara, Bangalore, New Delhi, *JAG*. Group participations: Balghandharvas Art Gallery & *Nag Foundation* Pune, National Kala Mela Mumbai & New Delhi, Chennai, *JAG, AIFACS, BAS, ASI*, HAS, *CKP*. Workshops: *Watercolour, painting, wood cut* workshop. Awards: HAS, *ASI*. Member: Faculty of Abhinav Kala Mahavidyalaya Pune. Collections: AP *LKA*, Davangere Art Gallery, Kritika Art Gallery Bangalore, pvt. & corporates Mumbai, Pune, Belgum; International: USA, Australia, France.

Milind Phadke prefers using *watercolour* in conjunction with *oil pastels* and *colour pencils* to create soft shimmering *landscapes*, which influences the overall mood of the work. Boats, rocks, village scenes and poetic viewpoints are some of the subjects he frequently *paints*.

He lives in Pune.

Photo-engraving A form of *relief* printing using *metal plates*, the *image* has been created using photographic light-sensitive methods. The prepared plate is inked and the *impression* taken in the usual way. In India it became a commercial activity especially when printing started in Goa, Bombay and Calcutta, where labels and boxes were printed. Some printmakers used this *technique* are *Jyoti Bhatt, Rm. Palaniappan*. Refer *FFA (MSU), Daguerre-otype/Daguerrotype, Engraving, Lithography, Monograph, Oleography, Photo-gravure, Photograph, Pointillism*; Illustrations–*Jyoti Bhatt, Rm. Palaniappan*.

Photo-etching A method of etching by using a photographic *light* with sensitive coating. The film *negative* is placed on the *plate*, which has been coated with a *light* sensitive material. The resist hardens when it is exposed to *light*. The *plate* is then cleaned, etched, inked and printed in the normal way. Refer *Etching, Printmaking, Jyoti Bhatt*.

Photograph A picture formed by the chemical action of light on sensitive coated film, which is then super-imposed on paper. It arrived in India in the late 19th century and slowly replaced portraiture. Indian colleges of *art* offered post-dip. courses in photography from 1950. Several *artists* explained this *medium*. Photography is commonly used in print advertising, *Gopal Damodar Deuskar* created photographic portraiture of live sitting personality.

Jyoti Bhatt has been working in different *media*, with photography and created photo-documenting of *folk* and *tribal art* in India. Photograpy has also found its way into *performance art* and *installation art*. Refer *Acid, Applied Art, Art, Commercial Art, Daguerreotype/Daguerrotype, Earth Art, Earth Works, Land Art, Environment Art, Found Object, Half-tone, Happening, Hyper-Realism, Ideal Art, Life-Mask, Lithography, Matte, Modernism, Modern Movement, Negative, New Realism, Photo-engraving, Photo-etching, Photo-engraving, Photo- montage, Photo-realism, Portrait, Positive, Print, Reproduction, Stencil, Super Realism, Yoga, Krishan Ahuja, Navjot Altaf, Suhas Bahulkar, Sadanandji Bakre, Siona Benjamin, Anant M. Bowleker, Shobha Broota, Chiru Chakravarty, Surjeet Kaur Choyal, Muhammed Abdur Rehman Chughtai, Avtarjeet S. Dhanjal, Shobha Ghare, Li Gotami, Ram Keote, Girish H. Khatri, Mahirwan Mamtani, Jaideep D. Mehrotra, Anjolie Ela Menon, Kahini (Arte) Merchant, Nasreen Mohamedi, Dashrath Patel, N. Pushpamala, Abalal Rahiman, Debi Prasad RoyChowdhury, Ali J. Sultan, Antonio X. Trindade, Umesh Varma, Zahoor Zargar, Haku Shah*.

Photogravure The *technique* is similar to the one employed in *photo-etching*. The *image* is printed from *intaglio* i.e. cut and etched rather than in *relief*, giving a *line* or *texture* and *half-tones* on the plate. At first this *technique* was used for textile *printing*. Later it became popular among *modern* printmakers/*artists*. Refer *Daguerreotype/ Dague-rrotype, Printmaking, Photo-engraving*; Illustration–*Jyoti Bhatt*.

Photo-montage A *collage* made by *overlapping photographs* or *fragments* of *photographs*, a *technique* used both in filmmaking and in *art*. In India it has been used by *artists* since the latter half of the 20th century. A new *image* is created by splicing together the *photographs*–effectively communicating the story line or the *composition*. Refer *Negative, New Realism, Pop Art, Super Realism, Krishan Ahuja, Jyoti Bhatt, Atul Dodiya, Dashrath Patel, K. Vasant Wankhede*.

Photo-realism Synonymous with *Super Realism. Artists* like C. Close and D. Hanson created work that were so photographically real that it fooled people into believing that the *sculptures* especially were live people. In India, *Jaideep D. Mehrotra* and *Bikash Bhattacharjee* have been experimenting with photo-realism in their otherwise surreal *compositions*. Refer *Surjeet Kaur Choyal, Dinkar V. Wadangekar*.

Picchwais=wall hangings or tapestries, usually of cotton or silk handspun and woven starched cloth, with *designs*, which are also hand painted using vegetable dyes with *outlines* and contrasting *colours*. Some works were also richly embroidered sometimes, with *silver* and *gold* threads. They usually come from RAJ and western India, especially the small pilgrimage town of Nathdwara. Many times they were used curtaining parts of the temple such as the main sanctum. The subject usually depict Lord KRISHNA and GOPIS in their beautiful surroundings, or the deity, Srinathji (a *form* of Lord KRISHNA). Refer RASA LILA, *Kailash Chandra Sharma*.

Pictorial Pictorial expression dates back to the cave *paintings* all over the world. In India, too the *rock-cut illustrations* at Bhimbetka date back to the Stone Age. As man evolved so did pictorial *design*. In the 2nd millennium the RAGAMALA *paintings* were wonderful examples of *illustrations* of sound/musical modes (RAGAS). Refer *Balance, Detailed Work*, HANUMAN, *Horizon, Illusion, Illusionism, Illustration, Kangra, Line, Mannerism*, RAGA, RAGAMALA, *Super Realism, Kartick Chandra Pyne Prabha Shah, Abdul Rahim Appabhai Almelkar, Biren De;* Illustrations– RAGINI, PARVATI, *Rini Dhumal, H.A. Gade, Ranjitsingh Gaekwad, Ganga Devi, Shaibal Ghosh, Asit K. Haldar, Ganesh Haloi, G. Narayana Pillai Kattur, Prabhakar Kolte, Jaidev Thakore, Kartick Chandra Pyne, Ganesh Pyne, Surya Prakash*.

Picture Space A *term* used in *painting*, to refer to the apparent *space* behind the picture plane–the surface of the *painting*, created by the use of *perspective* and other *painterly* devices. In *miniature paintings* the picture space was usually divided into sequences as in *narrative art* e.g. *Mewar* or *Malwa* miniatures where two or more incidents were portrayed in the same *painting*. *Mughal miniatures* were enlivened by the use of mixed *perspective*. *Contemporary painting* follows no particular rule. *Spaces* can flow into each other, *passages* can intersect. Several planes and *textures*, *patterns* and *colours* can enliven and interconnect. The term "picture space" has expanded in the 20th century, to include new *techniques* like *installation* and *video art*. Refer *Background*, *Jain Manuscript*, *Jain Manuscript Illumination*, *Narrative*, *Baburao Painter*, *Pestonjee Bomanjee*, *Kanu Desai;* Illustrations–BHAGAVATA PURANA, *Sudhir Patwardhan*.

Pigment These are small particles of coloured material that are suspended in water, *oils*, resins and other binders to *form paint*. They can be either **1.** *Inorganic* (naturally derived from mineral, chemical or *synthetic*). **2.** Organic (plant, animal or earth based). **3.** Metallic (*metal* based). Pigments were used in *prehistoric* period by cave *painters*, include coloured *clays*, soot and powdered bone. Some pigments are stable or permanent, while others are unstable and fade on exposure to *light*.

Tempera pigments are ground under water for 12 hours, the process being repeated for 24 hours after five days, then filtered and gum from the Neem (Azadirachta indica) tree added to it as a binder. This *colour* and its pigment study is one of the most important contexts in Indian *art* right from *Ajanta* and *miniature paintings*, and its *colour* application and its method of *painting*. Coloured *pencils* are *leads* composed of pigments, toners or metallic flakes and *clay* for binding and hardness. *Pastels*, usually encased, and are softer pigments. *Oil paints* a *paint*, in which the dry became the *techniques* followed from mid-19th century in India. *Artists* also used *oil* for the *finish* touch in *tempera* and early *portraits*. Around 1970s, in India, *acrylic* pigments were suspended in *synthetic* resin. Refer *Acrylics*, *Black*, *Canvas*, *Chalk*, *Crayon*, *Dragging*, *Drawing Inks*, *Dry Brush Painting*, *Drying Oils*, *Earth Colour*, *Egg-oil emulsion*, *Encaustic*, *Finish*, *Fresco*, *Gouache*, *Gestural Painting*, *Gum Arabic*, *India Ink*, *Matter*, *Media*, *Medium*, *Natural Colours*, *Neo-Impressionism*, *Oil Crayons*, *Opacity*, *Opaque*, *Sepia*, *Single Block Colour Printing*, *Space*, *Stippling*, *Viscous*, *Watercolours*, *White*, *Narendra Amin*, *Shanti Banerjea*, *Bikash Bhattacharjee*, *Santokba Dudhat*, *Prem Chandra Goswami*, *Rani Rai Mrityunjoy Chakraborty*, *Sisir Sahana*, *Rangaswamy Sarangan*, *Harendra Shah*, *G.S. Shenoy*, *Ved Pal Sharma*, *J. Swaminathan*, *D.B. "Deven" Seth*, *Sumatimohan*, *Sushil Vatsa;* Illustrations–*Ajanta*, *K.M. Adimoolam*, *Siona Benjamin*, *Natvar Bhavsar*, *Bal Chhabda*, *Rini Dhumal*, *Surendra Pal Joshi*, *Krishen Khanna*, *Sailoz Mookerjea*, *Kapu Rajaiah*, *Jamini Roy*, *Laxman Shreshtha*, *Pratima Sheth*, *Abanindranath Tagore*, *Nathu Lal Verma*.

Pithawalla, Manchershaw F. (1872–1937) b. Surat, GUJ. Education: Bombay School now *JJSA* under John Griffts. Solos: Simla Art Society, *BAS*; International: Dorc Gallery London–First Indian Artist's solo in UK. *Auctions*: Osians, Heart Mumbai, Heart New Delhi, Delhi Christie's. Awards: *BAS*, Gold Medals in 1907 to 1909 in India. Commissions: to produce album celebrating the flowers of Indian Woman-hood, which was presented by Indian ladies to Queen Mary during her visit to India. Coll-ections: *GC* Mumbai, *NGMA* New Delhi, *JJSA*, *PWM*; International: Trust-ees V&A, *portraits* in India & abroad.

Manchershaw F. Pithawalla was a fine portraitist in the *manner* of *Pestonjee Bomanjee*. He captured the likeness of the sitter. The face was rendered in great detail, his *handling* of *drapery* and other accessories was broader with a near impressionist array of short strokes and *highlights*. During his European sojourn in 1911 he produced quite a few *landscapes* and "sceneries" including quick spontaneous sketches in London.

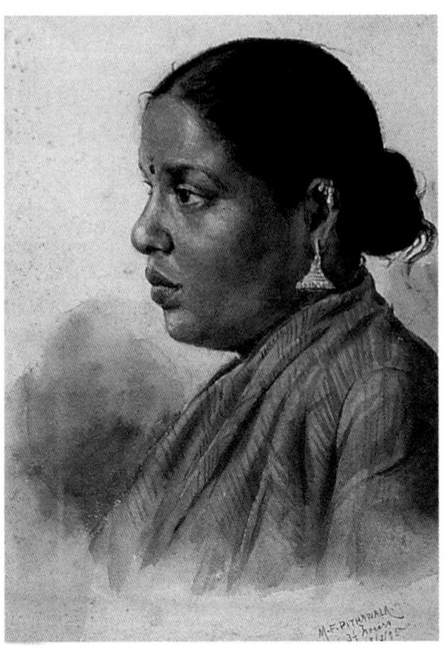

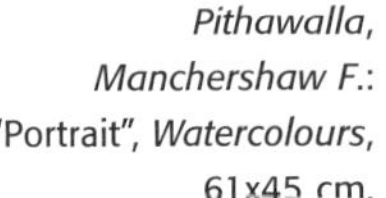

Pithawalla, Manchershaw F.: "Portrait", *Watercolours*, 61x45 cm.

Plaster A malleable material made from a mixture of limestone, sand and water, with a fibrous strengthener. It is used to coat walls, sometimes as a *ground* for *fresco*, and for mouldings and carved architectural ornamentation, or to make moulded *copies* of *sculpture*. Refer *Paper-Pulp Casting*, *Plaster of Paris*, *Sudha Arora*, *Ramkinkar Baij*, *Sankho Chaudhuri*, *Sadanandji Bakre*, *Sunirmal Chatterjee*, *Subrayalu Dhanapal*, *Balbir Singh Katt*, *Sunil Kumar Paul*, *Pilloo Pochkhanawalla*, *Himmat Shah*, *Bayaji Vasantrao Talim*, *K. Venkatappa;* Illustration–*Himmat Shah*.

Plaster Casting Refer *Casting*.

Plaster of Paris A fine *white* powder, becomes hard when mixed with water. Plaster of Paris–created in Paris, is an extensively used material by *sculptors*, due to its easy handling and *installation*. It literally, derives its name from the "Earth of Paris" as it contains a large percentage of *gypsum*. The most popularly used *forms* of plaster of Paris is alabaster which is *white*, fine grained, soft and *opaque*, and thus can be easily cut or carried. Refer *Plaster*, *Tensile Strength*, *Ganpatrao K. Mhatre*, *Aekka Yadagiri Rao*, *Debi Prasad RoyChowdhury;* Illustrations–*Art Education*, *Sadanandji Bakre*, *Bhagwant K. Goregaoker*, *Bayaji Vasantrao Talim*.

Plasticity **1.** The quality of appearing three-dimensional with respect to surrounding *space*, in the work of *art*. **2.** Malleability of soft but solid materials so that they can be shaped or modeled. A *sculpture* is called Plastic art. *Nandagopal's* work cannot be term plastic, as they are more angular and planner. Plastic or plasticity can be used to refer to the works of *Debi Prasad RoyChowdhury*, *Vinayak Pandurang Karmarkar*, *Raghav Kaneria*, *Ravinder G. Reddy* and all ancient Indian *sculpture*.

Plate The name used especially for a flat surface in *printmaking*. The *metal* sheet of the required thickness made of *copper*, *zinc* or *aluminium* is used for *etching*, *engraving* or *dry-point* respectively. These plates are used for printing different *tonal values* obtained by *acid* biting and aquatinting. *Prints* are then taken. *Printmaking* was introduced in India in the late 19th century by *Mukul Chandra Dey, Nandalal Bose, Rabindranath Tagore, Yagneshwar Kalyanji Shukla*, and many others. *Metal* sheets were also used by *sculptors. Shankar Nandgopal* used *enamelling* and *electroplating* to make his works colourful. Refer *Acid Resist, Bite, Biting in, Collography, Ground, Lithography, Metal Cut, Mezzotint, Monotype, Multi Block Colour Printing, Offset Printing, Oleography, Photo-engraving, Print, Relief, Soft Ground, Sugar Lift, Varnish, Viscosity Printmaking, V. Viswanadhan.*

Plein-Air (French)=open air. A *term* for a *painting* executed outdoors rather than in a studio. Impressionist *paintings* were done in plein-air. They are spontaneous and have a roughly brushed, unfinished look, as capturing the *light* of the moment was more important than mere likeness. In India, group of Bengal *artists*, Bombay *artists* and most *art* schools encouraged their students to work outdoors especially with *watercolour. Chittaprosad* did many impromptu *sketches* of the Bengal Famine Victims, which he would later *finish* with *ink* and *brush washes*. This *term* is also used to denote large *sculptures* installed in the open through *volume, mass* and *space*. Refer *Academic Art, Landscape, Aku, Ramkinkar Baij, Narayan S. Bendre, Shiavax Chavda, M. Dharmani, Bimal Kundu, Dhruva Mistry, Shankar Nandagopal, Natu J. Parikh, P.R. Thippeswamy.*

Pochkhanawalla, Pilloo (1923–1986) Mumbai, MAHA. Self-taught *sculptor*. Studied under N.G. Pansare. Over 12 solos: Mumbai, New Delhi. Group participations: *LKA*, Ashoka Gallery & *Triennale* New Delhi, *GC* Mumbai; International: USA, Yugoslavia, *Biennale* Belgium & Sao Paulo, on *Sculptures* Belgrade, Bangkok & Tokyo, Commonwealth London. *Auctions*: Heart Mumbai. Awards: *LKA* New Delhi, MAHA State Art Exhibition, *BAS* Exhibition & All India Sculptor's Association Silver Medal. Commissions: Outdoor *sculptures*, TV Centre, Ceat Tyres, Nehru Planetarium, The National Gas Company & Bombay Electric Supply & Transport Mumbai. Appointments: International, gave slide lectures & demonstrations at different venues in USA. Designed stage décor for following plays: "The Idiot", "The Book of Job", "Cyrus the Great", "Tughlaq", 'The Splendoured One'. Collections: *NGMA* & *LKA* New Delhi, *GC* Mumbai, University of PUJ Chandigarh, BARC, *PUAG, JNAG*; International: Gallery Surya Germany.

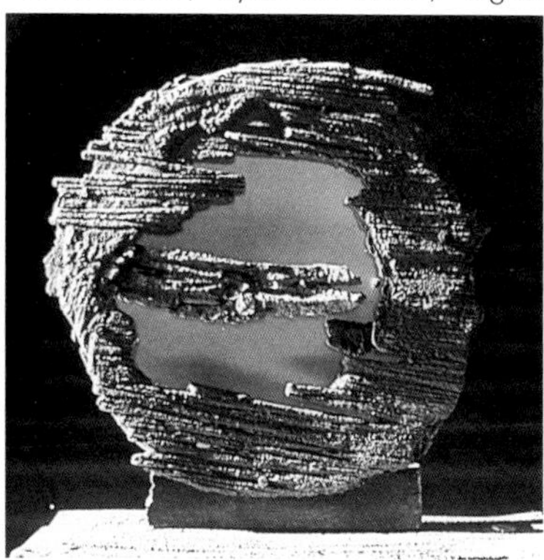

Pochkhanawalla, Pilloo: "Untitled", *Concrete*.

Pilloo Pochkhanawalla's early *sculptures* revealed both her Indian heritage and the *impression* that Henry Moore's organically shaped reclining *figures* had made on her. Soon, the "holes" in the works began to enlarge and the works became increasingly *abstract*. The works of the 70s and 80s partook of the same *abstract* spontaneity that is seen in the works of David Smith. She began to use *wax* and *plaster* to achieve the swirling movements and gestures of *abstract* expressionist *sculpture*. Like many others of the period, she began incorporating junk and scrap material into her works of the later period, when exploration of *space* and *texture* became her overriding concern. She has worked with several *media* including, welded *steel, copper, ceramic, wood, lead, cement* and *marble* chips, but *aluminium alloy*, especially *cast aluminium* remained her favourite.

Pointillism A *style* initiated by the scientifically precise *paintings* of 19th-century French painter, G. Seurat. He used closely spaced tiny precise dots of pure *colours* placing them in such a *manner* as to optically blend the *colours* into varied *shades* and *tints* especially when viewed from a distance. This was *optical mixing*, the scientific principle behind his *paintings*. In India, several 20th-century *artists* experimented with this *style*, the most famous examples being *Narayan S. Bendre* from 1966 onwards. Pointillist is a *painter* who uses this *technique*. Photographic *engraving* followed the principles of pointillism. Refer *Neo-Impressionism*; Illustration—*Narayan S. Bendre*.

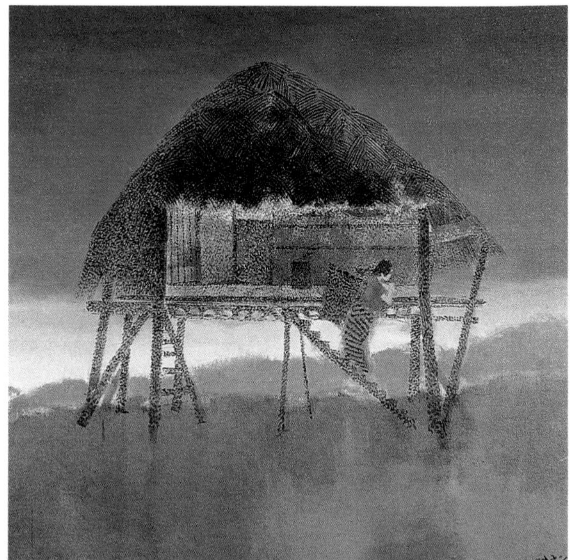

Pointillism: *Narayan S. Bendre*, "Arunodaya" at Arunachal, *Oil* on *Canvas*, 1989.

Polychromatic The use of many harmonious *colours*. Refer *Arun Bose, K.K. Hebbar, Vasudha Thozhur.*

Polychromatic Sculpture Essentially colourful *sculpture. Sculptures* were painted since Egyptian *times*. The Greeks also coloured their *sculptures*. During the *Renaissance colour* was applied to *stone* and *terracotta sculpture*. In the 20th century, new materials (i.e. vinyl) and ideas were incorporated into the field of *sculpture*. *Contemporary* examples of polychromatic sculptures are as diverse as minimalist industrial units and D. Hanson's hyper-realist *sculpture* with perfectly harmonized clothing. In India polychromatic sculpture is equally diverse as seen in the *paper* works of *C. Jagdish*, *fibreglass* of *Ravinder G. Reddy* and the *metal repousse* of *Nagesh Bhimrao Sabannavar* and *Shankar Nandagopal* among others. Polychromatic sculpture is versatile in its choice of in various *media*, such as *plaster of Paris*, *wood*, *terracotta*, *paper sculpture*, *ceramics*, *cement concete* and/or painted polyester resin *fibreglass*. Refer *M.J. Enas*, *Dhruva Mistry;* Illustrations–*Relief*, SHANKHA, *Navjot Altaf*, *Jyotsna Bhatt*, *C. Jagdish*, *Shankar Nandagopal*, *Ravinder G. Reddy*, *G. Reghu*.

Pop Art The name originates from the word popular (pop), standing for *mass culture*. The movement began in the 50s as a reaction against the formlessness of *Abstract Expressionism*. The mood was prevalent throughout the Western world. The basic concept was that of mass appeal. Pop art and *culture* included not only music and various *art forms*, but also used *themes* from films, advertising, literature, *mass* produced consumer goods and other *media* such as TV, newspapers etc. as materials in Pop arts. Indian *artists* like *Navjot Altaf*, *C. Jagdish*, *Bhupen Khakhar*, *Kanayi Kunhiraman*, *N. Pushpamala*, *Ravinder G. Reddy*, *Gulam Mohammed Sheikh*, *Vivan Sundaram* and others have experimented with Indian pop-type *imagery* in their works especially of religious *icons* and middle-class kitsch. Refer *Assemblages*, *Content*, *Dadaism*, *Ready-Made*, *Krishnamachari Bose*.

Portrait A drawn, painted, or photographed likeness of a person or animal. It could either be true to life or simply capture the essence of the subject. In India, portraiture became the force of several *artists* of the Mughal court. At times miniature portraits were executed on ivory pendants called "Shast". The Britishers introduced the Western *style* of portraiture into India. Artists from Britain and other European countries travelled around the Indian courts *painting* several portraits of the Rajahs and their harems. *Raja Ravi Varma* was to learn the *technique* of *oil painting* from Theodore Jensen, one such artist who visited the Kerala court. *Raja Ravi Varma* was to *paint* some of the finest court portraits especially that of the Baroda court. *Contemporary* Indian portraits were painted in *oils* with a photographic *finish*. The works were also judged in terms of *mass*, in addition to other elements such as *line*, *tone*, *colour* and *texture*. Indian *museums* have a good collection of portraits of all *styles* and period. Refer *Academic Art*, *M.T.V. Acharya*, *Muralidhar R. Achrekar*, *Vasudeo Adurkar*, *Shivananda P. Akki*, *Chetan Arya*, *Vidya Bhushan*, *Atul Bose*, *Adiveppa Murigeppa Chetty*, *Gajanan S. Haldankar*, *Manchershaw F. Pithawalla*, *Narayan R. Sardesai*, *Jyotirindranath Tagore*, *Antonio X. Trindade*, *Thotha Vaikun-tham*, *K. Venkatappa*, *Vinayakrao Venkatrao Wagh*, *K. Vasant Wankhede;* Illustrations–*Pestonjee Bomanjee*, *Rasiklal Parikh*, *Raja Ravi Varma*, *Shantilal M. Shah*, *Highlight–Anant M. Bowleker*.

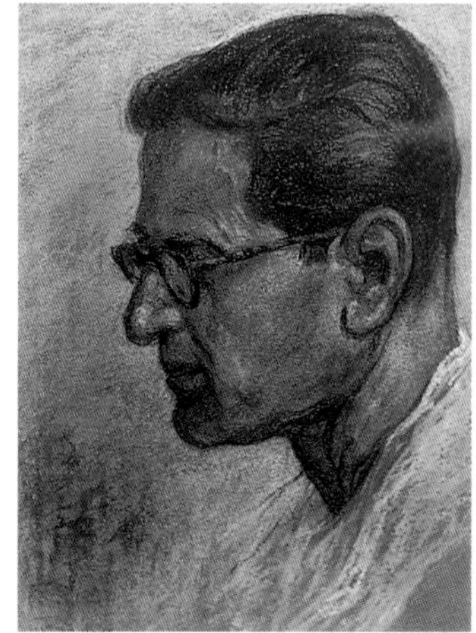

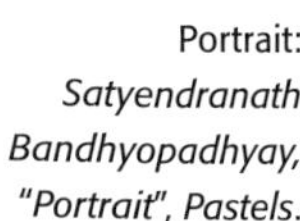

Portrait: *Satyendranath Bandhyopadhyay, "Portrait", Pastels.*

Positive 1. A *print* formed from a photographic *negative*. **2.** The object achieved by filling in a *negative* section with relevant material in *printmaking*, *sculpture* and *painting*. Refer *Chipping Mould*, *Copper*, *Daguerreotype/Daguerrotype*, *Photograph*, *Undercut*, *Waste-Mould*, *Wood Cut*, *Wood Cut Printing*, *Anju Chauduri*, *Jatin Das*.

Poster A *graphic design* for making signboards, handbills, placards or similar display. In Europe, earlier they were designed and hand painted by many prominent *artists* such as H. Toulouse-Lautrec, H. Matisse and P. Picasso.

In India *artists* worked for the film industry, producing posters & *hoardings* in the pre-Independence era e.g. *Maqbool Fida Husain*. Earlier *Nandalal Bose* painted the famous Haripura posters for the 1938 Congress session in GUJ. Poster making is essentially *commercial art* with *calligraphy* and *photo-montage*. Refer *Commercial Art*, *De'collage*, *Indian Film Industry*, Studio of *Mohile-Parikh Centre For The Visual Arts*, *Chetan Arya*, *Ashok Bhowmik*, *Manishi Dey*, *K. S. Kulkarni*, *Baburao Painter*, *Dashrath Patel*, *Prem Singh*.

Post-Impressionism A *term* coined by English *critic* R. Fry to describe the works of certain French *artists* immediately following the impressionist period. These *artists*, who included P. Cezanne, P. Gauguin, V. Van Gogh and others reacted against the impressionist preoccupation with *visual* appearances. Their *styles* were individual with no apparent common features except Gauguin's and Van Gogh's love of bright *colours* and *forms*.

The cosmopolitan *Bombay School* in 1934 came under the post-impressionist, fauvist influence. Refer *Abstract Impressionism*, *Fauvism*, *Modern*, *Maqbool Fida Husain*, *P.T. Reddy*, *Amrita Sher-Gil*.

Post-Independence In India, the *term* would refer to *art* after 1947. (India gained independence from Britian on August 15, 1947) Post-Independence *art* is *eclectic*, with borrowings and influences from the West as well as from indigenous sources. *Abstraction figurative*, *landscapes*, *abstract*, *figuration*, *printmaking*, *installations*, kinetic *sculpture* were all innovated and practised during this period of experimentation and appreciation of the *arts*. Refer *Abstract Movement*, *Art Criticism*, *Cubism*, *Mosaic*, *Narrative*, *Neo-Tantricism*, *Pastoral*, *Krishnaji Howlaji Ara*, *Vasudeo Adurkar*.

Post-Modern A *term* used to describe the *Contemporary period* as distinct from the *Modern* or Early and Mid 20th century *art*. It has *avant-garde* connotations. Refer *Art for Art's Sake, Art Nouveau, Arte Povera, Media, Video Art, Navjot Altaf, Avtarjeet S. Dhanjal, Shakuntala Kulkarni, Nalini Malani, Yashwant Mali, Chittrovanu Mazumdar, Ved Nayar, Saroj Gogi Pal, Dashrath Patel, Shantanu Ukil*.

Pottery Articles made of fired *clay* or earthenwares on potter's wheel, where he *moulds* the *clay* by the rapid spinning of the wheel. Refer *Casting, Ceramics, Crafts, Harappa, Islamic Art, Kiln, Neolithic Art, FFA* Vadodara, *RSA, Ramkinkar Baij, Jyotsna Bhatt, Kantibhai B. Kapadia, Jamini Roy, Vimoo Sanghvi, Mansimran Singh, Sardar Gurcharan Singh, Pratima Devi Tagore (Thakur)*.

Pouncing The *technique* of copying a *design* or *motif* by pricking holes in the *outline* and placing it on a sheet of *paper* or *canvas*, and dusting it with *chalk* or *graphite* powder. The *image* appearing as fine dots which are then connected with a *pencil* or *brush*. Mughal *artists* used the Charba (fine, *transparent* skin of gazelle) for tracing.

Prabasi This along with *Modern Review* were among the magazines edited, published and owned by Ramananda Chatterjee, one of the first practitioners of literary and illustrative journalism in India. The "Prabasi" (in Bengali) first appeared in 1901 and was essentially used by its editor to carry the nationalist messages to the Indian people. Along with *Modern Review*, it publicized the birth of the *Bengal School*, fostering National unity through *art*. Chatterjee introduced the practice of printing "A painting of the Month" in near naturalistic *half-tone* blocks along with a brief description of the work.

Prabhavali Refer ABHUSHANA, *Aureole, Halo*, NATARAJA, *Nimbus*,.

Pradhan, Niranjan (1940–) b. Midnapur, WB. Education: Dip. in *drawing* & *painting GCAC* Kolkata & Dip. in *sculpture* & *modelling GCAC* Kolkata, studied under *Chintamoni Kar*, *Art* appreciation course Calcutta University. Solos: Indo-American Society, Aurobindo Bhavan & *AIC* Kolkata, *JAG*. Group *exhibition*: Ashutosh Centenary Hall Kolkata. Group participations: Sculptor's Guild, *BAAC* & *AIC* Kolkata, *LKA* New Delhi, *AIFACS*. Awards: Received Silver Plaque *AIFACS, BAAC* Certificate of Merit & Award for *sculpture* Kolkata. Founder member: Sculptor's Guild Kolkata, Members *SCA*. Commissions: *Sculptures* & *bust portraits* for public places in Bengal; International: Bristol. Appointments: Asst. Prof. *GCAC* Kolkata. Seminars: *Khajuraho*, Kolkata, Tripura, Maldah. Collections: Birla Museum & Gallery La Mere Kolkata, *NGMA* New Delhi & pvt.

Niranjan Pradhan uses his *sculptures* to symbolically represent *nature's* eternal cycle along with vegetal growth and organic vitality. *Bronze* remains his favourite *medium*, though he has worked with *fibreglass, wood, stone* and *terracotta* as well. The fact that he has to *model* the *form* in *clay* before *casting*, allows Niranjan Pradhan the freedom to add or erase a detail or a plane or add *texture* as and when he pleases, which gives his *sculptures* a *painterly* quality.

He lives and works in Kolkata. Refer *Fibreglass*.

Prakash, Surya (1940–) b. Madhira, AP. Education: Advance Dip. in *painting* & *portrait* Govt. College of FA. Hyderabad; Worked under *Ram Kumar* New Delhi. Solos: KB & MMB Hyderabad, *LKA*, Kunika Chemould, *Art Heritage* & CMC New Delhi, *GC* Mumbai, Krithika Gallery Bangalore, *BAAC* Kolkata, *RBM*, CCMB, *Dhoomimal, GE*, TAG, *JAG, CYAG, SAI, CKP, CRAR, G88, ABC*; International: Germany, USA. Group Show: MMB & KB Hyderabad, *LKA* New Delhi, University Museum Chandigarh, MMB Kolkata, *PUAG, SAI, JAG* & *AIFACS*. Group participations: *Triennale LKA* & Husain Ki Sarai New Delhi, *BAAC* Kolkata, *ATG, Roopankar, G88, CYAG, BAS;* International: Germany, Washington, London. *Auction*: Helpage by Christie's Mumbai. Awards: Gold Medal HAS, AP *LKA*, National *LKA, AIFACS*. Fellowships: Senior Fellowship Govt. of India. Publications: A *monograph* & a book on his life & works by the Hyderabad *LKA* & *SUG;* A documentary has also been shot on his life & works by Amravathi Film Makers Hyderabad. Collections: AP Contemporary Museum, *NGMA, LKA* & *College of Art* New Delhi, KAR *LKA*, Air India Mumbai, CCMB, *SUG*, BARC, TIFR, *ABC* & other pvt., public; International: Institutional collections UK, Germany, USA.

Surya Prakash has been influenced greatly by the sunny, peaceful works of the French impressionist, Claude Monet. Like Monet's final reflective *paintings*, his works also contain *pictorial* elements taken from *nature*, simple yet specific, like floating leaves, water-lilies or dry rocky terrain or the reflection of foliage, the sky and clouds in glittering pools of still water. He uses thin *transparent* glazes of *oil colour* in subdued *shades* to create his romantic studies of *nature* at its best. He has recently painted round shaped *canvases*.

He lives and works in Hyderabad. (See illustration on page 257)

Prehistoric The period before written records.

Primary Colours The *colours* not obtained by mixing others. There are three primary colours: red, blue and yellow and the other *colours* are obtained by mixing these three *colours* or their *variants* in various *proportions*. Refer *Colour Wheel, Colour Circle, Company School/Company Painting, Manuscript Paintings, Secondary Colours, Dinanath Pathy*.

Priming The first coat on the *canvas, paper* or *metal* to make it impermeable. For *oil painting*, the *canvas* is primed with *white lead*, either plain or slightly tinted. Refer *Canvas*.

The primer for Indian *tempera painting* is either *stone white* or *zinc white* paste made of egg *emulsion* or organic glue. The *base canvas* or cloth is prepared with 8 to 10 thin coats of this mixture. Each coat is applied only after the earlier one has dried completely, and rubbed to a light polish with a paper-weight or conch shell. Refer *Art Education, Egg-oil emulsion, Facing, Finish, Gesso, Miniature Paintings, Palm Leaf, Size, Tensile Strength*.

Primitivism A *modern style* picked up from the primitive *art*. Primitivism and Indigenism came to be closely associated. *Artists* borrowed signs and *symbols* and *calligraphic* pictograms from primitive *art*. In many cases the neo-primitivists adopted an unfinished and unsophisticated *manner* of working that adds to the quality of Primitivism identified with *modernism*. The naive, childish, or even gauche appearance of the work of neo-primitive *artists* as also the folk-inspired *compositions* of *Jamini Roy* sometimes are confused with Primitivism, as also the *mask* wearing *monumental* and painted bodies of mother Goddesses executed by *Kanayi Kunhiraman* which tend to amalgamate primitive process, traditional execution and *modern* observation. Refer *Egyptian Art, Folk Inspiration, Symbolism, Tribal Art, Amit Ambalal, Santokba Dudhat*.

Prince of Wales Museum of Western India (PWM) (Mumbai, MAHA). Refer *Chhatrapati Shivaji Maharaj Vastu Sanghralaya (CSMVS)*.

Print A print is an *impression* in multiple *copies*, made from the original source such as a *wood* block, *lithography stone*, engraved *plate* a photographic *negative* or a silk screen *stencil*. It can also mean a typeset material. Printing press arrived in India in the 16th century though it did not flourish until the spread of printing technology 300 years later. The advent of *mass* prints eventually threatened the livelihood of Kalighat *artists*. Few of these *artists* then moved on to *lithography*. Refer *Abstract Expressionism, Aquatint, Artist's Proof, Bazaar Painting, Chequering, Collography, Collotype, Conservation Board, Engraving, Etching, Film, Half-tone, History Painting, Illustration, Impression, Kalamkari, Kalighat Pat, Kalighat Folk Painting, Key Block, Line, Line Engraving, Lino, Linocut, Maniere Noire, Mat, Mezzotint, Monograph, Monotype, Multi block colour printing, Offset Printing, Oleography, Photograph, Photogravure, Positive, Printmaking, Rabindra Bharati Museum, Ready-Made, Relief printing, Screen Printing, Silk Screen Printing, Single Block Colour Printing, Soft Ground, Tempering, Townscape, V Tool, Viscosity Printmaking, Wood Cut, Wood Cut Printing;* Illustrations–BHARATA, DIWALI, DIPAVALI, PARVATI, INDRA.

Printmaking The *technique* of making *prints*, using one of several *media* available to the printmaker. Each printmaking *medium* permits its own unique *visual* characteristics, which are exploited variously by different printmakers. There are three basic printmaking processes **1.** *relief* **2.** *intaglio* and **3.** planographic.

1. The *relief* process includes *wood cuts* and *engraving, metal cut* and *etching*, and *linocut*. **2.** *The intaglio* process includes *dry-point, engraving, etching, mezzotint*, and *aquatints*. **3.** *Lithography* is the most common *form* of planographic processes. Refer *Aquatint, Artist's Proof, Bite, Biting in, College of Art, Collography, Draughtsmanship, Engraving, Etching, Filler, Garhi Artist's Complex, Graphic, Ground, Gum Arabic, Half-Tone, Impression, Ink, Linocut, Lithography, Media, Metal, Monograph, Multiple Tool, Negative, Opaque, Outline, Photograph, Plate, Positive, Post-Independence, Screen Printing, Silk Screen Printing, Serigraphy, Society of Contemporary Artists, Tempering, Tensile Strength, Treatment, Varnish, Viscous, White Line Engraving, Wood, Wood Engraving, Zinc, Krishan Ahuja, Navjot Altaf, Dattatrey D. Apte, Yusuf Arakkal, Dipak Banerjee, Vidya Bhushan, Prayag Jha Chhillar, Chittaprosad, Swapan Kumar Das, Ajit R. Desai, Rini Dhumal, Seema Ghurayya, Somnath Hore, Paul A. Koli, Leela Mukherjee, Saroj Gogi Pal, Vasant Parab, Jayant Parikh, Sohan Qadri, Premalatha H. Seshadri, Lalu Prasad Shaw, Yagneshwar Kalyanji Shukla, K.S. Viswambhara, Shyamal Dutta Ray, D.L.N. Reddy;* Illustration–BHARATA, DIWALI, DIPAVALI, PARVATI, INDRA, *Amitabha Banerjee, R.B. Bhaskaran, Jyoti Bhatt, Rm. Palaniappan, Sohan Qadri, Krishna N. Reddy, Anupam Sud*.

Prithvi Gallery (PG) (Mumbai, MAHA). Though *exhibitions* by *artists* were held here in the 80s, the original gallery, in the foyer of the Prithvi Theatre was opened in 1994 by Sanjana Kapoor. *Deepak Shinde, Navjot Altaf* and *Lalitha Lajmi* are some of the *artists* who have exhibited here. The gallery also hosts travelling shows sponsored by other galleries in the city.

Progressive Artists Group (PAG) (Mumbai). The PAG was formed in Mumbai in 1947. It comprised *Francis Newton Souza, Sayed Haider Raza, Krishnaji Howlaji Ara, Maqbool Fida Husain, Sadanandji Bakre* and *H.A. Gade*. They met for discussions at several places, including the *BAS* Mumbai. The common denominator was *significant form*. They expressed themselves in highly individualized ways, had different visions of *art*, yet the concern for *significant form* unified them. In the catalogue of the Group's *exhibition* in 1948, *Francis Newton Souza* spoke of the laws that governed them, namely *aesthetic* order, plastic coordination and *colour composition*. The PAG was actively encouraged by several people, including three prominent Europeans, W. Langhammer, *Art* Dir. of the "Times of India", R.V. Leyden, *art critic* "Times of India" and E. Schelsinger who encouraged the *artists* by buying their work. The scientist Homi Bhabha also became a patron, buying several of their works, which now form part of the TIFR collection.

Progressive Artists Group (PAG) (Jaipur RAJ) Not to be mistaken for the *PAG* Mumbai. The PAG (RAJ) was formed in 1970 to promote *art* consciousness among the people of the state. The PAG (RAJ) *artist's* search for *contemporary* expressions has not blinded them to the pictorial tradition of their home state, namely *Miniature painting*. *Artists* belonging to the group include *Mohan Sharma, Kanhaiya Lal Verma*, Ranjeet Singh, *Prem Chandra Goswami* and others.

Proportion The relation or comparative *size* of one part with another. The word usually refers to proportion of *figures, forms* or *colours* within a *composition*. The Indian word is Praman and it refers to the proportion of *icons* and other *figures*. The Western *idea* of scale and proportion has its genesis in Greek Classicism. However in India, it is the CHITRASUTRA and the SHADANGA which lay down the rules of proportion; Indian *idols* have to strictly adhere to these rules deviation by as little as a finger's width, would bring misfortune upon both the artisan and the patron. These proportions along with the iconographical details were followed until the beginning of the *modern* period. With *Raja Ravi Varma* beginning to *paint* with *oils*, proportions too became Western oriented. In the *contemporary* period Indian proportions have less to do with reality and actual perception and more to do with conceptualization. Refer *Alloy*, *Canon of Proportion*, *Constructivism*, *Distortion*, *Hieratic Scaling*, *Ideal*, MANDALA, MURTI, *Neo-Classical Style*, *Primary Colours*, *Realistic*, *Secondary Colours;* Illustrations–*Jain Miniature*, *Jain Manuscript Illumination*.

Prositapatika One of the eight specific types of NAYIKAS (heroines) mentioned by ancient Indian writers and poets. Her lover has left on a long journey and she is depicted as mourning his departure in the company of her maids. This was a favorite topic of the *Basohli* and *Kangra* miniaturist. Refer ASHTANAYIKA, *Kangra*.

Pundole Art Gallery (PUAG) (Mumbai, MAHA). The PUAG was set up in 1963 by Kali Pundole in the heart of Mumbai's commercial area to exhibit and stock works of *contemporary* Indian *artists* including *Akbar Padamsee*, *Maqbool Fida Husain*, *Ram Kumar*, *Vasudeo Santu Gaitonde*, *Prabhakar Kolte*, *Babu Xavier*, *Sakti Burman*.

Purana=old *rituals*, old book. The Puranas are a distinct category of SANSKRIT religious literature, describing the stories and the exploits of the *gods* in several volumes. Each Purana is titled with the main name or the praise name of a *god* or his incarnation. The main Puranas are the BRAHMA, VISHNU, SHIVA, GARUDA, Vayu (wind), AGNI, Skanda (refer–PARVATI), Varaha (VARAHAVATARA-boar), Vamana (refer–VAMANA-TRIVIKRAMA,), Kurma (tortoise, the earth considered as a tortoise swimming on water), Matsya (MATSYA-AVATARA-fish), LINGA, Markandeya (winning over death), PADMA, Vaivarta ("metamorphoses of BRAHMA" who is identified with KRISHNA), BHAGAVATA-PURANA (referring to KRISHNA'S exploits) & including the principle of the TANTRAS and two *epics* i.e. the RAMAYANA & MAHABHARATA. Refer BHAGAVAN, BRAHMA-PURANA, CHITRASUTRA, *Devanagari Script*, *Illumination*, *Kangra Kalam*, *Kangra School*, *Kangra Miniatures*, KRISHNA, *Manuscript Paintings*, MATRIKAS, *Size*, *Spiritual*, *Visual*, *Nathu Lal Verma;* Illustrations– BHAGAVATA-PURANA, *Illuminated Manuscripts*, NATARAJA.

Puri, M.K. (1938–) b. Quetta (now Pakistan). Education: NDA *College of Art* New Delhi. Solos: *LKA*, Alliance Francaise & RB New Delhi, *JAG*, RB Hyderabad, UP *LKA* Lucknow, SRAG, TAG, *YBCAG*, *VEAG*, BHU; International: Paris. Group participations: *LKA* & *Triennale* New Delhi, In *painting*, *sculpture* & *graphic AIFACS*, TKS, SKP, *Dhoomimal*, *BAS*, HAS; International: Paris, Cuba, Mexico. *Art* workshop: *Ceramis LKA* at *GAC*, *Sculpture AIFACS*, PUJ *LKA*, WZCC Nagpur HP, MMB New Delhi; Participated in Theatre workshop by Yatrik. Awards: *AIFACS*, SKP. Founder members: Young Artist's League, Andretta Pottery & Crafts Society, Blue Ceramics Arts Society New Delhi. Commissions: Several *murals* in *ceramics* & other *media*; Designed sets for ballets. Collections: *NGMA* & *LKA* New Delhi, UP State *LKA*, AP AFA Hyderabad, PUJ State Museum Chandigarh, BHU, SKP; International: Smithsonian Foundation Washington D.C.

M.K. Puri is essentially a *figurative painter*, inspired by human behaviour and relationship. In the 60s, he worked in *oil paintings*, giving it up in favour of *drawing* after a decade. During this phase he came in contact with *ceramics* and started working with *mural design* as well, at times going on to make *sculptures* in the round. In the 80s, he developed the *technique* of *painting* with *waterproof ink* on *paper*, with the subject creating an interesting dialogue within the picture frame. It is the human visage and *hand gestures* that most interest him, possibly because he was in theatre involved. His later *medium* was *pencil* on *paper* and *acrylic* on *canvas*.

He lives and works in New Delhi.

Pushpamala, N. (1956–) b. Bangalore. Education: B.A. (Fine) & M.A. (Fine) *MSU*, Advance *sculpture* St. Martins School of Art London. Solos: *Sculpture* & *photographs* at *GC* Mumbai, Artist's studio Bangalore, *VEAG*. Group participations: 100 years of *NGMA*, RB & CMC Gallery New Delhi, *Gallery 7* & *GC* Mumbai, *VAG*, *VEAG*; International: Bangkok, Johannesburg, *Biennale*, Bath Festival Trust UK. Workshop: International in Modinagar UP & Open Circle Mumbai. Awards: Gold Medal *Triennale*. Commissions: Designed sets & costumes for theatre. Appointments: Curated *exhibition* of large specific works in Bangalore. Publications: Articles written on *art* for newspapers & journals.

She began her career as a *figurative sculptor*, working with witty observations of mundane people and places, mostly in the *terracotta medium*. Soon her work changed, with the concept behind it coming to the fore, rather than mere execution. Formally she uses a variety of *media*, including film photography and similar *ready-mades* as in her recent exhibitions "Phantom Lady" and "Golden Dreams". At times she uses the object in multiplicity, as in the "Labyrinth", adding text and working notes to make didactic statements.

She lives and works near Bangalore.

Pyne, Ganesh (1937–) b. Kolkata. Education: Dip. in *drawing* & *painting GCAC* Kolkata. Solos: VG New Delhi, *CIMA* & Retrospective Kolkata, MAHABHARATA *drawing* & other *exhibitions* at *NGMA* Mumbai, *VAG*. Group participations: 25 years in Indian Art & *Triennales* New Delhi, Freedom in India *AFA* & MMB Kolkata, *CKAG*; International: Contemporary Art of Asia & Travelling Exhibitions of Indian *Painting,* Fukuoka Museum of Art Japan, *Biennale* Paris, International Festival of Paintings France, *GC's* in Zurich, group shows RAA London, Germany, Japan & Washington. *Auction*: Heart Mumbai & New Delhi, Osian's Mumbai, Sotheby's London. Awards: Calcutta Art Society, *GCAC AFA* & *BAAC* Kolkata. Member: *SCA*. Publications: Ganesh Pyne Revelations–1999 by Geeti Sen, Ganesh Pyne portfolio. Collections: *NGMA* New Delhi, *AFA* & *BAAC* Kolkata, *Chandigarh Museum*; International: Gallery Surya Germany, pvt. & corporates.

Ganesh Pyne does small scale works in *tempera* on *canvas*, *watercolour* on *paper* and *gouache*. He *paints* microcosmic *images* and *motifs* from the world of Bengali fables and fairy tales, including the Thakurmar Jhuli and such similar sources. The music and lyrics of Baul singers and the poetry of Octario Paz find equal *space* in his works. His *figures* are toy-like and rich with allusions to wayside shrines, public houses and old buildings, woven dexterously into the *composition* with pale lyrical *colours* lending a touch of melancholy. He uses *white* judiciously to overlap a *form*, in one place and create a new *motif* elsewhere. Thus, his choice of *forms* is surreal, not their shapes; their presence together and their juxtaposition, lend *pictorial* validity. His most recent works, a pathbreaking series of *drawings* depicting scenes of the eternal Indian *epic*, "The Mahabharata", showed him in new light. These *illustrations*, in the *form* of *drawings* have a striking range of *form* and approach in a *painterly style*.

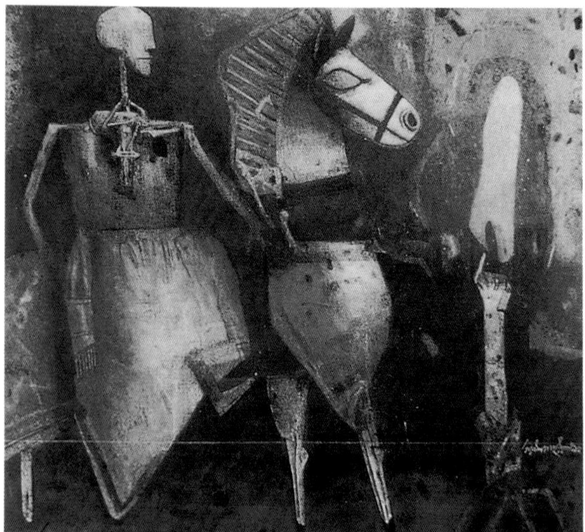

Pyne, Ganesh: "Night of The Rider", *Tempera* on *Canvas*, 1995, 44.4x50.8 cm.

Pyne, Kartick Chandra (1931–) b. Kolkata. Education: Dip. in *FA*. *GCAC* Kolkata. Solos: *AFA* Kolkata, *LKA* New Delhi, *CKAG*, *JAG*, *Dhoomimal*. Group participations: *AFA*, Gandhara Art Gallery & *BAAC* Kolkata, MKKP Raipur, *LKA Triennales* New Delhi, *CKAG*, *AIFACS*, *JAG*, BAG; International: Fukuoka Art Museum Japan, by ICCR Bangladesh, Asian Art by *CKAG* Singapore. Awards: *AFA* Kolkata & MKKP Raipur Scholarship *AFA* & India Culture Trust Kolkata. Commissions: *Frescoes* & *mural painting* Govt. of India, Home Publicity Govt. of WB. Publications: Articles published in periodicals & newspapers, *NGMA* New Delhi; International: Fukuoka Art Museum Japan. Collections: *NGMA* New Delhi, *BAAC* & Govt. of WB Gallery Kolkata; International: England, Italy, Japan, USA, Germany, UNESCO, Thailand, Singapore, pvt. & Institutional.

Kartick Chandra Pyne learnt the *techniques* of Western *style realistic painting* with the use of *perspective* and *chiaroscuro* in his *art* school. Gradually however, he moved toward the artistic expression of the Bengal *School*. His earlier works show his control over representational *drawing*. His later works however are an amalgamation of native *folk art* and *contemporary* Western art. This blend allows him to retain his distinctive identity, inspite of the experimentation. The *pictorial images* that surface in the works are culled from his subconscious, being fragments of daydreams and mythical *themes*. The *mediums* that he uses, be it *oils*, *watercolours* or *pastel*, contribute greatly to the final compositions and textural variation.

He lives and works in Kolkata.

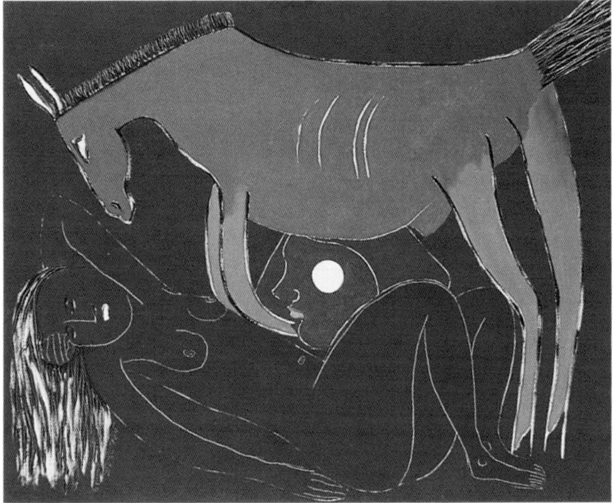

Pyne, Kartick Chandra: "Woman & Horse", *Oil* on *Canvas*, 1994, 91x109 cm.

Q

Qadir, Abdul (1956–) b. Indore. Self-taught; Worked under the guidance of *Maqbool Fida Husain*. Solos: MP *LKA* Bhopal, Indore FA. School, TAG Indore, *Tao Art Gallery* Mumbai, *JAG*. Group shows: Mumbai, *ATG* Chennai, New Delhi. Group participations: MP *LKA*, *Triennale* New Delhi, TAG Indore, *JAG*, *Biennale BB*; International: Germany & New York. Participated in *art* camps. Awards: Bhopal State award.

Abdul Qadir is a *figurative painter*, using dream *imagery* and mostly Indian *themes* in his expressionistic works. He uses the coloured scribble to fill in certain *forms* in contrast with the flatly coloured *backgrounds*. The *figures* are distorted in a naive *style*, at times sporting wings and elaborate headgear. There is also an element of the macabre, especially in the Ensor-like "Bomb-blast", where the various elements are scattered all over the *canvas*.

He lives and works in Indore and Bhopal.

Qadri, Sohan (1932–) b. Chachoki, PUJ. Education: Dip. *FA*. GCA Shimla. Over 40 solos: *GC* & *Gallery 7* Mumbai, PUJ University, FA. Museum Chandigarh, SRAG, *AIFACS*, *Dhoomimal*; International: Nairobi, Brussels, Zurich, Vienna, Poland, Munich, Basle, Copenhagen, London, Los Angeles, Toronto, Ottawa, Montreal, Finland, Stockholm. Group participations: National Exhibitions; International: Salon International Paris, Dusseldorf, Basle. *Art* workshops: Conducted International workshops with seminars & symposiums. Awards: *LKA* New Delhi; International: Toronto. Member: "Loose group" *painters* & poets, "La Fourmiere" Zurich. Publications: Books on poems, "Mitti Mitti" Punjabi Sutras translations New Delhi; A film "Journey into Silence" produced by Doordarshan; International: Artist's Reference Book London, "Tantra The Ancient Art of Energy" by TV2 Sweden & several interviews on Radio & TV; International workshops conducted on *aesthetics* & metaphysics. Collections: *NGMA*, *LKA* New Delhi; International: Bodo Glanb Museum Koln Germany, Slupks Museum of Modern Art Poland.

Sohan Qadri has allowed his initial exposure and belief in TANTRA and YOGA to influence his works. Technically he has evolved constantly, at times using *printmaking techniques* and dyes to create Rothko-like fields of *colour* and at other times exploiting the dichotomy between two *textures*, thickly impasted, rock-like formations and thin, fluid areas of brilliant *colour*. By stripping away extraneous detail, Sohan Qadri makes his works near *abstract* evocations of *colour*, *paper* and emotions. His recent works on *paper* involve the use of rows and columns of perforations; the dyes coagulating along these tears evoke the luxuriant feeling of embroidered velvet.

He lives and works in Denmark.

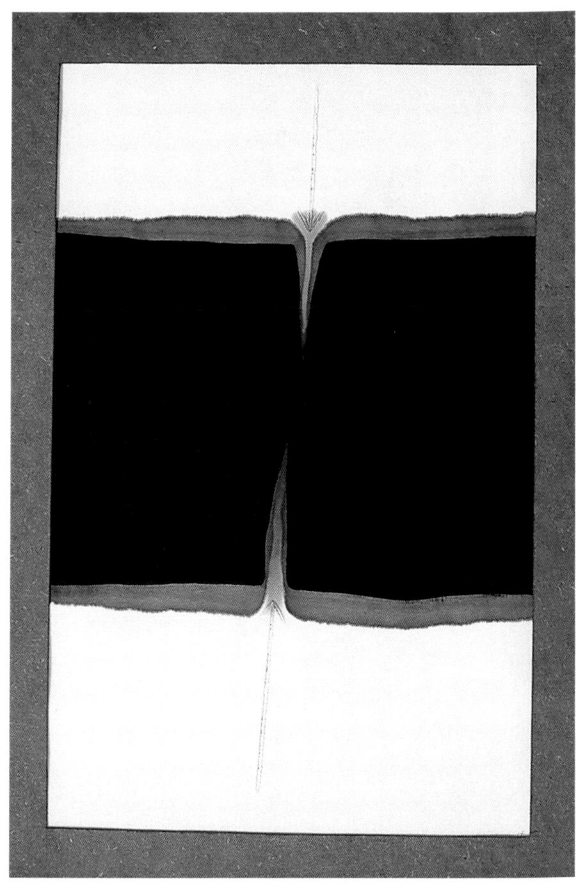

Qadri, Sohan: *Inks*, Dyes and *Tints* on *Paper* for Intaglio *Print*, 1993, 100x65 cm.

R

Raza, Sayed Haider: "Bindu", 1996, 120x120 cm. (See notes on page 298)

Rabindra Bharati Museum (RBM) (Kolkata) RBM was established in 1961 at the ancestral family home of the Tagores to perpetuate the memory of *Rabindranath Tagore's* life and work, to collect and preserve historical and other documentary material of the cultural *Renaissance* of Bengal. The *museum* also endeavoured to develop *exhibitions* on the *modern art* movement in India. Also displays *Rabindranath Tagore's paintings* as well as *art* showing British influence. There is an archive of manuscripts, documents, personal belongings, tape recordings of reminiscences and songs by *Rabindranath Tagore,* as well as first editions of books, journals, *photographs* and *prints*.

Rabindra Bharati University (RBU) (Kolkata) RBU was founded in 1972 as faculty of *"Visual Arts"*. Initially it offered a three-year Hons. course in *painting*, the first of its kind in Eastern India. In the 80s, the degree of Bachelor of Arts (B.A.) and Master of Arts (M.A.) were rechristened as Bachelor of Visual Arts (B.VA.) and Master of Visual Arts (M.VA.). The coverage too was expanded to include Dept. for *Portrait Painting*, *Painting*, *Graphics*, *Applied Art*, *Sculpture* and History of *Art*. The Founder Dean, Prof. Sovan Some, Vice Chancellor Dr. Rama Choudhury and their successors, such as Prof. *Shanu Lahiri* and Prof. *Dharmanarayan DasGupta* shaped over the years the institute which has done yeoman service to the Indian *art* world. The Dept. posseses a rich collection of slides and other *visual* materials and soon proposes to set up an *art* library and computer *graphics* section.

Radha Radha is one of the GOPIS (cowherdesses) in the myth of KRISHNA. Though the love story of Radha and KRISHNA is one of the most prolifically illustrated *themes* in the history of Indian miniatures, there are no references to her in any of the PURANAS or *epics*. She seems to be the creation of Jayadeva, the poet-writer of GITA-GOVINDA. Radha is a beautiful woman, and her dalliances with KRISHNA run into several romantic episodes, of which the most popular would be the "Cheerharana" (the stealing of her clothes) and the interludes in the forests of Vrindavan. However, on the *spiritual* plane, Radha would stand for the human soul yearning for her union with *god*. Radha was later worshipped as a goddess—as an AVATAR of LAKSHMI as KRISHNA is of VISHNU. Refer *Erotic Art*, *Kangra*, *Kishangarh*, *National Museum*, RITU, VIPRALABDHA, *White*, *Saroma Bhowmick*, *Muhammed Abdur Rehman Chughtai*, *Suhas Roy;* Illustrations—*Ganga Devi*, RASA LILA.

Raffic, Ahmed M.G. (1960–) b. Madurai. Self-taught in *art* & cinematography Dip. in pvt. Chandunu School of Art Chennai, Reference under *Subrayalu Dhanapal*, *Alphonso A. Doss*. Solos: India International Centre New Delhi, Govt. Museum & *LKA* sponsored Madurai, *SAI*, RAG. Group shows: Chola Art Society Thanjavur, Kasturi Srinivasam Art Gallery Coimbatore, Nova Art Gallery Madurai, Russian Culture Centre Chennai. Group participations: National Exhibition *LKA* & Rashtriya Kala Mela New Delhi, *LKA* Orissa, *Vijaya FA. Society* KAR, *LKA* Exhibition TN, *AIFACS*, *BAS;* International: *Triennale* Poland, *Biennale* Paris. *Art* camps: *LKA* camp Udagamangalam, SZCC & *LKA*,TN in Ooty. Awards: TN *LKA*, All India Drawing Pondicherry. Collections: Shimla *LKA*, TN *LKA*, *JAG*, *Dhoomimal*, *SAI;* International: France, England, Switzerland & USA, pvt. & corporates.

Ahmed M.G. Raffic deals with birth, death and everything in between. *Time* and *space mixed media* series entitled "Time" expresses the fast sweeping changes that are taking place around him, where man, machine and death dominate in his work. Cultivated from his subconscious, the *images* (which are created by rubber washers, *copper* wires, old *palm leaves* with scripts, etc.) emerge on the surface of the *painting*. His later *paintings* were titled "Nostalgia".

He lives and works in Madurai.

Raga=a selection of musical modes, where each mode has minimum of five notes up and down the scale, set in a certain order. Ragas are a uniquely Indian classical music tradition, where the state of the soul is expressed through a series of musical sounds (i.e. Ragas). Raga, especially when rendered by an expert, has the power to evoke in the listener, *rhythms* as well as certain *images*. This gives the Ragas *pictorial forms*, by personifying them into six principal male Ragas, namely Bhairava, Malkauns, Hindola, Deepak, Shree and Megha. Each of these male Ragas are further divided by depicting each one of them, as having five wives, the 30 RAGINIS. Further elaboration into Janya Ragas, Ragaputras (children modes) of eight each, brings about a total of 84 different musical modes. Each personification of these Ragas evokes a particular mood or sense of a particular season or *time* of the day and night; and many of these have been expressed in various *forms* of *paintings* especially RAGAMALA *paintings* from *Mewar*. These are based on the belief that each Raga or RAGINI has a sound body symbolized by a *god*, goddess or a beautiful lady. Refer *Malwa*, NAYAK-NAYAKA, *Pictorial*, RAGAMALA, RAGINI, *Om Prakash Sharma;* Illustration—*Mahadev V. Dhurandhar*.

Ragamala=necklace or string of RAGAS. **1.** In *terms* of music it is a composition where several RAGAS are sung one after other and they merge into each other smoothly. **2.** As applied to *visual art*, they refer to *miniature paintings* depicting life in the courts of Rajput Kingdoms of RAJ, especially *Mewar*, from the 17th century onwards. A unique feature of a Ragamala *painting*, is that it gives a *pictorial image* to the moods and sentiments of RAGAS. Thus it is a perfect marriage of literature, music and *painting*. Refer *Kangra*, NAYIKA, *Pictorial*, RAGINI, *Sakti Burman*, *Jagadish Dey*, *Laxman Pai*; Illustrations—*Mewar*, *Jayant Parikh*, *Sharma*, *M.K. Sumahendra*.

Raghuram, Bairu (1949–) b. Hyderabad. Education: B.A. & Dip. *drawing* & *painting* I.F.A.I Gulbarga KAR. Solos: Alliance Francaise Art Gallery Hyderabad, Atlier 2221 Gallery New Delhi, Right Line Art Gallery Bangalore *JAG*. Group participations: 1985 to 2005; Participated in several All India, national & international Art Exhibitions including 50 years of India's Independence. Group shows: Gulbarga, Visakhapatnam, New Delhi, Kolkata, Hyderabad, Chandigarh, Cochin, CCMB, *ATG*, *JAG*, *NCAG*. *Art* camps: *Graphics*—I.F.A.I

Gulbarga KAR, Alliance Francaise & CFA Hyderabad, *LKA* at Regional Centre Chennai; *Painting*–Bijapur KAR, Madapur, Hyderabad; Traditional *painting*–SZCC Nagpur & Thanjavur; International: USA, UK. Awards: National Award *LKA* New Delhi, HAS Gold Medal, Creative Akademi of Arts & Bharat Kala Parishad & Lalit Kala Samithi A.P. Collections: *LKA*–New Delhi, Chennai, Hyderabad, Luknow, *NGMA* New Delhi, *IFAS*'s Institute Gulbarga, *BB*; International: UK, USA, France, Switzerland, Germany, Canada & Bangladesh.

Bairu Raghuram has worked extensively with *etching*, producing delicate tonal variations in subtle *sepia* as well as *black* and *white*. His *images* are mostly set in the countryside, revealing a predilection for rural folk and country-life. His *painting* too abounds with *images* of Telangana folk, the colourful costumes in total contrast to the *black* and *white* print *images* of goat-herds and roosters. The same subject is portrayed in his *paintings* which are filled with riotous *colours*.

He lives in Hyderabad.

Ragini A female counterpart to the male RAGA. Certain configuration is followed for each Ragini e.g. Todi depicts a beautiful maiden playing the Veena (a musical instrument) in the forest and intoxicating the birds and animals with the sweet sound. She is shown feeding the deer at her feet. Refer RAGAMALA, *Malwa*, *Pictorial*, *Sakti Burman*.

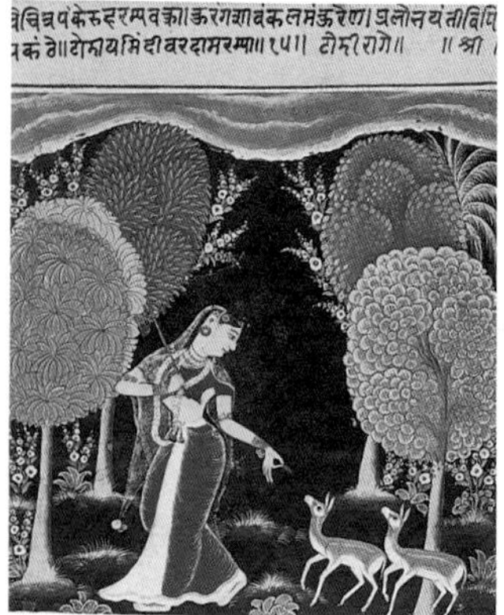

Ragini: "Todi Ragini".

Rahim, R. Abdul (1923–) Self-taught, also studied under V. Jagannathan & studied *Rajasthani miniature paintings* as well *Basohli*, *Kangra*, *Mughal miniatures* & *Bengal School*. Studied & copied some of the *paintings* of *Ajanta*. Solos: Pondicherry Museum, Lycee Francaise & Alliance Francaise Pondicherry. Group participations: Mysore DAE, *LKA* New Delhi, International & State Exhibition Pondicherry. Awards: DAE Medal, Gwalior prize. Member: *LKA* New Delhi. Collections: Pondicherry Museum & pvt. International: France & Canada.

R. Abdul Rahim was trained in the French impressionist *style* by V. Jagannathan. The *modern art* movement interested him and he produced serene *landscapes* in the impressionist *manner*. His views of the Indian countryside, the heat and dust of cows returning home in the evening and the lash of the rain in the coastal areas are among the more striking of his works.

R. Abdul Rahim lives in Pondicherry.

Rahiman, Abalal (1860– 1931) b. Kolhapur. Education: Dip. *JJSA*. Group participation: *BAS*. Appointments: Worked as *court artist* recording shooting expeditions & state occasions, executing mythological *paintings* & designing *stained glass*, *metal* & *ivory* objects for the Maharaja of Kolhapur; Taught *art* MAHA State. *Auctions*: Heart Mumbai. Collections: Museum in MAHA including Town Hall & New Palace Kolhapur, *Delhi Art Gallery*, *JJSA* and pvt.

Abalal Rahiman learnt Quranic *illustration* from his father before leaving for the school of *art*. He became well known for his *portrait drawings* in *chalk*. These *monochromatic portraits* were similar to those of *Mahadev V. Dhurandhar*. However when he returned to Kolhapur (after his mother's death) he gave up *portraits* in favour of miniature-sized *landscapes*. His poverty forced him to use scrap *paper* discarded by a nearby press and cheap *pigments*. Some of his best known works are *landscapes* of the lake at Sandhyamath at different times of the day. These works were near impressionistic in his negation of details in favour of *light* and *texture*. At a later stage he developed the *art* of *landscapes* which was inspired by various illustrated book studies, and also took up photography.

Rai, Mona b. Delhi. Education: *Art* classes at TKS. Solos: Chennai *AIC* & *Art Heritage* New Delhi, *GC* & *Gallery 7* Mumbai TKS, SRAG, *PUAG*, *GE*; International: Germany, Amsterdam. Group shows: Fine Art Company & *Group 7* Mumbai. Group participations: *LKA*, *NGMA* & Display Gallery New Delhi, Ghandhara Kolkata, *CYAG*, *JAG*, SKP, SRAG, *Dhoomimal*, HG, *GE*, *VAG*; International: *Biennale* in Germany, Japan, Norway & Yugoslavia, International Group in Dubai, Australia, Amsterdam. *Art* camps: Kasauli, Hyderabad, Coonoor, *College of Art* New Delhi, *GAC*. Collections: *NGMA* & *LKA* New Delhi, *BB*.

Mona Rai's *paintings* are based on *textures*, dots and dashes, circles and streaks, dashes and strokes forming her *images*. The exuberant scribbles and scratches release a burst of energy, they overlap and crisscross each other constantly in a play of *lines* and *colours*. This near *abstract* medley of *forms* and *colours* however, is solidly rooted in Indian *tradition* by Mona Rai's use of *titles* and *colours*. She has adopted the *technique* of *mixed media* with burnt charcoal, charcoal dust, gold dust and using unlikely materials as sequins and strings, in addition to the now popular powdered *pigments* and traditional *oils*, *watercolours*, *acrylics* and *pastels*.

She lives and works in New Delhi.

Raiba, A.A. (1922–) b. Mumbai. Education: GDA *Painting JJSA*. Solos: New Delhi, *GC*, Son-et-Lumiere, Mumbai *JAG*, TAG. Group participations: TAG, *JAG*; International: Russia, Egypt, Italy, Brazil, Japan. Awards: Received Scholarship, National Award *LKA*, Silver & Gold Medal *BAS*, Hon. MAHA Gaurav Puraskar & *ASI* Veteran artist of India Platinum Jubilee. Fellowship: *JJSA*. Commissions: *murals* for Expo-70 in Japan & Sydney Airport. Appointments: Briefly joined the film industry & the topics of his *sketches* were–rape, temptation & adultery; Visited *Ajanta* and *Ellora* & copied *frescoes*; Opened his Studio in 81 at Virar MAHA. Collections: *NGMA* New Delhi, Nagpur Museum, *JAG*. *Murals* in pvt. & public TIFR; International: Japan, Sydney.

A.A. Raiba is a senior *artist* who has serenely continued to paint in his old familiar *style*. He still *paints landscapes* and rural scenes in the same naive and simplified *manner*. He has painted several *themes* over the years. Among them are the "BARAMASA", the "Playing cards" and "Solha Shringar". Inspired by his travels and producing *paintings* in reaction to the places visited, has experimented with various *mediums*, including *glass painting*.

He lives and works in Mumbai. Refer *Stained Glass*.

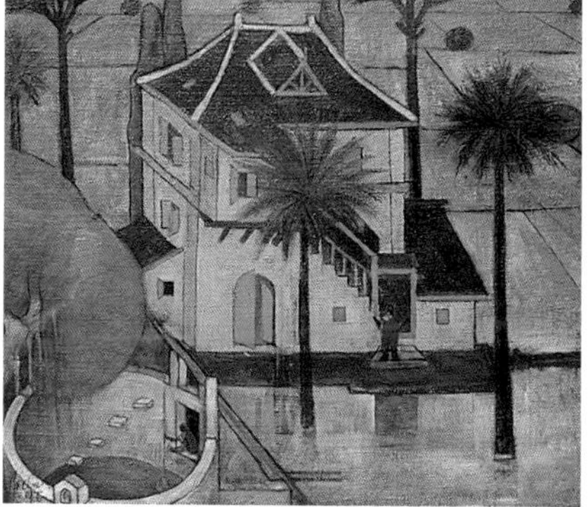

Raiba, A.A.: "Farm House", *Oil* on *Canvas* 1996, 76x76 cm.

Rajaiah, Kapu (1925–) b. Siddipet, AP. Education: Art Master's Certificate & Dip. in *art* Central School of Arts & Crafts Hyderabad. Dip. in *drawing* Chennai. Solos: Warangal, Siddipet, Karimnagar, Tirupati, Pantacheru, Raghupathipetha, Medak all in AP, Jangaon MAHA, *Dhoomimal*, HAS; International: Moscow. Retrospective: Lalit Kala Samithi KB Siddipet AP. Group participations: National Exhibitions, *LKA* & *Triennales* New Delhi; International: Czechoslovakia, Hungary, Romania, Bulgaria, USA, Cuba, Mexico, Seychelles. Awards: IAFA Amritsar, *LKA* New Delhi. All India Exhibitions & *LKA* AP, Gold Medal HAS, Three decades of Art of AP—Council of Artists Hyderabad, JNTU. Hon.: *AIFACS* as Veteran Artists of India; "Hamsa Award" Hyderabad AP. Senior Fellowship: by Govt. of India. Members: *LKA* New Delhi, HAS, JNTU, *AIFACS*. Appointments: President Lalit Kala Samiti Siddipet AP. Publications: *Monograph* of his works by the *LKA* AP, Coloured *reproduction* of one of his *paintings* by *LKA* New Delhi. Collections: *NGMA* & *LKA* New Delhi, State Museum AP & *LKA* Hyderabad, State Museum Mysore, Mangalore Museum, *SJM*, *CTAG;* International: Cultural Ministry, Moscow, Cuban National Museum Havana, pvt. & corporates.

Kapu Rajaiah has been constantly re-creating and reinterpreting the nuances of his folk heritage, without simplifying it in a contrived *manner*. Various village *crafts* provided the basic inspiration and *imagory* for him. His early works were in the *wash technique*, later he turned to *tempera* on *paper*, cardboard, plywood and cloth. He then started using *oil paints* in place of powdered *pigments*. His themes are always based on rural life in his part of the world i.e. local festivals, *rituals*, village *gods* and the day-to-day life of the masses. His *art* is characterized by its bold *outlines*, brilliant colouring and decorative iconic *figures* with large staring eyes.

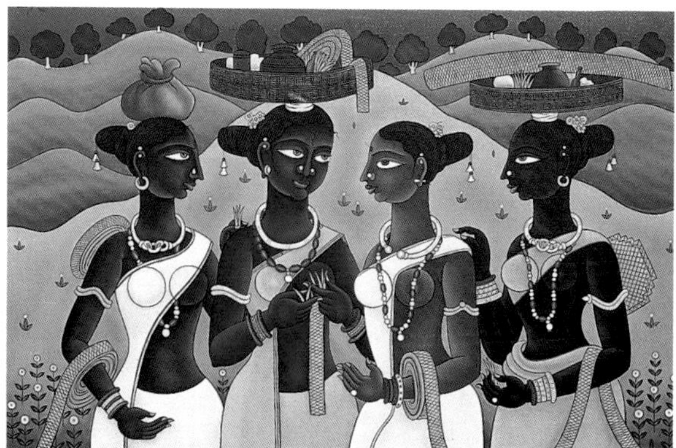

Rajaiah, Kapu: "Waddars", 1992, 86x133 cm.

He lives and works in Siddipet, AP.

Rajaram, C. Ponnappa (1927–1961) b. Coorg, KAR. Self-taught *sculptor*. Solos: Kunika Art Center New Delhi, *AIFACS*, *JAG;* International: Tokyo, Osaka & Tokohama Japan. Group participations: All India Sculpture Association, National *LKA* New Delhi, *BAS*. Awards: National *LKA* New Delhi, *BAS*, *VEAG* (*museum*). Appointments: Was Cadet—President of the Arts & Crafts Society of the Military College. Visited various *museums* & galleries in Europe & Japan. Collections: *LKA* New Delhi, *VEAG*.

C. Ponnappa Rajaram was a professional Army Officer who worked only with *wood carving*. He appreciated *wood* for the beauty of its shape, grain, *colour* and *texture*. In "Mother and Child", one of his early works, he exploited the grain while creating the smoothly finished ovoid *form*, while in "The Leap" the grain is lost within the roughly chiselled shape. His tour of Europe and Japan opened up further avenues of expression—his later works took on a modernistic *form* while remaining highly stylized and simplified. He was also interested in producing *masks* and textile printing.

Rajasthan School of Arts (RSA) (Jaipur). Rajasthan Vishwa Vidyalaya was founded by the ruler of Jaipur, Maharaja Sawai Jaisingh. It was initially called the Madersa Hunari (*arts* and handicrafts society) and was established as a commercial institute. Subsequently, between 1857 & 1880, Maharaja Sawai Ramsingh broadened its scope to include *art education* as well. The mansion that housed this institute was locally known as "Ajabghar" (The House of Wonders) and housed *art* and *craft* objects such as enamelled (Meenakari) blue *pottery*, and also those made by Maharaja Ramsingh himself. After 1921, the school received a facelift at the insistance of Jaipur's Prince Sawai Mansingh, who developed it into a *contemporary* school of *art*. *Sailendranath Dey* was offered the post of Principal, but he waived it in favour of *Asit K. Haldar*. Various Departments such as *Painting*, *Sculpture*, Blue *pottery*, *Metal* work and *Enamelling* (Meenakari), *Wood carving* and *Ivory carving* were added to the existing ones. In addition, students of *architecture* had to study *design*, *painting* and *sculpture*. Being a commercial institute, students were also paid half the amount from the sale of their works. Pandit Shivanand Sharma taught *painting* to the primary classes between 1931–33.

Rajasthani Miniature Painting The *term* applies to various schools that existed between 16th and early 19th century in the North-western Indian province of RAJ—Land of brave and valiant Princes. It was divided into many feudal states like *Mewar*, *Bundi*, Jaipur *Kishangarh*, *Kotah*, and

Malwa. Basic *themes* were Vaishnavite, with bright *colours* and bold, vigorous *forms*. The next phase brought in the influence of Mughal *art* patronized by Jaipur, Jaisalmer and Jodhpur. The hunting scenes of the *Kotah* School are the more popular *miniature paintings* with *Kishangarh* in its own distinctive *style*. Refer BARAMASA, *Erotic Art*, HARIVAMSA, HARIVANSA, *Kangra*, *Landscape*, NAYIKA, *Pahari Miniature Painting*, *Rajput Miniature Painting*, *Theme*, *Amit Ambalal*, *Nandalal Bose*, *R. Abdul Rahim*, *Prabha Shah*, *Gulam Mohammed Sheikh*, *Yashawant Shirwadkar*, *Rameshwar Singh*, *Kanhaiya Lal Verma*, *Ram Gopal Vijaivargiya;* Illustration–*Govardhan*, *Govardhanadhara*, HOLI, *B. Prabha*, *Nathu Lal Verma*.

Rajen b. India. Education: GDA *Painting* & *mural* decoration *JJSA*. Studied at RCA, later in Norway & Sweden. Over 35 solos all over India: *ABC*, *JAG*, TAG. Group participations: GUJ *LKA*, Jaipur; International: Brussels, Japan, USA, Denmark. Awards: GUJ *LKA*, for his *painting*, "Tapestry" All India Exhibition of Art Jaipur RAJ *LKA*. Appointments: Taught textile *design* at NID. Also makes exclusive furnishings at his studio Weavlab in Ahmedabad; He has created huge stage curtains in major auditoriums in the city of Ahmedabad; International: Worked on tapestry for United Nation in south Sweden. Collections: National & International corporates. & King of Norway's pvt.

Rajen is both a *painter* and weaver. He handles his tapestries in the *manner* of his *paintings*, *weaving* free-hand *drawings* in the impressionistic *style*, into it. A favourite *theme* is that of the elephant-*god*, GANESHA, which he has used in his *drawings* as well as his weaves. He has also done a series of *charcoal* and *pastel drawings* of the bull—the *line* in these works is forceful yet sensitive and vital, and has he also painted a series of *abstract* works.

He lives and works in Ahmedabad.

Rajendran, G. (1943–) b. Thiruvananthapuram, Kerala. Education: Dip. in *painting* GSAC Thiru-vananthapuram. Solos: Thiruvananthapuram, *CHAG*. Group participations: Mysore, National Exhibition New Delhi, Thiruvananthapuram Art Group, Kerala Kala Peetom, Kerala Kala Sangam, Kerala *LKA*, *CKP*. *Art* camps: *LKA* Kerala Thrissur & Bhootathan Kettu, Kerala Artists Camp, *Cartoon* camp Cochin, *Artists* camp Wynad, Manipal & SZCC Chennai. Awards: Kerala *LKA*, USIS Cultural Center Award, All India Exhibition Thiruvananthapuram. Fellowship: Kerala *LKA*. Member: Kerala *LKA*. Appointment: Instructor at the *CFA* Thiruvananthapuram. Collections: Kerala *LKA*, *CAG* Cochin, Sreechitra Art Gallery Thiruvananthapuram, *LKA* New Delhi & Regional Center Chennai, *CHAG* Ernakulam; Parliament House New Delhi, pvt. & public.

G. Rajendran's early works were characterized by a strong *linearity*, and pronounced *palette*, with an emphasis on Christian and Hindu *iconology*. The "Avastha" series was based on philosophy while the animal series was metaphorical in *nature*. His later works have veered towards the *abstract* in the melt-down of *forms* and *colours* and the use of *calligraphic* accents of *colour* at regular intervals. The appearance of winged couples and floating *figures* are reminiscent of the works of M. Chagall, as is the use of certain brilliant *hues*.

G. Rajendran lives in Thiruvananthapuram, where he is an *art* instructor at the *CFA*.

Rajput Miniature Painting The Rajputs descended from the Gurjars, Pratihars, Hunas and other central asian tribes. They put forth *legends* of their right to rule, and considered themselves champions of Hindu faith and *culture*. Their chief qualities were fierce loyalty, religious worship and great courage. The Rajput *paintings* are classified into two *styles*: the Rajasthani School and the Pahari School, each one of which comprise many sub-schools. Refer BHAKTI, GITA-GOVINDA, *Kangra*, *Miniature Painting*, NAYAK-NAYAKA, *Pahari Miniatures Paintings*, RAGAMALA, *Rajasthani Miniature Painting*, *Salar Jung Museum (SJM)* (Hyderabad), *K. Seshagiri Rao*, *Ishwari Rawal*.

Rama=omnipresent, all pervading, charming, enchanting. The seventh AVATAR of VISHNU—known as Ramachandra, son of Dashratha and Kausalya, husband of Sita and father of Lava and Kusha. This descendant of the Raghuvansha had three brothers, BHARATA, Laxmana and Shatrughna. He is the Hero of the RAMAYANA (subject in *sculpture* and *painting*) and an Uttamapurusha, the *ideal* man and brother and the perfect king. The RAMAYANA details the story of the vanquishing of the evil RAVANA, the king of ASURAS by Rama. In *miniature paintings* Rama is usually depicted in the garb of a simple forest dweller, with a top-knot encircled with flowers. As an AVATAR of VISHNU, he is blue-skinned, and is usually accompanied by his wife and brother. His *weapon* (AYUDHA) is the bow (Dhanush) and he holds an arrow (Bana) in his right hand. Refer CHITRAKATHI, DASAVATARA, *Ellora*, *Epic*, GANJIFA, *Government State Museum & National Art Gallery*, HANUMAN, *Madhubani*, RAVANA, *Santokba Dudhat*, *P. Vijyalakshmi*, *Laxman Pai*, *Jamini Roy*, *Gopal G. Subhedar*, *Raja Ravi Varma*, *Arnawaz Vasudev*, *Nathu Lal Verma;* Illustrations—BHARATA, DIWALI/ DIPAVALI, NAYAK-NAYAKA.

Ramachandran, A. (1935–) b. Kerala. Education: Dip. in FAC, Ph.D. *mural paintings* of Kerala, *KB*, *VBU*. Solos: Kumar Gallery & *Art Heritage* New Delhi, *BAAC* Kolkata, *LKA* Chennai, Kala Yatra Kolkata, Chennai, Bangalore, Mumbai & New Delhi, *Dhoomimal*, SRAG, *CKP*, *JAG*. Retrospective: New Delhi & *JAG*. Group participations: National *LKA* Exhibitions & *Triennales* New Delhi, *Sculpture BAAC* Kolkata; International: Brazil, Venezuela, USA, Canada, Yugoslavia, Poland, Bulgaria, Belgium, Menton, Tokyo, *Biennale* Sao Paulo & Havana. *Auctions*: Heart Mumbai, Christie's & Sotheby's. Awards: *LKA* National Award, Eminent *Artist* of *LKA*, Japan Foundation grant. Member: Chairman *LKA* Kerala. Commissions: Several *murals* at public places & executed *murals* on commission in New Delhi. Appointments: Prof. & HoD JMI *FA*. New Delhi. Publications: Written & published a thesis on *mural painting* of Kerala; Illustrated several books for children in India, Japan, England & USA. Ramachandran Art of the Mural—Rupika Chawla 1994; Also designed stamps for the postal department. Collections: *NGMA* & *LKA*

New Delhi, *Chandigarh Museum*, *BB*, *Painting & sculptures* in India & abroad including USA, Denmark, Germany, Switzerland, Canada, Norway & England.

Ramachandran A. is a *painter*, muralist and a *sculptor*. He *paints monumental mural*-sized *paintings*. His *imagery* is distinctive, with strong echoes of the past appearing in almost every series of works. However, the influence is integrated and assimilated to create these works with his personal vision stamped on them. In the early period one comes across *vignettes* of the Kerala *murals* painted in the *style* of Piero della Francesca or Michelangelo-like bodies tumbling out of a fiery sun. There is also a heavy use of *chiaroscuro* and *surrealism* in the negation of the face; instead a cowl or veil obscures it, leaving dense *shadow* behind.

His recent series of works owe their sinuousness of *line* and sensuousness of *form* to the *Ajanta frescoes*, floral and *miniature paintings*. A golden *light* pervades these large sized *compositions* with their voluptous half-clad women juxtaposed against vegetal and animal life, pulsating with mythical over *tones*.

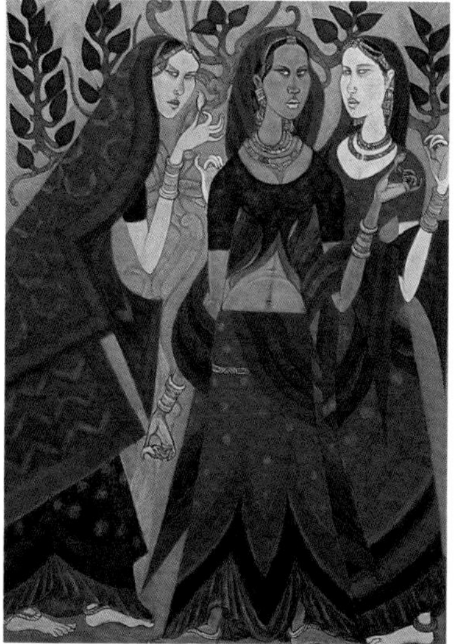

Ramachandran, A. "The Palas Tree & The Tribal Girls", 1991.

Ramachandran was inspired by the creative energy of *Ramkinkar Baij* and more recently practised *sculpture* as his *medium*.

He lives and works in New Delhi.

Ramayana The adventures of RAMA. one of the two major *epics* (other being the MAHABHARATA) in Indian *mythology*. The *epic* was composed by the sage (Rishi) Valmiki and it contains about 24,000 verses. The Ramayana relates to the life and exploits of Lord RAMA the 6th AVATAR (incarnation) of Lord VISHNU. The story is of RAMA, also known as Ramachandra, his love for his wife Sita; the abduction of Sita by RAVANA, the demon-king of Lanka; the war between RAMA and RAVANA; the dispatch to Lanka of HANUMAN, leader of the monkeys, who burnt the city ending in the destruction of RAVANA; the rescue of Sita; ending with RAMA ascending the throne of Ayodhya. The Ramayana was one of the sources of inspiration for *Rajastani miniature painting*. Several *modern artists* have also illustrated scenes from the *epic*. One of the most famous works was by *Raja Ravi Varma* and *K. Venkatappa's* "RAVANA & Jatayu". A dramatic *composition* full of *colour* and movement. Refer CHITRAKATHI, *Spiritual*, *Ellora*, GANJIFA, MAHABHARATA, *Manuscript Paintings*, PURANA, *Chittaprosad*, *Santokba Dudhat*, *Ganga Devi*, *Maqbool Fida Husain*, *Shrikant Gajanan Jadhav*, *Pilton Kothawalla*, *Reddeppa M. Naidu*, *P.L. Narasimha-Murti*, *Vijyalakshmi P.*, *Vamona A. Navelcar*, *Laxman Pai*, *Gopal G. Subhedar*, *Arnawaz Vasudev*, *Nathu Lal Verma*; Illustrations—BHARATA, DIWALI/DIPAVALI.

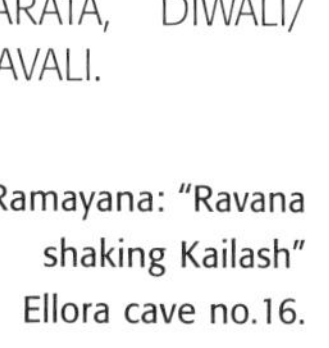

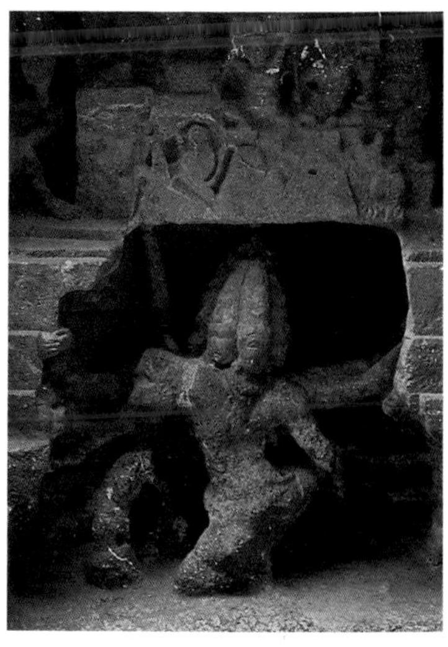

Ramayana: "Ravana shaking Kailash" Ellora cave no.16.

Ram Kumar (1924–) b. Shimla, HP. Education: Evening classes *SUSA* New Delhi, Received instructions from *Sailoz Mookerjea*; Studied under Andre Lhote Paris. Solos: Ahmedabad, YMCA Shimla, Kumar Gallery, Kunika Art Gallery, Chanakya, *Art Heritage & NGMA* New Delhi, Alliance Francaise, Gallery 59 & *GC* Mumbai, *Dhoomimal*, *VAG*, *PUAG*, *SAI*, *CKAG*. Retrospective: *NGMA*, *Art Heritage* New Delhi, *PUAG*, *VAG*; International: Poland, Paris, Colombo, London, Prague. Group participations: Mumbai, *LKA* New Delhi, SC; International: Prague, Sao Paulo, *Biennale* USA, Japan, Greece, Paris. *Auctions*: Heart & Osian's Mumbai, Heart New Delhi, Christie's New York, Christie's Hong Kong. Awards: *LKA* & Padma Shri New Delhi, Kalidas Samman MP; Fellowships International: J.D. Rockefeller III Fund Fellowship USA 1970. Publications: A *monograph* on the *artist* published by *LKA* in addition to the books on him. Ram Kumar by *NGMA* New Delhi; Cultural Profile of Varanasi written by him, collections of short series in English & Hindi. Appointments: Has curated a travelling *exhibition*, "Ten Indian Artists", to the USA. Collections: *NGMA* & *LKA* New Delhi, PUJ University, *Chandigarh Museum*, TIFR; International: National Museum Berlin & Prague, Washington, New York, pvt. & public.

Ram Kumar is an accomplished writer as well as a full-time *painter*, winning several awards for both his books and *paintings*. There is a strong affinity between the two *arts*, his *paintings* of a particular phase echoing the feelings apparent in his writing at the same time. However, there is one important difference—the emotional aspect. Emotions tend to be repressed in the *painting*, which are frozen evocations of the writing. Poverty and pain, for instance are apparent in the works, yet they do not evoke pathos, instead it is the *composition* with its marked grid-like structure that strikes one. *Distortion* and stylization of the *figures* and the *cityscape*-like *backgrounds* are the *key* note of his *paintings*.

While the *figure* was very prominent in the early works, after the 1960s it begins to merge with the *background*. By the time he painted the near-abstract Varanasi series, his role as a writer was relegated to the background. In a sense, Varanasi, the holy Hindu city of liberation, where the ashes of the dead are submerged, becomes a turning point for him; he liberates himself from the confines of *figuration*. His later *landscapes* and *cityscapes*, with the *colour palatte* mostly restricted to greys and browns, yellows and dull greens were an outcome of his training in Paris. His recent works are startling in comparision with the earlier *landscapes*, being literally laced with violent *colour* contrasts and *textures*, smacked on with the *palette knife*. They are also far more fragmentary than the earlier works, though the *landscape* elements still appear.

He lives and works in New Delhi.

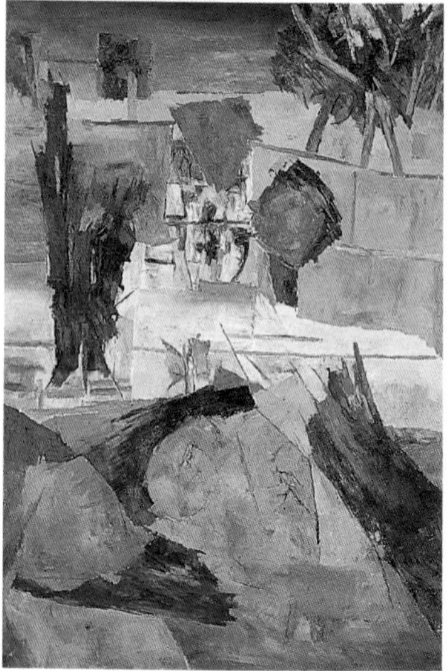

Ram Kumar: "Untitled", *Oil* on *Canvas*, 1998 90x60, cm.

Rane, Dattaprasanna S. (1952–) b. Talera, MAHA. Education: GDA, Art Master's certificate, Art Teacher's Dip., *JJSA* & *LSRSA*. Solos: The Gallery Chennai, *JAG, VAG*. Group participations: *LKA* New Delhi, GC, "50 years of Art in Mumbai" The Fine Art Company, Art Quest for CRY, *BAAC* & *NGMA*, Mumbai, *Nag Foundation* Pune, *TG, BAS, JAG, BB Biennales;* International: Hong Kong, South Korea, Japan, UK. *Art* camps: New Delhi, Bangalore, Mumbai. Awards: *Artists' Centre* Mumbai, *ASI, BAS*. Collections: *NGMA* New Delhi; International: La Salle Gallery Paris, National Museum & Art Forum Singapore, London Business School London & pvt.

The people from his birthplace appear constantly in Dattaprasanna S. Rane's *paintings*. They include the humble fisherfolk and farmers going about their daily business, with all the external trappings of their occupation. They wait patiently in shops, snooze gently on armchairs, play music at weddings or simply sit down to eat. While the subject may be mundane, Dattaprasanna S. Rane approaches it in an unconventional *manner*, almost giving his *oils* and *watercolours* a fresco-like feel. The *texture* is palpable, the *lines* wiry and the colouring subtle, with sudden accents of pure *colour*.

He lives in Mumbai.

Ranjan, Ghanshyam (1935–) b. Lucknow. Self-taught. Solos: Allahabad Lucknow. Group shows: Kanpur, Haldwani, Lakhimpurkheri, Lucknow, *AFA* Kolkata, IAFA Amritsar, *LKA* New Delhi. Group participations: UP Artist Association, State *LKA* & Young Artist in UP, *AFA* Kolkata, IAFA Amiritsar, Rashtriya Kala Mela Chennai & Bangalore, *AIFACS*. Founder member: Artists Group in Lucknow, Exhibition Committee UP, Member Adivory Board Rashtriya LKK Lucknow. Awards: Veteran Artist of India *AIFACS*. Appointments: Assisted with the *art* publications of UP *LKA* Lucknow. Collections: *LKA* New Delhi, UP *LKA* Lucknow & other pvt.

Ghanshyam Ranjan uses such unconventional *mediums* as sealing *wax* on *straw board* and *pen* and luxor *inks* on *paper*. The sealing *wax* which is applied on the grainy surface of the straw board with a *palette knife* creates a *tactile* feeling akin to surfaces impasted with *oil colours*. *Form* has to necessarily be simplistic yet *graphic* enough to excite the viewer's senses. His coloured *drawings* describe a *fantasy* world of lurking beasts and ghouls camouflaged as trees and shrubs.

Ghanshyam Ranjan lives in Lucknow.

Rao, Aekka Yadagiri (1938–) b. Hyderabad. Education: Dip. in *sculpture* CFA Hyderabad. Prof. at JNTU College. Solos: Hyderabad. Group participations: *Triennale* New Delhi over 8 National Exhibitions New Delhi & *SJM* Hyderabad. Participated in camps, *artist* conferences & seminar. Awards. *LKA*, AP State & All India including Gold Medal, HAS Hon. Eminent *Sculptor* & *Artist*, Kala Saraswathi & Visista Puraskaram Hyderabad & Govt. of AP. Members: *LKA* New Delhi & Hyderabad, Member Board of Studies BHU FFA. Life member HAS. Joint Secretary for Sculptors Forum of India New Delhi, President-Creative Art Society Hyderabad. Commissions: *Bronze bust* of Jawaharlal Nehru & Mahatma Ghandhi, modern sculptures & *mural* in *granite*, *bronze*, *copper*, *plaster of Paris* in Hyderabad, *NGMA* New Delhi; International: USSR, USA. Publications: Magazines, Newspapers & News Time Weekend, Monograph on life AP *LKA* Hyderabad. Collections: AP *LKA*, *NGMA* & *LKA* New Delhi *SJM*; International: Museum & Indian Embassy Moscow.

Aekka Yadagiri Rao had a deep attachment to *sculpture* right from his childhood days. He has produced welded *metal* of simple *forms*, and his *stone sculptures* move towards simplicity. Four types of NAYIKAS or heroines have been represented in *granite*. He expresses universal values and human feelings, also conveying the majesty of the animal kingdom with *modern forms* that are distorted in the Indian *manner*.

He lives in Hyderabad.

Rao, Bhaskar (1947–) b. Udupi, KAR. Self-taught. Over 12 solos: MMB, Bangalore,The Gallery Chennai *CRAR, JAG*. 52 Group shows: Udupi, KB Hyderabad, MMB, *LKA*, *Image Art Gallery* Bangalore, KAR Painters *LKA* Chennai, *VEAG, CYAG, JAG;* International: Hong Kong, Bangkok, Paris. Group Participations: *LKA* in Bangalore, Thrissur & Chennai, National Exhibition *LKA* New Delhi, All India Exhibition *BB*; International: Singapore, Hong Kong, Bangkok, Johannesberg, Paris & Dubai. *Art* camps: KAR Kala Mela Bangalore, All India *Artists* camp—Gulbarga, Bijapur, Regional Center *LKA* Chennai, CCMB, Hyderabad *ABC, CKP*. Awards: Four awards KAR *LKA* Bangalore. Commission: *Murals* in Bangalore. Collections: Kejriwal Galleries, *LKA* Bangalore, *LKA* New Delhi & *LKA* Chennai, Godrej Mumbai, *CRAR, CYAG, SUG;* pvt. India & abroad.

Bhaskar Rao's *paintings* are basically *figurative* and usually carry an underlying social message about the under-privileged. He portrays his surrounding with a great deal of accuracy, using acid greens and blues to heighten the sense of alienation and the pain of these people. He uses the quick drying *acrylic media* for his *paintings* and has also executed *sculptures* in *bronze* and *stone*.

Rao, K.S. (1936–) b. Mangalore, KAR. Education: Dip. *FA*. *JJSA*. Solos: MMB Chennai, SRAG, *SAI*, TAG. Group participations: British Council, Chennai, MMB & Progressive Painters of Mysore Bangalore, by *WSC* Mumbai, New Delhi, Chennai & Kolkata, *JAG*, *SAI*, *CRAR*; International: USA. *Art* camps & Mela: *LKA* Chennai & Bangalore; in Cochin by *LKA* Chennai. Awards: National Award *LKA* New Delhi, *AFA* Kolkata, *BAS*, *HAS*. Hon. Kala Mela & *LKA* KAR Bangalore. Appointments: Joined as an *art* designer with *WSC* Mumbai; Design Expert by Govt. of India to Govt. of Sri Lanka Colombo 1975 to 1980. Collections: Archaeology Museum Hyderabad, National Govt. Museum & Chennai, *LKA* & *NGMA* New Delhi, *LKA* Bangalore, *SAI*, *Dhoomimal*, *CRAR;* International: Texas USA.

An *eclectic* cublist *style* with impressionist brushstrokes is seen in his earlier *cityscapes*. His later works show *figures* stylized and simplified into geometric shapes, his work constantly interacting with his environment. He uses *mixed media–ink*, *oils* and *acrylic*. His statement about life is seen in context of emotion and rational direction in which the male and female are his central *theme*.

He lives and works in Chennai.

Rao, K. Sheshagiri (1924–) b. Warangal, AP. Education: Dip. *FA*. College of FA. & *Architecture* Hyderabad, Certificate study *VBU*, *Fresco painting Banasthali Vidyapith* RAJ. Solos: Hyderabad. Group shows: *LKA* in Hyderabad, Mumbai, Chennai, Kolkata, Mysore & New Delhi All India Arts Exhibition HAS; International: Cairo, Kabul, China, London; Studied Chinese & Japanese *techniques*. Awards: AP *LKA*, Mysore DAE, *AFA* Kolkata, Hon. by Govt. of AP, by Prime Minister of India for *portraits* New Delhi, Veteran Artist by *AIFACS*, HAS. Fellowship: Emeritus Fellowship Govt. of India HRD. Commissions: *backdrops* & *murals;* Painted *life-size portraits*. Appointments: Retired Prof., Vice-principal CFA, JNTU. Publications: Articles: Album "Sureka" the *drawing* on *sculptures* of Lepakshi, Tadipati & Hampi; Book: "Rekharnavam" principles of *line* & *design* with *illustration*; Illustrated "Abhignana Sakuntalam" 25 *paintings* with *wash* & *gouache technique*. Collection: Govt. Museum, Hyderabad, *SJM; Murals*–two in front of Bharatiya Vidya Bhavan Hyderabad.

K. Seshagiri Rao experimented with all *mediums* and *styles* between 1950 and 1965. He adopted *figuration* in the *realistic* traditional *style* of the *Bengal School*. Later he was influenced by *Abanindranath Tagore*, *Nandalal Bose*. *Ajanta*, Rajput *painting* and Lepakshi, which helped him to innovate in textural *forms* in *watercolours*. *Line* and *colour* are equally important in his works, which are replete with *images* of birds, animals, trees in addition to traditional human *figures*.

Rao, N. Chandrasekhar (1940–2004) b. Polasara, Ganjam, Dist. Orissa. Education: Dip. in *FA*. GSAC Khallikote Bhuvaneshwar University. Solos: *LKA* & Rabindra Mandap Bhubaneshwar, Museum of Art Chandigarh, *JAG*, BAG; International: San Diego USA. Group participations: *LKA* Orissa, *AFA* & *BAAC* Kolkata, National Exhibition, *Triennale* & RB New Delhi, *Nag Foundation* Pune, *LKA* Chandigarh, *AIFACS*, *BAS*, *JAG*; International: New Jersey, USA. *Art* camps: Orissa, *LKA* New Delhi, *Nag Foundation* Pune. Awards: State *LKA*, All India Fine Arts. & Hon. with Kala Bibhushana Orissa, SZCC Nagpur, *AIFACS*, *BAS*. Member: *LKA* New Delhi, Advisory Committee *LKA* Bhubaneshwar; Jury–for State *LKA* Orissa, National Research Award Scholarship *LKA* New Delhi. Commissions: *Murals* at the fairs in New Delhi, Nagpur & Ahmedabad; International Art Festival Sweden. Appointments: Seminars in Orissa on Pata (scrolls & panels) *Paintings*, *Filigree*, *Crafts* & *Contemporary Art* and *Artists*; In Bhubaneshwar on *Art Education*. Worked as handicraft designer at Handicrafts Design Center, Superintendent in State Institute of Handicraft Training, Deputy Dir. in Handicraft & Cottage Industries Orissa. Institute of Traditional Art, *LKA* New Delhi, Founder Dir. Creative School of Art Bhubaneshwar. Collections: *LKA* & *NGMA* New Delhi, *AFA*, *BAAC* Kolkata, *Orissa State Museum* Bhubaneshwar.

N. Chandrasekhar Rao rests on the back of traditional Indian *paintings* with *linear compositions*. The stylized *forms* signify the simplicity and often give the *impression* of *sculpture*. His *paintings* convey a lyrical sensation with some subjects being religious and others effecting a *modern* approach. He used the *medium* of water, *watercolour* and *mixed media* on *paper*. He lived and worked in Bhubaneshwar, Orissa.

Rao, Ramesh (1949–) b. Udupi, KAR. Education: Poorna Prajna College Udupi. 10 solos & 56 group shows: MMB Bangalore; Shrungar Art Gallery Udupi, Calicut University Chelari, Govt. Museum Mangalore, The Gallery Chennai, *VEAG*, *CRAR*, *CYAG*, *JAG*. Group participated: *LKA* Bangalore, Kerala, New Delhi & Chennai. Charitable Shows: Mumbai, Bangalore. International: Singapore, Hong Kong, Bangkok, Johannesberg, Paris & Dubai. *Art* camps All India: Kerala Kala Mela, Town Hall Bangalore, *LKA* Gulbarga & Chennai, SZCC Chennai, "Hasta Shilpa" Manipal. *Auctions:* Asprey's HelpAge India & Sotheby's Mumbai, *JAG*. Awards: *LKA* Bangalore, Thrissur & Chennai. Members: Founder member & President of Artist's Forum Udupi Manipal. Commissions: *Mural* Bangalore. Collections: Godrej Mumbai, *CYAG*, in India & abroad.

Paintings are part of living reality in Ramesh Rao's *theme* of human *figures* either at rest or in motion. They originate from and around his dreams. *Colours* are nuances that convey moods and interactions though they are

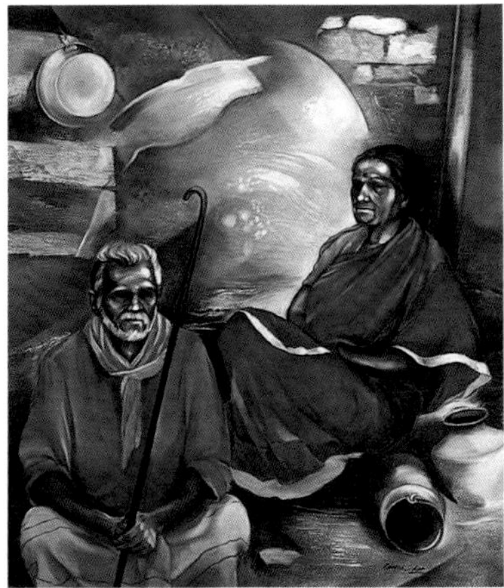

Rao, Ramesh: "Old Timers" *Oils*, 120x115 cm.

mystically *realistic*. He says *forms* and *colours*, *shades* and *light* dominate his *canvas*. The hazy *background* elements, *balances* the whole *composition*.

He lives and works in Udupi, KAR.

Rao, Rekha (1947–) b. Mumbai, MAHA. Studied *painting* under *artist* father *K.K. Hebbar*. Solos: *GC* Mumbai, *SG* Chennai & Bangalore, *JAG*, *Dhoomimal;* International: Australia, Germany, Los Angeles, USA. Group participations: 50 years of India's Independence Mumbai, *BAAC* & *Auction* Kolkata, *Triennale LKA* New Delhi, *BAS*, *JAG*, *NCAG*, *LTG*, *GE*. *Art* camp & workshop: *K.K. Hebbar's* camp Bangalore, *LKA* Goa, *Triennale LKA* in Jaipur, Conducted workshop *MPCVA*, *LKA* Lucknow. *Auctions*: Christie's, Sotheby's & Asprey's Helpage India Mumbai. Collections: *NGMA* & *LKA* New Delhi, MAHA State, Godrej & *VEAG*; International: Singapore Museum.

Rekha Rao's *paintings* are a conflation of associations—both for the viewer and for herself. Single isolated bits of memory are elaborated and connected to other reminiscences, recollections and turned into *visual* expression on *canvas*. Over the years, her *paintings*, though still *figurative* and inspired by *nature*, have gradually become a distillation of the broader reality of life itself. There is also a *calligraphic* element in her reduction of objects and *figures* with use of gestural brushstrokes. Rekha Rao has worked in *oils* as well as *acrylics* and other *media*.

She lives and works in Bangalore.

Rasa=**1.** A SANSKRIT word meaning sap, juice, extract from plants, fluid. **2.** To taste, or relish. **3.** In the world of Indian *art*, it refers to a state of bliss, emotions or *aesthetic* experience.

The theory of Rasa was first discussed by BHARATA in the Natya-shastra (Science/*Art* of dance). He applied Rasa theory to the stage, incorporating both dance and music. He divided them into eight emotions or sentiments, to which a ninth was added by later writers. **1.** Shringara–love, **2.** Hasya–comic, **3.** Karuna–pathetic, **4.** RAUDRA–furious **5.** Vira–*heroic*, **6.** Bhayanaka–terrible, **7.** Bibhatsa–odious, **8.** Adbhuta–wondrous or marvellous and **9.** Shanta–quiescent. Though Rasa is defined as being the whole and undivided BHAVA (emotion), it is through one or the other of these nine emotions, that an *aesthetic* experience occurs. As BHARATA stated, "Rasa is born from the union of the play with the performance of actors, and its reception by the audience." Rasa in *art*, would incorporate the *artist*, the *art* work and its elements, and the viewer, along with its supplementary and complementary moods and emotions. The experience itself would be termed as the tasting of flavour, "Rasaswadhana". The taster, i.e. the viewer would be the "Rasika" and the work of *art* involved would be "Rasavant". The Shringara Rasa, with its element of the erotic love was one of the most popular of the Rasas, being depicted in most of the miniatures. *Contemporary artists* like *Narendra Rai Shrivastar* have also used the Shringara Rasa as a *theme* for his 2005 series in *oils*. Refer *Aesthete*, *Art Criticism*, *Base*, *Colour*, *Empathy*, HANSA, HAMSA, NAVA RASA, *Performance Art*, RADHA, RUDRA, SANSKRIT, *Spiritual*, *Badri Narayan*, *Nand Katyal*, *Kshitendranath Mazumdar*, *Dhruva Mistry*, *Laxman Pai*, *Sultan Ali J.*, Illustrations–HOLI, KRISHNA.

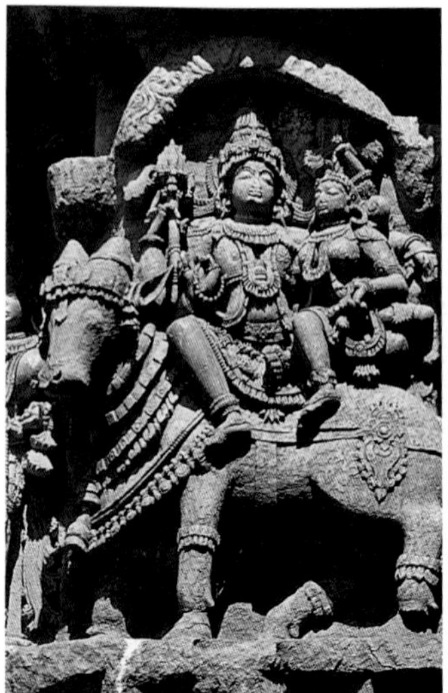

Rasa: Shringara Rasa, Shiv-Parvati Belur.

Rasa Lila is a devotional dance of KRISHNA with his consort, RADHA, and GOPIS. The dance symbolizes the universality of god and that every being is equally beloved (each GOPI thought that she was the favoured partner of KRISHNA). The Rasa Lila is depicted with this *theme* in *miniature paintings* as well as in textiles such as *Picchwais*. Refer GOPA, GOPI, GOPIKA, *Pastoral*.

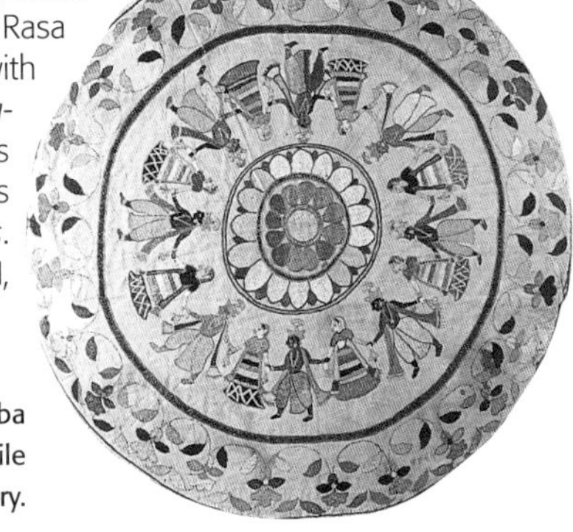

Rasa Lila: "Chamba Embroidery", Textile AD19th century.

Rasaja Foundation (New Delhi). The Rasaja Foundation was initiated by the writer-artist, *Jaya Appasamy* in an association of connoisseurs and scholar-historians who wished to document and preserve the artistic heritage of India as well as other countries. It is a registered society with its main focus on documentation and research of the *arts* and *crafts* of the country. The foundation proposes to open a *museum* called Manjusha, in which all the *art* objects will be donated by major collectors who wish to make them accessible to the public. It is hoped that these collectors will later think of donating manuscripts, *photographs*, books and catalogues.

Rasamanjari=cluster of delights. A 15th-century text by poet Bhanudatta, describing various types of lovers. It has been frequently illustrated through *miniature paintings*. Refer ASHTANAYIKA, *Basohli*.

Raval, Prem (1935–) b. Palanpur, GUJ. Education: GDFA & Art Master's Mumbai. Solos: Ahmedabad, Surat, Palanpur, Gandhinagar, Amritsar, New Delhi, Kolkata, Hyderabad, Jaipur, Bangalore, Nehru Centre Mumbai *PG*, TAG, *NCAG*; International: Germany USA. Group participation: Progress Painters Group Ahmedabad. Awards & Hons.:

Certificate *LKA* & Silver Medal *LKA* PUJ, Ahmedabad for Photography & *painting*, MPKP. Appointments: Art Dir. "Javanika Theater" as Interior Designer Since 1959 .

Painting for Prem Raval includes the indepth study of *colour*, *brushes* and *oils paint*, the subtlety of *colours*, the rhythmic movement of the *brush* and knife and perhaps most importantly the development of the *artist's* relationship with *colours* and *forms*. A certain amount of *Surrealism* is followed in the works with ladders leading nowhere and *figures* magically disappearing into a haze of *colour*. These works show his penchant for the *trompe l'oeil*. His *abstract* works are textured, with *blocks* of impasted *colour* appearing against a *background* of *monochrome colour*.

Raval, Rasik Durgashankar (1928–1980) b. Sardoi, GUJ. Education: GDA in *drawing* & *painting JJSA*. Solos: *JAG*, TAG; International: USA. Group participations: All Indian Exhibitions, National *LKA* & *NGMA* New Delhi, *AFA* Kolkata, Annual *BAS*. Awards: All Indian Exhibitions *NGMA* & *LKA* New Delhi, Kolkata; Scholarship for *mural painting*. Publications: In "The Illustrated Weekly of India" Mumbai, "Art of the World-India—500 years of Indian Art" by Herman Goetz. "Encyclopedia of Painting" 1956 Hutchson of London & Studio Magazine London. Collections: *LKA* Ahmedabad in the name of Rasik Durgashankar Raval, *NGMA* New Delhi & *Chandigarh Museum*.

Rasik Durgashankar Raval's *drawings* were simple, direct and human, with reds, greens, blues and occasional yellows serving as a nucleus for his *form* and *content*. His *figures* although rooted in folk *traditions* are stylized in a primitivist *manner*. These elongated semi-nude *figures*, seem almost alien in their negation of extraneous detail, appearing like *paper* cut-outs in his use of the coloured *silhouette*.

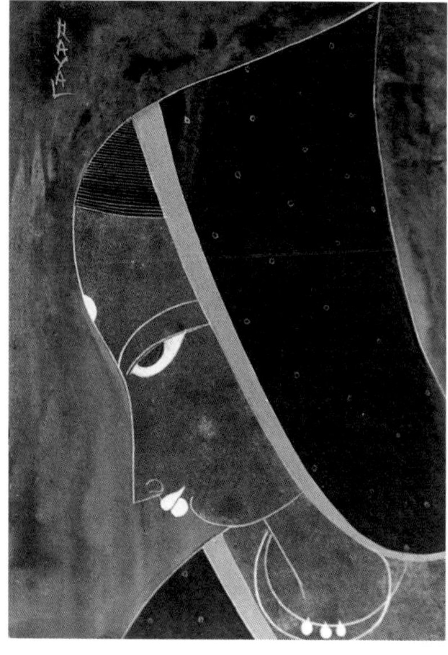

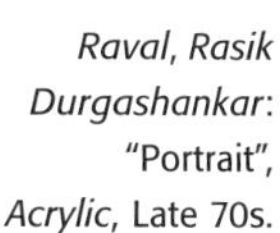

Raval, Rasik Durgashankar: "Portrait", *Acrylic*, Late 70s.

Raval, Ravishankar M. (1892–1979) (also known as Rawal) b. Bhavnagar, Saurashtra GUJ. Studied at *JJSA*. Group participation: in *exhibition* & worked at *Ajanta* for one month; Participations & member: Sahitya Parishad & Chitrakala Sangh GUJ, Kala Parishad Mumbai, *ASI;* Visited all North Indian Art Society, *artists*, *critics*, *museums* & as a Chief Guest at *Santiniketan*; Set up a Centre in Ahmedabad; Established "Kumar Magazine" Ahmedabad. Awards: Mayo Medal *JJSA*, Gold Medal *BAS*, Prize poster design Kolkata, Silver Medal Sahitya Parishad, Kalidas Prize, Ranjit Ram Gold Medal, Soviet-Land Nehru Award, Padma Shri, Fellowship & certificate *LKA* New Delhi. Publications: "Ajantana Kala Mandapo" a *monograph* of *Ajanta* caves, "Kalakarni Santaryatra" a book about his cultural trip to Japan & Northern India, Fine Art essays—"Kala Chintan" Collection of his paintings—"Mari Chitrasushi" & on his biography. Collections: at *museums* & galleries in India & pvt. in India & abroad.

As a child Ravishankar M. Raval was greatly inspired by *Raja Ravi Varma's style*. His years at the *BAS* resulted in him winning several medals, culminating in getting a commission to *paint* the European principal of a local college. However, he was greatly inspired by Mahatma Gandhi's call for freedom and total boycott of the British way of life. Giving up *academic art* was his contribution to the Mahatma's call. He later turned to oriental *art*, touring the Far East and meeting some of the best *artists* of Japan and China. His works are an amalgamation of the Far Eastern *wash technique* with the linear grace of *Ajanta*. His *themes* were mainly taken from classic and romantic literature.

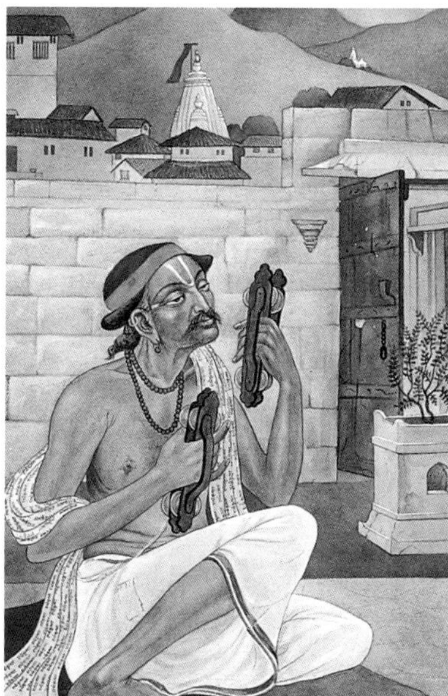

Raval, Ravishankar M.: "Painting".

Ravana Evil King of Rakshashas (*demons*) in Lanka, and son of Visravas and Kaikasi. He was supposed to be invulnerable and was described as Dashanana, having ten heads, twenty arms, burning eyes and sharp teeth. He had incredible strength, being able to break mountains, cause storms in the oceans and block the sun, moon and the course of wind with his hands and body. He could assume any *form*. INDRA and VISHNU tried to destroy him with Vajra—thunderbolt and Sudarshana CHAKRA (discus/wheel) without success. Finally VISHNU had to descend to earth in his 6th incarnation in the AVATAR (*form*) of RAMA to vanquish Ravana. This *forms* the basis of the *epic* RAMAYANA. Refer GANJIFA, GARUDA, HANUMAN, KAILASH, KAILASA, *Variant*; Illustration—*K. Venkatappa*.

Rawal, Ishwari (1944–) b. Barnawad, MP. Education: M.A. in *drawing* & *painting*. Solos: Jabalpur, Ujjain, MPKP Bhopal, Kala Vithika Indore, *JAG*, TAG, *AIFACS*. Group participations: MPKP, *Biennale*, Kala Mela, National Council of Educated Research & Training, Regional College Bhopal,

Kalidas Academy Ujjain, Rashtriya Kala Mela New Delhi & Indore, *BB*; International: By *Artists* of *"Halatol"*—Norway, Scotland & England. *Painting* camp: Mumbai. Workshop: On *Graphics* Bhopal. Award: Won Scholarship 1963. Member: President Group *"Halatol"*. Appointments: Organized Melwa Utsawa Exhibition 40 *artists*. Painted film *hoardings*; Miniature work on *Rajput miniature paintings*. Collections: Indore, *NGMA* & *LKA* New Delhi, MPKP Bhopal, Kalidas Academy Ujjain, *BB*, *CYAG*, TAG; International: USA, Uganda.

Ishwari Rawal's *landscapes* appear *fragmented* against neutrally coloured *backgrounds*. While small houses and streets are rendered in multi point *perspective*, the *figure* of a child is at times hazily rendered in a corner to heighten a surreal feeling. He uses lush greens and rich Vandyke browns to emphasize his *landscapes*. The prominence given to certain pieces of *drapery* and to certain objects in the *painting* give it a stage-set-like feeling.

Rawal, Jasu (1939–) b. India. Education: M.FA. in *painting MSU*, under the guidance of *K.G. Subramanyan* & *Vinod Shah*. Solos: MMB Bangalore, *JAG*, *CRAR*. Group shows: Kolkata, Chennai, Hyderabad, Lucknow, Bhuvaneshwar, Goa, Jaipur & Shimla. Group participated: National *LKA* New Delhi, Southern State Regional Academy Chennai, Kala Mela Bangalore. *Graphic artist* camp—National Kala Mela New Delhi, *GAC*. Awards: State *LKA* GUJ & KAR, DAE Mysore, *AIFACS* for traditional work. Commissions: Variously in *acrylics* and in *oils*. Collections: *NGMA* & *LKA* New Delhi, PUJ Museum Chandigarh, *LKA* Ahmedabad.

Jasu Rawal's *paintings* appear to be reflecting with *nature* and *still life*. Pots, pans and dishes are constantly depicted, though the arrangement may not all be on the same plane but in the *translucent* effect. The scattering of the *forms*, have an element of the accident in them.

Ray, Shyamal Dutta (1934–2005) b. Ranchi, Bihar. Education: *GCAC* Kolkata. Solos: Since 1962 Kolkata, Chennai, New Delhi & Mumbai. Retrospective: *BAAC* Kolkata. Group participations: National *LKA* & AFA New Delhi, *CIMA* Kolkata, *Graphic* Chandigarh, Kala Yantra Hyderabad, Harmony Mumbai, Indian *drawing* Today *JAG*, *AIFACS*; International: Poland, Algeria, Canada, Paris, Inter Grafik Germany, Indian Art Texas, *Prints* from India USA, *Biennale* London, Australia, Baghdad & Havana. Workshops: *LKA* New Delhi, *metal sculpture* camp *Santiniketan*, *CKAG*; International: Bangladesh. *Auctions:* Heart New Delhi, Osian's Mumbai. Awards: *BAAC* Gold Medal, *AFA* Kolkata, All India Graphics New Delhi, *RBU*, *CKP*. Member: Founder member *SCA*. Collections: *NGMA* & *LKA* New Delhi, *BAAC* Kolkata; International: V&A, Pratt Ghraphic Center New York, Museum Baghdad, Bangal Foundation Dhaka.

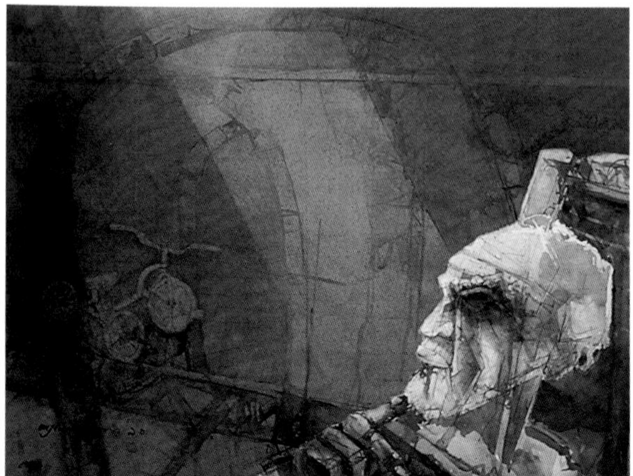

Ray, Shyamal Dutta: "Good Old Days", *Watercolours* 1993, 61x41 cm.

Shyamal Dutta Ray experimented widely with different *media*, including *printmaking* (*dry-point*, *etching*, collograph), *painting* and *drawing*. He has basically worked on *figurative*, with animals and surreal objects recurring in his works. He also did a series of puppet-like *figures* and textural *landscapes*. At times he employed a soft haziness of *texture* that is similar to *pastel*, at others the criss-crossing of vertical and horizontal *lines* gave his *landscapes* an expressionist quality.

Ray, Sita (1938–) b. India. Education: Dip. in *FA*. Delhi School of Art Delhi; Courses: Japanese/Chinese *brush painting* & *earth colours* in Japan; Influenced by *Sailoz Mookerjea*, *Biren De*, *Jaya Appasamy*. Solos: *AFA* Kolkata, TKS, SRAG, *CKAG*; International: Kobe, Tokyo, Hyogo Japan. Group participations: Bhubaneshwar, Contemporary Indian Artist New Delhi; International: Japan.

Sita Ray's extensive travels particularly to China and Korea have shaped her *style*. She was deeply influenced by *Japanese art* and *culture*. She is *eclectic*, using bold *forms* and startling *colours* as well as delicate *tints* and brushstrokes. She has painted in *media* as diverse as traditional Indian, traditional Japanese, *abstract*, and surrealist using a variety of subjects.

She lives and works in India and Japan.

Ray, Suchandra (1920–) Self-taught, practised from live *models AFA* Kolkata; studied under *Jamini P. Gangooly* & Malehon Dutta Gupta. She exhibited for over 40 years. Solos: Kolkata, Delhi, Jamshedpur; International: USA, Commonwealth Institute & Galleries London. Group participations: *AFA* Annual Exhibition, Women's Group & Sketch Club Exhibition Kolkata. Awards: Governor Padmaja Naidu Medal Kolkata. Publications: In "Anand Bazar Patrika", "Statesman". Collections: pvt. & public in India, UK, USA, Italy, Germany, Japan & Australia.

She is skilled at *portrait* and *landscape painting*. Her *canvases* are colourful, some portraying a dense darkness and yellow smudges of *light*. Others are filled with a gay energy, and vitality. Her subjects are chosen from RAJ, the Himalayas, Mathura and Varanasi. The *paintings* talk about the elementary pleasures of life: e.g. a couple working in the fields, a young woman holding a pigeon, women fetching water and other rural subjects.

Raza, Sayed Haider (1922–) b. Babaria, MP. India. Education: Studied *painting* at Nagpur School, *JJSA*; French Govt. Scholarship ENSBA. Solos: *Delhi Art Gallery*, *GC* Mumbai, MPKP, Bhopal, *BAS* & Institute of Foreign Language before leaving for Paris, *JAG*, *JNAG*, *BB*, *AIFACS;* International: New York Paris, Canada, San Fransisco, Norway, Bern, Cannes. Retrospective: *JAG* 2002; International: 1952–91

Museum of Menton France. Group shows: Venice, Sao Paulo, Senegal, Indian Artists Paris, RAA London, Museum Oxford, New York, ENSBA, others in Copenhagen, Denmark, Washington, Geneva Zurich, Tokyo, Milan & California. Group participations: *PAG* Mumbai, *Triennale* & *LKA* New Delhi, Marvel Art Gallery Ahmedabad, *BAS*; International: Paris, Washington DC, Norway, Linz, Milan, Zurich, Liverpool, Graham Gallery New York, Festival International Montreal, Art Now in India New Castle, *Biennale* Venice, Paris, Sao Paulo, Maro & Menton. *Auctions*: Heart, Osian's, Bowring's–Mumbai, Bowring's, Heart, Sotheby's New Delhi, Christie's, Sotheby's–London & New York, Bonham's London, Christie's Hong Kong & Singapore. Awards: Padma Shri by Indian President 1981; Prix de la Critique Paris. Members: Founder member *PAG* Mumbai 1947, Fellow member *LKA* New Delhi. Appointments: Visiting Lecturer University California 1962. Publications: *"Monograph" LKA* New Delhi, Raza Anthology 1980–90 *GC Mumbai*, "Bindu: Space and Time" in Raza's Vision by Geeti Sen. Collections: Museum of FA. Bhopal, *Maharaja Fatesingh Museum* Vadodara, Central Museum Nagpur, *NGMA* & *LKA* New Delhi, *Roopankar*, TIFR, *JNAG*; International: National Museum & Museum of Modern Art Paris, Asia Society New York.

Sayed Haider Raza's seminal work in the past three decades is aimed at pure plastic order and formal logic. Secondly it concerns the *theme* of *nature*. Both tenets have converged into a single point and have become inseparable. The point, the BINDU, symbolizes the seed bearing the potential of all life. The BINDU introduced to him by his schoolmaster in MP is also a visible *form* containing all the essential requisites of *line*, *tone*, *colour*, *texture* and *space*.

Sayed Haider Raza, who had been one of the original members of the *PAG* Mumbai originally painted impressionist *landscapes* in *gouache*. In Paris, this underwent a series of developments into the realm of *colour* field *painting* and finally to his present geometrically aligned *forms*. He lives and works in Paris. Refer *Plasticity*. (See illustration on page 288)

Ready-made A mass-produced object, usually a consumer item, selected by the *artist* to be an *art* object. The *term* was coined by the dadaist M. Duchamp. The ready-made differs from the *found object*, i.e. "objet trouve" in that the latter is incorporated into the final work whereas the former is part of an *art* work. *Installation art* of 1990s, apart from using *found objects* as an anti-aesthetic expression, also used the ready-made to lend creativity to the *compositions*. Indian *artists* have used *print reproductions* as ready-mades. *Vivan Sundaram* in 1988–89 included everything from simple *sketches* to loosely structured *forms*, glass boxes and strident *colours* and then went on to make elaborate *constructions* with *found objects* and ready-mades. Refer *Anti-Art*, *Dadaism*, *New Realism*, *Pop Art*, *Still life*, *Wood*, *N. Pushpamala*; Illustrations–*Aku*, *Vivan Sundaram*.

Realism A phase of French *Art* dating between 1860–70 when *artists* like G. Courbet rebelled against the subjectivity and emotion of *romanticism* and chose to portray only the truth i.e. reality and not the imaginary. Other *artists* include J. Millet and H. Daumier. A *term* generally used in *art* to describe works that are basically *realistic* in *technique*. The subjects would be real, the *colours* and the application of *paint* close to the native in the case of *painting;* while in *sculpture* it would denote an accurate, true to life rendering. In India, *Raja Ravi Varma* was among the earliest *artists* to achieve this degree of realism in his works; even though his setting and *landscape background* were stage-like. Refer *Art*, *Figuration*, *Figurative*, *Hyper-Realism*, *Naturalism*, *Roman Art*, *Sculptor*, SHAKTI, *Social Realism*, *Spiritual*, *Style*, *Super Realism*, *V.G. Andani*, *Aditya Basak*, *Bikash Bhattacharjee*, *Vidya Bhushan*, *Dayhalal K. Chauhan*, *Dwarika P. Dhuliya*, *Satyen Ghosal*, *Shamkant Jadhav*, *Ravindra Mestry*, *Ram Nath Pasricha*, *Balkrishna M. Patel*, *D.L.N. Reddy*, *Suhas Roy*; Illustrations–*Gobardhan Ash*, *Sadanandji Bakre*, *Pestonjee Bomanjee*, *Narayan S. Bendre*, *Manishi Dey*, *John Fernandes*, *Ranjitsingh Gaekwad*, *K.K. Hebbar*, *B.P. Kamboj*, *K. Khosa*, *Harkrishan Lall*, *Anilbaran Saha*, *Antonio X. Trindade*, *Raja Ravi Varma*.

Realistic Pertaining to *realism*, it refers to the *technique* in *painting*, in which the two-dimensional surface appears to be realistic and three-dimensional. **1.** *Art* with realistic *style* including *sketches*, *landscapes* and *portraits* were/are termed academic. The *media* used for representation included *pencil*, *pen*, *tempera*, *ink*, *gouache*, *watercolours*, *pastel* and *oil colours*. *Space* became an integral part of the *composition* during the British Raj. *Depth* and *anatomy* study was essential in *contemporary figurative art* which varied in *style* and *technique*. *Atmospheric effect* and clear *figures* in the *foreground* are seen in the works of *Raja Ravi Varma*, *Pestonjee Bomanjee*, *Hemendranath Mazumdar*, and *Jamini P. Gangooly*. **2.** Ancient Indian *sculpture* was not realistic in appearance. It had to conform to a set of canons not only iconographically but also in the *matter* of scale and *proportion*. It was only after the influence of Colonialism and the setting up of *art* academies, that realistic *sculpture* made an appearance in India. Soon *portraits* and full *figure* studies of political and social leaders become the norm. Different *media* were explored like *bronze casting stone* and *marble carving*. i.e. *Bhagwant K. Goregaoker*, *Vinayak Pandurang Karmarkar*. Refer *Backdrop*, *Fine Arts*, *Foreground*, *Hyper-Realism*, *Ideal*, *Nude*, *One-Point Perspective*, *Vanishing Point*, *Chandranath K. Achrekar*, *Shivananda P. Akki*, *K.C. Aryan*, *Vijaya Bagai*, *Gopal Damodar Deuskar*, *Usha Rani Hooja*, *Shrikant Gajanan Jadhav*, *K.B. Kulkarni*, *Vasant Parab*, *Sarbari RoyChowdhury*, *K. Sheshagiri Rao*, *B.D. Shirgaonkar*, *Laxman Narayan Taskar*, *K. Venkatappa*, *Vinayakrao Venkatrao Wagh;* Illustrations–*Art Education*, *Figure Painting*, *Life-Drawing*, *Portrait*, *Sadanandji Bakre*, *Vinayak Pandurang Karmarkar*, *Debi Prasad RoyChowdhury*, *Shantilal M. Shah*, *Abanindranath Tagore*, *Bayaji Vasantrao Talim*, *Antonio X. Trindade*, *Sarada Charan Ukil*, *Shantanu Ukil*, *Raja Ravi Varma*, *Brahman Vinayakrao Wagh*.

Reddy, Anjani P. (1952–) b. Hyderabad. Education: Grad. in *painting* College of FA. & *Architecture* JNTU. Solos: KB Hyderabad, *LKA* New Delhi, TAG, *JAG*. Group participations: KB, Women *Artists* by CCMB & L.B. Prasad Eye Institute Hyderabad, *Biennale* Jaipur, *Santiniketan*, *BAAC* Mumbai &

Kolkata, The Gallery Chennai, HAS, *AIFACS*, *CKP*, *ABC*; International: New York, London, Jakarta. Awards: Scholarship & Gold Medal AP *LKA*, Gold Medal HAS, The Elizabeth Greensheilds Foundation Grant Canada. *Art* camps & workshops: *Printmaking* Trends JNTU & Alliance Francaise, Traditional *painting* SZCC Nagpur. Appointments: Prof. & HoD *FA*. JNTU. Collections: AP Museum Hyderabad, Madras Museum Chennai, *NGMA* New Delhi & pvt. ATA Mumbai.

Anjani P. Reddy's *townscapes* are tightly structured in *oils*, and *mixed media*, *tempera*, with the vertical and horizontal grids, the occasional diagonals, breaking the monotony. Her use of *imagery* is consciously naive with multi-point *perspective* lending an air of old world charm to these works. She captures the reflections in the water, and the debris in a street with the same meticulous affection that she gives to the decorative grillwork and verandahs. Her recent works are more *realistic* being *symbolic self-portraits* with the middleclass and her mundane joys and pleasures being the central *theme*.

She lives and works in Hyderabad.

Reddy, D.L.N. (1949–) b. Nerada, AP. Education: Dip. in *drawing* & *painting* Govt. College of FA. Hyderabad. *Graphics MSU*. Solos: *Graphics* KB & MMB Hyderabad, *Gallery 7* Mumbai, *Oil* on *canvas* & *glass painting* New Delhi *JAG*, *PUAG*, *Drawing* & *watercolours SAI*. Group participations: MMB "German & Indian Art" Hyderabad, *CYAG*, Touring group *exhibition* in India; International: Germany. Participations: National Exhibition *Triennale* & *Biennale* New Delhi; Inter-national: UK, Germany, Yugoslavia, Germany, Switzerland. Workshops: *Painting* & *printmaking* in *BB* Bhopal & Kasauli, *Graphic* Vadodara, CCMB Hyderabad, KB Santiniketan; International: Germany. *Auctions*: Heart New Delhi. Awards: Scholarship & Gold Medal *LKA* AP, National Scholarship, Gold Medal HAS; International: Grant Elizabeth Greenshields Foundation Canada. Fellowship: Dept of Culture Govt. of India. Collections: *NGMA*, *College of Art* & *LKA* New Delhi, Govt. Museum Chandigarh, State Museum Hyderabad, *SJM*; International: Germany, USA.

D.L.N. Reddy is a versatile *artist*, straddling several methods of expression with great ease, having executed *paintings* on *canvas* and glass, *printmaking* and *sculptures*. His approach to *realism* is neither dramatic nor descriptive. His *imagery* is both subdued and sentimental. His *imagery*, though universal in the *manner* of *modern art*, is rooted in the local context. The sensuous attention to details speaks of his love for *form*, touched by a tinge of pathos. D.L.N. Reddy's *paintings* veer between brooding *self portraits*, vacant houses and the formal articulation of *landscapes*.

He lives and works in Hyderabad.

Reddy, Krishna N. (1925–) b. AP. Education: Dip. in *FA*. *Santiniketan*. Certificate in *FA*. Milan, Slade School London; AGC; Academy di Belle Arti di Brera Milan with Marino Marini for *sculpture*. Specialized in Gravure-Atelier 17, Founder-Dir., S.W. Hayter; International Center for Graphic Paris; Also apprenticeship with Henry Moore, O. Zadkine & Marino Marini for *sculpture* and Hayter in London, Paris, Rome, Milan respectively for seven years. Solos & Retrospective: *GC* Mumbai, AFA & *NGMA* New Delhi, *AFA* & *BAAC* Kolkata, State Academy of FA. & *LKA* Hyderabad, GCA Chandigarh, *LKA* New Delhi & Chennai *JJSA*, *Roopankar Museum*, *CKP;* International: USA, California, Japan, France, Mexico city, including series on "The Great Clown" in Sweden, "Clown Juggler" Improvisations New York, "Colour Intaglio" Yonkers & "Historic Intaglios" Bronxville. Group participations: *GC* Mumbai, CMC Art Gallery & *College of Art* New Delhi, *BAAC* Kolkata, *JAG*, *CKP;* International: USA, Germany, California. Participations: From 1954 onwards, including *Biennales*, *Triennales*, National Exhibitions, National Academi Graphics 85 *LKA* & Museum *BB* in India; International: USA, China, Japan, Germany, UK, France, Italy, Thailand & other countries. *Auctions*: Heart, Mumbai & New Delhi. Awards & Hons.: Philadelphia, Sweden, Art Festival Morocco, UN Stamp & Padma Shri by President of India 1972. Appointments: Special seminars & workshops as visiting Prof. at University & Prof. of *Art*, his subjects being *colour printing*, pointillist & broken-colours, *colour* structuring in *intaglio* surface *colour*, *nature* of materials in simultaneous *colour printing;* Dir. of Graphics & Printmaking Division, Dept. of *Art Education* New York University. Publications: Lectures & panel discussions: from 1955–1993—discussed on *print making* & "Krishna's Cosmos The Creativity of a Painter, Sculptor & Teacher" by Ratnottama Sengupta (Mapin Publishing) 2003. Collections: Dr. H. Bhaba & Tata Press Mumbai, *NGMA* New Delhi, *JJSA*, *VBU;* International: USA, UK, Japan, Switzerland, Canada, France, Italy, Royal Museum of FA. Copenhagen, Chester & Davida Herwitz collection 38 works Worcester, Mass, Portland Art Museum Oregon, V&A London, many other *museums* & galleries abroad, & pvt.

In the mid-70s, Krishna N. Reddy began developing the viscosity process of *intaglio printing*. He dispensed with the traditional *burin* and *acid* biting, and instead used mechanical devices, by which he created several layers of recession in the *plate*. The *relief* and textural effect is not just *visual* but also *tactile*. Nuances of *nature*, abstracted into repetitions of *form* can be discerned in the works. He has a *spiritual* curiosity about cosmos and *nature*, which led him to portray objects in their pure and essential *forms*, expressed through his viscosity *prints*.

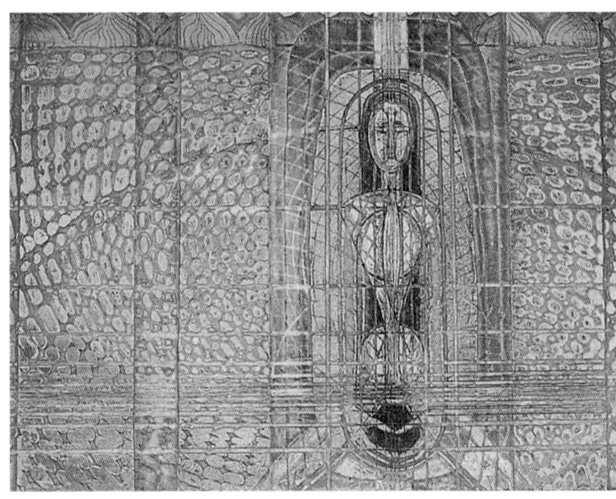

Reddy, Krishna N.: "The Woman of Sunflower", *Colour Engraving* 1995, 35x45 cm.

He lives and works in New York. Refer *Biting in*, *Viscosity Printmaking*.

Reddy, P.T. (1915–1997) b. Karimnagar, AP. Education: GDA in *drawing*, *painting* & *architecture JJSA*, *Madras School of Art* & *NKM*. Solos: *Artists' Centre* Bombay, Art Society Salon, Over 14 solos in Mumbai, New Delhi, Kolkata, Chennai, Lucknow & Hyderabad. Retrospective: 1935–79 Delhi, Lucknow, Mumbai, Chennai, Bangalore & Kolkata. Participa-tions: *Triennale* & National *LKA* New Delhi, Simla Art Society, *AFA* Kolkata, AP, Sculptor's Forum of India *BAS*, HAS; International: *Biennale* & Art Festival UK, Japan, Exhibitions Australia, Germany, USSR, USA, Sweden & Switzerland. Awards: Dolly Cursetjee & Mayo Scholarship for *murals*, Gold Medal HAS & AP *LKA* Hyderabad, Amritsar Art Society, *AFA* Kolkata, Simla Art Society *Silver* & *Bronze BAS*, Scholarship & Fellow *JJSA*. Appointments: In film industry, printing press. Publications: P.T. Reddy's Art Museum Hyderabad, *Drawings paintings* & *sculptures*, 40 *Drawings*, *Monograph* & 40 years of P.T. Reddy. Collections: P.T. Reddy's Art Museum Hyderabad, HAS, *SJM;* International: UK, USA, USSR, Japan, Germany, France, Australia, Greece, Rome, Iran.

P.T. Reddy's *landscapes* have the brilliant *colour* division of *post-impressionism*. However it is the *art* of *Ajanta*, miniatures and *folk art* that *form* the backbone of his *art*. Since 1967, he had concentrated on the neo-tantric *form* of *art* of which he was one of the most forceful exponents. His approach to TANTRA was holistic and not merely superficial. However he interpreted rather than imitated the traditional TANTRA philosophy and *iconography* in *terms* of his own work dealing with *contemporary themes*. He used *acrylics*, *watercolours*, *pen*, *ink* and *oils*. He lived and worked in Hyderabad.

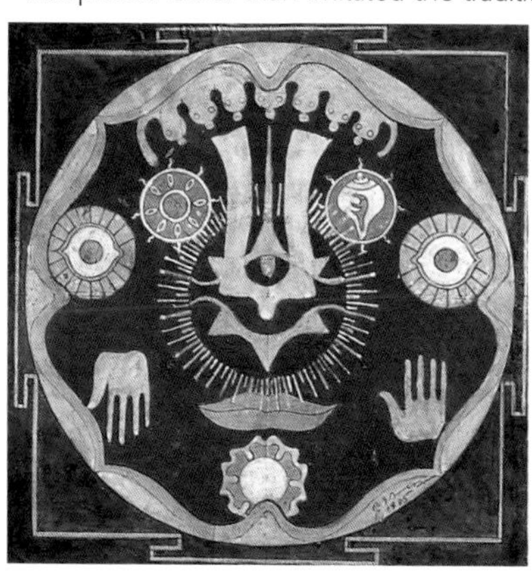

Reddy, P.T.: "*Painting*", 1985.

Reddy, Ravinder G. (1956–) Suryapet, AP. Education: B.A. & M.A. in *sculpture FFA* (*MSU*), Dip. in *art* & *design* Goldsmith College of Art London, Short course certificate in *ceramics* RCA. Solos: *Art Heritage* New Delhi, MMB Hyderabad, *SG* Bangalore & Chennai, CAG Ahmedabad, CCAG, *JAG*. Group participations: Timeless Art & *SG* Mumbai, *NGMA* New Delhi, *JAG*, HAS, *BAS*, *Biennale BB;* International: London, Australia. *Art* workshops & camps: *Sculptors* camp Ahmedabad, *LKA* Regional Centre Chennai, HG, *BB*, *wood carving* Vishakhapatnam. *Auction*: Sotheby's-Timeless Art Mumbai. Awards: National *LKA* & *NGMA* New Delhi, Ahmedabad. Scholarship: British Council UK. Fellowship: For *terracotta* & *ceramics* Junior & Senior Fellowship Dept. of Culture, Govt. of India New Delhi. Member: Faculty member & Assistant Dir. Kanoria Center for Arts Ahmedabad. Appointments: Visiting teachers School of *Architecture* Ahmedabad; Reader in *Sculpture* Dept. of FA. & Later Chairman Board of Studies Dept. of FA. Andra University Visakapatnam. Collections: National *LKA* & *NGMA* New Delhi; V&A London.

Ravinder G. Reddy's *sculptures* appear almost iconic in his use of large staring and brilliant eyes; though the *colours* sometimes looked unnatural. His females have a dexterous energy in their alertness, the *nudes* not titillating, but appearing sculptural in their *frontality*. *Clay* and *fibreglass* as a *medium*, helps him to visualize the physical presence of his work. He expresses his sensibilities, feelings and his reactions to present day situations through his *contemporary* renderings of the human *figure*.

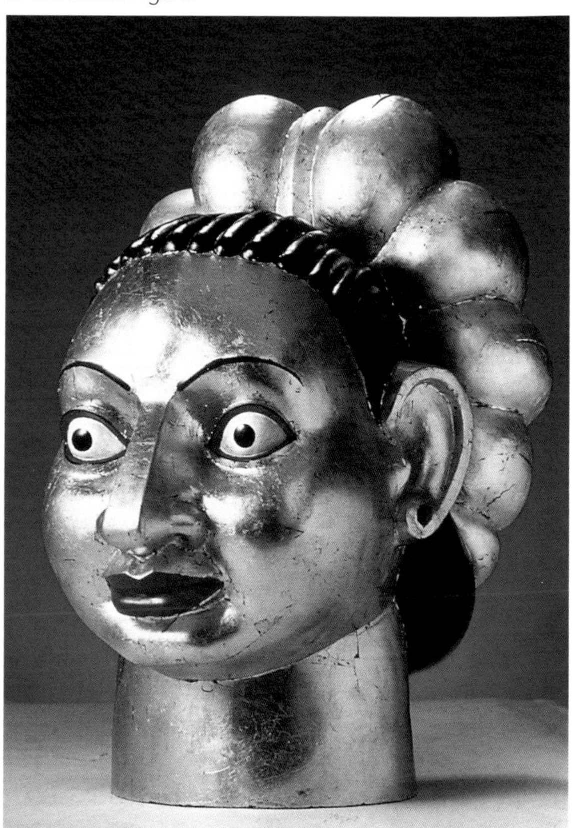

Reddy, Ravinder G.: "Head of The Gold Flower", Fiber Glass, 1996 28ht.x18wth.x25depth cm.

Reghu, G. (1959–) b. Kilimanoor, Kerala. Education: B.FA. College of Art Thiruvananthapuram in *sculpture*. Solos: *Art Heritage* & GC New Delhi, *SG* & Kala-Yantra Bangalore, Kanoria Center for Arts Ahmedabad, *JAG*. Group participations: *Images Art Gallery* Bangalore, *Roopankar Museum BB Biennale*, *VAG*, *LCAG*, *BAS*, *JAG;* National Exhibition: Chennai, New Delhi & Lucknow. *Art* camps: *LKA*, New Delhi, All India Sculpture *Roopankar BB*, *GAC*. Awards: *Biennale* Bhopal, *Roopankar BB*. Fellowship: HRD Govt. Fellowship. Collections: *NGMA*, RB New Delhi, MP Vidhan Sabha Bhavan Bhopal, *Roopankar Museum*.

G. Reghu uses *distortion* in a creative *manner*, while creating his strange humanoid creatures out of *clay*. Details, perhaps outlining a costume, or highlighting a piece of jewellery or straps going in and out of the outer *clay* fabric enliven his stolid, semi-bold creatures. They come in all shapes and *sizes*, their gestures oddly human in their playful grouping. Some of the *figures* are *assemblages* of fragmented body parts which can be interlinked or viewed independently. This fragmentation is especially useful while firing—considering the small *size* of the *kiln*.

Presently working in Bhopal, MP and Bangalore.

Relief 1. It is a sculptural *composition* that projects from a flat surface. It can either be low relief—in which the *composition* projects very slightly or *high relief*—where the *design* is raised high enough, so that it appears almost detached from the *background*. In India the relief work is seen first in the Indus Valley seals of steatite with life like representations of bulls, unicorns and Yogis. Later relief work becomes almost detached from the back wall as in the case of the Sanchi SHALEBHANJIKA. Relief work is an intrinsic part of temples and CHAITYAS, the *style* changing with the region and the age. **2.** A three-dimensional *illusion* was created in *drawing* and *painting* either in a *composition*, *still life*, *figurative* or a *landscape*. This was coloured in *grisaille*, leading to the *illusion* of a sculptural relief. Refer *Realism*, *Realistic*—with illustrations. **3.** Blind *embossing* also gives the effect of relief in *printmaking*—Refer *Relief printing*. Refer *Bas-Relief*, *Block Printing*, *Buddhist Art*, *Chisels*, *Collography*, *Constructivism*, *Continuous Representation*, *Depth*, *Dimension*, *Egyptian Art*, *Elephanta*, *Found Object*, *Fret Pattern*, *Fretwork*, *Frottage*, *Gandharan Art*, *Graphic Prints*, *Low Relief*, *Illusionism*, *Impasto*, *Indus Valley Civilization*, *Neo-Plasticism*, *Roman Art*, *Satish Gujral*, *Lalitha Lajmi*, *Sisir Sahana*, *Vishwanath M. Sholapurkar*, *K. Venkatappa;* Illustration—*Embroidery*, KAILASH, KAILASA, *Repousse*, *Shanti Dave*, *Shankar Nandagopal*, *Krishna N. Reddy*.

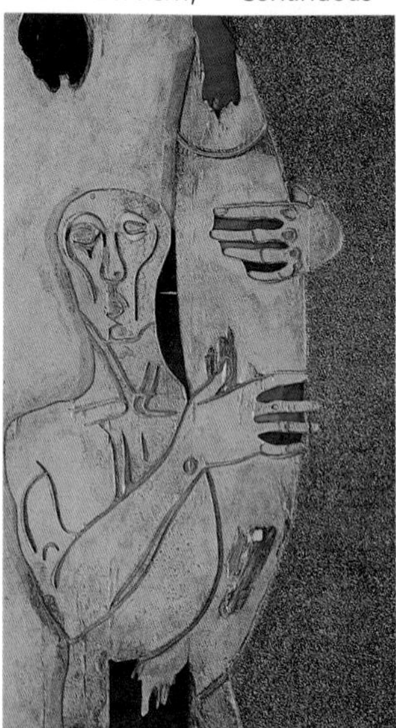

Relief: *Piraji Sagara*
"Man with Fish" *Wood Relief*
1970, 175x99 cm.

Relief Painting Refer *Collage*, *Enamel*, *Fat over lean*, *Impasto*, *Relief*.

Relief Printing A process of taking *prints* of an *image* created in a *relief form*, the areas, which are not to be printed, being cut back to a lower level. Materials used are *wood*, linoleum, *metal*. It has a variation in its *relief texture* as the printing *base*/block differs. Refer *Block Printing*, *Collography*, *Copper*, *Etching*, *Engraving*, *Frottage*, *Graphic*, *Ground*, *Intaglio*, *Linocut*, *Media*, *Metal Cut*, *Multiple Tool*, *Photo-engraving*, *Photo-etching*, *Photogravure*, *Printmaking*, *Single Block Colour Printing*, *V Tool*, *White Line Engraving*, *Wood Block Printing*, *Wood Engraving*, *Nandalal Bose*, *Mukul Chandra Dey*, *Somnath Hore*, *Paul A. Koli*, *Lalitha Lajmi*, *Basabendranath Tagore*, *Gaganendranath Tagore*, *Subhogendra Tagore;* Illustrations— *Rm. Palaniappan*, *Krishna N. Reddy*, *Anupam Sud*, *Wood Cut*, *Wood Cut Printing—Sudhir R. Khastgir*.

Relief Sculpture A *sculpture* made in a *relief form*. This method was used to prepare the *Mohenjo Daro* seals. The *relief sculptures* found at the Deogarh temple are theatrical with an *illusion* of *depth* and *space*. Sculptural *reliefs* of the *rock-cut cave* temples and *temple architecture* are decorated with flying mythological *figures*. The "continuous narration" method of *carving* is used in low *relief* and *high relief*. The *modern sculptor* has continued to use relief-work both in making *sculptures* and well as *mixed media compositions*. Refer *Brass*, *Chisels*, CHOLA, *Continuous Representation*, *Iron*, KAILASH, KAILASA, *Roman Art*, *Repousse*, *Ashutosh Museum of Indian Art*, *Ravinder G. Reddy*, *R.B. Bhaskaran*, *Reddeppa M. Naidu*; Illustrations—*Abu-Dilwara Group of Temples*, KAILASH, KAILASA, KAMA-SUTRA, *Terracotta*.

Renaissance (Italian/French) The Renaissance can be defined as the revival of *classical* ideas in the fields of *art*, literature, *architecture*, philosophy and social *culture*. Italy is the acknowledged birthplace of the Renaissance, though it quickly spread all over Europe and England. However, the Classicism inspired revival did not occur before the early 15th century with the humanist writings of L.B. Alberti echoed in the works of Masaccio (*painter*), Brunelleschi (architect) and Donatello (*sculptor*). Therefore, the period circa 1420–1500 is now termed Early Renaissance, which included *classical* studies in the fields of: human *anatomy*, the science of *perspective*, *classical* or Greco-Roman *architecture*, achieving balanced *harmony* and fidelity towards the physical rather than *spiritual* aspect of life and *art*. High Renaissance period of circa 1500–1530 started with *artists* like Leonardo de Vinci, Michelangelo Buonarroti and S. Raphael who achieved mastery and absolute control of their *techniques*, achieving a *classical* balanced *harmony* and elimination of superfluous details. Michelangelo's work was to be not only the culmination of the high point of the Renaissance, but also the fertile, breeding ground for *Mannerism*. Other *artists* associated with Renaissance: Botticelli, and Titian in Italy, Albrecht & Durer in Germany. In India the Bengal Movement (19th & 20th century) is also referred to as Indian Renaissance, reflecting the cultural efflorescence that took place in the Indian Society with the rising middle class asserting their tastes over wealthy, westernized upper classes. Renaissance is the turning point, at which no distinction between *fine arts* and *applied art* existed. Refer *Anatomy*, *Bengal School*, *Chiaroscuro*, *Christian Art*, *Closed Form*, *Fresco*, *Gothic*, *Transition*, *Polychromatic Sculpture*, *One-Point Perspective*, *Neo-Classicism*, *Mannerism*,

Asit K. Haldar, Maharaja Fatesingh Museum, Rabindra Bharati Museum (RBM) (Kolkata).

Renaissance Gallery (RG) (Bangalore) was established in 1993 and specializes in *exhibitions* of *contemporary* Indian *art*. It has about 850 sq.ft. of floor *space* with a wide glass frontage. RG holds curated shows in addition to the usual *exhibitions* where *G.S. Shenoy*, *Rekha Rao*, *Yashawant Shirwadkar* have exhibited. RG also has ample storage *space* to stock works of *artists*.

Replica An exact *copy* of a *painting* or *sculpture* or any work of *art*, prepared by the original *artist* or a *copy* made under his supervision. Replicas played an important role in popularizing *art* among the wealthy Indians. In the early part of 20th century, *engravings* and *copies* of *old masters* filtered through to elevate "native taste". *Copies* of the popular European/ Indian *artists'* works were in great demanded in the early 19th and 20th century. Refer *Mask*, *School of....*

Repousse (French)=pushed back. A *form* of *relief sculpture* in which sheets of *metal* are beaten into shape, by means of hammering from the back, so that certain portions of the sheet stand up in *relief*. Also termed *embossing*. Refer *Annealing, Cold Working, Copper, Polychromatic Sculpture, Chandrakant N. Mhatre, K. Jayapala Panicker, Nagesh Bhimrao Sabannavar*.

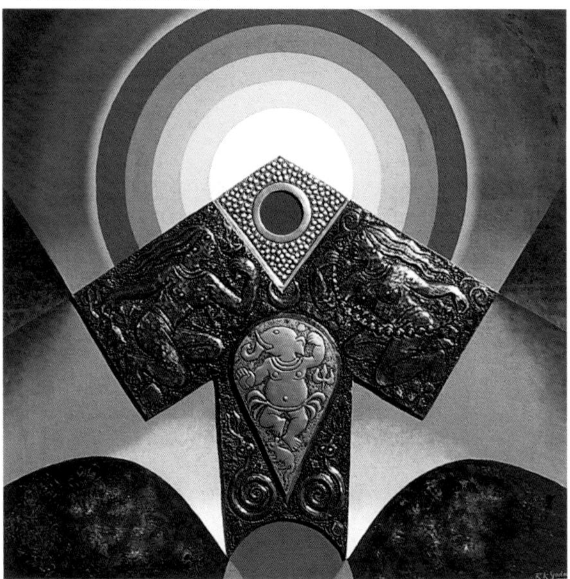

Repousse: *Ram Kishore Yadav*, "Worship of Ganesa", *Mixed media*.

Reproduction 1. A *copy* of a work of *art* made through mechanical means i.e. *oleography*, photography, *casting*, printing, photocopy and scanning. **2.** In case of *craft* objects, i.e. furniture, *ceramics*, textiles, or metalware, the word refers to an accurate *copy* of respective period piece.

The *compositions* at the *Ajanta* caves were rediscovered in 1819, and subsequently frequent visits were made by *artists* and students from Bombay School of *arts* in and around 1875 (now *JJSA*) and *Santiniketan*, especially *Nandalal Bose* and *Mukul Chandra Dey* for the purpose of reproducing the *frescoes*. *Pestonjee Bomanjee* spent twelve years in reproducing the *frescoes* at *Ajanta*. *Jaganath M. Ahivasi* was commissioned by *LKA* to *copy frescoes* from Badami & Sittanvasal. Refer *Anatomy, Modern Review, Multi Block Colour Printing, Pouncing, Ready-Made, Replica, Variant, Muhammed Abdur Rehman Chughtai, Vivan Sundaram, Gaganendranath Tagore, Raja Ravi Varma—Oleography*.

Restoration It means any action taken in order to try to return the object, as far as possible, to its *original* physical and *aesthetic* state. It attempts to rectify the results of deterioration. It has a limited purpose. Refer *Conservation, CIMA Gallery*, INTACH, *Vasudeo Adurkar, Prateep Ghosh, Kailash Chandra Sharma, Ved Pal Sharma;* Refer article "*Preservation of Art Objects*" by *O.P. Agrawal*, p. 383.

Revivalist Movement Refer *Artist Groups, Bengal Revivalism, Bengal School, Calcutta School, Modernism, Modern Movement, Neo-Classicism, Atul Bose*.

Rhythm A *pattern* or sequence of regular, repetitive sounds, movements or in the case of *visual arts*, shapes or *colours*, i.e. *lines* as well as *forms* or brushstrokes, which are rhythmic.

Indian *art* cultivates a subtle and sensitive understanding of rhythm and *harmony*. RAGA, especially when rendered by an expert, has the power to evoke in the listener, the rhythm as well as certain *visual imagery*. These *images* are created in the poetic sensitivity of *folk art* with linear *outlines* and *miniature paintings* with its rhythmic *pattern* in the movement of the leading and individual subjects of the *compositions*. Earlier, these were seen in the sculptural *forms* right from the 1st century. BUDDHA *sculpture*. The *contemporary* Indian *artist's* choice of *colours* bordered on the adventurous, while the *figures* added the essential touch of rhythm in the works. Yet others created *painting* and *sculpture* by mixing elements of *naive art* with folk rhythms, myths, *legends* in *compositions form*, *motifs* and scraps of *metals* welded together to create linear rhythms. Refer *Baroque, Calligraphy, Constructivism, Folk Inspiration, Shobha Broota, Vinod Dube, V. Hariram, Saroj Jain, Sailoz Mookerjea, Shankar Nandagopal, Balan Nambiar, Laxman Pai, D.P. Sibal, Premalatha Hanumanthiah Seshadri, V. Viswanadhan*.

Rig-Veda The most ancient and original of the four VEDAS, Rig-vedas were composed and transmitted orally, starting in circa 5000–2500 BC. It is a series of hymns reflecting mystical doctrines; which reveal faith in the elements, as well as simple concerns about the nomadic, *pastoral* life of Aryans in the early stages of their social evolution. The legendary stories of the *gods* in Rig-Veda and the Supernatural power are still the favoured *themes* of many Indian *artists* today. Refer *Erotic Art, Hinduism, Khajuraho, Legend, Metal*.

Ritu Literally meaning season. The earliest expressions of the six seasons of the year, which were based on the work Ritu-Samhara of poet Kalidas; and later described poetically by

Keshavadasa and Bihari. They are illustrated in *miniature painting* in sets of six, each depicting a particular season, as in Vasant (Spring), Grishma (Summer), Varsha (Rainy season), Sharad (Autumn), Hemanta (early winter), Shishir (late winter).

The mood of each season and climate change is accurately captured through festivities and celebrations. The festival of HOLI, with all its excitement, singing, dancing and smearing of *colour* and coloured water, heralds the arrival of Vasanta Ritu (spring season).

Art works about Grishma Ritu shows the sun beating down on a parched earth, while the divine lovers, RADHA and KRISHNA cool themselves in a pool under a large shady tree. etc. Refer *Ritual*, *Laxman Pai*.

Ritual (Kriya in Sanskrit) It refers to a ceremony or procedure (usually religious in nature) followed at certain times or for special occasions. In India, the entire span of human life, from birth to death, is marked by the appropriate rites. In its earliest *form*, ritual *art* was associated with the forces of *nature* and thus led to *nature*–worship. This was true, not just for India, but for the whole world. Evidence of tree-worship is depicted in some of the Indus Valley seals. Trees were also closely associated with Buddhism and Jainism. The Buddha is often represented in *relief sculptures* as being born under the Sal tree and gaining enlightenment under the Bodhi tree (Pipal [Ficus] tree).

The Sun (SURYA) and the Moon (CHANDRA) are worshipped as *gods*/ goddesses in many parts of the world. In India, in addition, AGNI or the *God* of Fire is associated with every rite that is performed. At times, AGNI is represented with raven tongues (referring to the tongues of flame). Illustration–AGNI.

Several rituals accompanied the initiation of a son into his father's occupation. This was true for Chitrakaras (*painters*), Shilpakaras (*sculptors*) and Vaasthukaras (architects) as well. *Iron* and *bronze* vessels were used to *cast* ritual vessels and *icons* of SHIVA and VISHNU. The rituals, ceremonies and festivals associated with the twelve months were beautifully rendered by the painters of the BARAMASA and the Ritu-Samhara (RITU). Painted and carved *masks* were also used during rituals to represent one's dead ancestors and various *gods* and goddesses. Refer *Art Education*, *Cire Perdue*, *Metal*, *Mural*, PURANA, *Sand Painting*, TANTRA, VEDA, YANTRA, *Shanti Dave*, *Kanayi Kunhiraman*, *Balan Nambiar*, *Saroj Gogi Pal*, *Kapu Rajaiah*, *Jehangir Sabavala*, *K.S. Sherigar*, *Rajendar Tiku*, *Radhika Vaidyanathan*; Illustration–*Folk Art*.

Rock-Cut Excavated from living rock. Medieval Indian temples were often hewn out of living rock, the excavation taking place from the top downwards. The sculptural decorations and architectural members were thus worked on in situ. The walls were sometimes prepared for *fresco* and then painted. Refer *Carving*, *Dravidian Style*, *Ellora*, *Elephanta*, *Gandharan Art*, *Mahabalipuram*, *Maurya Dynasty*, PALLAVAS, *Pallava Dynasty*, *Pictorial*, *Relief Sculpture*, *Visual*; Illustrations–*Ajanta*, CHAITYA, KAILASH, KAILASA, GANDHARVAS.

Roman Art Roman civilization extended from around 400 BC to AD 500. They became more powerful since the decline of brilliant Greek civilization after 5th century BC, and grew to a vast empire. The Romans had less concern for individual beauty of *form*, and more for its function, characterized by *monumental size*, massive and ornate columns and large inner *spaces*, unobstructed by *supports*. An innovative Roman structural system (used by the Indians, in the *Gupta* Period) was the arch system. This was seen typically in many of their major public works, as compared to the Colosseum in Rome, and in the famous arched bridge-aqueducts. The Romans used to commemorate war victories, in *relief sculpture* by the "continuous narration" method. e.g. Trajan's column, and *reliefs* from Ara Pacis Augustae, in Rome. It was the sense of *classical Realism*, which the Romans excelled in, especially in the *art* of sculpted *portraits* and full figurative *compostions*. Wall *frescoes* of mythological or literary scenes such as those seen at Pompeii, Herculaneum and Rome were the main kind of *paintings*. Romans used *perspective* to give *relief*, *depth* and three-dimensional effects, but they rarely made *portrait paintings* from real life. With their all-conquering sprees, the Romans left their influence on most ports of Europe, Asia Minor and Britain. In *architecture* especially, Roman Art enjoyed a new lease of life as Romanesque *architecture*. Churches were built in this *style* through out Europe, and after the British inroads into India, in India and the east as well. The plan of the church itself is taken from the Roman basilica. Thus Roman Art enjoys a lease of life even today, all over the world. Refer *Antique*, *Byzantine Art*, *Gandharan Art*, *Gothic*, *Greek Art*, *Maharaja Fatesingh Museum* (Vadodara), *Mural*, *Nationalism in Art*, *Neo-Classicism*, *Renaissance*, *Jehangir Sabavala;* Illustrations–*Still Life*, *Terracotta*, *Sakti Burman*, *Ganpatrao K. Mhatre*.

Romanticism At its height in the early 19th century, Romanticism was a revolt against the formality and intellectual discipline of the *neo-Classicism*. In a more positive and important aspect, it expresses individuality and commitment to feeling. It resulted in works of varying *techniques* and *styles*–e.g. J. Constable's pre-Impressionist *landscapes*, J.M.W. Turner's forays into abstraction, C.D. Friedrich's mystical expressions, and E. Delacroix's dramatic overtures. In general, Romanticism was an insistence on the rights of the imagination.

In India, it influenced the *Bengal School artists*, who adapted it with Japanese *wash techniques*, Ukiyo-e & Chinese *calligraphy*. Refer *Calligraphic Painting*, *Chinese Art*, *Japanese Art*, *Neo-Classicism*, *Realism*, *Sakti Burman*, *Dhirendrakrishna Deb Barman*, *Tapan Ghosh*, *Chhaganlal R. Jadav*; Illustrations–*Sankho Chaudhuri*, *Sakti Burman*.

Roopankar Museum (Roopankar) (Bhopal). Roopankar of *BB*–Bhopal, MP set up by *J. Swaminathan*. Refer *Bharat Bhavan* (Bhopal).

Roy, Ananda Gopal (1947–) b. WB. Education: Dip. in *FA*. *GCAC* Kolkata; American University Kolkata for Research work in *painting;* Teacher's Training Appreciation Calcutta University. Solos: *BAAC* & *AFA* Kolkata, *LKA* & Annual Art Exhibition, New Delhi, *AIFACS*. Group participations: American University Center, *AFA* & *BAAC* Kolkata, *VBU KB Santiniketan*, National *LKA*, *AIFACS* New Delhi, Millennium Show *LKA*, *JAG*.

Workshop: American University Center Kolkata; Initiated "Calcutta Art Fair", & also the Jury Art Competitions in Kolkata. Collections: Delhi, Mumbai, *BAAC* Kolkata; International: Japan, Canada, England, Singapore.

Ananda Gopal Roy's *paintings* are the result of *time* and *space* viewed perceptually and coloured by *fantasy* with use of illusionist *colours*. The *colours* create a radiance and distance through his succinct placement of *images*. *Space* is an integral part of his *composition*. He sifts through elements from the past, metamorphosing them into visions of *nature*. There is also an element of naivete in his use of child-like *drawing*.

He lives in Kolkata.

Roy, Avijit (1962–) b. WB. Education: Dip. in *drawing* & *painting RBU*, Post-Dip. in *graphics*, *MSU;* Certificate, Teacher's Training, *Commercial art* Calcutta University, *Fresco painting Banasthali Vidyapith* RAJ. Solos & group shows: Air India-Art Gallery Kolkata, *JAG*, *LTG*, SRAG. Group participations: *AFA*, *LKA* & British Council Kolkata, British Council & *Art Heritage* New Delhi, National Exhibition, BAG, *CYAG*, *PG;* International: UK, Germany, Australia. *Art* workshop & camps: Kanoria Centre for Arts Ahmedabad, *AAJ* Udaipur, *BB*, *MSU* ; British & American Printmaker. Awards & Scholarships: Indian College of Arts, All India Exhibition Kolkata, Bendre-Husain Award Mumbai, *LKA Garhi* New Delhi, *BAS*, *AIFACS*, *Biennale BB;* Junior Fellowship HRD Ministry & Dept. of Culture Govt. of India, *LKA* RAJ; International: Charles Wallace Indian Trust Fellowship UK, India Duchland Cultural Exchange Programme Germany. Collections: Godrej Mumbai, *LKA* New Delhi & Kolkata, *Roopankar BB*; International: Galleries in USA & Dubai, pvt. & corporates.

Avijit Roy is a printmaker, *painter* and *sculptor*, using the *form* of the bull to unleash violence. His lithographs are marked with a nervous vitality of *line* and energy i.e. expressionistic in force. His *sculptures* partake of this same readiness of action that characterizes his *prints*. He has also rendered *landscapes* in *paint*.

He is from Noida, WB.

Roy, Gopen (1920–) b. WB. Education: Grad. in *art GCAC* Kolkata reference *Mukul Chandra Dey*, *Atul Bose* & Romen Chakraborty. Solos: About 40 solos in Kolkata, Mumbai & New Delhi a stretch of 52 years, some at *AFA*, *ISOA* & his own Gallery "Rupkatha Art Gallery" Kolkata. Member: Vice President *ISOA;* Editor of the Journal of *ISOA*. Publications: Govt. of WB & *ISOA* subject New Dolls, Natun Putul, Anubhutir Roop, Graphics of Romen Chakraborty, Nakshi-Kantha, Classi-cal Art & Design of India in *modern* life, Indian traditional *design*.

His *paintings* are based on traditional Indian *art*. Some of his works have an element of *fantasy* as they are influenced by the fables and folk stories of his native Bengal. His *drawing* is rhythmic though stylized and is similar to the Bengal *style* of subtle *wash paintings*. He has also worked on *designs* for textiles.

Roy, Jamini (1887–1972) b. Bankura, Dist., WB. Education: Joined *GSAC* Kolkata, Grad. with European *techniques* of *painting*, learned *classical nudes* & *oil paintings*, 1921 New *style* inspired by folk sources. Solos: Exhibitions: *ISOA* & his own residence; International: London, New York; Experimented: 1925–1930s, *Bazaar painting* & sold them at the Kalighat temple in Kolkata; Returned to his Bengal country-side. Workshop: Started one on the artisanal principle. *Auctions*: Heart, Osian's, Bowring's—Mumbai, Sotheby's, Heart & Bowring's New Delhi, Bonham's, Christie's, Sotheby's—London, Christie's, Sotheby's New York, Christie's Hong Kong. Award: Elected Fellow *LKA* 1956; Hon.: State Award Padma Bhushan 1955. Publications: *LKA* New Delhi Lalit Kala Contemporary—2 & 3, *Bazaar painting* of Calcutta, "Jamini Roy" *LKA* 1973 reprinted 1987, Seminar Papers "Jamini Roy" *LKA* New Delhi 1992, Earlier Indian & Modern Art W.G. Archer on Jamini Roy-John Irwin & Bishnu Dey *ISOA*, catalogues *AFA* Samir Datta & Ranu Mookerjee Kolkata; International journals—"The Studio" & "Newsweek". Collections: *NGMA*, *LKA* & *Delhi Art Gallery* New Delhi, His residence & *Indian Museum* Kolkata, *CKAG*; International: New York, Europe, Chester & Davida Herwitz Trust collections USA & Trustees of the V&A.

Jamini Roy's exposure to the world of *folk art* was right since his childhood. He was born in Bankura village—with its *traditions* of folk *pottery*. His studies in the school were academic and he excelled at *painting landscapes* and *composition* in the impressionistic and post-Impressionistic *manner*. It was at 34 that he broke away from academicism to get back to his roots. The folk *tradition* of Bankura, his *empathy* for Bengal *crafts* like Kanthas (cloth quilting) Pata (scroll & panel *painting*) and Alpanas (floor *painting*) along with his knowledge of the Kalighat *painters* (who painted at KALI temples) was to lead the way to a new *style* that successfully amalgamated all the above ingredients, fleshing it with his use of home-made *pigments* and gum, including crushed rocks and tamarind seeds. His *palette* is emphatic without being clamorous, fine grained and chalky but not glossy or sleek. His *images* are simple. From 1935 to 1950, he painted *landscapes*, the *themes* painted were about people he saw around him—Santhals and the women with their children and singers. Mother and child *compositions*, including women going to the temple, the *symbolic* life of Christ from 1940 to 1970. Often worked in *drawings* as well as mythological characters e.g. RAMA and Sita, KRISHNA and Balarama,

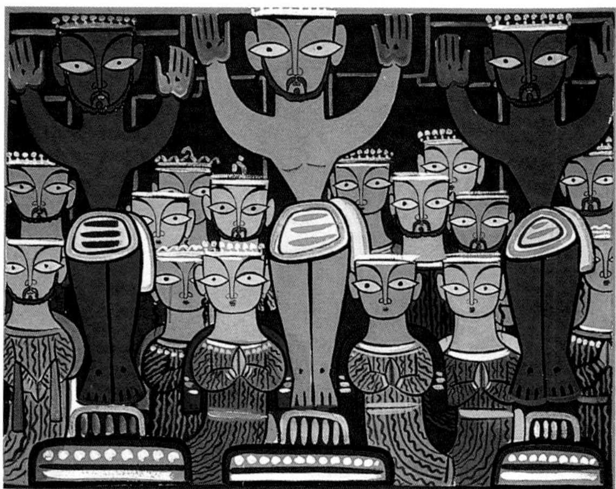

Roy, Jamini: "Crucifixion", *Tempera* on Cloth, 88.5x68.5 cm.

SHIVA and PARVATI and a series of animals in the decorative toy *form*. His *colours* are flat, with sweeping motion of textured *hues* among floral *motifs*. His mature *style* is marked by *frontality* and a simplification of *form* with attention to decorative detail with *lines* being echoed in subtler *shades*. He also worked as a *sculptor*, mostly in *wood*, his *themes* being rooted in the myths of his native village. Refer *Kalighat Pat*.

Roy, Sajal (1935–) b. Kolkata. Education: Dip. in *FA*. ICA&D Kolkata. Over 12 solos: Kolkata in *painting, drawing, graphics* & *gouache* from 1964–1993; International: Germany. Group participations: *AFA* from 1958–1965 & later, WBSA, *BAAC* &*LKA* Kolkata, 100 *artists* at *Delhi Art Gallery* & RB New Delhi, *JAG & NCAG, Biennale* Chandigarh Sahitya Parishad Kerala, AP *LKA*, Jadavpur University, Rashtriya *LKA*, Art Age & Young Artists' Society New Delhi; International: Texas USA, Germany & Berlin. Participated in seminar & conferences. Workshop: In Indo-German Artist's workshop Kolkata. *Auctions*: Christie's & Sotheby's London. Awards: "Indian Drawing" *Biennale* Chandigarh. Member: Academy Sketch Club, *AFA;* President Charukala Shilpi Sanstha 1968–74, Executive member *AFA*. Appointments: Part-time lecturer on *painting (applied art) RBU* 1985–1986; Examiner & paper setter GCAC Tripura, Jury WB State *FA*. Exhibition Govt. of WB. Publications: Newspapers, weekly magazines. Collections: *BAAC* Kolkata, Kerala Sahitya Parishad, other pvt. & public in India & abroad.

Sajal Roy tries to bare his inner psyche for the outside world through his *paintings*. There is an element of the dramatic in his use of distorted, grotesque *forms*. His *style* has evolved from a cubist *distortion* to *caricature* to a *monumental figuration* in the 90s. His *colours* are both muted and strident, with *texture* being an integral feature of the *painting*.

Roy, Shekhar (1957–) b. Kolkata. Education: Grad. *GCAC* Kolkata. Solos: *AFA* Kolkata, *G88, JAG, GE*. Group participations: British Council, *AFA*, Sanskriti, *BAAC* & Exhibition of *painting* with *Maqbool Fida Husain* Tata Centre Kolkata, Eastern Regional Art & *LKA* New Delhi, GAG, *G88, GK, JAG, AIFACS;* International: Germany. *Art* camps & workshop: Attended in Kolkata & New Delhi. Collections: *NGMA, LKA* & CMC New Delhi, pvt. & corporates, New Delhi, Mumbai & abroad.

Shekhar Roy's works reveal a successful mixture of *tradition* and his own individual persona, reacting to the life and the world around him. There is an element of *fantasy*, the formal and thematic *content* of the works expressing the *artist's* constant wandering. Reality in the *form* of social perception is also present in the works. His *colours* have an otherworldly effect in his use of blues and browns, highlighting *forms* floating in an underwater world.

He lives in Kolkata.

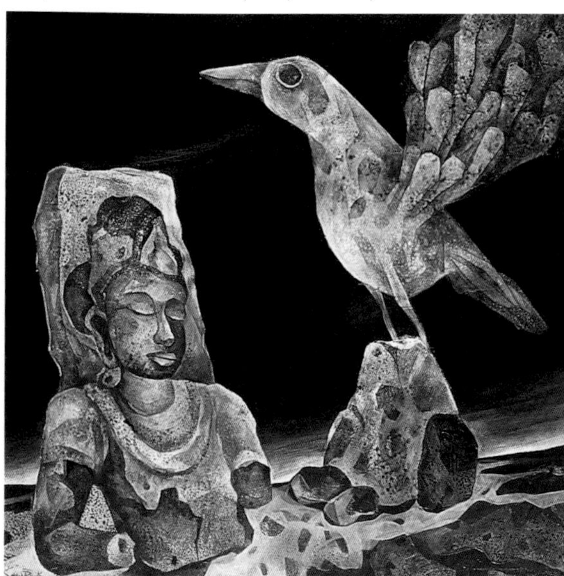

Roy, Shekhar: "Painting".

Roy, Suhas (1936–) b. Dacca, Bangladesh. Education: Dip. in FAC ICA&D Kolkata; *Graphic art* Atelier 17 Paris, ENSBA. Solos: *CKAG*, GAG, *Dhoomimal*. Group participations: WBSA, *CIMA*, Group 8, *AFA, BAAC* Kolkata, *LKA* in India, *CKP, Triennale* New Delhi, *SCA, Dhoomimal*; International: Prague, Paris, *Biennale* Tokyo, Exhibition of Indian Art Yugoslavia, Romania, Czechoslovakia & Hungary, *Graphics* Exhibition Poland. *Auctions*: Sotheby's & Helpage India New Delhi. Awards: ICA&D, WB Academy & *BAAC* Kolkata, *AIFACS*. Member: *SCA*. Appointments: Prof. & HoD of *Painting, KB, VBU*. Collection: *NGMA* & *LKA* New Delhi, *BAAC* Kolkata, PUJ Museum, *CYAG* Ministry of Eternal Affairs, pvt. & corporates, national & international: Japan, Germany, USA.

Suhas Roy is essentially a romanticist, introducing lyrical views of *nature* in his *paintings*. Plants, grass, flowers and birds find a place in his *paintings*. He has experimented with women. These ladies are not glamorous creatures, but have a certain innocence in their direct yet soft gaze. He saturates

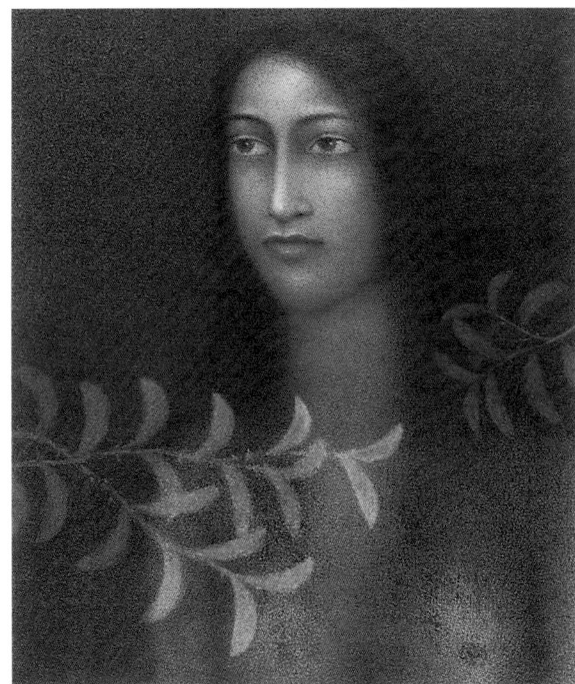

Roy, Suhas: "Radha", *Acrylic* on *Canvas*, 1995.

Realism with an electric change of the Romantic, semi-mystical *fantasy*, whereby his *imagery* of voluptuous long-tressed RADHAS entwined by floral vines reflects a sensual yet redolent vision.

He lives and works in Kolkata.

RoyChowdhury, Anita (1938–) b. Kolkata. Education: Qualified *GCAC* Kolkata. Solos: *AFA* & *BAAC* Kolkata, ISCA, *AIFACS*, *SAI*. Group participations: AFA, *LKA* New Delhi, *AFA*, *BAAC* & Center Art Gallery Kolkata, *KB Santiniketan*, MMB Hyderabad & Mumbai, *RBU*, *G88*, *AIFACS*, *ISOA*, ISCA, *CKP*; International: Tokyo Japan. *Art* camps & workshops: MMB Kolkata; FAR 1999. Members: Calcutta Painters Kolkata, ISCA, FAR.

Anita RoyChowdhury paints the essence of present day society and its ethos. She ploughs an individual furrow, different from other *artists*. Her *images* are outlined in a flurry of coloured strokes, the flecks and *pictographs* suggesting a greater reality. She uses the viscousness of the *oil medium* to gently glide her *brush* over the isolated *figures*.

RoyChowdhury, Debi Prasad (1899–1975) b. Tejhat, now Bangladesh. Studied under the tutelage of *Abanindranath Tagore* & Signor Boiess, an Italian *painter* taught *life-drawing* & portraiture. Taught Western *style painting* at the ISOAS, at the same time learning *modelling* from Hiranmoy Roy Chowdhury; Practised in both the Indian *style* of *modern art* (as epitomized by the *Bengal School*) & Western *technique* (as in *Impressionism*). *Auctions*: Heart–Mumbai & New Delhi. Awards: Among his many awards are an MBE from the British Govt., a D.Litt. (Hon.) by *RBU* and the Padma Bhushan; He was also the first Chairman of the *LKA*. Appointments: 1929 Principal of the Madras School of Arts and Crafts (*Madras School of Arts*) Chennai, post he held on for 30 years, in the course became one of India's more prominent *sculptor-painters*. Publications: in the *Prabasi* & *Modern Review*. Collections: *NGMA* & *LKA* New Delhi, H.K. Kejriwal Bangalore, *SJM*, *CKP*, several national & international *museums* & *sculptures* in public places in New Delhi, Kolkata, Chennai & Patna.

Debi Prasad RoyChowdhury started *painting* mythological subjects in the *wash technique*, with flowing sensitive *lines* and flat *tones*. Later he mastered both the study of *anatomy* and Western *technique*, combining them to create *realistic portraits* and *figure* studies of startling nationalism. His *paintings* were bathed in *chiaroscuro* in a Rembrandt-like fashion but it is for his *sculptures* that he is better known. In the *manner* of Rodin and Bourdelle, he "built up" rather than "carved in" employing the masters impressionistic *handling* with great ease. *Clay* and *plaster of Paris* were handled with expertize in making *realistic portrait* heads of which those of Percy Brown and Sir Jagdish Chandra Bose are particularly significant. Later in Chennai, he *cast portraits* and *monumental* statues of several leading personalities including the Maharajas of Travancore and Cochin and several Governors of Chennai. He also did *portraits* from *photographs* of which those of Dr. Annie Besant, Mahatma Gandhi and Motilal Nehru are exceptional. His sculptural *compositions* (in the outdoor) are among one of its kind, being both original in outlook and execution. The Martyr's Memorial especially, 4m. high and 29m. wide with 11 *figures* is installed in front of the Red Fort, while the "Triumph of Labour" with its straining heaving bodies is at the *NGMA* New Delhi.

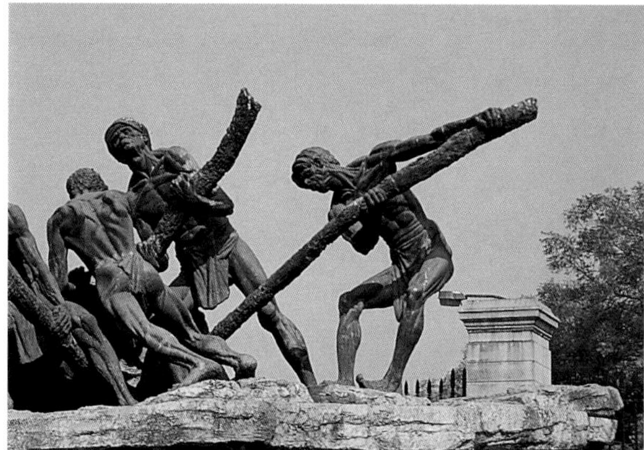

RoyChowdhury, Debi Prasad, " Triumph of Labour", *Bronze Sculpture.*

RoyChowdhury, Sarbari (1933–) b. East Bengal, Bangladesh. Education: Dip. in *sculpture GCAC* & Studied under Prodosh Gupta 1950 Kolkata, Post-Grad. *FFA* (*MSU*) under *Sankho Chaudhuri*, Studied Academy Belle Art Florence Italy. Solos: *Art Heritage* New Delhi, *SG* Chennai, *Dhoomimal*, *CYAG*; International: New York. Participated: All India Sculpture Exhibition New Delhi, *Biennale* Paris, *SG* Mumbai, *BAAC* Kolkata 1990–1992. Commissions: Works done in 1967 & 1971. Appointments: Prof. & HoD ICA&D Kolkata, Reader *Sculpture* Dept. *VBU* & Prof. at *KB University Santiniketan*. Collections: *NGMA* New Delhi; International: Henry Moore Collection UK, Alberto Giacommetti Paris, Madame Shenur Museum Florence.

Sarbari RoyChowdhury works exclusively with the *medium* of *bronze casting*. His works are almost always *figurative* with elements of abstraction creeping in quite strongly in the 70s, though the work is always grounded in reality. He began with sculpting *realistic portraits*, making several of prominent personalities. However it is of 1951 *portrait* titled "Gurudev" of *bronze* which is most exciting, because of the element of *caricature*. The influence of Henry Moore can be felt in several mid-career pieces, while the works of the 90s speak of fragmented views of reality. His recent works have an element of *fantasy* in the quaintness of the subject portrayed.

Rudra=howling, roaring, or angry. One of the NAVA-RASA'S or nine emotions, expressed in the early Indian *sculptures* at *Ellora*. The Vedic *god* of fury, father of the Rudras and Maruts (the sons), he was also identified with INDRA, AGNI and later with SHIVA; often invoked jointly as Rudra-Shiva. He is said to have sprung from BRAHMA's forehead and is likened to the dark smoke of the funeral pyres. Refer MUKUTA.

S

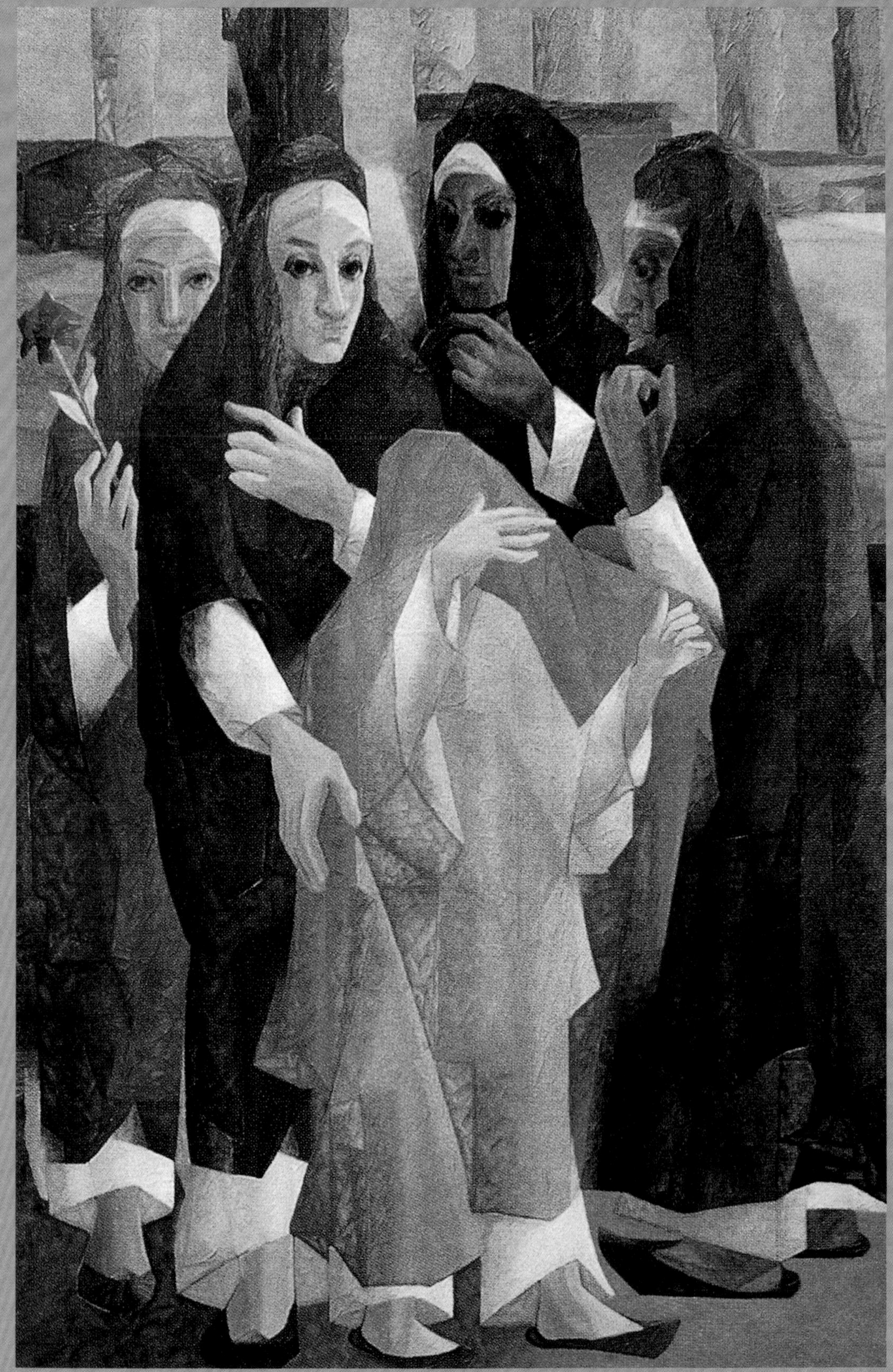

Sabavala, Jehangir: "The Rose", *Oil* on *Canvas*, 1981, 152x114 cm. (See notes on page 309)

Sabannavar, Nagesh Bhimrao (1925–2005) b. Belgaum KAR. Education: Junior B.A., Certificate in *Embossing* in *Metal* 1945 & Govt. Dip. in *painting* from *JJSA* and joined the teaching staff in Dept. of Lord Reay *Art* Workshop. Retrospective Solo: *NCAG*; Group participations: MAHA State Art Exhibitions. Awards: Several at MAHA State Art Exhibitions, KAR Rajya Prashasti. Publications: Edited article titled "Metal Work" for Marathi Vishwakosh 1976. Appointments: Designed and prepared mostly master-models for India Govt. Mint; Prepared Trophies for Sports, Trade Fair & Nehru Centre; Designed MAHA Gaurav Purashar Memento for Govt. of MAHA–1990. Commissions: *Silver* and *bronze* Trophy & plaque; Medal for the MAHA State Art Exhibition award, *Replica* of Meghadambari at Raigad in *bronze*.

Nagesh Bhimrao Sabannavar ex-Prof. and Head of Dept. of *Art* & Craft at *JJSA*, excelled in the *art* of repousse-work on *metal*, especially *copper*. His *images* of iconic *gods* and goddesses, both in the traditional decorative *manner* as well as in the stylized, *modern manner* show an attention to rhythmic detail and pleasing *harmony*. His master-models executed in *plaster of Paris* show the same attention to clarity of *line* and *form*. Sabannavar executed *designs* for several trophies, plaques and medallions in several *media* including *bronze*, *casting* and *wood*. He lived and worked in Mumbai. Refer *Tradition*, *Decorative Art*, *Style;* Illustrations–AGNI, MAKARA, Repousse.

Sabavala, Jehangir (1922–) b. Mumbai. Studied *JJSA*, Heatherly School of Art London, Academie Julien & Academie Andre Lhote Paris, AGC. Over 29 solos: Kolkata, Chennai, New Delhi, *Tao Art Gallery* Mumbai, *JAG*; International: Edinburgh, London. Group participations: National Exhibition, *Biennale*, *Triennale*, Art Mosaic CRY, *NGMA* & *LKA* New Delhi, MAHA State Exhibition, Art Trust & *NGMA* Mumbai, *CYAG*, *BAS*, *JAG*, other towns Ahmedabad, Chennai, Kolkata, Cochin, Bangalore, Pune; International: *Biennale* Venice, Commonwealth Art Festival London, "Asian Artists Today" at Fukuoka Art Museum Tokyo, other *exhibitions* in Paris, Sydney, Washington, Hong Kong, Boston, Teheran & London. *Auctions*: Osian's, Heart & Asprey's, Mumbai, Sotheby's & Christie's in Mumbai, New Delhi & London. Awards: Padma Shri 1977. Publications: "Sabavala"–Sadanga Series, "The Reasoning Vision"–Jehangir Sabavala's Painterly Universe, New Delhi; "Jehangir Sabavala" *LKA* New Delhi, "Pilgrim, Exile, Sorcerer"–The Painterly Evolution of Jehangir Sabavala by Ranjit Hoskote–1998; Articles published in newspapers and magazines, Talk on TV; Documentary Film in 1993. Collections: *NGMA* New Delhi, PUJ National Museum Chandigarh, TIFR; International: The National Gallery of South Australia Adelaide, Wycombe Abbey School England, pvt. & corporates.

Landscape has been a constant feature in Sabavala's career, though it has been interwoven with various phases, including that of academic portraiture, *figure* studies, *still lifes*, religious *compositions* and avian studies. His obsession with water, earth and the sky has an elemental, almost ritualistic quality. Stylistically he has evolved from academicism in the early part of his career to *self Impressionism* and later after his Paris soujourn, towards a stylized fusion of *Cubism* and *Impressionism*, highlighted by an attention to *classical balance* and *harmony*. Both *colour* and *light* emerge from his works in a subtle, poetic fusion of faceted strokes and delicately brushed whorls. While the early works pulsate with brilliant, prismatic *hues* and strong *colours* of "Roman Run" series; his recent works resonate with the interplay of *tones*, with as many as 50 *tones* of a single *colour* sometimes being used in one *painting*. The *figures* in his *figurative compositions* merge gracefully with the *landscape*, always being part of it, while in some *paintings* the birds sail serenely along with the clouds in the sky.

He lives and works in Mumbai. (See illustration on page 308)

Sable Hair Hair of a weasel-like furry animal, especially from the squirrel's tail. These *brushes* have a very fine point. Earlier Indian miniature *painters* used the finest sable hair *brushes*, for *watercolours*, which they made themselves. They are used in the modern period also for *tempera*, *water-colours* and for *glazing* and fine detailing in *oil paintings*. Refer *Brush*, *Manner*, *Mughal Miniatures*, *Vidya Bhushan*, *Ved Pal Sharma*, *Subhogendra Tagore*, *Sarada Chandra Ukil*, *Nathu Lal Verma*.

Sadwelkar, Baburao (1928–2000) b. Sawantwadi, MAHA. Education: GDA in *painting JJSA*. Solos: *JAG*, TAG; International: USA. Retrospective: "Over Three Decades in Art" 1951 to 1985 TAG. Group participations: Bombay Group 1956–1962, *LKA* New Delhi, other *exhibitions* in Kolkata, Bangalore, Mumbai; International: *Biennales*–Venice, Paris & Sao Paulo, Asian Artist's Tokyo, Indian Artist's Moscow, Contemporary Indian Artist's (*LKA*) Nairobi. Awards: MAHA State Mumbai, *BAS*; International: Fulbright Smith-Mundt Scholarship USA. Hon.: Gold Medal Academia Italy. Fellowship: *JJSA*. Member: Bombay Group (1956–62) *BAS*, *ASI*. Commissions: *Murals* in Mumbai, Pune, New Delhi; Inter-national: Texas, USA. Appointments: Ex. Dir. of Art MAHA; Compiled calendars for Govt. of MAHA, thematically based on *art* & *craft traditions* of MAHA, Mounted special *exhibition* for Govt. of MAHA & delivered lectures on *art;* Participated in seminars, symposiums & conferences on *art*; Talks on Radio & TV. Publications: Articles published in books, magazines & newspapers. Collections: *NGMA* & *LKA* New Delhi, PUJ National Museum Chandi-

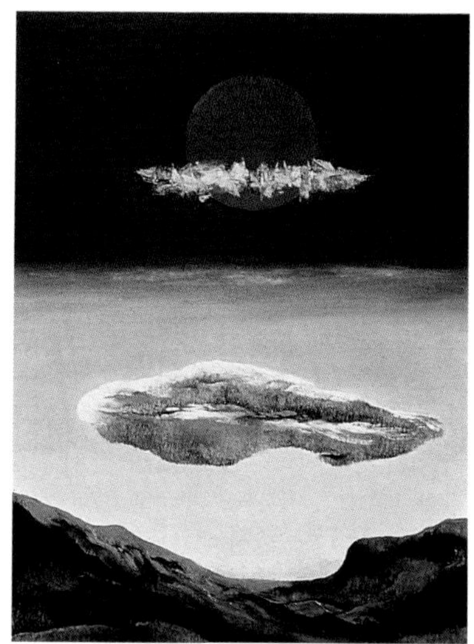

Sadwelkar, Baburao: "Flight Towards Crimson Planet" *Oil* on *Canvas*, 1986 100x75 cm.

garh, *GC* & TATA Mumbai, Town Hall Museum Kolhapur, TIFR, *JJSA*, pvt. & corporates. India, London, USA.

Baburao Sadwelkar was strongly influenced by the academic training offered by his alma-mater, *JJSA*, especially in the early part of his career. However, in spite of being a virtuoso portraitist, his interest in the last three decades veered towards the surreal *landscape*. A strange, uninhabited world in the *form* of islands floating in a chilly void, unlit by the cold red orb of the sun/moon. His *compositions* were landscape-like in character, being divided by the sharp *line* of the *horizon*. He experimented with diverse *media* and *techniques* with the *palette knife* being a special favourite.

Sagara, Piraji (1931–) b. Ahmedabad, GUJ. Education: *Drawing* Master & Dip. in Art Master *JJSA*. Solos: *GC* Mumbai, Kunika Art Gallery New Delhi, *Dhoomimal*. Retrospective: Ahmedabad 1983. Group participations: Sanskar Kendra Ahmedabad, *LKA* New Delhi; International: *Biennales*—Brazil, Tokyo, Cagnes Sur-Mes France. *Auctions*: Heart Mumbai. Awards: Gold Medal *AFA* Kolkata & *LKA* GUJ, *LKA* National Award New Delhi, Vishwa Gurjari, *Ravishankar M. Raval* Award GUJ. Hon.: Prof. School of *Architecture* Ahmedabad 1993. Members: Founder member Progressive Painters Group Ahmedabad, GUJ *LKA*. Commissions: *Murals* in Ahmedabad & Hyderabad. Collections: *NGMA* & *LKA* New Delhi, *BAAC* Kolkata, Baroda Museum, TIFR; International: Massachusetts Institute of Technology USA.

Sagara Piraji is not only a *painter*, using a variety of *media* but a *sculptor* as well. His early works show a tendency for *drawing*, with *ink*, *charcoal*, *pastel* and *pencil* being constantly used. *Watercolour* makes its first appearance in his works of the 60s. Gradually, he shifted to working with scrap and various *metals* such as *copper*, *brass* and *aluminium*. He also started using burnt *wood* as a base for his *metal collages*. His *sculptures* are mostly executed on *wood* or *stone*. Experi-menting with *techniques* and materials, at times he uses his fingers and nails in addition to the *brush* and knife while *painting*.

While his *themes* are mostly based on *nature* portraiture and *cityscapes*, his *oeuvre* is broadbased enough to embrace abstraction, with gestural strokes and bright *colours* enlivening the surface of his *canvas*. There is also a strong sense of folk based *imagery* in his *sculptures* and *metal reliefs*.

He lives and works in Ahmedabad. Refer *Relief*.

Saha, Anilbaran (1934–1999) b. Dacca, Bangladesh. Education: Dip. *GCAC* Kolkata. Solos: Over eight solos in Kolkata. Group participations: *Santiniketan*, *LKA* New Delhi, *AFA* & *BAAC* Kolkata, *AIFACS*, *BAS*; International: Toronto. Awards: *AFA* Kolkata. Founder member: *SCA*. Commissions: *Murals* in *wood*, *cement* & *mosaic* in WB & Bihar. Collections: *NGMA* & *LKA* New Delhi, *AFA* & *BAAC* Kolkata, pvt. & corporates.

The past *forms* the running *theme* in Anilbaran Saha's works. Certain objects culled from his memory, like cycle-rickshaws, ruined havelis and courtyards recur in many of the works, though stylistically, he has advanced from a cubo-surrealism to a cross-hatched *Realism*. His close association with *Gopal Ghose* led to an affinity for the *landscape*, not directly representing *nature*, but as *images* "recollected in tranquillity". Though he had worked with most *media*, his *pen* and *ink drawings* are evocative in their tenebristic use of *chiaroscuro*, while his *watercolours* are subtle in their use of pale *washes* of *colour*.

He lived in Kolkata.

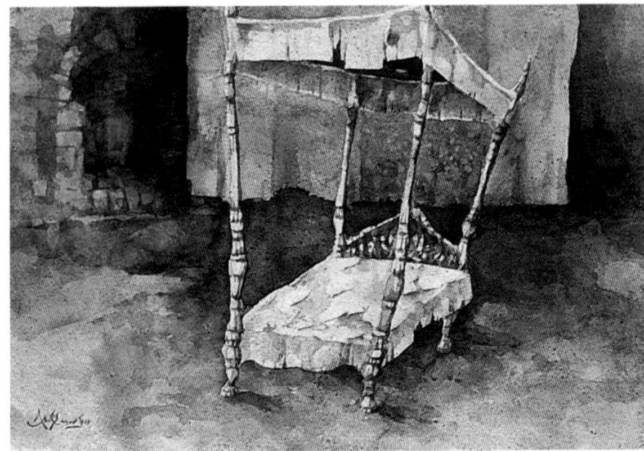

Saha, Anilbaran: "Bed", *Watercolour*, 50x75 cm.

Saha, Malay Chandan (1961–) b. Dacca, Bangladesh. Education: Grad. in *FA*. Kolkata. Solos: Tagore Art Gallery Kolkata, *ABC*, TKS. Group shows: *AFA* Kolkata, BAG, TAG, *JAG*, *NCAG*. Group participations: *Santiniketan*, CVA, *AFA* & *BAAC* Kolkata, National Exhibition *LKA* New Delhi, Lucknow & Chennai, Son-et-Lumiere Mumbai, *Biennale* Bhopal, *ISOA*, *JAG*, *NCAG*, *BAS*. Workshops: *Arts Acre* Kolkata. Awards: Shilpa Kala Parishad Patna, World Health Organization & All India Art Exhibition New Delhi, *BAS*. Member: *Arts Acre* Kolkata. Collections: *LKA* New Delhi, TATA Guwahati; International: Mithila Museum Tokyo & pvt. & public.

Nature's scintillating moments are captured with broken, gem-like flecks of *impasto colour* in Malay Chandan Saha's *landscapes*. Green predominates with yellow, red, mauve, blue and *black* all contributing to a rain-washed look of the *canvas*. He perceives the eternal cycle of life with its constant rejuvenation in *nature*. He has evolved with several *media* with a special preference for *mixed media*.

He lives and works in Kolkata.

Sahana, Sisir (1963–) b. Bankura, WB. Education: B.FA. & M.FA. *Painting KB Santiniketan*, Advance Dip. *Stained glass painting* Central Saint Martin's College of Art & Design London. Solos: *AFA* Kolkata, Heritage Chennai, Alliance Francaise Hyderabad, *SUG*, *GG*. Group participations: *BAAC*, *KB* & *AFA* Kolkata, *SNSPA* Hyderabad, Gallery Aurobindo New Delhi, *IFAS*, *CKP*, *BAS*, *JAG*, *GG*, HAS, *SUG*; International: London. *Art* camps: Hyderabad. Awards: *Santiniketan*, *BAS*, HAS; Junior Fellowship HRD Ministry; Commonwealth Scholarship nominated by HRD Ministry to UK. Appointments: Lecturer at the CFA, JNTU. Collections: pvt. India, England & USA.

Fascinated by the total integration of *light* and *colour* in glass, Sisir Sahana began experimenting with the *medium* of *glass painting*. He has evolved a special *technique* over the years, by scraping, abrading, gouging and heat bonding the *forms* in glass itself. Certain areas are etched for textural effect. He also *casts* and stains the glass itself aiming at glass *relief* rather than *glass painting*. His *style* is basically *figurative*, with the poorer sections of society being represented set against headless *idols* and ruined movements. The air is of a dissipated and dilapidated grandeur. *Black* makes a strong statement in the outlining of *forms* (as is usual in *stained glass* work). His *acrylics* too follow the same *pattern* with layers of *paper* and *pigment* crushed to create the relief-like look.

Sisir Sahana lives and works in Hyderabad.

Sahni, S.K. (1937–) b. Pakistan. Education: GDA *Painting JJSA*, M.A. *Drawing* & *painting* Meerut University. Solos: Srishti Art Gallery & Alliance Francaise New Delhi, *AFA* Kolkata, SRAG, *AIFACS*, TKS, *JAG*. Group participations: *LKA* & Srishti Art Gallery New Delhi, *JAG*, *AIFACS*; International: Paris, London. Keeper: *NGMA* New Delhi. Collections: *NGMA* & CFA New Delhi, *AFA* Kolkata, *GMAG* Chandigarh, SKP, pvt. & corporates.

S.K. Sahni has been exploring the possibilities of the straight *line* for the past two decades. The *line* is placed within the compositional area, allowed to develop and establish its identity in relation to the other *lines* already within the *picture space*. According to him, this ruler-straight *line* is devoid of emotion or feeling, but when seen in conjunction with other *lines*, a mood or sensibility may be experienced. He compares his *drawings* to music and its *abstract* mood. While the early works of the 90s had certain geometric *forms* highlighted by different *colour* accents, later works are essentially in *black* and *white* so as to enable the study of minute nuances of *tone* and direction.

He lives and works in New Delhi.

Saklat, Katayun (1938–) b. Kolkata. Education: Dip. in *drawing* & *painting* ICA&D Kolkata. Solos: *AFA* & British Council Kolkata, *GC* Mumbai, *ATG*. Group participations: *LKA* New Delhi, *BAAC* Kolkata, *SCA*, FAR. Awards: British Council Scholarship, Russian Govt. Scholarship & Buckin-ghamshire UK. *Art* teacher International School Kolkata; International: Taught *painting* at Burleighfield House Buckingham Shire 1974–75, Organized *Exhibitions* in India. Collections: AP *LKA* & pvt. India & abroad.

Katayun Saklat has experimented widely with a variety of *media*, including *oil* on *canvas*, *watercolour* and fabric *collage* before deciding to work with *stained*

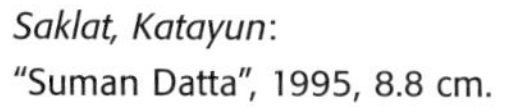

Saklat, Katayun:
"Suman Datta", 1995, 8.8 cm.

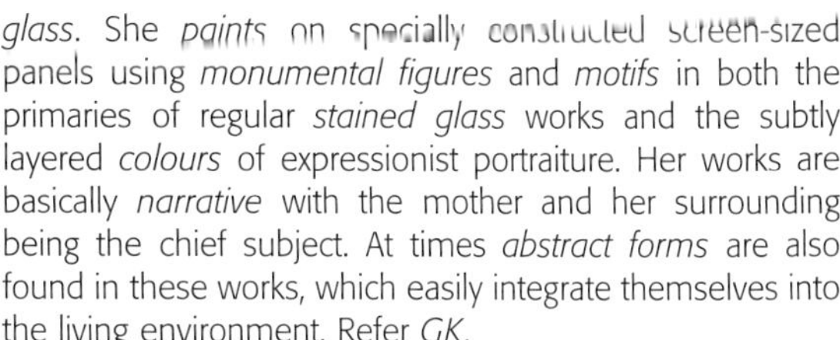

glass. She *paints* on specially constructed screen-sized panels using *monumental figures* and *motifs* in both the primaries of regular *stained glass* works and the subtly layered *colours* of expressionist portraiture. Her works are basically *narrative* with the mother and her surrounding being the chief subject. At times *abstract forms* are also found in these works, which easily integrate themselves into the living environment. Refer *GK*.

Sakshi Gallery (SG) A multi-location gallery, dealing with *contemporary art*, originally in Chennai, Bangalore and Mumbai. The Chennai gallery has since been closed down and a new branch opened at Pune, MAHA. The Mumbai Gallery shifted to a new venue in mid-1998. The 7000 sq.ft. warehouse in upper Worli, is now structured at three split levels, to create multi-functional areas, each independent of the other. One level is intended exclusively for previews and pvt. parties. SG houses *exhibitions* by both rising and established talents. *Artists* who have exhibited here include *Altaf*, *Krishen Khanna*, *Himmat Shah* and *Gulam Mohammed Sheikh*, *Laxman Shreshtha*.

Salar Jung Museum (SJM) (Hyderabad). Named after Salar Jung III the Prime minister of the Nizam of Hyderabad who was an avid collector of *art* and *art* objects. His palace was converted into the Salar Jung Museum in 1951. The collections were shifted to the present location in 1968. Apart from the one room housing some of Salar Jung's personal belongings, the rest of the ground floor is devoted to a vast selection of Indian *arts* and *crafts*, including textiles from Kashmir, *Kalamkari* from AP, Zardozi from Hyderabad and Phulkari from PUJ.

The Jade Room houses exquisite examples of jade *carving*, while the pride of the *museum* is the *miniature painting* gallery. The collection represents many different schools and *styles*, begining with *Jain illuminated manuscripts* and including examples from the Deccan and Rajput Schools. The Indian *sculptures* range from the 2nd century BC Bharhut *sculptures* to *bronze* of the *Chola* and *Pallava dynasties*.

The Western *art* galleries include the European Statuary Gallery, European porcelain, *copies* of Western masters and some *oils* attributed to J. Constable and J.M.N. Turner. There is also a collection of Venetian glass and West Asian carpets on view. The section on *Modern* Indian art includes works by the early modernists, like the two *paintings* by *Raja Ravi Varma*, "The Kerala Beauty" and "Stolen Interview". There are several *paintings* of the *Bengal School* on view here, including some by *Abanindranath Tagore*, *Nandalal Bose* and *Muhammed Abdur Rehman Chughtai*.

The works of *post-Independence artists*—like *K.K. Hebbar*, *Maqbool Fida Husain* and *Ramkinkar Baij* were acquired by the Art Purchase Committee after 1962.

Apart from this, there is a children's section, a library and a reading room. There is also a section devoted to rare manuscripts written in Arabic, Urdu and Persian.

Salve, Kashinath (1944–) b. Ahmednagar. Education: GDA in *drawing* & *painting* & *graphic* courses *JJSA*. Solos:

JAG, TAG, *NCAG*, TKS; International: USA, California. Group participations: MAHA State Art Exhibition Mumbai, *LKA* New Delhi & Lucknow, Shagun Art Gallery Mumbai *NCAG, BAS, JAG*, TAG, *AIFACS*, TKS, others in Kolkata, Pune & Chennai; International: USA. Workshops: *LKA* New Delhi, *mural, stained glass, enamelling* workshops with *NGMA* Mumbai. Awards: MAHA State Art Mumbai, Gold Medal *JJSA*, UP *LKA, BAS*. Commissions: Several *murals* in *wood, ceramic, copper* & *mixed media* in Mumbai & Nasik. Appointments: Lecturer Nagpur School of Art & *JJIAA*, Prof & HoD *JJSA*; Started workshop facility "Academy of Fine Arts" with the help of Bombay Diocesan Society/Robert Money Technical High School Mumbai in 2001. Collections: *NGMA & LKA* New Delhi, UP *LKA* Lucknow, *JJSA*.

Kashinath Salve's *painterly style* varies with the *technique* involved. While his large scale *murals* in *metal, ceramic* and *wood* are geometrical in their *imagery* and limited in their range of *colours*, the *paintings* in *oils* and *acrylics* are freely brushed in with *colours* and *forms* merging and re-emerging from the pale or dark *backgrounds*. He uses the roller to create panels of *neutral colours* against which the *landscape*-like elements and organic shapes are placed. The *collage*-like works reflect the decomposition of the *imagery* from the representative to the *abstract*. Salve's recent works have the *plaster* and hemp used to create robot-like shamsans in *relief*. The entire *motifs* span the length or breath of several framed boxes.

Salve lives and works in Mumbai.

Samant, Mohan (1924–2004) b. Mumbai. Education: GDA *Painting JJSA*. Solos: Kolkata, New Delhi, *GC* & *BAAC* Mumbai, TAG, *PUAG*; International: New York, Rome. Group participations: *Biennale* Venice, Tokyo & Sao Paulo, Comonwealth and Tate Gallery London, Museum of Modern Art Oxford, The Graham Gallery New York, Hirshhorn Museum Washington DC. *Auctions*: Osian's & Heart Mumbai. Awards: Italian Govt. Cultural Scholarship Rome, Asia Society Scholarship USA, National Awards, *BAS*. Publications: "Time Magazine", "Art News", "Art of India" & "Art of the World" series by N. Brown. Collections: *NGMA* & *LKA* New Delhi; International: Asia Society & Museum of Modern Art New York.

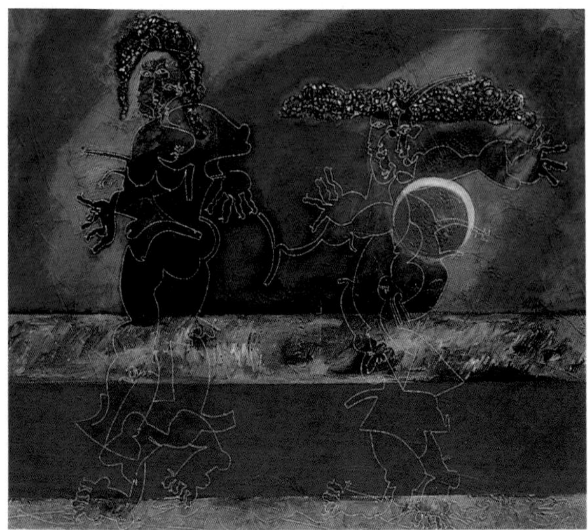

Samant, Mohan: "Moonlight Strolling"
Acrylic, Oil, Synthetic Hair & Wire *Drawing* on *Canvas*, 122x137 cm.

His *style* developed from his *aesthetic* relationship with the wide panorama of *visual* resources (from antiquity to the present age). At times, he gave up *painting* on regular *canvas*, and coated the *canvas* with *plaster* to get a rough primitive look. His works have evolved from the earlier with their linear *relief* and hieroglyphic aspect, inspired by *Egyptian art*, the *prehistoric* cave *paintings* at Lascaux, France and the bright *colours* of Indian *miniature paintings*. His later works have the added element of assemblage-like *drawings* in wire, which are affixed on the surface of the painted *canvas*. At times *plastic figures*, sand, sprakle and *crayon* are added to create a surreal element of *forms*, both emerging from and disappearing into the timeless *backdrop* created by the *canvas*. He lived and worked in New York, USA.

Sanathanan, M. (1943–2002) b. Kerala. Education: NDFA College of Art Chennai. Solos: Bangalore, Chennai, School of Art Gallery Thiruvananthapuram, Kala Mela New Delhi, *JAG*. Retrospective: Thiruvananthapuram in 1997. Group participations: Chennai, Thiruvananthapuram, National Exhibitions New Delhi, *AIFACS*. Awards: Kerala *LKA*, Bangladesh Art Exhibition, *AIFACS*. Member: Central *LKA* New Delhi, President *CKP*. Appointments: Lecturer & HoD Govt. *CFA* Thiruvananthapuram. Collections: Govt. Art Gallery AP, Kerala *LKA* Thrissur, *LKA* & *NGMA* New Delhi, *CHAG*, pvt. & corporates.

M. Sanathanan invoked the mysteries of the inner world through a conscious use of *colour symbolism* in his works. His *figurative abstracts* have developed from his early use of TANTRIC abstraction. *Space* division was enhanced by his use of *illusion*, conveying extreme *depth* on one hand and flat *space* on the other; this play of opposites was taken further with the contrasting use of *texture* a heavy *impasto* and thin, *transparent* glazes of *colour* coexist on the same *canvas*. He lived in Thiruvananthapuram.

Sand Blasting A method used for cleaning *stone* or *metal* and for decorating glass or *concrete* blocks, where fine sand or *iron* fillings are blasted onto the surface. The rest of the block is protected by covering it with a *stencil* or resist. Used by *sculptors* and glass workers. Refer *Art Brut, Bronze, Cire Perdue, Gold, Treatment, Mould, Radhika Vaidyanathan*.

Sand Moulding A *technique* of making *cast metal* objects, where hot liquid *metal* is poured into a *mould* of tightly bonded sand and then allowed to cool. Refer *Art Brut, Artefact, Assemblage, Bronze, Casting, Cire Perdue, Harappa, Iron, Junk Art, Mohenjo Daro, Matter, Papier Mache, Plaster, Treatment, South Indian Bronzes, Somnath Hore, C. Jagdish, Ratilal Kansodaria, Janak J. Narzary, Pilloo Pochkhanawalla, Himmat Shah, Radhika Vaidaynathan*.

Sand Painting A traditional, ritualistic method of making *designs* on the floor with different *colours* of sand, practised by tribes and diverse people all over the world. It must be prepared anew on each occasion because of its ephemeral nature. It is similar to Indian floor decorations, like Rangoli, Alpana and Kolam. These Indian *forms* are created with coloured *marble* dust, flower petals, grains and rice flour in various regions—with specific *motifs* and *colours* symbolising various events and religous or other festivals and ceremonies. Refer *Action Painting, Art Brut, Arte Povera, Artefact, Collage, Junk Art, Treatment, Siona Benjamin, Ramnik Bhavsar, Veerbala Bhavsar, Kavita Deuskar, Gold–Shanti Banerjea.*

Sanghvi, Vimoo (1920–) Studied in *pottery* in 1959 Williesden Art School London. Solos: *JAG*, TAG. Retrospective: Mumbai; Demonstrated at Greenwich House School New York, Hunslow School of Art London & Laboratory of Ceramics Tehran. Appointments: Invited lecturer at *JJSA*, Prof. at Sophia Polytechnic Mumbai.

Vimoo Sanghvi is a ceramist, having studied *pottery* under R. Cooper and M.A.D. Trey in London. Her works include pots and plates and a range of expressive figurines and mask-like faces. The *techniques* used are versatile and range from the slap-dash *handling* of glaze to the decorative use of repeated *forms*. The *colours* range from the earlier, westernized use of *pastels* to the raw use of *terracotta* influenced by tribal Gujarati *pottery*.

Vimoo Sanghvi lives and works in Mumbai.

Sankalan (Jaipur). The gallery was set up in 1995 to promote local *artists* by exhibiting their *sculptures* and *paintings* including Dwarka Prasad, *Deokinandan Sharma, Nathu Lal Verma, Rameshwar Singh* and others.

Sanskrit The ancient language of the Vedic people and the Hindus—the earliest literary works were in Sanskrit, which was the territory of the Brahmins as against the Pali (language used by BUDDHA for his sermons) spoken by the common people. Sanskrit is the mother language from which most present day Indian languages have evolved. It contains 12 vowels and 35 consonants. These are not all represented in the Latin alphabet, since Latin was a much simpler language.

Sanskrit died out circa 500 BC. BUDDHA already spoke Pali, the language in which the Buddhist scriptures are composed. A further development away from Sanskrit was Magadhi, the language of King Ashoka, which he used for his famous inscriptions. Sanskrit resurfaced later when study of the VEDAS and other ancient scriptures became more widespread. Refer BHARATA, BUDDHA, LOKA, PURANA, RASA, TANTRA, *Jamini P. Gangooly, Asit K. Haldar, Akbar Padamsee, P.L. NarasimhaMurti, P. Vijyalakshmi.*

Santiniketan (WB). The word literally means "abode of peace," Santiniketan was built in *Birbhum*, Bengal by *Rabindranath Tagore's* father Devendranath Tagore in the 1860s. In 1901, the poet started a small educational institution there with a new outlook and philosophy. The foremost aim of this school is to inculate a love of *nature* amongst its young pupils. Initially Santiniketan was meant only for educating children. Later however, *Rabindranath Tagore* realized that the study of *art*, music, *crafts* etc. was absolutely essential to make learning complete. Hence the school had an *art* teacher from the very begining. In 1919, he founded *KB*—the *art* school at Santiniketan and later in 1921, the Visva Bharati World University (*VBU*) which together formed the first *FFA* in an Indian University. Refer *KB, Banasthali Vidyapith, Bombay School* and *Madras School of Art*.

Santosh, Ghulam Rasool (1929–1997) b. Srinagar, J&K. Trained in *painting, weaving* & *papier-mache*, Studied in *painting* with Prof. *Narayan S. Bendre MSU*. Solos: Over 25, Srinagar, Kolkata, Kumar Gallery & Gallery Kunika Chemould New Delhi, *GC* Mumbai, *PUAG, JAG, Dhoomimal*, TKS, *LTG*; International: Tel-Aviv, Kabul, Los Angeles, Devorah Sherman Gallery Chicago, Revel Gallery New York. Group participations: *LKA, NGMA* & *Triennale* New Delhi, SKP, *Dhoomimal;* International: *Biennale* in Paris, Sao Paulo, Canada & Tokyo, *Tantra art* in Montreal, Contemporary Indian Painters in Japan, USA, Hong Kong, Singapore, France, Saudi Arabia, Bulgaria. *Auctions*: Sotheby's-Timeless Art, Osian's & Heart Mumbai, Sotheby's New Delhi, London & New York, Christie's London. Awards: *LKA* National Award, Padma Shri Govt. of India 1977, SKP *Artist* of the year. Members: J&K Cultural Academy, a poet, playwright & writer in Kashmiri & Urdu. Publications: Collection of poems "Besukh Ruh", Urdu novel "Samandar Pyasa Hai", an opera "Gulrez" & a play "Ze Butt"; Designed costumes & sets for stage. Collections: *NGMA* & *LKA* New Delhi, *BAAC* Kolkata, J&K Cultural Academy, *Chandigarh Museum*; International:

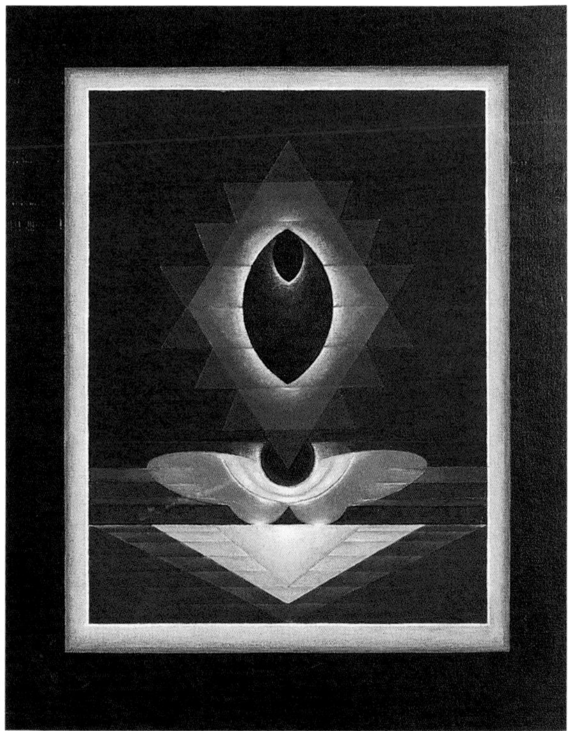

Santosh, Ghulam Rasool: "Light", *Oil* on *Canvas*.

Museum of Modern Art New York, Whitney Museum, Ben & Abbey Grey Foundation and Chester & Davida Herwitz USA, Masanori Fukuoka & Glenbarra Art Museum Japan.

Ghulam Rasool Santosh was inspired by *Sayed Haider Raza*. His early works of the 50s were cubistic exercises, with *landscapes* in *watercolours*. In the 60s he painted topographical abstractions in *oils* in memory of the white-capped mountain of his native Kashmir. He had also painted a few *portraits* in a semi-analytical cubist *style*. It was after his trip to the Amarnath caves in 1964, that he was spiritually and mystically moved to find his *content* from his Indian roots, rather than depend on the West. Ultimately, he found his *image* in the concept of the MITHUNA–the union of the male and female transformed into the *spiritual* concept of *creation*. This was the beginning of his "Tantrik" phase, which continued for more than two decades until his death. His TANTRA-inspired *paintings* are in the spirit of an inborn quest–a will to explore the *spiritual* basis of man's being. However, the geometrical configuration of the works, though closely linked with Tantric imagery, does not serve any specific magical functions that is normally ascribed to YANTRA diagrams.

Sanyal, Bhabesh Chandra (1902–2003) b. Dibrugarh, Assam. Education: Dip. in *FA*. Specialization *sculpture* GSA Kolkata. Solos: New Delhi, Mumbai *ABC*. Group participations: *LKA* New Delhi, SC; International: Salon de Mai Paris, *Biennales*–Venice, Sao Paulo & Brazil; International: Congress of Art USA & Europe, Cultural visit to China. *Auctions*: Heart Mumbai & New Delhi. Awards: Padma Bhushan, Gagan-Abani Award *VBU*, SKP Shield. Fellowship: *LKA* Fellowship Govt. of India, Emeritus Fellowship New Delhi. Members: *LKA* Secretary 1960, Founder member SC, Advisor on *Art Education* by Govt. of Nepal, Vice-Principal Lahore School of Art; Prof. & HoD Delhi Polytechnic (GCAC). Publication: "Vertical Women" authored by him. Collections: India & abroad.

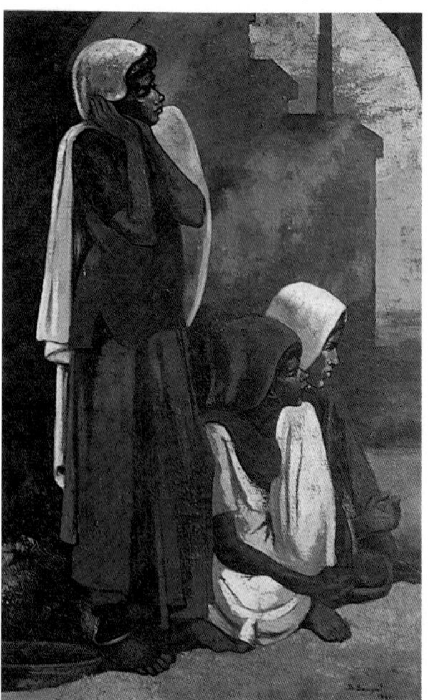

Sanyal, Bhabesh Chandra: "Three Women", *Oil* on *Canvas*, 1941, 143x91 cm.

Bhabesh Chandra Sanyal had always been fascinated by the folk-like *images* of DURGA made by his mother and other ladies in his native WB. Therefore, after completing his dip. in *painting*, he also specialized in *sculpture*. During the course of his long career, he worked with both *mediums*, *sculpture* and *painting*, in addition to his teaching, first at the Lahore School of Art and later after the partition, in the Delhi Polytechnic. He refused to be confined to any *style* as he believed that an *artist* should constantly experiment–with *technique*, *colour* and *texture*. He therefore used both the *figurative* and the *abstract*; his *drawings* have an expressive force which is in direct contrast with its extreme *minimalism*. Folk *motifs* and modernistic distortion and simplification are the hallmarks of some of his *styles*. His *sculptures*, especially his *portraits* share this trait, a few being impressionistic in the *manner* of Rodin and others being rhythmically simplified in the *manner* of Archipenko. Bhabesh Chandra Sanyal who lived for over 100 years, passed away in New Delhi.

Sanyal, Gopal (1933–) b. WB. Education: Dip. in *FA*. *GCAC* Kolkata. VG New Delhi. Solos: MMB Centre Gallery Kolkata, VG. Group participations: National Exhibition New Delhi, *BAAC* Kolkata, *AIFACS*. Award: *AIFACS*, National Scholarship, Govt. of India. Founder member: Calcutta Painters. Appointments: Lecturer at the ICA&D Kolkata. Publications: A film has been made on him & his works by Kolkata Doordarshan. Collections: *NGMA* New Delhi, PUJ Museum Chandigarh, *BAAC* Kolkata; International: USA, Germany.

Gopal Sanyal prefers *drawing* with *pen* and *ink* on *paper* to *painting* on *canvas*. He distorts *line* and *form* with his powerful strokes, using the naiveté of *folk art* and the bitterness of his own passion to create humans and animals of extraordinary strength. The horse is a favourite *motif*; in studies represented in a *symbolic manner* at times, it is heavily embellished with linear ornamentation. His *paintings* are few in number, but are succint examples of his mastery over *colour* and *colour symbolism*.

He lives and works in Kolkata.

Sarada Ukil School of Art (SUSA) (New Delhi). The school, set up in 1926, is the oldest *art* school in New Delhi. Started by *Sarada Charan Ukil*, the *modern* master and pupil of *Abanindranath Tagore*, the school since 1969, offers both a 3 years Dip. in *art* and a 1 year dip. in *applied art*. The school mainly trains students to become full-fledged *art* teachers. Refer *Sarada Charan Ukil*.

Sarala's Art International, Sarala's Art Centre, (SAI) (Chennai). The gallery, now called ArtWorld, which was established in 1965 by Soli J. Daruwalla deals with the work of *artists* from all over India since 40 years, and ArtWorld was established in 1997. The gallery deals with the *artists* since then–including *Chandranath K. Achrekar*, *K.M. Adimoolam*, *Balbhadra Agarwalla*, *Umesh Ahire*, *Dattatrey D. Apte*, *Prafulla Dahanukar*, *Dakoji Devraj*, *Sohini Dhar*, *Ram Keote*, *Paul A. Koli*, *P. Krishnamurthy*, *Lalitha Lajmi*, *Sachida Nagdev*, *P. Gouri Shanker*, *Saroj Gogi Pal*, *Arnawaz Vasudev*.

SAI has also arranged International *exhibitions* in Hong Kong, Tokyo and Singapore and are working on projects in Amsterdam and Canada.

Sarangan Rangaswamy (1929–1997) b. Thanjavur (Tanjore), Education: TN. Dip. in *FA*. & *Applied Art GCAC*

Chennai, Studied in *modelling*. Solos: Chennai, *LKA* New Delhi, *AIFACS*, TKS, SRAG, *JAG*. Group participations: National Exhibitions & Kumar Gallery New Delhi, HAS, South Indian Society of Painters & Progressive Painters Association Chennai, *AIFACS*, *JAG*. *Printmaking* workshops: USIS New Delhi; International: Second British International *Print Biennale* Bradford, Indian *Artist* San Francisco. Awards: *LKA* New Delhi, *AFA* Kolkata & Chennai, *AIFACS*. Member: South Indian Society of Painters Chennai. Collections: *NGMA* & *LKA* New Delhi, Chennai *LKA*, PUJ Govt. Museum Chandigarh, SKP.

Rangaswamy Sarangan's *paintings* incorporated the three-dimensional quality of *sculpture* in the *manner* in which he used semi-solid *paint*. He squeezes thin ribbons of *pigment* from the tube, directly *drawing* on the *canvas* or *paper*, creating both *texture* and *image*. He had also used *mixed media* (including *metal* sheets) to achieve similar relief-like *compositions*. His *images* have mythical overtones; animals, birds, TANTRIC symbols, folk-like *motifs* and *sculptures* are integrated into a patterned sequence that has the naiveté of floor *painting* (Rangoli) in its use of *colour* and decoration. He lived in New Delhi.

Sarasvati=Goddess of wisdom, science, *art* and music. Sarasvati is popular with the Hindus, the Buddhists and the *Jains*. She is variously represented in *painting* and *sculpture* as **1.** A river-goddess. **2.** The daughter of BRAHMA and later his consort, she also has the swan (HANSA, HAMSA) as her VAHANA. In the Brahmanas she is identified with Vacha (speech) and is later considered the goddess of learning or eloquence.

In addition to the swan, later *artists* have variously depicted her riding a peacock or sitting on a lotus throne. In *art*, she is represented as having four, eight or ten hands. In her four hands, she carries a Pustaka (book, symbol of learning), Akshamala (rosary), Veena (lute–a musical instrument) and PADMA (lotus). If she has eight hands, she carries a Dhanush (bow), GADA (mace), Pasha (noose), CHAKRA (wheel), SANKHA (conch shell), Musala (pestle), Ankusha (goad) and Veena (lute). Refer BRAHMA, *Devanagari Script*, *Maqbool Fida Husain*, *Ganpatrao K. Mhatre*, *Sunil Kumar Paul*, *Raja Ravi Varma;* Illustration–*Mrinalini Mukherjee*.

Sardesai, Narayan R. (1886–1954) b. Ratnagiri, MAHA. Education: Studied carpentry; *Drawing* & *painting KB* Vadodara; M.A. GDA *painting* & *Art* Master *JJSA*. Participated: Pune, Madras FA. Society, Simla FA. Society, Mysore DAE, Hyderabad FA. Society, *BAS*. Awards: Simla FA. Society, Gold Medal & Silver Medal *BAS*, Mayo Medal *JJSA*, Silver & Bronze Medal Madras FA. Society, 5 Silver Medal State of Mysore, Bronze Medals–Patna, Mysore, Mumbai. *Auction*: By Christie's. Appointments: Prof. *JJSA* for *drawing* & *painting*, later also a *drawing* teacher at Fort Propriety High School Mumbai. Collections: Bhavani Museum Aund, Nagpur Museum MAHA. *Delhi Art Gallery*, *JJSA*, *PWM*, pvt. & *museums*.

Narayan R. Sardesai specialized in *handling watercolour landscapes* as well as *figurative paintings* based on the *culture* of his home state, MAHA. His works were based more on *figurative art* & *compositions*, *oil painting* being his first *medium* of choice, though he also worked with *watercolours* and *charcoal*. He had a keen eye for capturing *vignettes* of small town life–with an extraordinary use of *light* and compostional detail, and *portrait* his subject. He commissioned for Govt. institutions and pvt. families.

He conducted Sunday classes at *ASI* & worked at Vadodara *KB*.

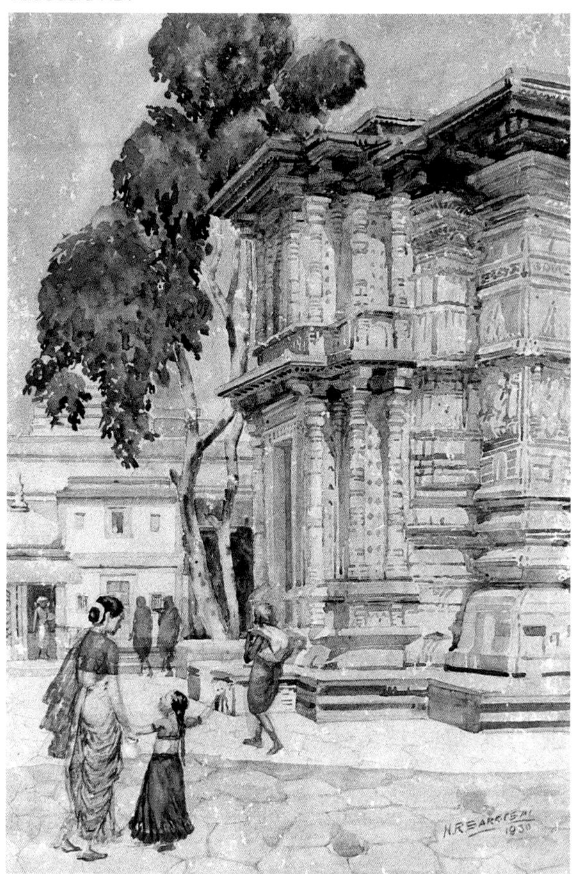

Sardesai, Narayan R.: "Women to the Temple, Kolhapur", *Watercolour*, 1930.

Sarojini Naidu School of Performing Arts, Fine Arts & Communication (SNSPA) (Hyderabad, AP). Established in 1990 in the residence of Sarojini Naidu, which was bequeathed to the University of Hyderabad, by her daughter, Padmaja Naidu. The school is multidisciplinary with post-grad. studies being offered in the performing and the plastic arts. Unlike conventional *art* schools there are no regular classes on a day to day basis. Instead the student is encouraged to work on his own and is assessed by a panel at the end of each month. In addition to the core faculty, there is a heavy reliance on visiting faculty, comprising eminent *artists* and performers, who are invited to spend one month in the campus, working and interacting with the students at will. There is no rigid demarcating line between listening and seeking guidance from the faculty of another discipline as the *aesthetics* of all the *arts* are shared. While *sculpture* is not yet offered in the school due to lack of space, specialization in both *painting* and *printmaking* is offered, as are two *styles* of South Indian Dance and Theatre. *Laxma Goud* was one of the founder members and former Dean of the school and other *artists* who still teach are S. Shyam Sunder, Alex Mathew, *D. L. N. Reddy*.

Saturation The brilliance or the degree of purity in a particular *colour*.

Satwalekar, Madhav (1915–2006) b. Lahore. Education: Dip. & Post-Grad. Scholarship *JJSA*, further studies in Florence Academy Italy, Slade School London AGC Paris. Solos: India, Europe, Uganda, Kenya, Tanganyika, Zanzibar. Group shows: *RG*. Founded Indian Art Institute Mumbai in 1954. Commissions: *Portraits* of national & international *figures*. Appointments: Had been Chairman *BAS* & Dir. of Art MAHA between 1969 and 75. Publications: Has written several articles on *art* in periodicals. Two booklets *"Oil Painting"* & "What's What in Art". Collections: pvt. & corporates.

Madhav Satwalekar's early training in *art* was under the guidance of his father, a noted turn-of-the-century *painter*, S.D. Satwalekar. However, unlike his father, who was academically *realistic*, Madhav Satwalekar himself used a more impressionistic *technique* and *palette*. His interiors with sensuous female *figures*, draped languorously over patterned bedspreads and curtains remind one of P. Bonnard, while his predominantly blue and yellow *landscapes* display his mastery over tonal *handling*. His work is in both *water-colour* and *oil* on *paper* and *canvas* respectively. At later stage in his *composition*, he adopted the *colour* and simplified *style* of V. Van Gogh.

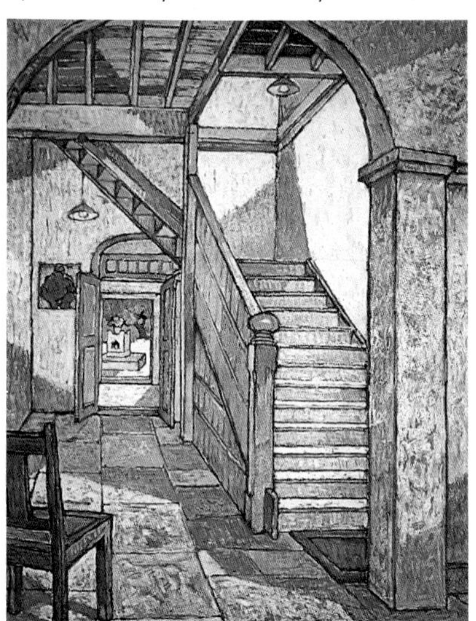

Satwalekar, Madhav: "Staircase", *Oil* on *Canvas*, 100x75 cm.

School of. . . This refers to the *style* or characteristics of an unidentified work of *art* from a particular school i.e. the Mughal School of... (atelier). The *style* represented the particular region, in India, which ranged from the states or a smaller territory, to a town; or a welknown *artists'* group. This means that an expert can usually detect with considerable accuracy, the provenance of a work of *art* with or without identifying a particular *artist*. Even later, *artists* (circa 18th–earlier19th century) painted in groups, where the master *artists* prepared the *composition* and others completed the work with the master always giving the finishing touch. *Raja Ravi Varma* was among the first *artists* who created individuality and changed the method, *style* and *techniques* in India. Refer *Mughal Dynasty*, *P.L. NarasimhaMurti*.

Scraperboard, Scratchboard A *drawing* surface made of board coated with *white gesso* which is later covered with *ink*. When dry, the *ink* can be scraped away with a sharp *point* to produce fine *white lines*. Refer *Burin*, *Burr*, *Dry-Point*, *Graffitti*, *Ground*, *Line Engraving*, *Sgraffito*, *Jyoti Bhatt*, *Siona Benjamin*, *Shobha Broota*, *C. Douglas*, *Satish Gujral*, *H.R. Kambli*, *Manu Parekh*, *Mona Rai*, *J. Swaminathan*, *Rabindranath Tagore*.

Screen Printing, Silk Screen Printing This is a method of *printmaking*. Screen printing, using *stencils*, dates back to around the 5th century, but the process of using a screen mesh did not arise until the late 19th century.

In India it is always known as hand printing, with various methods being used. In states like RAJ, GUJ, UP, MP, Bihar, the basic screen printing kit consists of a wooden *frame* with a silk mesh stretched taut on one side, a flat baseboard, the hingebar joining them and a flexible rubber or *synthetic* squeegee (rubber edged tool) to force the *colour* through the fine mesh to *print* on the *paper* registered on the baseboard. *Frames* can come in several *sizes* and are made from *wood*, plywood, tubular *steel* or *aluminium*. The mesh was originally of silk, though now nylon, terylene, polyester, *copper* and stainless *steel* are used. The fineness of the mesh governs the amount of *ink* that is deposited on the *paper* below. A *film stencil* is attached to the mesh. A liquid *filler* such as PVA (Polyvinyl Acetate *emulsion paint*), *acquer*, cellulose or *ink* is then applied with *brush*, scraper or finger for textural variation. Candles and *wax crayons* can also be used as *fillers*. The liquid *filler* is poured along one end of the *frame* while the *paper* is clamped to the baseboard. The squeegee then drags the liquid *filler* across the entire face of the mesh, forcing it through to *print* an *image*. In recent times, photo-stencils have also been used in screen printing. Refer *Chinese Art*, *Collotype*, *Half-Tone*, *Media*, *Serigraphy*, *Vijaya Bagai*, *Ramkinkar Baij*, *Jyoti Bhatt*, *Phalguni DasGupta*, *Y.D. Deolalikar*, *Gunen Ganguli*, *Maqbool Fida Husain*, *Benode Behari Mukherjee*, *Ajit S. Patel*, *Sharad Patel*, *Paramjeet Singh*, *Prem Singh*.

Sculptor=Shilpakara. A person who sculpts i.e. creates three-dimensional objects, by means of *casting*, *carving*, assembling or *modelling*. *Ramkinkar Baij* from *Santiniketan* and *Subrayalu Dhanapal* (1919) from Chennai were the first *modern* sculptors in the country to break away from academic *Realism*. *K.C. Aryan* was a *painter*, sculptor and *art* historian. Sculptors of the 20th century experimented with *assemblage*, using scrap *metal* and mesh wire and *synthetic* plastic. *Aluminium*, a lightweight silvery-white *metal*, *fibreglass* or *mixed media* are also used today. Refer *Abstract Sculpture*, *Direct Carving*, *Figurative Art*, *Masterpiece*, *Media*, *Model*, MURTI, *Plaster of Paris*, *Stone*, *Sculpture*; Illustrations–*K.C. Aryan*, *B. Vithal*, *Ramkinkar Baij*, *Sadanandji Bakre*, *Dhanraj Bhagat*, *R.B. Bhaskaran*, *Sankho Chaudhuri*,

C. Dakshina-moorthy, Gopal Ghose, Santosh Jadia, Ratilal Kansodaria, Chintamoni Kar, Vinayak Pandurang Karmarkar, Bimal Kundu, Meera Mukherjee, Balan Nambiar, Pilloo Pochkhanawalla, Shankar Nandagopal, P.S. Nandhan, A. Ramachandran, Krishna N. Reddy, Ravinder G. Reddy, Debi Prasad RoyChowdhury, Prabhas Sen, Brahman Vinayakrao Wagh.

Sculpture It refers to the *art* of consciously creating *forms* and *images* in the three-dimensional, also referred to as Plastic Art. This could either be in the round or in *relief*. Traditionally sculpture could be made in either of the two methods –i.e. by *carving* or by *modelling*. *Carving* is known as the substraction method–with the block (of *marble*, *stone*, different types of *wood*, *plaster*) being cut into, using various tools such as the *chisel*, hammer and *gouge* until the desired *form* is reached. In *modelling, clay* or *wax* are used as preliminary materials in creating a *form* before *casting* it in *metal* or *plaster*. In recent times, the distinction between *painting* and sculpture has become progressively finer, with *painting* taking on a heavy relief-like appearance and culpture becoming vividly coloured, *mobile* (as in Kinetic sculpture) or soft (as in the pneumatic vinyl Pop sculptures). *Assemblage*, *junk art*, *found objects*, conceptual sculpture and living sculpture are some of the three-dimensional *art* objects that defy definition in the *contemporary* world.

In India, sculpture has been a vibrant *art form* since the lively dancing girl of the *Indus Valley Civilization*. Through the ages sculpture has constantly evolved being either religious in *theme* or being used as architectural embellishment. In the *modern* age, however, *sculptors* have been free to interpret sculpture in new ways. They have used technology to sculpt using new materials with new concepts. While the traditionalist used every illusionistic trick to imitate human skin, hair, eyes and clothes, the conceptualist was happy making a phone call to a factory, dictating the *dimensions*, *colour* and shape of a *"sculpture"* that would be manufactured by the factory though credit was given to the *sculptor*. Traditionalists alone could differ as widely as the impressionist spontaneity of *Debi Prasad RoyChowdhury* and the Neo-classical *theme/style* of *Vinayak Pandurang Karmarkar*.

Twentieth century Indian *sculptors* experimented widely with material, using *cement* (*Ramkinkar Baij*), junk (*Pilloo Pochkhanawalla*) and *metal* plating and *enamelling* (*Nandagopal*). Other materials included glass, neon tubing (*light* sculpture) *plaster* and knotted hemp fibres. Refer *Architecture*, *Conceptual Art*, *Electroplating*, *Fibreglass*, *Illusion*, *Impressionism*, *Kinetic Art*, *Neo-Classical Style*, *Pop Art*, *Tradition;* Illustrations–*Navjot Altaf*, *Dhanraj Bhagat*, *Raghav Kaneria*, *Bishamber Khanna*, *Chandrakant N. Mhatre*, *Leela Mukherjee*, *Mrinalini Mukherjee*, *Shankar Nandagopal*, *Pilton Kothawalla*.

Scumbling A *technique* used in *oil* and *acrylics painting* where a thin layer of *opaque colour* is applied over an existing layer of different *colour*, so that the previous is not totally obliterated, giving the *painting* an uneven textural effect, sometimes creating a *matte* finish. e.g. *K.M. Adimoolam*, *Bikash Bhattacharjee*, *Surendra Pal Joshi*, *Akbar Padamsee*, *Chittrovanu Mazumdar*, *Gieve Patel*. Refer *Glazing*, *Texture*, *Underpainting*.

Seascape It is a view of the coastline, boats, seabirds etc. in which the sea, along with the sky forms the chief element. Refer *Cool Colour*, *Foreshortening*, *Horizon Landscape*, *Nature*, *Pralhad A. Dhond*, *Ino Gangooly*, *Jamini P. Gangooly*, *Gaganendranath Tagore*, *Bal Wad;* Illustration–*Form*–*Shiavax Chavda*.

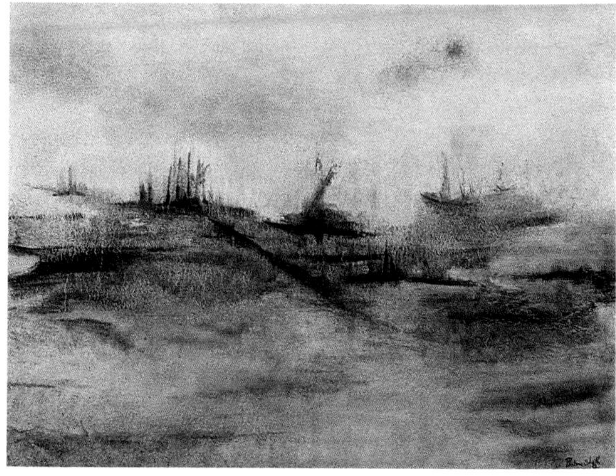

Seascape: *Pratima Sheth*, "New day", *Oil* on *Canvas*, 1997, 76x102 cm.

Secondary Colours *Colours* which are made by mixing two *primary colours* in equal *proportion*, i.e. Red + Yellow= Orange, Yellow + Blue=Green and Blue + Red=Violet. Refer *Colour Wheel*, *Colour Circle*, *Hue*, *Manuscript Paintings;* Illustration–*K.M. Adimoolam*, *K.V. Haridasan*, *Sayed Haider Raza*.

Self Portrait A *portrait* of the *artist* by the same *artist*. *Artists* painted *realistic* self portraits by watching themselves in a mirror with slightly narrowed eyes. However in the 20th century *artists* use their self *image* in an *abstract manner* to make highly personal statements e.g. *Atul Dodiya*, *Bhupen Khakhar*, *Lalitha Lajmi*, *A. Ramchandran*, *Paritosh Sen*, *Amrita Sher-Gil*. Refer *Broad Handling*, *Life-Mask*, *Life-Size*, *Shaibal Ghosh*, *Mahirwan Mamtani*, *Ratan Parimoo*.

Sen, Paritosh (1918–) b. Dacca, Bangladesh. Education: Dip. in *FA*. *GCAC* Chennai, Academie Andre Lhote, AGC, ENSBA *Painting*, History of *painting* Ecole de Louvre Paris. Over 20 solos: Mumbai, Kolkata, New Delhi; International: Brussels, Paris, London, Moscow. Group participations: Kolkata, Bangalore, *LKA* New Delhi, Timeless Art Mumbai, Marvel Art Gallery Ahmedabad, *CYAG*; International: Commonwealth Arts Festival London, Asahi Shimbun Exhibition Tokyo, *Biennale*–Havana, Sao Poulo & Sweden. *Auctions*: Sotheby's-Timeless Art, Heart & Osian Mumbai, Bowring's New Delhi; International: Christie's & Sotheby's London. Awards: Abanindra Puraskar for *painting* Govt. of WB, D.Litt. (hon.) by University of Burdwan WB, Shiromani Awards

LKA WB, Rockefeller III Grant, French Govt. Fellowship, Fellowship *LKA* New Delhi. Founder members: General Council *LKA* & Calcutta Group, *VBU*. Appointments: Lectured on Indian *contemporary painting* USA; Designed Bengali type-face based on the script of *Rabindranath Tagore* for French Govt., Artist-in-Residence NID. Publications: Written articles on *contemporary art* in journals & published four books in WB, documentary films on him were made by the WB Govt. & Doordarshan Kolkata. Collections: *NGMA*, *LKA*, Rashtrapati Bhavan & Palam Airport New Delhi, British Museum & *BAAC* Kolkata, PUJ University & Museum in Chandigarh, Godrej Mumbai, *BB*, *JAG*, *CYAG*, & pvt. in India & abroad.

There is a wild exuberance in Paritosh Sen's *paintings* of *modern* fables and human experience. His *images* are nearly surreal, in their fantastic delineation; his *colours* are nearly fauvist in their discordancy, yet the end result is both quaint and harmonious. *Colours* merge *forms* together, purple-skinned people coexist happily with red, yellow trees and wild-looking cats. His use of *oil paint* is particularly suited to his penchant for using heavily impasted *colours*.

He lives and works in Kolkata.

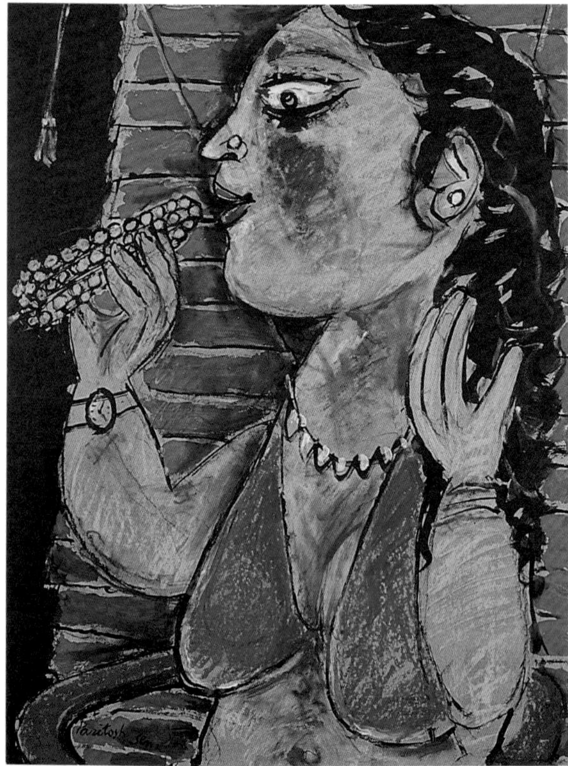

Sen, Paritosh: "Women eating Bhutta", *Mixed media*, 1996, 73x56 cm.

Sen, Prabhas (1919–2001) b. Bengal. Education: Dip. in *FA*. *VBU*, GSA Kolkata, Certificate Institute of Industrial Design Tokyo & later in Paris. Solos: Kolkata, Mumbai. Group participations: Kolkata & other centres in India; International: Smithsonian Institute Washington USA for *terracotta*, *Biennale*. Awards: WB *LKA*, State Abanindranath Award. Member: Calcutta Painters. Commissions: *Sculptures*; also involved in restoring *art* & *casting Ramkinkar Baij's monumental sculpture* jointly with Bipin Goswami. Appointments: Was Dir. of Regional Centre for Traditional Crafts Kolkata; Dir. of the Handicrafts Development Corporation & engaged in building up a collection of Bengal Handicrafts for the new Karuangan Museum; Written articles on Indian *arts* & *crafts*; Including monogram on the handicrafts of Orissa & a book on *crafts* of WB. Collections: In his own studio *Santiniketan*, and pvt. corporates.

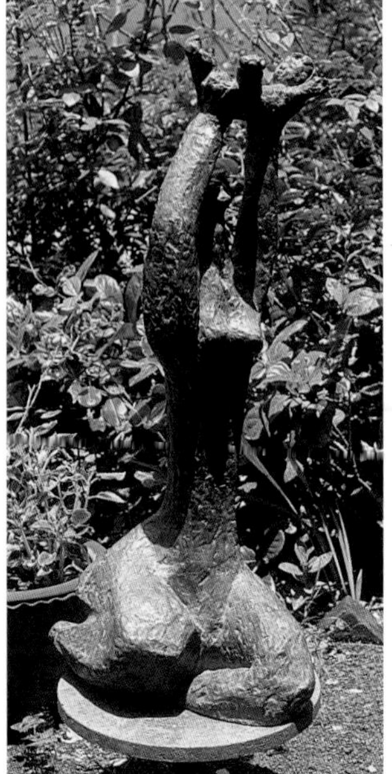

Sen, Prabhas: "Untitled", *Bronze*.

Prabhas Sen as a *sculptor* had worked mostly in *bronze*, *wood*, *terracotta* and *mixed media*. His *forms* were both expressionistic and *figurative*. There is an element of the primitive in his simplification and *distortion*.

Senathipathi, Manickam (1939–) b. Chennai, TN. Education: Dip. in *drawing* & *painting GCAC* Chennai. Solos: Grindlays Art Gallery, Regional Centre *LKA* & MMB Chennai, MMB Bangalore, *JAG*, *COAG*, *G88*, *SAI*. Group participations: *LKA* Bangalore & Kerala, *Triennale* New Delhi, Museum Gallery, Easel Gallery & Taj Coromandal Gallery Chennai, *AFA* & *BAAC* Kolkata, *JAG*, TAG, *VEAG*, SRAG; International: England, Holland, Morocco, Malaysia, Poland, Australia. *Art* camps: Kerala, TN *LKA* Kodaikanal, SZCC Chennai. *Auctions*: Osian's Mumbai. Awards: Senior Fellowship Dept. of Culture, Govt. of India New Delhi, TN *LKA*. Member: *LKA* Regional Center & Committe Member *LKA* Chennai; President–Artists' Handicrafts Association Chennai &

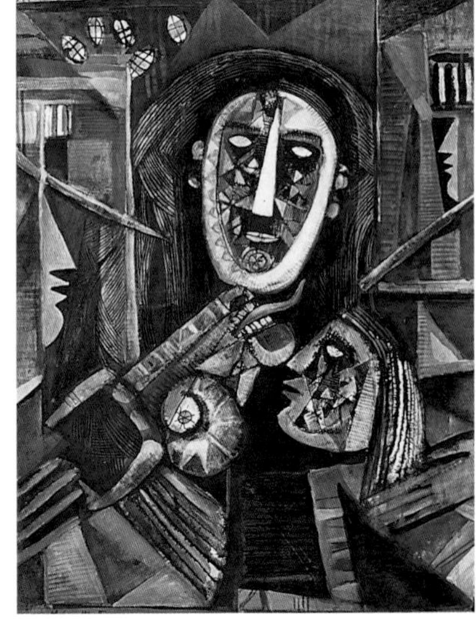

Senathipathi, Manickam: "Affection" *Mixed media* on *Paper*, 1996, 92x61 cm.

Cholamandal; General Council Member *LKA* New Delhi. Commissions: *Murals Mahabalipuram*. Collections: *NGMA* & *LKA* New Delhi, KAR & TN Govt. Muse-um, Air India Mumbai; International: Asia & Pacific Museum Poland, pvt. & corporates in Chennai & Ahmedabad.

From the very beginning, Manickam Senathipathi has been fascinated with the *images* of the various *gods* and goddesses forming the Hindu pantheon. There may be more than a touch of the *abstract* in his evocative use of multilimbed and multiheaded *figures*, but this is an abstraction born out of simplification and use of decorative *pattern*. Mythological *motifs* and symbols suffused with spirituality enliven the flat surface of the *background*, regardless of whether the *medium* is *pen* and *ink* or *metal*. The thin *metal* sheet lends itself admirably to the use of *texture*, while the *inks* enervate the surface of the *painting* with their translucence.

He lives and works in *Cholamandal*.

Sengupta, Siddhartha (1958–) b. Purulia, WB. Education: Dip. in *FA*. CVA Kolkata. Solos: *AFA & Arts Acre* Kolkata. Group participations: *AFA*, *BAAC*, *Arts Acre*, Tagore Art Gallery & *GC* Kolkata, Batra Art Gallery, *LKA* New Delhi, *NCAG*, TAG. Group pariticipation: *Arts Acre* India; International: London. *Art* camps & workshops: Gangotsav Art camp GUJ, Calcutta Dresden Artists workshop in MMB with *Arts Acre*, *Collage* workshop at *Arts Acre* with Alliance Francaise Kolkata. Awards: State *LKA* & AAI Award Kolkata. Member: *Arts Acre* Kolkata. Collections: *LKA* New Delhi, *GC* Mumbai; International: Fukuoka Museum Japan & pvt. & corporates.

Sengupta has experimented with several *media*, including *oil painting* and *mixed media* (*ink* and *watercolour*). His *style*, though basically *figurative*, has evolved from a linear patternization to a self-centred melting down of *form*. Though it is the people around him that inspire his *creations*, there is also a *spiritual* quality in his use of *colour*. He has a series of *paintings* based on the city of Varanasi, with pilgrims bathing in *ghats* and offering prayers around installed deities. These *paintings* appear almost supernatural in their softness and malleability of *form*.

He lives and works at *Arts Acre* village, Kolkata.

Sepia A dark brown *pigment* made from cuttle-fish secretions and used in *watercolours* and *inks* to create *monochrome wash drawings*. They were very popular in the latter half of the 19th century and the early years of the 20th century. Refer *Suhas Bahulkar*, *Surjeet Kaur Choyal*, *Lalitha Lajmi*.

Serial Imagery The repetition of the same *image*, sometimes with slight variations. The concept was used in the Pop *portraits* of A. Warhol and in the *abstracts* of D. Judd. Some Indian *artists* have used this type of *imagery* in their *paintings* and *sculptures* occasionally. This concept is also seen in the early *paintings* and *sculptures* of Indian *art*, e.g. *Ajanta* and *Ellora*. Refer *Flat Colour*, *Folk Art*, *Offset Printing*, *Buddhist Art*, *Navjot Altaf*, *Jogen Chowdhury*, *Pilloo Pochkhanawalla*, *N. Pushpamala*, *A. A. Raiba*.

Serigraphy Serigraphy comes from the root word Serikos, a Greek word meaning silk, another term for *screen printing*, *silk screen printing*. Earlier Chinese and Egyptians printed in this *technique*, and later developed in Europe and United States in 1930, originally adapted to flat *patterns; painterly* effects are a *modern* innovations. A stretched screen is also made from porous fabric such as nylon, silk or organdi, whose non-image area is covered with stopout *varnish*, which makes it a *stencil* for *printing*. Refer *Faculty of Fine Arts*, *Krishan Ahuja*, *Jyoti Bhatt*, *Devraj Dakoji*, *Kavita Nayar*.

Seshadri, Premalatha H. (1947–) b. Bangalore. Education: *GCAC* Chennai, Middlesex Polytechnic London. Solos: Alliance Francaise & Varma Art Gallery Bangalore, MMB Mumbai & Chennai, TAG, *JAG*, *CYAG*, *AIFACS;* International: London. Group participations: British Council Division & Madras State *LKA* Chennai, Kala Mela Bangalore, 50 years of India's Independence Chennai, *CKP*, *CYAG*, HAS; International: Festival of India USA, Festival of South British Museum London. Conducted workshop: Udagamangalam TN. Awards: Mysore State *LKA*, Mysore Alliance Francaise de Bangalore, British Council scholarship, Dept. of Culture Govt. of India Fellowship for *painting*, British Council Visitorship. Other activities: Worked on *printmaking* at *GAC;* Designed *block printing* Hyderabad, Dyeing & printing Madurai. Collections: In India & abroad.

Premalatha H. Seshadri's *eclectic* study of *printmaking techniques*, both conventional and otherwise was to influence her work greatly. The earlier works comprised *etchings*, *drawings* and *watercolours* teeming with fish, birds and animals. There was also a series devoted to man and her interpretation of the man-animal *form*. It is the primitive, and the *prehistoric* that has influenced her with its gestural *symbolism* and linear simplicity. Like the primitive *artists*, she too has limited her *colour palette* to the use of a few *earth colours*. Her creatures speak of her keen sense of observation, especially of *nature*, in their *rhythm* and *balance*.

She lives and works in Chennai.

Seth, D.B. "Deven" (1944–2000) b. Bareilly, UP. Education: GCAC Lucknow University, B.FA. *College of Art* Delhi University. Solos: The Heritage Chennai, TKS, *AIFACS*, SRAG, *Dhoomimal*, *JAG*, TAG. Group participations: *LKA* & RB New Delhi, IAFA Amritsar, SKP, *AIFACS*, TKS, *Dhoomimal*, *JAG*, *BAS*, *BB*; International: London, Sharjah, Singapore. Art Fairs: *LKA* New Delhi, *AIFACS*, SKP. *Art* camps: Bihar, *LKA* UP, Regional Centre Lucknow. Awards: Shilpa Kala Parishad Bihar, PUJ *LKA* Chandigarh, UP *LKA* Lucknow & *LKA* National Award, Was a Joint Hon. Secretary & awarded Kala Vibhushan by *AIFACS*, SKP. Collections: *NGMA* & SKP Museum New Delhi, *LKA* New Delhi & UP, Air India Mumbai, *AIFACS;* International: Columbia, Germany, Dubai, USA, pvt. & public.

Nature was the central *theme* of D.B. Seth's *paintings*. He termed the works an attempt at capturing the spirit of *nature*, earlier in *watercolours* and later due to the lack of good *paper*, in *oils*. His *oil paintings* include features like the use of thin glazes of *paint*, spontaneous *brushwork*, with *paint* thinned in *turpentine*, and brisk wiping. He also used the *palette knife* for *drawing* neatly incised *lines*. Again as in *watercolours*, he used the *white* of the *canvas* surface and never the *white pigment*. The results are a kind of *visual texture* created by the spontaneous yet contrived dashes of *pigment*. He lived and worked in Delhi, his subjects included *figures* and flowers, but it was underwater *imagery*, with fish and aquatic vegetation that inspired him most.

Sfumato (Italian)=having indistinct blurred *outlines*. Used to describe transitions of *colour*, especially from *light* to dark, so gradual as to be almost imperceptible. Leonardo da Vinci used this *technique* to achieve soft, romantic *images*, as if viewed in a smoky or misty haze.

Popularized by the *Bengal School*, strongly influenced by Japanese *techniques*. Works of *Abanindranath Tagore*, *Hemendranath Mazumdar* reflect the serene beauty of sfumato, as do the later works of Pratima Sheth. Refer *K. Khosa*.

Sgraffito (Italian)=scratched. It is a *technique* of scratching through or incising through one layer to expose the lower, differently coloured layer. The *burin* or the needle is the tool commonly used. Refer *Manu Parekh*, *Ambadas*, *Piraji Sagara*, *Setlur Gopal Vasudev*.

Shadanga (The six limbs/canons of Indian *art*). "Rupa-Bheda, Pramanani, BHAVA, Lavanya Yojanam, Sadrisyam, Varnika-Bhangam, Iti Chitram Sadangakam"–This verse from the CHITRASUTRA sums up the six rules that an ancient Indian *artist* had to follow. A *painting* or a *sculpture* would be deemed incomplete, if it lacked even one of the six canons.

1. Rupa *(form)* refers to the outward appearance of the *figure*; Rupa-Bheda is the difference in *form*.

2. Pramanani (scale and *proportion*) refers to the *size* and shape of the *figure*.

3. BHAVA (emotion) without which the *figure* would have no life.

4. Lavanya (grace) as in the lustre of the eye, the breath in the nostrils; Lavanya Yojanam–use of grace.

5. Sadrisyam (similitude) comparision of the various parts of the body with different elements of *nature*. i.e.–eyes shaped like a fish, a lotus or that of a deer, nose curved like a parrot's beak, thighs like the trunk of a banana tree and so on.

6. Varna *(colour)*–the influx of *colour*, either *symbolic* or naturalistic. i.e. blue skin denotes VISHNU or his various AVATARAS; Varnika-Bhangam–indicates use of *colour*, *brush-strokes*, even the caste of the subject.

Refer *Aesthetics*, *Canon of Proportion*, *Mathura Art*, *Abanindranath Tagore*.

Shade *Black* mixed with any *colour* creates a shade, opposite of *tint*. It is a dark *tone* of *colour* created especially with regard to the *depth* a *gradation* of *colour* known as shading. Shading is especially used in *academic art* like *portraits*, *life-drawings* and the *graphic arts*. In India, shading was used in *Ajanta* cave *paintings*. Shading with the monochromic effect was the *artists'* expression in single *tonal value* by *cross-hatching*. Refer *Bengal School*, *Background*, *Chiaroscuro*, *Contour Shading*, *Foreshortening*, *Hatching*, *Hue*, *Light*, *Modelling*, *Monochrome*, *Stippling*, *Thanjavur (Tanjore) Paintings on Glass*, *Tint*, *Narayan S. Bendre*, *Kailash Chandra Sharma*, *Ram Gopal Vijaivargiya;* Illustrations–*Academic Art*, *Thanjavur (Tanjore) Painting*, *Jyoti Bhatt*, *Nikhil Biswas*, *Chhaganlal D. Mistry*, *Surya Prakash*, *Vrindavan Solanki*, *Sarada Charan Ukil*.

Shadow Shadow is an area which is darker than its surroundings. Also a reflected *image*. Refer *Silhouette*, *Bengal Revivalism*, *Bengal School*, CHITRAKATHI, *Embroidery*, *Impressionism*, *Mughal Miniature*, *Bundi*, *A. Ramachandran*, *K. Vasant Wankhede*.

Shah, Bhanu (1935–) b. Ahmedabad. Education: B.A. (Fine) & Dip. in museology *FFA* (*MSU*). Over 24 solos: TAG, *PUAG*, Culture Centre Ahmedabad, Urja Art Gallery Vadodara; International: Canada. Group participations: National *LKA* New Delhi, *BAS*. Awards: National Award *LKA* New Delhi, GUJ State Art Exhibition, *BAS*; Gaurav Puraskar GUJ *LKA*. Fellowship: Senior Fellowship Dept. of Culture by Govt. of India New Delhi. Member: "Progressive Painters" Ahmedabad 1961–68, International Kite Festivals–Jury Ahmedabad, Dir. Umed Bhavan Palace Jodhpur; Kite being his subject, he represented India in other countries at International Festivals in France & Thailand; Art Kite *exhibitions*, public performances of kite flying as an *art*–national & international: Ahmedabad, Jodhpur, France, Holland, Philadelaphia USA. Appointments: Slide shows & lectures in India & abroad; Films, TV Interviews, Radio talks; Research from 1982–85 on History of Kite flying all over the world from 200 BC till the present day. Publications: "Stitch in Gujarat Embroidery", "Art Kites of India", "Wood Carvings of Gujarat", "Love Sculptures of India", "Step Wells of Gujarat", "Illustrated & Engraved Metal Objects of India", "Tribal Women of Gujarat"; Interviews & News in dailies & weeklies. Collections: *LKA* GUJ & New Delhi, Baroda Museum. Personal collections: Stitch *embroidery*, Sanji–stencil work of Mathura, *Art* Kites of India & Kites of other nations, and "My Poems" in Gujarati.

Bhanu Shah is a *painter* who has developed an interest in the *art* of kite-flying during MAKARA-SANKRANTI the festival celebrated on 14th January specially in GUJ. Unlike the decorative *pattern* of the kites, his recent *paintings* show an affinity for the *abstract* and the gestural, with its spontaneous sweeps of the *brush* creating the same swift currents of air that send his kites soaring sky-high.

He has also done *drawing* and stitching himself, with the machine stitch, in Saurashtra folk *embroidery style*.

He lives and works in Ahmedabad where he designed and founded the world's second International Kite Museum.

Shah, Haku (1934–) b. Valod, GUJ. Education: B.FA., M.A. (Fine) *MSU*. Solos: *GC* & *BAAC* Mumbai, *Art Heritage* New Delhi, Ashoka Gallery & *AFA* Kolkata, Marvel Art Gallery and Sanskar Kendra Museum Ahmedabad, *JAG*, *CYAG*. Retrospective: NID; International: New York, Berkeley, City Art Museum St.Louis & International House Philadelphia USA. Group participations: *LKA* New Delhi, *GC* & Coomarswamy Hall Mumbai. *Auctions*: Osian's Mumbai. Awards: Rockefeller

Grant USA, Nehru Fellowship (Research in *tribal art* of GUJ) & Padma Shri–Govt. of India. Appointments: Designer of Handlooms Govt. of India 1959–62; International: Regent Prof. in Davis School of Environmental Design University of California USA; Advisor at Mingei International San Diego USA; *Curator* Tribal Museum GUJ Vidhyapith Ahmedabad, Curated exhibition on *tribal art* in India & USA. Major Projects in New Delhi Udaipur; International: Amsterdam, London, Japan. Organized workshop & photo-documentary *exhibitions*. Gave Lectures & slide shows. Publications: Written & published Books & articles on Rural & Tribal Crafts & Anthropology; Made the film "Scraps". Collections: *NGMA* New Delhi, *BAAC* Kolkata, Chandigarh University Museum, Godrej Mumbai, *CYAG*.

Haku Shah's research into the *tribal arts* and *crafts* has influenced his *paintings*. His *images* are culled from his exposure to these people; his *figures* being stark and simple with large staring eyes and a timelessness that can only be felt in a village. Other elements–the trees, animals and flora–have also been reduced to near geometric, flat planes of *earth colour*. Though he has experimented with *lithography*, *wood cut* and *drawing*, he has settled down to *painting* with *oils* and digital *art*. His *compositions* too are basic, with *visual* elements like *space* division, *colour* and *line*, folk and tribal simplification inspiration being all important. He has recently experimented in a collaborative effort with vocalist Shubha Mudgal to encourage collaborational efforts of combining *art* and devotional poetry.

He lives and works in Ahmedabad.

Shah, Haku: "Cows Cowherd", 1993.

Shah, Harendra (1952–) b. Indore. Education: National Dip. in *painting* FA. College Indore. Solos: Bhopal, Delhi, Mumbai, Indore. Group participations: Bhopal, New Delhi, Chennai, Ujjain, Nagpur, Raipur, *Artists' Centre* Mumbai, *AFA* Kolkata, *JAG*, BAG. *Art* camps: Bhimbetka *Landscape* Camp MP, Youth Artists Camp Indore. Awards: State Award Indore, AIKS Ujjain, Youth Artists Exhibition Bhopal, Natraj Utsav Omkareshwar. Collections: MP State Art Gallery Bhopal, Lalbaug Palace Indore, *Gallery 7* Mumbai, *Roopankar BB* & pvt. abroad.

Black was the predominant *colour* in Harendra Shah's work in the first 10 years of *painting*. He used it to convey the various nuances of *landscape* before moving on almost automatically into abstraction. This element of abstraction always remained in his works even when the *figure* crept in. However he uses *warm colours*, *handling* them with the same finesse as his *black* works. In his recent works, he makes a substantial use of *texture*, thinning the *oil pigment* and loosely brushing it to achieve tonal variations, & spontaneous almost *calligraphic* strokes.

He lives and works in Indore.

Shah, Himmat (1933–) b. Lothal, GUJ. Studied under *Jagu Bhai Shah*, Drawing Teachers course *JJSA;* Dip. in *painting* under *Narayan S. Bendre MSU*; *Etching* under S.W. Hayter & *Krishna N. Reddy*. Solos: Kunika Chemould, Konark Art Gallery, MMB, IIT & *Art Heritage* New Delhi, *Art & Print* Gallery Kolkata, *SG* Mumbai, TKS, *Dhoomimal*, *GAC*, HCVA Ahmedabad. Group participations: *SG* & Timeless Art Mumbai, *LKA*, Kunika Chemould & *Group 1890* New Delhi, Progressive Painters Group Ahmedabad, *Dhoomimal*, *Roopankar BB*; International: *Biennales* Antwerp & Paris, Festival of India Royal Academy London. *Auctions*: Sotheby's-Timeless Art & Heart Mumbai. Awards: *AIFACS*, SKP Award, *LKA's* Research Grant at *GAC* & National *LKA* Award New Delhi, Gold Medal J&K Academy, *BAS;* International: French Govt. Scholarship. Fellowship: Emeritus Fellowship Govt. of India, Govt. of India Fellowship. Founder member: *Group 1890* New Delhi. Commissions: *Murals* in brick, *cement* & *concrete* Ahmedabad. Appointments: Designer *WSC* New Delhi. Collections: *NGMA* New Delhi, *CYAG*.

Terracotta, the sensuous *tactile medium* used both by the artisan and the *artist*, has fascinated Himmat Shah for the past several decades. He prepares the *clay*, himself, allowing it to mature over a period of years, until it becomes *viscous* enough for *slip casting*. The *slip* is mixed at times with brick or *marble* dust to create interesting *textures*. He also *casts* in *plaster* small *found objects* to create sophisticated *forms* and shapes. His recurring *motif* however is the head, which is nearly impersonal in his negation of facial features. Instead, these larger than life *terracotta* pieces, covered at times with metallic foil, *silver* leaf or simply texturized stand like mute, implacable entities of the past. He has also created interesting *reliefs*, treating them in the *manner* of *tactile paintings* using *plaster*, tar, cloth, *enamel paint* and *silver* foil.

He lives and works at *GAC*. Refer *Clay Water*.

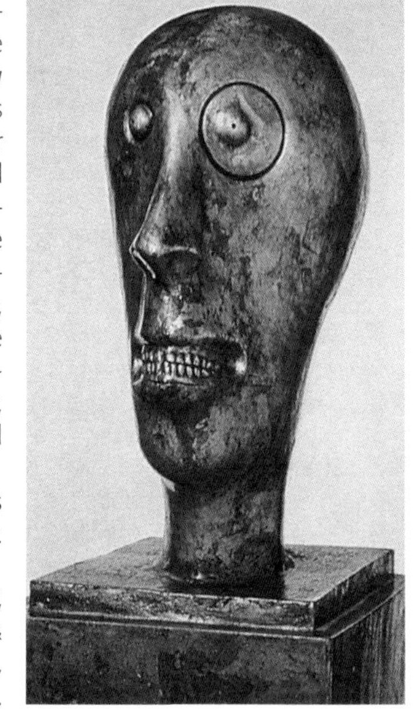

Shah, Himmat: "Head Z", *Plaster,* Linseed *Oil* & *Silver* foil, 1978, 98x24x33 cm.

Shah, Jagu Bhai (1916–) b. Saurashtra, GUJ. Education: GDA *JJSA*, Post-Dip. in *mural painting JJSA*, Adv. *sculpture* course Chennai, Senior Dip. in *Art* & *Art education* JMI, *Fresco painting Banasthali Vidyapith* RAJ. Solos: *LKA* & CMC New Delhi, *LKA* Ahmedabad, TKS, *AIFACS*. Group participations: National Exhibitions New Delhi, Group Exhibition in New Delhi & Mumbai, *AIFACS*, SKP. Awards: Dolly Cursetjee Award & Lord Willington Award Mumbai, International Art Exhibition London by *JJSA* & *AIFACS;* Hon.: *LKA* GUJ, International art & Veteran Artist *AIFACS*, Senior Fellowship Dept. of Culture SKP. Collections: *LKA* & *NGMA* New Delhi, Gandhi Smriti Museum Bhavnagar GUJ, *AIFACS*, JMI, SKP, *JJSA*, *BB*.

Jagu Bhai Shah painted *landscapes* (both in *tempera* and *watercolour*) of his native Saurashtra. He also painted street and *cityscapes* that documented the important events of India's struggle for freedom. He illustrated Gandhiji's teachings on the walls of the Swarajya Ashram near Bardoli. Later on, he switched to *oil paintings* effectively changing his *style* to an Indianized version of *Cubism*. His *compositions* represented an *eclectic* assimilation of the past-like the *Ajanta frescoes*, the folk-oriented *Picchwai paintings* on cloth and folk *paintings* based on Pata (scroll *painting*). The gestures he employed in his *narratives* are reminiscent of folk and street theatre.

He lives and works in New Delhi.

Shah, Prabha (1947–) b. Jodhpur, RAJ. Studied *painting* under *P.N. Choyal* University of Udaipur. Over 29 solos: Srishti Art Gallery & *LKA* New Delhi, C.P. Art Gallery Chennai, *BAAC* Kolkata, University Library Jaipur, SRAG, *JAG*, TAG *GMAG*; International: Canada. Group participations: *Triennale*, *LKA* & *NGMA* New Delhi, RAJ *LKA* Jaipur, Harmony Mumbai *Biennale BB*, *AIFACS*, SKP; International: New York, London. Awards: Silver Medal Udaipur RAJ *LKA* Jaipur, MKKP Raipur, *AAJ* Udaipur, *AIFACS;* International: Commonwealth Society for Deaf London. Member: Executive Council RAJ *LKA*. Appointments: Fellow Junior & Senior Dept. of Culture Govt. of India & *LKA* New Delhi. Collections: *NGMA* & *LKA* New Delhi, RAJ *LKA* Jaipur, TIFR.

Prabha Shah's earliest *images* were culled from *Rajasthani miniature paintings*, with their subtle mixture of the geometric and the curvilinear i.e. *architecture* and *figures*. Over the years, she has evolved a *pictorial vocabulary* that has become increasingly *abstract* though it is always grounded in reality. *Texture* is an integral part of her *comp-osition*. She often uses the roller to create subtle interplays of *light* and *shade*. She handles the *medium* in *oil painting* with the burst of flora and fauna, meticulously and realistically rendered, and with some accuracy.

She lives and works in New Delhi.

Shah, Shantilal M. (1922–1993) (Also known as Shanti Shah) b. Ahmedabad, GUJ. Studied in *art* training CNCFA, Dip. *Madras School of Art* (*GCAC*) Chennai, Studied in Munich Art Academy, Royal Academy of Amsterdam 1959–60. Solos: Kolkata, Chennai, Nainital, Udagamangalam, Kodaikanal, Darjeeling, Ahmedabad; International: Srilanka, Munich, Paris, Amsterdam, Rome, Hague, London, Washington, New York, Baltimore. Group participations: For *Portraits* Hyderabad, *BAS*. *Artists* camps: Haripura Congress met *Nandalal Bose*, *Mosaic murals* in GUJ & RAJ. Awards: State *LKA* Hon. Ahmedabad, *Portrait BAS* Mumbai, Mysore DAE *portrait* & *landscape*, Gold Medal Hyderabad, Received Felicitations for *portraits*; Scholarship Indian Govt. Culture Dept. New Delhi; International: Munich Germany, Netherland. Commissions: *Murals* & *portraits*. Publications: *Art Critic* Gujarat Samachar newspaper & a column on *Art* Activities "Aakar-Aakruti" for 12 years. Collections: Mysore State Chitralaya, Trivandrum Art Gallery & National Art Gallery Chennai, Sri Kasturbhai Lalbhai Ahmedabad; International: Ambassadors from Japan, Sri Lanka, London, Munich, Washington & Baltimore.

Shantilal M. Shah specialized in *portraits* and *mosaic murals*. His *portraits* were highly *realistic* with extreme attention to detail, right upto the wrinkles on the face and wisps of *white* hair. Brought up in the turmoil of the freedom struggle, his most prolific *drawings* were executed in prison. Later, with more European influence he paid greater attention to *forms* and painted a series of *nudes*. On the other hand his large *murals* were basically conceptual in *nature* but not totally *abstract* either.

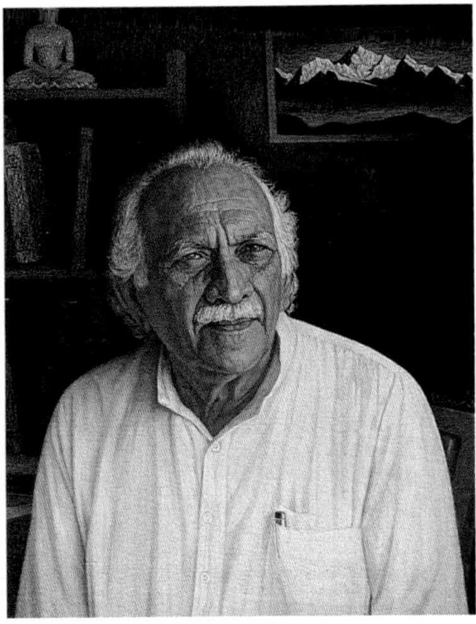

Shah, Shantilal M.: "Darshak, Portrait of Manubhai Pancholi", *Oils*.

Shah, Somalal Chunilal (1905–1994) b. Kapadvanj GUJ. Education: Vadodara *KB* under Pramodkumar Chatterjee, ISOAS under *Kshitendranath Mazumdar JJSA*. Solos: Mumbai, Vadodara, Ahmedabad, Bhavnagar, Rajkot. Group participations: Kolkata, Pune, Chennai, Rajkot *BAS*, Marvel Art Gallery Ahmedabad; International: UK. Awards: GUJ Sahitya Parishad Gold Medal, "Gujarat Nan Pankhio" Bombay State prize, Silver Medal Umareth, GUJ *LKA* Gaurav Puraskar & *Ravishankar M. Raval* Award, *AIFACS*. Publications: *Drawing* book for children, "Aapana Pankhio" 50 *drawings* by Somalal Shah, "Birds of Saurashtra & Kutch", "Rang Rekha– Album of *paintings*". Collections: *NGMA* New Delhi, GUJ *LKA* Gandhinagar, Rajkot Museum, Bhavnagar Museum, Vadodara Museum & pvt.

Somalal Chunilal Shah practised the *wash technique* of *painting* similar to the Bengal *style*, enriched with the bright *colours* of his native GUJ. He recorded the life of people living in the Saurashtra village influenced by the *landscape* and colourful costumes. He had the ability to bring to life ordinary scenes and characters, be they birds, animals, human beings or balconies of old ruined houses. In addition to the historical and mythological scenes, he also illustrated history books with *pen* and *ink drawings*.

Shah, Sumant V. (1933–) b. Chanava, GUJ. Education: B.FA. *MSU*. Solos: *Artists' Centre* Mumbai, PUJ University Museum Chandigarh, others in Jalandhar, Ahmedabad, Ludhiana, Kapurthala, *JAG*, TKS. Group participations: *LKA*, New Delhi, IAFA Amritsar, PUJ *LKA* Chandigarh, *AIFACS*, *BAS*, HAS, AIKS. *Art* camps & workshops: Patna *LKA* in New Delhi, PUJ *LKA* Chandigarh, *Printmaking* Jalandhar, Cultural Festival Chandigarh, NZCC Patiala. Awards: *AIFACS*, IAFA&C Society Amritsar, AIKS, HAS. Fellowship: *MSU*. Publications: Includes articles in newspapers, PUJ *LKA's* book on "Contemporary Artists working in PUJ"; Talks & interviews on Doordarshan & AIR. Collections: *NGMA* & *LKA* New Delhi, PUJ University Museum Chandigarh, *Murals* Palitana, GUJ & pvt.

Sumant Shah's early works revolved around the rural life in GUJ, with moving depictions of labourers, farmers and village folk engaged in their respective occupations. These works were quite representative. His later versions of similar subjects saw him developing his *style* with the use of *colours* such as yellow, sienna and *black*. His study of Jaipur *frescoes* during his fellowship was to effect another change: the *figures* became stylized and almost geometric with the *narrative* tightly woven around them. MAHAVIRA, the 24th *Jain* Tirthankara was his subject in the 70s, the large mural-like work had more than 300 *figures* of humans, animals, birds, *Gods* and the *demons* painted amongst trees, plants and *landscapes*. His later *abstracts* and *collage* were based on capturing *atmospheric effects*.

He lives and works in Vadodara, GUJ.

Shah, Vinod (1934–) b. GUJ. M.FA., 1961. Education: *FFA MSU*. Solos: Over 10 in Mumbai; International: Singapore, Boston, London, Edinburgh. Group participations: Mumbai, New Delhi, Bangalore, Nepal; Participations: *Triennale* New Delhi, Mount Abu, *BAS;* International: Bangladesh, *Biennale* Paris. *Art* camps: Conducted & participated in *art* workshops in India; International: London. Awards: National Awards, AIKS, *BAS*, HAS, *AIFACS*. Commissions: *Murals* For Parliament House New Delhi & Mount Abu. Collections: British Council New Delhi, *LKA* New Delhi & GUJ, TAG, *BB* pvt. India & abroad.

Vinod Shah's basic interest is simplified *landscapes* or interiors with *collages* in *mixed media*, using *watercolours* or *acrylics*. His *paintings* make eloquent use of man-made structures, human *forms*, animals or slum dwellers. His *form* interacts with the *colours* in his *collages* to create interesting surface variations.

He lives and works in Vadodara.

Shakila (1969–) b. 24 Parganas, WB. No formal training in *art*, self-taught, Studied under *B.R. Panesar*. Solos: *CKAG*. Group participations: *AFA*, *BAAC*, WBSA, LKK & *CIMA* Kolkata, National *LKA* & *NGMA* New Delhi, SCZC AP, MP & MAHA, *ISOA*, *GK*, *Biennale*, *BB*. Awards: WBSA & *AFA* Kolkata, UNESCO Award, *ISOA*; National Scholarship HRD New Delhi. Collections: *LKA* New Delhi; International: National Museum Singapore & pvt.

Shakila works with the *collage medium*. She is inspired by *painting exhibitions* held in and around where she lives. For her tearing a piece of *paper* is an *art*. She collects recycled *paper* bags, being fascinated by the *colours*, her surroundings and experimenting with various *forms* and subjects, such as Utopian *landscapes*, the goddess KALI and the street scenes.

She lives and works in 24 Parganas, WB.

Shakti=power, strength, might, energy. **1.** It refers to the feminine *form*—as against SHIVA the male principle. **2.** A synonym of PARVATI, DURGA and KALI, which embodies both the benevolent and the malevolent aspects of human *nature*. **3.** Shakti is both the symbol of fertility as well as ferocity.

Though religious and contradictory, the SHAKTI cult has always been represented in Indian *sculptures*, with the *stone engravings* in various temples, bazaar-type *paintings*, e.g. *Elephanta*, *Khajuraho*, *Thanjavur (Tanjore) paintings* and Patachitras. *Images* are sometimes used to signify the *form* showing energy that the *artist* wants to express. Later *paintings* veered towards the *abstract* with a cosmic effect, with just that touch of *Realism* and "*spiritual*" quality. Refer *Canvas*, NAYIKA, TANTRA, YONI, *Jalendu Dave*, *J. Srividya*; Illustrations—CHAMUNDA, CHANDI, CHANDIKA, DURGA, KALI, PARVATI, *Prafulla Mohanti*.

Shalebhanjikas They are voluptuous young women, represented standing next to a tree, either kicking it gently with a foot or touching a branch or tendril with one hand. This action supposedly causes a tree to bear flowers or fruits. These women are thus symbols of fertility. They are seen at both Bharhut and Sanchi, though they may be confused with YAKSHIS. Refer *Archaeological Museum*, *Sunga Dynasty or Style*, *Jatin Das*.

Shankha The conch shell carried by VISHNU and his incarnations. It is called Panchajaneya, and is sounded by VISHNU at the *time* of going to battle. In *sculpture* it is usually depicted as a plain conch or a heavily decorated one with tassels of pearls dangling from it. Along the PADMA, CHAKRA and GADA the Shankha is always held in one of VISHNU'S four hands. Refer *Attribute*, CHATUR BHUJA, *Ecological Art*, *Gupta*, MATRIKAS.

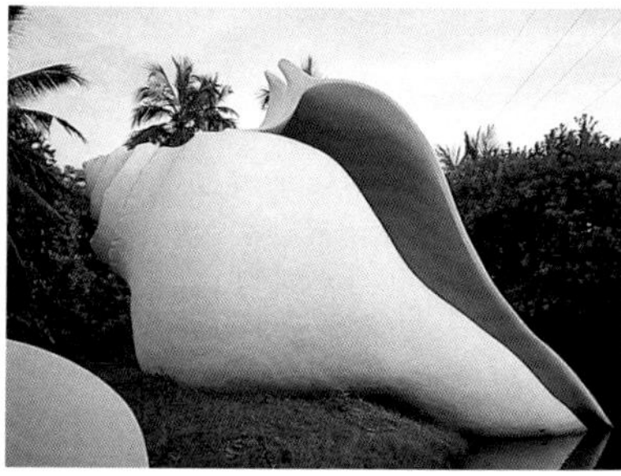

Shankha: *Sculpture* by *Kanayi Kunhiraman*, *Cement Concrete*.

Sharma, Bhawani S. (1945–) b. Banasthali, RAJ. Education: M.FA. in *painting* & M.FA. in *graphic MSU*, *Fresco* training *Banasthali Vidyapith* RAJ, studied in *painting* & history of *art* Milano Italy, Ph.D. Kanpur University. Solos: Jaipur, Chandigarh, Mumbai; International: California USA,

Milano Italy. Group participations: International Cultural Centre New Delhi, *PAG* of Jaipur, *LKA* RAJ, Artists Group in New Delhi, Lucknow, Ahmedabad, Mumbai & Banasthali RAJ, *CYAG*. Participated: *LKA* New Delhi, *AFA* Kolkata, *AIFACS*, SKP, *BAS*, *JAG*; International: Japan, USA, Holland. Workshops, *Artist* camps & seminars: RAJ , Agra, UP, New Delhi. Awards: *LKA* RAJ, Scholarship to Vadodara; International: Italian Scholarship. Members: Board of Studies RAJ University Jaipur, FFA Academy Council *Banasthali Vidyapith*, Executive Council & General Council of RAJ *LKA*, RSA. Appointments: External Examiner in Various Universities, Prof. & HoD at Visual Art Dept. *Banasthali Vidyapith* RAJ. Publications: *Drawings* & articles in newspapers & magazines. Collections: *NGMA* New Delhi, PUJ University Museum Chandigarh, *LKA* New Delhi, UP & RAJ, MMB Mumbai & pvt.

Bhawani S. Sharma not only worked in *graphics* but also *drawing* in *oils* with *forms* observed from *nature*. These *forms* developed and changed their shapes according to the *harmony* of their formal values. Working in *oils*, *watercolours*, *frescoes* and *graphic mediums* he has simplified and stylized them to suit his coloured and sketchy *compositions*.

He works and lives in Jaipur/*Banasthali Vidyapith* RAJ.

Sharma, Bulbul (1952–) Education: Dip. New Delhi Women's Polytechnic, Moscow State University; An *art* teacher for street children. Solos: IIC, TKS, VG, *JAG*. Group participations: National Exhibition & *LKA*, New Delhi, *BAAC* Kolkata, *Triennale* Goa, VG, *AIFACS*, *VAG*, *Dhoomimal*, HG, *LTG*, *PUAG*, *BB Biennale*. Workshop: For disabled children UNICEF, Safdar Hashmi Memorial Trust New Delhi. Publications: Books on "Indian Birds for Children", "My Sainted Aunt"; Illustrates for newspapers & magazine. Collections: *NGMA* & *LKA* New Delhi, UNICEF; International: Washington & pvt.

Texture is important in Bulbul Sharma's works. She cuts, engraves and generally builds up the surface raising it before *painting* her *images*. Her *compositions* are based on elements of *nature* especially flowers and leaves.

She works and lives in New Delhi.

Sharma, Charan (1950–) b. Nathdwara, RAJ. Education: M.A. FA. University Udaipur, *Graphic JJSA*. Solos: Udaipur, Jaipur, *JAG;* International: Singapore. Group participations: Udaipur, Jaipur, Chennai, New Delhi, Mumbai; International: Yugoslavia, Singapore. Participated: International Experimental Art Exhi-bition Budapest, Group show Vienna. *Auction*: Aspary-Helpage India *JAG*. Awards: For *painting* compition *LKA* RAJ & Singapore; Appointments: Taught at Govt. College Nathdwara RAJ; Book designer "The Thousand Moon" on J. Krishnamurthy & also working as a chief designer. Collections: India & Abroad.

Charan Sharma's *canvases* show arches under wooden rafters. He earlier used to *paint landscapes* which depict piles of *stones* and rocks framed with carved arched windows, wooden frames, the sky, *white* clouds and the *light* effects–all are realistic–stylized to his native Nathdwara region in RAJ.

Now he lives and works in Mumbai.

Sharma, Deokinandan (1917–2005) b. RAJ. Education: Dip. in *drawing* & *painting* Maharaja School of Art Jaipur, Special training in *fresco* & *painting Santiniketan* under *Nandalal Bose* & *Benode Behari Mukherjee*. Solos: *LKA* New Delhi, National History Society Mumbai, Jawahar Kala Kendra & Kala Vithi Banasthali, Mussorie, *JAG*; International: Art Gallery of Greater Victoria Canada. Group participations: RB & Kala Mela New Delhi, Govt. Museum Chandigarh, *AIFACS*; International: Canada, London, Tokyo. Organized *fresco* workshops: Khairagarh, Agra; International: Victoria & Saanichton, Canada. Awards: RAJ *LKA*; Fellowship RAJ *LKA*; Senior Fellowship HRD Ministry. Hon.: *AIFACS*. Member: Board of Studies, *Drawing* & *painting* Academic Councils & Faculty Member of University of RAJ, Was a Gen. Council, Executive Committee & Vice President *LKA* RAJ. Appointments: Prof. & HoD at *Banasthali Vidyapith* RAJ for more than 40 years; Prof. Emeritus Award by UGC 1978 to 1980. Commissions: Several *frescoes* in India. Collections: RAJ Central Museum Jaipur, Patiala Museum, *LKA* New Delhi.

Deokinandan Sharma learnt the *techniques* of *wash painting* and *fresco* from *Sailendranath Dey*, *Nandalal Bose* and *Benode Behari Mukherjee* of the *Bengal School*. His works are essentially inspired by both traditional and *folk art*, his subjects being taken from *nature*. While villagers toiling with their animals in fields and *Ajanta*-like lotus ponds abound in his works, it is for his depiction of 'birds' that he is most known. Honoured as one of the best bird *artists* of the world in 1963, his *paintings* were exhibited at the Natural History Society in Mumbai. His *landscapes* in *wash* and *ink* are influenced by his *Bengal School* mentors. He had worked in both *watercolour* and *tempera* in addition to his *frescoes*.

He lived and worked in Banasthali, RAJ.

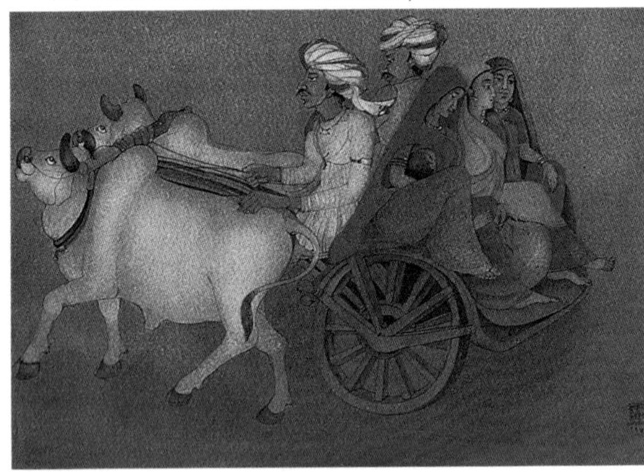

Sharma, Deokinandan: **"Bullock Cart"**, ***Wash Painting***.

Sharma, Kailash Chandra (1944–) b. Jaipur, RAJ. Education: *Art* Dip. IGD MAHA, Dip. in *architecture* RAJ Shiksha Vibhag Bikaner. Solos & group participations: Jawahar Kala Kendra, Kala Mela Jaipur; International: "Contemporary Indian Painting"–*Tradition* to Modernity at Fulda Germany by BHU Varanasi. *Art* camp: RAJ *LKA*, Traditinal *art* camp Jawar Kala Kendra Jaipur–50 years of RAJ Kala Kendra 1999. Awards: Kalidas Samman Ujjain. Scholarship RAJ *LKA*. All India Art Award RAJ *LKA*. Fellowships: Junior & Senior Fellowship HRD Ministry New Delhi. Commissions: *Restoration* works; *Murals* done in Jaipur Raj Gorana; Others in *glass mosaic*, woodstick, *paper*, *ivory*, *Picchwais*, *Kalamkari*, *oil painting* & *watercolours*. Appointments: Teacher in Moheshwari School Jaipur. Collections: RAJ *LKA*; several *frescoes oil painting* at temples trusts Jaipur Palitana GUJ, & pvt.

Kailash Chandra Sharma, belongs to the fifth generation of a family of miniature *painters* (Mussibvir Gharana). Studied *art* from his renowned father Shyam Sunder Lal Sharma and an exponent of the Bengal *style* from *Ram Gopal Vijaivargiya*. His *paintings* are an *eclectic* fusion of several miniature *traditions*, with the added advantage of his Westernized training. *Perspective* and *colour* shading are thus important additions to some of his works, which at times reveal the naiveté of the *Jain miniature tradition* in its use of the "farther" eye and brilliant, *primary colours*. The minute rendering of detail, however imparts a static, almost schematized quality to the works.

He lives and works in Jaipur, where he trains students in the *art* of *miniature painting*.

Sharma, Mohan (1942–d.) b. Nathdwara, RAJ. Education: Govt. Dip. in *art JJSA* with Honours, Dip. *Art* Educated London. Solos: Delhi, Jaipur, Mumbai; International: London. Group participations: National Exhibitions New Delhi, *AIFACS*. Awards: National Award New Delhi, *AIFACS*. Fellowship: *LKA* RAJ. Member: *PAG* RAJ. Appointments: Lecturer of *Painting RSA*. Collections: *NGMA* & *LKA* New Delhi, State Gallery of Modern Art Jaipur.

Mohan Sharma's *paintings* are essentially cubist in their *construction*, with razor-sharp *lines* creating planes and square facets of *light* and *colour*. The *forms* are hard-edged, the *tones* subtle, while *texture* makes its appearance in the *drawings*. Though seemingly *abstract*, the *forms* are essentially representational, with *still lifes* of interiors and *cityscapes* being the chief source of inspiration. Mohan Sharma used a sophisticated *palette* of limited textiary *colours*, with dull yellows and blue-greys predominating.

Sharma, Om Prakash (1932–) b. Bawal, Haryana. Education: Grad. in *drawing* & *painting* Meerut College UP, NDFA Delhi Polytechnic, Post-Grad. in *FA*. Columbia University and Art Students League New York. Over 51solos: Kumar Gallery, Gallery Chanakya, Gallery Aurobindo & Gallery Romain Rolland New Delhi, *GC* Mumbai, Ashoka Gallery Kolkata, *AIFACS*, *Dhoomimal*, SRAG, *PUAG*, GAG; International: USA, Moscow Russia. Group participations: National Exhibitions, *LKA* & *Triennales* New Delhi, *GC* Mumbai, *AIFACS*; International: Tokyo, *Biennale* Bangladesh, "Tantra" *exhibition* German Museum, Neo-Tantra Exhibition Los Angeles & Australia, Contemporary Indian Art Exhibition International Book Fair Frankfurt & Poland. Awards: National Award New Delhi, *AIFACS;* Fulbright Scholarship USA. Commissions: *Murals* for national & international Trade Fairs & Exhibitions. Appointments: Designed 4 *exhibitions* on various political *themes* in New Delhi; Lecture delivered on works; Taught *art* since 1951, Dean of *College of Art* New Delhi. Publications: Written about *art* in magazines and *art* columns; Talks on *art* in India & abroad; Advisor to *Art Education*; Two TV films have been made on his life & works–"On the Journey of Art", "Om Prakash!", "Neo–Tantra". Collections: *NGMA* & *LKA* New Delhi; International: Grey Art Gallery & New York University USA, Berlin Museum Berlin and pvt.

Om Prakash Sharma's works have evolved considerably over the past four decades from *figurative* works, *portraits* and *landscapes* in a Westernized cubistic or impressionistic *style* to geometiricized TANTRIC *motifs* and lastly towards *abstract* expression.

His *paintings* of the 80s, were characterized by the use of the female *nude*, especially in the RAGA series. In the late 80s he painted a series on the MANDALAS. These were *compositions* with a geometric character based on certain cosmic principles–albeit with a *modern* interpretation. However, the crucial element for the *artist* is the emanation of the primordial sound, with numerous vibrating *tones* which have different corresponding *colours* and *hues*.

His recent works entitled "Rite of Colours" shows the unconventional use of *colour*, ranging from baby pink, pure *white*, off *white* to *light* green, applied in a flat *manner*. The works are a consummate mixture of the exotic and the *spiritual*.

He lives and works in New Delhi.

Sharma, Ved Pal (1943–2002) b. Jaipur. Traditional *artist*, learnt *painting* from Mahipalji, his father & Mohanlalji his grandfather, all *court painters* in Jaipur. Solos: RAJ *LKA*, French Embassy New Delhi; International: Switzerland, London, New York. Group exhibitions: Indian Festival USA. Award: National Award. Appointments: Has restored several Indian miniatures; Trained students in India, & abroad directly by the Universities in UK & USA. Publications: Works published in books including "A Second Paradise" & magazines; International: "Vogue" & "New York Times". Collections: *Art* Galleries & pvt. & corporates, national & international.

Ved Pal Sharma, popularly known as Bannu, studied the *art* of *miniature painting* from his father and grandfather. Unlike the traditional miniature *painters* who were limited to the *style* of their court, Bannu experimented with various *styles*, though still adhering to the traditional *pigments* and materials. He had been most influenced by the *Kishangarh* and the *Basohli* School. For his *restoration* work, he uses *hand-made paper* over a 100 years old. He used to prepare his *colours* himself, using semiprecious *stones*, minerals,

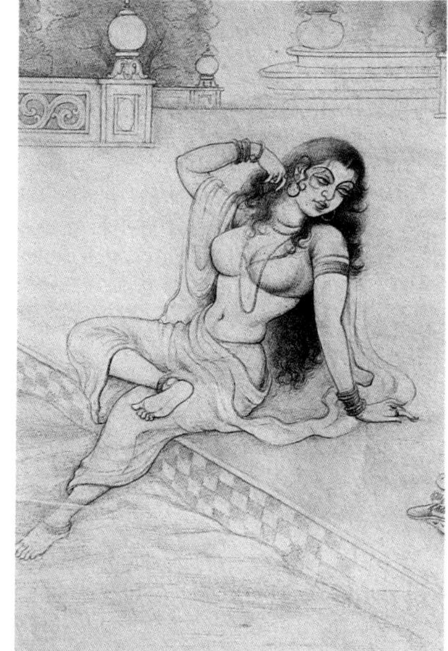

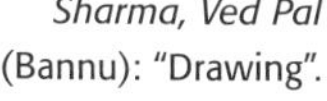

Sharma, Ved Pal (Bannu): "Drawing".

vegetable and insect derivatives. Like the early miniaturists, he too prepared a brilliant yellow from the urine of a cow, fed a diet of mango leaves. In addition, he used *silver* and *gold leaf* for embellishing his *figures* with jewellery. He used clam shells as *palettes* and *bru-shes* made from squirrel hair.

His favourite subject was the human *figure*, especially the voluptuous, half-clad female *form* in romantic situations. His *paintings* are characterized by his fine detailing and soft colouring. He lived and worked in Jaipur, RAJ. Refer *Tempera*.

Shashi (1947–) b. Mumbai. Education: Dip. in *painting JJSA* Dip. in *painting, ceramic* & *sculpture* Polish University Poland. Solos: Kolkata, New Delhi, Mumbai; International: Poland, Estonia. Group participations: *NGMA* New Delhi, *Biennale* Bhopal, TKS, *VAG, AIFACS*, SKP; International: Poland. *Art* camps: Bhopal, Haryana, RAJ, *GAC*, SKP; International: *Ceramic* & *sculpture* in Poland. Awards & Merits: *JJSA*, Consolation Prize GUJ State. Commission: Works done in Vishakapatam & New Delhi. Collections: *NGMA*, New Delhi, Bombay University, *VAG*, SKP; International: Polland & pvt.

Shashi works with *clay/terracotta*. Her *forms* are based on the humanistic *tradition*. She *moulds clay* with circular movements into hewn *figures* representing the Earth Mother. Her plaques are full of expressive power.

She works at *GAC* and lives in New Delhi.

Shaw, Lalu Prasad (1937–) b. Suri, WB. Education: Dip. in *FA*. *GCAC* Kolkata, Experimented in *etching* & *lithography*. Solos: *Painting* & *graphic* at Kolkata, & *Graphic* at *Art Heritage* New Delhi, Bangalore, Udipi & *SAI*. Group participations: *BAAC* Kolkata, *LKA* New Delhi, *SCA, AIFACS, BAS, Triennale* New Dellhi; International: Texas, Poland, Paris, Italy, Norway, USA, UK, *Biennale* London, Yugoslavia, Norway, Baghdad & Bangladesh, Youth Festival Art Exhibition Prague, Whiteley's Art Gallery London. *Auctions*: Osian's Mumbai; International: Christie's London. Awards: National award New Delhi, *LKA* state WB, *BAAC* Kolkata. Member: *SCA*. Appointments: Over 16 years serving *VBU*, Lecturer/Reader in *graphic art*. Collections: *LKA* & *BAAC* Kolkata, *NGMA* New Delhi; International: Art Forum Singapore.

His first works were painted in *watercolours* and *oils*. These works were basically flat, geometric and non-figurative. It was when he started experimenting with *etching* and other *printmaking techniques* that the geometric rigidity gave way to more flexible, less detailed *motifs* in *black* and *white*. With *lithography*, he incorporated a *calligraphic* touch to the works. His *gouache paintings* are two-dimensional, with the *space* being divided by the *contour lines* of the single *figure composition*.

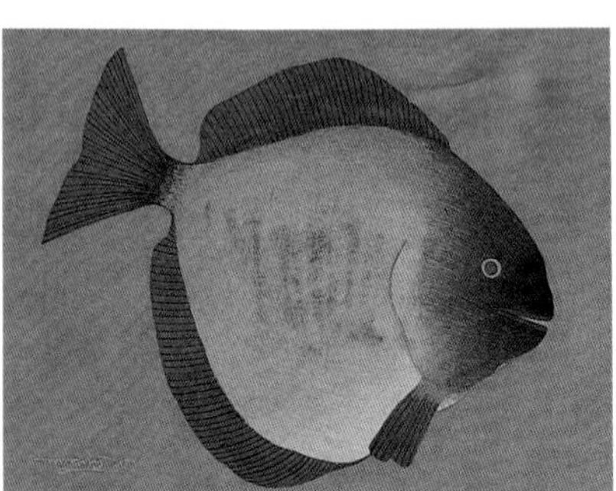

Shaw, Lalu Prasad: "Fish", *Tempera*, 33.5x42.5 cm.

He lives and works in Kolkata.

Sheikh, Gulam Mohammed (1937–) b. Surendranagar, GUJ. Education: *FFA* (*MSU*) & studied at RCA. Solos: Kunika Chemould & *Art Heritage* New Delhi, *JAG*, TAG; International: Pompidou, Musee National d'Art Moderne Paris. Group participations: *Triennale, Group 1890*, RB & *LKA* New Delhi, *SG* Mumbai, Marvel Art Gallery Ahmedabad, *AIFACS, VAG*, VG, *JAG, Roopankar BB;* International: *Biennale*, Art Festival Tokyo & Paris, Contemporary Indian Art London & Washington. *Auctions*: Osian's & Heart Mumbai, Heart New Delhi & abroad. Awards: National Award, Gallery 8 awards including Padma Shri Govt. of India New Delhi. Appointments: Prof. & HoD *MSU*. Publications: A poet, writer & a journalist, articles on *art* published in Gujarati, Hindi & English. Collections: *NGMA* & *LKA* New Delhi, PUJ University Museum.

Gulam Mohammed Sheikh's *paintings* are a study in narrativity. They address complex spatial and intellectual reltionships, between people, *culture*, *art* and poetry. The influences are many and *eclectic*: *Rajasthani miniature paintings*, Sufi poetry, Indian *mythology* and *sculpture* as well as *paintings* by Western masters. *Colours* in his early works had the jewel-like brightness of Western Indian *painting*, while recently, *acid* bright *colours* like blue, purple and pink have made an appearance in his works. In the 1990s he started working in *gouache* after years of *painting* in *oils*. More recently, he has experimented with *installations* as well as digital *collage*.

He lives and works in Vadodara.

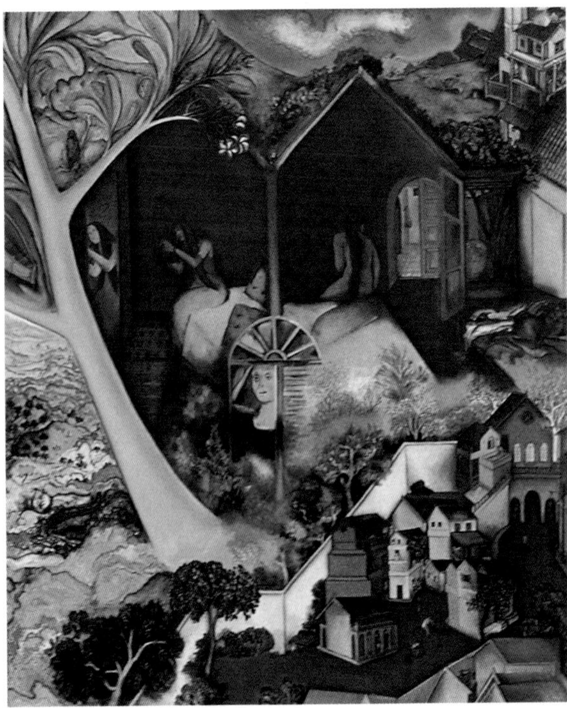

Sheikh, Gulam Mohammed: "About Waiting & Wandering", *Oil* on *Canvas*, 1981, 135x112.5 cm.

Sheikh, Nilima G. (1945–) b. New Delhi. Education: B.FA. & M.A. *FFA* (*MSU*), Studied in Indian *miniature painting* & the traditions of *tempera painting*. Solos: *GC* & MMB Mumbai, CAG Ahmedabad, *GE;* International: Asian Society New York. Group participations: Kunika Chemould, RB New Delhi, Timeless Art Mumbai, *ATG*, *GE*, *AIFACS*, VG; International: Germany, Yugoslavia, UK, South Africa, GBP. *Art* camps & workshop: *Graphic* Vadodara, *Picchwai painting* of Nathdwara, Handicraft Museum New Delhi, *Painting Roopankar BB;* International: Germany & Italy. *Auctions*: Christie's Mumbai, Heart New Delhi. Appointments: Under took theatre design. Collections: *NGMA* New Delhi, PUJ Museum Chandigarh, *Roopankar BB;* International: UK.

Nilima G. Sheikh has constantly explored the possibilities of *tempera painting*, preferring the *matte texture* of that *medium* to the glossiness of *oil painting*. *Casein* too offers her the same muted elegance of Indian oranges and reds, without the loud appeal of bright *colours*. Her subjects, whether taken from deeply felt personal experiences such as the "Champa" series, or *legends* and myths handed down over the ages, all show the same use of *vignettes* and *fragments* of expression, much like the jotting of thoughts rather than final statements of morality. Her use of insets appears much like a *painting* within a *painting*, clouds and streams of *colour* being another favourite *motif*.

She lives and works in Vadodara.

Shenoy, G.S. (1938–1994) b. Udipi, KAR. Education: Dip. in *painting JJSA*. Solos: Mangalore, Mysore, Chennai, Udipi, MMB & Gallery Windsor Manor Bangalore, *VEAG*, *CRAR*, *JAG*, TAG; International: Singapore. Group participations: Mumbai, Chennai, KAR *LKA*, Progress Painter of Coastal Mysore, KAR Painters, Kritika Art Gallery, Kala Mela Bangalore, National Exhibition, *Triennale* New Delhi & *BB*, *CRAR;* International: Amsterdam, Denmark, *Art Biennale* Turkey, *Art* Exhibition Manchester UK. *Artist* camps: Thanjavur, Goa, Mysore, Manipal, Mangalore, Bangalore, *LKA* & SZCC Chennai, *BAS*. Awards: KAR *LKA*, *BAS*. Commissions: *Murals* Bangalore Mumbai, Mysore, Mangalore. Collections: *LKA* Chennai, Bangalore & New Delhi, Govt. Museum, MMB & KAR Tourism Bangalore, BARC; International: Singapore, Germany, USA.

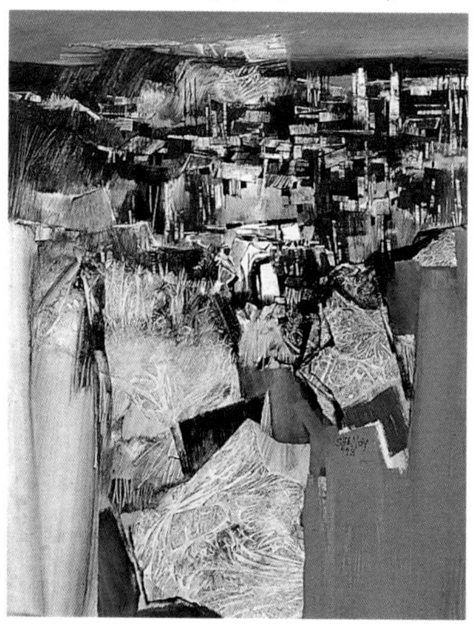

Shenoy, G.S.: "Hampi *Landscape*", *Mixed media,* 1993, 70x35 cm.

G.S. Shenoy's *motifs* in his earlier works were derived from elements of *folk art* and by *painterly* arrangements of the *pigment*. He moved towards this type of *abstract imagery*, by using succinct strokes of the *palette knife* and rollers. The topography of his homeland, the rocks and mountains; the rivers and streams; the home town and its surrounding; these were the elements from *nature* that inspired him in his *paintings*, which blend strength and *Mannerism* of *colour* and *texture*.

Shenoy, Gurudas (1965–) b. Udipi, KAR. Education: B.FA. *MSU*. Solos: *VEAG*, *RG*, *JAG*. Group participations: Chandigarh, Udipi, Mangalore Museum, GUJ State *LKA* Exhibition, Mysore DAE, Gallery Sumukha Windsor Manor & *LKA* Bangalore, *VEAG*, *BAS*, *JAG*, *YBCAG*, *CKP*; International: Hong Kong. *Artist* camps: Bangalore, Art Mela Vadodara. Award: Mangalore Museum, Bendre-Husain National Scholarship *BAS*. Member: Life member *BAS*. Commissions: *Mural* in *metal* & *terracotta* Bangalore. Appointments: *Curator*, Husain's Museum "Husain Sankalana" Bangalore. Collections: *LKA* Chennai & New Delhi, Mangalore Museum, pvt. & public in India & abroad.

Gurudas Shenoy uses the *landscape* format on a large scale, though his elements are based on his father's *style*. He uses *palette knife* to render his subjects in *oils*. He also works in *metal*, *terracotta*, *wood cut* and *lino engraving*. His *compositions* are large with *colours* of *nature* showing *depth* and *perspective* being plain rather than Renaissance-like.

He lives and works in Bangalore.

Shenoy, K.M. (1932–2005) b. Udipi KAR. *Art Education NKM* & later *GCAC* Kolkata; Self-taught with tremendous experimentation. Solos: *AFA* Kolkata, *Artists' Centre* Mumbai, *JAG*; Group Show of Art Plaza Mumbai—exhibited; International: Jataka. Large number of group shows & participations. Founder Member of Art Plaza in Mumbai; Member: *Artists Centre* Mumbai, *BAS*, Indian Artists Network. Awards: Felicitation *ASI*, *BAS* for his life time achievement & service to young Indian *artists*.

K.M. Shenoy's works show his masterly control over the line; he made his *drawing* speak for itself, the alternately thick and thin sinuous strokes capturing *light* and *shade* with minimum effort. His restless, almost impressionistic brush-strokes dissolve his *images* into a medley of *colour* and *texture*. He was also known for his brightly coloured *figurative landscapes* in the *wash (technique)*.

However, his most important contribution is as the founder of Art Plaza, the street art gallery outside *JAG*. This proved to be a boon for young, struggling *artists*, giving them a platform to exhibit their works at a very nominal rate.

Sher-Gil, Amrita (1913–1941) b. Budapest, Hungary. Studied *painting* ENSBA, studied *murals* & *sculpture*; Returned to India 1934; Went to Lahore 1941. Solos: New Delhi, Mumbai, Hyderabad, Allahabad, Lahore, Simla FA. Society, other exhibitions in *NGMA* & RB New Delhi & abroad. *Auction*: Sotheby's New Delhi. Received Awards; Travelled & painted in Shimla, Gorakhpur UP, *Ajanta*, *Ellora*, South India & Cochin. Publications: *LKA* New Delhi, Press, Catalogues, Books. Collections: *NGMA* New Delhi, pvt. *Vivan Sundaram*.

Amrita Sher-Gil's academic education in the West had exposed her to the works of the *modern* masters. She was especially enamoured by the simplicity of *form* in P. Cezanne's work and the disassociation of *colour* from reality in P. Gauguin's and V. Van Gogh's work. She returned to India, because as she said, Paris belonged to H. Matisse and P. Picasso, whereas India was hers. Her first attempts at finding an Indian *idiom* was tentative with each exposure to Indian *art tradition* leaving its mark on her. i.e. the *Mathura art sculptures* of the *Kushana dynasty* which was to influence her in the rendition of the *drapery* in her "Hill-Men and Hill-Women". The compositional feature at *Ajanta* with a lighter or darker skinned person in the center being offset by a ring of darker/ lighter skinned people was incorporated into "Brahmacharis"and "Brides Toilette". The Kerala *murals* with their bright *hues* and decorative *patterns* found its way into her "Villagers going to Market" while *Basohli colours* were soon incorporated into her interpretation of NAYIKAS and Sakhis.

Amrita Sher-Gil's influence has been manifold. She shook Indian *art* out of its lethargic allegiance to British academicism and servile imitation of the *Bengal School*. She made *artists* aware of the basic tenets of *Modernism*, simplicity and stylization. She was to influence several generations of Indian *artists*.

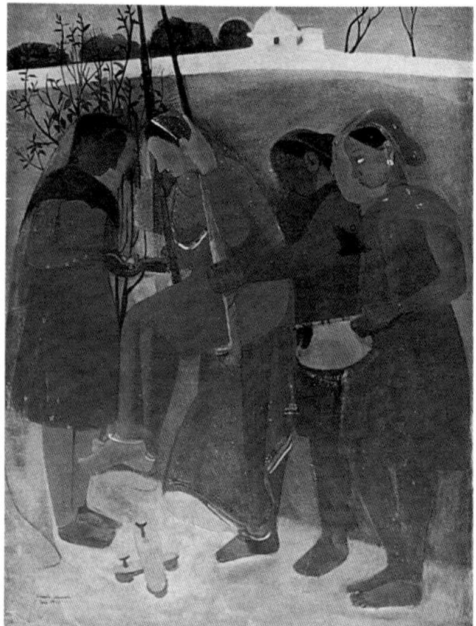

Sher-Gil, Amrita: "The Swing", *Oil* on *Canvas*, 1940, 91x70 cm.

Sherigar, K.S. (1947–) b. Udupi, KAR. Education: Dip. in *drawing* & *painting* Udupi KAR, Reference under *G.S. Shenoy*. Solos: Udupi, Shimoga, Manipal, *VEAG*. Group participations: Udupi, Bangalore, Mangalore, *LKA* Bangalore. *Art* camps: Dharwar, *LKA* KAR, Kala Mela New Delhi. Awards: KAR *LKA*, Mangalore Museum. Collections: *LKA* Bangalore, pvt. in India, Australia, California, Paris, UK, USA.

Paintings, *drawings* are based on *folk art* of Bhootharadhana and Nagamandala from the south coastal region—KAR. K.S. Sherigar's views are of *ritual* scenes based on festivals, dances and costumes with *forms* and vibrant *colours*. His earlier works were basically *ink drawing* on cloth incorporating folk *motifs* in a symmetrical *manner*.

He lives and works in Udupi, KAR.

Shikhara=mountain peak. The towering structure, usually built over the Garbhagriha (sanctum sanctorum) in an Indian temple. The Kalasha (pot of nectar) placed on the Shikhara, is aligned perfectly with the *icon* (MURTI) placed in the shrine below. Refer *Dravidian Style*, *Hinduism*, *Nagara Style*, PARVATI, *Vesara Style*, *Ranvir Singh Bisht*, *Ino Gangooly*, *Sayed A.G.M. Kazi*, *Ghulam Rasool Santosh*; Illustration—KAILASH, KAILASA.

Shinde, Deepak (1946–) b. Yavatmal, MAHA. Education: GDA in *drawing* & *painting JJSA*. Solos: *LKA* & Centre of Con-temporary Art New Delhi, *PG*, TAG, *SAI*, *ABC*, *G88*, 25 years of *Painting JAG*; International: Dubai, Sydney. Group participations: *GC*, *BAAC* & *Artists' Centre* Mumbai. National Exhibition *LKA*, CMC & *Triennale* New Delhi, *BAAC* Kolkata, *JAG*, *CYAG*, *BAS*, *DG*, others in Chennai, Hyderabad, Thrissur, Jaipur, Bhubaneshwar, Patna, Lucknow; International: *Biennale* Japan & Havana, World Trade Centre Amsterdam, Netherlands. *Art* camps: Mumbai, Goa, Harihareshwar, *AAJ Painters* camp Udaipur. *Auctions*: Safdar Hashmi Memorial Trust New Delhi, Sotheby's Mumbai & London. Awards: *Artists' Centre* Mumbai, *ASI;* Senior Fellowship Govt. of India. Collections: Gwalior & Jammu, *NGMA*, Rashtra Bhavan & *LKA* New Delhi, Vidhan Bhavan & Godrej Mumbai; International: Fokuoka Masanori Japan.

Deepak Shinde began by meticulously copying *portraits* of important leaders or pictures in magazines. He watched people at work in the country noting the rich, rugged *patterns* of the countryside which was to surface later in his use of heavy impasted *paint*. *Line*, *colour*, *form* and expression are all equally important in his works, which was based on *figuration*. An aggressive stylist, Deepak Shinde's works bring forth celebrations in *style*, honesty in *compositions* and heat in his choice of *colours*. More recently, his passion for *texture* has become subdued, with the smooth, plain expanse of the *canvas* in contrast relation to the textural *paint* he used a few years ago. Deepak Shinde's vision trajectory then turned to *abstracts* and then on to *figuration*, contemplative *figuration* as he calls it, where it now rests. His latest works seem like parables— a *modern* Panchatantra of sorts, with human and animal life, interwoven in a medley of *texture* and *colour*.

He lives in Mumbai.

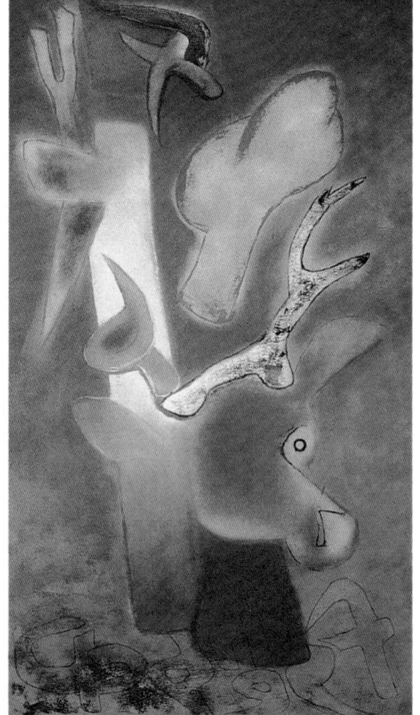

Shinde, Deepak: "The Musk", *Mixed media*, 150x90 cm.

Shirgaonkar, B.D. (1909–) b. Tarle, Kolhapur, MAHA. Education: Dip. in *drawing & painting* & Art Master's Certificate *JJSA* & Kolhapur, Teacher training *JJSA*, Specialized in *arts* and *crafts*, *VBU*. Solos: *KB Santiniketan*, Chetana Art Gallery Mumbai, BAG, TAG, *JAG* & Retrospective. Participated: In various regional & All India Art Exhibition. Awards: *AFA* WB, *BAS* & All India *Exhibition*–won prizes. Scholarship in *mural*, Fellowship *JJSA*. Hon. by *AIFACS* as "Veteran Artist". Member: Managing Committee *BAS* Board of Studies in "Art & Painting" of SNDT Women's College Mumbai & BHU. Appointments: Prof. & HoD of *Drawing* & *Painting JJSA*, Examiner & Moderator for Govt. of MAHA at various Universities, Lecturer & Writer. Collections: In New Vidhan Bhavan Mumbai, various *art* galleries, pvt & public national & international.

B.D. Shirgaonkar was schooled in the academic *tradition* of the *Bombay School*. His works mirror the output of the school in the matter of *landscapes*, both *realistic* and impressionistic, *portraits* and later on a *gestural abstraction* based on the *technique* of *watercolour* and *landscapes*.

He lives and works in Mumbai.

Shirwadkar, Yashawant (1951–) b. Mumbai. Education: GDA in *drawing* & *painting* MAHA. Over 60 solo & group shows: Bangalore, Kolkata, New Delhi, Varanasi, Mumbai, Chennai, Marvel Art Gallery Ahmedabad; International: France, Germany, Switzerland. Group participations: *Artists' Centre* Mumbai, All India Fine Arts. Kolkata, Kala Mela New Delhi, *JAG*, *BAS*, *AIFACS*, others in Bangalore, Pune, Ahmed-nagar; International: Belgium, London, Germany, Nepal, USA. *Auctions*: Sotheby's 1998, Christie's 2001–02. Collections: Kathmandu, KAR Tourism, *AFA* Kolkata, pvt. in India & abroad.

Yashawant Shirwadkar has concentrated on the traditional *landscape*, working with both *oils* and *watercolours*. He works outdoors, choosing his subjects from the towns he visits. Old ruined buildings, colonial or Indian *architecture*, Banaras *ghats,* Varanasi and Rajasthani *vignettes* are some of the scenes depicted in his *canvases*.

He lives and works in Mumbai.

Shiva=The Auspicious One. Shiva the Destroyer is the third *god* of the Hindu Trinity; the other two are BRAHMA the Creator, and VISHNU the Preserver. He is symbolized and worshipped as the LINGAM or phallus, because He personifies reproduction; and the Hindu philosophy believes in regeneration and change to new form of life after death, destruction and annihilation. The CHANDRA (crescent moon) on Jata Mukuta (top knot) of his Jatadhara (matted hair) marks the passing of months; the serpent around his neck, the passing of years; and the necklace of skulls and serpents, the passing generations. He has three eyes, the third one in the centrel of his forehead is open only to destroy the world. The three eyes are said to symbolize three divisions of *time* i.e. past, present and future. His throat is dark blue from drinking the poison occurring at the churning of ocean, to save the world; and hence the name Nilkanth (blue throat). Thus He became Supreme *god*, being known as Mahadeva or Maheshvara (the Great *God*). He is also called Gangadhara, because he intercepted the descent of proud river GANGA, to prevent the earth being crushed under her weight and speed; and so Shiva bound her in his hair, and let her out as a trickle. His *weapon* is the TRISHULA (Trident) which he holds in his hand, which, according to some devotees is the great *attribute* of the Creator, Destroyer and Regenerator. A small Damaru (SHIVA's drum) is used by Shiva to express his triumph, and the rope to bind sinners. His VAHANA (vehicle) is the NANDI, the bull.

Shiva's consort is GANGA's sister PARVATI (born from mountains) also known as DURGA, KALI, Uma, Gauri and Bhairavi; and she is held to be the supreme manifestation of cosmic SHAKTI (energy). He has two sons, GANESHA and Kartikeya, and lives on Mount KAILASH, in the Himalayas. Shiva is also regarded as the greatest yogi and Lord of the Dance (NATARAJA) and in the dance (Tandava) he performed, he is said to have energized *creation* and the secret syllable "OM", the deepest vibration of the cosmos.

Though he has no incarnations, (AVATARA) the 1008 names specified in the Shiva PURANA, such as Shambu, Shankara, Isa, Ishwara, Bhairava and HARA (single SHIVA) signify various aspects of his nature and deeds. Thus Yogisvara refers to his Yogic prowess, Ardhanarisvara (the half-male and half-female *form*) signifies the union of the male and female for purpose of procreation; the various Anugraha-murtis (*idols* of grace) describe his boon giving *forms* and the Samhara-murtis describe his destructive capacities. Refer AYUDHAS, ABHUSHANA, AGNI, AYUDHAS, BHAGAVAN, BHAKTI, CHATUR BHUJA, CHOLA, *Chola Dynasty*, *Cire Perdue*, DASHA-BAHU, DASHA-BHUJA, Elephanta, GAJA-HASTA, GANA, *Gupta*, Hinduism, KALA/KAAL, *Khajuraho*, LINGA, MATRIKAS, MUKUTA, *Nagara Style*, NANDI, PURANA, *Ritual*, RUDRA, SHULA, *South Indian Bronzes*, *Spiritual*, TANTRA, *Thanjavur (Tanjore) Paintings*, *Wood Block Printing*, YOGA, YONI, *Dhanraj Bhagat*, *Sunayani Devi Chattopadhyay*, *Adiveppa Murigeppa Chetty*, *Alphonso A. Doss*, *Prafulla Mohanti*, *Jamini Roy;* Illustration–*Ganga Devi*, MUKUTA, NANDI, NATARAJA, OM, PARVATI.

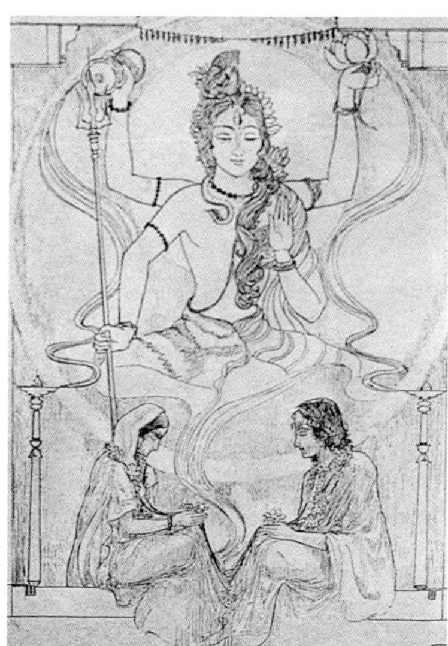

Shiva: *Desai, Kanu*, "Blessings", *Drawing*.

Sholapurkar, Vishwanath M. (1931–) b. Bijapur, KAR. *Art Education NKM*, GDA in *painting* & Art Master *JJSA*. Solos: Bangalore, Kala Academy Goa, *JAG*, *CHAG*. Awards: National Awards for excellence in designing *art* magazine "Roopa-Bheda" *JJSA;* On the Faculty of *JJSA* between 1957–79.

Founder: Dean of Chamarajendra Academy of Visual Art (CAVA) Mysore; Has been *art critic* for Free Press & Times of India Mumbai. Collections: pvt. & corporates in Mysore, Bangalore, Mumbai; International: UK, Spain & Australia.

Vishwanath M. Sholapurkar was basically a *painter* until 1990, when he changed his *medium* of expression to *wood*. He works with *wood sculpture* both in the round, and in *relief*, using a collage-like *technique* called marquetry to create his *compositions*. He saws *wood* into 3mm slices and later cuts them into intricate shapes that fit into one another in jig-saw fashion to become *landscapes*, *still lifes*, birds and flying men. *Texture* and *colour*, through the grain and *colour* of the *wood*, are an important part of his works. His wooden *sculptures* with *inlay* work are more *abstract*, with *symbolic* shapes enlivening the surface rather than creating a new *form*.

He lives and works in Mysore. Refer *Inlaid*, *End-Grain*.

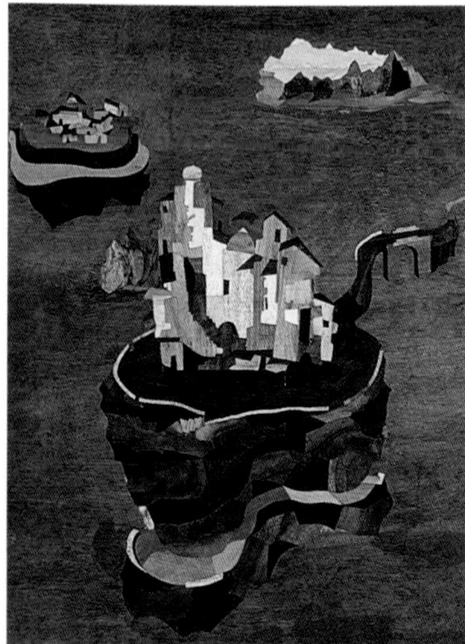

Sholapurkar, Vishwanath M.: "Himalayan Landscape", Marquetry (*Wood Collage*), 1993, 120x90 cm.

Shreshtha, Laxman (1939–) b. Siraha, Nepal. Education: Continued GDA in *drawing* & *painting JJSA;* ENSBA, AGC & Atelier 17 Paris, Central School of Art London. Solos: *GC* Mumbai, TAG, *JAG*, *PG;* International: Kathmandu, USA, Germany, Kenya. Group participations: Chennai, *GC*, *Gallery 7* & *SG* Mumbai, *Triennale*, RB & *NGMA* New Delhi, *Arts Acre* & *CIMA* Kolkata, *CYAG*, *PUAG*, *JAG*, *VAG*; International: Paris, Cologne, USA. *Auctions*: Osian's & Heart Mumbai; International: Christie's London. Awards: French Govt. School Boursiers Exhibition Prize Paris, Prix d' Honneur New York, Gorkh Dakshin Bahu Medal Nepal, Inter Nations Invitation Germany, International Grant USA. Collections: pvt. & public including Glenbarra Art Museum Japan.

They may resemble *landscapes*, particularly of his native mountains, but Laxman Shreshtha *terms* his *paintings* as relationships based on his experiences. *Nature* becomes a pretext for expression of the subtleties of emotion. He does not need the human *form* to express emotion. The long thin *lines* of *charcoal*, the juxtapositioning of *colours*, the tonal palpitations reflect the complexities of life. While his works may overtly appear similar; his *techniques* have evolved over the years. In the 70s and the 80s he had shunned the *white pigment*, preferring to leave the *canvas* bare to convey that particular *colour*. *Transparent colours* were used to convey the subtleties of relationships. In the 90s however, he began using thick *opaque oil colours* including blobs of *white*, thus grounding his *composition* in reality. His *watercolours* and *charcoals* reveal his mastery of *texture*. These smaller works automatically, almost unconsciously, insinuate themselves into the later *oils*. His works are usually untitled because he wishes to leave the subject open to personal interpretation.

Laxman Shreshtha lives and works in Mumbai.

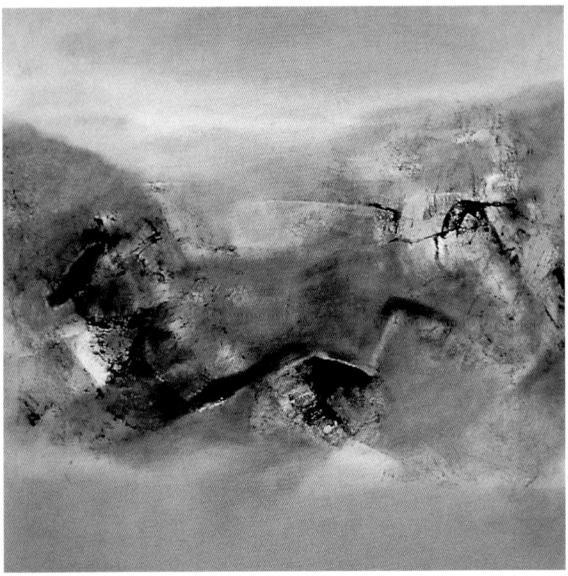

Shreshtha, Laxman: "Painting XVIII", 153x153 cm.

Shukla, Shiv Dutt (1945–) b. Jabalpur. Self-taught *painter*. Solos: Indore, Jabalpur, MPKP Bhopal, *JAG*, *Dhoomimal*. Group participations: Indore, *JAG*, RB New Delhi, *BB*. *Artists* camp: Jabalpur. Award: Kalidas National Ujjain. Appointments: Prof. in the Gandhi Medical College. Collections: *Roopankar* & pvt.

Shiv Dutt Shukla prefers to paint on *paper*, using a variety of *mediums* including *watercolour*, *ink* and *oil paint*. His *paintings* resemble *landscapes*, albeit in a loose, deconstructed *manner*, with elements floating in a textured *space*. *Space* division is his forte and the strong diagonals and *diptychs* form an abstracted *horizon* in his new versions of the *landscape* format.

He lives and works in Bhopal.

Shukla, Yagneshwar Kalyanji (1907–1986) b. Porbander, GUJ. Education: GDA *JJSA* Dip. with Hon. Royal Academy of FA. Rome, Italy in *murals*, *etching* & *engraving* on *metal* & *wood*, Dip. National Institute of FA. Peking China. Solos: Vadodara, Mumbai, Ahmedabad, New Delhi, Rajkot, Varanasi; International: Rome, Perugia, Peking. Group participations: Pune, Kolkata, Shimla, Mumbai, Delhi, Amritsar; International: London, Rome, Paris, Tokyo, Cairo, Kenya, Sao Paulo, Leipzig, England. Awards: GUJ *LKA*, Gold Medal Poona FA. Society & Calcutta FA. Society, Silver Medal Simla FA. Society, Governor's prize Mumbai, Delhi FAC Society, Amritsar FA. Society, UGC Grant, Award for Research Work in *Fresco Paintings* RAJ. Member: Secretary GUJ *LKA*. Commissions: Several *murals* New Delhi, GUJ & Mumbai. *Portraits* of National Leaders for State Assemblies, Sets &

costumes for mythological films. Publications: Including "Art of Shukla", "Painting by Y.K. Shukla", & several articles in magazines & newsletters; also written books in Gujarati, including "Story of Art" & "Wall Paintings of Rajasthan". Collections: *NGMA* & *LKA* New Delhi, *Maharaja Fatesingh Museum* Vadodara, *GMAG* Chandigarh, *PWM*, *JJSA* & other collection.

Yagneshwar Kalyanji Shukla's study of Indian, Western and *Chinese art* has resulted in him producing works of an *eclectic nature* in the fields of both *painting* and *printmaking*. His study of the Western masters, got him the knowledge of *anatomy* and *chiaroscuro*, while his year in China introduced him to the nuances of *painting* in a single *colour*, i.e. *black ink*, as also sharpened his understanding of *line*. His *etchings* also display this characteristic, with *tonal values* being expressed with *cross-hatching*. Yagneshwar Kalyanji Shukla was interested in the field of *art education* too, being Prof. at BHU Varanasi and *Banasthali Vidyapith* RAJ.

Shula, Trishula or Trisula The trident, the favourite *weapon* of SHIVA, usually represented as a triple *metal* spike mounted on a long wooden handle. It is also seen on top of Shaivite temples. Refer MATRIKAS, PARVATI; Illustration—GANGA.

Shuvaprasanna (1947–) b. Kolkata, WB. Education: Grad. Indian College of Art *RBU*. Solos: *BAAC*, MMB, Decor Art Gallery, Calcutta Art Gallery, *Indian Museum*, Art Age Gallery & *CIMA* Kolkata, The Gallery Chennai, TKS, SRAG, *JAG;* International: Switzerland, France, Germany, Singapore, Bangladesh. Group participations: Chennai, *BAAC* Kolkata, *LKA* New Delhi, *JAG*; International: Germany, Cuba, Turkey, Bangladesh. Workshops: Kolkata, Chennai; International: London, Dresden, Munich. *Auctions*: Heart Mumbai. Awards: *BAAC* Kolkata, State *LKA* WB, *AIFACS*. Member: Calcutta Painters, Art & Artists Group, CVA Kolkata. Founder member: *Arts Acre* Kolkata. Publications: Published & Edited several journals, "Art Today", "Artists", a collection of *wood cut prints*, "Dream and Reality", a collection of *drawings*. Collections & portfolios of *prints* & *drawings*. Collections: *NGMA*, *LKA* & GCAC New Delhi, UP *LKA* Lucknow, WB *LKA* & *BAAC* Kolkata, *Chandigarh Museum*, PUJ University; International: Glenbarra Art Museum Japan.

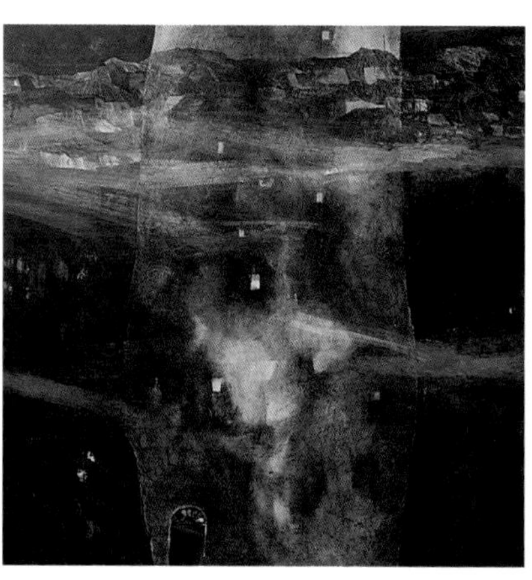

Shuvaprasanna: "Middletone", *Charcoal* & *Oil*, 1995, 112x130 cm.

His early works were reflections on the cosmos and man's position in it, the *colours* prominently used were deep brown, grey and moss green. Later he experimented with a variety of *media*, his subjects centering on mankind, the city of Kolkata and symbolic birds. These works, though thematically representative, approached abstraction in his use of *texture*, *chiaroscuro* and the *colour black*. This reliance on *black* was to induce him to start working with *charcoal*.

Shuvaprasanna's forte lies in his *draughtsmanship*, *distortions* and etherialization of *form* lending his works their distinctive air.

He lives and works in Kolkata.

Sibal, D.P. (1934–) b. Sargodha, (now Pakistan). Education: Dip. Interior Design & Decorrhodes International London. Solos: *LKA*, New Delhi, *AIFACS*. Group pariticipations: *LKA* New Delhi, All India Drawing Chandigarh, *AIFACS*, SKP, *Dhoomimal*, *Biennale BB;* International: *Triennale* Japan; Group *art* activities & *art* fairs Tokyo, California, London & Paris. Seminars, workshops & camps: IIC, British Council, *NGMA* & *LKA Triennale* Exhibition New Delhi, *AIFACS*. Awards: *AIFACS*, SKP, UNESCO; A Life Fellow: International Institute of Arts & Letters Switzerland. Publications: Several articles in newsletters; Written on *art*, *architecture* & interior decoration. Collections: *NGMA* & *LKA* New Delhi, *AIFACS*, *BB;* International: California & other pvt.

D.P. Sibal's background as an architect and interior designer has worked its way into his *art*, which is a fusion of interiors and exteriors and the *atmosphere* created by the intermingling of various *colours* and the *rhythm* thus generated. He is also an environmentalist, transmitting several issues of worldwide importance into his *paintings*.

He lives and works in New Delhi.

Siddhanta, Uma (1933–) Education: Dip. in FAC *GCAC* Kolkata for *sculpture*. Had few solos & won awards: B.M. Birla Gold Medal, *AFA* Kolkata, *LKA* Award New Delhi, also won awards for publishing information on *Art Education*. Public commissions: *Sculptures* at Bidhan Sabha, Hazra Park (WB). Appointments: Served as *art* teacher & lecturer in several institutions. Publications: Articles & *paintings* published in several newsletters & press bulletin of Asiatic Society & Ananda Bazar Group Kolkata. Collections: *NGMA* New Delhi.

Uma Siddhanta has worked mostly with *terracotta* and *cement*. Her smaller works in *clay* have a raw earthiness, the *texture* coming from a rough *handling* of the *medium* in addition to the decorative striations and *patterns* etched on the surface. Her public works are large in scale and have a rhythmic flow in their arrangement of *form*. "Mother Cactus"especially has a H. Moore-like organic quality that makes the *sculpture* almost part of its *background*.

She lives and works in Kolkata.

Significant Form The *term* coined by English aesthetician and *critic* C. Bell to describe the essence of a work of *art*; i.e. *forms* and relationships of *forms*. According to this doctrine, in any work of *art*, *form* itself is the true *content* and other kinds of *content*, i.e. the *narrative*, iconographic and *symbolic* elements were secondary. It was this theory that was to be a major influence on the *PAG* Mumbai.

Silhouette A dark *outline shadow* in profile against a lighter *background*. It is named after Etienne de Silhouette, an 18th-century French politician whose hobby was cut-out portraiture. It was originally made by tracing the *shadow* of a person, cast by a bright *light* and *painting* it solid *black*. By extension, the word silhouette is applicable to any object or scene rendered in *opaque black*. Refer *Amarjit Chadha, J. Srividya;* Illustration–*B. Prabha, R.B.Bhaskaran, Rasik Durgashankar Raval*.

Silk Screen Printing Refer *Screen Printing*.

Silver Greyish-white metallic *shade*. It is a shining malleable *metal*, which is used for coating or plating. It is also available as silver foil. In Indian *art*, *gold* and silver foils were used for embellishing *painting* and *sculpture*. Silver was used by *Kangra* and *Bundi artists* to represent water. Refer *Bidri*, CHANDRA, *Codex*, *Electroplating*, *Embroidery*, *Enamel*, *Harappa*, *Illuminated Manuscripts*, *Kangra*, *Miniature Painting*, *Pala Miniatures*, *Picchwais*, *Ved Pal Sharma*, *Arnawaz Vasudev*, *V. Viswanadhan;* Illustrations–KAILASH, KAILASA, *Balan Nambiar*, *Himmat Shah*.

Simultaneous Contrast The instantaneous increase or decrease in the intensity of *colours*, when they are placed in adjacent position. i.e. two *complementary colours* enhance each other, while any other combination would have a modifying or cancelling effect on each other. e.g. *Saroj Gopi Pal*, *Krishna N. Reddy*. Refer *Illusion*, *Illusionism*, *Mixed Contrast*, *Op or Optical Art*, *Tonal Values*; Illustration–*Thanjavur (Tanjore) Paintings*, *Narayan S. Bendre*, *Chhaganlal D. Mistry*.

Singh, Arpita (1937–) b. Bara Nagar, WB. Education: School of Art Delhi Polytechnic New Delhi. Solos: Kunika Chemould & *Art Heritage* New Delhi, *Gallery 7* & *GC* Mumbai, *CIMA* Kolkata, *Dhoomimal*, *VAG*, CCAG, *PUAG*; International: Werl Germany, Schoo's Gallery Amsterdam. Group participations: The Unknown, Kunika Chemould, *LKA*, RB, *Triennale* & Safdar Hashmi Memorial Trust New Delhi, *GC* & *SG* Mumbai, Kala Yantra Bangalore, *CIMA* Kolkata, SRAG, *VAG*, CCAG, *JAG*, *BB;* International: Istanbul Ankara, Belgrade, Paris, Havana, Geneva, Algeria, Kuwait, New South Wales, New York, RAA London. *Auctions*: Heart & Christie's Mumbai, Sotheby's New Delhi; International: Christie's New York. Awards: *Chandigarh Museum*, SKP; International: Algeria *Biennale*. Members: The Unknown & *LKA* New Delhi. Collections: *NGMA* New Delhi, *Roopankar BB;* International: V&A London, National Museum Malaysia, Indian Cultural Centre Fiji, pvt. & public.

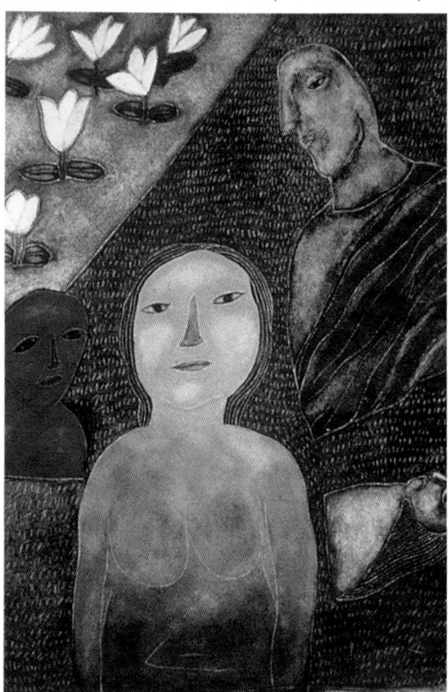

Singh, Arpita: "Figures by the Water", Mixed media, 1985, 36x48 cm.

Arpita Singh, wife of *Paramjeet Singh*, has usually worked her surreal sagas around the female *figure*, surrounded with the paraphernalia of daily life. While there was an element of the fantastic or the playful in her early works, her 1997–98 works have dark undertones and a foreboding, even menacing air. The subject is overwhelmingly sexual with references to the male and female organ appearing explicitly in much the same *manner* as the fans, fish and clocks in her early texturized works. Her *style* changes with her *medium*, the *oil paintings* being heavily impasted while her *watercolours* are thin *washes* of *colour* layered one over the other.

She lives and works in New Delhi.

Singh, Jaspal (1959–) b. Jarhat, Assam. Education: Bachelor of Visual Arts (BVA) *GCAC* Kolkata. Solos: *BAAC* Kolkata, TAG, *JAG*, TKS. Group participations: *AFA*, *BAAC*, *Arts Acre* & *GC* Kolkata, RB, *LKA* & Art Age New Delhi, The Gallery Chennai, Balgandharva Gallery Pune, *JAG*, *NCAG*, VG; International: UK, USA. Workshops: *Arts Acre* & MMB Kolkata *RBU*; International: *Graphic* workshop *Art Acre* and Washington DC, Calcutta Dresden Artists' at *Arts Arce* Kolkata. Member: *Arts Acre* WB. Collections: *LKA* New Delhi, *ABC*, *Arts Acre* WB; International: Glenbarra Art Museum Japan & other pvt. & corporates.

Jaspal Singh's *medium* is primarily *watercolour*, though he has also worked with *oil painting* on *paper* and on *canvas*. It is the urban situation, with the chaos, noise and pollution that appears through *overlapping images* of buildings and vehicles. The objects and *images* merge into one another in bursts of liquid *colour*, creating *atmospheric effect* of fog and smoke, with human beings appearing as mere abbreviated presences in the general vicinity. There is also a resemblance to P. Klee's works in these *cityscapes*.

He lives and works mostly at *Arts Acre* WB Mumbai.

Singh, Mansimran (1939–) b. Lahore. Education: Studied Delhi Blue Art Pottery under the tutelage of his father, *Sardar Gurcharan Singh*; Later worked under Bernard Leach & Geoffrey Whiting England. Solos: Jaipur, Mumbai, Kolkata, Delhi, Chennai; International: Commonwealth Institute London. Group participations: *CYAG;* Directed workshops for *LKA* Lucknow. Awards: British Council visitorship.

Mansimran Singh, a potter and ceramicist worked under the guidance of his father, renowned potter *Sardar Gurcharan Singh*. Further training under the English potters introduced him to the work of the *abstract*. His present work includes graceful narrow-necked pots with large bellies and high shoulders. The glazes are usually allowed to drip in an *abstract manner*, creating interesting *lines* and merged areas. After working with English, French and German potters he returned to work at the New Delhi Blue Art Pottery. Later he went to *Santiniketan* as a visiting expert. He also set the *pottery* studios at *GAC*, in 1984 moved to Andretta, in HP with his wife, where they now teach three-month courses of studio *pottery*, using local *clay*. The work is mostly functional tableware. They have built a *museum* in Andretta where they intend to document and display Himachal *pottery*.

Singh, Paramjeet (1941–) b. Jamshedpur, Bihar. Education: NDA *College of Art* New Delhi. Solos: Gallery 42 New Delhi, TKS, SC; International: Czechoslovakia. Group participations: *LKA* & Alliance Francaise New Delhi, *VAG*, *AIFACS*, SKP; International: Czechoslovakia, UK, UAE, Berlin, Dubai, Tehran, Cairo, Cuba, Australia. *Artists* camps & workshops: *Wood cut printmaking* Udaipur. Awards: Kala Shree & Kala Vibhusan to promate *art AIFACS*, National *LKA* New Delhi, PUJ *LKA*, UNESCO Bronze Medal, Group 8 Medals, *AIFACS* Silver Plaque, SKP. Members: Group 8 New Delhi, *AIFACS*, SC. Collections: *LKA* & *NGMA* New Delhi, pvt. & corporates.

Paramjeet Singh is primarily a printmaker, specializing in *silk screen printing*, though he also *paints*. The silk screen process has greatly influenced his *tonal values*, which is predominantly flat with *shades* limited within the *contour* of his simplistic *imagery* of *figures* within a specific *space*. *Nature* makes its appearance in the simplified *landscapes* appearing through windows or as bunches of flowers or potted plants within interiors. His *paintings* have a slightly more texturized surface, with the brushstroke enlivening the *forms*.

He lives and works in New Delhi, retired as Prof. at the *College of Art*.

Singh, Paramjit (1935–) b. Amritsar. School of Art Delhi Polytechnic New Delhi, Worked *printmaking* Atelier Nord Oslo in Norway. Solos: Gallery Chanakya & Kunika Chemould New Delhi, *GC* Mumbai, TKS, *VAG*, *Dhoomimal*; International: Norway, Brussels, Germany. Group participations: Kunika Chemould, *Triennale* & *NGMA* New Delhi, *GC* Mumbai, The Gallery Chennai, *CIMA* Kolkata, Marvel Art Gallery Ahmedabad, *ATG*, *JAG*, *BB;* International: Japan, Norway, Germany, Iraq, Commissioner of Indian participation Pakistan Art Festival. *Artists* camps: Srinagar, Faridabad, Dasauli, Kodaikanal, Kolkata, Coonoor, Dalhousie, Vadodara, Bhopal; International: Thailand, Kalimpong. *Auctions*: Sotheby's & Christie's in New Delhi, Christie's London, Heart & Helpage India Asprey UK in Mumbai; 1990–1993 Painted 450 sq.ft. area for an environmental room in Mumbai. Awards: *LKA* National Award. Founder member: "The Unknown" New Delhi. Appointments: Prof. in FA. JMI. Collections: *NGMA* & *LKA* New Delhi, *Chandigarh Museum* & PUJ University Museum Chandigarh, Punjabi University Patiala, *BB*, corporates, Govt. & pvt. Co. HUDCO, TELCO, TISCO, ITDC.

Paramjit Singh arrived at his present fascination with the eternal *landscape* in the 70s, having plumbed the *depths* of the *still life* and the almost surreal floating stores. His *landscape* is animated by a mysterious life-like quality in its wavering shimmer and shafts of sunlight. It is both *colour* and *light* that lift these *paintings* beyond the merely representational towards an abstraction of both *form* and *content*. Therefore the various elements of a *landscape*–the sky, water, grass, the trees do not exist as themselves, but are merged almost impressionistically into atmospheric hazes of *colour*, *light* and *texture*, while in his *oil paintings*, it is his brushstroke that animates his surface, his recent *pastels* have him exploiting the irregular *texture* of the high-quality *paper* (Kalipong, Arches or Kent) to create velvety *shadows* and *highlights*.

After nearly three decades of teaching *painting* in the *FA*. Dept. JMI, he now lives in New Delhi/Srinagar.

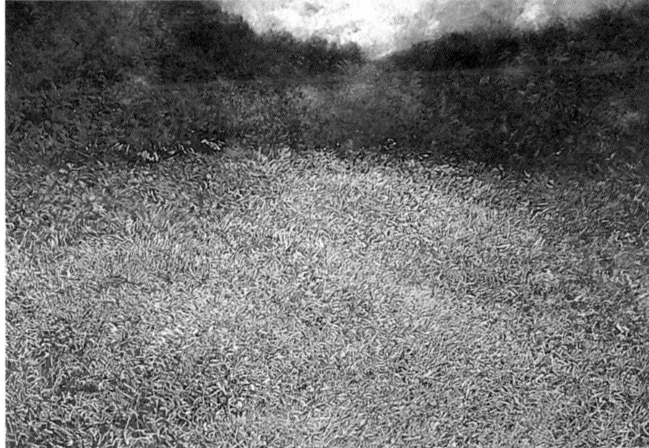

Singh, Paramjit: "Ochre Fields", *Oil* on *Canvas*, 1996, 120x180 cm.

Singh, Prem (1943–) b. Patiala, PUJ. Education: Dip. in *FA*. GCA Chandigarh, M.A. in *FA*. PUJ University Patiala. Solos: Gallery Aurobindo New Delhi, FA. Museum, Alliance Francaise, Gallery Form Function, PUJ KB Chandigarh, CAG Ahmedabad, *AFA* Kolkata, TAG, TKS, SC, *VAG*, *LTG*. Group participations: *LKA*, Gallery Safdar Hashmi Memorial Trust, *NGMA* & Gallery Chanakya New Delhi; International: UK, Bangladesh. *Art* workshops & camps: *Printmaking* USIS New Delhi, *Silk screen printing poster designer GAC; Painters* camp: HRD, *NGMA* New Delhi, Jammu Academy of Art Patnitop, RAJ *LKA* Pushkar, NZCC Patiala, PUJ *LKA* Chandigarh, *Artists* camp Dept. of Culture Haryana (Chandigarh, Panchkuia, Kurukshetra, Hissar). Awards: PUJ *LKA*, IAFA Amritsar, *AFA* Kolkata, *Triennale* & *LKA* New Delhi, *Artist* of The Year Art Society of India Ludhiana, Om Prakash Memorial Award Prakash Kala Sangam Chandigarh, *GMAG*. Member: *LKA*, NZCC Patiala, Chandigarh *LKA*, Founder Secretary, The Solids Chandigarh; *Art critic* for Chandigarh newspaper. Collections: *NGMA*, *LKA* & *College of Art* New Delhi, State Museum Chennai, PUJ University FA. Museum Chandigarh, PUJ University FA. Museum Patiala, J&K Academy of Art & Culture Jammu, RAJ *LKA* Jaipur, *GMAG*, Govt. & corporates.

It is the female *figure*, either pensive, cowled or shrouded which *forms* the central focus of Prem Singh's *paintings*. His statements, like his *images* are direct and simple with a negation of detail and a centralized *composition*. His *colours*, in *gouache*, *watercolour* or *oil* on *canvas* are sombre and sparingly applied.

He lives and works in Chandigarh.

Singh, Rameshwar (1948–) b. Deogarh, RAJ. Education: M.A. in *drawing* & *painting* Udaipur University. Over 35 solos: Bangalore, Gallery Aurobindo New Delhi,

Kala Mela, Jawahar Kala Kendra & School of Art Jaipur, Gallery Chetana, Mumbai, Art Gallery *MSU*, Information Centre Udaipur, CAG Ahmedabad. TKS, *AIFACS*, SRAG, *Dhoomimal*, *JAG*, BAG, TAG, *CKAG*. Group participations: *LKA* New Delhi, RAJ *LKA* Jaipur, Orissa *LKA* Bhubaneshwar, *AIFACS*, *BAS*, *BB*; International: Tokyo. *Art* camps: RAJ *LKA*, *AAJ* Udaipur, SZCC Nagpur. Awards: National *LKA* Awards, RAJ *LKA*, UP *LKA*, SZCC Nagpur, Chandigarh *Biennale*, *BAS*. Collections: *NGMA*, *LKA* & *College of Art* New Delhi, Modern Art Gallery, Jawahar Kala Kendra Jaipur, WZCC Udaipur, SZCC Nagpur, *Chandigarh Museum*, SKP, pvt. & govt.

Rameshwar Singh's interest in the traditional *art* of his native RAJ was not just limited to its *forms*, *colours* and *imagery*, but included the *calligraphic* insets in the miniatures as well as the colourful edges (Hashiyas). His *paintings* have the appearance of *antique* works in his use of *trompe l'oeil* tears and creases in the *paper* in addition to a collage-like effect of fragmentation. Carefully torn pieces of aged *paintings* seem to be pieced together in his works, creating creatures that appear more startling than the multi- limbed Hindu *gods* and goddesses. The introduction of the Mughal element, serves to *highlight* his observation of *Rajasthani miniatures paintings* with its fusion of Mughal and Western Indian *tradition*. Rameshwar Singh mostly works with *acrylics*, *tempera* and *oil painting* to achieve his desired effects.

He lives and works in Jaipur, RAJ.

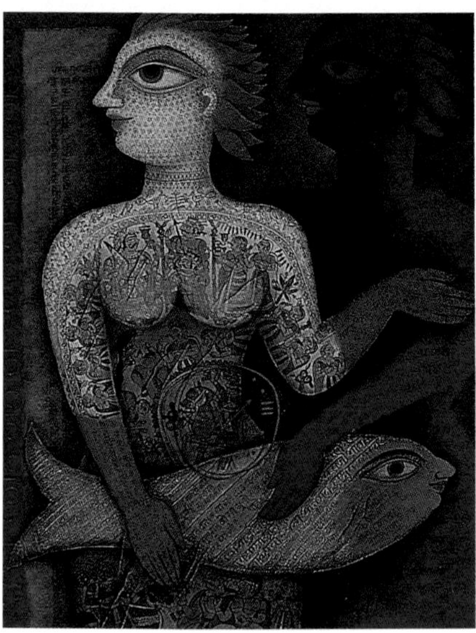

Singh, Rameshwar: "The Tattoo Fantasy Series" *Mixed media.*

Singh, Sardar Gurcharan (1896–1995) b. Srinagar, J&K. Education: Prince of Wales College Jammu, Traditional *sculpture* & *pottery* training & guidance under Pathan Abdula, Studied two years under senior *artists* in Tokyo Japan. Solos: First in Japan Tokyo 1922, London through *AIFACS*. Group participations: Abroad & India–*CYAG*. Workshops: Started Delhi Blue Pottery New Delhi 1991–1992 completed 50 years in 2002 & Second for students. Awards: Felicitation, Fellowship *AIFACS*, Padma Shri Govt. of India New Delhi. Appoint-ments: Taught in Lahore Govt. Potters Institute, Ambala, Return to Delhi 1953. Collections: India & abroad.

Sardar Gurcharan Singh's *pottery* conforms to his ideals of thinking in the *abstract*, while concentrating on the simple and the functional. He had a large repertoire of shapes and *sizes*, not developing outlandish *styles* and decorativeness, but a constant exploration, a steady expansion of his basic *style*. The *patterns* that he used, to decorate his pots, both on-glaze and incised, were *modern* in their simplicity and directness. It was the subtle detail that interested him, be it an unusual curving out at the bottom or the expressionistic surface of salt-glaze ware or the simple vertical drips of a dark glaze against a *light body*, they all speak of his characteristic touch. There is also an element of Far Eastern *pottery* in some of his works.

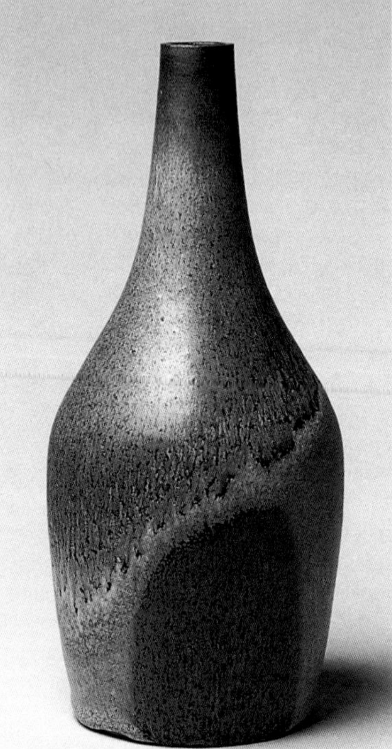

Singh, Sardar Gurcharan: "Tall Bottle", with a Titanium glaze.

Singh, Saroj Kumar R.K. (1952–) b. Imphal, Manipur. Education: Dip. in *FA*. Imphal Art College Imphal, Higher studies *MSU*, B.FA. Lucknow University. Solos: *MSU*, UP *LKA*, College Arts & Crafts Gallery Lucknow, *LKA* New Delhi, *JAG*. Group participations: Nainital, Bhopal, Chandigarh, Manipur State Museum Imphal, UP *LKA*, Rashtriya *LKA* Lucknow, *LKA* New Delhi, *CYAG*, *JAG*, *ABC*. *Artists* camps: Imphal, Kanpur, Jaipur, Jammu, Udaipur, *GAC*. Awards: State Kala Grant, State Kala Fellowship, State Kala Academy Award, Sahitya Parishad & Art Society Manipur, All India Drawing Award Patiala, Gold Medal Gauhati University. National Scholarship & National Fellowship New Delhi. Appointments: External Examiner at BHU, Lucknow University, Aligarh University; Ex-secretary Manipur Art Society; Demonstrated programmers & Slide Shows; Supervisor for *graphics* at the Rashtriya *LKA* Lucknow. Collections: State Kala Academy & State Museum Manipal, Mutuwa Museum Imphal, UP *LKA* Lucknow, KAR *LKA* Bangalore, National *LKA* New Delhi & pvt. in India & abroad.

It is his love of *nature*, of *flora & fauna paintings*, specifically aquatic life, that surfaces in Saroj Kumar R.K. Singh's *prints* and *etchings*. It is not one fish or one bird alone that appears in his works, but an *abstract* medley of *lines* and *patterns* that enervates the *composition*. He has also painted a few *portraits* of his native people, being fascinated with tribal features.

He lives and works in Lucknow.

Singh, V. P. (Vishwanath Pratap Singh) (1931–) b. Allahabad, U.P. No formal training in *art*, Stated *painting* in 1994. Solos: Arpana Gallery of the Academy of Literature & Fine Art New Delhi, Durbar Art Gallery Kochi–Titled "Random Impulses", *JAG*. Group participations: Delhi, Mumbai. Publications: "Frontline Magazine", "The Tribune"–Chandigarh, "The Hindu"–Kochi, "Telegraph"–Kolkata, "Asian Age", "Navabharat Times", "Rashtriya Sahara", "Afternoon" and "Sunday Mid-Day". Catalogues and books on poems.

V. P. Singh was the seventh Prime Minister of India (1989–1990). *Art* being his first interest, he has experimented with several *media* in the field of *painting*, in addition to writing poetry. He has worked with *pastels*, *oil painting*, *watercolours*, *pencil* and *charcoal drawing* and *acrylics*. His works are mostly *figurative*, capturing fleeting expressions and diverse moment in the life of different people. His *doodles* and spontaneous brushstrokes are reminiscent of the works of *Rabindranath Tagore*. His *pastel drawing* of a pet dog reveals his understanding of *texture* and *form*. His *portraits* reveal the inner character of the sitters, while his *watercolours* have a *calligraphic rhythm* in their spontaneity.

He lives and works in New Delhi.

Single Block Colour Printing Is through single block either in *lino*, *wood* or litho for multi *colour printing*. The single block method is simpler to use, and in this, it involves *colour printing* process, *colour* application, which goes light to dark, step by step until a final *print image* is achieved. It is preferable not to *print* more than three or four *colours*, as the *pigment* tends to build up. Refer *Artist's Proof*, *Block Printing*, *Colour Printing & Four Colour Process*, *Key Block*, *Lithography*, *Printmaking*, *Viscosity Printmaking*, *Rini Dhumal*, *Gaganendranath Tagore;* Illustrations–*Wood Cut Printing*, *Krishna N. Reddy*.

Sinha, Beohar Ram Manohar (1929–) b. Jabalpur. Education: Dip. in FAC *VBU*, Post Dip. in *mural painting*, Indian Govt. Scholarship, Institute of FA. Peking China. Solos: *AIFACS*, *BB*, TAG; International: England, France. Group participations: *Santiniketan*, *BAAC* Kolkata, *LKA* & Kala Mela New Delhi, *BB*, TAG, *JAG*, *AIFACS*, IIC; International: China. *Artists* camp: Gwalior, Jabalpur, *BB;* Seminars: *LKA* New Delhi, Khairagarh University BHU, MPKP. *Auctions*: Sotheby's London. Awards: "Shikhar Samman" Govt. of MP, *AIFACS* Special Award, Hon. as a Veteran Artist *AIFACS* New Delhi. Member: *INTACH*, Shikhar Samman, Govt. of MP. Commissions: *Murals KB Santiniketan* & Martyr's Memorial Jabalpur. Appointments: Principal of Govt. Kalaniketan & Govt. Institute of FA. Jabalpur, Dean of Faculty of Painting, University of Art & Music Khairagarh, Adhyapaka (teacher) *KB VBU*.

Beohar Ram Manohar Sinha's years of training at *Santiniketan* and at the Central Institute of Fine Arts, Beijing have influenced his *style* of *painting*. His brushstrokes are both *calligraphic* and lyrical in their spontaneity and brevity. With a few strokes he manages to convey both subject and surface. *Tone*, *depth* and *texture* all flow out of these few strokes. Water with its wavering surface and boats and the Varanasi sun-umbrellas seem to be a perennial favourite with Beohar Ram Manohar Sinha, with rocks and lotus flowers being a close second.

Presently he lives and works in Jabalpur.

Sinha, Rohini (1938–) Education: GDA & *Mural* decoration *JJSA*. Solos: MMB, Mumbai, *JAG*, SRAG. Group participations: Chandigarh, Kala Melas Mumbai, National *LKA* New Delhi, MAHA State Art Exhibition, *BAS*, *LTG*, *BB*. Awards: MAHA State Art Award. Collections: *LKA* New Delhi, Godrej Mumbai, *BB* & pvt.

Rohini Sinha usually *paints* large abstracted *landscapes* in *acrylics* or does *pen* and *ink drawings*. She achieves a sense of *volume* and *space* without relying on conventional *perspective*. It is by layering and *overlapping tints* and *shade* that she conveys *light* and *shade*, *texture* being important in these *abstract* bursts of *colour* and *pigment*.

She lives and works in Mumbai.

Size 1. Refers to the *dimensions* of the work and material. **2.** A gelatinous solution or glue made from animal skin. Size is available in the *form* of rough, leathery sheets, granules or powder. It is mixed with hot water to make a powerful adhesive which is brushed on to the *support* i.e. *canvas* for *oil painting*, certain types of *paper* and fabric. The size will permeate the surface without coating it. It protects the surface and makes it resistant to deterioration.

The "Vishnudharmottara Purana" gives instructions on the use of buffalo hide, in the making of size. The PURANA recommends the use of size as a binder, stating that "it fixes and tempers *colour* and stops them from flaking." Refer *Glue Size*.

Size Colour A form of painting. It is used almost exclusively for stage scene or as binder for distemper in which the powdered pigment is mixed with hot glue size or size.

Sketch=rough draft, general *outline*. It refers to a quick *drawing* or *painting*. It is also a preliminary study of the envisioned *composition*, for a *landscape painter*. A sketch is probably made on the spot itself, usually in *watercolour*, while the finished *painting* might be rendered in *oil colours* in the studio. For the *sculptor*, a sketch would help in deciding the *composition*, while for the *painter* it would help in deciding certain aspects like *size*, scale, *composition*, *texture* and placement of *colour*. Refer Illustrations–*Erotic Art*, *Hatching– Laxma Goud*, *Life-Drawing–Muralidhar R. Achrekar*, *Line– Shiavax Chavda*, *Still Life*–Pratima Sheth, *Ranjitsingh Gaekwad*, *Rathin Mitra*, *Mohan Samant*, *Ved Pal Sharma*, SHIVA–*Kanu Desai*, *Vrindavan Solanki*.

Slip Refer *Casting*, *Clay Water*, *Sudha Arora*, *Himmat Shah*.

Soak-stain Technique A *technique* in *oil painting*, *watercolour* and *tempera*, which produces soft stains or blots of *colour* through the use of thin, running *paint* on unsized *canvas* or *paper*. Refer *Bengal School*, *Jaganath M. Ahivasi*, *Jamini P. Gangooly*, *Kanu Desai*, *Baburao Painter*, *Ali J. Sultan*, *Abanindranath Tagore*, *Ram Gopal Vijaivargiya;*

Illustrations–*Seascape, Muhammed Abdur Rehman Chughtai, Pralhad A. Dhond, John Fernandes, Asit K. Haldar, K. Khosa, K.B. Kulkarni–Drapery, Hemendranath Mazumdar, Kshitendranath Mazumdar, Paresh Maity, Sarada Charan Ukil.*

Social Realism Refers to *contemporary art* about life *styles* of the working class usually projecting socialist or leftist viewpoints. As seen in "The Eight" and "Kitchen Sink" schools of the West; in India it is exemplified by works of *Satish Gujral* and several other *artist* of *Calcutta School* from 50s to 80s and 90s and other works in the *Maharaja Fatesingh Museum*.

Society of Contemporary Artists (SCA) (Kolkata) The society was founded in 1960, after Ahibhusan Malik, a cartoonist and *art critic* of Anand Bazar Patrika brought together a group of *artists* for an exhibition in Kolkata and Mumbai. The success of these exhibitions led to the formation of the society, which was initially housed in the residence of one of the members, *Anilbaran Saha*. They held their first *exhibition* at the Artistry House Gallery Kolkata. Later the society was shifted to its present premises in *Ajit Chakravarti's* studio at Lenin Sarani.

Here, they became involved in *printmaking*, hosting international *exhibitions*, printing limited edition *portfolios* and offering studio facilities even to non-members. They also helped to setup the *graphics* studio of the Dacca Sahitya Kala Parishad after their exhibition in Bangladesh.

The society holds regular *exhibitions* of the members' works all over the country.

Soft Ground A *ground* that remains soft and malleable even after it has been applied onto the *plate*. Subtle effects and textural *impressions* are possible in this *technique* of *etching* as against the linear quality of *hard ground prints*. The *ground* is usually made by adding one part of tallow or grease to three parts *hard ground*. It is applied with a roller, the *plate* being heated at first. The remaining procedure is the same, with the exception that extreme care has to be taken not to smudge the *ground*. Refer *Acid Resist, Bite, Biting in, Amitabha Banerjee, Jyoti Bhatt, H.R. Kambli, Rm. Palaniappan, Krishna N. Reddy.*

Soft-Sculpture Which began in 1960. C. Oldenburg a "Pop Artist" made soft-sculptures of *canvas* filled with foam rubber, based on red objects, took on distorted appearance, through both their scale and their response to gravity; other material used were rope, *leather*, vinyl, latex, cloth etc. This has also developed in India by using a lot of throw-away material (in their *installations*, both for their *visual* appearance and *symbolic* connotations). Refer *Mrinalini Mukherjee*.

Solanki, Vrindavan (1942–) b. Junagadh, GUJ. Education: Dip. in *painting*, Post-Dip. in *graphics MSU*. Over 30 solos: MMB Mumbai, *Art Heritage* New Delhi, Marvel Art Gallery, CAG & *LKA* Ahmedabad, Vithi Art Gallery Vadodara, The Gallery Chennai *JAG*, TAG, *DG*, *CYAG*, TKS; International: USA, Mauritius. Group participations: *LKA* New Delhi, Harmony Mumbai, *CYAG*, *GMAG JAG*. *Art* camps & workshops: Chennai, New Delhi, The Art Trust Mumbai, Linoprint workshop Ahmedabad. *Auctions*: Osian's Mumbai. Awards: GUJ *LKA*, Kalidas Art Exhibition Ujjain, Graphics Exhibition Hyderabad, "Takman 28" Prize Udaipur, UP *LKA*, *ASI*, *BAS*. Member: *LKA* GUJ. Commissions: *murals* New York USA; designed TISCO Calender. Appointments: Visiting Faculty NID. Collections: Godrej Mumbai, *CYAG*, & pvt.

For the first 25 years of his career, Vrindavan Solanki only worked in *ink* on *paper*, using a variety of *pens*, including traditional bamboo sticks used by the traders in his native GUJ to write their accounts. He also uses Chinese bamboo holders and fine nibs from New York that range from two inches width to a quarter of an inch. In his recent works, he has used *acrylic paint*, watered down to an inky consistency, preparing his *canvases* with rabbit glue and *gesso* to achieve a smooth working surface for his *monochromatic* renderings of men and women from his native Saurashtra. The absence of *colour* is not noticeable in the rich *chiaroscuro* of cross-hatched strokes.

He lives and works in Ahmedabad, GUJ.

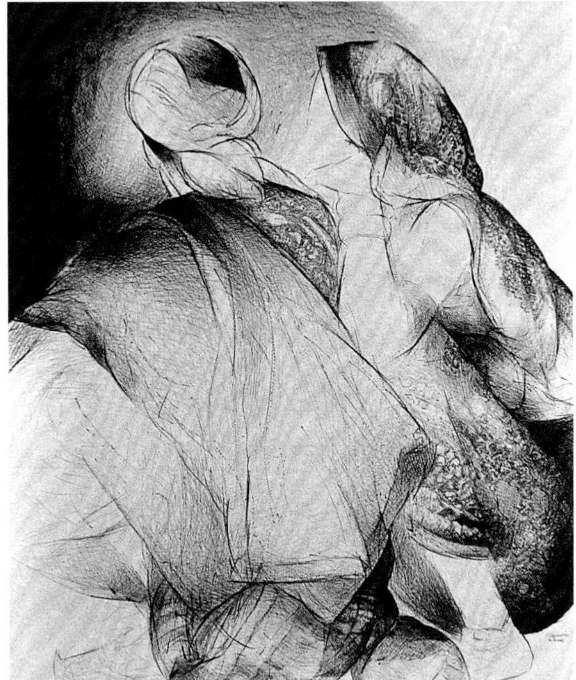

Solanki, Vrindavan: "Couple Series II", *Drawing* No.1, *Pen-Ink* on *Paper*, 1993, 102.5x90 cm.

Som, Sovon (1932–) b. Silchar, Assam. Education: Dip. in *FA*. *KB Santiniketan*, under *Nandalal Bose* & *Ramkinkar Baij RBU*. Solos: Nagpur, *KB Santiniketan* & *AFA* Kolkata; International: Jordan, Cuba, USA, La Galerie Bangladesh. Group participations: *AFA* & Gallery Shivam Kolkata. Participated: In seminars. Member: WB Academy of Dance, Drama, Music & FA. Appointments: Prof. of history of *art* at *RBU*, Also International University at Havana University, Visiting Prof. Cuba. Publication: Writes on *art* for several Bengali magazines. Collections: University in USA, Geneva & pvt.

Though he was known more as an *art* historian, Som Sovon has been exhibiting his *paintings* since the early 50s. He gave up *oil painting* in the 70s for the grace of *watercolour*, as he believed that the shine of the linseed *oil* was alien to the reflective quality of Eastern light. It is the human predicament that interests him. He tries to transform these situations into metaphorical and allegorical statements, in which symbols and *ciphers* play a major role.

He lives and works in Kolkata.

Sonavane, Shamendu N. (1956–) b. Mehunbare, MAHA. Education: GDA in *painting* & Art Master *JJSA*. Solos: *JAG*, TAG, BAG. Group participations: Aurangabad, *Artists' Centre*, Gallery Mahalsa & MAHA State Exhibition, Mumbai, *WSC* Artist Group Mumbai, Kolkata & Chennai, *LKA* New Delhi, SZCC Nagpur, *Triennale* New Delhi & Goa, TAG, *JAG*, *DG*, BAG, *ASI*, *JJSA*, *CRAR*, *BAS*. Participated: Tapestries Exhibition UK, Designed Tapestries Japan & France, Wall hanging Sweden, International Trade Fair-Hand painted mega *size* tapestries. Awards: National *LKA* New Delhi, Award & Gold Medal *JJSA*. Collections: *NGMA* & *LKA* New Delhi, Air India Mumbai, SZCC Nagpur, pvt. & corporates in India & abroad.

A designer at the *WSC*, he is fascinated by the possibilities of impasted *oil painting*. He uses his *painting knife* gesturally, creating vortexes of warm *transparent colours* which are cocooned within the confines of almost plastered slabs of *paint*.

The *paint* is relief-like in conception with the excess forming ridges at the edge of each stroke. He has worked in both *oils* and *watercolours*, but it is obiviously *oil painting* and its dense, *viscous* quality that is his forte.

He lives and works in Mumbai.

Sonavani, Vasant S. (1943–) Niphad, Nashik MAHA. Education: *JJSA*. Solos: *JAG*. Group participations: MAHA State Exhibition Mumbai, MAHA Contemporary Artists & FAIM Exhibition New Delhi, *BAAC* Kolkata, *Mural* designed Nasik, *JAG*, TAG, *BAS*, *Dhoomimal*. Awards: MAHA State Exhibition, *BAS*. Member: Nominated Member of *Art Education* Committee *LKA* New Delhi & General Council. Appointments: HoD *Art* Teacher's Training *JJSA*. Collections: *LKA* & *NGMA* New Delhi, *BAAC* Kolkata, pvt. & corporates in Mumbai, Pune & abroad.

It is *nature*, specifically *landscape* and the effect of natural *light* on the elements of the universe that interests Vasant S. Sonavani. He observes the effects of *light* dispersing from hard-edged objects while forming a rayonist *pattern*. The vertical divisions in some works is a residue of his observation of the rays of the sun intercepted at certain *points*. He never uses the *brush*. He applies *paint* on the *canvas*, sometimes using *painting knife*, but usually working with the roller.

He lives and works in Mumbai.

South Indian Bronzes *Metal sculpture* have been made in India & other countries. *Brass*, *copper* and *bronze* are the most popularly used *metals*. Of particular significance are South Indian bronzes mainly *cast* during the CHOLA period. Using the *"lost wax process"*, these were made of *bronze* alloyed with a large percentage of copper. The *figures* ranged from small temple *idols* to standing *figures* as tall as 1.5m. SHIVA was the most popular subject, particularly his dancing *form* called the NATARAJA. Additionally, all the deities and their AVATARAS have been *cast*. The South Indian bronze not only stand out for the mastery of *technique* of the Sthapathis (craftsmen) but also for their grace and beauty. Refer *Cire Perdue*, BHAKTI.

Souza, Francis Newton (1924–2002) b. Goa. Education: *JJSA;* Central School of Art London, ENSBA. Solos: *Delhi Art Gallery* New Delhi, *BAS*, *PUAG*, *Dhoomimal*, CCAG, *LTG*; International: Zurich, Venice, Johannesburg, Geneva, Sweden, Germany, Canada, Commonwealth & Indian Institute of Contemporary Art London, Gallery Creuze Paris, UAE, GBP. Retrospective: New Delhi, Mumbai, London. Participated: *PAG* Mumbai 1949; International: Sao Paulo, Tate Gallery & Commonwealth Exhibition in London, Indian Independence Exhibition Washington DC, Festival of India, Museum of Modern Art Oxford, V&A & others. *Auctions*: Heart, Osian's Mumbai & New Delhi. Bonhams, Christie's & Sotheby's–London, Sotheby's New York. Award: Italian Govt. Scholarship. Founder member: *PAG* Mumbai. Publications: "Times of India", "Sunday Observer"; International: Art News & Review, Auto-biography "Words & Lines" London. Collections: Vadodara Museum, *NGMA* New Delhi; International: Tate Gallery London, Wakefield City Museum, National Gallery of Victoria Melbourne, passed away in Mumbai.

Francis Newton Souza was the founder member and the most vocal of the *PAG* Mumbai. "Francis Newton Souza straddled many *traditions*, but served none" is an apt description of his *modern* Indian erotica. His NAYIKAS have the full bodies, sensuality of the MITHUNA *figures* in *Khajuraho* and Konarak, with the added vitality of his *line*. Though the *eclectic* human *form* remains the most memorable in his repertoire of *images*, Francis Newton Souza had also worked with *landscapes*, *still lifes* and Biblical subjects. He used *distortion* freely, his *colours* have the brilliance of *stained glass*. *Oil painting* was clearly his preferred *medium* of expression. Refer *Erotic Art*, *Nude*.

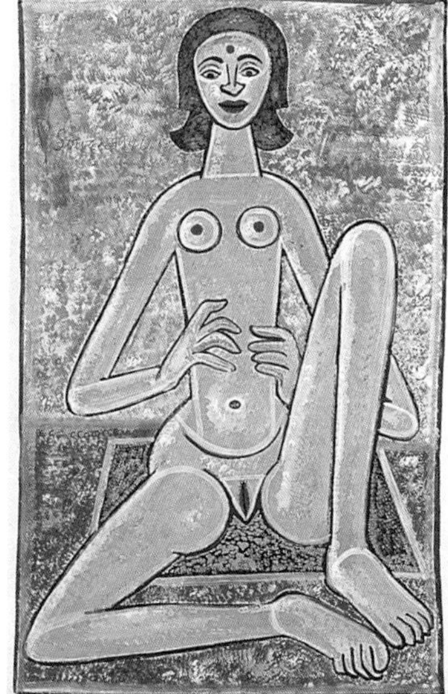

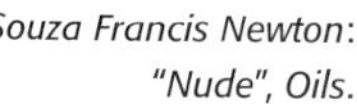

Souza Francis Newton: "Nude", Oils.

Space It is a continuous expanse, area. In *art*, the word refers to the area portrayed or felt in the work. i.e. the illusionary *depth* created by the use of *one-point perspective* in *figurative paintings*, the *depth* occupied by *forms* and *colours* in *abstract art*, the space displaced by three-dimensional *sculpture*. In India spatial *illusion* was first introduced by the British and from then onward, space became an integral part of the *composition*.

In Indian *miniature painting*, space was mostly flat. The early *Pala* and *Jain manuscript paintings* rarely depicted space, with the human *figure* dominating against a flat blue or red *background*. *Mewar* and *Basohli* miniatures too use flat dark-red and orange accents to depict incidents. The Mughals were the first to introduce *background* elements, like trees and rocks to open up space. Unlike Western *paintings* where the *foreground images* were larger and more sharply defined than the *background,* the Mughal *artist* preferred to place the *foreground figures* in the lower *register* and the *background figure* in the upper part of the *folio*.

In *abstract art* space refers to the actual area of the *canvas*, *paper* or other material used. i.e. *Ambadas' transparent* drips of *pigment* contain an *illusion* of *depth* as do *K.M. Adimoolam's* geometric accents of *colour*. Later, large abstracted *compostions* in *sculpture*, *painting* and *installation* achieved a sense of *volume* and space without relying on conventional *perspective*. Refer *Aerial Perspective, Atmosphere/Atmospheric Effects, Backdrop, Background, Bindu, Closed Form, Junk Art, Landscape, Narrative, Neo-Plasticism, Op or Optical Art, Two-Point Perspective, Ramkinkar Baij, Kanchan Chander, Nagjibhai V. Chauhan, Bhagwan Chavan, Jamini P. Gangooly, Shaibal Ghosh, V. Hariram, Janak J. Narzary, K. Jayapala Panicker, Dashrath Patel, Ahmed M.G. Raffic, K.G. Subramanyan;* Illustrations—*Abstract Geometric, Accidental Light, Figure Painting, Alphonso A. Doss, Kanayi Kunhiraman—Earth Art, Earth Work, Land Art, Mass, Shakuntala Kulkarni, Tyeb Mehta, Shankar Nandagopal, Amrut Patel, Pilloo Pochkhanawalla, Sayed Haider Raza, Raja Ravi Varma*.

Spiritual Religious, divine, mystic. Refers to that quality in a work of *art* that appeals to the *metaphysical* rather than the physical plane. In Indian *art*, the earliest *sculptures* have a spiritual quality. *Art* was basically spiritual or religious being full of didactic symbols and infused with spiritual and philosophical significance, e.g. *Ajanta/Ellora*, *Khajuraho*. *Images* drawn from different *cultures* are sometimes used to signify philosophical or spiritual indicators. Later *paintings* veered towards the *abstract*, with just that touch of *Realism* and "spiritual" quality.

From TANTRIC *Art* to *contemporary paintings*, Indian *artists* have constantly attempted to explore the *theme*, both on the spiritual and *abstract* plane. They constructed strong geometric *forms*, which producing a spiritual *background*. There is also a spiritual quality in the use of *colours*. Refer *Bundi*, CHATUR-BHUJA, DASAVATARA, KALPA-SUTRA, MITHUNA, RADHA, SARASVATI, SURYA, *Tree of Life*, Illustrations—APSARA, ASANAS, BHAGAVATA-PURANA, BHARATA, BRAHMA, BUDDHA, CHAKRA, CHAMUNDA, DIWALI/DIPAVALI, DURGA, DIGAMDARA, *Erotic Art*, GANDHARVAS, GANESHA, GARUDA, *Glass Painting*, GOVARDHAN, HOLI, *Illuminated Manuscripts*, INDRA, JATAKA, KAILASH, KAILASA, KALI, KALKI (KALKIN), KARMA, KRISHNA, LAKSHMI, LINGA, LINGAM, MAHAVIRA, MAKARA, *Mewar*, *Mosaic*, NANDI, NARASIMHA, NATARAJA, NAYAK-NAYAKA, OM, *Palm Leaf*, PARAVTI, RAGINI, RAMAYANA, RASA, RASA LILA, *Repousse*, SHANKHA, SWASTIKA, *Thanjavur (Tanjore) Painting, Manjit Bawa, Madhukar B. Bhat, Ganga Devi, K.V. Haridasan, K.K. Hebbar, Tyeb Mehta, Chhaganlal D. Mistry, Mrinalini Mukherjee, Reddeppa M Naidu, Rathin Mitra, Laxman Pai, K.C.S. Paniker, Jamini Roy, Suhas Roy, Ali J. Sultan, Sarada Charan Ukil, Shantanu Ukil, Christian Art—Francis Newton Souza,* SHIVA- *Kanu Desai, Tantra art—Ghulam Rasool Santosh*, YANTRA—*Rekha Krishnan*.

Srinivasan, P. (1951–) b. Chennai. Education: Grad. in *arts* University of Chennai, Dip. in *FA. painting* & Post. Dip. *GCAC* Chennai, *Fresco* training *Banasthali Vidyapith* RAJ. Solos: Pondicherry, PUJ University Museum Chandigarh, *LKA* Chennai, *AFA* Kolkata, *JAG*, RAG, TKS. Group participations: Over 60 participations & 20 group shows including National Exhibition, *LKA* & *Triennale* New Delhi, *BAAC* Kolkata & Mumbai, *CKP, AIFACS*; International: International Mini Print Spain, Brazil & Japan, Festival of India Japan, *Biennale* Tokyo & Brazil, Contemporary Art Yugoslavia & Denmark organized by Art World—Chennai. Workshops & camps: All India Painters Patna, *GAC* New Delhi, Southern Regional Painters Nandi Hills. State Academy Camp Kodaikanal. Awards: Research Grant & National Exhibition *LKA* New Delhi, Victoria Technical Institute Scholarship Chennai, Bharat Kala Parishad Hyderabad, State *LKA* Chennai, *CKP*. Fellowship: Junior Fellowship Govt. of India. Collections: *Garhi Studio's*, *LKA* & *NGMA* New Delhi, PUJ University Museum Chandigarh, Govt. Museum, *LKA* Chennai, *BAAC* Kolkata, UP *LKA* Lucknow, *GAC, CYAG;* International: Spain, Japan,Brazil & Poland.

Srinivasan P. is deeply interested in *texture* and its various elements. Though storytelling was an integral part of his *paintings* in the late 70s and 80s, his present work entirely shuns the *figure* or even curvilinear *lines*. Instead he practises Frank Stella-like *hard-edged paintings*, using the comb to create parallel incisions in his thick, impasted geometric divisions in *oil*.

He lives & works in Chennai.

Srivastav, Narendra Rai (1943–) b. Hyderabad. Education: Dip. in *painting JJSA* Higher degree, JNTU. Solos: Hyderabad. Group participations: Bombay Group Hyderabad, National Exhibition New Delhi, HAS; International: USA, *Biennale* Havana Cuba & Japan. Workshops & *artists* camps: *Painting*, KB Hyderabad & JNTU, *Graphic* Chennai. Awards: Felicitated by organizations Gold Medals AP *LKA*, National Award & HAS. Publications: Poems, invited by Doordarshan TV, AIR. Collections: Govt. *museums* & *academies*, pvt. & corporates, national & international.

Narendra Rai Srivastav has moved from a surrealistic rendering of *figures* in the 80s to an *eclectic*, even mixed group of works in the 90s. His work of the 90s includes miniature like stylized NAYAKA and NAYIKAS standing amidst naive *landscape* and expressionistically painted and distorted *fragments* of reality. His *technique* with *oils*, *watercolours*, *mixed media* and *tempera* using both *brush* and *painting knife*, results in flat and brilliantly coloured *compositions*.

He lives in Hyderabad.

Srivastava, Harish (1941–) b. Baroli, UP. Education: Grad. Meerut University, Dip. in *FA*, *College of Art* New Delhi, Art Master GCAC, Lucknow Textile *Design*. Solos & group shows: Green wood Gallery, Russian Cultural Center *College of Art*, *LKA* & RB New Delhi, *JAG*, SRAG, TKS. Participations: Bangalore, Ahmedabad, Lucknow, National *LKA*, *Triennale* & Kala Mela New Delhi, *LKA* Orissa, UP & Bihar, *AIFACS*, SKP; International: Mexico, Czechoslovakia, National Museum Havana Cuba. Camps: All India Camp *LKA* Patna, Jammu State Academi. Awards: National *LKA* New Delhi, *LKA* in Bihar & Orissa, *AIFACS*. Fellowship: HRD Ministry Govt. of India. Collections: SKP, *Dhoomimal*, *College of Art* & Gallery Aurobindo New Delhi, *LKA* New Delhi, Orissa, UP, KAR, Himachal State & abroad.

Harish Srivastava has worked exclusively with *oil colours*, using them in heavy, impasted strokes of the *brush* and knife, building up his mountainous *landscapes*. He tries to capture the warmth of the sunlight falling on these cool, snow-capped peaks.

He lives in New Delhi.

Srividya, J. (1939–) b. Thuraiyur, Chennai. Education: Dip. in *FA. painting*, Post-Dip. in *commercial art* Italy, Florence Academy Belli Arti, Bennett College UK *commercial art*. Solos & group participations: New Delhi, Mumbai, Hyderabad, Chennai; International: Zurich, Oxford, Basel, Florence, Milan. Participated: *Biennale*, National Exhibitions, *LKA* & *NGMA* New Delhi, Progress Painters Chennai; International: Basel Art Fair, UNESO, USSR, USA, Japan, UK; listed in World Art Directory. Awards: Fellowship Italy, National *LKA* New Delhi. Member: In International Art Society & India. Collections: *LKA* & *NGMA* New Delhi; International: Switzerland, Korea.

His works are based on TANTRA, specifically on Kundalini and Tantricism. He creates brilliant *patterns* on *paper*, using *images* like the *silhouette* with TANTRIC energy flowing into decorative compartments. He uses the *mixed media technique*, with *acrylic colours*.

He is from Indore.

Stained Glass Coloured pieces of glass stained with *metal* oxides and then joined together with strips of *lead* to *form* colourful *patterns*. This *technique* dates back to Medieval period and its finest examples are seen in cathedrals and churches in Europe and later in India. The *patterns* in stained glass are illuminated by diaphanous *light*. In *contemporary* period stained glass has also been used by expressionist *artists* using new *technique* developed in Denmark. In India *artist* like *Katayun Saklat* have also used stained glass as a *medium*. Refer *A.A. Raiba*, *Back-Glass Painting*, *Christian Art*, *Glass Painting*, *Gothic*, *Sukumar Das*, *P. Khemraj*, *Sisir Sahana*.

State Museum (Patna, Bihar) one of the most important example of Mauryan *sculpture*, the Didarganj YAKSHINI is to be found at this *museum*. She has a voluptuous *figure*, with a Chauri (fly whisk) held over one shoulder. The *sculpture* has the typical Mauryan polish, a *technique* which has so far eluded discovery by *modern sculptors*.

The *museum* itself was established in 1917. It has an outstanding collection of Indian *art*, including the above mentioned *sculpture* in the *sculpture* galleries, the *bronze* gallery and the *terracotta* collection all belonging to various *periods* in Indian history.

Steel Steel is an industrial material. *Contemporary artists* create new *form* of work in *art* with different materials, steel being one of them in the *form* of *plates* and coils. Mild steel can be twisted, turned, shaped, cut and polished on lathe machines. Earlier the process was done of steel and cowdung, or pre-stressed thin *metal* sheets welded into behemoth like shapes.

Old artisans created most of their works and *masterpieces* in *stone*, *cement*, *plaster of Paris*, *metal-bronze* and *copper*. Steel being the material of the 20th century, it can be *cast*, welded and used in conjunction with different *metals*, *alloys* and *mixed media*. *Artists* have used steel sheets, solid blocks and geometrical shapes to depict *abstract forms*. Refer *Assemblages*, *Media*, *Screen Printing*, *Silk Screen Printing*, *Welding*, *Navjot Altaf*, *Pilloo Pochkhanawalla*, *Vivan Sundaram*; Illustrations—*Sankho Chaudhuri*, *Raghav Kaneria*.

Stencil It is a method of transferring *designs* where *paper*, card, thin, *metal*, *wood* or stretched gauze are cut in the required shape and then sprayed or brushed with *ink*, *paint* or are printed. There are two methods of stenciling, direct and indirect. In the direct method a cut out shape of an *image* is placed on a *base*, and the *paint* is brushed, sprayed or printed in the cut out area to create this *image*.

In the indirect method, a stencil is first made in the cut out shape required on thin strong *paper*, placed on the screen mesh and then the *paint* is brushed, sprayed or printed around it. The stencil is lifted to leave a *negative image*. e.g. as in *silk screen printing* or photographic stencil. Refer *Air Brushing*, *Monotype*, *Print*, *Sand Blasting*, *Serigraphy*, *Screen Printing*, *Silk Screen Printing*, *Wax*, *Seema Ghurayya*, *Mahadeo Bhanaji Ingle*.

Still Life *Paintings* containing arrangements of inanimate objects: domestic tableware, flowers, food and books in particular. This was popular in the Graeco-Roman *mosaics*. In India, it was first taught as a subject in the *academic art* school, it often appeared in the *form* of *background* in the *compositions* of *Krishnaji Howlaji Ara*, *K.G. Subramanyan*, *B. Prabha*. Still life could either be realistically rendered or simplified in an *abstract manner*. e.g. *Akbar Padamsee*. Refer *Assemblage*, *Cubism*,

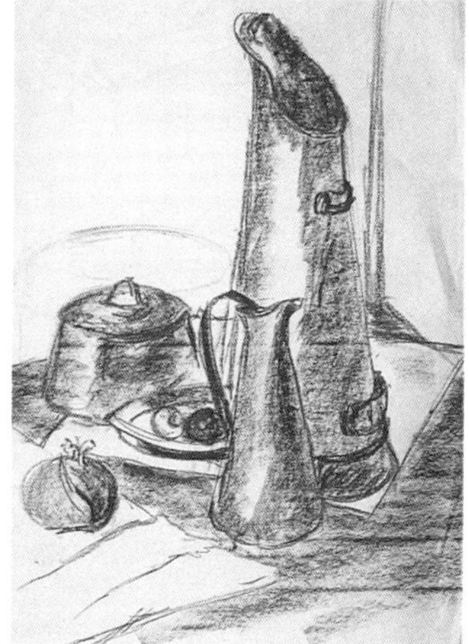

Still Life: *Pratima Sheth*, *Charcoal* on *Paper*, 1984, 58.15x45 cm.

Flora & Fauna Paintings, Found Object, Highlight, Op or Optical Art, Realistic, Vasudeo Adurkar, Navjot Altaf, R.B. Bhaskaran, Ramnik Bhavsar, Vishnu Chinchalkar, R.S. Dhir, Mohan Sharma, Paramjeet Singh, Francis Newton Souza, Rathindranath Tagore; Illustration–*Aku*.

Stippling A *technique* of *modelling form* using small dots or short strokes instead of shading. The process is used in *drawing, painting, engraving* and printing. *Narayan S. Bendre's* pointillist *paintings*, though stippled with pure dots of *pigment* achieved the *tonal value* of mixed *colours*. Refer *Neo-Impressionism, Pointillism, Print, Chhaganlal D. Mistry*.

Stone A piece or *fragment* of a solid, non-metallic, mineral *matter* i.e. rock. Other than *marble*, there is an extensive variety of stones available. Stones are of three types: igneous or volcanic rocks, like *granite*, metamorphic such as *marble* and sedimentary rocks, like sandstone and limestone or Portland stone and related igneous rocks. Stone is well preserved or fresh from the mine as opposed to dead stone. This material is perfect for sculptural use and gives out a clear, ringing sound. A pointed metallic hammer or single or multiple-pointed pick is used, to crack and chip away large masses of stone as required. They are usually quarried in large rectangular blocks used by both *sculptors* and builders. They vary in hardness from soft alabastres to dense *granites* and present a huge variety of *textures* and *colours*. The factors that determine their respective usability are their suitability for tools like bush chisel, claw chisel, driller (which are hand-held tools used in *stone carving*), the desired effect and their durability with reference to the ultimate site of *installation*. Refer *Acrylics, Antique, Architecture, Arte Povera, Artefact, Bas-Relief, Block Printing, Boucharde, Bronze, Bust, Carving, Cast Stone, Cave Art,* CHAITYA, *Chisels, Colour, Conte Pencil, Copper, Direct Carving, Dravidian Style, Egyptian Art, Filler, Finish, Found Object, Gandharan Art, Gouge, Gum Arabic,* HANUMAN, *Harappa, Hoysala, Inlay, Jali Work,* JATAKA, *Junk Art, Khajuraho,* LINGA, LINGAM, *Lithography, Mahabalipuram,* MANDAPA, *Maniere Noire, Mathura Art, Maurya Dynasty, Media, Mohenjo Daro, Monotype, Mughal Dynasty,* MURTI, *Nagara Style, Natural Colours, Neolithic Art, New Realism, Nude, Oil, Oleography,* PALLAVAS, *Pallava Dynasty, Pictorial, Plaster, Polychromatic sculpture, Print, Realistic, Sand Blasting, Sculpture,* SHAKTI, *Stone Carving, Stupa, Tensile Strength, Thanjavur (Tanjore) Paintings*–used limestone, *Vesara Style,* VIHARA, *Visual, Wetting Down, White, Sudha Arora, Ramkinkar Baij, Sadanandji Bakre, Pushp Betala, Ajit Chakravarti, Sunirmal Chatterjee, Sankho Chaudhuri, Dakoji Devraj, Adi M. Davierwala, Subrayalu Dhanapal, M. Dharmani, M.J. Enas, Sukhen Ganguly, Bhagwant K. Goregaokar, Satish Gujral, Kantibhai B. Kapadia, Balbir Singh Katt, Latika Katt, Nilkanth P. Khanvilkar, P. Khemraj, D.G. Kulkarni, Anil Kumar, Janak J. Narzary, Mahendra Pandya, Goverdhan S. Panwar, Raj Kumar Panwar, S.L. Parasher, Choudhary Satyanarayan Patnaik, L. Anand Patole, Niranjan Pradhan, Sunil Kumar Paul, Aekka Yadagiri Rao, Bhaskar Rao, Ved Pal Sharma (Bannu), Sharma M.K. Sumahendra, Vivan Sundaram, J. Swaminathan, Nathu Lal Verma*–used precious stones; Illustration–DIWALI/DIPAVALI, NARASIMHA/NARASINHA, *Avtarjeet S. Dhanjal, C. Dakshinamoorthy,* GANDHARVAS, GANESHA, *P.S. Nandhan, Nagji Patel, Ceramics–Jyotsna Bhatt, Ellora*–KAILASH, *Mosaic–Shanti Shah, Relief–Piraji Sagara*.

Stone Carving The *art* of cutting into *stone* to create a desired *form* or shape. The *artist* first draws an *outline* as a guide on a *block* of generally rectilinear *stone*. Using *chisel* and hammer, large pieces of chips are knocked off the *stone*; the *artist* then defines the broad *form* with multi pointed claw chisel and later removes the rough edges to get as close as possible to the final shape he wants to achieve. Various tools are then used, such as *boucharde* or bushhammer, punch, *chisels*, file, drill and rasp etc. to impact *shadows* and put life (expression) in the finished sculpted *form*. The Indian *architecture* evolved with heavily decorated *stone* pillars, *carvings*, and larger than *life-size images* of *gods* and goddesses, at *Ajanta* and *Ellora*, Bagh, Badami, Aihole, *Mahabalipuram* and *Elephanta*. Refer *Direct Carving, Finish, Found Object, Gandharan Art, Junk Art, Maurya Dynasty, Media,* MURTI, *Mosaic, Neolithic Art, Oleography, Polychromatic Sculpture, Rock-cut, Sculpture, Temple Architecture, Texture, Wetting Down, Ramkinkar Baij, Sadanandji Bakre, Adi M. Davierwala, Subrayalu Dhanapal, M. J. Enas, Sukhen Ganguly, Bhagwant K. Goregaoker, Satish Gujral, Nilkanth P. Khanvilkar, D.G. Kulkarni, Choudhary Satyanarayan Patnaik, Aekka Yadagiri Rao, Bhaskar Rao, J. Swaminathan;* Illustrations–*Jali Work,* JATAKA, LINGA, LINGAM, MANDAPA, NARASIMHA, *C. Dakshinamoorthy, Avtarjeet S. Dhanjal, P.S. Nandhan, Nagji Patel, Bayaji Vasantrao Talim*.

Studio of. . . Indicates that the work of *art* has been executed in the atelier (studio), and, or under the personal supervision of a particular *artist*, and at most, it is only partly executed by him. *Mughal miniatures artists* were studio *painters*. Later in *modern* period large scale *compositions*, especially for *film* theatres, *posters, backdrops*, large scale *sculptures* were produced in this *manner*. Refer *Attribution, Society of Contemporary Artists, Kanu Desai, Nilkanth P. Khanvilkar, S.L. Parasher, Vinayak Pandurang Karmarkar*.

Stupa The stupa was a dome erected by the Buddhists. It obviously evolved from the simple burial mound of prehistory. The BUDDHA's remains were enshrined under eight such artificial mounds of earth and brick. The chief purpose of the stupa was thus to enshrine body relics or personal belongings of the BUDDHA or Buddhist teachers. These objects were placed in reliquaries made of precious materials, enclosed in a *stone* box and placed in a small chamber that was totally enclosed by the solid masonry of the stupa. At *times* a smaller stupa was built to commemorate some event at places sacred to *Buddhism*. It soon became a symbol of BUDDHA's Parinirvana (death) and thus an object of worship.

Structurally, the stupa consists of a solid dome called Anda (egg-mound). It stands on a Medhi (circular/square base) with a Harmika (balcony) above it containing a Chhattravali (umbrella). A Vedika (fence) surrounds the stupa, creating a Pradakshina Patha (promenade), with four

Toranas (hanging decoration of an entrance) facing the four cardinal directions. Later another Vedika (fence) was built on the Medhi, creating a Pradakshina Patha that was reached by climbing two Sopanas (stairway). The Vedika and the Toranas were richly decorated with sculptural groups. They resembled *stone copies* of wooden village gates and fencing. The stupa was made of large bricks and rubble, covered with a thick layer of *white plaster* coated with *colour* and gilt. It was richly decorated with festoons, flowers and banners during celebrations. Bharhut and Sanchi are some of the places where stupas have been built in as early as 1230 BC–500 BC. Refer *Sunga Dynasty or Style*, VIHARA, *Bas-Relief*, *Buddhism*, *Buddhist Art*, CHAITYA, *Conservation*, *Ellora*, *Icon*, *Maurya Dynasty*.

Style Is a *term* for expression or exact knowledge of the characteristics of any period/*school of. . .art* or the personal way of doing the work of *art* by any *artist*. *Miniature painting* schools, *Company School* refered to styles of Indian *paintings* by Indian *painters*. Later style changed in mid-19th leading to the forming of *contemporary* style schools, such as the *Bengal School*, *Santiniketan*, *Bombay School*, *Madras School of Art*, *Calcutta School*, *Banasthali Vidyapith* RAJ were formed.

Raja Ravi Varma did the initial exploratory forays into *oil painting* during which he mastered the *technique*, evolving a personal style from his exposure to Western *Art*. *Figurative art* was called academic *realism*. Earlier, *Vinayak Pandurag Karmarkar's* creative *sculptures* followed the neo-classically graceful and *realistic ideas*. *Ramkinkar Baij* was the first one who adopted a new *abstract style* and *technique* in the *art* of *sculpture*. *Krishna N. Reddy* in the mid-70s began developing the viscosity process of *intaglio printing*.

Style became increasingly personal in the 20th century. Various *techniques* and *media* were explored in the process of evolving *imagery* and *design*. However, even through the new *images* and *techniques*, the quintessential Indianness still is inherent in the works. Refer *Abstraction Geometric*, *Bengal School*, *Creation*, *Cubism*, *Decorative Art*, *Distortion*, *Draughtsmanship*, *Figurative Art*, *Landscape*, *Life-Size*, *Manner*, *Medium*, *Miniature Painting*, *Symbolic Art*, *Synthetism*, TANTRIC, *Tradition*, *Transition*, *Wash (Technique)*, *Jamini P. Gangooly*, *Bhaskar Rao*, *Bhanu Shah*, *Somalal Chunilal Shah*, *Sumant V. Shah*, *Om Prakash Sharma*, *Gaganendranath Tagore*, *Rathindranath Tagore*, *Nathu Lal Verma*, *Vinayakrao Venkatrao Wagh*; Illustrations–*Academic Art*, *Embroidery*, *Life-Drawing*, *Portraits*, *Thanjavur (Tanjore) Paintings on Glass*, *Sailendranath Dey*, *Ramesh Rao*, *Ghulam Rasool Santosh*, *Bhabesh Chandra Sanyal*, *Sardar Gurcharan Singh*, *Sarada Charan Ukil*, *K. Venkatappa*, *V. Viswanadhan*, *Kanhiyalal R. Yadav*.

Subhedar, Gopal G. (1938–) b. KAR. Studied *NKM*, GDA in *drawing* & *painting* & specialized in *glass painting* KAR & MAHA. Solos & group shows: Hyderabad, Mumbai, Bangalore, Kolkata, Ahmedabad, New Delhi, Hyderabad, Pune, Chennai; International: London, New York. Participated: *LKA* & *NGMA* New Delhi, All India Exhibition Nasik, *AIFACS*, *ASI*, *Murals* in New Delhi, Mumbai & USA, Muscat. Workshops & *artist* camps: Kala Mela, All India *Artist* Camps all over India. Awards: Bronze Medal Mumbai, Art Exhibition Nasik, *AIFACS*, *ASI*; Felicitation By Giants International 1998. Lectures & Demonstrations: KAR School; International: California USA. Collections: *LKA* & *NGMA* New Delhi, Mumbai, Institutions in India & abroad.

His *style* of *painting* is derived from Indian miniatures as well as *Thanjavur (Tanjore) painting on glass*. He *paints* on glass using *oil paints* to achieve a high gloss. His *forms* are fragmented with *figures* placed in an indeterminate *space* with collage-like pieces of *calligraphy* nestling the main *figures*. His subjects are basically taken from the RAMAYANA, MAHABHARATA or from historical events. His later works of rural woman and small chindren are similar in *style* and *content* to the works of *Thotha Vaikuntham*.

He lives in Mumbai.

Subramanyan, K.G. (1924–) b. Kerala. Dip. in *FA*. Education: *VBU*, Studied at *KB Santiniketan* under *Benode Behari Mukherjee*, *Nandalal Bose*, *Ramkinkar Baij* & others, Slade School of Art London, D.Litt. *RBU*. Solos: Vadodara, Bangalore, Kolkata, *Art Heritage* New Delhi, *Gallery 7*, *GC*, *SG* Mumbai, CCAG, *CYAG;* International: New York, Oxford. Retrospective: *BAAC* Kolkata, *Art Heritage* & *NGMA* New Delhi, *BB*. Group participations: National Exhibitions, *Triennale* New Delhi, SC, *BAS*; International: *Beinnale* in Sao Paulo, Menton & Tokyo, Fukuoka Museum Japan, others in Tate Gallery & RAA London, Museum of Modern Art Oxford, Mural World Fair New York; Also experimented & exhibited on fibre hangings and *sculpture*, *weaving*, textile *painting*, *murals*; Toy making at Toy Design Fair Vadodara. *Auctions*: India & abroad including Christie's, Sotheby's, Osian's, Heart, in New Delhi & Mumbai. Awards: National Award, Gold Medal *Triennale*, Padma Shri, Kalidas Samman, Fellow *LKA* & *RBU* Award New Delhi, MAHA State Art Mumbai, Kerala *LKA*, *BAS*; International: JDR IIIrd Fund Fellowship USA, British Council Scholarship to Slade School UK, Sao Paulo *Biennale*. Commissions: Stage sets and costume designer of *Rabindranath Tagore's* play; *Murals* in *terracotta;* Reverse-side *glass painting*. Appointments: Seminars & Lectures at *MPCVA*, *FFA* (*MSU*) & all over India; Visiting Lecturer McGill University, Concordia University & Canadian Universities; Later Deputy Dir. (*design*) *WSC* Mumbai; Was Prof. of *painting* and Dean at *FFA* (*MSU*) and Prof. of *paintings* at *KB Santiniketan*. Publications: Written fables, journals, essays, Indian *Art* & also a foundation for the study of *contemporary* Indian Art; Designed and illustrated children's books; Delegate at Asian Assembly of World Craft Council Sydney & World Assembly Council Mexico. Collections: Godrej & TATA Mumbai, *LKA* & *NGMA* New Delhi, *CYAG*; International: Hood Museum Hanover, USA.

K.G. Subramanyan has successfully straddled the *media* of *sculpture* and *painting*, working with both at the same time, using *imagery* filled with a modernist spirit. His *terracotta* plaques of the 70s appear both lyrical and decorative, but actually incorporate the violence of war. His trademark fragmented *forms* and decorative appendages like trees, tile borders and decorative punched and combed *textures* are also seen in his *patterns*. K.G. Subramanyan began with a P. Picasso-like *cubism* in the 50s, moving towards *surrealism* and *painting* with *colour* in the 60s; his *still lifes* especially taking on a relief-like character. Since the 80s, K.G. Subramanyan has been working with several *paintings* on glass and more recently perspex. The *medium* relates to the traditional school of *glass painting*, but the *imagery* and *narratives* are his own. *Space* is both flat and tilted upwards at an angle in the *manner* of both H. Matisse and *Mughal miniatures*. His recent works which tilt toward earthy *hues*, rather than the brilliant *colours* once associated with him are *modern* day versions of fables and fairy tales. *Texture* still plays an important role in his works.

He lives & works in *Santiniketan*.

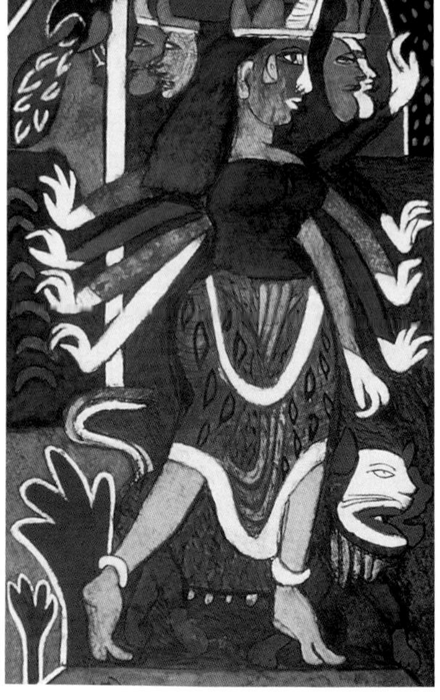

Subramanyan, K.G.: "Bahurupee 1", 1994, 104x64x2 cm.

Sud, Anupam (1944–) b. Hoshiarpur, PUJ. Education: National Diploma in FA. New Delhi, Studied at printmaking Slade School of Art London. Solos: Art Heritage New Delhi, LTG, CKAG; International: GBP. Retrospective: Art Heritage New Delhi. Group participations: National Exhibition, Triennale & Biennale New Delhi, GCA Chandigarh, AIFACS, SKP, HAS, CYAG, JAG; International: Italy, Frankfurt, Manchester, Biennale Florence, Turkey & Algiers, Giza, Triennale Switzerland & Berlin, Third World Art London. Group shows: USA, Finland. Workshops & camps: New Delhi Krishna Reddy, Vadodara, LKA camp Kolkata, BB; International: Canada. Auctions: Osian's Mumbai. Awards: National LKA, Biennale, All India Exhibition, President of India's Gold Medal & Women's International Art Exhibition New Delhi, Indian Academy Amritsar, AIFACS, SKP, HAS; Intern-ational: British Council Scholarship London, Certificate Biennale Havana, Medal Giza. Founder Member: Group 8 New Delhi. Appointments; Graphic HoD College of Art New Delhi. Collections: LKA & NGMA New Delhi, Godrej Mumbai, IMTMA, CYAG; International: Library of Congress Washington, V&A.

Anupam Sud uses her perfect draughtsmanship and understanding of anatomy to create compositions in which the figure plays a prominent role. She uses several printmaking techniques in creating her fragmented world of tortured souls and masked figures. Cross-hatching in particular opens the possibilities of the near sculptural appearance of her fallen heads and nudes. She has also worked with the medium of collage, using fragments and cut outs of her etchings and engravings to make statements on the condition of humanity. Her figures rarely meet the viewer's gaze, preferring the contemplative inner gaze.

She lives and works in New Delhi.

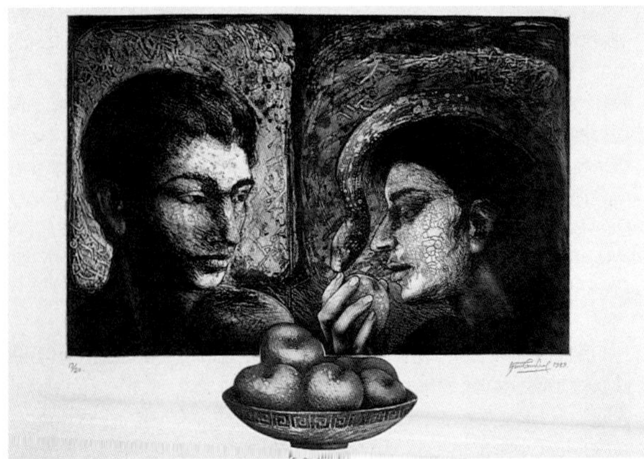

Sud, Anupam: "For you apple only", *Graphic/Print*, 1989, Coloured *Etching*, 46.5x54 cm.

Sufism A mystical branch of Islam, which originated in the 8th century, dedicated to the elimination of the self and to union with *god*. It made its tenets known through poetry, using analogies of human love to express the striving of the soul towards the creator. Similar to the BHAKTI cult, entwined with the KRISHNA *legend*. Refer *Manjit Bawa*, *Gulam Mohammed Sheikh*; Illustration–*Abanindranath Tagore*.

Sugar Lift Also known as lift ground. A *technique* used in *aquatint etching*. A solution made of five parts sugar to four parts Indian *ink* with a few grains of soap powder and a drop of *gum arabic* is stirred and used to *paint* directly on the cleaned *plate*. The stop-out *varnish* or *ground* is brushed onto the entire *plate* even covering the *design*. The *plate* is then immersed in hot water and lightly brushed until the sugar solution melts and lifts the *varnish*. The exposed area is then prepared for *aquatint* in the usual *manner*. Refer *Intaglio*, *Printmaking*, *Jyoti Bhatt*, *Naina Dalal*, *Mukul Chandra Dey*; Illustrations–*Amitabha Banerjee*, *Somnath Hore*, *Krishna N. Reddy*, *Anupam Sud*.

Sultan, Ali J. (1920–1990) b. Mumbai. Studied under *Debi Prasad RoyChowdhury*, Dip. in *painting GCAC* Chennai, Studied Govt. Textile Institute Chennai, Dip. in photography Lingham. Solos: Over 22 between 1946–1986 including Chennai, Madanpalle, New Delhi, Mumbai; International: California, Papua New Guinea. Group participations: *LKA* & Artists Handicraft New Delhi, Marvel Art Gallery Ahmedabad, SKP, *AIFACS*; International: National & International *drawing*, *painting* & *engravings* Lugano & Switzerland, *Triennale* & *Biennale* in Italy, Brazil, China & Bangladesh, Fukuoka Museum Japan. *Auctions*: Heart & Osian's Mumbai, Heart New Delhi, Sotheby's London & New York. Awards: SKP, President of India's Silver Plaque *AIFACS*, National Award for *oil painting* & *drawing*. Fellowship: TN *LKA*. Member: Progressive Painters Association & Vice President

Cholamandal. Collections: *NGMA*, *LKA* & IICC, Ford Foundation New Delhi, PUJ Museum Chandigarh, AP State Museum Hyderabad, *BKD* Varanasi, National Art Gallery Chennai; International: Commonwealth Institute of Australia Sydney, Berlin Museum of Indian Art, Royal Tropical Museum Holland, University Museum Nigeria, pvt. & corporates.

Ali J. Sultan became interested in the *art* of the Indian tribals, travelling to several such centres as Bastar, Korapur, Jagdalpur, Narayanpur, Bhandara, Raipur and other places in Orissa and MP. His *imagery* was culled from this assimilation of *figures* and *forms*, resulting in his fantastic creatures and symbols of power, peace and destruction. The bull, which was the epitome of beauty, power, fierceness and motion, was one of his important *motifs*, as were men, women, snakes, owls, plants and other such vibrant elements of *nature*. More than the *image*, it that was the emotion, the RASA evoked by it was important to him. However, it is his stark, *grapic images* of *folk art* that endures.

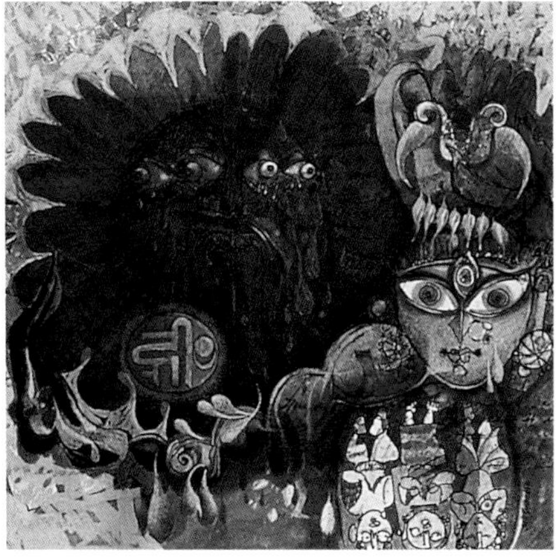

Sultan, Ali J.: "Surya", *Watercolour, Painting* 1990.

Sumahendra, Sharma M.K. (1943–) b. Jaipur, RAJ. Education: Dip. & M.A. in *drawing* & *painting* & Ph.D. Ragamala *painting* University of RAJ. Solos: *LKA* New Delhi, *LKA* for *sculpture* Jaipur, UP *LKA* Lucknow, PUJ University Gallery Chandigarh, *LKA* Cochin, *AIFACS*, TKS *JAG*, BHU, *CKP*; International: Switzerland, Austria, ENSBA Paris. Group participations: *RSA* Udaipur & Jaipur, Art Festival Mount Abu, *Triennale LKA* New Delhi, *Biennale BB;* International: Germany, Japan. *Art* camps & workshop: *Fresco* camps Banasthali, *Sculptors* & *painters* at University RAJ Jaipur, *LKA* New Delhi, Jaisalmer & NZCC Gurgaon. Awards: *LKA* New Delhi & RAJ, Gold Medal University of RAJ. Members: *LKA* New Delhi & RAJ. Commissions: *Sculptures* in Jaipur & Bikaner. Appointments: Lectures & Demonstrations at France, Switzerland, Austria, for *sculpture* & *modelling*; Talk on Radio & TV on Jaipur *Wall Painting*, BARAHMASA & RAGAMALA; Principal *RSA* Jaipur. Publications: Press, magazine & *LKA* information India & abroad. Collections: Of *painting* & *sculpture* India & abroad UK, USA France, Switzerland.

He is both a *painter* and *sculptor*, working in *watercolours*, *oils* and *metal*, *stone* and *marble*. The *sculptures* are small in scale, being almost relief-like in their embossed and grained appearance. He is preoccupied with the *figure* and the *abstract portrait*, the *bronzes* having been *cast* from pinched *forms* in *clay*. His *paintings* are facile *colour* studies of young, rural women set against timeless *landscapes*. The broadness of execution of the *background* is offset by the more detailed appearance of the single, isolated *figure*.

He lives in Jaipur.

Sumatimohan (1937–) b. India. Education: Dip. GDA, Art Master State MAHA Mumbai, M.FA. Pratt Institute New York. Solos: *Artists' Centre* Mumbai,TAG, *JAG,SAI;* International: Quogue, Albuquerque (Mexico) San Francisco, Pratt Institute Gallery, Limer Gallery & Avanti Galleries New York, Engelwood Library New Jersey. Group participations: Indian Consulate, Sheroton Centre New York USA. Hon. & Awards: Ahmedabad, Certificate of Merit *NKM*; Invited Radio & TV New Delhi, Radio Mumbai. Publications: "Times of India", "Statesman", India & International: Art Magazine New York. Collections: Gandhi Museum New Delhi, GUJ State Govt. Ahmedabad, *PUAG*; International: New York, West Land, San Francisco, Antwerp, Netherlands.

Sumatimohan works on square *canvases* creating *colour* fields, which subtly change from dark to *light*. He uses hand-ground *pigment*, applying it with the *palette knife* to produce a scaly, gestural surface that is refined by his delicate *pattern*. The dark *forms* surge up in frozen flame-like *forms* and dissolve into *light*. His *paintings* are based on spirituality, though they are *abstract*. They present a universal message through the philosophy of *light*. He uses both *oil* and *watercolour*, using the *brush* and the knife to render his *abstract colour* visions.

He lives in New York.

Sundaram, Vivan (1943–) b. Shimla. Education: B.A. in *FA*. *MSU* Post. Grad. in *painting* & history of cinema Slade School London. Over 25 solos: *SG* & "The Sher-Gil Archive" an *installation GC* Mumbai, Hungarian Information & Cultural Centre, Kunika Chemould, RB & British Council New Delhi, *AFA* & *BAAC* Kolkata, CAG Ahmedabad, *SG* Bangalore, MMB Hyderabad, TAG, *JAG*, TKS, *LTG*, *AIFACS*, *Dhoomimal*, *MSU;* International: London, Montreal, Winnipeg, Vancouver. Group participations: *LKA*, RB & *NGMA* New Delhi, *GC*, Timeless Art, & *SG* Mumbai, *Arts Acre* Kolkata, TKS, *LTG*, *AIFACS*, *JAG*, TAG, *PUAG G88*, *Roopankar BB;* International: *Graphic prints* Slade School & RAA London, Indian Graphics Poland, Festival & Indian Art London, *Biennale* Tokyo & Havana, Fukuoka Art Museum Japan, other countries Germany, USA. Attended camps & workshop. Also member, founder member & trustee of *art* organization. *Auctions*: Osian's Mumbai. Awards: Commonwealth Scholarship London, Gold Medal at International Festival. Appointments: Silent Video films taken, travelled & organized retrospective & *monograph* on *Amrita Sher-Gil* & collaborated in scripting the film on her; His films are prepared with other *artists*. Collections: In galleries, *museum*, pvt. & public.

One of the few *artists* to have consciously broken away from the constraits of *painting* on *canvas*, Vivan Sundaram is constantly exploring new, tangible materials in his quest with the *installation form*. His *art* had always been replete with quotations and references to sources as varied as Octavio Paz's poems, the Mumbai Riots, autobiographical and political statements and experiments with burning, assembling and constructing. His *paintings* (of the early years to the mid-80s) were essentially *narratives* in the Vadodara *manner*, with expressive *brushwork* and naturalistic rendering. His *forms* become looser and the *colours* more strident and expressionistic in 1988–89 before he switched to making elaborate *constructions* in sandstone, *terracotta*, *acrylic* sheet, *steel*, mirrors, and *ready-mades* like postcards, engine oil and *print reproductions*. This was followed by "Memorial", his scathing analysis of the Mumbai riots and the "Sher-Gil Archives", with his documentation of both family and *art*–both topics highly personal, yet historically important. He lives & works in New Delhi. Refer *Assemblage*, *Environment Art*, *Happening*.

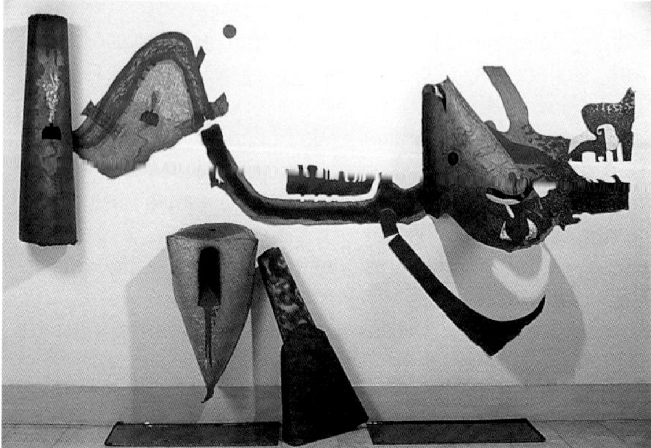

Sundaram, Vivan: "Arwer carries its Past" Enqine Oil & Burn Marks on Kalamkush *Handmade Paper, Oil* & Water in *Zinc* Trays, 1992, 203x305x30 cm.

Sunga Dynasty or Style The Sunga dynasty was founded by Pushyamitra Sunga, a general who overthrew the *Maurya dynasty* by assassinating the Maurya King, Brihadratha. They ruled for just over a century (circa 188 BC–76 BC) and although Brahmanas by faith, did not persecute the Buddhists. This enabled the *stupas* at Bharhut and Sanchi to be erected during this period. Although most of the people were Buddhists, worship of indigenous *gods* (Devatas) and nature spirits (YAKSHAS, Gram-Devatas, SHALEBHANJIKAS) was common during this period. This resulted in the prolific representation of such spirits and damsels on the Toranas (hanging decoration of an entrance) at Sanchi and Bharhut. Refer *Stupa*, YAKSHA, YAKSHINIS.

Sunkad, M.K. (1930–) b. Hubli. Education: Dip. in *drawing* & *painting*, *FA*., Art Master's School of Art Hubli KAR. Solo & group participations: Indian Institute of World Culture, State *LKA* & Teachers' College Bangalore, *LKA* Hubli, *AIFACS*. Group *artists*: *LKA*. Member: Rashtreeya Vidyashala Education Institute Bangalore. Appointments: Prof.: KAR *FA*. Education Hubli Bangalore.

M.K. Sunkad is basically a landscapist, capturing the sculptural grandeur of the temples at Badami, Aihole and Pattadakal. He renders these *landscapes* in a naturalistic *manner*, akin to Constable's, yet their surface quality gives them an essentially Indian character. His portraitist *landscapes* also have this typical Indian *atmosphere*, filled with a bright tropical *light*. M.K. Sunkad has also run the gamut of *folk* and *modern art* inspired *compositions*, using a fractured surface to add to the decorativeness of the *imagery*.

He lives and works in Bangalore.

Super Realism A synonym of *photo-realism* in *painting* and *hyper-realism* in *sculpture*. It describes a popular *art* movement in the 1970s in which *paintings* are based on *photographs* and *sculpture* from direct *casts* of the human *figure*. Minute attention is paid to details, even the *colours* are accurately portrayed in both *painting* and *sculpture*, the final *painting* is near the *pictorial* quality of the *photograph*. The *artists* associated with the movement included C. Close and D. Hanson. Super Realism also refers to the *technique* itself, which is practised by a few Indian *artists* in a sporadic *manner*. Refer *Surjeet Kaur Choyal*, *Jaideep D. Mehrotra*, *Dinkar V. Wadangekar*.

Support Is the *base*, the *ground*, the surface of material on which the work of *art* is created, e.g. **1.** Surface that is used to *paint* on, including *canvas*, *canvas board* and *paper*. **2.** For a *bust* model, a wooden support is attached vertically in a base board to *form* the basic foundation upon which also called lead peg. **3.** Glueing or nailing of wooden strips vertically and horizontally to the back of the wooden panel to strengthen it, from the expansion and contraction caused by changes in humidity and temperature. Refer ARDHA-MANDAPA, *Casing*, *Collotype*, *Elephanta*, *Facing*, *Ground*, *Gupta*, *Painting*, *Paper-Pulp Casting*, *Roman Art*, *Size*, VIHARA, VISHNU, *Manjit Bawa*.

Surinder (Kaur) (1947–) b. India. Grad. *College of Art* New Delhi, Joined TKS in 1975. Solos: SRAG, *JAG*. Group participations: "Indian Women Artists" *NGMA* & National Exhibition New Delhi, HG, SKP, *AIFACS*, *JAG*, *Biennale BB;* International: New York, USA, Netherland, London. Awards: Women's Year SKP, Annual Exhibitions *AIFACS*. Collections: *NGMA*, *LKA* & *College of Art* New Delhi, PUJ University, SKP, *BB;* International: France, London, Netherland, Holland, Italy, Canada, New York.

The geometrical shape and precision of the square has always fascinated Surinder and has over the years come to symbolize the entire universe in her *paintings*. The quadrangle is used to recall different elements of *nature* and urban life. Her *landscapes* based on the square, evoke associations with *aerial perspective* and other such *visual* experiences. Her preoccupation is with *paint*, *texture*, *colour* and *composition* evoking the intangible quality of air, and *space*. Her use of *transparent overlapping colours* create scintillating fields of *colour* in which small objects like chairs, beds and human *figures* flit in peripherally. She has worked with both *oils* and *watercolours*.

She lives and works in New Delhi at TKS.

Surrealism A *term* coined originally in 1924 to describe *art* influenced by Freudian theory of liberating the subconscious through dream *imagery* and the suspension of conscious control (*Automatism*). Surrealist works are of two different types, the super-realistically rendered dream *images*, and the inventive and the accidental effects. The

Indian *artists* associated with the movement were as diverse as *Bikash Bhattacharjee*, and *Jaideep Mehrotru* with their fragmented yet realistically rendered *figures* and *Rabindranath Tagore* with his *fantasy* based *doodles* of beaked and clawed flying creatures, while *K.G. Subramanyan* moved towards Surrealism in the 60s. Refer *Abstract Expressionism, Biomorphic, Blot Drawing, Decalcomania, Dadaism, Frottage, Modern, Realistic, Vijaya Bagai, Aditya Basak, Pushp Betala, Alok Bhattacharya, Paul A. Koli, Sanjay Kumar, Babu K. Namboodiri, Animesh Nandi, Sita Ray, Narendra Rai Srivastav;* Illustrations–*Collage, Ramkinkar Baij, Bal Chhabda, K. Khosa, Ganesh Pyne, A. Ramachandran, Anilbaran Saha, K.G. Subramanyan.*

Surya=the sun. The Sun *god*, Surya or Savitar the stimulalor, is regarded as part of the Vedic triad with AGNI on earth, INDRA in the *atmosphere* and his place in the sky. He rides through the sky in a chariot drawn by seven red mares driven by Aruna or the Dawn. He holds a lotus in each of his two hands and wears a KIRITA MUKUTA as seen at the Konark Temple in Orissa. He has several wives and two sons, the Ashvin-kumaras, who preceded him in the golden chariot of their own as rays of the rising Sun. Other important Surya temples include the Sun Temple at Modhera GUJ. Refer MAKARA-SANKRANTI, *Orissa State Museum*, RITU, SWASTIKA, VEDA, *Ganga Devi, Baburao Sadwelkar, Raja Ravi Varma;* Illustrations–CHAKRA, INDRA, *Mosaic, Sultan Ali J., Shantanu Ukil.*

Surya Gallery (SUG) (Hyderabad). The SUG was set up in 1993 in Hyderabad, the city of colourful contrasts. The one-man shows and group shows held by the gallery were *eclectic* in their *style* and thematic *content* of *artists* including *Akhilesh, Sunil Das, C. Jagdish, Choudhary Satyanarayan Patnaik, Surya Prakash, Bhaskar Rao, Sisir Sahana, Thotha Vaikuntham, Zahoor Zargar.* They held slide shows, workshops and discussions on *art* and *culture*.

Svethambara Second sect in *Jainism*, Svethambara literally means clad or clothed. Refer DIGAMBARA, *Jain Jainism*, MAHAVIRA; Illustrations–KALPA-SUTRA, *Jain Miniature, Jain Manuscript Illumination.*

Swadeshi Movement A political movement, Swadeshi encouraged people of India to boycot foreign goods and promote Indian products born out of traditional raw materials and processes such as Khadi, a cotton handspun and handwoven cloth. Popularized by Mahatma Gandhi, father of the nation, it galvanized the masses to voice their demand for freedom from foreign rule. The nationalist fervour it unleashed had an impact on all walks of life including *art*.

However, when applied to *art*, the *term* Swadeshi meant rejection of Western influence on Indian *art* and emphasis on *art* abounding in true Indian *tradition* and *mythology*. *Abanindranath Tagore* was among the pioneers of the trend in Indian *art*, encouraged and supported by E.B. Havell, Principal of the Calcutta School of Art. To him Swadeshi meant to use traditional *themes*, express traditional sentiments and employ traditional *styles*. *Abanindranath Tagore's* "Bharat Mata" symbolizes *Bengal School* and *Bengal Revivalism*, both influenced heavily by this Swadeshi Movement. Refer *Bombay School*.

Swadhinapatika One of the eight specific types of NAYIKAS (heroines) mentioned by ancient Indian writers and poets. She is confident of her lover's devotion and dominates him entirely. The NAYAK (hero) is usually depicted in *miniature paintings* as washing or *painting* her feet. Refer ASHTANAYIKA, NAYAK-NAYAKA.

Swaminathan, J. (1928–1994) b. Shimla, HP. Education: Delhi Polytechnic (CFA New Delhi), AFA Warsaw Poland. Over 30 solos: Shimla, *GC* Mumbai, *BB, Dhoomimal*, last *exhibition VAG*. Group participations: *Triennale, Biennale, LKA* & *NGMA* New Delhi, *Roopankar*. Participated: In important national & international exhibitions, & with *artist* colleague created a monument in Bhopal in the memory of the great poet Iqbal, also participated in *stone carving* and *sculpture*. *Auctions*: Heart, Sotheby's New Delhi, Osians & Heart Mumbai; International: Christie's London. Awards: Jawaharlal Nehru Fellowship 1968–70, Govt. of MP Hon. him by posthumously awarding the Kalidas Samman. Members: International Jury of *Biennale* Sao Paulo, Was elected General Council of *LKA* Artist's Constituency and member of the Akademi's Executive Board, Founder member of *Group 1890*, Dir. of *Roopankar*, Member for the Craft Museum Committee, Programme Committee NZCC, Member SC; Was a Commissioner for the Adivasi Art at Festival of India Japan. Publications: Poems in Hindi, Text on *tribal art* MP, Founder & editor of monthly journal on art "Contra". Collections: *NGMA* & *LKA* New Delhi, *Roopankar BB, GC* Mumbai, *VAG, JNAG;* International: Masanori Fukuoka & Glenbarra Museum Hemeji Japan.

Swaminathan J. disliked *narrative* or didactic morals in *painting*, preferring instead to work in the poetic, automatist *manner* of Paul Klee. His early works contain certain highly simplified *images* that appear constantly in his works. These birds, insects, water bodies, trees and strange buildings are primarily structures, that float in a serene, unworldly brilliantly coloured *space*. Their relationship follows no laws, real or otherwise. It is chance that has placed them together in an

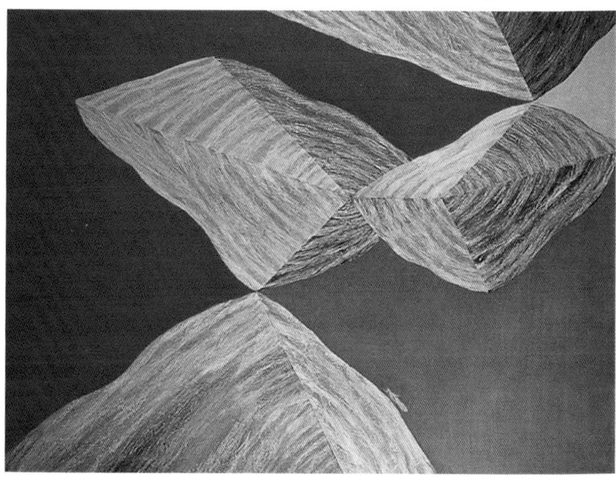

Swaminathan, J.: "Journey–I", *Oil* on *Canvas*, 102.5x105 cm.

atmosphere that is almost surreal in its *colour*, *form* and succint juxtapositions of textural and flat areas. His later works, based on his exposure to the tribal way of life was a magnification of the small textural areas in the earlier *canvas*. He used a *wax*-based *medium* to carry his natural *pigments*, red, yellow ochre and *charcoal* dust. By subtly changing the pressure on the rollers he varied the intensity of the *colours*, scratching and incising the surface into decorative repetitions that are influenced by representations of tribal and god-heads.

Swastika A kind of cross inscripted on objects to denote good luck. It consists of four spokes crossing each other at right angles with short parts of the periphery at the end of each spoke turning around in one direction. This direction usually stands for movement of the sun. The symbol of swastika has been ritualistically used from early *times* for warding off evil, invoking good luck, wishing for welfare or as a sign of respect and worship. In *art*, Swastika is used as a sign, gesture, posture and a symbol covering various areas of communication such as *painting*, *sculpture* and dance. Refer *Abstract*, *Abstract Art*, LOKA, *Spiritual*, SURYA, *Symbolic*.

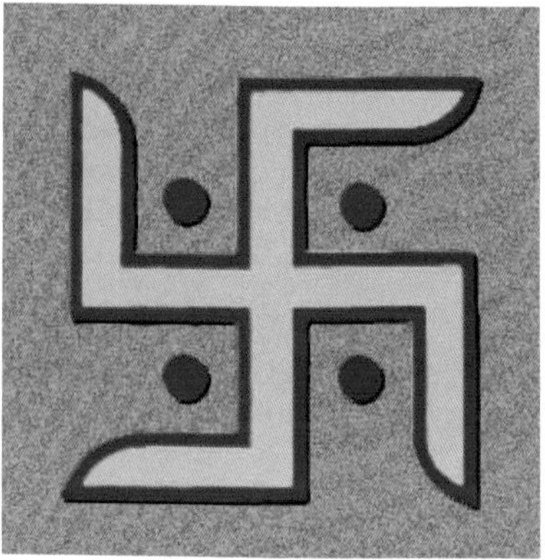

Illustration: Swastika.

Symbolic Refer to *Attribute*, *Buddhist Art*, *Conceptual Art*, *Concept Art*, *Composition*, *Emblem*, *Gupta*, *Symbolism*, *Symbolic Art*, TANTRA, *Sunil Das*, *Amal Ghosh*, *Nirode Mazumdar*, *Gopal Sanyal*, *K. S. Viswambhara*, *Vishwanath M. Sholapurkar*.

Symbolic Art A *style* of *art* that employs symbols to express certain ideas, emotions or state of the world. Symbols were used in ancient times to express stories and religious *themes*. Indian Art has always been *symbolic* in *nature*. Every gesture, attitude and *attribute* had a corresponding meaning. In fact, it is possible to "read" ancient Indian *painting* and *sculpture*, through knowledge of the symbols used. *Contemporary* Indian *artists* also use *Symbolism* in their work. This could vary from direct analogies to literary or even cinematic references. Performance *artists* also include *Symbolism* in their works. Refer *Abstract Art*, *Cold Working*, *Figurative Art*, *Gesture Painting*, *Isms*, *Neo-Tantricism*, *Significant Form*, *Tantra Art*, *Vesara Style*, *Visual*, *Dipak Banerjee*, *Prabhakar Barwe*, *Ghulam Rasool Santosh;* Illustrations—*Tantra Art*, *Biren De*, *Surendra Pal Joshi*, *Laxman Pai*.

Symbolism Refer Symbolic Art.

Synthetic The compounds or materials that are produced through non-natural means or artificially. Synthetic plastic is available in different *forms*, used by *sculptors*, *painters* and printers. In India, it is used in *acrylics* (1970s) when it is mixed with *pigment* and resin; combination of synthetic resin and filaments of glass produces *fibreglass*. When the works are done in *charcoal*, *chalk* and *pastel drawings* are created on it, it is fixed with *fixative*, which protects against accidental smudges. Many Indian *painters* use synthetic material in *mixed media* to create new *art* influence and impulses in the *art* of today. Refer *Gel*, *Kinetic Art*, *Lacquer*, *Media*, *Medium*, *Mobile*, *Mural*, *Oil Paint*, *Over Lapping*, *Screen Printing*, *Silk Screen Printing*, *Sculpture*, *Wax*, *Yusuf Arakkal*, *Sujata Bajaj*, *Krishnamachari Bose*, *Madhu Champaneria*, *Sunirmal Chatterjee*, *M.J. Enas*, *Usha Rani Hooja*, *Maqbool Fida Husain*, *Tyeb Mehta*, *Kishen Khanna*, *Mahendra Pandya*, *Amrut Patel*, *Ankit Patel*, *Ravinder G. Reddy*, *Vivan Sundaram*.

Synthetism A *style* of *painting* prevalent for a short period in the 1890s in Europe, when flat areas of bright *colour*, were thickly outlined with *black*. The *artists* believed that they should synthesize their *impressions* and *paint* from memory, rather than depict directly from *nature*, as the preceding Impressionists did. In India *abstract* expressionist *painters* use gestural slashes of *paint*, to *outline* the human *form*. There may be more than a hint of the *Kalighat Pat style painting* in the use of soft *outlines* and *distortions*. *Artists'* works blend of with traditional *style* and *modern* subjects. The *artists*, included were *Jamini Roy*, *Nandalal Bose*, *Vajubhai D. Bhagat*, *Phalguni DasGupta*. Refer *Back-Glass Painting*, *Folk Art*, *Miniature Painting*, *Thanjavur (Tanjore) Painting*, *Surinder K. Bhardwaj*, *R.B. Bhaskaran*, *Muhammed Abdur Rehman Chughtai*, *S. Krishnappa*, *K. Madhava Menon*, *Sailoz Mookerjea*.

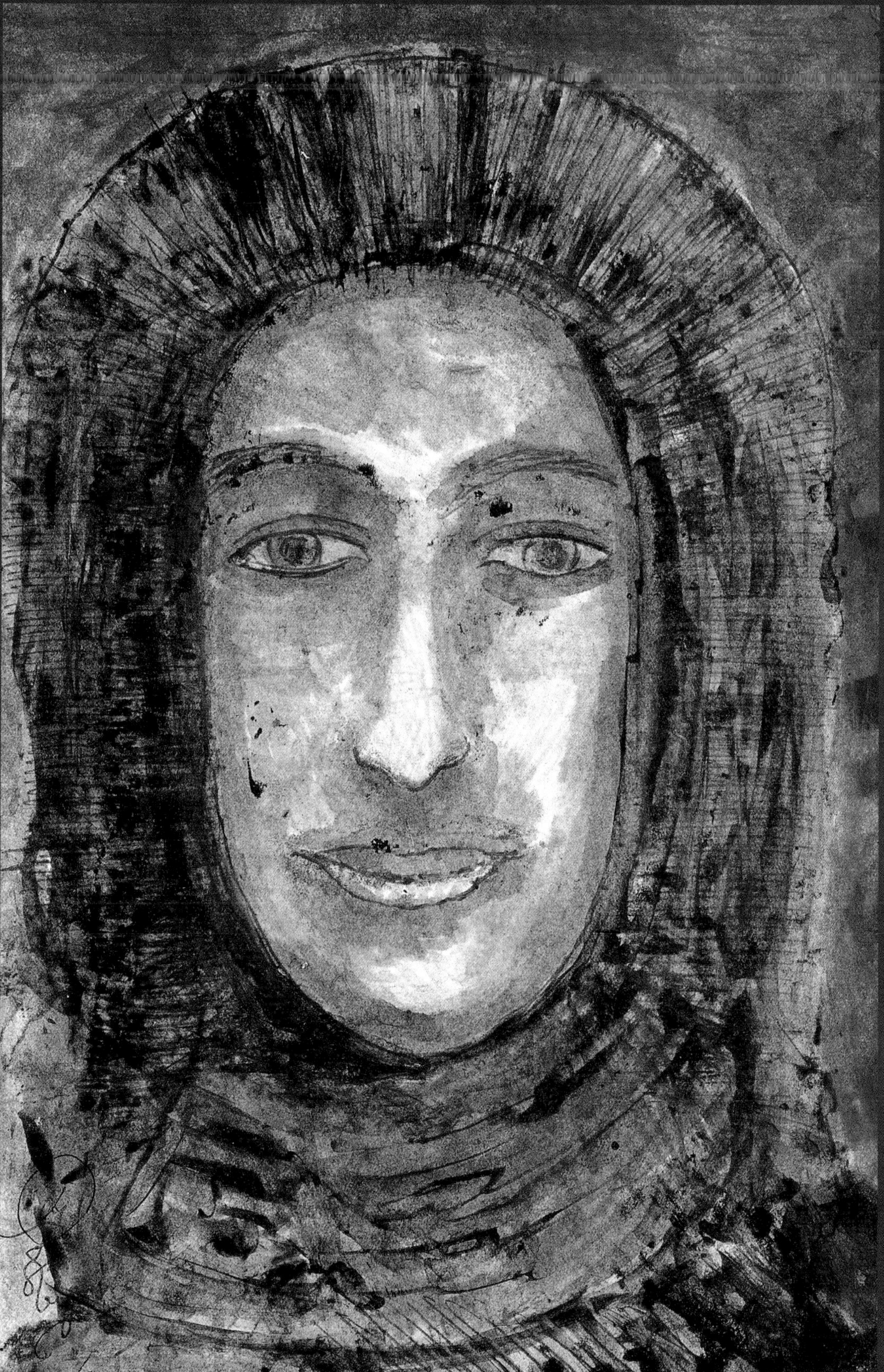

Tagore, Rabindranath: "Head of a Woman", *Pen & Ink*, *Gouache* & Coloured *Ink on Pape*r, circa 1928/30, 28.75x20 cm.
(See notes on page 350)

Tactile The sense of touch. In *painting* it refers to *illusion* or the *trompe l'oeil* effect of contrasting *textures* and the simple feel of *texture* in an *abstract* work. In *sculpture* it denotes the *finish*, whether smooth and sensual, or rough and earthy. The *artists'* attempt to capture the sense of weight, *relief* and *texture* in the *sculpture.* Refer *Fibreglass, Kinetic Art, Dhiraj Choudhury, Adi M. Davierwala, Shobha Ghare, Paresh C. Hazra, D.G. Kulkarni, Jayant Parikh, Ghanshyam Ranjan*; Illustrations–*Somnath Hore, Prokash Karmarkar, Krishna N. Reddy, Himmat Shah, Jai Zharotia.*

Tagore, Abanindranath (1871–1951) b. *Jorasanko*, Kolkata. Abanindranath Tagore, the nephew of *Rabindranath Tagore*, the poet-painter, began by learning the elements of Western *painting* under the guidance of the Italian artist, O. Gilhardi and English painter C. Palmer. At that time he was an admirer of *Raja Ravi Varma's* work. However, with the growing consciousness of Indian Nationalism, Abanindranath Tagore too, felt the need for an Indian identity in the field of *Art*. In this, he was more than amply aided by E.B. Havell, the principal of *Madras School of Art*, and later, of the Calcutta School of Arts Kolkata. In spite of being an Englishman, E.B. Havell was enlightened enough to realize the importance of an Indian ethos in the works of Indian *artists*. To this end, he requested Abanindranath Tagore to step in as Vice-Principal of Calcutta School of Arts. In 1907, Abanindranath Tagore established *Indian Society of Oriental Art (ISOA)*, which soon became an important platform for the nurturing of the new Indian *style*. By 1919, the society had produced an *art* journal, "Rupam" which stimulated interest in Asian cultural studies. In 1921, he was appointed to the Chair of Bageswari Prof. of *FA.* by Calcutta University. The Bageshwari lectures comprise articles on *nature* of *art* and the *artist*, the perception and creativity in *art*, the theory of beauty & other such discussions. He also authored "An Introduction to Indian Artistic Anatomy & SHADANGA" (six principal limbs of Indian *Art*).

Abanindranath Tagore's Indian *style* was marked by *eclectic* borrowings from ancient sources. From the *Ajanta frescoes*, came the MUDRAS, (gestures) of hands and limbs and the graceful *linearity*; from the Mughal and the Pahadi, the sophisticated *colours*, formal *balance* and love of architectural details. To this he added some elements from the Japanese School of Painting. Many *artists* were invited to *Jorasanko*, the hub of cultural activity in Kolkata. Among these were Okakara Kakuzo, Hishida and Y. Taikan. It was from these Japanese artists, that Abanindranath Tagore got the inspiration to develop the famous *Bengal School "wash style"*. Unlike the spontaneous *brush paintings* of the Japanese however, Abanindranath Tagore's *wash technique* was quite different. After the *painting* was nearly complete, he would dip it in a bath of water and go over it with a flat brush. This resulted in much of the *pigment* being washed out and the others merging into each other in a muted *harmony* of *colours*. His subjects at this point, were also romantic and based on literary sources. The Omar Khayyam series especially, shows Abanindranath Tagore's *style* at its best, with luminously bright *pigments* blending harmoniously with deep, dark *shadows*.

He constantly explored new *styles*, including the folk *idiom* in his "Krishna Mangal" series, with its few *primary colours*, applied mostly in a flat *manner*, and bold and heavy *contours*. Towards the end of his life he embarked in a new direction–the making of small toys or *sculptures* from *found objects*, such as dry twigs, acorns, bits of string, wires and *wood*. He called them his "Katum-Kutum" toys because of the ordinariness and ephemeral nature of the materials used. Abanindranath Tagore's vast *oeuvre* included *realistic* portraiture in *oils*, *pastels* and *landscapes*. His works have been put on *auctions* at Heart, Osian's, Bowring's–Mumbai, Bowring's–New Delhi, Bonham's, Christie's, Sotheby's–London, Sotheby's–New York.

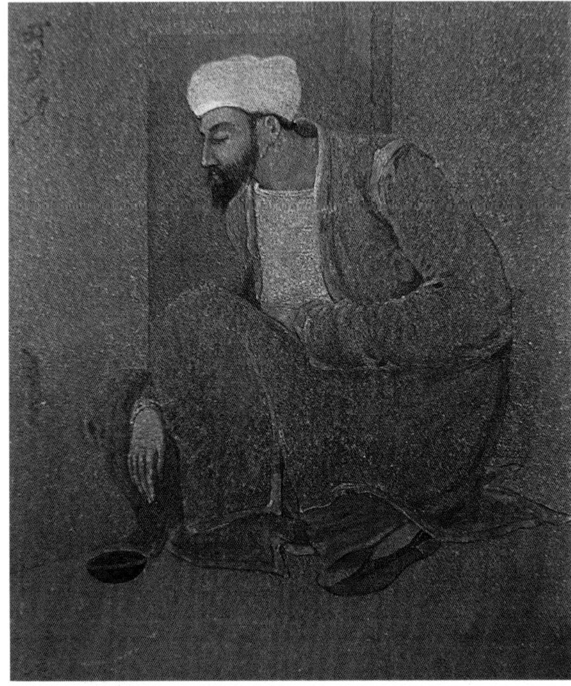

Tagore, Abanindranath: "Sufi", *Watercolour*, early 20th century, 33x28 cm.

Tagore, Alokendranath (1896–1971) b. Bengal. The eldest son of *Abanindranath Tagore*, who received his first lessons in *art* from his father. He learnt *fresco painting* from a Nepalese *artist*, Lakshman Prasad and *sculpture* from Giridhar Mahapatra, an Orissan *sculptor*. He exhibited at the *ISOA* Kolkata and received Award. Collection: *RBM* Kolkata.

Tagore, Basabendranath (1916–d.) b. Kolkata. The younger brother of *Subhogendra Tagore*. He studied at the Calcutta School of Arts Kolkata and at the RAA London; Later, he became a restorer and interior designer; and also qualified as a *sculptor*. His *relief*, "Harvest Time" dated 1956, has an indigenous *folk art* character.

He painted in *watercolour* and *oils*. In the 60s he brought out a tri-monthly newsletter on *art* called "The Art World".

Tagore, Gaganendranath (1867–1938) b. *Jorasanko*, Kolkata. He was the elder brother of *Abanindranath Tagore* & nephew of *Rabindranath Tagore*. He started *painting* fairly late in life, although there are *sketches*, attributed to him dating from 1905. Like *Abanindranath Tagore*, he too became interested in the works of the Japanese painters, Y. Taikan and H. Shunso and adapted their *technique* in the series of *illustrations* that he did for *Rabindranath Tagore's* "Jivansmruti" (My Reminiscences) in 1912. He also began teaching at the *ISOA*.

Gaganendranath Tagore can also be compared to the French artist H. Daumier, for his love of *caricature*. Unlike H. Daumier, whose output was political in *nature*, Gaganendranath Tagore however, preferred to make comments on the social scene, then prevalent in Bengal. His favourite subject was "Bhadra Lok", the first true middle-class gentry in India. He got his inspiration from the incongruity of these Bhadra Lok, trying to imitate their British master while attempting at the same time to preserve their Indian mode of life and religion. The hallmark of his *cartoons*, was an essential simplicity of *line*. Some of his *cartoons* were reproduced by means of *lithography*. Two volumes of *reproduction*, "Virupa Vajra" and "Advoot Lok" were published. He also wrote a book, "Bhodor Bahadur" (Otter the Great), for children.

Gaganendranath Tagore was tutored in the rudiments of *watercolour* by Harinarayan Bandopadhyay. It is quite likely that his *landscapes* and *seascapes* at Puri were a result of this training. But Gaganendranath Tagore's true contribution to Indian *art*, (as he has been termed the "first modern artist" in India) came later, in the decade of 1920–30, with his experiments in the cubistic *manner*. The first of these *paintings* were published in "Rupam", an *art* magazine along with an article by Stella Kramrisch in 1922. Unlike the Western cubists however, Gaganendranath Tagore was more interested in recording the properties of *light* rather than *volume*. He shows a proclivity for diagonal divisions rather than the horizontal-verticals used by P. Picasso. and G. Braque.

This use of *light* and interpenetrative planes extended into his other interest, namely stage decor and costume designing for *Rabindranath Tagore's* plays. In this, he may have been inspired by the *designs* of Gordon Craig and other revolutionary scenographists who adapted cubist, futurist and constructivist ideas, to set designing.

His later *style* of *painting*, dating from 1925–1930 (when he had to stop *painting* due to illness) has been termed "post-cubist" and is distinguished by a compact structure and spatial alignment closely derived from his cubist phase. What marks these *paintings* as different, is the strong element of *fantasy* and predominance of *black* and *white* over *colour*. His works have been auctioned at Heart, Osian's, Bowring's—Mumbai, Heart, New Delhi, Bonham's, Christie's, Sotheby's—London, Sotheby's—New York. Refer *Abstraction Geometric*.

Tagore, Gunendranath (1847–1881) b. Bengal. Father of *Gaganendranath Tagore* and *Abanindranath Tagore*. With the rest of the Tagores, he also acted, composed music and was interested in the stage, all in the short life span of 34 years. He was trained in *art* along with his cousin, *Jyotirindranath Tagore*. His favourite subject was decorative *landscape painting*.

Tagore, Hitendranath (1867–1908) b. *Jorasanko*. English tutor, Charles Palmer taught him to *paint* mainly *portraits*. Though a poet, he joined the Calcutta School of Arts Kolkata, to study chromolithography. When E.B. Havell was appointed as British principal of the college, he changed the syllabus and chromolithography was no longer offered at the school. Hitendranath Tagore left, and started a litho press by himself. He, along with *Gaganendranath Tagore* is credited with doing pioneering work in the field of *lithography* in India. His *oil paintings* were mostly *landscapes* based on *fantasy*. The *manner* in which he painted *landscapes* were: atmospheric, moody, formal, Academic and non-Indian.

He was the co-editor of "Dunya" journal, doing most of the *illustrations*. He also illustrated other periodicals including "Bharati" and "Sahitya", and wrote articles in "Tattva Bhodini Patrika". Collections: *RBU/RBM*. Refer *Lithography*.

Tagore, Jyotirindranath (1849–1925) b. *Jorasanko*, Kolkata. Jyotirindranath Tagore, the elder brother of the poet-painter *Rabindranath Tagore*, had private lessons in *drawing* in the city of Ahmedabad in 1867. His forte was portraiture, and he excelled in making *portraits* of most of his family members and acquaintances. For some years he had also been interested in phrenology, the science through which mental faculties and disposition of the sitter could be gauged through the shape of his or her skull. His sitters included *Rabindranath Tagore*, Mahatma Gandhi, Stella Kramrisch as well as the Japanese artists Y. Taikan, S. Hishida and O. Kakuzo, who were to influence *Abanindranath Tagore* in the development of the Bengal *style*. The book, "Twenty Five Collotypes from the Original Drawing by Jyotirindranath Tagore" was published in 1914.

His other achievements included translating by Molier, T. Gautier and P. Loti, from French into Bengali. He also translated Lokmanya Tilak's "Srimadbhagvata Gita Rahasya" from Marathi into Bengali. He was also a well-known singer and played violin, sitar and piano.

Tagore, Nabendranath (1910–1965) b. Bengal. A son of *Gaganendranath Tagore*, he followed *Abanindranath Tagore's style*, even though he was essentially self-taught. His *paintings* were based on Puranic *themes* and *landscapes*. He exhibited his works through *ISOA*, of which he was the secretary. His *paintings* were published in various periodicals, including *Prabasi*, Bichitra, Barrgashi and Rupam. He also did some of the *illustrations*, for *Rabindranath Tagore's* "Gitanjali". Collections: RB Society Kolkata *RBU/RBM*.

Tagore, Pratima Devi, (Thakur) (1893–1969) b. Bengal. She was the wife of *Rathindranath Tagore*, *Rabindranath Tagore's* only son. She was educated in *Fine Arts*. by Surendranath Kar and *Nandalal Bose*. Her preferred *medium* of expression was *watercolour*, as a result of the immediate influence of *Abanindranath Tagore* and through him, of Y. Taikan and S. Hishida. She learnt the *art* of *fresco painting* in Paris. The *paintings* she exhibited at the *ISOA*, had a distinct stamp of *Ajanta*, not only in the choice of subject, but also in the *style*. Some of her better known works are the "Departure of Siddhartha" and "Siddhartha and

Devadutta". There is a distinct influence of Japanese *painting* in these works. She was also credited with popularizing the *art* of *batik painting* and working with several *mediums* including *leather craft*, *ceramics* and *pottery*. Collections: *RB*, *AFA* & RB Society Kolkata *RBM*.

Tagore, Rabindranath (1861–1941) b. *Jorasanko*, Kolkata. Poet, novelist, song-writer and toward the end of his life a *painter* as well, Rabindranath Tagore was the most accomplished *artist* in a family of *artists*. He was knighted by the British in 1915 and was awarded the Nobel Prize in Literature and Poetry in 1913. He founded the *Santiniketan* School on the family lands in 1901, adding the *art* school *KB*, in 1919.

Rabindranath Tagore received elementary lessons in *drawing* along with his siblings from a *drawing* master in the 1860s. His predilection for doodling was observed at an early age, and all his manuscripts contain some *form* of it. His *doodles* were recognized as serious *art* by Victoria Ocampo, his Argentinian hostess in the mid-1920s. By this time, the erasures and scratches of his early works had changed in format from a delicate floriated or vine-like *pattern* to more menacing and grotesque shapes, in the *form* of birds and animals of prey with sharp hooked beaks, claws and beady eyes. By 1928, when he was 67 years old, he began *painting* in earnest, giving up the practice of *drawing doodles* and erasures. These closed, self-contained shapes were in *monochrome*, being worked on *paper* with a fountainpen. There was an element of *fantasy* in these works, which were soon followed by two-toned and three-toned *drawings*. The *pen* was used along with the finger and bits of rag to spread the *ink*. Finally, he also used *brush* to *paint* his predominantly *calligraphic images* (inspired in part by Far Eastern Art).

Being a writer, *paper* was his favourite *Medium*, though there are works on *leather* as well. From around 1932, he experimented with *crayons*, corrosive *inks*, vegetable dyes and *varnishes*. His *imagery* included expressionistic *lines*, hybrid flowers and birds and beasts, reptiles, amphibians, as well as serene *landscapes* and head studies. A recurring *image* is that of the face of a woman fitted within a phallic *outline*. While the earlier examples are delicate and pensive, the later ones are increasingly dramatic with a strongly lit forehead, and an exaggerated bridge and brow painted with strong *colours* as against the opalescent *colours* of the former.

Rabindranath Tagore executed more than 3000-odd *drawings* and *paintings* between 1928–1940. The major part of these works are housed in the *RB* Kolkata, *VBU* and *Santiniketan*. The first exhibition of his works was held during his lifetime at the Gallerie Pigalle in Paris (1930). Since then, his works have been exhibited in most of the major metropolitan cities in India and the world. His works have been auctioned at Heart New Delhi, Osian's and Heart Mumbai. Countless books have been published about his achievements both as a writer and a *painter*. He is now considered as one of India's premier *modern artist*, along with his nephew *Gaganendra-nath Tagore*. (See illustration on page 347)

Tagore, Rathindranath (1888–1961) b. Bengal. The oldest son of *Rabindranath Tagore*, and husband of *Pratima Devi Tagore*, Rathindranath Tagore was both a *painter* and craftsman. Being a biologist trained in agriculture, he loved *painting* flowers. He used various *media* and *styles*, and loved to *paint* flowers from the garden he himself planted in the *Santiniketan*. He also loved *painting landscapes*, mostly of the terrace gardens of Kolkata. *Wood* work was his favourite *craft*. He carved tiny objects such as caskets, cigarette cases, trays and stands, from ebony, Gambhar and other jungle *woods*, finishing them with *textures* ranging from rough and rustic to a smoothened surface exposing the grain of the *wood*. Most of these objects are displayed in *Santiniketan* and *VBU* which was exhibited at *AIFACS* New Delhi.

Tagore, Samarendranath (1870–1951) b. Bengal. Brother to the more illustrious *Gaganendranath Tagore* and *Abanindranath Tagore*, he was instrumental in turning Dakshiner Varandah (southern lobby) of Dwarkanath Tagore's (the head of the family and their great-grandfather) house into a studio. He concentrated on *landscapes* in *chalk* and *pastel*, though a few *figure drawings* by him have also survived. Founder member of *ISOA*. Collections: RB Society Kolkata *RBU/RBM*.

Tagore, Subhogendra (1912–) b. Bengal. Learnt *painting* from Nepalese *artist* Bekaraj, Studied Indian *painting* at Calcutta Art School & Central School London. Solos: Kolkata. Founder member: Calcutta Group. Editor: Bengali *art* journal "Sundaram": Collection: *RBM*.

Subhogendra Tagore learnt *wash painting* in the *manner* of *Abanindranath Tagore*. His commemorative *paintings* show a strong influence of *Chinese*, *Japanese* and Indonesian *art*. His later works *highlight* the use of a decorative *Cubism*. He has experimented with different *mediums*, including *oils*, *tempera*, *watercolour* and tapestry making. He was also a *sculptor*, incorporating handloom *motifs* and Alpana (Rangoli–floor *design*) *designs* in his *reliefs*. One of his best known works depicts *Rabindranath Tagore* in a naive cubistic *style* with decorative angular *lines*.

Taj Mahal Refer *Inlay*, *Marble*, *Monumental*, *Mughal Dynasty*; Illustration–*Kanhiyalal R. Yadav*

Talim, Bayaji Vasantrao (1888–1970) b. Hyderabad. Education: GDA, *JJSA*. Group participations: *BAS*; International: London. Awards: Gold Medals *BAS* and also in Vadodara; Later Dolly Cursetjee Prize and Mayo Medal Mumbai. Commissions: Several public commission, inclu-ding *life-size sculptures* of Dadabhai Navroji & other judicial *figures* in Mumbai.

Bayaji Vasantrao Talim was a student of Gladstone Solomon, the Principal of *JJSA* Mumbai. In 1928, he built his own Talim's Art Studio, executing *commissioned work* for interested patrons. "Takli" depicts a young woman spinning thread in emulation of one of the patriotic duties suggested by Mahatma Gandhi–executed in *marble*, the *sculpture* is elaborately posed and has the contrived grace of neo-classical works. "In tune with the Almighty" a work in *plaster*, depicts an emaciated ascetic playing a religious tune on a

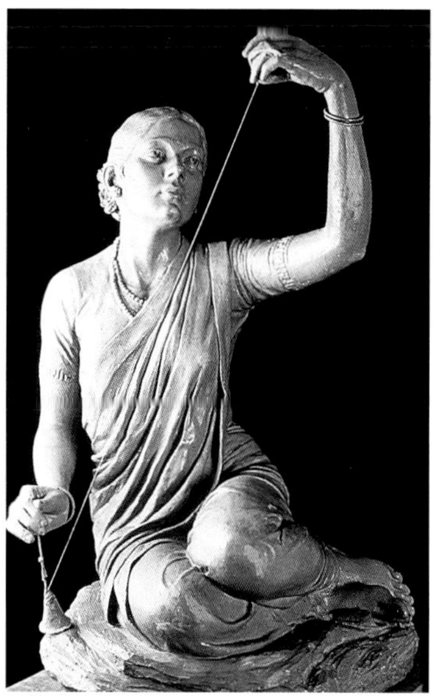

one-stringed instrument. Most of Bayaji Vasantrao Talim's creative works were limited to a period of about ten years, after which he only executed commissioned *portraits*. While the *bronze portrait* of Dadabhai Navroji was Victorian in conception, the *marble sculpture* of Sai Baba was both casual and effective.

Talim, Bayaji Vasantrao: "Takli", *Plaster of Paris*, 1923.

Tanjore Paintings Refer *Thanjavur (Tanjore) Painting*.

Tanjore Paintings on Glass Refer *Thanjavur (Tanjore) Painting on Glass*.

Tantra TANTRIC *culture* dates back to *Indus Valley Civilization* (circa 3500 BC). The word Tantra is composed of SANSKRIT words 1) "Tan" and 2) "Trai"—meaning "A doctrine of faith". The origin of Tantras were supposed to be in the form of a dialogue between SHIVA and his consort; when detailed methods and instructions of worship were laid down, to achieve control over natural forces and self. It is a regulated path to reach *god* and the deities through specified modes of worship and prayer. It incorporates elements of Samkhya philosophy, emphasising the union of opposites, and the notion that the universe is manifested out of the copulation of the divine couple. Some of the practices include a few with a strong sexual connotation.

Rituals which may be physical or *metaphysical* and mystical, were composed in 6th century AD. Ultimate goal was to achieve human amelioration and consummation. Tantra is of universal nature, and allows for individual adjustments, so that any person, of any faith can achieve realization of pure and perfect experience. Refer CHAKRA, *Culture, Decorative Art, Design, Modern Style, Neo-Tantricism, Open Form*, SHAKTI, *Spiritual, Tantra Art, Dipak Banerjee, Jyoti Bhatt, Biren De, Murli Lahoti, K.C.S. Paniker, Shankar Patil, Sohan Qadri, P.T. Reddy, Ghulam Rasool Santosh, Om Prakash Sharma, J. Srividya, Bal Wad, Ram Kishore Yadav.*

Tantra Art is rooted in *spiritual* values, the *artist* being in a constant process of discovery, of the origins and the roots of the cosmos—art being not a profession but a path towards truth and self-realization. Certain neo-tantric *artists* of the 20th century practising TANTRA have taken the geometric configurations of the YANTRA as their basic *image* and have worked around certain specific diagrams. Yet others have taken the sexual energy from TANTRA, using specific objects with sexual undertones (LINGAM-YONI) as leitmotifs in their *paintings*. In the 60s, the Indian *painters* who worked on colourful *compositions symbolic* of TANTRA were *Ghulam Rasool Santosh, Biren De, Mahirwan Mamtani, Sayed Haider Raza, Sultan Ali J., Prafulla Mohanti, K.V. Haridasan, Om Prakash Sharma, Sohan Qadri, K.C.S. Paniker* and *Shankar Palsikar*. Refer *Composition, Emblem, Form, Hard-Edge Painting, Neo-Tantricism, Open Form, Painting, Pattern*, PURANA, *Symbolic Art, Warm Colours*, YONI, *J. Srividya.*

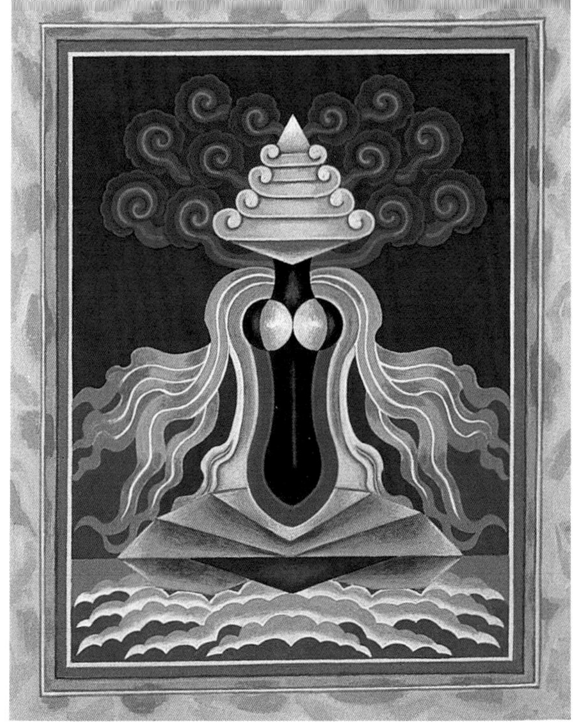

Tantra Art: *Ghulam Rasool Santosh*, "Untitled", 1995, 75x60 cm.

Tantric Pertaining to TANTRA. One who practises TANTRA. Refer *Art*, ATMA, *Cold Working, Erotic Art*, HANUMAN, *Khajuraho*, MANDALA, *Manuscript Paintings, Neo-Tantricism, Spiritual, Style, Ramnik Bhavsar, Roop Chand, Bimal DasGupta, Jalendu Dave, Natver Mistry, M. Sanathanan, Rangaswamy Saranagan, Om Prakash Sharma;* Illustrations—AGNI, OM, YANTRA, *Madhukar Bhatt, Biren De, K.V. Haridasan, Laxman Pai, K.C.S Panicker, Ghulam Rasool Santosh*

Tantric Composition Refer *Abstract Symbolism*, TANTRA, *Tantra Art*, TANTRIC, YANTRA, *Narayanan Akkitham, Shankar Palsikar.*

Tao Art Gallery Housed in the plush Sarjan Plaza, Worli Mumbai. Tao, which means "path" or "way", has been owned and managed by Kalpana Shah, since 2000. The first group of *artists* were *Sujata Bajaj, Prabhakar Kolte*, Anant Nikam, *Sayed Haider Raza*, Vijay Shinde. Gallery II which is an extension, opened in February 2005 with approx. 5000sq.ft. The gallery focuses on powerful displays to create latent experience out of artistic innovation and creativity.

Tao's exhibitions and events aim to invite dialogues about contemporary *culture*, politics, *aesthetics* and *traditions* of *visual art*. Group shows have included *Brinda C. Miller*, *Paresh Maity*, *Sudhir Patwardhan*, *Vasudeo Santu Gaitonde*, *Maqbool Fida Husain*, *Tyeb Mehta*, *RamKumar*, *Bal Chhabda*, and solos including *Sayed Haider Raza*, *Manu Parekh*, *Lalitha Lajmi*, *Viswanadhan*, *Surya Prakash*, *Dasharat Patel*, and other *artists*.

Taskar, Laxman Narayan (1870–1937) b. Mumbai, MAHA. Studied, *JJSA*. Solos: in India, Pune 1904–1935; International: Later in England. *Auctions*: Osian's Mumbai. Awards: Mayo Medal *JJSA*, *BAS*, Madras FA. Society, Simla FA. Society; International: Royal Imperial Exhibition London. Appointments: Teacher in 1898. Collections: In India, UK and Europe.

Laxman Narayan Taskar, though well versed in *oil paintings* and *pencil drawings*, was most interested in *watercolour landscapes* and *figurative paintings*. Concentrating on mythological and *contemporary* subjects he showed middleclass men and women in typical Maharashtrian costumes. He made effective use of *gouache* and *chiaroscuro techniques* to lend *perspective* to his works. His *paintings* of the *ghats* (mountain slopes) of Nasik, street scenes and temples with tonal presentation of the *horizon*, lend them their characteristic touch of rustic charm.

Technique It refers to the mechanical skill in the execution of a work of *art*. The *artist* usually blends his inner feelings with creative energies and techniques to express himself and communicate with viewers.

Technique usually changes with the *media* used. It evolves with the skill and dexterity of the *artist*. In ancient India, the miniature *painters* had to learn to painstakingly grind *colours* to perfection, make *brushes* and *paint* small areas of the *painting*. Young *sculptors* would probably work on small parts of the statuary like the jewellery or costume, honing their technique before being allowed to sculpt large *sculptures*.

A thorough knowledge of technique is equally important for the *contemporary artist*. At times technique dominates the *style* and *imagery*. A good work of *art* is one where technique, *style* and *imagery* work harmoniously together. Refer *Abstract*, *Acid Resist*, *All-over*, *Aquarelle*, *Back-Glass Painting*, *Batik*, *Bazaar Painting*, *Bengal Revivalism*, BHITTI-CHITRA, *Bidri*, *Bite*, *Biting in*, *Black*, *Collography*, *Composition*, *Graphic*, *Harmony*, *Miniature Painting*, *Sculpture*, *Tempera*, *Transition*, *Viscosity Printmaking*, *Wash (Technique)*, *Satyendranath Bandhyopadhyay*, *Nandalal Bose*, *Samar N. Bhowmik*, *Vidya Bhushan*, *P.N. Choyal*, *Asit K. Haldar*, *Somnath Hore*, *Maqbool Fida Husain*, *Meera Mukherjee*, *Amrut Patel*, *Jamini Roy*, *Vivan Sundaram*, *Gaganendranath Tagore*, *Nathu Lal Verma*, *Ram Gopal Vijaivargiya*.

Tempera A *technique* in which binders such as whole egg, egg-yolk or different kinds of glue are used to mix with powder *colour* to make it workable, on a dry *plaster* surface with the help of water. The result is that the *paint film* dries very quickly and gives a tough and longlasting finish. Only the final touches are then applied in *oil* for *glazing*. Later, from this method, the whole *techniques* of *oil painting* developed. In India, a type of glue, made from tamarind seeds was used as a binder in *miniature paintings*. In the *modern* period, certain *artists* from the *Bengal School* used tempera, notably *Nandalal Bose*, and *Sarada Charan Ukil*. The Haripura panels with their quick spontaneous brush-strokes were executed in this *medium*. Refer *Abstract Impressionism*, *Albumen*, *Back-Glass Painting*, *Banasthali Vidyapith*, *Bazaar Painting*, *Bengal Revivalism*, *Bengal School*, BHITTI-CHITRA, *Blocking In*, *Cityscape*, *Cubism*, *Dead Colour*, *Egg-oil emulsion*, *Egyptian Art*, *Facing*, *Finish*, *Folk Inspiration*, *Fresco*, *Gesso*, *Illumination*, *Japanese Art*, *Line and Wash*, *Local Colour*, *Manner*, *Media*, *Mixed Media*, *Modern Style*, *Oil*, *Outline*, *Painting*, *Palette*, *Pigment*, *Priming*, *Realistic*, *Sable Hair*, *Soak-stain Technique*, *Term*, *Thanjavur (Tanjore) Paintings on Glass*, *Transparent*, *Wash (Technique)*, *White*, *K.C. Aryan*, *Satyendranath Bandhyopadhyay*, *Gautam Basu*, *Narayan S. Bendre*, *Bikash Bhattacharjee*, *Vidya Bhushan*, *Adiveppa Murigeppa Chetty*, *P.N. Choyal*, *Muhammed Abdur Chughtai*, *Dharmanarayan DasGupta*, *Dhirendrakrishna Deb Barman*, *Kavita Deuskar*, *Mukul Chandra Dey*, *H.A. Gade*, *Sukhen Ganguly*, *Asit K. Haldar*, *Paresh C. Hazra*, *Goverdhanlal Joshi*, *Sanat Kar*, *Kshitendranath Mazumdar*, *Sukhamoy Mitra*, *Benode Behari Mukherjee*, *Leela Mukherjee*, *L. Munuswamy*, *Shankar Palsikar*, *Khodidas Parmar*, *Sushil Paul*, *P. Perumal*, *Kapu Rajaiah*, *Anjani P. Reddy*, *Jagu Bhai Shah*, *Ved Pal Sharma*, *Nilima G. Sheikh*, *Rameshwar Singh*, *Narendra Rai Srivastav*, *Subhogendra Tagore*, *Sarada Charan Ukil*, *K. Venkatappa*, *Nathu Lal Verma*; Illustrations—*Ajanta*, DURGA , *Gandharvas*, GANJIFA, *Pastoral—Nathu Lal Verma*, *Thanjavur (Tanjore) Painting*, *Nandalal Bose*, *Manishi Dey*, *Ganesh Pyne*, *Jamini Roy*, *Deokinandan Sharma*, *Lalu Prasad Shaw*, *Nathu Lal Verma*.

Tempering **1.** It is the mixing of *colours* to produce intermediate *hues*—by multi-coloured strokes or splashes of *colour*. Even the *watercolour palette* has a number of indentations for holding the *colours*. e.g. *Jehangir Sabavala*, Pratima Sheth, *Bharati Kapadia*. The *colour* viscosity *technique* in *printmaking* is to obtain the subtle variations of *hue* in the *prints*. e.g. *Krishna N. Reddy*. **2.** The *annealing* of *clay*, *metal*, glass etc., regulating its degree of hardness. Refer *Medium*, *Sankho Chaudhuri*, *Shankar Nandagopal*.

Temple Architecture Refer HANSA, HAMSA, *Dravidian Style*, *Nagara Style*, *Relief Sculpture*, *Vesara Style*.

Tensile Strength The degree (strength) of any material under stretching. Among the *metals*, *bronze* has been extensively used in *sculpture*, because of its high degree of tensile strength. *Stone*, *marble*, *granite*, *plaster of Paris* and other such materials have a lesser degree of tensile strength when compared to *metals*. e.g *Concrete* is strengthened and reinforced with *steel* and *iron* bars or mesh when used both in *sculpture* and *architecture*. Refer *Aluminium*, *Canvas*,

Canvas Board, Handmade Paper, Frame, Screen Printing, Stencil, Somnath Hore, Vasudha Thozhur, K. Vasant Wankhede

Term 1. A particular period of *time*. **2.** A word or a group of words used to express a particular conception. In *art,* term which describes a body of work or *style* or *technique*. e.g. *Isms, Modernism, Modern Movement, Ready-Made, Post-Modern, Miniature Painting, Installation, Tempera,* TANTRA. Refer *Canvas, Realistic, Style, Trompe L'oeil, K. Khosa, Bhupen Khakhar, Kanayi Kunhiraman, Ved Nayar, P.T. Reddy.*

Terracotta Literally baked earth, it is a fired *clay* which is unglazed and used most commonly in building materials such as tiles and *sculptures*. Earliest example of terracotta go back to *Indus Valley Civilization*. In Neolithic period it was used for making both utilitarian and decorative objects. Greeks and Romans also used it for making many statues. In India, most of the temples in Bishnupur in WB are constructed out of terracotta bricks and decorated with terracotta plaques and *sculptures*, while in the South massive terracotta horses are dedicated to the *god* Ayyanar (TN). In Molela, a small village in RAJ, craftsmen create terracotta wall-plaques depicting a host of local deities, including Dev Narayan, Nag Devta, Devi DURGA and local heroes such as Pabuji.

Terracotta is also the most commonly used *ceramic medium* due to its *plasticity* and pleasing *colour*, though it is fragile and disintegrates quickly. Refer *Archaeological Museum, Armature, Artefact, Ashutosh Museum of Indian Art, Bharat Kala Bhavan (BKB), Birbhum, Dadaism, Found Object, Gandharan Art, Government Museum, Harappa, Jagdish & Kamla Mittal Museum of Indian Art, Media, Mohenjo Daro,* MURTI, *New Realism, Polychromatic Sculpture, State Museum, Texture, Prayag Jha Chhillar, C. Dakshinamoorthy, Ranen Datta, Partha Pratim Deb, Kavita Deuskar, Subrayalu Dhanapal, Bhanu Dudhat, M.J. Enas, Paresh C. Hazra, Reba Hore, Raghav Kaneria, Kantibhai B. Kapadia, Latika Katt, P.S. Nandhan, Mahendra Pandya, Goverdhan S. Panwar, Raj Kumar Panwar, Choudhary Satyanarayan Patnaik, Niranjan Pradhan, N. Pushpamala, Vimoo Sanghvi, Prabhas Sen, Himmat Shah, Shashi, Gurudas Shenoy, Uma Siddhanta, K.G. Subramanyan, Vivan Sundaram, Rajendar Tiku, Radhika Vaidaynathan, J.R. Yaduvu.*

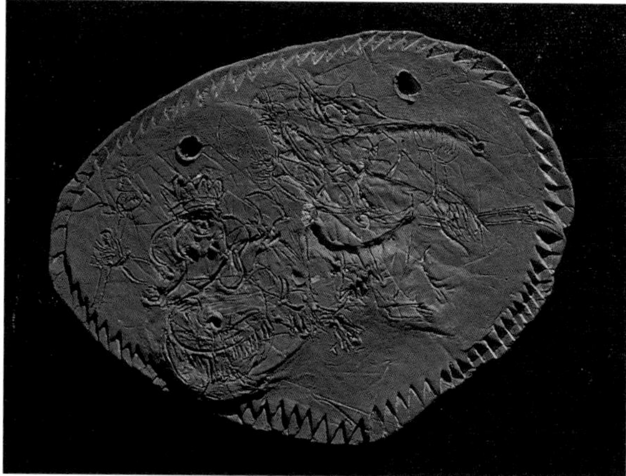

Terracotta: Sudha Arora, "Aale Main Baithe Ganesh", 1995, 30.5x45.75 cm.

Texture The *nature* of the surface of **1.** *Painting*—it depends upon the brushstroke and the *medium* used, which can be smooth, ridged, thin, *transparent* or *opaque*. e.g. *Amit Ambalal, Bikash Bhattacharjee, Rabindranath Tagore, Shantanu Ukil.* **2.** *Sculpture*—it depends upon the type of *chisel* marks on a *stone*, the thumb marks on a piece of *clay* or *terracotta*, and the sheen of the *bronze*. e.g. *Ramkinkar Baij, Dhanraj Bhagat, Girish C. Bhatt, Ajit Chakravarti* **3.** *Architecture*—the indentations on entrances, windows, pillars, balconies and doors on the facade of the building can create an exciting surface *pattern* that contributes to the textural quality at a distance. At a closer level the *nature* of the wall *finish (paint*, material etc.) contributes to texture. e.g. *Abu-Dilwara Temples.* Refer *Balance, Canvas, Cast Stone, Chequering, Combing, Contour, Crayon Manner, De'collage, Draughtsmanship, Dry Brush Painting, Encaustic—Eric Bowen, Fibreglass, Frottage, Glazing, Graphic, Hand-made Paper, Hardboard, Harmony, Junk Art, Line, Linearity, Linear Composition, Linearly, Linocut, Landscape Format, Line, Linocut, Marble, Mass, Monotype, Oil Painting, Passage, Patina, Photogravure, Picture Space, Sketch, Stone Carving, Tactile, Thumb Impression, Relief printing;* Illustration—*Amit Ambalal, Ramkinkar Baij, Amitabha Banerjee, Dhanraj Bhagat, Natvar Bhavsar, Vasudeo Santu Gaitonde, Ganesh Haloi, Paresh C. Hazra, Surendra Pal Joshi, Sanat Kar, K.B. Kulkarni, Bimal Kundu, Chittrovanu Mazumdar, Chhaganlal D. Mistry, Sailoz Mookerjea, Mrinalini Mukherjee, Sachida Nagdev, B.P. Paliwal, Shankar Palsikar, Manu Parekh, Nagji Patel, Pilloo Pochkhanawalla, Pointillism—Narayan S. Bendre, Sohan Qadri, Shyamal Dutta Ray, Sayed Haider Raza, Jamini Roy, Bhabesh Chandra Sanyal, Manickam Senathipathi, G.S. Shenoy, Deepak Shinde, Shuvaprasanna, Paramjit Singh Vishwanath M. Sholapurkar, Laxman Shreshtha, K.G. Subramanyan, Setlur Gopal Vasudev, Portrait—Satyendranath Bandhyopadhyay, Wood Cut—Sudhir R. Khastgir.*

Thadani, Sheila (1934–) b. India. Education: Dip. in interior decoration, *JJSA*, She joined TKS and worked under *K.S. Kulkarni*. Over 23 solos: Mumbai, New Delhi, Kanpur. Group participations: Kanpur, Lucknow, *LKA* New Delhi, SKP, *AIFACS, VEAG.* Publications: "The Statesman", "Hindustan Times", "Delhi Diary" New Delhi. Collections: *LKA & College of Art* New Delhi, pvt. & corporates in TATA; International: Cairo, Canada, USA, Yugoslavia, Italy, UK.

Sheila Thadani began her career as a *painter*, but over the years, she has added *batik painting* and *sculpture* to her *oeuvre*. Her *themes* in all three *mediums* however, have remained predominantly Indian, both in simplification and the use of decorative *patterns.* Her *paintings* show fascination with *colour*, *form* and *line*, in her *landscapes* with creative *compositions*. Her *bronzes* on the other hand, show the use of imaginative *figure forms*, being built up in a spontaneous *manner*.

She lives and works in New Delhi.

Thaker, Sanat (1917–1990) b. Jodiya, Saurashtra. Education: Dip. in *painting JJSA*; Informal training in portraiture & *landscape* under M.D. Trivedi in Karachi, now Pakistan. Solos: Srinagar, Udagamangalam, *AFA* Kolkata, TAG, *JAG*. Group artists: *Painting* & *graphic* Mumbai & Kolkata. Group participations: National Exhibitions, Govt. Museum FA. Chandigarh, AFA Amritsar, *BAS*, *AIFACS*. *Art* camps: Chorward GUJ, Mandavgadh MP. Awards: *LKA* GUJ, *BAS*, *AIFACS*. Member: *LKA* GUJ. Collections: Vakils, TATA Mumbai, Indian Railway New Delhi, Home Science College Chandigarh, *LKA* Ahmedabad, Colleges, Mission & University in Rajkot; International: Sweden, USA.

Sanat Thaker's early works were greatly influenced by his initial exposure to the works of Western masters like M.V.R. Rembrandt and J.M.W. Turner. An element of *Eclecticism* was added to his *oeuvre* by his later fascination for the works of a Bengali *painter*. He experimented with different *mediums* and modes of expression, evolving from an obsession with Classicism early in his career, an impressionist *technique* for his *watercolour landscapes*, towards abstraction (which he deemed richer and greater than traditional *art*) in the twilight of his career. *Nature*, especially the changing face of the Himalayas, have always been his primary thematic concern.

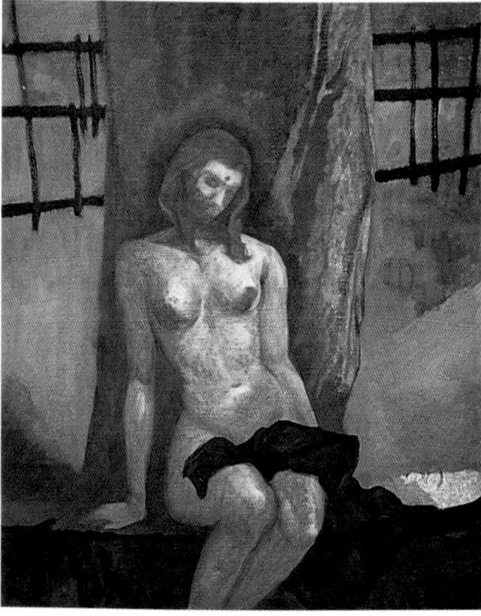

Thaker, Sanat: "Untitled", *Oil* on *Canvas*, 115x80 cm.

Thakore, Jaidev (1943–) b. Vadodara. Dip. in *painting* & Certificate in *graphics*, *MSU*. Solos: *GC* Mumbai, *Art Heritage* New Delhi, CAG Ahmedabad, Vithi Vadodara, *JAG*, *PUAG*, TKS, *SAI*. Group participations: National *LKA* GUJ, other *exhibitions* in Vadodara, Mumbai, Ahmedabad, Lucknow, Chandigarh. *Art* camps: *MSU*. Workshops: *Printmaking* workshop *FFA* Vadodara, in Saputara by *LKA*, Amrita Sher-Gil Trust 1972–1973, Conducted workshops: Jaipur School of Art Jaipur, NID. Awards: HRD Ministry New Delhi. Fellowship: *LKA* GUJ. Commissions: *Murals* Vadodara, Chennai. Collections: *LKA* & Times of India New Delhi; MMB Mumbai, *Chandigarh Museum*; International: British Museum London.

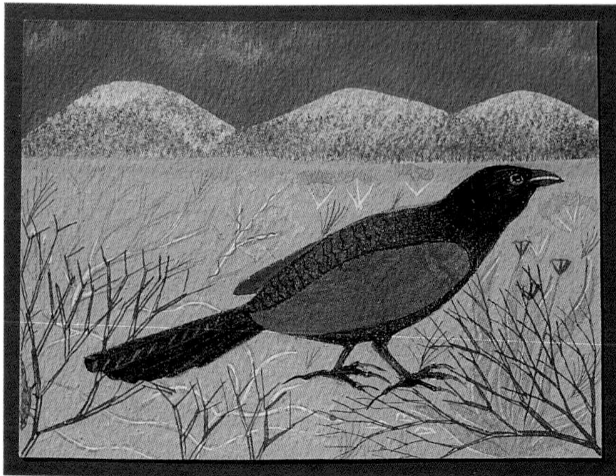

Thakore, Jaidev: "Crow Pheasant", *Watercolours*, 1988, 7.5x10 cm.

The simplicity of *form* and brilliant *colours* of Jaidev Thakore's near miniature sized works border on the naive, with the *distortion* in *perspective* and premeditated compositional and *pictorial* scheme lending the requisite element of wit. His thematic concerns with various animals and birds point to the influence of the French naive *painter*, H. Rousseau, while the decorative patternizing is taken from H. Matisse.

He lives and works in Vadodara.

Thakore, Nita (1958–) b. India. Education: M.A. in *painting*, *MSU*, Goldsmith's College of Art & Design, Textile Art London. Solos: Vadodara, British Council Gallery & Sonet-Lumiere Mumbai, TKS, *CYAG*. Group participations: Annual shows Ahmedabad, Harmony Reliance Mumbai, Gallery Jharokha New Delhi, BAG, *CYAG*; International: Smith Gallery London. *Art* camps: New Delhi; International: Austria; Hon.: International: Charles Wallace India Trust Award London. *LKA* GUJ. Commissions: Textile *mural* Mumbai. Appointments: Taught at NID, Visiting Lecturer at NID, National Institute of Fasion Technology Gandhinagar, Chandigarh & New Delhi. Collections: GUJ *LKA*, *Art Heritage* New Delhi, Jindal, *INTACH* & British Council Mumbai, *CYAG*, *PUAG*; International: British Museum London.

Nita Thakore began her career as an *artist* using *pastels* and *oils* to execute her *compositions* for some years. Her training in textile *art* in London, led to her experimenting with both hand and machine *embroidery*, using the same *imagery*. From the near expressionist tendencies in the 1992 works, Nita Thakore has now resorted to juxtaposing sharply defined areas with minute detailing against ambigious, almost *monochromatic backdrops* sometimes continuing the same *composition*. Her later works are based on Indian *mythology*, with its range of animal, bird life and human *forms*.

She lives and works in Vadodara along with her *artist* husband, *Jaidev Thakore*. Refer *Embroidery*.

Thanjavur (Tanjore) Paintings Thanjavur lies about 300 km from Chennai in TN. It is renowned for its Thanjavur (Tanjore) *style paintings*, which flourished in the 17th–18th centuries under the patronage of the Marathas. The same *style* was also seen in Mysore under the rule of Krishnaraja Wodeyar. The subjects were taken from *Hinduism* and generally represented episodes surrounding *gods* like SHIVA, VISHNU and KRISHNA. KRISHNA especially was a favourite, with scenes from his childhood being usually depicted, the *figures* which are *monumental* and robust, unlike the slimmer *figures* in Indian miniatures, adhered strictly to iconographic canons, as the *paintings* were made for the purpose of worship. They were usually kept in the Puja-room (prayer room) and not displayed. The *colours* used were pure and the application was flat. The *background* was always red and/or green. Green was also commonly used for furnishings and curtains. The *figures* followed iconographic dictates, with KRISHNA invariably being painted blue as an adult, but *white* as a baby. The *figures* were outlined in a dark reddish brown and *gold*, gems and cut glass were profusely used to decorate the *paintings*. It takes about three weeks to complete one *painting* in the Thanjavur (Tanjore) *style*. The base is usually of jackwood, then the unbleached cloth is pasted on it. On this an *outline* of the *idol* is sketched out then a mixture of limestone, *chalk* powder, gum and honey is applied in layers on the *sketch*. Thousands of dots are embossed with the paste. Certain areas, such as furniture, sari borders, *drapery* and jewellery are raised with extra coats of the same paste. Once dry, the gems were set into the *plaster* and the *colours* were painted and smoothened and *outlines* were etched. Earlier, real diamonds, pearls and rubies were used and pure *gold leaf* applied with a glue made of tamarind, gum and jaggery. The Thanjavur (Tanjore) painting *craft* is being revived once again, though more for their *style* rather than religious feeling. Refer *Glass Painting, Museums*, SHAKTI, *Thanjavur (Tanjore) Paintings on Glass.*

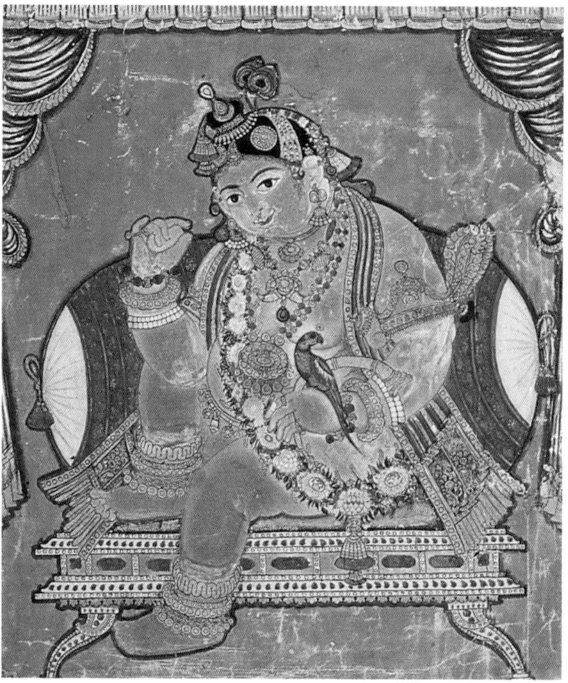

Thanjavur (Tanjore) Painting: "Navneetha Krishna", *Tempera* on *Paper*, 30x25.5 cm.

Thanjavur (Tanjore) Paintings on Glass Thanjavur was also an important centre of *glass painting* in the South. The *style* is clearly related to the *Thanjavur (Tanjore) paintings* done on *wood*. The *painters* however belonged to the Raju caste from AP. They also practiced in neighbouring towns in South India such as Tiruchirapalli, Madurai and Pudukottai. The *technique*, however differed from *painting* on *wood*. The *theme* was coloured in the *tempera technique*, using *opaque colours* thickened with *white*. The usual *technique* was reversed, with details, such as *outlines* and jewellery done first, as the *composition* was painted on the back of the glass. *Gold leaf* sequins and other shining objects were used to imitate jewellery and sari borders. At times small portions of the glass were mirrored with mercury, and at other, parts of the glass was left bare and *gold* foil or *paper* was fixed behind the glass. The larger areas are skilfully brushed in, so as not to disturb the painted *outlines*. Shading is used but only to indicate roundness of the *figures* which contrasts well with the patterned areas of the *composition*. As in *Thanjavur (Tanjore) paintings* on *wood*, the *themes* included the *epics*, *icons* and *portraits* of kings and heroes. Refer *Back-Glass Painting.*

Theme The subject of a work of *art*. The theme of the *wall paintings* at *Ajanta* are Buddhist JATAKAS and the life of the BUDDHA. Most of the *Rajasthani miniature paintings* are based on the theme of KRISHNA BHAKTI. Closer to our times, *Raja Ravi Varma* used mythological themes even though his characters were dressed in contemporary costume. *Contemporary compositions* may be based thematically on *abstract* concepts and ideas, such as *Maqbool Fida Husain's* "Svetambari" and *Vivan Sundaram's* "Memorial" and "The Shergil Archives". Refer AHIMSA, *Altarpiece, Art Nouveau, Bengal Oil Painting, Bengal Revivalism, Buddhist Art, Chinese Art, Content, Decadent Art, Detailed Work, Exhibition (Art), Glass Painting, Idiom, Kotah, Mewar, Miniature Painting, Motif, Multi block colour printing, Narrative, Naturalism*, NAYIKA, *Performance Art, Pop Art*, RADHA, RASA LILA, *Sculpture, Spiritual, Still Life, Swadeshi Movement, Symbolic Art, Thanjavur (Tanjore) Paintings on Glass, Tree of Life*; Illustrations–*Basohli, Erotic Art*, GANJIFA, *Glass Painting*, JATAKA, *Kangra*, RASA LILA, *Thanjavur (Tanjore) Paintings, B. Vithal, Manjit Bawa, Shiavax Chavda, Muhammed Abdur Rehman Chughtai, Jatin Das, Manishi Dey, Satish Gujral, K.K. Hebbar, Sukhen Ganguly, Somnath Hore, B.P. Kamboj, Bhupen Khakhar, Bimal Kundu, Paresh Maity, Mahirwan Mamtani, Prafulla Mohanti, Reddeppa M. Naidu, Madhavi Parekh, Ratan Parimoo, Gieve Patel, Shankar Patil, Sudhir Patwardhan, Kartick Chandra Pyne, A.A. Raiba, Ramesh Rao, Sayed Haider Raza, P.T. Reddy, Jamini Roy, Anilbaran Saha, Ghulam Rasool Santosh, Sarada Charan Ukil, Christian Art–Francis Newton Souza, Mas–S. Fyzee-Rahamin, Relief–Sagara Piraji, Repousse–Ram Kishore Yadav, Terracotta–Sudha Arora*, YANTRA–*Rekha Krishnan*,

Thippeswamy, P.R. (1922–) b. Harthikote, KAR. Edu-cation: Dip. in *FA.*, Chamarajendra Technical Institute Mysore. Solos: Mysore, Bangalore. Group participations: Mysore DAE, *AIFACS, CKP*. Awards: KAR State *LKA*, Mysore DAE. Member: Founder Secretary Chitra Shilpi Academy Mysore; Chairman KAR *LKA*. Publications: Books published "Bharateeya Chitrakala" (Indian Art), *Monographs* on *K. Venkatappa*, M.V. Veerappa, K. Kenchappa, S. Nanjunda-swamy & several articles on *art* & *artists*. Collections: Bangalore Art Museum, *Folklore Museum* Mysore, KAR *LKA* & pvt.

P.R. Thippeswamy is a landscapist, *painting* in "*Plein-air*", using *transparent watercolour washes* to accurately record the beauty of the Indian countryside. He also shows a predilection for crumbling ruins and ancient monuments, recording them with a zeal of a topographer.

He lives and works in Mysore.

Thozhur, Vasudha (1956–) b. Mysore. Education: Dip. in *painting*, *GCAC* Chennai, Advanced certificate in *painting* Croydon School of Art & Design UK. Solos: Alliance Francaise Chennai & Pondicherry, *SG* Chennai, Mumbai & Bangalore, MMB Hyderabad; International: Paris, London. Group participations: Chennai, Eicher Gallery, *LKA* & National Exhibitions New Delhi, *SG* Mumbai, *LTG*, SRAG, *BB*, *JAG*; International: Delfina, London, Castlegate Cumbria, Cite Internationale Des Arts Paris. *Art* camps & workshops: Kerala, Hyderabad, Painter's camp MMB Chennai, *LKA* New Delhi, Women's *artists GAC*, *Printmaking* TN; International: Cite Internationale Des Arts Paris Residency. *Auction*: Osian's Mumbai. Awards: French Govt. Scholarship, Charles Wallace Grant, *LKA* Research Grant New Delhi. Fellowship: HRD Ministry. Appointments: Cumbria College of Art & Design Carlisle, Charlotte Mason College Ambleside. Collections: *LKA* & *NGMA* New Delhi, Godrej & *SG* Mumbai, pvt. & corporates in Hyderabad & Chennai.

Vasudha Thozhur's *paintings* develop from fragmented memories, in varying *sizes* of conception and execution. They could be both *monochromatic* and colourful as in accents of *black* and *white* in a *polychromatic background*. She calls it a continually unfolding panorama of *time* and being. Most of her works display a trait as unimportant for empty or *"negative" spaces*, with *images* and reminiscences filling the *canvas* to capacity and an adventurous use of *colour*, *line* and scale. She has also varied her *technique* to achieve different results, i.e. the sponge for spontaneity and the *brush* for emphasis. She has worked with diverse materials, including *canvases* stitched to resemble tarpaulin, unstretched *canvases*, *palm leaf*, newspaper and *paper*, colouring and *painting* with *oils*, *acrylics*, *gouache*, *pastels*, *earth colours* and *charcoal*.

She lives and works in Chennai and Vadodara.

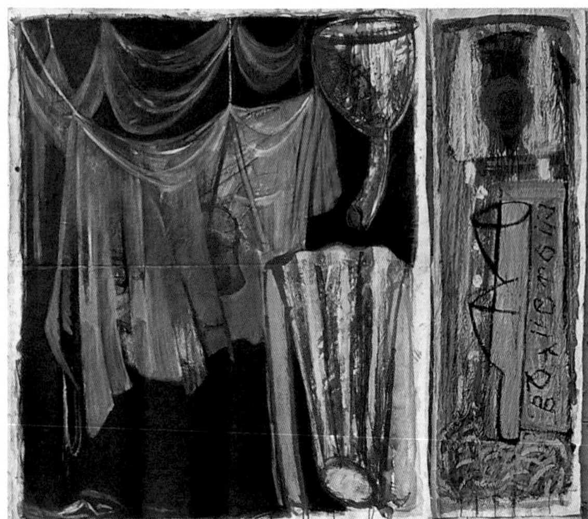

Thozhur, Vasudha: "The Rites of Passage", *Acrylic* & *Oil* on *Canvas*, 1997, 150x180 cm.

Thumb Impression An inked imprint of the thumb. Usually stands for a signature by an illiterate person. Certain *artists* may prefer signing their works in this *manner*. It may also be used to generate *texture* in *sculpture* and *painting*; the *texture* of the fingers used in all *mediums* by the *artists* to convey ideas and feelings. *Rabindranath Tagore* used a *pen* along with fingers and bits of rag to spread the *ink* and also used *brush* to *paint* his main *calligraphic images*. Refer *Impression*, *Screen Printing*, *Silk Screen Printing*, *Sunil Kumar Paul*.

Tie and Dyed Fabrics Known in India as *Bandhani* fabrics, the intricate and cultural *style* found in Bhuj, Jamnagar and Mandavi (Saurashtra and Kutch). This is a process of decorating textiles by the method of resist dyeing. The fabric is tied with threads and other materials, including strips of rubber, and later dyed to give interesting *patterns*. This process is repeated with various *colours* so as to produce multi-hued fabrics, which are worn as sarees, shawls and dress materials. This traditional *craft* has now been adapted by various *artists*, to create *patterns* and *installations* that take tie-dyeing beyond the realm of just garment making. Refer *Batik*, *Biharilal C. Barbhaiya*, *Prabha Panwar*, *Pratima Devi (Thakur) Tagore*, *Sheila Thadani*, *Arnawaz Vasudev*.

Tiku, Rajendar (1953–) b. Wadwan, Kashmir. Education: Dip. in *sculpture* Institute of Music & FA. Srinagar. Solos: *Art Heritage* New Delhi. Group participations: National *LKA* exhibitions & *Triennale*, New Delhi, *BAAC* Kolkata, Harmony Mumbai *VAG*, *GE*, VG, *BB Biennales*, other towns Srinagar, Jammu, Mumbai. Camps & symposiums: All India Sculpture Camp J&K & Gwalior, International Sculptors Symposium MAHA, Clay Symposium India at Goa. Awards: J&K State, National *LKA*, *Triennale*, New Delhi. Fellowship: HRD Ministry. Member: Kala Gram NZCC. Appointments: Lecturer of *sculpture* at the Institute of FA. Srinagar. Collections: J&K Cultural Academy, *LKA*, *NGMA* & *Art Heritage* New Delhi, *LKA* MP.

Rajendar Tiku draws inspiration from simple sources, including *visual* stimuli from man made objects, both *imaginary* and tangible happenings, experiences, fragments of memories and the nostalgia they evoke. He tries to combine various shapes, including such contrasting ones as organic and geometric objects, simple and intricate *patterns* to arrive at his *sculptures*, in *terracotta* and stained *wood*. He compares making *sculpture* to performing *rituals*, the *artist* being a primitive shaman, creating shapes and *forms* which become objects of faith, surrounded by an aura of sacred silence. *Colour* also performs a significant role in his *sculpture*. It generates a positive relationship between his work and the spectator.

He lives and works in Srinagar.

Time Refer KALA/KAAL.

Tint *White*, when mixed with any other *colour*, is known as a tint of that particular *colour*, as in reddish-white or reddish tint. *Gouache* is *white filler* used to make *paint opaque*, used by the miniature *painters*. *Artists* used heavy *opaque colours* mixed with *white* both in *oil paint* and *watercolours* applying the material with thick *impasto* brushstrokes or preferring a smooth *finish*. Many *artists* use an overall tint as a *background* for their *painting*. e.g. *C. Douglas, Shaibal Ghosh, K. Jayapala Panicker, Saroj Gogi Pal.* Refer *Brush, Brush Drawing, Key, Mixed Contrast, Mono-chrome, Opacity, Overlapping, Shades, Dipak Banerjee.*

Titles The name given to the work of *art*. In the past, viewers tended to identify and admire *paintings* and *sculptures* by reading its title. This was even true in the case of allegorical or cryptic *symbolic* titles. All this was to change with the advent of abstraction. V. Kandinsky was to do away with titles altogether, titling his works as consecutively numbered "*compositions*" and "improvisations"; many *contemporary artists* like *Laxman Shreshtha* use numbers instead of titles, thus offering no clue to the viewers who would rather "identify" the work than enjoy it.

Tonal Values The *light* and dark variations. The contrast produced by the different *tones* in a work of *art*. These contrasts can be extreme as in the case of works like *Antonio X. Trindade's* "Flora" or they can be relatively faint as in the *wash paintings* of *Abanindranath Tagore*. Tonal variation are seen in the *paintings* at *Ajanta*, though not in the Indian miniatures. The Western *technique* was again introduced to indigenous *artists* during the 18th century resulting in the *Company School.* Refer *Balance, Chiaroscuro, Complementary Colours, Cool Colour, Draughtsmanship, Etching, Figure-Ground Relationship, Graphite, Key, Modelling, Maniere Noire, Negative, Plate, Stippling, Underpainting, Value, Vocabulary, Prem Chandra Goswami, Dattatray B. Pardeshi, Yagneshwar Kalyanji Shukla, Paramjeet Singh;* Illustrations–*Shiavax Chavda.*

Tone The composite impact of an overall colouration in *paint/colours*. Also known as *value*. It is the degree of lightness or darkness of *colours* in the whole *painting*.The skill of the *artist* determines the tonal *harmony*. e.g. *Yusuf Arakkal's paintings* are usually dark in tone, while *J. Swaminathan's* works are warm and bright in *tonal value*. The desire to achieve *depth* and *tone* by the first generation of *modern* Indian *artists* are seen in most *paintings* of late 19th followed by the 20th century. In printing method, tones are generally created by *aquatint*, photo process or manually printed, etc. Refer *Bite, Biting in, Hue, Collotype, Key, Mass, Miniature Painting, Neutral Colours, Printmaking, Tint, Narayan S. Bendre, Atul Bose, Shiavax Chavda, Dhirendrakrishna Deb Barman, Seema Ghurayya, Subrata Kundu*; Illustrations –*Mukul Chandra Dey, Shaibal Ghosh, A. Ramachandran, Sayed Haider Raza, Jehangir Sabavala.*

Torso 1. The trunk of the human body. **2.** A piece of *sculpture* representing the body, lacking the head, arms and legs. Refer *Contrapposto, Figure*, TRIBHANGA, *Girish C. Bhatt*; Illustration–*Kshitendranath Mazumdar.*

Townscape A *landscape painting, drawing* or *print* depicting views of a town or a city as seen in the cubist *cityscapes* of *Ram Kumar*. Refer *Abstract Geometric, Anjani P Reddy, G.S. Shenoy, Yashwant Shirwadkar.*

Tradition 1. The customs and beliefs of a people, or country or region carried through generations. **2.** As in traditional *art*, the *art forms* and canons conceived and followed by *artists* of a by gone era, in a specific region. In Indian traditional *art*, it would include the *art* under various dynasties which ruled India in the past.

Tradition plays an important role in the works of *contemporary artists* too. Signs, symbols, even thought process could add significantly to *abstract* works and newer modes of expression, such as *installation* and *conceptual art.* e.g. *K.K. Hebbar, Maqbool Fida Husain, Sayed Haider Raza*. There are several *artists* who still practise working in the traditional *manner*. e.g. Banasthali, the idol-makers of Maharashtra, and Kolkata. Indian *artists*, who practised traditional *style* in *all-over technique* are seen in *contemporary art.* Refer *Banasthali Vidyapith* RAJ, *Icon*, KALPA-SUTRA, *Natural Colours, Wood Carving, Sculpture, K.C. Aryan, Jamini Roy, Kailash Chandra Sharma, Rameshwar Singh, Nathu Lal Verma.*

Transition 1. *Passage* or period of change between a place or *style* from one to another. **2.** In *art*, it refers to an intermediary *style* between two *styles* or periods of *art* e.g. the period between the archaic and the *classical* in Greek *sculpture*. *Mannerism* is referred to as the transition between the *Renaissance* and the *Baroque styles*.

It is seen in the evolution of Indian *sculpture* and *miniature paintings*, which vary from region to region and also from period to period. e.g. During the *Gupta* era (the golden age of Ancient Indian Art) the *Ajanta* caves were decorated with *wall paintings* and *sculptures* describing the Buddhist way of life. As they were painted over a long period of *time*, circa 200 BC to AD 728, the *style* kept evolving and changing. Refer *Bengal Revivalism, Erotic Art, Folk Art, Gupta, Mythology*, TANTRIC, *Tantra Art, Ramkinkar Baij, Pestonjee Bomanjee, Nandalal P. Bose, Mahadev V. Dhurandhar, Sailendranath Dey, Savlaram L. Haldankar, Manchershaw F. Pithawalla, Abalal Rahiman, Ravishankar M. Raval, Jamini Roy, Ghulam Rasool Santosh, Narayan R. Sardesai, Amrita Sher-Gil, Vivan Sundaram, Abanindranath Tagore, Gaganendranath Tagore, Rabindranath Tagore, Bayaji Vasantrao Talim, Laxman Narayan Taskar, Antonio X. Trindade, Raja Ravi Varma, Vinayakrao Venkatrao Wagh.*

Translucent Semi-transparent allowing the *light* to pass partially through or become diffused, so that the object lying beyond is visible through a haze but not clearly and sharply. It can be found in *Ajanta* and is the chief characteristic of the *wash technique* of the *Bengal School*. Refer *Abstract Impressionism, Bengal Revivalism, Bundi, Colour, Enamels, Gum Arabic, Imagery, Tempera*; Illustrations–*Madhukar B. Bhat, Hemendranath Mazumdar, P.T. Reddy, Abanindranath Tagore.*

Transparent Allowing the *light* to pass through completely so that the objects lying beyond are fully visible.

In *painting* it refers to the method of using *overlapping*, transparent, thin *washes* or glazes, of *watercolour*, *ink* or *oil paint*, so as to let the lower layers be visible. Long-established *artists* used layers of transparent *colours* especially in *egg-tempera technique* and *oils* to build up their *composition*; e.g. *Jaganath M. Ahivasi*, *Hemendranath Mazumdar.* Refer *Acrylic Plastic*, *Aquarelle*, *Back-Glass Painting*, *Black*, *Blocking In*, *Egg-oil emulsion*, *Enamels*, *Film*, *Fresco*, *Glazing*, *India Ink*, *Wash (Technique)*, *Vidya Bhushan*, *Muhammed Abdur Rehman Chughtai*, *Arup Das*, *Dilip DasGupta*, *Pralhad A. Dhond*, *Sailoz Mookerjea*, *Bhanwar Singh Panwar*, *Surya Prakash*, *Pratima Sheth*, *Laxman Shreshtha*, *P.R. Thippeswamy.*

Treatment It is a method/process of making a work of *art*, and refers to the *creation* of a surface either in *painting*, *sculpture*, *graphic* or *printmaking*. e.g. *clay* could be moulded, *cement* could be sand blasted, *oil paintings* could be combed or dragged and *mixed media* used for *found objects* and *installation*. *Modern artists,* including *Nandalal Bose*, *Ramkinkar Baij*, *Abanindranath Tagore,* used different methods of treatment in the *creation* of *art.* Refer *Art Education*, *Bengal Revivalism*, *Narayanan Akkitham*, *Dashrath Patel*; Illustrations–*Ajanta*, *Aku*, *Nagji Patel*, *Embroidery*, *Hemendranath Mazumdar*, *Sailoz Mookerjea*, *Laxman Pai*, *Setlur Gopal Vasudev.*

Tree of Life The idea of Tree of Life has pervaded almost all ancient *cultures* of the world, ranging from Sumerian, Mesopotamian, Greek, Judeo-Christian, Mayan, Near and Middle Eastern, to Far Eastern, in their mythological and *spiritual* accounts. The Tree, in its various *forms*, but essentially the same significant characteristics, signifies eternal life, presence and unity with *god*, giver of *spiritual* wisdom, and a link between Heaven, Earth and the world beneath. The seeds and fruits of the Tree are symbols of immortality and continuous regeneration.

Thus, the Tree of Life is depicted in many different types of *art* works from different *cultures*, though symbolizing a common *theme*. Examples are:

Egyptian coffin covers depicting the dead, eating and drinking from The Tree; and other *artefacts* showing pharaohs being fed from the Tree of Life.

The Jewish Menorah (seven branched candlestand) is supposed to have originated from the Tree of Life myth.

In *Greek art*, the sacred palm symbol on the *gold* Vapphio cups from Crete; and *black* and red vases, showing Dionysius kneeling before a palm.

Tree of Life *designs* in near and middle eastern textiles and carpets.

Tree of Life *patterns*, adopted by Indian Calico printers and used in decorative textiles such as painted and dyed cotton bedspreads etc. in the 17th century.

Tribal Art The *art* of various indigenous tribes. A primitive, *spiritual* and decorative quality permeates the works which are mostly utilitarian. *Contemporary artists* have been influenced by the *images* and *motifs* of specific tribes, often incorporating its rough and ready character into their works. *Dokra casting* by the Bastars, and Warli rice-flour *painting* by the Warli Tribe of MAHA are among the most popularly known tribial art *forms*. Refer *Art*, *Cipher*, *Colour Wheel*, *Colour Circle*, *Culture*, *Decorative Art*, *Design*, *Idiom*, *Installation*, *Modern Style*, *Papier Mache*, *Patina*, *Warli Paintings*, *Arts and Crafts Movement*, *Bharat Bhavan*, *National Handicrafts & Handlooms Museum National Museum*, *Jyoti Bhatt*, *Ajit Chakravarti*, *Y.D. Deolalikar*, *Jamini Roy*, *P. Krishnamurthy*, *P.S. Nandhan*, *Vinod R. Parul*, *Jyoti Bhatt*, *Haku Shah.*

Tribhanga=Tri means "three" and Bhanga means "bend". The *classical* human *figure* in traditional Indian *painting* and *sculpture*, showing the pose at rest. It denotes bending of the body, at neck and the hips–so as to show the *figure* in a sinuous pose; similar to the 'S' bend of *Greek art./* Classical Refer *Ajanta* (BODDHISATTVA Padmapani), *Contrapposto*, *Gandharan Art.*

Triennale An *exhibition* of *art*, usually at the international level, which is held every three years by *LKA* who first hosted the Triennale India in 1968. The idea is to provide a forum to the *artists* of the world to gather on a common platform. So far ten triennales have been held in India.

Trindade, Antonio X. (1870–1935) b. Goa. Education: *JJSA*. Group participations: *BAS exhibitions*. Awards: Mayo Silver Medal *JJSA*, *BAS* Gold Medals, Governor's Prize. Commissions: Several *portraits*. *Auctions*: Christie's London. Collections: *NGMA* New Delhi, *JJSA.*

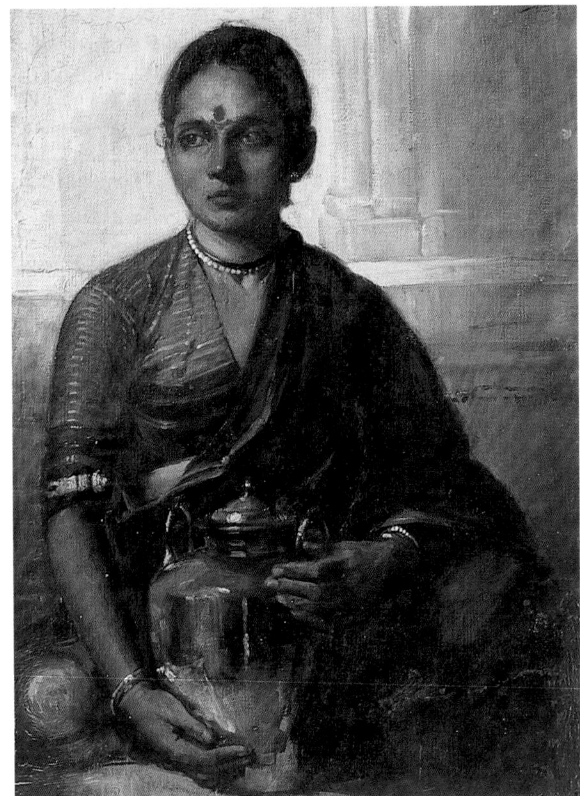

Trindade, Antonio X.: "A Hindu Girl", *Oils*, 1925, 72x52.5 cm.

After studying *art* at *JJSA*, he began teaching at his alma-mater, in addition to the work he did with Raja Deen Dayal, a leading photographer, as a commissioned *painter* of *portraits*. His mastery over Western *styles* and *techniques*, with his use of Tenebrism (name given to the *technique* of extreme *chiaroscuro* used by the mannerist and *Baroque* artists in the 17th century) and *compositions* akin to the early works of the Spanish *Baroque painter*, D.R. des Velasquez made him a popular figure with his patrons, especially the Nawabs of Hyderabad. Other than *portraits*, his forte was intimate interiors featuring his wife and daughters. Being a Christian, he also painted Biblical subjects, one of which was "Ecce Homo". It was an elegant conception of the face of Christ.

Triptych Three painted panels, usually of *wood*, hinged together, to either *form* one single *composition* or three separate compatible *compositions*. Two outer panels can sometimes be closed over the center panel. *Altarpieces* were frequently made in a *form* of a triptych. In India, carved or painted, decorative *wood* panels also made a triptych. Refer *Diptych*, *Arpana Caur*, *Kanchan Chander*.

Trivedi, P. Vinay (1929– d.) b. Bhavnagar, Education: GUJ. B.A. in *FA*. *MSU*. Solos: *JAG*. Group shows: TAG, *JAG*. Group participations: National *LKA* exhibitions. *Art* camp: GUJ *artists* camp. Awards: Saurashtra Govt. Scholarship. Member: Baroda group of *artists* 1956–60. Commissions: Several for pvt. & public institutions Vadodara, New Delhi, Nagda; A *painting* for Parliament House New Delhi; International: Canada. Appointments: Lectures *FFA* Dept. *Applied Art MSU*. Publications: "Indian Express" & on "Folk Traditions"–"Times of India" Mumbai. Collections: *LKA* GUJ, *BKB* Varanasi.

Vinay P. Trivedi attempted a judicious blend of folk inspired *art* with Pop *imagery*. The *motifs* originate from Saurashtrian *embroidery*. His *paintings* are basically simple, decorative *narratives* with folk songs and film songs deftly interwoven into the flat *compositions*. His main *medium* was *waterproof ink* and *oils*, with the *themes* exploring the KRISHNA *legend*. He lived and worked in Vadodara, where he retired as a Reader from the *FFA* (*MSU*), in 1989.

Trompe L'oeil (French)=deceiving the eye, *illusion*. This *term* refers to a type of *painting*, in which the two-dimensional surface appears to be *realistic* giving a three-dimensional effect. While this was commonly soon in the West, from the Roman times, Indian *art* was *symbolic* rather than *realistic*. However with the British arriving in India, this *technique* seen became widely used and admired. *Portraits* done by *Raja Ravi Varma* were much sought after not only because of the likeness of the sitter, but because of his *realistic handling* of sari borders and the illusionistic gleam of pearls and gold jewellery. This type of *painting* is especially perfect for e.g. D.C. Jogleker, *K.B. Kulkarni*, *Muhammed Abdur Rehman Chughtai* and many others. Refer *Fine Arts*, *Depth*, *Dimension*, *Drapery*, *Foreshortening*, *Landscape*, *Monocular Vision*, *Value*, *Jamini P. Gangooly*.

Turpentine It is a moderately toxic, anhydrous and colourless or slightly yellow solvent. Along with linseed *oil*, it is used for mixing *colours*, and for varnishing. It has a distinctive sharp odour and evaporates, leaving a gummy residue that does not detract from the brightness of the *pigment*. Turpentine is also used in *modelling wax*.

Dilute turpentine is mixed with the *paint* in order to make it dry quickly. The process is also used by the *artists* to feature thin glazes of *paint*, spontaneous *brushwork*, and brisk wiping. Various experiments and *techniques* are used by *artists* to create subtle blends of *light* and *shade*, e.g. *Hemendranath Mazumdar*. The first extensive use of *oil paints* with turpentine in India was found in the *Bengal School* in 19th century. Refer *Canvas Test*, *Fat over lean*, *Lean*, *Oil Painting*, *Overlapping*, *Treatment*, *Transparent*, *Translucent*, *Varnish*, *D.B. "Deven" Seth*, *Abanindranath Tagore*, *Raja Ravi Varma*, *V. Viswanadhan*; *"Preservation of Art Objects"–O.P. Agrawal*, p. 383.

Two-Point Perspective A *composition*, which uses two *vanishing points* to create a three-dimensional effect, instead of a traditional single *vanishing point*. Refer *Backdrop*, *Bengal School*, *Company School*, *Eye-Level*, *Horizon*, *Illusion*, *Illusionism*, *One-Point Perspective*, *Orthogonal*, *Perspective*, *Picture Space*; Illustration–*Pralhad A. Dhond*, *Paresh Maity*, *Baburao Painter*, *Amrut Patel*, *Sudhir Patwardhan*, *Ramesh Rao*, *Gaganendranath Tagore*, *Sarada Charan Ukil*.

Tyagi, Haripal (1934–) b. Bijnor, UP. Self-taught *artist*. Over 11 solos: Kala Mela Moradabad, at a Club Nainital, SRAG, TKS, *AIFACS*. Group participations: Garhwal, National *LKA* exhibitions, *AIFACS*. Workshop: Garhwal UP All India Senior Camps *AIFACS*. Awards: RAJ *LKA*, All India Exhibitions.

Haripal Tyagi is basically a *figurative painter*, using *distortion* and simplification of *form* where he deems important. Both *colour* and *line* act independently in his works, yet the general effect is that of a unified, balanced *composition*. The animals and birds in his works are the survivors of a chaotic world, they are the innocent victims of mankind's greed and vanity. The diagonal slashes across the *canvas* indicate this passion for destruction, while the short, impasted *brush* and knife strokes herald the beginning of a new day.

He lives and works in New Delhi.

U

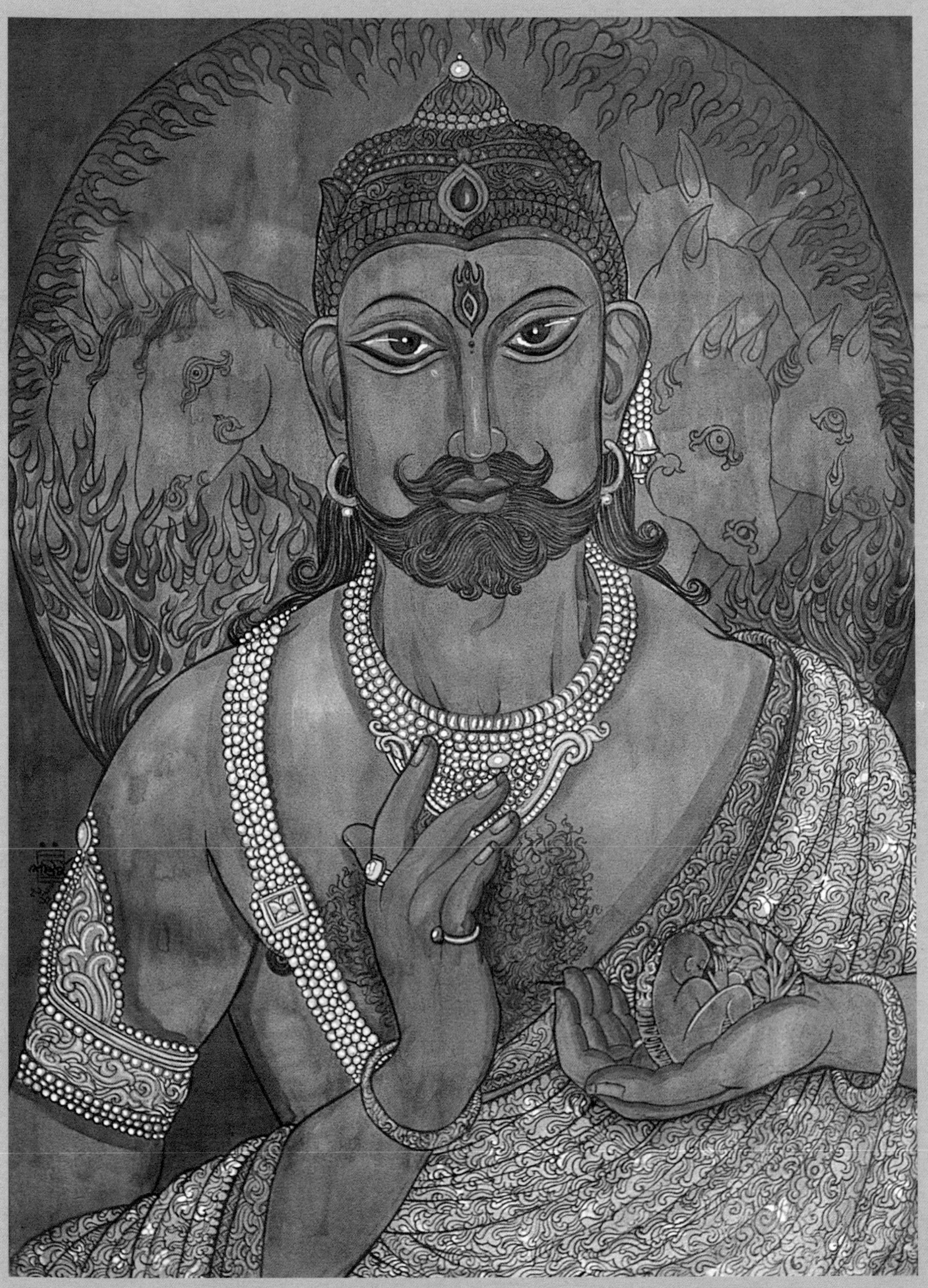

Ukil, Shantanu: "Sun God", *Watercolour Wash*, 100x75 cm. (See notes on page 361)

Ukil, Sarada Charan (1888–1940) b. Dhaka, now Bangladesh. Education: GSA Kolkata; Later studied *painting* under *Abanindranath Tagore*. Solos & group participations: Delhi, Mysore, *ISOA, BAS*; International: Paris, London, Geneva, Dublin, New York. *Auctions*: Christie's & Sotheby's London, Sotheby's New York, Bowring's New Delhi & Mumbai. Awards: Viceroys Cup Delhi, Maharaja Mysore prize at DAE, Gold Medal *BAS, AIFACS*. Member: *AIFACS*, Founder member *SUSA* 1926 New Delhi. Commissions: *Murals* in *egg-tempera* for the Maharaja of Bilaspur. Publications: In "Roop-Lekha" New Delhi, *AIFACS*. Collections: New Delhi, Vadodara, Harad-pur, Patiala, Mysore Art Gallery, pvt. & royal in India & England.

Sarada Charan Ukil's early works were all produced in the *manner* of the *Bengal School*, first outlining the *design* with light strokes of the *brush* and later laying the principal *colours* in *watercolours*. The whole *painting* was later washed with water, causing the *colours* to blend. The whole process was repeated time and again until the desired *depth* and *tone* were achieved with fine linear *brushwork*.

Sarada Charan Ukil's *line drawings* were not mere *sketches*, but look like his finished works. His *figures* were delicately rendered in a *manner* similar to the *Ajanta style* of *draughtsmanship*, with an element of romanticized *form* and *colour*. His women were like ethereal, personalized visions of clinging creepers and vine-like branches. Sarada Charan Ukil was also a practitioner of *egg-tempera* and *painting* on silk, executing one of the largest silk *paintings* on the KRISHNA *theme*. Mythological and literary subjects were the *themes* that he drew from most often. His mastery is obvious from the fact that his *painting* on silk can be seen from both sides of the screen.

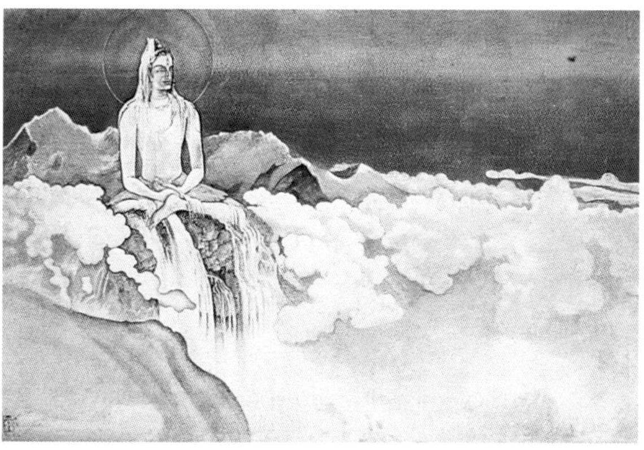

Ukil, Sarada Charan: "Mount Kailash", *Watercolours*, early 20th century, 49.5x72.4 cm.

Ukil, Shantanu (1927–) b. Kolkata. Education: *SUSA* New Delhi; Advance study in *FA*. Kyoto Japan; Post-Dip. *FA*. Germany. Solos: Son-et-Lumiere Mumbai, TAG. Group participations: *LKA* New Delhi; International: Dresden, Germany. Awards: India and abroad including USA, Cambridge England. Founder member: Indian Art Association, National Committees; International: Association of Art in India. Commi-ssions: *Frescoes* & *murals* in Delhi. Appointments: Delivered slide shows & lectures on Modern & Contemporary Indian Art in Europe & Japan. Collections: Mysore Museum, *Chandigarh Museum*; International: Heritage Gallery USSR, Museum of Finland, France, Germany, Denmark, Cairo, Poland, Japan, USA, China & pvt.

Shantanu Ukil, the son of *Sarada Charan Ukil*, was educated in the family-run *SUSA* in New Delhi. The *style* practised there was a romanticized rendering of *colour*. His *watercolours* are enlivened by small linear detailing of *drapery* and the flowing tresses of *gods* and goddesses. He later started using *gouache*, *acrylic*, affecting a drastic change of *texture* and *form* in his works. These works have a strong sense of the *post-Modern* in their abbreviated use of *line* and *discordant* use of *texture*, yet they remain Indian in ethos. "The song of the Baul" is one example of this assimilation of the East and the West.

Shantanu Ukil lives and works in both *Santiniketan* and New Delhi. (See illustration on page 360)

Undercut 1. In *casting*, that part or projecting portion of a three-dimensional object or *mould* that prevents easy removal of the *positive* impression. Refer *Bronze, Cast, Cire Perdue, Copper*. **2.** Undercutting, in *etching*, refers to the fault or accident, which occurs when *acid* erodes or eats through fine *pattern*, causing *lines* or separate areas to merge or widen. e.g. *Krishna N. Reddy*. Refer *Printmaking, Intagleo, Jyoti Bhatt, Arun Bose, Naina Dalal*.

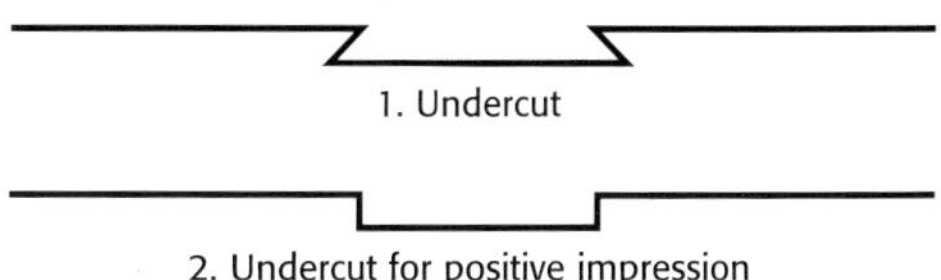

Underpainting A *term* used in *oil painting*. It is the laying in of *forms* and *tonal values* in *monochrome* before applying the areas of *local colour*. The underpainting is done only after the *canvas* is prepared. The word can also be applied to a layer of *colour* over which a glaze is applied or *scumbling* is done. Refer *Back-Glass Painting, Blocking in, Colour Ground, Facing, Fat over lean, Fresco, Glazing, Opacity, Overlapping, Sgraffito*.

Upanishad Upa=near, ni=down, shad=sit. It tells us that VEDAS, history, science and other studies mean progression by *god*. This is achieved by a group of pupils who sit down near the teacher to learn from his secret doctrines. Upanishad is a text in prose and verse, composed between 600 BC–200 BC. They mark the beginning of mysticism and Hindu philosophy. Refer *Hinduism*.

Ushnisha The protuberance, which usually appears as a top-knot on BUDDHA's head. It is one of the 32 Mahapurusha Lakshana (signs of a great being) and signifies his superior knowledge and self-control. It is usually covered with small snail-shell curls in Satavahana *sculpture* while the Mathura *sculptures* depict it as a simple twisted knot. Also a turban. Refer *Buddhist Art, Gandharan Art, Icon, Mathura Art*.

Utkanthita, Utka One of the eight specific types of NAYIKAS (heroines) mentioned by ancient Indian writers and poets. She is depicted as sitting on a large bed of leaves in the forest, yearning for her lover, who has been inadvertently delayed elsewhere. Refer ASHTANAYIKA.

V

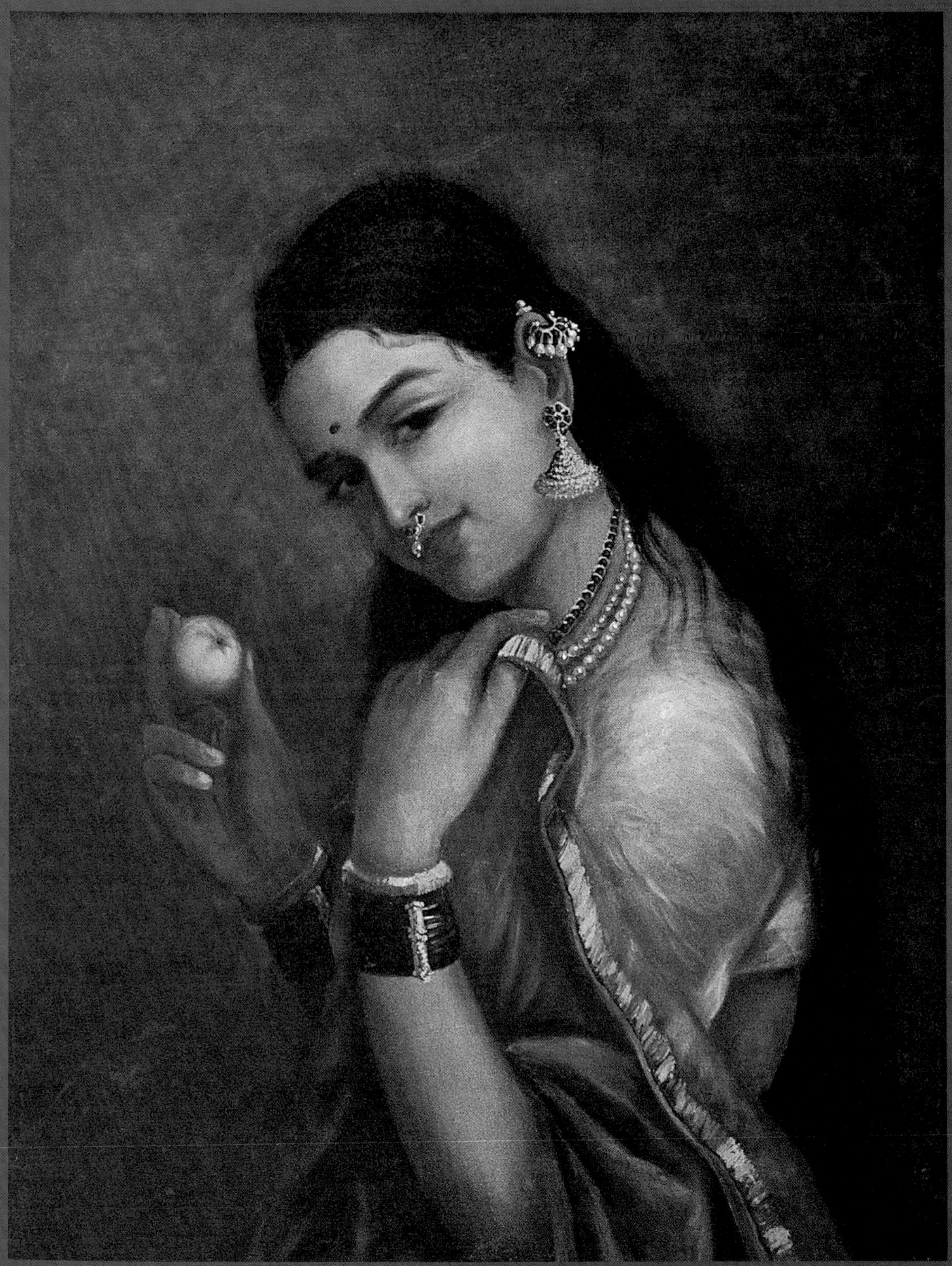

Varma, *Raja Ravi*: "A Woman holding a Fruit", *Oil* on *Canvas*, 45x60 cm. (See notes on page 364)

V Tool A V-shaped cutting edge with a wooden handle used for linoleum cutting, and *engraving* to create a rich and simple *black* and *white* and multi-colour *prints*. *Nandalal Bose's designs* were based on simple *motifs* and *design*, clear arrangement with space and *balance* of *black* and *white*. This was as early as 1930. Refer *Block Printing, Gouge, Linocut, Relief Printing, Rani Chanda, Shanti Dave, Rini Dhumal, Somnath Hore, Paul A. Koli, Sukhamoy Mitra, Ashit Paul.*

Vadehra Art Gallery (VAG) (New Delhi). VAG promotes *contemporary* Indian *art* and also has permanent collections of *paintings* by both young and established Indian *artists* of India and abroad, by which they have taken part in *auctions*. VAG has held retrospectives of eminent Indian *painters* such as *Ram Kumar, Sayed Haider Raza* and Raghu Rai. It has an active publication activity concentrating on *post-Independence art*. Other *artists* who held their *exhibitions* at VAG include *J. Swaminathan, K.K. Hebbar, Maqbool Fida Husain, Jogen Chowdhury, Arup Das, Arpita Singh, Manu Parekh, Paramjit Singh, Tyeb Mehta, Prabhakar Kolte, Bhupen Khakhar.*

Vahana The mount or vehicle of various *gods* and deities. In the case of VISHNU, it is GARUDA, the half-man half-eagle, though VISHNU also reclines on ANANTA or Shesha, the multi-hooded snake. SHIVA's vehicle is NANDI (bull), whose seated *sculpture* adorns every SHIVA temple, while BRAHMA's is HAMSA (swan), so also SARASVATI. The Goddess LAKSHMI is usually represented on a lotus, while INDRA, the King of *Gods* is mounted on the *white* elephant, Airavata. Refer MAKARA, PADMA; Illustration— *Mrinalini Mukherjee.*

Vaidyanathan, Radhika (1963–) b. Madurai, TN. Education: Dip. in *industrial design* (*ceramics*) NID, M.FA. Tama Art University Tokyo Japan. Group participations: *LKA* & *GE* New Delhi, *LCAG*; International: Kyoto, Tokyo Japan. Awards: Japanese Govt. Scholarship to study *ceramics* in Japan; "Saji Prize" Tokyo Japan, *Artist* of the Month MMB Chennai. Editorial Assistant: Catalogue of *exhibition* "Form & Many Forms of Mother Clay" by *Haku Shah* New Delhi; Documented the process of *ritual terracotta* in TN. Worked: in *ceramics* Pondicherry & *LKA* Chennai; International: Japan. Collections: Suntory Museum Japan, pvt. & corporates.

While a student of *industrial design*, Radhika Vaidyanathan worked with *ceramics*, explored the creative possibilities of *clay*. Working with surface *textures*, *firing* methods and glazes, she used materials such as sand, *metal* sheets and pieces to complete her *sculptures*. *Nature* and its many *forms* shape her ideas, which incorporate her interest in *ritual* and functional *terracottas*. It is Indian *terracotta* with its *balance* of relationship between man, society, material and expression of the *spiritual* and the *metaphysical* that especially manifests itself in her *installations* of standing and suspended *forms*. The titles too suggest this continuous relationship between earth, sky, water and fire.

She lives in Chennai.

Vaij, Ramkinkar Refer *Ramkinkar Baij.*

Vaikuntham, Thotha (1942–) b. Boorugupalli, AP. Education: Dip. in *painting* College of FA. & *Architecture* Hyderabad. Solos: Chennai, KB & MMB Hyderabad, HAS, *SUG, CYAG, GE, AIFACS, G88, CRAR*; International: London. Group participations: MMB Hyderabad, *Triennales* New Delhi, Marvel Art Gallery Ahmedabad, *SJM*. *Art* camps & workshops: *GAC*, *Graphic* workshop All India Artists camp, *Terracotta* workshop Hyderabad. *Auctions*: Heart Mumbai & New Delhi. Awards: *AFA* Kolkata, Mahakoshal Kala Samiti MP, National *LKA* New Delhi HAS, *BB*. Fellowship: AP *LKA* Hyderabad to study *painting* in *MSU*. Collections: Hyderabad, *NGMA* & *LKA* New Delhi, *SJM*; International: Glenbarra Museum Japan, Chester & Davida Herwitz Charitable Trust USA & pvt.

Thotha Vaikuntham is known for his *acrylic* and *mixed media portraits* of his native Telangana women with their dark-complexioned faces accented by bright red vermilion dots against a sandalwood smeared forehead. Their voluptuous pot-bellied bodies are draped in brightly coloured polka-dotted sarees, adorned with glinting nose-rings and an array of bangles making them more sensuous and dynamic. Thotha Vaikuntham's work is singular for the application of linear *detail*, with meticulous attention being paid to coiffure and jewellery. These small-sized *paper* works are

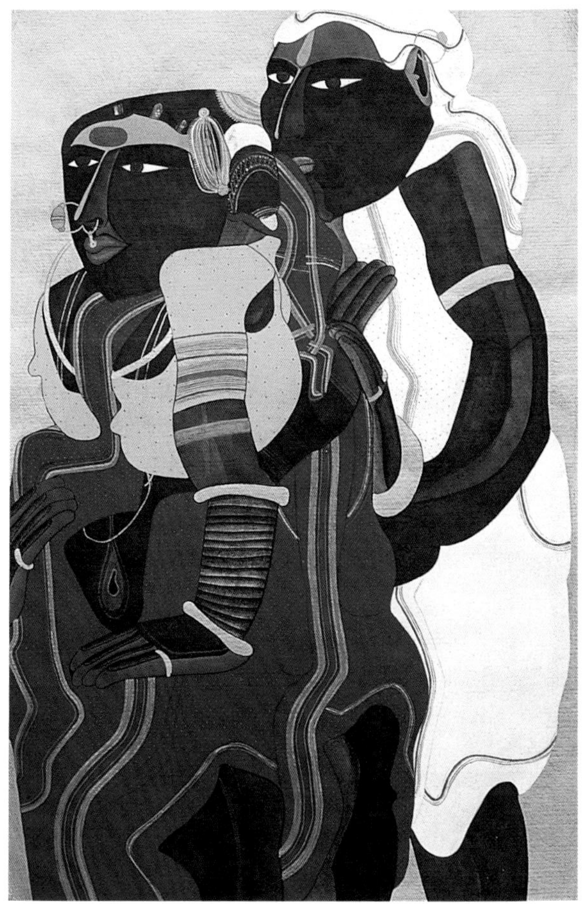

Vaikuntham, Thotha: "Nayika and Nayaka", 75x45 cm.

painted in twos or threes. He has recently included male *figures* in his repertoire of *images*.

He lives and works in Hyderabad, and also the staff of Jawahar Bal Bhavan.

Value As in *tonal values*, this refers to the relationship between variations in *gradation* or *tones*, i.e. from *light* to dark, seen in any object. For example the *tonal value* of *black* is low, while that of *white* is high. In Indian art traditional value of *balance*, *harmony* and *composition* was accomplished more in *painting* than in *sculpture*. The *creation* of a three-dimensional effect in primary *sketches* of *painting and drawing gives tonal value* on a flat surface. This was first seen in the Mughal miniatures of the Jehangiri period. Later, *artists* of the *Company School*, being influenced by European *artists* used *cross-hatching* and other *techniques* to achieve *tonal values*. Refer *Colour*, *Hue*, *Mughal Dynasty*, *Tint*, *Narayan S. Bendre*, *Prem Chandra Goswami*, *Dattatray B. Pardeshi*, *Abanindranath Tagore*, *Gaganendranath Tagore*.

Vamana-Trivikrama Refer DASAVATARA, PURANA; Illustration–VISHNU.

Vanishing Point It is an illusory fixed point in the system of *perspective* where parallel *lines* receding from the picture plane, appear to converge. In India, with subjects such as *portraits*, *figurative art*, *realistic landscapes*, *perspective* was popularized by the *artists* of the Academic Schools. Refer *Aerial Perspective*, *Atmosphere*, *Backdrop*, *Balance*, *Space*, *Bengal School*, *Bombay School*, *Calcutta School*, *Madras School of Art*, *Jaganath M. Ahivasi*, *Shanti Banerjea*, *Pestonjee Bomanjee*, *Nandalal Bose*, *Vidya Bhushan*, *Kanu Desai*, *Asit K. Haldar*, *Baburao Painter*, *Gaganendranath Tagore*.

Varada-Mudra Refer *Buddhist Art*, MUDRAS or Hastas, VISHNU.

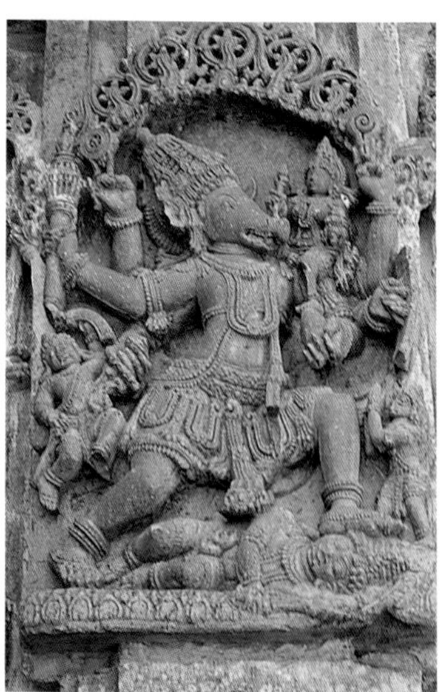

Varahavatara One of the ten incarnations of VISHNU the giant boar *form* created to lift the earth, BHUDEVI, from the *depths* of the ocean. It is represented in PALLAVA *sculpture* with the face of a boar and the body of a man with BHUDEVI clinging to his tusks. Refer BHUDEVI, *Iconography*, *Iconology*, PURANA.

Varahavatara: "The Giant Boar", Belur.

Variant Usually denotes a *copy*, or a slightly different version of a work of *art*, with minor variation in *composition* or execution. It may be made by the same *artist*, like *Raja Ravi Varma's* variations of "Ravana killing Jatayu"; by his assistants under supervision, or by different *artists*. Refer *Reproduction*.

Varma, Raja Ravi (1848–1906) b. Killmanoor, Princely State of Travancore, Kerala. Self-taught *painter*, studied *techniques* of Theodore Jansen, Ramaswami Nayadu, his uncle Raja Raja Varma & Frank Brooks (RAA). Solos & selected *exhibition* Chennai (Madras), *Maharaja Fatesingh Museum* of Baroda Vadodara, *Mewar* Udaipur, *BAS*, *CTAG*, 1993 *exhibition* of the collection from *CHAG*, *NGMA* & pvt. collections *National Museum* New Delhi; International: 1893 World's Columbian Exhibition Chicago, Vienna Italy. Group participations: Chennai, Pune, Mumbai, Kolkata, New Delhi. *Auctions*: Christie's, Sotheby's, Heart & Osian's. Awards: First prize & Gold Medal Chennai, Medal Chicago. Hon. & Certificate: First honour Maharaja of Travancore in Madras, Gaekwad Gold Medal Vadodara; International: Vienna, British Govt. London. Commssions: Mumbai, *Maharaja Fatesingh Museum* of Baroda Vadodara, *paintings* & *portraits* at Royal Palaces Vadodara & Mysore. Publications: *Prints* of his works; Later books & catalogues by *CTAG*; Printed oleographs at his press in Mumbai in 1894–1901; A film "Raja Ravi Varma" was made on his life; Publications include several books and articles. Collections: Pranlal Bhogilal Mumbai, Dept. of Archaeology Museum MAHA State, Laxmi Vilas Palace Vadodara, Jaganmohan Art Gallery & Mysore Palace Mysore, Udaipur Palace, *NGMA* New Delhi, *CTAG*, *PWM*, *SJM*; International: V&A.

Raja Ravi Varma was one of the first Indian *painters* to use the *medium* of *oil* on *canvas* in *painting*. After the initial exploratory forays, he mastered the *technique*, evolving a personal *style* from his exposure to Western *Art*. Raja Ravi Varma's *paintings*, though thematically Indian, were basically influenced by Western academicism, specifically the use of *perspective* and *chiaroscuro* in addition to the study of *anatomy* and balanced *composition*. His subjects included scenes from the *epics*, especially the RAMAYANA and MAHABHARATA and *classical* literature by Kalidas; he was specially commissioned to *paint portraits* for several royal families while his *compositions* of *contemporary* women were famed for their grace and femininity. His *portraits* are majestic, with the *drapery*, costumes and jewellery rendered in great *detail*. His *compositions* are always harmoniously balanced, being pyramidal in structure and his colouring *realistic*. In 1890s, Raja Ravi Varma set up a press in partnership with Mumbai merchants. He specialized in lithographic *reproductions* of Indian *gods* and goddesses particularly LAKSHMI, SARASVATI and KRISHNA. In later life he took up ceremonial duties as guardian of the Prince of Travancore, thereby, reducing his output of *art* works. Of all the *artists* of *modern* India, he was the one who made the maximum trend setting-impact. His work was impressive and became highly debated, sponsored and patronized. He infringed upon the artistic conventions of his time, allowed his creative faculty to soar above the commonplace and created an artistic world so very much his own that it was incomparable with any that prevailed in the *contemporary* artistic vision. He stood before the world as vindicator of both *realism* and symbology. His *paintings* are often finished to the extreme thereby *drawing* closer even the most uninterested observer. So intense was his idealism that the heat and radiance of his *colours* comes through even though cloaked under the weight of *realism*.

Raja Ravi Varma's contribution is not just restricted to the field of *art*, but was also apparent in theatre, in set *design*, posture, advertisments and indeed in the entire cultural field in India. His *paintings* which were oleographed, adorned the walls of nearly every Indian home and Hindu Puja rooms in the early 20th century; colouring the Hindu perception of *gods*. Refer *Oleography*. (See illustration on page 362)

Varma, Umesh (1935–) b. Banda, UP. Education: NDFA New Delhi Polytechnic. Solos: SC, TKS, *VAG*, *Dhoomimal*; International: Japan. Group participations: *LKA* & Kunika New Delhi, *AIFACS*, SC, SRAG, *VAG*, TAG, *JAG*, other *exhibitions* in Ambala, Ludhiana, Bangalore; International: Japan, Philipines, USA, Russia. *Art* camps & workshops: SKP *painting*, Dept. of Culture Allahabad, Hardwar camp, Gallery Aurobindo Mussoori, Paul Lingren's *graphic* workshop New Delhi, USIS *printmaking* workshop, Creative Photography workshop *GAC*. Awards: Ludhiana, All India FA. Gold Medal Ambala, *Sailoz Mookerjea's* Prize & *LKA* Research Grant New Delhi. Senior Fellowship: Dept. of Culture Govt. of India, *AIFACS*. Appointments: Assistant Editor Contemporary *LKA* & Visiting Lecturer *College of Art* New Delhi; Also Educationist & Freelance *art critic*. Collections: PUJ University Museum, Govt. Museum Chandigarh, *College of Art*, *LKA* & *NGMA* New Delhi, SKP; Institutions: Japan, USA, Switzerland.

Umesh Varma's works are related to the social milieu that he hails from with his personal *symbolism*. It is his repertoire of grotesque *images* that strikes the eye first; with humans briefly becoming bulls, cows, tigers and wolves. He identifies these decorative *figures* to the animal or its trait, running within each human. His works are thus private *allegories* in *colour* or in *black* and *white*. Umesh Varma, who is a poet and a printmaker as well, has also researched folk *techniques* in Japanese *ceramics*.

He lives in New Delhi.

Varnish Varnish is *transparent* liquid substance of natural or *synthetic* resins. When applied to a surface, it dries to *form* a strong and glossy protective coating. A varnish is applied to a *plate* as an *acid* resisting *film* in *etching*. e.g. *Printmaking*, *Intaglio*, *Jyoti Bhatt*, *Naina Dalal*, *Amitabha Banerjee*, *Anupam Sud*, *Somnath Hore*, *Krishna N. Reddy*. There are many different types of varnish, used for different purposes e.g. **1.** Resin dissolved in a solvent, commonly used in *oil paintings*, which dries by evaporation of the solvent. **2.** Resin cooked in *drying oil* and thinned with *turpentine*, which dries by a more complex process similar to drying of *oil paint*. e.g. *Raja Ravi Varma*. **3.** *Lacquers*, based on vinyl resin are also used as varnish, as are *enamels*, which are combinations of varnish and *oil*. e.g. *Shankar Nandagopal*, *Bhanwar Singh Panwar*, *Setlur Gopal Vasudev*, *Siona Benjamin*, *Balan Nambiar*, *Bishamber Khanna*. **4.** *Wax* based varnish also gives a *matte* finish. e.g. *Encaustic*, *Eric Brown*, *Shanti Dave*, *Ramlal Dhar*. Refer Aquatint, *Brass*, *Bite*, *Biting in*, *Cire Perdue*, *Crayon Manner*, *Etching*, *Film*, *Fixative Lacquer*, *Fresco*, *Oil*, *Sugar Lift*, *Tempera*, *Rabindranath Tagore*.

Vasakasajja Vasaka=bed chamber, Sajja or Sajjika= A woman ready to receive her lover. One of the eight specific types of NAYIKAS (heroines) mentioned by ancient Indian writers and poets. She eagerly awaits her lover, having dressed and perfumed herself. A bed decorated with flowers and garlands is usually depicted as well. Refer ASHTANAYIKA.

Vasudev, Arnawaz (1945–1988) b. Chennai, TN. Education: Dip. *GCAC* Chennai. Solos: New Delhi, Bangalore, *CYAG*, International: Canada, USA. Group shows: Chennai, Mumbai, Hyderabad, Kolkata, Bangalore, New Delhi. Group participations: British council & *LKA* Chennai, *LKA* New Delhi, *SAI*; International: Italy, Japan. *Auctions*: Heart Mumbai. Award: *LKA* Chennai. Commissions: *Murals* for banks in Chennai. Collections: *NGMA* & *LKA* New Delhi, Shaw Wallace Chennai; International: Smithsonian Institute USA.

Arnawaz Vasudev *drawings* in *pen* and *ink washes* are based on *fantasy*. The wiry, curvilinear *lines* combined with lightly stained and marbled areas of coloured *wash technique*, suggesting *space* and *depth*, in addition to the decorative folk inspired aspect of her *imagery*. She was inspired by traditional *crafts*, including Kolam—a type of floor decoration and *nature*; incorporating the cactii and other plant shapes that she found around her. In addition to her *drawings*, she also worked with *batik*, at the *COAG craft* counter; as well as delicate *copper* and *silver* bowls, embossed and stamped with her personal *imagery* of lotus blossoms and other organic shapes. Her series of works inspired by the RAMAYANA *paintings* belonging to the medieval era stands out for its energetic use of *pattern* and notation.

Vasudev, Setlur Gopal (1941–) b. Mysore. Education: Govt. Dip. in *FA*. *GCAC* Chennai. Solos: Bangalore, Chennai, Mumbai, New Delhi, Dharwad, Marvel Art Gallery Ahmedabad; International: Canada, USA, Germany. Group shows: COAG, *CYAG*, others in New Delhi, Goa, Bangalore. Group participations: *LKA* & *Triennales* New Delhi, *AFA* Kolkata, KAR *LKA* Bangalore; International: Norway, Denmark, London, Belgium, National Gallery of Modern Art USA, *Biennale* France & Cuba, Festival of India Japan. *Art* camps: KAR *CKP* & *LKA*, in all Kala Mela Bangalore, other camps also in Hyderabad, Mangalore, Kolkata, Chennai & Srinagar. Awards: Govt. of India Scholarship *Painting*, National Award *LKA* New Delhi, State Award KAR *LKA* Bangalore, TN *LKA*. Founder member: *Cholamandal*. Commissions: Several *murals* in *copper*, powdered glass & *enamel* in Chennai & Bangalore; International: New York. Collections: *NGMA* & *LKA* New Delhi, KAR *LKA* Bangalore, TN *LKA* & National Art Gallery Chennai, *Chandigarh Museum*, *GC* & *SG* Mumbai, Chanakya New Delhi, *VEAG*, *SJM*, *PUAG*, *CRAR*, corporates & pvt.

Setlur Gopal Vasudev's *paintings* are based on myths drawn from various sources including folklore, *legend* and Indian *mythology*. It is the concept of the MITHUNA (the loving couple) that forms his main thematic concern, however this is not just limited to the relationships between man and woman, it also encompasses the relationship between the sun, moon, earth, sky, stars and clouds; bird, reptile, fish, fowl, seed and fruit. These various elements along with his Kalpavriksha (*Tree of Life*) animate his *painting* with its emphasis on *drawing* and importance in colouring. His *pen* and *ink drawings* reveal his mastery over *texture* and *pattern*, while his *oil paintings* are his spontaneous brushstrokes, and other textural *techniques*, all filling in and carving out of fluid *colour*.

Setlur Gopal Vasudev lives and works in Bangalore.

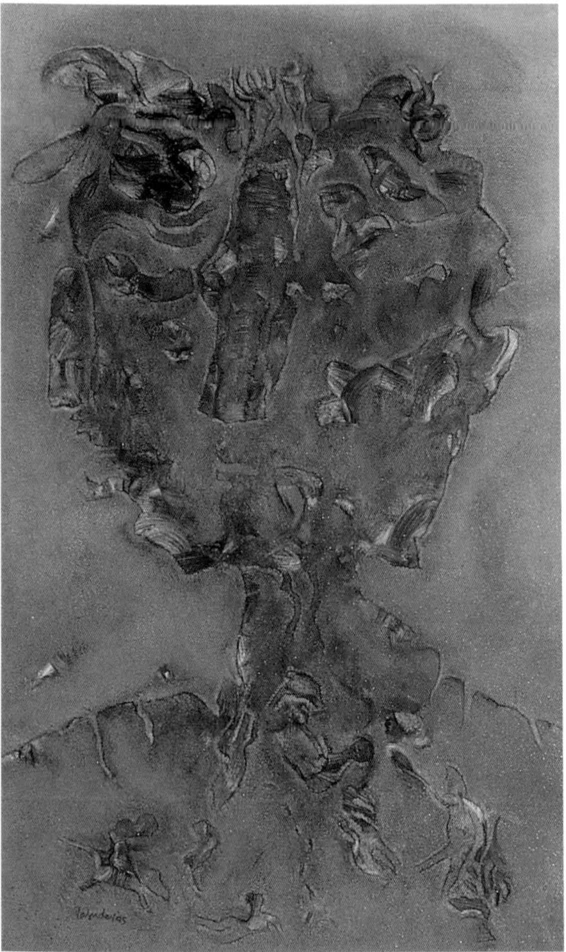

Vasudev, Setlur Gopal: "Humanscape", *Oil* on *Canvas*, 1995.

Vatsa, Sushil (1930–) b. UP. Self-taught *painter*, *sculptor* & writer. Solos: Mussoorie, IAFA Amritsar, Kunika Chemould & *LKA* New Delhi, SC, *AIFACS*, SRAG, TKS, TAG; International: Germany. Group participations: *LKA* & Kala Mela New Delhi, IAFA Amritsar, *AIFACS*, SKP, *BAS*; International: Tokyo, London, Alabama USA. Awards: National *LKA* Award, Veteran Artist *AIFACS*, IAFA Amritsar Gold Medal, "Kala Pujari" title by World Council of Art Culture New Delhi, *AIFACS*, SKP. Fellowship: UNESCO. Commissions: *Murals* New Delhi, Allahabad, UP. Appointments: President (Group of All Indian Artists) New Delhi. Collections: *NGMA*, *LKA* & *College of Art* New Delhi, PUJ Museum Chandigarh, *Roopankar BB*, *AIFACS*.

A centrifugal force seems to hold Sushil Vatsa's *forms* in the centre of the *canvas*, which seems ready to release the imprisioned blobs of *pigment*; a virtual whirpool-like effect can be seen in most of his works whether they be *paintings* in *oils*, *acrylics* or litho *prints*. Sushil Vatsa speaks of these ovoids as rockscapes and inscapes in a dream world. His *drawings* capture fractured *fragments* of rocky terrains and landscape-like *forms*.

He lives and works in New Delhi and California.

Veda SANSKRIT word meaning knowledge. The vedas were the Ancient Indian texts of prayers, hymns, *rituals* and doctrines of worship to the elements and *gods* like AGNI (fire), Vayu (wind), Varuna (sky), INDRA (moon) and SURYA (sun). They were thought to have been composed and transmitted in oral *tradition*, between circa 5000 and 2500 BC. Initially there were three Vedic texts: **1.** RIG-VEDA **2.** Yajur-Veda and **3.** Sama-Veda. Subsequently a fourth veda i.e. Atharva-Veda was added. Each Veda essentially consists of two parts: **1.** Samhitas or collection of MANTRAS—Hymns and prayers and **2.** Brahmanas—explanations and meanings of religious rules, *rituals* and formulae. Attached to each Brahmana, is an UPANISHAD, which is a mystical doctrine on nature of *God* and relationship between soul and matter. Refer *Hinduism*, VISHNU.

Vegad, Amrit Lal (1928–) b. Jabalpur, MP. Education: Dip. in *FA.* & *Mural* specialist *KB Santiniketan*. Solos: *AFA* Kolkata, *LKA* by NZCC in New Delhi, Museum Bhopal, Indore, *JAG*. Group participations: *BAAC* Kolkata, Art from MP in New Delhi, *BB*. *Art* camps: AIKS & All India Graphics camp *BB*, *Artists* camp Allahabad, Rajahmundry. Awards: MPKP Bhopal, Veteran *Artist AIFACS*. Appointments: Lecturer at Govt. Kalaniketan Jabapur. Publications: Book in Hindi. Collection: MKKP Central India.

Amrit Lal Vegad's works are concerned with people and their environs, which capture the interaction between these two elemental forces of *nature* in his *collages* or as he *terms* them, "collatings" (*collage paintings*). The river Narmada, has formed his chief subject for the past two decades. The *sketches* that he executed while trekking the 1800 km stretch of the river were later developed into exquisitely detailed *collages*, that pulsate with vibrant *colour*s and *texture*.

He lives and works in Jabalpur MP.

Vehicle is a fluid *medium* in which the *pigments* are suspended, with the result they adhere to the surface. It may be combined with a binder or other additives such as solvents, driers, or preservatives. Refer *Dyestuff*, *Egg-oil emulsion*, *Miniature Painting*, *Nature*, *Paint*.

Venkatapathy, D. (1935–) b. Vellore, TN. Education: *Fresco painting Banasthali Vidyapith* RAJ, Dip. *painting GCAC* Chennai. Group participations: *LKA*, Kala Mela & *Triennales*

New Delhi, TN *LKA*, British Council & *LKA* Regional Centre Chennai, *JAG*, *CKP*, *BB*, other group shows Pune, Lucknow, Mumbai & Kerala; International: Morocco, Australia, Poland. *Painters* camps: Udagamangalam, SZCC Chennai, Nandi Hills KAR. Awards: *AIFACS* Silver Plaque, Veteran Artist New Delhi, *AFA* Kolkata, TN *LKA*, South Indian Society Painters Chennai, *LKA* New Delhi, *CKP*. Member: *Cholamandal*. Collections: *NGMA* New Delhi, TN State Academy, *LKA* Regional Centre & National Art Gallery Chennai, Jawahar Kala Kendra RAJ; International: USA, Asia, Pacific Museum Poland, Artists Village Holland, pvt. & corporates.

A member of the *Cholamandal* Artists Group for the past three decades, D. Venkatapathy's early works were based on myths and *epics*. These folk-inspired *figures* were rendered mainly in *ink* and *oils*. He has also executed *drawings* in *pen* and *ink*. His later work is largely textural, the *theme* being hilly or rocky landscape/terrain.

He lives and works in the *Cholamandal* village and exhibits with the group.

Venkatappa Art Gallery (VEAG) In the premises of Karnataka Govt. Museum in Bangalore, the Foundation stone was laid in 1967. The gallery was inaugurated in 1975 and dedicated to central education. It consists of five floors, where the ground floor exhibits *K. Venkatappa's* works donated by his son. There are other galleries which exhibit works of *K.K. Hebbar* and *C. Ponnappa Rajaram* works collected before 1975. All these sections are in the control of the Archeology and Museum Dept. KAR.

Venkatappa, K. (1887–1965) b. Mysore, KAR. Education: Dip. in *FA*. Chamaraja Technical Institute Mysore. *FA*. GSA Chennai, Advance study *FA*. *GSFAC* Kolkata. Solos: Held solos in India & his own *VEAG*. Group participations: later in Central *LKA* KAR, *CKP*. Awards: *LKA*, Mysore Maharaja Scholarship. Collections: Tagore collection, Raja of Digapathia, Mysore Chitrasala, *VEAG*.

K. Venkatappa was born into a family of *court artists* in Mysore, his father, Krishappa being a palace *artist*. He was initially trained in *art* under K. Ramakrishna at the Chamaraja Technique Institute Mysore. Besides, he was exposed to the works of several *artists* and artisans, working on the new palace. The Maharaja sponsored his studies at the GSA Chennai, where he mastered the Western *style* of *art*. Later he was sent to the *Calcutta School*, where he studied not only *painting*, but also *drawing*, *sculpture* and music, under Percy Brown and *Abanindranath Tagore*. While at the school, he and *Nandalal Bose* were deputed to make *copies* of the *Ajanta frescoes* for Lady Herringham.

On his return to Mysore, he was appointed to work at the palace itself, first making *reliefs* on *plaster*, some of which are on the palace walls. Though he began working in the *manner* of the *Bengal School*, in the course of time he developed an individual *style*. He was an expert colourist, often making his own *colours*, while working in *tempera*. His *landscapes* of Udagamangalam and the Himalayas are *realistic* in the *manner* of the West. His Indian subjects based on mythology and *epics* are executed in the Bengal *style*, with sharp *outlines* and misty colouring. He has also executed *Flora & Fauna Paintings* studies after the *manner* of the Mughal miniaturist, Mansur, a Mughal *painter* of Jahangir's reign. A skillful blending of traditional Indian *space* division and Western neo-classical *figure* rendering is characteristic of several of his works, including the *reliefs* in *plaster*. He has also painted *portraits* on *ivory*. After the demise of his patron, Krishna Raja Wodeyar IV, he left Mysore to settle in Bangalore. The Govt. of KAR built the *VEAG* in Bangalore to house his collection after his death in 1965.

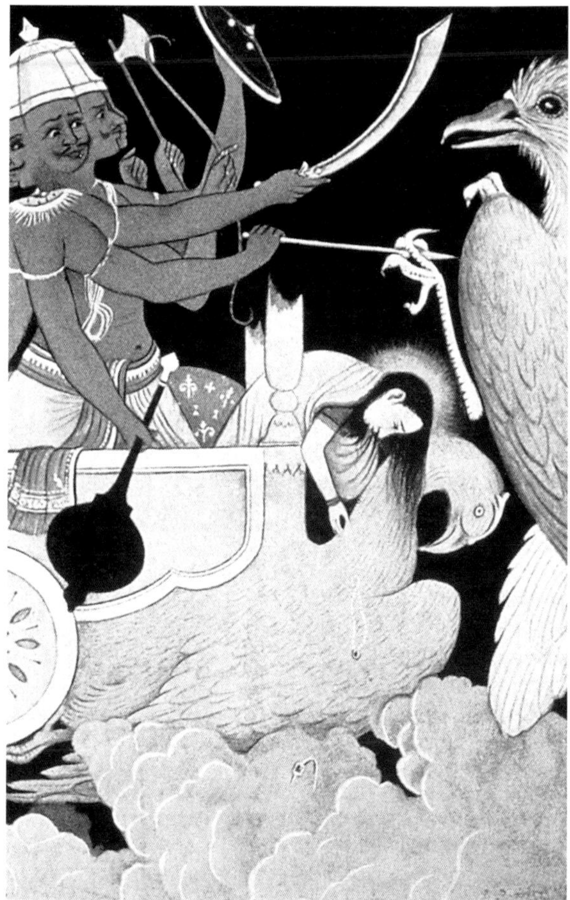

Venkatappa, K.: "Ravana and Jatayu".

Vent It refers to the *passage* that is formed for the air/gas/liquid to escape from a *mould*. Refer *Air Vents*, *Cire Perdue*, *Somnath Hore*, *Ratilal Kansodaria*, *Meera Mukherjee*.

Verma, Kanhaiya Lal (1943–) b. Sambhar, RAJ. Education: B.A. in *drawing* & *painting* RAJ University. Solos: RAJ *LKA* Gallery, *Banasthali Vidyapith*, Govt. College, Jawahar Kala Kendra RAJ, *RSA*. Group participations: RAJ *LKA* Jaipur 1971 to 2002, Progressive Painters Group RAJ, *LKA* New Delhi, Kalidas Academy Ujjain, UP *LKA* Lucknow, *JAG*, *AIFACS* *BB*. *Art* camps: Pushkar Fair, Collograpy camp, Jaipur, and others in Jaisalmer, Dundcod & Mount Abu. Awards: RAJ *LKA*, Progressive Painters Association Jaipur, SZCC Nagpur, *AIFACS*. Hon.: Best Teacher—President of India. Fellowship: National

Govt. of India for *miniature paintings*. Publications: Postcards published by RAJ *LKA*, "Ten Contemporary Artists of India" RAJ *LKA*. Collections: *LKA* New Delhi, RAJ *LKA*, Modern Art Gallery Jaipur, UP *LKA* Lucknow, SZCC Nagpur & many pvt.

Kanhaiya Lal Verma's *paintings* are a naive adaptation of the traditional *Rajasthani miniature painting style*. They combine the hot, burning *colours* of the *Mewar, Mewar Kalam*; the tall, slim *figures* of the *Bundi;* and the Pahari Kalams resulting in hard-edged *contours* and decorative *patterns*. At times the frilly, spiralled clouds of the Tibetan Thankas and electric blues and greens are used to set off small inset panels of *calligraphy*.

He lives and works in Sambhar Lake RAJ, where he was a lecturer in *drawing* and *painting*.

Verma, Nathu Lal (1946–) b. Jaipur, RAJ. Education: M.A. in *drawing & painting* & Ph.D. University of RAJ. Solos: Jaipur, Agra, Jodhpur, *JAG, NCAG*; International: Germany. Group participations: RAJ *LKA*, *PAG*—Jaipur in Mumbai, *LKA* New Delhi, *AIFACS*, other *exhibitions* in Kolkata, New Delhi, Chennai & Bhopal; Demonstrations of *fresco painting* & *miniature paintings MSU*, Indra Kala Sangeet Sansthan MP, Agra University, RAJ University. *Art* camps: Pushkar, Jaisalmer, Palampur, Jawahar Kala Kendra & *Graphic* camp Jaipur. Awards: RAJ *LKA*, All India Handicrafts Board, Kalidas Academy Ujjain, *AIFACS*. Member: General Council RAJ *LKA*, Secretary *PAG* Jaipur. Appointments: Was assistant Prof. HoD in Art Faculty RAJ University; Demonstrations—*miniature painting* at *FFA* and on *fresco paintings* Jaipur RAJ University. Collections: Govt. & pvt. in India; International: UK, USA, France, Canada, Germany.

Nathu Lal Verma has combined the *motifs* and *styles* of the *Mewar, Mewar Kalam* and the *Ajanta frescoes* in his colorful miniature like *paintings*. The subjects are taken from the Rajasthani *traditions* of the BHAGAVATA-PURANA, MAHABHARATA, RAMAYANA and GITA-GOVINDA. He is a follower of the renowned *painter* Kripal Singh Shekhawat and grinds his own *pigments* from minerals, plants, precious and semi-precious stones. The *forms* are intricately outlined and painted in the *tempera technique*. Some of the works have *calligraphic* panels inset in the *manner* of traditional miniatures.

He lives and works in Jaipur RAJ. Refer Illustration—*Pastoral*.

Vesara Style Vesara literally means a "Mule", born out of heterogeneous parents, it essentially denotes a mixed *style*. Vesara temples were built by later Chalukyas of Kanarese district and by the *Hoysala* dynasty of Mysore. The special features of these temples are the juxtaposition of *Nagara detail* to DRAVIDA *constructions.* Badami, Aihole and Pattadakal temples indicate the prevalence of Vesara style. It refers to a type of Vimana, which has a circular, ellipsoidal or apsidal elevation. It also refers to the group of temples, built in Nalini Gulm Vimana Ranakpur RAJ, and the Halebid-Belur area by the *Hoysala* rulers in the South. The plan of these temples is usually Asthabhadra i.e. star-shaped, obtained by a number of rotated squares. The temple itself is in three parts, the Vimana, the Garbhagriha (sanctum sanctorum), the Sukhanasika (connecting vestibule), and the Navaranga (new designed pillared hall). Sometimes a Mukha MANDAPA (open-pillared pavilion) stands in front of the Navaranga. At times three Vimanas fronted by their Sukhanasika surround the same Navaranga. The Kesava temple at Somnathpur shows this Trikutachala (three shrines) plan; it is also surrounded by a courtyard with cellars fronted by pillared verandahs. The *Hoysala* temples are carved out of greenish-grey chloritic schist (soapstone) which is quite soft when quarried, but later turns hard on oxidation. This advantage has led the craftsmen to turn out exquisitely detailed *sculpture*. The various *gods* and goddesses are covered with the profuse ornamentation, replete with lacelike arches, loads of jewellery with heavy Kiritas (*crowns*), necklaces, arm-bands and over-hanging girdles. The striking aspect of this sculptural exuberance is especially noticeable in the elevated basements with its bands of symbolically carved friezes. The Gaja-Patti (row of elephants) at the bottom denotes strength, with the horsemen scrollwork, Yallis (hybrid monsters) HAMSA (geese) and Pauranic (stories from the PURANAS) episodes. The crowning feature of the temple, the SHIKHARA has been destroyed in several of these temples, where the SHIKHARA followed the general star shaped plan to its pinnacle. Refer *Temple Architecture*.

Victoria Memorial Museum (VMM) (Kolkata, WB). This *museum*, located in the Victoria Memorial Building houses a collection, which is almost exclusively related to the colonial period. The *white marble* building designed by William Emerson and some modification done by R.N Mukerji was opened in 1921and completed in 1934. The distinguishing feature of the dome is 19 feet high of *bronze*, revolving "Angel of Victory".

The garden is dotted with *sculpture*; Sir Thomas Brocks, *life-size* statue of the Empress as a young woman is placed in the central hall. The Royal Gallery has huge *oil paintings*, depicting the life of the Empress, as well as a few personal belongings. The *portrait* gallery contains *paintings* of British administrators and some manuscripts and books related to the RAJ. There is a *sculpture* gallery in the south entrance hall. The *museum* also has some *paintings* of Indian scenes and *portraits* done by British *artists* like W. Hodges, T. Daniells, J. Zoffany and T. Kettle who travelled to India in the late 18th and 19th century.

Video Art The *post-Modern* period in India opened the possibilities of using several non-traditional *media* in the making of *art*. Video is another *medium* used in *installations* and by "Performance" or "*Happening*" *artists*. This allows the recording of performances, acts or simple tableaux that are played to the spectators at galleries. Video *art* can also be used by *artists* as part of an overall *exhibition* or series of works. Refer *Action Painting, Base, Body Art, Installation, Life-Mask, New Realism, Performance Art, Post-Modern,* YOGA, *Amdavad ni Gufa & Herwitz Gallery* Ahmedabad, *Navjot Altaf, Shobha Ghare, Nalini Malani, Yashwant Mali, Mahirwan Mamtani, Vivan Sundaram, MPCVA*.

Vignette In *modern art*, the *term* would loosely refer to fragments of form or *landscape* that crop up collage-like, in *painting*. It could also refer to phases of life in *genre painting*. **1.** A decorative and usually small *design* filling a blank surrounding *space* on a page in a book. **2.** An *image*, in a work of *art*, which fades off in the surrounding area diffusely and without a clear edge. **3.** It also means a dark *background* surrounding an object in a *drawing*, which fades to lighter *tones*, as it moves away from the centre of the *image*. Refer *Company School/Company Painting, Reddeppa M. Naidu, Nilima G. Sheikh, Yashawant Shirwadkar, Ram Gopal Vijaivargiya;* Illustration–*Abstract Landscape, Jain Miniature, Ganga Devi, Shaibal Ghosh, C. Jagdish, Ratilal Kansodaria, A. Ramachandran.*

Vihara=The Vihara, along with the CHAITYA and the stupa were among the earliest examples of Buddhist *architecture*. They were the living quarters of the Buddhist monks (BHIKSHUS) during the rainy season. The earliest Viharas were free-standing structures of *wood* or *stone*. Later on they, too were excavated from living rock, as at *Ajanta*. Although according to Pali (language used by BUDDHA for his sermons) texts, the fully developed Vihara included not just the living rooms but also private dwellings (Parivenas), halls (MANDAPAS), service corridors (Upattana Salas), halls with fireplaces (Agni Salas), porches (Kottakas), promenades (Chankamas), storehouses (Kappiya Kutis), privies (Vaccha Kuties), room for bathing (Janta Gharas), wells (Udapanas) and tanks (Pokkharani). The Vihara was usually a series of small cells opening out on three sides of a wide hall, could be entered through a vestibule or a doorway. Each of these tiny cells had a raised *stone* bed on one side. The hall was used for conducting group prayers or discourse, while the BHIKSHUS retired for the night to each of the small cells. The Vihara was usually not decorated with painted *frescoes*, though the pillars supporting the hallway or vestibule could be sculpturally embellished. They can be seen at Nasik, Kondone Pithalkhore, and *Ajanta* among others. Refer *Ellora*.

Vijaivargiya, Ram Gopal (1905–2003) b. Baler, RAJ. Education: Dip. Maharaja School of Arts & Crafts RAJ. Solos: FA. Society Kolkata, Roerich Centre of Art Allahabad, RAJ *LKA* Jaipur, *LKA* & RB New Delhi, UP *LKA* Lucknow, Lalbhai Dalpatbhai Museum Ahmedabad, Kalidas Academy Ujjain. Group participations: *LKA* New Delhi, RAJ *LKA*, *AIFACS*. Awards: Maharaja of Patiala Medal, Indore School of Art Certificate, *Abanindranath Tagore* Certificate, "Kalavid" RAJ *LKA*, "Kala Ratna" *AIFACS*, Padma Shri, Sahitya Academy Award New Delhi. Fellowships: *LKA* 1988 & HRD Ministry for two years New Delhi. Publications: Works & *illustrations* published in several Gujarati, Hindi, Urdu & Bengali magazines including "Vishal Bharat", *"Modern Review"*, "Sarasvati", "Chand" & "Madhuri"; Released "Roopankar" Volume Jaipur; Published several books & articles on *art* & literature. Collections: *BKB* Varanasi, *Maharaja Fatesingh Museum* Vadodara, City Palace Museum & Modern Art Gallery Jaipur, Allahabad Museum; International: Kuwait, Japan, Germany, USA.

Ram Gopal Vijaivargiya was trained in the *Abanindranath Tagore style* of *painting* by *Sailendranath Dey*, with *wash (technique)* of the *Bengal School* in the *art* school. Though he developed a more *modern* approach in the mid-50s, his early *style* with its typical *Ajanta* characteristics such as sensuous and sinuous bodies, *contour shading* and half-closed eyes was more prominent. Ram Gopal Vijaivargiya also studied and classified the various schools in traditional *Rajasthani miniature painting*. He adopted some of the features of *Rajasthani miniature paintings* especially the *Kishangarh* profile and Jaipur costume in his *vignettes* of village life. Though he used *oils* at times, his forte was *watercolour*.

Ram Gopal Vijaivargiya had been Principal of the Rajasthan Kala Mandir and of the *RSA* at different times.

Vijaya Fine Art Society (Vijaya Kalamandira) (Gadag, KAR) The school was founded by *artist Takappa P. Akki* in 1947, to encourage *art education* in the state and to facilitate the holding of *art* examinations. Later Vijaya Natya Sangha was also an institute to teach dance, drama, music and bring the school on par with the status of *Santiniketan*. Well over sixty percent of KAR's *drawing* teachers were educated at this institute. In 1985–86 it became the first school to offer a degree in *art* in North KAR. There are plans for the M.FA. course as well. The present principal is Ashok Akki, also an *artist*, the son of the founder.

Vipralabdha One of the eight specific types of NAYIKAS (heroines) mentioned by ancient Indian writers and poets. She is both angry and dejected at her lover's failure to meet her and is depicted in *miniature paintings* as loosening her tresses and flinging away her jewels. RADHA is frequently represented as a Vipralabdhanayika. Refer ASHTANAYIKA.

Viscosity Printmaking The word refers to the *technique* of printing several *colours* at the same time from one single etched *plate*, using *oil* based *colours* of different viscosities or consistencies. The *plate* is etched at different levels, and separate *colours* are used for each level. The rollers (used for inking the *plate*) are of varying degrees of hardness, the soft roller will reach into the deepest levels, while the hardest will *ink* only the topmost layer. There will also be a certain amount of *colour* mixing resulting in greens, violets and browns. The whole *plate* is then placed on the press and the *print* taken. *Krishna N. Reddy* was amongst the earliest masters of this process. Refer *Etching, Offset Printing, Overlapping, Printmaking, Single Block Colour Printing, Viscous, Zinc.*

Viscous (sticky consistency) **1.** In the *oil painting medium*, refers to the *texture* of the sticky, glutinous mixture of the *pigment* with *oils*. **2.** Also refers to the viscosity or density of the printing *ink* in *printmaking*. **3.** *Clay*, *wax*, and *fibreglass* that are used in *sculpture* are all viscous in semi-solid state, harden on exposure to air. Refer *Brushwork, Cire Perdue, Lost Wax Process, Himmat Shah, Shamendu N. Sonavane.*

Vishnu The protector, the preserver is the most humane of the *gods* forming the Hindu trinity. The other two being SHIVA (the destroyer) and BRAHMA (the creator). He is usually depicted as having four arms each holding an *attribute*:

SHANKHA (conch shell), GADA (club), CHAKRA (discus), and PADMA (lotus). Vishnu maintains the balance of the Universe. He is normally represented in three postures: the standing *image* (Sthanaka-Murti), sitting *image* (Asana-Murti) or reclining (Sayana-Murti).

The last is the most popularly worshipped posture—resting in the ocean of milk on the back of a many-hooded snake with his consort LAKSHMI by his side. Half-man, half-eagle, GARUDA, is his VAHANA (vehicle). Vishnu is usually depicted in dark blue *colour*.

Dasavataras: The ten incarnations of Vishnu, declared to have been assumed by him on 10 different occasions with a view to destroy certain ASURAS and set right the havoc created by them in the world. These 10 AVATARAS are MATSYA-AVATARA (fish), KURMAVATARA (tortoise), VARAHAVATARA (boar), NARASIMHA/NARASINHA (man-lion), VAMANA-TRIVIKRAMA (dwarf), PARASURAMA, RAMA, KRISHNA, BUDDHA and KALKI.

MATSYA-AVATARA: The fish incarnation of Vishnu, assumed by the *God* to recover the VEDAS from Hayagriva, a *demon* who had snatched it from BRAHMA. It is usually depicted in *miniature painting* as a large, one-horned fish, or as half-fish, half-man. The *image* is given four hands, two of which carry the SHANKHA and CHAKRA and the other two in VARADA MUDRA and ABHAYA MUDRA.

KURMAVATARA: The tortoise *form* assumed by Vishnu for the purpose of supporting (on its back) the Mandara employed in the churning of the ocean (Sagara-Manthana, Amrita-Manthana) to obtain nectar (Amrita) for the *gods*. It is represented in *miniature painting* as a half-man, half-tortoise, with two hands carrying the SHANKHA and CHAKRA with the front two hands in the VARADA MUDRA and ABHAYA MUDRA. The *image* is adorned with *ornaments* and crowned with KIRITA MUKUTA.

VARAHAVATARA: The giant boar *form* assumed by Vishnu to lift the earth, BHUDEVI, from the *depths* of the ocean. It is represented with the face of a boar and the body of a man with BHUDEVI clinging to his tusk.

NARASIMHA/NARASINHA: The man-lion *form* assumed by Vishnu to fight the *demons* Hiranyaksha and Hiranyakasipu. He is represented as being with a lion's face and the body of a man and shown springing out of a pillar or placing the *demon* on his lap and ripping his chest apart.

VAMANA-TRIVIKRAMA: Vishnu as a young boy/dwarf, born to Aditi to subjugate Bali. He is depicted as a young Brahmin boy with shaven head and carrying a straw umbrella. He asked Bali to grant him three pieces of land, which was immediately bestowed on him. At this, Vamana assumed the gigantic *form* of Trivikrama and measured the whole of Bhuloka (earth) with one stride and Svarga or heavens with his second stride. There was no *space* left for his third stride and therefore Bali offered his own head to Trivikrama. Immediately by the pressure of his foot Trivikrama sent Bali to Patalaloka (or nether world) where he ruled over all the ASURAS (*demons*). Trivikrama may be represented with the left foot raised to the level of (a) the right-knee (b) the navel (c) the forehead. He has either four or eight hands. If he is represented with four hands, then he carries the CHAKRA and the SHANKHA and stretches one arm out parallel to the lifted leg and the other in VARADA-MUDRA, ABHAYA pose, if he has eight hands then he carries the SANKHA, CHAKRA, GADA, Saranga (bow), Hala, the other three being the same. He is as dark as the rain clouds and is clothed in red garments and decorated with *ornaments*. The Kalpataru tree is represented behind him and INDRA holds an umbrella over him. Varuna and Vayu have Chamaras (fly-whisks) on either side.

Parasurama: Is attributed with the feat of subduing the Kshatriyas and cutting off the throat and arms of Satasta bahu Kartavirya Arjuna. Refer RAMA.

Krishna: Refer KRISHNA.

Buddha: Refer BUDDHA.

Kalki: Refer KALKI.

Refer ABHUSHANA, *Aesthetics*, ANANTA SHAYANA, AYUDHA-PURUSHA, BHAGAVAD GITA, BHAGAVATA-PURANA, CHATUR BHUJA, DASAVATARA, DIWALI, DIPAVALI, *Ellora*, GANJIFA, *Gupta*, HARI-VAMSA, *Heroic*, HINDUISM, HOIL, *iconography*, *iconology*, KALA/KAAL, KALA, KALKIN, *Khajuraho*, MATRIKAS, MUKUTA, *Nagara Style*, PURANA, RADHA, RAMAYANA, RAVANA, *Ritual*, SHADANGA, *Thanjavur (Tanjore) Paintings*, VAHANA; Illustration—CHAKRA, GARUDA, NARASIMHA/NARASINHA, OM, PADMA (Flower), SHANKHA, VARAHAVATARA.

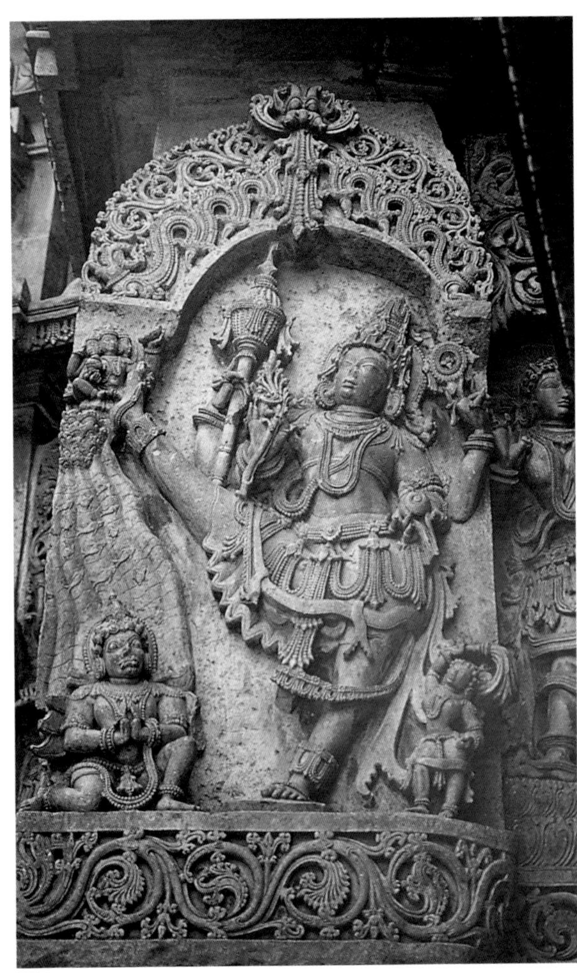

Vishnu: "Vamana-Trivikrama", Belur.

Vismaya Refer MUDRAS.

Visual The word refers to "seeing". It usually means the impact of a scene or *composition* as registered in the eyes, rather than on the mind. In visual *arts*, different *mediums* of expression are seen from *stone* and *canvas* to celluloid and computers. India has a rich *tradition* of the visual *arts* dating back to Bhimbetka rock *carving* in MP, and the dancing girl, bearded priest and steatite seals found in *Mohenjo Daro* and *Harappa*. The Visual Arts include *painting*, *sculpture* and *architecture* as opposed to the *Performance Arts*, such as dance, drama, theatre and music. e.g. Illustration–BHAGAVATA-PURANA, PARVATI–*Raja Ravi Varma*, *Dhanraj Bhagat*, *Arpana Caur*, *Bimal DasGupta*, *Asit K. Haldar*, *Ganesh Haloi*, *Somnath Hore*, *Surendra Pal Joshi*, *Bishamber Khanna*, *Meera Mukherjee*, *Mrinalini Mukherjee*, *Ved Nayar*, *Laxman Pai*, *Nagji Patel*, *Krishna N. Reddy*, *Mohan Samant*, *Haku Shah*, *Anupam Sud*, *Vrindavan Solanki*, *Vivan Sundaram*. Refer *Content*, *Creation*, *Imagery*, *Lettrism*, *Lettrisme*, *Miniature Paintings*, *Model*, *Neo-Tantricism*, *Rhythm*, *Symbolic Art*.

Visva Bharati (WB) Refer to *KB* and *Santiniketan*.

Viswambhara, K.S. (1940–) b. Shimoga, KAR. Education: Dip. in Music & Dip. in FAC *Visva Bharati Santiniketan*. Solos & International: Gallery 6 USA. Retrospective: Goa 1994. Group participations: Nanadan & *KB Santiniketan*, *AFA* Kolkata, *LKA* & *Triennales* New Delhi, *GC* Mumbai, Kala Academy, The Goan Art Forum Goa, *Graphic* & *drawing* Chandigarh, RAJ *LKA* Jaipur *AIFACS*, *GAC*, *CYAG*, *JAG*, *BAS*, *CKP*, *Roopankar*, *CHAG*; International: Japan, Egypt. *Artists* camps, workshops, seminars: British Council Kolkata; *Printmaking* summer workshop: Govt. of Goa, *Intaglio* (*Krishna N. Reddy*) *CKP*, Camps in Bangalore, WZCC Goa College of Art. WZCC Udaipur, *LKA printmaking* camp Bhubaneshwar, *Lithography* workshop WZCC Udaipur, *IFAS*, *MSU*; International: *Printmaking* summer workshop Kansas USA. Awards: Scholarship Mysore Govt. Museum, Kala Academy Goa, Research Grant *LKA* New Delhi, RAJ *LKA*. Fellowship: HRD Ministry Senior Fellowship. Collections: *NGMA* & *LKA* New Delhi, SZCC Chennai, WZCC RAJ, *BB*; International: USA, Brazil, Poland, Japan, Egypt.

K.S. Viswambhara initially worked with *sculpture*, using a wide range of materials. However, his early exposure to the world of printing (His father being a printer, he was one of the first three to own a printing machine in Mysore) soon told on him and he rediscovered *printmaking* around 1975 when he settled down in Goa.

At first he experimented, exploring the possibilities of several *media* including *wood cut*, *etching* and *lithography*. Earlier he concentrated on *etching*, on *intaglio printing* and later between 1991–94 on *lithography*. His *imagery* is based on the *figurative*, with an indirect reference the tragic and the fear aspen of life. *Form* itself is stylized and well integrated with *texture*. The *figure* is highly simplified to the point of being *symbolic ciphers* with several iconographic interpretation laid open. Some *etchings* do have a sense of the humorous in their portrayal of life. The *colours* that he employs especially in his *intaglios* are both subtle and subdued, though his later lithographs reveal the distinct use of direct *hues* as well.

K.S. Viswambhara is presently living in Goa and Bangalore.

Viswanadhan, V. (1940–) b. Kerala. Education: Dip. in *FA*. *GCAC* Chennai. Solos: Chennai, Gallery Chanakya & *NGMA* New Delhi, *GC* Mumbai *GE*, *VAG*, *CKAG*; International: Denmark, France, Italy, Germany, Sweden, Mexico, USA. Group participations: *Triennales*, *LKA* & *NGMA* New Delhi, *BAAC* & *CIMA* Kolkata, *GC* Mumbai, *AIFACS*, *GE*; International: UK, France, Japan, Germany, Italy, Switzerland, South Korea, Greece. *Auctions*: Osian's & Heart Mumbai, Heart New Delhi. Awards: National Award *LKA* & Graphics Medal New Delhi; International: Festival & Gallerie France Paris. Prepared four films & participated in film festivals. Collections: *BB*, *BAAC* Kolkata, Mysore State Museum Bangalore, *LKA* & *NGMA* New Delhi, PUJ State University Chandigarh, TN *LKA* Chennai; International: Musee d'Art Moderne de la Ville de Paris France, Germany, Sweden, Venezuela & pvt. & corporates.

V. Viswanadhan believes that the basis of his *creations* on *paper*, *canvas* and *metal plate* has been on *drawing* the inner spirit from the matter. He has been constantly interested in exploring *space*, not only within the *painting* but, in the very action, the gestural act of *painting*, with his characteristic diagonal slashes of *pigment*. He experimented with a variety of *techniques* as well working with *turpentine* and a *metal* stylus, mixing *watercolour* and *oils* at times to create subtle blends of *light* and *shade*. He used *gold* and *silver watercolour* in the 70s. The 70s and the 80s also saw him "sewing" strong *handmade paper* into *patterns*, creating coherent *compositions* out of autonomous parts. The recent *drawings* in Indian *ink* were done using a bamboo *style*. Both the large, horizontal works and the smaller square *drawings* reveal a supreme freedom and dynamic inner *rhythm*.

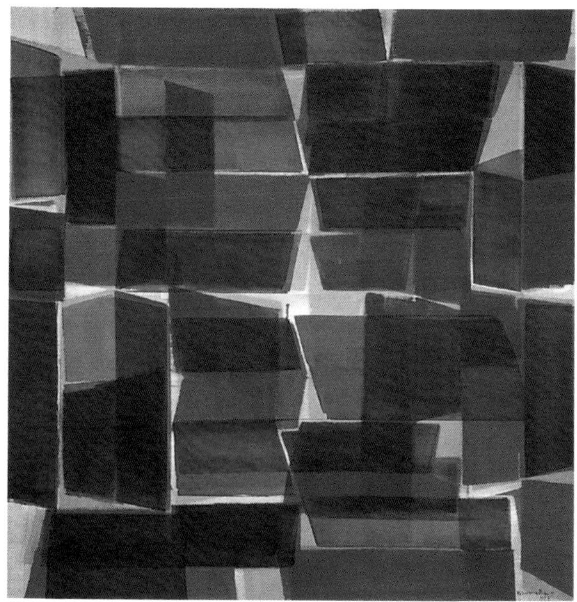

Viswanadhan, V.: "Untitled", *Casein* on *Canvas*, 1997, 202x202 cm.

His works more geometric almost like the MANDALAS and cosmic diagrams which he learnt to experiment with *space* from his teacher, *K.C.S. Paniker*.

He lives and works in Paris, France.

Vocabulary In *art*, the word refers to various elements that make up the *painting*, *sculpture* or *graphics*. This pertains not just to the *image* portrayed, but also to the *tonal values*, *texture*, *colour*, *line* and *form*. Indian *art* is influenced by Indian *culture*, e.g. Indian ornamental *sculpture*, and *miniature paintings* with its *style*, *technique*, and materials used. Refer *Landscape;* Illustrations–*B. Prabha*, *Jogen Chowdhury*, *Rini Dhumal*, *Bhagwant K. Goregaoker*, *Chittrovanu Mazumdar*, *Benode Behari Mukherjee*, *Akbar Padamsee*, *Madhvi Parekh*.

Volume A synonym for *mass*, it refers to **1.** The *space* displaced by a *sculpture* or three-dimensional object. **2.** The imaginary *space* occupied by a painted *figure*, object or subject. In *abstract art*, *artists*, *painters* and *sculptors* achieved a sense of volume and *space* without relying on conventional *perspective*. *Sayed Haider Raza's colour* sense and form placement create powerful and voluminious effect; so also in *Tantra art*. Refer *Form*, *Opaque*, *Printmaking*, *Om Prakash Sharma*; Illustrations– *Ramkinkar Baij*, *Manjit Bawa*, *Muhammed Abdur Rehman Chughtai*, *Mukul Chandra Dey*, *Shaibal Ghosh*, *Janak J. Narzary*, *P.T. Reddy*, *Ghulam Rasool Santosh*, *J. Srividya*.

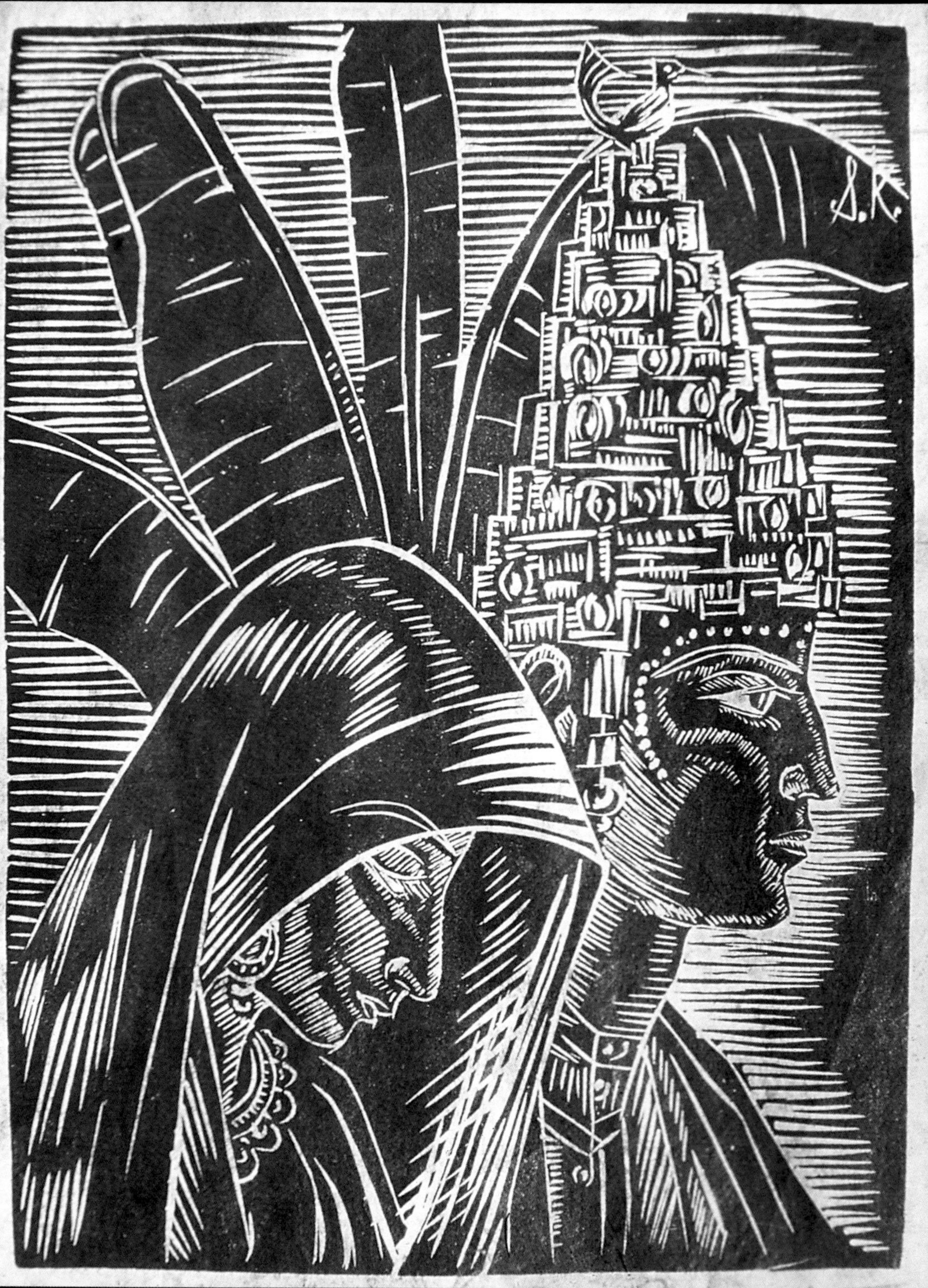

Wood Cut, Wood Cut Printing: *Sudhir R. Khastgir*, "Couple", mid20th century, 19x16.5 cm. (See notes on page 378)

Wad, Bal (Gangardhar Balkrishna Wad) (1926–2004) Education: Govt. Dip. in *drawing* and *painting* England, National Dip. in design Yugoslavia, Dip. in *Applied Art*, Dip. in Conservation & Preservation of old monuments old painting, Govt. Scholarship (1960), study tour of National Museums USA (1974). Solos and Group shows: Pune, Shrinagar, Shimla, New Delhi, Mumbai, *TAG*, *JAG*; International: London, Wimbeldon, Denmark & Galeria–Taj Caribe New York (Glimpses of RAJ). Founder member: Creative Club Pune an *arts* and *crafts* institution, & opened an Art Gallery which is now conducted by his daughter *artist* Sujata Dharap. Presented: 8 huge *canvases* on the Indo-Pak War 1971–72 to the then Prime Minister. Commissions: Large *murals*–Pune, Mumbai worked with his daughter. Appointments: Demonstrations on *acrylic medium* and how to use it–1970 onwards. Publications: Books on how to *paint–landscapes* on fabric, "Dream Land–Flora of Himachal".

Bal Wad was mostly known for his role in promoting new *painting* products in his capacity as Art Director for Camlin. He gave many public demonstrations of *painting* with the then new *medium*, *acrylic*. In addition to studying *painting* Bal Wad worked for two years in the Museum of Belgrade on "Conservation and Preservation of Art". *Nature*, as in *flora and fauna painting* studies and *seascapes* were the chief source of inspiration in his works. He has experimented with several *media* and has also executed two large *murals* in *acrylic* and *mosaic*. In 1996 he worked on three large 22x10" *Kalamkari* based on *nature*, and two–10x10" *Kalamkari*. His later works have taken a new direction being inspired by his fascination for Reiki, meditation and TANTRA. These heavily *symbolic* works are displayed flat on the ground, enabling the spectator to walk around them, and experience them at all levels and see them from above. He worked in Mumbai and later settled in Pune. Refer Illustration–*Kalamkari*.

Wadangekar, Dinkar V. (1932–) b. MAHA. Education: GDA in *drawing* & *painting* & Art Master's certificate *JJSA*. Group participation: *JAG*. Awards: Gold Medal MAHA State Awards. Member: *LKA* New Delhi, *BAS*. Collections: pvt. & public.

Dinkar Wadangekar's *art* is based on *nature* and natural *forms*. Though he does not use *photo-realism*, recognizable objects and *vignettes* of *nature* are creatively juxtaposed in his *compositions*. The play of *light* and *shade* is also apparent. He has worked mostly with *oils* and *watercolours*, occasionally using *pastel* as well.

He lives in Kolhapur, since his retirement as a Prof. at the *JJSA*.

Wagh, Brahman Vinayakrao (1917–1993) b. Mumbai, MAHA. Education: GDA in *modelling* I.T. School of Art Mumbai, GDA *JJSA*, studied *portrait sculpture* under father *Vinayakrao Venkatrao Wagh*, *marble carving* & *bronze casting* under Italian masters. Awards: Gold Medal All India Arts & Crafts *exhibition* Karachi. Member: Founder member & Chairman Indian Sculptors' Association (1962–70), Board of Examiners (1973–75); Dir. of Art MAHA. Commissions: Prepared *busts* & statues of National leaders & dignitaries from India & abroad. Collections: India, abroad & at the Chowpatty Art Studio Mumbai with the collection of his grandfather. Presently his son works at the studio.

Brahman Vinayakrao Wagh set up Wagh's Fine Arts. Studio in Mumbai which was to turn out many commissioned works. He worked mostly in *bronze* erecting *heroic size busts* of National leaders like Dr. Rajendra Prasad, Pandit Jawaharlal Nehru, Lal Bahadur Shastri and Dr. Zakir Hussain at Rashtrapati Bhavan, New Delhi as well as in Hyderabad, Nanded, Chandrapur, Mumbai, Raj Bhavan Patna, Bhopal, Nagpur, Kanpur, Yawatmal, Porbandar and Chanda. Prominent industrialists like the Tatas and Birlas *commissioned work* from the Wagh studio. A record number of memorial *bronze busts* and statues of Dr. B.R. Ambedkar have been executed for prominent locations in India and abroad.

Apart from national leaders, Brahman Vinayakrao Wagh also made a *bronze* statue of King Tribhuvana of Nepal, and *bronze busts* of Robert Kennedy and Martin Luther King (USA). His *bronze busts* of Mahatma Gandhi are installed in Canada and East Africa and of Pandit Jawaharlal Nehru in Germany.

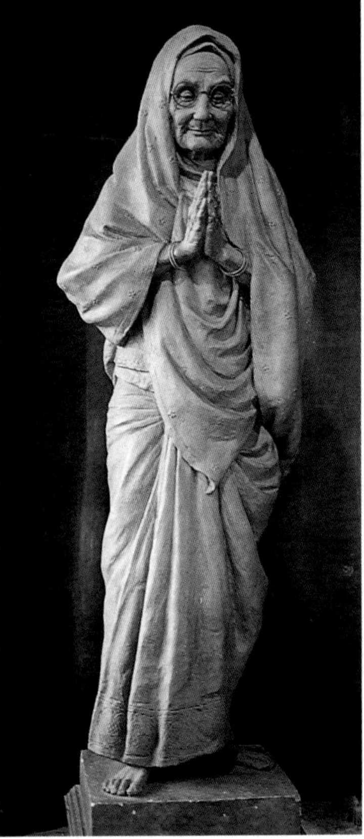

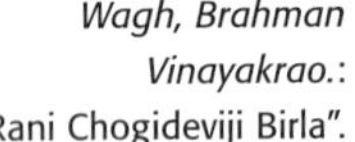

Wagh, Brahman Vinayakrao.: "Rani Chogideviji Birla".

Wagh, Vinayakrao Venkatrao (1883–1958) b. Karwar, KAR. Education: Course in *sculpture* & *modelling JJSA*; *Black & white drawing* under Ganpatrao Kedare, studied *sculpture* & *modelling* under Prof. Agarkar who was HoD *JJSA*, *Drawing & painting* under *Antonio X. Trindade*. Awards: From *BAS* for *portraits sculpture* & a Silver Medal in 1926 for *sculpture*. Member: Life member of *BAS*, *ASI*. Commissions: In Chennai, Mumbai, Myore and other states.

Vinayakrao Venkatrao Wagh's field of specialization was life-like portraiture in bold *style* and he was an authority on head study. After completing his course at *JJSA* he was invited by Lord Hardinge, then Viceroy & Governor General of India to prepare his *bust* from sittings and was then given a Warrant of Appointment. He was commissioned to prepare *busts* and statues of Rulers of various states & Lord Willingdon Governor of Madras, Sir George Lloyd and Sir Leslie Wilson—the Governers of Bombay; Dr. Rajendra Prasad, First President of the Republic of India and other Govt. dignitaries.

However, after the arrest of Mahatma Gandhi in 1930 he renounced all the diplomas conferred on him by the British Govt. He then made *busts* of national leaders from *line* sittings viz. Lokmanya Tilak, Mahatma Gandhi, Lala Lajpat Rai, *Rabindranath Tagore*, Surendranath Bannerji, Vitthalbhai Patel, Madan Mohan Malaviya, M. Visweswarayya, Dr. Rajendra Prasad and many others. He was awarded by the Presidency of Bengal with an order for a *marble* statue of Babu Girish Chandra Ghosh. Many saints also gave him sittings and he made *busts*/statues of Ramakrishna Paramahansa, Shri Sai Baba of Shirdi, Sadhu T.L. Vaswani and many others. Nobel Laureate *Rabindranath Tagore* favoured him with live sittings for a *bust*. Apart from *sculptures* Vinayakrao Venkatrao Wagh also learnt to play the Veena (lute—a musical instrument) and Sitar.

He became so proficient in the *art* that he gave public demonstrations of *modelling busts* in *clay* from live sittings of eminent personalities in one/two hours at the Town Hall, at his studio and other places in Mumbai. The same procedure is followed by his grandson Vinay Wagh, Mumbai.

Wall Painting Refer *Ajanta*, *Banasthali Vidyapith*—RAJ, BHITTI-CHITRA, *Chalk*, *Distemper*, *Fresco*, *Mural*, *Theme*, *Transition*, *Warli Paintings*.

Wankhede, K. Vasant (1936–) b. MAHA. Education: Dip. in *drawing* & *painting JJSA*. Over 10 solos: Mumbai, New Delhi, Chennai, including *BAAC* Mumbai. Group participations: New Delhi, *BAAC* & *NGMA* Mumbai, *BB*; International: UK. Awards: Five awards for *painting* MAHA State Art & *BAS*, National Awards for Films including the film on "*Warli Paintings*". Appointment: Art Dir. of five films including "Woman" & "Siddarth". Collection: *NGMA* New Delhi; International: Milan Museum Italy, Glenbarra Art Museum Japan, pvt. Holland.

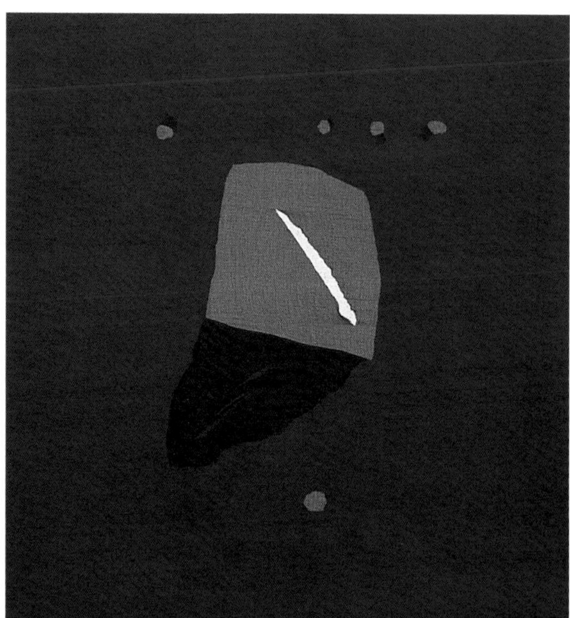

Wankhede, K. Vasant: "Collage 98-H", Fabric on *Canvas*, 1998, 90x85 cm.

K. Vasant Wankhede an *artist* of the *Bombay School*, progressed in a predictable *manner*, through the usual phases of *painting modern landscapes*, quick, spontaneously rendered *portraits* and romantic architectural ruins, that were studies of *light* and *shadow* rather than topographical views. It is his *collages* dated from 70s, when he started working at the Govt. Press that mark him as an innovative *artist*. The waste *paper* that he found inspired him to experiment, exploring the various possibilities of the material in relation with other non-traditional materials like cyclostyling *ink*, photo-painting cut outs, *plastic* sheets, used notebooks, etc. The *paper* would be torn delicately, folded, pasted in thin *overlapping* layers, and coloured over with sienna and greens. Sometimes sentences from torn newsprint appear through the overlaid *colours*. Since the 80s he has been using cloth in the same *manner*. These sheer layers of fabric-voiles, muslins, thin silks are stretched, lacerated, slashed and have *found objects* mounted on them. His recent works show fabric being used as *collage* on *canvas backgrounds*. These multiple layers are puckered and gathered creating subtle folds and blisters. The *images* created are *abstract*, the *colours* used sophisticated and elegant.

He lives and works in Mumbai.

Warli Paintings Also called Warli *murals*, are executed by tribal people of Warli, MAHA, on the mud-plastered reed walls of huts and rock shelters. The purpose behind them is to propitiate the *gods* and ward off evil spirits on occasions like marriage and "Navakhai"—the collective consuming of newly-harvested grain. Semi-liquid rice paste is the *medium* used with a rice stem as a *brush*. The Warli *images* are direct and naive with *nature* in its unadorned and seasonal glory being the principal subject. Strict adherence to basic *forms* of geometry e.g. squares, triangles and circles, portrays an amazing directness and child-like innocence. Thus, they are stylistically similar to *wall paintings* in other parts of rural India such as Saora (Orissa—Andhra border), villages of Deccan and Gangetic plains. Refer *Ajanta*, *Folk Art*, *Media*, *Wall Painting*, *Tribal Art*.

Warm Colours They belong to the reddish part of the *colour* spectrum, the *colours* being red, orange, yellow and their *shades*. They appear to advance from the picture plane and create a feeling of warmth.

Miniature *painters* have used mostly *tints* and *shades* of warm colours along with large accents of *white* in *painting*. In *Tantra art* and neo-tantric *art* warm colours convey energy. Refer *Advancing Colours*, AGNI, *Amitabha Banerjee*, *Ashok Bhowmik*, *Harendra Shah;* Illustrations—*Abstraction Lyrical*, *Colour Wheel*, HOLI, *Jain Miniature*, *Jain Manuscript Illumination*, *Mewar*, *Mewar Kalam*, *K.M. Adimoolam*, *Aparna Caur*, *K.V. Haridasan*, *K. Khosa*, *Ved Nayar Amrut Patel*, *Mona Rai*, *Sayed Haider Raza*, *Chittrovanu Mazumdar*.

Wash (Technique) 1. A thin, *transparent* layer of *colour* in *watercolours, gouache* or diluted *ink*. **2.** Some of the Indian *artists* used *tempera*, a *technique* where layers of *colours* are applied and later washed off. The sequence is repeated so that the repeated *overlapping* and merging of *colours* produce a muted and hazy effect. *Details* are then highlighted and *outlines* painted in, for the completion of the *composition*. This *technique* was adopted by *Abanindranath Tagore*.

Waste-Mould The *negative mould* made of *plaster of Paris*. It is the *mould* from which the *positive* is *cast*. When broken and destroyed, it frees the *positive cast* in one-off process. The advantage in using the waste-mould is that it reduces or eliminates the seams that occur when a piece of *mould* is used. Refer *Air Vent, Casing, Cire Perdue, Sadanandji Bakre, Ramkinkar Baij, Somnath Hore, Vinayak Pandurang Karmarkar, Himmat Shah, Vinayakrao Venkatrao Wagh.*

Watercolours It refers to the *technique* of *painting* with *colour pigments ground* with water soluble gums such as *gum arabic*. They are usually painted on *paper, handmade paper* or otherwise; they can be *opaque* as in *gouache* or relatively *transparent* as in *wash painting*. The classic *technique* is to use the *base white paper* as the *highlight* and apply *transparent, overlapping washes* of *colour* to obtain *colour gradation*. Many *painters* of *Bombay School, Bengal School* and *Madras School of Art* painted impressionistic *watercolour landscapes* and *figurative* works using both *opaque* and *transparent wash techniques*. Refer *Aquarelle, Bazaar Painting, Bengal Revivalism, Bengal School, Blocking in, Blot Drawing, Chinese Art, Cubism, Drip Painting, Film, Gouache, Ink, Japanese Art, Landscape, Line and Wash, Linearity, Linear Composition, Linearly, Lyricism, Monograph, Overlapping, Pastel Shades, Pencil, Plein-air, Romanticism, Sepia, Shade, Style, Technique, Tempera, Tonal Values, Translucent, Transparent, Watercolours, Muralidhar R. Achrekar, Vasudeo Adurkar, V.G. Andani, Satyendranath Bandhyopadhyay, Ramananda Bandyopadhyay, Dhirendrakrishna Deb Barman, Atasi Barua, Prithvi Nath Bhargava, Samar N. Bhowmik, Ranvir Singh Bisht, Nandalal Bose, Matilal Chakrabarti, Mrityunjoy Chakraborty, Sunayani Devi Chatto-padhyay, Bal Chhabda, K.P. Chidambarakrishnan, P.N. Choyal, Muhammed Abdur Rehman Chughtai, Arup Das, Dilip DasGupta, Manishi Dey, Sailendranath Dey, Dhanapal Ravi, R.S. Dhir, Dwarika P. Dhuliya, Gopal Ghose, Jyotish Dutta Gupta, Gajanan S. Haldankar, Paresh C. Hazra, S. Krishnappa, K.S. Kulkarni, Paresh Maity, Kshitendranath Mazumdar, Nirode Mazumdar, Sukhamoy Mitra, Benode Behari Mukherjee, Sachida Nagdev, Prabha Panwar, Kapu Rajaiah, K. Seshagiri Rao, Ravishankar M. Raval, Gopen Roy, Debi Prasad RoyChowdhury, Anilbaran Saha, Somalal Chunilal Shah, K.M. Shenoy, Arpita Singh, Abanindranath Tagore, Subhogendra Tagore, P.R. Thippeswamy, Arnawaz Vasudev, Ram Gopal Vijaivargiya;* Illustrations—*Muhammed Abdur Rehman Chughtai, Asit K. Haldar, Deokinandan Sharma, Abanindranath Tagore, Sarada Charan Ukil, Shantanu Ukil.*

Waterproof The *term* refers to *paper, paint, ink* or any such material that is impervious to water. *Oil paper* when prepared gives a *transparent finish* and is both waterproof and *oil* proof and is used for *oil painting, pastel, crayons*, waterproof *ink, egg-oil emulsion painting*. All over India various types of waterproof, oil and *handmade paper* are still made manually. Refer *Back-Glass Painting, Kraft Paper, Papier Mache, Mewar, Mezzotint, Nude, Portrait, Still Life, Wash (Technique), Watercolours, Bengal School, Neo-Bengal School, Aditya Basak, Rekha Krishnan, S. Krishnappa, Dinanath Pathy, Manchershaw F. Pithawalla, M.K. Puri, G. Reghu, Shekhar Roy, Jehangir Sabavala, S.K. Sahni, Paramjit Singh, Rameshwar Singh, Vinay P. Trivedi, Subhogendra Tagore, Babu Xavier.*

Wax Natural or *synthetic* sticky substance, pale yellow in *colour*, which may be *viscous* or in solid state, and lustrous or *translucent* in appearance. It is insoluble in water and softens and melts at higher temperatures. Natural waxes are of animal and vegetable origin, and *synthetic* ones are derived from *oil* and petroleum distillates. It is used for surface coating during the lithographic process in India, started in Kolkata. The *cire perdue* or *lost wax process* of *casting metal* was practiced in India since *Indus Valley Civilization*, and flourished during the CHOLA period. In *painting medium, batik* is made by using the wax resists process. A special blend of plastic wax is used recently in *modelling* and *carving* three-dimensional objects. Refer *Crayon Manner, Dyestuff, Lithography, Mould, Oil Painting, Paper-Pulp Casting, Screen printing, Stencil, Varnish, Amit Ambalal, Anis Farooqi, Somnath Hore, Meera Mukherjee, B.R. Panesar, Pilloo Pochkhanawalla, Ghanshyam Ranjan, J. Swaminathan, Abanindranath Tagore.*

Weapons Refer *Attributes*, AYUDHAS, CHAKRA, GADA, AGNI, SHULA, TRISHULA, SHAKTI.

Weaver's Service Centres (WSCs) (Head office: New Delhi). The centre were established in 1956 by Govt. of India. They function under the Development Commissioner (Handlooms) New Delhi. Here weavers and *fine art artists* work together in close collaboration along with the dye laboratory and the *weaving* shed, to produce new *designs* and *motifs*. The *design* here is dictated by the limitations of the yarn, the dyes and *weaving techniques*. *Artists* associated with the centres include *Prabhakar Barwe, K.G. Subramanyan, Harkrishan Lall, Jeram Patel* of Mumbai, Dinesh Kurekar of Aurangabad has woven *abstract* tapestries. There are WSCs at Hyderabad, Nagpur, Vijayawada, Guwahati, Bhagalpur and *Madhubani* in Bihar, Bangalore, Ahmedabad, Cannanore, Indore, Jaipur, Bhubaneshwar, Chennai, Kanchipuram, Panipat, Raigarh, Imphal, Agartala, Chamoli, Meerut, Varanasi and Kolkata.

Weaving A *technique* of making fabric by interlacing a continuous thread horizontally (weft), across a set of threads strung lengthwise (wrap). Many different natural and *synthetic* fibres are used such as cotton, silk, wool, nylon, polyester etc. Different methods produce various types of tight or loose weaves such as plain, twill, tapestry, pile carpeting. An unusual example in *arts* and *crafts*, is *Mrinalini Mukherjee's* work of *sculptures* knotted in hemp fibre. Refer *Abstract Sculpture, Art, Folk Decoration, Matter, Roshan M. Mullan, Saroj Gogi Pal, K. Jayapala Panicker, Rajen, Ghulam Rasool Santosh, WSC.*

Welding Is joining and fusing edges of pieces of *metal*, using an oxy-acetylene torch. Indian *sculptors* have used welding in making *assemblages* of junk and machine parts, utilizing their strange *form* and rusty surfaces to create overwhelming and expressive *images* full of force and energy. Refer *Facing, Steel, Wrought Metal, Sudha Arora, Adi M. Davierwala, P.S. Nandhan;* Illustrations–*Somnath Hore, Raghav Kaneria, Shankar Nandagopal.*

West Bengal Artists' Federation (WBAF) This is an organization comprising of *painters* and *sculptors* affiliated to the *LKA*. The *artists* exhibit as a group in All India Exhibitions including the *AIFACS*, *BAS's* Annual exhibition, *BAAC* Kolkata and *LKA* National *exhibition*. The group includes *Simlai Barun*, Dilip Bannerjee, Kajal Dasgupta and Bankiar Bannerjee among others.

Wetting Down **1.** A process of watering the surface of a *stone* to identify veins and other flaws so that final effect after *carving*, and or polishing the *stone*, could be gauged. **2.** A method of keeping the *clay model* moist and workable by spraying it with water and wrapping with a damp cloth or polyethylene. Refer *Cast Stone, Chasis, China Clay, Clay Water, Indirect Carving, Pottery, Sculpture, Terracotta, Texture, Sadanandji Bakre, Jyotsna Bhatt, Avtarjeet S. Dhanjal, Vinayak Pandurang Karmarkar, Balbir Singh Katt, Sunil Kumar Paul, Ravinder G. Reddy, Mansimran Singh, Himmat Shah, Radhika Vaidyanathan, Vinayakrao Venkatrao Wagh*; Illustration–*Ceramics*, NARASIMHA, *P.S. Nandhan, Nagji Patel, Sardar Gurcharan Singh.*

White It is the *colour* seen by reflection or transfer of sunlight. White is derived from different ingredients. In India, *transparent* white has always been used in *tempera*; while with *gouache* (1790 onwards), it is used in a relatively heavy and *opaque manner.* White is chiefly used to depict architectural pavillions and domed turrets in Indian miniatures. The high burnishing makes the dots of white *pigment* into near perfect *trompe l'oeil* representations of pearl necklaces especially in *Kishangarh Miniatures*, e.g. *portrait* of RADHA of *Kishangarh*.

In *oil colours*–**1.** Flake white is quick drying, and flexible. **2.** Titanium white is the most commonly used white, and is the whitest and most *opaque* of all three. **3.** Zinc white is the least *opaque* of the three, and tends to dry slowly.

Coats of *acrylic* white can be applied on *canvas, wood, paper*, cardboard, fibreboard, *plaster, metal, stone* and *concrete* with treatment with a special *ground* to render its capability of holding the *pigment*. White mixing is the *technique* to achieve *opaque*. Refer *Gesso, Sukumar Chatterjee*; Illustration–*Gobardhan Ash, Manjit Bawa, Bal Chhabda, Ganesh Haloi, Ram Kumar, Tyeb Mehta, Bhabesh Chandra Sanyal, Laxman Shreshtha.*

White Line Engraving An *impression* made from an *engraving* on *wood* block or *lino*, printed as *relief* so that the *image* is formed as a *white line* on a coloured *background*. The *wood cut* and *linocut line engraving* done by the Bengali *artists*, the *Kalighat Pat* and the work of *artists* of *Kala Bhavan Santiniketan*, clearly represent this. Indian *artists* took interest in *graphic art* with *wood* and *lino printmaking*. Refer *Graphic, Relief Printing, Nandalal Bose, Mukul Chandra Dey, Somnath Hore, Paul A. Koli;* Illustration–*Wood Cut, Wood Cut Printing–Sudhir R. Khastgir.*

Wood A material that is used in both *sculpture* and *printmaking*, as well as for *murals*. It is used in the *form* of large blocks or planks taken from various trees. Rosewood, ebony and mahogany are some of the popular woods used. The grain of the wooden block or plank plays an important role in *sculpture*, which is carved, by using the scauper/scalper tool to remove areas of wood around an *image*. Later the *chisel, gouge* and hammer are used. For *wood engravings* and *wood cut*, special tools are needed to make cuts across the grain. Wood is also used as a *base* in place of a *canvas*. The latter half of 20th-century *art* in India has seen the influx of *mixed media assemblages* with *metal* and wood in addition to *ready-made* objects and various other objects. Refer *Acrylic, Arte Povera, Bas-Relief, Block Printing, Burin, Carving, Collage, End-Grain, Found Object, Fretwork, Gouge, Hardboard, Inlay, Mobile, Paper, Printmaking, Relief Printing, Shanti Dave, Satish Gujral, Somnath Hore, Pilton Kothawalla, Chittrovanu Mazumdar;* Illustration–*Navjot Altaf, Aku, Dhanraj Bhagat, Kanchan Chander, Laxma Goud, Santosh Jadia, Bimal Kundu, Vishwanath M. Sholapurkar, Relief–Piraji Sagara, Wood Cut, Wood Cut Printing–Sudhir R. Khastgir.*

Wood Block Printing Company painters used the wood block printing process for making *illustrations* for Bengali books. They also printed iconic representations of SHAKTI, SHIVA and VISHNU. There were some depictions of some interesting syncretistic *images*. The important subject was DURGA. The basic *technique* was simple, with fine *engraving lines* to yield good *prints*. Wood block printing, was also the preferred *medium* textile printing from the early 14th century. Key centres for *block printing* of textiles were Sanganer, Jaipur, Nagru and Barmer in Rajasthan, and Anjar, Deesa, Ahmedabad, Jetpur, Rajkot, Porbandar and Bhavnagar in Gujarat. Refer *Company School, Culture, Dyestuff, Icon, Kalamkari, Multi Block Colour Printing, Single Block Colour Printing, Wood Engraving, Wood Cut Printing, Jyoti Bhatt, Nandalal Bose, Mukul Chandra Dey, Somnath Hore, Paul A. Koli, Vasant Parab.*

Wood Carving *Carving* done on *wood* by cutting and shaping of a block of *wood*. The *tradition* of wood carving in India can be traced to the earliest Buddhist period, especially in Northern India and GUJ. These were intricate carved *frames* of doors, windows, facades and balconies of temples and house, as well as carved *figures* of *gods* and goddesses. A very important example is of 17th to 19th century, *wood sculptures* of Patan, GUJ noted for *carvings* of homes and

Jain homes and temples. Refer *Engraving*, HANUMAN, *Wood Engraving, Wood Cut, Balwant Singh Kushawaha, Leela Mukherjee, Mahendra Pandya, C. Ponnappa Rajaram, Ravinder G. Reddy, Bhanu Shah;* Illustration–*Dhanraj Bhagat, Santosh Jadia, Bimal Kundu, Vishwanath M. Sholapurkar, Relief–Piraji Sagara.*

Wood Cut, Wood Cut Printing One of the *relief printing techniques* which came into use in the late 14th century for printing from *wood* blocks. It had become an artistic *medium* within the course of a century, with meticulous wood cut *drawings* by A. Durer. In India, the earliest wood cuts were made in the 19th century in Bengal. Bharat Chandra's "Anandamangal" being the first Bengali book to be illustrated with wood cuts (1816). Calcutta wood cuts were printed from circa 1860 on loose rectangular sheets of *paper*.

A wood cut is executed in a *manner* similar to the *linocut*, with the plank engraved along the grain. The *design* is traced onto the plank and *gouges* and *chisels* are used to remove the non-printing areas, leaving only those areas to be printed in *relief*.

Ink is then rolled on the plank and it is pushed through the press with a suitably dampened sheet of *paper*. The *design* will appear in reverse. In the case of *multi block colour printing*, more than one block is used, the *positive* areas of each block being used to *print* in a different *colour*. Refer *History Painting, Metal Cut, Metal Block Monograph, Multiple Tool, Printmaking, Single Block Colour Printing, Texture, White Line Engraving, Wood Block Printing, Wood Carving, Wood Engraving, Dattatrey D. Apte, Sujata Bajaj, Chittaprosad, Shanti Dave, Somnath Hore, Sudhir R. Khastgir, Paul A. Koli, Chittrovanu Mazumdar, Sharad Patel, Haku Shah, Gurudas Shenoy, K.S. Viswambhara;* Illustration–*Kanchan Chander*. (See illustration on page 373)

Wood Engraving It is a variation of the *wood cut*; however it differs from the *wood cut*, here the *wood* is cut across the grain rather than along the grain; and the *engraving* and detailing is very fine because a *burin* or needle is used. It was developed in mid-19th century. "Company" painters were employed to produce block printed *illustrations* in *white line engraving*. The *relief* process, including *woodcuts* and *engraving* process is also used in *intaglio* method of *printmaking*. Refer *Company School/Company Paintings, Kalamkari, AFA, GCAG & RBU* Kolkata, *College of Art* New Delhi, *JJSA, Kala Bhavan Santiniketan, MSU, GCAC* Chennai, *Jyoti Bhatt, Nandalal Bose, Mukul Chandra Dey, Devraj Dakoji, Laxma Goud, Somnath Hore, Paul A. Koli, Vasant Parab, Rm. Palaniappan, Yagneshwar Kalyanji Shukla;* Illustrations–*Wood Cut, Wood Cut Printing–Sudhir R. Khastgir* & *Kanchan Chander.*

Wrought Metal Rough *form* of a *metal* which is beaten or shaped when sufficiently cool to allow *handling*, after *casting* in *mould* when hot. Refer *Bidri, Brass, Bronze, Cast, Cloison, Gold, Iron, Mobile, Repousse, Welding, Sculpture, South Indian Bronzes, Somnath Hore, Raghav Kaneria, Shankar Nandagopal, Ankit Patel, Pilloo Pochkhanawalla;* Illustration–*K.C. Aryan.*

X Y Z

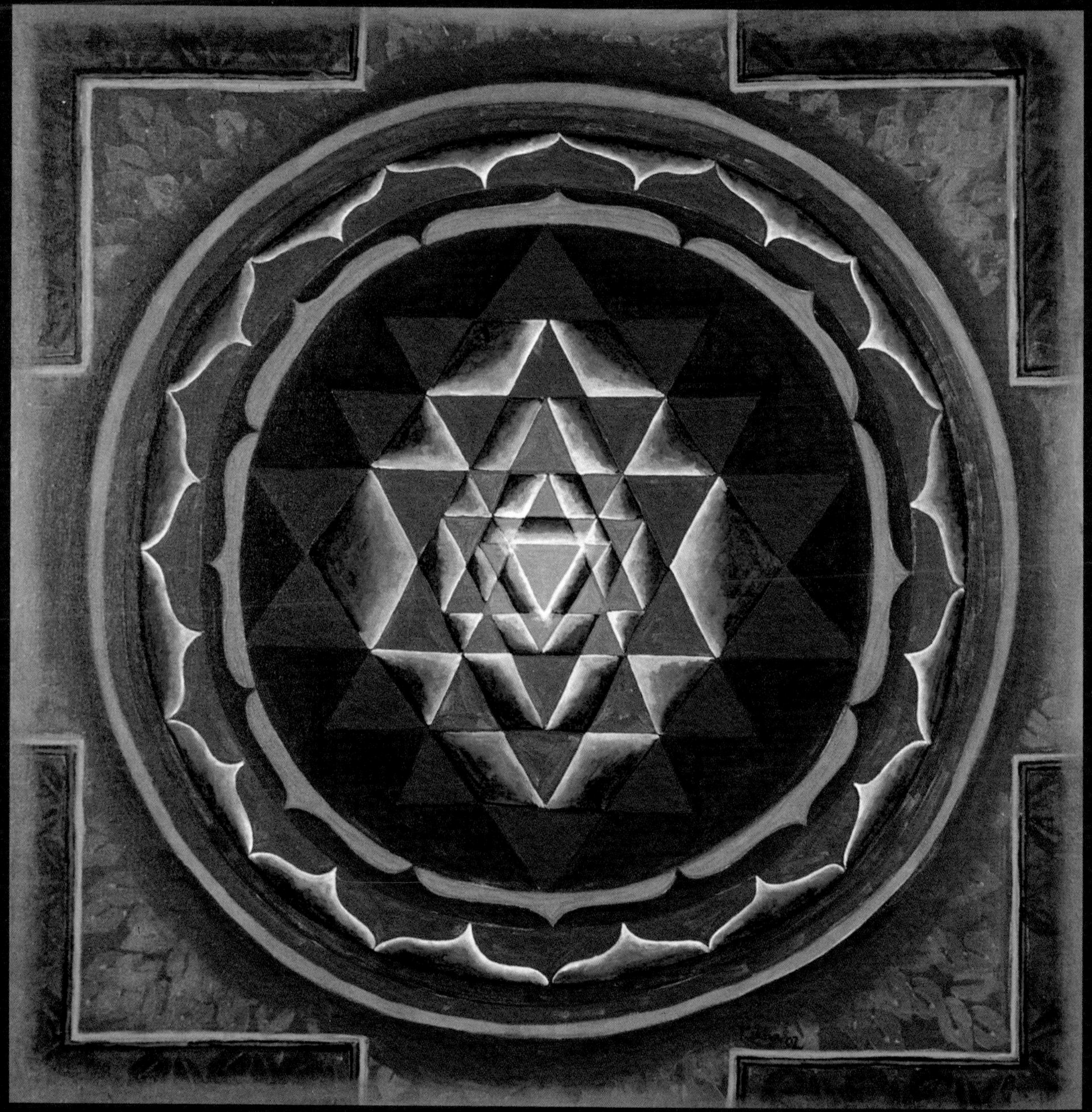

YANTRA: *Rekha Krishnan*, "Sri Yantra 1", 2001, 92x92 cm. (See notes on page 381)

Xavier, Babu (1960–) b. Kottayam, Kerala. Self-taught, having practised *painting* with *K. Jayapala Panicker* of *Cholamandal* for some years. Solos: Bangalore, *SG* Art World Chennai, Kalapeedom Cochin, *PUAG*, *RG*, SAG, *GG*; International: Germany, Switzerland, Denmark. Group parti cipations: Kerala *LKA*, *BAAC* Kolkata, *Triennale* New Delhi, *BB Biennales*, *JAG*, *BAS;* International: London. *Art* camps: Goa, Kolkata, Kerala *LKA* camp. Award: Kerala *LKA*. Publications: A book of poems "Clairvoyant". Collections: *NGMA* & *LKA* New Delhi, *BB*, *PUAG*; International: V&A, Chester Herwitz collection USA, pvt. & corporates.

Babu Xavier's early training in zoology opened a world peopled by animals, each intricately created so as to seem real. Plants and animals, clocks and metre-scales all merge together in a welter of *colours* to make up his *compositions*, with a series of works inspired by the Bible. He uses jewel-like bursts of *colour* to enliven his pseudo-realistic *compositions*. He has worked with several *media*, including *oils*, *acrylics*, *waterproof ink* and *pastels*.

He lives and works in Kovalam, Thiruvananthapuram.

Y. B. Chavan Art Gallery (YBCAG) (Mumbai) was launched by Yashavantrao Chavan Pratishthan, Mumbai on the 2nd of February, 1992 to promote *FA.* and help young and upcoming *artists*. The gallery has a display area of 1800 sq.ft., 188 running ft. wall and movable screen *space*, with 462 sq.ft. display area.

Yadav, Kanhiyalal R. (1932–1992) b. Ratlam, MP. Education: GDA in *drawing* & *painting*, Art Master's certificate Mumbai, Studied under *Rasiklal Parikh*; Inspired by his own visit to *JJSA.* Solos: Mumbai. Group participations & National *Exhibitions*: *LKA* & Nagpur, *BAS*. Awards: Creative *painting* prize Mumbai, Mysore DAE, IAFA Kolkata, *BAS*. Commissions: *Paintings* & *portraits* in temples. Appointments: Lecturer in CNCFA. Collections: *LKA* New Delhi, *LKA* GUJ & Nagpur Museum.

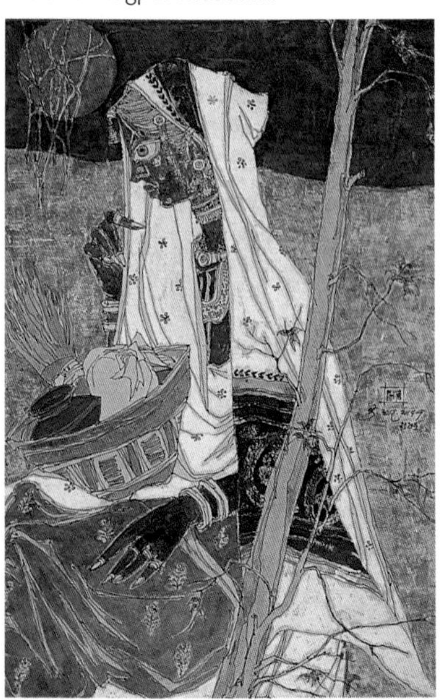

Yadav, Kanhiyalal R.: "Untitled", *Watercolours,* 1976.

Kanhiyalal R. Yadav's *style* was *eclectic*, though it had its formal roots in traditional *art*. His *landscapes* in *watercolour* are serene with near impressionistic *wash* and planes of soft *colour*. His *"Taj Mahal"* captures the reflection of the monument in the water. He painted several spontaneous *sketches* of birds and other creatures. His studies of village life, with *perspective landscapes* of his slum-dwelling as well as bejewelled women are folk-like in his use of wiry, descriptive *lines* and sparse *colour* areas.

Yadav Ram Kishore (1937–) b. Pratap Pura, Agra. Education: National Dip. in *commercial art College of Art* New Delhi. Over 60 solos: *LKA* New Delhi & Chennai, *BAAC* & Gallery Sanskriti Kolkata, FA. Museum Chandigarh, TKS, *AIFACS*, SRAG, *Dhoomimal*, *VAG*, BAG, *JAG*, TAG; International: 12 solos Belgium, Germany, Poland, Luxembourg, USA. Group participations: *LKA* New Delhi, AP Council of Arts Hyderabad, *AIFACS*, SKP, *BAS*, *NCAG*. *Art* camps & workshops: Nathdwara, Agra, camp SKP, workshop *AIFACS*. Awards: Kalidas Academy MP, Gold Jubliee Governer of RAJ for solo, National Award in commemorative stamp *design* on Mahatma Gandhi, *AIFACS*, NID; International: Bulgaria New Jersey USA. Fellowships: Senior at Dept. of Culture Govt. of India; International: From British Council London. Collect-ions: *LKA* & *NGMA* New Delhi, PUJ *LKA*, *FA*. Museum Chandigarh, *GMAG*, pvt. & corporates.

Ram Kishore Yadav has worked with several *mediums*, but *embossing* and beating *patterns* on *metal* sheets is a clear favourite. His early *oil paintings* picked *themes* from the rural as well as urban environment of India. With *embossing* however, *folk art*, religious *themes* and symbols became predominant, patterned neatly into geometric shapes and Tantra-inspired *colours*.

His *pastels* are more iconic with female *figures* set against idyllic, *pastoral backgrounds*. The *colours* here are more subtle, elegant, as is the *texture*.

He lives and works in New Delhi. Refer Illustration–*Repousse*.

Yadava, J.R. (1933–) b. Hansi, Haryana. Education: Dip. in *FA*. PUJ University Chandigarh. Solos: FA. Museum PUJ, KB Chandigarh, Town Hall Shimla, *AIFACS*, *GMAG*. Group participations: *LKA* New Delhi, PUJ *LKA* Chandigarh, *AIFACS*. Award: *AIFACS*. Collections: FA. Museum Chandigarh, *GMAG*.

J.R. Yadava is both a *painter*, working with *oils* and *watercolours,* and a *graphic artist*. *Texture* is an important element in his works, lending an ominous quality to his *drawings* of knotted tree-trunks and rock formations. His *sculptures* in *terracotta* show the use of similar *imagery*, with the human *form* seeming to emerge out of the convoluted *mass* of heaving shapes.

He lives and works in Chandigarh, PUJ.

Yaksha=spirit, living supernatural being. Male earth spirit, nature spirit, semi-divine being. The sculpted *images* of the Yakshas have certain physical characteristics in common. These include a powerful physique, an earthy quality, with powerful arms and legs. They are mostly pot-bellied, and convey the essence of life i.e. breath. In the case of Kubera Yaksha, the belly is an indication of prosperity. Most of the *sculptures* depict the Yakshas as wearing only a lower garment. They were executed chiefly during the Mauryan and Sunga period. Refer YAKSHI, YAKSHINI.

Yakshi, Yakshini The female counterpart of the YAKSHA, she is a female earth or nature spirit. They are both native or folk deities, being worshipped and propitiated by the indigenous people, even when *Buddhism* or *Hinduism* became popular. In fact some of the most beautiful Yakshini *figures* are found adorning the Buddhist monuments. The Yakshini is represented as a beautiful woman, with a voluptuous *figure* and a sensuous smile. At *times*, the concept of the Yakshini became similar to that of the SHALEBHANJIKA. At Bharhut and Sanchi especially, the SHALEBHANJIKA Yakshini *form* has been repeatedly used. The Didarganj Yakshini is an elegant e.g. of Mauryan *art*. She is tall, heavy breasted and large hipped with a narrow tapering waist. She also holds a Chauri (fly whisk) in one hand. Refer *Ecological Art, Mathura Art, Maurya Dynasty, Sunga Dynasty or Style, State Museum* (Patna, Bihar), *Jatin Das, B.P. Kamboj;* Illustration–*Earth Art, Earth Work, Land Art, Kanayi Kunhiraman*.

Yantra An instrument, a spell or a certain mystic geometrical diagram, incised and raised on a *metal plate*. The Yantras are believed to possess power to fulfil one's desire and ambitions speedily. A Vedic practice, ancient Rishis used them as focal points for concentration of thoughts to attain complete peace of mind so essential on the path towards self-realization and communion with *god*. The *rituals* were adapted to specific requirement of the religion; and were used in conjunction with sacred syllables known as the Mantras. Thus, Yantras are the *visual* equivalent of Mantra. Each deity is typified by the use of a specific Yantra to depict his/her power. These diagrams and their *spiritual* undertones are generally used by neo-tantric *artists*. Refer *Abstract, Abstract Art, Design, Neo-Tantricism, Spiritual, Tantric Composition, Theme, Jyoti Bhatt;* Illustrations–*Tantra Art, K.V. Haridasan, Ghulam Rasool Santosh.* (See illustration on page 379)

Yoga Yoga is an ancient system dating circa150 BC of a *spiritual* discipline that brings together the combined powers of the body, mind and soul and dedicates the forces so generated to *god*. Originally meant only for self-contemplation it later became an efficient system of self-discipline. Training in Yoga is gradually imparted, from stage to stage, in eight steps: Yama–the act of purity in one's approach to life; Niyama–is the purification of the body and mind with will-power; ASANAS–sitting in a dignified agreeable posture with concentration; Pranayama–controlled breathing; Pratyahara–deep breathing in a complete controlled manner to cleanse the mind of all senses; Dharana–fixed concentration on an object; Dhyana–meditation through contemplation; and Samadhi–absorption through meditation to a stage of super consciousness. The practice of Yoga is said to unite the individual self with the universal self. Ancient Indian *sculpture* was influenced by the various Yogic postures, e.g. BUDDHA, MAHAVIRA, BRAHMA, *Ellora, Ajanta, Gandharan Art, Mathura Art*. Yoga, along with other *art forms* like dance, theatre, *Video art* photography have at times been incorporated into *art performance* and other *contemporary art forms.* Refer Illustration–ASANA, BRAHMA, MAHAVIRA, SHIVA.

Yoni= vagina, female organs of generation. The Yoni is the female principle, symbolizing the Devi (goddess). It is often represented as encircling the LINGAM in Indian *sculpture*. Just as the LINGAM signifies SHIVA and is worshipped by Shaivites, the Yoni is worshiped by the Shaktas (followers of Devi SHAKTI). It is one of the *key motifs* in neo-tantric and *Tantra art*.

Young Turks A group of *artists* from *JJSA*, who preceded the *PAG* by about eight years. They included E. Mogul, *P.T. Reddy*, M.Y. Kulkarni, C. Baptista, M.P. Bhople and A.A. Majeed. The group was possibly named by R. Leyden. They were also among the earliest *artists* in India to propagate *modernism*. However unlike the later *PAG artists*, they were still using *colour* in the academic *manner* of late 19th-century British *painting*. However, they experimented with their *techniques*, E. Mogul especially using thick expressionist strokes with the *palette knife*.

Yuga A period of astronomical and/or historical cycles. Refers to Ages of years of existence of which there are four **(i)** Satya or Krita: Age of truth or accomplishment; **(ii)** Treta: Age of Triad; **(iii)** Dvapara: Age of the world, comprising 2400 years; and **(iv)** Kali: Kaliyuga, the present age, the age of darkness.

The first three having passed, the world is supposed to be passing through Kaliyuga which is supposed to have begun in 3102 BC. Refer KALI, KALKI, KALKIN.

Yusuf (1952–) b. Gwalior. Education: NDFA & National Dip. in *sculpture* Gwalior. Solos: Gwalior, Bhopal, New Delhi, Jabalpur, Indore, Ahmedabad, Kolkata, *Tao Art Gallery* Mumbai. Group participations: *Triennale* New Delhi, *CYAG, JAG, BB*; International: Dhaka. *Art* camps: All India *Sculpture*, Gwalior *Artists, Mural, Metal casting* & *Graphic* Gwalior, *LKA Graphic* Bhubaneshwar, All India Painters New Delhi; India International *Artists* camp: New Delhi, Goa, Manipur, Pune, Bhubaneshwar, Lucknow. Awards: MP State Award, Raza Award Bhopal, National *LKA, BB*. Govt. of India Fellowship New Delhi; International: *Biennale* Turkey. Member: *LKA* New Delhi. Appointments: By MP Govt. nominee for *LKA*

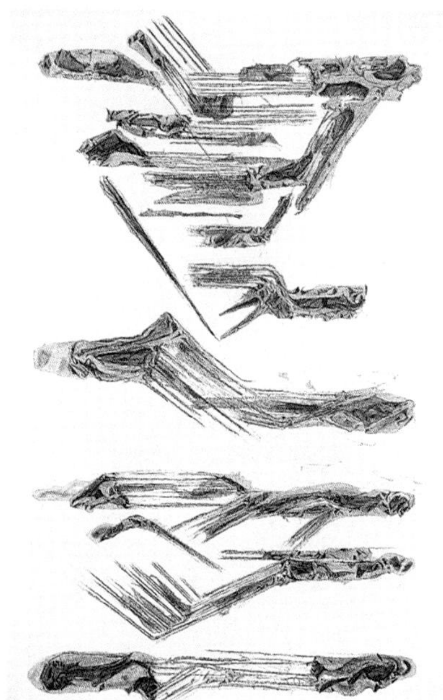

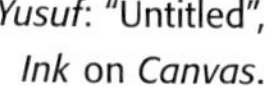

Yusuf: "Untitled", *Ink* on *Canvas*.

& by Govt. of India nominee *LKA* New Delhi; Collected *Folk & Tribal Art* for *Roopankar BB* & for Festival of India in Japan. Collections: *NGMA*, *LKA* & Sanskriti Pratishtan New Delhi, MPKP Bhopal, *LKA* Bhubaneshwar, Impal & Lucknow, *Nag Foundation* Pune, *CYAG*, *GAC*, *BB*.

Line plays an important role in Yusuf's *art*. The *line* or more accurately the group of *lines* are the basic element around which his *paintings* evolve. They maintain their essentially linear character, alternately running, turning, sustaining, joining, rising, flying, breaking and sometimes creating a net-like *texture*. The works also convey a horizontal structure against a subtle vertical *background*, unified by slashing, short diagonals at regular intervals. The *colours* are stormy yet subtle. Yusuf also incises *lines* at regular intervals, bringing out the whiteness of the *hand-made paper* that he works on.

He lives and works in Bhopal.

Zahoor, Zargar (1950–) b. Srinagar, Kashmir. Edu-cation: M.FA. in *applied arts MSU*. Solos: Srinagar, Alliance Francaise New Delhi, SRAG, *LTG*, TAG, *JAG*. Group participations: MMB New Delhi, *CIMA* Kolkata, *SUG*, HG, *LTG*, *Dhoomimal*, SKP, *JAG*. *Artist* camps: Hyderabad; Workshops: *LKA* Photographic, Alliance Francaise New Delhi, *GAC*. Awards: GUJ *LKA*, J&K Academy. Appointments: Reader at JMI; Designed Books. Collections: *LKA* New Delhi; Inter-national: World Bank Germany, France, USA, pvt. & corporates.

Zahoor Zargar can be called a landscapist for the speckled brushstroke that he employs evoking an impressionist feeling. The diffused *light* in his works in *gouache*, *oils*, *watercolours* and *mixed media* eliminates strong *shadows* and merges *forms* into nearly *abstract* fields of flecked *colour*.

He lives and works in New Delhi.

Zharotia, Jai (1945–) b. New Delhi. Education: *College of Art* New Delhi, *SUSA* New Delhi. Solos: Kunika Chemould, *LKA* & *Art Heritage* New Delhi, Aakar Chandigarh, TKS, *Dhoomimal*, *VAG*, *CYAG*, *CKAG*, GAG, *G88*, BHU. Group participations: *Triennale*, RB & Gallery Aurobindo New Delhi, *AIFACS*, SC, *VAG*, *LTG*, SRAG, *JAG*; International: Cuba, Bonn, Frankfurt, Poland, Hamburg. *Art* camps: *Santiniketan*, *Graphics* Vadodara, *LKA* & CMC *art* camps New Delhi, *AIFACS*, *GAC*, SKP; International: Japan. *Auctions*: Heart New Delhi. Awards: National Award New Delhi, SKP, *AIFACS*. Founder member: New Group. Appointments: Prof. of *Painting* & HoD M.FA. *CFA* New Delhi. Collections: Godrej Mumbai, *NGMA* New Delhi, Chandigarh University Museum, *BKB*, *CYAG*, SKP.

Jai Zharotia creates a fantasy-filled world, peopled with clowns, masked and flying *figures*, centaurs and other beasts floating in a limbo-like *space* of *colour* and *lights* in his works. *Watercolour* with its inherent fluidity is most suited to his *technique*, but he does use other *techniques* as well. The *colour* contrasts beguile the senses with sparks of shocking pink and yellow enlivening staid blues and greys. The simplifications of *form* and *colour* comparable to *Basohli* miniatures, but the *imagery* is purely modernistic. His *sculptures* allow him to explore the relationship of his chosen *form* to the *space* within which it is set. *Texture* is equally important in these works, evoking the *tactile* sense as well as the *visual*.

He lives and works in New Delhi.

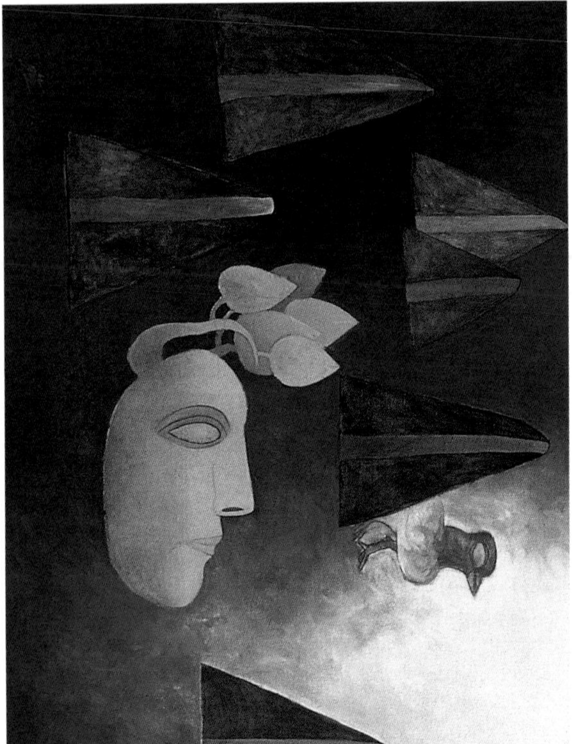

Zharotia, Jai: "Untitled", *Oil* on *Canvas*, 1995, 75x95 cm.

Zinc (Metal) (Sanskrit=Dasta) It was known to European metallurgists in the 1720s. Recent excavations at Southern RAJ have discovered evidence of zinc probably in the 14th century. Zinc is used to prepare a metallic yellow *alloy*, *brass*, which often used in *sculpture*. Zinc or *aluminium plates* are also used for *lithography*. While the zinc *plate* is used for *engraving* and *etching*, by Ramachand Roy (18th century) in Calcutta was one of the earliest printmakers to use *metal plates*. The *artist* used it for *intaglio printing* among which *etching* was easier with *acid resist ground* and its application on the *metal* surface. In the mid-70s, *Krishna N. Reddy* developed the *viscosity printmaking* on the zinc *plates*. Refer *Acid Bath*, *Alum*, *Ground*, *White*, *Jyoti Bhatt*, *Mukul Chandra Dey*, *Vivan Sundaram*.

Introduction

India has a very ancient and rich tradition of art and craft in the form of sculptures, metal images, wooden objects, textiles, miniature paintings, canvas paintings, paper manuscripts and so on, belonging to different periods and regions. In the contemporary scene also, there are thousands of paintings, sculptures and art objects of various types. Such artistic creativity is supported quite often by places of worship like temples and churches. On important festive occasions, paintings were executed on walls, on panels and on paper. In every walk of life in India, art has always played a dominant role.

This legacy handed down to us in various forms is housed today in museums, libraries, and private collections and with individuals. Art objects in one form or another are found in almost every household.

Damage and Deterioration of Art Objects

Unfortunately art objects, in whatever form they exist, do not remain immune to the ravages of time and natural deterioration. There are many factors, which cause art objects to deteriorate for some reason or the other. There are some types of objects that are more susceptible to deterioration, while others are more durable. The rate of decay depends upon the nature of the object, the material of which it is made and also the nature of the damaging agency. In order to preserve art objects for a longer duration, one has to under-stand the nature of the material of which the objects are made and also the nature and type of the deterioration, which has affected the object.

Nature of Materials

The materials of which art objects are made can be classified broadly as inorganic and organic. All substances like stone, clay, metals that are derived from the earth, are termed inorganic, and all substances which are derived from plants and animals, like wood, paper, leather, textiles, canvas are known as organic material. As a general rule inorganic materials are more hardy and durable than the organic ones. We know by experience, and also on scientific principles, that substances like stone, clay and metals are less affected by natural agencies than materials like paper manuscripts, books, textiles fabrics, and wooden objects. This is the fundamental basic principle of preservation. One has to take more care of organic objects than of inorganic objects. This does not mean that art objects made of inorganic materials are totally immune to deterioration. They also get damaged, particularly during transportation or handling. But the chances of decay are fewer. On the other hand paper, textiles, leather, and wood are affected continuously by many agencies.

Paintings, whether ancient or modern, fall into a different category. A painting has at least two layers—one is the support, like canvas, paper, metal, ivory, etc., on which the painting is done and another the paint layer. A painting is thus a complex structure and therefore the phenomenon of deterioration is also complex. Chemically, both the components, namely the support and the paint remain inert but there are chances that the paint might crumble and flake off from the support. Hence, paintings demand a lot of attention with regard to preservation.

The Nature of Decay and Damage

External factors harmful to art objects may be classified into natural and manmade. The natural causes include the effect of climate, light, micro-organisms of various types and insects. Manmade causes are war, theft, vandalism, improper storage and mishandling. The public can cause damage and professionals out of ignorance can also cause it. They may be instant damage through earthquake or floods. One has to prepare for all these eventualities.

Art of Preservation

The techniques of preservation are both an art and science, which involve certain basic principles of decay and chemical laws. On the other hand it depends on the art of applying those principles in practice. The important thing is a full understanding of the nature of the objects on the one hand and the factors causing decay on the other.

Factors of Damage

As stated earlier, there are several factors which cause damage and we propose to deal with them one by one, pointing out their effects and how they can be controlled.

Climate: The climate of a place tells us how hot it is and what the humidity level is. Is it high or low? Tropical regions have hot and humid climates. Desert areas have a hot but dry climate. High humidity of the atmosphere would give rise to several problems like the growth of fungi and proliferation of different types of insects. Paper objects in high humidity become limp and attract fungi. Hot climate with a high temperature accelerates all types of chemical reactions, causing the materials to decay fast. A dry climate on the other hand causes objects to turn brittle.

Variations during the day and night, or even the seasonal fluctuations of climate, are harmful to art objects. Wooden sculptures crack on this account. One of the main reasons for the flaking of paint in paintings is the fluctuations in the climatic conditions of the place where the paintings are exhibited or stored.

It is therefore necessary that art objects are protected from high humidity, high temperature and also from frequent changes in climatic conditions. Quite often air conditioning of the storage or exhibition areas is recommended. However, if air conditioning is expensive, and the running cost is high, alternative methods can be considered. For example, paintings on paper like miniature paintings if stored in hardboard boxes are protected from climatic variations, dust, etc., to a certain extent. Objects inside showcases keep better than those which are exhibited outside. The design of the building also has great influence on the climate inside. The orientation of the buil-ding, its plan, shape, the thickness of the walls, the ventilation system and so on, influence the microclimate inside. Roofs and external walls if painted white, or near white, deflect much of the solar radiation. Provision of external shades can keep the building cool. Trees planted outside the building can also provide some shade.

Thermal insulation of roofs or the provision of false ceilings can reduce solar radiation considerably. By shading the windows, the penetration of solar heat can be greatly reduced. Proper ventilation inside the storage and the exhibition areas is therefore important.

In case it is possible to provide air conditioning, the standards and norms for air conditioning in museums must be followed. Air conditioning should be on all the time throughout the year. Recommended temperatures are bet-ween 20 to

22°C and the relative humidity between 45 to 55 per cent. There should be as little variation in these as possible.

Light: Light also has a tremendous effect on the physical strength of art objects, especially water-colour paintings, miniature paintings, coloured textiles. All susceptible objects should be protected from light. However, for viewing an object, a light source is very necessary. Therefore one has to take into consideration certain important properties of light. Light has two main components–one is visible and the other is invisible. This means that the component, which is necessary for viewing an object is what is visible, while the other, although present in the light, is not required for looking at an object. Ultra-violet rays are an example of an invisible property of light. It is also known that ultra-violet rays are extremely harmful to organic materials like paper, fabrics, colour, paintings, feathers and so on.

Based on the above analysis, we draw the following important conclusions for the protection of objects from the dangerous effect of light:

• The objects should be exposed to light for a minimum period of time. Excess exposure to light would mean more likelyhood of damage to the object.

• The intensity of the light should be kept low, and only as much as is required for a comfortable viewing of the paintings and other objects.

• The ultra-violet rays should be filtered by using ultra-violet absorbing filters in front of the light source.

These are some very simple but very effective precautions against the effect of light.

Quite often excessive light is used for photographing paintings. Sometimes paintings are even brought out in bright sunlight for this purpose. This must be avoided. Even the use of photoflood lamps for long periods may harm delicate objects. It is safest to use a flash.

Insects: Insects of various types also damage art objects and paintings. Objects of an organic nature like wooden sculptures, costumes, fabrics, manuscripts, palm-leaf manuscripts, and books are particularly liable to be damaged by insects. They feed on the material and produce holes in it.

There are various types of insects but the most damaging are termites, commonly known as white ants. Other insects like bookworms, silver fish, cockroaches also harm art materials.

To control insects it is better to use insect-proof materials for the construction of buildings. When a new building is constructed for a museum or an art gallery it should be made termite-proof by introducing anti-termite chemicals in the foundation. In old buildings anti-termite chemicals, available in hardware stores, are introduced by drilling holes in the floor of the building and introducing the protective solution under pressure.

Insect repellents are used for the storage of art objects, paintings, books, etc. In the case of active infestation, fumigation in a fumigation chamber may be the only effective remedy. Fumigation chambers are of various types: simple units and vacuum fumigation chambers. A simple fumigant is the chemical paradichlo-benzene, which comes in the form of crystals.

For the control of cockroaches crystals of sodium floride or pyrethrum mixed with wheat flour are sprinkled on the floor. Wheat flour is mixed to attract the insects.

Naphthalene balls or bricks placed on storage shelves may also control insects.

Fungus: In humid countries like India, fungi and other types of micro-organisms may also grow on art objects and may damage them. In outside locations, algae, bacteria, lichen and moss are very active. Fungi on the other hand are a serious threat to art objects displayed indoors. Fungi when they develop on paper, leather paintings or textiles not only degrade them but also cause stains. They break down the structure of the materials and bring about changes in the chemical properties of objects. Sometimes a fungus may grow beneath the surface and is not visible on the surface layer. Quite often it is found to grow in between the paper layers of a miniature painting. It may also grow on books, manuscripts and leather bindings. Fungi might affect oil paintings stored in a wet basement even in the period of a few days.

To prevent fungi, control of humidity is essential. If air-conditioning is not possible, good ventilation and circulation of air are helpful. Cleanliness of objects and the building where they are stored and exhibited is important. Manuscripts, books, paintings and other art objects should be taken out of the shelves and dusted from time to time.

Disinfecting the stores and cupboards where objects are stored might also control the growth of fungi. For this purpose a ten per cent solution of thymol in rectified spirit is sprayed inside the room to disinfect it.

Storage: For the physical safety of art objects, proper storage is of considerable significance. A survey conducted by the Museum Development Cell of the Indian Council of Conservation Institutes has revealed that improper storage is one of the main reasons for damage to art objects. For planning the storage of museum art objects or library mate-rials, the following points have to be kept in mind.

• Objects should not be placed one over the other to avoid their rubbing against each other and causing physical pressure.

• Objects should be placed in such a manner, properly labelled so that they are easily traceable.

• There should be a proper record of the location of objects.

• They should be fully protected from climate, fungus, insects, light, etc.

Objects or paintings that should not rub against one another and should not be placed one over the other also include:

- Scroll paintings
- Thangkhas
- Canvas paintings
- Water colours and miniature paintings
- Sculptures, bronze images and other three dimensional objects
- Textiles
- Small objects like medals, seals and coins

Miniature paintings should be stored in specially prepared cardboard boxes. Manuscripts are kept wrapped in pieces of cotton, generally of a red or yellow colour.

Flat textiles like saris and shawls are rolled over rollers for storage. The roller should be of slightly bigger length than the width of the fabric. The rollers in turn are stored in properly designed cupboards.

Scroll paintings and Thangkhas are stored in such a manner that they do not crumble under their own weight. They are best stored in cardboard boxes, which in turn are kept in a cupboard. Or else, they may be kept in shallow drawers with appropriate separators in between.

Special cabinets with shallow drawers and slots are prepared for storing small objects like coins, seals, medals, beads and so on.

Loose single sheet documents, watercolour

paintings or miniature paintings can be stored in one of the following methods:

- Inside specially prepared portfolios
- Windows-cut mount boards
- Between two mount boards

Palm-leaf manuscripts should always be kept between two wooden boards slightly bigger than the size of the leaves. In palm-leaf manuscripts normally there are two holes on either side through which a cord is passed and then brought over the two boards and tied around tightly. The bundles of manuscripts are then stored in specially constructed cupboards with pigeonhole slots in each of which one manuscript is kept.

There are certain general precautions for storage, which may be enumerated as follows:

• The stores must be kept absolutely clean, not only the objects but also the areas. Dust attracts fungus and insects. Wherever it settles, it is a source of attracting moisture.

• No food or drink should be allowed inside the store.

• Smoking must be strictly prohibited inside the storage area.

• There should always be insect repellent kept at appropriate places in the store.

Improper Handling: Although natural causes like climate, light, fungi, insects, and so on damage art objects, equally damaging is the improper handling and transportation. Art objects and paintings should never be touched with unclean hands; it often transmits oil, grease and perspi-ration to the object. In turn, it attracts dust. Hands should never touch painted surfaces. Photographs, negatives and prints should also be handled with great care; they should be handled at the edges and not at the surface.

A trolley should be used while moving an object from one place to another. Small objects should be kept on trays for transporting. Large paintings should also be moved on specially padded trolleys. If such facilities are not available, at least two persons should be available to support the painting. While keeping the objects in trays or trolleys, enough padding should be placed below the objects to avoid physical damage. A ceramic item, or a sculpture should never be lifted by holding it at the beck or rim; it may be weak and These are common precautions. The idea is to handle paintings and other art objects with care.

Conclusion

It will be seen from the above description that the preservation of art objects is based on a set of certain principles to minimize the effect of dama-ging forces, which may be described as aggressors of art objects. All artists, and art collectors should know about them and should follow them in actual practice. Only then can precious art objects be saved from destruction.

O. P. Agrawal

Founder Director of the National Research Laboratory for the Conservation of Cultural Property in Lucknow; Director General of INTACH Indian Conservation Institute; b.1931 and educated at University of Allahabad; Acquired training in the technique of conservation at Central Institute of Restoration, Rome. Has written books and articles. He is a Fellow of the International Institute of Conservation, London.

Credits

To all those who helped prepare this Dictionary
My personal thanks to

Kamal Abhyankar, Mumbai, for Sanskrit
O.P. Agrawal , Lucknow
Amit Ambalal, Ahmedabad
Amroliwala Aban, Mumbai
Nalini G. Bhagwat, Mumbai
Rashmi Doshi, Pune
Saryuben Doshi, Mumbai
Suken Ganguly, Santiniketan
S.K. Gorakshkar, Mumbai
Kishore N. Gordhandas, Mumbai
(for Ganjifa information)
Anella Jasuja, Mumbai
Dr. Jyotindra Jain
Sanat Kar, Santiniketan
Jyoti Khambatta, Mumbai
Rekha Krishnan, Mumbai
Yeshwant Mahale, Mumbai
C.D. Mistry, Ahmedabad
Partha Mitter, London
N.B. Patel, Mumbai, for Sanskrit
Rohit Pombra, Kolkata
Perin Pombra, Kolkata
Sayed Raza Haider, Paris
Rita Rebello, Mumbai
Pauline Rohtagi, Mumbai
Malay Chandan Saha, Kolkata
(Late) D.B. 'Deven' Seth, New Delhi
Arvindbhai Shah, Vadodara
Malthiben Shah, Vadodara
Siddhartha Tagore, New Delhi
Mahatab Tarapore, Mumbai
Veena Thimmaiah, Bangalore
Dr. Nathu Lal Verma, Jaipur
Babu Xavier, Thiruvananthapurum
R.K. Yadav, New Delhi

For slides, photographs, information, permission, and courtesy:

Aziz Khan, California, USA.
Babu Anichandji Panalalji Adishwar
Walkeshwar Temple, Mumbai
Bharat Kala Bhavan Museum, Varanasi
Benoy Behl, Photographic Credit for
Ajanta Slides, New Delhi
Prof. A. Bowlekar, Special thanks for
Photography & Illustration
Delhi Art Gallery, New Delhi
Gallery 7, Mumbai
Gallery Chemould, Mumbai
Sankalana Husain, Mumbai
Pasricha Indar, London, U.K.
Jain Temple Charitable Trust, Mumbai
Jehangir Art Gallery, Mumbai
Kala Bhavan, Santiniketan, West Bengal
Harkishore Kejriwal, Chitrakala Parishad,
Bangalore
Prakash Kejriwal, Chitrakoot, Calcutta
Lalit Kala Akademi, New Delhi
Mohile Parikh Centre for the Visual Art
(MPCVA), Mumbai
National Gallery of Modern Arts (NGMA),
New Delhi
Pundole Art Gallery, Mumbai
Sakshi Gallery, Mumbai
(Sir) J.J. School of Art, Mumbai
(Sri) Jayachamarajendra Art Gallery Trust,
Mysore

A special word of thanks also to all those unnamed above, who worked, helped and assisted behind the scenes and whose goodwill and encouragement led this arduous task to its happy and logical end–its publication.

Bibliography

20 Artists. New Delhi: All India Fine Arts & Crafts Society, January 1994.

25th Anniversary Exhibition of Calcutta Painters. Kolkata: Birla Academy of Art & Culture, 1990.

30th National Exhibition of Art. New Delhi: Lalit Kala Akademi, 1987.

32nd National Exhibition of Art. New Delhi: Lalit Kala Akademi, 1989.

33rd National Exhibition of Art. New Delhi: Lalit Kala Akademi, 1990.

34th National Exhibition of Art. New Delhi: Lalit Kala Akademi, 1990–1991.

35th National Exhibition of Art. New Delhi: Lalit Kala Akademi, March 1992.

37th National Exhibition of Art. New Delhi: Lalit Kala Akademi, New Delhi, n.d.

A Centenary Volume R.T. Sahitya Akademi (1861–1961). New Delhi: Sahitya Akademi, 1996.

A Guide to Mamallapuram. Mamallapuram: Studio Mahendra, Krishnaveni Printers, n.d.

A Historical Epic India in The Making 1757–1950. Ahmedabad & Mumbai: Mapin Publishing Pvt.Ltd. & Osian's, 2002.

A Historical Mela: The ABC of India, The Art, Book & Cinema. Ahmedabad & Mumbai: Mapin Publishing Pvt. Ltd & Osian's, 2002.

A Magazine of the Arts–Odissi. Context and Continuity. Vol. XLII No.2. Mumbai: Marg Publications, n.d.

A Retrospective of Umesh Varma 1955 to 95, (English/Hindi). New Delhi: Dhoomimal Gallery, 1995.

A. Ramachandran. Virendra Kumar, 1965.

Abanindranath Tagore. New Delhi: NGMA,1988.

Acharekar, M.R. *Elephanta*. Mumbai: Rekha Publications, 1983.

——. *Female Nude*. Mumbai: 1960.

Advani, Ashok H. *The India Magazine*. Vol. 13. Mumbai: 1993.

Aekka Yadagiri Rao. Hyderabad: Andhra Pradesh LKA, 1984.

Agarwala, R.A. *Bundi: The City of Painted Wall*. Agam Kala Prakashan, 1996.

Agrawal, O.P. *Preservation of Art Objects and Library Materials*. New Delhi: National Book Trust, 1993.

Ajanta Ellora. Mumbai: Maharashtra Tourism Development Corporation, n.d.

Alfred, Daniels. *Enjoying Acrylics*. Great Britain: William Luscan Book Publishers Ltd., 1976.

Amrita Sher-Gil. New Delhi: Rabindra Bhavan Gallerie, 1970.

Anand, Mulk Raj. *Ajanta*. Mumbai: Marg Publications, 1971.

——. Ed. Marg Graphics–*A Magazine of the Art. Vol. XIX*, No. 4. Mumbai: Tata Enterprise, Marg Publications, September 1966.

——. *Madhubani Painting*. New Delhi: Ministry of Information and Broadcasting, Government of India, 1984.

——. *Marg Magazine*, Vol. 54, No. 3; Vol. 55, No. 1; Vol. 55, No. 2. Mumbai: Marg Publications, 2003.

Anand, Mulk Raj. *The Single Line–Drawing by K.K. Hebber*. New Delhi: Abhinav Publications, 1982.

——. *Treasure of Indian Museum*. Mumbai: Marg Publications, n.d.

Anatomy of Sculpture. Mumbai: JJSA, n.d.

Appasamy, Jaya. *Contemporary Indian Art Series* (Jamini Roy). New Delhi: LKA, 1987.

——. Ed. *Lalit Kala Contemporary*. New Delhi: LKA, n.d.

——. *Indian Paintings on Glass*. New Delhi: ICCR, 1980.

——. *Lalit Kala Contemporary 5*. New Delhi: LKA, n.d.

——. *The Critical Vision*. New Delhi: LKA, 1985.

Apte, Vaman Shivram. Reprint. *The Student's English & Sanskrit Dictionary*. New Delhi: Motilal Banarsidass Publishers Pvt. Ltd., 1997.

Arpita Singh—Femine Fables. Mumbai: Gallery Chemould, 1997.

Art and the Artist. Vol. 2. Kolkata: Academy of Fine Arts by Mookerjee R., n.d.

Art and the Artist. Vol. 3. Kolkata: Academy of Fine Arts by Mookerjee R., n.d.

Art and the Artist. Vol. 4. Kolkata: Academy of Fine Arts by Mookerjee R., n.d.

Art and the Artist. Vol. 6. Kolkata: Academy of Fine Arts by Mookerjee R., n.d.

Art and the Artist. Vol. 7. Kolkata: Academy of Fine Arts by Mookerjee R., n.d.

Art and the Artist. Vol. 21. Kolkata: Academy of Fine Arts by Mookerjee R., n.d.

Art of Basab Tagore: In Retrospective. Kolkata: Asiatic Society, 1984.

Art of Bengal: Whitechapel Art Gallery. London & Bradford: Trustees of the Whitechapel Art Gallery, 1979.

Asher, Frederick M. & G.S. Gai. *Indian Epigraphy*. New Delhi: Oxford & IBH Publishing Co, 1985.

B.C. Gue. Rajasthan: LKA, 1974.

Bahadur, Om Lata. *The Book of Hindu Festivals & Ceremonies*. New Delhi: UBS Publishers' Distributors Ltd., 1998.

Bazin, Germain. *A Concise History of Art—Part Two*. London: Thames & Hudson, 1968.

Beaver, R.P., Dr. J. Bergmas et al. *The World's Religions*. England: Lion Publishing, 1992.

Bhatnagar, R.K. *Contemporary Indian Art Series*. Gaganendranath Tagore, 1986.

———. *Gaganendranath Tagore—Contemporary Indian Art Series*. New Delhi: LKA, 1964.

Bhattacherjee, S.B. *Encyclopaedia of Indian Events & Dates*. New Delhi: Sterling Publishers Pvt. Ltd., 1999.

Bhide, G.R. and Gajabar Baba. *Kalamaharshi Baburao Painter* (Baburao Krishnarao Mestry). Kolhapur: 1978.

Bhoumik Samar N. *Contribution of Tagore Family of Jorasanko in Art of India*. Kolkata: RBM, 1984.

Bhupen among Friends. Mumbai: Gallery Chemould, 2005.

Bickelmann, Ursula and Ezekiel Nissim. Ed. *Artists Today*. Mumbai: Marg Publications, 1987.

Birla Academy of Art & Culture: Celebrates Silver Jubilee: Northern India—1967–1992, Eastern India—1967–1992, Southern India—1967–1992, Western India—1967–1992. Kolkata: BAAC.

Bisht, R.S. *In Search of Self*. Lucknow: Ratan P. Hingorani/Nand K. Khanna Pustak Kendra, 1966.

Bisht, Ranbir Singh. *Contemporary Indian Art Series*. New Delhi: LKA, 1988.

Borjeson, Per-Olov. *The Great Clown—Krishna Reddy*. Sweden: Borjeson Galerie, n.d.

Bose, Nandalal. *Haripura Panels*. New Delhi: National Gallery of Modern Art, 1988.

Bose, Uttam Kumar. *Xpressions*. New Delhi: November 2003, October 2003.

Brijbhusan, Jamila. *The World of Indian Miniatures*. Tokyo, New York & San Francisco: Kodansha International Ltd., 1979.

Brown, David A. *The Guide to Religions*. Delhi: ISPCK, 1991.

Burton, Richard & Arbuthnot F.F. *Kama Sutra of Vatsyana*. Ed. Anand Mulk Raj, Lance Dane. Translated from the Original Sanskrit & adapted from the first English translation of 1883.

Calcutta Black & White. An Exhibition of Drawings by Shuvaprasanna. Kolkata: RPG Enterprises Limited, 1990.

Calcutta through The Eyes of Painters. Kolkata: BAAC, 1990.

Cavendish, Richard. *Mythology*. London: 1980.

Celebrating 25 Years—Surya Prakash. Mumbai: Cymroza Art Gallery, 1997.

Chakravorty, Ramendranath. *Abanindranath Tagore—His Early Work*. Kolkata: Indian Museum, 1964.

Chandrasekhar S.N. *M.A. Chetti*. Bangalore: Karnataka Lalitha Kala Academy, 1985.

Chattopadhyay, Kamaladevi. *Handicrafts of India*. Kolkata: 1975.

Chaudri, L.R. *Secrets of Yantra Mantra and Tantra*. New Delhi: Sterling Publishers Pvt. Ltd., 1998.

Chawla, Rupika. *Surface & Depth*. Delhi: Viking 1995.

———. *Ramachandran—Art of the Muralist*. New Delhi: Kala Yatra & Sistas Publication, 1994.

Chopra, Jagmohan. *Roopa-Lekha*. Ashok H. Advan Vol. LXIII. New Delhi: AIFACS,1993.

Christie's London Indian Contemporary Art. London: 1997.

Christie's Twentieth Century Indian Art. London: 1998.

Chughtai's Paintings. Lahore: Jahangir Book Club Chabuk Sanaran, n.d.

Collection of Works. New Delhi: Vadehra Art Gallery, n.d.

Contemporary Art. Ahmedabad: Mapin Publishing Pvt. Ltd, 1995.

Contemporary Artists of UP. Lucknow: State LKA UP, 1990.

Contemporary Indian Art Series—Bhagat. New Delhi: LKA, 1986.

Contemporary Indian Art Series—K.S. Kulkarni. New Delhi: LKA New Delhi, 1988.

Contemporary Indian Art Series—M. Reddeppa Naidu. New Delhi: New Delhi, 1994.

Contemporary Indian Art Series—Raza. New Delhi: LKA, 1990.

Contemporary Indian Art Series—Vinayak Pandurang Karmarkar. New Delhi: LKA, 1989.

Contemporary Indian Art Series—Y.K. Shukla. New Delhi: LKA, 1987.

Contemporary Indian Art. London: RAA-London, Indian Advisory Committee, Festival of India-UK, 1982.

Contemporary Series of Indian Art—Chavda. New Delhi: LKA. n.d.

Contemporary Series of Indian Art—L. Munuswamy. New Delhi: New Delhi, 1985.

Contemporary Series of Indian Art—Sher-Gil. New Delhi, 1965.

Coomaraswamy Ananda K. *Christian & Oriental Philosophy of Art*. New York: Dover Publications, Inc., 1956.

——— and Sister Nivedita, *Myths of The Hindus And Buddhists*. Mumbai: Jaico Publishing House, 1999.

Cooper, Ilay and John Gillow. *Arts And Crafts of India*. London: Thames and Hudson Ltd., 1996.

Craven, Roy C. *Indian Art*. London: Thames & Hudso, 1976.

Dalley, Terence. Ed. *The Complete Guide to Illustration & Design Techniques and Materials Consultant*. Oxford: Phaidon Press Ltd., QED. Publishing Ltd.,1980.

Daniel, Scott, Singh. *Ramkumar A Retrospective*. Kottayam: The Ashram Press, n.d.

Das, Asok Kumar. *Dawn of Mughal Painting*. Mumbai: Vakils, Feffer and Simons Ltd.,1982.

Dasgupta, Bimal. *Contemporary Indian Art Series*. New Delhi: LKA, 1989.

Dave, Ramesh. *Kanaiyalal Yadav—A Memory Sketch*.

Daw, Prasanta. *Art and Aesthetics of Deviprasa*. Kolkata: ISOA, 1998.

———. *Atul Bose*. Kolkata: Chaudhuri Indira Nag, Indian Society of Oriental Art, 1990.

Dawson, John. *The Complete Guide to Prints & Print Making Technique & Material*. London: Phaidon Press Ltd., 1981.

De Biren, Mookerjee Ajit. *Contemporary Indian Art Series*. New Delhi: LKA, 1985.

Deneck, Marguerite-Marie. *Indian Art*. London: Paul Hamlyn Ltd., 1967.

Deshmukh, S.D. *Shankar Palsikar*. Mumbai: 1987.

Dey, Mukul. *Birbhum Terracottas*. New Delhi: LKA, 1959.

Doctor, Geeta. *Arnawaz*. Chennai: Arnawaz Vasudev Charities Cholamandal Artists' Village, 1989/1991.

Doshi, Saryu. *MARG: Master Pieces on Jain Painting*. Mumbai: Marg Publications, 1985.

Dowson, John. *A Classical Dictionary of Hindu Mythology & Religion*. Kolkata, Ahmedabad, Mumbai & New Delhi: Rupa & Co./Harper Collins,1982/1997.

Dubois Abbe, J.D. and Henry K. Beaucham. *Hindu Manners Customs & Ceremonies*. Delhi: C.I.E., 1978.

Face To Face. Delhi: LKA, 1998.

FAIM—*Federation of Artists Institutions of Maharashtra*. Mumbai: Lawate S.K., 1992.

Fine Sculptor's Tools Materials, and Accessories. New York: Sculpture Associates Ltd., n.d.

Fourth Triennale India 1978. New Delhi: LKA, n.d.

Fukuoka, Masanori. *Contemporary Indian Art*. Japan: Glenberra Japan Co. Ltd., 1993.

Gaganendranath Tagore. Assam: Rabindra Bharati Society, Assam Book Depot, 1964.

Gaganendranath Tagore. New Delhi: NGMA, 1996.

Gandhi, Maneka. *The Penguin Book of Hindu Names*. New Delhi: Penguin Book India (P) Ltd., 1993.

Garga, B.D. *So Many Cinemas: The Motion Picture in India*. Mumbai: Eminence Design Pvt. Ltd., 1996.

Garrette, John. *A Classical Dictionary of India*. Kolkata, Ahmedabad, Mumbai & New Delhi: Rupa & Co. and Harper Collins, 1871.

Genesis of Ramkinkar. Kolkata: BAAC, 2000.

Ghose, D.C. *Bibliography of Modern Indian Art*. New Delhi: LKA, 1980.

Ghose, Vijaya. Ed. *Tirtha, The Treasury of Indian Expressions*. Delhi: CMC. Ltd., 1992.

Gillow, John and Barnard Nicholas. *Traditional Indian Textile*. London: Thames & Hudson, 1993.

Goltsegen, Mark David. *The Painters Handbook*. New York: Watson Guotell Publications, 1993.

Goswamy, B.N. *Essence of Indian Art*. San Francisco: Asian Art Museum of San Francisco; The Festival of India, 1986.

Goyal, Naresh. *Jetwings Magazine*. Mumbai: October 2003—Vol 3. Issue 10; January 2004—Vol 4. Issue 1; March 2004—Vol 4. Issue 3; April 2004—Vol 4. Issue 4.

Graphic Workshop '95. New Delhi: Udayan Care, n.d.

Gray, Basil. *The Arts of India*. New York: Cornell University Press, 1981.

Guha-Thakurta, Tapati. *The Making of the New "Indian" Art: 1850–1920*. USA: Cambridge University Press, 1992.

Guide to Ajanta Frescoes. Rev. ed. Hyderabad: Archeological Dept. A.E.H. The Nizam's Govt. Hyderabad-Deccan, 1935.

Gupte, R.S. *Iconography of Hindus Buddhists and Jains*. Mumbai: B. Taraporevala Sons & Co. Pvt. Ltd., 1972.

Handa, O.C. *Shiva in Art*. New Delhi: Indus, 1992.

Hebbar K.K. *Tulsidas*. New Delhi: Abhinav Publications, 1989.

——. *Hebbar*. New Delhi: LKA, n.d.

——. *Voyage in Images*. Mumbai: Jehangir Art Gallery, n.d.

Hoskote, Ranjit. *Pilgrim Exile, Sorcerer, The Painterly Evolution of Jehangir Sabavala*. Mumbai: Eminence Designs Pvt. Ltd., 1998.

Husain Ki Sarai. New Delhi: Vadhera Art Gallery, n.d.

Ilango, Chandra. Ed. *Madras: An Emotion*. Chennai: Org. Values Art Foundations, 1996.

Image—Beyond Image. From the collection of Glenbarra Art Museum, Japan. New Delhi/Mumbai: NGMA, 1997.

Impressionism. New Delhi: College of Art, 1994.

Indian Drawing Today. Mumbai: JAG, 1987.

Indian Painting Today. Mumbai: JAG, 1981.

Indian Print Making Today. Mumbai: JAG, 1985.

Jai Zharotia/Moti Zharotia. Mumbai: Cymroza Art Gallery, 1992.

Jamini Roy at Jehangir. Mumbai: JAG, 1980.

Jamini Roy—Contemporary Indian Art Series. New Delhi: LKA, 1987.

Jindal, Sangita. *Art India*. Mumbai: 2004.

Joshi, Goverdhan Lal and M.K. Sharma. *Contemporary Indian Art Series*. New Delhi: LKA, 1992.

K. Madhava Menon. Lalit Kala Series of Contemporary Indian Art. New Delhi: LKA, 1992.

K. Venkatappa (Kannada/English). Bangalore: Karnataka Lalit Kala Academy, 1983.

K.B. Kulkarni and His Art. Mumbai: Navneet Publications (India) Ltd., 1999.

K.G. Subramanyan. New Delhi: Vadehra Art Gallery, 2000.

K.G. Subramanyan: *Retrospective*. Kolkata: BAAC, 1983.

Kapoor, Kamala. *Indian Artists*. Ahmedabad: Mapin Publishing Pvt. Ltd. n.d.

Kapoor, Kamala. *Laxman Shreshtha*. Mumbai: JAG, 1994.

Kapur, Geeta. *R.G. Subramanyan*. New Delhi: LKA, 1987.

Kaul, Manohar. *Kala Darshan*. Vol. 2, No. 2. New Delhi: 1989.

——. *Kala Darshan*. Vol. 5, No. 1. New Delhi: n.d.

——. *Kala Darshan*. Vol. 5, No. 3. New Delhi: n.d.

——. *Kala Darshan*. Vol. 6, No.1. New Delhi: n.d.

Knappert, Jan. *Indian Mythology*. Borgo Press, 1991.

Kolte, Prabhakar Mahadeo. *Kolte*. 1993.

Kossak, Steven. *Indian Court Painting 16th–19th Century*. London: Thames & Hudson, 1997.

Koushik, Dinkar. *Nandalal Bose Centenary*. New Delhi: National Book Trust, India, 1985.

Kramrisch, Stella. *The Hindu Temple 1 & 2*. 1976.

Krishnan, Gauri Parimoo. Ed. *Ratan Parimoo, Ceaseless. Creativity Paintings, Prints, Drawings*. New Delhi: Gauri Parimoo Krishnan, 1999.

Krishnan, Gauri Parimoo. Ed. *Religious Traditions of India—1988*. Vadodara: Gauri Parimoo Krishnan, 1999.

Krishnan, S.A. *Artist Directory*. New Delhi: LKA, 1981.

Kulkarni, Shakuntala. *Beyond Proscenium*.

——. *Godhadi*. Mumbai: Gallery Chemould, 1999.

——. Mumbai: 1996.

Kumar, R. Shiva. *Santiniketan: The Making of a Contextual Modernism*. Delhi: NGMA, 1997.

Kumar, Ram. *A Retrospective*. New Delhi: JAG & Vadehra Art Gallery, 1994.

Lalit Kala Contemporary 1. New Delhi: LKA, 1968.

Lalit Kala Contemporary 3. New Delhi: LKA, 1965.

Lalit Kala Contemporary 30. New Delhi: LKA, n.d.

Lalit Kala Contemporary 35. New Delhi: LKA, September 1987.

Lalit Kala Contemporary 36. New Delhi: LKA, September 1990.

Lalit Kala Contemporary 37. New Delhi: LKA, March 1991.

Lalit Kala Contemporary 38. New Delhi: LKA, March 1993.

Lalit Kala Contemporary 39. New Delhi: LKA, March 1994.

Lalit Kala Contemporary 40. New Delhi: LKA, March 1995.

Lalit Kala Contemporary Art 41. New Delhi: LKA,1995.

Lalit Kala Contemporary. New Delhi: LKA,1993.

Lalu Shaw. New Delhi: Centre for Contemporary Art, 1990.

Langland, Tuck. *From Clay to Bronze, A Studio Guide to Figurative Sculpture*. New York: Watson-Guptill Publications, 1999.

LKA Information from Contemporaries. New Delhi: LKA, n.d.

LKA Information from Monographs. New Delhi: LKA, n.d.

LKA—VII Triennale. New Delhi: LKA, 1991.

Losos, Ludvik. *Painting Techniques*. London: Octopus Books Ltd., 1987.

Lucie-Smith, Edward. *Movements in Art since 1945*. London: Thames & Hudson, 1996.

——. *The Thames and Hudson Dictionary of- Art Terms*. London: 1984.

Lucis, R. *Krishna Reddy*: A Retrospective 1982. New York: Bronx Museum of the Arts, 1981.

Mago, P.N. *Vision—Recaptured*. New Delhi: The British Council, 1997.

Mago, Pran Nath. *Contemporary Art in India*. New Delhi: National Book Trust, 2000.

Majumdar R.C., Raychaudhuri H.C. & Datta Kalikinkar. *An Advanced History of India*. Chennai: Macmillan India Ltd.,1996.

Masters—Best of Some Outstanding Delhi Artists. New Delhi: Vadehra Art Gallery, 1991.

Mehta, Anupa. Ed. *The Jehangir Nicholson Collection*. Mumbai: Jehangir Nicholson-NGMA, 1998.

Mehta, Chinmay. Ed. *Contemporary Artists of Rajasthan*. Jaipur: LKA, 1992.

Mehta, Tyeb. *Celebration*. Mumbai: Times Bank Ltd., 1996.

Meister, Michael W. *Discourses on Siva, Proceedings of a Symposium on the Nature of Religious Imagery*. Philadelphia, Mumbai: University of Pennsylvania Press and Vakils, Feffer & Simons, 1984.

Millennium Show: *A Century of Art from Maharashtra*. Mumbai: NCAG, 2000/2001.

Mistry, Dhruva. *Work 1990–1995*. London: Anthony Wilkinson Fine Art, 1995.

Mitchell, A.G. *Hindu Gods & Goddesses*. New Delhi: UBSPD, 1998.

Mitra, Debala. *Ajanta—1983. New Delhi:* Gen. Archeological Survey of India, n.d.

Mitter, Partha. *Art Nationalism Colonial India 1850–1922*. Occidental Orientation and Cambridge University Press, 1994.

Mitter, Partha. *Indian Art*. New York: Oxford University Press, 2001.

Moitra, Dwijendra. *The Academy Of Fine Arts*. Kolkata: AFA, 1983.

Mona Rai: Paintings. New Delhi: Art Heritage, 1997.

Monier M., Williams. *A Sanskrit English Dictionary*. New Delhi: Motilal Banarsidass Publishers Pvt. Ltd., 1977.

Mookerjee, Ajit. *Ritual Art of India*. London: Thames & Hudson, n.d.

Movements in Indian Art Attribute (50 years). Bangalore: CKP, 1997–1998.

Mukherjee, Binode Behari. *Abanindranath Tagore*. Translated from Bengali by Kshitis Roy. New Delhi: NGMA, 1998.

Mukhopadhya, Amit. *Petals of Offering—Sanyal B.C.* New Delhi: LKA, 1992.

—— and B.P. Kamboj. *Ten Contemporary Graphic Printers*. New Delhi: LKA: n.d.

Murray, Peter and Linda Murray. *Dictionary of Art & Artist*. UK: Penguin, 1985.

Murthi, A.N.S. Ed. And compiled. *The Life and Art of C.P. Rajaram*.

Murty, K. Satya. *Handbook of Indian Architecture*. New Delhi: Ashish Publishing House, 1991.

Nagji, Patel. *Animals-Seeds-Deities Sculptures 1960–1994*.

Naik, Bapurao S. *Typography of Devanagari*. Vol. 1. Mumbai: Directorate of Publishing of Govt. of India, 1971.

Naik, Satish. *Kala Kird*. Mumbai: Chinha Publication, 1986.

Nair, C.V. Balan. *The India Magazine*. Vol. 13. Kerala: 1992.

Nandalal Bose. Vol. 1983. New Delhi: LKA, n.d.

National Exhibition of Art 1955–1990. New Delhi: LKA.

National Exhibition of Art 1973. New Delhi: LKA.

National Exhibition of Art 1976. New Delhi: LKA.

National Exhibition of Art 1978. New Delhi: LKA.

National Exhibition of Art 1981. New Delhi: LKA.

National Gallery of Modern Art, New Delhi, Acc. No.1224, 1840, 2557.

National Gallery of Modern Art. Catalogue of Collections, Vol. 1. New Delhi: 1989.

O'Flaherty, Wendy Doniger. *Hindu Myths*. England: Penguin Books Ltd., 1975.

Oddiyan—Contemporary paintings from Orissa. Mumbai & New Jersey: JAG, 1994.

P.T. Reddy. *Contemporary Indian Art Series*. New Delhi: LKA, 1992.

Padamsee, Akbar, Laxman Shreshtha, Jogen Showdhury. Mumbai: Pundole Art Gallery, December 1992.

Pai, Laxman. *My Search My Evolution*. Delhi: Purnima Pai & Laxman Pai, 1999.

Paintings and Graphics by Shyamal Dutta Ray. Kolkata: BAAC, 1993.

Pal D.N.G. *Silk Screen Printing*. Chennai: Pioneer Publication, 2003.

Pal, Ila. *Beyond the Canvas: An Unfinished Portrait of M.F. Husain*. New Delhi: INDUS and HarperCollins, 1994.

Palsikar, Shankar. *Lyrical Line*. Mumbai: Gangal Publications, 1967.

Palsikar, Shankar. *Memorial Exhibition 20th–26th December 1984*. Mumbai.

Panjabi, Camellia. Ed. *The Taj Magazine*. Mumbai: Vol. 22 No. 1, January–March 1993 & Vol. 25 No. 1, July–September 1996.

Pant, Pushpesh. *Ajanta & Ellora—Cave Temples of Ancient India*. Holland: Roli & Janssen BV, 2003

Paramjit Singh—Oil Pastels. Mumbai: Gallery Chemould, 1996.

Parikh, Urmi. *Kalaguru Rashiklal Parikh* (Gujarati). Ahmedabad: 2000.

Parimoo, Ratan. *Studies in Modern Indian Art*. New Delhi: Krishnan Gauri Parimoo, 1975.

Patnaik, D.P. *Abanindranath And His Art*. Kolkata: Rabindra Bharati Society, 1995.

Paul, Ashit. Ed. *Woodcut Prints of Nineteenth Century Calcutta*. Kolkata: Seagull Books, 1983.

Philippe, Joseph. *Glass Chambers*. Edinburgh: W & R Chambers Ltd, 1978

Pilloo Pochkhanawala. New Delhi: LKA, n.d.

Piraji Sagara. *Contemporary Indian Art Series*. New Delhi: LKA, 1995.

Prakash, Surya. *Surya Prakash*. Hyderabad: Surya Gallery, 1994.

Punja, Shobita. *Museums of India—An Illustrated Guide*. Hong Kong: The Guide Book Company Ltd., 1990.

Purohit, Vinayak. *Art of Transitional India by 20th Century*. Vol. I & II. Bombay: Bombay Popular Prakashan Pvt. Ltd., 1988.

Qadri, Sohan. *The Dot and the Dots*. Sweden: Galerie International, 1960.

——. *The Seer*. New Delhi: Art & Deal, 1999.

Radhakrishan, S. *The Hindu View of Life*. New Delhi: Rupa & Co. and Harper Collins, 1927.

Rado, N. Chadrashekar. *Krishna Theme in Orissan Painting*. Bhubaneshwar: Working Artists' Association, n.d.

Ram Gopal Vijaivargiya. *Contemporary Indian Art Series*. New Delhi: LKA, 1988.

Ram Kishore Yadav—Paintings (Oil Pastels). 1996.

Raman, A.S. *Contemporary Indian Art Series*. New Delhi: LKA,1992.

Raman, A.S. *The Critical Vision*. New Delhi:LKA, 1993.

Ramananda Bandyopadhyay. Kolkata: BAAC, 1993.

Ramanujacharya, C.R. *Ravi Varma's Hamsa Damayanthi–A Critical Study*. Nagpur: Philosophical Society–Nagpur, n.d.

Ramkumar. *A Retrospective*. Mumbai: JAG, 1994.

Randhawa, M.S. *Kangra Paintings of the Bihari Sat Sai*. New Delhi: National Museum,1962.

—— and D.S. Randhawa. *Kishangarh Painting*. Mumbai: Vakils, Feffer and Simons Ltd, 1980.

——. *Basohli Paintings*. New Delhi: Ministry of Information and Broadcasting, Government of India, 1959.

——. *Kangra Paintings of the Gita Govinda*. New Delhi: National Museum, 1982.

——. *Paintings of the Babur Namah*. New Delhi: National Museum, 1983.

Rao, T.A. Gopinatha. *Elements of Hindu Iconography*. Vol. 1, Part 1. New Delhi: Motilal Banarsidass Publishers Pvt. Ltd, 1914.

Raval, Prem. *Chitra Sangi*. Ahmedabad: 1990.

Raval, Ravishankar. *Gujratma Kalana Prakran*. Gujarat: Kala Ravi Trust & Archer, 1998.

Raza, Sayed Haider. *Raza Anthology 1980–90* (Hindi and English). Mumbai: Gallery Chemould, 1991.

Raza. Mumbai: 1979.

Read, Herbert. Ed. *Dictionary of Art & Artists*. London: Thames & Hudson, 1989.

Reddy, A.K.V.S. *Guide Book*. Hyderabad: 1998.

Reddy, G.V. Bhaskara. *Erotic Sculptures of Ancient India: A Critical Study (From the Earliest Times to AD 1200)*. New Delhi: Inter-India Publication, 1991.

Reddy, Krishna. *A Retrospective*. Kolkata: BAAC, 1984–1985.

Reddy, N. Krishna. *New Ways Of Colour Printmaking*. New Delhi: Ajanta Offset & Packagings Ltd. & Vadhera Art Gallery, 1998.

Rege, Nina. *S.L. Haldankar-G.S. Haldankar*. Mumbai: Nehru Centre Art Gallery, 1999.

——. *Gopal D. Deuskar*. Mumbai: Nehru Centre Art Gallery, 1995.

——. *Padmashri Vinayak Pandurang Karmarkar* (Marathi and English). 1997.

——– and K.D. Kawadkar. *Ravindra Mestry, A Master Painter & Sculptor*. Mumbai: Nehru Centre Art Gallery, 1997.

Rekha Rao. Mumbai: Cymroza Art Gallery, 1995.

Roaf, Peggy. *Looking At Paintings*. New York: Hyperion Books for Children, 1993.

Rowland, Benjamin. *The Ajanta Caves: Early Buddhist Paintings from India*. Collins-UNESCO, 1963.

——. *The Pelican History of Art. The Art & Architecture of India, Buddhist-Hindu-Jain*. Britain: Pelican, 1953.

Roy, Kshitish. *Rabindranath Tagore*. New Delhi: NGMA, 1988.

Roy, Yamini, Punya Nagpal, Ritu Jaggia, Minal Vazirani and Dinesh Vazirani. *Saffronart Online Auction*. Mumbai: n.d.

Sailoz Mookerjea. Lalit Kala Series of Contemporary Indian Art (Hindi). New Delhi: LKA, 1987.

Sarkar, Pabitra Prabaha. *Exhibition of Art of Bengal 1850 to 1999*. Kolkata: Art Sub-Committee, Biswa Banga Samme, Millennium Festival, 2000.

Sarma, I.K. Ed. *Salar Jung Museum B 1. Annual Reasearch Journal*. Vol. XXXII. Hyderabad: 1996.

Sastry, B.V.K. *Murals of Karnataka*. Karnataka: LKA, 1983.

Saxton, Colin. *Art School–An Instructional Guide Based on the Teaching of Leading Art Colleges*. London: QED Publishing Ltd., 1981.

Sen, Geeti. *Bindu. Space and Time in Raza's Vision*. New Delhi: Media Transasia Ltd., 1982.

Sen, Geeti. *Image and Imagination: Five Contemporary Artists in India*. Ahmedabad: Mapin Publishing Pvt. Ltd., 1996.

Sengupta, Kajal and Sohini Sen. Ed. *Album 1960–1991*. Kolkata: SCA, n.d.

Sengupta, Kajal and Prakash Kejriwal. *H.K. Kejriwal–Collection 1830–1995*. Bangalore: CKP, 1996.

Serigraph Prints of 16 Drawings by Dhanraj Bhagat. New Delhi: CMC Ltd., 1988.

Seth, Deven. *'92–Search of Nature*. Mumbai: Taj Art Gallery, 1992.

Seth, Mira. *Wall Paintings of the Western Himalayas*. New Delhi: Dir. Publication Division Govt. of India, 1976.

Shah, Himmat. *A Profile*. New Delhi: Art Heritage, n.d.

Shah, Natubhai. *Jainism*. UK: Jain Samaj-Europe, n.d.

Shah, Prabha. *The Mirror Inside Me Shows*. 2000.

Shakila–A Truly Barefoot Artist. The Telegraph Magazine. 1993.

Sharma, Mohan. *Mohan*. Jaipur: PAG and LKA, 1992.

Sharma, Om Prakash. *Om Prakash*. New Delhi: 1988.

Sheth, Pratima. *Perspective*. Mumbai: 2000.

Shinde, Deepak. *25 Years of Painting 1971–1996*. Mumbai: 1997.

Shivananda P. Akki (Kannada). *Karnataka Lalit Kala Academy*. Bangalore: Mukundan K., 1994.

Shuvaprasanna. Kolkata: BAAC, 1992.

Shuvaprasanna–Expression 1971–1986. Kolkata: Artist's Home Gallery, 1986.

Shyamal Dutta Ray. New Delhi: 2001.

Singh, B.P. *The Modern*. Mumbai: NGMA, 1996.

Singh, Gurcharan. *Contemporary Indian Art Series* (Hindi). New Delhi: LKA, 1995.

Sinha, Gayatri. *Indian Art An Overview*. New Delhi: Rupa & Co., 2003

Sivaramamurti, C. *Indian Painting*. New Delhi: National Book Trust, 1970.

Six Triennale–India 1986. LKA: New Delhi, 1986.

Sixth Indian Oil Art Exhibition 1992. Mumbai: Indian Oil Corporation Ltd. n.d.

Solanki, Vrindavan. Mumbai: Cymroza Art Gallery, 1997.

Somnath Hore. New Delhi: LKA, n.d.

Sotheby's Foundation Indian, European and Oriental Paintings and Works of Art. New Delhi: 1992.

Souza, Francis Newton. *Souza 1940's–1990's*. New Delhi: Dhoomimal Gallery, 1990.

——. *Souza in the Forties*. New Delhi: Dhoomimal Gallery, 1983.

——. *The Demonic Line–An Exhibition of Drawings 1940–1964*. New Delhi: Delhi Art Gallery, 2001.

Srikant. *Alphabet of Reality 2: The Sun-God Soorya*. Kerala: Integral Books, December 1996.

Stangos, Nikos. *Concepts of Modern Art*. UK: Thames & Hudson, 1995.

Sthapati, V. Ganapati. *Indian Sculpture and Iconography*. Ahmedabad: Mapin Publishing and Sri Aurobindo Institute of Research in Social Sciences, 2002.

Stilled Lives (with details) Manu Parekh. New Delhi: LKA & Seagull Foundation for the Arts, Rabindra Bhavan, 1995.

Story of Sir J.J. School of Art 1857–1957. Mumbai: JJSA, n.d.

Subramanyan, K.G. *Of Myth and Fairytale*. Kolkata: BAAC & Seagull Foundation for the Arts, 1989.

——. *Jyotsna Bhatt: Ceramics*. New Delhi: Art Heritage, 1997.

——. *Paintings and Drawings*. Seagull Foundation for the Arts, 1998.

——. *The Living Tradition–Perspectives on Modern Indian Art*. Kolkata: Seagull Books,1987.

Sud, Anupam. Mumbai: Cymroza Art Gallery, 1994.

Sud, Halle. *Coups De Coeur*. Geneva: Aux Halles de l'Ile, 1987.

Sudhir Patwardhan—Paintings and Drawings. Mumbai & Bangalore: Sakshi Gallery and Synergy Art Foundation Ltd., n.d.

Sultan Ali. New Delhi: LKA, 1983.

Sultan Ali: Paintings. New Delhi: Art Heritage, 1997.

Sundaram, Vivan. *Collaboration/Combines.* Catalogue. 1992.

——. *Long Night: Drawings in Charcoal.* 1988.

——. *River Scape 1992–1993.*

Sundaram, Vivan. *Engine Oil and Charcoal: Works on Paper.* 1991.

——. *Journeys—Soft Pastel on Paper.* 1988.

Sundaram, Vivan. *Memorial—An installation with Photographs and sculpture.* 1993.

——. *The Sher-Gil Archive—An Installation.* 1995.

Swaminathan, J. *Contemporary Indian Art Series.* New Delhi: LKA, 1995.

——. *Exhibition of Paintings.* New Delhi: Vadehra Art Gallery, 1993.

T. Vaikuntam. Mumbai: Cymroza Art Gallery, 1997.

T.P. Akki (Kannada). *Karnataka Lalit Kala Academy.* Bangalore: Mukundan K., 1994.

Tagore, Abanindranath and Kramrisch Stella. Ed. *Journal of the Indian Society of Oriental Art.* Vol XVI. Kolkata: ISOA, 1948.

Tagore, Jyotirindranath. *Faces Unforgettable—Studies from Life.* Kolkata: Rabindra Bharati Society, January 1995.

Tagore, Rabindranath. *Bichitra—An Exhibition of Paintings.* Mumbai: NGMA, 2000.

——. *Drawings and Paintings, Centenary 1861–1961.* New Delhi: LKA, n.d.

——. *The Meaning of Art.* Reprint. New Delhi: LKA, Visva-Bharati, Santiniketan, 1983.

Tagore, Siddhartha. Ed. *Art & Deal.* New Delhi: 1999–2002.

Tamil Nadu Ovia Nunkalai Kuzhu. LKA, 1995.

Tandon, Rajkumar. *Indian Miniature Painting 16th through 19th Centuries.* Bangalore: 1982.

Teachers. Sir J.J. School of Art. Mumbai.

Teachers' Government College of Art & Craft—Kolkata. Mumbai: JAG, 1996.

Thacker, Manu and G. Venkatachalam. *Present-Day Painters of India.* Mumbai: Sudhangshu Publications, n.d.

The Art of Ram Kishore Yadav (Metal and Pastel Work).

The Downtrodden and We. New Delhi: LKA, 1991.

The Illustrated Weekly of India. Mumbai: Times of India, 1989.

The Meaning of Art. London: Faber & Faber Ltd., 1931.

The Presence of the Past. The British Council & INTACH, 1998.

The Treasures of Castle Park. No. 9. Leicester: The Jain Centre, n.d.

Third Triennale—India 1975. New Delhi: LKA, n.d.

Thoshur, Vasudha. *Paintings and Drawings 1989–90.*

——. *An Impression.* Mumbai: Cymroza Art Gallery, 1991–92.

Tokuriki, Tomikichiro. *Wood-block Print Primer.* Japan: Japan Publication INC., 1970.

Tomory, Edith. *A History of Fine Arts in India and the West 1982.* Chennai: Orient Longman Ltd., 1999.

Treasures of Indian Museum. Mumbai: Marg Publications, n.d.

Trends in Bengal Art. London: Commonwealth Institute, 1986.

Tripathi, Ramashankar. *History of Ancient India.* New Delhi: Motilal Banarsidass Publishers Pvt. Ltd., 1999.

Tuli, Neville. *Intuitive Logic.* Ahmedabad: Mapin Publishing Pvt. Ltd, First Published by Heart in 1999.

Tuli, Neville. *Osian's.* Ahmedabad: Mapin Publishing Pvt. Ltd., 2003.

V.K. Wankhede. Mumbai: BAAC, 1999.

Varma, Raja Ravi. Thiruvananthapuram: Chitra Art Gallery, n.d.

Vasudev, S.G. Bangalore: Crimson–The Art Resource, n.d.

——. *Copper Extracts–Soliloquies in Sheet-metal*. 2003

——. *Future Recollections–Fragments Between Myth and Fable*.1999.

——. *Inscape–Paintings by Vasudev*.

Venkatachalam, G. *Contemporary Indian Painters*. Mumbai: Nalanda and Marg, 1947.

Venniyoor, E.N.J. *Raja Ravi Varma*. New Delhi: The Govt. of Kerala–LKA, n.d.

Verma, Umendra. *Aurangabad-Daultabad-Ellora-Ajanta*.

VII Triennale India 1991. New Delhi: LKA, n.d.

Viswanadhan. (French/English). New Delhi: NGMA, 1998.

Walls and Floors. The Living Traditions of Village India. Photography by Jyoti Bhatt.

Water Colours and Contemporary Indian Painting. New Delhi: Gallery Art Motif, 1999.

Weavers' Service Centres. New Delhi: Development Commissioner for Handlooms, 1985.

Wheeler, Daniel. *Art Since Mid-Century–1945 to The Present 1991*. London: Thames & Hudson, 1991.

Who's Who of Karnataka Artists. Bangalore: Karnataka LKA, 1983.

Yusuf. *Recent Paintings and Drawings*. 1996.

Zimmer, Heinrich. *Myths and Symbols in Indian Art & Civilization*. Princeton: Princeton University Press, 1946.

——. *The Art of Indian Asia*. Vol. 1 & 2. New York: Bollingen Foundation Inc., 1955.

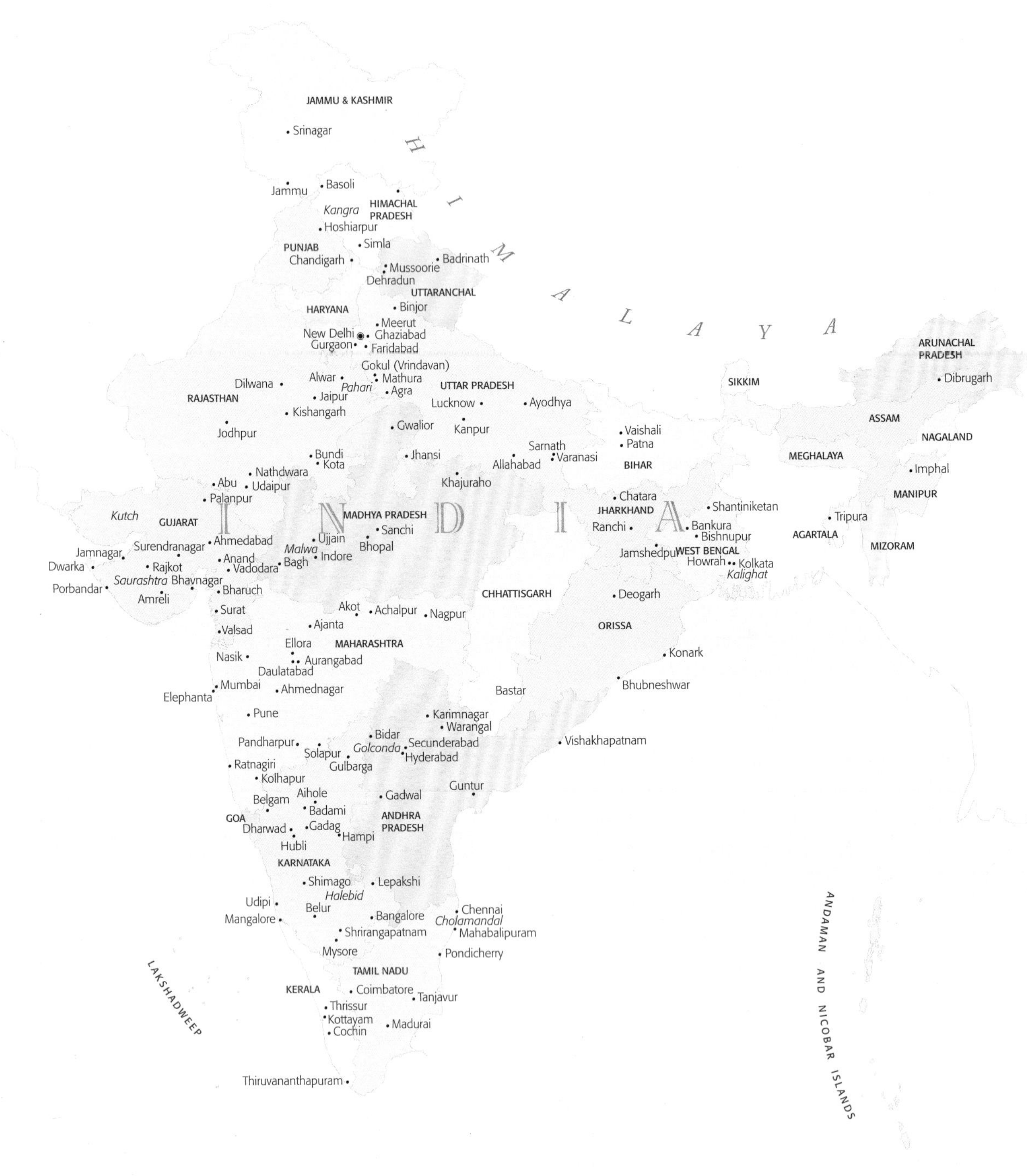

Map by Gopal Limbad

Based upon Survey of India maps with the permission of the Surveyor General of India.

Responsibility for the correctness of internal details shown on the main map rests with the publisher.